PROBLEMS, CASES, AND READINGS

ENVIRONMENTAL POLICY LAW

SIXTH EDITION

by

HOLLY DOREMUS
Professor of Law
University of California at Berkeley
School of Law

ALBERT C. LIN
Professor of Law
University of California at Davis
School of Law

RONALD H. ROSENBERG
Associate Dean for Academic Affairs and Chancellor Professor of Law
William and Mary Law School
College of William and Mary

FOUNDATION PRESS
2012

THOMSON REUTERS™

© 1982, 1985, 1991, 1996, 2002 FOUNDATION PRESS

© 2008 By THOMSON REUTERS/FOUNDATION PRESS

© 2012 By THOMSON REUTERS/FOUNDATION PRESS

      1 New York Plaza, 34th Floor

      New York, NY 10004

      Phone Toll Free 1–877–888–1330

      Fax 646–424–5201

      foundation–press.com

Printed in the United States of America

ISBN 978–1–60930–173–6

Mat #41289913

PREFACE

Environmental law is no longer a new field. Few people today would be surprised to learn that the law addresses a variety of environmental problems. Many attorneys consider at least a portion of their practice to be "environmental" in some sense; personal injury litigation, real estate transactions, corporate counseling and other practices all raise environmental issues. Environmental law proved its staying power in the mid-1990s, when advocates of deregulation gained a majority in Congress but were unable to significantly relax federal environmental laws.

Although it has in some respects matured over the last two decades, environmental law remains an exciting and controversial field. Environmental problems typically share a number of characteristics that complicate attempts to find legal solutions to them. Human activities can affect the environment at great distances, crossing state and international boundaries. Environmental harms often result from the combination of a number of different actions, and even different types of action, none of which would be problematic in isolation. It is frequently difficult to predict the environmental consequences of action, or even to measure them. It is equally difficult to agree on the value of environmental harm, or how it should be compared with the economic costs of preventing it. Because of the threat of irreversible or catastrophic harm, environmentalists often argue for early, precautionary, responses. On the other hand, proposals for economically costly regulation face substantial resistance where their benefits cannot be clearly demonstrated.

We take a very broad view of environmental law, encompassing the regulation of private and public land use and protection of wildlife as well as pollution control and remediation. We believe that artificially separating pollution law from the regulation of natural resources can obscure important conceptual similarities. Each instructor, of course, must determine the appropriate scope of coverage for his or her class. This casebook is designed to facilitate that kind of selection. It provides sufficient breadth for any introductory environmental or natural resources law course.

Environmental law remains highly complex. Students who aspire to practice environmental law must gain a sense of that complexity, and the confidence to address it. They must learn something of the science, economics, and philosophy used to evaluate environmental controversies. They must become familiar with regulations and the basics of administrative law, as well as statutes and judicial opinions. They must understand that state and local law, although still not as important as federal law, plays an increasingly important role as the federal courts take an increasingly restrictive view of federal powers.

At the same time, environmental law remains subject to continual modification. Although there have been few amendments to the major federal environmental statutes in the last few years, judicial opinions and regulatory changes have continued apace. Since the details will surely change, we believe it is most productive for teachers and students to focus on the larger picture. We have struck a balance by focusing in detail on those portions of the statutes covered that raise particularly interesting or important conceptual issues. Throughout, we highlight perpetual controversies such as the nature of human relationships to nature, the appropriate extent of individual control over natural resource use, and the degree of certainty needed to support regulatory intervention.

We have included in each chapter a number of problems designed to provide a concrete focus for classroom discussion. These problems help students develop and test their facility with the materials in the text and the concepts underlying those materials.

The development of such a comprehensive set of materials necessarily reflects the combined efforts of many people. Berkeley Law, the University of California, Davis, School of Law, and the William and Mary Law School provided invaluable institutional and financial support. Finally, we owe a tremendous debt to Gordon Anthon, Linh Thai, and Yanfang Tang for their patience and support during the course of this project.

HOLLY DOREMUS
Berkeley, California

ALBERT C. LIN
Davis, California

RONALD H. ROSENBERG
Williamsburg, Virginia

ACKNOWLEDGEMENTS

The following copyrighted material has been reproduced with permission of the copyright holder:

Adler, Robert W., Integrated Approaches to Water Pollution: Lessons from the Clean Air Act, 23 Harv. Envtl. L. Rev. 203, 228 (1999), reprinted with permission.

Andreen, William L., In Pursuit of NEPA's Promise: The Role of Executive Oversight in the Implementation of Environmental Policy, 64 Ind. L.J. 205, 245–247 (1989), reprinted with permission.

Andreen, William L., The Evolution of Water Pollution Control in the United States: State, Local and Federal Efforts, 1789–1972, Part I, 22 Stan. Envtl. L. J. 145, 161 (2003), reprinted with permission.

Andreen, William L., Water Quality Today—Has the Clean Water Act Been a Success?, 55 Ala. L. Rev. 537 (2004), reprinted with permission.

Andrews, Richard N.L., The Unfinished Business of National Environmental Policy, in Environmental Policy and NEPA: Past, Present, and Future, 85 (Ray Clark and Larry Canter eds, 1997), reprinted with permission.

Applegate, John S., Synthesizing TSCA and REACH: Practical Principles for Chemical Regulation Reform, 35 Ecology L.Q. 721 (2008), reprinted with permission of the Regents of the University of California.

Bachmann, John, Will the Circle Be Unbroken: A History of the U.S. National Ambient Air Quality Standards, 57 Journal of the Air and Waste Management Association 652 (2007), reprinted with permission.

Baxter, William F., People or Penguins: The Case for Optimal Pollution, 4–12 (Columbia University Press 1974), reprinted with permission.

Bear, Dinah, NEPA at 19: A Primer on an "Old" Law with Solutions to New Problems, 19 Envtl. L. Rep. 10060, 10061–10065 (1989). Copyright 1989, Environmental Law Institute, reprinted with permission.

Brunet, Edward, Debunking Wholesale Pivate Envorcement of Environmental Rights, 15 Harv. J.L. & Pub. Pol'y 311, 313–323 (1992), reprinted with permission.

Bryner, Gary C., Carbon Markets: Reducing Greenhouse Gas Emissions Through Emissions Trading, 17 Tul. Envtl. L. J. 267 (2004).

Cannon, Jonathan Z., Adaptive Management in Superfund: Thinking like a Contaminated Site, 13 N.Y.U. Envtl. L. J. 561 (2005), reprinted with permission.

Charnovitz, Steve, Free Trade, Fair Trade, Green Trade: Defogging the Debate, 27 Cornell Int'l L.J. 459, 462–65 (1994), reprinted with permission.

Cole, Luke W. and Caroline Farrell, Structural Racism, Structural Pollution and the Need for a New Paradigm, 20 Wash. U. J. L. & Pol'y 265, 268–273 (2006).

Commission for Racial Justice, United Church of Christ, Toxic Wastes and Race in the United States, 13 (1987), reprinted with permission.

Coquillette, Daniel R., Mosses from an Old Manse: Another Look at Some Historic Property Cases About the Environment, 64 Cornell L. Rev. 761, 792 (1979), reprinted with permission.

Cross, Frank B., Common Law Conceits: A Comment on Meiners & Yandle, 7 Geo. Mason L. Rev. 965, 966–981 (1999), reprinted with permission.

Doremus, Holly, Patching the Ark: Improving Legal Protection of Biological Diversity, 18 Ecology L.Q. 265, 269–281 (1991), reprinted with permission.

Driesen, David M., Is Emissions Trading an Economic Incentive Program?: Replacing the Command and Control/Economic Incentive Dichotomy, 55 Washington & Lee Law Review 289, 313–319, 324–338 (1998), reprinted with permission.

Drury, Richard Toshiyuki, Michael E. Belliveau, J. Scott Kuhn & Shipra Bansal, Pollution Trading and Environmental Injustice: Los Angeles' Failed Experiment in Air Quality Policy, 9 Duke Envtl. L. & Pol'y Forum 231 (1999).

Fine, James D. and Dave Owen, Technocracy and Democracy: Conflicts Between Models and Participation in Environmental Law and Planning, 56 Hastings L. J. 901, 949–965 (2005), reprinted with permission.

Fischman, Robert L., Cooperative Federalism and Natural Resources Law, 14 N.Y.U. Envtl L.J. 179 (2005), reprinted with permission.

Germany's Polluter Pays Concept Could Be Applied to U.S. Industry, 17 Int'l Env't Rptr. (BNA) 368 (1994), reproduced with permission from International Environment Reporter, Vol. 17, No. 8, p. 368 (April 20, 1994). Copyright 1994 by The Bureau of National Affairs, Inc. (800–372–1033) http//www.bna.com.

Hamilton, James T. & W. Kip Viscusi, Calculating Risks: The Spatial and Political Dimensions of Hazardous Waste Policy 240–43 (The MIT Press, 1999).

Hardin, Garrett, The Tragedy of the Commons, reprinted with permission from 162 Science 1243, 1244–1245, 1247 (1968). Copyright 1968 American Association for the Advancement of Science.

Heinzerling, Lisa, Discounting Our Future, 34 Land & Water L. Rev. 39, 44 (1999), reprinted with permission.

Hill, Randolph L., An Overview of RCRA: The "Mind-Numbing" Provisions of the Most Complicated Environmental Statute, 21 Envtl. L. Rep. 10254, 10268–10269 (1991), copyright © 1991 Environmental Law

Institute®, Washington, DC. Reprinted with permission from **ELR® – The Environmental Law Reporter®**. All rights reserved.

Houck, Oliver A. Houck, The Clean Water Act TMDL Program: Law, Policy, and Implementation, 2d ed., 87–92 (ELI Press 2002).

Hsu, Shi–Ling, Reducing Emissions from the Electricity Generation Industry: Can We Finally Do It?, 14 Tulane Envtl. L. J. 427 (2001), reprinted with permission.

Karkkainen, Bradley C., Information as Environmental Regulation: TRI and Performance Benchmarking, Precursor to a New Paradigm? 89 Geo. L.J. 257, 287–333 (2000), reprinted with permission. Reprinted with permission of the publisher, Georgetown Law Journal © 2000.

Krieger, Martin H., What's Wrong With Plastic Trees, reprinted with permission from 179 Science 446, 446–453 (1973). Copyright 1973 American Association for the Advancement of Science.

Lazarus, Richard J., Restoring What's Environmental About Environmental Law in the Supreme Court, 47 UCLA L. Rev. 703, 744–748 (2000), reprinted with permission.

Lazarus, Richard J., Meeting the Demands of Integration in the Evolution of Environmental Law: Reforming Environmental Criminal Law, 83 Geo. L.J. 2407, 2423–38 (1995), reprinted with permission of the publisher, Georgetown Law Journal © 1995.

Leopold, Aldo, A Sand County Almanac: with other Essays on Conservation from Round River, 218–240, copyright 1949, 1953, 1966, renewed 1977, 1981 by Oxford University Press. Used by permission of Oxford University Press, Inc.

Lin, Albert C., Size Matters: Regulating Nanotechnology, 32 Harv. Envtl. L. Rev. 349 (2007), reprinted with permission.

McCauley, Douglas J., Selling Out on Nature, 443 Nature 27, 27–28 (2006). Reprinted by permission from Macmillan Publishers Ltd.: Nature 443:27, copyright 2006.

McGarity, Thomas O., Missing Milestones: A Critical Look at the Clean Air Act's VOC Emissions Reduction Program in Non–Attainment Areas, 18 Virginia Environmental Law Journal 41 (1999).

Meiners, Roger & Yandle, Bruce, Common Law and the Conceit of Modern Environmental Policy, 7 Geo. Mason L. Rev. 923, 946–959 (1999), reprinted with permission.

Meyer, Judy L., The Dance of Nature: New Concepts in Ecology, 69 Chi.-Kent L. Rev. 875, 875–886 (1994), reprinted with permission.

Noss, Reed F., Some Principles of Conservation Biology, As They Apply to Environmental Law, 69 Chi.-Kent L. Rev. 893, 895 (1994), reprinted with permission.

Pacala, S. and R. Socolow, Stabilization Wedges: Solving the Climate Problem for the Next 50 Years with Current Technologies, 305 Science 968–72 (2004).

Pedersen, William F. Pedersen, Jr., Turning the Tide on Water Quality, 15 Ecology L.Q. 69, 82–83 (1988), reprinted with permission.

Rechtschaffen, Clifford, The Warning Game: Evaluating Warnings Under California's Proposition 65, 23 Ecology L.Q. 303, 313–348 (1996), reprinted with permission.

Rechtschaffen, Clifford, Deterrence vs. Cooperation and the Evolving Theory of Environmental Enforcement, 71 S. Cal. L. Rev. 1181, 1186–89 (1998), reprinted with the permission of the Southern California Law Review.

Sagoff, Mark, We Have Met the Enemy and He Is Us or Conflict and Contradiction in Environmental Law, 12 Envtl. L. 283, 283–308 (1982), reprinted with permission.

Salzman, James, Sustainable Consumption and the Law, 27 Envtl. L. 1243, 1273 (1997), reprinted with permission.

Salzman, James, Thompson, Barton H. & Daily, Gretchen, Protecting Ecosystem Services: Science, Economics, and Law, 20 Stan. Envtl. L.J. 309, 312 (2001), reprinted with permission.

Sax, Joseph, Introduction to Symposium: Environmental Law: More Than Just a Passing Fad, 19 U. Mich. J.L. Ref. 797, 804 (1986), reprinted with permission.

Setear, John K., Ozone, Iteration, and International Law, 40 Va. J. Int'l L. 193, 195–216 (1999), reprinted with permission.

Shavell, Steven, Liability for Harm Versus Regulation of Safety, 13 J. Legal Stud. 357, 357–365 (1984). Copyright 1984 by The University of Chicago. All rights reserved.

Sigman, Hilary, The Pace of Progress at Superfund Sites: Policy Goals and Interest Group Influence, 44 J. L. & Econ. 315 (2001), reprinted with permission.

Slovic, Paul, The Risk Game, 86 J. Hazardous Materials 17 (2001), reprinted with permission from Elsevier.

Stavins, Robert N., Vintage Differentiated Environmental Regulation, 25 Stan. Envtl. L. J. 29, 30 (2006), reprinted with permission.

Stewart, Richard B., Pyramids of Sacrifice? Problems of Federalism in Mandating State Implementation of National Environmental Policy. Reprinted by permission of The Yale Law Journal Company and William S. Hein Company from The Yale Law Journal, Vol. 86, pages 1196–1272.

Sunstein, Cass R., Of Montreal and Kyoto: A Tale of Two Protocols, 31 Harv. Envtl. L. Rev. 1 (2007), reprinted with permission.

Tarlock, A. Dan, Environmental Law: Ethics or Science? 7 Duke Envtl. L. & Pol'y F. 193, 194–195, 221–223 (1996).

Thornton, Robert D., Searching for Consensus and Predictability: Habitat Conservation Planning Under the Endangered Species Act of 1973, 21 Envtl. L. 605, 621–624 (1991), reprinted with permission.

Torres, Gerald, Introduction: Understanding Environmental Racism, 63 U. Colo. L. Rev. 839, 839–840 (1992), reprinted with permission.

Uhlmann, David M., Environmental Crime Comes of Age: The Evolution of Criminal Enforcement in the Environmental Regulatory Scheme, 2009 Utah L. Rev. 1223 (2009), reprinted with permission.

SUMMARY OF CONTENTS

TABLE OF CONTENTS

TABLE OF CASES

Principal cases are in bold type. Non-principal cases are in roman type. References are to Pages.

xxix

GLOSSARY OF ACRONYMS

2,4–D	2,4–dichlorophenoxyacetic acid
2,4,5–T	2,4,5–trichlorophenoxyacetic acid
AAIA	Airport and Airway Improvement Act
ADEC	Alaska Department of Enviromental Conservation
AID	Agency for International Development
ALJ	Administrative Law Judge
AMC	American Mining Congress
APA	Administrative Procedure Act
API	American Petroleum Institute
ARAR	applicable or relevant and appropriate requirements
AWD	American Waste Disposal
BACT	best available control technology
BAT	best available technology economically achievable
BAU	business as usual
BCT	best conventional pollutant control technology
BDAT	best demonstrated available technology
BDT	best demonstrated technology
BFPP	bona fide prospective purchaser
BOD	biological oxygen demand
BPT	best practicable control technology currently available
CAA	Clean Air Act
CAFE	Corporate Average Fuel Economy
CARB	California Air Resources Board
CASAC	Clean Air Scientific Advisory Council
CEM	continuous emission monitor
CEO	chief executive officer
CEQ	Council on Environmental Quality
CERCLA	Comprehensive Environmental Response, Compensation and Liability Act
CERCLIS	Comprehensive Environmental Response, Compensation and Liability Information System
CFCs	chloroflurocarbons
CFR	Code of Federal Regulations
CH_4	methane
CMA	Chemical Manufacturers Association
CML	chronic myelogenous leukemia
CMR	carcinogenic, mutagenic or toxic to reproduction
CO	carbon monoxide
CO_2	carbon dioxide
CRS	Congressional Research Service
CSDG	Chemclene Site Defense Group

CSR	chemical safety report
CTG	control technique guideline
CWA	Clean Water Act
CWMII	Chemical Waste Management of Indiana, Inc.
DDT	dichlorodiphenyltrichloroethane
DEC	Department of Environmental Conservation
DEP	New Jersey Department of Environmental Protection
DMR	discharge monitoring reports
DNA	deoxyribonucleic acid
DOE	Department of Energy
DOI	Department of Interior
DOT	Department of Transportation
DSD	Duales System Deutschland
DTF	Dithiocarbamate Task Force
DWS	County of Hawaii Department of Water Supply
EA	environmental assessment
EAB	Environmental Appeals Board
ECF	elemental chlorine free
EIS	environmental impact statement
ELI	Environmental Law Institute
EP	extraction procedure
EPA	Environmental Protection Agency
EPCA	Energy Policy and Conservation Act
EPCRA	Emergency Planning and Community Right-to-Know Act
ESA	Endangered Species Act
ETP	Eastern Tropical Pacific
EU	European Union
FAA	Federal Aviation Administration
FDA	Food and Drug Administration
FEIS	final environmental impact statement
FERC	Federal Energy Regulatory Commission
FDCA	Food, Drug and Cosmetic Act
FHA	Federal Highway Administration
FIFRA	Federal Insecticide, Fungicide, and Rodenticide Act
FIP	federal implementation plan
FMCSA	Federal Motor Carrier Safety Administration
FOE	Friends of the Earth
FONSI	finding of no significant impact
FPC	Federal Power Commission
FQPA	Food Quality Protection Act
FWPCA	Federal Water Pollution Control Act
FWS	Fish and Wildlife Service
GATT	General Agreement on Tariffs and Trade
GAO	Government Accountability Office
GDP	gross domestic product

GGS	giant garter snake
gpm	grams per mile
GtC	gigatons of carbon emitted
HCP	habitat conservation plan
HPV	high production volume
HSWA	Hazardous and Solid Waste Amendments of 1984
HUD	Department of Housing and Urban Development
ICJ	International Court of Justice
I/M	inspection and maintenance
IPCC	Intergovernmental Panel on Climate Change
ITP	incidental take permit
IWC	International Whaling Commission
LAER	lowest achievable emission rate
LDR	land disposal restriction
LHC	Lovely Harbor Company
LULU	locally undesirable land use
LFAS	low frequency active sonar
MCC	Minnesota Conservation Club
MCLs	maximum contaminant levels
MDNR	Missouri Department of Natural Resources
MEI	maximally exposed individual
MM & R	machinery manufacturing and rebuilding
MMPA	Marine Mammal Protection Act
MOA	memorandum of agreement
MSDS	material safety data sheet
MSW	municipal solid waste
NAAQS	National Ambient Air Quality Standard
NAFTA	North American Free Trade Agreement
NAHB	National Association of Home Builders
NBC	Natomas Basin Conservancy
NCP	National Contingency Plan
NED	New England Development Company
NEPA	National Environmental Policy Act
NHPA	National Historic Preservation Act
NIMBY	not in my back yard
NMFS	National Marine Fisheries Service
NPL	National Priorities List
NRC	National Research Council
NRDC	Natural Resources Defense Council
NO_2	nitrogen dioxide
NOAA	National Oceanic and Atmospheric Administration
NOI	notice of intent
NO_x	nitrogen oxides
NPDES	National Pollutant Discharge Elimination System
NSPS	new source performance standard

NSR	new source review
NWF	National Wildlife Federation
O_3	ozone
OIRA	Office of Information and, Regulatory Affairs
OMB	Office of Management and Budget
ONRW	outstanding national resource water
OPIC	Overseas Private Investment Corporation
OSH	Occupational Safety and Health
OSHA	Occupational Safety and Health Administration
OTC	organic toxicity characteristics
PA/SI	preliminary assessment/site inspection
PBT	persistent, bioaccumulative and toxic
PCBs	polychlorinated biphenyls
PEL	permissibly exposure limit
PM	particulate matter
PMN	premanufacture notification
POTW	publicly owned treatment works
PPMs	processes and production methods
PRPs	potentially responsible parties
PSD	prevention of significant deterioration
RACT	reasonably available control technology
RCRA	Resource Conservation and Recovery Act
REACH	Registration, Evaluation and Authorization of Chemicals
RECLAIM	Regional Clean Air Incentives Market
RFP	reasonable further progress
RI/FS	remedial investigation/feasibility study
ROD	record of decision
SARA	Superfund Amendments and Reauthorization Act of 1986
SCAQMD	South Coast Air Quality Management District
SCR	selective catalytic reduction
SCRAP	Students Challenging Regulatory Agency Procedures
SDWA	Safe Drinking Water Act
SEP	supplemental environmental project
SEC	Securities Exchange Commission
SFWMD	South Florida Water Management District
SIP	state implementation plan
SJVUAPCD	San Joaquin Valley Unified Air Pollution Control District
SLC	St. Lawrence Cement Company
SNUN	significant new use notice
SO_2	sulfur dioxide
SO_x	sulfur oxides
SWANCC	Solid Waste Agency of Northern Cook County
TCA	trichloroethane
TCE	trichloroethylene
TCF	total chlorine free

TCLP	Toxicity Characteristic Leaching Procedure
TCM	transportation control measure
TERP	Texas Emissions Reduction Plan
TKN	total Kjeldahl nitrogen
TMDL	total maximum daily load
TNRCC	Texas Natural Resources Conservation Commission
TPD	tons per day
TPH	total petroleum hydrocarbons
TRI	Toxic Release Inventory
TSCA	Toxic Substances Control Act
TSDF	treatment, storage and disposal facility
TSS	total suspended solids
TVA	Tennessee Valley Authority
USGS	United States Geological Survey
UWC	Universal Widget Company
vPvB	very persistent and very bioaccumulative
VDRs	vintage differentiated regulations
VMEP	Voluntary Mobile Emission Reduction Programs
VOCs	volatile organic compounds
WAC	Washington Administrative Code
WQS	water quality standards
WTO	World Trade Organization
ZEV	zero emission vehicle

PROBLEMS, CASES, AND READINGS

ENVIRONMENTAL POLICY LAW

PART I

INTRODUCTION

In this part we present the background themes and legal underpinnings of environmental law. Chapter 1 begins with an explanation of what sets environmental law apart from other areas of law, identifies tools from natural science and economics that can be used to address environmental conflicts, and highlights the role of values in determining what constitutes an environmental problem and what solutions may be available.

In Chapter 2 we look at the earliest legal tools for addressing environmental conflicts—common law tort actions. We examine both the shortcomings and the strengths of the common law, then consider its appropriate role in modern environmental conflict resolution.

Although the common law remains important, modern environmental law relies primarily on complex statutes administered by federal and state governmental agencies. Understanding environmental law, therefore, requires some exposure to the basics of administrative law. Chapter 3 provides that background.

Decisions affecting the environment are made by individuals and by government at all levels. Chapter 4 explores the allocation of regulatory power between federal and state and local governments.

CHAPTER ONE

ENVIRONMENTAL POLICY PERSPECTIVES

SECTION 1. WHAT IS ENVIRONMENTAL LAW?

The environment is where we live; it encompasses all our surroundings, physical, biological, and social. The physical environment includes such things as the air we breathe; the water we drink, grow crops with, and use in industrial processes; the soils that nourish our agriculture and support our buildings; and the storms, floods, and earthquakes that disrupt our lives. The biological environment includes the plants, animals, and micro-organisms that provide food, clothing, beauty, and companionship as well as disease and, occasionally, danger. Our surroundings also include the social and cultural environment—the form of our cities, the economic and ethnic diversity of their human population, and the relationships among individuals and groups.

Environmental law is the regulation of human activities affecting the physical and biological environment, "a set of rules for managing the interface between humans and * * * the larger ecological systems within which human social and economic systems are nested." Jonathan Baert Wiener, Law and the New Ecology: Evolution, Categories, and Consequences, 22 Ecology L.Q. 325, 337 (1995). It includes governmentally-imposed limitations on pollution of the air, water and land; requirements that past pollution be remediated; protection of various aspects of nature, including wetlands and endangered species; and allocation of natural resources among competing uses. Although not directly aimed at the social and cultural environment, environmental law inevitably affects those aspects of our surroundings as well. Choices we make about air pollution, for example, affect the cost of electricity, the types of automobiles available, and the compactness of our cities. Concerns about the socio-cultural environment may also determine how we choose to attack environmental problems. In deciding how and where to dispose of hazardous wastes, for instance, we may want not only to protect the air and water but also to treat communities equitably.

This casebook concentrates on federal environmental law, both to avoid becoming mired in the variable details of state programs and because federal initiatives have been the major driving force behind the great expansion of environmental regulation that began in the 1970s. It is important to keep in mind, however, that environmental law occurs at both larger and smaller geographic scales. A number of treaties and international agreements address environmental concerns that cross international boundaries, such as emissions of ozone-destroying chemicals and distribution of the waters of international rivers. State law operates in combination with federal law in many environmental contexts, imposing additional limitations as well as implementing federally-determined goals. Local governments also play an important role, one which originated as an outgrowth of their traditional regulation of land use and waste disposal. In recent years, state and local governments have been more active than the federal government in attempting to address new environmental problems, and indeed there have been a series of disputes over the authority of the states to step in where they believe the federal government is not doing enough.

Environmental law encompasses a wide range of problems, each of which could be addressed by multiple regulatory strategies. It is easy to get lost in the bewildering details of environmental regulation. The details are vitally important to the outcome of particular disputes, and anyone who wishes to become an environmental lawyer must learn how to master them. But to understand environmental policy, you must also see the larger picture. A good place to begin is to look for common characteristics of environmental problems that affect policy choices.

Richard J. Lazarus, Restoring What's Environmental About Environmental Law in the Supreme Court

47 UCLA L. Rev. 703, 744–48 (2000).

What makes environmental law distinctive is largely traceable to the nature of the injury that environmental protection law seeks to reduce, minimize, or sometimes prevent altogether. Environmental law is concerned, in the first instance, with impacts on the natural environment. Hence, although some environmental laws are concerned about human health effects, as are many other types of laws (e.g., food and drug, worker safety, Medicare, and food stamp programs), environmental law is concerned only about human health effects resulting from impacts on the natural environment. And, of course, many environmental laws are concerned only with those impacts and not with possible human health effects at all.

A common denominator, therefore, for environmental law is the *ecological injury* that serves as the law's threshold and often exclusive focus. That common denominator is also the primary source of the special challenges environmental law presents for lawmaking. Ecological injury has several recurring features that render its redress through law especially difficult. * * *

1. *Irreversible, Catastrophic, and Continuing Injury*: Environmental law is often concerned about the avoidance of irreversible, catastrophic results. The destruction of an aquifer upon which a community depends for drinking water, the erosion of soil necessary for farming that required

centuries to develop, and the destruction of the ozone layer are not possibilities to be lightly taken. Such potential downsides render enormously costly any errors in decision making. Yet, while errors are costly, so too can be delays in decision making. Even the best resolution is worth little if it is developed too late to prevent a chain of events inexorably leading to ecological disaster.

Finally, a closely related trait of some environmental injury is its continuing nature. Environmental law must address harm that increases over time. The harm is dynamic and not static in character. An oil spill addressed quickly may be confined to manageable dimensions. But conversely, if not quickly addressed, it may rapidly and exponentially increase in scope to overwhelming dimensions. Legal regimes that are inherently cautious and slow to react do not readily lend themselves to the quick action often necessary in the ecological context.

2. *Physically Distant Injury*: Ecological injury is often not physically confineable. Actions in one location may have substantial adverse effects in very distant locations. This may be because the pollutants actually travel from one place to another. Or it may be as the result of the adverse impacts of activities in one locale on a global commons, upon the viability of which many regions are dependent.

Long-range transportation of airborne pollutants is an example of the former. The ozone layer in the upper atmosphere exemplifies the transboundary implications of degradation of a commons resource, as the destruction of the ozone layer by activities in one part of the world can have serious environmental and human health effects in other parts of the world. Global warming presents a similar physical dimension.

For each, the associated challenges for the establishment of any legal regime are great, especially because the costs of control are imposed in one area and the benefits are enjoyed in a very different area. Such a distributional mismatch renders the adoption, implementation, and enforcement of the necessary transboundary legal rules very difficult. This is certainly true in the international arenas, but even far more localized spreadings of causes and effects between states and counties resist ready political resolutions.

3. *Temporally Distant Injury*: Much of the injury environmental law seeks to address is not imminent. Sometimes actions now may trigger the injury, but the injury itself will be realized only in the distant future. Sometimes the injury will be realized now and will increase, inexorably, over time. To the extent that the latter is occurring, this temporal character to some environmental injury may become, as a practical matter, irreversible and thus collapse into the first feature of ecological injury described above.

This temporal feature of ecological injuries poses challenges to legal doctrine and lawmaking analogous to those presented by the "physically distant" characteristic discussed above. The same distributional mismatch is presented but even more problematically, because the benefits to be enjoyed will generally inure only to future generations lacking any representation in current lawmaking fora. Such intergenerational effects raise issues regarding the propriety of "discounting" the value of future benefits (including human lives) in selecting environmental controls today. Even more fundamentally, however, the intergenerational dimension to ecological injury raises basic questions regarding the moral responsibilities that current generations have to safeguard the interests of future generations.

4. *Uncertainty and Risk*: There is much uncertainty associated with environmental injury, which poses even further challenges for lawmaking. The primary source of this uncertainty is the sheer complexity of the natural environment and, accordingly, how much is still unknown about it. This uncertainty expresses itself in our inability to know beforehand the environmental impact of certain actions. It equally undermines our ability to apprehend, after the fact, what precisely caused certain environmental impacts.

The inevitable upshot is that environmental laws that seek to prevent harm are directed to risk rather than to actual impact. It similarly means that environmental laws that seek to assign responsibility for harm that has already occurred are limited in their ability to do so.

Because, moreover, environmental law is concerned with risk, there is an inherently psychological dimension to the injury being redressed. The injury is not confined to that which occurs if the risk is itself realized. There is often psychological harm resulting from the risk itself, whether or not ever realized. For this same reason, by failing to address that mental dimension, one can increase the associated injury even if the numerical probability of the risk's physical realization remains the same.

5. *Multiple Causes*: Ecological injuries are rarely the product of a single action at an isolated moment of time. Putting aside the pervasive uncertainty issues, environmental harms are more typically the cumulative and synergistic result of multiple actions, often spread over significant time and space. This is primarily traceable to the sharing inherent in any common natural resource base, which is the object of so many simultaneous and sporadic actions over time and space.

6. *Noneconomic, Nonhuman Character*: Many of the ecological injuries resulting from environmental degradation are not readily susceptible to monetary valuation and have a distinctively nonhuman character. There is simply no readily available market analogue. The nonexclusive nature of the natural resources at stake is often one factor prompting resistance of valuation. Even more generally, the decision to protect the ecological interest in question may have been deliberately made notwithstanding any notion of economic value. It could, of course, be ultimately rooted in notions of uncertainty and concerns about adverse human health affects— e.g., the after-the-fact discovery that the DNA of a subspecies of fly would have cured the common cold. But it may instead be, and often is, based on the deeper notion that there are certain results—such as species extinction or resource destruction—that humankind should strive to avoid because they fall beyond its legitimate authority.

Other kinds of injury that resist ready monetary valuation are the adverse human health effects that can result from environmental degradation, although these valuation issues are shared by all laws designed to safeguard human health. For some economists, *all* human health effects of this kind must be susceptible to such valuation for the simple reason that tradeoffs are inevitably made in any allocation of limited societal resources. Nothing has infinite value, and each decision has opportunity costs related to opportunities thereby foregone. But some environmental laws reflect a very different philosophy, which posits that there are some adverse human health effects that are presumptively out of bounds for policymakers. For those who share that policy view, economic valuation and tradeoffs are therefore not legitimate topics for policy discussion.

NOTES AND QUESTIONS

1. *Characteristics of environmental problems.* What characteristics does Professor Lazarus identify as typical of environmental problems? Do all environmental problems share all these characteristics? Is any one characteristic common to all environmental problems? Do you agree with Lazarus that these characteristics make "redress through law especially difficult"? How do they complicate the search for legal solutions to environmental problems?

Can you think of any other characteristics that should be added to the list? Are there often many victims as well as many causes of environmental harm? How might that make legal redress more difficult to obtain? Another common feature, implicit in Lazarus' discussion of the non-economic, non-human character of environmental harms, is that environmental problems frequently implicate difficult tradeoffs between conflicting, deeply-held values. These values are explored in more detail in Section 4 below. It is worth thinking for a moment at this point, however, about the difficulty of arriving at public policy positions in the face of deep moral divisions in society. Consider, for example, the struggles over abortion, rights to die, and other issues that are the subject of strong moral beliefs. How should individual values be translated into public policy? Should a strong societal consensus be required before coercive measures are implemented? To what extent does such a consensus exist with respect to environmental problems?

2. *The precautionary principle.* As Professor Lazarus points out, two common features of environmental problems are the possibility of irreversible or catastrophic harm, and the existence of substantial uncertainty about the likelihood of such harm. One possible response to those conditions is application of the "precautionary principle," a general exhortation to proceed cautiously which can be framed in various ways. A classic statement of the precautionary principle is given in Principle 15 of the 1992 Rio Declaration on Environment and Development: "Where there are threats of serious or irreversible damage, lack of full scientific certainty shall not be used a reason for postponing cost-effective measures to prevent environmental degradation." The precautionary principle shifts the burden of proof from regulators to the proponents of environmentally risky activities.

The precautionary principle has many proponents, particularly in international law. It has been incorporated, in various forms, into a large number of treaties and international agreements. But it also has its critics.

Interpreted too broadly, the principle could lead to paralysis, since adverse impacts are rarely fully understood and proving the absence of harm is almost impossible. See Christopher D. Stone, Is There a Precautionary Principle?, 31 Envtl. L. Rep. 10790 (2001).

Who should bear the burden of proof in environmental decisions? Your answer is likely to depend on the relative values you assign to economic activity and the environment. The precautionary principle can be seen as a healthy recognition of our ignorance, designed to encourage additional inquiry and learning where the value of information is very high. It can also be seen as an unwarranted block on development, placing an unjustified premium on environmental values compared to others. Do we need a special rule for dealing with low or uncertain probabilities of catastrophic or irreversible harm? Are the tools used to evaluate ordinary risks (discussed further in Chapter 7) sufficient for extra-ordinary risks?

3. *Psychological harm.* Professor Lazarus argues that because "environmental law is concerned with risk, there is an inherently psychological dimension to the injury being redressed." Should environmental law concern itself with psychological harms? Consider first bystanders who inhale a chemical suspected to be toxic in the wake of a train derailment. Even if they never develop physical symptoms as a result, should they be compensated for their fear of cancer? Does it matter how rational that fear is, that is, whether and to what extent it is supported by evidence that the inhaled chemical may indeed cause cancer? Next, consider the desire of people who will never visit Alaska to have the Arctic National Wildlife Refuge remain pristine. Should that desire be factored into the decision to allow or forbid oil drilling in the refuge? If so, how should it be weighed against the economic needs, or even the esthetic preferences, of local residents?

SECTION 2.   INSIGHTS FROM ECOLOGY

Because the defining characteristic of environmental problems is injury, or threatened injury, to the non-human natural world, environmental law has long looked to ecology for insight and justification. In the 1960s and 1970s, a major inspiration for environmental law was the image of humankind upsetting the "balance of nature," with potentially disastrous results.

Ecology began to move away from that image many years ago. Law has only recently followed.

Judy L. Meyer, The Dance of Nature: New Concepts in Ecology

69 Chi.–Kent L. Rev. 875, 875–886 (1994).

I.   NATURAL SYSTEMS ARE OPEN AND CONTINUOUSLY CHANGING; THEY ARE NOT AT EQUILIBRIUM.

The classical paradigm in ecology conceives of an ideal ecosystem that is either at equilibrium, stable, or moving toward stability. * * * [E]arly ecological thinkers conceived of an ideal system that was stable, and they viewed nature as striving to achieve that ideal. In the field of plant ecology, individuals sought to identify the stable, self-perpetuating, climax community in an area and the well-defined stages leading to that climax. In the field of theoretical ecology, mathematical modelers solved their equations for the equilibrium condition.

Empirical data in several disciplines of ecology did not necessarily fit this classical paradigm. Natural communities were found to have multiple persistent states rather than a local climax, and there were multiple successional pathways—that is, several ways of getting there. Ecologists recognized that terrestrial and aquatic ecosystems in nature were frequently subjected to a wide range of disturbances including fires, windstorms, insect outbreaks, floods, and droughts. These disturbances alter succession and influence the distribution and abundance of species in the ecosystem.

* * * Discoveries like these have led to a paradigm shift in ecology.

The contemporary paradigm recognizes that ecosystems are open and not necessarily in equilibrium. It recognizes disturbance to be a natural and necessary part of ecosystems. It recognizes that systems are influenced by and can, in fact, be controlled by events occurring in neighboring or even distant ecosystems. The focus of the contemporary paradigm is on process rather than endpoint—on the trajectory of change rather than on the final endpoint. It recognizes historical contingency: the state of the system today depends on what happened yesterday as well as decades ago.

* * *

The classical view of nature is of a system striving for equilibrium, which implies that systems will maintain themselves in balance if they are protected from human disturbance. This view results in a very different conservation and management strategy than the strategy that would result from the non-equilibrium paradigm. * * * Rather than simply protecting the endpoint, we need to preserve the processes that generate the desired result. Disturbance * * * is an essential part of the process.

* * *

The lack of stable endpoints in nature has implications for how we write regulations and assess the impacts of human activity. Consider the issue of preserving water quality. Over the past decade, we have achieved considerable water quality improvement by strict end-of-pipe regulations. As we begin to tackle the problems of nonpoint pollution, it will be necessary to shift our regulatory emphasis to maintaining the ecological integrity of the rivers receiving the runoff. We cannot do this by establishing some threshold value of a metric or series of metrics that rivers have to achieve to be considered of high quality. Regardless of what we choose for this metric, it will vary with region, season, and year. * * *

Danger lurks in misinterpretation of the new paradigm: if change is a part of nature, then can we view anthropogenic change as just part of the natural way? Absolutely not; the new paradigm is not a license for environmental abuse. Anthropogenic change differs from natural change in both quality and rate. It is more rapid and often of a type never before experienced by natural ecosystems. Anthropogenic change is acceptable only if that change is within limits. * * * We can use natural rates of change to help set acceptable limits for anthropogenic change. One important role for ecological science is to determine natural rates of change—to understand intrinsic variation in ecological phenomena over long periods of time.

II. Linkages are Extensive in the Landscape * * *

* * * Our history of dealing with problems of eutrophication or acidification of lakes has taught us that activities in one part of the landscape greatly influence other parts. * * * Our laws need to recognize these natural connections in the landscape. As an example, we know that in many landscapes, streams and groundwater are linked physically, chemically and biologically. Yet * * * [i]n some cases, a pipe that pumps water from a stream is subject to a different set of laws than a pipe that pumps water from the ground a few feet from the channel. This makes little ecological sense. * * *

III. Indirect Effects can be as Significant as Direct Effects in Natural Systems.

This concept is another expression of the connectedness of ecological systems. Ecologists have long observed the importance of direct effects in ecosystems: for example, the response of lakes to nutrient additions from municipal wastewater. Yet it is not just these direct, "bottom-up" effects that influence aquatic ecosystems. "Top-down" and indirect effects are often equally important; altering higher trophic levels affects lower trophic levels in a "trophic cascade." A simple description of a lake food web illustrates how this trophic cascade can be manipulated by lake managers. In a lake, algae are fed on by herbivorous zooplankton, which are fed on by planktivorous (plankton eating) fish like bluegill, which become food for piscivorous fish like bass. As bass numbers increase (for example, from stocking), bluegill numbers decrease, large herbivorous zooplankton like Daphnia increase and graze heavily on algae, which then decrease.

* * * It is important that regulators and managers recognize the multiplicity of control points in natural systems. Controlling nutrient inputs is important, but the structure of the food web will influence the effectiveness of that control measure.

* * *

V. Organisms not only Adapt to the Environment, They Modify it.

* * * [W]e often forget how interdependent the physical and biological systems are on our planet. We readily accept a determining role for physical factors (for example, climatic influences on vegetation), but we forget the extent to which physical factors are influenced by biological activity. * * *

* * * A global circulation model does a decent job of predicting global patterns of temperature and rainfall when rates of evapotranspiration are what one would expect from a vegetated planet. But if the effects of plant evapotranspiration are removed from the model, it no longer provides reasonable predictions of global patterns of rainfall and temperature: it predicts no rain in Scotland and summer temperatures of forty-five degrees Celsius (one hundred and thirteen degrees Fahrenheit) in Chicago. Clearly the biosphere has a marked influence on our climate.

This example of global temperature and precipitation patterns brings me to my final point, which is that ecology is global. Humans are altering a highly interconnected biosphere, and the actions of another state or nation can have major implications for our environment in the United States. Even if United States resource management were fully enlightened and environmental laws rigorously enforced, we would not be guaranteed a sustainable biosphere. It is critical that environmental law maintain a global perspective.

NOTES AND QUESTIONS

1. *Insights from the "old ecology."* Despite its revolutionary nature, the non-equilibrium paradigm leaves undisturbed, and may even reinforce, several key concepts from the "old ecology." One is the idea of *interconnectedness*. Ecology, old and new, teaches that there are many important interconnections in the ecological landscape, not all of which are obvious at first glance. The flow of energy, water, and nutrients through ecosystems forms a complex web of linkages connecting communities and individuals across time, space, and species lines.

While it is not precisely true that everything is connected to everything else, there are enough connections that impacts can propagate across the landscape. A well-known example is the effect of removing the starfish *Pisaster ochraceus* from the rocky intertidal zone on the Pacific coast. The starfish is the top predator in these systems, preying on sessile, filter-feeding barnacles and mussels. In the presence of the starfish, these communities include some fifteen species. When starfish are removed from an area, the barnacles move in, and are eventually crowded out by the mussels. More surprisingly, the overall number of species in the intertidal community falls to eight, as algae are physically crowded out, and invertebrates cannot find either space or food. See R.T. Paine, Food Web Complexity and Species Diversity, 100 American Naturalist 65 (1966).

A second, related, concept is that of *complexity*. Ecosystems are complicated and, almost without exception, poorly understood. It is often difficult to predict with any confidence the effects, quantitative and qualitative, of perturbations. Prior to the starfish experiment described above, for example, scientists would not have expected starfish removal to dramatically alter the community's algal composition.

A third concept is *the importance of scale*, in terms of time, geography, and extent of impacts. While disturbance on one scale may be an integral part of ecosystem functioning, the same disturbance on a larger scale may drastically alter the system. For example, small fires distributed across a landscape may increase the diversity of habitats and, therefore, of species. A large fire in the same area, however, may have a very different effect, eliminating species that depend on forested habitat. As the scale of reserves shrinks, managing them to allow disturbance at an appropriate scale while at the same time preventing disturbance at a catastrophic scale becomes increasingly complicated. The temporal scale of disturbances is also important. Global temperatures have always fluctuated; the earth has gone through both warmer and cooler periods in the past. The ability of animals and plants to respond to temperature changes depends critically not only upon the ultimate extent of the change, but also upon the rapidity with which that change occurs.

2. *People and nature.* An enduring puzzle for environmental policy is how to deal with the dual status of people as 1) product of, and part of, nature; and 2) conqueror of nature, with far greater ability to control and alter nature than any other species. What implications did the old "balance-of-nature" paradigm have for the role of human beings in and with respect to nature? Precisely how do the implications of the non-equilibrium paradigm differ? Are human effects on other species or the natural world generally different from other "natural" effects in ways relevant to environmental policy and, in particular, the role of law?

SECTION 3.   INSIGHTS FROM ECONOMICS

A.   ALLOCATING SCARCE RESOURCES: EFFICIENCY AND MARKETS

Environmental problems are problems of competition among conflicting demands for scarce resources. Air pollution would not be a problem if the atmosphere were large enough to provide a sink for all the waste people want to vent to it, and at the same time provide clean air for all who wish to breathe it. The same is true of endangered species—if there were enough habitat to satisfy both development and conservation desires, there would be no endangered species controversies.

Given that natural resources are scarce compared to human demands, we must make choices about their allocation. Welfare economists tell us that under certain circumstances a well-functioning decentralized market, driven by the self-interested decisions of individual participants, will allocate scarce resources efficiently. Efficiency in this sense has a particular meaning. An efficient allocation maximizes individual preference satisfaction, aggregated across society. The most stringent definition of efficiency is "Pareto efficiency." An allocation is Pareto-efficient if any change in that allocation would reduce at least one person's preference satisfaction. A change that makes at least one person better off and no one worse off (because the winners compensate the losers) is "Pareto-superior." Perfect markets should achieve Pareto-efficient allocation of resources because transactions are voluntary. The fact that Seller is willing to sell, and Buyer to buy, a resource at a given price in a voluntary market exchange proves that Seller prefers the money to the resource, and Buyer prefers the resource to the money. Assuming an ideal market, their transaction makes both better off and no one else worse off. The market achieves levels of efficiency that would be very difficult to duplicate by central government regulation because individuals, who know their own preferences best, make the key decisions.

In order for a market to allocate resources efficiently, it must meet several criteria. Buyers and sellers must have *full information* about all relevant characteristics of the goods or services exchanged. There must be large numbers of buyers and sellers in the market, so that there is *no collusion or monopoly power*. There must be *no externalities*, that is costs or benefits of the transaction that are not paid or realized by the participants. There must be *well-defined and enforceable property rights* to the resources traded. Finally, *transaction costs* must be sufficiently low to allow mutually beneficial transactions to occur. See Steven C. Hackett, Environmental and Natural Resources Economics: Theory, Policy, and the Sustainable Society 33–34 (1998).

Reliance on the market to allocate environmental resources is subject to two major criticisms. The first, explored in Section 3(B), below, is that markets for environmental resources rarely satisfy the criteria for efficient allocation. The second, considered in Section 4, is that efficiency is not the only, or necessarily the highest, societal goal.

B. MARKET FAILURE AND MARKET CORRECTION

Garrett Hardin, The Tragedy of the Commons

162 Science 1243, 1244–45, 1247 (1968).

The Tragedy of Freedom in a Commons

The tragedy of the commons develops in this way. Picture a pasture open to all. It is to be expected that each herdsman will try to keep as many cattle as possible on the commons. * * *

As a rational being, each herdsman seeks to maximize his gain. Explicitly or implicitly, more or less consciously, he asks, "What is the utility *to me* of adding one more animal to my herd?" This utility has one negative and one positive component.

1.   The positive component is a function of the increment of one animal. Since the herdsman receives all the proceeds from the sale of the additional animal, the positive utility is nearly + 1.

2.   The negative component is a function of the additional overgrazing created by one more animal. Since, however, the effects of overgrazing are shared by all the herdsmen, the negative utility for any particular decision-making herdsman is only a fraction of–1.

Adding together the component partial utilities, the rational herdsman concludes that the only sensible course for him to pursue is to add another animal to his herd. And another; and another.... But this is the conclusion reached by each and every rational herdsman sharing a commons. Therein is the tragedy. Each man is locked into a system that compels him to increase his herd without limit—in a world that is limited. Ruin is the destination toward which all men rush, each pursuing his own best interest in a society that believes in the freedom of the commons. Freedom in a commons brings ruin to all.

* * *

In an approximate way, the logic of the commons has been understood for a long time, perhaps since the discovery of agriculture or the invention of private property in real estate. But it is understood mostly only in special cases which are not sufficiently generalized. Even at this late date, cattlemen leasing national land on the western ranges demonstrate no more than an ambivalent understanding, in constantly pressuring federal authorities to increase the head count to the point where overgrazing produces erosion and weed-dominance. Likewise, the oceans of the world continue to suffer from the survival of the philosophy of the commons. Maritime nations still respond automatically to the shibboleth of the "freedom of the seas." Professing to believe in the "inexhaustible resources of the oceans," they bring species after species of fish and whales closer to extinction.

The national parks present another instance of the working out of the tragedy of the commons. At present, they are open to all, without limit. The parks themselves are limited in extent—there is only one Yosemite Valley—whereas population seems to grow without limit. The values that visitors seek in the parks are steadily eroded. Plainly, we must soon cease to treat the parks as commons or they will be of no value to anyone.

What shall we do? We have several options. We might sell them off as private property. We might keep them as public property, but allocate the right to enter them. The allocation might be on the basis of wealth, by the use of an auction system. It might be on the basis of merit, as defined by some agreed-upon standards. It might be by lottery. Or it might be on a first-come, first-served basis, administered to long queues. These, I think, are all the reasonable possibilities. They are all objectionable. But we must choose—or acquiesce in the destruction of the commons that we call our national parks.

Pollution

In a reverse way, the tragedy of the commons reappears in problems of pollution. Here it is not a question of taking something out of the commons, but of putting something in—sewage, or chemical, radioactive, and heat wastes into water; noxious and dangerous fumes into the air; and distracting and unpleasant advertising signs into the line of sight. The calculations of utility are much the same as before. The rational man finds that his share of the cost of the wastes he discharges into the commons is less than the cost of purifying his wastes before releasing them. Since this is true for everyone, we are locked into a system of "fouling our own nest," so long as we behave only as independent, rational, free-enterprisers.

The tragedy of the commons as a food basket is averted by private property, or something formally like it. But the air and waters surrounding us cannot readily be fenced, and so the tragedy of the commons as a cesspool must be prevented by different means, by coercive laws or taxing devices that make it cheaper for the polluter to treat his pollutants than to discharge them untreated. We have not progressed as far with the solution of this problem as we have with the first. Indeed, our particular concept of private property, which deters us from exhausting the positive resources of the earth, favors pollution. The owner of a factory on the bank of a stream—whose property extends to the middle of the stream—often has difficulty seeing why it is not his natural right to muddy the waters flowing past his door. The law, always behind the times, requires elaborate stitching and fitting to adapt it to this newly perceived aspect of the commons.

* * *

Mutual Coercion Mutually Agreed Upon

The social arrangements that produce responsibility are arrangements that create coercion, of some sort. Consider bank-robbing. The man who takes money from a bank acts as if the bank were a commons. How do we prevent such action? Certainly not by trying to control his behavior solely by a verbal appeal to his sense of responsibility. * * *

The morality of bank robbing is particularly easy to understand because we accept complete prohibition of this activity. We are willing to say "Thou shalt not rob banks," without providing for exceptions. But temperance also can be created by coercion. Taxing is a good coercive device. To keep downtown shoppers temperate in their use of parking space we introduce parking meters for short periods, and traffic fines for longer ones. We need not actually forbid a citizen to park as long as he wants to; we need merely make it increasingly expensive for him to do so. * * *

* * * To many, the word coercion implies arbitrary decisions of distant and irresponsible bureaucrats; but this is not a necessary part of its meaning. The only kind of coercion I recommend is mutual coercion, mutually agreed upon by the majority of the people affected.

To say that we mutually agree to coercion is not to say that we are required to enjoy it, or even to pretend we enjoy it. Who enjoys taxes? We all grumble about them. But we accept compulsory taxes because we recognize that voluntary taxes would favor the conscienceless. We institute and (grumblingly) support taxes and other coercive devices to escape the horror of the commons. * * *

The Tragedy of the Commons illustrates the consequences of market failure. The grazing commons in Hardin's essay violates two of the requirements for efficient markets: it lacks well-defined property rights, and it permits externalization of costs. These two flaws are connected. In the absence of defined, enforceable limits on each herder's rights to the commons, herders can externalize a portion of the costs of their use, while internalizing the full benefits. As a result, every herder has an incentive to overutilize the resource.

The commons example can be generalized to all "collective" or "public" goods, defined as goods which cannot be supplied to one person without also making them available to others. The classic example of a collective good is national defense, since one person cannot be protected against a missile strike without also protecting her neighbors. Clean air is another obvious example—if the air is healthy for one person, it is necessarily healthy for others nearby. Can you think of other environmental collective goods?

Because the supply of collective goods cannot be limited to those who pay, the market system breaks down. No one consumer will pay the full price of the good, because no one consumer can realize the full benefit. Moreover, individual consumers expecting that others will pay may rationally decide to "free ride," paying nothing but expecting to enjoy the benefits because others will pay. If everyone thinks that way no one will pay, and the good simply will not be supplied. Collective goods are therefore overconsumed and undersupplied in the market.

How can collective good problems like the tragedy of the commons be solved? What solutions does Hardin suggest in the national park context? In the pollution context? Why are those suggestions different?

Because the problem is one of market failure, the solution is societal intervention in some form to correct that failure. Intervention can take many different forms.

1. *Command-and-control regulation.* The government (or any other authority with the power to impose sanctions) can step in to create enforceable standards for use of or access to the commons. In the pollution context, the government sets standards for allowable emissions. To be effective, those standards must be backed by mechanisms for detecting and punishing violations, which may impose significant administrative costs.

Command-and-control is the predominant strategy employed by our current environmental law system. Environmentalists have traditionally favored the command-and-control system, while economists have long questioned the efficiency of centrally-determined, uniform standards.

2. *Privatizing the commons.* Property owners who realize both the costs and the benefits associated with caring for and exploiting resources have incentives to use those resources efficiently. If the grazing commons is divided into individual property allotments, from which the owner can exclude other herders' livestock, the perverse incentives to over-exploit the resource should disappear. This solution is promoted by advocates of "free-

market environmentalism." See generally Terry L. Anderson & Donald R. Leal, Free Market Environmentalism (2001).

Of course, some resources are more easily privatized than others. Although it certainly entails costs, fencing portions of a pasture is straightforward. Dividing the air into individual allotments seems much more difficult. With some ingenuity, though, it can be done, at least for some purposes. The Clean Air Act shows how, creating a system of tradable permits for emissions of SO_2, a major cause of acid rain. The program essentially sets a cap on the extent to which power plants and other major sources can use the atmosphere to dispose of their SO_2, allocates the allowable SO_2 increment among existing sources, and allows those sources to trade with one another, setting up a market for SO_2 emissions.

Clear, secure, tradable property rights allow a private market, with the benefits of decentralized decisionmaking, to flourish. Under a command-and-control system, all polluters must install the same equipment or control pollution to the same level. Tradable permits allow those able to control pollution at less cost to profit from that ability by selling their excess credits to those less able to reduce emissions. If the market works well, the same level of pollution control will be reached at less cost than under a command-and-control regime.

This type of market also allows environmentalists to satisfy their preferences for clean air, provided they are willing to pay the going price. They can purchase credits in order to retire them, thereby reducing allowable emissions. Various nonprofit organizations, including environmental law societies at several law schools, have taken advantage of this market opportunity.

3. *Economic incentives.* Instead of establishing standards and issuing permits, government can force users of collective goods to bear the costs of their actions through taxes or fines. Taxes have the drawback of not assuring a specific level of control. It can also be difficult to determine the appropriate amount of a tax or charge if the goal is to induce specific levels of behavior modification. But taxes offer the advantage of facilitating individually adaptive responses much the same way that private rights do. Firms able to reduce emissions pay lower taxes, and therefore enjoy a competitive advantage. Investment and innovation in pollution control is directly rewarded.

Fines, taxes, and fees are negative economic incentives, designed to force the producers of environmental costs to internalize those costs in their decisions. Government can also use positive economic incentives, subsidies, to help the producers of environmental benefits internalize the value of those benefits. Environmental subsidies include federal payments to local governments for wastewater treatment plants and tax credits for pollution control equipment.

C. COST-BENEFIT ANALYSIS

To many economists, the proper goal of regulation is correction of market failure or, put another way, achievement of the efficient distribution of resources in the absence of an ideal market. Cost-benefit analysis provides, in theory at least, an objective mechanism for determining whether a proposed regulation is efficient.

The concept of efficiency employed in cost-benefit analysis differs from the Pareto efficiency described earlier. Without a market, it can be exceedingly difficult to ensure that no one is made worse off by a regulation (economists would say the transaction costs of arranging for winners to compensate losers can be very high). Recognizing that, economists have developed an alternative, less stringent, efficiency criterion known as Kaldor–Hicks efficiency. An allocation decision satisfies this criterion if the aggregate gains in preference satisfaction exceed the aggregate losses. A change that imposes heavy losses on a small number of people will nonetheless be efficient in the Kaldor–Hicks sense if it provides a very small benefit to a large number of people.

While this might seem unfair at first glance, it has substantial intuitive appeal if resources seem to be inappropriately distributed, but transaction costs or other factors prevent the market from redistributing them efficiently. Consider, for example, land reform in nations where ownership is concentrated in a small elite class. Government redistribution of land to the larger peasant class would be Kaldor–Hicks efficient if the new owners would value the land more highly than the old ones. Yet lack of resources, and perhaps social taboos, would prevent the peasants from ever obtaining the land in the market. Under the circumstances, it may seem appropriate for government to step in and transfer the land to the peasants, particularly if the wealthy owners are allowing the land to sit idle. It may not even seem unfair if the government does not compensate the gentry for the loss of their land.

Cost-benefit analysis tests for Kaldor–Hicks efficiency by comparing the total societal costs of a policy with the total societal benefits, using dollars as the common metric. Future costs and benefits are typically *discounted* to present value. When both costs and benefits are strictly monetary, discounting is non-controversial (although there may be fierce arguments about the discount rate). It simply reflects the uncontroverted fact that money received later is worth less than money received earlier. If you doubt that, consider being asked to choose between getting $500 today and getting $500 five years from now. Most people would opt for the former without hesitation. Discounting becomes highly controversial, however, when applied to non-monetary benefits such as years of life saved by restricting use of a toxic chemical, or a river left free-running by not building a dam. Will those be worth more or less in the future than today? The answer is not obvious: we could not "invest" a river today to generate more rivers in the future. On the other hand, keeping the river free may cost us money we could otherwise invest, or foreclose opportunities to generate money.

The discounting decision, and the choice of discount rate, often have enormous impacts on the outcome of cost-benefit analyses because environmental costs and benefits are typically realized over long time frames.

> [T]he present value of a benefit of $1 million to be received in ten years from now is $900,000 if one uses a 1% discount rate, but only $390,000 if one applies a 10% discount rate. Discounted at 10%, one dollar received fifty years from now is worth slightly less than a penny today—a difference of two orders of magnitude. Even more dramatic, "if one discounts present world GNP [gross national product] over two hundred years at 5% per annum, it is worth only a few hundred thousand dollars, the price of a good apartment. Discounted at 10%, it is equivalent to a used car."

Lisa Heinzerling, Discounting Our Future, 34 Land & Water L. Rev. 39, 44 (1999), quoting Geoffrey Heal, Interpreting Sustainability, in Sustainability: Dynamics and Uncertainty 7 (Graciela Chichilnisky et al., eds., 1998).

Like discounting, cost-benefit analysis itself is straightforward and non-controversial when both costs and benefits are readily measured in dollars. But in the environmental context, many costs and benefits are not readily monetizable. Many, perhaps most, environmental amenities are not traded in any existing market, and many people are uncomfortable with assigning a monetary price to those amenities. What is the value, for example, of a clean river, an unspoiled view, or healthy air? Many people would intuitively describe those things as priceless.

Nonetheless, economists have developed techniques for assigning prices to a wide range of environmental amenities. The normative objections to using such prices to make policy decisions are considered below, in Section 4. Setting those aside for the moment, a major technical challenge remains. How can we estimate the monetary value of environmental goods and services for which no market exists? *Contingent valuation* and *hedonic pricing* are two techniques economists have developed for this purpose. We describe them very briefly here. For a more detailed explanation, see Steven C. Hackett, Environmental and Natural Resources Economics: Theory, Policy, and the Sustainable Society 110–117 (1998).

Contingent valuation relies on surveys asking respondents whether they would be willing to pay specified amounts to ensure a specific policy outcome. For example, to determine the value of protecting salmon runs from extinction, residents of the Pacific northwest might be asked if they would pay $5, $50, or $500 annually to protect salmon. Contingent valuation has been criticized on several grounds, including: that people who have never thought about the question may simply pick an answer at random, revealing little about their true preferences; that people may not be prepared to express their environmental values in terms of money; and that people may overstate their willingness to pay because they do not actually have to come up with the money.

Hedonic pricing uses information from actual markets to infer the value of environmental amenities. Analysts can compare the value of parcels of land as closely matched as possible except for one characteristic, such as scenic beauty, air quality, or access to environmental amenities. The price differential between the parcels should reflect the value of the environmental characteristic. This method has the advantage of reflecting real market behavior, but it cannot be applied to many environmental goods. In particular, it cannot reflect existence values, the extent to which people care about aspects of the environment they do not expect ever to use. No real market can be used to estimate the value of the Arctic National Wildlife Refuge to residents of the continental United States who do not wish to go to Alaska but enjoy knowing that the refuge exists in a relatively pristine condition.

Assuming the technical challenges can be surmounted, many environmentalists remain uncomfortable about using cost-benefit analysis to evaluate environmentally protective regulations. Critics of cost-benefit analysis are skeptical that environmental values can, or should, be monetized. They fear that benefits for which no monetary value can be generated will be effectively ignored in the decision. They also point out that cost-benefit analysis is as much art as science, leaving a great deal of room for subjective guesses. As Professor Daniel A. Farber points out: "Except in extreme cases, the result of a cost-benefit analysis often turns on a series of discretionary judgments; competent, reasonable analysts can come up with quite different but equally defensible answers." Daniel A. Farber, Revitalizing Regulation, 91 Mich. L. Rev. 1278, 1282 (1993). Particularly when it is carried out by the Office of Management and Budget, an agency widely regarded during the Reagan–Bush years as hostile to regulation, environmentalists suspect that cost-benefit analysis may be slanted against environmental protection.

D.   THE INTERFACE OF ECONOMICS AND ECOLOGY: ECOSYSTEM SERVICES

In addition to a range of material goods, nature supplies humanity with an array of useful services, such as waste decomposition and detoxification, air and water purification, crop pollination, pest control, and flood control. The importance of these ecosystem services was recognized long ago; the national forest system was established in the late 19th century not only to ensure the nation a lasting timber supply, but also to protect water supplies and reduce flood danger.

Recently, ecologists and economists have worked to bring ecosystem services systematically into environmental policy decisions. This effort may help increase public awareness of ecosystem functions which are easily taken for granted. Because ecosystem services are collective goods for which markets do not currently exist and cannot easily be created, however, properly valuing them in environmental decisions is extraordinarily difficult. In addition to facing the usual difficulties of non-market valuation, it requires a level of ecological understanding that may be difficult to obtain. For discussions of the valuation problem, see, e.g., Rudolph S. DeGroot et al., A Typology for the Classification, Description and Valuation of Ecosystem Functions, Goods and Services, 41 Ecological Economics 393 (2002); Gretchen C. Daily et al., The Value of Nature and the Nature of Value, 289 Science 395 (2000); R.K. Turner et al., Ecosystem Services Value, Research Needs, and Policy Relevance: A Commentary, 25 Ecological

Economics 61 (1998); Robert Costanza et al., The Value of the World's Ecosystem Services and Natural Capital, 387 Nature 253 (1997).

Despite the challenges, many economists, ecologists, and policy analysts are enthusiastic about the ecosystem services approach. As one group explains:

> An explicit ecosystem services perspective provides two obvious benefits. The first is political. Understanding the role of ecosystem services powerfully justifies why habitat preservation and biodiversity conservation are vital, though often overlooked, policy objectives. While a wetland surely provides existence and option values to some people, the benefits provided by the wetland's nutrient retention and flood protection services are both universal and undeniable. Tastes may differ over beauty, but they are in firm accord over the high costs of polluted water and flooded homes.

> The second benefit is instrumental. Efforts to capture the value of ecosystem services may spur institutional designs and market mechanisms that effectively promote environmental protection at the local, regional, national, and international levels. To realize this potential, however, we must first create market mechanisms and institutions that can capture and maximize service values. If given the opportunity, natural systems can, in many cases, quite literally "pay their way." The key challenge is how to make this happen.

James Salzman, Barton H. Thompson & Gretchen Daily, Protecting Ecosystem Services: Science, Economics, and Law, 20 Stan. Envtl. L.J. 309, 312 (2001).

Not everyone shares this enthusiasm, however. Knowledge of ecosystem services can provide greater accuracy to cost-benefit determinations, but does not necessarily overcome skepticism about whether cost-benefit analysis is an appropriate basis for environmental policy decisions. As one ecologist has recently put it:

> [M]arket-based mechanisms for conservation are not a panacea for our current conservation ills. If we mean to make significant and long-lasting gains in conservation, we must strongly assert the primacy of ethics and aesthetics in conservation. We must act quickly to redirect much of the effort now being devoted to the commodification of nature back towards instilling a love for nature in more people. . . .

> As conservation tolls, ecosystem services are limited in four fundamental ways. First, the logic of ecosystem-service-based conservation rests on the implicit assumption that the biosphere is benevolent—that it provides us with useful services and protects us from malevolent abiotic forces such as hurricanes, floods and rising temperatures. This reasoning ignores basic ecology . . . There are myriad examples of what might be labelled "ecosystem disservices." . . .

> Second, although most conservationists would argue that nature should be conserved in perpetuity, the strength and direction of market

forces that are now being called upon to motivate nature conservation are anything but perpetual. . . .

Third, conservation based on ecosystem services commits the folly of betting against human ingenuity. The entire history of technology and human "progress" is one of producing artificial substitutes for what we once obtained from nature, or domesticating once-natural services. . . .

Lastly, although it has been suggested that in most cases the services that come from nature are valuable enough to make conservation profitable, making money and protecting nature are all too often mutually exclusive goals. Take the case of Africa's Lake Victoria, where the introduction of the invasive Nile perch (*Lates niloticus*) contributed significantly to the decimation of local biodiversity while dramatically boosting the economic value of the lake. Local people profiting from trade in the fish hail its introduction as a success, whereas biologists have condemned the event as "the most catastrophic extinction episode of recent history."

Douglas J. McCauley, Selling Out on Nature, 443 Nature 27, 27–28 (2006).

NOTES AND QUESTIONS

1. *Cost-benefit analysis in agency decisions.* As we shall see in subsequent chapters, some environmental laws forbid consideration of costs in setting environmental standards. In a world of scarce resources, can a policy forbidding consideration of costs ever be justified? Does Congress truly expect agencies to impose regulations that will wreak economic havoc?

Since 1981, federal agencies have been required by executive order to prepare cost-benefit analyses of major regulations. Executive Order 12,866, issued by Bill Clinton and currently in effect (with some modifications), mandates that each agency "assess both the costs and the benefits of the intended regulation and, recognizing that some costs and benefits are difficult to quantify, propose or adopt a regulation only upon a reasoned determination that the benefits of the intended regulation justify its costs." Exec. Ord. 12,866, § 1(b)(6) (Sept. 30, 1993).

Executive Order 13,563, issued by President Obama (76 Fed. Reg. 3821, Jan. 18, 2011) supplements E.O. 12,866. In addition to reaffirming the principles from the earlier order that regulations should be adopted only when their benefits justify their costs and that they should be tailored "to impose the least burden on society consistent with obtaining regulatory objectives," the 2011 executive order calls on agencies to "consider regulatory approaches that reduce burdens and maintain flexibility and freedom of choice for the public," including warnings and information disclosure mandates, as alternatives to prescriptive regulation.

The executive orders requiring cost-benefit analysis do not purport to alter agencies' statutory responsibilities or authority, nor could they do so. If a statute forbids consideration of costs, the agency must prepare a cost-benefit analysis but may not base its regulatory decision on that analysis. Is there any point to requiring cost-benefit analysis in that situation? Where the applicable statute does not forbid consideration of costs, what role should cost-benefit analysis play in regulatory decisions? Should cost-benefit analysis be required? Should it be determinative? Can you think of circumstances under which it would be appropriate to adopt a regulation that failed a cost-benefit analysis?

2. *Is market failure necessary to justify regulation?* President George W. Bush twice modified Executive Order 12,866. The second amendment, subsequently revoked by President Obama, added the following requirement: "Each agency shall identify in writing the specific market failure (such as externalities, market power, lack of information) or other specific problem that it intends to address (including where applicable, the failures of public institutions) that warrant new agency action, as well as assess the significance of that problem, to enable assessment of whether any new regulation is warranted." Exec. Ord. 13,422, § 1(a) (Jan. 18, 2007), revoked by Exec. Ord. 13,497 (Jan. 30, 2009). Should agencies be required to identify a relevant market failure prior to issuing new regulations? What else (if anything) might justify government intervention?

3. *Discounting and obligations to future generations.* Should discounting be applied to non-monetary costs and benefits in evaluating environmental policy? Do obligations to future generations argue for or against discounting? For discussion of these issues, see David Weisbach & Cass R. Sunstein, Climate Change and Discounting the Future: A Guide for the Perplexed, 27 Yale L. & Pol'y Rev. 433 (2009); Symposium, Intergenerational Equity and Discounting, 74 U. Chi. L. Rev. 1 (2007); Lisa Heinzerling, Discounting Our Future, 34 Land & Water L. Rev. 39 (1999); Richard L. Revesz, Environmental Regulation, Cost-benefit Analysis, and the Discounting of Human Lives, 99 Col. L. Rev. 941 (1999); Daniel A. Farber & Paul A. Hemmersbaugh, the Shadow of the Future: Discount Rates, Later Generations, and the Environment, 46 Vand. L. Rev. 267 (1993).

SECTION 4. THE ROLE OF VALUES

Ecology and economics are useful tools for understanding the natural world and human behavior, both integral aspects of environmental problems. They are widely accepted, by persons on both sides of the political spectrum, as means to improve the odds of achieving societally-determined ends. When their practitioners tout them, implicitly or explicitly, as methods for determining societal goals, however, they become controversial. A key reason for the continuing controversy over environmentally protective regulation is that it implicates a fundamental clash of deeply held values. As the following excerpts illustrate, ecologists and economists often find themselves on opposite sides of this value divide.

Aldo Leopold, A Sand County Almanac: With other Essays on Conservation From Round River

218–240 (Oxford University Press 1949, 1977, 1981).

The first ethics dealt with the relation between individuals; the Mosaic Decalogue is an example. Later accretions dealt with the relation between the individual and society. The Golden Rule tries to integrate the individual to society; democracy to integrate social organization to the individual.

There is as yet no ethic dealing with man's relation to land and to the animals and plants which grow upon it. * * * The land-relation is still strictly economic, entailing privileges but not obligations.

The extension of ethics to this third element in human environment is, if I read the evidence correctly, an evolutionary possibility and an ecological necessity. * * *

All ethics so far evolved rest upon a single premise: that the individual is a member of a community of interdependent parts. His instincts prompt him to compete for his place in the community, but his ethics prompt him also to co-operate (perhaps in order that there may be a place to compete for).

The land ethic simply enlarges the boundaries of the community to include soils, waters, plants, and animals, or collectively, the land.

This sounds simple: do we not already sing our love for and obligation to the land of the free and the home of the brave? Yes, but just what and whom do we love? Certainly not the soil, which we are sending helter-skelter downriver. Certainly not the waters, which we assume have no function except to turn turbines, float barges, and carry off sewage. Certainly not the plants, of which we exterminate whole communities without batting an eye. Certainly not the animals, of which we have already extirpated many of the largest and most beautiful species. A land ethic of course cannot prevent the alteration, management, and use of these "resources," but it does affirm their right to continued existence, and, at least in spots, their continued existence in a natural state.

In short, a land ethic changes the role of *Homo sapiens* from conqueror of the land-community to plain member and citizen of it. It implies respect for his fellow-members, and also respect for the community as such.

* * *

One basic weakness in a conservation system based wholly on economic motives is that most members of the land community have no economic value. Wildflowers and songbirds are examples. Of the 22,000 higher plants and animals native to Wisconsin, it is doubtful whether more than 5 per cent can be sold, fed, eaten, or otherwise put to economic use. Yet these creatures are members of the biotic community, and if (as I believe) its stability depends on its integrity, they are entitled to continuance.

When one of these non-economic categories is threatened, and if we happen to love it, we invent subterfuges to give it economic importance. At the beginning of the century songbirds were supposed to be disappearing. Ornithologists jumped to the rescue with some distinctly shaky evidence to the effect that insects would eat us up if birds failed to control them. The evidence had to be economic in order to be valid.

It is painful to read these circumlocutions today. We have no land ethic yet, but we have at least drawn nearer the point of admitting that birds should continue as a matter of biotic right, regardless of the presence or absence of economic advantage to us.

* * *

To sum up: a system of conservation based solely on economic self-interest is hopelessly lopsided. It tends to ignore, and thus eventually to eliminate, many elements in the land community that lack commercial value, but that are (as far as we know) essential to its healthy functioning. It assumes, falsely, I think, that the economic parts of the biotic clock will function without the uneconomic parts. * * *

A land ethic, then, reflects the existence of an ecological conscience, and this in turn reflects a conviction of individual responsibility for the health of the land. Health is the capacity of the land for self-renewal. Conservation is our effort to understand and preserve this capacity.

* * *

The "key-log" which must be moved to release the evolutionary process for an ethic is simply this: quit thinking about decent land-use as solely an economic problem. Examine each question in terms of what is ethically and esthetically right, as well as what is economically expedient. A thing is right when it tends to preserve the integrity, stability, and beauty of the biotic community. It is wrong when it tends otherwise.

William F. Baxter, People or Penguins: The Case for Optimal Pollution

4–12 (Columbia University Press 1974).

* * * Recently scientists have informed us that use of DDT in food production is causing damage to the penguin population. For the present purposes let us accept that assertion as an indisputable scientific fact. The scientific fact is often asserted as if the correct implication—that we must stop agricultural use of DDT—followed from the mere statement of the fact of penguin damage. But plainly it does not follow if my criteria are employed.

My criteria are oriented to people, not penguins. Damage to penguins, or sugar pines, or geological marvels is, without more, simply irrelevant. One must go further, by my criteria, and say: Penguins are important because people enjoy seeing them walk about rocks; and furthermore, the well-being of people would be less impaired by halting use of DDT than by giving up penguins. * * *

[T]his attitude does not portend any massive destruction of nonhuman flora and fauna, for people depend on them in many obvious ways, and they will be preserved because and to the degree that humans do depend on them.

* * *

I reject the proposition that we *ought* to respect the "balance of nature" or to "preserve the environment" unless the reason for doing so, express or implied, is the benefit of man.

I reject the idea that there is a "right" or "morally correct" state of nature to which we should return. The word "nature" has no normative connotation. Was it "right" or "wrong" for the earth's crust to heave in contortion and create mountains and seas? Was it "right" for the first amphibian to crawl up out of the primordial ooze? Was it "wrong" for plants to reproduce themselves and alter the atmospheric composition in favor of oxygen? For animals to alter the atmosphere in favor of carbon dioxide both by breathing oxygen and eating plants? No answers can be given to these questions because they are meaningless questions.

* * *

From the fact that there is no normative definition of the natural state, it follows that there is no normative definition of clean air or pure water— hence no definition of polluted air—or of pollution—except by reference to the needs of man. The "right" composition of the atmosphere is one which has some dust in it and some lead in it and some hydrogen sulfide in it— just those amounts that attend a sensibly organized society thoughtfully and knowledgeably pursuing the greatest possible satisfaction for its human members.

* * *

People enjoy watching penguins. They enjoy relatively clean air and smog-free vistas. Their health is improved by relatively clean water and air. Each of these benefits is a type of good or service. As a society we would be well advised to give up one washing machine if the resources that would have gone into that washing machine can yield greater human satisfaction when diverted into pollution control. We should give up one hospital if the resources thereby freed would yield more human satisfaction when devoted to elimination of noise in our cities. And so on, trade-off by trade-off, we should divert our productive capacities from the production of existing goods and services to the production of a cleaner, quieter, more pastoral nation up to—and no further than—the point at which we value more highly the next washing machine or hospital that we would have to do without than we value the next unit of environmental improvement that the diverted resources would create.

Mark Sagoff, We Have Met the Enemy and He Is Us *or* Conflict and Contradiction in Environmental Law

12 Envtl. L. 283, 283–308 (1982).

In a course I teach on environmental ethics, I ask students to read the Supreme Court opinion in *Sierra Club v. Morton* [405 U.S. 727 (1972)]. In that case environmentalists challenged a decision by the Forest Service to lease the Mineral King Valley, a wilderness area in the middle of Sequoia National Park, to Walt Disney Enterprises, to develop a ski resort. But let the Court describe the facts:

> The final Disney plan, approved by the Forest Service in January 1969, outlines a $35 million complex of motels, restaurants, swimming pools, parking lots, and other structures designed to accommodate 14,000 visitors daily.... Other facilities, including ski lifts, ski trails, a cog-assisted railway, and utility installations, are to be constructed on the mountain slopes and in other parts of the valley.... To provide access to the resort, the State of California proposes to construct a highway 20 miles in length. A section of this road would traverse Sequoia National Park, as would a proposed high-voltage power line....

I asked how many of the students had visited the wilderness at Mineral King or thought they would visit it as long as it remained a wilderness. No one raised a hand. Why not? Too many mosquitoes, someone said. Not enough movies, said another. Another offered to explain in technical detail the difference between chillblain and trench foot. * * *

Then I asked how many students would like to visit the Mineral King Valley if it were developed in the way Disney planned. Every hand went up. * * *

I brought the students to order by asking if they thought the government did the right thing in giving Disney Enterprises a lease to develop Mineral King. I asked them, in other words, whether they thought that environmental policy, at least in this instance, should be based on the principle of maximizing the satisfaction of consumer demand. Was there a connection between what the students as individuals wanted for themselves and what they thought we should do, collectively, as a nation?

The response was unanimous, visceral, and grim. All of the students believed that the Disney plan was loathsome and despicable; that the Forest Service had violated a public trust by approving it; and that the values for which we stand as a nation compel us to preserve the little wilderness we have for its own sake and as an historical heritage for future generations.

The consumer interests or preferences of my students are typical of those of Americans in general. Most Americans like a warm bed better than a pile of wet leaves. They would rather have their meals prepared in a kitchen than to cook them over a campstove. Disney's market analysts knew all this. They found that the resort would attract over 14,000 tourists a day, in summer and winter alike, which is a lot more people than now hike into Mineral King. Moreover, tourists would pay to use the valley; backpackers just walk in.

You might suppose that most Americans approved of the Disney proposal; after all, it would service their consumer demands. * * *

Yet the public's response to the Disney project was like that of my students—visceral and grim. Public opinion was so unfavorable that Congress acted in 1978 to prohibit the project, by making the Mineral King Valley a part of Sequoia National Park. * * *

Economists have given us a sophisticated array of tools for measuring the costs and benefits associated with various public works projects. These techniques generally help us to determine "consumer surplus"—that is, the amount that consumers are willing to pay for a project less the amount that the project will cost. The idea behind these techniques seems to be this: the use of resources that generates the greatest consumer surplus over the long run is the use that ought to be made of them. One such use, I believe, would be the development of a Disney resort at Mineral King.

One problem with economic techniques of "cost-benefit analysis," however, is that they may fail to register ideological or ethical convictions citizens entertain about the very things that interest them as consumers. * * *

The things we cherish, admire, or respect are not always the things we are willing to pay for. Indeed they may be cheapened by being associated with money. It is fair to say that the worth of the things we love is better measured by our *unwillingness* to pay for them. Consider love itself. A civilized person may climb the highest mountain, swim the deepest sea, or cross the hottest desert for love, sweet love. He might do anything, indeed, except be willing to pay for it.

* * *

The things we are unwilling to pay for are not worthless to us. We simply think we ought not to pay for them. Love is not worthless. We would make all kinds of sacrifices for it. Yet a market in love—or in anything we consider "sacred"—is totally inappropriate. These things have a *dignity* rather than a *price*. The things that have a dignity, I believe, are in general the things that help us to define our relationship with one another. The environment we share has such a dignity. The way we use and the way we preserve our common natural heritage helps to define our relation or association with each other. It also helps to define our association with generations in the future and in the past.

A. Dan Tarlock, Environmental Law: Ethics or Science?

7 Duke Envtl. L. & Pol'y F. 193, 194–95, 221–23 (1996).

The principal argument of this article is that environmental law and management should derive their primary political power and legitimacy from science, not ethics. This is a deliberately provocative statement because it runs counter to the pluralistic justification for environmental law, which posits that environmentalism can be sustained from multiple sources of legitimacy all of which are equal. * * * Pluralism has served the environmental movement well. If science does not support a position, the problem may be reclassified as ethical. As environmentalism matures, however, questions of legitimacy become more important and the pluralistic basis of environmentalism becomes more problematic by making legitimacy too contingent. The easy regulatory actions have been taken, and future actions intrude more deeply into personal choice and conflict more directly with the pursuit of other firmly rooted cultural interests.

* * *

Ethics are not a substitute for scientific analysis, and thus environmental law and environmentalism are more contingent than many would prefer them to be. Any principles derived from science remain subject to revision in light of new evidence. Ethics can legitimately, however, bridge the gap between scientific uncertainty and the risks of inaction pending further research through the adoption of the cautionary principle. Environmentalism does represent a profound shift in our world-view of our physical surroundings. Through science we have increasingly come to see natural processes as phenomena to be respected rather than manipulated. This new-found respect can support laws, enacted in advance of conclusive scientific evidence, which recognize the value of new resource functions. * * * However, as long as we value rationality (an open question with respect to some strains of modern environmentalism), science will continue to serve an important checking function. The need for some scientific justification, however probabilistic, for environmental regulation is necessary to constrain the potential arbitrariness and unfairness that can result from the substitution of intuition for verification.

* * *

The central project of environmental law has been to marry wonder to power. Environmentalism's central insight has been to demonstrate the need to supplant the Enlightenment view that humans are sovereign over nature with one which appreciates the many instrumental as well as intrinsic values of nature. In short, nature is both a commodity and a source of delight and wonder to be valued by different standards from the past. Environmental law's mission has been to counter the traditional bias in favor of the early and rapid exploitation of nature by using principles and procedures which try to sustain biodiversity over time. To many environmentalists this seems a modest if not incorrect objective, but it is Herculean in light of the continued dominance of the view that nature is a commodity for present consumption. * * * Biodiversity management can be informed by values which reflect the heightened appreciation of the functions that natural systems perform, but the management choices that are made must be grounded in science and recognized as contingent. Modification of management strategies and adjustment to new information, not the recognition of the rights of nature, will characterize the future of environmental law.

NOTES AND QUESTIONS

1. *Ecology and values.* Does the new ecology undermine Leopold's call for a land ethic? His description of that ethic?

2. *Economics and values.* To what extent do Leopold and Baxter agree? Exactly how do their views differ? Is Baxter's view of "economic" value broader than Leopold's? Is it broad enough to support Leopold's call for a land ethic? Environmentalists often criticize the implicit goal of cost-benefit analysis, which is maximizing aggregate societal welfare. Why might environmentalists disagree with efficiency as a decision criterion? What other goals might environmental regulation have?

3. *Obligations to future generations and the possibility of substitution.* Many people agree that the present generation has some obligation to take the needs of future generations into account. There is disagreement, however, about the definition of intergenerational equity. Economists tend to think of it as obliging us to consider future human welfare, in the sense of the opportunity to satisfy aggregate individual preferences. They also tend to view environmental resources, like others, as subject to substitution. If oil or scenic vistas run short, they argue, people will find something else to satisfy their desires for energy and esthetic pleasure. Viewed in this light, intergenerational equity requires only that the current generation provide the future with a robust stock of aggregate capital; it does not matter how much of that capital is natural. Ecologists are far less likely to see natural capital as replaceable by means of human ingenuity. They therefore believe that intergenerational equity requires the protection of natural capital for future generations. This same disagreement haunts debates over "sustainable development." See, e.g., Bryan G. Norton & Michael A. Toman, Sustainability: Ecological and Economic Perspectives, 73 Land Econ. 553, 555 (1997).

4. *Are citizens different from consumers?* Do you agree with Professor Sagoff that people approach decisions differently, and may arrive at different conclusions, in the contexts of consumer and societal choices? Would you patronize a ski resort at Mineral King? Would you vote in favor of permitting development of a ski resort there? What accounts for the willingness of Sagoff's students to visit the ski resort, but their unwillingness to allow its construction? Can economics account for "citizen preferences"? Will willingness-to-pay surveys include those preferences? How else might they be measured? Should societal decisions depend only upon the *intensity* of preferences, or is their *basis* and *justification* at least equally important?

5. *Preference shaping.* The quest for economic efficiency depends upon two assumptions: that individuals know their own preferences best, and that individual preferences deserve societal respect. Does the fact that preferences are shaped by experiences and information, and can be manipulated by advertising, make efficiency a less appealing goal?

The malleability of preferences complicates the setting of environmental goals. Consider the following excerpt:

> * * * What a society takes to be a natural environment is one.
> * * *

It is likely that we shall want to apply our technology to the creation of artificial environments. It may be possible to create environments that are evocative of other environments in other times and places. It is possible that, by manipulating memory through the rewriting of history, environments will come to have new meaning. Finally, we may want to create proxy environments by means of substitution and simulation. In order to create substitutes, we must endow new objects with significance by means of advertising and by social practice. Sophistication about differentiation will become very important for appreciating the substitute environments. We may simulate the environment by means of photographs, recordings, models, and perhaps even manipulations in the brain. What we experience in natural environments may actually be more controllable than we imagine. Artificial prairies and wildernesses have been created, and there is no reason to believe that these artificial environments need be unsatisfactory for those who experience them.

* * *

What's wrong with plastic trees? My guess is that there is very little wrong with them. Much more can be done with plastic trees and the like to give most people the feeling that they are experiencing nature. We will have to realize that the way in which we experience nature is conditioned by our society—which more and more is seen to be receptive to responsible interventions.

Martin H. Krieger, What's Wrong With Plastic Trees?, 179 Science 446, 446–53 (1973). Is there something wrong with plastic trees, even if people could be persuaded to enjoy them as much as the real thing? Does the malleability of preferences make it more or less important to protect the environment?

6. *The search for rationality.* Economists and ecological scientists tend to share the view that environmental policy decisions should be "rational" in a particular sense—that they should be arrived at and defended on objective grounds. Economists tend to look to cost-benefit analysis to provide that rationality. Professor Tarlock, and many natural scientists, look to science. Do you agree that environmental (or other) policy decisions must be grounded in some objective measure? What are the benefits of objective decisionmaking? What might be its shortcomings?

To what extent can science make environmental decisions more rational? Precisely what role does Tarlock suggest should be assigned to science? What role(s) would Leopold and Baxter have science play?

One well-known practitioner of conservation biology, a discipline devoted to determining how biological resources might best be protected, writes:

A distinguishing feature of conservation biology is that it is mission oriented. Underlying any mission is a set of values. Philosophers of science now recognize that no science is value free, despite all we were taught in school about the strict objectivity of the scientific method. Conservation biology is more value-laden than most sciences because it is not concerned with knowledge for its own sake but rather is directed toward particular goals. Maintaining biodiversity is an unquestioned goal of conservation biologists. * * *

Reed F. Noss, Some Principles of Conservation Biology, As They Apply to Environmental Law, 69 Chi.-Kent L. Rev. 893, 895 (1994). Does this confession undermine the usefulness of science as a basis for environmental decisionmaking? As an assurance that environmental policy is "rational"?

7. *Environmental justice.* Environmental hazards and access to environmental benefits are not evenly distributed. In the 1980s, a series of studies finding that racial minorities in the United States are disproportionately likely to live near hazardous waste facilities sparked charges of "environmental racism," triggering the environmental justice movement. See, e.g., Rachel D. Godsil, Environmental Justice and the Integration Ideal, 49 N.Y. L. Sch. L. Rev. 1109 (2004–2005); Clifford Rechtschaffen and Eileen Gauna, Environmental Justice: Law, Policy & Regulation (2002); Luke Cole and Sheila Foster, From the Ground Up: Environmental Racism and the Rise of the Environmental Justice Movement (2001); Richard J. Lazarus, "Environmental Racism! That's What It Is," 2000 U. Ill. L. Rev. 255; Robert D. Bullard, ed., Confronting Environmental Racism: Voices from the Grassroots (1993).

In addition to being the victims of hazardous facility siting decisions, racial and cultural minorities are sometimes forgotten when general standards are set to control environmental risk. In setting standards for acceptable amounts of toxins in water, for example, state and federal agencies make certain assumptions about the amount of contaminated fish people are likely to consume. If those assumptions are based on average fish consumption across the entire national population, they will systematically underprotect people who consume large quantities of fish, such as some Native American and recent immigrant communities. See Catherine A. O'Neill, Variable Justice: Environmental Standards, Contaminated Fish, and "Acceptable" Risks to Native Peoples, 19 Stanford Environmental Law Journal 3 (2000).

Environmental justice has proven difficult to define. The United States Environmental Protection Agency ("EPA") currently describes it in the following terms:

> Environmental Justice is the fair treatment and meaningful involvement of all people regardless of race, color, national origin, or income with respect to the development, implementation, and enforcement of environmental laws, regulations, and policies. EPA has this goal for all communities and persons across this Nation. It will be achieved when everyone enjoys the same degree of protection from environmental and health hazards and equal access to the decision-making process to have a healthy environment in which to live, learn, and work.

EPA, Environmental Justice, http://www.epa.gov/compliance/environmentaljustice/index.html. What exactly, though, is "fair treatment" or "meaningful involvement"? Is the treatment of a minority neighborhood fair if it is chosen to site the only hazardous waste facility in a metropolitan area, so long as the facility must comply with generally applicable substantive standards? What if a low-income neighborhood is chosen because the costs of the land needed to develop the facility are low? Must environmental hazards be evenly distributed across the landscape to achieve fairness? Can compensation of a minority community ever make the siting of an environmental hazard fair? Is involvement of the community "meaningful" if environmental documents are produced in the majority language of the community, even if the documents are highly technical and difficult to understand?

SECTION 5. CHOOSING POLICY TOOLS

Environmental problems can be addressed through a range of policy instruments, each with its own political and practical strengths and weaknesses. Throughout this course, we will look in detail at various policy strategies that have been used in environmental law, and the results of those efforts. It may be helpful at the outset, however, to briefly list the available choices and some criteria that might be used to choose among them in a specific context. There is no reason to think, of course, that only a single strategy can or should be employed. Sometimes the best results may come from creatively combining several different strategies.

In a 1995 report, the congressional Office of Technology Assessment identified twelve major policy tools for addressing pollution; with the addition of protected lands, these are also the major tools for natural resource protection.

Office of Technology Assessment, Congress of the United States, Environmental Policy Tools

September 1995; pp. 84–85.

- *Harm-based standards*. A harm-based standard prescribes the end results, not the means, of regulatory compliance. Regulated entities are responsible for meeting some regulatory target but are largely free to choose or invent the easiest or cheapest methods to comply, Sometimes referred to as health-based standards or performance standards, harm-based standards are widely used, primarily in combination with design standards.

- *Design standards*. A design standard is a requirement expressed in terms of the state of the art of pollution abatement at some point in time, for example, "best available" or "reasonably available" technology. In a permit, design standard requirements are typically, but not always, stated as the level of emissions control the model approach is capable of achieving. Design standards written as emission limits allow individual sources the freedom to achieve the required emissions control by using the model approach or equivalent means. Design standards are very widely used, most often as part of a technology-based strategy.

- *Technology specifications.* A technology specification is a requirement expressed in terms of specific equipment or techniques, The standard is to be met by all entities; facilities are not free to choose their means of pollution abatement or prevention. Explicit technology specifications in statutes or regulations are very rare. However, some designs standards can be considered de facto technology specifications when it is extremely difficult to prove to the regulatory agency that an alternative to the model technology is equivalent.

- *Product bans and limitations.* This regulatory approach bans or restricts production, processing, distribution, use, or disposal of substances that present unacceptable risks to health or the environment. It focuses on the commodity itself rather than polluting by-products. As a result, the instrument is used most heavily under the Federal Insecticide, Fungicide, and Rodenticide Act (FIFRA) and other statutes where the hazard is the commodity.

- *Tradeable emissions.* Emissions trading is achieved through government-issued permits that allow the owner to emit a specific quantity of pollutants over a specified period, and which can be bought from and sold to others. The government typically caps aggregate emissions from sources within a geographic region by issuing only the number of permits consistent with environmental goals. A relatively new approach to tradeable emissions is an "open market," in which unregulated sources may opt into the program voluntarily. Emissions trading has been used most widely under the Clean Air Act and to a more limited degree to address water quality issues.

- *Integrated permitting.* Integrated permits contain facility-wide emission limits, either for a single pollutant across multiple individual sources or media, or for several pollutants emitted to a single medium. An integrated permit might use one or several other environmental policy instruments. "Bubble" permits are used under the Clean Air Act, and to a very limited extent under the Clean Water Act. Other types of integrated permits are uncommon but are under study as part of several state pilot projects.

- *Challenge regulation.* Challenge regulations ask target groups to change their behavior and work toward a specific environmental goal, with mandatory requirements imposed if the goal is not reached. The government identifies a goal and gives the groups time to select and implement an effective means of achieving it. Challenge regulations have the potential to be a less-intrusive way to achieve environmental goals. The concept of challenge regulation is attracting interest but is still uncommon as a stand-alone regulatory tool.

- *Pollution charges.* With pollution charges, a regulated entity must pay a fixed dollar amount for each unit of pollution emitted or disposed. Pollution charges do not set a limit on emissions or production. Instead, the government must calculate what level of charge will change the behavior of regulated entities enough to achieve environmental objectives. Sources are free to choose whether to emit pollution and pay the charge or pay for the installation of controls to reduce emissions. * * * In the United States, pollution charges have been used for solid waste control but rarely for control of other types of pollution.

- *Liability*. Liability provisions require entities that cause environmental harm to pay those who are harmed to the extent of the damage. Liability can provide a significant motivation for behavioral change because the dollar amounts involved can be huge. * * * Several environmental statutes impose statutory liability, including CERCLA and the Oil Pollution Act.

- *Information reporting*. Information reporting requires targeted entities to provide specified types of information to a government agency or to the public directly. Required information typically involves activities affecting environmental quality, such as emissions, product characteristics, or whether risk to the public exceeds a threshold. Information programs are widely used.

- *Subsidies*. Subsidies are financial assistance given to entities as an incentive to change their behavior, or to help defray costs of mandatory standards. Subsidies might be provided by the government or by other parties, who thus bear part of the cost of environmentally beneficial controls or behavior. Government subsidies have historically been widely used, particularly in wastewater treatment. Subsidies from other parties are becoming more common as government budgets shrink.

- *Technical assistance*. The government offers technical assistance to help targeted entities prevent or reduce pollution. These programs educate sources that might not be fully aware of the environmental consequences of their actions or of techniques or equipment to reduce those consequences. Technical assistance may take many forms, including manuals and guidance, training programs, and information clearinghouses. Some types of technical assistance, such as facility evaluations, are conditioned on facilities agreeing to respond with environmentally beneficial behavior. Technical assistance is very common, particularly in combination with other tools.

In the same report, OTA identified three overarching themes for environmental policy: environmental results; costs and burdens; and change. Within those themes, it listed seven criteria for comparing policy tools:

1. *Assurance of meeting environmental goals*, which is higher for prescriptive standards and lower for voluntary or informational strategies.

2. *Prevention*, that is whether the strategy can prevent problems before they occur rather than simply control or remedy them later.

3. *Environmental equity and justice*, which focuses on distributional outcomes and effective participation by affected communities.

4. *Cost-effectiveness and fairness*, for both the public and regulated sources.

5. *Demands on government*, including both government costs and the ability to produce needed information.

6. *Adaptability*, meaning the ability to modify the strategy to keep up with changes in circumstances or knowledge.

7. *Technology innovation and diffusion*, that is the extent to which the strategy encourages development and diffusion of new or improved technologies.

Id. at 145. Of course, for any individual tool, high performance on one factor may be balanced by poor performs on another. When faced with a choice among policy instruments, therefore, society often also must decide which factors are most important in the specific context.

CLASS DISCUSSION PROBLEM: GLOBAL WARMING

The earth receives a constant barrage of solar radiation. Some of that is reflected directly back by clouds or from the surface of the earth, but much of it is absorbed and later emitted back into space as infrared radiation. So-called "greenhouse gases," which include (among others) water vapor, carbon dioxide (CO_2), methane (CH_4), and nitrogen oxides, absorb infrared radiation, in effect trapping the sun's heat in the earth's atmosphere. Greenhouse gases are produced by a variety of natural processes, and at background levels are responsible for the earth's relatively moderate climate. Without greenhouse gases, the earth would be a very cold and inhospitable place. But while some greenhouse gas in the atmosphere is good, more is not necessarily better.

There is now broad scientific consensus that human activities, which over the last century or so have greatly increased the accumulation of several greenhouse gases in the atmosphere, are the primary (though perhaps not the only) cause of global warming. Most climate scientists agree that the effects of anthropogenic climate change are already observable. The earth's temperature increased about 1° Fahrenheit from 1900 to 2000. Arctic sea ice has receded, permafrost has thawed in some locations, and glaciers are noticeably retreating in, for example, Glacier National Park.

In 2007, the Intergovernmental Panel on Climate Change predicted that global temperatures would increase roughly another 0.7°F over the next two decades. By the end of the 21st century, average global temperatures could increase by anywhere from 2 to 11.5°F, depending on emission levels. Temperatures in parts of the United States may increase even more than the global average change, although precise local impacts are still difficult to predict.

Increases in global temperatures will cause a variety of impacts. One of the most confident predictions is that global sea level will rise, by as much as two feet under high-emission scenarios. Sea level rise would cause increased flooding and threaten fresh water supplies in coastal areas. Heat waves are also very likely, as is an increase in the intensity of tropical storms. Precipitation is likely to increase at high latitudes and decrease near the equator, although precise local effects on precipitation are still difficult to forecast. In the arid western United States, increased temperatures are expected to decrease the proportion of precipitation that falls as snow. That will cause a severe problem for states like California, which rely on the snowpack as an inexpensive water storage "reservoir." For people and other organisms, heat stress will increase, as will smog-induced respiratory illness, but cold stress could decrease. Some infectious human diseases, such as malaria, could spread to places where they are not now found. It is virtually certain that global warming will radically alter the distribution of plant and wildlife species, and highly likely that it will cause widespread loss of biodiversity.

There has, of course, always been some variability in the earth's climate. It is thought that anthropogenic climate change has already exceeded the level of natural variation, however, and it is accelerating. Human-induced climate change is occurring much more rapidly than most natural climatic events. Many scientists now believe that "[t]hresholds likely exist that, if crossed, could abruptly and perhaps almost irreversibly switch the climate to a different regime." Thomas R. Karl and Kevin E. Trenberth, Modern Global Climate Change, 302 Science 1719 (2003). A report prepared in 2003 for the Pentagon (available at http://www.ems.org/climate/ pentagon_climate_change.html#report) concluded that "because of the potentially dire consequences, the risk of abrupt climate change, although uncertain and quite possibly small, should be elevated beyond a scientific debate to a U.S. national security concern."

Carbon dioxide (CO_2) is the most important anthropogenic greenhouse gas; CO_2 emissions account for about 80% of climate change potential. Historic concentrations of atmospheric carbon dioxide varied from about 190 ppm (parts per million by volume) during the last ice age to about 280 ppm. By the middle of the 20th century, atmospheric CO_2 had risen to 315 ppm, and by 2011 it was over 394 ppm (NOAA provides recent CO_2 concentration data at http://www.esrl.noaa.gov/gmd/ccgg/trends/ index.html#global). Human activities, particularly the burning of fossil fuels, are largely responsible for this increase. Once emitted, CO_2 persists in the atmosphere for hundreds of years. Although research is ongoing on ways to "sequester" emitted CO_2 below ground or chemically trap it, at the moment there is no practicable technology for CO_2 emission control. In the absence of such a technology, the only way to reduce CO_2 emissions is to burn less fuel.

Although China has overtaken the United States as the largest emitter of greenhouse gases in the world, the United States is still responsible for just under 20% of global greenhouse gas emissions. Emissions per capita are about three to four times higher in the U.S. than in China, although that ratio is changing rapidly. (The highest per capita emissions are in a handful of small oil-rich nations.) In the United States, major contributors to greenhouse gas emissions are transportation (about 33%, the majority of that from automobiles), electricity production (about 41%), and industrial operations (about 13%, putting aside industrial electricity consumption). EPA, *supra*, at ES–7 to ES–8.

The United States, state and local governments, and the global community are currently facing the challenge of deciding what to do to address global warming. At the international level, the United States has been reluctant to accept aggressive emission reduction requirements unless similar requirements are applied to developing nations. That is why the U.S. did not join the 1997 Kyoto Protocol, which called on developed nations to reduce their emissions below 1990 levels, but imposed no restrictions on emissions from developing nations. The Kyoto Protocol expires in 2012, but the parties have agreed to extend it another 5–8 years while negotiating a succesor.

How should a successor treaty be framed? Should equivalent proportional reductions be required of all countries? Should they have to achieve equivalent per capita reductions, or reduce to equal per capita levels? Should developed countries (which are responsible for more of the historic emissions that have brought the globe to the current situation) have to reduce more than others? Note that international agreements cannot be imposed on any nation. To succeed, agreements must gain the voluntary adherence of a critical mass of nations. Negotiators face the daunting task of satisfying enough nations to get an agreement done without emptying the agreement of all substance.

How should the world decide on a goal for emission reductions? How much CO_2 in the atmosphere is acceptable? How much temperature increase is "too much"? Might low-lying flood-prone nations have a different view of that than others?

Domestically, how should the United States respond to global warming? Should it wait for an international agreement before enacting domestic law? Will acting to reduce emissions now help or hinder its international negotiating position? Is there a role for state and local governments in crafting a response to climate change, or must action, to be effective, originate at the federal or international level? Will states necessarily see themselves as in competition with one another for economic development? Might regional agreements enable states to take meaningful action even without a federal mandate? Might a proliferation of state or local steps encourage industry to support federal action? Which policy tools seem most likely to prove effective in this context and why? Which of OTA's suggested evaluative criteria seems most important?

NOTES AND QUESTIONS

1. *Characteristic features.* Which of the features Professor Lazarus identifies as characteristic of environmental disputes does the issue of global warming display? How do those features complicate responses to the problem?

2. *Cost-benefit analysis*. Would cost-benefit analysis be helpful in deciding what action to take in response to global warming? How readily could the costs of global warming be quantified? What about the costs of reducing emissions? Would cost-benefit analysis overlook any factors important to the decision? Because past emissions have already committed the world to temperature increases, most of the benefits of reducing emissions today will accrue decades into the future and many will be enjoyed by very distant future generations. Should those benefits be discounted in a cost-benefit analysis? Why or why not? What obligations do current people owe to future generations with respect to global climate?

3. *Regulation versus markets versus taxes*. What strategies might law (at any level) take to reduce carbon emissions? The three major strategies currently being debated are: 1) command-and-control regulation, that is, ordering emitters to reduce emissions or adopt available technologies; 2) marketable permits to emit, which allow sources better able to control their emissions to sell emission credits to others; or 3) emission taxes. How might each be used to address global warming? Which do you think is the most promising, or how might they be combined? Can you think of other possible approaches?

4. *Choosing regulatory targets*. Should emissions from all sectors be addressed in the same way? Can they be? Should some sectors be expected to reduce emissions more than others? Which?

5. *Making voluntary measures possible*. Even without regulatory intervention, some people want to reduce their "carbon footprint." What could motivate such reductions? What steps can individuals take to reduce their responsibility for global warming? A market has developed for "carbon offsets," designed to allow people to reduce their global warming impact without changing their behavior. Suppose, for example, that you have relatives across the country, and limited vacation time. Flying may be the only practical way to make the trip in the time available, but you know that air travel consumes a great deal of fuel and therefore produces substantial carbon emissions. You might buy an "offset" from a vendor who promises to use the money to fund reforestation (young trees take up carbon dioxide), emissions-free energy production (solar power, for example), or energy efficiency projects.

How do you know offset payments are used effectively? A number of offset sellers belong to the Chicago Climate Exchange, which sets certain requirements. Still, it can be very difficult for a purchaser of carbon offset credits to know what, exactly, she is buying. Environmental and consumer groups have called for stronger regulation of the carbon offset industry.

6. *Scientific uncertainty*. Like many environmental problems, decisions about global warming involve areas of substantial scientific uncertainty and disagreement, particularly when it comes to the local effects of climate change. Many of these uncertainties cannot be resolved by experiments or additional observations in the short term, because they require forecasts into the distant future. How should these uncertainties be factored into the decision? Should the precautionary principle be applied? What exactly would that mean in this case? Should we be "cautious" about impacts to the earth's climate, impacts to the economy, or both? What degree of caution is appropriate?

7. *An abortive attempt at federal climate change legislation.* On June 26, 2009, the House of Representatives narrowly passed H.R. 2454, the American Clean Energy and Security Act of 2009, also known as Waxman–Markey after its principal sponsors. The bill ran more than 1400 pages in the Government Printing Office's print. Its centerpiece was a federal cap-and-trade program for greenhouse gas emissions, which would reduce emissions nationwide 17% by 2020 and 80% by 2050 compared to 2005 levels. Other provisions would have established a federal renewable energy standard and federal energy efficiency standards for new buildings, and tightened appliance efficiency standards. It would have required EPA to set greenhouse gas emission standards for large trucks and offroad vehicles, but removed EPA's authority to regulate greenhouse gas emissions from stationary sources under the Clean Air Act.

Environmental groups struggled to decide whether or not to support Waxman–Markey, which they viewed as weak but perhaps politically the best deal they could get. Conservative groups opposed it. Businesses split. The US Chamber of Commerce was strongly opposed, but many businesses, from Starbucks to clean tech startups, supported Waxman–Markey. Some opponents said that it would bankrupt the economy, but an economic analysis by the U.S. Energy Information Agency estimated the average cost per household at about $83 annually. Whatever its virtues and flaws may have been, the Waxman–Markey bill died in the Senate in 2010, and Congress has shown no interest since in taking up a climate bill.

CHAPTER TWO

ENVIRONMENTAL COMMON LAW

Before enactment of the numerous federal and state statutes that currently form the backbone of environmental law, environmental problems were addressed, if at all, by the common law. Today, despite the existence of many detailed environmental statutes, the common law remains relevant. It provides the flexibility to address new technologies or newly-recognized harms, and it allows recovery of compensatory damages, a remedy generally not available through environmental statutes.

CLASS DISCUSSION PROBLEM: POLLUTION ON THE PIGEON RIVER

James Collins owns a 200–acre farm located along the Pigeon River near Hartford, Tennessee, a few miles west of the border with North Carolina. James diverts water directly from the river for his livestock and, in dry periods, to irrigate his crops. A shallow well located close to the river provides the family's water. Tennessee law gives riparian owners the right to divert water for domestic and agricultural purposes.

The Pigeon River was once a popular trout-fishing stream, but it now runs the color of coffee past James's farm, and frequently exudes the odor of rotten eggs. Fish populations are down substantially, and state authorities have advised people not to eat fish caught in the Pigeon River. In addition, several area residents have been diagnosed with leukemia or other cancers. James fears for his health and that of his family. He also worries that the value of the farm, the family's only substantial economic asset, is sharply declining.

James and his neighbors blame the Fox Pulp and Paper Mill, located about 30 miles upstream in Canton, North Carolina, for the pollution. Pulp and paper production is a water-intensive process. Fox, the largest employer in its county, diverts about 90% of the flow of the Pigeon River in Canton, returning it to the river laden with organic waste which makes the water brown and murky. In addition to being unattractive, the dark color interferes with the growth of aquatic plants, and as it decomposes the dissolved organic matter reduces the availability of oxygen for aquatic life. Fox's wastewater also contains chlorine and chlorinated organic compounds produced by its bleaching process. Some chlorinated organic compounds are classified as potential human carcinogens, although the precise extent of cancer risk they pose is fiercely contested.

Fox has a discharge permit issued by North Carolina's Department of Natural Resources. The permit requires the mill to control the color and smell of its discharge but does not address chlorine or chlorinated compounds. State and federal statutes, as well as a Canton town ordinance, forbid the discharge of dangerous chemicals to waters. State and local officials, however, have told James nothing can be done about the chemical discharges.

Does James have a remedy under the common law? What barriers will a common law action face? If James came to you for legal advice, what counsel would you offer? In answering those questions, consider the following cases and materials.

SECTION 1. COMMON LAW ENVIRONMENTAL DOCTRINES

A. NUISANCE

Nuisance, which potentially covers pollution of air, water, or land by almost any route, has been called the "common law backbone" of modern environmental law. William H. Rodgers, Environmental Law 113 (2d ed. 1994). The common law recognizes two distinct but related causes of action, for private nuisance and public nuisance.

1. PRIVATE NUISANCE

A private nuisance is an unreasonable and substantial interference with the use and enjoyment of land. The influential Restatement (2d) of Torts, § 822, calls for liability for acts that are either: (a) intentional and unreasonable, or (b) unintentional and otherwise actionable under the rules controlling liability for negligent or reckless conduct, or for abnormally dangerous conditions or activities. Acts are considered "intentional" if they are substantially certain to produce harm, whether or not the actor desires that harm. Intention is therefore established if an invasion continues after the defendant has been made aware of the harm. Id. § 825.

An invasion is "unreasonable" if the gravity of the harm outweighs the utility of the conduct or the harm is serious and the economic burden of compensation would not make the conduct infeasible. Id. § 826. Factors to be considered in determining the gravity of the harm and the utility of the conduct include: the extent and character of the harm; the social value of the plaintiff's use of land and defendant's conduct; the suitability of each to the character of the locality; and the burdens on plaintiff and defendant, respectively, of avoiding the harm. Id. §§ 827–28.

This balancing of utilities rule, followed in most American jurisdictions, is a 19th-century modification of the old common law rule of *sic utere tuo ut alienum non laedas* (use your own property so as not to injure that of another). Prior to the industrial revolution, substantial injury to the enjoyment of property was actionable without regard to fault or the social utility of the defendant's conduct. As expanding populations led to increasingly frequent land use conflicts and industrial uses took on greater economic importance, courts adjusted the doctrine of nuisance. The location and social utility of defendant's conduct became important elements in determining whether there was a nuisance and, if so, what relief would be granted. *See* Louise A. Halper, Untangling the Nuisance Knot, 26 B.C. Envtl. Aff. L. Rev. 89, 101–115 (1998); Joel Franklin Brenner, Nuisance Law and the Industrial Revolution, 3 J. Legal Stud. 403, 408–420 (1974). Activities that might be a nuisance in a rural agricultural area could now continue in the industrial towns. In the famous words of Justice Sutherland, a nuisance came to be seen as "merely a right thing in the wrong place, like a pig in the parlor instead of the barnyard." Euclid v. Ambler Realty Co., 272 U.S. 365, 388 (1926). Even in a relatively unsullied area, an activity with great economic or social value might be found not to be a nuisance, or not to justify injunctive relief.

Were these changes a necessary adjustment to a changed economy, or an unjustified subsidy for wealthy entrepreneurs? Consider the following statement from Daniel R. Coquillette, Mosses from an Old Manse: Another Look at Some Historic Property Cases About the Environment, 64 Cornell L. Rev. 761, 792 (1979):

> This old common law doctrine was decent and humane compared to the hardened attitudes of the nineteenth century. The balancing of utilities doctrine * * * permitted the industrial user to externalize the costs of his pollution. Such a legal doctrine offered no economic incentive for the active user of property to develop technology that would prevent such side effects. * * * It was an unjust way of forcing public investment in industrial growth, regardless of how desirable that investment might have seemed.

2. PUBLIC NUISANCE

A public nuisance is an unreasonable interference with the interest of the community or the rights of the general public. The doctrine has been used to protect public health, safety, and even morality (there are many public nuisance cases dealing with prostitution, drug use, and gambling). Traditionally, public nuisance actions could be brought only by public authorities, or by a private citizen who had suffered injury different in kind from that suffered by the general public. The Restatement (2d) of Torts, § 821C, would allow a private citizen who has standing to sue "as a representative of the general public, as a citizen in a citizen's action or as a member of a class in a class action" to maintain an action to abate a public nuisance (but not to recover damages) without having to satisfy the special injury requirement.

B. Trespass

Whereas nuisance protects the right to use and enjoyment of land, trespass protects the right to exclusive possession. Knowing physical invasion of land without the possessor's permission is a trespass. The trespasser is liable for actual damages done, and for nominal damages if there is no actual harm. William B. Stoebuck & Dale A. Whitman, The Law of Property 411 (3d ed. 2000).

Trespass and nuisance shade into one another in environmental pollution cases. Both claims may be available. In Bradley v. American Smelting
& Refining Co., 709 P.2d 782 (Wash. 1985), for example, the court held that
a group of landowners could sue in both trespass and nuisance for damages
to their property caused by microscopic airborne particles from a nearby
copper smelter. Jurisdictions which allow trespass claims for pollution,
however, typically add a requirement that the plaintiff demonstrate substantial damage. *See* id. at 790–91. Other jurisdictions continue to insist
that trespass actions are not available without a tangible physical invasion.
See Adams v. Cleveland–Cliffs Iron Co., 237 Mich.App. 51, 602 N.W.2d 215
(1999) (holding that Michigan law does not permit trespass action for
"intangible" intrusions by airborne particles, noise, or vibrations).

C.   NEGLIGENCE

An important limitation of trespass doctrine in most jurisdictions is
that the defendant must either intend the intrusion or act with knowledge
that it is substantially certain to result. *See* United Proteins, Inc. v.
Farmland Industries, Inc., 259 Kan. 725, 915 P.2d 80 (1996). Trespass,
therefore, does not cover isolated accidents which release hazardous materials or contaminate property. Negligence and strict liability fill that gap, and
inform modern nuisance law. Negligence and strict liability remain substantially broader than nuisance, since they are not limited to harm to
interests in land.

Conduct is negligent if it creates an unreasonable risk of harm to
others. A cause of action based on negligence has four elements:

(1) a legal duty owed by the defendant to the plaintiff;

(2) a breach of that duty;

(3) harm; and

(4) a causal relationship between the breach and the harm.

D.   STRICT LIABILITY

Most jurisdictions recognize liability for damages caused to persons or
property by abnormally dangerous activities without requiring any showing
of fault. The Restatement (2d) of Torts, § 520, calls for consideration of the
following factors in order to determine whether an activity is abnormally
dangerous:

(a) whether the activity poses a high degree of risk of some harm to
people, land, or personal property;

(b) the likelihood of grave harm;

(c) whether the risk can be eliminated by the exercise of reasonable
care;

(d) whether the activity is common or not;

(e) whether it is appropriate to the place where it is carried on; and

(f) the extent to which its value to the community is outweighed by the danger it poses.

Justifications for imposing liability without fault include: forcing those who engage in dangerous activities to internalize the costs of those activities; spreading the costs of otherwise devastating individual losses across a large group; avoiding unfairness by imposing the costs of injury on the person who benefits from the injurious activity; deterring highly dangerous activities; and reducing the administrative costs associated with proving negligence. *See* Joseph H. King, Jr., A Goals–Oriented Approach to Strict Tort Liability for Abnormally Dangerous Activities, 48 Baylor L. Rev. 341, 350–61 (1996). By contrast to negligence, which is a determination for the jury, whether or not an activity is abnormally dangerous is a matter of law decided by the court. Restatement (2d) of Torts, § 520, comment l.

Indiana Harbor Belt Railroad Co. v. American Cyanamid Co.

United States Court of Appeals, Seventh Circuit, 1990.
916 F.2d 1174.

■ P<small>OSNER</small>, C<small>IRCUIT</small> J<small>UDGE</small>.

American Cyanamid Company, the defendant in this diversity tort suit governed by Illinois law, is a major manufacturer of chemicals, including acrylonitrile, a chemical used in large quantities in making acrylic fibers, plastics, dyes, pharmaceutical chemicals, and other intermediate and final goods. On January 2, 1979, at its manufacturing plant in Louisiana, Cyanamid loaded 20,000 gallons of liquid acrylonitrile into a railroad tank car that it had leased from the North American Car Corporation. The next day, a train of the Missouri Pacific Railroad picked up the car at Cyanamid's siding. The car's ultimate destination was a Cyanamid plant in New Jersey served by Conrail rather than by Missouri Pacific. The Missouri Pacific train carried the car north to the Blue Island railroad yard of Indiana Harbor Belt Railroad, the plaintiff in this case, a small switching line that has a contract with Conrail to switch cars from other lines to Conrail, in this case for travel east. The Blue Island yard is in the Village of Riverdale, which is just south of Chicago and part of the Chicago metropolitan area.

The car arrived in the Blue Island yard on the morning of January 9, 1979. Several hours after it arrived, employees of the switching line noticed fluid gushing from the bottom outlet of the car. The lid on the outlet was broken. After two hours, the line's supervisor of equipment was able to stop the leak by closing a shut-off valve controlled from the top of the car. No one was sure at the time just how much of the contents of the car had leaked, but it was feared that all 20,000 gallons had, and since acrylonitrile is flammable at a temperature of 30° Fahrenheit or above, highly toxic, and possibly carcinogenic, the local authorities ordered the homes near the yard evacuated. The evacuation lasted only a few hours, until the car was moved to a remote part of the yard and it was discovered that only about a quarter of the acrylonitrile had leaked. Concerned nevertheless that there had been some contamination of soil and water, the Illinois Department of Environmental Protection ordered the switching line to take decontamination measures that cost the line $981,022.75, which it sought to recover by this suit.

* * * * *

The question whether the shipper of a hazardous chemical by rail should be strictly liable for the consequences of a spill or other accident to the shipment en route is a novel one in Illinois * * *.

The parties agree that the question whether placing acrylonitrile in a rail shipment that will pass through a metropolitan area subjects the shipper to strict liability is, as recommended in Restatement (2d) of Torts § 520, comment l (1977), a question of law, so that we owe no particular deference to the conclusion of the district court. They also agree * * * that the Supreme Court of Illinois would treat as authoritative the provisions of the Restatement governing abnormally dangerous activities. The key provision is section 520, which sets forth six factors to be considered in deciding whether an activity is abnormally dangerous and the actor therefore strictly liable.

The roots of section 520 are in nineteenth-century cases. The most famous one is Rylands v. Fletcher, 1 Ex. 265, *aff'd*, L.R. 3 H.L. 300 (1868), but a more illuminating one in the present context is Guille v. Swan, 19 Johns. (N.Y.) 381 (1822). A man took off in a hot-air balloon and landed, without intending to, in a vegetable garden in New York City. A crowd that had been anxiously watching his involuntary descent trampled the vegetables in their endeavor to rescue him when he landed. The owner of the garden sued the balloonist for the resulting damage, and won. Yet the balloonist had not been careless. In the then state of ballooning it was impossible to make a pinpoint landing.

Guille is a paradigmatic case for strict liability. (a) The risk (probability) of harm was great, and (b) the harm that would ensue if the risk materialized could be, although luckily was not, great (the balloonist could have crashed into the crowd rather than into the vegetables). The confluence of these two factors established the urgency of seeking to prevent such accidents. (c) Yet such accidents could not be prevented by the exercise of due care; the technology of care in ballooning was insufficiently developed. (d) The activity was not a matter of common usage, so there was no presumption that it was a highly valuable activity despite its unavoidable riskiness. (e) The activity was inappropriate to the place in which it took place—densely populated New York City. The risk of serious harm to others (other than the balloonist himself, that is) could have been reduced by shifting the activity to the sparsely inhabited areas that surrounded the city in those days. (f) Reinforcing (d), the value to the community of the activity of recreational ballooning did not appear to be great enough to offset its unavoidable risks.

These are, of course, the six factors in section 520. They are related to each other in that each is a different facet of a common quest for a proper legal regime to govern accidents that negligence liability cannot adequately control. The interrelations might be more perspicuous if the six factors were reordered. One might for example start with (c), inability to eliminate the risk of accident by the exercise of due care. The baseline common law regime of tort liability is negligence. When it is a workable regime, because the hazards of an activity can be avoided by being careful (which is to say, nonnegligent), there is no need to switch to strict liability. Sometimes, however, a particular type of accident cannot be prevented by taking care but can be avoided, or its consequences minimized, by shifting the activity in which the accident occurs to another locale, where the risk or harm of an accident will be less ((e)), or by reducing the scale of the activity in order to minimize the number of accidents caused by it ((f)). By making the actor strictly liable—by denying him in other words an excuse based on his inability to avoid accidents by being more careful—we give him an incentive, missing in a negligence regime, to experiment with methods of preventing accidents that involve not greater exertions of care, assumed to be futile, but instead relocating, changing, or reducing (perhaps to the vanishing point) the activity giving rise to the accident. The greater the risk of an accident ((a)) and the costs of an accident if one occurs ((b)), the more we want the actor to consider the possibility of making accident-reducing activity changes; the stronger, therefore, is the case for strict liability. Finally, if an activity is extremely common ((d)), like driving an automobile, it is unlikely either that its hazards are perceived as great or that there is no technology of care available to minimize them; so the case for strict liability is weakened. * * *

Against this background we turn to the particulars of acrylonitrile. Acrylonitrile is one of a large number of chemicals that are hazardous in the sense of being flammable, toxic, or both; acrylonitrile is both, as are many others. A table in the record * * * contains a list of the 125 hazardous materials that are shipped in highest volume on the nation's railroads. Acrylonitrile is the fifty-third most hazardous on the list. * * * The plaintiff's lawyer acknowledged at argument that the logic of the district court's opinion dictated strict liability for all 52 materials that rank higher than acrylonitrile on the list, and quite possibly for the 72 that rank lower as well, since all are hazardous if spilled in quantity while being shipped by rail. Every shipper of any of these materials would therefore be strictly liable for the consequences of a spill or other accident that occurred while the material was being shipped through a metropolitan area. * * *

[W]e can get little help from precedent, and might as well apply section 520 to the acrylonitrile problem from the ground up. To begin with, we have been given no reason * * * for believing that a negligence regime is not perfectly adequate to remedy and deter, at reasonable cost, the accidental spillage of acrylonitrile from rail cars. [A]lthough acrylonitrile is flammable even at relatively low temperatures, and toxic, it is not so corrosive or otherwise destructive that it will eat through or otherwise damage or weaken a tank car's valves although they are maintained with due (which essentially means, with average) care. No one suggests, therefore, that the leak in this case was caused by the inherent properties of acrylonitrile. It was caused by carelessness—whether that of the North American Car Corporation in failing to maintain or inspect the car properly, or that of Cyanamid in failing to maintain or inspect it, or that of the Missouri Pacific when it had custody of the car, or that of the switching line itself in failing to notice the ruptured lid, or some combination of these possible failures of care. Accidents that are due to a lack of care can be prevented by taking care; and when a lack of care can * * * be shown in court, such accidents are adequately deterred by the threat of liability for negligence. * * *

The district judge and the plaintiff's lawyer make much of the fact that the spill occurred in a densely inhabited metropolitan area. Only 4,000 gallons spilled; what if all 20,000 had done so? Isn't the risk that this might happen even if everybody were careful sufficient to warrant giving the shipper an incentive to explore alternative routes? Strict liability would supply that incentive. But this argument overlooks the fact that, like other transportation networks, the railroad network is a hub-and-spoke system. And the hubs are in metropolitan areas. Chicago is one of the nation's largest railroad hubs. In 1983, the latest year for which we have figures, Chicago's railroad yards handled the third highest volume of hazardous-material shipments in the nation. * * * With most hazardous chemicals (by volume of shipments) being at least as hazardous as acrylonitrile, it is unlikely—and certainly not demonstrated by the plaintiff—that they can be rerouted around all the metropolitan areas in the country, except at prohibitive cost. Even if it were feasible to reroute them one would hardly expect shippers, as distinct from carriers, to be the firms best situated to do the rerouting. * * * It is no more realistic to propose to reroute the shipment of all hazardous materials around Chicago than it is to propose the relocation of homes adjacent to the Blue Island switching yard to more distant suburbs. It may be less realistic. Brutal though it may seem to say it, the inappropriate use to which land is being put in the Blue Island yard and neighborhood may be, not the transportation of hazardous chemicals, but residential living. The analogy is to building your home between the runways at O'Hare.

The case for strict liability has not been made. * * *

Leaf River Forest Products, Inc. v. Ferguson

Supreme Court of Mississippi, 1995.
662 So.2d 648.

■ PITTMAN, JUSTICE.

* * *

In 1984 the Leaf River Paper Mill began operation in New Augusta, Perry County, Mississippi. The mill is located on the Leaf River, which eventually combines with the Chickasawhay River to form the Pascagoula River. The mill processes timber into a paper pulp product for domestic and foreign sale. In 1985 2,3,7,8–tetrachlorodibenzo-p-dioxin ("dioxin"), a toxic substance, was detected in the sludge, or solid waste material, produced by certain paper mills in Maine. It was subsequently determined that this type of dioxin was a by-product of the pulp-making process, particularly resulting where chlorine was used to bleach pulp to make it whiter. Dioxin was eventually found in the effluent, or waste water, and sludge produced by the Leaf River mill. Testing for dioxin was subsequently performed on fish caught in the Leaf River. As a result of these tests the Mississippi Department of Wildlife and Fisheries closed the Leaf, Pascagoula and Escatawpa Rivers to commercial fishing from October 1990 to January 1991, and issued consumption advisories for fish caught from the Leaf and Pascagoula Rivers. The consumption advisory for the Pascagoula was lifted in December 1990, but remained in effect for the Leaf River.

On March 1, 1991, [plaintiffs] filed suit * * *. The plaintiffs alleged that the defendants, through the operation of the Leaf River mill, had discharged toxic chemicals into the Leaf River, causing injury to the plaintiffs, who lived along the Pascagoula River. The complaint was based on negligence, strict liability, nuisance and trespass. The plaintiffs alleged that they had suffered emotional distress and were entitled to actual and punitive damages totaling approximately $560,000,000.00. [T]he Fergusons' property was approximately one hundred twenty-five miles downriver from the mill. * * *

PLAINTIFFS/APPELLEES

Thomas Ferguson, Jr., was born in Georgia but had lived in south Mississippi since 1945. In 1960, Ferguson purchased fifteen acres of land on the Pascagoula River. He cleared the land and built bayous, two boat sheds, a house, a bait shop and a trailer park. He had hoped to leave the property to his son. He stated that he could no longer swim or fish in the river and he had developed a fear of cancer, as he had eaten large amounts of fish caught in the Pascagoula before knowing about the dioxin problem. Ferguson also stated that his property had flooded several times recently and this had worsened his fear that his property was contaminated with dioxin.

Ferguson testified that if he had known that the mill was discharging dioxin into the river, he would have made "different arrangements with [his] lifestyle." He had first noticed the river water getting darker in 1986–87. Ferguson had seen Dr. Charlton Stanley, a psychologist, and Dr. Donald Guild, a psychiatrist, but had not taken the medicine prescribed for him. He had not been informed of any kind of evaluation or diagnosis until his pretrial deposition was taken. Ferguson had not had his property or his well water tested for dioxin, and had not tried to sell his property. He had not had his blood tested for determination of dioxin levels....

Bonnie Jane Ferguson, wife of Thomas Ferguson, Jr., was born and raised in south Mississippi. She was a housewife and she also ran their marina, which included collecting the rent and keeping the records of the rent money. She stated that over the past few years the river had gotten darker, a light coffee color, and the fish did not bite like they once had. She had first noticed the change in the color of the river in 1985. Her greatest sense of loss came from the belief that the property she and her husband had planned to leave to their son was now worthless. She had declined Leaf River's offer to pay for her blood to be tested, stating that if dioxin was in her system and could not be removed she did not want to know about it. She claimed to have developed a fear of cancer because of the large amount of catfish she had eaten which had been caught in the Pascagoula. The fear was not something that paralyzed her or kept her from functioning.

* * * * *

APPELLEES' EXPERTS

Dr. Arnold Schecter, physician and professor of preventative medicine at the State University of New York, Binghamton, referred to 2,3,7,8–tetrachlorodibenzodioxin, or dioxin, as a "super toxin," because a very tiny amount would produce increased ill effects in an animal. Schecter testified that dioxin was fat-soluble, that it could enter the body through breathing, ingestion or through contact with the skin; that the dioxin in food that was eaten and not eliminated through waste would be absorbed into the bloodstream and throughout the body's organs; and that dioxin was a persistent compound, with an estimated half-life of seven years. Schecter testified that studies showed that human health effects resulting from exposure to dioxin included several different cancers; malformation and death of unborn children; weakening of the immune system; liver damage; lipid alteration; damage to the central nervous system; skin rashes; and learning disabilities. Schecter felt that there was no doubt that dioxin caused cancer in humans. He had visited with the appellees for less than an hour before trial and had reviewed a number of fish studies performed by the State of Mississippi as well as medical and psychological tests concerning the appellees. He stated that he felt that, based on a reasonable degree of medical probability, the appellees' fear of developing cancer from eating fish from the Pascagoula River was reasonable. Schecter agreed that a comprehensive medical evaluation, including blood tests, was the best method of determining exposure to dioxin, and stated that he had his own blood and fat tested for dioxin after he became involved with a chemical cleanup in Binghamton, New York. He could not say that the appellees' health was actually at risk because of their exposure to dioxin. He also did not know the level of dioxin in the appellees' bodies, either before or after their alleged exposure due to eating fish from the river.

* * *

Dr. Charlton Stanley, a psychologist, was admitted as an expert in the field of human psychology and particularly in the area of human psychological effect of environmental disasters. Dr. Stanley had seen the Fergusons on May 13, 1991. He interviewed them jointly, and took a history. He found that the Fergusons' primary fear besides contracting cancer was not being able to leave something of value, their property, to their son. Stanley believed that the Fergusons suffered from an adjustment disorder. He believed that the Fergusons' fears and distress were genuine and reasonable under the circumstances. Dr. Stanley had not informed the Fergusons of his findings concerning them and it was his understanding that they had not sought any follow-up psychotherapy or counseling.

Guy Blankinship was accepted as an expert in the field of real estate appraisal. Blankinship based his appraisal of the Ferguson property, totaling approximately 14 acres, on 6.1 acres facing the Pascagoula. He estimated a market value of $12,000.00 per acre, for a total of $73,200.00, and stated that the diminution in value of the property due to the presence of dioxin in the Leaf River and the stigma involved with the river was $65,000.00. Blankinship did not know whether dioxin was actually on the Fergusons' property. He had recommended to them that they have the property tested, but they had not tested the property.

TESTING FOR DIOXIN

As the Fergusons did not have themselves or their property tested for the presence of dioxin, they relied on tests of wildlife in the area of the Leaf River to support their claims of emotional distress and nuisance. Appellants used the same test results in an effort to repudiate these claims. The testing took place from 1988 to 1990. The majority of the test results dealt with fish caught in the vicinity of the Leaf River mill. The earlier results showed detectable levels, in parts per trillion or quadrillion, of dioxin in fish caught on the Leaf River. Some of the later results showed a reduction of dioxin levels in the fish tested. None of the testing of fish took place in the vicinity of the Fergusons' property. The testing sites closest to the Fergusons' property were at Merrill, approximately eighty miles upriver from the Fergusons. * * *

APPELLANTS' EXPERTS

* * * * *

Dr. Kenneth Dickson served as a professor of aquatic ecology at the University of North Texas in Denton, Texas. He was accepted as an expert in the fields of aquatic ecology and aquatic biology. Dickson testified that he had examined several studies done concerning the Leaf and Pascagoula Rivers and offered the following conclusions: (1) the Leaf and Pascagoula Rivers were in good condition; (2) the rivers had made a remarkable recovery from pollution problems of the 1950s–60s; (3) there was "no impact on the ecological health of the aquatic communities downstream of the mill, compared to upstream of the mill." He stated that it was extremely unlikely that the mill's effluent could have any effect on aquatic life 100 to 125 miles below the mill. He also labeled as unlikely the effluent from the mill causing a color change in the river 100 miles down river.

James Davis, Jr. was called as an expert real estate appraiser. Davis denied that the Ferguson property had decreased in value due to alleged dioxin contamination or to the 1990 fishing advisory, saying that this had not been born [sic] out by comparable sales in the area.

Dr. Wood Hiatt, professor of psychiatry at the University of Mississippi, had reviewed Dr. Stanley's file and the tests that Dr. Stanley had administered to the Fergusons. Dr. Hiatt found it unacceptable that the Fergusons had been seen together by Dr. Stanley instead of being evaluated as individuals. Dr. Hiatt found that the Fergusons' fear of cancer was not reasonable, as they had refused to have themselves tested to determine if they had potentially dangerous levels of dioxin in their bodies.

* * *

Dr. Renate Kimbrough, a physician who had worked for several governmental agencies, including the Center for Disease Control, the Food and Drug Administration, and the Environmental Protection Agency, was accepted as an expert in public health and epidemiology. She was familiar with the ten to fifteen major studies done on dioxin exposure. Kimbrough testified that there had been no convincing study showing an excess of cancer in those exposed to many times the levels of dioxin alleged to be present in the Leaf and Pascagoula Rivers. She further stated that it would be important to test the blood of the plaintiffs to see whether they had been exposed at all, and to see whether their levels were any different than a normal person's. * * * Kimbrough testified that, assuming dioxin levels of four parts per trillion in fish around the Leaf River mill, and assuming that the plaintiffs lived one hundred miles downriver, she would not expect the plaintiffs to have anything other than normal background exposure. She denied that eating fish from the Leaf or Pascagoula River would pose any health risk. Kimbrough agreed that people who ate large amounts of fish regularly would get higher exposure rates, but not necessarily increased risk. * * *

The jury found in favor of the defendants on the trespass count. As to nuisance, the jury found for the Fergusons, awarding $10,000.00 each. On the emotional distress count the jury found for the Fergusons, awarding $90,000.00 each. In addition, the jury awarded $3,000,000.00 in punitive damages to the Fergusons. * * *

I. WHETHER THE EMOTIONAL DISTRESS VERDICT BELOW MUST BE REVERSED * * *

Appellants argue both that the Fergusons failed to show that they were exposed to dioxin and that the cause of action for fear of future disease does not exist or is not compensable. Assuming there is such a cause of action, appellants argue that there is insufficient evidence to show that appellees' fear is reasonable.

This state recognizes recovery for both negligently and intentionally inflicted emotional distress * * *.

It would be impossible to enumerate all the ways in which emotional distress could be inflicted. However, this Court has never allowed or affirmed a claim of emotional distress based on a fear of contracting a disease or illness in the future, however reasonable.

In this case, there is a lack of evidence proving exposure of the appellees to a dangerous or harmful agent and the record is devoid of any medical evidence pointing to possible or probable future illness. Certainly, if one is to recover for emotional distress predicated on potential future illness there must be substantial proof of exposure and medical evidence that would indicate possible future illness. * * *

II.   WHETHER THE NUISANCE VERDICT BELOW MUST BE REVERSED * * *

The appellees alleged, in their second amended complaint, that the appellants had discharged "into the waters of the Leaf River, and the East and West Pascagoula Rivers dark and foul smelling effluent in sufficient quantities that the color of the river is often altered as far downstream as waters adjacent to plaintiffs' property in Jackson County, Mississippi." * * *

The Fergusons argue that their nuisance claim was based not only on "the dioxin problem, but is also based on the unsightly discoloration of the water, river banks, and sand bars caused by Defendants' injection of the darkening effluent into the Leaf River." * * *

There was testimony that the Pascagoula had darkened, and river banks and sand bars had also been discolored. * * * There was no testimony that the Fergusons' property had been darkened, or that the river had left a dark residue on their land or their buildings. There was no testimony showing the appellants to be the cause of this color change except that the change had been noticed after the appellants began operation of the mill. Some of the appellees' witnesses noticed the color change around 1985; others did not until 1990. Guy Blankinship never mentioned any damage to the property except for the condition of the river and the resulting stigma. We find that the evidence presented is insufficient to constitute a significant interference with the Fergusons' use and enjoyment of their property. We further find that mere stigma, supported by tests showing dioxin contamination no closer than eighty river miles north of the alleged damage, is not sufficient evidence of compensable injury.

* * *

■ McRae, Justice, dissenting:

The majority's ruling is contradictory to the long established principal [sic] of law in this state that physical impact or injury is not necessary to prove intentional, or even negligent infliction of emotional distress. * * *

In concluding that the plaintiffs' fears are too remote, the majority incorrectly distinguished the plaintiffs' fears from their emotional distress. The plaintiffs' emotional distress in this case is the fear that they will become sick in the future. The fear and the emotional distress are merely two different ways of describing the same injury. The fear of future illness is only a more specific way of characterizing the emotional distress suffered by the plaintiffs. The emotional distress in the present case is not "based on the fear of a future illness" as indicated by the majority. The emotional distress, or fear, is instead based on the fish kills, discoloration of the water, and foul odors among other things caused by the Leaf River pollution.

* * *

The majority reverses the nuisance claim for lack of sufficient evidence demonstrating that the contamination existed as far downstream as the Ferguson property. Again, the majority fails to afford the Fergusons the benefit of all favorable inferences that may be reasonably drawn from the evidence. * * * Both Bonnie and Thomas Ferguson testified that the water changed color at the location of their property. * * * The wildlife consumption advisories and commercial fishing ban directly impacted the Ferguson property, and signs were posted to that effect both north and south of the property.

It was reasonable for the jury to conclude from this evidence that dioxin was present in the area of the Ferguson property despite the absence of scientific data specifically from the site of their property. Giving the plaintiffs the benefit of all favorable inferences to be drawn, as is required where the jury has returned a verdict for the plaintiffs, we must conclude that the evidence sufficiently established all of the elements of private nuisance.

NOTES AND QUESTIONS

1. *Economic welfare analysis.* As Ronald Coase demonstrated in his landmark paper, The Problem of Social Cost, 3 J.L. & Econ. 1 (1960), from an economic welfare standpoint nuisance cases present a reciprocal conflict. Neighbors of a pulp mill are hurt if the mill is permitted to pollute the surrounding air and water. But the mill is hurt if the neighbors are given the right to block its polluting activities. The ultimate question is which of the conflicting activities should prevail. Economists typically answer that the efficient result, in which the more valuable activity prevails, should be preferred.

Coase demonstrated that private bargaining against a background of clear legal rules will produce the economically efficient result no matter who begins with the entitlement, provided there are no barriers to a voluntary transaction between the parties. Economists call the costs of surmounting these barriers, which can include the costs of gathering information, making contact with the other affected parties, conducting negotiations, and enforcing the negotiated result, "transaction costs."

Consider a conflict between a sewage treatment plant and nearby residences. Suppose odors from the plant affect 25 homes, lowering the value of each by $20,000. Suppose also that the plant could eliminate those odors through use of a new treatment method at a cost of $450,000. If the law gives neighbors an entitlement to be free of unpleasant odors, how will the conflict be resolved? The plant's operators will either have to eliminate the odor or pay the neighbors enough so that they will choose not to complain. Since in our example it is cheaper to control the odors ($450,000) than to compensate the neighbors (25 x $20,000 = $500,000), the efficient solution is for the plant to adopt the new treatment method. Assuming the plant is managed by well-informed economically rational actors, it will choose to do so.

If instead the law permits the plant to vent its odors without liability, the Coase theorem predicts that the same outcome will result, provided there are no transaction costs. In this case, the neighbors will have to pay the plant to control its odors. Operators of the plant will agree to adopt the new treatment method if the neighbors together can pay a total of at least $450,000. That would require a contribution of $18,000 from each neighbor ($450,000 / 25 = $18,000). Since each neighbor suffers $20,000 worth of harm from the odors, each should be willing to make that contribution.

Will the plant actually adopt the new method in this second example? Coase recognized that, in the real world, transaction costs are frequently significant. What transaction costs might prevent bargaining in this example? Aside from transaction costs, can you see any other possible barriers to achieving the efficient result?

Even if transaction costs are sufficiently low for the Coase theorem to apply, society may not be indifferent to the choice of entitlements, which can have powerful distributional consequences. In the example above, assigning the entitlement to either the plant or the neighbors may result in adoption of the new odor control technology, the efficient solution. But placement of the entitlement will determine who bears the costs of resolving the conflict.

Another limitation of the Coase theorem (and economic efficiency analysis in general) is that it does not effectively account for costs and benefits that are not readily translated into monetary terms. Expert testimony from a real estate appraiser can establish the effect of the plant on the market value of neighboring homes. But does that value capture the full effect on the neighbors? Would a neighbor who does not wish to leave the community be indifferent between the plant eliminating its odors and giving her $20,000? Or suppose the dispute is over water pollution rather than odors, and the neighbors are concerned not only with their property values, but with the health of their children and the ecological integrity of the river. Can and should those values be monetized to determine the preferred outcome?

2. *Strict liability and its limits.* The approach taken by the Seventh Circuit to strict liability in *Indiana Harbor Belt* is fairly typical. Outside the context of products liability, strict liability is typically available only in unusual circumstances, where the activity in question cannot be carried out safely through the exercise of ordinary care, but can be moved to a location where it poses less of a threat. The common law doctrine is not often applied to environmental harms, but it has been imported into statutory law by the Comprehensive Environmental Response, Compensation, and Liability Act (CERCLA), which imposes strict liability for improper disposal of hazardous wastes. CERCLA is discussed in detail in Chapter 9.

3. *Interstate disputes.* In the discussion problem, pollution from the mill crossed state boundaries. Because both air and water are mobile, that is not unusual. What law should govern such disputes?

In two important cases early in the twentieth century, the Supreme Court recognized a federal common law of nuisance, which states could invoke against interstate pollution. In Missouri v. Illinois, 200 U.S. 496 (1906), Missouri complained that the city of Chicago had polluted the Mississippi River. Chicago's sewer system had originally been designed to empty into Lake Michigan. City officials soon realized that was a bad idea, because Lake Michigan was also the source of the city's drinking water. Chicago's engineers devised a plan to reverse the flow of the Chicago River, which carried the sewer discharge, away from Lake Michigan to the Des Plaines River, which eventually flowed to the Mississippi River. Some 357 miles downstream of Chicago, St. Louis drew its drinking water from the Mississippi. Justice Holmes, writing for the Court, observed that, in a case of "serious magnitude, clearly and fully proved," nuisance might provide a remedy for a downstream state. The Court concluded, however, that Missouri, which allowed its own cities to discharge sewage into the river, had failed to prove that Chicago's discharges had caused any harm to St. Louis.

The next year, in Georgia v. Tennessee Copper Co., 206 U.S. 230 (1907), the Court held that Georgia was entitled to an injunction against the operation of two copper smelters located just across the border in Tennessee, fumes from which were damaging forests and crops in Georgia. Justice Holmes again wrote for the Court:

> It is a fair and reasonable demand on the part of a sovereign that the air over its territory should not be polluted on a great scale by sulphurous acid gas, that the forest on its mountains, be they better or worse, and whatever domestic destruction they have suffered, should not be further destroyed or threatened by the act of persons beyond its control, that the crops and orchards on its hills should not be endangered from the same source.

Id. at 238. The parties agreed to postpone entry of a final decree while they attempted to settle the dispute. The state reached a settlement with one of the two smelters, but in 1914 applied for a permanent injunction against the other. In the interim, operators of the smelter had spent more than $600,000, and managed to reduce sulfur emissions by more than half. Nonetheless, the Court concluded that the remaining emissions, which averaged more than 30 tons of sulfur per day, continued to cause damage in Georgia. It therefore imposed emissions limitations, ordering the smelter to limit emissions to no more than 20 tons per day during the summer months, and 40 tons per day at other times. Georgia v. Tennessee Copper Co., 237 U.S. 474 (1915).

In the modern era, the Supreme Court has held that statutory law limits the reach of the federal common law of nuisance. The interplay of federal statutes with federal and state nuisance law is considered in Section 3 of this Chapter.

4. *Remedies in nuisance actions.* Historically, a plaintiff who proved a nuisance was entitled to injunctive relief. Since the industrial revolution, however, courts have been reluctant to enjoin economically valuable polluting activities. In the famous case of Boomer v. Atlantic Cement Co., 26 N.Y.2d 219, 257 N.E.2d 870 (1970), the court found that air pollution from a cement plant constituted a nuisance, but allowed the operator to escape an injunction by paying compensatory damages. Today, American courts typically "balance the equities" to determine if injunctive relief is justified in a nuisance case.

It is important to keep in mind that an injunction need not be a simple command to stop all pollution, and that injunctive and monetary relief are not mutually exclusive. Courts enjoy considerable discretion to combine compensatory and injunctive remedies, and to tailor injunctions to the circumstances of the particular case. A court can retain jurisdiction or appoint a special master to oversee long-term compliance with an injunction.

How might the *Boomer* court have structured an injunction, taking into account both the value of the plant's operations and the plaintiffs' interest in being free of pollution? What difficulties would the court face in crafting and implementing such an injunction? What advantages would a carefully-tailored injunction offer over compensatory damages alone?

5. *The scope of monetary damages.* In the Class Discussion Problem, assuming that James Collins could prove all the elements of nuisance, the common law would have no trouble awarding him compensatory damages for the reduction in value of his property, for any demonstrable present harm to his health, and for the discomfort and annoyance associated with the discoloration and unpleasant aroma of the river. As you can see from the *Leaf River Forest Products* case, property value reduction does become problematic where it results from "stigma," that is reputational harm not connected to actual contamination or remaining after the contamination is removed. Although the economic damage from stigma is real, it is in some sense irrational. Should a polluter bear responsibility for the effect of public fear on property values, even if that fear is misplaced? On the other hand, as between the polluter and the property owner, who is more responsible for that harm?

Other forms of economic damages are even more problematic. Recreational use of the Pigeon River would surely be affected by the pollution detailed in the problem. Should the owner of a rafting outfitter or of a rural campground frequented by fishermen and rafters be able to bring a claim against Fox? What about the owner of a sporting goods store whose business depends on sales of recreational fishing equipment? A nuisance claim would not be available to those people because the damage they suffer is not to the use of real property. Although negligence claims are broader, courts have struggled to find principled bases for addressing the claims of those who are economically dependent upon a natural resource but lack a proprietary interest in affected land. One approach is to distinguish compensable "direct" harm to interests such as commercial fishing from non-compensable "indirect" harm to processors, restaurateurs, and others. *See* Pruitt v. Allied Chemical, 523 F.Supp. 975 (E.D. Va. 1981); Union Oil Co. v. Oppen, 501 F.2d 558 (9th Cir. 1974). Can this distinction be defended? If not, should both or neither type of interest be remediable?

As the *Leaf River* excerpt makes clear, the risk of future health consequences and the fear likely to accompany that risk have also proved challenging for courts. Treatment of fear of disease in tort cases is discussed in more detail in the notes at the end of Section 2 of this chapter.

What about those who would raft or fish the Pigeon River if it were less polluted, or those who simply like to observe its wildlife? Common law historically limited tort recovery to economic damages. In general, that remains true even under modern statutory schemes. Recreational interests could challenge the mill's permit under the Clean Water Act or seek an injunction to force compliance with that permit, but they could not seek compensatory damages for the harm to their recreational interests. Under the Clean Water Act and Comprehensive Environmental Response, Compensation, and Liability Act, however, federal and state governments can recover for damages to natural resources, including lost existence and option values. Natural resource damage actions are discussed further in Chapter 9.

Punitive damages may be awarded in pollution cases if the defendant's conduct is sufficiently wrongful, but the size of the punitive damages award may be limited by statutory, common law, or constitutional doctrines. Perhaps the best known, and certainly the most drawn-out, environmental law punitive damages dispute followed the 1989 grounding of the Exxon Valdez, which spilled 11,000,000 gallons of oil into Alaska's Prince William Sound. After finding that Exxon had recklessly caused the accident, a jury awarded commercial fishermen and native Alaskans $5 billion in punitive damages. A lengthy series of appeals and remands followed. In 2007, the Ninth Circuit approved a punitive damages award of $2.5 billion. In re Exxon Valdez, 490 F.3d 1066 (9th Cir. 2007). With Justice Alito taking no part in the decision, an equally divided Supreme Court ruled that punitive damages could be assessed for reckless acts by company officials. The Court went on, however, to hold by a 5–3 vote that under maritime common law punitive damages could not exceed compensatory damages, which in this case were $507 million. Exxon Shipping Co. v. Baker, 554 U.S. 471 (2008). In the *Leaf River* case, do you think the large punitive damages award, far in excess of the compensatory damages, played a role in the court's decision to reverse the nuisance finding?

6. *The interplay of litigation and political action.* Persons who believe they have been harmed by pollution are not limited to litigation. They can (and do) also seek remedies through the political process and the market. In the actual dispute on which the Pigeon River problem is based, the downstream residents and environmental advocates posted signs in prominent areas along the River pointedly blaming the paper mill for its condition, persuaded the state of Tennessee to sue North Carolina over the terms of the permit issued to the mill, and pushed the US EPA to take over permitting authority. All of those steps contributed to the mill's eventual agreement to significant tightening of its permit and installation of costly pollution control equipment. By 2007, dioxin contamination below the mill had declined sufficiently that the states of North Carolina and Tennessee were able to lift longstanding advisories against consumption of fish from the Pigeon River, although local environmental activists still think the new permit allows the mill to discharge too much pollution.

SECTION 2.   TOXIC TORTS

Toxic torts are personal injury actions based on exposure to substances that present an unusually high risk to human health or the environment. Toxic tort actions arise in a variety of contexts, including occupational and environmental exposure.

As the excerpt from *Leaf River* in the previous Section suggests, toxic tort actions often present difficult issues of causation. To prevail, plaintiffs must show: 1) that they were exposed to chemicals released by the defendants; 2) that those chemicals can cause the types of harm they suffered; and 3) that the chemicals in fact did cause their harm.

Each of these elements may require expert testimony and expensive tests, making toxic tort cases costly and time-consuming to litigate. Plaintiffs in *Leaf River* failed to satisfy the first element, because they did not offer tests showing dioxin contamination of their property or themselves. In a later case involving the same mill, plaintiffs provided proof of exposure, but were unable to trace the dioxins to defendant's mill. Anglado v. Leaf River Forest Products, 716 So.2d 543 (Miss. 1998). As the following excerpt illustrates, however, often the most difficult hurdle for toxic tort plaintiffs is proof that exposure has caused their injury.

In re "Agent Orange" Product Liability Litigation

United States District Court, Eastern District of New York, 1985.
611 F.Supp. 1223.

[Veterans of the Vietnam war filed a class action alleging that exposure to "Agent Orange" manufactured by the chemical company defendants had caused them various health problems. Agent Orange, a mix of the herbicides 2,4–D and 2,4,5–T, which contained dioxin as a contaminant, was used as a defoliant during the war. It got its nickname from the bright label on its containers.

The case was assigned to Chief Judge Jack Weinstein. Judge Weinstein brokered a $180 million settlement, the largest tort recovery to that date in the United States. The settlement authorized recovery by all service persons and their biological children without any showing of causation. Judge Weinstein approved the settlement in a lengthy opinion, 597 F.

Supp. 740 (E.D.N.Y. 1984), despite expressing reservations about the causation issue. Id. at 745–46.

Many veterans groups opposed the settlement, however, because it limited each member of the extremely large class to a maximum recovery of $12,700. Several hundred claimants elected to opt out of the class action to pursue their individual claims. In the following opinion, Judge Weinstein rejected their claims.]

■ WEINSTEIN, DISTRICT JUDGE.

Defendants, seven chemical companies, have moved to dismiss or in the alternative for summary judgment. Plaintiffs are Vietnam veterans and members of their families who have opted out of the class previously certified by the court * * *. They allege that as a result of the veterans' exposure to Agent Orange, a herbicide manufactured by the defendants, they suffer from various health problems. * * *

Plaintiff Vietnam veterans do suffer. Many deserve help from the government. They cannot obtain aid through this suit against private corporations. * * *

The most serious deficiency in plaintiffs' case is their failure to present credible evidence of a causal link between exposure to Agent Orange and the various diseases from which they are allegedly suffering. * * *

In support of their contention that Agent Orange did not cause the various ailments that allegedly afflict the veteran plaintiffs, defendants rest upon a number of epidemiological studies. As this court has indicated in extensive and repeated recorded colloquy with counsel and in prior opinions, all reliable studies of the effect of Agent Orange on members of the class so far published provide no support for plaintiffs' claims of causation.

Epidemiological studies rely on "statistical methods to detect abnormally high incidences of disease in a study population and to associate these incidences with unusual exposures to suspect environmental factors." Dore, "A Commentary on the Use of Epidemiological Evidence in Demonstrating Cause-in-Fact," 7 Harv. Envtl. L. Rev. 429, 431 (1983). In their study of diseases in human populations, epidemiologists use data from surveys, death certificates, and medical and clinical observations. Id.

A number of sound epidemiological studies have been conducted on the health effects of exposure to Agent Orange. These are the only useful studies having any bearing on causation.

All the other data supplied by the parties rests on surmise and inapposite extrapolations from animal studies and industrial accidents. It is hypothesized that, predicated on this experience, adverse effects of Agent Orange on plaintiffs might at some time in the future be shown to some degree of probability.

The available relevant studies have addressed the direct effects of exposure on servicepersons and the indirect effects of exposure on spouses and children of servicepersons. No acceptable study to date of Vietnam veterans and their families concludes that there is a causal connection between exposure to Agent Orange and the serious adverse health effects claimed by plaintiffs. * * *

Plaintiffs cite a number of studies conducted on animals and industrial workers as evidence of a causal link between exposure to [dioxin] and the development of various hepatotoxic, hematotoxic, genotoxic, and enzymatic responses. None of these studies do more than show that there may be a causal connection between dioxin and disease. None show such a connection between plaintiffs and Agent Orange. * * *

Even most of plaintiffs' experts express doubt about causation, except for some ill-defined possible "association" as compared with associations with any specific other products or natural carcinogens; none supports the conclusion that present evidence permits a scientifically acceptable conclusion that Agent Orange did cause a specific plaintiff's specific disease. * * *

Plaintiffs offer the opinion of two experts who conclude that in the cases of the specific opt-out plaintiffs before the court, exposure to Agent Orange caused adverse health effects. * * *

Dr. Singer, who is board certified in internal medicine, hematology, and oncology, reaches a number of conclusions based on his review of the numerous form affidavits with their attached checklists. He bases his opinion on his medical background, a review of the literature on the biomedical effects of Agent Orange, and an examination of the individual affidavits. He apparently did not examine any medical records or any plaintiffs. * * *

Dr. Singer notes at the outset that 2,4–D, 2,4,5–T, and 2,3,7,8–tetra-chlorodibenzo-p-dioxin ("dioxin") "are potent and toxic agents capable of inducing a wide variety of adverse effects both in animals and in man." Dr. Singer then analyzes the various ailments suffered by the individual affiants. * * *

As a review of Dr. Singer's affidavit reveals, he attributes some 37 separate diseases, disorders, and symptoms—including baldness and diarrhea—to exposure to Agent Orange. * * *

Stripped of its verbiage, Dr. Singer summarizes his overall conclusion by stating that *if* the affiants are telling the truth and *if* there is no cause for their complaints other than Agent Orange, then Agent Orange must have caused their problems. Dr. Singer states:

> *Assuming the truth of the affidavits submitted, and absent any evidence of pre-existing, intervening, or superseding causes for the symptoms and diseases* complained of in these affidavits, it is my opinion to a reasonable degree of medical probability (that is, more likely than not) that the medical difficulties described by the affiants were proximately caused by exposure to Agent Orange. (Emphasis supplied.)

Put differently, Dr. Singer's analysis amounts to this: the affiants complain of various medical problems; animals and workers exposed to extensive dosages of [dioxin] have suffered from related difficulties; therefore, assuming nothing else caused the affiants' afflictions, Agent Orange caused them. One need hardly be a doctor of medicine to make the statement that if X is a possible cause of Y, and if there is no other possible cause of Y, X must have caused Y. Dr. Singer's formulation avoids the problem before us: which of myriad possible causes of Y created a particular veteran's problems. To take just one of the diseases reported by plaintiffs in an undifferentiated form, and relied upon by Dr. Singer, hepatitis: this is a disease common in the civilian population and there is not the slightest evidence that its incidence is greater among those exposed to Agent Orange than those not exposed. * * *

Plaintiffs belatedly submitted affidavits by Dr. Samuel S. Epstein. He has been specially trained in the fields of pathology, bacteriology, and public health. * * *

* * * Dr. Epstein attributes some fourteen different diseases and afflictions to exposure to Agent Orange of fifteen plaintiffs. Dr. Epstein's affidavits, even if considered timely, are insufficient to oppose the motion for summary judgment. All the diseases in the cases he relies upon are found in the general population of those who were never exposed to Agent Orange. There is no showing that the incidence of the diseases relied upon are greater in the Agent Orange-exposed population than in the population generally. * * *

Central to the inadequacy of plaintiffs' case is their inability to exclude other possible causes of plaintiffs' illnesses—those arising out of their service in Vietnam as well as those that all of us face in military and civilian life. For example, the largest number of plaintiffs considered by Dr. Singer suffer from symptoms such as exhaustion, depression, sleep disturbances, anxiety and anger. He concludes that these symptoms are "compatible with" exposure to dioxin. As scientific literature establishes, such symptoms are also frequently identified with Vietnam stress syndrome due to battle and other military stresses. Dr. Singer in no way rules out stress syndrome as the cause of plaintiffs' neurological symptoms. * * *

After careful scrutiny of all available evidence in this protracted litigation, there is no doubt that a directed verdict at the close of each of plaintiffs' cases would be required. Such careful scrutiny of proposed evidence is especially appropriate in the toxic tort area. * * *

Having voluntarily given up the advantages of the class action, each plaintiff is in the position of being unable to prove either (1) that his disease is due to Agent Orange, or (2) that any particular defendant produced the Agent Orange to which he may have been exposed. No case has ever permitted recovery in such a situation. There is no possible theory of law on which these individual opt-out plaintiffs can recover. * * *

The cases of the veterans and any other members of the class who opted out of the class are dismissed.

NOTES AND QUESTIONS

1. *Causation.* Proving causation is often exceedingly difficult in toxic tort cases. As the New Jersey Supreme Court has explained:

In toxic tort cases, the task of proving causation is invariably more complex because of the long latency period of illness caused by carcinogens or other toxic chemicals. The fact that ten or twenty years or more may intervene between the exposure and the manifestation of the disease highlights the practical difficulties encountered in the effort to prove causation. Moreover, the fact that segments of the entire population are afflicted by cancer and other toxically-induced diseases requires plaintiffs, years after their exposure, to counter the argument that other intervening exposures or forces were the "cause" of their injury.

Ayers v. Jackson, 106 N.J. 557, 585, 525 A.2d 287, 301 (1987).

Plaintiffs must prove both "general causation," i.e., that the substance to which they were exposed is capable of causing the type of injury they suffered, and "specific causation," i.e., that the substance caused their specific injury. Scientific uncertainty complicates both tasks.

For obvious reasons, controlled tests of the effects of deliberate exposure of humans to substances suspected of toxicity are hardly ever available. Plaintiffs therefore must rely on other types of evidence to prove causation. They commonly offer one or more of the following, listed in order of increasing probative value: 1) expert testimony about structure-activity relationships (predictions about the toxicity of a given substance based on information about the effects of chemically related compounds); 2) experimental studies using isolated animal tissues ("in vitro" studies); 3) experimental studies on live animals ("in vivo" studies); and 4) epidemiological studies of human disease.

Structure-activity evidence rests on educated guesses that similar compounds will produce similar types and levels of harm. In vitro studies can illuminate biological pathways of harm. Effects produced in a test tube, however, may not occur in live animals. Because human beings are biologically similar in many respects to other mammals, in vivo tests on animals such as rats or mice often provide useful models for medical research. Nonetheless, it is difficult to extrapolate from animal toxicity tests, which are often performed using high doses and animal strains known to be especially susceptible to disease, to low dose exposure of human beings.

Epidemiological studies compare the incidence of disease in populations exposed at different levels to a potential toxin or the exposure levels of sick persons to those of healthy ones. Because they directly relate human exposure to disease, epidemiological studies provide the strongest evidence that a substance does or does not produce a particular disease. When available, they are often given more weight by courts than other evidence. But the results of these studies can also be difficult to interpret. The scope of epidemiological studies is limited by cost and the chance occurrence of exposure. Studies of a small exposed population may miss a weak, but real, association. Studies of the effects of high exposure, as often occurs in occupational settings, may be difficult to apply to lower environmental doses. Often, epidemiological studies are not undertaken until litigation draws attention to a potential effect. In that situation they are necessarily short term, and may not reveal an effect with a long latent period.

Well-designed and implemented epidemiological studies generate relative risk factors that can be used to prove causation. Suppose 10 of every 10,000 persons in the general population develops chronic myelogenous leukemia, a rare form of cancer. If 21 of 10,000 persons exposed to substance X develop chronic myelogenous leukemia, the relative risk factor (incidence in the exposed population divided by incidence in the control population) for substance X would be 2.1 (21/10). Since the risk of leukemia is more than twice as high in the exposed group, there is a better than 50% probability (i.e., it is more likely than not), that any leukemia in the exposed group is attributable to exposure.

On the other hand, if only 16 of 10,000 exposed persons develop chronic myelogenous leukemia, the relative risk factor is 1.6. In this group, only six of 16 leukemias would be attributable to substance X, and the probability that any individual case is due to substance X would be 37.5%. Differential diagnosis, where a physician testifies that other causes are unlikely based on the case history or clinical evidence, may allow a jury to find specific causation. In the absence of additional evidence implicating substance X or ruling out other possible leukemia causes, however, ordinary legal standards would not allow a finding that any leukemia in this group was due to substance X.

In these circumstances, application of ordinary tort principles leads to either over- or under-compensation. In the first example above, all twenty-one plaintiffs would recover, although only eleven cases were caused by substance X. On the other hand, in the second example, no plaintiff would recover, although six have been harmed by substance X. Faced with the probabilistic nature of toxic tort cases, courts have struggled to find a balance between excessive generosity to plaintiffs, which discourages socially valuable activities that require or produce toxic substances, and excessive generosity to defendants, which leaves injured plaintiffs uncompensated and provides too little deterrence.

Can the choice between over- and under-deterrence be avoided? Some observers have suggested that each member of the exposed group be compensated in proportion to the increased risk of disease. *See* Richard Delgado, Beyond Sindell: Relaxation of Cause–In–Fact Rules for Indeterminate Plaintiffs, 70 Calif. L. Rev. 881 (1982); Glen O. Robinson, Pobabilistic Causation and Compensation for Tortious Risk, 14 J. Legal Stud. 779, 787 (1985); Christopher H. Schroeder, Corrective Justice and Liability for Increasing Risks, 37 UCLA L. Rev. 439 (1990). In the first example above, each plaintiff would recover 11/21 (the proportion of cancers attributable to substance X) of the damages attributable to a cancer. In the second case, each would recover 6/16 of that amount. What advantages would this approach have over the traditional requirement that each plaintiff individually prove harm? What disadvantages? Should it apply in a lawsuit brought not as a class action but by an individual plaintiff? Should some minimum level of increased risk be required before liability is imposed?

2. *Statistical significance.* There is still another complication to consider. In any study, the observed incidence of disease will include chance variation within the population as well as the effects of exposure to the substance at issue. By convention, epidemiologists regard an effect as proven only if statistical tests show a very low probability (typically 5% or less) that the observed outcome resulted from chance variation. The power of studies to distinguish real from chance variation goes up as the number of test subjects goes up. If the exposed population is small or the background rate high, it may be impossible to obtain statistically significant results. Should courts allow plaintiffs to bring in evidence of epidemiologic studies which suggest an effect but do not meet conventional scientific standards for statistical significance? Should such evidence ever be sufficient to establish causation? Compare Brock v. Merrell Dow Pharmaceuticals, Inc., 884 F.2d 166, 167 (5th Cir. 1989) (finding plaintiffs' failure to present statistically significant epidemiological evidence fatal to their case) with DeLuca v. Merrell Dow Pharmaceuticals, Inc., 911 F.2d 941, 955 (3d Cir. 1990) (describing statistical significance as only one factor in the evaluation of epidemiological evidence).

3. *The substantial factor test.* Some courts have loosened the causation requirements for toxic tort plaintiffs by applying the "substantial factor" test, originally developed for multiple tort-feasor situations. Under this test, a plaintiff can prevail on a showing that the defendant's action was a substantial factor in the injury, without having to prove that the injury would not have occurred absent defendant's action. *See* Elam v. Alcolac, Inc., 765 S.W.2d 42, 174 (Mo. App. 1988). A toxic substance may be considered a substantial factor in the injury if its contribution to the harm is "more than negligible or theoretical." Rutherford v. Owens–Illinois, Inc., 16 Cal. 4th 953, 978, 941 P.2d 1203 (1997). In Kennedy v. Southern California Edison, 219 F.3d 988 (9th Cir. 2000), a panel of the Ninth Circuit, applying California law, initially concluded that a jury could reasonably find that radiation exposure was a "substantial factor" in plaintiff's disease in the face of uncontroverted expert testimony that there was only a 1 in 100,000 chance that the exposure caused the disease, reversed itself. The court explained:

> Presented perhaps more concretely, if the entire U.S. population were exposed to the amount of radiation in appellee's hypothetical upon which its expert based his statistical opinion, then approximately 2,500 people would contract [plaintiff's disease]. While this number is relatively small, it is more than "negligible."

Id. at 999. Subsequently, though, the panel reversed itself, noting:

> At trial, the defendants introduced uncontroverted expert testimony that [even assuming plaintiffs' claims of exposure to radioactive "fuel fleas" were correct], there is only a one in 100,000 chance that her CML [chronic myelogenous leukemia] was caused by the exposure. Indeed the testimony went further—even assuming that we knew for certain that Mrs. Kennedy's CML was caused by radiation (rather than some other source), there would only be a one in 30,000 chance that

"fuel flea" radiation would have been the actual cause. On these facts, the contribution of the "fuel fleas," even assuming exposure and ingestion and with full knowledge that the person in question actually developed CML, only played an infinitesimal or theoretical part in bringing about [the] injury."

Kennedy v. Southern California Edison, 268 F.3d 763 (9th Cir. 2001). Was the court right the first time or the second about what constitutes a negligible risk?

Critics of the substantial factor test argue that focusing on risk alone is inappropriate. "[R]isk does not equate with cause. If ten people shoot at a deer, each contributes to the risk that the deer will be hit, but if a single bullet strikes the animal, only one person caused its death." Bert Black and David H. Hollander Jr., Unravelling Causation: Back to the Basics, 3 U. Balt. J. Envtl. L. 1, 21 (1993). Is this an apt analogy to toxic exposure cases?

4. *Eliminating cause-in-fact?* Should standard causation analysis be relaxed more radically in toxic tort cases? Professor Margaret Berger argues that requiring proof that defendant's substance caused plaintiff's harm encourages defendants to avoid developing or disclosing information about potential health risks. She suggests imposing liability instead for failure to provide the public with information about the risks posed by a substance, subject to an affirmative defense that the adverse health reactions could not plausibly have been caused by exposure to defendant's product or substance. She would protect defendants who release sufficient information from liability. Margaret A. Berger, Eliminating General Causation: Notes Towards a New Theory of Justice and Toxic Torts, 97 Columbia L. Rev. 2117 (1997). Is this proposal appealing? Does it rest on unproven assumptions that most chemicals are harmful? That most cancers are attributable to artificial chemicals? In light of the difficulties of obtaining clear scientific proof that a substance is or is not toxic, how would courts define the standards for testing? How should they factor in the dose to which defendant exposes plaintiffs? The ability or inability of a plaintiff to avoid exposure? Would this proposal over-deter the use of relatively safe substances?

5. *Expert witness testimony under the Federal Rules of Evidence.* Concerned that juries may not be able to evaluate scientific evidence and may be improperly swayed by the emotional appeals of injured plaintiffs, courts have devised special admissibility tests for expert witness testimony. For many years the federal courts used the *Frye* test, so called after the case in which it was first enunciated, Frye v. United States, 293 F. 1013 (D.C. Cir. 1923), to determine admissibility. *Frye* allowed expert testimony only if the technique concerned was generally accepted in the relevant scientific community.

In Daubert v. Merrell Dow Pharmaceuticals, 509 U.S. 579 (1993), the Supreme Court ruled that the Federal Rules of Evidence, adopted in 1975, superseded the *Frye* test. Under the Federal Rules, the Court explained, the trial judge must determine whether expert testimony will assist the trier of fact. "This entails a preliminary assessment of whether the reasoning or methodology underlying the testimony is scientifically valid and of whether that reasoning or methodology properly can be applied to the facts in issue. * * * The focus, of course, must be solely on principles and methodology, not on the conclusions that they generate." Id. at 592–95. Factors to be considered include whether the theory or technique has been tested; whether it has been subjected to peer review; the known or potential error rate; and general acceptance in the relevant scientific community. Id. at 593–94.

Daubert offered a partial victory to both plaintiffs and defendants. Plaintiffs at least nominally won relief from *Frye*'s general acceptance test, which the Supreme Court described as "rigid," and "at odds with the liberal thrust" of the Federal Rules of Evidence. Id at 588. Defendants, on the other hand, gained a strong endorsement of the role of the trial judge as evidentiary gatekeeper, shielding the jury from unreliable expert evidence. Surveys of federal judges and attorneys before and after *Daubert* suggest that *Daubert* has led to closer scrutiny and more frequent exclusion of expert testimony. *See* Molly Treadwell Johnson et al., Expert Testimony in Federal Civil Trials: A Preliminary Analysis (Federal Judicial Center 2000).

State courts have split on *Daubert*. According to a detailed study, as of mid–2003 twenty-seven states had adopted a test for admission of expert testimony "consistent with" *Daubert* in a broad sense. David E. Bernsteing & Jeffrey D. Jackson, The Daubert Trilogy in the States, 44 Jurimetrics J. 351, 356 (2004). Only nine had adopted *Daubert* and its progeny precisely as applied in the federal courts. *Id.* at 357.

6. *Accrual of the cause of action.* Virtually all jurisdictions now apply the "discovery rule" to claims based on development of disease long after exposure. The statute of limitations runs not from the time of exposure but from the time when the plaintiff knew or should have known of the injury. Determining that date may not be easy.

Suppose a train derails near a construction site, releasing a substance which can cause lung cancer. Three years later Alicia, who was working at the construction site on the day of the derailment, develops shortness of breath. She attributes her symptoms to the general effects of aging, a new sedentary job, and recent weight gain. Two years after that, a physical exam reveals that Alicia has a lung tumor. The statute of limitations for negligence in this jurisdiction is 1 year. Can Alicia bring suit? Does it matter whether the derailment and resulting release were widely reported in the local media? Whether Alicia actually knew of the derailment or the release?

7. *Defining compensable injury.* Suppose Brad works at the train yard where the derailment occurs. Aware of his exposure to a toxic substance, Brad consults his doctor, who opines that the exposure has increased Brad's risk of lung cancer from 1 in 1,000 to roughly 1 in 100. The doctor suggests annual chest X-rays to ensure that the disease, if it develops, will be caught early. Brad is not suffering any current symptoms. Does he have a present claim for the increased risk of cancer? For his fear that he will become a cancer victim? For the costs of medical monitoring?

Courts have generally refused to allow recovery solely on the basis of an increased risk of developing cancer or other diseases in the future. Many courts, however, have allowed recovery on a slightly different theory for fear of future disease, which is recognized as a form of emotional distress. For a claim of negligent infliction of emotional distress, many jurisdictions require proof of some present physical impact or injury other than mere exposure to the toxic substance. *See*, e.g., Ball v. Joy Technologies, 958 F.2d 36, 38 (4th Cir. 1991). A few have done away with the need for physical injury or allowed recovery based on the impact of exposure alone. *See* Hagerty v. L & L Marine Serv., 788 F.2d 315, 318, *modified on denial of rehearing en banc*, 797 F.2d 256 (5th Cir. 1986); Herber v. Johns–Manville Corp., 785 F.2d 79, 85 (3d Cir. 1986).

Which is the better approach? Is the answer different for toxic torts than traditional ones? Consider another hypothetical. Christine buys a container of defendant's yogurt which, due to defendant's negligence, contains broken glass. Christine discovers the glass when she puts the first spoonful in her mouth. She is not cut but is upset, and fears that she may have swallowed some glass. Cf. Restatement (2d) of Torts, § 436A, illus. 1. Is Christine's emotional distress claim equivalent to Brad's? If not, which is stronger and why?

Fear of future disease must be "reasonable" to support recovery. Is Brad's fear reasonable? Should reasonableness depend on the extent to which exposure has increased the risk, or only on the absolute magnitude of the risk? Is it relevant that surveys show that cancer is a particularly "dread" disease? The California Supreme Court has limited recovery for fear of future disease to plaintiffs who can show that they are more likely than not to develop disease in the future. The Court explained:

> We cannot say that it would never be reasonable for a person who has ingested toxic substances to harbor a genuine and serious fear of cancer where reliable medical or scientific opinion indicates that such ingestion has significantly increased his or her risk of cancer, but not to a probable likelihood. Indeed, we would be very hard pressed to find that, as a matter of law, a plaintiff faced with a 20 percent or 30 percent chance of developing cancer cannot genuinely, seriously, and reasonably fear the prospect of cancer. Nonetheless, we conclude * * * that emotional distress caused by the fear of cancer that is not probable should generally not be compensable in a negligence action.

> As a starting point in our analysis, we recognize the indisputable fact that all of us are exposed to carcinogens every day. * * *

> Thus, all of us are potential fear of cancer plaintiffs, provided we are sufficiently aware of and worried about the possibility of developing cancer from exposure to or ingestion of a carcinogenic exposure. The enormity of the class of potential plaintiffs cannot be overstated * * *.

Potter v. Firestone Tire & Rubber Co., 6 Cal.4th 965, 863 P.2d 795 (1993).

Some, but not all, courts have allowed recovery of the costs of medical monitoring following toxic exposure. What arguments can you think of for and against awards of medical monitoring costs? Do the concerns about a potential flood of litigation expressed in the excerpt from *Potter* apply equally to medical monitoring claims? Does it matter whether the plaintiff has medical insurance which would pay for the tests? Might a medical monitoring award reduce the potential future damages, should plaintiff develop disease? Where medical monitoring costs are recoverable, plaintiffs typically are required to show a significantly increased risk of contracting a serious latent disease, and that early detection and treatment of the disease is beneficial. *See* In re Paoli R.R. Yard PCB Litigation, 916 F.2d 829, 852 (3d Cir. 1990); *Potter*, 863 P.2d at 821.

SECTION 3.   THE INTERPLAY OF STATUTES AND COMMON LAW

Federal pollution laws (and their state analogues) impose substantive standards on polluting sources. Violation of a statutory or regulatory standard or failure to obtain a required permit, may be a nuisance or negligence per se, automatically subjecting the violator to common-law liability in addition to whatever consequences are imposed by statute. *See*, e.g., Gill v. LDI, 19 F. Supp. 2d 1188, 1198–99 (W.D. Wash. 1998) (holding that violation of Clean Water Act permit amounts to nuisance per se under Washington law).

Compliance with statutory and regulatory standards, on the other hand, is not an automatic bar to a tort action. *See*, e.g., Galaxy Carpet Mills v. Massengill, 255 Ga. 360, 338 S.E.2d 428 (1986) (polluting boilers could be declared a nuisance even though operated in accordance with state permit); Village of Wilsonville v. SCA Servs., 86 Ill.2d 1, 426 N.E.2d 824 (1981) (enjoining operation of hazardous waste disposal as public and private nuisance notwithstanding state permit). Compliance may, however, be evidence of reasonableness or of the expected standard of care.

Statutes may explicitly displace or explicitly allow concurrent operation of common law nuisance doctrine. Often, however, environmental statutes are not entirely clear about the role nuisance may or may not continue to play. The next two cases address the role of federal and state common law in areas addressed by environmental statutes.

American Electric Power Company, Inc. v. Connecticut

United States Supreme Court, 2011.
__ U.S. __, 131 S.Ct. 2527.

■ GINSBURG, J. delivered the opinion of the Court.

We address in this opinion the question whether the plaintiffs (several States, the city of New York, and three private land trusts) can maintain federal common law public nuisance claims against carbon-dioxide emitters (four private power companies and the federal Tennessee Valley Authority).

As relief, the plaintiffs ask for a decree setting carbon-dioxide emissions for each defendant at an initial cap, to be further reduced annually. The Clean Air Act and the Environmental Protection Agency action the Act authorizes, we hold, displace the claims the plaintiffs seek to pursue.

I

In *Massachusetts v. EPA*, 549 U.S. 497 (2007) [excerpted in Chapter 10], this Court held that the Clean Air Act authorizes federal regulation of emissions of carbon dioxide and other greenhouse gases. * * * Because EPA had authority to set greenhouse gas emission standards and had offered no "reasoned explanation" for failing to do so, we concluded that the agency had not acted "in accordance with law" when it denied the requested rulemaking. Id., at 534–535.

Responding to our decision in *Massachusetts*, EPA undertook greenhouse gas regulation. In December 2009, the agency concluded that greenhouse gas emissions from motor vehicles "cause, or contribute to, air pollution which may reasonably be anticipated to endanger public health or welfare," the Act's regulatory trigger. * * *

EPA and the Department of Transportation subsequently issued a joint final rule regulating emissions from light-duty vehicles, and initiated a joint rulemaking covering medium- and heavy-duty vehicles. EPA also began phasing in requirements that new or modified "[m]ajor [greenhouse gas] emitting facilities" use the "best available control technology." Finally, EPA commenced a rulemaking under § 111 of the Act, 42 U.S.C. § 7411, to set limits on greenhouse gas emissions from new, modified, and existing fossil-fuel fired power plants. Pursuant to a settlement finalized in March 2011, EPA has committed to issuing a proposed rule by July 2011, and a final rule by May 2012.

II

The lawsuits we consider here began well before EPA initiated the efforts to regulate greenhouse gases just described. In July 2004, two groups of plaintiffs filed separate complaints in the Southern District of New York against the same five major electric power companies. The first group of plaintiffs included eight States and New York City, the second joined three nonprofit land trusts; both groups are respondents here. The defendants, now petitioners, are four private companies and the Tennessee Valley Authority, a federally owned corporation that operates fossil-fuel fired power plants in several States. According to the complaints, the defendants "are the five largest emitters of carbon dioxide in the United States." Their collective annual emissions of 650 million tons constitute 25 percent of emissions from the domestic electric power sector, 10 percent of emissions from all domestic human activities, and 2.5 percent of all anthropogenic emissions worldwide.

By contributing to global warming, the plaintiffs asserted, the defendants' carbon-dioxide emissions created a "substantial and unreasonable interference with public rights," in violation of the federal common law of interstate nuisance, or, in the alternative, of state tort law. The States and New York City alleged that public lands, infrastructure, and health were at risk from climate change. The trusts urged that climate change would destroy habitats for animals and rare species of trees and plants on land the trusts owned and conserved. All plaintiffs sought injunctive relief requiring each defendant "to cap its carbon dioxide emissions and then reduce them by a specified percentage each year for at least a decade."

* * * * *

III

[With Justice Sotomayor not participating because she sat on the Second Circuit panel that produced the decision appealed from, an equally divided Court affirmed that at least some plaintiffs had standing under *Massachusetts v. EPA*, and that the political question doctrine did not bar judicial review.]

IV

A

"There is no federal general common law," *Erie R. Co. v. Tompkins*, 304 U.S. 64, 78 (1938), famously recognized. In the wake of *Erie*, however, a keener understanding developed. See generally Friendly, In Praise of Erie—And of the New Federal Common Law, 39 N.Y.U.L.Rev. 383 (1964). *Erie* "le[ft] to the states what ought be left to them," id., at 405, and thus required "federal courts [to] follow state decisions on matters of substantive law appropriately cognizable by the states," id., at 422. *Erie* also sparked "the emergence of a federal decisional law in areas of national concern." Id., at 405. The "new" federal common law addresses "subjects within national legislative power where Congress has so directed" or where the basic scheme of the Constitution so demands. Id., at 408, n. 119, 421–422. Environmental protection is undoubtedly an area "within national legislative power," one in which federal courts may fill in "statutory interstices," and, if necessary, even "fashion federal law." Id., at 421–422. As the Court stated in Milwaukee I: "When we deal with air and water in their ambient or interstate aspects, there is a federal common law." 406 U.S., at 103.

Decisions of this Court predating Erie, but compatible with the distinction emerging from that decision between "general common law" and "specialized federal common law," Friendly, supra, at 405, have approved federal common law suits brought by one State to abate pollution emanating from another State. See, e.g., Missouri v. Illinois, 180 U.S. 208, 241–243 (1901) (permitting suit by Missouri to enjoin Chicago from discharging untreated sewage into interstate waters); New Jersey v. City of New York, 283 U.S. 473, 477, 481–483 (1931) (ordering New York City to stop dumping garbage off New Jersey coast); Georgia v. Tennessee Copper Co., 240 U.S. 650 (1916) (ordering private copper companies to curtail sulfur-dioxide discharges in Tennessee that caused harm in Georgia). See also Milwaukee I, 406 U.S., at 107 (post-Erie decision upholding suit by Illinois to abate sewage discharges into Lake Michigan). The plaintiffs contend that their right to maintain this suit follows inexorably from that line of decisions.

Recognition that a subject is meet for federal law governance, however, does not necessarily mean that federal courts should create the controlling law. Absent a demonstrated need for a federal rule of decision, the Court has taken "the prudent course" of "adopt[ing] the readymade body of state law as the federal rule of decision until Congress strikes a different accommodation." United States v. Kimbell Foods, Inc., 440 U.S. 715, 740 (1979). And where, as here, borrowing the law of a particular State would be inappropriate, the Court remains mindful that it does not have creative power akin to that vested in Congress.

In the cases on which the plaintiffs heavily rely, States were permitted to sue to challenge activity harmful to their citizens' health and welfare. We have not yet decided whether private citizens (here, the land trusts) or political subdivisions (New York City) of a State may invoke the federal common law of nuisance to abate out-of-state pollution. Nor have we ever held that a State may sue to abate any and all manner of pollution originating outside its borders.

The defendants argue that considerations of scale and complexity distinguish global warming from the more bounded pollution giving rise to past federal nuisance suits. Greenhouse gases once emitted become well mixed in the atmosphere; emissions in New Jersey may contribute no more to flooding in New York than emissions in China. The plaintiffs, on the other hand, contend that an equitable remedy against the largest emitters of carbon dioxide in the United States is in order and not beyond judicial competence. And we have recognized that public nuisance law, like common law generally, adapts to changing scientific and factual circumstances. Missouri, 200 U.S., at 522 (adjudicating claim though it did not concern "nuisance of the simple kind that was known to the older common law").

We need not address the parties' dispute in this regard. For it is an academic question whether, in the absence of the Clean Air Act and the EPA actions the Act authorizes, the plaintiffs could state a federal common law claim for curtailment of greenhouse gas emissions because of their contribution to global warming. Any such claim would be displaced by the federal legislation authorizing EPA to regulate carbon-dioxide emissions.

B

"[W]hen Congress addresses a question previously governed by a decision rested on federal common law," the Court has explained, "the need for such an unusual exercise of law-making by federal courts disappears." Milwaukee II, 451 U.S., at 314 (holding that amendments to the Clean Water Act displaced the nuisance claim recognized in Milwaukee I). Legislative displacement of federal common law does not require the same sort of evidence of a clear and manifest [congressional] purpose demanded for preemption of state law. Due regard for the presuppositions of our embracing federal system as a promoter of democracy does not enter the calculus, for it is primarily the office of Congress, not the federal courts, to prescribe national policy in areas of special federal interest. The test for whether congressional legislation excludes the declaration of federal common law is simply whether the statute "speak[s] directly to [the] question" at issue. Mobil Oil Corp. v. Higginbotham, 436 U.S. 618, 625 (1978).

We hold that the Clean Air Act and the EPA actions it authorizes displace any federal common law right to seek abatement of carbon-dioxide emissions from fossil-fuel fired power plants. *Massachusetts* made plain that emissions of carbon dioxide qualify as air pollution subject to regulation under the Act. And we think it equally plain that the Act "speaks directly" to emissions of carbon dioxide from the defendants' plants.

Section 111 of the Act directs the EPA Administrator to list "categories of stationary sources" that "in [her] judgment . . . caus[e], or contribut[e] significantly to, air pollution which may reasonably be anticipated to endanger public health or welfare." § 7411(b)(1)(A). Once EPA lists a category, the agency must establish standards of performance for emission of pollutants from new or modified sources within that category. § 7411(b)(1)(B); see also § 7411(a)(2). And, most relevant here, § 7411(d) then requires regulation of existing sources within the same category.[7] For existing sources, EPA issues emissions guidelines; in compliance with those guidelines and subject to federal oversight, the States then issue performance standards for stationary sources within their jurisdiction.

The Act provides multiple avenues for enforcement. See County of Oneida, 470 U.S., at 237–239 (reach of remedial provisions is important to determination whether statute displaces federal common law). EPA may delegate implementation and enforcement authority to the States, but the agency retains the power to inspect and monitor regulated sources, to impose administrative penalties for noncompliance, and to commence civil actions against polluters in federal court. In specified circumstances, the Act imposes criminal penalties on any person who knowingly violates emissions standards issued under § 7411. And the Act provides for private enforcement. If States (or EPA) fail to enforce emissions limits against regulated sources, the Act permits "any person" to bring a civil enforcement action in federal court. § 7604(a).

If EPA does not set emissions limits for a particular pollutant or source of pollution, States and private parties may petition for a rulemaking on the matter, and EPA's response will be reviewable in federal court. See § 7607(b)(1); *Massachusetts*, 549 U.S., at 516–517, 529. As earlier noted, EPA is currently engaged in a § 7411 rulemaking to set standards for greenhouse gas emissions from fossil-fuel fired power plants. To settle litigation brought under § 7607(b) by a group that included the majority of the plaintiffs in this very case, the agency agreed to complete that rulemaking by May 2012. The Act itself thus provides a means to seek limits on

---

7. There is an exception: EPA may not employ § 7411(d) if existing stationary sources of the pollutant in question are regulated under the national ambient air quality standard program, §§ 7408–7410, or the "hazardous air pollutants" program, § 7412. See § 7411(d)(1).

emissions of carbon dioxide from domestic power plants—the same relief the plaintiffs seek by invoking federal common law. We see no room for a parallel track.

C

The plaintiffs argue, as the Second Circuit held, that federal common law is not displaced until EPA actually exercises its regulatory authority, i.e., until it sets standards governing emissions from the defendants' plants. We disagree.

The sewage discharges at issue in *Milwaukee II*, we do not overlook, were subject to effluent limits set by EPA; under the displacing statute, every point source discharge of water pollution was prohibited unless covered by a permit. 451 U.S., at 318–320. As *Milwaukee II* made clear, however, the relevant question for purposes of displacement is "whether the field has been occupied, not whether it has been occupied in a particular manner." Id., at 324. Of necessity, Congress selects different regulatory regimes to address different problems. Congress could hardly preemptively prohibit every discharge of carbon dioxide unless covered by a permit. After all, we each emit carbon dioxide merely by breathing.

The Clean Air Act is no less an exercise of the legislature's considered judgment concerning the regulation of air pollution because it permits emissions until EPA acts. The critical point is that Congress delegated to EPA the decision whether and how to regulate carbon-dioxide emissions from power plants; the delegation is what displaces federal common law. Indeed, were EPA to decline to regulate carbon-dioxide emissions altogether at the conclusion of its ongoing § 7411 rulemaking, the federal courts would have no warrant to employ the federal common law of nuisance to upset the agency's expert determination.

EPA's judgment, we hasten to add, would not escape judicial review. Federal courts, we earlier observed, can review agency action (or a final rule declining to take action) to ensure compliance with the statute Congress enacted. As we have noted, the Clean Air Act directs EPA to establish emissions standards for categories of stationary sources that, "in [the Administrator's] judgment," "caus[e], or contribut[e] significantly to, air pollution which may reasonably be anticipated to endanger public health or welfare." § 7411(b)(1)(A). "[T]he use of the word judgment," we explained in *Massachusetts*, "is not a roving license to ignore the statutory text." 549 U.S., at 533. "It is but a direction to exercise discretion within defined statutory limits." Ibid. EPA may not decline to regulate carbon-dioxide emissions from power plants if refusal to act would be "arbitrary, capricious, an abuse of discretion, or otherwise not in accordance with law." § 7607(d)(9)(A). If the plaintiffs in this case are dissatisfied with the outcome of EPA's forthcoming rulemaking, their recourse under federal law is to seek Court of Appeals review, and, ultimately, to petition for certiorari in this Court.

Indeed, this prescribed order of decisionmaking—the first decider under the Act is the expert administrative agency, the second, federal judges—is yet another reason to resist setting emissions standards by judicial decree under federal tort law. The appropriate amount of regulation in any particular greenhouse gas-producing sector cannot be prescribed in a vacuum: as with other questions of national or international policy, informed assessment of competing interests is required. Along with the environmental benefit potentially achievable, our Nation's energy needs and the possibility of economic disruption must weigh in the balance.

The Clean Air Act entrusts such complex balancing to EPA in the first instance, in combination with state regulators. Each standard of performance EPA sets must "tak[e] into account the cost of achieving [emissions] reduction and any nonair quality health and environmental impact and energy requirements." § 7411(a)(1), (b)(1)(B), (d)(1). EPA may "distinguish among classes, types, and sizes" of stationary sources in apportioning responsibility for emissions reductions. § 7411(b)(2), (d). And the agency may waive compliance with emission limits to permit a facility to test drive an "innovative technological system" that has "not [yet] been adequately demonstrated." § 7411(j)(1)(A). The Act envisions extensive cooperation between federal and state authorities, see § 7401(a), (b), generally permitting each State to take the first cut at determining how best to achieve EPA emissions standards within its domain, see § 7411(c)(1), (d)(1)–(2).

It is altogether fitting that Congress designated an expert agency, here, EPA, as best suited to serve as primary regulator of greenhouse gas emissions. The expert agency is surely better equipped to do the job than individual district judges issuing ad hoc, case-by-case injunctions. Federal judges lack the scientific, economic, and technological resources an agency can utilize in coping with issues of this order. Judges may not commission scientific studies or convene groups of experts for advice, or issue rules under notice-and-comment procedures inviting input by any interested person, or seek the counsel of regulators in the States where the defendants are located. Rather, judges are confined by a record comprising the evidence the parties present. Moreover, federal district judges, sitting as sole adjudicators, lack authority to render precedential decisions binding other judges, even members of the same court.

* * * * *

The judgments the plaintiffs would commit to federal judges, in suits that could be filed in any federal district, cannot be reconciled with the decisionmaking scheme Congress enacted. The Second Circuit erred, we hold, in ruling that federal judges may set limits on greenhouse gas emissions in face of a law empowering EPA to set the same limits, subject to judicial review only to ensure against action "arbitrary, capricious, . . . or otherwise not in accordance with law." § 7607(d)(9).

V

The plaintiffs also sought relief under state law, in particular, the law of each State where the defendants operate power plants. The Second Circuit did not reach the state law claims because it held that federal common law governed. In light of our holding that the Clean Air Act displaces federal common law, the availability *vel non* of a state lawsuit depends, *inter alia*, on the preemptive effect of the federal Act. None of the parties have briefed preemption or otherwise addressed the availability of a claim under state nuisance law. We therefore leave the matter open for consideration on remand.

North Carolina v. Tennessee Valley Authority

United States Court of Appeals, Fourth Circuit, 2010.
615 F.3d 291.

■ WILKINSON, CIRCUIT JUDGE:

The Tennessee Valley Authority (TVA) appeals an injunction requiring immediate installation of emissions controls at four TVA electricity generating plants in Alabama and Tennessee. The injunction was based on the district court's determination that the TVA plants' emissions constitute a public nuisance in North Carolina. As a result, the court imposed specific emissions caps and emissions control technologies that must be completed by 2013.

*   *   *   *   *

I.

The Tennessee Valley Authority (TVA) is a federal executive branch agency, established in 1933 and tasked with promoting economic development in the Tennessee Valley region. One of TVA's "primary objectives" is to "produce, distribute, and sell electric power." 16 U.S.C. §§ 831d(l), 831i, & 831n–4(f). As a result of this mandate, TVA provides electricity to citizens in parts of seven states. Much of this power is generated by eleven TVA owned and operated coal-fired power plants located in Tennessee, Alabama, and Kentucky.

As a natural byproduct of the power generation process, coal-fired power plants emit sulfur dioxide (SO_2) and nitrous oxides (NO_x). In the atmosphere, both compounds can transform into microscopic particles known as "fine particulate matter" or "$PM_{2.5}$" (particulate matter less than 2.5 micrometers in diameter) that cause health problems if inhaled. When exposed to sunlight, NO_x also assists in the creation of ozone, which is known to cause respiratory ailments.

SO_2, NO_x, $PM_{2.5}$, and ozone are among the air pollutants extensively regulated through the Clean Air Act. Pursuant to the Act, the Environmental Protection Agency (EPA) has issued numerous regulations, and states have enacted further rules implementing the Act and the EPA requirements. Together, these laws and regulations form a system that seeks to keep air pollutants at or below safe levels.

In order to comply with requirements under the Clean Air Act, a number of controls can be fitted to coal-fired power plants to reduce the amounts of SO_2 and NO_x they emit and, by extension, the amounts of $PM_{2.5}$

and ozone created. One of the ways SO_2 can be reduced, for example, is by installing a flue gas desulfurization system, or "scrubber." Scrubbers are large chemical plants—often larger than the power plants themselves—that remove SO_2 from plant exhaust and cost hundreds of millions of dollars.

To control NO_x emissions, plants may use selective catalytic reduction (SCR). Like scrubbers, SCRs are building-sized plants that can cost hundreds of millions of dollars to construct. However, they can remove approximately 90% of the NO_x from the flue gasses a coal power plant produces. NO_x emissions can also be reduced in alternative ways, such as retrofitting plants with burners that result in lower NO_x emissions, burning types of coal that have low NO_x output, and installing selective non-catalytic reduction (SNCR) controls. * * *

TVA has already installed numerous pollution controls at its coal-fired plants. SO_2 scrubbers already operating cover 43% of TVA's coal-fired electricity generation capacity, while scrubbers under construction and anticipated to be completed this year will bring that number above 50%. Nationwide, only one-third to one-half of the country's coal plants are equipped with scrubbers. Similarly, while one-third to one-half of the country's coal plants have SCRs to control NO_x, TVA has installed SCRs on 60% of its coal-fired electricity generation capacity. At several plants that do not currently have SCRs, TVA is installing SNCRs and is also burning low NO_x coal.

Unlike TVA, power plants in North Carolina historically had not put sufficient controls on their emissions, choosing instead to purchase emissions allowances under an EPA cap and trade program implemented by Congress in 1990 to address acid rain. As a result, North Carolina decided to implement more stringent controls on in-state coal-fired plants as a matter of state law, as it is allowed to do under the Clean Air Act. See 42 U.S.C. § 7416. It passed the North Carolina Clean Smokestacks Act, which requires investor-owned public utilities that operate coal-fired generating units to reduce their emissions of NO_x and SO_2 to levels even lower than those specified in EPA regulations promulgated pursuant to the Clean Air Act.

Not all emissions are generated by in-state sources, however. Prevailing high pressure weather systems in the states where TVA operates tend to cause emissions to move eastward into North Carolina and other states. Although there are lengthy Clean Air Act provisions and regulations controlling such interstate emissions, North Carolina chose to bring a public nuisance suit against TVA in the Western District of North Carolina, seeking an injunction against all eleven of TVA's coal-fired power plants. [After ruling that TVA was not immune from Clean Air Act regulation, the district court held a bench trial. Finding that operation of four of TVA's power plants, each located within 100 miles of the North Carolina border, created a public nuisance, the court ordered TVA to install scrubbers and SCRs at these plants, and imposed SO_2 and NO_x emission limits.]

II.

The desirability of reducing air pollution is widely acknowledged, but the most effective means of doing so remains, not surprisingly, a matter of dispute. The system of statutes and regulations addressing the problem represents decades of thought by legislative bodies and agencies and the vast array of interests seeking to press upon them a variety of air pollution policies. To say this regulatory and permitting regime is comprehensive would be an understatement. To say it embodies carefully wrought compromises states the obvious. But the framework is the work of many, many people, and it is in place.

The district court's well-meaning attempt to reduce air pollution cannot alter the fact that its decision threatens to scuttle the extensive system of anti-pollution mandates that promote clean air in this country. If courts across the nation were to use the vagaries of public nuisance doctrine to overturn the carefully enacted rules governing airborne emissions, it would be increasingly difficult for anyone to determine what standards govern. Energy policy cannot be set, and the environment cannot prosper, in this way.

North Carolina attempts to frame this case in terms of protecting public health and saving the environment from dirty air. But the problem is not a neglected one. In fact, emissions have been extensively regulated nationwide by the Clean Air Act for four decades. The real question in this case is whether individual states will be allowed to supplant the cooperative federal-state framework that Congress through the EPA has refined over many years.

[The court explained that under the Clean Air Act, EPA sets national air quality standards for pollutants including SO_2 and NO_x, that states implement those standards through implementation plans and state permit requirements, and that state plans and permits must not contribute to air quality violations in other states. TVA had permits issued by Alabama and Tennessee under that framework for the plants in question. North Carolina had not challenged either those permits or TVA's compliance with them.]

III.

* * * * *

Dissatisfied with the air quality standards authorized by Congress, established by the EPA, and implemented through Alabama and Tennessee permits, North Carolina has requested the federal courts to impose a different set of standards. The pitfalls of such an approach are all too evident. It ill behooves the judiciary to set aside a congressionally sanctioned scheme of many years' duration—a scheme, moreover, that reflects the extensive application of scientific expertise and that has set in motion reliance interests and expectations on the part of those states and enterprises that have complied with its requirements. To replace duly promulgated ambient air quality standards with standards whose content must await the uncertain twists and turns of litigation will leave whole states and industries at sea and potentially expose them to a welter of conflicting court orders across the country.

The Supreme Court addressed this precise problem of multiplicity in International Paper Co. v. Ouellette, 479 U.S. 481 (1987). It emphasized that allowing "a number of different states to have independent and plenary regulatory authority over a single discharge would lead to chaotic confrontation between sovereign states." Id. at 496–97. This problem is only exacerbated if state nuisance law is the mechanism used, because "nuisance standards often are vague and indeterminate." Id. at 496.

* * * * *

Indeed, a patchwork of nuisance injunctions could well lead to increased air pollution. Differing standards could create perverse incentives for power companies to increase utilization of plants in regions subject to less stringent judicial decrees. Similarly, rushed plant alterations triggered by injunctions are likely inferior to system-wide analysis of where changes will do the most good. Injunction-driven demand for such artificial changes could channel a limited pool of specialized construction expertise away from the plants most in need of pollution controls to those with the most pressing legal demands. * * *

We need not hold flatly that Congress has entirely preempted the field of emissions regulation. In *TVA I*, for example, we held that the savings clause of the Clean Air Act may allow for some common law nuisance suits, although we did not address whether a nuisance action brought under these circumstances is barred by preemption under the Supremacy Clause. The *Ouellette* Court itself explicitly refrained from categorically preempting every nuisance action brought under source state law. At the same time, however, the *Ouellette* Court was emphatic that a state law is preempted "if it interferes with the methods by which the federal statute was designed to reach [its] goal," id. at 494, admonished against the "tolerat[ion]" of "common-law suits that have the potential to undermine [the] regulatory structure," id. at 497, and singled out nuisance standards in particular as "vague" and "indeterminate," id. at 496. The upshot of all this is that we cannot state categorically that the *Ouellette* Court intended a flat-out preemption of each and every conceivable suit under nuisance law. We can state, however, with assurance that *Ouellette* recognized the considerable potential mischief in those nuisance actions seeking to establish emissions standards different from federal and state regulatory law and created the strongest cautionary presumption against them.

* * * * *

It is true, as North Carolina argues, that the Clean Air Act's savings clause states that "[n]othing in this section shall restrict any right which any person (or class of persons) may have under any statute or common law to seek enforcement of any emission standard or limitation or to seek any other relief." 42 U.S.C. § 7604(e). * * *

* * * Ouellette held that the Clean Water Act's savings clause, which is similar to the one found in the Clean Air Act, did not preserve a broad right for states to "undermine this carefully drawn statute through a general savings clause." Ouellette, 479 U.S. at 494. The Court indicated that the clause was ambiguous as to which state actions were preserved and noted that "if affected States were allowed to impose separate discharge standards on a single point source, the inevitable result would be a serious interference with the achievement of the full purposes and objectives of Congress." Id. at 493–94. * * *

The difficulties with North Carolina's approach in this litigation do not end with the prospect of multiplicitous decrees or vague and uncertain nuisance standards. In addition to envisioning a role for the states that the Clean Air Act did not contemplate, North Carolina's approach would reorder the respective functions of courts and agencies. * * *

It is crucial * * * that courts in this highly technical arena respect the strengths of the agency processes on which Congress has placed its imprimatur. Regulations and permits, while hardly perfect, provide an opportunity for predictable standards that are scientifically grounded and thus give rise to broad reliance interests. TVA, for example, spent billions of dollars on power generation units that supply electricity to seven different states in the belief that its permits allowed it to do so. * * * Without a single system of permitting, "[i]t would be virtually impossible to predict the standard" for lawful emissions, and "[a]ny permit issued ... would be rendered meaningless." Ouellette, 479 U.S. at 497. * * * A company, no matter how well-meaning, would be simply unable to determine its obligations *ex ante* under such a system, for any judge in any nuisance suit could modify them dramatically.

* * * * *

In addition to the problems noted above, the district court's decision compromised principles of federalism by applying North Carolina law extraterritorially to TVA plants located in Alabama and Tennessee. There is no question that the law of the states where emissions sources are located, in this case Alabama and Tennessee, applies in an interstate nuisance dispute. The Supreme Court's decision in *Ouellette* is explicit: a "court must apply the law of the State in which the point source is located." 479 U.S. at 487. While *Ouellette* involved a nuisance suit against a source regulated under the Clean Water Act, all parties agree its holding is equally applicable to the Clean Air Act.

Unfortunately, while the district court acknowledged the proper standard, it for all practical purposes applied North Carolina's Clean Smokestacks Act extraterritorially in Alabama and Tennessee. The decision below does little more than mention the black letter nuisance law of Alabama and Tennessee on its way to crafting a remedy derived entirely from the North Carolina Act.

* * * * *

Even were we to accept North Carolina's claim that the district court actually applied source state law from Alabama and Tennessee, it would be difficult to uphold the injunctions because TVA's electricity-generating operations are expressly permitted by the states in which they are located. It would be odd, to say the least, for specific state laws and regulations to expressly permit a power plant to operate and then have a generic statute countermand those permissions on public nuisance grounds. As the Supreme Court has made clear, "[s]tates can be expected to take into account their own nuisance laws in setting permit requirements." *Ouellette*, 479 U.S. at 499.

While North Carolina points out that an activity need not be illegal in order to be a nuisance, that is not the situation before us. There is a distinction between an activity that is merely not illegal versus one that is explicitly granted a permit to operate in a particular fashion. "Courts traditionally have been reluctant to enjoin as a public nuisance activities which have been considered and specifically authorized by the government." New England Legal Found. v. Castle, 666 F.2d 30, 33 (2d Cir. 1981). This is especially true "where the conduct sought to be enjoined implicates the technically complex area of environmental law." Id.; see also Restatement (Second) of Torts § 821B cmt. f. ("Although it would be a nuisance at common law, conduct that is fully authorized by statute, ordinance or administrative regulation does not subject the actor to tort liability.").

* * * * *

In sum, TVA's plants cannot logically be public nuisances under Alabama and Tennessee law where TVA is in compliance with EPA NAAQS, the corresponding state SIPs, and the permits that implement them. These standards impose more stringent requirements than source state nuisance law. Alabama and Tennessee nuisance law only prohibits activities that substantially interfere with the average person—for example, a person of *ordinary* health and sensibilities, and *ordinary* modes of living, or an *ordinary* reasonable man.

In contrast, the EPA's regulations regarding NAAQS and the SIPs implementing them are understandably designed to protect even those individuals particularly sensitive to emissions. * * * This case does not join the issue of whether TVA is in compliance with the various permits under which it operates, and we assume, without deciding, that it is. If TVA is in compliance with the more demanding federal EPA requirements and state law SIPs, it cannot be in violation of less-stringent state law nuisance standards.

NOTES AND QUESTIONS

1. *Displacement of federal common law.* Federal common law is a gap filler used only when necessary; the federal courts recognize that Congress is the primary and usual federal lawmaker. Common law is therefore displaced when the legislature addresses a problem or delegates power to do so to a federal agency. The key question, of course, is how directly and explicitly Congress must act.

In *City of Milwaukee v. Illinois*, 451 U.S. 304 (1981), the Supreme Court held that the Clean Water Act had displaced the federal common law of nuisance with respect to Illinois' complaint about discharges from Milwaukee's sewage treatment plant. The Court wrote:

> We conclude that, at least so far as concerns the claims of respondents, Congress has not left the formulation of appropriate federal standards to the courts through the application of often vague and indeterminate nuisance concepts and maxims of equity jurisprudence, but rather has occupied the field through the establishment of a comprehensive regulatory program supervised by an expert administrative agency.

Id. at 317. The Court applied the same rationale in Middlesex County Sewerage Authority v. National Sea Clammers Association, 453 U.S. 1 (1981), holding that fishermen could not maintain a federal common law nuisance claim based on harm to fisheries caused by ocean dumping of sewage. In that case, the Court described the federal common law of nuisance as entirely preempted by the Clean Water Act in the area of water pollution.

In *AEP*, the Second Circuit held that the Clean Air Act did not preclude a federal common law nuisance claim against five large utilities based on their emissions of greenhouse gases. At the time of that decision, the Supreme Court had ruled in *Massachusetts v. EPA* that greenhouse gases were pollutants for purposes of the Clean Air Act. EPA had proposed to find that greenhouse gas emissions from motor vehicles endanger public health and welfare, and therefore would be regulated under the Clean Air Act, but had not yet issued its final endangerment determination. No regulation of greenhouse gases was yet in effect, nor had any regulation of emissions from stationary sources been proposed.

By the time the case reached the Supreme Court, the regulatory landscape had changed. EPA had finalized its endangerment finding for greenhouse gas emissions from motor vehicles; issued (jointly with the Department of Transportation) a final rule regulating greenhouse gas emissions from cars; begun work on rules for trucks; and issued rules governing emissions from new and modified large stationary sources. EPA had also agreed, in settlement of a lawsuit brought by several states, to issue emission guidelines under Clean Air Act § 111(d), 42 U.S.C. § 7411(d), which tells EPA to establish a procedure for states to issue and implement performance standards for existing sources of for pollutants not covered by national air quality criteria.

What exactly did the Supreme Court hold had displaced common law for purposes of this suit? The Clean Air Act alone? The Court's ruling in *Massachusetts v. EPA* that the Act applies to greenhouse gases? EPA's endangerment finding? The issuance of final regulations governing motor vehicles? EPA's agreement to begin a rulemaking under § 111? Should displacement apply before any actual regulation of these sources is in place?

How important to the Court's ruling was it that the Clean Air Act provides a mechanism for these plaintiffs to challenge EPA's failure to regulate greenhouse gas emissions from these sources, or more accurately EPA's failure to force the states to regulate them?

2. *Preemption of state common law.* State nuisance claims stand on a different footing than federal nuisance claims. Conflicting federal law preempts state law, but the test for preemption is generally described as more demanding than that for displacement of federal common law. The Supreme Court ordinarily presumes that state law is not preempted "unless that was the clear and manifest purpose of Congress." Rice v. Santa Fe Elevator Corp., 331 U.S. 218, 230 (1947). Nonetheless, in recent years the Court has applied preemption broadly in several environmental law cases. Preemption of state law is considered in more detail in Chapter 4, Section 4B.

The Clean Air Act contains a "savings clause" which states that its citizen suit provision does not "restrict any right which any person (or class of persons) may have under any statute or common law to seek enforcement of any emission standard or limitation or to seek any other relief." 42 U.S.C. § 7604(e). The Clean Water Act contains an identical savings clause; most federal environmental statutes include similar provisions. Courts have generally read those savings clauses as evidence that Congress did not intend to preempt state law nuisance actions, which therefore remain viable. It is common for plaintiffs to bring federal statutory and state law nuisance claims in the same action.

How does the Fourth Circuit, in *North Carolina v. TVA*, treat the Clean Air Act's savings clause? Does it hold that state law nuisance suits can never be brought? Does it provide any basis for deciding when such claims would or would not be preempted? In *AEP*, the Second Circuit did not reach the state law nuisance claim because it decided that federal common law governed. With that holding now overturned by the Supreme Court, those claims have been remanded to the appellate court. How should the Second Circuit address them? What barriers, if any, might those claims face? How likely do you think they are to succeed?

3. *Choice of law in interstate disputes.* To the extent state law nuisance claims are not preempted by the Clean Air or Clean Water Act, the Supreme Court has made it clear that such claims are governed by the law of the source state rather than of the receiving state. In International Paper v. Ouellette, 479 U.S. 481 (1987), a nuisance suit filed by property owners on the Vermont side of Lake Champlain against a paper mill on the New York side, the Court explained:

> After examining the [Clean Water Act] as a whole, its purposes and history, we are convinced that if affected States were allowed to impose separate discharge standards on a single point source, the inevitable result would be a serious interference with the achievement of the full purposes and objectives of Congress. Because we do not believe Congress intended to undermine this carefully drawn statute, we conclude

that the CWA precludes a court from applying the law of an affected State against an out-of-state source. * * *

Our conclusion that Vermont nuisance law is inapplicable to a New York point source does not leave respondents without a remedy. The CWA precludes only those suits that may require standards of effluent control that are incompatible with those established by the procedures set forth in the Act. The saving clause specifically preserves other state actions, and therefore nothing in the Act bars aggrieved individuals from bringing a nuisance claim pursuant to the law of the *source* State. * * *

An action brought against [International Paper Co.] under New York nuisance law would not frustrate the goals of the CWA as would a suit governed by Vermont law. First, application of the source State's law does not disturb the balance among federal, source-state, and affected-state interests. Because the Act specifically allows source States to impose stricter standards, the imposition of source-state law does not disrupt the regulatory partnership established by the permit system. Second, the restriction of suits to those brought under source-state nuisance law prevents a source from being subject to an indeterminate number of potential regulations. Although New York nuisance law may impose separate standards and thus create some tension with the permit system, a source only is required to look to a single additional authority, whose rules should be relatively predictable. Moreover, States can be expected to take into account their own nuisance laws in setting permit requirements.

International Paper asked the Court to go further and hold that nuisance actions could only be brought in the courts of the source state. The Court declined to adopt that rule.

Does it make sense to limit nuisance actions to the law of the source state? That rule provides practical benefits to sources, which need only comply with the law of one state. Does it unfairly allow upwind or upriver states to take advantage of a geographical accident to externalize their pollution on downwind and downriver states? We shall see in Chapters 10 and 11 that the Clean Air and Clean Water Acts, respectively, require source states to take at least some account of effects on downwind and downstream states.

4. *The effect of permit compliance.* Whether a defendant who is in compliance with a permit will nonetheless be liable in nuisance may depend upon a variety of factors, including whether the permit directly addresses the alleged nuisance and the extent to which the concerns of neighbors were accounted for in permit proceedings. *See* New England Legal Found'n v. Costle, 666 F.2d 30 (2d Cir. 1981) (holding nuisance claim precluded where EPA had specifically authorized use of high-sulfur coals); Twitty v. North Carolina, 527 F.Supp. 778 (E.D. N.C. 1981) (rejecting nuisance suit against state for storing PCBs in landfill and against EPA for authorizing storage).

The *North Carolina v. TVA* court says activities which are expressly permitted cannot be a nuisance under the laws of Tennessee or Alabama. What does it mean for an activity to be "expressly permitted"? Does the court mean that nothing about operation of these plants could be considered a nuisance, so long as they are in compliance with their permits? Or does it mean that emissions of SO_2 and NO_x at permitted levels cannot be a nuisance? Currently, the permits under which the power plants at issue in *AEP* operate do not include emission limits for greenhouse gases. Are those permits relevant to state law nuisance claims?

Should regulatory compliance protect against a tort action? Will allowing such a defense encourage defendants to ignore hazards not recognized by the regulations? Will it increase industry incentives to lobby for lax regulations? On the other hand, without such a defense might defendants be found liable even when their actions were reasonable at the time? Psychologists have found that people who know the outcome tend to overestimate the predictability of past events, a phenomenon known as "hindsight bias." Where a defendant's actions have proven insufficient, in retrospect, to prevent harm, hindsight bias makes it more difficult for judges and juries to view those precautions as reasonable even if everyone would have agreed that they were at the time. *See* Jeffrey Rachlinski, Regulating in Foresight Versus Judging Liability in Hindsight: The Case of Tobacco, 33 Ga. L. Rev. 813 (1999).

5. *The Kivalina case.* Another public nuisance suit remained pending in the Ninth Circuit as of July 2011. It was filed in 2008 by the Native Village of Kivalina, Alaska, against Exxon, other major oil companies, the largest producers of electricity from fossil fuels, and major coal producers. Kivalina is located on a barrier reef in northwest Alaska. It has been told by the US Army Corps of Engineers that it must relocate, at a cost of $95 to $400 million, because the loss of sea ice in the area has left it too vulnerable to winter storms. The complaint alleged that defendants are responsible for a substantial portion of the greenhouse gases in the atmosphere that have caused global warming, and that defendants conspired to deceive the public by creating "a false scientific debate about global warming." The Village sought to hold the defendants jointly and severally liable for its monetary damages from global warming.

The District Court dismissed the Village's complaint, ruling that it raised a nonjusticiable political question. Native Village of Kivalina v. ExxonMobil Corp., 663 F. Supp. 2d 863 (N.D. Cal. 2009). The Village appealed. The Supreme Court's affirmance (by an equally divided court) of the contrary ruling in *American Electric Power* seems to take the political question issue off the table. Assuming the Ninth Circuit holds that the Village has standing (an issue that is not free from doubt, by any means), how do you think the Village's case would fare on the merits? The complaint put forth both federal and state law nuisance claims. Following *American Electric Power*, are the federal law claims displaced by the Clean Air Act? Note that they do not rest on the operation of major stationary sources, as the *AEP* case did, but rather on the defendants' production of fossil fuels. Are the state law claims preempted? How would you decide? If either federal or state claims are justiciable, what other barriers might they face?

SECTION 4. THE ROLES OF PUBLIC AND COMMON LAW

As we shall see in more detail in later chapters, statutes and regulations have overtaken the common law as the primary mechanism for controlling environmental harm. Common law liability can substitute for, supplement, or be pre-empted by prescriptive (sometimes called "command and control") regulation. The appropriate role of private and public law in the environmental context, both generally and in specific circumstances, remains a subject of intense debate.

Steven Shavell, Liability for Harm Versus Regulation of Safety

13 J. Legal Stud. 357, 357–65 (1984).

Liability in tort and the regulation of safety represent two very different approaches for controlling activities that create risks of harm to others. Tort liability is private in nature and works not by social command but rather indirectly, through the deterrent effect of damage actions that may be brought once harm occurs. Standards, prohibitions, and other forms of safety regulation, in contrast, are public in character and modify behavior in an immediate way through requirements that are imposed before, or at least independently of, the actual occurrence of harm. * * *

To identify and assess the factors determining the social desirability of liability and regulation, it is necessary to set out a measure of social welfare; and here that measure is assumed to equal the benefits parties derive from engaging in their activities, less the sum of the costs of precautions, the harms done, and the administrative expenses associated with the means of social control. The formal problem is to employ the means of control to maximize the measure of welfare.

We can now examine four determinants that influence the solution to this problem. The first determinant is the possibility of a *difference in knowledge about risky activities* as between private parties and a regulatory authority. This difference could relate to the benefits of activities, the costs of reducing risks, or the probability or severity of the risks.

Where private parties have superior knowledge of these elements, it would be better for them to decide about the control of risks, indicating an advantage of liability rules, other things being equal. * * *

The second of the determinants of the relative desirability of liability and regulation is that *private parties might be incapable of paying for the full magnitude of the harm done.* Where this is the case, liability would not furnish adequate incentives to control risk, because private parties would treat losses caused that exceeded their assets as imposing liabilities only equal to their assets. But under regulation inability to pay for harm done would be irrelevant, assuming that parties would be made to take steps to reduce risk as a precondition for engaging in their activities. * * *

Let us turn next to the third of the four general determinants, the chance that *parties would not face the threat of suit for harm done*. Like incapacity to pay for harm, such a possibility results in a dilution of the incentives to reduce risk created by liability, but is of no import under regulation.

* * * One reason that a defendant can escape tort liability is that the harms he generates are widely dispersed, making it unattractive for any victim individually to initiate legal action. This danger can be offset to a degree if victims are allowed to maintain class actions * * *. A second cause of failure to sue is the passage of a long period of time before harm manifests itself. This raises the possibility that by the time suit is contemplated, the evidence necessary for a successful action will be stale or the responsible parties out of business. A third reason for failure to sue is difficulty in attributing harm to the parties who are in fact responsible for producing it. This problem could arise from simple ignorance that a given harm or disease was caused by a human agency (as opposed to being "natural" in origin) or from inability to identify which one or several out of many parties was the cause of the harm. * * *

The last of the determinants is the magnitude of the *administrative costs incurred by private parties and by the public* in using the tort system or direct regulation. Of course, the costs of the tort system must be broadly defined to include the time, effort, and legal expenses borne by private parties in the course of litigation or in coming to settlements, as well as the public expenses of conducting trials, employing judges, empaneling juries, and the like. Similarly, the administrative costs of regulation include the public expense of maintaining the regulatory establishment and the private costs of compliance.

[Professor Shavell concludes that two of these factors—differential knowledge and administrative costs—will generally favor liability approaches whereas the other two—incapacity to pay for harm done and likelihood of escaping suit—favor regulation.] This suggests not only that neither tort liability nor regulation could uniformly dominate the other as a solution to the problem of controlling risks, but also that they should not be viewed as mutually exclusive solutions to it. A complete solution to the problem of the control of risk evidently should involve the joint use of liability and regulation, with the balance between them reflecting the importance of the determinants.

Roger Meiners & Bruce Yandle, Common Law and the Conceit of Modern Environmental Policy

7 Geo. Mason L. Rev. 923, 946–59 (1999).

The standard economic justification for federal intervention is based on the notion of externality. Under this classification, pollution is a spillover from otherwise beneficial activities that imposes costs on people who did not agree to incur those costs. Since the polluter does not take the spillover costs into account when producing and pricing products, the outcome leads to an inefficient allocation of resources. It is then the business of the state to correct the mispricing of environmental assets. While elegant models can be constructed to illuminate the problem, the difficulty comes in identifying actual situations where state intervention can be justified on economic grounds. How much pollution (or anything else that irritates someone) is too much? Economic literature provides little operational guidance as to when the state should intervene to "internalize" a perceived externality. A sharp theoretical focus provides ways of thinking about benefits and costs, and there is a suggestion, at least, that taking regulatory actions to deal with externalities may be more costly than the gains obtained from doing so. We note that evidence to the contrary notwithstanding, these discussions implicitly assume that politicians are driven primarily by a desire to make the world more efficient.

In recent years, a competing line of inquiry has focused on property rights, which yields a logical framework where the common law tort of nuisance converges with the economic concept of unpaid opportunity cost. Pollution that has meaning in law and economics occurs when property rights are not well specified or effectively enforced. It is then the state's responsibility to enforce property rights and related agreements. When property rights are defined and enforced, economic agents who seek to use an environmental asset must deal with holders of the related rights. Bargaining between parties allows for the transfer of rights, and at common law, contracting around the common law rule. Contracting allows for activities that might otherwise provide a cause of action against a polluter, and the contracting parties bear the cost of their actions. Common law and property rights convert a commons to a managed asset that is treated with owner-like concern. * * *

Critics of the common law approach to solving environmental problems deride the process as unworkable. It is a quaint historical relic that could be better replaced by bright people putting their minds to devising rules, enforced by the EPA and its minions in the states, that would protect us against a host of environmental ills. If correct, there is no reason why that logic should not apply to other areas largely governed by the common law. * * *

We presume that many truly believed that the pre–1970 legal structure regarding the environment, a combination of common law, state and local rules, and a few federal rules, was simply inadequate. Horror stories of pre-EPA environmental ruin, ranging from the burning of the Cuyahoga River to the tragedy at Love Canal seemingly support this presumption, as does the parade of horribles trotted out by political leaders seeking to expand federal environmental programs. * * *

In 1969, the sight of flames leaping from the Cuyahoga River in Ohio shocked many Americans, but it was not big news in Cleveland. An oil slick on the river caught fire and that fire lit wooden train trusses. There had been fires in the river before; the Cuyahoga, an industrial sewer, was biologically dead. A few years before the fire, Bar Realty Corporation sued the city of Cleveland for allowing the river to deteriorate to such a condition. The trial court ordered the city to investigate the causes of the pollution and ordered "such nuisances * * * to be abated." The Supreme Court of Ohio reversed, holding that the river was under the control of state authorities. The Ohio Water Pollution Control Board erased common law protections by granting various industries permissions to discharge wastes into the Cuyahoga and, thereby, Lake Erie. When regulation takes precedent [sic] over common law rights, the result can be destructive to the environment. * * *

The erection of a massive federal environmental bureaucracy came at significant cost. By the EPA's own estimates, federal environmental regulations cost as much as $200 billion per year in current dollars. Yet the cost of federal regulations is not only one of dollars and cents. Federal regulations have also curtailed traditional common law remedies for pollution.

In general, the various federal statutes did not eliminate the right to bring common law actions; they created an alternative that is, in general, much easier to bring (and win). One advantage for defendants is that if they can show compliance with statutory standards, whether the standards are related to likelihood of injury or not, that presents strong evidence to the jury that the defendant must be complying with "the law." * * *

The various federal regulatory schemes have had a clear impact on common law, especially in its application to interstate pollution cases. As early as 1981, courts held that federal acts preempted federal common law with respect to water discharge effluent standards. These decisions held that federal courts lacked the authority to impose more stringent effluent limitation standards than those imposed by the federal agencies responsible for determining appropriate standards. * * *

* * * Perhaps the greatest effect that regulatory standards (either state or federal) may have on common law claims is on the plaintiffs' ability to establish the element of their tort claim related to harm or damage. Arguably, if an agency has blessed the quantity and quality of a discharge either to air or water (i.e., a permit stipulates release of specific pollutants), it may be more difficult for a plaintiff to successfully prove damage. Thus, even if the courts in a jurisdiction do not hold that statutory standards preempt common law claims, decision-makers hearing such actions (e.g., juries, judges) may, nonetheless, reach decisions that give that effect. * * *

Statute law displaced common law for precisely the opposite reasons generally offered by those who extol statute law's virtues. Critics of common law argue that common law protection is unreliable in that bad consequences still happen despite the law, that evidence of cause and effect is difficult to provide, and that enforcement is subject to unpredictable whims of common law judges and juries. Without asking "Relative to What?" common law is seen as providing uneasy and unreliable environmental protection, making it possible for polluters to impose environmental costs with impunity. We contend that common law environmental protection was, if anything, too strict for those who wanted to generate pollution with greater impunity. At common law, there were no EPA permits or uniform technology requirements that sanctioned the actions of the polluter.

Common law remedies varied across the states. That is, common law judges reflected on the customs and traditions of their communities. No "one suit fits all" could evolve from common law courts. And no group of nationally organized rent seekers could ever simultaneously obtain cartel-forming judge-made law. Common law does not fit in a rent-seeking world. Common law evolved to protect rights, not to protect interest groups.

Statute law, on the other hand, provides an escape for polluters. One is hard pressed to find a single instance where a major industrial polluter who violated EPA permits was shut down under statute law. Fines are levied instead (and the fines are often trivial compared to jury verdicts), and the polluters are given more time, under a sternly worded consent decree, to reduce discharges to levels permitted by statute.

* * *

[S]tatute writing is a batch process where information is assembled periodically and durable statutes are written and implemented. As the world evolves and changes, the informational underpinnings of statutes still in force become obsolete. On the other hand, the common law process is continuous; it draws together information on controversies as they occur; and evolves as the world changes. While errors may be made in either case, in statute writing the cost of error is logically higher, because statutes are all-encompassing and more costly to change.

Frank B. Cross, Common Law Conceits: A Comment on Meiners & Yandle

7 Geo. Mason L. Rev. 965, 966–81 (1999).

Meiners and Yandle claim that the effectiveness of the common law was destroyed or at least undermined significantly by the intervention of federal environmental legislation and regulation. The most obvious problem with this theory is that common law has not generally been preempted by such legislation. Virtually every major piece of federal environmental legislation contains a savings clause stating that the statute would not "restrict any right that any person (or class of persons) may have under any statute or common law." Because of such savings clauses, common law actions remain much as they did before the passage of the environmental protection statutes. * * *

Perhaps recognizing the limitations of their preemption claims, Meiners and Yandle suggest that federal regulation makes it harder to win common law claims. Thus, they suggest the common law, insofar as it survives at all, is frail. They must concede that compliance with federal regulation is generally not a recognized defense to a common law action, but contend that compliance must be a "strong evidence to the jury" or that courts would "defer to administrative agencies'" determinations or that plaintiffs would be unable to prove damages. These claims, however, are unsupported by so much as a single citation and thus appear wrong. * * *

While regulatory compliance is not an effective defense to common law liability, regulatory noncompliance is a powerful tool for common law plaintiffs. Meiners and Yandle overlook this key point. A violation of environmental regulations is commonly regarded as proof of negligence or nuisance per se, thus easing considerably a plaintiff's burden of proof in a tort action. Therefore, rather than weakening the common law, statutory requirements may actually strengthen its application.

Any vitality that the common law ever had is still present. The four billion dollar judgment in the Exxon Valdez oil spill is but the most obvious example of the continuance of common law remedies. * * * A quick check of litigation records demonstrates the continued vitality of the common law, particularly the nuisance remedy favored by Meiners and Yandle. A Westlaw survey found that the number of nuisance actions associated with pollution or hazardous substances has grown since the passage of federal environmental legislation [from a total of 259 environmental nuisance cases reported in federal and state courts for the period 1965–70 to 1,114 for the period 1990–95]. * * *

Meiners and Yandle's theoretical claim is readily amenable to empirical testing. If, as they say, a less effective public law system supplanted a more effective common law system of environmental protection in the 1970s, one would expect the environment to have deteriorated as a result. In fact, the vast majority of environmental problems have been alleviated, while most national pollution problems were at their peak in the common law era.

The common law era saw some of the most dramatic pollution episodes. It was during this time that the Cuyahoga River caught fire and that Donora, Pennsylvania and New York City suffered from "killer smogs." The era before federal legislation was marked by "massive oil spills, killer smogs, rivers burning, fish kills, the impending death of Lake Erie." A historical analysis of nuisance law in England found that it was "ineffectual" in dealing with "pollution of the air and water." * * *

The environment became considerably cleaner following the passage of federal environmental legislation. * * *

Reliance on the common law might be defended on economic efficiency grounds, though I am dubious of broad claims to this effect. The free market environmentalists want to capture the environment for themselves, though, and make expansive claims that the common law would be stricter or more protective of the environment than is current regulation. If they were right and sincere in these claims, greater reliance on the common law would probably be a bad thing—more strictness in environmental protection is not generally advisable. I suspect they are wrong, however. The evidence suggests that reliance on the common law would roll back environmental protection considerably, overshooting the mark and resulting in too little environmental protection. Even if the rollback proved desirable as a policy matter, its occurrence would certainly destroy the credibility of those who advocated the common law as a tool to strengthen environmental regulation.

Edward Brunet, Debunking Wholesale Private Enforcement of Environmental Rights

15 Harv. J. L. & Pub. Pol'y 311, 313–23 (1992).

A shift to a scheme of private enforcement of environmental rights in property, tort, or contract will face a number of obstacles. * * *

The high transaction costs of individual suits will often prevent necessary enforcement. Many environmental breaches of property and contract rights are likely to be modest property damage injuries, above the threshold of a small claims court but not large enough to interest a plaintiffs' attorney seeking a contingent fee. Such claims may cost more to enforce than damages or injunctive recovery would warrant. * * * Consequently, small injuries may go unremedied, because individual plaintiffs would not themselves have a sufficient economic stake in the litigation to incur the litigation costs.

Furthermore, even *de minimis* environmental claims will often raise complex issues of causation. It may be clear that fish in a private property owner's stream have been killed, but at the same time there may be uncertainty over the identity of the cause or water polluter. Resolution of such causation issues is complex and expensive. * * *

Private litigants funding their own environmental enforcement actions are likely to have difficulty proving that defendants have violated established substantive standards of environmental conduct. The necessity of proving on-going, site-specific violations of environmental standards is very difficult and costly [because] it often requires the alleged or suspected violator's cooperation, which is rarely forthcoming. Private citizens who suffer some type of environmental injury but lack litigation experience or resources will have difficulty overcoming these obstacles. * * *

[T]here are reasons to be skeptical of systematic use of even high-stakes personal injury suits as a means of environmental enforcement. * * * First, individual suits bring highly inconsistent judgments. * * * Second, a high percentage of damage recovery goes to attorneys rather than to victims. * * * Third, those fortunate enough to sue early often recover more than those unfortunate enough to suffer belated damages. * * *

One of the main reasons for the birth of the modern administrative agency was the inability of private individuals to protect themselves effectively when in conflict with more powerful and experienced opponents in the business world. Examination of the origin of New Deal agencies reveals that agency prosecution was partially premised on the notion that the vigorously managed, fully equipped, and experienced litigation unit of an administrative agency was a far superior litigant than victimized private individuals.

NOTES AND QUESTIONS

1. *Public and private law.* As Professor Shavell points out, public and private law can both play a role in addressing environmental (and other) problems. Furthermore, as we shall see, public law can take a wide variety of forms, and can be implemented at the local, state, or federal level. Shavell identifies several factors to consider in deciding whether liability or regulation should play the primary role, including the availability of information, ability to pay, likelihood that a private suit will be pursued, and administrative costs. Can you think of other factors important to the choice? What about the ability of the decisionmaker to evaluate available information? The need for uniform decisions or local flexibility? Flexibility in response to new circumstances or new knowledge? The likelihood that government enforcement might be inhibited by the political resistance of influential polluters? The desirability of forestalling harm before it occurs, rather than paying for it afterwards?

Note that Shavell's stated goal is to determine which strategy (or combination of strategies) will maximize social welfare, in other words, to design the most efficient regulatory system. Is that the only relevant goal? Should distributional factors, such as the importance of providing compensation to injured parties or the distribution of enforcement costs between public and private actors, also be considered? Does it make a difference whether standards for environmental quality are set through a conscious political process or through the accretion of individual market decisions overseen by case-by-case litigation? In that regard, recall Sagoff's distinction between "consumers" and "citizens" and see Christopher H. Schroeder, Lost in the Translation: What Environmental Regulation Does that Tort Cannot Duplicate, 41 Washburn L. J. 583, 584–586 (2002).

Given the characteristics of environmental problems identified in Chapter 1, Section 1, how effective would you expect private law to be against environmental harms? If the tort system is not effective, does that automatically mean that regulatory regimes are the only solution? Might there also be ways to make the tort system more responsive? Might other types of common law, such as property law, be useful? Note also that regulation is not monolithic. In addition to the paradigmatic "command-and-control" regulatory systems, public law can (among other things): mandate tort-like liability for environmental harm; require proof of financial responsibility as a prerequisite for engaging in risky activities; command disclosure of information that may be useful for political or market decisions; establish subsidies or fines; and create or correct markets for trading environmental goods or services.

2. *Free market environmentalism.* Professors Meiners and Yandle advocate a free market approach to environmental protection. Perhaps the best known defense of the free market position is the book *Free Market*

Environmentalism by Terry L. Anderson and Donald R. Leal, first published in 1991. Free market environmentalists believe the government's primary role in environmental protection should be the creation and enforcement of clear property rights in natural resources, rather than prescriptive regulation. Recall the discussion of the tragedy of the commons in Chapter 1. Individual property rights can solve the tragedy of the commons if the property owner internalizes all costs and benefits. Why did Hardin recommend coercion (i.e., government regulation) rather than private property interests as the solution to environmental pollution? Can property rights play a role in reducing pollution? How?

3. *Skepticism about motivations.* Some critics charge that those who call themselves free market environmentalists are not always sincere about seeking to advance environmental protection. It has been pointed out, for example, that many of the same groups that profess to support free market environmentalism have called for tort reform measures that would reduce the ability of plaintiffs to recover in common law actions. *See* Andrew McFee Thompson, Free Market Environmentalism and the Common Law: Confusion, Nostalgia, and Inconsistency, 45 Emory L. J. 1329, 1363 (1996). Do Professors Meiners and Yandle regard environmental regulations as too lax or too stringent? Do you find their claim that the growth of statutory environmental law has actually harmed the environment persuasive? For a very different view of history *see* Joel Franklin Brenner, Nuisance Law and the Industrial Revolution, 3 J. Legal Stud. 403, 408–420 (1974) (concluding that the law of nuisance was ineffective against air and water pollution in 19th-century England); J.R. McNeill, Something New Under the Sun: An Environmental History of the Twentieth–Century World 58–72 (2000) (concluding that only with the rise of statutes did the law begin to effectively address the air pollution problems of the early 20th century).

There are specific areas, however, where environmental law does preempt state tort law, and in doing so may well have increased the "acceptable" level of exposure to environmental harms. The Federal Insecticide, Fungicide, and Rodenticide Act, which regulates pesticide sale and use, is the best-known example. Because the law relies heavily on information supplied by pesticide manufacturers and makes enforcement difficult, courts and commentators have agreed that it is "not nearly as protective of persons exposed to pesticides as state tort law." Burke v. Dow Chemical Co., 797 F.Supp. 1128, 1135 (E.D. N.Y. 1992); Tseming Yang, Environmental Regulation, Tort Law and Environmental Justice: What Could Have Been, 41 Washburn L. J. 607, 623 (2002).

4. *The environmental case for a vigorous common law.* Although many traditional environmentalists are skeptical of the call to replace environmental statutes with a return to the common law, that does not mean they are altogether skeptical of the common law. It is possible to view statutes as essential but still celebrate the power and virtues of the common law, and even see it as providing opportunities for better enforcement of environmental policy in some contexts. One leading environmental trial lawyer puts it this way:

The common law, by contrast [to statutory environmental law], is not subject to political pressures and bureaucratic inertia. Plaintiffs in common law actions often have stronger incentives for initiating and prosecuting such actions, such as the immediate risk of personal harm and the potential to recover economic damages. Moreover, although proof of causation is required in common law cases, judges and juries still have flexibility to act in the face of uncertainty. The "more probable than not" standard of proof, for example, allows juries to make decisions in the face of uncertainty far greater than would be tolerated in the scientific arena. The fact that jury decisions may be based on less than complete information does not mean that such decisions are more likely to be wrong. In fact, instinct, experience, and "group" decisionmaking may lead to not only more rapid, but more accurate, social decisions. . . .

Although the common law is, in theory, anchored by stare decisis and fidelity to precedent, the greatest strength of the common law is its flexibility and ability to achieve justice and fairness in individual cases.

Michael D. Axline, The Limits of Statutory Law and the Wisdom of the Common Law, 38 Envtl. L. Rep. 10268 (2008).

4. *Strategies for tackling global warming.* Is global warming a problem that should be primarily addressed by common law or public law strategies? Why? Might both have a role to play? Should other strategies, such as incentives or subsidies, be included? Can you think of ways that regulatory and common law might be effectively combined to combat global warming?

CHAPTER THREE

THE ADMINISTRATIVE LAW OF THE ENVIRONMENT

SECTION 1. THE ADMINISTRATIVE DECISIONMAKING PROCESS

A. INTRODUCTION

Environmental law is inextricably intertwined with administrative law. While common law doctrines serve as the foundation of environmental law and continue to play an important role, statutes and regulations have come to dominate environmental law today. Legislatures set general norms and standards in federal and state environmental statutes, leaving the details of policymaking to regulatory agencies that can devote time, resources, and expertise to specific policy matters. At the federal level, agencies such as the Environmental Protection Agency (EPA) implement the general policies set by Congress by promulgating regulations, issuing agency guidance interpreting those regulations, adjudicating individual matters, and enforcing statutory and regulatory requirements. Administrative law is the body of law that governs agency decisionmaking, orders the relationships between the three branches of government, and ensures that private parties affected by agency decisions receive the protection of constitutional and statutory standards.

Administrative agencies can affect the environment in three principal ways:

- by undertaking actions themselves that have environmental effects;
- by licensing or permitting activities undertaken by individuals, private firms, or other government agencies; and
- by adopting regulations or other policies that impact environmental quality.

The primary environmental regulatory agency at the federal level is the EPA, which was created in 1970. Other federal agencies, such as the Department of the Interior and the Department of Commerce, have important environmental responsibilities as well, and under the National Environmental Policy Act (NEPA), 42 U.S.C. §§ 4321–4370f, all federal agencies have an obligation to incorporate environmental concerns into their decisionmaking processes and to prepare an environmental impact statement for all "major Federal actions significantly affecting the quality of the human environment." 42 U.S.C. § 4332(C). Most states have a department of environmental quality or department of natural resources that functions in a manner similar to the federal EPA.

Although administrative agencies have long existed within the federal government, the administrative state arose during the 20th century with the formation of various agencies under the New Deal. The role of these agencies in regulating markets and in administering programs that affect ordinary citizens (such as Social Security) led to growing concerns about the creation of a increasingly powerful "fourth branch" of government not directly accountable to the people. The Administrative Procedure Act (APA), enacted in 1946, sought to address these concerns by prescribing procedures that federal agencies must follow and by delineating the role of courts in reviewing agency actions. Other important sources of administrative law include: the Constitution, which establishes important principles of separation of powers and due process; the common law; and specific statutes that govern particular agencies or particular types of agency actions. At the state level, agencies are subject to analogous procedural and substantive rules based upon state law.

B.   AGENCY POLICYMAKING ALTERNATIVES

Administrative agencies such as the Environmental Protection Agency make policy in two principal ways: 1) by rulemaking, issuing general, forward-looking rules that announce policy applicable to a range of individual circumstances; and 2) by adjudication, making individual decisions applying policy to particular situations. Congress may specify in a particular statute which method an agency must follow; in the absence of such direction, the agency must adhere to the requirements of the APA. Constitutional due process may also mandate adjudicatory procedures in certain circumstances. See Londoner v. Denver, 210 U.S. 373 (1908) (requiring opportunity for taxpayer to be heard before tax imposed on relatively small number of property owners).

1.   AGENCY RULEMAKING

An important way in which agencies act is by making rules (also referred to as regulations). The APA defines a rule as "the whole or a part of an agency statement of general or particular applicability and future effect designed to implement, interpret, or prescribe law or policy" or to establish rules of practice. 5 U.S.C. § 551(4). Agencies use rules to set policies for several reasons. Through a rule, an agency can announce a coherent and comprehensive policy response in an area under its authority, rather than making policy incrementally through case-by-case determinations. In the rulemaking process, an agency can solicit and obtain input from regulated entities, other interested parties, and the general public concerning the subject matter of regulation, regulatory options, and potential implications. And once a rule is established, regulated parties know of their legal responsibilities as well as the potential sanctions for noncompliance.

There are two basic types of rulemaking: informal and formal.

a. Informal or Notice and Comment Rulemaking.

Excerpts From the Administrative Procedure Act

5 U.S.C. § 553.

§ 553. Rulemaking

* * *

(b) General notice of proposed rulemaking shall be published in the Federal Register, unless persons subject thereto are named and either personally served or otherwise have actual notice thereof in accordance with law. The notice shall include—

(1) a statement of the time, place, and nature of public rulemaking proceedings;

(2) reference to the legal authority under which the rule is proposed; and

(3) either the terms or substance of the proposed rule or a description of the subjects and issues involved.

Except when notice or hearing is required by statute, this subsection does not apply—

(A) to interpretative rules, general statements of policy, or rules of agency organization, procedure, or practice; or

(B) when the agency for good cause finds (and incorporates the finding and a brief statement of reasons therefor in the rules issued) that notice and public procedure thereon are impracticable, unnecessary, or contrary to the public interest.

* * *

(c) After notice required by this section, the agency shall give interested persons an opportunity to participate in the rulemaking through submission of written data, views, or arguments with or without opportunity for oral presentation. After consideration of the relevant matter presented, the agency shall incorporate in the rules adopted a concise general statement of their basis and purpose. * * *

(d) The required publication or service of a substantive rule shall be made not less than 30 days before its effective date, except

(1) a substantive rule which grants or recognizes an exemption or relieves a restriction;

(2) interpretive rules and statements of policy; or

(3) as otherwise provided by the agency for good cause found and published with the rule.

(e) Each agency shall give an interested person the right to petition for the issuance, amendment, or repeal of a rule.

Informal rulemaking, the most common and most significant method of rulemaking, refers to the promulgation of rules under APA § 553. Also known as "notice and comment" rulemaking, this process begins with publication of a general notice of the proposed rule in the Federal Register. This is followed by a reasonable time period during which the agency receives and considers written comments from all interested parties. After giving consideration to the comments presented, the agency must publish the final rule adopted along with a "concise general statement of [its] basis and purpose" in the Federal Register.

The question of what constitutes adequate notice presents an interesting legal problem since the APA does not demand a very detailed form of notice. The key seems to be sufficient information to provide interested parties an opportunity to comment effectively and in a timely manner. What if the final regulation deviates in a significant way from the rule proposed in the original notice? Courts have adopted a "logical outgrowth" test to determine the adequacy of the APA notice. See Environmental Integrity Project v. EPA, 425 F.3d 992 (D.C. Cir. 2005) (overturning EPA's revised Clean Air Act monitoring rule as not being a logical outgrowth of the proposed rule). Challenges to EPA rulemaking have been unsuccessful when the agency gave those commenting information about various rule alternatives that might be adopted in the final regulation. See Arizona Pub. Serv. Co. v. EPA, 211 F.3d 1280 (D.C. Cir. 2000). But how close must the final rule be to the original proposal? When an agency does not adequately connect the final rule to the initial proposal, courts will invalidate the rule. See Council Tree Comm. V. FCC, 619 F.3d 235 (3d Cir. 2010).

The requirement that final rules be published with a statement of their basis and purpose helps to ensure that regulations are supported by an explanation of how they were selected from alternatives. See Automotive Parts & Accessories v. Boyd, 407 F.2d 330, 338 (D.C. Cir. 1968) (emphasizing the need to "see what major issues of policy were ventilated by the informal proceedings and why the agency reacted to them as it did"). Courts have also insisted that EPA explain regulatory structure and categorization so that the public can understand the basis for the rule. See Northeast Md. Waste Disposal Auth. v. EPA, 358 F.3d 936 (D.C. Cir. 2004).

As this discussion demonstrates, the APA prescribes only minimal procedural requirements for informal rulemaking. Can courts order an agency to follow procedures in addition to those required by the APA, such as additional comment opportunities, cross-examination rights, or an opportunity to use experts to challenge evidence in the administrative record? In the oft-cited *Vermont Yankee* decision, the U.S. Supreme Court ruled that although such "hybrid" procedures could be voluntarily adopted by an agency, they could not be judicially imposed on top of procedures mandated by the APA or agency statutes. Vermont Yankee Nuclear Power Corp. v. Natural Res. Def. Council, 435 U.S. 519 (1978).

Although the procedures mandated by the APA appear relatively straightforward, informal rulemaking is often difficult, expensive, and time-consuming. Keenly aware of the potential for their rules to be challenged in

court, agencies often feel compelled to buttress their rulemaking records
with detailed explanations and responses to public comments. See Sidney
A. Shapiro & Thomas O. McGarity, Reorienting OSHA, Regulatory Alternatives and Legislative Reform, 6 Yale J. on Reg. 1 (1989) (noting that the
Occupational Safety and Health Administration "completed only twenty-
four substance-specific health regulations" in the first seventeen years of
its existence and describing factors that make health and safety regulation
difficult).

b. Formal Rulemaking

Informal rulemaking is the norm in modern administrative practice.
However, an agency's authorizing statute may sometimes require that rules
be made "on the record" following a hearing. That language invokes APA
§ 553(c), which provides that "[w]hen rules are required by statute to be
made on the record after opportunity for an agency hearing," the agency
must follow sections 556 and 557 of the APA. Rulemaking under these
provisions, referred to as formal rulemaking, resembles an adjudicative
process. Before issuing a rule, the agency must, in addition to publishing
the proposed rule in the Federal Register, conduct a trial-type hearing and
provide interested persons an opportunity to testify, submit evidence, and
cross-examine adverse witnesses.

c. Exempt Rulemaking

Section 553 of the APA exempts certain types of rules from even the
minimal notice and comment requirements of informal rulemaking. Exemptions exist for (a) interpretive rules, (b) general policy statements, (c)
procedural rules, and (d) when the agency finds for "good cause" that
notice and public procedures are "impractical, unnecessary, or contrary to
the public interest." These are usually described as "non-legislative rules."

"[L]egislative rules are those which create law, . . . whereas interpretive rules are statements as to what [an] administrative officer thinks the
statute or regulation means." American Hosp. Ass'n v. Bowen, 834 F.2d
1037, 1045 (D.C. Cir. 1987). The key threshold issue is whether an agency's
statement can be reasonably shown to interpret the underlying federal
statute or a regulation issued under it. Interpretive rules and policy
statements nevertheless can be very important because they set forth how
an agency views its existing legal authorities. These rules and other
"guidance" documents are often subject to legal challenge by parties
arguing that their issuance circumvented notice and comment rulemaking
requirements. In such cases, courts often must make difficult case-by-case
assessments of whether a rule is being applied in a binding way as a rule of
law. See Appalachian Power Co. v. EPA, 208 F.3d 1015 (D.C. Cir. 2000)
(holding that an EPA guidance, which broadened a preexisting rule, was
legislative, not interpretive). Agency procedural rules are not subject to
review as long as they are a "legitimate means of structuring [the agency's]
enforcement authority." See United States v. Gonzales Bonds & Ins.
Agency, Inc., 728 F.Supp.2d 1077 (N.D. Cal. 2010). Finally, agencies also

rely upon the "good cause" exception to avoid notice and comment requirements imposed under § 553.

d. *Negotiated Rulemaking*

An agency, whether undertaking informal or formal rulemaking, typically determines the substance of a proposed rule on its own. Under the Negotiated Rulemaking Act of 1990, however, federal agencies may conduct negotiations among interested parties to develop regulatory proposals. See 5 U.S.C. §§ 561–570. This practice of "regulatory negotiation" reflects a recognition that rules are often a compromise among interest groups, and that it may be desirable to enter into a structured bargaining process to develop certain rules. The negotiation involves the rulemaking agency conducting a thorough examination and revision of a proposed rule with interest groups that will be affected directly by the rule. The process allows interest groups to have greater control over the content of proposed rules, while giving agencies a more accurate picture of the costs and benefits of policy alternatives. If the negotiation process results in an agreement, the agency issues the agreed-upon language as a proposed rule, and then follows the usual procedure for notice and comment (or formal) rulemaking.

In today's atmosphere, regulatory negotiation can be an attractive option for agencies and interest groups. Agencies hope that groups given the opportunity to participate in the rulemaking will be less inclined to challenge the final rule. Regulatory negotiation is, however, an exceptionally political process, not to be undertaken unless a party is prepared to do battle over issues of science and policy under the glaring heat of the media spotlight. Moreover, the practice has come under criticism for its potential to substitute private bargains for reasoned agency decisionmaking. See William Funk, Bargaining Toward the New Millenium: Regulatory Negotiation and the Subversion of the Public Interest, 46 Duke L.J. 1351 (1997).

2. AGENCY ADJUDICATION

In addition to making rules, an agency adjudicates individual cases, decides whether a person's conduct complies with the laws and rules the agency administers, and imposes sanctions for violations. Adjudication, which encompasses these varied activities, differs from rulemaking in two significant ways. First, adjudication resolves disputes among specific individuals in specific cases, whereas rulemaking affects the rights of broad classes of individuals. Second, because adjudication involves concrete disputes, it has an immediate impact on specific entities.

a. *Formal Adjudication*

Under § 554(a) of the APA, the standards for "formal" adjudication apply when adjudication is "required by statute to be determined on the record after opportunity for an agency hearing." 5 U.S.C. § 554(a). For formal, "on the record" adjudication, Section 554 requires notice and an opportunity for the submission and consideration of facts, in addition to a hearing and decision in accordance with Sections 556 and 557 of the APA.

These latter provisions, discussed above in connection with formal rule-making, require a trial-type hearing and an opportunity to testify, submit evidence, and cross-examine adverse witnesses. Note that the process of decisionmaking in an agency is often hierarchical: the hearing may be conducted by an officer known as an administrative law judge, who prepares an initial decision, whereas the final decision may be made by an agency head or board. A formal adjudication concludes with a written decision that "shall include * * * findings and conclusions, and the reason or basis therefor, on all the material issues of fact, law, or discretion presented on the record." APA § 557(c).

What if a statute requires a "hearing" or "public hearing," but does not use the talismanic phrase, "on the record"? While some courts reject a simple "magic words" approach in favor of a contextual approach that considers whether a decision is adjudicative in nature, courts will often defer to an agency's choice of procedures. See Alfred C. Aman, Jr. & William T. Mayton, Administrative Law 201–04 (2d ed. 2001); Chemical Waste Management, Inc. v. EPA, 873 F.2d 1477, 1482 (D.C. Cir. 1989) (deferring to agency's choice of adjudicatory procedures where statute required a "public hearing"); Dominion Energy Brayton Point, LLC v. Johnson, 443 F.3d 12, 17–18 (1st Cir. 2006) (same).

b. Informal Adjudication

Most agency decisions affecting the environment are made by "informal" means. These may be quite important decisions: processing claims, issuing licenses or permits, awarding contracts or grants, releasing entitlement funds to states or individuals, or deciding on the method of implementing a government program.

Such decisions do not constitute rulemaking since they apply only to a particular individual or case. See 5 U.S.C. § 551 (defining "adjudication" as the "agency process for the formulation of an order" and defining "order" as "the whole or a part of a final disposition . . . in a matter other than rule making . . ."). And because most such decisions need not be "on the record," they are not formal adjudications, but rather are termed "informal adjudications." Although the APA does not explicitly cover this category of agency actions, agencies have developed their own procedures and the courts have imposed certain minimum standards of due process to enable judicial review: an administrative record and a contemporaneous explanation of the decision. See Citizens to Preserve Overton Park v. Volpe, 401 U.S. 402 (1971) (excerpted later in this chapter). However, one APA provision—section 558(c)—provides a limit on the informal adjudication process. It limits sanctions imposed on federal licensees by requiring that before revoking or suspending a federal license, the agency must give the licensee written notice of the facts or conduct that may warrant the punitive action and an opportunity to demonstrate compliance with all lawful requirements. See Buckingham v. Secretary, 603 F.3d 1073 (9th Cir. 2010). More generally, section 555(a) requires a "brief statement of the grounds for denial" of an application, petition or other agency request. This seldom enforced section is one of the few APA provisions applicable to informal adjudication.

c. *Adjudication at EPA*

Much of environmental law focuses on the growth of regulatory policy and on the efforts of EPA and other agencies to develop and apply environmental policies through rulemaking ultimately reviewed by the courts. Increasingly, however, EPA undertakes agency adjudication in the enforcement and implementation of the environmental laws for which it has responsibility. EPA's system of adjudication applies to two important aspects of its environmental programs: 1) permitting appeals and 2) challenges to administratively-imposed penalties. In addition, the agency conducts administrative hearings for a broad range of other decisions, including debarment from government contracting, ocean dumping permits, and RCRA Corrective Action Orders.

EPA's administrative judicial system has two levels: 1) Administrative Law Judges (ALJs) and 2) an Environmental Appeals Board (EAB). ALJs preside over matters that are required by APA § 554(a) to be "determined on the record after an opportunity for an agency hearing." The ALJs, called Presiding Officers, act as trial judges making findings of fact, drawing conclusions of law and issuing judgments in the form of decisions. One important function they serve is to rule in administrative enforcement actions on EPA requests for civil penalties against polluters under various environmental statutes.

Following EPA's Consolidated Rules of Practice, the ALJ conducts a quasi-judicial proceeding involving the government's complaint, settlement negotiations, answers, discovery, motions, hearings and decisions. *See* 40 C.F.R. Part 22. The government must prove its case by "a preponderance of the evidence." *Id.* at § 22.24. Appeals from an ALJ decision may be taken to EPA's Environmental Appeals Board, which is the agency's final decisionmaker in administrative appeals. Formed in 1992 to better deal with an expanding administrative docket, the EAB conducts *de novo* review of ALJ decisions and may reverse, modify, or affirm penalty determinations. Appeal from the EAB to the federal courts is determined by the specific environmental statute involved.

C. AGENCY POWER AND ITS LIMITS

The APA is vitally important in spelling out the basic procedural requirements for agency action. In this section, we will examine several other sources of constraints on agency action: the nondelegation doctrine, which limits Congress's ability to delegate its legislative power to executive agencies; congressional supervision of agencies; and presidential supervision of agencies.

1. THE NONDELEGATION DOCTRINE

How do agencies obtain the authority to make environmental decisions? Although Article I of the United States Constitution provides that "all legislative powers shall be vested in a Congress of the United States," Congress routinely delegates broad powers to administrative agencies, including the EPA. This is constitutionally permissible as long as the legislation prescribes basic policy and contains criteria that are sufficiently clear to enable Congress, the courts, and the public to ascertain whether the agency has conformed with those standards. Mills v. United States, 36 F.3d 1052 (11th Cir. 1994). This requirement, known as the nondelegation doctrine, bars the excessive delegation of discretionary authority from Congress to administrative agencies.

The doctrine arguably implements the constitutional separation of powers by preventing Congress from shifting untethered legislative power to executive agencies. Prior to the New Deal, courts acknowledged the existence of limits to Congress' ability to delegate authority, but consistently upheld challenged delegations of power as allowing executive agencies merely to fill in the details of policy set by Congress. See Marshall Field & Co. v. Clark, 143 U.S. 649, 693 (1892); United States v. Grimaud, 220 U.S. 506 (1911). Whether a delegation was permissible depended on whether Congress had established "an intelligible principle to which the person or body authorized [to act] is directed to conform." J.W. Hampton, Jr., & Co. v. United States, 276 U.S. 394, 409 (1928).

The nondelegation doctrine achieved its greatest force during the 1930s, when it served as the basis for invalidating several New Deal statutes that granted federal agencies broad economic authority. See Panama Ref. Co. v. Ryan, 293 U.S. 388 (1935); A.L.A. Schechter Poultry Corp. v. United States, 295 U.S. 495 (1935); Carter v. Carter Coal Co., 298 U.S. 238 (1936). In *Schechter Poultry*, for instance, the Supreme Court struck down a delegation that authorized the National Recovery Administration to establish "codes of fair competition" for various business and industries. As the Court explained,

> [The statute] supplies no standards for any trade, industry, or activity. It does not undertake to prescribe rules of conduct to be applied to particular states of fact determined by appropriate administrative procedure. Instead of prescribing rules of conduct, it authorizes the making of codes to prescribe them. For that legislative undertaking, section 3 sets up no standards, aside from the statement of the general aims of rehabilitation, correction, and expansion described in section 1. In view of the scope of that broad declaration and of the nature of the few restrictions that are imposed, the discretion of the President in approving or prescribing codes, and thus enacting laws for the government of trade and industry throughout the country, is virtually unfettered. We think that the code-making authority thus conferred is an unconstitutional delegation of legislative power.

295 U.S. at 541–42.

Following this active period, the nondelegation doctrine entered a period of dormancy in which the Court repeatedly approved broad delegations of power. See, e.g., Yakus v. United States, 321 U.S. 414 (1944) (upholding price controls and explaining that standards provided in the statute were "sufficiently definite and precise to enable Congress, the courts and the public to ascertain whether the Administrator, in fixing the designated prices, has conformed to those standards"); Mistretta v. United States, 488 U.S. 361 (1989) (upholding delegation to U.S. Sentencing Commission of authority to develop mandatory sentencing guidelines).

Justice Rehnquist's concurring opinion in *Industrial Union Dept., AFL–CIO v. American Petroleum Institute*, 448 U.S. 607 (1980) (the "Benzene case"), however, rekindled interest in the nondelegation principle. The Benzene case involved a challenge to an agency rule limiting workplace exposure to benzene. The rule had been promulgated pursuant to Section 6(b)(5) of the Occupational Safety and Health Act, which directed the Secretary of Labor to set health and safety standards which would "most adequately assure[], to the extent feasible, on the basis of the best available evidence, that no employee will suffer material impairment of health or functional capacity. . . ." Although a majority of the Court found no delegation problem, Justice Rehnquist contended that the Congress had provided insufficient standards in the statute:

> Read literally, the relevant portion of § 6(b)(5) is completely precatory, admonishing the Secretary to adopt the most protective standard if he can, but excusing him from that duty if he cannot. In the case of a hazardous substance for which a "safe" level is either unknown or impractical, the language of 6(b)(5) gives the Secretary absolutely no indication where on the continuum of relative safety he should draw his line. Especially in light of the importance of the interests at stake, I have no doubt that the provision at issue, standing alone, would violate the doctrine against uncanalized delegations of legislative power.

448 U.S. at 675. Justice Rehnquist went on to articulate three functions of the nondelegation doctrine: "it ensures . . . that important choices of social policy are made by Congress, the branch of our Government most responsive to the popular will"; it "provides the recipient of that authority with an 'intelligible principle' to guide the exercise of the delegated discretion"; and it "ensures that courts charged with reviewing the exercise of delegated legislative discretion will be able to test that exercise against ascertainable standards." Id. at 685–86. The doctrine thus helps prevents Congress from ducking hard political choices and shifting responsibility for those choices to administrative agencies.

Speculation that Justice Rehnquist's concurrence would reinvigorate the nondelegation doctrine, however, has not been borne out by subsequent cases. Rather, in *Whitman v. American Trucking Associations, Inc.*, 531 U.S. 457 (2001), the Supreme Court reaffirmed Congress' ability to delegate broad authority to agencies. In an opinion by Justice Scalia, the Court unanimously overruled the D.C. Circuit's holding that § 109 of the Clean Air Act, which directs EPA to determine national ambient air quality standards (NAAQS), delegated too much legislative power to EPA. Applying the "intelligible principle" standard from *J.W. Hampton v. United States*, the Court upheld the Clean Air Act's rather vague delegation, stating that:

requiring the EPA to set air quality standards at a level that is "requisite"—that is, not lower or higher than is necessary—to protect the public health with an adequate margin of safety, fits comfortably within the scope of discretion permitted by our precedent.

531 U.S. at 475–76. With this sweeping language, the Court reaffirmed the "intelligible principle" concept and broad agency discretion in implementing protective environmental and public health policy.

In the end, courts apparently have concluded that broad delegation to agencies is beneficial, taking advantage of administrative flexibility, responsiveness, and expertise, and perhaps unavoidable, given the multitude of issues Congress must address and the complexity of modern society. Courts have also found it difficult to formulate a workable judicial test for determining whether a particular delegation goes too far. Ultimately, broad delegations may be consistent with democratic values in that they reflect congressional intent and permit the democratically elected Chief Executive to achieve policy goals.

2. CONGRESSIONAL SUPERVISION OF ADMINISTRATIVE AGENCIES

Congress can supervise and influence agency conduct in various ways. Congress controls the establishment of agencies, their statutory mandates, agency appropriations, and how agencies are governed. Individual members or committees of Congress can also affect agency conduct. Congressional members may have informal contacts with agencies in hopes of influencing specific decisions (e.g., funding a local project) or shaping regulations of importance to an industry (e.g., coal mining reclamation rules). Members of Congress may use formal or informal channels to support or to block certain executive appointments to key positions in federal agencies. More formally, Congress acts through its committee structure to exercise oversight of agencies, including an agency's budget, substantive authority, and operations.

Congress also has the opportunity to review agency rules before they take effect. Under 5 U.S.C. § 801, enacted in 1996 as part of the Small Business Regulatory Enforcement Fairness Act, agencies must submit to Congress each regulation, along with a report containing a cost-benefit analysis and other information pertaining to the regulation. Although "non-major" rules can take effect once the rule and report are provided to Congress, major rules do not take effect for sixty days, during which Congress can pass a joint resolution disapproving the rule. Unless the President vetoes such a resolution, the agency must withdraw the rule.

Congress also can pass statutes designed to shape the way agencies make decisions. The National Environmental Policy Act of 1969, for example, requires federal agencies to consider and to disclose the environmental impact of their actions. 42 U.S.C. §§ 4321–4370f. The Regulatory Flexibility Act of 1980 requires that agencies determine the effects of their actions on small businesses. 5 U.S.C. §§ 601–612. And the Unfunded Mandates

Reform Act of 1995 requires agencies to prepare a regulatory analysis of any rulemaking likely to impose more than $100 million in costs on the private sector or on state, local, and tribal governments. 2 U.S.C. § 1532.

3. EXECUTIVE SUPERVISION OF ADMINISTRATIVE AGENCIES

Article II, § 1 of the U.S. Constitution vests executive power in the President, but the term "executive power" is undefined. As the chief administrator of the executive branch of government, the President can influence agency policy through the appointment and removal of agency officials. The appointment of these "officers of the United States" must be done in conformity with the procedures set out in the Appointments Clause, Art. II, § 2, of the U.S. Constitution. "Principal" officers, and some "inferior" officers, must be appointed with the advice and consent of the Senate. Removal of these officers, with the exception of independent agencies, can occur at the will of the President.

All Presidents, however, seek direct influence over agency policy as well. They may exercise policy supervision informally through conversations with agency heads or more formally through the issuance of executive orders. From the standpoint of administrative agencies, one of the most important executive orders is Executive Order (E.O.) 12,866, issued by President Clinton in 1993. E.O. 12,866 is a critical means for the White House to exercise control over the rulemaking activities of federal agencies.

Building on earlier orders issued by President Reagan, E.O. 12,866 requires agencies to submit "significant regulatory actions" for review by the Office of Information and Regulatory Affairs (OIRA), an office within the Office of Management and Budget. The agency's submission must include the proposed rule, a description of the need for the regulatory action and an explanation of how the regulatory action will meet that need, and an assessment of the potential costs and benefits of the regulatory action. OIRA review may result in changes in the scope, impact, costs, or benefits of a regulation, and perhaps even withdrawal of the regulation. A 2003 study by the U.S. General Accounting Office found that the most frequent changes resulting from OIRA review occurred with respect to EPA's rules, and that these changes often occurred after "outside parties (most commonly representatives of regulated entities) had contacted OIRA." U.S. General Accounting Office, Rulemaking: OMB's Role in Review of Agencies' Draft Rules and the Transparency of Those Reviews 9–11 (2003). Indeed, critics have charged that OIRA review has sometimes resulted in the imposition of cost-benefit criteria upon regulatory schemes that were designed by Congress to exclude consideration of costs. See, e.g., Lisa Heinzerling, Statutory Interpretation in the Era of OIRA, 33 Fordham Urban L.J. 1097 (2006).

SECTION 2. JUDICIAL REVIEW OF AGENCY ACTION

Congress and the Executive are not the only branches of government exercising control over agency decisionmaking. The courts also play an important role. Judicial review of agencies may involve determinations of whether an agency has acted beyond its delegated authority or beyond constitutional limits, whether an agency's findings of fact are adequately supported, whether an agency's interpretation of the law is proper, and whether an agency has made reasonable judgments.

A litigant wishing to obtain judicial review of an agency's action (or non-action) must demonstrate not only that the court has jurisdiction over the disputed claim, but also that standing and other justiciability requirements are satisfied. This section examines these prerequisites to judicial review.

A.   JURISDICTION

Subject-matter jurisdiction involves the power of a court to review an agency action. Such jurisdiction may be based on either a general jurisdictional statute (such as federal question jurisdiction provided for under 28 U.S.C. § 1331) or on a specific statute that confers jurisdiction for a particular form of review. The Clean Air Act, for instance, provides for judicial review of certain EPA rules by the U.S. Court of Appeals for the D.C. Circuit. See 42 U.S.C. § 7607. Only in the absence of special statutory review may an action be brought under a general jurisdiction statute. The general jurisdiction statute most frequently relied on as the basis for reviewing agency action, 28 U.S.C. § 1331, vests district courts with "jurisdiction of all civil actions arising under the Constitution, laws, or treaties of the United States." Given the jurisdictional provisions often found in environmental statutes, as well as the broad jurisdiction granted by 28 U.S.C. § 1331, lack of subject-matter jurisdiction is rarely a problem for those seeking review of agency action.

B.   REVIEWABILITY AND SCOPE OF REVIEW

The judicial review provisions of the Administrative Procedure Act, excerpted below, further define the circumstances under which judicial review is available and set out standards governing that review. As you read these provisions, consider what sort of agency actions are reviewable, as well as the amount of deference a court will give to agency determinations.

Excerpts From the Administrative Procedure Act

5 U.S.C. §§ 701–706.

Sec. 701   Application: Definitions

(a) This chapter applies according to the provisions thereof except to the extent that—

  (1) statutes preclude judicial review; or

(2) agency action is committed to agency discretion by law.

* * *

Sec. 702   Right of Review

A person suffering legal wrong because of agency action, or adversely affected or aggrieved by agency action within the meaning of a relevant statute, is entitled to judicial review thereof.

Sec. 703   Form and Venue of Proceedings

The form of proceeding for judicial review is the special statutory review proceeding relevant to the subject matter in a court specified by statute or in the absence or inadequacy thereof any applicable form of legal action, including actions for declaratory judgements or writs of prohibitory or mandatory injunction or habeas corpus in a court of competent jurisdiction.

Sec. 704   Actions Reviewable

Agency action made reviewable by statute and final agency action for which there is no other adequate remedy in a court are subject to judicial review.

* * *

Sec. 706   Scope of review

To the extent necessary to decision and when presented, the reviewing court shall decide all relevant questions of law, interpret constitutional and statutory provisions, and determine the meaning or applicability of the terms of an agency action. The reviewing court shall—

(1) compel agency action unlawfully withheld or unreasonably delayed; and

(2) hold unlawful and set aside agency action, findings, and conclusions found to be—

(A) arbitrary, capricious, an abuse of discretion, or otherwise not in accordance with law;

(B) contrary to constitutional right, power, privilege, or immunity;

(C) in excess of statutory jurisdiction, authority, or limitations, or short of statutory right;

(D) without observance of procedure required by law;

(E) unsupported by substantial evidence in a case subject to sections 556 and 557 of this title or otherwise reviewed on the record of an agency hearing provided by statute; or

(F) unwarranted by the facts to the extent that the facts are subject to trial de novo by the reviewing court.

* * *

The APA provides for judicial review of "[a]gency action made reviewable by statute and final agency action for which there is no other adequate remedy in a court." 5 U.S.C. § 704. This section has been read to create a presumption in favor of judicial review. See Abbott Labs. v. Gardner, 387 U.S. 136, 140–41 (1967). A statute may preclude review, however, see 5 U.S.C. § 701(a)(1), and the extent to which "a particular statute precludes judicial review is determined not only from its express language, but also from the structure of the statutory scheme, its objectives, its legislative history, and the nature of the administrative action involved." Block v. Community Nutrition Inst., 467 U.S. 340, 345 (1984). Judicial review is also unavailable where "agency action is committed to agency discretion by law." 5 U.S.C. § 701(a)(2). This exception to reviewability is a narrow one, exemplified by the exercise of prosecutorial discretion, which "often involves a complicated balancing of a number of factors which are peculiarly within its expertise." Heckler v. Chaney, 470 U.S. 821, 831 (1985).

The following case considers whether the "committed to agency discretion" exception applies to other types of agency action. More importantly, the case establishes important principles regarding the scope of review of informal agency action.

Citizens to Preserve Overton Park, Inc. v. Volpe

United States Supreme Court, 1971.
401 U.S. 402.

■ Opinion of the Court by MR. JUSTICE MARSHALL, announced by MR. JUSTICE STEWART.

The growing public concern about the quality of our natural environment has prompted Congress in recent years to enact legislation designed to curb the accelerating destruction of our country's natural beauty. We are concerned in this case with § 4(f) of the Department of Transportation Act of 1966, as amended, and § 18(a) of the Federal–Aid Highway Act of 1968, 82 Stat. 823, 23 U.S.C. § 138 (1964 ed. Supp. V)(hereafter, § 138). These statutes prohibit the Secretary of Transportation from authorizing the use of federal funds to finance the construction of highways through public parks if a "feasible and prudent" alternative route exists. If no such route is available, the statutes allow him to approve construction through parks only if there has been "all possible planning to minimize harm" to the park.

Petitioners, private citizens as well as local and national conservation organizations, contend that the Secretary has violated these statutes by authorizing the expenditure of federal funds for the construction of a six-lane interstate highway through a public park in Memphis, Tennessee. Their claim was rejected by the District Court, which granted the Secretary's motion for summary judgment, and the Court of Appeals for the Sixth Circuit affirmed. After oral argument, this Court granted a stay that halted construction and, treating the application for the stay as a petition for certiorari, granted review. We now reverse the judgment below and remand for further proceedings in the District Court.

Overton Park is a 342 acre city park located near the center of Memphis. The park contains a zoo, a nine-hole municipal golf course, an outdoor theater, nature trails, a bridle path, an art academy, picnic areas, and 170 acres of forest. The proposed highway, which is to be a six-lane, high-speed, expressway, will sever the zoo from the rest of the park. Although the roadway will be depressed below ground level except where it crosses a small creek, 26 acres of the park will be destroyed. The highway is to be a segment of Interstate Highway I–40, part of the National System of Interstate and Defense Highways. I–40 will provide Memphis with a major east-west expressway which will allow easier access to downtown Memphis from the residential areas on the eastern edge of the city.

Although the route through the park was approved by the Bureau of Public Roads in 1956 and by the Federal Highway Administrator in 1966, the enactment of § 4(f) of the Department of Transportation Act prevented distribution of federal funds for the section of the highway designated to go through Overton Park until the Secretary of Transportation determined whether the requirements of § 4(f) had been met. Federal funding for the rest of the project was, however, available; and the state acquired a right-of-way on both sides of the park. In April 1968, the Secretary announced that he concurred in the judgment of local officials that I–40 should be built through the park. And in September 1969 the state acquired the right-of-way inside Overton Park from the city. Final approval for the project—the route as well as the design—was not announced until November 1969, after Congress had reiterated in § 138 of the Federal–Aid Highway Act that highway construction through public parks was to be restricted. Neither announcement approving the route and design of I–40 was accompanied by a statement of the Secretary's factual findings. He did not indicate why he believed there were no feasible and prudent alternative routes or why design changes could not be made to reduce the harm to the park.

Petitioners contend that the Secretary's action is invalid without such formal findings and that the Secretary did not make an independent determination but merely relied on the judgment of the Memphis City Council. They also contend that it would be "feasible and prudent" to route I–40 around Overton Park either to the north or to the south. And they argue that if these alternative routes are not "feasible and prudent," the present plan does not include "all possible" methods for reducing harm to the park. Petitioners claim that I–40 could be built under the park by using either of two possible tunneling methods, and they claim that, at a minimum, by using advanced drainage techniques the expressway could be depressed below ground level along the entire route through the park including the section that crosses the small creek.

Respondents argue that it was unnecessary for the Secretary to make formal findings, and that he did, in fact, exercise his own independent judgment which was supported by the facts. In the District Court, respondents introduced affidavits, prepared specifically for this litigation, which indicated that the Secretary had made the decision and that the decision was supportable. These affidavits were contradicted by affidavits introduced by petitioners, who also sought to take the deposition of a former Federal Highway Administrator who had participated in the decision to route I–40 through Overton Park.

The District Court and the Court of Appeals found that formal findings by the Secretary were not necessary and refused to order the deposition of the former Federal Highway Administrator because those courts believed that probing of the mental processes of an administrative decisionmaker was prohibited. And, believing that the Secretary's authority was wide and reviewing courts' authority narrow in the approval of highway routes, the lower courts held that the affidavits contained no basis for a determination that the Secretary had exceeded his authority.

We agree that formal findings were not required. But we do not believe that in this case judicial review based solely on litigation affidavits was adequate.

A threshold question—whether petitioners are entitled to any judicial review—is easily answered. Section 701 of the Administrative Procedure Act, 5 U.S.C. § 701, provides that the action of "each authority of the government of the United States," which includes the Department of Transportation, is subject to judicial review except where there is a statutory prohibition on review or where "agency action is committed to agency discretion by law." In this case, there is no indication that Congress sought to prohibit judicial review and there is most certainly no "showing of 'clear and convincing evidence' of a ... legislative intent" to restrict access to judicial review. Abbott Laboratories v. Gardner, 387 U.S. 136, 141 (1967). * * *

Similarly, the Secretary's decision here does not fall within the exception for action "committed to agency discretion." This is a very narrow exception. Berger, Administrative Arbitrariness and Judicial Review, 65 Col.L.Rev. 55 (1965). The legislative history of the Administrative Procedure Act indicates that it is applicable in those rare instances where "statutes are drawn in such broad terms that in a given case there is no law to apply." S.Rep. No. 752, 79th Cong., 1st Sess., at 26 (1945).

Section 4(f) of the Department of Transportation Act and § 138 of the Federal–Aid Highway Act are clear and specific directives. Both the Department of Transportation Act and the Federal–Aid to Highway Act provide that the Secretary "shall not approve any program or project" that requires the use of any public parkland "unless (1) there is no feasible and prudent alternative to the use of such land, and (2) such program includes all possible planning to minimize harm to such park. . . ." This language is a plain and explicit bar to the use of federal funds for construction of highways through parks—only the most unusual situations are exempted.

Despite the clarity of the statutory language, respondents argue that the Secretary has wide discretion. They recognize that the requirement that there be no "feasible" alternative route admits of little administrative discretion. For this exemption to apply the Secretary must find that as a matter of sound engineering it would not be feasible to build the highway along any other route. Respondents argue, however, that the requirement that there be no other "prudent" route requires the Secretary to engage in a wide-ranging balancing of competing interests. They contend that the Secretary should weigh the detriment resulting from the destruction of parkland against the cost of other routes, safety considerations, and other factors, and determine on the basis of the importance that he attaches to these other factors whether, on balance, alternative feasible routes, would be "prudent."

But no such wide-ranging endeavor was intended. It is obvious that in most cases considerations of cost, directness of route, and community disruption will indicate that parkland should be used for highway construction whenever possible. Although it may be necessary to transfer funds from one jurisdiction to another, there will always be a smaller outlay required from the public purse when parkland is used since the public already owns the land and there will be no need to pay for right-of-way. And since people do not live or work in parks, if a highway is built on parkland no one will have to leave his home or give up his business. Such factors are common to substantially all highway construction. Thus, if Congress intended these factors to be on an equal footing with preservation of parkland there would have been no need for the statutes.

Congress clearly did not intend that cost and disruption of the community were to be ignored by the Secretary. But the very existence of the statutes indicates that protection of parkland was to be given paramount importance. The few green havens that are public parks were not to be lost unless there were truly unusual factors present in a particular case or the cost or community disruption resulting from alternative routes reached extraordinary magnitudes. If the statutes are to have any meaning, the Secretary cannot approve the destruction of parkland unless he finds that alternative routes present unique problems.

Plainly, there is "law to apply" and thus the exemption for action "committed to agency discretion" is inapplicable. But the existence of judicial review is only the start: the standard for review must also be determined. For that we must look to § 706 of the Administrative Procedure Act, 5 U.S.C. § 706. A "reviewing court shall ... hold unlawful and set aside agency action, findings, and conclusions found" not to meet six separate standards. In all cases agency action must be set aside if the action was "arbitrary, capricious, an abuse of discretion, or otherwise not in accordance with law" or if the action failed to meet statutory, procedural, or constitutional requirements. In certain narrow, specifically limited situations, the agency action is to be set aside if the action was not supported by "substantial evidence." And in other equally narrow circumstances the reviewing court is to engage in a de novo review of the action and set it aside if it was "unwarranted by the facts."

Petitioners argue that the Secretary's approval of the construction of I–40 through Overton Park is subject to one or the other of these latter two standards of limited applicability. First, they contend that the "substantial evidence" standard of § 706(2)(E) must be applied. In the alternative, they claim that § 706(2)(F) applies and that there must be a de novo review to determine if the Secretary's action was "unwarranted by the facts." Neither of these standards is, however, applicable.

Review under the substantial-evidence test is authorized only when the agency action is taken pursuant to a rulemaking provision of the Administrative Procedure Act itself, 5 U.S.C. § 553, or when the agency action is based on a public adjudicatory hearing. *See* 5 U.S.C. §§ 556, 557. The Secretary's decision to allow the expenditure of federal funds to build I–40 through Overton Park was plainly not an exercise of a rulemaking function. And the only hearing that is required by either the Administrative Procedure Act or the statutes regulating the distribution of federal funds for highway construction is a public hearing conducted by local officials for the purpose of informing the community about the proposed project and eliciting community views on the design and route. The hearing is nonadjudicatory, quasi-legislative in nature. It is not designed to produce a record that is to be the basis of agency action—the basic requirement for substantial-evidence review.

Petitioner's alternative argument also fails. De novo review of whether the Secretary's decision was "unwarranted by the facts" is authorized by § 706(2)(F) in only two circumstances. First, such de novo review is authorized when the action is adjudicatory in nature and the agency fact-finding procedures are inadequate. And, there may be independent judicial fact-finding when issues that were not before the agency are raised in a proceeding to enforce nonadjudicatory agency action. Neither situation exists here.

Even though there is no de novo review in this case and the Secretary's approval of the route of I–40 does not have ultimately to meet the substantial-evidence test, the generally applicable standards of § 706 require the reviewing court to engage in a substantial inquiry. Certainly, the Secretary's decision is entitled to a presumption of regularity. But that presumption is not to shield his action from a thorough, probing, in-depth review.

The court is first required to decide whether the Secretary acted within the scope of his authority. This determination naturally begins with a delineation of the scope of the Secretary's authority and discretion. As has been shown, Congress has specified only a small range of choices that the Secretary can make. Also involved in this initial inquiry is a determination of whether on the facts the Secretary's decision can reasonably be said to be within that range. The reviewing court must consider whether the Secretary properly construed his authority to approve the use of parkland as limited to situations where there are no feasible alternative routes or where feasible alternative routes involve uniquely difficult problems. And the reviewing court must be able to find that the Secretary could have reasonably believed that in this case there are no feasible alternatives or that alternatives do involve unique problems.

Scrutiny of the facts does not end, however, with the determination that the Secretary has acted within the scope of his statutory authority. Section 706(2)(A) requires a finding that the actual choice made was not "arbitrary, capricious, an abuse of discretion, or otherwise not in accordance with law." To make this finding the court must consider whether the decision was based on a consideration of the relevant factors and whether there has been a clear error of judgment. Although this inquiry into the facts is to be searching and careful, the ultimate standard of review is a narrow one. The court is not empowered to substitute its judgment for that of the agency.

The final inquiry is whether the Secretary's action followed the necessary procedural requirements. Here the only procedural error alleged is the failure of the Secretary to make formal findings and state his reason for allowing the highway to be built through the park.

Undoubtedly, review of the Secretary's action is hampered by his failure to make such findings, but the absence of formal findings does not necessarily require that the case be remanded to the Secretary. Neither the Department of Transportation Act nor the Federal–Aid Highway Act requires such formal findings. Moreover, the Administrative Procedure Act requirements that there be formal findings in certain rulemaking and adjudicatory proceedings do not apply to the Secretary's action here. *See* 5 U.S.C. §§ 553(a)(2), 554(a). And, although formal findings may be required in some cases in the absence of statutory directives when the nature of the agency action is ambiguous, those situations are rare. Plainly, there is no ambiguity here; the Secretary has approved the construction of I–40 through Overton Park and has approved a specific design for the project.

Thus it is necessary to remand this case to the District Court for plenary review of the Secretary's decision. That review is to be based on the full administrative record that was before the Secretary at the time he made his decision. But since the bare record may not disclose the factors that were considered or the Secretary's construction of the evidence it may be necessary for the District Court to require some explanation in order to determine if the Secretary acted within the scope of his authority and if the Secretary's action was justifiable under the applicable standard.

The court may require the administrative officials who participated in the decision to give testimony explaining their action. Of course, such inquiry into the mental processes of administrative decisionmakers is usually to be avoided. And where there are administrative findings that were made at the same time as the decision, there must be a strong showing of bad faith or improper behavior before such inquiry may be made. But here there are no such formal findings and it may be that the only way there can be effective judicial review is by examining the decisionmakers themselves.

The District Court is not, however, required to make such an inquiry. It may be that the Secretary can prepare formal findings that will provide an adequate explanation for his action. Such an explanation will, to some extent, be a *"post hoc* rationalization" and thus must be viewed critically.

If the District Court decides that additional explanation is necessary, that court should consider which method will prove the most expeditious so that full review may be had as soon as possible.

NOTES AND QUESTIONS

1. *Reviewability. Overton Park* involved the type of agency decisionmaking known as "informal agency adjudication." Such decisions are generally reviewable. Under what circumstances is judicial review unavailable? When, if ever, should court review be entirely precluded?

2. *The Overton Park test.* What inquiry does *Overton Park* require courts to undertake? What result would you expect it to produce in *Overton Park* itself? On remand, the District Court, after a 25–day trial that involved affidavits by the Secretary of Transportation and the testimony of his subordinates, reversed the Secretary's decision and remanded the case to the agency for yet another determination. The Secretary was ultimately unable to show that there was no prudent or feasible alternative, and the road was not built.

3. *The administrative record.* For a court to exercise judicial review, there must be some kind of administrative record. In formal agency decisionmaking, whether rulemaking or adjudicatory, there will be an administrative record consisting of all the transcripts, exhibits, and papers filed in the proceeding. Did an administrative record exist to support the informal agency action in *Overton Park*? Read carefully the Supreme Court's instruction that the District Court exercise "plenary review" of the Secretary's decision. Upon what is this "plenary review" to be based?

Overton Park requires agencies to compile an administrative record even in informal adjudicatory and informal rule-making proceedings. What must the administrative record contain? Must the agency create formal and contemporaneous findings of fact and conclusions of law? In *Camp v. Pitts*, 411 U.S. 138 (1973), the Supreme Court answered this question by accepting a very brief explanation by the Comptroller of Currency for denying a branch bank application. The denial was based upon facts showing no need for additional banking services in the particular community. The Court noted that "[u]nlike *Overton Park*, in the present case there was contemporaneous explanation of the agency decision. The explanation may have been curt, but it surely indicated the determinative reason for the final action taken: the finding that a new bank was an uneconomic venture * * *." *Id.* at 143.

4. *Standards of judicial review.* Consider again the different standards of judicial review discussed in the *Overton Park* case. The court quotes from APA § 706, which contains the following six standards:

(A) arbitrary, capricious, an abuse of discretion, or otherwise not in accordance with law;

(B) contrary to constitutional right, power, privilege, or immunity;

(C) in excess of statutory jurisdiction, authority, or limitations, or short of statutory right;

(D) without observance of procedure required by law;

(E) unsupported by substantial evidence in a case subject to sections 556 and 557 of this title or otherwise reviewed on the record of an agency hearing provided by statute; or

(F) unwarranted by the facts to the extent that the facts are subject to trial de novo by the reviewing court.

Note that "substantial evidence review" is tied to sections 556 and 557 of the APA, which means that it is applicable if the agency decision was made after a trial-type hearing on the record, characteristic of both formal adjudication and formal "on the record" rulemaking. Substantial evidence review means that the court should not assess the facts of the matter itself, but should evaluate the *reasonableness* of the agency's fact finding. A court should consider the "whole record," which means it should evaluate not only evidence that supports the agency but also the relevant evidence both for and against the decision. Universal Camera Corp. v. NLRB, 340 U.S. 474 (1951).

A second important standard of review is "abuse of discretion" review under APA § 706(A). This standard of review is applied both to informal rulemaking under APA § 553 and informal adjudication such as the *Overton Park* decision. Under this standard of review the courts will demand a clear statement of the basis and purpose of the agency action. A spin-off of "abuse of discretion" review is the "hard look" or "reasoned decisionmaking" approach, which requires that the agency's decision fall within the bounds of reasoned decisionmaking and involves relatively close judicial oversight. See, e.g., Baltimore Gas & Elec. Co. v. Natural Res. Def. Council, 462 U.S. 87 (1983) (upholding a Nuclear Regulatory Commission rule which did not place any negative environmental weight on the risks of long-term spent fuel storage in connection with the licensing of nuclear power plants.)

A third standard is de novo judicial review, in which the reviewing court gives no deference to the agency's decision. Since *Overton Park*, de novo review has limited application. According to the Supreme Court, in what two instances is it still viable?

5. *Review of procedure versus review of substance.* Both agency procedure and agency action are subject to judicial review. The APA specifically provides that courts may set aside agency actions that are "without observance of procedure required by law." 5 U.S.C. § 706(2)(D). Agency failure to follow the procedural requirements of its own authorizing statute, its own rules, or the APA can result in a court remand. Should an agency's substantive decision be reversed and remanded for every possible procedural violation, including minor, non-prejudicial ones? Should judicial intervention depend on the nature of the agency's action?

Moreover, should courts scrutinize agency procedures more carefully than the substance of agency decisions? Many EPA decisions involve the analysis of scientific and engineering information and result in the making of important regulatory decisions based upon these analyses. When these technically complex and economically expensive judgments are later challenged in court, judges must evaluate both the agency's procedure and substantive choices. The substantive review of EPA decisions asks federal judges, who are legal generalists by training and experience, to evaluate expert agency choices. This deep judicial involvement in highly technical matters has been the source of controversy throughout the modern history of environmental law. During the first decade of EPA's Clean Air Act regulation, two respected appellate judges—Harold Leventhal and David Bazelon—debated this issue in *Ethyl Corp. v. EPA*, 541 F.2d 1 (D.C. Cir. 1976).

> Judge Bazelon argued that "technically illiterate" judges should not get involved in the substance of agency decisions. His solution to the need for courts to supervise agency decisionmaking was purely procedural: "in cases of great technological complexity, the best way for courts to guard against unreasonable or erroneous administrative decisions is not for the judges themselves to scrutinize the technical merits of each decision. Rather, it is to establish a decisionmaking process that assures a reasoned decision that can be held up to the scrutiny of the scientific community."

> Judge Leventhal disagreed. He argued that substantive review was, in fact, necessary if judges were to carry out their statutory and constitutional duties: "The substantive review of administrative action is modest, but it cannot be carried out in a vacuum of understanding. Better no judicial review at all than a charade that gives the imprimatur without the substance of judicial confirmation that the agency is not acting unreasonably." Judge Leventhal went on to emphasize that he was not advocating wholesale substitution of judicial judgements for that of the agency. He concluded, however, that: "on issues of substantive review, on conformance to statutory standards and requirements of rationality, the judges must act with restraint. Restraint, yes, abdication, no."

Alfred C. Aman & William T. Mayton, Administrative Law 506–07 (2d ed. 2001). Should judges focus on agency processes to assure a "reasoned decision" as Judge Bazelon suggested? Or, should judges employ the "modest" substantive review of administrative action recommended by Judge Leventhal? Should judges "second-guess" technical choices made by agencies following modern administrative procedures and practices? Or should a "science and technology court" manned by technically trained judges consider these cases? How can a legal generalist determine the "rationality" of a scientifically-based agency choice?

In adopting regulations, adjudicating disputes, and taking other actions, agencies often decide questions of law. How should courts review an agency's interpretation of a statute? Do courts owe any deference to the agency? Or should courts, as the arbiters of questions of law, conduct an independent inquiry? The following case, a landmark Supreme Court decision on how courts are to review agency interpretations of law, sets out a two-pronged analysis for judicial review. As you read *Chevron v. NRDC*, identify this analytical framework, consider the rationale behind it, and assess whether it is appropriate.

Chevron, U.S.A., Inc. v. Natural Resources Defense Council

United States Supreme Court, 1984.
467 U.S. 837.

■ JUSTICE STEVENS delivered the opinion of the Court.

In the Clean Air Act Amendments of 1977, Congress enacted certain requirements applicable to States that had not achieved the national air quality standards established by the Environmental Protection Agency (EPA) pursuant to earlier legislation. The amended Clean Air Act required these "nonattainment" States to establish a permit program regulating "new or modified major stationary sources" of air pollution. Generally, a permit may not be issued for a new or modified major stationary source unless several stringent conditions are met. The EPA regulation promulgated to implement this permit requirement allows a State to adopt a plantwide definition of the term "stationary source." Under this definition, an existing plant that contains several pollution-emitting devices may install or modify one piece of equipment without meeting the permit conditions if the alteration will not increase the total emissions from the plant. The question presented by these cases is whether EPA's decision to allow States to treat all of the pollution-emitting devices within the same industrial grouping as though they were encased within a single "bubble" is based on a reasonable construction of the statutory term "stationary source."

I

The EPA regulations containing the plantwide definition of the term stationary source were promulgated on October 14, 1981. Respondents filed a timely petition for review in the United States Court of Appeals for the District of Columbia Circuit. The Court of Appeals set aside the regulations. * * *

II

When a court reviews an agency's construction of the statute which it administers, it is confronted with two questions. First, always, is the question whether Congress has directly spoken to the precise question at issue. If the intent of Congress is clear, that is the end of the matter; for the court, as well as the agency, must give effect to the unambiguously expressed intent of Congress. If, however, the court determines Congress has not directly addressed the precise question at issue, the court does not simply impose its own construction on the statute, as would be necessary in the absence of an administrative interpretation. Rather, if the statute is silent or ambiguous with respect to the specific issue, the question for the court is whether the agency's answer is based on a permissible construction of the statute.[11]

"The power of an administrative agency to administer a congressionally created ... program necessarily requires the formulation of policy and the making of rules to fill any gap left, implicitly or explicitly, by Congress." Morton v. Ruiz, 415 U.S. 199, 231 (1974). If Congress has explicitly left a gap for the agency to fill, there is an express delegation of authority to the agency to elucidate a specific provision of the statute by regulation. Such legislative regulations are given controlling weight unless they are arbitrary, capricious, or manifestly contrary to the statute. Sometimes the legislative delegation to an agency on a particular question is implicit rather than explicit. In such a case, a court may not substitute its own construction of a statutory provision for a reasonable interpretation made by the administrator of an agency.

We have long recognized that considerable weight should be accorded to an executive department's construction of a statutory scheme it is entrusted to administer, and the principle of deference to administrative interpretations

> has been consistently followed by this Court whenever decision as to the meaning or reach of a statute has involved reconciling conflicting policies, and a full understanding of the force of the statutory policy in the given situation has depended upon more than ordinary knowledge respecting the matters subjected to agency regulations.

> ... If this choice represents a reasonable accommodation of conflicting policies that were committed to the agency's care by the statute, we should not disturb it unless it appears from the statute or its legislative history that the accommodation is not one that Congress would have sanctioned. United States v. Shimer, 367 U.S. 374, 382, 383 (1961).

In light of these well-settled principles it is clear that the Court of Appeals misconceived the nature of its role in reviewing the regulations at issue. Once it determined, after its own examination of the legislation, that Congress did not actually have an intent regarding the applicability of the bubble concept to the permit program, the question before it was not whether in its view the concept is "inappropriate" in the general context of a program designed to improve air quality, but whether the Administrator's view that it is appropriate in the context of this particular program is a reasonable one. Based on the examination of the legislation and its history which follows, we agree with the Court of Appeals that Congress did not have a specific intention on the applicability of the bubble concept in these

---

11. The court need not conclude that the agency construction was the only one it permissibly could have adopted to uphold the construction, or even the reading the court would have reached if the question initially had arisen in a judicial proceeding.

cases, and conclude that the EPA's use of that concept here is a reasonable policy choice for the agency to make.

* * *

IV

The Clean Air Act Amendments of 1977 are a lengthy, detailed, technical, complex, and comprehensive response to a major social issue. A small portion of the statute expressly deals with nonattainment areas. The focal point of this controversy is one phrase in that portion of the Amendments [i.e., the meaning of the term "major stationary source"—Eds.]

Basically, the statute required each State in a nonattainment area to prepare and obtain approval of a new SIP by July 1, 1979. In the interim those States were required to comply with the EPA's interpretative Ruling of December 21, 1976. The deadline for attainment of the primary NAAQS's was extended until December 31, 1982, and in some cases until December 31, 1987, but the SIP's were required to contain a number of provisions designed to achieve the goals as expeditiously as possible.

Most significantly for our purposes, the statute provided that each plan shall

"(6) require permits for the construction and operation of new or modified major stationary sources in accordance with section 173...."

Before issuing a permit, § 173 requires (1) the state agency to determine that there will be sufficient emissions reductions in the region to offset the emissions from the new source and also to allow for reasonable further progress toward attainment, or that the increased emissions will not exceed an allowance for growth, (2) the applicant to certify that his other sources in the State are in compliance with the SIP, (3) the agency must determine that the applicable SIP is otherwise being implemented, and (4) the proposed source to comply with the lowest achievable emission rate (LAER).

The 1977 Amendments contain no specific reference to the "bubble concept." Nor do they contain a specific definition of the term "stationary source," though they did not disturb the definition of "stationary source" applicable by the terms of the Act to the NSPS [new source performance standard] program.

VI

As previously noted, prior to the 1977 Amendments, the EPA had adhered to a plantwide definition of the term "source" under a NSPS program. [After the Amendments, EPA considered changing its plantwide definition, but decided against it.]

In August 1980, however, the EPA adopted a regulation that, in essence, applied the basic reasoning of the Court of Appeals in these cases. The EPA took particular note of the two then-recent Court of Appeals decisions, which had created the bright-line rule that the "bubble concept" should be employed in a program designed to maintain air quality but not in one designed to enhance air quality. Relying heavily on those cases, EPA adopted a dual definition of "source" for nonattainment areas that required a permit whenever a change in either the entire plant, or one of its components, would result in a significant increase in emissions even if the increase was completely offset by reductions elsewhere in the plant. The EPA expressed the opinion that this interpretation was "more consistent with congressional intent" than the plantwide definition because it "would bring in more sources or modifications for review," 45 Fed. Reg. 52697 (1980), but its primary legal analysis was predicated on the two Court of Appeals decisions.

In 1981 a new administration took office and initiated a "Government-wide reexamination of regulatory burdens and complexities." In the context of that review, the EPA reevaluated the various arguments that had been advanced in connection with the proper definition of the term "source" and concluded that the term should be given the same definition in both nonattainment areas and PSD areas.

In explaining its conclusion, the EPA first noted that the definitional issue was not squarely addressed in either the statute or its legislative history and therefore that the issue involved an agency "judgment as how to best carry out the Act." It then set forth several reasons for concluding that the plantwide definition was more appropriate. It pointed out that the dual definition "can act as a disincentive to new investment and modernization by discouraging modifications to existing facilities" and "can actually retard progress in air pollution control by discouraging replacement of older, dirtier processes or pieces of equipment with new, cleaner ones." Moreover, the new definition "would simplify EPA's rules by using the same definition of 'source' for PSD, nonattainment new source review and the construction moratorium. This reduces confusion and inconsistency." Finally, the agency explained that additional requirements that remained in place would accomplish the fundamental purposes of achieving attainment with NAAQS's as expeditiously as possible. These conclusions were expressed in a proposed rulemaking in August 1981 that was formally promulgated in October.

VII

In this Court respondents expressly reject the basic rationale of the Court of Appeals' decision. That court viewed the statutory definition of the term "source" as sufficiently flexible to cover either a plantwide definition, a narrower definition covering each unit within a plant, or a dual definition that could apply to both the entire "bubble" and its components. It interpreted the policies of the statute, however, to mandate the plantwide definition in programs designed to maintain clean air and to forbid it in programs designed to improve air quality. Respondents place a fundamentally different construction on the statute. They contend that the text of the Act requires the EPA to use a dual definition—if either a component of a plant, or the plant as a whole, emits over 100 tons of pollutant, it is a major stationary source. They thus contend that the EPA rules adopted in

1980, insofar as they apply to the maintenance of the quality of clean air, as well as the 1981 rules which apply to nonattainment areas, violate the statute.

Statutory Language

The definition of the term "stationary source" in § 111(a)(3) refers to "any building, structure, facility, or installation" which emits air pollution. This definition is applicable only to the NSPS program by the express terms of the statute; the text of the statute does not make this definition applicable to the permit program. * * *

* * * Although the definition in that section is not literally applicable to the permit program, it sheds as much light on the meaning of the word "source" as anything in the statute. As respondents point out, use of the words "building, structure, facility, or installation," as the definition of source, could be read to impose the permit conditions on an individual building that is a part of a plant. A "word may have a character of its own not to be submerged by its association." Russell Motor Car Co. v. United States, 261 U.S. 514, 519 (1923). On the other hand, the meaning of a word must be ascertained in the context of achieving particular objectives, and the words associated with it may indicate that the true meaning of a word must be ascertained in the context of achieving particular objectives, and the words associated with it may indicate that the true meaning of the series is to convey a common idea. The language may reasonably be interpreted to impose the requirement on any discrete, but integrated, operation which pollutes. This gives meaning to all of the terms—a single building, not part of a larger operation, would be covered if it emits more than 100 tons of pollution, as would any facility, structure, or installation. Indeed, the language itself implies a "bubble concept" of sorts: each enumerated item would seem to be treated as if it were encased in a bubble. * * *

We are not persuaded that parsing of general terms in the text of the statute will reveal an actual intent of Congress. We know full well that this language is not dispositive; the terms are overlapping and the language is not precisely directed to the question of the applicability of a given term in the context of a larger operation. To the extent any congressional "intent" can be discerned from this language, it would appear that the listing of overlapping, illustrative terms was intended to enlarge, rather than to confine, the scope of the agency's power to regulate particular sources in order to effectuate the policies of the Act.

Legislative History

In addition, respondents argue that the legislative history and policies of the Act foreclose the plantwide definition, and that the EPA's interpretation is not entitled to deference because it represents a sharp break with prior interpretations of the Act.

Based on our examination of the legislative history, we agree with the Court of Appeals that it is unilluminating. * * * We find that the legislative history as a whole is silent on the precise issue before us. It is, however, consistent with the view that the EPA should have broad discretion in implementing the policies of the 1977 Amendments.

More importantly, that history plainly identifies the policy concerns that motivated the enactment; the plantwide definition is fully consistent with one of those concerns—the allowance of reasonable economic growth—and, whether or not we believe it most effectively implements the other, we must recognize that the EPA has advanced a reasonable explanation for its conclusion that the regulations serve the environmental objectives as well. Indeed, its reasoning is supported by the public record developed in the rulemaking process, as well as by certain private studies.

Our review of the EPA's varying interpretations of the word "source"—both before and after the 1977 Amendments—convinces us that the agency primarily responsible for administering this important legislation has consistently interpreted it flexibly—not in a sterile textual vacuum, but in the context of implementing policy decisions in a technical and complex arena. The fact that the agency has from time to time changed its interpretation of the term "source" does not, as respondents argue, lead us to conclude that no deference should be accorded the agency's interpretation of the statute. An initial agency interpretation is not instantly carved in stone. On the contrary, the agency, to engage in informed rulemaking, must consider varying interpretations and the wisdom of its policy on a continuing basis. Moreover, the fact that the agency has adopted different definitions in different contexts adds force to the argument that the definition itself is flexible, particularly since Congress has never indicated any disapproval of a flexible reading of the statute.

Significantly, it was not the agency in 1980, but rather the Court of Appeals that read the statute inflexibly to command a plantwide definition for programs designed to maintain clean air and to forbid such a definition for programs designed to improve air quality. The distinction the court drew may well be a sensible one, but our labored review of the problem has surely disclosed that it is not a distinction that Congress ever articulated itself, or one that the EPA found in the statute before the courts began to review the legislative work product. We conclude that it was the Court of Appeals, rather than Congress or any of the decision-makers who are authorized by Congress to administer this legislation, that was primarily responsible for the 1980 position taken by the agency.

The arguments over policy that are advanced in the parties' briefs create the impression that respondents are now waging in a judicial forum a specific policy battle which they ultimately lost in the agency and in the 32 jurisdictions opting for the "bubble concept," but one which was never waged in the Congress. Such policy arguments are more properly addressed to legislators or administrators, not to judges.

In these cases the Administrator's interpretation represents a reasonable accommodation of manifestly competing interests and is entitled to deference: the regulatory scheme is technical and complex, the agency considered the matter in a detailed and reasoned fashion, and the decision involves reconciling conflicting policies. Congress intended to accommodate both interests, but did not do so itself on the level of specificity presented by these cases. Perhaps that body consciously desired the Administrator to strike the balance at this level, thinking that those with great expertise and charged with responsibility for administering the provision would be in a better position to do so; perhaps it simply did not consider the question at this level; and perhaps Congress was unable to forge a coalition on either side of the question, and those on each side decided to take their chances with the scheme devised by the agency. For judicial purposes, it matters not which of these things occurred.

Judges are not experts in the field, and are not part of either political branch of the Government. Courts must, in some cases, reconcile competing political interests, but not on the basis of the judges' personal policy preferences. In contrast, an agency to which Congress has delegated policy making responsibilities may, within the limits of that delegation, properly rely upon the incumbent administration's views of wise policy to inform its judgments. While agencies are not directly accountable to the people, the Chief Executive is, and it is entirely appropriate for this political branch of the Government to make such policy choices—resolving the competing interests which Congress itself either inadvertently did not resolve, or intentionally left to be resolved by the agency charged with the administration of the statute in light of everyday realities.

When a challenge to an agency construction of a statutory provision, fairly conceptualized, really centers on the wisdom of the agency's policy, rather than whether it is a reasonable choice within a gap left open by Congress, the challenge must fail. In such a case, federal judges—who have no constituency—have a duty to respect legitimate policy choices made by those who do. The responsibilities for assessing the wisdom of such policy choices and resolving the struggle between competing views of the public interest are not judicial ones: "Our Constitution vests such responsibilities in the political branches."

We hold that the EPA's definition of the term "source" is a permissible construction of the statute which seeks to accommodate progress in reducing air pollution with economic growth. * * *

NOTES AND QUESTIONS

1. *Judicial review of questions of law.* *Chevron* is one of the most frequently cited administrative law cases. There is good reason for this fact—agencies frequently must find statutory support for the things they do and for the ways they do them. Those adversely affected by an agency action often challenge agency legal interpretations in an effort to delay or block the action. *Chevron* analysis is common because it provides a framework for this judicial review. Should courts, as generalists, be reluctant to intrude into the complex and controversial policy making of specialized, expert agencies? Does the Supreme Court's test allow a court to refuse deference to an agency's interpretation of the law? Under what circumstances? Cutting through the legal verbiage, what policies support judicial review of agency actions, and to what extent do those policies justify or permit deference to the agency on matters of statutory interpretation? Does judicial review improve the rationality of government decisionmaking? Do the courts exercise a "quality control" function? Is such review worth the cost in terms of administrative efficiency? Consider the following possible benefits:

1. Preventing agencies from ignoring their statutory mandate.
2. Ensuring that all required procedures are followed.
3. Protecting against undue political influence or other bias.
4. Ensuring the openness ("transparency") of agency decisions.
5. Improving the quality of an agency's technical judgments.

Is close judicial scrutiny of agency action more appropriate or less so for environmental decisions, as opposed to decisions in other areas? Why?

2. *The scope of Chevron.* Subsequent Supreme Court cases have focused on identifying the limits of *Chevron* deference owed to administrative practice in applying a statute. These cases are of potential importance for EPA and other agencies because they issue a large number of regulations, guidance documents, and interpretations, and take other actions involving interpretation of statutory authorities.

In *United States v. Mead Corp.*, 533 U.S. 218 (2001), the Court considered a challenge brought by an importer of day planners over the tariff classification given the product by the U.S. Customs Service. The tariff ruling was issued by way of a "ruling letter" to Mead which had the effect of reclassifying imported day planners and making them subject to a tariff when previously there had been none. Mead challenged the tariff classification, contending that the agency's ruling deserved no judicial deference. Although the Court agreed that the ruling should not receive *Chevron* deference, it acknowledged that a lesser amount of deference might still be warranted. *Chevron* thus appears to represent a high degree of insulation from close judicial review that will apply only in some circumstances. As the Court explained in *Mead*:

> Administrative implementation of a particular statutory provision qualifies for *Chevron* deference when it appears that Congress delegated authority to the agency generally to make rules carrying the force of law, and that the agency interpretation claiming deference was promulgated in the exercise of that authority.

Id. at 226–27.

How can an agency demonstrate the delegation required? The Court went on to explain that "[d]elegation of such authority may be shown in a variety of ways, as by an agency's power to engage in adjudication or notice-and-comment rulemaking, or by some other indication of a comparable congressional intent." Id. at 227. It seems then, that this highest degree of judicial deference carrying with it the "force of law" stems from express congressional authorizations providing for relatively formal administrative procedure "tending to foster fairness and deliberation." Id. at 230. On the facts presented by *Mead*, the Court refused to grant *Chevron* deference in light of the lack of explicit delegation of rulemaking authority, the lack of precedential impact, and the nonbinding effect of the action on third parties.

The *Mead* decision nevertheless noted that different levels of judicial deference could be given to administrative interpretations of authority, with *Chevron* representing the highest level of deference. Deference may be warranted even in the absence of delegation of rulemaking authority, "given the 'specialized experience and broader investigations and information' available to the agency, and given the value of uniformity in its administrative and judicial understandings of what a national law requires." Id. at 234. This lesser deference, sometimes referred to as *Skidmore* "respect" (as discussed in *Skidmore v. Swift & Co.*, 323 U.S. 134 (1944)), is appropriate when "the regulatory scheme is highly detailed, and [the agency] can bring the benefit of specialized experience to bear on the subtle question." Mead, 533 U.S. at 235. The degree of deference under *Skidmore* depends upon the agency's "power to persuade," in particular "the [agency] writer's thoroughness, logic, and expertness, its fit with prior interpretations, and any other sources of weight." Id. How would EPA defend an attack on an interpretive guidance document if *Skidmore* deference was all that would be accorded to it?

Notwithstanding *Mead*, in Coeur Alaska v. Southeast Alaska Conservation Council, 557 U.S. 261 (2009), the Supreme Court was quite deferential to an agency guidance memorandum that had not undergone the rulemaking process. Justice Scalia, who dissented in *Mead*, wrote in a concurrence in *Coeur Alaska*:

> The Court's deference to the EPA and the Corps of Engineers in today's cases is eminently reasonable. It is quite impossible to achieve predictable (and relatively litigation-free) administration of the vast body of complex laws committed to the charge of executive agencies without the assurance that reviewing courts will accept reasonable and authoritative agency interpretation of ambiguous provisions. If we must not call that practice *Chevron* deference, then we have to rechristen the rose. Of course the only reason a new name is required is our misguided opinion in *Mead*, whose incomprehensible criteria for *Chevron* deference have produced so much confusion in the lower courts that there has now appeared the phenomenon of *Chevron* avoidance— the practice of declining to opine whether Chevron applies or not. See Bressman, How Mead Has Muddled Judicial Review of Agency Action, 58 Vand. L. Rev. 1443, 1464 (2005).
>
> I favor overruling Mead. Failing that, I am pleased to join an opinion that effectively ignores it.

C. STANDING

How does a person or an organization obtain access to the courts to question administrative behavior? Only a party with standing to sue may challenge agency action in federal court. While the law of standing is complicated and has been subject to frequent revision in recent years, the basic structure for the law of standing originates from two sources: 1) constitutional standing, based on the "case or controversy" requirement of Article III of the U.S. Constitution; and 2) prudential standing, developed by courts as an aspect of court management. At the state level, courts have developed their own standing doctrines which may be more lenient or more restrictive than federal standing doctrine.

1. CONSTITUTIONAL STANDING

Constitutional standing doctrine is based on the language of Article III, § 2, which limits federal judicial power to "cases or controversies." The American judicial system relies on litigants to identify disputes warranting judicial attention and to provide the necessary data upon which to rule. The "cases" or "controversies" requirement limits the exercise of judicial power to those disputes where parties have a particular stake. In general, the modern framework for constitutional standing requires a plaintiff to demonstrate that: 1) "injury-in-fact," or a "concrete and particularized" invasion of a legally protected interest, 2) "causation," indicating that the injury was caused by and is "fairly traceable" to the defendant's action, and 3) "redressability," showing that it is "likely and not merely speculative" that the injury can be "redressed" by a judicial remedy awarded to the plaintiff. See Sprint Communications Co. v. APCC Services, Inc., 554 U.S. 269 (2008). As you read the following cases, consider how a plaintiff can satisfy these requirements.

Lujan v. Defenders of Wildlife

United States Supreme Court, 1992.
504 U.S. 555.

■ JUSTICE SCALIA delivered the opinion of the Court with respect to Parts I, II, III–A, and IV, and an opinion with respect to Part III–B in which the CHIEF JUSTICE, JUSTICE WHITE, and JUSTICE THOMAS join.

This case involves a challenge to a rule promulgated by the Secretary of the Interior interpreting § 7 of the Endangered Species Act of 1973 (ESA), 87 Stat. 884, 892, as amended, 16 U.S.C. § 1536, in such fashion as to render it applicable only to actions within the United States or on the high seas. The preliminary issue, and the only one we reach, is whether the respondents here, plaintiffs below, have standing to seek judicial review of the rule.

I.

Section 7(a)(2) of the Act provides, in pertinent part:

Each Federal agency shall, in consultation, with and with the assistance of the Secretary [of the Interior], insure that any action authorized, funded, or carried out by such agency.... is not likely to jeopardize the continued existence of any endangered species or threatened species or result in the destruction or adverse modification of habitat of such species which is determined by the Secretary, after consultation as appropriate with affected States, to be critical.

16 U.S.C. § 1536(a)(2).

In 1978, the Fish and Wildlife Service (FWS) and National Marine Fisheries Service (NMFS), on behalf of the Secretary of the Interior and the Secretary of Commerce respectively, promulgated a joint regulation stating that the obligations imposed by § 7(a)(2) extend to actions taken in foreign nations. 43 Fed. Reg. 874 (1978). The next year, however, the Interior Department began to reexamine its position. Letter from Leo Kuliz, Solicitor, Department of the Interior, to Assistant Secretary, Fish and Wildlife and Parks, Aug. 8, 1979. A revised joint regulation, reinterpreting § 7(a)(2) to require consultation only for actions taken in the United States or on the high seas, was proposed in 1983, 48 Fed. Reg. 29990 (1983), and promulgated in 1986, 51 Fed. Reg. 19926 (1986); 50 C.F.R. 402.01 (1991).

Shortly thereafter, respondents, organizations dedicated to wildlife conservation and other environmental causes, filed this action against the Secretary of the Interior, seeking a declaratory judgment that the new regulation is in error as to the geographic scope of § 7(a)(2), and an injunction requiring the Secretary to promulgate a new regulation restoring the initial interpretation.

II

Over the years, our cases have established that the irreducible constitutional minimum of standing contains three elements: *First*, the plaintiff must have suffered an "injury-in-fact"—an invasion of a legally-protected interest which is (a) concrete and particularized, and (b) actual or imminent, not conjectural or hypothetical. *Second*, there must be a causal connection between the injury and the conduct complained of—the injury has to be "fairly ... trace[able] to the challenged action of the defendant, and not ... th[e] result [of] the independent action of some third party not before the court." Simon v. Eastern Ky. Welfare Rights Org., 426 U.S. 26, 41–42 (1976). *Third*, it must be "likely," as opposed to merely "speculative," that the injury will be "redressed by a favorable decision." Id. at 38, 43.

The party invoking federal jurisdiction bears the burden of establishing these elements. Since they are not mere pleading requirements but rather an indispensable part of the plaintiff's case, each element must be supported in the same way as any other matter on which the plaintiff bears the burden of proof, *i.e.,* with the manner and degree of evidence required at the successive stages of the litigation.

When the suit is one challenging the legality of government action or inaction, the nature and extent of facts that must be averred (at the summary judgment stage) or proved (at the trial stage) in order to establish standing depends considerably upon whether the plaintiff is himself an object of the action (or foregone action) at issue. If he is, there is ordinarily little question that the action or inaction has caused him injury, and that a judgment preventing or requiring the action will redress it. When, however, as in this case, a plaintiff's asserted injury arises from the government's allegedly unlawful regulation (or lack of regulation) of *someone else*, much more is needed. In that circumstance, causation and redressability ordinarily hinge on the response of the regulated (or regulable) third party to the government action, or inaction—and perhaps on the response of others as well.

III

A

Respondents' claim to injury is that the lack of consultation with respect to certain funded activities abroad "increas[es] the rate of extinction of endangered and threatened species." Of course, the desire to use or observe an animal species, even for purely aesthetic purposes, is undeniably a cognizable interest for purpose of standing. But the "injury in fact" test requires more than an injury to a cognizable interest. It requires that the party seeking review be himself among the injured. To survive the Secretary's summary judgment motion, respondents had to submit affidavits or other evidence showing, through specific facts, not only that listed species were in fact being threatened by funded activities abroad, but also that one or more of respondents' members would thereby be "directly" affected apart from their special interest in th[e] subject." Sierra Club v. Morton, 405 U.S. at 735.

With respect to this aspect of the case, the Court of Appeals focused on the affidavits of two Defenders' members—Joyce Kelly and Amy Skilbred. Ms. Kelly stated that she traveled to Egypt in 1986 and "observed the traditional habitat of the endangered nile crocodile there and intend[s] to do so again, and hope(s) to observe the crocodile directly," and that she "will suffer harm in fact as a result of [the] American ... role ... in overseeing the rehabilitation of the Aswan High Dam on the Nile ... and [in] develop[ing] ... Egypt's ... Master Water Plan." Ms. Skilbred averred that she traveled to Sri Lanka in 1981 and "observed th[e] habitat" of "endangered species such as the Asian elephant and the leopard" at what is now the site of the Mahaweli Project funded by the Agency for International Development (AID), although she "was unable to see any of the endangered species;" "this development project," she continued, "will seriously reduce endangered, threatened, and endemic species habitat including areas that I visited ... [which] may severely shorten the future of these species;" that threat, she concluded, harmed her because she "intend[s] to return to Sri Lanka in the future and hope[s] to be more fortunate in spotting at least the endangered elephant and leopard." When Ms. Skilbred was asked at a subsequent deposition if and when she had any plans to return to Sri Lanka, she reiterated that "I intend to go back to Sri Lanka," but confessed that she had no current plans: "I don't know

[when]. There is a civil war going on right now. I don't know. Not next year, I will say. In the future."

We shall assume for the sake of argument that these affidavits contain facts showing that certain agency-funded projects threaten listed species—though that is questionable. They plainly contain no facts, however, showing how damage to the species will produce "imminent" injury to Ms. Kelly and Skilbred. That the women "had visited" the areas of the projects before the projects commenced proves nothing. As we have said in a related context, "[p]ast exposure to illegal conduct does not in itself show a present case or controversy regarding injunctive relief . . . if unaccompanied by any continuing, present adverse effects." Lyons, 461 U.S. at 102.

And the affiants' profession of an "inten[t]" to return to the places they had visited before—where they will presumably, this time, be deprived of the opportunity to observe animals of the endangered species—is simply not enough. Such "some day" intentions—without any description of concrete plans, or indeed even any specification of *when* the some day will be—do not support a finding of the "actual or imminent" injury that our cases require.

Besides relying upon the Kelly and Skilbred affidavits, respondents propose a series of novel standing theories. The first, inelegantly styled "ecosystem nexus," proposes that any person who uses *any part* of a "contiguous ecosystem" adversely affected by a funded activity has standing even if the activity is located a great distance away. This approach, as the Court of Appeals correctly observed, is inconsistent with our opinion in *National Wildlife Federation*, which held that a plaintiff claiming injury from environmental damage must use the area affected by the challenged activity and not an area roughly "in the vicinity" of it. 497 U.S., at 887–889. It makes no difference that the general-purpose section of the ESA states that the Act was intended in part "to provide a means whereby the ecosystems upon which endangered species and threatened species depend may be conserved," 16 U.S.C. § 1531(b). To say that the Act protects ecosystems is not to say that the Act creates (if it were possible) rights of action in persons who have not been injured in fact, that is, persons who use portions of an ecosystem not perceptibly affected by the unlawful action in question.

Respondents' other theories are called, alas, the "animal nexus" approach, whereby anyone who has an interest in studying or seeing the endangered animals anywhere on the globe has standing; and the "vocational nexus" approach, under which anyone with a professional interest in such animals can sue. Under these theories, anyone who goes to see Asian elephants in the Bronx Zoo, and anyone who is a keeper of Asian elephants in the Bronx Zoo, has standing to sue because the Director of AID did not consult with the Secretary regarding the AID-funded project in Sri Lanka. This is beyond all reason. Standing is not "an ingenious academic exercise in the conceivable," United States v. Students Challenging Regulatory Agency Procedures (SCRAP), 412 U.S. 669, 688 (1973), but as we have said requires, at the summary judgment stage, a factual showing of perceptible harm. It is clear that the person who observes or works with a particular animal threatened by a federal decision is facing perceptible harm, since the very subject of his interest will no longer exist. It is even plausible—though it goes to the outermost limit of plausibility—to think that a person who observes or works with animals of a particular species in the very area of the world where that species is threatened by a federal decision is facing such harm, since some animals that might have been the subject of his interest will no longer exist. It goes beyond the limit, however, and into pure speculation and fantasy, to say that anyone who observes or works with an endangered species, anywhere in the world, is appreciably harmed by a single project affecting some portion of that species with which he has no more specific connection.

B

The most obvious problem in the present case is redressability. Since the agencies funding the projects were not parties to the case, the District Court could accord relief only against the Secretary: He could be ordered to revise his regulation to require consultation for foreign projects. But this would not remedy respondents' alleged injury unless the funding agencies were bound by the Secretary's regulation, which is very much an open question. Whereas in other contexts the ESA is quite explicit as to the Secretary's controlling authority, *see*, e.g., 16 U.S.C. § 1533(a)(1) ("The Secretary shall" promulgate regulations determining endangered species); § 1535(d)(1) ("The Secretary is authorized to provide financial assistance to any State"), with respect to consultation the initiative, and hence arguably the initial responsibility for determining statutory necessity, lies with the agencies, *see* § 1536(a)(2) *("Each Federal agency shall*, in consultation with and with the assistance of the Secretary, insure that any" funded action is not likely to jeopardize endangered or threatened species) (emphasis added). When the Secretary promulgated the regulation at issue here, he thought it was binding on the agencies. The Solicitor General, however, has repudiated that position here, and the agencies themselves apparently deny the Secretary's authority. (During the period when the Secretary took the view that § 7(a)(2) did apply abroad, AID and FWS engaged in a running controversy over whether consultation was required with respect to the Mahaweli project, AID insisting that consultation applied only to domestic actions.)

Respondents assert that this legal uncertainty did not affect redressability (and hence standing) because the District Court itself could resolve the issue of the Secretary's authority as a necessary part of its standing inquiry. Assuming that it is appropriate to resolve an issue of law such as this in connection with a threshold standing inquiry, resolution by the District Court would not have remedied respondents' alleged injury anyway, because it would not have been binding upon the agencies. They were not parties to the suit, and there is no reason they should be obliged to honor an incidental legal determination the suit produced.

A further impediment to redressability is the fact that the agencies generally supply only a fraction of the funding for a foreign project. AID, for example, has provided less than 10% of the funding for the Mahaweli Project. Respondents have produced nothing to indicate that the projects they have named will either be suspended, or do less harm to listed species, if that fraction is eliminated. [I]t is entirely conjectural whether the nonagency activity that affects respondents will be altered or affected by the agency activity they seek to achieve. There is no standing.

IV

The Court of Appeals found that respondents had standing for an additional reason: because they had suffered a procedural injury. The so-called "citizen suit" provision of the ESA provides, in pertinent part, that "any person may commence a civil suit on his own behalf (A) to enjoin any person, including the United States and any other governmental instrumentality or agency ... who is alleged to be in violation of any provision of this chapter." 16 U.S.C. § 1540(g). The court held that because § 7(a)(2) requires interagency consultation, the citizen-suit provision creates a "procedural righ[t]" to consultation in all "persons"—so that *anyone* can file suit in federal court to challenge the Secretary's (or presumably any other official's) failure to follow the assertedly correct consultative procedure, notwithstanding their inability to allege any discrete injury flowing from that failure. To understand the remarkable nature of this holding one must be clear about what it does *not* rest upon: This is not a case where plaintiffs are seeking to enforce a procedural requirement the disregard of which could impair a separate concrete interest of theirs (*e.g.*, the procedural requirement for a hearing prior to denial of their license application, or the procedural requirement for an environmental impact statement before a federal facility is constructed next door to them).[7] Nor is it simply a case where concrete injury has been suffered by many persons, as in mass fraud or mass tort situations. Nor, finally, is it the unusual case in which Congress has created a concrete private interest in the outcome of a suit against a private party for the government's benefit, by providing a cash bounty for the victorious plaintiff. Rather, the court held that the injury-in-fact requirement had been satisfied by congressional conferral upon all

---

7. There is this much truth to the assertion that "procedural rights" are special: The person who has been accorded a procedural right to protect his concrete interests can assert that right without meeting all the normal standards for redressability and immediacy. Thus, under our case law, one living adjacent to the site for proposed construction of a federally licensed dam has standing to challenge the licensing agency's failure to prepare an environmental impact statement, even though he cannot establish with any certainty that the statement will cause the license to be withheld or altered, and even though the dam will not be completed for many years. (That is why we do not rely, in the present case, upon the Government's argument that, even if the other agencies were obliged to consult with the Secretary, they might not have followed his advice.) What respondents' "procedural rights" argument seeks, however, is quite different from this: standing for persons who have no concrete interests affected—persons who live (and propose to live) at the other end of the country from the dam.

persons of an abstract, self-contained, noninstrumental "right" to have the Executive observe the procedures required by law. We reject this view.[8]

We have consistently held that a plaintiff raising only a generally available grievance about government—claiming only harm to his and every citizen's interest in proper application of the Constitution and laws, and seeking relief that no more directly and tangibly benefits him than it does the public at large does not state an Article III, case or controversy.

* * *

■ JUSTICE KENNEDY, with whom JUSTICE SOUTER joins, concurring in part and concurring in the judgment.

Although I agree with the essential parts of the Court's analysis, I write separately to make several observations.

In my view, Congress has the power to define injuries and articulate chains of causation that will give rise to a case or controversy where none existed before, and I do not read the Court's opinion to suggest a contrary view. In exercising this power, however, Congress must at the very least identify the injury it seeks to vindicate and relate the injury to the class of persons entitled to bring suit. The citizen-suit provision of the Endangered Species Act does not meet these minimal requirements, because while the statute purports to confer a right on "any person . . . to enjoin . . . the United States, and any other governmental instrumentality or agency . . . who is alleged to be in violation of any provision of this chapter," it does not of its own force establish that there is an injury in "any person" by virtue of any "violation." 16 U.S.C. 1540(g)(1)(A).

The Court's holding that there is an outer limit to the power of Congress to confer rights of action is a direct and necessary consequence of the case and controversy limitations found in Article III. I agree, that it would exceed those limitations if, at the behest of Congress and in the absence of any showing of concrete injury, we were to entertain citizen-suits to vindicate the public's nonconcrete interest in the proper administration of the laws. While it does not matter how may persons have been injured by the challenged action, the party bringing suit must show that the action injures him in a concrete and personal way. This requirement is not just an empty formality. It preserves the vitality of the adversarial process by assuring both that the parties before the court have an actual, as opposed to professed, stake in the outcome and that "the legal questions

---

8. The dissent's discussion of this aspect of the case distorts our opinion. We do *not* hold that an individual cannot enforce procedural rights; he assuredly can, so long as the procedures in question are designed to protect some threatened concrete interest of his that is the ultimate basis of his standing. The dissent, however, asserts that there exist "classes of procedural duties . . . so enmeshed with the prevention of a substantive, concrete harm that an individual plaintiff may be able to demonstrate a sufficient likelihood of injury just through the breach of that procedural duty." If we understand this correctly, it means that the Government's violation of a certain (undescribed) class of procedural duty satisfies the concrete-injury requirement by itself, without any showing that the procedural violation endangers a concrete interest of the plaintiff (apart from his interest in having the procedure observed). We cannot agree.

presented . . . will be resolved, not in the refined atmosphere of a debating society, but in a concrete factual context conducive to a realistic appreciation of the consequence of judicial action.''

■ JUSTICE STEVENS, concurring in the judgment.

I

In my opinion a person who has visited the critical habitat of an endangered species, has a professional interest in preserving the species and its habitat, and intends to revisit them in the future has standing to challenge agency action that threatens their destruction. Congress has found that a wide variety of endangered species of fish, wildlife, and plants are of "aesthetic, ecological, educational, historical, recreational, and scientific value to the Nation and its people." 16 U.S.C. § 1531(a)(8). Given that finding, we have no license to demean the importance of the interest that particular individuals may have in observing any species or its habitat, whether those individuals are motivated by aesthetic enjoyment, an interest in professional research, or an economic interest in preservation of the species. Indeed, this Court has often held that injuries to such interests are sufficient to confer standing, and the Court reiterates that holding today.

The Court nevertheless concludes that respondents have not suffered "injury in fact" because they have not shown that the harm to the endangered species will produce "imminent" injury to them. I disagree. An injury to an individual's interest in studying or enjoying a species and its natural habitat occurs when someone (whether it be the government or a private party) takes action that harms that species and habitat. In my judgment therefore, the "imminence" of such an injury would be measured by the timing and likelihood of the threatened environmental harm, rather than—as the Court seems to suggest—by the time that might elapse between the present and the time when the individuals would visit the area if no such injury should occur.

In this case the likelihood that respondents will be injured by the destruction of the endangered species is not speculative. If respondents are genuinely interested in the preservation of the endangered species and intend to study or observe these animals in the future, their injury will occur as soon as the animals are destroyed. Thus the only potential source of "speculation" in this case is whether respondents' intent to study or observe the animals is genuine.[2] In my view, Joyce Kelly and Amy Skilbred

---

2. As we recognized in *Sierra Club v. Morton*, 405 U.S. at 735, the impact of changes in the aesthetics or ecology of a particular area does "not fall indiscriminately upon every citizen". The alleged injury will be felt directly only by those who use [the area], and for whom the aesthetic and recreational values of the area will be lessened. . . . Thus respondents would not be injured by the challenged projects if they had not visited the sites or studied the threatened species and habitat. But, as discussed above, respondents did visit the sites; moreover, they have expressed an intent to do it again. This intent to revisit the area is significant evidence tending to confirm the genuine character of respondents' interests but I am not at all sure that an intent to revisit would be indispensable in every case. The interest that confers standing in a case of this kind is comparable, though by no means equivalent, to the interest in a relationship among family members that can be immediately harmed by the

have introduced sufficient evidence to negate petitioner's contention that their claims of injury are "speculative" or "conjectural."

The plurality also concludes that respondents' injuries are not redressable in this litigation for two reasons. First, respondents have sought only a declaratory judgment that the Secretary of the Interior's regulation interpreting § 7(a)(2) to require consultation only for agency actions in the United States or on the high seas is invalid and an injunction requiring him to promulgate a new regulation requiring consultation for agency actions abroad as well. But, the plurality opines, even if respondents succeed and a new regulation is promulgated, there is no guarantee that federal agencies that are not parties to this case will actually consult with the Secretary. Furthermore, the plurality continues, respondents have not demonstrated that federal agencies can influence the behavior of the foreign governments where the affected projects are located. Thus, even if the agencies consult with the Secretary and terminate funding for foreign projects, the foreign governments might nonetheless pursue the projects and jeopardize the endangered species. Neither of these reasons is persuasive.

We must presume that if this Court holds that § 7(a)(2) requires consultation, all affected agencies would abide by that interpretation and engage in the requisite consultations. Certainly the Executive Branch cannot be heard to argue that an authoritative construction of the governing statute by this Court may simply be ignored by any agency head. Moreover, if Congress has required consultation between agencies, we must presume that such consultation will have a serious purpose that is likely to produce tangible results. As Justice Blackmun explains, it is not mere speculation to think that foreign governments, when faced with the threatened withdrawal of United States assistance, will modify their projects to mitigate the harm to endangered species.

II

Although I believe that respondents have standing, I nevertheless concur in the judgment of reversal because I am persuaded that the Government is correct in its submission that § 7(a)(2) does not apply to activities in foreign countries.* * *

■ JUSTICE BLACKMUN, with whom JUSTICE O'CONNOR joins, dissenting.

I part company with the Court in this case in two respects. First, I believe that respondents have raised genuine issues of fact—sufficient to survive summary judgment—both as to injury and as to redressability. Second, I question the Court's breadth of language in rejecting standing for "procedural" injuries. I fear the Court seeks to impose fresh limitations on the constitutional authority of Congress to allow citizen suits in the federal courts for injuries deemed "procedural" in nature. I dissent.

---

death of an absent member, regardless of when, if ever, a family reunion is planned to occur. Thus, if the facts of this case had shown repeated and regular visits by the respondents, proof of an intent to revisit might well be superfluous.

I think a reasonable finder of fact could conclude from the information in the affidavits and deposition testimony that either Kelly or Skilbred will soon return to the project sites, thereby satisfying the "actual or imminent" injury standard. The Court dismisses Kelly's and Skilbred's general statements that they intended to revisit the project sites as "simply not enough." But those statements did not stand alone. A reasonable finder of fact could conclude, based not only upon their statements of intent to return, but upon their past visits to the project sites, as well as their professional backgrounds, that it was likely that Kelly and Skilbred would make a return trip to the project areas.

By requiring a "description of concrete plans" or "specification of *when* the some day [for a return visit] will be," the Court, in my view, demands what is likely an empty formality. No substantial barriers prevent Kelly or Skilbred from simply purchasing plane tickets to return to the Aswan and Mahaweli projects. This case differs from other cases in which the imminence of harm turned largely on the affirmative actions of third parties beyond a plaintiff's control.

The Court also concludes that injury is lacking, because respondents' allegations of "ecosystem nexus" failed to demonstrate sufficient proximity to the site of the environmental harm. To support that conclusion, the Court mischaracterizes our decision in Lujan v. National Wildlife Federation, 497 U.S. 871 (1990), as establishing a general rule that "a plaintiff claiming injury from environmental damage must use the area affected by the challenged activity." In *National Wildlife Federation* the Court required specific geographical proximity because of the particular type of harm alleged in that case: harm to the plaintiff's visual enjoyment of nature from mining activities. One cannot suffer from the sight of a ruined landscape without being close enough to see the sites actually being mined. Many environmental injuries, however, cause harm distant from the immediately affected by the challenged action. Environmental destruction may affect animals traveling over vast geographical ranges, *see*, e.g., Japan Whaling Assn. v. American Cetacean Soc., 478 U.S. 221 (1986) (harm to American whale watchers from Japanese whaling activities), or rivers running long geographical courses, *see*, e.g., Arkansas v. Oklahoma, 503 U.S. 91 (1992) (harm to Oklahoma residents from wastewater treatment plant 39 miles from border). It cannot seriously be contended that a litigant's failure to use the precise or exact site where animals are slaughtered or where toxic waste is dumped into a river means he or she cannot show injury.

The Court also rejects respondents' claim of vocational or professional injury. The Court says that it is "beyond all reason" that a zoo "keeper" of Asian elephants would have standing to contest his government's participation in the eradication of all the Asian elephants in another part of the world. I am unable to see how the distant location of the destruction *necessarily* (for purposes of ruling at summary judgment) mitigates the harm to the elephant keeper. If there is no more access to a future supply of the animal that sustains a keeper's livelihood, surely there is harm.

The Court concludes that any "procedural injury" suffered by respondents is insufficient to confer standing. It rejects the view that the "injury-in-fact requirement ... [is] satisfied by congressional conferral upon *all* person of an abstract, self-contained, noninstrumental 'right' to have the Executive observe the procedures required by law." Whatever the Court might mean with that very broad language it cannot be saying that "procedural injuries" *as a class* are necessarily insufficient for purposes of Article III standing.

It is to be hoped that over time the Court will acknowledge that some classes of procedural duties are so enmeshed with the prevention of a substantive, concrete harm that an individual plaintiff may be able to demonstrate a sufficient likelihood of injury just through the breach of that procedural duty. For example, in the context of the NEPA requirement of environmental impact statements, this Court has acknowledged "it is now well settled that NEPA itself does not mandate particular results [and] simply prescribes the necessary process," but "these procedures are almost certain to affect the agency's substantive decision." Robertson v. Methow Valley Citizens Council, 490 U.S., 332, 350 (1989). This acknowledgment of an inextricable link between procedural and substantive harm does not reflect improper appellate fact-finding. It reflects nothing more than the proper deference owed to the judgment of a coordinate branch—Congress—that certain procedures are directly tied to protection against a substantive harm.

In conclusion, I cannot join the Court on what amounts to a slash-and-burn expedition through the law of environmental standing. * * *

NOTES AND QUESTIONS

1. *Injury in fact.* What would the plaintiffs in *Lujan* have to demonstrate in order to establish injury in fact? How difficult would it be for these plaintiffs to do so? Injury in fact includes not only damage to a legally-protected right, but also harm to economic, environmental, recreational, and aesthetic interests. Mere interest in a problem, however, is not sufficient.

What about the increased risk of an injury which, if it occurs, would satisfy standing requirements? In Summers v. Earth Island Institute, 555 U.S. 488 (2009), the Court considered a challenge to U.S. Forest Service regulations exempting some logging projects, including one in the Sequoia National Forest, from generally applicable notice, comment, and appeal procedures. After the parties settled their dispute about that logging project, the Court refused to allow plaintiffs to pursue a nationwide challenge to the regulations. Justice Scalia, writing for a five-justice majority, held that the probability that some members of the plaintiff organizations would visit areas affected by the challenged regulations in the future was insufficient to establish constitutional standing in the absence of specification of who would be affected where.

Uncertainty, however, does not necessarily negate standing. In Monsanto Co. v. Geertson Seed Farms, ___ U.S. ___, 130 S.Ct. 2743 (2010), growers of conventional alfalfa challenged the Department of Agriculture's decision to deregulate "Roundup–Ready alfalfa," a variety genetically engineered to resist the herbicide Roundup. The Supreme Court agreed that plaintiffs had standing, despite uncertainty about whether their crops would become tainted by genes from the Roundup–Ready variety because plaintiffs showed that the risk of genetic contamination would induce them to test their crops and seek new sources of seed.

Can animals satisfy constitutional standing requirements? See Cetacean Cmty. v. Bush, 386 F.3d 1169 (9th Cir. 2004) (suggesting there is "no reason why Article III prevents Congress from authorizing a suit in the name of an animal," but ultimately concluding that animals lacked prudential standing).

2. *Justice Kennedy's concurrence.* To what extent does Justice Kennedy disagree with Justice Scalia in *Lujan*? If Kennedy's view of standing were to prevail, how much of a difference would that make for potential plaintiffs?

3. *Procedural injury.* Does *Lujan* indicate whether the standing analysis differs with respect to procedural injuries, such as injuries alleged by NEPA plaintiffs, as opposed to substantive injuries? The Supreme Court has occasionally suggested that being deprived of information can support the injury in fact requirement. See, e.g., FEC v. Akins, 524 U.S. 11, 13 (1998) and Public Citizen v. U.S. DOJ, 491 U.S. 440, 449 (1989). However, in Wilderness Society, Inc. v. Rey, 622 F.3d 1251 (9th Cir. 2010), the appeals court ruled that informational injury could not support a claim of standing adopting the Seventh Circuit's view that this kind of injury can only be sufficient for standing purposes if the goal of the statute being allegedly violated is to provide the public with information. See Bensman v. U.S. Forest Serv., 408 F.3d 945, 958 (7th Cir. 2005).

4. *Organizational standing.* With standing law requiring an individualized injury-in-fact, how can an organization such as an environmental group satisfy this requirement? An organization seeking to vindicate its own interests or the interests of its individual members can demonstrate injury-in-fact in two ways. First, an environmental group might sue to vindicate its own interests. Second, groups can vindicate the interests of their members if they can satisfy the three-part test set out in *Hunt v. Washington State Apple Advertising Commission*, 432 U.S. 333 (1977). Under *Hunt*, an association has standing to bring suit on behalf of its members when: (a) its members would otherwise have standing to sue in their own right; (b) the interests it seeks to protect are germane to the organization's purpose; and (c) neither the claim asserted nor the relief requested requires the participation of individual members in the lawsuit.

5. *"Fairly traceable" or causation requirement.* A plaintiff must establish that the injury it suffers is "fairly traceable" to the challenged agency conduct. This is more commonly known as the causation requirement of standing doctrine. The Supreme Court has ruled inconsistently on the strength of the causal link required. For a more relaxed view of the "fairly traceable" standing requirement, see *United States v. Students Challenging Regulatory Agency Procedures (SCRAP)*, 412 U.S. 669 (1973) and *Northeastern Fla. Chapter of Assn. of Gen. Contractors v. Jacksonville*, 508 U.S. 656 (1993). For a more restrictive view, see *Warth v. Seldin*, 422 U.S. 490 (1975).

6. *Redressability.* Redressability requires that a plaintiff demonstrate a "substantial likelihood" that a favorable court ruling would actually redress the harm alleged to result from the challenged action. This element of standing can be difficult to establish where redress depends in part on the choices of third parties not before a court. See, e.g., Simon v. Eastern Ky. Welfare Rights Org., 426 U.S. 26 (1976) (organization representing indigents lacked standing to challenge an IRS ruling reducing the amount of indigent care that hospitals were required to provide in order to qualify for charitable, tax-exempt status because a court ruling overturning the IRS interpretation might lead hospitals to forgo tax exemption rather than provide greater indigent care); Allen v. Wright, 468 U.S. 737 (1984) (similar ruling regarding tax-exempt status for racially discriminatory private school).

Environmental citizen suits have also turned on redressability concerns. In *Steel Co. v. Citizens for a Better Environment*, 523 U.S. 83, 106–107 (1998), the Court held that the plaintiffs lacked standing because neither prospective injunctive relief nor civil penalties payable to the U.S. Treasury, the only remedies available under the statute, would redress the injury caused by the defendant's past statutory violations. The Court limited the scope of *Steel Company* two years later in *Friends of the Earth v. Laidlaw Environmental Services*, 528 U.S. 167 (2000). There, the Court found the plaintiffs had standing to seek civil penalties for violations of the Clean Water Act that were alleged to be ongoing when the plaintiffs filed suit. Distinguishing the *Steel Company* case on the grounds that it involved "wholly past violations," rather than "violations that are ongoing at the time of the complaint and that could continue into the future if undeterred," the Court explained that civil penalties provide redress to plaintiffs who are threatened with injury from ongoing unlawful conduct because "they encourage defendants to discontinue current violations and deter them from committing future ones." *Id.* at 186, 188.

Note that in *Lujan* only four justices concurred in the portion of Justice Scalia's opinion on redressability (Part III.B). In the following case, a majority of the Court continued to reject Justice Scalia's narrow view of redressability.

Massachusetts v. EPA

United States Supreme Court, 2007.
549 U.S. 497.

■ JUSTICE STEVENS delivered the opinion of the Court.

Calling global warming "the most pressing environmental challenge of our time," a group of States, local governments, and private organizations, alleged in a petition for certiorari that the Environmental Protection Agency (EPA) has abdicated its responsibility under the Clean Air Act to regulate the emissions of four greenhouse gases, including carbon dioxide. Specifically, petitioners asked us to answer two questions concerning the meaning of § 202(a)(1) of the Act: whether EPA has the statutory authority to regulate greenhouse gas emissions from new motor vehicles; and if so, whether its stated reasons for refusing to do so are consistent with the statute.

In response, EPA, supported by 10 intervening States and six trade associations, correctly argued that we may not address those two questions unless at least one petitioner has standing to invoke our jurisdiction under Article III of the Constitution.

* * *

IV

Article III of the Constitution limits federal-court jurisdiction to "Cases" and "Controversies." Those two words confine "the business of federal courts to questions presented in an adversary context and in a form historically viewed as capable of resolution through the judicial process." It is therefore familiar learning that no justiciable "controversy" exists when parties seek adjudication of a political question, when they ask for an advisory opinion, or when the question sought to be adjudicated has been mooted by subsequent developments. This case suffers from none of these defects.

The parties' dispute turns on the proper construction of a congressional statute, a question eminently suitable to resolution in federal court. Congress has moreover authorized this type of challenge to EPA action. See 42 U.S.C. § 7607(b)(1). That authorization is of critical importance to the standing inquiry: "Congress has the power to define injuries and articulate chains of causation that will give rise to a case or controversy where none existed before." *Lujan,* 504 U.S., at 580, (Kennedy, J., concurring in part and concurring in judgment). "In exercising this power, however, Congress must at the very least identify the injury it seeks to vindicate and relate the injury to the class of persons entitled to bring suit." *Ibid.* We will not, therefore, "entertain citizen suits to vindicate the public's nonconcrete interest in the proper administration of the laws." *Id.,* at 581.

EPA maintains that because greenhouse gas emissions inflict widespread harm, the doctrine of standing presents an insuperable jurisdictional obstacle. We do not agree. At bottom, "the gist of the question of standing" is whether petitioners have "such a personal stake in the outcome of the controversy as to assure that concrete adverseness which sharpens the presentation of issues upon which the court so largely depends for illumination." Baker v. Carr, 369 U.S. 186 (1962). As Justice Kennedy explained in his *Lujan* concurrence:

While it does not matter how many persons have been injured by the challenged action, the party bringing suit must show that the action injures him in a concrete and personal way. This requirement is not just an empty formality. It preserves the vitality of the adversarial process by assuring both that the parties before the court have an actual, as opposed to professed, stake in the outcome, and that the legal questions presented ... will be resolved, not in the rarified atmosphere of a debating society, but in a concrete factual context conducive to a realistic appreciation of the consequences of judicial action.

504 U.S. at 581.

To ensure the proper adversarial presentation, *Lujan* holds that a litigant must demonstrate that it has suffered a concrete and particularized injury that is either actual or imminent, that the injury is fairly traceable to the defendant, and that it is likely that a favorable decision will redress that injury. See *id.*, at 560–561. However, a litigant to whom Congress has "accorded a procedural right to protect his concrete interests," *id.*, at 572, n.7—here, the right to challenge agency action unlawfully withheld, § 7607(b)(1)—"can assert that right without meeting all the normal standards for redressability and immediacy," *ibid.* When a litigant is vested with a procedural right, that litigant has standing if there is some possibility that the requested relief will prompt the injury-causing party to reconsider the decision that allegedly harmed the litigant. *Ibid.*

We stress here, as did Judge Tatel below, the special position and interest of Massachusetts. It is of considerable relevance that the party seeking review here is a sovereign State and not, as it was in *Lujan,* a private individual.

Well before the creation of the modern administrative state, we recognized that States are not normal litigants for the purposes of invoking federal jurisdiction. As Justice Holmes explained in *Georgia v. Tennessee Copper Co.,* 206 U.S. 230, 237 (1907), a case in which Georgia sought to protect its citizens from air pollution originating outside its borders:

> The case has been argued largely as if it were one between two private parties; but it is not. The very elements that would be relied upon in a suit between fellow-citizens as a ground for equitable relief are wanting here. The State owns very little of the territory alleged to be affected, and the damage to it capable of estimate in money, possibly, at least, is small. This is a suit by a State for an injury to it in its capacity of *quasi*-sovereign. In that capacity the State has an interest independent of and behind the titles of its citizens, in all the earth and air within its domain. It has the last word as to whether its mountains shall be stripped of their forests and its inhabitants shall breathe pure air.

Just as Georgia's "independent interest ... in all the earth and air within its domain" supported federal jurisdiction a century ago, so too does Massachusetts' well-founded desire to preserve its sovereign territory today. That Massachusetts does in fact own a great deal of the "territory alleged to be affected" only reinforces the conclusion that its stake in the outcome of this case is sufficiently concrete to warrant the exercise of federal judicial power.

When a State enters the Union, it surrenders certain sovereign prerogatives. Massachusetts cannot invade Rhode Island to force reductions in greenhouse gas emissions, it cannot negotiate an emissions treaty with China or India, and in some circumstances the exercise of its police powers to reduce in-state motor-vehicle emissions might well be pre-empted.

These sovereign prerogatives are now lodged in the Federal Government, and Congress has ordered EPA to protect Massachusetts (among others) by prescribing standards applicable to the "emission of any air pollutant from any class or classes of new motor vehicle engines, which in [the Administrator's] judgment cause, or contribute to, air pollution which may reasonably be anticipated to endanger public health or welfare." 42 U.S.C. § 7521(a)(1). Congress has moreover recognized a concomitant procedural right to challenge the rejection of its rulemaking petition as arbitrary and capricious. § 7607(b)(1). Given that procedural right and Massachusetts' stake in protecting its quasi-sovereign interests, the Commonwealth is entitled to special solicitude in our standing analysis.[17]

With that in mind, it is clear that petitioners' submissions as they pertain to Massachusetts have satisfied the most demanding standards of the adversarial process. EPA's steadfast refusal to regulate greenhouse gas emissions presents a risk of harm to Massachusetts that is both "actual" and "imminent." *Lujan*, 504 U.S., at 560. There is, moreover, a "substantial likelihood that the judicial relief requested" will prompt EPA to take steps to reduce that risk. Duke Power Co. v. Carolina Environmental Study Group, Inc., 438 U.S. 59, 79 (1978).

The Injury

The harms associated with climate change are serious and well recognized. [Here, the Court summarized evidence of climate change.]

That these climate-change risks are "widely shared" does not minimize Massachusetts' interest in the outcome of this litigation. According to petitioners' unchallenged affidavits, global sea levels rose somewhere between 10 and 20 centimeters over the 20th century as a result of global

---

17. The Chief Justice accuses the Court of misreading *Georgia v. Tennessee Copper Co.,* 206 U.S. 230 (1907), and "devis[ing] a new doctrine of state standing." But no less an authority than Hart & Wechsler's The Federal Courts and the Federal System understands *Tennessee Copper* as a standing decision. R. Fallon, D. Meltzer, & D. Shapiro, Hart & Wechsler's The Federal Courts and the Federal System 290 (5th ed. 2003). Indeed, it devotes an entire section to chronicling the long development of cases permitting States "to litigate as *parens patriae* to protect quasi-sovereign interests—*i.e.,* public or governmental interests that concern the state as a whole." *Id.,* at 289; see, *e.g.,* Missouri v. Illinois, 180 U.S. 208, 240–241 (1901) (finding federal jurisdiction appropriate not only "in cases involving boundaries and jurisdiction over lands and their inhabitants, and in cases directly affecting the property rights and interests of a state," but also when the "substantial impairment of the health and prosperity of the towns and cities of the state" are at stake)....

warming. These rising seas have already begun to swallow Massachusetts' coastal land. Because the Commonwealth "owns a substantial portion of the state's coastal property," it has alleged a particularized injury in its capacity as a landowner. The severity of that injury will only increase over the course of the next century: If sea levels continue to rise as predicted, one Massachusetts official believes that a significant fraction of coastal property will be "either permanently lost through inundation or temporarily lost through periodic storm surge and flooding events." Remediation costs alone, petitioners allege, could run well into the hundreds of millions of dollars.[21]

Causation

EPA does not dispute the existence of a causal connection between man-made greenhouse gas emissions and global warming. At a minimum, therefore, EPA's refusal to regulate such emissions "contributes" to Massachusetts' injuries.

EPA nevertheless maintains that its decision not to regulate greenhouse gas emissions from new motor vehicles contributes so insignificantly to petitioners' injuries that the agency cannot be haled into federal court to answer for them. For the same reason, EPA does not believe that any realistic possibility exists that the relief petitioners seek would mitigate global climate change and remedy their injuries. That is especially so because predicted increases in greenhouse gas emissions from developing nations, particularly China and India, are likely to offset any marginal domestic decrease.

But EPA overstates its case. Its argument rests on the erroneous assumption that a small incremental step, because it is incremental, can never be attacked in a federal judicial forum. Yet accepting that premise would doom most challenges to regulatory action. Agencies, like legislatures, do not generally resolve massive problems in one fell regulatory swoop. They instead whittle away at them over time, refining their preferred approach as circumstances change and as they develop a more-nuanced understanding of how best to proceed. That a first step might be tentative does not by itself support the notion that federal courts lack jurisdiction to determine whether that step conforms to law.

And reducing domestic automobile emissions is hardly a tentative step. Even leaving aside the other greenhouse gases, the United States transportation sector emits an enormous quantity of carbon dioxide into the atmosphere-according to the MacCracken affidavit, more than 1.7 billion

---

21. In dissent, the Chief Justice dismisses petitioners' submissions as "conclusory," presumably because they do not quantify Massachusetts' land loss with the exactitude he would prefer. He therefore asserts that the Commonwealth's injury is "conjectur[al]." Yet the likelihood that Massachusetts' coastline will recede has nothing to do with whether petitioners have determined the precise metes and bounds of their soon-to-be-flooded land. Petitioners maintain that the seas are rising and will continue to rise, and have alleged that such a rise will lead to the loss of Massachusetts' sovereign territory. No one, save perhaps the dissenters, disputes those allegations. Our cases require nothing more.

metric tons in 1999 alone. That accounts for more than 6% of worldwide carbon dioxide emissions. To put this in perspective: Considering just emissions from the transportation sector, which represent less than one-third of this country's total carbon dioxide emissions, the United States would still rank as the third-largest emitter of carbon dioxide in the world, outpaced only by the European Union and China. Judged by any standard, U.S. motor-vehicle emissions make a meaningful contribution to greenhouse gas concentrations and hence, according to petitioners, to global warming.

The Remedy

While it may be true that regulating motor-vehicle emissions will not by itself *reverse* global warming, it by no means follows that we lack jurisdiction to decide whether EPA has a duty to take steps to *slow* or *reduce* it. Because of the enormity of the potential consequences associated with man-made climate change, the fact that the effectiveness of a remedy might be delayed during the (relatively short) time it takes for a new motor-vehicle fleet to replace an older one is essentially irrelevant. Nor is it dispositive that developing countries such as China and India are poised to increase greenhouse gas emissions substantially over the next century: A reduction in domestic emissions would slow the pace of global emissions increases, no matter what happens elsewhere.

We moreover attach considerable significance to EPA's "agree[ment] with the President that 'we must address the issue of global climate change,'" 68 Fed. Reg. 52929 (quoting remarks announcing Clear Skies and Global Climate Initiatives, 2002 Public Papers of George W. Bush, Vol. 1, Feb. 14, p. 227 (2004)), and to EPA's ardent support for various voluntary emission-reduction programs, 68 Fed. Reg. 52932. As Judge Tatel observed in dissent below, "EPA would presumably not bother with such efforts if it thought emissions reductions would have no discernable impact on future global warming." 415 F.3d, at 66.

In sum—at least according to petitioners' uncontested affidavits—the rise in sea levels associated with global warming has already harmed and will continue to harm Massachusetts. The risk of catastrophic harm, though remote, is nevertheless real. That risk would be reduced to some extent if petitioners received the relief they seek. We therefore hold that petitioners have standing to challenge the EPA's denial of their rulemaking petition.

* * *

■ CHIEF JUSTICE ROBERTS, with whom JUSTICE SCALIA, JUSTICE THOMAS, and JUSTICE ALITO join, dissenting.

Apparently dissatisfied with the pace of progress on this issue in the elected branches, petitioners have come to the courts claiming broad-ranging injury, and attempting to tie that injury to the Government's alleged failure to comply with a rather narrow statutory provision. I would reject these challenges as nonjusticiable. Such a conclusion involves no judgment on whether global warming exists, what causes it, or the extent of the problem. Nor does it render petitioners without recourse. This Court's standing jurisprudence simply recognizes that redress of grievances of the sort at issue here "is the function of Congress and the Chief Executive," not the federal courts. Lujan v. Defenders of Wildlife, 504 U.S. 555, 576 (1992). I would vacate the judgment below and remand for dismissal of the petitions for review.

I

* * * [P]etitioners bear the burden of alleging an injury that is fairly traceable to the Environmental Protection Agency's failure to promulgate new motor vehicle greenhouse gas emission standards, and that is likely to be redressed by the prospective issuance of such standards.

Before determining whether petitioners can meet this familiar test, however, the Court changes the rules. It asserts that "States are not normal litigants for the purposes of invoking federal jurisdiction," and that given "Massachusetts' stake in protecting its quasi-sovereign interests, the Commonwealth is entitled to *special solicitude* in our standing analysis." (emphasis added).

Relaxing Article III standing requirements because asserted injuries are pressed by a State, however, has no basis in our jurisprudence, and support for any such "special solicitude" is conspicuously absent from the Court's opinion. The general judicial review provision cited by the Court, 42 U.S.C. § 7607(b)(1), affords States no special rights or status. Under the law on which petitioners rely, Congress treated public and private litigants exactly the same.

Nor does the case law cited by the Court provide any support for the notion that Article III somehow implicitly treats public and private litigants differently. The Court has to go back a full century in an attempt to justify its novel standing rule, but even there it comes up short. The Court's analysis hinges on *Georgia v. Tennessee Copper Co.,* 206 U.S. 230 (1907)—a case that did indeed draw a distinction between a State and private litigants, but solely with respect to available remedies. The case had nothing to do with Article III standing.

In *Tennessee Copper,* the State of Georgia sought to enjoin copper companies in neighboring Tennessee from discharging pollutants that were inflicting "a wholesale destruction of forests, orchards and crops" in bordering Georgia counties. Although the State owned very little of the territory allegedly affected, the Court reasoned that Georgia-in its capacity as a "*quasi*-sovereign"—"has an interest independent of and behind the titles of its citizens, in all the earth and air within its domain." The Court explained that while "[t]he very elements that would be relied upon in a suit between fellow-citizens as a ground for equitable relief [were] wanting," a State "is not lightly to be required to give up *quasi*-sovereign rights for pay." Thus while a complaining private litigant would have to make do with a *legal* remedy—one "for pay"—the State was entitled to *equitable* relief.

In contrast to the present case, there was no question in *Tennessee Copper* about Article III injury. There was certainly no suggestion that the State could show standing where the private parties could not; there was no dispute, after all, that the private landowners had "an action at law." *Tennessee Copper* has since stood for nothing more than a State's right, in an original jurisdiction action, to sue in a representative capacity as *parens patriae*. Nothing about a State's ability to sue in that capacity dilutes the bedrock requirement of showing injury, causation, and redressability to satisfy Article III.

What is more, the Court's reasoning falters on its own terms. The Court asserts that Massachusetts is entitled to "special solicitude" due to its "quasi-sovereign interests," but then applies our Article III standing test to the asserted injury of the State's loss of coastal property. In the context of *parens patriae* standing, however, we have characterized state ownership of land as a "nonsovereign interes[t]" because a State "is likely to have the same interests as other similarly situated proprietors." *Alfred L. Snapp & Son, supra,* at 601.

II

* * * When the Court actually applies the three-part test, it focuses, as did the dissent below, on the State's asserted loss of coastal land as the injury in fact. If petitioners rely on loss of land as the Article III injury, however, they must ground the rest of the standing analysis in that specific injury. That alleged injury must be "concrete and particularized," *Defenders of Wildlife,* 504 U.S., at 560, and "distinct and palpable," *Allen,* 468 U.S., at 751. Central to this concept of "particularized" injury is the requirement that a plaintiff be affected in a "personal and individual way," *Defenders of Wildlife,* 504 U.S., at 560, n. 1, and seek relief that "directly and tangibly benefits him" in a manner distinct from its impact on "the public at large," *id.,* at 573–574.

The very concept of global warming seems inconsistent with this particularization requirement. Global warming is a phenomenon "harmful to humanity at large," 415 F.3d, at 60 (Sentelle, J., dissenting in part and concurring in judgment), and the redress petitioners seek is focused no more on them than on the public generally-it is literally to change the atmosphere around the world.

If petitioners' particularized injury is loss of coastal land, it is also that injury that must be "actual or imminent, not conjectural or hypothetical," *Defenders of Wildlife, supra,* at 560, "real and immediate," *Los Angeles v. Lyons,* 461 U.S. 95, 102 (1983), and "certainly impending," *Whitmore v. Arkansas,* 495 U.S. 149, 158 (1990).

As to "actual" injury, the Court observes that "global sea levels rose somewhere between 10 and 20 centimeters over the 20th century as a result of global warming" and that "[t]hese rising seas have already begun to swallow Massachusetts' coastal land." But none of petitioners' declarations supports that connection. * * *

The Court's attempts to identify "imminent" or "certainly impending" loss of Massachusetts coastal land fares no better. One of petitioners' declarants predicts global warming will cause sea level to rise by 20 to 70 centimeters *by the year 2100*. Another uses a computer modeling program to map the Commonwealth's coastal land and its current elevation, and calculates that the high-end estimate of sea level rise would result in the loss of significant state-owned coastal land. But the computer modeling program has a conceded average error of about 30 centimeters and a maximum observed error of 70 centimeters. As an initial matter, if it is possible that the model underrepresents the elevation of coastal land to an extent equal to or in excess of the projected sea level rise, it is difficult to put much stock in the predicted loss of land. But even placing that problem to the side, accepting a century-long time horizon and a series of compounded estimates renders requirements of imminence and immediacy utterly toothless.

III

Petitioners' reliance on Massachusetts's loss of coastal land as their injury in fact for standing purposes creates insurmountable problems for them with respect to causation and redressability. To establish standing, petitioners must show a causal connection between that specific injury and the lack of new motor vehicle greenhouse gas emission standards, and that the promulgation of such standards would likely redress that injury. As is often the case, the questions of causation and redressability overlap.

The Court ignores the complexities of global warming, and does so by now disregarding the "particularized" injury it relied on in step one, and using the dire nature of global warming itself as a bootstrap for finding causation and redressability. First, it is important to recognize the extent of the emissions at issue here. Because local greenhouse gas emissions disperse throughout the atmosphere and remain there for anywhere from 50 to 200 years, it is global emissions data that are relevant. According to one of petitioners' declarations, domestic motor vehicles contribute about 6 percent of global carbon dioxide emissions and 4 percent of global greenhouse gas emissions. The amount of global emissions at issue here is smaller still; § 202(a)(1) of the Clean Air Act covers only *new* motor vehicles and *new* motor vehicle engines, so petitioners' desired emission standards might reduce only a fraction of 4 percent of global emissions.

This gets us only to the relevant greenhouse gas emissions; linking them to global warming and ultimately to petitioners' alleged injuries next requires consideration of further complexities. As EPA explained in its denial of petitioners' request for rulemaking,

> [P]redicting future climate change necessarily involves a complex web of economic and physical factors including: our ability to predict future global anthropogenic emissions of [greenhouse gases] and aerosols; the fate of these emissions once they enter the atmosphere (e.g., what percentage are absorbed by vegetation or are taken up by the oceans); the impact of those emissions that remain in the atmosphere on the

radiative properties of the atmosphere; changes in critically important climate feedbacks (e.g., changes in cloud cover and ocean circulation); changes in temperature characteristics (e.g., average temperatures, shifts in daytime and evening temperatures); changes in other climatic parameters (e.g., shifts in precipitation, storms); and ultimately the impact of such changes on human health and welfare (e.g., increases or decreases in agricultural productivity, human health impacts).

Petitioners are never able to trace their alleged injuries back through this complex web to the fractional amount of global emissions that might have been limited with EPA standards. In light of the bit-part domestic new motor vehicle greenhouse gas emissions have played in what petitioners describe as a 150–year global phenomenon, and the myriad additional factors bearing on petitioners' alleged injury—the loss of Massachusetts coastal land—the connection is far too speculative to establish causation.

IV

Redressability is even more problematic. To the tenuous link between petitioners' alleged injury and the indeterminate fractional domestic emissions at issue here, add the fact that petitioners cannot meaningfully predict what will come of the 80 percent of global greenhouse gas emissions that originate outside the United States.

Petitioners offer declarations attempting to address this uncertainty, contending that "[i]f the U.S. takes steps to reduce motor vehicle emissions, other countries are very likely to take similar actions regarding their own motor vehicles using technology developed in response to the U.S. program." In other words, do not worry that other countries will contribute far more to global warming than will U.S. automobile emissions; someone is bound to invent something, and places like the People's Republic of China or India will surely require use of the new technology, regardless of cost. The Court previously has explained that when the existence of an element of standing "depends on the unfettered choices made by independent actors not before the courts and whose exercise of broad and legitimate discretion the courts cannot presume either to control or to predict," a party must present facts supporting an assertion that the actor will proceed in such a manner. *Defenders of Wildlife,* 504 U.S., at 562 (opinion of Kennedy, J.). The declarations' conclusory (not to say fanciful) statements do not even come close.

The Court's sleight-of-hand is in failing to link up the different elements of the three-part standing test. What must be *likely* to be redressed is the particular injury in fact. The injury the Court looks to is the asserted loss of land. The Court contends that regulating domestic motor vehicle emissions will reduce carbon dioxide in the atmosphere, *and therefore* redress Massachusetts's injury. But even if regulation *does* reduce emissions—to some indeterminate degree, given events elsewhere in the world—the Court never explains why that makes it *likely* that the injury in fact—the loss of land—will be redressed. Schoolchildren know that a kingdom might be lost "all for the want of a horseshoe nail," but "likely" redressability is a different matter. The realities make it pure conjecture to suppose that EPA regulation of new automobile emissions will *likely* prevent the loss of Massachusetts coastal land.

NOTES AND QUESTIONS

1. *The effect of Massachusetts v. EPA on standing analysis.* Does *Massachusetts v. EPA* change the standing inquiry laid out in *Lujan*? Does the fact that the plaintiffs in *Massachusetts v. EPA* are states affect the standing analysis? If so, how? Should states be able to satisfy standing requirements more readily than individuals?

2. *Congress' power to create standing.* In light of *Lujan* and *Massachusetts v. EPA*, how much authority does Congress have to create standing by defining injury in fact, causation, and redressability?

3. *Will it last?* In *Massachusetts v. EPA*, Justice Stevens was able to muster only five votes for the proposition that the states had constitutional standing. It is too soon to tell how durable that holding will be, or how broadly the Court will interpret it. In American Electric Power Co. v. Connecticut, ___ U.S. ___, 131 S.Ct. 2527 (2011) (excerpted in Chapter 2), the Supreme Court divided four to four on whether states and environmental groups had standing to pursue a public nuisance case against electric power producers. The result of that tie vote was to affirm the lower court's finding that plaintiffs did have standing.

2.   NON–CONSTITUTIONAL OR PRUDENTIAL STANDING

In addition to constitutional standing, the Supreme Court has developed other requirements, generally referred to as prudential standing requirements, to advance values important to the federal judiciary. Because they are discretionary and not dictated by the Constitution, these prudential considerations can be changed by congressional legislation.

One important prudential concern for plaintiffs seeking to raise claims under environmental statutes is the zone of interests test. Section 702 of the Administrative Procedure Act provides for judicial review at the behest of "[a] person suffering legal wrong because of agency action or adversely affected or aggrieved by agency action within the meaning of a relevant statute...." In *Association of Data Processing Service Organizations, Inc. v. Camp*, 397 U.S. 150 (1970), the Court interpreted that provision to require that a plaintiff's asserted injury fall arguably within the zone of interests to be protected by the statute under which the claim was asserted. To determine whether a plaintiff satisfies the zone of interests test, a court should examine whether the plaintiff's interest is "arguably" related to the statute in question. Congressional intent to benefit the plaintiff may suffice, but is not necessarily required. See National Credit Union Admin. v. First Nat'l Bank & Trust Co., 522 U.S. 479, 492 (1998).

Environmental cases sometimes turn on this issue. Compare Grand Council of the Crees v. FERC, 198 F.3d 950 (D.C. Cir. 2000) (native groups' challenge to a FERC decision allowing a Quebec utility to sell electricity in the U.S. at higher rates not within the zone of interest of the Federal Power Act), and Central S.D. Coop. Grazing Dist. v. Secretary of the U.S. Dept. of Agric., 266 F.3d 889 (8th Cir. 2001) (grazing district whose only interest in grazing lands was economic not within zone of interest of NEPA) with New Mexico Cattle Growers Ass'n v. U.S. Fish & Wildlife Serv., 81 F. Supp 2d 1141 (D.N.M. 1999), rev'd on other grounds, 248 F.3d 1277 (10th Cir. 2001) (organization of ranchers and farmers fell within zone of interests of NEPA because it sought to protect members' consumptive interests in the land and water at issue and to prevent environmental damage on other lands).

There are two other potential prudential standing barriers to environmental plaintiffs. First, litigants may not use the federal courts as a forum to air "generalized grievances" about the conduct of government, which, according to the Court, are properly submitted to the political branches. Taxpayers suits are frequently blocked by the "generalized grievance" doctrine under rules set out in *Flast v. Cohen*, 392 U.S. 83 (1968) and *Frothingham v. Mellon*, 262 U.S. 447 (1923). Taxpayers generally do not have standing to contest specific government spending because the effect of the spending on their tax liability is likely to be "minute and indeterminable." See DaimlerChrysler Corp. v. Cuno, 547 U.S. 332 (2006).

Second, a party generally must represent her own rights and not those of third persons not before the court. This prudential rule is, of course, subject to the principles allowing organizational standing and also to exceptions when the plaintiff will effectively represent the rights of a third party who cannot effectively protect his own rights.

Bennett v. Spear

United States Supreme Court, 1997.
520 U.S. 154.

■ JUSTICE SCALIA delivered the opinion of the Court.

[The Endangered Species Act (ESA), covered in more detail in Chapter 6, calls upon the Secretary of the Interior to identify "critical habitat" for threatened or endangered species. Although final decisionmaking authority rests with the Secretary, he is required to consult the Fish and Wildlife Service (FWS), which must provide a written "Biological Opinion." The Biological Opinion explains how a proposed action might affect the species and provides for mitigation measures. The Bureau of Reclamation informed the FWS that the operation of the Klamath Irrigation Project might harm two endangered species of fish (the Lost River and shortnose suckers). The FWS issued a Biological Opinion agreeing with this concern and recommended that the Bureau of Reclamation maintain minimum water levels in reservoirs. The Bureau of Reclamation then agreed to do so. The plaintiffs were irrigation districts and ranchers who claimed that the Biological Opinion violated various provisions of the ESA and the Administrative Procedure Act. The Ninth Circuit held that the plaintiffs lacked standing because their economic interests did not lie within the "zone of interests" protected by the ESA.]

We first turn to the question the Court of Appeals found dispositive: whether petitioners lack standing by virtue of the zone-of-interests test. Although petitioners contend that their claims lie both under the ESA and the APA, we look first at the ESA because it may permit petitioners to recover their litigation costs, *see* 16 U.S.C. § 1540(g)(4), and because the APA by its terms independently authorizes review only when "there is no other adequate remedy in a court," 5 U.S.C. § 704.

The question of standing "involves both constitutional limitations on federal-court jurisdiction and prudential limitations on its exercise." To satisfy the "case" or "controversy" requirement of Article III, which is the "irreducible constitutional minimum" of standing, a plaintiff must, generally speaking, demonstrate that he has suffered "injury in fact," that the injury is "fairly traceable" to the actions of the defendant, and that the injury will likely be redressed by a favorable decision. In addition to the immutable requirements of Article III, "the federal judiciary has also adhered to a set of prudential principles that bear on the question of standing." Like their constitutional counterparts, these "judicially self-imposed limits on the exercise of federal jurisdiction," are "founded in concern about the proper—and properly limited—role of the courts in a democratic society," but unlike their constitutional counterparts, they can be modified or abrogated by Congress. Numbered among these prudential requirements is the doctrine of particular concern in this case: that a plaintiffs grievance must arguably fall within the zone of interests protected or regulated by the statutory provision or constitutional guarantee invoked in the suit.

The "zone of interests" formulation was first employed in *Association of Data Processing Service Organizations, Inc. v. Camp.* There, certain data processors sought to invalidate a ruling by the Comptroller of the Currency authorizing national banks to sell data processing services on the ground that it violated, inter alia, § 4 of the Bank Service Corporation Act of 1962, which prohibited bank service corporations from engaging in "any activity other than the performance of bank services for banks." The Court of Appeals had held that the banks' data-processing competitors were without standing to challenge the alleged violation of § 4. In reversing, we stated the applicable prudential standing requirement to be "whether the interest sought to be protected by the complainant is arguably within the zone of interests to be protected or regulated by the statute or constitutional guarantee in question." *Data Processing,* and its companion case, *Barlow v. Collins,* applied the zone-of-interests test to suits under the APA, but later cases have applied it also in suits not involving review of federal administrative action, and have specifically listed it among other prudential standing requirements of general application. We have made clear, however, that the breadth of the zone of interests varies according to the provisions of law at issue, so that what comes within the zone of interests of a statute for purposes of obtaining judicial review of administrative action under the "generous review provisions" of the APA may not do so for other purposes.

Congress legislates against the background of our prudential standing doctrine, which applies unless it is expressly negated. The first question in the present case is whether the ESA's citizen-suit provision, * * * negates the zone-of-interests test (or, perhaps more accurately, expands the zone of interests). We think it does. The first operative portion of the provision says that "any person may commence a civil suit"—an authorization of remarkable breadth when compared with the language Congress ordinarily uses. Even in some other environmental statutes, Congress has used more restrictive formulations, such as "[any person] having an interest which is or may be adversely affected," 33 U.S.C. § 1365(g) (Clean Water Act).

Our readiness to take the term "any person" at face value is greatly augmented by two interrelated considerations: that the overall subject matter of this legislation is the environment (a matter in which it is common to think all persons have an interest) and that the obvious purpose of the particular provision in question is to encourage enforcement by so-called "private attorneys general"—evidenced by its elimination of the usual amount-in-controversy and diversity-of-citizenship requirements, its provision for recovery of the costs of litigation (including even expert witness fees), and its reservation to the Government of a right of first refusal to pursue the action initially and a right to intervene later. Given these factors, we think the conclusion of expanded standing follows a fortiori from our decision in *Trafficante v. Metropolitan Life Ins. Co.,* which held that standing was expanded to the full extent permitted under Article III by a provision of the Civil Rights Act of 1968 that authorized "[a]ny person who claims to have been injured by a discriminatory housing practice" to sue for violations of the Act. There also we relied on textual evidence of a statutory scheme to rely on private litigation to ensure compliance with the Act. The statutory language here is even clearer, and the subject of the legislation makes the intent to permit enforcement by everyman even more plausible.

It is true that the plaintiffs here are seeking to prevent application of environmental restrictions rather than to implement them. But the "any person" formulation applies to all the causes of action authorized by § 1540(g)—not only to actions against private violators of environmental restrictions, and not only to actions against the Secretary asserting under-enforcement under § 1533, but also to actions against the Secretary asserting over-enforcement under § 1533. As we shall discuss below, the citizen-suit provision does favor environmentalists in that it covers all private violations of the Act but not all failures of the Secretary to meet his administrative responsibilities; but there is no textual basis for saying that its expansion of standing requirements applies to environmentalists alone. The Court of Appeals therefore erred in concluding that petitioners lacked standing under the zone-of-interests test to bring their claims under the ESA's citizen-suit provision.

[The Court held that the citizen suit provision did reach the claim that the federal government had effectively designated critical habitat without considering economic factors at all, but not to the plaintiffs' other claims. The Court then considered whether these other claims could be brought under the APA.]

No one contends (and it would not be maintainable) that the causes of action against the Secretary set forth in the ESA's citizen-suit provision are exclusive, supplanting those provided by the APA. The APA, by its terms, provides a right to judicial review of all "final agency action for which there is no other adequate remedy in a court," 5 U.S.C. § 704, and applies universally "except to the extent that—(1) statutes preclude judicial review; or (2) agency action is committed to agency discretion by law," § 701(a). Nothing in the ESA's citizen-suit provision expressly precludes review under the APA, nor do we detect anything in the statutory scheme suggesting a purpose to do so. And any contention that the relevant provision of 16 U.S.C. § 1536(a)(2) is discretionary would fly in the face of its text, which uses the imperative "shall."

In determining whether the petitioners have standing under the zone-of-interests test to bring their APA claims, we look not to the terms of the ESA's citizen-suit provision, but to the substantive provisions of the ESA, the alleged violations of which serve as the gravamen of the complaint. The classic formulation of the zone-of-interests test is set forth in *Data Processing*: "whether the interest sought to be protected by the complainant is arguably within the zone of interests to be protected or regulated by the statute or constitutional guarantee in question." The Court of Appeals concluded that this test was not met here, since petitioners are neither directly regulated by the ESA nor seek to vindicate its overarching purpose of species preservation. That conclusion was error.

Whether a plaintiff's interest is "arguably . . . protected . . . by the statute" within the meaning of the zone-of-interests test is to be determined not by reference to the overall purpose of the Act in question (here, species preservation), but by reference to the particular provision of law upon which the plaintiff relies. It is difficult to understand how the Ninth Circuit could have failed to see this from our cases. In *Data Processing* itself, for example, we did not require that the plaintiffs' suit vindicate the overall purpose of the Bank Service Corporation Act of 1962, but found it sufficient that their commercial interest was sought to be protected by the anti-competition limitation contained in § 4 of the Act—the specific provision which they alleged had been violated. As we said with the utmost clarity in *National Wildlife Federation*, "the plaintiff must establish that the injury he complains of . . . falls within the 'zone of interests' sought to be protected by the statutory provision whose violation forms the legal basis for his complaint."

In the claims that we have found not to be covered by the ESA's citizen-suit provision, petitioners allege a violation of § 7 of the ESA, which requires, inter alia, that each agency "use the best scientific and commercial data available." Petitioners contend that the available scientific and commercial data show that the continued operation of the Klamath Project will not have a detrimental impact on the endangered suckers, that the imposition of minimum lake levels is not necessary to protect the fish, and that by issuing a Biological Opinion which makes unsubstantiated findings to the contrary the defendants have acted arbitrarily and in violation of § 1536(a)(2). The obvious purpose of the requirement that each agency "use the best scientific and commercial data available" is to ensure that the ESA not be implemented haphazardly, on the basis of speculation or surmise. While this no doubt serves to advance the ESA's overall goal of species preservation, we think it readily apparent that another objective (if not indeed the primary one) is to avoid needless economic dislocation produced by agency officials zealously but unintelligently pursuing their environmental objectives. That economic consequences are an explicit concern of the Act is evidenced by § 1536(h), which provides exemption from § 1536(a)(2)'s no jeopardy mandate where there are no reasonable and prudent alternatives to the agency action and the benefits of the agency action clearly outweigh the benefits of any alternatives. We believe the "best scientific and commercial data" provision is similarly intended, at least in part, to prevent uneconomic (because erroneous) jeopardy determinations. Petitioners' claim that they are victims of such a mistake is plainly within the zone of interests that the provision protects.

* * *

D.   Ripeness, Exhaustion and Mootness

There are three important concepts related to the timing of judicial review: 1) ripeness, 2) exhaustion of administrative remedies, and 3) mootness.

1.   RIPENESS

The ripeness and mootness doctrines, like the doctrine of constitutional standing, spring from the Article III "case or controversy" requirement. Ripeness and mootness focus on the timing of a plaintiff's claim: a claim brought too early is not ripe for review, and a claim brought too late is moot. The policies underlying ripeness doctrine are incorporated into APA § 704, which limits judicial review to "final agency action for which there is no other adequate remedy in court" unless otherwise provided for by statute. But when is an agency's action sufficiently "final" to be judicially reviewed? *Bennett v. Spear*, 520 U.S. 154 (1997), which held that a biological opinion issued by the FWS pursuant to the Endangered Species Act was a final agency action subject to review, set out a frequently-quoted test for finality: 1) the agency's action must mark the consummation of the agency's decisionmaking process, and should not be merely a tentative determination; and 2) the action must be one by which rights or obligations have been determined or from which legal consequences will flow. The application of the second prong of the *Bennett v. Spear* test has drawn appellate courts into a murky area of determining whether opinion letters or interpretive rules are "legal" enough to satisfy the test. See, e.g., Independent Equip. Dealers Ass'n. v. EPA, 372 F.3d 420 (D.C. Cir. 2004).

Certain agency acts are clearly final, such as agency adjudications where there is no further right of internal agency appeal. Promulgation of a final regulation at the conclusion of the agency rulemaking process would also seem to be final. However, absent special statutory authorization, courts have held that regulations generally cannot be judicially reviewed until they are enforced against a party. This rule means that, in general, pre-enforcement review of agency regulations *is not* allowed. Most environmental statutes, however, run counter to this general rule by specifically authorizing pre-enforcement judicial review of agency regulations, but only for a limited time period 60 or 120 days after their issuance or promulgation. Section 307(b) of the Clean Air Act and section 509(b) of the Clean Water Act are good examples. Why do you suppose these statutes are designed in this way? These laws also contain the proviso that regulations cannot be challenged during individual enforcement proceedings. Why is that?

What about situations where an agency fails to act? Is this subject to judicial review? Can non-action be a "final agency action?" In *Norton v. Southern Utah Wilderness Alliance*, for example, environmental plaintiffs challenged the Bureau of Land Management's failure to take action to address the environmental damage caused by off-road vehicle use on lands managed by the agency. 542 U.S. 55 (2004). The Supreme Court ruled that an agency's failure to act is reviewable only when 1) the non-action was "discrete" and 2) agency action was required by law. See id. at 62–64. Applying these principles, the Court held that the plaintiffs were not entitled to relief due to the broad discretion that Congress had granted the agency in managing the lands at issue and the lack of a statutory prohibition on off-road vehicles.

Even if an agency action is final, it may not be ripe for judicial review. In *Ohio Forestry Ass'n v. Sierra Club*, 523 U.S. 726 (1998), the Sierra Club challenged the forest management plan developed for the Wayne National Forest. The organization alleged that the plan permitted excessive timber harvest and excessive clear-cutting. The plan had been formally adopted, and it had legal consequences because all forest management actions had to be consistent with it. Nonetheless, a unanimous Court held that the challenge was not ripe. In doing so, it considered: "1) whether delayed review would cause hardship to the plaintiffs; 2) whether judicial intervention would inappropriately interfere with further administrative action; and (3) whether the courts would benefit from further factual development of the issues presented." Id. at 733. The Court noted that the Sierra Club would have the opportunity to challenge site-specific timber harvest plans before any trees could be cut, and that judicial review would be aided by the focus that a particular logging proposal could provide. The Court also pointed out that Congress had not specifically provided for pre-implementation review of forest plans.

2. EXHAUSTION OF ADMINISTRATIVE REMEDIES

A second doctrine affecting the timing and availability of judicial review is the principle that the litigant must exhaust administrative remedies prior to seeking court review. There are a number of policy justifications for the exhaustion doctrine, including: limiting unnecessary judicial intervention into agency matters, preventing parties from blocking agency proceedings, clarifying legal and factual issues prior to court review, and allowing agencies the opportunity to correct their errors. Myers v. Bethlehem Shipbuilding Corp., 303 U.S. 41 (1938). Nonetheless, the Supreme Court held in *Darby v. Cisneros*, 509 U.S. 137 (1993), that there is no general exhaustion element beyond the Administrative Procedure Act's § 704 requirement of "finality" unless an agency's authorizing statute or regulations require it. Finality and exhaustion inquiries thus often overlap. Most environmental statutes do not specifically require intra-agency appeal as a precondition of obtaining judicial review. See, e.g., Clean Water Act § 509(b)(1) (review of EPA action under the CWA); Washington Toxics Coal. v. EPA, 413 F.3d 1024 (9th Cir. 2005) (administrative exhaustion of remedies available under Federal Insecticide, Fungicide, and Rodenticide Act was not required before plaintiffs could file citizen suit under Endangered Species Act); but see Shawnee Trail Conservancy v. U.S. Dep't of Agric., 222 F.3d 383 (7th Cir. 2000) (upholding requirement of Forest Service regulations that plaintiff pursue agency appeal before seeking judicial review).

3. MOOTNESS

If it is too late to obtain judicial review, the case is said to be moot. When is a matter moot? A case is moot when there is no live or active controversy between the parties. For example, an industry's challenge to an air pollution control regulation may become moot if EPA repeals or amends the rule. Or a citizen suit alleging permit violations may become moot if a polluter comes into compliance with its permit conditions after the suit is filed. Alternatively, the suit may become moot if the polluting facility is sold to another party, closed, and dismantled. Such events raise the possibility that the court should dismiss the action on grounds of mootness.

The Supreme Court has made clear, however, that dismissal for mootness is more difficult for defendants to achieve than dismissal for lack of standing. In *Friends of the Earth v. Laidlaw Environmental Services*, 528 U.S. 167 (2000), plaintiff Friends of the Earth (FOE) filed a CWA citizen suit alleging that the operator of a wastewater treatment plant was violating the discharge limits of its NPDES permit. After finding that FOE had standing to pursue civil penalties as well as injunctive relief, the district court imposed a $405,800 civil penalty. The district court declined to order injunctive relief, however, because Laidlaw had achieved "substantial compliance" with its permit, and on appeal, the Fourth Circuit concluded that the penalties had also become moot because "the only remedy currently available to [FOE]—civil penalties payable to the government—would not redress any injury [FOE has] suffered." 149 F.3d at 307.

After the Fourth Circuit issued its opinion, but before the Supreme Court decided the case, Laidlaw closed and dismantled the facility. Notwithstanding these facts, the Court concluded that neither the request for injunctive relief nor the request for penalties was moot:

> The only conceivable basis for a finding of mootness in this case is Laidlaw's voluntary conduct—either its achievement by August 1992 of substantial compliance with its NPDES permit or its more recent shutdown of the Roebuck facility. It is well settled that "a defendant's voluntary cessation of a challenged practice does not deprive a federal court of its power to determine the legality of the practice" City of Mesquite, 455 U.S. at 289. "If it did, the courts would be compelled to 'leave the defendant ... free to return to his old ways.'" 455 U.S. at 289, n. 10. In accordance with this principle, the standard we have announced for determining whether a case has been mooted by the defendant's voluntary conduct is stringent: "A case might become moot if subsequent events made it absolutely clear that the allegedly wrongful behavior could not reasonably be expected to recur." United States v. Concentrated Phosphate Export Ass'n, Inc., 393 U.S. 199, 203 (1968). The "heavy burden of persuading" the court that the challenged conduct cannot reasonably be expected to start up again lies with the party asserting mootness. Ibid.

* * *

In its brief, Laidlaw appears to argue that, regardless of the effect of Laidlaw's compliance, FOE doomed its own civil penalty claim to mootness by failing to appeal the District Court's denial of injunctive relief. This argument misconceives the statutory scheme. Under § 1365(a), the district court has discretion to determine which form of relief is best suited, in the particular case, to abate current violations and deter future ones. "[A] federal judge sitting as chancellor is not mechanically obligated to grant an injunction for every violation of law." Weinberger v. Romero–Barcelo, 456 U.S. 305, 313 (1982). Denial of injunctive relief does not necessarily mean that the district court has concluded there is no prospect of future violations for civil penalties to deter. Indeed, it meant no such thing in this case. The District Court denied injunctive relief, but expressly based its award of civil penalties on the need for deterrence. As the dissent notes, federal courts should aim to ensure "the framing of relief no broader than required by the precise facts." Schlesinger v. Reservists Comm. to Stop the War, 418 U.S. 208, 222 (1974). In accordance with this aim, a district court in a Clean Water Act citizen suit properly may conclude that an injunction would be an excessively intrusive remedy, because it could entail continuing superintendence of the permit holder's activities by a federal court—a process burdensome to court and permit holder alike.

Laidlaw also asserts, in a supplemental suggestion of mootness, that the closure of its Roebuck facility, which took place after the Court of Appeals issued its decision, mooted the case. The facility closure, like Laidlaw's earlier achievement of substantial compliance with its permit requirements, might moot the case, but—we once more reiterate—only if one or the other of these events made it absolutely clear that Laidlaw's permit violations could not reasonably be expected to recur. The effect of both Laidlaw's compliance and the facility closure on the prospect of future violations is a disputed factual matter. FOE points out, for example—and Laidlaw does not appear to contest—that Laidlaw retains its NPDES permit. These issues have not been aired in the lower courts; they remain open for consideration on remand.

528 U.S. at 189, 192–94.

NOTES AND QUESTIONS

1. *Demonstrating mootness.* Consider *Laidlaw* in conjunction with the possible compliance measures a defendant may take after the filing of a citizen suit. When would it be "absolutely clear" that wrongful behavior would not reoccur? What steps would or should satisfy this mootness test? Installation of pollution control equipment? Adoption of thorough facility operation and maintenance training? Consent agreements with substantial financial penalties for later noncompliance? Sale of the facility to another company? Plant shutdown and demolition? Relinquishment of the environmental permit?

2. *Remedies. Laidlaw* suggests that once standing has been established by a plaintiff showing that there was a substantial likelihood of a continuing violation, federal judges possess a range of remedial options to deter future misbehavior by the defendant. Whereas a plaintiff has the burden of proving each element of standing, the defendant bears the burden of proving that a case is moot. In *Laidlaw*, unless it was "absolutely clear" that permit violations could not be reasonably expected to recur, the suit was *not* moot, and the judge had discretion to frame remedies.

3. *Capable of repetition, yet evading review.* An important exception to mootness doctrine applies to conduct that is "capable of repetition, yet evading review." If a challenged action does not remain in effect long enough to be fully litigated prior to its cessation or expiration, and there is a reasonable expectation that the same complaining party will be subjected to similar action again, litigation may proceed even after the action ceases or expires. Weinstein v. Bradford, 423 U.S. 147, 149 (1975). Thus, for example, a challenge to an annual catch limit for a commercial fishery does not become moot when the limit expires. See Greenpeace Action v. Franklin, 14 F.3d 1324 (9th Cir. 1992).

CLASS DISCUSSION PROBLEM: A FREEWAY IN DULUTH

In Duluth, Minnesota a proposed new highway is generating great controversy. In order to relieve the extremely heavy traffic demand in the downtown area, state and city officials have proposed the construction of a two-lane freeway from 10th Avenue East through 26th Avenue East. At its beginning point near 10th Avenue East the freeway will enter a tunnel and pass beneath Leif Erikson Park, for which it will be necessary to utilize 0.2 acres of parkland. After passing through the park, the freeway will follow the shore of Lake Superior to its terminus at 26th Avenue East.

Because the freeway is to be constructed with federal funds, the proposal calls into play the decision-making process under the Federal–Aid Highway Act, 23 U.S.C. §§ 101–156. Under this law the U.S. Secretary of Transportation cannot approve any state or local highway project for federal funding unless she finds that "such projects are based upon a continuing and comprehensive transportation planning process carried on cooperatively by States and local communities. . . ." 23 U.S.C. § 134. The state and local sponsors must develop transportation improvement plans which consider social, economic, environmental, and energy conservation goals as well as the probable effect on land use and future development. In addition, 23 U.S.C. § 138 of the Federal–Aid Highway Act states that before the Secretary of Transportation can approve any project involving the use of any publicly owned park, recreation area, wildlife refuge, or historic site, she must find that there is "no feasible or prudent alternative" to such use and that "all possible planning" has been carried out to minimize harm to the site.

The Secretary of Transportation has determined that the National Environmental Policy Act (NEPA) also applies to the freeway project, and to comply with both section 138 and NEPA a composite final environmental impact/section 4(f) statement (EIS) has been prepared (the origin of the section 138 requirements was section 4(f) of the Department of Transportation Act of 1966).

The EIS gives a detailed description of the affected parkland and lists seven alternative routes that avoid the park and explains why each of those was either infeasible or imprudent. The EIS also describes mitigation measures that are planned: when construction is completed, vegetation in and around the park will be replanted, and the Minnesota Department of Transportation has agreed to acquire an additional 2.3 acres of usable parkland from private owners, thus increasing the park's total size by 2.1 acres. The EIS also discusses plans for noise reduction and additional pedestrian' and bicycle trails.

Leif Erikson Park is also a historic site that is listed on the National Register of Historic Places pursuant to the National Historic Preservation Act (NHPA), 16 U.S.C. §§ 470 et seq.

In addition to the environmental review provided by NEPA, § 106 of the National Historic Preservation Act requires federal agencies, "prior to the approval of any Federal funds" for any project, to take into account sites and properties eligible for or included in the National Register and to ask for comment from the Advisory Council on Historic Preservation. 16 U.S.C. § 470f. Federal agencies are under an express obligation to locate all possible eligible sites that may be affected by any "undertaking." To fulfill this requirement they are to consult with the State Historic Preservation Officer. Section 110(f) of the NHPA requires that agencies, to the maximum extent possible, undertake such planning and actions as may be necessary to minimize harm to any National Historic Landmark that may be adversely affected by a project and to provide the Council with an opportunity for comment. 16 U.S.C. § 470f. An agency, however, is not legally required to follow the Council's advice. 36 C.F.R. § 800.6(c)(2). Section 106 does not indicate what action an agency should take.

Several individuals and groups still oppose the new freeway. First, the Northern Bell Telephone Company is protesting that the proposed tunnel will result in damage to its telephone equipment, leading to severe service disruptions to customers during and after construction. Second, the Minnesota Conservation Club (MCC), which has 856 members who live within a 100–mile radius of Leif Erikson Park, opposes both the tunnel under the park and the use of the city-owned shoreline of Lake Superior, which constitutes the last significant stretch of vacant shore lands within the city limits. The MCC argues that although the EIS/4(f) statement discusses alternatives to the use of 0.2 acres of parkland, there is no consideration of the impact of building the highway along the shore of Lake Superior, which will have a much greater adverse impact on the environment.

Northern Bell and MCC plan to file suit to ask for injunctive relief from the building of the freeway. What are their chances of success?

CHAPTER FOUR

ENVIRONMENTAL FEDERALISM

In the U.S. federal system, responsibility for and control over decisions affecting the environment are shared among federal, state and local governments. This chapter examines the contours and controversies over that distribution of power. The federal government obtains its regulatory power from the federal constitution. States possess, as an attribute of sovereignty, a generalized police power that supports environmental regulation in the absence of countervailing federal law. Local governments obtain their authority from the states. They often have primary responsibility for land use decisions.

SECTION 1. HISTORICAL AND THEORETICAL BACKGROUND

The appropriate division of power over environmental policy between national and state or local governments has long been debated. Environmental problems were once virtually the exclusive province of state and local law. Despite judicial expansion of federal powers in the early to mid-twentieth century, not until the 1970s did federal environmental regulation become pervasive. The explosion of federal environmental law in the 1970s was driven by growing recognition of the interstate effects of pollution, coupled with the widespread perception that states were not adequately controlling environmental harms. Although they imposed federal minimum environmental requirements and erected a substantial federal regulatory structure, the federal environmental laws of the 1970s retained an important role for the states. Many of them, including the Clean Air Act, Clean Water Act, and Resource Conservation and Recovery Act, relied on "cooperative federalism," setting minimum environmental standards but allowing states to assume responsibility for implementing those standards.

In the 1990s, the tides of federalism reversed. Beginning in 1995, the Supreme Court decided a series of cases cutting back on the scope of federal power. At the same time, political pressures for "devolution" of environmental authority to the states increased. These pressures helped drive the Republican takeover of Congress in 1994, and the "Contract with America" Republican agenda, centered on reducing the federal regulatory presence. Although the "Contract" did not produce any major environmental legislation, devolution of environmental power remains a major political issue, played out not only in the legislature but in the environmental agencies. States began to take up the slack, experimenting with a variety of environmental innovations even without the driving force of federal mandates, and sometimes even in open opposition to federal policy. Over the last ten to twenty years, the states have arguably been responsible for the bulk of innovation in environmental policy.

Decisions about the division of authority between federal and state government involve several elements. There are, as explained in detail in Sections 3 and 4 of this Chapter, legal limitations on the scope of both federal and state authority. Often, however, those limits are broad enough to encompass a range of possible choices about how to divide or combine authority. Choices among legally permissible alternatives might be made on the basis of judgments about the relative significance of state and federal interests, the relative capacity of state and federal institutions to address the problem, or some combination of the two. The excerpt below, from a groundbreaking early article, considers some of the challenges of identifying relevant interests and capacities.

Richard B. Stewart, Pyramids of Sacrifice? Problems of Federalism in Mandating State Implementation of National Environmental Policy

86 Yale L.J. 1196, 1210–22 (1977).

As a nation, we have traditionally favored noncentralized decisions regarding the use and development of the physical environment. This presumption serves utilitarian values because decisionmaking by state and local governments can better reflect geographical variations in preferences for collective goods like environmental quality and similar variations in the costs of providing such goods. Noncentralized decisions also facilitate experimentation with differing governmental policies, and enhance individuals' capacities to satisfy their different tastes in conditions of work and residence by fostering environmental diversity.

Important nonutilitarian values are also served by noncentralized decisionmaking. It encourages self-determination by fragmenting governmental power into local units of a scale conducive to active participation in or vicarious identification with the processes of public choice. This stimulus to individual and collective education and self-development is enriched by the wide range of social, cultural and physical environments which noncentralized decisionmaking encourages. * * * [T]he moral virtues of diversity have special force in the realm of environmental policy, for the condition of the natural environment and the corresponding nature and extent of commercial and industrial development profoundly shape patterns of life and perception.

In our nation, the factors favoring noncentralized decisionmaking have been powerfully reinforced by geography, history, and the structure of our politics. Nonetheless, the presumption in favor of decentralization has in recent years been repeatedly overridden by congressional legislation imposing federal standards and federal measures to control environmental degradation. * * *

A. *The Rationales for Centralization*

* * *

1. *The Tragedy of the Commons and National Economies of Scale*

The Tragedy of the Commons arises in noncentralized decisionmaking under conditions in which the rational but independent pursuit by each decisionmaker of its own self-interest leads to results that leave all decisionmakers worse off than they would have been had they been able to agree collectively on a different set of policies. States and local communities whose citizens desire environmental quality are also concerned with employment and economic growth. Given the mobility of industry and commerce, any individual state or community may rationally decline unilaterally to adopt high environmental standards that entail substantial costs for industry and obstacles to economic development for fear that the resulting environmental gains will be more than offset by movement of capital to other areas with lower standards. If each locality reasons in the same way, all will adopt lower standards of environmental quality than they would prefer if there were some binding mechanism that enabled them simultaneously to enact higher standards, thus eliminating the threatened loss of industry or development. * * *

The characteristic insistence in federal environmental legislation upon geographically uniform standards and controls strongly suggests that escape from the Tragedy of the Commons by reduction of transactions [sic] costs has been an important reason for such legislation. The statutory structure of federal environmental programs also reflects other economies of scale that help explain centralizing tendencies. Collection of data and analysis of environmental problems, standard setting, and (in some instances) selection of control measures involve recurring, technically complex issues; such steps can often be taken far more cheaply once on the national level than repeatedly at the state and local level.

2. *Disparities in Effective Representation*

* * *

Industrial firms, developers, union and others with incentives to avoid environmental controls are typically well-organized economic units with a large stake in particular decisions. The countervailing interest in environmental quality is shared by individuals whose personal stake is small and who face formidable transaction costs in organizing for concerted action. These factors tend to produce more effective and informed representation before legislative and administrative decisionmakers of interests favoring economic development as opposed to those favoring environmental quality. The technical complexity of environmental issues exacerbates this disparity by placing a premium on access to scarce and expensive scientific, economic, and other technical information and analytical skill.

The comparative disadvantage of environmental groups will often be reduced, however, if policy decisions are made at the national level. In order to have effective influence with respect to state and local decisions, environmental interests would be required to organize on a multiple basis, incurring overwhelming transaction costs. Given such barriers, environmental interests can exert far more leverage by organizing into one or a few units at the national level.

Centralized decisionmaking may imply similar scale economies for industrial firms, but these are likely to be of lesser magnitude—particularly if such firms are already national in scope. Moreover, effective representation may be less a function of comparative resources than of attainment of a critical mass of skills, resources, and experience. Industry and development interests can probably deploy these requisites regardless of whether decision is local or national. But a national forum for decision may greatly lessen the barriers to environmental interests' achievement of organizational critical mass, sharply reducing the disparity in effective representation.

* * *

3. *Spillovers*

Even if the "commons" problem were eliminated, decentralized environmental decisionmaking would remain flawed because spillover impacts of decisions in one jurisdiction on well-being in other jurisdictions generate conflicts and welfare losses not easily remedied under a decentralized regime.

The most obvious form of spillover is physical pollution. Prevailing winds or river flows may transport pollution generated in one state to another and visit damage there. These spillovers are in many instances pervasive and far-reaching. For example, a significant percentage of sulfate pollution in the eastern states is attributable to emissions originating hundreds of miles westward. Spillovers can also be psychic and economic. Environmental degradation in pristine areas often imposes substantial welfare losses on individuals in other states who value the option of visiting such areas or who take ideological satisfaction in their preservation. * * *

4. *Moral Ideals and the Politics of Sacrifice*

The groundswell of public concern with environmental quality that arose in the late 1960s had undeniable aspects of a moral crusade with powerful emotional, even religious, undercurrents. This development cannot be fully explained by utilitarian models that explain individual behavior in terms of calculated preference satisfaction. On the contrary, it partially reflects the sacrifice of preference-satisfaction in order to fulfill duties to others, or to transform existing preference structures in the direction of lessened dependence upon consumption of material goods and greater harmony with the natural environment. * * * The preservation of pristine areas may be understood in part as reflecting a special obligation to future generations (despite the fact that they may, in economic terms, be wealthier than we) to prevent the potentially irreversible loss of important categories of human experience. These measures to preserve natural environments, together with programs to protect endangered species, could also be viewed as an assumption of duties to nature. Alternatively, they could be understood as a deliberate renunciation of maximum economic progress in order to affirm a different view of the ends of human life to which the society should aspire.

National mechanisms for determining environmental policies facilitate, to a greater degree than their state and local counterparts, the achievement of commitments entailing material sacrifice; the moral content of rising environmental concern thus helps explain the increasing resort to centralized decision. Communities no less than individuals may be far more willing to undertake sacrifices for a common ideal if there are effective assurances that others are making sacrifices too. National policies can provide such assurances and also facilitate appeals to sublimate parochial interests in an embracing national crusade. * * *

B. *The Antithetical Rationales: Local Resistance to National Environmental Policies*

* * * Having catalogued the reasons favoring centralized determination of environmental policies, we are now in a position to understand more precisely the corresponding grounds of state and local resistance to such policies. For the virtues of federal dictation are matched by corresponding vices.

1. *Diseconomies of Scale*

While centralized decisionmaking may be necessary in order to overcome the commons problem and deal with spillovers, it also often generates burdens that are or will appear to be unjustified in particular localities. Federal environmental programs typically place heavy reliance on nationally uniform standards or controls. These uniformities, which reflect both political and administrative constraints in federal decisionmaking, impose economic and social costs on certain areas that are unnecessary or excessive in relation to the benefits obtained. For example, * * * [t]he nationally uniform technology-based discharge limitations in the [Clean Water Act] create regulatory "overkill" in many areas. Although the aggregate advantages of federal environmental measures may exceed the costs, particular localities will be loathe to enforce such measures when they involve local burdens that are not offset by local gains.

* * *

2. *The Impairment of Self–Determination*

Environmental interests may well enjoy relatively more influence if environmental decisions are shifted from the state and local to the national level. But this shift is accomplished at the expense of local political self-determination. Decisions about environmental quality have far-reaching implications for economic activity, transportation patterns, land use, and other matters of profound concern to local citizens. Federal dictation of environmental policies depreciates the opportunity for and value of participation in local decisions on such matters. The impairment of local self-determination is considerably aggravated when * * * local fiscal resources and governmental powers are conscripted by federal agencies. Nor is it clear that this loss of self-determination always purchases a net gain in social welfare. Even if unorganized interests (such as environmentalists) are underrepresented at the local level, they may well be * * * overrepresented at the national level.

    3. *National Ideals as "Pyramids of Sacrifice"*

    Moral crusades enjoy little credit with the nonbelievers who are taxed to underwrite such ventures. * * * Resistance and resentment may be heightened by the fact that many environmental programs distribute the costs of controls in a regressive pattern while providing disproportionate benefits for the educated and wealthy, who can better afford to indulge an acquired taste for environmental quality than the poor, who have more pressing needs and fewer resources with which to satisfy them. These circumstances may foster, and in part justify, a cynical attitude towards the moral justifications advanced by upper-middle class advocates for environmental programs which benefit that class disproportionately. The impairment of local political mechanisms of self-determination and official accountability involved in federally dictated environmental programs affords further grounds for resentment.

    * * * Aspects of national environmental policy might * * * be viewed as the insensitive imposition of sacrifices on local communities * * * (in particular the poor communities), for the sake of a national elite's vision of a better society. * * *

NOTES AND QUESTIONS

1. *National versus local regulation.* What rationales does Professor Stewart offer in favor of national environmental regulation? What counterarguments does he recognize in favor of local regulation? Which do you find more persuasive? Does it depend upon the problem? For which of the following environmental problems would you regard regulation at the national level as appropriate: drinking water quality; air quality; endangered species protection (does the answer depend upon the species?); preservation of open space; drilling for oil in federally-owned lands on the outer continental shelf, several miles offshore of the Gulf Coast states?

2. *Race to the bottom or healthy competition?* Professor Stewart describes the competition among states that may result in inefficiently low environmental standards as a tragedy of the commons. Others have dubbed this kind of destructive competition a "race to the bottom." Is the competition among states for economic development a "prisoners' dilemma," in which all states would be better off if they could cooperate, but each individually faces incentives to defect, reducing environmental and perhaps other standards to undesirably low levels? If so, one way to solve the dilemma would be to take away the defection option by imposing national minimum environmental standards.

    Although the race-to-the-bottom rationale is a common justification for national regulation, not everyone agrees that the states are locked into a prisoners' dilemma. Professor Richard Revesz argues that states set environmental standards on the basis of their citizens' willingness to trade environmental quality for changes in wages, taxes, and other goods. If that competition results in lower environmental standards in particular states, Revesz concludes, it does so not because of an inefficient race to the bottom but rather because the citizens are unwilling to bear the costs of higher standards. Richard L. Revesz, Rehabilitating Interstate Competition: Rethinking the "Race-to-the-Bottom" Rationale for Federal Environmental Regulation, 67 N.Y.U. L. Rev. 1210 (1992). Even if there is a race to the bottom, Professor Revesz contends that federal environmental regulation will only shift that race to another venue, such as taxes or worker safety.

Neither Stewart nor Revesz offers any empirical evidence to support their conflicting views about the likelihood that states will engage in a detrimental race to the environmental bottom. What factors might contribute to such a race? Is there competition among states for industrial facilities and other forms of development? Are developers in a position to bargain strategically, hiding from the states their willingness to comply with environmental regulations in order to induce the states to under-regulate? Based on a survey of regulators, Professor Kirsten Engel argues that policymakers overestimate the effect of environmental standards on industries' choices of location. Consequently, she contends, states may relax their standards more than necessary in their effort to attract industrial facilities. Kirsten H. Engel, State Environmental Standard–Setting: Is There a "Race" and Is It "to the Bottom"?, 48 Hastings L.J. 271 (1997).

One other piece of data is available. Although most federal environmental laws allow the states to adopt more protective standards, few have chosen to do so. Does that suggest that there is a race to the bottom, or that the federal standards are at least as stringent as the public desire?

3. *Uneven political power.* Professor Stewart argues that environmental groups may have more political clout at the national than at the local level. What might account for a stronger environmental voice at the national level? One possibility is that local decisions underestimate the environmental interest because the environmentally concerned public is unable to effectively organize at the local level. Another possibility, however, is that the electorate in some localities simply has less interest in the environment relative to other goods than the national electorate. A small logging community in Oregon, for example, may not value old-growth forests and their associated species as highly as the national population does. In the latter case, is it legitimate for the national electorate to impose its views on the locality? Under what circumstances?

Professor Revesz is skeptical of the claim that difficulties in organizing make national fora systematically more sympathetic to environmental interests than their state counterparts. Richard L. Revesz, Federalism and Environmental Regulation: A Public Choice Analysis, 115 Harv. L. Rev. 553 (2001). He argues that national organization is at least as challenging for environmental groups as organization at a state or local level, and that industry may even enjoy an advantage at the national level. He points out that at least some federal environmental regulation, such as tailpipe emission standards for automobiles, responded to industry's fears that state initiatives might lead to a proliferation of disparate standards. Finding that state records on environmental innovation correspond closely to the environmental voting records of their congressional delegations, Revesz concludes that states whose voters are committed to environmental protection are not disabled by "public choice pathologies" from responding to that commitment.

Is there any reason to suppose that one level of government or another will systematically be more friendly to environmental regulation over time? Might views at both levels fluctuate with electoral results? See William W. Buzbee, Contextual Environmental Federalism, 14 N.Y.U. Envtl. L. J. 108, 113 (2005). Nonetheless, Buzbee sees some consistent differences in state and federal incentives. States, he believes, are systematically more inclined than the federal government to favor economic growth because their revenues are more dependent upon that growth. Id. at 121.

4. *Spillovers.* It is widely agreed that interstate environmental externalities, such as air or water pollution that physically spills over state borders, justify national intervention. Stewart suggests that economic spillovers also play a role, through the race to the bottom. Further, he points out that there may be psychic spillovers from intrastate actions. Extensive development of Alaska's coastal plain, for example, would upset many people who have never visited Alaska. Is it legitimate to impose federal environmental standards on Alaska to prevent that sort of harm? Does it matter whether the federal government owns the land in question? Whether the people of Alaska had any effective say in which lands the federal government retains?

What about intrastate externalities? Suppose, for example, that prevailing winds carry air pollutants from a heavily populated coastal portion of a state to a less populous area, but not across a state border (something like this happens in California, where the winds carry pollution east from the San Francisco Bay Area to the Central Valley, but not beyond the Sierra Nevada mountains). Would federal intervention be justified to aid the citizens of the less populous area? What other avenues of relief might be open to them?

5. *Laboratories of experimentation.* Stewart does not mention one of the most frequently cited justifications for devolving power to the states: that they can act as laboratories for policy experiments, testing various approaches to common problems. Proponents of providing room for state-level experiments argue that failures are less costly at that level, and that interstate competition for people and businesses can provide an incentive for states to seek "optimal social policy." See, e.g., Robert A. Schapiro, The Varieties of Federalisms, in Navigating Climate Change Policy: The Opportunities of Federalism 35, 41 (Edella C. Schlager, Kirsten H. Engel and Sally Rider, eds., 2011). Other states and the federal government can learn from each others' experiences, allowing successful policies to diffuse from one jurisdiction to another. Continual experimentation may be especially important for environmental policy, because of the prevalence of uncertainty and ongoing change. See Kirsten H. Engel, Harnessing the Benefits of Dynamic Federalism in Environmental Law, 56 Emory L. J. 159, 182 (2006).

6. *Combining state and federal efforts.* The early debate about environmental federalism focused on a choice between federal or state and local authority, seeking to identify the best regulatory fit, either at a general level or for specific problems. Many environmental and constitutional scholars today, however, would argue that, for doctrinal, institutional and practical reasons, environmental problems typically cannot be resolved without the exercise of regulatory authority at both levels. Federal and state interests, authority, and capacities often overlap. See, e.g., Erin Ryan, Federalism and the Tug of War Within: Seeking Checks and Balance in the Interjurisdictional Gray Area, 66 Md. L. Rev. 503, 572–573 (2007); Robert V. Percival, Environmental Federalism: Historical Roots and Contemporary Models, 54 Md. L. Rev. 1141, 1178 (1995). The next Section focuses on "cooperative federalism," the dominant paradigm for combining state and federal regulation in the environmental arena.

7. *Climate federalism.* A topic of considerable interest right now is the roles federal and state (not to mention international) governments should play in addressing greenhouse gas emissions and adaptation to a changing climate. So far in the United States, Congress has been unable to produce any climate-change-specific legislation. Nonetheless, because some of the established environmental laws turn out to unintentionally address or have consequences for greenhouse gas emissions, some federal regulatory efforts are now underway. Some states and local governments have been quite active, adopting emission limits, cap-and-trade systems, planning requirements, renewable energy portfolio mandates, energy efficiency requirements, and other measures. Other states have so far sat on the sidelines, or even pulled back from previously adopted measures.

We will discuss limits on the legal authority of state and federal governments below. For now, assume that both levels have considerable authority to address both climate change mitigation (greenhouse gas emission limits) and adaptation (responses to environmental change caused by the accumulation of greenhouse gases in the atmosphere). What roles should be assigned to each level? What federal interests are at stake? What state or local interests? What special capacities or expertise could each bring to the problems of climate mitigation and adaptation? For discussion of both what has been happening and what should happen in terms of climate federalism, see, e.g., Vivian E. Thomson and Vicki Arroyo, Upside–Down Cooperative Federalism: Climate Change Policymaking and the States, 29 Va. Envtl. L. J. 1 (2011); Robert L. Glicksman, Climate Change Adaptation: A Collective Action Perspective on Federalism Considerations, 40 Envtl. L. 1159 (2010); Patricia E. Salkin, Cooperative Federalism and Climate Change: New Meaning to "Think Globally—Act Locally," 40 Envtl. L. Rep. 10562 (2010); Ann E. Carlson, Iterative Federalism and Climate Change, 103 Nw. U. L. Rev. 1097 (2009); Daniel A. Farber, Climate Adaptation and Federalism: Mapping the Issues, 1 S.D. J. Climate &

Energy L. 259 (2009); Richard B. Stewart, States and Cities as Actors in Global Climate Regulation: Unitary vs. Plural Architectures, 50 Ariz. L. Rev. 681 (2008); Holly Doremus & W. Michael Hanemann, Of Babies and Bathwater: Why the Clean Air Act's Cooperative Federalism Framework Is Useful for Addressing Global Warming, 50 Ariz. L. Rev. 799 (2008).

SECTION 2.   COOPERATIVE FEDERALISM

Many federal environmental statutes, notably including the Clean Air and Clean Water Acts, operate through a system known as "cooperative federalism" which "allows the States, within limits established by federal minimum standards, to enact and administer their own regulatory programs, structured to meet their own particular needs." Hodel v. Virginia Surface Mining and Reclamation Ass'n, 452 U.S. 264, 289 (1981). First developed in the context of federal benefits programs, cooperative federalism expanded to the regulatory arena with the environmental laws of the early 1970s, and became the regulatory model of choice in the late 20th century. It is now employed in contexts ranging from telecommunications regulation to health care. Philip J. Weiser, *Towards a Constitutional Architecture for Cooperative Federalism*, 79 N.C. L. REV. 663 (2001).

Cooperative federalism offers the promise of the best of both worlds: tapping centralized expertise, taking advantage of economies of scale and preventing destructive competition between states, while remaining sensitive to local conditions and desires. In practice, of course, the overlapping and sometimes imprecisely defined authorities typical of a cooperative federalism system can produce significant tensions. There are conflicts over who plays the primary role in interpreting standards, who has the final say in enforcement decisions, and whether challenges to state action must proceed through state institutions. Tensions may be both substantive, that is state and federal authorities may have different views about how the relevant law should be interpreted and applied, and dignitary, that is state authorities may feel that the state is not being accorded the respect it is due as a sovereign in its own right.

That sense may be exacerbated by the fact that, despite its label, cooperative federalism in practice rarely involves a truly equal partnership. Typically the federal government remains firmly in charge of setting policy goals, overseeing state progress, and in many cases even determining the range of policy tools states may employ. As the following case illustrates, federal dominance is often met with state resistance and resentment.

Alaska Department of Environmental Conservation v. U.S. Environmental Protection Agency

United States Supreme Court, 2004.
540 U.S. 461.

■ JUSTICE GINSBURG delivered the opinion of the Court.

This case concerns the authority of the Environmental Protection Agency (EPA or Agency) to enforce the provisions of the Clean Air Act's (CAA or Act) Prevention of Significant Deterioration (PSD) program. * * *

In the case before us, "the permitting authority" under § 7479(3) is the State of Alaska, acting through Alaska's Department of Environmental Conservation (ADEC). The question presented is what role EPA has with respect to ADEC's BACT determinations. * * *

I

* * *

The PSD program imposes on States a regime governing areas "designated pursuant to [42 U.S.C. § 7407] as attainment or unclassifiable." § 7471. An attainment area is one in which the air "meets the national primary or secondary ambient air quality standard for [a regulated pollutant]." § 7407(d)(1)(A)(ii). Air in an unclassifiable area "cannot be classified on the basis of available information as meeting or not meeting the national primary or secondary ambient air quality standard for the pollutant." § 7407(d)(1)(A)(iii). Northwest Alaska, the region this case concerns, is classified as an attainment or unclassifiable area for nitrogen dioxide, 40 CFR § 81.302 (2002), therefore, the PSD program applies to emissions of that pollutant in the region. * * *

Section 165 of the Act, 42 U.S.C. § 7475, installs a permitting requirement for any "major emitting facility," defined to include any source emitting more than 250 tons of nitrogen oxides per year, § 7479(1). No such facility may be constructed or modified unless a permit prescribing emission limitations has been issued for the facility. § 7475(a)(1). * * *

The Act sets out preconditions for the issuance of PSD permits. *Inter alia,* no PSD permit may issue unless "the proposed facility is subject to the best available control technology for each pollutant subject to [CAA] regulation ... emitted from ... [the] facility." 42 U.S.C. § 7475(a)(4). As described in the Act's definitional provisions, "best available control technology" (BACT) means:

> [A]n emission limitation based on the maximum degree of reduction of each pollutant subject to regulation under this chapter emitted from or which results from any major emitting facility, which the permitting authority, on a case-by-case basis, taking into account energy, environmental, and economic impacts and other costs, determines is achievable for such facility through application of production processes and available methods, systems, and techniques...."

§ 7479(3). * * *

Among measures EPA may take to ensure compliance with the PSD program, two have special relevance here. The first prescription, § 113(a)(5) of the Act, provides that "[w]henever, on the basis of any available information, [EPA] finds that a State is not acting in compliance with any requirement or prohibition of the chapter relating to the construction of new sources or the modification of existing sources," EPA may "issue an order prohibiting the construction or modification of any major stationary source in any area to which such requirement applies." 42 U.S.C. § 7413(a)(5)(A). The second measure, § 167 of the Act, trains on enforcement of the PSD program; it requires EPA to "take such measures, including issuance of an order, or seeking injunctive relief, as necessary to prevent the construction or modification of a major emitting facility which does not conform to the [PSD] requirements." § 7477.

Teck Cominco Alaska, Inc. (Cominco), operates a zinc concentrate mine, the Red Dog Mine, in northwest Alaska approximately 100 miles north of the Arctic Circle and close to the native Alaskan villages of Kivalina and Noatak. The mine is the region's largest private employer. It supplies a quarter of the area's wage base. * * *

In 1988, Cominco obtained authorization to operate the mine, a "major emitting facility" under the Act and Alaska's SIP. The mine's PSD permit authorized five 5,000 kilowatt Wartsila diesel electric generators, MG–1 through MG–5, subject to operating restrictions; two of the five generators were permitted to operate only in standby status. Petitioner Alaska Department of Environmental Conservation (ADEC) issued a second PSD permit in 1994 allowing addition of a sixth full-time generator (MG–6), removing standby status from MG–2, and imposing a new operational cap that allowed all but one generator to run full time.

In 1996, Cominco initiated a project, with funding from the State, to expand zinc production by 40%. [Cominco applied to ADEC for a PSD permit to allow increased operation of its standby generator, MG–5. ADEC proposed as BACT an emission control technology known as selective catalytic reduction (SCR), which reduces nitrogen oxide emissions by 90%. Cominco proposed an alternative which would add a seventh generator, and proposed as BACT an alternative control technology—Low NO_x—that reduces emissions by 30%. ADEC issued a draft permit applying Low NO_x as BACT for MG–5 and the additional generator.]

* * * "[W]ith an estimated reduction of 90%," ADEC stated, SCR "is the most stringent" technology. Finding SCR "technically and economically feasible," ADEC characterized as "overstated" Cominco's cost estimate of $5,643 per ton of nitrogen oxide removed by SCR. Using Cominco's data, ADEC reached a cost estimate running between $1,586 and $2,279 per ton. Costs in that range, ADEC observed, "are well within what ADEC and EPA conside[r] economically feasible." Responding to Cominco's comments on the preliminary permit, engineering staff in ADEC's Air Permits Program pointed out that, according to information Cominco provided to ADEC, "SCR has been installed on similar diesel-fired engines throughout the world."

[Nonetheless,] ADEC endorsed the alternative proffered by Cominco. To achieve nitrogen oxide emission reductions commensurate with SCR's 90% impact, Cominco proposed fitting the new generator MG–17 and the six existing generators with Low NO_x. Cominco asserted that it could lower net emissions by 396 tons per year if it fitted all seven generators with Low

NO_x rather than fitting two (MG–5 and MG–17) with SCR and choosing one of them as the standby unit. Cominco's proposal hinged on the "assumption ... that under typical operating conditions one or more engines will not be running due to maintenance of standby-generation capacity." If all seven generators ran continuously, however, Cominco's alternative would increase emissions by 79 tons per year. Accepting Cominco's submission, ADEC stated that Cominco's Low NO_x solution "achieve[d] a similar maximum NO_x reduction as the most stringent controls; [could] potentially result in a greater NO_x reduction; and is logistically and economically less onerous to Cominco."

[EPA wrote to ADEC, commenting that it must require SCR, having found it economically and technologically feasible. ADEC issued a second draft permit, again finding Low NO_x to be BACT.] ADEC conceded that, lacking data from Cominco, it had made "no judgment ... as to the impact of ... [SCR] on the operation, profitability, and competitiveness of the Red Dog Mine." Contradicting its May 1999 conclusion that SCR was "technically and economically feasible," ADEC found in September 1999 that SCR imposed "a disproportionate cost" on the mine. ADEC concluded, on a "cursory review," that requiring SCR for a rural Alaska utility would lead to a 20% price increase, and that in comparison with other BACT technologies, SCR came at a "significantly higher" cost. No economic basis for a comparison between the mine and a rural utility appeared in ADEC's technical analysis.

[EPA again protested. It suggested that ADEC include an analysis of the specific economic impacts of SCR on Cominco's operation. Cominco, however, declined to submit financial data, simply asserting that its debt load remained high despite continuing profits. ADEC issued the permit, approving Low NO_x as BACT. EPA immediately issued an order prohibiting ADEC from issuing the permit, and Cominco from making the modifications.]

* * *

III

Centrally at issue in this case is the question whether EPA's oversight role, described * * * extends to ensuring that a state permitting authority's BACT determination is reasonable in light of the statutory guides. Sections 113(a)(5) and 167 lodge in the Agency encompassing supervisory responsibility over the construction and modification of pollutant emitting facilities in areas covered by the PSD program. In notably capacious terms, Congress armed EPA with authority to issue orders stopping construction when "a State is not acting in compliance with any [CAA] requirement or prohibition ... relating to the construction of new sources or the modification of existing sources," § 7413(a)(5), or when "construction or modification of a major emitting facility ... does not conform to the requirements of [the PSD program]," § 7477.

* * *

All parties agree that one of the "many requirements in the PSD provisions that the EPA may enforce" is "that a [PSD] permit contain a BACT limitation." It is therefore undisputed that the Agency may issue an order to stop a facility's construction if a PSD permit contains no BACT designation.

EPA reads the Act's definition of BACT, together with CAA's explicit listing of BACT as a "[p]reconstruction requiremen[t]," to mandate not simply *a* BACT designation, but a determination of BACT faithful to the statute's definition. In keeping with the broad oversight role §§ 113(a)(5) and 167 vest in EPA, the Agency maintains, it may review permits to ensure that a State's BACT determination is reasonably moored to the Act's provisions. We hold, as elaborated below, that the Agency has rationally construed the Act's text and that EPA's construction warrants our respect and approbation.

BACT's statutory definition requires selection of an emission control technology that results in the "maximum" reduction of a pollutant "achievable for [a] facility" in view of "energy, environmental, and economic impacts, and other costs." 42 U.S.C. § 7479(3). This instruction, EPA submits, cabins state permitting authorities' discretion by granting only "authority to make *reasonable* BACT determinations," *i.e.,* decisions made with fidelity to the Act's purpose "to insure that economic growth will occur in a manner consistent with the preservation of existing clean air resources," 42 U.S.C. § 7470(3). Noting that state permitting authorities' statutory discretion is constrained by CAA's strong, normative terms "maximum" and "achievable," § 7479(3), EPA reads §§ 113(a)(5) and 167 to empower the federal Agency to check a state agency's unreasonably lax BACT designation.

EPA stresses Congress' reason for enacting the PSD program—to prevent significant deterioration of air quality in clean-air areas within a State and in neighboring States. That aim, EPA urges, is unlikely to be realized absent an EPA surveillance role that extends to BACT determinations. The Agency notes in this regard a House Report observation:

> Without national guidelines for the prevention of significant deterioration a State deciding to protect its clean air resources will face a double threat. The prospect is very real that such a State would lose existing industrial plants to more permissive States. But additionally the State will likely become the target of "economic-environmental blackmail" from new industrial plants that will play one State off against another with threats to locate in whichever State adopts the most permissive pollution controls.

H.R. Rep. No. 95–294, p. 134 (1977).

* * *

ADEC argues that the statutory definition of BACT unambiguously assigns to "the permitting authority" alone determination of the control technology qualifying as "best available." Because the Act places responsibility for determining BACT with "the permitting authority," ADEC urges,

CAA excludes federal Agency surveillance reaching the substance of the BACT decision. EPA's enforcement role, ADEC maintains, is restricted to the requirement "that the permit contain a BACT limitation."

Understandably, Congress entrusted state permitting authorities with initial responsibility to make BACT determinations "case-by-case." A state agency, no doubt, is best positioned to adjust for local differences in raw materials or plant configurations, differences that might make a technology "unavailable" in a particular area. But the fact that the relevant statutory guides—"maximum" pollution reduction, considerations of energy, environmental, and economic impacts—may not yield a "single, objectively correct BACT determination," surely does not signify that there can be no *unreasonable* determinations. * * * EPA claims no prerogative to designate the correct BACT; the Agency asserts only the authority to guard against unreasonable designations.

* * * We fail to see why Congress, having expressly endorsed an expansive surveillance role for EPA in two independent CAA provisions, would then implicitly preclude the Agency from verifying substantive compliance with the BACT provisions and, instead, limit EPA's superintendence to the insubstantial question whether the state permitting authority had uttered the key words "BACT."

We emphasize, however, that EPA's rendition of the Act's less than crystalline text leaves the "permitting authority" considerable leeway. The Agency acknowledges "the need to accord appropriate deference" to States' BACT designations, and disclaims any intention to "second guess state decisions," 63 Fed. Reg., at 13797. Only when a state agency's BACT determination is "not based on a reasoned analysis," may EPA step in to ensure that the statutory requirements are honored.[14] EPA adhered to that limited role here, explaining why ADEC's BACT determination was "arbitrary" and contrary to ADEC's own findings. * * *

Even if the Act imposes a requirement of reasoned justification for a BACT determination, ADEC ultimately argues, such a requirement may be enforced only through state administrative and judicial processes. State review of BACT decisions, according to ADEC, allows development of an adequate factual record, properly imposes the burden of persuasion on EPA when it challenges a State's BACT determination, and promotes certainty. Unless EPA review of BACT determinations is channeled into state administrative and judicial forums, ADEC suggests, "there is nothing to prevent the EPA from invalidating a BACT determination at any time—months, even years, after a permit has been issued."

It would be unusual, to say the least, for Congress to remit a federal agency enforcing federal law solely to state court. We decline to read such

14. According to the Agency, "[i]t has proven to be relatively rare that a state agency has put EPA in the position of having to exercise [its] authority," noting that only two other reported judicial decisions concern EPA orders occasioned by States' faulty BACT determinations. EPA's restrained and moderate use of its authority hardly supports the dissent's speculation that the federal Agency will "displac[e]" or "degrad[e]" state agencies or relegate them to the performance of "ministerial" functions. * * *

an uncommon regime into the Act's silence. EPA, the expert federal agency charged with enforcing the Act, has interpreted the BACT provisions and its own enforcement powers not to require recourse to state processes before stopping a facility's construction. That rational interpretation, we agree, is surely permissible.

* * *

Nor do we find compelling ADEC's suggestion, reiterated by the dissent, that, if state courts are not the exclusive judicial arbiters, EPA would be free to invalidate a BACT determination "months, even years, after a permit has been issued." This case threatens no such development. It involves preconstruction orders issued by EPA, not postconstruction federal Agency directives. EPA itself regards it as "imperative" to act on a timely basis, recognizing that courts are "less likely to require new sources to accept more stringent permit conditions the farther planning and construction have progressed." (July 15, 1988, EPA guidance memorandum). In the one instance of untimely EPA action ADEC identifies, the federal courts declined to permit enforcement to proceed. See *States v. AM General Corp.*, 34 F.3d 472, 475 (C.A. 7 1994). EPA, we are confident, could not indulge in the inequitable conduct ADEC and the dissent hypothesize while the federal courts sit to review EPA's actions.

* * *

IV

We turn finally, and more particularly, to the reasons why we conclude that EPA properly exercised its statutory authority in this case. * * *

EPA concluded that ADEC's switch from finding SCR economically feasible in May 1999 to finding SCR economically infeasible in September 1999 had no factual basis in the record. In the September and December 1999 technical analyses, ADEC acknowledged that "no judgment [could then] be made as to the impact of [SCR's] cost on the operation, profitability, and competitiveness of the Red Dog Mine." ADEC nevertheless concluded that SCR would threaten both the Red Dog Mine's "unique and continuing impact on the economic diversity" of northwest Alaska and the mine's "world competitiveness." ADEC also stressed the mine's role as employer in an area with "historical high unemployment and limited permanent year-round job opportunities."

We do not see how ADEC, having acknowledged that no determination "[could] be made as to the impact of [SCR's] cost on the operation . . . and competitiveness of the [mine]," could simultaneously proffer threats to the mine's operation or competitiveness as reasons for declaring SCR economically infeasible. ADEC, indeed, forthrightly explained why it was disarmed from reaching any judgment on whether, or to what extent, implementation of SCR would adversely affect the mine's operation or profitability: Cominco had declined to provide the relevant financial data, disputing the need for such information and citing "confidentiality" concerns. No record evidence suggests that the mine, were it to use SCR for its new generator, would be obliged to cut personnel, or raise zinc prices. Absent evidence of that order, ADEC lacked cause for selecting Low NO_x as BACT based on the more stringent control's impact on the mine's operation or competitiveness.

Nor has ADEC otherwise justified its choice of Low NO_x. To bolster its assertion that SCR was too expensive, ADEC invoked four BACT determinations made in regard to diesel generators used for primary power production; BACT's cost, in those instances, ranged from $0 to $936 per ton of nitrogen oxide removed. ADEC itself, however, had previously found SCR's per-ton cost, then estimated as $2,279, to be "well within what ADEC and EPA considers economically feasible." No reasoned explanation for ADEC's retreat from this position appears in the final permit. Tellingly, as to examples of low-cost BACT urged by Cominco, ADEC acknowledged: "The cited examples of engines permitted in Alaska without requiring SCR are not valid examples as they either took place over 18 months ago or were not used for similar purposes." ADEC added that it has indeed "permitted [Alaska] projects requiring SCR." Further, EPA rejected ADEC's comparison between the mine and a rural utility because "no facts exist to suggest that the 'economic impact' of the incrementally higher cost of SCR on the world's largest producer of zinc concentrates would be anything like its impact on a rural, non-profit utility that must pass costs on to a small base of individual consumers."

ADEC's basis for selecting Low NO_x thus reduces to a readiness "[t]o support Cominco's Red Dog Mine Production Rate Increase Project, and its contributions to the region." This justification, however, hardly meets ADEC's own standard of a "source-specific ... economic impac[t] which demonstrate[s] [SCR] to be inappropriate as BACT." In short, as the Ninth Circuit determined, EPA validly issued stop orders because ADEC's BACT designation simply did not qualify as reasonable in light of the statutory guides.

In its briefs to this Court, ADEC nonetheless justifies its selection of Low NO_x as BACT for MG–17 on the ground that lower aggregate emissions would result from Cominco's "agree[ment] to install Low NO_x on *all* its generators." We need not dwell on ADEC's attempt to resurrect Cominco's emissions-offsetting suggestion adopted in the initial May 1999 draft permit, but thereafter dropped. As ADEC acknowledges, the final PSD permit did not offset MG–17s emissions against those of the mine's six existing generators, installations that were not subject to BACT. * * *

We emphasize that today's disposition does not impede ADEC from revisiting the BACT determination in question. In letters and orders throughout the permitting process, EPA repeatedly commented that it was open to ADEC to prepare "an appropriate record" supporting its selection of Low NO_x as BACT. At oral argument, counsel for EPA reaffirmed that, "absolutely," ADEC could reconsider the matter and, on an "appropriate record," endeavor to support Low NO_x as BACT. We see no reason not to take EPA at its word.

■ JUSTICE KENNEDY with whom THE CHIEF JUSTICE, JUSTICE SCALIA, and JUSTICE THOMAS join, dissenting.

* * *

The majority holds that, under the CAA, state agencies are vested with "initial responsibility for identifying BACT in line with the Act's definition of that term" and that EPA has a "broad oversight role" to ensure that a State's BACT determination is "reasonably moored to the Act's provisions." The statute, however, contemplates no such arrangement. It directs the "permitting authority"—here, the Alaska Department of Environmental Conservation (ADEC)—to "determine" what constitutes BACT. To "determine" is not simply to make an initial recommendation that can later be overturned. It is "[t]o decide or settle . . . conclusively and authoritatively." American Heritage Dictionary 495 (4th ed. 2000).

The BACT definition presumes that the permitting authority will exercise discretion. It presumes, in addition, that the BACT decision will accord full consideration to the statutory factors and other relevant and necessary criteria. Contrary to the majority's holding, the statute does not direct the State to find as BACT the technology that results in the "maximum reduction of a pollutant achievable for [a] facility" in the abstract. Indeed, for a State to do so without regard to the other mandatory criteria would be to ignore the words of the statute. The Act requires a more comprehensive judgment. It provides that the permitting authority must "tak[e] into account" a set of contextual considerations—"energy, environmental, and economic impacts and other costs"—to identify the best control technology "on a case-by-case basis." 42 U.S.C. § 7479(3). * * *

To be sure, §§ 113(a)(5) and 167 authorize EPA to enforce requirements of the Act. These provisions, however, do not limit the States' latitude and responsibility to balance all the statutory factors in making their discretionary judgments. * * * When the statute is read as a whole, it is clear that the CAA commits BACT determinations to the discretion of the relevant permitting authorities. Unless an objecting party, including EPA, prevails on judicial review, the determinations are conclusive.

* * *

EPA insists it needs oversight authority to prevent a "race to the bottom," where jurisdictions compete with each other to lower environmental standards to attract new industries and keep existing businesses within their borders. Whatever the merits of these arguments as a general matter, EPA's distrust of state agencies is inconsistent with the Act's clear mandate that States bear the primary role in controlling pollution and, here, the exclusive role in making BACT determinations. In "cho[osing] not to dictate a Federal response to balancing sometimes conflicting goals" at the expense of "[m]aximum flexibility and State discretion," H.R. Rep. No. 95–294, p. 146 (1977), Congress made the overriding judgment that States are more responsive to local conditions and can strike the right balance between preserving environmental quality and advancing competing objectives. By assigning certain functions to the States, Congress assumed they would have a stake in implementing the environmental objectives of the Act. * * *

The presumption that state agencies are not to be trusted to do their part is unwarranted in another respect: EPA itself said so. As EPA concedes, States, by and large, take their statutory responsibility seriously, and EPA sees no reason to intervene in the vast majority of cases. In light of this concession, EPA and *amici* not only fail to overcome the established presumption that States act in good faith, but also admit that their fears about a race to the bottom bear little relation to the real-world experience under the statute.

The statute contains safeguards to correct arbitrary and capricious BACT decisions when they do occur. Before EPA approves a State's PSD permit program that allows a state agency to make BACT determinations, EPA must be satisfied that the State provides "an opportunity for state judicial review." 61 Fed. Reg. 1882 (1996). Furthermore, before an individual permit may issue, the State must allow all "interested persons," including "representatives of the [EPA] Administrator," to submit comments on, among other things, "control technology requirements." 42 U.S.C. § 7475(a)(2). To facilitate EPA's participation in the State's public comment process, the statute further provides that specific procedures be followed to inform the EPA Administrator of "every action" taken in the course of the permit approval process. § 7475(d). Any person who participated in the comment process can pursue an administrative appeal of the State's decision, followed, as mentioned, by judicial review in state courts.

* * *

* * * In the proper discharge of their responsibilities to implement the CAA in different conditions and localities nationwide, the States maintain permanent staffs within special agencies. These state employees, who no doubt take pride in their own resourcefulness, expertise, and commitment to the law, are the officials directed by Congress to make case-by-case, site-specific, determinations under the Act. Regulated persons and entities should be able to consult an agency staff with certainty and confidence, giving due consideration to agency recommendations and guidance. After today's decision, however, a state agency can no longer represent itself as the real governing body. No matter how much time was spent in consultation and negotiation, a single federal administrator can in the end set all aside by a unilateral order. This is a great step backward in Congress' design to grant States a significant stake in developing and enforcing national environmental objectives.

* * *

The broader implication of today's decision is more unfortunate still. The CAA is not the only statute that relies on a close and equal partnership between federal and state authorities to accomplish congressional objectives. Under the majority's reasoning, these other statutes, too, could be said to confer on federal agencies ultimate decisionmaking authority, relegating States to the role of mere provinces or political corporations, instead of coequal sovereigns entitled to the same dignity and respect. If cooperative federalism is to achieve Congress' goal of allowing state governments to be accountable to the democratic process in implementing environmental policies, federal agencies cannot consign States to the ministerial tasks of information gathering and making initial recommendations, while reserving to themselves the authority to make final judgments under the guise of surveillance and oversight.

NOTES AND QUESTIONS

1. *ADEC's position.* What precisely did ADEC seek? Did it claim authority to determine BACT free of any review or oversight? Would its position, if accepted by the courts, change the substantive outcome of this conflict, in other words, under ADEC's position would its determination that the "Low NOx" technology was BACT survive review?

2. *Practical exercise of oversight.* The dissent contends that review of ADEC's BACT determination should be confined to the state process, which was approved by EPA as part of the state's SIP. What problems would that holding pose for EPA? Is it feasible for EPA to follow and participate in state administrative proceedings on every permit application in every state? Should it be required to do so, at the risk of losing its opportunity for input? On the other hand, if EPA is not subject to the state's statute of limitations, will that create problems for state agencies and permittees? When would it be too late for EPA to challenge a state permit decision in federal court?

3. *Standards of review.* What standard of review applies to EPA's decision to approve or disapprove ADEC's determination? What standard of review applies to that decision? Should Alaska bear the burden of demonstrating that its preferred control technology is BACT, or should EPA have to show that the state's choice is not BACT? What are the potential advantages and disadvantages of placing the burden of proof on the state? On the federal government?

4. *The views of other states.* Other states were closely divided on this case. Thirteen, including California, joined an amicus brief supporting EPA, while eleven others supported Alaska. Why would states like California support an EPA decision that seems to limit state authority?

5. *Authority to interpret the law.* In general, as you know, federal courts give some deference to a federal agency's considered interpretation of the statutes it implements. Cooperative federalism adds a twist. SIPs under the Clean Air Act and water quality standards under the Clean Water Act are produced by the states but must be reviewed and approved by EPA, and become key elements of the federal regulatory scheme. Suppose the language of a SIP or a WQS is ambiguous and state and federal authorities adopt differing interpretations. Should a federal court defer to either view? If so, should the state or federal view prevail? In Arkansas v. Oklahoma, 503 U.S. 91 (1992), the Supreme Court held that EPA's reasonable interpretation of state water quality standards was entitled to deference despite the contrary view of the state because those standards "have a federal character." Do you agree? Does workable cooperative federalism require that holding? Could EPA require states to clarify any ambiguous provisions when it reviews SIPs and water quality standards?

6. *Federal funding and other incentives.* The federal government often makes funding available to the states as one "carrot" to induce them to play their role in a cooperative federalism statutory scheme. The extent of federal money available may play a critical role in determining the fervor with which states respond:

> The sad truth about the implementation of environmental law is that it is largely limited by what agencies (and sometimes third parties, such as private attorneys general) can afford to do. While the legal structure of cooperative federalism is very important, it is the funding for it that most controls the extent of participation by states. The strength of the inducement in cooperative federal relationships will depend on the significance of the funds at stake. Some programs such as [Clean Water Act] nonpoint source planning, are notoriously weak due to paltry funding. In contrast, the highway funds at stake in the [Clean Air Act] do induce states to participate in comprehensive planning and regional cooperation.

Robert L. Fischman, Cooperative Federalism and Natural Resources Law, 14 N.Y.U. Envtl. L.J. 179 (2005).

Although money is often crucial, it is not the only benefit states stand to gain from participation in federal environmental programs. They may also gain an increased measure of self-determination, as the Clean Air Act provides by allowing states substantial discretion in deciding how they will meet national air quality standards (see Chapter 10, Section 2B). They may even gain increased authority over federal actions. The Clean Water Act, for example, makes state certification that approved state water quality standards will not be violated a prerequisite to federal approval of activities which may result in a discharge to navigable waters. CWA § 401(a) (33 U.S.C. § 1341(a)). The Coastal Zone Management Act requires that federal actions be consistent with approved state coastal zone management plans. 16 U.S.C. § 1456(c).

7. *The benefits and costs of cooperative federalism.* Why did Congress choose a cooperative federalism approach in the CAA, CWA, and other federal environmental statutes? What does the federal government gain from this approach? What do the states gain? What, if anything, is lost, and by whom?

> Consider two opposing views. Michael Greve argues that:
>
> cooperative federalism is a rotten idea, its political popularity notwith-standing. Cooperative federalism undermines political transparency and accountability, thereby heightening civic disaffection and cynicism; diminishes policy competition among the states; and erodes self-government and liberty.

Michael S. Greve, Against Cooperative Federalism, 70 Miss. L. J. 557, 559 (2000). He would prefer a system that clearly assigned responsibility to either the state or the federal government. By contrast, William Buzbee emphasizes the benefits of cooperative federalism:

> A first benefit * * * is * * * the learning function. Federal and state actors learn from each other. Similar, but often slightly varied legal regimes, allow for some experimentation in implementation and enforcement, as well as mimicking of successes. * * * Overlap and interaction also provide structural and enforcement benefits. A federal minimum required level of protection, or bottom, allows states to resist race-to-the-bottom temptations. [T]his undoubtedly constrains some states that would prefer not to trade off other amenities or regulatory protections in their quest for economic vitality. However, for those states concerned with environmental degradation, federal standards create a benefit. During periods of lax implementation and enforcement, overlapping roles also keep the law meaningful and discourage wholesale legal disobedience. * * * Overlap of regulatory turfs * * * can provide a valuable antidote to inaction incentives. With numerous potential regulators, plus a citizen role under most laws, those most concerned about an environmental ill can assess which level of government might be best suited to take a desired action.

William W. Buzbee, Contextual Environmental Federalism, 14 N.Y.U. Envtl. L.J. 108, 122–127 (2005).

Which perspective is more compelling? With respect to the particular decision at issue in the *ADEC* case, what are the benefits of and drawbacks to allowing the states primary authority to identify BACT pollution control measures? To giving EPA the ability to oversee that decision to the extent permitted by the Supreme Court? To relegating EPA to the avenues for permit challenges provided by state law?

In general, does the current cooperative federalism approach take adequate account of federal and local interests, and of federal and local expertise and capacity? Are multiple diverse regulatory regimes desirable both to facilitate adaptation to local conditions and to facilitate future adaptation to changing conditions, much as genetic variation provides adaptive potential for animal and plant species? See David E. Adelman and Kirsten H. Engel, Adaptive Federalism: The Case Against Reallocating Environmental Regulatory Authority, 92 Minn. L. Rev. 1796 (2007). Does the current model allow too little room and incentive for development of effective state capacity? Can (and should) state leadership be encouraged without facilitating foot-dragging by states less interested in environmental protection?

SECTION 3.   SOURCES OF AND LIMITS ON FEDERAL POWER

Federal regulatory power must be grounded in the federal constitution. In the early years of the twentieth century, concerns about lack of constitutional authority inhibited robust federal regulation. Beginning with the New Deal, however, judicial decisions greatly expanded federal powers, allowing the expansion of federal environmental law in the 1960s and 1970s. By the 1980s, it was widely perceived that the constitution imposed virtually no limits on federal power to protect the environment. The pendulum swung back in 1995 when for the first time in 60 years the Supreme Court struck down a federal statute on grounds that it exceeded the constitutional limits of federal power. Today, there remains substantial uncertainty about where precisely the limits of federal authority lie.

CLASS DISCUSSION PROBLEM: PLEASANTVILLE SCHOOL

The city of Pleasantville wishes to construct a new high school to accommodate recent population growth. Pleasantville has identified only one suitable site, a 40–acre vacant parcel close to the population to be served, and has succeeded in passing a bond issue to fund construction.

A few days before the scheduled groundbreaking ceremony, Pleasantville learned that the school site harbors two rare birds, the jewel-necked hummingbird and the drab flycatcher. The hummingbird, which is found only within a twenty-mile region in and around Pleasantville, is tiny but visually spectacular, with iridescent blue, red, and purple markings on its head and neck. It draws birders from across the country and beyond to the nearby Hummingbird National Wildlife Refuge. Scientists have been studying the hummingbird's distinctive coloration, hoping to duplicate the unusual iridescence for paints. The flycatcher, as its name suggests, is nondescript. Only a very small number of highly dedicated birders have any interest in seeing it. So far as Pleasantville is aware, there are no ongoing scientific studies of the flycatcher. But its range is not as limited as the hummingbird's. The flycatcher is sparsely distributed across several states. It is believed that at least a few birds each year migrate from one population to another, crossing state lines to do so.

As the City Attorney for Pleasantville, you are in a difficult situation. The U.S. Fish and Wildlife Service asserts that the school cannot be built on this site without illegally "taking" the hummingbird and flycatcher, both of which are listed as endangered under the federal Endangered Species Act. The Mayor and City Council insist that a new high school is desperately needed, and this is the only available site. Can you successfully argue that the United States lacks authority to protect the birds against this project?

A. SOURCES OF FEDERAL POWER

1. THE COMMERCE CLAUSE

Among the powers of Congress enumerated in the federal constitution is the power "[t]o regulate Commerce * * * among the several States." Art. I, § 8, cl. 3. In the late 19th and early 20th centuries, the Supreme Court resisted congressional efforts to expand federal regulatory authority under the commerce clause. The battle came to a head over New Deal statutes governing wages and working hours of intrastate businesses. The Court at first held those statutes unconstitutional, ruling that Congress could only regulate activities with a direct effect on interstate commerce. A.L.A. Schechter Poultry Corp. v. United States, 295 U.S. 495 (1935). Shortly thereafter, however, faced with Roosevelt's Court-packing threat, the Court sharply reversed course. See, e.g., National Labor Relations Bd. v. Jones & Laughlin Steel Corp., 301 U.S. 1 (1937) (upholding the National Labor Relations Act against a commerce clause challenge). For sixty years after *Schechter Poultry*, the Court interpreted the commerce clause expansively.

In 1995, the Court reversed course, surprising many observers by ruling that a federal statute exceeded the commerce power. A 5–4 majority struck down the Gun–Free School Zones Act of 1990, which had made it a federal crime knowingly to possess a gun near a school. United States v. Lopez, 514 U.S. 549 (1995). The Court emphasized the need to find some judicially-enforceable limit to the commerce power. Id. at 567.

Five years later, in *United States v. Morrison*, 529 U.S. 598 (2000), the Court issued another 5–4 decision striking down a federal statute under the Commerce clause. *Morrison* dealt with the Violence Against Women Act, which created a federal cause of action for victims of crimes of violence motivated by gender. Noting that "[g]ender-motivated crimes of violence are not, in any sense of the phrase, economic activity," the Court rejected the claim that their aggregate effect on interstate commerce supported federal intervention. Again the Court emphasized the need to impose limits on the commerce power, lest it "completely obliterate the Constitution's distinction between national and local authority." Id. at 615.

The most recent Supreme Court case interpreting the Commerce clause may indicate that the Court has lost enthusiasm for narrowing federal powers. In Gonzales v. Raich, 545 U.S. 1 (2005), the Court upheld enforcement of the federal Controlled Substances Act against those who grow and use marijuana for medicinal purposes. While the challengers emphasized the local nature of their individual activities, the Court emphasized that those local activities are part of a larger economic class that together have a substantial effect on interstate commerce.

Raich has not greatly reassured the advocates of strong federal environmental regulation. The vote in *Raich* was 5–4, indicating that the law in this area is far from settled, and it is difficult to know how much it owed to the particular context of drug regulation. It has not silenced speculation in recent years that the Supreme Court's narrowed view of the Commerce clause could undermine federal environmental regulation. Most federal environmental law stands on indisputably solid constitutional foundations. Operations that produce goods for interstate commerce, or that produce air or water pollution that spills over across state lines, are clearly subject to federal regulation under the commerce clause. See Hodel v. Virginia Surface Mining and Reclamation Ass'n, 452 U.S. 264 (1981) (upholding federal Surface Mining Control and Reclamation Act on grounds that surface mining of coal diminishes usefulness of land and causes pollution and other environmental impacts that affect interstate commerce). Laws which extend to non-commercial activities and more local environmental impacts, however, may be more vulnerable to constitutional challenge.

Rancho Viejo, LLC v. Norton

United States Court of Appeals, District of Columbia Circuit, 2003.
323 F.3d 1062.

■ GARLAND, CIRCUIT JUDGE:

* * *

The Endangered Species Act (ESA), 16 U.S.C. §§ 1531 *et seq.*, is "the most comprehensive legislation for the preservation of endangered species ever enacted by any nation." *Tennessee Valley Auth. v. Hill,* 437 U.S. 153, 180 (1978). Finding that "various species of fish, wildlife, and plants in the United States have been rendered extinct as a consequence of economic growth and development untempered by adequate concern and conservation," 16 U.S.C. § 1531(a)(1), Congress passed the ESA "to provide a means whereby the ecosystems upon which endangered species and threatened species depend may be conserved," *id.* § 1531(b).

The ESA directs the Secretary of the Interior to list fish, wildlife, or plant species that she determines are endangered or threatened. 16 U.S.C. § 1533(a). Section 9 of the Act makes it unlawful to "take" any such listed species without a permit. *Id.* § 1538(a)(1)(B). "The term 'take' means to harass, harm, pursue, hunt, shoot, wound, kill, trap, capture, or collect, or to attempt to engage in any such conduct." *Id.* § 1532(19). The Secretary has promulgated, and the Supreme Court has upheld, a regulation that defines "harm" as including "significant habitat modification or degradation where it actually kills or injures wildlife by significantly impairing essential behavioral patterns, including breeding." 50 C.F.R. § 17.3.

* * *

The Secretary listed the arroyo toad as an endangered species on December 16, 1994. The toads live in scattered populations from California's Monterey County in the north to Mexico's Baja California in the south. They breed in shallow, sandy, or gravelly pools along streams, and spend most of their adult lives in upland habitats. The toads range no farther than 1.2 miles from the streams where they breed, and none in the area at issue in this case travel outside the state of California. Habitat destruction has driven the toad from approximately 76% of its former California range.

Plaintiff Rancho Viejo plans to build a 280–home residential development on a 202–acre site in San Diego County. The property is bordered on the south by Keys Creek, a major tributary of the San Luis Rey River, and is just east of Interstate 15. The company's construction plan is to build homes in an upland area of approximately 52 acres, and to use an additional 77 acres of its upland property and portions of the Keys Creek streambed as a "borrow area" to provide fill for the project. Rancho Viejo wants to remove six feet or more of soil from the surface of the borrow area, amounting to approximately 750,000 cubic yards of material, and to transport that soil to the 52–acre housing site to the north. Surveys of Keys Creek have confirmed the presence of arroyo toads on and adjacent to the project site.

* * *

In May 2000, Rancho Viejo excavated a trench and erected a fence, each running parallel to the bank of Keys Creek. Arroyo toads were observed on the upland side of the fence. In the FWS's view, the fence has prevented and may continue to impede movement of the toads between their upland habitat and their breeding habitat in the creek. On May 22, the FWS informed Rancho Viejo that construction of the fence has resulted in the illegal take and will result in the future illegal take of federally endangered arroyo toads in violation of the Endangered Species Act.

[FWS also] determined that excavation of the 77–acre borrow area would result in the taking of arroyo toads * * *.

Rancho Viejo [filed suit], alleging that the listing of the arroyo toad as an endangered species under the ESA, and the application of the ESA to Rancho Viejo's construction plans, exceeded the federal government's power under the Commerce Clause.

* * *

In *Lopez,* the Supreme Court considered whether a provision of the Gun–Free School Zones Act, 18 U.S.C. § 922(q)(1)(A), which made it a federal offense to possess a firearm near a school, exceeded Congress' authority under the Commerce Clause. 514 U.S. at 551. The Court held that the clause authorizes Congress to regulate "three broad categories of activity":

> First, Congress may regulate the use of the channels of interstate commerce. Second, Congress is empowered to regulate and protect the instrumentalities of interstate commerce, or persons or things in interstate commerce, even though the threat may come only from intrastate activities. Finally, Congress' commerce authority includes the power to regulate those activities having a substantial relation to interstate commerce, *i.e.,* those activities that substantially affect interstate commerce.

Id. at 558–59. With respect to the third category, the Court discussed four factors that led it to conclude that the activities regulated by the Gun–Free School Zones Act did not substantially affect interstate commerce.

First, the Court said, "the possession of a gun in a school zone ... has nothing to do with 'commerce' or any sort of economic enterprise, however broadly one might define those terms." *Lopez,* 514 U.S. at 560–61. Second, the Court observed that the Act "has no express jurisdictional element which might limit its reach to a discrete set of firearm possessions that additionally have an explicit connection with or effect on interstate commerce." *Id.* at 562. Third, *Lopez* noted that, "[a]lthough as part of our independent evaluation of constitutionality under the Commerce Clause we of course consider legislative findings, and indeed even congressional committee findings, ... neither the statute nor its legislative history contains express congressional findings regarding the effects upon interstate commerce of gun possession in a school zone." *Id.* Finally, the Court determined that the relationship between gun possession and interstate commerce was simply too tenuous to be regarded as substantial, and that if the government's arguments were accepted, the Court would be "hard pressed to posit any activity by an individual that Congress is without power to regulate." *Id.* at 564.

In [National Association of Home Builders v. Babbitt, 130 F.3d 1041 (D.C. Cir. 1997)], this circuit applied *Lopez* in a case challenging the application of the ESA to a construction project in an area that contained the habitat of the Delhi Sands Flower–Loving Fly. The fly, an endangered species, is found in only two counties, both in California. One of those counties reported to the FWS that it planned to construct a hospital and power plant on a site occupied by the fly, and to expand a highway intersection in connection with that work. The FWS informed the county that the expansion of the intersection would likely lead to a take of the fly in violation of section 9 of the ESA. Thereafter, the county filed suit against the Secretary of the Interior, contending that application of the ESA in those circumstances exceeded the authority of the federal government under the Commerce Clause.

A majority of the *NAHB* court held that the take provision of ESA § 9, and its application to the facts of that case, constituted a valid exercise of Congress' commerce power. The court found that application of the ESA fell within the third *Lopez* category, concluding that the regulated activity "substantially affects" interstate commerce. In so holding, the majority agreed upon two rationales: (1) "the loss of biodiversity itself has a substantial effect on our ecosystem and likewise on interstate commerce"; and (2) "the Department's protection of the flies regulates and substantially affects commercial development activity which is plainly interstate." *Id.* at 1058 (Henderson, J., concurring); *see id.* at 1046 n. 3, 1056 (Wald, J.). * * * Because the second *NAHB* rationale readily resolves this case, it is the focus of the balance of our discussion.[2]

* * *

The first *Lopez* factor is whether the regulated activity has anything "to do with commerce or any sort of economic enterprise, however broadly one might define those terms." *Lopez,* 514 U.S. at 561. The regulated activity at issue in *NAHB*—the construction of a hospital, power plant, and supporting infrastructure—was plainly an economic enterprise. * * * The

---

2. In focusing on the second NAHB rationale, we do not mean to discredit the first. Nor do we mean to discredit rationales that other circuits have relied upon in upholding endangered species legislation. We simply have no need to consider those other rationales to dispose of the case before us.

same is true here, where the regulated activity is the construction of a 202 acre commercial housing development.

Second, the court must consider whether the statute in question contains an "express jurisdictional element." *Lopez,* 514 U.S. at 561–62. Section 9 of the ESA has no express jurisdictional hook that limits its application, for example, to takes "in or affecting commerce." *Lopez* did not indicate that such a hook is required, however, and its absence did not dissuade the *NAHB* court from finding application of the ESA constitutional. * * * Rather, in a case like this, "[t]he absence of such a jurisdictional element simply means that courts must determine independently whether the statute regulates activities that arise out of or are connected with a commercial transaction, which viewed in the aggregate, substantially affect[ ] interstate commerce." *United States v. Moghadam,* 175 F.3d 1269, 1276 (11th Cir. 1999).

The third *Lopez* factor looks to whether there are "express congressional findings" or legislative history "regarding the effects upon interstate commerce" of the regulated activity. *Lopez,* 514 U.S. at 561–62. There are no such findings or history with respect to the specific rationale that we rely upon here, the effect of commercial housing construction on interstate commerce. But neither findings nor legislative history is necessary. * * * Rather, such evidence merely "enable[s] [the court] to evaluate the legislative judgment that the activity in question substantially affected interstate commerce, even though no such substantial effect was visible to the naked eye." *Lopez,* 514 U.S. at 563. As we discuss in the remainder of this section, the naked eye requires no assistance here.

The fourth *Lopez* factor is whether the relationship between the regulated activity and interstate commerce is too attenuated to be regarded as substantial. *See Lopez,* 514 U.S. at 563–67. Although Rancho Viejo avers that the effect on interstate commerce of preserving endangered species is too tenuous to satisfy this test, it does not argue that the effect of commercial construction projects is similarly attenuated. Because the rationale upon which we rely focuses on the activity that the federal government seeks to regulate in this case (the construction of Rancho Viejo's housing development), and because we are required to accord congressional legislation a "presumption of constitutionality," *Morrison,* 529 U.S. at 607, plaintiff's failure to demonstrate (or even to argue) that its project and those like it are without substantial interstate effect is fatal to its cause.

This conclusion is not diminished by the fact that the arroyo toad, like the Flower–Loving Fly, does not travel outside of California, or that Rancho Viejo's development, like the San Bernardino hospital, is located wholly within the state. As Judge Henderson said in *NAHB,* the regulation of commercial land development, quite "apart from the characteristics or range of the specific endangered species involved, has a plain and substantial effect on interstate commerce." [NAHB] at 1059. * * * Here, Rancho Viejo's 202-acre project, located near a major interstate highway, is likewise one that "is presumably being constructed using materials and people from outside the state and which will attract" construction workers and purchasers "from both inside and outside the state." *Id.* at 1048 (Wald, J.).

* * *

In *Morrison,* the Court considered a challenge to a section of the Violence Against Women Act, 42 U.S.C. § 13981, which provided a federal civil remedy for victims of gender-motivated violence. Concluding that the case was "controlled by our decision[ ] in *United States v. Lopez,*" the Court held that Congress lacked authority to enact the provision under the Commerce Clause. *Morrison,* 529 U.S. at 602. * * *

Rancho Viejo contends that *Morrison* stands for the proposition that whether the regulated activity is economic is not simply a factor in the analysis, but instead is outcome-determinative: that noneconomic activity, whatever its *effect* on interstate commerce, cannot be regulated under the Commerce Clause. Although plaintiff acknowledges that *Morrison* expressly declined to adopt a categorical rule against aggregating the effects of any noneconomic activity because a categorical rule was unnecessary to the outcome of that case, it argues that the Court "came pretty close" to adopting such a rule. Because the arroyo toad is not itself "the subject of commercial activity," *id.* at 15, Rancho Viejo argues that regulation of the toad fails *Morrison*'s (and *Lopez*'s) first factor.

But how close the Court came to embracing plaintiff's view is irrelevant to the disposition of this appeal, because the ESA *regulates takings, not toads.* * * *

* * * The ESA does not purport to tell toads what they may or may not do. Rather, section 9 limits the taking of listed species, and its prohibitions and corresponding penalties apply to the persons who do the taking, not to the species that are taken. In this case, the prohibited taking is accomplished by commercial construction, and the unlawful taker is Rancho Viejo.

Nothing in the facts of *Morrison* or *Lopez* suggests that focusing on plaintiff's construction project is inappropriate or insufficient as a basis for sustaining this application of the ESA. Both of those cases involved the regulation of purely noneconomic activity: the statute in *Morrison* regulated gender-motivated violence; the one in *Lopez* regulated gun possession. * * *

Here, by contrast, both the "actor," a real estate company, and its "conduct," the construction of a housing development, have a plainly commercial character. So too does the "design" of the statute: the ESA seeks in part to regulate "economic growth and development untempered by adequate concern and conservation," which, Congress found, had the consequence of rendering "various species ... extinct." 16 U.S.C. § 1531(a)(1). * * *

Rancho Viejo suggests that even if the regulated activity here is the taking of the toads through economic activity, that fact still does not end the matter. Although the ESA may *regulate* economic activity, plaintiff insists that the statute has a noneconomic *purpose*: the preservation of biodiversity, and, in this case, the preservation of toads that Rancho Viejo maintains are without commercial value. Asserting that to survive Commerce Clause scrutiny a statute must be aimed at economic activity and not simply regulate it for some other purpose, Rancho Viejo concludes that the ESA (at least as applied to its project) must fall. This argument suffers from a number of serious defects.

First, the ESA, like many statutes, has multiple purposes. Whether or not economic considerations were the primary motivation for the Act, there is no question that the commercial value of preserving species diversity played an important role in Congress' deliberations. As Judge Wald described in *NAHB*,"[t]he Committee Reports on the ESA reveal that one of the primary reasons that Congress sought to protect endangered species from 'takings' was the importance of the continuing availability of a wide variety of species to interstate commerce." 130 F.3d at 1050. Likewise, the Fourth Circuit has noted that "[c]ommittee reports and legislative debates have emphasized the importance of endangered species to interstate commerce." *Gibbs*, 214 F.3d at 494 n. 3.

* * *

Moreover, the Supreme Court has long held that Congress may act under the Commerce Clause to achieve noneconomic ends through the regulation of commercial activity. The first case in this line is *Champion v. Ames*, in which the Court upheld the constitutionality of a statute prohibiting the interstate transportation of lottery tickets, notwithstanding that Congress passed the statute "for the protection of public morals." 188 U.S. 321, 355–57 (1903). * * * Perhaps the most important of the subsequent cases is *Heart of Atlanta Motel, Inc. v. United States,* 379 U.S. 241, 261–62 (1964), in which the Court rebuffed a Commerce Clause attack on Title II of the Civil Rights Act of 1964. The Court acknowledged that "[t]he Senate Commerce Committee made it quite clear that the fundamental object of Title II was to vindicate the deprivation of personal dignity that surely accompanies denials of equal access to public establishments." *Id.* at 250. But the fact that Congress passed the statute to attack the moral outrage of racial discrimination did not lead the Supreme Court to find it unconstitutional. To the contrary, citing several of the cases discussed above, the Court held that the fact "[t]hat Congress was legislating against moral wrongs . . . render[s] its enactments no less valid." *Id.* at 257.

* * *

Rancho Viejo next argues that even if the taking regulated in this case is commercial in character, the ESA bans other takings that are not. Because the ESA's prohibition on takings applies as much to a hiker's "casual walk in the woods" as to the commercial activities of a real estate company, Rancho Viejo contends that the statute cannot constitutionally be applied to its taking of arroyo toads. Plaintiff's "overbreadth" argument is unavailing.

In *Lopez,* the Supreme Court noted that "where a general regulatory statute bears a substantial relation to commerce, the de minimis character of individual instances arising under that statute is of no consequence." 514 U.S. at 558. Hence, because much activity regulated by the ESA does bear a substantial relation to commerce, it may well be that the hiker hypothetical proffered by the plaintiff is "of no consequence" to the statute's constitutionality.

But we need not decide that question here because there is a more basic answer to Rancho Viejo's hiker hypothetical: it is not this case. Plaintiff characterizes its complaint as "fundamentally ... an as-applied challenge to the constitutionality of the Defendants' regulation of the 'taking' of arroyo toads under the ESA." And as we have already discussed, the particular application before us involves the regulation of Rancho Viejo's commercial real estate development, which falls well within the powers granted Congress under the Commerce Clause.

At oral argument, Rancho Viejo asserted that it has a different kind of "as-applied" challenge in mind. Plaintiff's objection, it said, is not confined to the application of the ESA to its development project, but "to the listing of this particular endangered species," the arroyo toad. In effect, plaintiff explained, "[w]e are facially challenging the listing of the arroyo toad." But this curious characterization is simply the plaintiff's attempt to have its cake and eat it too. The company would like us to consider its challenge to the ESA only as applied to the arroyo toad, which it says has no "known commercial value"—unlike, for example, Mark Twain's celebrated jumping frogs of Calaveras County. Yet it would also like us to regard that narrow challenge as a facial one, unconstrained by the fact that plaintiff is a commercial developer.

This artificially constructed "facial" challenge must fail. [T]o mount a successful facial challenge, the challenger must establish that no set of circumstances exists under which the Act would be valid. Because Rancho Viejo's own case represents a "set of circumstances" under which the ESA may constitutionally be applied—even to the lowly arroyo toad—plaintiff cannot shoulder the "heavy burden" required to prevail in a facial challenge. In effect, Rancho Viejo seeks to trade the shoes of a commercial developer for those of a weekend hiker. But permitting plaintiff to stand in the hiker's shoes would mean recognizing the kind of overbreadth challenge the Supreme Court has expressly forsworn.

* * *

Finally, Rancho Viejo draws our attention to *Morrison*'s declaration that "[t]he Constitution requires a distinction between what is truly national and what is truly local." 529 U.S. at 617–18. Plaintiff argues that the ESA represents an unlawful assertion of congressional power over local land use decisions, which it describes as an area of traditional state regulation. The ESA, however, does not constitute a general regulation of land use. Far from encroaching upon territory that has traditionally been the domain of state and local government, the ESA represents a national response to a specific problem of "truly national" concern.

In making these points, we can do little to improve upon the Fourth Circuit's opinion in *Gibbs,* which upheld, as a valid exercise of federal power under the Commerce Clause, an FWS regulation that limited the taking of red wolves. 214 F.3d at 487. As Chief Judge Wilkinson explained, regulation of the taking of endangered species "does not involve an area of traditional state concern, one to which States lay claim by right of history and expertise." *Id.* at 499. Rather, as the Supreme Court acknowledged in *Minnesota v. Mille Lacs Band of Chippewa Indians,* "[a]lthough States have important interests in regulating wildlife and natural resources within their borders, this authority is shared with the Federal Government when the Federal Government exercises one of its enumerated constitutional powers." 526 U.S. 172, 204 (1999). Moreover, while "states and localities possess broad regulatory and zoning authority over land within their jurisdictions, . . . [i]t is well established . . . that Congress can regulate even private land use for environmental and wildlife conservation." *Gibbs,* 214 F.3d at 500. Tracing a hundred-year history of congressional involvement in natural resource conservation, Chief Judge Wilkinson concluded that "it is clear from our laws and precedent that federal regulation of endangered wildlife does not trench impermissibly upon state powers." *Id.* at 500–01.

The Fourth Circuit also recognized the national scope of the problem posed by species conservation. Citing the ESA's legislative history, the court noted Congress' concern that "protection of endangered species is not a matter that can be handled in the absence of coherent national and international policies: the results of a series of unconnected and disorganized policies and programs by various states might well be confusion compounded." *Gibbs,* 214 F.3d at 502. As the *Gibbs* court explained: "States may decide to forego or limit conservation efforts in order to lower these costs, and other states may be forced to follow suit in order to compete." *Id.* at 501. And the Supreme Court, as the Fourth Circuit observed, "has held that Congress may take cognizance of this dynamic and arrest the 'race to the bottom' in order to prevent interstate competition whose overall effect would damage the quality of the national environment." *Gibbs,* 214 F.3d at 501 (citing *Hodel v. Virginia Surface Mining & Reclamation Ass'n,* 452 U.S. 264 (1981)).

For these reasons, the protection of endangered species cannot fairly be described as a power "which the Founders denied the National Government and reposed in the States." *Morrison,* 529 U.S. at 618. Rather, "the preservation of endangered species is historically a federal function," *Gibbs,* 214 F.3d at 505, and invalidating this application of the ESA "would call into question the historic power of the federal government to preserve scarce resources in one locality for the future benefit of all Americans," *id.* at 492. We therefore agree with Chief Judge Wilkinson that to sustain challenges of this nature "would require courts to move abruptly from preserving traditional state roles to dismantling historic federal ones." *Id.* at 504.

"Due respect for the decisions of a coordinate branch of Government demands that we invalidate a congressional enactment only upon a plain showing that Congress has exceeded its constitutional bounds." *Morrison,* 529 U.S. at 607. Rancho Viejo has not made that "plain showing" here.
* * *

■ GINSBURG, CHIEF JUDGE, concurring:

Although I do not disagree with anything in the opinion of the court, I write separately because I do not believe our opinion makes clear, as the Supreme Court requires, that there is a logical stopping point to our rationale for upholding the constitutionality of the exercise of the Congress's power under the Commerce Clause here challenged.

In this case I think it clear that our rationale for concluding the take of the arroyo toad affects interstate commerce does indeed have a logical stopping point, though it goes unremarked in the opinion of the court. Our rationale is that, with respect to a species that is not an article in interstate commerce and does not affect interstate commerce, a take can be regulated if—but only if—the take itself substantially affects interstate commerce. The large-scale residential development that is the take in this case clearly does affect interstate commerce. Just as important, however, the lone hiker in the woods, or the homeowner who moves dirt in order to landscape his property, though he takes the toad, does not affect interstate commerce.

Without this limitation, the Government could regulate as a take any kind of activity, regardless whether that activity had any connection with interstate commerce. With this understanding of the rationale of the case, I concur in the opinion of the court.

Rancho Viejo, LLC v. Norton

United States Court of Appeals, District of Columbia Circuit, 2003.
334 F.3d 1158.

■ JOHN ROBERTS, CIRCUIT JUDGE, dissenting from denial of rehearing en banc:

The panel's opinion in effect asks whether the challenged *regulation* substantially affects interstate commerce, rather than whether the *activity* being regulated does so. Thus, the panel sustains the application of the Act in this case because Rancho Viejo's commercial development constitutes interstate commerce and the regulation impinges on that development, not because the incidental taking of arroyo toads can be said to be interstate commerce.

Such an approach seems inconsistent with the Supreme Court's holdings in *United States v. Lopez,* 514 U.S. 549 (1995) and *United States v. Morrison,* 529 U.S. 598 (2000). The Court in those cases upheld facial Commerce Clause challenges to legislation prohibiting the possession of firearms in school zones and violence against women. Given *United States v. Salerno,* 481 U.S. 739 (1987), such a facial challenge can succeed only if there are no circumstances in which the Act at issue can be applied without violating the Commerce Clause. Under the panel's approach in this case, however, if the defendant in *Lopez* possessed the firearm because he was part of an interstate ring and had brought it to the school to sell it, or the defendant in *Morrison* assaulted his victims to promote interstate extortion, then clearly the challenged *regulations* in those cases would have substantially affected interstate commerce, and the facial Commerce Clause challenges would have failed.

* * *

The panel's approach in this case leads to the result that regulating the taking of a hapless toad that, for reasons of its own, lives its entire life in California constitutes regulating "Commerce ... among the several States." U.S. Const. art. I, § 8, cl. 3. To be fair, the panel faithfully applied *National Association of Home Builders v. Babbitt,* 130 F.3d 1041 (D.C. Cir. 1997). En banc review * * * would also afford the opportunity to consider alternative grounds for sustaining application of the Act that may be more consistent with Supreme Court precedent. *See Rancho Viejo, LLC v. Norton,* 323 F.3d at 1067–68 n. 2.

NOTES AND QUESTIONS

1. *Scope of the commerce power.* According to *Lopez*, what three categories of activities does the commerce clause permit Congress to regulate? Which of these categories is most likely to support environmental regulation?

2. *Aggregation of individually small effects.* Under what circumstances may activities whose individual effect on commerce is small be aggregated to find a substantial effect justifying federal intervention? Is it permissible to aggregate the effects of extinction of multiple species, or of all the activities that might "take" a single species? Should the focus be on the protected species or on the activities that might "take" it?

3. *Regulation of economic activity.* Because the criminal statute challenged in *Lopez* had "nothing to do with commerce or any sort of economic enterprise, however broadly one might define those terms," the Supreme Court concluded that it was "not an essential part of a larger regulation of economic activity, in which the regulatory scheme could be undercut unless the intrastate activity were regulated," and could not be upheld under the line of cases dealing with activities which, viewed in the aggregate, substantially affect interstate commerce. 514 U.S. 549, 561 (1995). Does the ESA have the requisite connection to commerce? How does the *Rancho Viejo* panel answer that question? Why does then-judge, now Chief Justice, Roberts disagree? For purposes of this question, is the relevant activity construction of a large-scale residential development; construction of a fence and excavation of a borrow pit; or the harming of arroyo toads? Does it matter?

4. *Historical pigeon-holing.* The majority in *Rancho Viejo* felt compelled to discuss at some length whether federal endangered species protection encroaches too far "upon territory that has traditionally been the domain of state and local government." The Supreme Court has encouraged that kind of distinction; federalism jurisprudence frequently seems to be trying to divide authority (and interests) into two distinct boxes: the national and the state or local. That may not be a very useful exercise, both because interests often overlap and because the historic locus of authority is often difficult to objectively identify. In *Rancho Viejo*, for example, the answer to the question of whether the federal government was stepping on entrenched state power or exercising its own traditional powers depends upon whether the power in question is defined as land use regulation (a traditional state power) or wildlife preservation (an area where both federal and state governments have been active for over a hundred years). Or consider the argument in Pacific Merchant Shipping v. Goldstene, 639 F.3d 1154 (9th Cir. 2011) (petition for certiorari filed, June 23, 2011), about whether California has the authority to regulate fuel use by vessels traveling beyond state waters in order to control air pollution. Should that be treated as air pollution regulation (an area where state regulation has the longer pedigree) or maritime commerce (long an area of exclusive or near-exclusive federal regulation)? Environmental regulation often straddles historic boundaries, limiting the usefulness of efforts to find the right historic box for resolving disputes about state versus federal power.

5. *The ESA and the commerce power.* Since 1997, five federal circuits have addressed the constitutional scope of federal power under the Endangered Species Act. All have upheld the challenged regulations, but they have not settled on a common rationale. In National Ass'n of Home Builders v. Babbitt, 130 F.3d 1041 (D.C. Cir. 1997), a fractured panel of the D.C. Circuit held that protection of the Delhi Sands flower-loving fly, a species found only within a small segment of California, was constitutionally permissible. In Gibbs v. Babbitt, the Fourth Circuit upheld an ESA regulation restricting the taking of reintroduced red wolves on private property by ranchers seeking to protect their livestock. In GDF Realty Investments v. Norton, 326 F.3d 622 (5th Cir. 2003), the Fifth Circuit upheld the protection of six species of cave-dwelling invertebrates, ruling that the taking of all endangered species could be aggregated to find a substantial effect on commerce. Each of these cases drew a vigorous dissent. The Eleventh Circuit, aggregating the effects of the ESA in total on commerce, upheld protection of the Alabama sturgeon (which it described as "one homely-looking fish to be found only with the greatest effort in one river system in one state") against a commerce clause challenge. Alabama–Tombigbee Rivers Coalition v. Kempthorne, 477 F.3d 1250, 1272 (11th Cir. 2007). Most recently the Ninth Circuit, in San Luis & Delta–Mendota Water Authority v. Salazar, 638 F.3d 1163 (9th Cir. 2011), upheld protection of the delta smelt, another species found in only one state, on the grounds that the ESA sets forth a comprehensive regulatory scheme with a substantial relation to commerce. Under *Raich*, the Ninth Circuit held, such a scheme is constitutional even as applied to some purely intrastate activity.

6. *Wetlands regulation and the commerce power.* Most commentators agree that wetlands protection is the other federal environmental program vulnerable under the commerce clause. Regulations adopted by the Army

Corps of Engineers and Environmental Protection Agency under section 404 of the Clean Water Act assert federal jurisdiction over all wetlands "the use, degradation or destruction of which could affect interstate or foreign commerce." 33 C.F.R. § 328.3(a)(3) (1999). In a 1986 interpretation referred to as the "migratory bird rule," the agencies explained that federal jurisdiction extended to wetlands used as habitat by birds which migrate across state lines, or by any endangered species. Is the migratory bird rule constitutional? Before *Lopez* and *Morrison*, two federal circuits upheld it. See Hoffman Homes, Inc. v. Administrator, 999 F.2d 256 (7th Cir. 1993); Leslie Salt Co. v. United States, 896 F.2d 354 (9th Cir. 1990). In Solid Waste Agency of Northern Cook County v. U.S. Army Corps of Engineers, 531 U.S. 159 (2001), the Supreme Court avoided the constitutional question, ruling as a matter of statutory interpretation that the Clean Water Act did not authorize the migratory bird rule. The scope of federal jurisdiction under the Clean Water Act is discussed in more depth in Chapter 11.

7. *Justifications for federal intervention.* Assuming that Congress *can* regulate to protect wholly intrastate species or wetlands, what principled ground is there for arguing that it *should* do so? Are there any circumstances in which the decision to protect intrastate resources should be left to the states? If Congress does mandate protection, who should bear the costs, including the opportunity costs of foregone development?

8. *Other environmental laws and the commerce power.* To date, no federal court has struck down any federal environmental law under the commerce clause. In addition to the ESA cases, post-*Lopez* decisions include United States v. Olin Corp., 107 F.3d 1506 (11th Cir. 1997) (upholding Comprehensive Environmental Response, Compensation, and Liability Act (CERCLA), which makes owners and operators of facilities contaminated with hazardous substances responsible for cleanup costs), and Allied Local and Regional Manufacturers Caucus v. U.S. EPA, 215 F.3d 61 (D.C. Cir. 2000) (upholding regulations under the Clean Air Act limiting the content of volatile organic compounds in paint and other architectural coatings).

2.   OTHER SOURCES OF FEDERAL POWER

The commerce clause has been the primary constitutional basis for most federal environmental regulation. Several other enumerated federal powers support environmental regulation, however. If the Supreme Court continues to restrict the commerce power, these other powers may become increasingly important.

The Treaty Power. The federal constitution grants the President, with the advice and consent of the Senate, power to make treaties. Art. II, § 2, cl. 1. Under the necessary and proper clause, Art. I, § 8, cl. 18, Congress has the power to make laws implementing treaties. The treaty power has long been thought to be above federalism concerns, such that legislation implementing treaties can extend into areas that otherwise would be beyond federal power. See Missouri v. Holland, 252 U.S. 416 (1920) (upholding the Migratory Bird Treaty Act under the treaty power, notwithstanding lack of federal authority to protect migratory birds before execution of the treaty). The treaty power is often cited in support of the Endangered Species Act, which was enacted in part to implement several international agreements. See 16 U.S.C. § 1531(a)(4); Gavin R. Villareal, Comment, One Leg to Stand On: The Treaty Power and Congressional Authority for the Endangered Species Act After *United States v. Lopez*, 76 Tex. L. Rev. 1125 (1998); Omar N. White, Comment, The Endangered Species Act's Precarious Perch: A Constitutional Analysis Under the Commerce Clause and the Treaty Power, 27 Ecology L.Q. 215 (2000).

The Property Power. Congress enjoys plenary power to "make all needful Rules and Regulations respecting the Territory or other Property belonging to the United States." Art. IV, § 3, cl. 2. This power allows Congress to protect natural resources, including wildlife, on federal lands. Kleppe v. New Mexico, 426 U.S. 529 (1976).

The Spending Power. The spending clause, Art. I, § 8, cl. 1, may be the broadest alternative to the commerce power. It gives Congress great discretion to expend funds to advance the general welfare, and permits it to impose conditions on the use of those funds. Conditions need not be within Congress' other powers, but they must be related to the purposes for which funds are expended. South Dakota v. Dole, 483 U.S. 203 (1987). Congress provides substantial funding to the states for a variety of environmental programs. It could couple that funding with environmental protection conditions, giving the states the choice of accepting the conditions or declining the funds.

B. LIMITS ON FEDERAL POWER

New York v. United States

United States Supreme Court, 1992.
505 U.S. 144.

■ JUSTICE O'CONNOR delivered the opinion of the Court.

* * *

I

We live in a world full of low level radioactive waste. Radioactive material is present in luminous watch dials, smoke alarms, measurement devices, medical fluids, research materials, and the protective gear and construction materials used by workers at nuclear power plants. Low level radioactive waste is generated by the Government, by hospitals, by research institutions, and by various industries. The waste must be isolated from humans for long periods of time, often for hundreds of years. Millions of cubic feet of low level radioactive waste must be disposed of each year.

Our Nation's first site for the land disposal of commercial low level radioactive waste opened in 1962 in Beatty, Nevada. Five more sites opened in the following decade: Maxey Flats, Kentucky (1963), West Valley, New York (1963), Hanford, Washington (1965), Sheffield, Illinois (1967), and

Barnwell, South Carolina (1971). Between 1975 and 1978, the Illinois site closed because it was full, and water management problems caused the closure of the sites in Kentucky and New York. As a result, since 1979 only three disposal sites—those in Nevada, Washington, and South Carolina—have been in operation. Waste generated in the rest of the country must be shipped to one of these three sites for disposal.

In 1979, both the Washington and Nevada sites were forced to shut down temporarily, leaving South Carolina to shoulder the responsibility of storing low level radioactive waste produced in every part of the country. The Governor of South Carolina, understandably perturbed, ordered a 50% reduction in the quantity of waste accepted at the Barnwell site. The Governors of Washington and Nevada announced plans to shut their sites permanently.

Faced with the possibility that the Nation would be left with no disposal sites for low level radioactive waste, Congress responded by enacting the Low–Level Radioactive Waste Policy Act. Relying largely on a report submitted by the National Governors' Association, Congress declared a federal policy of holding each State "responsible for providing for the availability of capacity either within or outside the State for the disposal of low-level radioactive waste generated within its borders," and found that such waste could be disposed of "most safely and efficiently . . . on a regional basis." § 4(a)(1), 94 Stat. 3348. The 1980 Act authorized States to enter into regional compacts that, once ratified by Congress, would have the authority beginning in 1986 to restrict the use of their disposal facilities to waste generated within member States. The 1980 Act included no penalties for States that failed to participate in this plan.

By 1985, only three approved regional compacts had operational disposal facilities; not surprisingly, these were the compacts formed around South Carolina, Nevada, and Washington, the three sited States. The following year, the 1980 Act would have given these three compacts the ability to exclude waste from nonmembers, and the remaining 31 States would have had no assured outlet for their low level radioactive waste. With this prospect looming, Congress once again took up the issue of waste disposal. The result was the legislation challenged here, the Low–Level Radioactive Waste Policy Amendments Act of 1985.

The 1985 Act was * * * based largely on a proposal submitted by the National Governors' Association. In broad outline, the Act embodies a compromise among the sited and unsited States. The sited States agreed to extend for seven years the period in which they would accept low level radioactive waste from other States. In exchange, the unsited States agreed to end their reliance on the sited States by 1992.

* * *

The Act provides three types of incentives to encourage the States to comply with their statutory obligation to provide for the disposal of waste generated within their borders.

1. *Monetary incentives*. One quarter of the surcharges collected by the sited States must be transferred to an escrow account held by the Secretary of Energy. The Secretary then makes payments from this account to each State that has complied with a series of deadlines. * * *

2. *Access incentives*. The second type of incentive involves the denial of access to disposal sites. States that fail to meet the [progressive deadlines established by the Act may be assessed increasing surcharges and eventually denied access].

3. *The take title provision*. The third type of incentive is the most severe. The Act provides:

> "If a State (or, where applicable, a compact region) in which low-level radioactive waste is generated is unable to provide for the disposal of all such waste generated within such State or compact region by January 1, 1996, each State in which such waste is generated, upon the request of the generator or owner of the waste, shall take title to the waste, be obligated to take possession of the waste, and shall be liable for all damages directly or indirectly incurred by such generator or owner as a consequence of the failure of the State to take possession of the waste as soon after January 1, 1996, as the generator or owner notifies the State that the waste is available for shipment." 42 U.S.C. § 2021e(d)(2)(C).

* * *

II

* * *

Petitioners do not contend that Congress lacks the power to regulate the disposal of low level radioactive waste. Space in radioactive waste disposal sites is frequently sold by residents of one State to residents of another. Regulation of the resulting interstate market in waste disposal is therefore well within Congress' authority under the Commerce Clause. Petitioners likewise do not dispute that under the Supremacy Clause Congress could, if it wished, pre-empt State radioactive waste regulation. Petitioners contend only that the Tenth Amendment limits the power of Congress to regulate in the way it has chosen. Rather than addressing the problem of waste disposal by directly regulating the generators and disposers of waste, petitioners argue, Congress has impermissibly directed the States to regulate in this field.

* * *

As an initial matter, Congress may not simply "commandee[r] the legislative processes of the States by directly compelling them to enact and enforce a federal regulatory program." Hodel v. Virginia Surface Mining & Reclamation Assn., Inc., 452 U.S. 264, 288 (1981). * * *

* * * We have always understood that even where Congress has the authority under the Constitution to pass laws requiring or prohibiting certain acts, it lacks the power directly to compel the States to require or

prohibit those acts. The allocation of power contained in the Commerce Clause, for example, authorizes Congress to regulate interstate commerce directly; it does not authorize Congress to regulate state governments' regulation of interstate commerce.

This is not to say that Congress lacks the ability to encourage a State to regulate in a particular way, or that Congress may not hold out incentives to the States as a method of influencing a State's policy choices. Our cases have identified a variety of methods, short of outright coercion, by which Congress may urge a State to adopt a legislative program consistent with federal interests. Two of these methods are of particular relevance here.

First, under Congress' spending power, "Congress may attach conditions on the receipt of federal funds." South Dakota v. Dole, 483 U.S. 203, 206 (1987). Such conditions must (among other requirements) bear some relationship to the purpose of the federal spending; otherwise, of course, the spending power could render academic the Constitution's other grants and limits of federal authority. Where the recipient of federal funds is a State, as is not unusual today, the conditions attached to the funds by Congress may influence a State's legislative choices. * * *

Second, where Congress has the authority to regulate private activity under the Commerce Clause, we have recognized Congress' power to offer States the choice of regulating that activity according to federal standards or having state law pre-empted by federal regulation. Hodel v. Virginia Surface Mining & Reclamation Assn., Inc., supra, 452 U.S., at 288. This arrangement, which has been termed "a program of cooperative federalism," Hodel, supra, 452 U.S. at 289, is replicated in numerous federal statutory schemes.

By either of these two methods, as by any other permissible method of encouraging a State to conform to federal policy choices, the residents of the State retain the ultimate decision as to whether or not the State will comply. * * * Where Congress encourages state regulation rather than compelling it, state governments remain responsive to the local electorate's preferences; state officials remain accountable to the people.

By contrast, where the Federal Government compels States to regulate, the accountability of both state and federal officials is diminished. If the citizens of New York, for example, do not consider that making provision for the disposal of radioactive waste is in their best interest, they may elect state officials who share their view. That view can always be preempted under the Supremacy Clause if it is contrary to the national view, but in such a case it is the Federal Government that makes the decision in full view of the public, and it will be federal officials that suffer the consequences if the decision turns out to be detrimental or unpopular. But where the Federal Government directs the States to regulate, it may be state officials who will bear the brunt of public disapproval, while the federal officials who devised the regulatory program may remain insulated from the electoral ramifications of their decision. Accountability is thus diminished when, due to federal coercion, elected state officials cannot regulate in accordance with the views of the local electorate in matters not pre-empted by federal regulation.

* * *

III

* * * Construed as a whole, the Act comprises three sets of "incentives" for the States to provide for the disposal of low level radioactive waste generated within their borders. We consider each in turn.

* * *

The Act's first set of incentives, in which Congress has conditioned grants to the States upon the States' attainment of a series of milestones, is thus well within the authority of Congress under the Commerce and Spending Clauses. Because the first set of incentives is supported by affirmative constitutional grants of power to Congress, it is not inconsistent with the Tenth Amendment.

In the second set of incentives, Congress has authorized States and regional compacts with disposal sites gradually to increase the cost of access to the sites, and then to deny access altogether, to radioactive waste generated in States that do not meet federal deadlines. As a simple regulation, this provision would be within the power of Congress to authorize the States to discriminate against interstate commerce. Where federal regulation of private activity is within the scope of the Commerce Clause, we have recognized the ability of Congress to offer states the choice of regulating that activity according to federal standards or having state law pre-empted by federal regulation.

* * *

The Act's second set of incentives thus represents a conditional exercise of Congress' commerce power, along the lines of those we have held to be within Congress' authority. As a result, the second set of incentives does not intrude on the sovereignty reserved to the States by the Tenth Amendment.

The take title provision is of a different character. This third so-called "incentive" offers States, as an alternative to regulating pursuant to Congress' direction, the option of taking title to and possession of the low level radioactive waste generated within their borders and becoming liable for all damages waste generators suffer as a result of the States' failure to do so promptly. In this provision, Congress has crossed the line distinguishing encouragement from coercion.

* * *

The take title provision offers state governments a "choice" of either accepting ownership of waste or regulating according to the instructions of Congress. Respondents do not claim that the Constitution would authorize Congress to impose either option as a freestanding requirement. On one hand, the Constitution would not permit Congress simply to transfer radioactive waste from generators to state governments. Such a forced transfer, standing alone, would in principle be no different than a congressionally compelled subsidy from state governments to radioactive waste producers. The same is true of the provision requiring the States to become liable for the generators' damages. Standing alone, this provision would be indistinguishable from an Act of Congress directing the States to assume the liabilities of certain state residents. Either type of federal action would "commandeer" state governments into the service of federal regulatory purposes, and would for this reason be inconsistent with the Constitution's division of authority between federal and state governments. On the other hand, the second alternative held out to state governments—regulating pursuant to Congress' direction—would, standing alone, present a simple command to state governments to implement legislation enacted by Congress. As we have seen, the Constitution does not empower Congress to subject state governments to this type of instruction.

Because an instruction to state governments to take title to waste, standing alone, would be beyond the authority of Congress, and because a direct order to regulate, standing alone, would also be beyond the authority of Congress, it follows that Congress lacks the power to offer the States a choice between the two. * * *

Respondents emphasize the latitude given to the States to implement Congress' plan. The Act enables the States to regulate pursuant to Congress' instructions in any number of different ways. States may avoid taking title by contracting with sited regional compacts, by building a disposal site alone or as part of a compact, or by permitting private parties to build a disposal site. States that host sites may employ a wide range of designs and disposal methods, subject only to broad federal regulatory limits. This line of reasoning, however, only underscores the critical alternative a State lacks: A State may not decline to administer the federal program. No matter which path the State chooses, it must follow the direction of Congress.

* * * Whether one views the take title provision as lying outside Congress' enumerated powers, or as infringing upon the core of state sovereignty reserved by the Tenth Amendment, the provision is inconsistent with the federal structure of our Government established by the Constitution.

IV

* * * [T]he United States argues that the Constitution's prohibition of congressional directives to state governments can be overcome where the federal interest is sufficiently important to justify state submission. * * * [But n]o matter how powerful the federal interest involved, the Constitution simply does not give Congress the authority to require the States to regulate. The Constitution instead gives Congress the authority to regulate matters directly and to pre-empt contrary state regulation. Where a federal

interest is sufficiently strong to cause Congress to legislate, it must do so directly; it may not conscript state governments as its agents.

* * *

The sited State respondents focus their attention on the process by which the Act was formulated. They correctly observe that public officials representing the State of New York lent their support to the Act's enactment. Respondents note that the Act embodies a bargain among the sited and unsited States, a compromise to which New York was a willing participant and from which New York has reaped much benefit. Respondents then pose what appears at first to be a troubling question: How can a federal statute be found an unconstitutional infringement of State sovereignty when state officials consented to the statute's enactment?

The answer follows from an understanding of the fundamental purpose served by our Government's federal structure. The Constitution does not protect the sovereignty of States for the benefit of the States or state governments as abstract political entities, or even for the benefit of the public officials governing the States. To the contrary, the Constitution divides authority between federal and state governments for the protection of individuals. * * *

[T]he facts of these cases raise the possibility that powerful incentives might lead both federal and state officials to view departures from the federal structure to be in their personal interests. Most citizens recognize the need for radioactive waste disposal sites, but few want sites near their homes. As a result, while it would be well within the authority of either federal or state officials to choose where the disposal sites will be, it is likely to be in the political interest of each individual official to avoid being held accountable to the voters for the choice of location. If a federal official is faced with the alternatives of choosing a location or directing the States to do it, the official may well prefer the latter, as a means of shifting responsibility for the eventual decision. If a state official is faced with the same set of alternatives—choosing a location or having Congress direct the choice of a location—the state official may also prefer the latter, as it may permit the avoidance of personal responsibility. The interests of public officials thus may not coincide with the Constitution's intergovernmental allocation of authority. Where state officials purport to submit to the direction of Congress in this manner, federalism is hardly being advanced.

* * *

■ JUSTICE WHITE, with whom JUSTICE BLACKMUN and JUSTICE STEVENS join, concurring in part and dissenting in part.

* * *

My disagreement with the Court's analysis begins at the basic descriptive level of how the legislation at issue in this case came to be enacted. * * * The Low–Level Radioactive Waste Policy Act of 1980 (1980 Act) and its amendatory Act of 1985 resulted from the efforts of state leaders to achieve a state-based set of remedies to the waste problem. They sought not federal pre-emption or intervention, but rather congressional sanction of interstate compromises they had reached.

* * *

Ultimately, I suppose, the entire structure of our federal constitutional government can be traced to an interest in establishing checks and balances to prevent the exercise of tyranny against individuals. But these fears seem extremely far distant to me in a situation such as this. We face a crisis of national proportions in the disposal of low-level radioactive waste, and Congress has acceded to the wishes of the States by permitting local decisionmaking rather than imposing a solution from Washington. New York itself participated and supported passage of this legislation at both the gubernatorial and federal representative levels, and then enacted state laws specifically to comply with the deadlines and timetables agreed upon by the States in the 1985 Act. For me, the Court's civics lecture has a decidedly hollow ring at a time when action, rather than rhetoric, is needed to solve a national problem.

* * *

■ JUSTICE STEVENS, concurring in part and dissenting in part.

* * *

The notion that Congress does not have the power to issue "a simple command to state governments to implement legislation enacted by Congress," is incorrect and unsound. There is no such limitation in the Constitution. * * * To the contrary, the Federal Government directs state governments in many realms. The Government regulates state-operated railroads, state school systems, state prisons, state elections, and a host of other state functions. I see no reason why Congress may not also command the States to enforce federal water and air quality standards or federal standards for the disposition of low-level radioactive wastes.

NOTES AND QUESTIONS

1. *A national problem?* Is the problem of low-level radioactive waste disposal one that demands a national solution? Why? Does it pose a prisoner's dilemma for the states?

2. *Finding a solution.* What options did Congress have to solve this problem? Why do you think the Low Level Radioactive Waste Policy Act and the 1985 amendments to the Act took the particular form they did? *New York* upheld the Act's monetary incentives for siting, as well as the provision allowing sited states to deny unsited states access to disposal facilities, but invalidated the take title provision. Would you expect the Act to be effective without its heaviest regulatory "stick"? Does Congress have any other sticks it might use to apply pressure on unsited states?

Since *New York v. U.S.*, only one new low-level radioactive waste disposal facility has been licensed in the U.S. That facility, located in Clive,

Utah, and operated by EnergySolutions, currently disposes of most of the low-level radioactive waste generated in the U.S. by volume. Under the terms of the Northwest Interstate Compact on Low–Level Radioactive Waste, to which Utah belongs, the Clive facility may not accept waste from outside the Compact states without an affirmative vote of two-thirds of the member states, and any decision to accept out-of-compact waste is subject to the host state's veto. Seven states and the District of Columbia are currently not members of any compact; several of the non-compact states withdrew or were expelled from compacts after they were chosen as site hosts. Those withdrawals have in some cases led to litigation that is not yet fully resolved. See Alabama v. North Carolina, ___ U.S. ___, 130 S.Ct. 2295 (2010).

3. *Political accountability and the Tenth Amendment.* In *New York*, the Court wrote that allowing the federal government to compel state regulation diminishes the accountability of both state and federal officials. Do you agree that state officials "will bear the brunt of public disapproval" under those circumstances, while federal officials "remain insulated from the electoral ramifications of their decision"? Does use of the spending power to "encourage" state legislation create the same accountability problems?

4. *Enforcing state compromises.* The majority concedes that New York supported enactment of the statute it challenged in this case. Why doesn't that bar the Tenth Amendment claim? Could the Court have distinguished "compromise" legislation imposed at the request of the states from legislation imposed by the federal government contrary to the wishes of the states, or imposed at the request of some states over the objection of others? Could this problem be solved by a nationwide interstate compact?

5. *Encouragement versus coercion.* The Tenth Amendment permits federal "encouragement" of state regulation but prohibits federal "coercion." As the Fifth Circuit has put it, so long as "the fact that the alternative [to implementing a federal regulatory program] is difficult, expensive or otherwise unappealing is insufficient to establish a Tenth Amendment violation." City of Abilene v. EPA, 325 F.3d 657, 662 (5th Cir. 2003). According to the *New York* majority, what distinguishes impermissible coercion from permissible encouragement? Do you find the distinction persuasive? Could withdrawal of federal funds ever amount to "coercion"? See South Dakota v. Dole, 483 U.S. 203, 211 (1987).

6. *Co-opting state actors.* In Printz v. United States, 521 U.S. 898 (1997), a 5–4 majority of the Court invalidated a federal statute requiring local law enforcement officers to perform background checks on prospective handgun purchasers. The Court rejected the government's argument that although states could not be compelled to make policy (under *New York*), they could be compelled to undertake ministerial acts to implement federal policy.

7. *The Tenth Amendment and other environmental statutes.* Can Congress require that states establish a program for detecting and remedying lead contamination in water coolers in schools and day-care centers? See ACORN v. Edwards, 81 F.3d 1387 (5th Cir. 1996) (no). That they relax their general rules of judicial standing in air pollution cases, on pain of loss

of federal highway funds, limitations on construction of new pollution sources, and federal assumption of the state's air pollution control program? See Commonwealth of Virginia v. Browner, 80 F.3d 869 (4th Cir. 1996) (yes). That, if they regulate fishing activity within their boundaries, they prohibit fishing methods harmful to endangered species, or themselves face liability under of the Endangered Species Act? See Strahan v. Coxe, 127 F.3d 155 (1st Cir. 1997) (yes). That municipalities obtain NPDES permits for their storm sewer system discharges, and that EPA's preferred permit format requires that permittees implement specific steps to detect and eliminate illicit discharges? See Environmental Defense Center v. EPA, 344 F.3d 832 (9th Cir. 2003) (yes, because municipalities can pursue an alternate permitting procedure under which they would be subject only to end-of-the-pipe numeric discharge limits). In the last example, would the permit requirement violate the Tenth Amendment if EPA eliminated the alternate procedure, or is the fact that a municipality could choose not to have a storm sewer system sufficient to avoid a constitutional problem?

SECTION 4. LIMITS ON STATE POWER

A. THE DORMANT COMMERCE CLAUSE

United Haulers Association v. Oneida–Herkimer Solid Waste Management Authority

United States Supreme Court, 2007.
550 U.S. 330.

■ CHIEF JUSTICE ROBERTS delivered the opinion of the Court * * *.

* * *

Located in central New York, Oneida and Herkimer Counties span over 2,600 square miles and are home to about 306,000 residents. Traditionally, each city, town, or village within the Counties has been responsible for disposing of its own waste. Many had relied on local landfills, some in a more environmentally responsible fashion than others.

By the 1980s, the Counties confronted what they could credibly call a solid waste "crisis." Many local landfills were operating without permits and in violation of state regulations. Sixteen were ordered to close and remediate the surrounding environment, costing the public tens of millions of dollars. These environmental problems culminated in a federal clean-up action against a landfill in Oneida County; the defendants in that case named over 600 local businesses and several municipalities and school districts as third-party defendants.

The "crisis" extended beyond health and safety concerns. The Counties had an uneasy relationship with local waste management companies, enduring price fixing, pervasive overcharging, and the influence of organized crime. Dramatic price hikes were not uncommon: In 1986, for example, a county contractor doubled its waste disposal rate on six weeks' notice.

Responding to these problems, the Counties requested and New York's Legislature and Governor created the Oneida–Herkimer Solid Waste Management Authority (Authority), a public benefit corporation. The Authority is empowered to collect, process, and dispose of solid waste generated in the Counties. * * *

In 1989, the Authority and the Counties entered into a Solid Waste Management Agreement, under which the Authority agreed to manage all solid waste within the Counties. Private haulers would remain free to pick up citizens' trash from the curb, but the Authority would take over the job of processing the trash, sorting it, and sending it off for disposal. To fulfill its part of the bargain, the Authority agreed to purchase and develop facilities for the processing and disposal of solid waste and recyclables generated in the Counties.

The Authority collected "tipping fees" to cover its operating and maintenance costs for these facilities.[3] The tipping fees significantly exceeded those charged for waste removal on the open market, but they allowed the Authority to do more than the average private waste disposer. In addition to landfill transportation and solid waste disposal, the fees enabled the Authority to provide recycling of 33 kinds of materials, as well as composting, household hazardous waste disposal, and a number of other services. If the Authority's operating costs and debt service were not recouped through tipping fees and other charges, the agreement provided that the Counties would make up the difference.

As described, the agreement had a flaw: Citizens might opt to have their waste hauled to facilities with lower tipping fees. To avoid being stuck with the bill for facilities that citizens voted for but then chose not to use, the Counties enacted "flow control" ordinances requiring that all solid waste generated within the Counties be delivered to the Authority's processing sites. Private haulers must obtain a permit from the Authority to collect waste in the Counties. Penalties for noncompliance with the ordinances include permit revocation, fines, and imprisonment.

Petitioners are United Haulers Association, Inc., a trade association made up of solid waste management companies, and six haulers that operated in Oneida and Herkimer Counties when this action was filed. In 1995, they sued the Counties and the Authority under 42 U.S.C. § 1983, alleging that the flow control laws violate the Commerce Clause by discriminating against interstate commerce. They submitted evidence that without the flow control laws and the associated $86–per–ton tipping fees, they

---

3. Tipping fees are disposal charges levied against collectors who drop off waste at a processing facility. They are called "tipping" fees because garbage trucks literally tip their back end to dump out the carried waste. As of 1995, haulers in the Counties had to pay tipping fees of at least $86 per ton, a price that ballooned to as much as $172 per ton if a particular load contained more than 25% recyclables.

could dispose of solid waste at out-of-state facilities for between $37 and $55 per ton, including transportation.

* * *

The Commerce Clause provides that "Congress shall have Power . . . [t]o regulate Commerce with foreign Nations, and among the several States." U.S. Const., Art. I, § 8, cl. 3. Although the Constitution does not in terms limit the power of States to regulate commerce, we have long interpreted the Commerce Clause as an implicit restraint on state authority, even in the absence of a conflicting federal statute.

To determine whether a law violates this so-called "dormant" aspect of the Commerce Clause, we first ask whether it discriminates on its face against interstate commerce. In this context, "discrimination simply means differential treatment of in-state and out-of-state economic interests that benefits the former and burdens the latter." *Oregon Waste Systems, Inc. v. Department of Environmental Quality of Ore.*, 511 U.S. 93, 99 (1994). Discriminatory laws motivated by "simple economic protectionism" are subject to a "virtually *per se* rule of invalidity," *Philadelphia v. New Jersey*, 437 U.S. 617, 624 (1978), which can only be overcome by a showing that the State has no other means to advance a legitimate local purpose, *Maine v. Taylor*, 477 U.S. 131, 138 (1986).

* * * [T]he haulers argue vigorously that the Counties' ordinances discriminate against interstate commerce under *Carbone*. In *Carbone*, the town of Clarkstown, New York, hired a private contractor to build a waste transfer station. According to the terms of the deal, the contractor would operate the facility for five years, charging an above-market tipping fee of $81 per ton; after five years, the town would buy the facility for one dollar. The town guaranteed that the facility would receive a certain volume of trash per year. To make good on its promise, Clarkstown passed a flow control ordinance requiring that all nonhazardous solid waste within the town be deposited at the transfer facility.

This Court struck down the ordinance, holding that it discriminated against interstate commerce by "hoard[ing] solid waste, and the demand to get rid of it, for the benefit of the preferred processing facility." *Id.*, at 392. The dissent pointed out that all of this Court's local processing cases involved laws that discriminated in favor of *private* entities, not public ones. *Id.*, at 411 (opinion of Souter, J.). According to the dissent, Clarkstown's ostensibly private transfer station was essentially a municipal facility, and this distinction should have saved Clarkstown's ordinance because favoring local government is by its nature different from favoring a particular private company. The majority did not comment on the dissent's public-private distinction.

The parties in this case draw opposite inferences from the majority's silence. The haulers say it proves that the majority agreed with the dissent's characterization of the facility, but thought there was no difference under the dormant Commerce Clause between laws favoring private entities and those favoring public ones. The Counties disagree, arguing that the majority studiously avoided the issue because the facility in *Carbone* was private, and therefore the question whether *public* facilities may be favored was not properly before the Court.

We believe the latter interpretation of *Carbone* is correct. As the Second Circuit explained, "in *Carbone* the Justices were divided over the *fact of whether* the favored facility was public or private, rather than on the import of that distinction." 261 F.3d, at 259 (emphasis in original). The *Carbone* dissent offered a number of reasons why public entities should be treated differently from private ones under the dormant Commerce Clause. It is hard to suppose that the *Carbone* majority definitively rejected these arguments without explaining why.

The *Carbone* majority viewed Clarkstown's flow control ordinance as "just one more instance of local processing requirements that we long have held invalid." *Id.,* at 391. It then cited six local processing cases, every one of which involved discrimination in favor of *private* enterprise. The Court's own description of the cases acknowledges that the "offending local laws hoard a local resource—be it meat, shrimp, or milk—for the benefit of *local businesses* that treat it." *Id.,* at 392 (emphasis added). If the Court were extending this line of local processing cases to cover discrimination in favor of local government, one would expect it to have said so.

* * *

The flow control ordinances in this case benefit a clearly public facility, while treating all private companies exactly the same. Because the question is now squarely presented on the facts of the case before us, we decide that such flow control ordinances do not discriminate against interstate commerce for purposes of the dormant Commerce Clause.

Compelling reasons justify treating these laws differently from laws favoring particular private businesses over their competitors. "Conceptually, of course, any notion of discrimination assumes a comparison of substantially similar entities." *General Motors Corp. v. Tracy,* 519 U.S. 278, 298 (1997). But States and municipalities are not private businesses—far from it. Unlike private enterprise, government is vested with the responsibility of protecting the health, safety, and welfare of its citizens. These important responsibilities set state and local government apart from a typical private business.

Given these differences, it does not make sense to regard laws favoring local government and laws favoring private industry with equal skepticism. As our local processing cases demonstrate, when a law favors in-state business over out-of-state competition, rigorous scrutiny is appropriate because the law is often the product of "simple economic protectionism." *Wyoming v. Oklahoma,* 502 U.S. 437, 454 (1992). Laws favoring local government, by contrast, may be directed toward any number of legitimate goals unrelated to protectionism. Here the flow control ordinances enable the Counties to pursue particular policies with respect to the handling and treatment of waste generated in the Counties, while allocating the costs of those policies on citizens and businesses according to the volume of waste they generate.

The contrary approach of treating public and private entities the same under the dormant Commerce Clause would lead to unprecedented and unbounded interference by the courts with state and local government. The dormant Commerce Clause is not a roving license for federal courts to decide what activities are appropriate for state and local government to undertake, and what activities must be the province of private market competition. In this case, the citizens of Oneida and Herkimer Counties have chosen the government to provide waste management services, with a limited role for the private sector in arranging for transport of waste from the curb to the public facilities. The citizens could have left the entire matter for the private sector, in which case any regulation they undertook could not discriminate against interstate commerce. But it was also open to them to vest responsibility for the matter with their government, and to adopt flow control ordinances to support the government effort. It is not the office of the Commerce Clause to control the decision of the voters on whether government or the private sector should provide waste management services. "The Commerce Clause significantly limits the ability of States and localities to regulate or otherwise burden the flow of interstate commerce, but it does not elevate free trade above all other values." *Maine v. Taylor,* 477 U.S., at 151.

We should be particularly hesitant to interfere with the Counties' efforts under the guise of the Commerce Clause because "[w]aste disposal is both typically and traditionally a local government function." 261 F.3d, at 264 (case below) (Calabresi, J., concurring). Congress itself has recognized local government's vital role in waste management, making clear that "collection and disposal of solid wastes should continue to be primarily the function of State, regional, and local agencies." Resource Conservation and Recovery Act of 1976, 90 Stat. 2797, 42 U.S.C. § 6901(a)(4). The policy of the State of New York favors "displac[ing] competition with regulation or monopoly control" in this area. N.Y. Pub. Auth. Law Ann. § 2049–tt(3). We may or may not agree with that approach, but nothing in the Commerce Clause vests the responsibility for that policy judgment with the Federal Judiciary.

Finally, it bears mentioning that the most palpable harm imposed by the ordinances—more expensive trash removal—is likely to fall upon the very people who voted for the laws. Our dormant Commerce Clause cases often find discrimination when a State shifts the costs of regulation to other States, because when "the burden of state regulation falls on interests outside the state, it is unlikely to be alleviated by the operation of those political restraints normally exerted when interests within the state are affected." *Southern Pacific Co. v. Arizona ex rel. Sullivan,* 325 U.S. 761, 767–768, n. 2 (1945). Here, the citizens and businesses of the Counties bear the costs of the ordinances. There is no reason to step in and hand local businesses a victory they could not obtain through the political process.

We hold that the Counties' flow control ordinances, which treat in-state private business interests exactly the same as out-of-state ones, do not "discriminate against interstate commerce" for purposes of the dormant Commerce Clause.[7]

The Counties' flow control ordinances are properly analyzed under the test set forth in *Pike v. Bruce Church, Inc.*, 397 U.S. 137, 142 (1970), which is reserved for laws "directed to legitimate local concerns, with effects upon interstate commerce that are only incidental." *Philadelphia v. New Jersey*, 437 U.S., at 624. Under the *Pike* test, we will uphold a nondiscriminatory statute like this one "unless the burden imposed on [interstate] commerce is clearly excessive in relation to the putative local benefits." 397 U.S., at 142.

After years of discovery, both the Magistrate Judge and the District Court could not detect *any* disparate impact on out-of-state as opposed to in-state businesses. The Second Circuit alluded to, but did not endorse, a "rather abstract harm" that may exist because "the Counties' flow control ordinances have removed the waste generated in Oneida and Herkimer Counties from the national marketplace for waste processing services." 438 F.3d, at 160. We find it unnecessary to decide whether the ordinances impose any incidental burden on interstate commerce because any arguable burden does not exceed the public benefits of the ordinances.

The ordinances give the Counties a convenient and effective way to finance their integrated package of waste-disposal services. While "revenue generation is not a local interest that can justify *discrimination* against interstate commerce," *Carbone*, 511 U.S., at 393 (emphasis added), we think it is a cognizable benefit for purposes of the *Pike* test.

At the same time, the ordinances are more than financing tools. They increase recycling in at least two ways, conferring significant health and environmental benefits upon the citizens of the Counties. First, they create enhanced incentives for recycling and proper disposal of other kinds of waste. Solid waste disposal is expensive in Oneida–Herkimer, but the Counties accept recyclables and many forms of hazardous waste for free, effectively encouraging their citizens to sort their own trash. Second, by requiring all waste to be deposited at Authority facilities, the Counties have markedly increased their ability to enforce recycling laws. If the haulers could take waste to any disposal site, achieving an equal level of enforcement would be much more costly, if not impossible. For these reasons, any

---

7. The Counties and their amicus were asked at oral argument if affirmance would lead to the "Oneida–Herkimer Hamburger Stand," accompanied by a "flow control" law requiring citizens to purchase their burgers only from the state-owned producer. We doubt it. "The existence of major in-state interests adversely affected by [a law] is a powerful safeguard against legislative abuse." Minnesota v. Clover Leaf Creamery Co., 449 U.S. 456, 473, n. 17 (1981). Recognizing that local government may facilitate a customary and traditional government function such as waste disposal, without running afoul of the Commerce Clause, is hardly a prescription for state control of the economy. In any event, Congress retains authority under the Commerce Clause as written to regulate interstate commerce, whether engaged in by private or public entities. It can use this power, as it has in the past, to limit state use of exclusive franchises.

arguable burden the ordinances impose on interstate commerce does not exceed their public benefits.

* * *

■ Justice Scalia, concurring in part.

I write separately to reaffirm my view that "the so-called 'negative' Commerce Clause is an unjustified judicial invention, not to be expanded beyond its existing domain." *General Motors Corp. v. Tracy,* 519 U.S. 278, 312 (1997) (Scalia, J., concurring). "The historical record provides no grounds for reading the Commerce Clause to be other than what it says—an authorization for Congress to regulate commerce." *Tyler Pipe Industries, Inc. v. Washington State Dept. of Revenue,* 483 U.S. 232, 263 (1987) (Scalia, J., concurring in part and dissenting in part).

I have been willing to enforce on *stare decisis* grounds a "negative" self-executing Commerce Clause in two situations: "(1) against a state law that facially discriminates against interstate commerce, and (2) against a state law that is indistinguishable from a type of law previously held unconstitutional by the Court." *West Lynn Creamery, Inc. v. Healy,* 512 U.S. 186, 210 (1994) (Scalia, J., concurring in judgment). As today's opinion makes clear, the flow-control law at issue in this case meets neither condition. * * *

I am unable to join Part II–D of the principal opinion, in which the plurality performs so-called *"Pike* balancing." Generally speaking, the balancing of various values is left to Congress—which is precisely what the Commerce Clause (the *real* Commerce Clause) envisions.

■ Justice Thomas, concurring in the judgment.

I concur in the judgment. Although I joined *C & A Carbone, Inc. v. Clarkstown,* 511 U.S. 383 (1994), I no longer believe it was correctly decided. The negative Commerce Clause has no basis in the Constitution and has proved unworkable in practice. As the debate between the majority and dissent shows, application of the negative Commerce Clause turns solely on policy considerations, not on the Constitution. Because this Court has no policy role in regulating interstate commerce, I would discard the Court's negative Commerce Clause jurisprudence.

* * *

■ Justice Alito, with whom Justice Stevens and Justice Kennedy join, dissenting.

In *C & A Carbone, Inc. v. Clarkstown,* 511 U.S. 383 (1994), we held that "a so-called flow control ordinance, which require[d] all solid waste to be processed at a designated transfer station before leaving the municipality," discriminated against interstate commerce and was invalid under the Commerce Clause because it "depriv[ed] competitors, including out-of-state firms, of access to a local market." *Id.,* at 386. Because the provisions challenged in this case are essentially identical to the ordinance invalidated in *Carbone,* I respectfully dissent.

* * *

The fact that the flow control laws at issue discriminate in favor of a government-owned enterprise does not meaningfully distinguish this case from *Carbone.* * * *

The only real difference between the facility at issue in *Carbone* and its counterpart in this case is that title to the former had not yet formally passed to the municipality. The Court exalts form over substance in adopting a test that turns on this technical distinction, particularly since, barring any obstacle presented by state law, the transaction in *Carbone* could have been restructured to provide for the passage of title at the beginning, rather than the end, of the 5–year period.

* * *

In any event, we have never treated discriminatory legislation with greater deference simply because the entity favored by that legislation was a government-owned enterprise. * * *

* * * To be sure, state-owned entities are accorded special status under the market-participant doctrine. But that doctrine is not applicable here.

* * * Respondents are doing exactly what the market-participant doctrine says they cannot: While acting as market participants by operating a fee-for-service business enterprise in an area in which there is an established interstate market, respondents are also regulating that market in a discriminatory manner and claiming that their special governmental status somehow insulates them from a dormant Commerce Clause challenge.

* * *

I see no basis for the Court's assumption that discrimination in favor of an in-state facility owned by the government is likely to serve "legitimate goals unrelated to protectionism." Discrimination in favor of an in-state government facility serves "local economic interests," *Carbone,* 511 U.S., at 404 (O'Connor, J., concurring in judgment), inuring to the benefit of local residents who are employed at the facility, local businesses that supply the facility with goods and services, and local workers employed by such businesses. It is therefore surprising to read in the opinion of the Court that state discrimination in favor of a state-owned business is not likely to be motivated by economic protectionism. * * *

Proper analysis under the dormant Commerce Clause involves more than an inquiry into whether the challenged Act is in some sense directed toward legitimate goals unrelated to protectionism; equally important are the means by which those goals are realized. If the chosen means take the form of a statute that discriminates against interstate commerce—either on its face or in practical effect—then the burden falls on the enacting government to demonstrate both that the statute serves a legitimate local purpose, and that this purpose could not be served as well by available nondiscriminatory means.

Thus, if the legislative *means* are themselves discriminatory, then regardless of how legitimate and nonprotectionist the underlying legislative *goals* may be, the legislation is subject to strict scrutiny. Similarly, the fact that a discriminatory law "may [in some sense] be directed toward any number of legitimate goals unrelated to protectionism" does not make the law nondiscriminatory. The existence of such goals is relevant, not to whether the law is discriminatory, but to whether the law can be allowed to stand even though it discriminates against interstate commerce. * * *

* * * [W]hile I do not question that the laws at issue in this case serve legitimate goals, the laws offend the dormant Commerce Clause because those goals could be attained effectively through nondiscriminatory means. Indeed, no less than in *Carbone,* those goals could be achieved through "uniform [health and] safety regulations enacted without the object to discriminate" that "would ensure that competitors [to the municipal program] do not underprice the market by cutting corners on environmental safety." 511 U.S., at 393. Respondents would also be free, of course, to "subsidize the[ir] [program] through general taxes or municipal bonds." *Id.,* at 394. "But having elected to use the open market to earn revenues for" their waste management program, respondents "may not employ discriminatory regulation to give that [program] an advantage over rival businesses from out of State." *Ibid.*

The Court next suggests that deference to legislation discriminating in favor of a municipal landfill is especially appropriate considering that "waste disposal is both typically and traditionally a local government function." I disagree on two grounds.

First, this Court has previously recognized that any standard "that turns on a judicial appraisal of whether a particular governmental function is integral or traditional" is "unsound in principle and unworkable in practice." *Garcia v. San Antonio Metropolitan Transit Authority,* 469 U.S. 528, 546–547 (1985). * * *

Second, although many municipalities in this country have long assumed responsibility for disposing of local garbage, most of the garbage produced in this country is still managed by the private sector. In that respect, the Court is simply mistaken in concluding that waste disposal is "typically" a local government function.

Moreover, * * * a "traditional" municipal landfill is for present purposes entirely different from a monopolistic landfill supported by the kind of discriminatory legislation at issue in this case and in *Carbone.* While the former may be rooted in history and tradition, the latter has been deemed unconstitutional until today. It is therefore far from clear that the laws at issue here can fairly be described as serving a function "typically and traditionally" performed by local governments.

NOTES AND QUESTIONS

1. *The dormant commerce clause.* In addition to serving as an affirmative grant of federal power, the commerce clause has been interpreted to restrict state power. The "dormant" (or "negative") commerce clause prohibits state interference with interstate commerce absent congressional authorization. Two different tests apply, depending upon whether the state or local law treats interstate and intrastate commerce differently. Discriminatory laws are presumptively invalid; they will be upheld only if the state or locality shows that no less discriminatory strategy could achieve its legitimate goal. By contrast, laws which treat interstate and intrastate commerce evenhandedly will be upheld, unless the burdens they place on interstate commerce are clearly excessive compared to the local benefits. Sometimes it is difficult to tell the two apart. Which test did the Supreme Court apply in *United Haulers*?

2. *Commerce and garbage.* The flow of solid and hazardous waste across state lines has become one of the primary dormant commerce clause litigation battlegrounds. The Supreme Court has addressed the topic six times since 1978, in Philadelphia v. New Jersey, 437 U.S. 617 (1978); Chemical Waste Mgmt. v. Hunt, 504 U.S. 334 (1992); Fort Gratiot Sanitary Landfill, Inc. v. Michigan Dept. of Natural Resources, 504 U.S. 353 (1992); Oregon Waste Sys. v. Department of Envtl. Quality, 511 U.S. 93 (1994); *Carbone*; and most recently *United Haulers*. Lower federal courts have been virtually swamped with litigation over garbage import and export.

What accounts for this abundance of disputes about interstate shipment of waste? State and local governments can face pressures to restrict the flow of solid waste either into or out of the jurisdiction. Providing for waste disposal is a traditional local police power function. Jurisdictions concerned about preserving scarce landfill space, minimizing the environmental and economic externalities their citizens experience near landfills, or simply not appearing to be available as dumping grounds for wealthier states may seek to restrict the import of waste. On the other hand, municipalities which have financed the construction of expensive incinerators, landfills, or transfer stations, may restrict export by enacting "flow control" measures requiring disposal of locally-generated waste at local facilities in order to ensure the flow of sufficient waste to pay for those facilities. Are either or both of these legitimate local goals? Do they conflict with national needs?

3. *Flow control after United Haulers.* What precisely is the holding of *United Haulers*? Do you agree that the burden on interstate commerce in *United Haulers* was outweighed by the local benefits? Could the counties have achieved their goals through other measures? Were those goals legitimate? Do you agree with the majority that it is significant that the ordinance challenged in *United Haulers* benefitted a municipal, rather than a private, business? That it related to a traditional government function, disposing of waste?

4. *Blocking garbage import.* In Fort Gratiot Sanitary Landfill, Inc. v. Michigan Dept. of Natural Resources, 504 U.S. 353 (1992), the Court struck down a state law that required counties to plan for twenty years of solid waste disposal capacity, and banned disposal of out-of-county wastes unless a permit was obtained from the county. Does that holding penalize the state and its counties for trying to address a problem, and plan for it? What else could the state have done to achieve its goals without running afoul of the dormant commerce clause? The majority suggested that Michigan could cap the total amount of waste accepted at landfills. Would that serve the same goals? Would it be constitutionally permissible? See Waste Mgmt. Holdings v. Gilmore, 252 F.3d 316 (4th Cir. 2001) (holding invalid cap that affected only large regional landfills which relied almost entirely on out-of-state waste). Could Michigan constitutionally ban the import of waste from states lacking effective source reduction or recycling programs? See National Solid Wastes Mgmt. Ass'n v. Meyer, 165 F.3d 1151 (7th Cir. 1999) (invalidating a Wisconsin statute prohibiting disposal of solid waste unless source community had a recycling ordinance meeting Wisconsin specifications). Could Michigan ban waste from states lacking some threshold level of landfill space per capita, on the grounds that those states have failed to shoulder their fair share of the landfill burden?

5. *The "market participant" exception.* State and local governments are not subject to the strictures of the dormant commerce clause when they act as participants in the ordinary marketplace, rather than as regulators. Accordingly, a state or local government which owns a landfill can refuse to accept non-local waste. However, the exemption can be lost if the state acts both as market participant and as regulator. The federal courts have divided over whether municipalities can evade dormant commerce clause limits on export restrictions through franchise agreements, contracts under which a single hauler has the exclusive right to collect and process all municipal solid waste in the jurisdiction, and agrees to dispose of that waste at the local facility. See, e.g., USA Recycling v. Town of Babylon, 66 F.3d 1272 (2d Cir. 1995); Houlton Citizens' Coalition v. Town of Holton, 175 F.3d 178 (1st Cir. 1999); Huish Detergents, Inc. v. Warren County, 214 F.3d 707 (6th Cir. 2000).

6. *Is federal legislation desirable?* Congress can authorize states to regulate in ways that interfere with interstate commerce. States have unsuccessfully sought legislation authorizing waste import restrictions and flow control requirements. Is this an area where federal regulation is appropriate? Why do you suppose Congress has so far declined to legislate in this area? Are decisions about *where* solid waste generated within a jurisdiction should be processed and disposed of appropriately left to local decisionmakers? Are those decisions separable from decisions about *how* solid waste generated within the jurisdiction should be treated?

7. *Acid rain and the dormant commerce clause.* Although garbage is a frequent subject of commerce clause disputes, it is not the only commodity whose interstate trade implicates environmental concerns. The Clean Air Act creates tradable permits for emissions of SO_2, a primary component of acid rain, between utilities, with the goal of encouraging economically efficient reductions in SO_2 emissions. The state of New York, which is convinced that SO_2 emissions in upwind states contribute to acid rain harmful to New York's environment, enacted a statute requiring any New York utility that sells SO_2 allowances to an upwind state to pay the state a fee equal to the price of the allowances. N.Y. Pub. Serv. Law § 66–k. A utility industry group challenged the statute on dormant commerce clause grounds. In Clean Air Markets Group v. Pataki, 338 F.3d 82 (2d Cir. 2003), excerpted below, the Second Circuit avoided the constitutional question by holding that the New York restriction was preempted by the Clean Air Act. If the constitutional question were reached, would the state law survive dormant commerce clause analysis?

B. PREEMPTION

Clean Air Markets Group v. Pataki

United States Court of Appeals, Second Circuit, 2003.
338 F.3d 82.

■ CABRANES, CIRCUIT JUDGE.

BACKGROUND

* * * In 1990, Congress amended the Clean Air Act of 1970, 42 U.S.C. §§ 7401 *et seq.* Title IV of the Clean Air Act Amendments of 1990 has the express purpose of "reduc[ing] the adverse effects of acid deposition through reductions in annual emissions of sulfur dioxide." 42 U.S.C. § 7651(b). According to Title IV's statement of purpose, "it is the intent of [Title IV] to effectuate such reductions ... through ... an emission allocation and transfer system." *Id.* In other words, the purpose of Title IV is to implement a "cap-and-trade" system in order to reduce sulfur dioxide ("SO_2") emission, which is a leading cause of "acid rain" and other forms of acid deposition that are harmful to the environment. Under the cap-and-trade system created by Title IV, electricity-generating utilities are each allocated a certain number of emission allowances per year and each allowance authorizes the utility to emit one ton of SO_2. Every successive year, the total cap on allowable SO_2 emissions is reduced, and fewer allowances are allocated. Pursuant to the system created by Title IV, SO_2 allowances "may be transferred ... [to] *any other person* who holds such allowances." 42 U.S.C. § 7651b(b) (emphasis added). By permitting the sale of unnecessary allowances, the cap-and-trade system creates a financial incentive for utilities to reduce their SO_2 emissions.

Title IV's cap-and-trade system seeks to minimize "acid deposition," the most common form of which is "acid rain." Acid deposition has been particularly problematic in the Adirondack region of New York State. The thin, calcium-poor soils and igneous rocks in this area make it highly susceptible to acidification. Acid deposition in this region has caused substantial harm to aquatic life and other natural resources.

Because SO_2 emissions can travel hundreds of miles in the wind, much of the acid deposition in the Adirondacks results not from SO_2 emissions in New York, but, rather, from SO_2 emissions in fourteen "upwind" states. These states include New Jersey, Pennsylvania, Maryland, Delaware, Virginia, North Carolina, Tennessee, West Virginia, Ohio, Michigan, Illinois, Kentucky, Indiana, and Wisconsin.

In 2000, the New York legislature sought to address this problem by passing the Air Pollution Mitigation Law, N.Y. Pub. Serv. L. § 66–k. Pursuant to this statute, the New York State Public Service Commission ("PSC") is required to assess "an air pollution mitigation offset" upon any New York utility whose SO_2 allowances are sold or traded to one of the fourteen upwind states. N.Y. Pub. Serv. L. § 66–k(2). The amount assessed is equal to the amount of money received by the New York utility in exchange for the allowances. Moreover, the assessment is made regardless of whether the allowances are sold directly to a utility in an upwind state or are subsequently transferred there. Accordingly, in order to avoid the assessment, New York utilities must attach a restrictive covenant to any allowances they sell that prohibits their subsequent transfer to any of the fourteen upwind states.

Plaintiff–Appellant CAMG is an association of electricity generation companies, SO_2 emissions allowance brokers, mining companies, and trade associations. On November 15, 2000, CAMG filed the instant action against Governor Pataki and the Commissioners of the New York Public Service Commission. The complaint sought to enjoin the enforcement of section 66–k on the grounds that it is preempted by Title IV of the Clean Air Act Amendments of 1990 * * *.

DISCUSSION

* * *

On appeal, defendants first argue that the District Court erred in holding that section 66–k violates the Supremacy Clause of the Constitution. The Supreme Court has instructed that the Supremacy Clause "invalidates state laws that interfere with, or are contrary to, federal law."[8] *Hillsborough County, Florida v. Automated Med. Labs., Inc.*, 471 U.S. 707, 712 (1985). Federal law may supercede state laws under the Supremacy Clause in three ways. First, "Congress is empowered to pre-empt state law by so stating in express terms." *Id.* Second, preemption of all state law in a particular field "may be inferred where the scheme of federal regulation is sufficiently comprehensive to make reasonable the inference that Congress left no room for supplementary state regulation." *Id.* Finally, "[e]ven where Congress has not completely displaced state regulation in a specific area, state law is nullified to the extent that it *actually conflicts* with

---

8. The Supremacy Clause states: "This Constitution, and the Laws of the United States which shall be made in Pursuance thereof; and all Treaties made, or which shall be made, under the Authority of the United States, shall be the supreme Law of the Land; and the Judges in every State shall be bound thereby, any Thing in the Constitution or Laws of any State to the Contrary notwithstanding." U.S. Const. art. VI, cl. 2.

federal law." *Id.* (emphasis added). Such a conflict necessarily arises where "compliance with both federal and state regulations is a physical impossibility." *Id.* Moreover, an actual conflict exists when a state law "stands as an obstacle to the accomplishment and execution of the full purposes and objectives of Congress," in enacting federal legislation. *Id.*

The District Court held that section 66–k is preempted by Title IV because section 66–k stands as an obstacle to the accomplishment and execution of the full purposes and objectives of Title IV. Defendants disagree, arguing that section 66–k supports the ultimate purpose of Title IV by helping to protect natural resources.

The Supreme Court has held, however, that "[i]n determining whether [a state law] stands as an obstacle to the full implementation of [a federal statute], it is not enough to say that the ultimate goal of both federal and state law is [the same]." *International Paper Co. v. Ouellette,* 479 U.S. 481, 494 (1987). Even where federal and state statutes have a common goal, a state law will be preempted "if it interferes with the *methods* by which the federal statute was designed to reach this goal." *Id.* (emphasis added).

There can be no doubt that section 66–k interferes with the method selected by Congress for regulating SO_2 emissions. Title IV expressly states that "it is the intent of [Title IV] to effectuate [SO_2 emission] reductions ... *through* ... *an emission allocation and transfer system.*" 42 U.S.C. § 7651(b) (emphasis added). In creating this system, Congress sought to grant utilities "the opportunity to reallocate among themselves their total emissions reduction obligations *in the most efficient and cost-effective way possible.*" S. Rep. 101–228, at 303 (1989) (emphasis added). In the words of the District of Columbia Circuit: "The basic idea of [Title IV's allowance trading system] is that if polluters for which cutbacks are relatively costly can buy pollution entitlements from ones for which cutbacks are relatively cheap, *the nation* can achieve a much greater overall cutback for a given expenditure of resources (or achieve a given cutback for a lower expenditure)." *Texas Mun. Power Agency v. EPA,* 89 F.3d 858, 861 (D.C. Cir. 1996) (emphasis added). In order to implement this scheme on a national scale, Title IV permits allowances to "be transferred ... [to] *any other person* who holds such allowances." 42 U.S.C. § 7651b(b) (emphasis added).

The legislative history of Title IV provides further support for the fact that Congress intended the allowance transfer system to be nationwide. In implementing Title IV, the House of Representatives initially proposed and passed a bill that would have divided the nation into two geographic regions and would have required the transferring utility and the receiving utility to have been located in the same region. This geographic restriction also appeared in the bill passed by the Senate Committee on Environment and Public Works. However, the bill passed by the Senate contained no geographic restrictions, instead providing for a national allowance trading system, and the bill that ultimately emerged from the House–Senate Conference, and that was signed by the President, also included no geographic restrictions on the allowance trading system. Instead, the enacted bill clearly states that allowances "may be transferred ... [to] *any other person* who holds such allowances," anywhere in the United States.

The regulations adopted by the Environmental Protection Agency in order to implement Title IV further support the conclusion that the nationwide allowance trading system is an essential element of Title IV. In particular, the EPA regulations expressly mandate that state programs for granting "acid rain permits" pursuant to Title V of the Clean Air Act Amendments "shall not restrict or interfere with allowance trading." 40 C.F.R. § 72.72(a). These regulations were adopted over the objection of New York State, which argued vigorously in favor of a scheme that permitted allowance trading to be geographically restricted. In rejecting New York's arguments, the EPA explained that "[t]he national transfer of allowances was clearly contemplated by the drafters of the act." 58 Fed. Reg. 3590, 3614–15 (Jan. 11, 1993). Accordingly, the EPA structured the regulations implementing Title IV to "create ... a national system of tradable pollution permits." *Madison Gas & Elec. Co. v. EPA,* 4 F.3d 529, 530 (7th Cir. 1993).

Although section 66–k does not technically limit the authority of New York utilities to transfer their allowances, it clearly interferes with their ability to effectuate such transfers. First, by requiring utilities to forfeit one hundred percent of their proceeds from any allowance sale to a utility in an upwind state, section 66–k effectively bans such sales. Moreover, the only way for New York utilities to ensure that they will not be assessed pursuant to section 66–k is to attach to every allowance they sell a restrictive covenant that prohibits the subsequent transfer of the allowance to an upwind state. Because such a restrictive covenant indisputably decreases the value of the allowances, section 66–k clearly "restrict[s] or interfere[s] with allowance trading," 40 C.F.R. § 72.72(a). In sum, section 66–k impermissibly interferes with the *methods* by which Title IV was designed to reach the goal of decreasing SO_2 emissions, and therefore it stands as an obstacle to the execution of Title IV's objectives.

* * *

Engine Manufacturers Ass'n v. South Coast Air Quality Mgmt. Dist.

United States Supreme Court, 2004.
541 U.S. 246.

■ JUSTICE SCALIA delivered the opinion of the Court.

Respondent South Coast Air Quality Management District (District) is a political subdivision of California responsible for air pollution control in the Los Angeles metropolitan area and parts of surrounding counties that make up the South Coast Air Basin. It enacted six Fleet Rules that generally prohibit the purchase or lease by various public and private fleet operators of vehicles that do not comply with stringent emission requirements. The question in this case is whether these local Fleet Rules escape pre-emption under § 209(a) of the Clean Air Act (CAA) because they address the purchase of vehicles, rather than their manufacture or sale.

I

The District is responsible under state law for developing and implementing a "comprehensive basinwide air quality management plan" to reduce emission levels and thereby achieve and maintain "state and federal ambient air quality standards." Cal. Health & Safety Code Ann. § 40402(e) (West 1996). Between June and October 2000, the District adopted six Fleet Rules. The Rules govern operators of fleets of street sweepers, of passenger cars, light-duty trucks, and medium-duty vehicles, of public transit vehicles and urban buses, of solid waste collection vehicles, of airport passenger transportation vehicles, including shuttles and taxicabs picking up airline passengers, and of heavy-duty on-road vehicles. All six Rules apply to public operators; three apply to private operators as well.

The Fleet Rules contain detailed prescriptions regarding the types of vehicles that fleet operators must purchase or lease when adding or replacing fleet vehicles. Four of the Rules require the purchase or lease of "alternative-fuel vehicles," and the other two require the purchase or lease of either "alternative-fueled vehicles" or vehicles that meet certain emission specifications established by the California Air Resources Board (CARB). CARB is a statewide regulatory body that California law designates as "the air pollution control agency for all purposes set forth in federal law." Cal. Health & Safety Code Ann. § 39602 (West 1996). The Rules require operators to keep records of their purchases and leases and provide access to them upon request. Violations expose fleet operators to fines and other sanctions.

* * *

II

Section 209(a) of the CAA states:

> No State or any political subdivision thereof shall adopt or attempt to enforce any standard relating to the control of emissions from new motor vehicles or new motor vehicle engines subject to this part. No State shall require certification, inspection, or any other approval relating to the control of emissions ... as condition precedent to the initial retail sale, titling (if any), or registration of such motor vehicle, motor vehicle engine, or equipment.

42 U.S.C. § 7543(a).

> The District Court's determination that this express pre-emption provision did not invalidate the Fleet Rules hinged on its interpretation of the word "standard" to include only regulations that compel manufacturers to meet specified emission limits. This interpretation of "standard" in turn caused the court to draw a distinction between purchase restrictions (not pre-empted) and sale restrictions (pre-empted). Neither the manufacturer-specific interpretation of "standard" nor the

resulting distinction between purchase and sale restrictions finds support in the text of § 209(a) or the structure of the CAA.

"Statutory construction must begin with the language employed by Congress and the assumption that the ordinary meaning of that language accurately expresses the legislative purpose." Park 'N Fly, Inc. v. Dollar Park & Fly, Inc., 469 U.S. 189, 194 (1985). Today, as in 1967 when § 209(a) became law, "standard" is defined as that which "is established by authority, custom, or general consent, as a model or example; criterion; test." Webster's Second New International Dictionary 2455 (1945). The criteria referred to in § 209(a) relate to the emission characteristics of a vehicle or engine. To meet them the vehicle or engine must not emit more than a certain amount of a given pollutant, must be equipped with a certain type of pollution-control device, or must have some other design feature related to the control of emissions. This interpretation is consistent with the use of "standard" throughout Title II of the CAA (which governs emissions from moving sources) to denote requirements such as numerical emission levels with which vehicles or engines must comply, e.g., 42 U.S.C. § 7521(a)(1)(B)(ii), or emission-control technology with which they must be equipped, e.g., § 7521(a)(6).

Respondents, like the courts below, engraft onto this meaning of "standard" a limiting component, defining it as only "[a] production mandat[e] that require [s] manufacturers to ensure that the vehicles they produce have particular emissions characteristics, whether individually or in the aggregate." This confuses standards with the means of enforcing standards. Manufacturers (or purchasers) can be made responsible for ensuring that vehicles comply with emission standards, but the standards themselves are separate from those enforcement techniques. While standards target vehicles or engines, standard-enforcement efforts that are proscribed by § 209 can be directed to manufacturers or purchasers.

* * *

That a standard is a standard even when not enforced through manufacturer-directed regulation can be seen in Congress's use of the term in another portion of the CAA. As the District Court recognized, CAA § 246 (in conjunction with its accompanying provisions) requires state-adopted and federally approved "restrictions on the purchase of fleet vehicles to meet clean-air standards." (Respondents do not defend the District's Fleet Rules as authorized by this provision; the Rules do not comply with all of the requirements that it contains.) Clearly, Congress contemplated the enforcement of emission standards through purchase requirements.[6]

Respondents contend that their qualified meaning of "standard" is necessary to prevent § 209(a) from pre-empting "far too much" by "en-

---

6. The District Court reasoned that "[i]t is not rational to conclude that the CAA would authorize purchasing restrictions on the one hand, and prohibit them, as a prohibited adoption of a 'standard,' on the other." This reasoning is flawed; it is not irrational to view Congress's prescription of numerous detailed requirements for such programs as inconsistent with unconstrained state authority to enact programs that ignore those requirements.

compass [ing] a broad range of state-level clean-air initiatives" such as voluntary incentive programs. But it is hard to see why limitation to mandates on manufacturers is necessary for this purpose; limitation to mandates on manufacturers and purchasers, or to mandates on anyone, would have the same salvific effect. We need not resolve application of § 209(a) to voluntary incentive programs in this case, since all the Fleet Rules are mandates.

In addition to having no basis in the text of the statute, treating sales restrictions and purchase restrictions differently for pre-emption purposes would make no sense. The manufacturer's right to sell federally approved vehicles is meaningless in the absence of a purchaser's right to buy them. It is true that the Fleet Rules at issue here cover only certain purchasers and certain federally certified vehicles, and thus do not eliminate all demand for covered vehicles. But if one State or political subdivision may enact such rules, then so may any other; and the end result would undo Congress's carefully calibrated regulatory scheme.

A command, accompanied by sanctions, that certain purchasers may buy only vehicles with particular emission characteristics is as much an "attempt to enforce" a "standard" as a command, accompanied by sanctions, that a certain percentage of a manufacturer's sales volume must consist of such vehicles. We decline to read into § 209(a) a purchase/sale distinction that is not to be found in the text of § 209(a) or the structure of the CAA.

III

The dissent expresses many areas of disagreement with our interpretation, but this should not obscure its agreement with our answer to the question "whether these local Fleet Rules escape pre-emption ... because they address the purchase of vehicles, rather than their manufacture or sale." The dissent joins us in answering "no." It reaches a different outcome in the case because (1) it feels free to read into the unconditional words of the statute a requirement for the courts to determine which purchase restrictions in fact coerce manufacture and which do not; and (2) because it believes that Fleet Rules containing a "commercial availability" proviso do not coerce manufacture.

As to the first point: The language of § 209(a) is categorical. It is (as we have discussed) impossible to find in it an exception for standards imposed through purchase restrictions rather than directly upon manufacturers; it is even more inventive to discover an exception for only that subcategory of standards-imposed-through-purchase-restrictions that does not coerce manufacture. But even if one accepts that invention, one cannot conclude that these "provisos" save the day. For if a vehicle of the mandated type were commercially available, thus eliminating application of the proviso, the need to sell vehicles to persons governed by the Rule would effectively coerce manufacturers into meeting the artificially created demand. To say, as the dissent does, that this would be merely the consequence of "market demand and free competition," is fanciful. The demand is a demand, not generated by the market but compelled by the Rules, which in turn effectively compels production. To think that the Rules are invalid until such time as one manufacturer makes a compliant vehicle available, whereupon they become binding, seems to us quite bizarre.

* * * The textual obstacles to the strained interpretation that would validate the Rules by reason of the "commercial availability" provisos are insurmountable—principally, the categorical words of § 209(a). The dissent contends that giving these words their natural meaning of barring implementation of standards at the purchase and sale stage renders superfluous the second sentence of § 209(a), which provides: "No State shall require certification, inspection, or any other approval relating to the control of emissions from any new motor vehicle or new motor vehicle engine as condition precedent to the initial retail sale, titling (if any), or registration of such motor vehicle, motor vehicle engine, or equipment." 42 U.S.C. § 7543(a). We think it not superfluous, since it makes clear that the term "attempt to enforce" in the first sentence is not limited to the actual imposition of penalties for violation, but includes steps preliminary to that action. The sentence is, however, fatal to the dissent's interpretation of the statute. It categorically prohibits "certification, inspection, or any other approval" as conditions precedent to sale. Why in the world would it do that if it had no categorical objection to standards imposed at the sale stage? Why disable the States from assuring compliance with requirements that they are authorized to impose?

The dissent next charges that our interpretation attributes carelessness to Congress because § 246 mandates fleet purchasing restrictions, but does so without specifying "notwithstanding" § 209(a). That addition might have been nice, but hardly seems necessary. It is obvious, after all, that the principal sales restrictions against which § 209(a) is directed are those requiring compliance with state-imposed standards. What § 246 mandates are fleet purchase restrictions under federal standards designed precisely for federally required clean-fuel fleet vehicle programs—which programs, in turn, must be federally approved as meeting detailed federal specifications. It is not surprising that a "notwithstanding" § 209(a) did not come to mind. Far from casting doubt upon our interpretation, § 246 is impossible to reconcile with the dissent's interpretation. The fleet purchase standards it mandates must comply strictly with federal specifications, being neither more lenient nor more demanding. But what is the use of imposing such a limitation if the States are entirely free to impose their own fleet purchase standards with entirely different specifications?

Finally, the dissent says that we should "admit" that our opinion pre-empts voluntary incentive programs. Voluntary programs are not at issue in this case, and are significantly different from command-and-control regulation. Suffice it to say that nothing in the present opinion necessarily entails pre-emption of voluntary programs. It is at least arguable that the phrase "adopt or attempt to enforce any standard" refers only to standards that are enforceable—a possibility reinforced by the fact that the prohibition is imposed only on entities (States and political subdivisions) that have power to enforce.

IV

The courts below held all six of the Fleet Rules to be entirely outside the pre-emptive reach of § 209(a) based on reasoning that does not withstand scrutiny. In light of the principles articulated above, it appears likely that at least certain aspects of the Fleet Rules are pre-empted. * * *

It does not necessarily follow, however, that the Fleet Rules are pre-empted in toto. We have not addressed a number of issues that may affect the ultimate disposition of petitioners' suit, including the scope of petitioners' challenge, whether some of the Fleet Rules (or some applications of them) can be characterized as internal state purchase decisions (and, if so, whether a different standard for pre-emption applies), and whether § 209(a) pre-empts the Fleet Rules even as applied beyond the purchase of new vehicles (e.g., to lease arrangements or to the purchase of used vehicles). These questions were neither passed on below nor presented in the petition for certiorari. They are best addressed in the first instance by the lower courts in light of the principles articulated above.

The judgment is vacated, and the case is remanded for further proceedings consistent with this opinion.

■ JUSTICE SOUTER, dissenting.

The Court holds that preemption by the Clean Air Act prohibits one of the most polluted regions in the United States from requiring private fleet operators to buy clean engines that are readily available on the commercial market. I respectfully dissent and would hold that the South Coast Air Quality Management District Fleet Rules are not preempted by the Act.

I

* * *

First, "[i]n all pre-emption cases, and particularly in those [where] Congress has legislated ... in a field which the States have traditionally occupied, we start with the assumption that the historic police powers of the States were not to be superseded by the Federal Act unless that was the clear and manifest purpose of Congress." Medtronic, Inc. v. Lohr, 518 U.S. 470, 485 (1996). The pertinence of this presumption against federal pre-emption is clear enough from the terms of the Act itself: § 101 states that "air pollution prevention (that is, the reduction or elimination, through any measures, of the amount of pollutants produced or created at the source) and air pollution control at its source is the primary responsibility of States and local governments." 42 U.S.C. § 7401(a)(3). The resulting presumption against displacing law enacted or authorized by a State applies both to the "question whether Congress intended any pre-emption at all" and to "questions concerning the scope of [§ 209(a)'s] intended invalidation of state law." Medtronic, supra, at 485.

Second, legislative history should inform interpretive choice, and the legislative history of this preemption provision shows that Congress's purpose in passing it was to stop States from imposing regulatory requirements that directly limited what manufacturers could sell. During the hearings leading up to the 1967 amendments, "[t]he auto industry ... was adamant that the nature of their manufacturing mechanism required a single national standard in order to eliminate undue economic strain on the industry." S. Rep. No. 403, 90th Cong., 1st Sess., 32 (1967). Auto manufacturers sought to safeguard "[t]he ability of those engaged in the manufacture of automobiles to obtain clear and consistent answers concerning emission controls," and to prevent "a chaotic situation from developing in interstate commerce in new motor vehicles." H.R. Rep. No. 728, 90th Cong., 1st Sess., 20 (1967). Congress was not responding to concerns about varying regional appetites for whatever vehicle models the manufacturers did produce; it was addressing the industry's fear that States would bar manufacturers from selling engines that failed to meet specifications that might be different in each State.

Section 209(a) can easily be read to give full effect to both principles. As amended in 1967, § 202 of the Act authorized federal regulators to promulgate emissions standards for "any class or classes of new motor vehicles or new motor vehicle engines." § 202(a), 81 Stat. 499. The 1967 amendments in turn defined "new motor vehicle" as "a motor vehicle the equitable or legal title to which has never been transferred to an ultimate purchaser," and a "new motor vehicle engine" as "an engine in a new motor vehicle or a motor vehicle engine the equitable or legal title to which has never been transferred to the ultimate purchaser." § 212(3), 81 Stat. 503. Section 202 of the 1967 Act, in other words, is naturally understood as concerning itself with vehicles prior to sale and eligible to be sold. * * *

On this permissible reading of the 1967 amendments, § 209(a) has no preemptive application to South Coast's fleet purchase requirement. The National Government took over the direct regulation of manufacturers' design specifications addressing tailpipe emissions, and disabled States (the California exception aside) from engaging in the same project. The "standards" that § 209(a) preempts, accordingly, are production mandates imposed directly on manufacturers as a condition of sale. Section 209(a) simply does not speak to regulations that govern a vehicle buyer's choice between various commercially available options.

This is not to say that every conceivable purchase restriction would be categorically free from preemption. A state law prohibiting any purchase by any buyer of any vehicle that failed to meet novel, state-specified emissions criteria would have the same effect as direct regulation of car manufacturers, and would be preempted by § 209(a) as an "attempt to enforce [a] standard relating to the control of emissions from new motor vehicles." 42 U.S.C. § 7543(a). But that fantasy is of no concern here, owing to a third central point that the majority passes over: South Coast's Fleet Rules require the purchase of cleaner engines only if cleaner engines are commercially available. If no one is selling cleaner engines, fleet owners are free to

buy any vehicles they desire. The manufacturers would, of course, understand that a market existed for cleaner engines, and if one auto maker
began producing them, others might well be induced to do the same; but
that would not matter under the Act, which was not adopted to exempt
producers from market demand and free competition. So long as a purchase
requirement is subject to a commercial availability proviso, there is no basis
to condemn that kind of market-based limitation along with the state
command-and-control regulation of production specifications that prompted
the passage of § 209.

* * *

II

Reading the statute this way not only does a better job of honoring
preemption principles consistently with congressional intent, but avoids
some difficulties on the majority's contrary interpretation. To begin with,
the Court's broad definition of an "attempt to enforce any standard
relating to the control of emissions" renders superfluous the second sentence of § 209(a), which provides that "[n]o State shall require certification, inspection, or any other approval relating to the control of emissions
from any new motor vehicle ... as condition precedent to the initial retail
sale, titling (if any), or registration of such motor vehicle." 42 U.S.C.
§ 7543(a). At the very least, on the majority's view, it is hard to imagine
any state inspection requirement going to the control of emissions from a
new motor vehicle that would not be struck down anyway as an attempt to
enforce an emissions standard.

Next, on the majority's broad interpretation of "standard," Congress
would seem to have been careless in drafting a critical section of the Act. In
the one clear instance of which we are aware in which the Act authorizes
States to enact laws that would otherwise be preempted by § 209, Congress
expressly provided that the authorization is effective notwithstanding that
preemption section. The natural negative implication is that, if a statutory
authorization does not include such a "notwithstanding" clause or something similar, its subject matter would not otherwise be preempted by
§ 209(a). Given that, the majority's interpretation of the scope of § 209(a)
is difficult to square with § 246, which requires States to establish fleet
purchasing requirements for "covered fleet operator[s]" in ozone and
carbon monoxide "nonattainment areas" (that is, regions struggling with
especially intractable pollution), 42 U.S.C. § 7586. Section 246 thus requires States, in some cases, to establish precisely the kind of purchaser
regulations (adopted here by a lower level governmental authority) that the
majority claims have been preempted by § 209(a). But § 246 gives no
indication that its subject matter would otherwise be preempted; there is
certainly no "notwithstanding" clause. This silence suggests that Congress
never thought § 209(a) would have any preemptive effect on fleet purchasing requirements like the ones at issue.

Finally, the Court suggests that both voluntary incentive programs,
and internal state purchasing decisions may well be permissible on its

reading of § 209(a). These suggestions are important in avoiding apparent implausibility in the majority's position; if a State were said to be barred even from deciding to run a cleaner fleet than the National Government required, it would take an airtight argument to convince anyone that Congress could have meant such a thing. But it is difficult, when actually applying the majority's expansive sense of forbidden "standard," to explain how the specification of emissions characteristics in a State's internal procurement guidelines could escape being considered an impermissible "adopt [ion of a] standard," 42 U.S.C. § 7543(a), even if the standard only guided local purchasing decisions. By the same token, it is not obvious how, without some legal sleight of hand, the majority can avoid preempting voluntary incentive programs aimed at the private sector; the benefit proffered by such schemes hinges on the recipient's willingness to buy a vehicle or engine that complies with an emissions standard. Such a program clearly "adopt[s]" an emissions standard as the majority defines it. The Court should, then, admit to preemption of state programs that even petitioners concede are not barred by § 209(a). That is not a strong recommendation for the majority's reading.

III

These objections to the Court's interpretation are not, to be sure, dispositive, standing alone. They call attention to untidy details, and rightly understood legislation can be untidy: statutes can be unsystematic, redundant, and fuzzy about drawing lines. As a purely textual matter, both the majority's reading and mine have strengths and weaknesses. The point is that the tiebreakers cut in favor of sustaining the South Coast Fleet Rules. My reading adheres more closely to the legislative history of § 209(a). It takes proper account of the fact that the Fleet Rules with this commercial availability condition do not require manufacturers, even indirectly, to produce a new kind of engine. And, most importantly, my reading adheres to the well-established presumption against preemption.

NOTES AND QUESTIONS

1. *Federal supremacy and preemption.* Valid federal law prevails over conflicting state or local law under the supremacy clause of the federal Constitution, Art. VI, cl. 2. Congress can expressly preempt state regulation, as it has in the Federal Insecticide, Fungicide, and Rodenticide Act, which explicitly precludes state regulation of pesticide labeling. 7 U.S.C. § 136v(b). The Supreme Court also recognizes two forms of implied preemption. Field preemption occurs when Congress intends to fully occupy a particular regulatory field, leaving no room for state action, or where the federal interest is so dominant that it precludes state regulation. That does not necessarily mean that federal regulation is more restrictive; Congress may intend to leave some portions of a field unregulated. Conflict preemption occurs where compliance with both federal and state standards is impossible, or where a state law stands in the way of fulfillment of congressional objectives. Identifying either express or implied preemption requires detailed evaluation of the federal and state statutes or regulations at issue, their purposes, and their legislative history. The Court has frequently said that it applies a presumption against preemption, particularly in areas of traditional state or local responsibility. See, e.g., Wyeth v. Levine, 555 U.S. 555, 565 (2009). That presumption, however, is not always even acknowledged, much less followed. Robert S. Peck, A Separation-of-Powers Defense of the "Presumption Against Preemption," 84 Tulane L. Rev. 1185, 1185 (2010).

In recent years, the Supreme Court has applied preemption rules broadly in several environmental cases. For example, in United States v. Locke, 529 U.S. 89 (2000), the Court held that federal law preempted Washington state regulations governing operation of oil tankers in Washington waters. While some commentators see the Court's recent preemption cases as inconsistent with its federalism jurisprudence, others point out that broad preemption may be preferred by business interests operating in multiple jurisdictions. See Stephen R. McAllister and Robert L. Glicksman, Federal Environmental Law in the "New" Federalism Era, 30 Envtl. L. Rep. 11122, 11143 (2000).

Which type of preemption was found in *Clean Air Markets*? Did the New York law interfere with federal efforts to address a national problem? In what way? If all downwind states imposed a regulation like section 66–k, would that complicate federal efforts to address acid rain? What kind of preemption did the majority find in *Engine Manufacturers*?

2. *Preemption and federalism.* Does aggressive federal preemption of state environmental laws threaten the benefits of cooperative federalism? See Kirsten H. Engel, Harnessing the Benefits of Dynamic Federalism in Environmental Law, 56 Emory L.J. 159, 184–187 (2006). Should the courts be reluctant to find preemption in an area where policy experimentation and overlapping regulatory jurisdiction seem particularly valuable? How can such areas be identified? Should courts be more reluctant to find federal preemption of state environmental standards exceeding federal standards ("ceiling preemption") than of state standards below federal thresholds ("floor preemption")? Does ceiling preemption serve legitimate interests?

3. *Clean Air Act waivers.* As you know, the Clean Air Act allows EPA to waive preemption of California mobile source regulations. Why didn't SCAQMD (or the California Air Resources Board) seek such a waiver for its Fleet Rules, which were explicitly authorized by state legislation?

4. *Preemption in Engine Manufacturers.* Who has the better of the argument about preemption in *Engine Manufacturers*, Justice Scalia or Justice Souter? Should the Court apply a presumption against preemption here, because the states under their police powers have the traditional authority to regulate pollution? Or does the fact that Congress obviously intended to negate *some* state regulation of mobile sources make that presumption inapplicable? Are regulations that require certain buyers to purchase clean vehicles if those vehicles are commercially available "standards relating to the control of emissions from new vehicles"? Are they attempts to enforce standards? Is the purpose of the CAA's preemption provision relevant, or is the statutory language sufficiently clear that the Court need not inquire into its purpose? How far does the preemption found in *Engine Manufacturers* extend? Does the CAA preempt regulations requiring that fleets which choose to lease (rather than buy) new vehicles lease clean ones? Tax rebates for the purchase of low-emission or alternative-fuel vehicles?

On remand the Ninth Circuit, relying on the market participant exception, concluded that the fleet rules are not preempted to the extent that they regulate the purchasing or leasing decisions of state and local government entities. It remanded to the District Court for further evaluation of the remaining Fleet Rules. Engine Manufacturers Ass'n v. SCAQMD, 498 F.3d 1031 (9th Cir. 2007).

5. *Preemption of mobile source regulation.* A current hotbed of preemption litigation concerns the status of California's regulation of greenhouse gas emissions from automobiles. In 2002, California passed a law requiring that the California Air Resources Board develop regulations that will "achieve the maximum feasible and cost-effective reduction of greenhouse gases from motor vehicles." Cal. Health & Safety Code 43018.5. California sought a waiver of preemption for those standards under Clean Air Act § 209 shortly after they were enacted. EPA initially denied the waiver request, but reversed itself after a change of administrations. 74 Fed. Reg. 32744 (July 8, 2009).

Before EPA approved California's waiver request, auto manufacturers challenged California's standards in three different lawsuits. They argued primarily that the state's greenhouse gas emission standards are preempted by the Energy Policy and Conservation Act (EPCA), which sets federal corporate average fuel economy (CAFE) standards. EPCA provides: "a State or a political subdivision of a State may not adopt or enforce a law or regulation related to fuel economy standards or average fuel economy standards for automobiles covered by an average fuel economy standard under this chapter." 49 U.S.C. § 32919(a). There is currently no method for controlling tailpipe emissions of greenhouse gases; the only way to reduce emissions per mile traveled is to reduce fuel consumption. California's greenhouse gas emission limits, the manufacturers argued, therefore essentially amount to fuel efficiency standards. Following the Supreme Court's decision in Massachusetts v. EPA, 549 U.S. 497 (2007) (excerpted in Chapter 10, Section 3), two district courts held that EPCA does not preempt the California greenhouse gas emission standards. Green Mountain Chrysler–Plymouth v. Crombie, 508 F. Supp. 2d 295 (D. Vt. 2007); Central Valley Chrysler–Jeep v. Goldstene, 529 F. Supp. 2d 1151 (E.D. Cal. 2007).

Following the grant of California's waiver request, EPA and the Department of Transportation issued joint greenhouse gas emission and fuel economy rules. California agreed to accept compliance with those national regulations as meeting its greenhouse gas standards, and in return automobile manufacturers dropped their preemption litigation. 75 Fed. Reg. 25324, 25328 (May 7, 2010).

6. *Preemption under FIFRA.* Another context in which manufacturers have sought strong preemption in order to maintain national uniformity is the Federal Insecticide, Fungicide and Rodenticide Act (FIFRA). FIFRA allows states to impose additional regulations on the sale and use of pesticides but does not allow states to impose labeling or packaging requirements different from or in addition to federal requirements. 7 U.S.C. § 136v. In Wisconsin Public Intervenor v. Mortier, 501 U.S. 597 (1991), the Supreme Court held that FIFRA does not occupy the field of pesticide regulation, concluding that a local ordinance requiring a special permit for aerial pesticide application was not preempted. Subsequently, in Bates v. Dow Agrosciences LLC, 544 U.S. 431 (2005), the Court held that state law tort claims for based on the design and manufacture of the product are not preempted, even if success on those claims might induce the manufacturer to supplement the label. The Court also ruled that state-law fraud and failure to warn claims were not preempted to the extent they proscribed conduct also prohibited by FIFRA's ban on false or misleading label statements.

7. *Preemption at the state level.* Because local governments are creatures of state law, states enjoy broad power to preempt local legislation. Most states recognize both express and implied preemption. Constitutional or legislative "home rule" provisions may limit the state's preemptive power by giving some or all local governments primary authority over local matters. The details of state and local powers vary from state to state. For detailed discussion of the extent and limits of state control over municipal governments, see Osborne M. Reynolds, Local Government Law 76–137 (2d ed. 2001).

PART II

NATURAL RESOURCES

A recurring theme of environmental law is the conflict between economic pressures to use and develop natural resources and the urge to preserve their ecological integrity and scenic beauty. Environmental law imposes both procedural requirements and substantive limits on decisions to alter the environmental status quo. Chapter 5 explores the National Environmental Policy Act, which requires that federal agencies consider environmental impacts before taking action, and other informational strategies. Chapter 6 looks at substantive limits on decisions affecting public resources, as well as privately-owned resources with a public dimension.

CHAPTER FIVE

NEPA AND THE POWER OF INFORMATION

SECTION 1. INTRODUCTION TO NEPA

Excerpts From the National Environmental Policy Act

42 U.S.C. §§ 4321–4335.

Sec. 2. Congressional declaration of purpose

The purposes of this chapter are: To declare a national policy which will encourage productive and enjoyable harmony between man and his environment; to promote efforts which will prevent or eliminate damage to the environment and biosphere and stimulate the health and welfare of man; to enrich the understanding of the ecological systems and natural resources important to the Nation; and to establish a Council on Environmental Quality.

Sec. 101. Congressional declaration of national environmental policy

(a) The Congress, recognizing the profound impact of man's activity on the interrelations of all components of the natural environment, particularly the profound influences of population growth, high-density urbanization, industrial expansion, resource exploitation, and new and expanding technological advances and recognizing further the critical importance of restoring and maintaining environmental quality to the overall welfare and development of man, declares that it is the continuing policy of the Federal Government, in cooperation with State and local governments, and other concerned public and private organizations, to use all practicable means and measures, including financial and technical assistance, in a manner calculated to foster and promote the general welfare, to create and maintain conditions under which man and nature can exist in productive harmony, and fulfill the social, economic, and other requirements of present and future generations of Americans.

(b) In order to carry out the policy set forth in this chapter, it is the continuing responsibility of the Federal Government to use all practicable means, consistent with other essential considerations of national policy, to improve and coordinate Federal plans, functions, programs, and resources to the end that the Nation may—

(1) fulfill the responsibilities of each generation as trustee of the environment for succeeding generations;

(2) assure for all Americans safe, healthful, productive, and aesthetically and culturally pleasing surroundings;

(3) attain the widest range of beneficial uses of the environment without degradation, risk to health or safety, or other undesirable and unintended consequences;

(4) preserve important historic, cultural, and natural aspects of our national heritage, and maintain, wherever possible, an environment which supports diversity, and variety of individual choice;

(5) achieve a balance between population and resource use which will permit high standards of living and a wide sharing of life's amenities; and

(6) enhance the quality of renewable resources and approach the maximum attainable recycling of depletable resources.

(c) The Congress recognizes that each person should enjoy a healthful environment and that each person has a responsibility to contribute to the preservation and enhancement of the environment.

Sec. 102. Cooperation of agencies; reports * * *

The Congress authorizes and directs that, to the fullest extent possible: (1) the policies, regulations, and public laws of the United States shall be interpreted and administered in accordance with the policies set forth in this chapter, and (2) all agencies of the Federal Government shall—

* * *

(C) include in every recommendation or report on proposals for legislation and other major Federal actions significantly affecting the quality of the human environment, a detailed statement by the responsible official on—

(i)   the environmental impact of the proposed action;

(ii)   any adverse environmental effects which cannot be avoided should the proposal be implemented;

(iii) alternatives to the proposed action;

(iv)   the relationship between local short-term uses of man's environment and the maintenance and enhancement of long-term productivity; and

(v)   any irreversible and irretrievable commitments of resources which would be involved in the proposed action should it be implemented.

Prior to making any detailed statement, the responsible Federal official shall consult with and obtain the comments of any Federal agency which has jurisdiction by law or special expertise with respect to any environmental impact involved. Copies of such statement and the comments and views of the appropriate Federal, State, and local agencies, which are authorized to develop and enforce environmental standards, shall be made available to the President, the Council on Environmental Quality and to the public * * *, and shall accompany the proposal through the existing agency review processes;

* * *

(E) study, develop, and describe appropriate alternatives to recommended courses of action in any proposal which involves unresolved conflicts concerning alternative uses of available resources * * *

Dinah Bear, NEPA at 19: A Primer on an "Old" Law With Solutions to New Problems

19 Envtl. L. Rep. 10060, 10061–65 (1989).

Title II of NEPA created the Council on Environmental Quality (CEQ) in the Executive Office of the President, composed of three Members appointed by the President with the advice and consent of the Senate. CEQ has a number of responsibilities, including preparation of an annual report on environmental quality, developing and recommending to the President national environmental policies, and documenting and defining environmental trends.

CEQ Guidance and Regulations

Shortly after NEPA was signed into law, President Nixon issued Executive Order 11514 which, among other things, directed CEQ to issue guidelines on preparation of environmental impact statements. Beginning in 1970, CEQ issued a series of these guidelines, which addressed the basic requirements of environmental impact assessment and administratively interpreted the thrust of the considerable case law that was occurring throughout the 1970s.

While the guidelines were useful, the environmental impact assessment process, or "NEPA process," as it frequently is referred to in the federal establishment, acquired some unfortunate "barnacles" during the mid–1970s. The most frequent complaints were the length of EISs and the delays that the NEPA process was perceived to cause in the decisionmaking process. Observers believed that the lack of uniformity throughout the government and uncertainty about what was required accounted to a large degree for these problems. Consequently, in 1977 President Carter issued Executive Order 11991, directing CEQ to issue binding regulations to federal agencies in an effort to make the process more uniform and efficient. * * *

Regulatory Structure

The CEQ regulations implementing the procedural provisions of NEPA [found at 40 C.F.R. Parts 1500–1508] apply to all agencies of the federal government, excluding Congress and any of its institutions, the judiciary, and the President, including the performance of staff functions for the President. The CEQ regulations are generic in nature, and do not address the applicability of the various procedural requirements to specific agency actions. Instead, each federal department and agency is required to prepare its own NEPA procedures that address that agency's compliance in relation to its particular mission. CEQ reviews and approves all agency procedures and amendments to those procedures.

The agency procedures are required to establish specific criteria for and identification of three classes of actions: those that require preparation of an environmental impact statement; those that require preparation of an environmental assessment; and those that are categorically excluded from further NEPA review. * * *

Categorical Exclusions

"Categorical exclusions" refer to acts falling within a predesignated category of actions that do not individually or cumulatively have a significant effect on the human environment. Thus, no documentation of environmental analysis is required. Agencies may list either very specific actions, or a broader class of actions with criteria and examples for guidance. However, federal officials must be alert to extraordinary circumstances in which a normally excluded action may have a significant environmental effect. A categorical exclusion is *not* an exemption from compliance with NEPA, but merely an administrative tool to avoid paperwork for those actions without significant environmental effects.

Environmental Assessments

An environmental assessment (EA) is supposed to be a concise public document that may be prepared to achieve any of the following purposes: to provide sufficient evidence and analysis for determining whether to prepare an EIS; to aid an agency's compliance with NEPA when no EIS is necessary; and to facilitate preparation of an EIS if one is necessary. An EA should include a brief discussion of the need for the proposal, of alternatives as required by NEPA § 102(2)(E), and of the environmental impacts of the proposed action and alternatives. * * * An EA is followed by one of two conclusions: either a Finding of No Significant Impact (FONSI) or a decision to prepare an EIS. A FONSI briefly presents the reasons why an action, not otherwise categorically excluded, will not have a significant effect on the human environment. * * *

While the EA and FONSI process is a valuable and even essential tool, it has been subjected, far too often, to two types of abuse. On the one hand, some compliance has reduced the EA analysis to a one-page form that is so cursory that it is questionable whether the underlying decision about whether to prepare an EIS is sound. On the other hand, an EA all too frequently takes on the look, feel, and form of an EIS, complete with the same qualitative contents and volume and weight. There can be several reasons for this, but certainly one unfortunate rationale has been to avoid as much public involvement as an EIS would stimulate, while being prepared to turn the EA into an EIS rapidly if a court would so order. * * *

Environmental Impact Statements

The primary purpose of an EIS is to serve as an action-forcing device to ensure that the policies and goals defined in NEPA are infused into the ongoing programs and actions of the federal government. It must provide full and fair discussion of significant environmental impacts and shall inform decisionmakers and the public of the reasonable alternatives that would avoid or minimize adverse impacts or enhance the quality of the human environment. In preparing EISs, *agencies should focus on significant environmental issues and alternatives and reduce paperwork and the accumulation of extraneous background data.* Texts should be concise, clear, and to the point, and should be supported by evidence that the agency has made the necessary environmental analyses. An EIS is *more* than a disclosure document; it should be used by federal officials to plan actions and make decisions.

* * *

Once the decision is made to prepare an EIS of any type, the proponent federal agency publishes a Notice of Intent (NOI) in the Federal Register. The NOI should describe the proper action and possible alternatives, the agency's intent to prepare an EIS, the agency's proposed scoping process, and any planned scoping meetings and the name and address of a contact person in the agency.

The agency must then engage in the "scoping process," a process to determine the scope of issues to be addressed in the EIS and for identifying the significant issues related to a proposed action. Scoping may or may not include meetings, but the process should involve interested parties at all levels of government, and all interested private citizens and organizations. * * *

The next step is preparation of a draft EIS. The EIS may be prepared either by the lead agency, with assistance from any cooperating agencies, or by a contractor. * * * The agency may accept information from any party, including the applicant, but it *always* has the duty to independently evaluate such information.

* * *

Once the draft EIS is prepared, it must be circulated for at least 45 days for public comment and review. Federal agencies with jurisdiction by law or special expertise with respect to any of the relevant environmental impacts are expected to comment, although this may take the form of a "no comment" letter. At the conclusion of the comment period, the agency must evaluate the comment letters and respond to the substantive comments in the final EIS. The final EIS is sent to all parties who commented on the draft EIS. No decision may be made concerning the proposed action until at least 30 days after the Notice of Availability of the final EIS or 90 days after the publication of the Notice of Availability of the draft EIS, whichever is later.

At the time of decision, the decisionmaker must sign a Record of Decision (ROD). The ROD states what the decision is, identifies which alternatives were considered by the agency in making the decision, specifies which alternatives were considered to be environmentally preferable, and discusses factors that were balanced by the decisionmaker. Further, the ROD states whether all practical methods to avoid or minimize environmental harm are being adopted, and if not, why not. The ROD also includes a description of any applicable enforcement and monitoring programs.

Calvert Cliffs' Coordinating Committee, Inc. v. United States Atomic Energy Commission

United States Court of Appeals, District of Columbia Circuit, 1971.
449 F.2d 1109.

[This case involved judicial review of several rules of the Atomic Energy Commission. The discussion of the rules themselves is now of largely historical interest. The case is still noteworthy, however, as the first important judicial interpretation of NEPA.]

■ J. Skelly Wright, Circuit Judge.

* * *

[NEPA] Section 101 sets forth the Act's basic substantive policy: that the federal government "use all practicable means and measures" to protect environmental values. Congress did not establish environmental protection as an exclusive goal; rather, it desired a reordering of priorities, so that environmental costs and benefits will assume their proper place along with other considerations. In Section 101(b), imposing an explicit duty on federal officials, the Act provides that "it is the continuing responsibility of the Federal Government to use all practicable means, consistent with other essential considerations of national policy," to avoid environmental degradation, preserve "historic, cultural, and natural" resources, and promote "the widest range of beneficial uses of the environment without . . . undesirable and unintended consequences."

Thus the general substantive policy of the Act is a flexible one. It leaves room for a responsible exercise of discretion and may not require particular substantive results in particular problematic instances. However, the Act also contains very important "procedural" provisions—provisions which are designed to see that all federal agencies do in fact exercise the substantive discretion given them. These provisions are not highly flexible. Indeed, they establish a strict standard of compliance.

NEPA, first of all, makes environmental protection a part of the mandate of every federal agency and department. The Atomic Energy Commission, for example, had continually asserted, prior to NEPA, that it had no statutory authority to concern itself with the adverse environmental effects of its actions. Now, however, its hands are no longer tied. It is not only permitted, but compelled, to take environmental values into account. Perhaps the greatest importance of NEPA is to require the Atomic Energy Commission and other agencies to *consider* environmental issues just as they consider other matters within their mandates. This compulsion is most plainly stated in Section 102. There, "Congress authorizes and directs that, to the fullest extent possible: (1) the policies, regulations, and public laws of the United States shall be interpreted and administered in accordance with the policies set forth in this Act. . . ." * * *

The sort of consideration of environmental values which NEPA compels is clarified in Section 102(2)(A) and (B). In general, all agencies must use a "systematic, interdisciplinary approach" to environmental planning and evaluation "in decisionmaking which may have an impact on man's environment." In order to include all possible environmental factors in the decisional equation, agencies must "identify and develop methods and procedures . . . which will insure that presently unquantified environmental amenities and values may be given appropriate consideration in decisionmaking along with economic and technical considerations." "Environmental amenities" will often be in conflict with "economic and technical considerations." To "consider" the former "along with" the latter must involve a balancing process. In some instances environmental costs may outweigh economic and technical benefits and in other instances they may not. But NEPA mandates a rather finely tuned and "systematic" balancing analysis in each instance.

To ensure that the balancing analysis is carried out and given full effect, Section 102(2)(C) requires that responsible officials of all agencies prepare a "detailed statement" covering the impact of particular actions on the environment, the environmental costs which might be avoided, and alternative measures which might alter the cost-benefit equation. The apparent purpose of the "detailed statement" is to aid in the agencies' own decision making processes and to advise other interested agencies and the public of the environmental consequences of planned federal action. Beyond the "detailed statement," Section 102(2)(D)* requires all agencies specifically to "study, develop, and describe appropriate alternatives to recommended courses of action in any proposal which involves unresolved conflicts concerning alternative uses of available resources." This requirement, like the "detailed statement" requirement, seeks to ensure that each agency decision maker has before him and takes into proper account all possible approaches to a particular project (including total abandonment of the project) which would alter the environmental impact and the cost-benefit balance. Only in that fashion is it likely that the most intelligent, optimally beneficial decision will ultimately be made. Moreover, by compelling a formal "detailed statement" and a description of alternatives, NEPA provides evidence that the mandated decision making process has in fact taken place and, most importantly, allows those removed from the initial process to evaluate and balance the factors on their own.

---

* [Now section 102(2)(E)—Eds.]

Of course, all of these Section 102 duties are qualified by the phrase "to the fullest extent possible." We must stress as forcefully as possible that this language does not provide an escape hatch for footdragging agencies; it does not make NEPA's procedural requirements somehow "discretionary." Congress did not intend the Act to be such a paper tiger. Indeed, the requirement of environmental consideration "to the fullest extent possible" sets a high standard for the agencies, a standard which must be rigorously enforced by the reviewing courts.

* * *

Thus the Section 102 duties are not inherently flexible. They must be complied with to the fullest extent, unless there is a clear conflict of *statutory* authority. Considerations of administrative difficulty, delay or economic cost will not suffice to strip the section of its fundamental importance.

We conclude, then, that Section 102 of NEPA mandates a particular sort of careful and informed decisionmaking process and creates judicially enforceable duties. The reviewing courts probably cannot reverse a substantive decision on its merits, under Section 101, unless it be shown that the actual balance of costs and benefits that was struck was arbitrary or clearly gave insufficient weight to environmental values. But if the decision was reached procedurally without individualized consideration and balancing of environmental factors—conducted fully and in good faith—it is the responsibility of the courts to reverse. As one District Court has said of Section 102 requirements: "It is hard to imagine a clearer or stronger mandate to the Courts."

Strycker's Bay Neighborhood Council, Inc. v. Karlen

United States Supreme Court, 1980.
444 U.S. 223.

■ Per Curiam.

[The New York City Planning Commission, together with the United States Department of Housing and Urban Development planned a joint redevelopment project in Manhattan. The project was originally envisioned as a mix of 70% middle-income and 30% low-income housing, but later revised to 100% low-income. Trinity Episcopal School, which had built a combination school and middle-income housing development nearby, and a group of neighbors sued in federal court to enjoin the construction of low-income housing on a portion of the project known as Site 30. In the first round of litigation, the District Court found no violation of NEPA, but the Second Circuit reversed, holding that HUD had not adequately studied alternatives to the project.]

On remand, HUD prepared a lengthy report entitled Special Environmental Clearance (1977). After marshaling the data, the report asserted that, "while the choice of Site 30 for development as a 100 percent low-income project has raised valid questions about the potential social environmental impacts involved, the problems associated with the impact on social fabric and community structures are not considered so serious as to require that this component be rated as unacceptable." The last portion of the report incorporated a study wherein the Commission evaluated nine alternative locations for the project and found none of them acceptable. While HUD's report conceded that this study may not have considered all possible alternatives, it credited the Commission's conclusion that any relocation of the units would entail an unacceptable delay of two years or more. According to HUD, "[m]easured against the environmental costs associated with the minimum two-year delay, the benefits seem insufficient to justify a mandated substitution of sites."

[The District Court again ruled in favor of HUD, and the Second Circuit again reversed.] The appellate court focused upon that part of HUD's report where the agency considered and rejected alternative sites, and in particular upon HUD's reliance on the delay such a relocation would entail. The Court of Appeals purported to recognize that its role in reviewing HUD's decision was defined by the Administrative Procedure Act (APA), 5 U.S.C. § 706(2)(A), which provides that agency actions should be set aside if found to be "arbitrary, capricious, an abuse of discretion, or otherwise not in accordance with law...." Additionally, however, the Court of Appeals looked to "[t]he provisions of NEPA" for "the substantive standards necessary to review the merits of agency decisions...." The Court of Appeals conceded that HUD had "given 'consideration' to alternatives" to redesignating the site. Nevertheless, the court believed that " 'consideration' is not an end in itself." Concentrating on HUD's finding that development of an alternative location would entail an unacceptable delay, the appellate court held that such delay could not be "an overriding factor" in HUD's decision to proceed with the development. According to the court, when HUD considers such projects, "environmental factors, such as crowding low-income housing into a concentrated area, should be given determinative weight." The Court of Appeals therefore remanded the case to the District Court, instructing HUD to attack the shortage of low-income housing in a manner that would avoid the "concentration" of such housing on Site 30.

In *Vermont Yankee Nuclear Power Corp. v. NRDC*, 435 U.S. 519, 558 (1978), we stated that NEPA, while establishing "significant substantive goals for the Nation," imposes upon agencies duties that are "essentially procedural." As we stressed in that case, NEPA was designed "to insure a fully informed and well-considered decision," but not necessarily "a decision the judges of the Court of Appeals or of this Court would have reached had they been members of the decisionmaking unit of the agency." *Vermont Yankee* cuts sharply against the Court of Appeals' conclusion that an agency, in selecting a course of action, must elevate environmental concerns over other appropriate considerations. On the contrary, once an agency has made a decision subject to NEPA's procedural requirements, the only role for a court is to insure that the agency has considered the environmental consequences; it cannot " 'interject itself within the area of

discretion of the executive as to the choice of the action to be taken.' "
Kleppe v. Sierra Club, 427 U.S. 390, 410 n.21 (1976).[2]

In the present litigation there is no doubt that HUD considered the
environmental consequences of its decision to redesignate the proposed site
for low-income housing. NEPA requires no more. The petitions for certiorari are granted, and the judgment of the Court of Appeals is therefore

Reversed.

■ JUSTICE MARSHALL, dissenting.

The issue raised by these cases is far more difficult than the *per
curiam* opinion suggests. The Court of Appeals held that the Secretary of
Housing and Urban Development (HUD) had acted arbitrarily in concluding that prevention of a delay in the construction process justified the
selection of a housing site which could produce adverse social environmental effects, including racial and economic concentration. * * *

In the present case, the Court of Appeals did not "substitute its
judgment for that of the agency as to the environmental consequences of its
actions," for HUD in its Special Environmental Clearance Report acknowledged the adverse environmental consequences of its proposed action: "the
choice of Site 30 for development as a 100 percent low-income project has
raised valid questions about the potential social environmental impacts
involved." These valid questions arise from the fact that 68% of all public
housing units would be sited on only one crosstown axis in this area of New
York City. * * * The environmental "impact . . . on social fabric and
community structures" was given a B rating in the report, indicating that
from this perspective the project is "questionable" and ameliorative measures are "mandated." * * * The report also discusses two alternatives,
Sites 9 and 41, both of which are the appropriate size for the project and
require "only minimal" amounts of relocation and clearance. Concerning
Site 9 the report explicitly concludes that "[f]rom the standpoint of social
environmental impact, this location would be superior to Site 30 for the
development of low-rent public housing." The sole reason for rejecting the
environmentally superior site was the fact that if the location were shifted
to Site 9, there would be a projected delay of two years in the construction
of the housing.

The issue before the Court of Appeals, therefore, was whether HUD
was free under NEPA to reject an alternative acknowledged to be environmentally preferable solely on the ground that any change in sites would
cause delay. * * * Whether NEPA, which sets forth "significant substantive goals," *Vermont Yankee*, 435 U.S., at 558, permits a projected two-year

---

2. If we could agree with the dissent that the Court of Appeals held that HUD had acted
"arbitrarily" in redesignating the site for low-income housing, we might also agree that
plenary review is warranted. But the District Court expressly concluded that HUD had not
acted arbitrarily or capriciously and our reading of the opinion of the Court of Appeals
satisfies us that it did not overturn that finding. Instead, the appellate court required HUD to
elevate environmental concerns over other, admittedly legitimate, considerations. Neither
NEPA nor the APA provides any support for such a reordering of priorities by a reviewing
court.

time difference to be controlling over environmental superiority is by no means clear. Resolution of the issue, however, is certainly within the normal scope of review of agency action to determine if it is arbitrary, capricious, or an abuse of discretion. * * *

NOTES AND QUESTIONS

1. *The role of the courts.* Because NEPA does not contain a judicial review provision, review is conducted under the Administrative Procedure Act provisions discussed in Chapter 3. The Supreme Court, beginning with the *Strycker's Bay* decision, has consistently refused to permit substantive judicial review of agency decisions under NEPA. In *Robertson v. Methow Valley Citizens Council*, 490 U.S. 332, 350–51 (1989), the Court stated:

> [I]t is now well settled that NEPA itself does not mandate particular results, but simply prescribes the necessary process. If the adverse environmental effects of the proposed action are adequately identified and evaluated, the agency is not constrained by NEPA from deciding that other values outweigh the environmental costs. * * * Other statutes may impose substantive environmental obligations on federal agencies, but NEPA merely prohibits uninformed—rather than un-wise—agency action.

Does that conclusion follow from *Strycker's Bay*? Note that *Calvert Cliffs* mentions Section 101 of NEPA. Does that section provide any basis for substantive judicial review? How would a court determine whether an agency decision, for example to construct a ski resort on national forest land (the issue in *Robertson*), was arbitrary or capricious under NEPA?

2. *The value of process.* In the absence of substantive judicial review of agency decisions, what purpose(s) does NEPA serve? Does the preparation of an EIS alone improve the likelihood that environmental impacts will receive appropriate consideration? That the agency will become more sensitive to environmental concerns? Is there any point to public disclosure other than to assure the public that the agency is aware of the impacts? Might the EIS serve as a rallying point for the public to bring political pressure to bear to change the decision?

3. *NEPA and agency authority.* Does NEPA expand agency authority to take environmentally protective action? In Natural Resources Defense Council v. U.S. EPA, 859 F.2d 156 (D.C. Cir. 1988), the court held that it does not. Do you agree? Even if it does not provide an additional grant of authority, might § 101 provide the justification for a more environmentally-protective interpretation of agency organic statutes?

SECTION 2.   THE DUTY TO PREPARE AN EIS

Whether and when an EIS must be prepared are often highly contentious. In this section we consider in turn the three most common issues related to the duty to prepare an EIS: when that duty attaches, what constitutes a "major federal action," and whether the resulting environmental impacts are "significant."

A. "RECOMMENDATION OR REPORT ON PROPOSALS"

Excerpts From Council on Environmental Quality Regulations

40 C.F.R. Parts 1500–1517.

Sec. 1502.5 Timing

An agency shall commence preparation of an environmental impact statement as close as possible to the time the agency is developing or is presented with a proposal so that preparation can be completed in time for the final statement to be included in any recommendation or report on the proposal. The statement shall be prepared early enough so that it can serve practically as an important contribution to the decisionmaking process and will not be used to rationalize or justify decisions already made. For instance:

(a) For projects directly undertaken by Federal agencies the environmental impact statement shall be prepared at the feasibility analysis (go-no go) stage and may be supplemented at a later stage if necessary.

(b) For applications to the agency appropriate environmental assessments or statements shall be commenced no later than immediately after the application is received. Federal agencies are encouraged to begin preparation of such assessments or statements earlier, preferably jointly with applicable State or local agencies.

Sec. 1508.23. Proposal

Proposal exists at that stage in the development of an action when an agency subject to the Act has a goal and is actively preparing to make a decision on one or more alternative means of accomplishing that goal and the effects can be meaningfully evaluated. Preparation of an environmental impact statement should be timed (§ 1502.5) so that the final statement may be completed in time for the statement to be included in any recommendation or report on the proposal. A proposal may exist in fact as well as by agency declaration that one exists.

Kleppe v. Sierra Club

United States Supreme Court, 1976.
427 U.S. 390.

■ JUSTICE POWELL delivered the opinion of the Court.

[This controversy involved actions of the Department of Interior regarding coal development on public lands. Plaintiff environmental groups contended that federal officials were required to prepare a comprehensive environmental impact statement on coal development in the Northern

Great Plains region. The Department was in the process of completing a nationwide programmatic EIS on coal-related activities. During that process, the Department had committed to limiting new leasing activities, and preparing project-specific environmental analyses as required by NEPA.

Justice Powell first explained that plaintiffs had failed to produce any evidence of an action of regional scope. He then went on to address the Court of Appeals' conclusion that an EIS was required because the Department "contemplated" a regional program.]

We conclude that the Court of Appeals erred in both its factual assumptions and its interpretation of NEPA. We think the court was mistaken in concluding, on the record before it, that the petitioners were "contemplating" a regional development plan or program. * * *

Even had the record justified a finding that a regional program was contemplated by the petitioners, the legal conclusion drawn by the Court of Appeals cannot be squared with the Act. The court recognized that the mere "contemplation" of certain action is not sufficient to require an impact statement. But it believed the statute nevertheless empowers a court to require the preparation of an impact statement to begin at some point prior to the formal recommendation or report on a proposal. The Court of Appeals accordingly devised its own four-part "balancing" test for determining when during the contemplation of a plan or other type of federal action, an agency must begin a statement. The factors to be considered were identified as the likelihood and imminence of the program's coming to fruition, the extent to which information is available on the effects of implementing the expected program and on alternatives thereto, the extent to which irretrievable commitments are being made and options precluded "as refinement of the proposal progresses," and the severity of the environmental effects should the action be implemented.

* * *

The Court's reasoning and action find no support in the language or legislative history of NEPA. The statute clearly states when an impact statement is required, and mentions nothing about a balancing of factors. Rather, as we noted last Term, under the first sentence of § 102(2)(C) the moment at which an agency must have a final statement ready "is the time at which it makes a recommendation or report on a *proposal* for federal action." Aberdeen & Rockfish R. Co. v. SCRAP, 422 U.S. 289, 320 (1975) (emphasis in original). The procedural duty imposed upon agencies by this section is quite precise, and the role of the courts in enforcing that duty is similarly precise. A court has no authority to depart from the statutory language and, by a balancing of court-devised factors, determine a point during the germination process of a potential proposal at which an impact statement *should be prepared*. Such an assertion of judicial authority would leave the agencies uncertain as to their procedural duties under NEPA, would invite judicial involvement in the day-to-day decisionmaking process of the agencies, and would invite litigation. As the contemplation of a project and the accompanying study thereof do not necessarily result in a proposal for major federal action, it may be assumed that the balancing process devised by the Court of Appeals also would result in the preparation of a good many unnecessary impact statements.[15]

■ JUSTICE MARSHALL, with whom JUSTICE BRENNAN joins, concurring in part and dissenting in part.

While I agree with much of the Court's opinion, I must dissent from Part IV, which holds that the federal courts may not remedy violations of the National Environmental Policy Act of 1969 (NEPA)—no matter how blatant—until it is too late for an adequate remedy to be formulated. As the Court today recognizes, NEPA contemplates agency consideration of environmental factors throughout the decisionmaking process. Since NEPA's enactment, however, litigation has been brought primarily at the end of that process—challenging agency decisions to act made without adequate environmental impact statements or without any statements at all. In such situations, the courts have had to content themselves with the largely unsatisfactory remedy of enjoining the proposed federal action and ordering the preparation of an adequate impact statement. This remedy is insufficient because, except by deterrence, it does nothing to further early consideration of environmental factors. And, as with all after-the-fact remedies, a remand for preparation of an impact statement after the basic decision to act has been made invites *post hoc* rationalizations, rather than the candid and balanced environmental assessments envisioned by NEPA. Moreover, the remedy is wasteful of resources and time, causing fully developed plans for action to be laid aside while an impact statement is prepared.

Nonetheless, until this lawsuit, such belated remedies were all the federal courts had had the opportunity to impose under NEPA. In this case, confronted with a situation in which, according to respondents' allegations, federal agencies were violating NEPA prior to their basic decision to act, the Court of Appeals for the District of Columbia Circuit seized the opportunity to devise a different and effective remedy. It recognized a narrow class of cases, essentially those where both the likelihood of eventual agency action and the danger posed by nonpreparation of an environmental impact statement were great, in which it would allow judicial intervention prior to the time at which an impact statement must be ready. The Court today loses sight of the inadequacy of other remedies and the narrowness of the category constructed by the Court of Appeals,

---

15. This is not to say that § 102(2)(C) imposes no duties upon an agency prior to its making a report or recommendation on a proposal for action. This section states that prior to preparing the impact statement the responsible official "shall consult with and obtain the comments of any Federal agency which has jurisdiction by law or special expertise with respect to any environmental impact involved." Thus, the section contemplates a consideration of environmental factors by agencies during the evolution of a report or recommendation on a proposal. But the time at which a court enters the process is when the report or recommendation on the proposal is made, and someone protests either the absence or the adequacy of the final impact statement. This is the point at which an agency's action has reached sufficient maturity to assure that judicial intervention will not hazard unnecessary disruption.

and construes NEPA so as to preclude a court from ever intervening prior to a formal agency proposal. This decision, which unnecessarily limits the ability of the federal courts to effectuate the intent of NEPA, is mandated neither by the statute nor by the various equitable considerations upon which the Court relies.

* * *

Metcalf v. Daley

United States Court of Appeals, Ninth Circuit, 2000.
214 F.3d 1135.

■ TROTT, CIRCUIT JUDGE.

* * *

I FACTUAL BACKGROUND

The Makah, who reside in Washington state on the northwestern Olympic Peninsula, have a 1500 year tradition of hunting whales. In particular, the Makah target the California gray whale ("gray whale"), which annually migrates between the North Pacific and the coast of Mexico. * * *

In 1855, the United States and the Makah entered into the Treaty of Neah Bay, whereby the Makah ceded most of their land on the Olympic Peninsula to the United States in exchange for "[t]he right of taking fish and of whaling or sealing at usual and accustomed grounds and stations...." Treaty of Neah Bay, 12 Stat. 939, 940 (1855). Despite their long history of whaling and the Treaty of Neah Bay, however, the Makah ceased whaling in the 1920s because widespread commercial whaling had devastated the population of gray whales almost to extinction. * * *

Because the gray whale had become virtually extinct, the United States signed in 1946 the International Convention for the Regulation of Whaling * * *. The International Convention for the Regulation of Whaling enacted a schedule of whaling regulations ("Schedule") and established the International Whaling Commission ("IWC"), which was to be composed of one member from each signatory nation. * * *

Subsequently, in 1949, Congress passed the Whaling Convention Act to implement domestically the International Convention for the Regulation of Whaling. See 16 U.S.C.A. § 916 et seq. (1985). The Whaling Convention Act prohibits whaling in violation of the International Convention for the Regulation of Whaling, the Schedule, or any whaling regulation adopted by the Secretary of Commerce. * * *

When the IWC was established on December 2, 1946, it took immediate action to protect the beleaguered mammal. Specifically, the IWC amended the Schedule to impose a complete ban on the taking or killing of gray whales. However, the IWC included an exception to the ban "when the meat and products of such whales are to be used exclusively for local consumption by the aborigines." This qualification is referred to as the "aboriginal subsistence exception."

In addition to being shielded from commercial whaling under international law, the gray whale received increased protection in 1970 when the United States designated the species as endangered under the Endangered Species Conservation Act of 1969, the predecessor to the Endangered Species Act of 1973 ("ESA"). In 1993, however, NMFS [the National Marine Fisheries Service] determined that the eastern North Pacific stock of gray whales had recovered to near its estimated original population size and was no longer in danger of extinction. As such, this stock of gray whales was removed from the endangered species list in 1994. * * *

After these gray whales were removed from the endangered species list, the Makah decided to resume the hunting of whales * * *. The Tribe asked representatives from the Department of Commerce to represent it in seeking approval from the IWC for an annual quota of up to five gray whales.

As evidenced in an internal e-mail message written by an NMFS representative, the United States agreed in 1995 to "work with" the Makah in obtaining an aboriginal subsistence quota from the IWC. * * *

In January 1996, Will Martin, an NOAA [National Oceanic and Atmospheric Administration, the parent agency of NMFS] representative, sent an e-mail message to his colleagues informing them that "we now have interagency agreement to support the Makah's application in IWC for a whaling quota of 5 grey whales." Shortly thereafter, on March 22, 1996, NOAA entered into a formal written Agreement with the Tribe, which provided that "[a]fter an adequate statement of need is prepared [by the Makah], NOAA, through the U.S. Commissioner to the IWC, will make a formal proposal to the IWC for a quota of gray whales for subsistence and ceremonial use by the Makah Tribe." * * * [T]he Agreement provided that within thirty days of IWC approval of a quota, "NOAA will revise its regulations to address subsistence whaling by the Makah Tribe, and the Council will adopt a management plan and regulations to govern the harvest...." * * *

Pursuant to the Agreement, the Makah prepared an adequate statement of need, and the United States presented a formal proposal to the IWC for a quota of gray whales for the Tribe at the IWC annual meeting in June 1996. * * * Ultimately, the United States realized that it did not have the three-quarters majority required to approve it. Thus, after consulting with the Makah, the United States withdrew the proposal * * *.

In June 1997, an attorney representing the organizations Australians for Animals and BEACH Marine Protection wrote a letter to NOAA and NMFS alleging that the United States Government had violated NEPA by authorizing and promoting the Makah whaling proposal without preparing an EA or an EIS. In response, the Administrator for NOAA wrote to Australians for Animals and BEACH Marine Protection on July 25, 1997, informing them that an EA would be prepared. Twenty-eight days later, on August 22, 1997, a draft EA was distributed for public comment.

On October 13, 1997, NOAA and the Makah entered into a new written Agreement, which, in most respects, was identical to the Agreement signed in 1996. * * * Four days later, and after the signing of this new Agreement, NOAA/NMFS issued, on October 17, 1997, a final EA and a Finding of No Significant Impact ("FONSI").

The 1997 IWC annual meeting was held on October 18, 1997, one day after the final EA had been issued. Before this meeting, however, the United States (representing the Makah) and the Russian Federation (representing a Siberian aboriginal group called the Chukotka) had met to discuss the possibility of submitting a joint proposal for a gray whale quota, as the IWC previously had granted a gray whale quota for the benefit of the Chukotka. After conferring, the United States and the Russian Federation decided to submit a joint proposal for a five-year block quota of 620 whales. The total quota of 620 assumed an average annual harvest of 120 whales by the Chukotka and an average annual harvest of four whales by the Makah. We note in passing that because "not every gray whale struck will be landed," the EA eventually concluded that the cumulative impact of the removal of injured gray whales by the Makah would total not just twenty whales over a five-year period, but forty-one. * * *

At the meeting * * * the quota was approved by consensus with no objections.

On April 6, 1998, NOAA issued a Federal Register Notice setting the domestic subsistence whaling quotas for 1998. [T]he Notice allowed the Makah to engage in whaling pursuant to the IWC-approved quota * * *.

IV NEPA CLAIM

NEPA sets forth a "national policy which will encourage productive and enjoyable harmony between man and his environment ... [and] promote efforts which will prevent or eliminate damage to the environment and biosphere and stimulate the health and welfare of man." 42 U.S.C.A. § 4321 (1994). NEPA does not set out substantive environmental standards, but instead establishes "action-forcing" procedures that require agencies to take a "hard look" at environmental consequences. We have characterized the statute as "primarily procedural," and held that "agency action taken without observance of the procedure required by law will be set aside." Save the Yaak [Comm. v. Block, 840 F.2d 714,] 717 [(9th Cir. 1988)]. In this respect, we have observed in connection with the preparation of an EA that "[p]roper timing is one of NEPA's central themes. An assessment must be 'prepared early enough so that it can serve practically as an important contribution to the decisionmaking process and will not be used to rationalize or justify decisions already made.'" Id. at 718.

The phrase "early enough" means "at the earliest possible time to insure that planning and decisions reflect environmental values." Andrus v. Sierra Club, 442 U.S. 347, 351 (1979). The Supreme Court in referring to

NEPA's requirements as "action forcing" has embraced the rule that for projects directly undertaken by Federal agencies, environmental impact statements "shall be prepared at the feasibility analysis (go-no go) stage and may be supplemented at a later stage if necessary." *Id.* at 351 n. 3.

All of these rules notwithstanding, NEPA does not require that agency officials be "subjectively impartial." Environmental Defense Fund v. Corps of Eng'rs of the U.S. Army, 470 F.2d 289, 295 (8th Cir. 1972). The statute does require, however, that projects be objectively evaluated.

> NEPA assumes as inevitable an institutional bias within an agency proposing a project and erects the procedural requirements of § 102 to insure that there is no way [the decision-maker] can fail to note the facts and understand the very serious arguments advanced by the plaintiff if he carefully reviews the entire environmental impact statement.

Id.

In summary, the comprehensive "hard look" mandated by Congress and required by the statute must be timely, and it must be taken objectively and in good faith, not as an exercise in form over substance, and not as a subterfuge designed to rationalize a decision already made. * * *

* * * In the case at bar, the Makah first asked the Federal Defendants to help them secure IWC approval for a gray whale quota in 1995; however, NOAA/NMFS did not prepare an EA until 1997. During these two years, the United States and the Makah worked together toward obtaining a gray whale quota from the IWC. * * *

The Federal Defendants did not engage the NEPA process "at the earliest possible time." Instead, the record makes clear that the Federal Defendants did not even consider the potential environmental effects of the proposed action until long after they had already committed in writing to support the Makah whaling proposal. The "point of commitment" in this case came when NOAA signed the contract with the Makah in March 1996 and then worked to effectuate the agreement. It was at this juncture that it made an "irreversible and irretrievable commitment of resources." * * * Although it could have, NOAA did not make its promise to seek a quota from the IWC and to participate in the harvest conditional upon a NEPA determination that the Makah whaling proposal would not significantly affect the environment.

* * *

It is highly likely that because of the Federal Defendants' prior written commitment to the Makah and concrete efforts on their behalf, the EA was slanted in favor of finding that the Makah whaling proposal would not significantly affect the environment. * * *

We want to make clear, however, that this case does not stand for the general proposition that an agency cannot begin preliminary consideration of an action without first preparing an EA, or that an agency must always prepare an EA before it can lend support to any proposal. * * * Rather, our holding here is limited to the unusual facts and circumstances of this case where the defendants already had made an "irreversible and irretrievable commitment of resources"—i.e., by entering into a contract with the Makah before they considered its environmental consequences and prepared the EA.

V REMEDY

Appellees argue that, even if the Federal Defendants did violate NEPA by preparing the EA after deciding to support Makah whaling, the issue is moot because the only relief that the court could order is the preparation of an adequate EA, which, appellees contend, already has been done. In making this argument, appellees rely on Realty Income Trust v. Eckerd, 564 F.2d 447 (D.C. Cir. 1977), in which the court refused to remand to the district court because an adequate EIS had been prepared before any action was taken that might harm the environment. Id. at 457. The *Eckerd* court explained:

> The problem here, to repeat, was simply one of timing, that is, that there was not a timely filing of an EIS with Congress. No complaint remains on appeal that the statements in substance were inadequate in any way.

Id.

We conclude that the case at bar is distinguishable from *Eckerd* and, therefore, appellees' reliance on that case is misplaced. Unlike in *Eckerd*, appellants do not concede that the EA that ultimately was prepared is adequate. To the contrary, appellants contend that the EA is demonstrably suspect because the process under which the EA was prepared was fatally defective—i.e., the Federal Defendants were predisposed to finding that the Makah whaling proposal would not significantly affect the environment. We agree. Moreover, appellants vigorously maintain that the EA is deficient with respect to its content and conclusions.

Our conclusions about the EA in this case raise an obvious question: Having already committed in writing to support the Makah's whaling proposal, can the Federal Defendants now be trusted to take the clear-eyed hard look at the whaling proposal's consequences required by the law, or will a new EA be a classic Wonderland case of first-the-verdict, then-the-trial? In order to avoid this problem and to ensure that the law is respected, must we—and can we—set aside the FONSI and require the Federal Defendants to proceed directly to the preparation of an Environmental Impact Statement? On reflection, and in consideration of our limited role in this process, we have decided that it is appropriate only to require a new EA, but to require that it be done under circumstances that ensure an objective evaluation free of the previous taint. * * *

■ KLEINFELD, CIRCUIT JUDGE, dissenting.

* * * The majority opinion errs in three respects: (1) it imposes a novel version of the "objectivity" requirement that cannot be applied in a predictable, consistent manner by other panels in other cases; (2) it

misconstrues the regulation that controls the time when an environmental assessment ought to be prepared; (3) it requires that a new environmental assessment be prepared without finding anything wrong with the old one. Obviously the agency did not prepare the environmental assessment until its officials had already decided that they wanted to let the Makah Indians hunt whales. Why else would they have gone to the trouble of preparing an environmental assessment? But without identifying something wrong with the environmental assessment (and we have not), we have no warrant for setting it aside.

First, "objectivity." * * * All the majority shows is that the agency knew the answer it wanted before it asked the question. But * * * that "institutional bias" does not vitiate the environmental assessment's "objectivity". To show that the environmental assessment is not objective, an objector must show that there is something wrong with the assessment, not just that the agency that prepared it wanted a particular result.

* * *

Second, timing. The majority holds that the "at the earliest possible time" requirement in the regulations means before "making an irreversible and irretrievable commitment of resources." I agree with that proposition of law. But then the majority goes on to say that because the agency's commitment to the Makah tribe preceded the environmental assessment, the environmental assessment came too late. I respectfully disagree with the application of law to facts, though the issue is close.

The commitment to allow the Makah tribe to hunt whales was not an "irreversible and irretrievable commitment," despite the contract. * * * [T]here was a subsequent regulatory process before the first harpoon could be fired, so the environmental assessment was not untimely. * * * The timing requirement of the statute and regulations required that the agency prepare an environmental assessment before the Makah tribe was allowed to hunt whales. It did. * * *

Preparation of an environmental assessment, and, if necessary, an environmental impact statement, is itself a major commitment of resources, and it does not make practical sense to require that these resources be wasted where the agency is not yet in a position to implement a policy choice requiring that expenditure. * * *

Third, remedy. The majority's remedy brings us into conflict with the only other circuit to have considered the issue. In *Realty Income Trust v. Eckerd*, the agency made a proposal to Congress, which involved moving a stream, before preparing its environmental impact statement. * * * The District of Columbia Circuit held that construction could proceed without a second environmental impact statement, despite the unlawful timing, because "equity should not require the doing of a vain or useless thing." That is to say, even if the environmental impact statement was prepared too late, the agency would not be required to prepare a new one in the absence of a showing that the statement was substantively inadequate.

The majority purports to distinguish *Eckerd* on the basis that in the case at bar, the environmental advocacy groups contend that the environmental assessment was "demonstrably suspect because the process under which the EA was prepared was fatally defective—i.e., the federal defendants were predisposed to finding that the Makah whaling proposal would not significantly affect the environment." But that does not distinguish *Eckerd* at all. * * * True, there is a challenge to the substantive adequacy of the environmental assessment in this case and not in *Eckerd*. But we do not rule upon the challenge. * * * In the absence of a judicial determination that the environmental assessment really *was* inadequate. * * * we cannot conclude that preparing another environmental assessment would be other than what *Eckerd* terms "a vain or useless thing."

* * *

The value of the environmental assessments and impact statements comes mostly after the agency has settled on a policy choice. The process of preparing them mobilizes groups that may generate political pressure sufficient to defeat the executive initiative. Exploration of the alternatives, and the facts brought out in preparation, may educate the agency, so that the initiative is modified in a useful way. * * * The quality of the statement may persuade Congress or others who must pass on the agency proposal that the agency was wrong in its policy choice. The statement also stands as an archive with which the public may evaluate the correctness of the agency's policy choices after implementation, to decide whether the agency has done what it promised during implementation, and whether to repose more or less confidence in the agency's policy choices in the future. Preparation and publication of the statements eliminate the agency's monopoly of information, thus enabling other participants in the political process to use the information to overcome the agency's policy choice. None of these values were subverted in this case by the agency's commitment to the Makah Tribe. * * * We have no warrant in this case to interfere.

NOTES AND QUESTIONS

1. *Timing.* The question of when an EIS must be prepared goes to the heart of the NEPA process. Does the holding in *Kleppe* mean that environmental factors need not be considered before a final proposal is made? Is there statutory authority for review of the environmental factors prior to the proposal stage? If so, what mechanism is to be employed? When do the CEQ regulations (promulgated after *Kleppe*) require that an EIS be prepared? Are the regulations consistent with *Kleppe*?

Is it either practical or useful to demand that an agency prepare an EIS before it has decided whether to take action and what action to take? Do you agree with Judge Kleinfeld's assertion that the "value of the environmental assessments and impact statements comes mostly after the agency has settled on a policy choice"? If so, is that what Congress intended? Is it possible to ensure that environmental study informs the policy choice, rather than follows it?

2. *Irreversible commitment.* The majority and dissent in *Metcalf* agree that NEPA environmental analysis must be undertaken prior to "any irreversible and irretrievable commitment of resources." Where does that standard come from? Is it an appropriate test? What does the majority conclude amounted to an irreversible commitment? Why does the dissent disagree? Who has the better of the argument? Is it relevant that the Whaling Convention Act, 16 U.S.C. § 916k (not cited in either opinion), provides that regulations issued by the IWC "shall be submitted for ... publication in the Federal Register by the Secretary of Commerce and shall become effective with respect to all persons and vessels subject to the jurisdiction of the United States in accordance with the terms of such regulations and the provisions of article V of the convention [dealing with the schedule of allowable harvest]."

3. *Postscript on Makah whaling.* The Makah are the only tribe in the U.S. with a treaty right to hunt whales. Whaling was the cornerstone of traditional Makah culture and spiritual life. The tribe voluntarily stopped whale hunting in the 1920s, after commercial (non-tribal) whaling decimated the whale population. On May 17, 1999, a Makah whaling crew, with the approval of NMFS, set out for the first time in more than 70 years. The successful hunt "electrified the Makahs and fueled a cultural renaissance in Neah Bay, a village of about 2,000 people that has been devastated by substance abuse and a 60 percent unemployment rate." Paul Shukovsky, Makah "Treaty Warriors": Heroes or Criminals?, Seattle Post–Intelligencer, Mar. 16, 2008.

After *Metcalf v. Daley*, NMFS withdrew from its agreement with Makah and began a new EA. The second EA was finalized in 2001. It again concluded that the Makah whale hunt would have no significant environmental impact. NMFS announced a quota allowing the Makah to land 5 gray whales in 2001 and 2002. 66 Fed. Reg. 64,378 (Dec. 13, 2001). Again anti-whaling groups sued. This time, the Ninth Circuit concluded that NMFS was required to prepare a full EIS. Anderson v. Evans, 371 F.3d 475 (9th Cir. 2004). In addition, the court concluded that approval of a whaling quota for the Makah violated the Marine Mammal Protection Act (MMPA), 16 U.S.C. 1361 et seq., notwithstanding approval of the quota by the IWC. Early in 2005, the Tribe applied for a waiver from the MMPA's prohibitions on the taking of gray whales. NMFS determined that it must prepare an EIS before it could make a decision on the waiver request.

NMFS released a draft EIS in May 2008. As of July 2011, the draft, which proposes to authorize the tribe to harvest an average of four whales each year, had not been finalized. For more on the status of the Makah's whaling proposals, see NMFS's web page on the topic, at http://www.nwr. noaa.gov/Marine–Mammals/Whales–Dolphins–Porpoise/Gray–Whales/ Makah–Whale–Hunt.cfm, and the Makah Tribe's, at http://www.makah. com/whaling.html.

Meanwhile, in September 2007 five Makah tribal members, acting without authorization from either the tribe or federal authorities, decided to go on a whale hunt. They were arrested by the Coast Guard after putting four harpoons and sixteen bullet holes in a gray whale. The whale died several hours later. The hunters were charged with misdemeanor violations of the Marine Mammal Protection Act. Tribal leaders sympathized with the hunters' frustration, but viewed the unauthorized hunt as a major political mistake. Although the tribe believes it should not need executive branch approval to exercise its treaty hunting rights, it has been trying to work within the system. Shukovsky, *supra.*

Three of the hunters pleaded guilty to a single misdemeanor count under the MMPA and were placed on probation for two years. The other two were convicted after a bench trial, and sentenced to three and five months in federal prison (more than prosecutors had recommended).

4.   *Exemptions from NEPA.*

(a) *Statutory conflict.* Because section 104 of NEPA preserves the specific statutory obligations of federal agencies, NEPA duties are not applicable where there is a clear and unavoidable statutory conflict. Strict statutory deadlines can create such a conflict. See Flint Ridge Development Co. v. Scenic Rivers Association, 426 U.S. 776 (1976).

(b) *Statutory exemptions.* Congress has exempted actions taken by EPA under the Clean Air Act and most EPA actions under the Clean Water Act from the EIS requirement by declaring that those actions shall not be deemed major federal actions significantly affecting the environment. See 15 U.S.C. § 793(c)(1); 33 U.S.C. § 1371(c)(1). What might justify those exemptions?

(c) *Functional equivalence.* In Portland Cement Ass'n v. Ruckelshaus, 486 F.2d 375 (D.C. Cir. 1973), decided before enactment of the statutory exemption under the Clean Air Act, the court held that no EIS was required for an EPA regulation setting air pollution performance standards for new cement plants. According to the court, the legislative history and purposes of NEPA raised serious questions about the applicability of NEPA to "environmentally protective regulatory agencies" such as EPA. The EIS requirement might delay environmentally beneficial actions. But applying NEPA would assure consideration of effects on other resources, provide an opportunity for input by other federal agencies, and open the decision to the public. Unwilling to grant EPA a blanket exemption from NEPA, the court determined that this particular action was exempt because it provided for "the functional equivalent of a NEPA impact statement." In reaching that conclusion, the court noted that EPA was required to consider counter-productive environmental effects as well as the economic costs of regulation; that other agencies and the public had the opportunity to comment on the regulation; and that the decision was subject to judicial review.

The functional equivalence doctrine has since been applied to relieve EPA of the EIS mandate with respect to such actions as: an exemption from the Safe Drinking Water Act, Western Nebraska Resources Council v. U.S. EPA, 943 F.2d 867 (8th Cir. 1991); a Resource Conservation and Recovery Act permit for "the nation's largest hazardous waste facility," State of Alabama ex rel. Siegelman v. U.S. EPA, 911 F.2d 499 (11th Cir. 1990); registration of a pesticide under the Federal Insecticide, Fungicide and Rodenticide Act (FIFRA), permitting its marketing and use, Merrell v. Thomas, 807 F.2d 776 (9th Cir. 1986); and deregistration under the FIFRA, taking a pesticide off the market, State of Wyoming v. Hathaway, 525 F.2d

66 (10th Cir. 1975). Should this exemption apply only when the action being taken unequivocally strengthens environmental protections? Should it be limited to EPA, or extended to other agencies when they are acting to protect the environment? To what extent should it depend on the details of procedural correspondence with NEPA?

(d) *Ministerial acts.* NEPA does not apply when the federal agency has no discretion to take environmental effects into account. See, e.g., American Airlines v. Department of Transportation, 202 F.3d 788 (5th Cir. 2000); Sugarloaf Citizens Ass'n v. FERC, 959 F.2d 508 (4th Cir. 1992). This exemption is discussed in more detail below, in connection with Department of Transportation v. Public Citizen, 541 U.S. 752 (2004).

(e) *Categorical exclusions.* Neither an EIS nor an EA is required for any class of actions "which do not individually or cumulatively have a significant effect on the human environment." 40 C.F.R. § 1508.4. In order to take advantage of this exemption, the action agency must go through a formal procedure to determine that the class of actions in question does not have a significant environmental effect. Environmental documentation must be prepared in the "extraordinary circumstances in which a normally excluded action may have a significant environmental effect." Id. The George W. Bush administration has made aggressive use of categorical exclusions, particularly for national forest management. The Government Accountability Office has reported that:

> The Forest Service approved 3,018 vegetation management projects to treat about 6.3 million acres during calendar years 2003 through 2005. Of these projects, the agency approved about 28 percent using an EA or EIS to treat about 3.4 million acres, while it approved the remainder using categorical exclusions. Although 72 percent of the projects were approved using categorical exclusions, these projects accounted for less than half—46 percent—of the total treatment acres.

GAO, Forest Service: Vegetation Management Projects Approved During Calendar Years 2003 Through 2005 Using Categorical Exclusions, GAO–07–1016T (June 28, 2007). Does the sheer volume of "vegetation management" (primarily timber harvest) approved under categorical exclusions undermine the argument that, individually and collectively, those actions do not have a significant environmental impact? On the other hand, if some timber harvest operations do not have any significant environmental impact, isn't it preferable to concentrate on analyzing the effects of the others? For a decision upholding one forest management categorical exclusion against a facial challenge, but also detailing the amount of effort that went into establishing the categorical exclusion, see Colorado Wild v. United States Forest Service, 435 F.3d 1204 (10th Cir. 2006).

B. "Major Federal Actions"

CLASS DISCUSSION PROBLEM: THE CHAD–CAMEROON OIL PIPELINE PROJECT, PART 1

The Overseas Private Investment Corporation (OPIC) is an agency of the United States government which, according to its web site, "helps U.S.

businesses invest overseas, fosters economic development in new and emerging markets, complements the private sector in managing risks associated with foreign direct investment, and supports U.S. foreign policy." Among other things, OPIC provides "political risk insurance" to U.S. investors, contractors, and financial institutions doing business overseas. The insurance covers risks associated with political instability, including property expropriation and political violence. OPIC has considerable discretion in choosing projects for which to provide financing or insurance. It typically does limited environmental screening of applications, and can include environmental conditions in its loan or insurance contracts.

In 1998, OPIC approved $100 million in political risk insurance coverage for Pride International, Inc., a subcontractor on the Chad/Cameroon Petroleum Development and Pipeline Project. Pride pays an annual premium of $1.1 million for the insurance. Overall, the project involves development of oil fields in southern Chad, construction of an oil pipeline running more than 600 miles from those oil fields to the Atlantic Ocean off Cameroon, and construction of an offshore terminal where oil from the pipeline can be loaded into tankers for shipment around the world. The total cost of the project is estimated at about $3.5 billion. Its major sponsors are ExxonMobil, Chevron–Texaco, and Petronas, a Malaysian oil company. Pride's role is to provide drilling and related services at the oil fields. In a separate decision, the Export–Import Bank, a US government-owned corporation that provides financing in various forms to support exports from the United States, provided a $200 million loan guarantee for the pipeline portion of the project.

Chad, a landlocked country in north-central Africa, is among the poorest countries in the world. Political instability, including a long-running civil war in the northern part of the country and periodic civil unrest and open civil war in the south, has severely limited foreign private investment. Crossing Cameroon, the pipeline will run through a largely intact rainforest and across several major rivers. Ultimately, the project could produce as much as $2 billion in revenue for Chad and $500 million for Cameroon.

Neither OPIC nor the Export–Import Bank prepared either an EA or an EIS prior to issuing insurance coverage. Friends of the Earth filed suit against both under NEPA and the APA. Has NEPA been violated? What, precisely, is the "federal action" whose environmental impacts must be analyzed?

Excerpts From Council on Environmental Quality Regulations

40 C.F.R. Parts 1500–1517.

Sec. 1502.4.   Major Federal actions requiring the preparation of environmental impact statements

(a) Agencies shall make sure the proposal which is the subject of an environmental impact statement is properly defined. Agencies shall use the criteria for scope (§ 1508.25) to determine which proposal(s) shall be the subject of a particular statement. Proposals or parts of proposals which are related to each other closely enough to be, in effect, a single course of action shall be evaluated in a single impact statement. * * *

Sec. 1508.18.   Major Federal action

Major Federal action includes actions with effects that may be major and which are potentially subject to Federal control and responsibility. Major reinforces but does not have a meaning independent of significantly (§ 1508.27). Actions include the circumstance where the responsible officials fail to act and that failure to act is reviewable by courts or administrative tribunals under the Administrative Procedure Act or other applicable law as agency action. * * *

Sec. 1508.25.   Scope

Scope consists of the range of actions, alternatives, and impacts to be considered in an environmental impact statement. * * * To determine the scope of environmental impact statements, agencies shall consider 3 types of actions, 3 types of alternatives, and 3 types of impacts. They include:

(a) Actions * * * which may be:

    (1) Connected actions, which means that they are closely related and therefore should be discussed in the same impact statement. Actions are connected if they:

        (i) Automatically trigger other actions which may require environmental impact statements.

        (ii) Cannot or will not proceed unless other actions are taken previously or simultaneously.

        (iii) Are interdependent parts of a larger action and depend on the larger action for their justification.

    (2) Cumulative actions, which when viewed with other proposed actions have cumulatively significant impacts and should therefore be discussed in the same impact statement.

    (3) Similar actions, which when viewed with other reasonably foreseeable or proposed agency actions, have similarities that provide a basis for evaluating their environmental consequences together, such as common timing or geography. An agency may wish to analyze these actions in the same impact statement. It should do so when the best way to assess adequately the combined impacts of similar actions or reasonable alternatives to such actions is to treat them in a single impact statement.

(b) Alternatives, which include:

    (1) No action alternative.

    (2) Other reasonable courses of actions.

(3) Mitigation measures (not in the proposed action).

(c) Impacts, which may be:

(1) Direct;

(2) indirect;

(3) cumulative.

South Carolina ex rel. Campbell v. O'Leary

United States Court of Appeals, Fourth Circuit, 1995.
64 F.3d 892.

■ NIEMEYER, CIRCUIT JUDGE.

* * *

As an important aspect of the United States' longstanding policy for the nonproliferation of nuclear weapons, the United States has sought to convert foreign nuclear reactors from using highly-enriched uranium, which may readily be employed in the construction of nuclear weapons, to low-enriched uranium, which cannot be so employed. Adopting a formal program to encourage that conversion, known as the Reduced Enrichment for Research and Test Reactors program (the "Reduced Enrichment program"), the United States has committed to accept highly-enriched spent nuclear fuel rods from European research reactors for storage in facilities in the United States. * * *

Because recently enacted statutes and regulations require that the modified Reduced Enrichment program receive environmental review before the Department of Energy can officially implement the policy, foreign nuclear reactors have been forced to retain spent fuel rods at their sites. Over time, storage space for spent fuel rods at foreign reactor sites began to run out, creating the risk that the foreign reactors would transfer their spent fuel rods to other countries for reprocessing, thus perpetuating the use of highly-enriched uranium in nuclear fuel in contravention of the United States' nonproliferation policy. A market in highly-enriched uranium would promote the fabrication of nuclear weapons.

In July 1993, * * * the Department of Energy recommended: (1) the preparation of an Environmental Impact Statement in connection with a long term plan of selecting a site and constructing a facility to receive 24,000 spent fuel rods from European research reactors; [and] (2) the preparation of an Environmental Assessment in connection with the immediate receipt of a few hundred spent fuel rods in urgent need of shipment for storage at the Department of Energy's existing storage facility at the Savannah River Site * * *.

[T]he Department of Energy released a final Environmental Assessment in April 1994, determining that 409 spent fuel rods were in urgent need of shipment and that there would be no significant environmental impact if these rods were shipped to the Savannah River Site. * * *

In September 1994, South Carolina filed this action, seeking an injunction to prohibit receipt of the 409 fuel rods. [The district court granted the injunction.]

South Carolina does not argue, nor can it, that the Department of Energy is dividing the importation of European spent fuel rods into several minor shipments in order to avoid the preparation of any Environmental Impact Statement, for the Department of Energy is already conducting an Environmental Impact Statement for the importation of the 24,000 spent fuel rods. Instead, South Carolina argues that there is no meaningful distinction between the urgent relief shipments of 409 rods and the total proposed shipment of 24,000 rods and that if an Environmental Impact Statement is required for the total shipment, the Department of Energy should likewise be required to prepare an Environmental Impact Statement for the "segmented" urgent relief shipments.

However, South Carolina apparently fails to appreciate the significance of the fact that there is no site or facility in the United States to receive the 24,000 rods and that an Environmental Impact Statement must be prepared for such a major endeavor. With respect to the 409 rods in need of urgent relief, however, the plan is to store them at existing and approved facilities at the Department of Energy's Savannah River Site. That site is currently being used on a continuing basis to receive spent nuclear fuel rods from U.S. research reactors, and no Environmental Assessment or Environmental Impact Statement is demanded for each domestic shipment of those rods to the Savannah River Site. The fact that the 409 rods under consideration originate in Europe, instead of the United States, has not been shown to impose a meaningfully different environmental impact.
* * *

Furthermore, as we held in State of North Carolina v. City of Virginia Beach, 951 F.2d 596 (4th Cir. 1991), the segmentation of one phase of a larger project prior to the completion of the environmental review of the entire project constitutes impermissible segmentation only if the component action has a "direct and substantial probability of influencing [the agency's] decision" on the larger project. Id. at 603. These urgent relief shipments fail to pose such an influence; they do not in any way commit the government to accepting the larger shipment of 24,000 rods nor do they determine the outcome of the Environmental Impact Statement that is currently being prepared for the larger shipment.

Finally, the district court held that the urgent relief shipments of 409 rods and the larger, proposed 24,000–rod shipments qualify as "connected actions," "cumulative actions," and "similar actions" within the meaning of 40 C.F.R. § 1508.25(a). If the district court were correct, then the applicable NEPA regulations would require that such related actions be considered in the same Environmental Impact Statement. However, a careful reading of the regulations fails to support the district court's conclusion.

Separate actions are considered "connected" if they (1) "[a]utomatically trigger other actions which may require Environmental Impact Statements''; (2) ''[c]annot or will not proceed unless other actions are taken previously or simultaneously''; or (3) ''[a]re interdependent parts of a larger action and depend on the larger action for their justification.'' See 40 C.F.R. § 1508.25(a)(1). The urgent relief shipments of 409 rods do not qualify as ''connected actions'' under any of these three definitions. The shipments involving 409 rods do not ''automatically trigger'' the acceptance of the larger 24,000–rod shipments, nor does their utility depend upon the viability of the larger shipment. The urgent relief shipments are independent and separable, and merely preserve the Department of Energy's option to accept the larger shipments.

The urgent relief shipments of 409 rods and the larger proposed shipments of 24,000 rods also do not qualify as ''cumulative actions,'' which are defined as actions ''which when viewed with other proposed actions have cumulatively significant impacts.'' 40 C.F.R. § 1508.25(a)(2). By itself, the proposed shipment of 24,000 spent fuel rods has a significant impact requiring an Environmental Impact Statement. Such a shipment will necessitate the construction of a new domestic storage facility regardless of whether the Department of Energy is permitted to accept the urgent relief shipments. Furthermore, the cumulative impact of accepting the urgent relief shipments is not ''significant,'' in that it does not require the construction of a new facility or even materially deprive the United States of existing storage facilities. The Department of Energy has projected that it will run out of storage spaces at the Savannah River Site in May 1999 if it does not receive the urgent relief shipments, and in January 1999 if it does receive them.

We also disagree with the district court's characterization of the two separate projects as ''similar actions.'' Similar actions are defined as having ''similarities that provide a basis for evaluating their environmental consequences together, such as common timing or geography.'' 40 C.F.R. § 1508.25(a)(3). Other than the fact that both the urgent relief shipments and the larger 24,000–rod shipments involve spent nuclear fuel, the two shipments are dissimilar. The timing of the shipments is different, since the urgent relief shipments are scheduled to conclude within the next few months and the larger shipments will not begin for several years, if ever. Moreover, since a site for the larger facility has not been selected, it may be constructed at an entirely different area of the country with no geographic similarity to the Savannah River Site.

Accordingly, we conclude that the district court's segmentation argument is not supported in fact or by law.

■ DONALD RUSSELL, CIRCUIT JUDGE, dissenting:

* * *

I continue to adhere to my position that the shipment of 409 spent nuclear fuel elements, or any portion of that amount, constitutes an improper segmentation from the Department of Energy's larger plan to accept 24,000 spent fuel elements from foreign research reactors over the next ten to thirteen years.

* * *

[T]he EIS studies three different alternatives for managing the spent nuclear fuel from foreign research reactors. The most ambitious management alternative, Management Alternative 1, would involve the acceptance of roughly 24,000 spent nuclear fuel elements over a ten to thirteen year period. Management Alternative 2 would involve the management of spent nuclear fuel overseas either by providing assistance, incentives, and coordination for the storage of spent fuel at one or more locations overseas, or by providing nontechnical assistance, incentives, and coordination for the reprocessing of spent nuclear fuel at overseas reprocessing facilities. Management Alternative 3, the hybrid alternative, would involve a combination of accepting spent fuel elements for storage in the United States and providing assistance for the management of spent fuel overseas. The Draft EIS also considers the alternative of taking no action.

The EIS does not propose a permanent solution to the storage of the 24,000 spent fuel elements that would be accepted under Management Alternative 1. Instead, the EIS proposes a two-phase storage plan for managing the accepted spent fuel for a 40–year period. In phase 1, spent nuclear fuel elements would be shipped to existing facilities for interim storage while the Department of Energy constructs a more permanent storage facility. The EIS explains that only two facilities could serve as potential phase 1 sites: the Savannah River Site and the Idaho National Engineering Laboratory. Phase 2 would begin when the DOE constructs a new facility or refurbishes an existing facility for the 40–year storage of the spent fuel elements. The Draft EIS considers five possible sites for such a phase 2 storage facility: the Savannah River Site, the Idaho National Engineering Laboratory, the Hanford Site, the Oak Ridge Reservation, and the Nevada Test Site.

* * *

The DOE insists that it will not select a management alternative until it issues the final EIS, which it claims will be completed in September 1995. In fact, the DOE has already begun implementation of Management Alternative 1. In September 1994, this Court allowed the government to accept a shipment of 153 spent nuclear fuel elements from foreign research reactors for storage at the Savannah River Site. In lifting the district court's injunction in this case, this Court authorizes the government to accept a second shipment of 157 rods to be stored at Savannah River. Although the DOE insists that these "urgent" shipments are part of a separate program, the fact remains that under Management Alternative 1, the government proposes to import the same type of spent fuel elements from the same set of research reactors and to store them at the same facility. The only difference between these "urgent" shipments and the shipments under Management Alternative 1 is the timing. By segmenting the "urgent" shipments from its larger plan to accept 24,000 rods, the DOE has begun implementing Management Alternative 1 before it has completed the EIS.

* * * It undermines the purposes of NEPA, and is a bit unseemly, for the DOE to begin implementation of its proposed action while it claims to be studying the environmental impacts and considering other alternatives. The EIS should be more than a formality. Before the DOE begins importing large amounts of spent nuclear fuel, which rank among the most dangerous material that humanity has ever tried to control, we should require the DOE to complete its environmental review.

* * *

Ka Makani 'O Kohala Ohana Inc. v. County of Hawai'i Department of Water Supply

United States Court of Appeals, Ninth Circuit, 2002.
295 F.3d 955.

■ TASHIMA, CIRCUIT JUDGE.

In 1987, the [County of Hawaii Department of Water Supply (DWS)] began planning for the Kohala Project, a transbasin water diversion system on the Big Island of Hawaii that would transfer up to 20 million gallons of groundwater per day (in Phases I and II, combined) from the northern part of Kohala to South Kohala through an arrangement of groundwater wells, gravity flow pipelines, and storage reservoirs, to provide a reliable supply of potable water for the development of coastal resorts.

[United States Geological Survey (USGS)] involvement in the Kohala Project consisted primarily of the partial funding of and participation in a series of preliminary studies designed to assess the groundwater availability in the basal aquifer of the North Kohala area and a program of test drilling and test pumping in the aquifer. DWS and USGS entered into four Joint Funding Agreements in 1988, dividing the costs of the studies and an interpretative analysis of the data collected evenly between the two, in the amount of $800,000 each. The studies resulted in the publication of two reports in 1995 and were used by the DWS to prove the merits of the project. In addition to the initial studies, the DWS consulted with the USGS about the design of the Kohala Project and requested that the USGS conduct further studies on the impact of the proposed wells on the streamflow of the Polulu Valley Stream, the Kohakohau Stream, the Waikoloa Stream, and the Olaa Flume Spring.

In 1991, [the U.S. Department of Housing and Urban Development (HUD)] became involved in the Kohala Project when Congress passed an appropriations bill allocating $500,000 to the County of Hawaii for an EIS for the development of a water resource system for the community of Kohala. HUD provided the County with application materials for the special purpose grant and gave the County advice regarding its application, including a recommendation to restrict the scope of the activities proposed to be funded by the grant to those exempted from NEPA requirements in order to expedite the approval process. While it is unclear from the record whether HUD restricted the use of the grant funds to the preparation of an EIS alone or had informally approved of its use in the other activities set forth in the County's revised application, there is no doubt that the activities to be funded by the grant were limited to those of a preliminary nature.

The DWS only drew upon the grant account once, in 1995, for $30,000 to cover a portion of the payments made to contractors working on the state EIS for the Kohala Project. In 1998, the DWS notified HUD that the Kohala Project had been placed on hold due to the poor economic climate, but maintained that the project would be resumed at the appropriate time. HUD initially agreed to extend the three-year time limit for use of the grant funds, but later recommended the closing out of the grant. In 1999, Congress authorized Hawaii County to transfer the remaining balance for use in other water system improvement projects subject to HUD's approval. In April 2000, the DWS proposed to use the remaining $470,000 for an unrelated project in South Hilo.

* * *

NEPA requires a federal agency to prepare a detailed EIS for all "major Federal actions significantly affecting the quality of the human environment." 42 U.S.C. § 4332(2)(C). Among other things, the EIS must set forth the unavoidable adverse environmental effects of the proposed action and alternatives to the proposed action. *Id.* The primary issue in this appeal is whether the USGS and HUD involvement in the Kohala Project is sufficiently major to transform it into a "major Federal action," triggering the EIS requirement of NEPA. We conclude that it is not.

"There are no clear standards for defining the point at which federal participation transforms a state or local project into a major federal action." *Almond Hill Sch. v. United States Dep't of Agric.,* 768 F.2d 1030, 1039 (9th Cir.1985). "The matter is simply one of degree." *Id.* "Marginal federal action will not render otherwise local action federal." *Id.* To make this determination, we look "to the nature of the federal funds used and the extent of federal involvement." *Sierra Club v. Penfold,* 857 F.2d 1307, 1314 (9th Cir. 1988).

While "significant federal funding" can turn "what would otherwise be" a state or local project into a "major federal action," *Alaska v. Andrus,* 591 F.2d 537, 540 (9th Cir. 1979), consideration must be given to a "great disparity in the expenditures forecast for the state [and county] and federal portions of the *entire* program." *See Friends of the Earth, Inc. v. Coleman,* 518 F.2d 323, 329 (9th Cir. 1975). In the present case, the sum total of all of the federal funding that was ever offered to the Kohala Project is $1.3 million,[4] which is less than two percent of the estimated total project cost of

---

4. The $1.3 million figure is based on $800,000 provided by USGS for preliminary studies and $500,000 offered under the HUD grant. Because $470,000 of the HUD grant has been transferred for use on other projects, the total amount of federal funding actually spent is only $830,000.

$80 million.[5] At this point, the State of Hawaii and DWS have spent $3,453,161 on the Kohala Project and intend to fund the rest of the project, when it is ready to proceed, with the proceeds of bonds issued by the State and/or County. We therefore conclude that the federal funding contribution alone could not transform the entire Kohala Project into a "major federal action."

The USGS and HUD also lacked the degree of decision-making power, authority, or control over the Kohala Project needed to render it a major federal action. The purpose of NEPA is to "bring environmental considerations to the attention of *federal* decision-makers." *Friends of the Earth,* 518 F.2d at 329 (emphasis added). * * *

Although the USGS played an advisory role in the planning of the Kohala Project because of the agency's expertise and participation in the preliminary research studies, the USGS was not "placed in a decisionmaking role." *See Almond Hill Sch.,* 768 F.2d at 1039. Because the final decision-making power remained at all times with DWS, we conclude that the USGS involvement was not sufficient to constitute "major federal action." *See Village of Los Ranchos,* 906 F.2d at 1482 (stating that in order to have "major federal action," a federal agency's authority to influence "must be more than the power to give nonbinding advice to the nonfederal actor ... the federal agency must possess actual power to control the nonfederal activity").

Similarly, HUD's provision of advice and information to the DWS regarding its application for HUD's special purpose grant "did not constitute discretionary involvement or control over" the entire Kohala Project, and therefore, was not "major federal action" for the purposes of NEPA.

Finally, Ka Makani's heavy reliance on *Scottsdale Mall v. Indiana,* 549 F.2d 484 (7th Cir. 1977), and *Ross v. Fed. Highway Admin.,* 162 F.3d 1046 (10th Cir. 1998), is misplaced. Both *Scottsdale* and *Ross* are distinguishable from the present case because of the extent and nature of the federal involvement in those two federal-aid highway project cases. In those cases, the projects were conceived of as federal from the outset and had already been subjected to a high degree of federal oversight and control. Furthermore, the federal involvement, including federal funds, had continued long after the preliminary planning stages. In the present case, federal involvement in the Kohala Project was restricted to the support and funding of preliminary activities such as the EIS and scientific background studies. Moreover, the Kohala Project was always under the total control of nonfederal actors and agencies.

In sum, we hold that the actions of HUD and USGS, taken together, in the preliminary stages of the Kohala Project did not constitute "major federal action" within the scope of NEPA.

---

5. Although there is no evidence that the money was ever spent, for summary judgment purposes, it is reasonable to infer that an additional $61,200 in federal funding was anticipated to go towards a USGS study requested by the DWS on the streamflow of the Pololu Valley Stream and three other streams. This additional amount, however, would only raise the federal portion of the total project cost to 2.5 percent and would not alter our analysis.

NOTES AND QUESTIONS

1. *Segmentation.* Narrowly defining a project may allow an agency to avoid preparing an EIS for any part of the project, or may result in a series of separate environmental documents, none of which considers all the environmental impacts of the project. What guidance do the CEQ regulations offer for determining whether actions must be considered together in a single environmental document? What test did the Fourth Circuit apply in *South Carolina v. O'Leary*? Why does the dissent disagree? Will the shipment of 409 fuel rods to Savannah River affect the agency's decision on the larger question of what to do in the future about spent fuel from foreign reactors? Is that the right question to ask? Would the dissent have allowed the shipment of twenty fuel rods, or two, without preparation of an EIS?

In the Class Discussion Problem, must the question of whether environmental documentation is required be answered for the OPIC insurance and Export–Import Bank loan guarantee together, or can they be treated as separate?

2. *Small handles.* The flip side of the segmentation problem arises when federal funding is sought or federal authorization is required for one portion of a larger non-federal project. The problem in these cases, sometimes called the "small handles" problem, is whether federal responsibility, and therefore federal procedural requirements, should swallow the entire project. Are additional concerns important in the small handles situation? According to the *Ka Makani* court, what test determines whether federal agency funding "federalizes" a larger project for NEPA purposes? Is the court's approach consistent with the CEQ regulations? Is it sensible? In the Class Discussion Problem, does the federal funding make the entire Development Project a federal action for NEPA purposes? Would you analyze the "small handles" problem differently if it involved a federal permit rather than federal funding? Suppose, for example, that a private utility company proposes to construct a 67–mile long electric power transmission line. The line will cross the Missouri River. That requires a permit from the Army Corps of Engineers under the Rivers and Harbors Act, 33 U.S.C. § 403. Is the "federal action" for NEPA purposes only the 1.25 mile river crossing, or is it the entire 67 mile line? See Winnebago v. Ray, 621 F.2d 269 (8th Cir. 1980).

The small handles problem arises frequently in connection with the issuance of permits under Clean Water Act § 404. Two recent cases in that line are Ohio Valley Environmental Coalition v. Aracoma Coal Co., 556 F.3d 177 (4th Cir. 2009) (holding that Corps properly limited its NEPA analysis for a § 404 permit authorizing valley fills in connection with mountaintop removal mining to the specific effects of placing fill in federal jurisdictional waters) and White Tanks Concerned Citizens v. Strock, 563 F.3d 1033 (9th Cir. 2009) (holding that NEPA analysis for a § 404 permit to fill twenty-nine acres of washes dispersed across the site of a master-planned development must consider the impacts of the entire proposed development, because without the proposed fill the area could not be developed as a single connected community.)

3. *Highway projects.* Courts are reluctant to allow state or local governments to determine the route of a highway prior to NEPA analysis by building the nonfederal segments before seeking federal approval or funding. See, e.g., Maryland Conservation Council, Inc. v. Gilchrist, 808 F.2d 1039 (4th Cir. 1986). However, a portion of a larger highway project may be considered in isolation if it has independent utility and logical termini. See 23 C.F.R. § 771.111(f) (Federal Highway Administration NEPA guidelines); Preserve Endangered Areas of Cobb's History, Inc. v. U.S. Army Corps of Engineers, 87 F.3d 1242 (11th Cir. 1996). Is this an appropriate test? Is it consistent with that applied in other segmentation and small handles cases?

4. *NEPA and agency inaction.* Is NEPA compliance ever required when an agency declines to take action? How do the CEQ regulations treat that question? What accounts for the different treatment of action and inaction? Does NEPA apply to: (a) a decision by the U.S. Forest Service not to use herbicides in a national forest (see Minnesota Pesticide Information & Education, Inc. v. Espy, 29 F.3d 442 (8th Cir. 1994)); (b) U.S. refusal to regulate transport of nuclear waste through the waters of the U.S. Exclusive Economic Zone, where the scope of U.S. authority over those waters is uncertain (see Mayaguezanos por la Salud y el Ambiente v. United States, 198 F.3d 297 (1st Cir. 1999); (c) a decision by the Food and Drug Administration not to issue blanket regulations regarding genetically modified food crops (see Alliance for Bio-Integrity v. Shalala, 116 F. Supp. 2d 166 (D.D.C. 2000))?

5. *Application of NEPA abroad.* In general, there is a presumption against the extraterritorial application of domestic US law, meaning that absent a clear statement to the contrary it is presumed that Congress intends only to reach conduct occurring in or having effects in the United States. In Environmental Defense Fund v. Massey, 986 F.2d 528 (D.C. Cir. 1993), the D.C. Circuit held that presumption inapplicable to a decision by the National Science Foundation to incinerate food wastes at an Antarctic research station. The court noted that the regulated conduct, NSF's decisionmaking, occurred "primarily, if not exclusively, in the United States, and the alleged extraterritorial effect of the statute will be felt in Antarctica—a continent without a sovereign, and an area over which the United States has a great measure of legislative control." On the other hand, the same court concluded in NRDC v. Nuclear Regulatory Commission, 647 F.2d 1345 (D.C. Cir. 1981), that the decision to allow export of a nuclear reactor to the Philippines, although made wholly in the United States, was not subject to NEPA because its environmental impacts would be felt solely in the Philippines. See also NEPA Coalition of Japan v. Aspin, 837 F.Supp. 466 (D.D.C. 1993), holding that NEPA did not apply to US military installations in Japan because of "the substantial likelihood that treaty relations [would] be affected." If the only environmental impacts of the

Chad–Cameroon project would occur in Africa, should it be subject to NEPA? Might there be impacts in the United States?

C.   "SIGNIFICANTLY AFFECTING THE QUALITY OF THE HUMAN ENVIRONMENT"

CLASS DISCUSSION PROBLEM: THE CHAD–CAMEROON OIL PIPELINE PROJECT, PART 2

Assuming that the OPIC insurance or Export–Import Bank loan guarantee (or both) is a "federal action" for NEPA purposes, what is the scope of the environmental impacts that must be considered in an EA or EIS? Could the analysis be limited to Pride's drilling activities and the direct effect of pipeline construction? Must it also consider the global warming impacts of consumption of the oil that will be produced in Chad and exported through the pipeline? The additional CO_2 emissions, and associated global warming effects, of economic development in Chad and Cameroon that will follow pipeline development?

Excerpts From Council on Environmental Quality Regulations

40 C.F.R. Parts 1500–1517.

Sec. 1508.7.   Cumulative impact

Cumulative impact is the impact on the environment which results from the incremental impact of the action when added to other past, present, and reasonably foreseeable future actions regardless of what agency (Federal or non-Federal) or person undertakes such other actions. Cumulative impacts can result from individually minor but collectively significant actions taking place over a period of time.

Sec. 1508.8.   Effects

"Effects" include:

(a) Direct effects, which are caused by the action and occur at the same time and place.

(b) Indirect effects, which are caused by the action and are later in time or farther removed in distance, but are still reasonably foreseeable. Indirect effects may include growth inducing effects and other effects related to induced changes in the pattern of land use, population density or growth rate, and related effects on air and water and other natural systems, including ecosystems.

Effects and impacts as used in these regulations are synonymous. Effects includes ecological (such as the effects on natural resources and on the components, structures, and functioning of affected ecosystems), aesthetic, historic, cultural, economic, social, or health [effects], whether direct, indirect, or cumulative. Effects may also include those resulting from actions which may have both beneficial and detrimental effects, even if on balance the agency believes that the effect will be beneficial.

Sec. 1508.27.   Significantly

Significantly as used in NEPA requires considerations of both context and intensity:

(a) *Context.* This means that the significance of an action must be analyzed in several contexts such as society as a whole (human, national), the affected region, the affected interests, and the locality. * * * Both short- and long-term effects are relevant.

(b) *Intensity.* This refers to the severity of impact. * * * The following should be considered in evaluating intensity:

> (1) Impacts that may be both beneficial and adverse. A significant effect may exist even if the Federal agency believes that on balance the effect will be beneficial.

> (2) The degree to which the proposed action affects public health or safety.

> (3) Unique characteristics of the geographic area such as proximity to historic or cultural resources, park lands, prime farmlands, wetlands, wild and scenic rivers, or ecologically critical areas.

> (4) The degree to which the effects on the quality of the human environment are likely to be highly controversial.

> (5) The degree to which the possible effects on the human environment are highly uncertain or involve unique or unknown risks.

> (6) The degree to which the action may establish a precedent for future actions with significant effects or represents a decision in principle about a future consideration.

> (7) Whether the action is related to other actions with individually insignificant but cumulatively significant impacts. Significance exists if it is reasonable to anticipate a cumulatively significant impact on the environment. Significance cannot be avoided by terming an action temporary or by breaking it down into small component parts.

* * *

Department of Transportation v. Public Citizen

United States Supreme Court, 2004.
541 U.S. 752.

■ Justice Thomas delivered the opinion of the Court.

In this case, we confront the question whether the National Environmental Policy Act of 1969 (NEPA) * * * require[s] the Federal Motor

Carrier Safety Administration (FMCSA) to evaluate the environmental effects of cross-border operations of Mexican-domiciled motor carriers, where FMCSA's promulgation of certain regulations would allow such cross-border operations to occur. Because FMCSA lacks discretion to prevent these cross-border operations, we conclude that [NEPA imposes] no such requirement on FMCSA.

I

* * *

FMCSA, an agency within the Department of Transportation (DOT), is responsible for motor carrier safety and registration. See 49 U.S.C. § 113(f). FMCSA has a variety of statutory mandates, including "ensur[ing]" safety, § 31136, establishing minimum levels of financial responsibility for motor carriers, § 31139, and prescribing federal standards for safety inspections of commercial motor vehicles, § 31142. Importantly, FMCSA has only limited discretion regarding motor vehicle carrier registration: It must grant registration to all domestic or foreign motor carriers that are "willing and able to comply with" the applicable safety, fitness, and financial-responsibility requirements. § 13902(a)(1). FMCSA has no statutory authority to impose or enforce emissions controls or to establish environmental requirements unrelated to motor carrier safety.

We now turn to the factual and procedural background of this case. Before 1982, motor carriers domiciled in Canada and Mexico could obtain certification to operate within the United States from the Interstate Commerce Commission (ICC).[6] In 1982, Congress, concerned about discriminatory treatment of United States motor carriers in Mexico and Canada, enacted a 2–year moratorium on new grants of operating authority. Congress authorized the President to extend the moratorium beyond the 2–year period if Canada or Mexico continued to interfere with United States motor carriers, and also authorized the President to lift or modify the moratorium if he determined that doing so was in the national interest. Although the moratorium on Canadian motor carriers was quickly lifted, the moratorium on Mexican motor carriers remained, and was extended by the President.

In December 1992, the leaders of Mexico, Canada, and the United States signed the North American Free Trade Agreement (NAFTA), 32 I.L.M. 605 (1993). As part of NAFTA, the United States agreed to phase out the moratorium and permit Mexican motor carriers to obtain operating authority within the United States' interior by January 2000. On NAFTA's effective date (January 1, 1994), the President began to lift the trade moratorium by allowing the licensing of Mexican carriers to provide some bus services in the United States. The President, however, did not continue

---

6. In 1995, Congress abolished the ICC and transferred most of its responsibilities to the Secretary of Transportation. In 1999, Congress transferred responsibility for motor carrier safety within DOT to the newly created FMCSA.

to ease the moratorium on the timetable specified by NAFTA, as concerns about the adequacy of Mexico's regulation of motor carrier safety remained.

The Government of Mexico challenged the United States' implementation of NAFTA's motor carrier provisions under NAFTA's dispute-resolution process, and in February 2001, an international arbitration panel determined that the United States' "blanket refusal" of Mexican motor carrier applications breached the United States' obligations under NAFTA. Shortly thereafter, the President made clear his intention to lift the moratorium on Mexican motor carrier certification following the preparation of new regulations governing grants of operating authority to Mexican motor carriers.

In May 2001, FMCSA published for comment proposed rules concerning safety regulation of Mexican motor carriers. One rule (the Application Rule) addressed the establishment of a new application form for Mexican motor carriers that seek authorization to operate within the United States. Another rule (the Safety Monitoring Rule) addressed the establishment of a safety-inspection regime for all Mexican motor carriers that would receive operating authority under the Application Rule.

In December 2001, Congress enacted the Department of Transportation and Related Agencies Appropriations Act, 2002, 115 Stat. 833. Section 350 of this Act provided that no funds appropriated under the Act could be obligated or expended to review or to process any application by a Mexican motor carrier for authority to operate in the interior of the United States until FMCSA implemented specific application and safety-monitoring requirements for Mexican carriers. Some of these requirements went beyond those proposed by FMCSA in the Application and Safety Monitoring Rules. Congress extended the § 350 conditions to appropriations for Fiscal Years 2003 and 2004.

In January 2002, acting pursuant to NEPA's mandates, FMCSA issued a programmatic EA for the proposed Application and Safety Monitoring Rules. FMCSA's EA evaluated the environmental impact associated with three separate scenarios: where the President did not lift the moratorium; where the President did but where (contrary to what was legally possible) FMCSA did not issue any new regulations; and the Proposed Action Alternative, where the President would modify the moratorium and where FMCSA would adopt the proposed regulations. The EA considered the environmental impact in the categories of traffic and congestion, public safety and health, air quality, noise, socioeconomic factors, and environmental justice. Vital to the EA's analysis, however, was the assumption that there would be no change in trade volume between the United States and Mexico due to the issuance of the regulations. FMCSA did note that § 350's restrictions made it impossible for Mexican motor carriers to operate in the interior of the United States before FMCSA's issuance of the regulations. But, FMCSA determined that "this and any other associated effects in trade characteristics would be the result of the modification of the moratorium" by the President, not a result of FMCSA's implementation of the proposed safety regulations. Because FMCSA concluded that the entry of the Mexican trucks was not an "effect" of its regulations, it did not consider any environmental impact that might be caused by the increased presence of Mexican trucks within the United States.

The particular environmental effects on which the EA focused, then, were those likely to arise from the increase in the number of roadside inspections of Mexican trucks and buses due to the proposed regulations. The EA concluded that these effects (such as a slight increase in emissions, noise from the trucks, and possible danger to passing motorists) were minor and could be addressed and avoided in the inspections process itself. The EA also noted that the increase of inspection-related emissions would be at least partially offset by the fact that the safety requirements would reduce the number of Mexican trucks operating in the United States. Due to these calculations, the EA concluded that the issuance of the proposed regulations would have no significant impact on the environment, and hence FMCSA, on the same day as it released the EA, issued a FONSI.

On March 19, 2002, FMCSA issued the two interim rules, delaying their effective date until May 3, 2002, to allow public comment on provisions that FMCSA added to satisfy the requirements of § 350. In the regulatory preambles, FMCSA relied on its EA and its FONSI to demonstrate compliance with NEPA. * * *

In November 2002, the President lifted the moratorium on qualified Mexican motor carriers. Before this action, however, respondents filed petitions for judicial review of the Application and Safety Monitoring Rules, arguing that the rules were promulgated in violation of NEPA and the CAA. The Court of Appeals agreed with respondents, granted the petitions, and set aside the rules.

* * *

II

An agency's decision not to prepare an EIS can be set aside only upon a showing that it was "arbitrary, capricious, an abuse of discretion, or otherwise not in accordance with law." 5 U.S.C. § 706(2)(A). Here, FMCSA based its FONSI upon the analysis contained within its EA; respondents argue that the issuance of the FONSI was arbitrary and capricious because the EA's analysis was flawed. In particular, respondents criticize the EA's failure to take into account the various environmental effects caused by the increase in cross-border operations of Mexican motor carriers.

Under NEPA, an agency is required to provide an EIS only if it will be undertaking a "major Federal actio[n]," which "significantly affect[s] the quality of the human environment." 42 U.S.C. § 4332(2)(C). Under applicable CEQ regulations, "[m]ajor Federal action" is defined to "includ[e] actions with effects that may be major and which are potentially subject to Federal control and responsibility." 40 CFR § 1508.18 (2003). "Effects" is defined to "include: (a) Direct effects, which are caused by the action and occur at the same time and place," and "(b) Indirect effects, which are caused by the action and are later in time or farther removed in distance, but are still reasonably foreseeable." § 1508.8. Thus, the relevant question is whether the increase in cross-border operations of Mexican motor carriers, with the correlative release of emissions by Mexican trucks, is an "effect" of FMCSA's issuance of the Application and Safety Monitoring Rules; if not, FMCSA's failure to address these effects in its EA did not violate NEPA, and so FMCSA's issuance of a FONSI cannot be arbitrary and capricious.

* * *

[R]espondents have only one complaint with respect to the EA: It did not take into account the environmental effects of increased cross-border operations of Mexican motor carriers. Respondents' argument that FMCSA was required to consider these effects is simple. Under § 350, FMCSA is barred from expending any funds to process or review any applications by Mexican motor carriers until FMCSA implemented a variety of specific application and safety-monitoring requirements for Mexican carriers. This expenditure bar makes it impossible for any Mexican motor carrier to receive authorization to operate within the United States until FMCSA issued the regulations challenged here. The promulgation of the regulations, the argument goes, would cause the entry of Mexican trucks (and hence also cause any emissions such trucks would produce), and the entry of the trucks is reasonably foreseeable. Thus, the argument concludes, under the relevant CEQ regulations, FMCSA must take these emissions into account in its EA when evaluating whether to produce an EIS.

Respondents' argument, however, overlooks a critical feature of this case: FMCSA has no ability to countermand the President's lifting of the moratorium or otherwise categorically to exclude Mexican motor carriers from operating within the United States. To be sure, § 350 did restrict the ability of FMCSA to authorize cross-border operations of Mexican motor carriers, but Congress did not otherwise modify FMCSA's statutory mandates. In particular, FMCSA remains subject to the mandate of 49 U.S.C. § 13902(a)(1), that FMCSA "*shall* register a person to provide transportation ... as a motor carrier if [it] finds that the person is willing and able to comply with" the safety and financial responsibility requirements established by the Department of Transportation. (Emphasis added.) Under FMCSA's entirely reasonable reading of this provision, it must certify any motor carrier that can show that it is willing and able to comply with the various substantive requirements for safety and financial responsibility contained in DOT regulations; only the moratorium prevented it from doing so for Mexican motor carriers before 2001. Thus, upon the lifting of the moratorium, if FMCSA refused to authorize a Mexican motor carrier for cross-border services, where the Mexican motor carrier was willing and able to comply with the various substantive safety and financial responsibilities rules, it would violate § 13902(a)(1).

If it were truly impossible for FMCSA to comply with both § 350 and § 13902(a)(1), then we would be presented with an irreconcilable conflict of laws. As the later enacted provision, § 350 would quite possibly win out. But FMCSA can easily satisfy both mandates: It can issue the application and safety inspection rules required by § 350, and start processing applications by Mexican motor carriers and authorize those that satisfy § 13902(a)(1)'s conditions. Without a conflict, then, FMCSA must comply with all of its statutory mandates.

Respondents must rest, then, on a particularly unyielding variation of "but for" causation, where an agency's action is considered a cause of an environmental effect even when the agency has no authority to prevent the effect. However, a "but for" causal relationship is insufficient to make an agency responsible for a particular effect under NEPA and the relevant regulations. As this Court held in Metropolitan Edison Co. v. People Against Nuclear Energy, 460 U.S. 766, 774 (1983), NEPA requires "a reasonably close causal relationship" between the environmental effect and the alleged cause. The Court analogized this requirement to the "familiar doctrine of proximate cause from tort law." Ibid. In particular, "courts must look to the underlying policies or legislative intent in order to draw a manageable line between those causal changes that may make an actor responsible for an effect and those that do not." Id., at 774, n. 7.

Also, inherent in NEPA and its implementing regulations is a "rule of reason," which ensures that agencies determine whether and to what extent to prepare an EIS based on the usefulness of any new potential information to the decisionmaking process. Where the preparation of an EIS would serve no purpose in light of NEPA's regulatory scheme as a whole, no rule of reason worthy of that title would require an agency to prepare an EIS.

In these circumstances, the underlying policies behind NEPA and Congress' intent, as informed by the rule of reason, make clear that the causal connection between FMCSA's issuance of the proposed regulations and the entry of the Mexican trucks is insufficient to make FMCSA responsible under NEPA to consider the environmental effects of the entry. The NEPA EIS requirement serves two purposes. First, "[i]t ensures that the agency, in reaching its decision, will have available, and will carefully consider, detailed information concerning significant environmental impacts." Robertson, 490 U.S., at 349. Second, it "guarantees that the relevant information will be made available to the larger audience that may also play a role in both the decisionmaking process and the implementation of that decision." Ibid. Requiring FMCSA to consider the environmental effects of the entry of Mexican trucks would fulfill neither of these statutory purposes. Since FMCSA has no ability categorically to prevent the cross-border operations of Mexican motor carriers, the environmental impact of the cross-border operations would have no effect on FMCSA's decisionmaking—FMCSA simply lacks the power to act on whatever information might be contained in the EIS.

Similarly, the informational purpose is not served. The "informational role" of an EIS is to "giv[e] the public the assurance that the agency has indeed considered environmental concerns in its decisionmaking process, and, perhaps more significantly, provid[e] a springboard for public comment" in the agency decisionmaking process itself, ibid. The purpose here is to ensure that the "larger audience," ibid., can provide input as necessary to the agency making the relevant decisions. But here, the "larger audience" can have no impact on FMCSA's decisionmaking, since, as just noted, FMCSA simply could not act on whatever input this "larger audience" could provide.

It would not, therefore, satisfy NEPA's "rule of reason" to require an agency to prepare a full EIS due to the environmental impact of an action it could not refuse to perform. Put another way, the legally relevant cause of the entry of the Mexican trucks is not FMCSA's action, but instead the actions of the President in lifting the moratorium and those of Congress in granting the President this authority while simultaneously limiting FMCSA's discretion.

Consideration of the CEQ's "cumulative impact" regulation does not change this analysis. An agency is required to evaluate the "[c]umulative impact" of its action, which is defined as "the impact on the environment which results from the incremental impact of the action when added to other past, present, and reasonably foreseeable future actions regardless of what agency (Federal or non-Federal) or person undertakes such other actions." § 1508.7. The "cumulative impact" regulation required FMCSA to consider the "incremental impact" of the safety rules themselves, in the context of the President's lifting of the moratorium and other relevant circumstances. But this is exactly what FMCSA did in its EA. FMCSA appropriately and reasonably examined the incremental impact of its safety rules assuming the President's modification of the moratorium (and, hence, assuming the increase in cross-border operations of Mexican motor carriers). The "cumulative impact" regulation does not require FMCSA to treat the lifting of the moratorium itself, or consequences from the lifting of the moratorium, as an effect of its promulgation of its Application and Safety Monitoring Rules.

We hold that where an agency has no ability to prevent a certain effect due to its limited statutory authority over the relevant actions, the agency cannot be considered a legally relevant "cause" of the effect. Hence, under NEPA and the implementing CEQ regulations, the agency need not consider these effects in its EA when determining whether its action is a "major Federal action." Because the President, not FMCSA, could authorize (or not authorize) cross-border operations from Mexican motor carriers, and because FMCSA has no discretion to prevent the entry of Mexican trucks, its EA did not need to consider the environmental effects arising from the entry.

* * *

Sierra Club v. Marsh

United States Court of Appeals, First Circuit, 1985.
769 F.2d 868.

■ BREYER, CIRCUIT JUDGE.

This case embodies an argument about whether a cargo port and a causeway that Maine plans to build at Sears Island will significantly affect the environment. * * *

The record shows that Sears Island is an undeveloped, wooded 940–acre island in upper Penobscot Bay. The island is connected to the mainland by a gravel bar exposed only at low tide. The mainland area adjacent to the island has been developed for industrial use: a chemical plant and a petroleum storage area sit on either side of the point leading to the gravel bar. Indeed, Searsport (where the island is located) is one of the busiest ports in Maine. * * * The most recent proposal for Sears Island consists of three parts: (1) a 1,200–foot solid-fill causeway that would connect Sears Island to the mainland with a railroad line and a two-lane road; (2) a dry-cargo marine terminal designed principally for the shipping of lumber and agricultural products, containerized cargo, and, possibly at a later stage in the project, coal; and (3) an industrial park in an area adjacent to the cargo port. The precise nature of the industrial park is now uncertain, for the park's eventual shape depends on what businesses choose to locate there. The plans for the other two components, however, are definite, and the impact of those plans has been discussed in great detail by various federal agencies which have examined the proposal.

Maine voters and government agencies have shown considerable support for the Sears Island project. Maine voters have twice approved bond referenda to finance the state's share of costs for the causeway and port. State agencies have recommended reconciling concerns about the environment with those about economic growth by concentrating industrial development in Maine within several selected coastal areas; these agencies have designated the Searsport area (and two other municipal areas in Maine) "for the 'most constraining' heavy industrial development" (Maine DOT EA, vol. 3, at 4). The town of Searsport has prepared "A Municipal Response Plan for the Industrial Development of Sears Island," which predicts substantial economic benefits from the causeway/port/industrial park project but recommends that the town enact appropriate land use laws to control the level of industrial development. The town has recently enacted such laws and has zoned the island for industrial use. The town has also borrowed $400,000 for its share of the cost of constructing the causeway.

[In 1981 the Maine DOT prepared an EA focused only on the causeway, which required a permit from the Corps of Engineers and was partially funded by the Federal Highway Administration (FHA). The FHA adopted this EA], issued a FONSI, and approved federal funding for the causeway. At this point, at least four federal agencies objected—three "environmental" agencies (the Fish and Wildlife Service, EPA, the National Marine Fisheries Service) and the Coast Guard. These four agencies said that the EA was inadequate and that all three parts of the proposed development (causeway, port, and industrial development) should be considered together in an EIS.

Maine DOT then prepared another EA, this time on the port facility alone; the Federal Highway Administration adopted this EA and then issued another FONSI. Again, the three federal environmental agencies objected * * *. Responding to this criticism, the Federal Highway Administration adopted a new document, prepared by Maine DOT, called an "Environmental Assessment Summary." The new document considered both causeway and port, but it expressly disclaimed any need for consideration of "development on Sears Island outside of the current marine terminal project." On December 16, 1983 the Federal Highway Administration issued yet another FONSI for the causeway/port project.

On the same day, the Army Corps of Engineers (the agency responsible for issuing permits for the project) released its own EA, in respect to port and causeway, and, on the basis of that EA, issued a FONSI. * * * Then, without preparing an EIS, it issued a permit allowing causeway and port construction to begin. At that point, the Sierra Club filed suit.

* * *

The EAs before us concern the likely environmental effects of building the causeway and the port. Our reading of the record indicates that the major environmental bones of contention have included the following:

1. *Clam flats.* Building the causeway will eliminate 1.5 to 2 acres of clam flats; construction of the port will eliminate another 1.5 to 2 acres. Maine's DOT, however, will replace 2.14 acres of this habitat by seeding an area east of the causeway. * * *

2. *Lobsters, scallops, and other marine animals.* Building the marine terminal will require dredging and filling 90 acres now inhabited by lobsters, scallops, and other marine animals. * * * Maine's DOT, however, noted that many of the lobsters can move elsewhere and the scallop grounds are not very productive. * * *

3. *Waterfowl.* The appellants and several environmental agencies said the project would adversely affect certain birds by encroaching on their current habitat. Maine's DOT, after consulting with Maine wildlife agencies, concluded that it would not do so because the birds' winter feeding on the island is limited to areas that do not freeze, and the project will not deprive them of a significant amount of such habitat.

4. *Seals.* One of the federal environmental agencies argued that the project would drive seals from the area. Maine's DOT, however, concluded that the harbor seals are already accustomed to the shipping traffic and would not be significantly disturbed.

5. *Upland habitat.* The parties agree that the port terminal would eliminate at least 40 acres of wooded upland habitat which supports several kinds of mammals and birds (including foxes, whitetailed deer, osprey, and woodcock). Maine's DOT and the Corps concluded, however, that the loss was not significant because the 40 acres represent only 4 percent of the

island's total "upland habitat"; displaced animals could go elsewhere; and the area has an abundance of such resources.

* * *

8. *Dredging and "spoil" disposal.* Construction of the port will require the disposal of over 2 million cubic yards of dredged material (called "spoils")—1.3 million in the initial phases of the project; 750,000 in the later stages. The Fish and Wildlife Service feared that Maine's plan to dump the spoils at a special ocean dump site would destroy a "benthic community"—organisms on which fish and other sea animals feed. The Corps concluded that this possibility was not environmentally significant because the dredged material would cover only 65 acres, the "communities" could reestablish themselves, and Maine agreed to consider other ways of disposing of some of the material.

Whether or not these environmental effects, when considered together, do, or do not, show a "significant impact" is arguable. We note that the federal agencies, including the project's agency sponsors, differ among themselves about the significance of some of these effects. * * * [T]he Corps evidently believes that *promises* to mitigate certain environmental impacts in the future mean that these impacts lack significance. The CEQ, however, has written:

> Mitigation measures may be relied upon to make a finding of no significant impact only if they are imposed by statute or regulation, or submitted by an applicant or agency as part of the original proposal. As a general rule, the regulations contemplate that agencies ... should not rely on the possibility of mitigation to avoid the EIS requirement.

> If a proposal appears to have adverse effects which would be significant, and certain mitigation measures are then developed during the scoping or EA stages, the existence of such *possible* mitigation does not obviate the need for an EIS.... [Preparation of an EIS] is essential to ensure that the final decision is based on all the relevant factors and that the full NEPA process will result in enforceable mitigation measures through the Record of Decision.

Forty Most Asked Questions, 46 Fed. Reg. 18028, 18038 (1981) (emphasis in original). Regardless, were *only* the above-mentioned impacts at issue, we doubt that we could say that the "FONSI" conclusions of the Corps and the Federal Highway Administration were "arbitrary, capricious, an abuse of discretion." 5 U.S.C. § 706(2)(A).

The problems just noted become significant, however, when combined with a more serious omission by the Corps and the Federal Highway Administration—their failure to consider adequately the fact that building a port and causeway may lead to the further industrial development of Sears Island, and that further development will significantly affect the environment. The CEQ says that agencies must take account of such "indirect effects," which it defines as those that are caused by the action and are later in time or farther removed in distance, but are still reasonably foreseeable. Indirect effects may include *growth inducing effects* and other effects related to *induced changes in the pattern of land use, population density, or growth rate,* and related effects on air and water and other natural systems, including ecosystems.

40 C.F.R. § 1508.8 (emphasis added). Of course, agencies need not consider highly speculative or indefinite impacts. But, here the "impacts" seem neither speculative nor indefinite.

Whether a particular set of impacts is definite enough to take into account, or too speculative to warrant consideration, reflects several different factors. With what confidence can one say that the impacts are likely to occur? Can one describe them "now" with sufficient specificity to make their consideration useful? If the decisionmaker does not take them into account "now," will the decisionmaker be able to take account of them before the agency is so firmly committed to the project that further environmental knowledge, as a practical matter, will prove irrelevant to the government's decision?

In this case, the record contains clear answers to these questions. And those answers show that the agencies should have taken account of the "secondary impacts." First, the record makes it nearly impossible to doubt that building the causeway and port will lead to further development of Sears Island. Local planners have considered the port, causeway, and industrial park to be components of an integrated plan. * * *

Second, the plans for further development are precise enough for an EIS usefully to take them into account. The record contains, for example, a 35–page "Land Use Plan/Industrial Marketing Study" prepared for the owner of the southern half of the island, and the town's 50–page "Municipal Response Plan for the Industrial Development of Sears Island." * * *

Third, once Maine completes the causeway and port, pressure to develop the rest of the island could well prove irreversible. * * *

In sum, given the likely secondary effects of the Sears Island project and the other effects previously described, the record in this case cannot support a FONSI, and therefore an EIS must be prepared. We reach this conclusion not because preparation of an EIS is merely a technical requirement which, under NEPA and its implementing regulations, we must here enforce. Rather, this requirement reflects NEPA's underlying purpose in requiring agencies to determine and assess environmental effects in a systematic way—namely, having decisionmakers focus on these effects when they make major decisions. That is to say, the requirement flows not only from the letter, but also from the spirit, of NEPA.

* * *

NOTES AND QUESTIONS

1. *NEPA and nondiscretionary decisions.* The *Mexican Trucks* decision can be seen as joining a well-established line of cases holding that NEPA simply does not apply to non-discretionary federal decisions. See, e.g., American Airlines v. Department of Transportation, 202 F.3d 788, 803 (5th Cir. 2000) (agency decisions which do not entail the exercise of significant discretion do not require an EIS); Sugarloaf Citizens Ass'n v. FERC, 959 F.2d 508 (4th Cir. 1992); Atlanta Coalition on Transp. Crisis, Inc. v. Atlanta Regional Comm'n, 599 F.2d 1333, 1344–45 (5th Cir.1979). The justification for this exception is that NEPA is intended to bring environmental considerations into the decisionmaking process. Where the agency has no discretion to alter a decision on the basis of environmental considerations, NEPA analysis, it is thought, serves no purpose.

2. *The environmental baseline or status quo.* An action that does not change the environmental status quo does not require an EIS. Does transfer of land out of federal ownership, without an immediate change in use, alter the status quo? Suppose the federal government acquires a cattle ranch by foreclosure. Can it sell the ranch without an EIS? See National Wildlife Fed'n v. Espy, 45 F.3d 1337 (9th Cir. 1995). Must the National Park Service complete an EIS before transferring land to a local government which intends to develop an amusement park? Does it matter whether additional federal approvals will be required before the park can be built? See Anacostia Watershed Soc'y v. Babbitt, 871 F.Supp. 475 (D.D.C. 1994).

3. *NEPA and the President.* Because NEPA does not establish a private right of action, suits challenging NEPA compliance must be brought under the APA. The President of the United States is not an "agency" subject to suit under the Administrative Procedure Act, so the President's compliance with NEPA cannot be challenged directly. See Public Citizen v. U.S. Trade Representative, 5 F.3d 549 (D.C. Cir. 1993). Public Citizen therefore could not sue the President directly for lifting the moratorium on Mexican trucks without preparing an EIS.

4. *Proximate cause analysis.* In *Mexican Trucks*, the Supreme Court held that in order to prevail NEPA plaintiffs must show more than "but for" causation of an environmental impact by an agency action. The action challenged must be the proximate cause of the environmental impact. In other words, it must be reasonable to blame the agency. Does the proximate cause formulation provide a useful mode of analysis for "segmentation" cases such as *South Carolina v. O'Leary* or "small handle" cases such as *Ka Makani*?

5. *Timing redux.* The question of whether the impacts of a federal action surpass the threshold of significance is closely related to the question of when NEPA analysis must be done. Environmental analysis must precede the point at which the agency action becomes the cause of significant environmental impacts. In Sierra Club v. Peterson, 717 F.2d 1409 (D.C. Cir. 1983), the court drew a distinction on the basis of stipulations in leases issued by the Forest Service for oil and gas exploration. So long as the leases required additional agency approval prior to any surface-disturbing activity no EIS was required at the leasing stage, but an EIS had to be done before the agency could issue leases which allowed disturbance of the surface.

6. *"Significantly."* How do the CEQ regulations define the term "significantly"? What test did the court apply in *Sierra Club v. Marsh?* Setting aside the possibility that development of the port and causeway would encourage further industrial development of Sears Island, would the direct effects have been sufficient to require an EIS?

7. *Judicial review.* What standard governs judicial review of an agency decision not to prepare an EIS? In Marsh v. Oregon Natural Resources Council, 490 U.S. 360, 375–77 (1989), reviewing a decision not to supplement an EIS based on new information, the Supreme Court explained:

> In determining the proper standard of review, we look to § 10(e) of the Administrative Procedure Act (APA), 5 U.S.C. § 706, which empowers federal courts to "hold unlawful and set aside agency action, findings, and conclusions" if they fail to conform with any of six specified standards. We conclude that review of the narrow question before us of whether the Corps' determination that the FEIS need not be supplemented should be set aside is controlled by the "arbitrary and capricious" standard of § 706(2)(A).
>
> Respondents contend that the determination of whether the new information suffices to establish a "significant" effect is either a question of law or, at a minimum, a question of ultimate fact and, as such, "deserves no deference" on review. Apparently, respondents maintain that the question for review centers on the legal meaning of the term "significant" or, in the alternative, the predominantly legal question of whether established and uncontested historical facts presented by the administrative record satisfy this standard. Characterizing the dispute in this manner, they posit that strict review is appropriate under the "in accordance with law" clause of § 706(2)(A) or the "without observance of procedure required by law" provision of § 706(2)(D). We disagree.
>
> The question presented for review in this case is a classic example of a factual dispute the resolution of which implicates substantial agency expertise. The dispute thus does not turn on the meaning of the term "significant" or on an application of this legal standard to settled facts. Rather, resolution of this dispute involves primarily issues of fact. Because analysis of the relevant documents "requires a high level of technical expertise," we must defer to "the informed discretion of the responsible federal agencies." Kleppe v. Sierra Club, 427 U.S. 390, 412 (1976).

Is this decision consistent with the purposes of the EIS requirement? Should the same standards apply when the issue is whether an EIS is required at all, rather then whether it must be supplemented? The circuits had split after *Marsh*, with some continuing to apply a somewhat more demanding "reasonableness" test to the threshold EIS decision. *Public*

Citizen has settled the issue, explicitly holding that the decision not to prepare an EIS is reviewed under the "arbitrary and capricious" standard.

8. *Mitigation and significance.* Can mitigation measures be used to justify a FONSI for an action that, in the absence of those measures, would have significant environmental impacts? If the answer is no, will substantial time and resources be wasted in the preparation of environmental documents for actions that ultimately will not have a significant effect? Could allowing the use of mitigation to support a FONSI encourage agencies to undertake mitigation? But recall that the environmental assessment process is less visible to the public than the EIS process. Will agencies tend to overestimate the effectiveness of mitigation measures? What assurance does the public have that such measures will actually be implemented?

9. *Indirect impacts.* On what basis did the court in *Sierra Club v. Marsh* conclude that the agency was required to consider the effects of future industrial development on Sears Island? Was the the court's treatment of this issue consistent with *South Carolina v. O'Leary* and *Ka Makani*? Did it impermissibly expand the scope of federal control? Is *Sierra Club v. Marsh* good law after *Public Citizen*? Why weren't the environmental impacts of increased Mexican trucks "indirect effects" of the FMCSA decision or reasonably foreseeable cumulative impacts?

SECTION 3. CONTENTS OF THE EIS

Excerpts From Council on Environmental Quality Regulations

40 C.F.R. Parts 1500–1517.

Sec. 1502.14. Alternatives including the proposed action.

This section is the heart of the environmental impact statement. * * * In this section agencies shall:

(a) Rigorously explore and objectively evaluate all reasonable alternatives, and for alternatives which were eliminated from detailed study, briefly discuss the reasons for their having been eliminated.

(b) Devote substantial treatment to each alternative considered in detail including the proposed action so that reviewers may evaluate their comparative merits.

(c) Include reasonable alternatives not within the jurisdiction of the lead agency.

(d) Include the alternative of no action.

* * *

Sec. 1502.15. Affected environment.

The environmental impact statement shall succinctly describe the environment of the area(s) to be affected or created by the alternatives under consideration. The descriptions shall be no longer than is necessary to understand the effects of the alternatives. * * *

Citizens Against Burlington, Inc. v. Busey

United States Court of Appeals, District of Columbia Circuit, 1991.
938 F.2d 190.

■ CLARENCE THOMAS, CIRCUIT JUDGE.

The city of Toledo decided to expand one of its airports, and the Federal Aviation Administration decided to approve the city's plan. In this petition for review of the FAA's order, an alliance of people who live near the airport contends that the FAA has violated several environmental statutes and regulations. * * *

The Toledo Express Airport, object of the controversy in this case, lies about twenty-five miles to the west of downtown Toledo. * * *

Citizens Against Burlington first materialized about a year after the [Toledo–Lucas County] Port Authority * * * began to consider the possibility of the airport's expansion. The Port Authority soon heard from Burlington Air Express, which had been flying its planes out of an old World War II hangar at Baer Field, an Air National Guard airport in Fort Wayne. After looking at seventeen sites in four midwestern states, Burlington chose the Toledo Express Airport. Among Burlington's reasons were the quality of Toledo's work force and the airport's prior operating record, zoning advantages, and location (near major highways and close to Detroit and Chicago). For its part, the Port Authority expects the new hub to create one thousand new jobs in metropolitan Toledo and to contribute almost $68 million per year to the local economy after three years of the hub's operation. * * *

* * * This case concerns the most important responsibility that NEPA demands—that an agency reviewing proposals for action prepare an environmental impact statement, and, more specifically, that the agency discuss in its statement alternatives to the action proposed. We consider here whether the FAA has complied with NEPA in publishing an environmental impact statement that discussed in depth two alternatives: approving the expansion of the Toledo Express Airport, and not approving the expansion of the Toledo Express Airport.

Federal agencies must prepare environmental impact statements when they contemplate "major Federal actions significantly affecting the quality of the human environment." NEPA § 102(2)(C). An EIS must discuss, among other things, "alternatives to the proposed action," NEPA § 102(2)(C)(iii), and the discussion of alternatives forms "the heart of the environmental impact statement." 40 C.F.R. § 1502.14.

The problem for agencies is that "the term 'alternatives' is not self-defining." Vermont Yankee Nuclear Power Corp. v. Natural Resources Defense Council, Inc., 435 U.S. 519, 551 (1978). Suppose, for example, that a utility applies for permission to build a nuclear reactor in Vernon,

Vermont. Free-floating "alternatives" to the proposal for federal action might conceivably include everything from licensing a reactor in Pecos, Texas, to promoting imports of hydropower from Quebec. If the Nuclear Regulatory Commission had to discuss these and other imaginable courses of action, its statement would wither into "frivolous boilerplate" * * *. If, therefore, the consideration of alternatives is to inform both the public and the agency decisionmaker, the discussion must be moored to "some notion of feasibility." Id., 435 U.S. at 551.

Recognizing the harm that an unbounded understanding of alternatives might cause, CEQ regulations oblige agencies to discuss only alternatives that are feasible, or (much the same thing) reasonable. 40 C.F.R. §§ 1502.14(a)–(c), 1508.25(b)(2). But the adjective "reasonable" is no more self-defining than the noun that it modifies. Consider two possible alternatives to our nuclear reactor in Vernon. Funding research in cold fusion might be an unreasonable alternative by virtue of the theory's scientific implausibility. But licensing a reactor in Lake Placid, New York might also be unreasonable, even though it passes some objective test of scientific worth. In either case, the proposed alternative is reasonable only if it will bring about the ends of the federal action—only if it will do what the licensing of the reactor in Vernon is meant to do. If licensing the Vernon reactor is meant to help supply energy to New England, licensing a reactor in northern New York might make equal sense. If licensing the Vernon reactor is meant as well to stimulate the Vernon job market, licensing a reactor in Lake Placid would be far less effective. * * *

* * * When an agency is asked to sanction a specific plan, the agency should take into account the needs and goals of the parties involved in the application. Perhaps more importantly, an agency should always consider the views of Congress, expressed, to the extent that the agency can determine them, in the agency's statutory authorization to act, as well as in other congressional directives.

* * *

In the first chapter of its environmental impact statement, the FAA begins by noting that the Port Authority had requested the agency's approval of the plan to develop Toledo Express. The agency then explains that "[t]he purpose and need for this action lies in [the] FAA's responsibility to review the airport design and runway configuration with respect to its safety, efficiency and utility within the national airspace system and its environmental impact on the surrounding area." After surveying the engineering reasons that justify an extended runway and new facilities, the FAA concludes by stating that the agency "has a statutory mandate to facilitate the establishment of air cargo hubs under Section 502(a)(7) [of the Airport and Airway Improvement Act of 1982 (AAIA), 49 U.S.C. app. § 2201(a)(7)] and to undertake capacity enhancement projects under Section 502(a)(11) [of the AAIA, 49 U.S.C. app. § 2201(a)(11)]."*

---

* [The provisions referenced by the FAA, now codified at 49 U.S.C. § 47101(a) read: "It is the policy of the United States * * * (7) that airport construction and improvement projects

In the second chapter of the environmental impact statement, the FAA begins by stating:

> The scope of alternatives considered by the sponsoring Federal agency, where the Federal government acts as a proprietor, is wide ranging and comprehensive. Where the Federal government acts, not as a proprietor, but to approve and support a project being sponsored by a local government or private applicant, the Federal agency is necessarily more limited. In the latter instance, the Federal government's consideration of alternatives may accord substantial weight to the preferences of the applicant and/or sponsor in the siting and design of the project.

The agency goes on to explain:

> In the present system of federalism, the FAA does not determine where to build and develop civilian airports, as an owner/operator. Rather, the FAA facilitates airport development by providing Federal financial assistance, and reviews and approves or disapproves revisions to Airport Layout Plans at Federally funded airports.... Similarly, under the Airline Deregulation Act of 1978, the FAA does not regulate rates, routes, and services of air carriers or cargo operators. Airline managements are free to decide which cities to serve based on market forces.

The EIS then describes five alternatives: approving the Port Authority's plan for expanding Toledo Express, approving other geometric configurations for expanding Toledo Express, approving other ways of channelling airplane traffic at Toledo Express, no action by the agency at all, and approving plans for other airports both in the Toledo metropolitan area and out of it, including Baer Field in Fort Wayne. Finally, the EIS briefly explains why the agency eliminated all the alternatives but the first and the fourth. See 40 C.F.R. § 1502.14(a).

The FAA's reasoning fully supports its decision to evaluate only the preferred and do-nothing alternatives. The agency first examined Congress's views on how this country is to build its civilian airports. As the agency explained, Congress has told the FAA to nurture aspiring cargo hubs. See AAIA § 502(a)(7), (11), 49 U.S.C. app. § 2201(a)(7), (11). At the same time, however, Congress has also said that the free market, not an ersatz Gosplan for aviation, should determine the siting of the nation's airports. See Airline Deregulation Act of 1978, Pub.L. No. 95–504, 92 Stat. 1705. Congress has expressed its intent by statute, and the FAA took both of Congress's messages seriously.

The FAA also took into account the Port Authority's reasons for wanting a cargo hub in Toledo. In recent years, more than fifty major

---

that increase the capacity of facilities to accommodate passenger and cargo traffic be undertaken to the maximum feasible extent so that safety and efficiency increase and delays decrease; * * * (11) that the airport improvement program should be administered to encourage projects that employ innovative technology * * *, concepts, and approaches that will promote safety, capacity, and efficiency improvements in the construction of airports and in the air transportation system * * *.—Eds.]

companies have left the Toledo metropolitan area, and with them, over seven thousand jobs. The Port Authority expects the cargo hub at Toledo Express to create immediately more than two hundred permanent and six hundred part-time jobs with a total payroll value of more than $10 million. After three years, according to the Port Authority, the hub should create directly more than one thousand permanent jobs at the airport and one hundred and fifty other, airport-related jobs. The University of Toledo estimates that the new Toledo Express will contribute at least $42 million to the local economy after one full year of operation and nearly $68 million per year after three. In addition, the Port Authority expects the expanded airport, and Burlington's presence there, to attract other companies to Toledo. All of those factors, the Port Authority hopes, will lead to a renaissance in the Toledo metropolitan region.

Having thought hard about these appropriate factors, the FAA defined the goal for its action as helping to launch a new cargo hub in Toledo and thereby helping to fuel the Toledo economy. The agency then eliminated from detailed discussion the alternatives that would not accomplish this goal. Each of the different geometric configurations would mean technological problems and extravagant costs. So would plans to route traffic differently at Toledo Express, or to build a hub at one of the other airports in the city of Toledo. None of the airports outside of the Toledo area would serve the purpose of the agency's action. The FAA thus evaluated the environmental impacts of the only proposal that might reasonably accomplish that goal—approving the construction and operation of a cargo hub at Toledo Express. It did so with the thoroughness required by law.

We conclude that the FAA acted reasonably in defining the purpose of its action, in eliminating alternatives that would not achieve it, and in discussing (with the required do-nothing option) the proposal that would. The agency has therefore complied with NEPA.

Citizens agree that the FAA need only discuss reasonable, not all, alternatives to Toledo Express. Relying on Van Abbema v. Fornell, 807 F.2d 633 (7th Cir. 1986), however, Citizens argues that "the evaluation of 'alternatives' mandated by NEPA is to be an evaluation of alternative means to accomplish the *general* goal of an action; it is not an evaluation of the alternative means by which a particular applicant can reach his goals." *Id.* at 638. According to Citizens, the "general goal" of the Port Authority's proposal is to build a permanent cargo hub for Burlington [Air Express, Inc.]. Since, in Citizens' view, Fort Wayne (and perhaps Peoria) will accomplish this general goal just as well as Toledo, if not better, Baer Field is a reasonable alternative to Toledo Express, and the FAA should have discussed it in depth. * * *

We see two critical flaws in *Van Abbema*, and therefore in Citizens' argument. The first is that the *Van Abbema* court misconstrued the language of NEPA. *Van Abbema* involved a private businessman who had applied to the Army Corps of Engineers for permission to build a place to "transload" coal from trucks to barges. The panel decided that the Corps had to survey "feasible alternatives ... to the applicant's proposal," or alternative ways of accomplishing "the general goal [of] deliver[ing] coal from mine to utility." In commanding agencies to discuss "alternatives to the proposed action," however, NEPA plainly refers to alternatives to the "major *Federal* actions significantly affecting the quality of the human environment," and not to alternatives to the applicant's proposal. NEPA § 102(2)(C) (emphasis added). An agency cannot redefine the goals of the proposal that arouses the call for action; it must evaluate alternative ways of achieving *its* goals, shaped by the application at issue and by the function that the agency plays in the decisional process. Congress did expect agencies to consider an applicant's wants when the agency formulates the goals of its own proposed action. Congress did not expect agencies to determine for the applicant what the goals of the applicant's proposal should be.

The second problem with *Van Abbema* lies in the court's assertion that an agency must evaluate "alternative means to accomplish the general goal of an action," 807 F.2d at 638—a statement that troubles us even if we assume that the panel was alluding to the general goals of the federal action instead of to the goals of the private proposal. Left unanswered in *Van Abbema* and Citizens' brief (and at oral argument) is why and how to distinguish general goals from specific ones and just who does the distinguishing. *Someone* has to define the purpose of the agency action. Implicit in *Van Abbema* is that the body responsible is the reviewing court. As we explained, however, NEPA and binding case law provide otherwise.

■ Buckley, Circuit Judge, dissenting in part.

* * *

I cannot fault the FAA for the attention given Burlington and its preferences. While both Toledo and Burlington are indispensable to the enterprise, Burlington is plainly the dominant partner; its requirements and desires shaped the project from the start. As the agency points out in its Record of Decision ("ROD"), "[t]he demand for this project is clearly based on a business decision by Burlington Air Express and the interest of a local airport sponsor, the Toledo–Lucas County Port Authority, in accommodating and facilitating this decision."

I do fault the agency for failing to attend to its own business, which is to examine all alternatives "that are practical or feasible from the technical and economic standpoint . . . rather than simply desirable from the standpoint of the applicant." Forty Most Asked Questions Concerning CEQ's National Environmental Policy Act Regulations, 46 Fed. Reg. 18,026, 18,027 (1981). As far as I can tell, the FAA never questioned Burlington's assertions that of the ones considered, Toledo Express is the only airport suitable to its purposes. * * *

I do not suggest that Burlington is untrustworthy, only that the FAA had the duty under NEPA to exercise a degree of skepticism in dealing with self-serving statements from a prime beneficiary of the project. It may well be that none of the sixteen other alternatives examined by Burlington and its consultants could be converted into a viable air cargo hub at acceptable cost. That, however, was something that the FAA should have determined for itself instead of accepting as a given. Under NEPA, "the federal agency must itself determine what is reasonably available." Trinity Episcopal School Corp. v. Romney, 523 F.2d 88, 94 (2d Cir.1975). By allowing the FAA to abandon this requirement, the majority establishes a precedent that will permit an applicant and a third-party beneficiary of federal action to define the limits of the EIS inquiry and thus to frustrate one of the principal safeguards of the NEPA process, the mandatory consideration of reasonable alternatives.

*   *   *

NOTES AND QUESTIONS

1. *Consideration of alternatives.* NEPA's requirement that a federal agency consider alternatives to its proposed actions is somewhat broader than the EIS requirement. NEPA § 102(2)(E) requires that all agencies "study, develop, and describe appropriate alternatives to recommended courses of action in any proposal which involves unresolved conflicts concerning alternative uses of available resources."

What legal standard must the agency fulfill in considering alternatives under NEPA? Must alternatives be within the power of the action agency? Must each alternative fully achieve all goals of the proposed action? In Natural Resources Defense Council v. Morton, 458 F.2d 827 (D.C. Cir. 1972), the proposed action was the sale of off-shore oil and gas leases. The D.C. Circuit found the EIS inadequate, in part because it did not consider alternatives that would supply less energy than the proposed leases. More recently, however, the same court ruled that the Federal Highway Administration need not consider a ten-lane alternative to a proposed twelve-lane highway bridge because ten lanes would not accommodate the traffic expected over the next twenty years. City of Alexandria v. Slater, 198 F.3d 862 (D.C. Cir. 1999). Are these two decisions reconcilable? If not, which is more consistent with the purposes of NEPA?

The extent to which an EIS must consider alternatives substantially different from the proposed project remains a vexing question. To take just one recent example, suppose that the U.S. Army decides to transform a combat brigade into an armored vehicle brigade to make it "more responsive, deployable, agile, versatile, lethal, survivable, and sustainable." Must the EIS consider moving the brigade from its current location to another, where the environmental impacts of armored vehicle training maneuvers might be less severe? See 'Ilio'ulaokalani Coalition v. Rumsfeld, 464 F.3d 1083 (9th Cir. 2006).

2. *Defining goals.* As *Citizens Against Burlington* illustrates, delineation of the goals of the project determines the scope of the required discussion of alternatives. Should goals be more broadly construed for fully federal actions than for federal approvals of non-federal activities? Is this issue similar to the "small handles" problem? To what extent should the federal agency (and reviewing courts) defer to the applicant's goals? How much practical difference does it make? In *Citizens Against Burlington*, how would the EIS have been different if the FAA had fully considered alternative sites such as Fort Wayne? Would the ultimate decision have been different? Would public understanding of, and reaction to, the decision have been altered?

The D.C. Circuit acknowledged in *Citizens Against Burlington* that the Seventh Circuit uses a different approach. The latter court justified its more aggressive review of the choice of alternatives for examination in Simmons v. U.S. Army Corps of Engineers, 120 F.3d 664, 666–67 (7th Cir. 1997):

> The "purpose" of a project is a slippery concept, susceptible of no hard-and-fast definition. One obvious way for an agency to slip past the strictures of NEPA is to contrive a purpose so slender as to define competing "reasonable alternatives" out of consideration (and even out of existence). The federal courts cannot condone an agency's frustration of Congressional will. If the agency constricts the definition of the project's purpose and thereby excludes what truly are reasonable alternatives, the EIS cannot fulfill its role. Nor can the agency satisfy the Act.

> We are confronted here with an example of this defining-away of alternatives. In 1989, the City of Marion applied to the U.S. Army Corps of Engineers (the Corps) for permission to build a dam and reservoir, as required by § 404 of the Clean Water Act, 33 U.S.C. § 1344. The dam would block up Sugar Creek, a free-flowing stream in southern Illinois running seven miles southeast of Marion. Marion envisioned that the resulting Sugar Creek Lake would supply water not just to Marion, but to the Lake of Egypt Water District, which encompasses six counties and 15,000 rural customers. Sugar Creek Lake would drown a substantial area, with the usual environmental effects of drowning, including the transformation or obliteration of the riverine habitats of several species.

> * * * From the beginning, Marion and the Corps have defined the project's purpose as supplying two users (Marion and the Water District) from a single source—namely, a new lake. Accordingly, when the Corps prepared an environmental impact statement, it confined the analysis to single-source alternatives. And therein lies the difficulty. At no time has the Corps studied whether this single-source idea is the best one—or even a good one. Marion and the Lake of Egypt Water District share a common problem, a thirst for water. From this fact the Corps adduces the imperative for a common solution. We disagree. A single source may well be the best solution to the putative water shortages of Marion and the Lake of Egypt Water District. The Corps' error is in accepting this parameter as a given. To conclude that a common problem necessarily demands a common solution defies common sense. We conclude that the U.S. Army Corps of Engineers defined an impermissibly narrow purpose for the contemplated project.

3. *Chad–Cameroon pipeline problem.* In the Class Discussion Problem, assuming that OPIC and the Export–Import Bank conceded that an EIS was required, what alternatives must that EIS consider? What is the purpose of the federal action? How else might that action be accomplished?

4. *Mitigation promises.* In Robertson v. Methow Valley Citizens Council, 490 U.S. 332 (1989), the Supreme Court held that NEPA requires a discussion of the extent to which adverse effects can be mitigated or avoided, but that it does not mandate adoption of a mitigation plan. If an agency promises in an EIS to take mitigation actions, is that promise subsequently enforceable in court? Consider the following excerpt from William L. Andreen, In Pursuit of NEPA's Promise: The Role of Executive Oversight in the Implementation of Environmental Policy, 64 Ind. L.J. 205, 245–47 (1989):

It should come as no surprise, considering the judicial reluctance to review an agency's substantive decision, that the courts have refused to enforce "commitments" found in an EIS. However misleading representations contained in an EIS may seem when viewed in light of actual agency performance,[281] the fact remains that those representations do not amount to enforceable duties. As the CEQ regulations amply demonstrate, an EIS is simply a planning document which is intended to inform the ultimate decisionmaker. Therefore, any attempt to enforce a mitigation measure or any other condition found in an EIS is, in reality, an effort to force a particular decision upon an agency by transforming a planning tool into a final decision. If any document generated during the NEPA process could give rise to such an action for enforcement, it would have to be an agency's ROD.

While CEQ has expressed its belief that "the terms of a ROD are enforceable by * * * private parties," the regulations promulgated by CEQ reveal that the enforceable duties arising from a record of decision are more circumscribed. The regulations do not direct an agency to implement every aspect of a decision. Rather, CEQ chose only to require an agency to perform the "mitigation * * * and other conditions" identified during the EIS process and adopted in the agency's decision.[284] A court, consequently, could find a failure to implement such mitigation a breach of an agency's legal duty and order the agency to comply.

An agency, however, has no duty to adopt mitigation measures or other impact reducing conditions in its ROD. As a result, a potential litigant may find little to enforce. Moreover, a citizen will likely be

281. *City of Blue Ash v. McLucas,* 596 F.2d 709 (6th Cir. 1979), involved an especially egregious example of an agency turning its back on an impact-reducing representation contained in its EIS. The Federal Aviation Administration (FAA) had prepared an EIS for its funding of an airport expansion in suburban Cincinnati. The EIS indicated that, due to public opposition, jet aircraft would be barred from using the renovated facility. Soon after the project was completed, however, the FAA reversed itself and declared that certain types of jets would, in fact, be granted access to the airport. Id. at 710–11.

284. CEQ Regulations, 40 C.F.R. § 1505.3 (1987) * * *.

unaware of whether an agency has ever performed its obligations to mitigate environmental damage. And even if one becomes aware of an implementation failure, the discovery may come so late in the process that a suit cannot be brought until after the project has been completed. In such a case, a court might be inclined to dismiss the action for mootness or to deny injunctive relief on account of laches.

SECTION 4.   REMEDIES FOR **NEPA** VIOLATIONS

Plaintiffs bringing a NEPA challenge normally seek an injunction prohibiting the agency from taking the proposed action pending preparation of an adequate EA or EIS. In light of the federal courts' refusal to review the substance of environmental choices under NEPA, is injunctive relief especially important in NEPA cases? How likely is that relief to affect the ultimate decision? Even if it does not prompt the agency to change its mind, might delay itself benefit environmental plaintiffs? How?

According to the Supreme Court, "the balance of harms will usually favor the issuance of an injunction to protect the environment" if injury is found to be sufficiently likely because "environmental injury, by its nature, can seldom be adequately remedied by money damages and is often permanent or at least of long duration, i.e., irreparable." Amoco Prod. Co. v. Village of Gambell, 480 U.S. 531, 545 (1987). Still, injunctions are not automatic, as the Supreme Court emphasized in the following case.

Winter v. Natural Resources Defense Council

United States Supreme Court, 2008.
555 U.S. 7.

■ CHIEF JUSTICE ROBERTS delivered the opinion of the Court.

"To be prepared for war is one of the most effectual means of preserving peace." 1 Messages and Papers of the Presidents 57 (J. Richardson comp. 1897). So said George Washington in his first Annual Address to Congress, 218 years ago. One of the most important ways the Navy prepares for war is through integrated training exercises at sea. These exercises include training in the use of modern sonar to detect and track enemy submarines, something the Navy has done for the past 40 years. The plaintiffs complained that the Navy's sonar training program harmed marine mammals, and that the Navy should have prepared an environmental impact statement before commencing its latest round of training exercises. The Court of Appeals upheld a preliminary injunction imposing restrictions on the Navy's sonar training, even though that court acknowledged that "the record contains no evidence that marine mammals have been harmed" by the Navy's exercises.

The Court of Appeals was wrong, and its decision is reversed.

I

The Navy deploys its forces in "strike groups," which are groups of surface ships, submarines, and aircraft centered around either an aircraft carrier or an amphibious assault ship. Seamless coordination among strike-group assets is critical. Before deploying a strike group, the Navy requires extensive integrated training in analysis and prioritization of threats, execution of military missions, and maintenance of force protection.

Antisubmarine warfare is currently the Pacific Fleet's top war-fighting priority. Modern diesel-electric submarines pose a significant threat to Navy vessels because they can operate almost silently, making them extremely difficult to detect and track. Potential adversaries of the United States possess at least 300 of these submarines.

The most effective technology for identifying submerged diesel-electric submarines within their torpedo range is active sonar, which involves emitting pulses of sound underwater and then receiving the acoustic waves that echo off the target. Active sonar is a particularly useful tool because it provides both the bearing and the distance of target submarines; it is also sensitive enough to allow the Navy to track enemy submarines that are quieter than the surrounding marine environment.[285] This case concerns the Navy's use of "mid-frequency active" (MFA) sonar, which transmits sound waves at frequencies between 1 kHz and 10 kHz.

Not surprisingly, MFA sonar is a complex technology, and sonar operators must undergo extensive training to become proficient in its use. Sonar reception can be affected by countless different factors, including the time of day, water density, salinity, currents, weather conditions, and the contours of the sea floor. When working as part of a strike group, sonar operators must be able to coordinate with other Navy ships and planes while avoiding interference. The Navy conducts regular training exercises under realistic conditions to ensure that sonar operators are thoroughly skilled in its use in a variety of situations.

The waters off the coast of southern California (SOCAL) are an ideal location for conducting integrated training exercises, as this is the only area on the west coast that is relatively close to land, air, and sea bases, as well as amphibious landing areas. At issue in this case are the Composite Training Unit Exercises and the Joint Tactical Force Exercises, in which individual naval units (ships, submarines, and aircraft) train together as members of a strike group. A strike group cannot be certified for deployment until it has successfully completed the integrated training exercises, including a demonstration of its ability to operate under simulated hostile conditions. In light of the threat posed by enemy submarines, all strike groups must demonstrate proficiency in antisubmarine warfare. Accordingly, the SOCAL exercises include extensive training in detecting, tracking,

---

285. In contrast, passive sonar "listens" for sound waves but does not introduce sound into the water. Passive sonar is not effective for tracking diesel-electric submarines because those vessels can operate almost silently. Passive sonar also has a more limited range than active sonar, and cannot identify the exact location of an enemy submarine.

and neutralizing enemy submarines. The use of MFA sonar during these exercises is "mission-critical," given that MFA sonar is the only proven method of identifying submerged diesel-electric submarines operating on battery power.

Sharing the waters in the SOCAL operating area are at least 37 species of marine mammals, including dolphins, whales, and sea lions. The parties strongly dispute the extent to which the Navy's training activities will harm those animals or disrupt their behavioral patterns. The Navy emphasizes that it has used MFA sonar during training exercises in SOCAL for 40 years, without a single documented sonar-related injury to any marine mammal. The Navy asserts that, at most, MFA sonar may cause temporary hearing loss or brief disruptions of marine mammals' behavioral patterns.

The plaintiffs are the Natural Resources Defense Council, Jean–Michael Cousteau (an environmental enthusiast and filmmaker), and several other groups devoted to the protection of marine mammals and ocean habitats. They contend that MFA sonar can cause much more serious injuries to marine mammals than the Navy acknowledges, including permanent hearing loss, decompression sickness, and major behavioral disruptions. According to the plaintiffs, several mass strandings of marine mammals (outside of SOCAL) have been "associated" with the use of active sonar. They argue that certain species of marine mammals—such as beaked whales—are uniquely susceptible to injury from active sonar; these injuries would not necessarily be detected by the Navy, given that beaked whales are "very deep divers" that spend little time at the surface.

II

The procedural history of this case is rather complicated. The Marine Mammal Protection Act of 1972 (MMPA) generally prohibits any individual from "taking" a marine mammal, defined as harassing, hunting, capturing, or killing it. 16 U.S.C. §§ 1362(13), 1372(a). The Secretary of Defense may "exempt any action or category of actions" from the MMPA if such actions are "necessary for national defense." § 1371(f)(1). In January 2007, the Deputy Secretary of Defense—acting for the Secretary—granted the Navy a 2–year exemption from the MMPA for the training exercises at issue in this case. The exemption was conditioned on the Navy adopting several mitigation procedures, including: (1) training lookouts and officers to watch for marine mammals; (2) requiring at least five lookouts with binoculars on each vessel to watch for anomalies on the water surface (including marine mammals); (3) requiring aircraft and sonar operators to report detected marine mammals in the vicinity of the training exercises; (4) requiring reduction of active sonar transmission levels by 6 dB if a marine mammal is detected within 1,000 yards of the bow of the vessel, or by 10 dB if detected within 500 yards; (5) requiring complete shutdown of active sonar transmission if a marine mammal is detected within 200 yards of the vessel; (6) requiring active sonar to be operated at the "lowest practicable level"; and (7) adopting coordination and reporting procedures.

The National Environmental Policy Act of 1969 (NEPA) requires federal agencies "to the fullest extent possible" to prepare an environmental impact statement (EIS) for "every . . . major Federal action significantly affecting the quality of the human environment." 42 U.S.C. § 4332(2)(C). An agency is not required to prepare a full EIS if it determines—based on a shorter environmental assessment (EA)—that the proposed action will not have a significant impact on the environment.

In February 2007, the Navy issued an EA concluding that the 14 SOCAL training exercises scheduled through January 2009 would not have a significant impact on the environment. The EA divided potential injury to marine mammals into two categories: Level A harassment, defined as the potential destruction or loss of biological tissue (*i.e.*, physical injury), and Level B harassment, defined as temporary injury or disruption of behavioral patterns such as migration, feeding, surfacing, and breeding.

The Navy's computer models predicted that the SOCAL training exercises would cause only eight Level A harassments of common dolphins each year, and that even these injuries could be avoided through the Navy's voluntary mitigation measures, given that dolphins travel in large pods easily located by Navy lookouts. The EA also predicted 274 Level B harassments of beaked whales per year, none of which would result in permanent injury. Beaked whales spend little time at the surface, so the precise effect of active sonar on these mammals is unclear. Erring on the side of caution, the Navy classified all projected harassments of beaked whales as Level A. In light of its conclusion that the SOCAL training exercises would not have a significant impact on the environment, the Navy determined that it was unnecessary to prepare a full EIS.

Shortly after the Navy released its EA, the plaintiffs sued the Navy, seeking declaratory and injunctive relief on the grounds that the Navy's SOCAL training exercises violated NEPA * * * and the Coastal Zone Management Act of 1972 (CZMA). The District Court granted plaintiffs' motion for a preliminary injunction and prohibited the Navy from using MFA sonar during its remaining training exercises. The court held that plaintiffs had "demonstrated a probability of success" on their claims under NEPA and the CZMA. The court also determined that equitable relief was appropriate because, under Ninth Circuit precedent, plaintiffs had established at least a "possibility" of irreparable harm to the environment. Based on scientific studies, declarations from experts, and other evidence in the record, the District Court concluded that there was in fact a "near certainty" of irreparable injury to the environment, and that this injury outweighed any possible harm to the Navy.

The Navy filed an emergency appeal, and the Ninth Circuit stayed the injunction pending appeal. After hearing oral argument, the Court of Appeals agreed with the District Court that preliminary injunctive relief was appropriate. The appellate court concluded, however, that a blanket injunction prohibiting the Navy from using MFA sonar in SOCAL was overbroad, and remanded the case to the District Court "to narrow its injunction so as to provide mitigation conditions under which the Navy may conduct its training exercises." 508 F.3d 885, 887 (2007).

On remand, the District Court entered a new preliminary injunction allowing the Navy to use MFA sonar only as long as it implemented the following mitigation measures (in addition to the measures the Navy had adopted pursuant to its MMPA exemption): (1) imposing a 12–mile "exclusion zone" from the coastline; (2) using lookouts to conduct additional monitoring for marine mammals; (3) restricting the use of "helicopter-dipping" sonar; (4) limiting the use of MFA sonar in geographic "choke points"; (5) shutting down MFA sonar when a marine mammal is spotted within 2,200 yards of a vessel; and (6) powering down MFA sonar by 6 dB during significant surface ducting conditions, in which sound travels further than it otherwise would due to temperature differences in adjacent layers of water. The Navy filed a notice of appeal, challenging only the last two restrictions.

The Navy then sought relief from the Executive Branch. The President, pursuant to 16 U.S.C. § 1456(c)(1)(B), granted the Navy an exemption from the CZMA. Section 1456(c)(1)(B) permits such exemptions if the activity in question is "in the paramount interest of the United States." The President determined that continuation of the exercises as limited by the Navy was "essential to national security." He concluded that compliance with the District Court's injunction would "undermine the Navy's ability to conduct realistic training exercises that are necessary to ensure the combat effectiveness of . . . strike groups."

Simultaneously, the Council on Environmental Quality (CEQ) authorized the Navy to implement "alternative arrangements" to NEPA compliance in light of "emergency circumstances." See 40 CFR § 1506.11.[3] The CEQ determined that alternative arrangements were appropriate because the District Court's injunction "create[s] a significant and unreasonable risk that Strike Groups will not be able to train and be certified as fully mission capable." Under the alternative arrangements, the Navy would be permitted to conduct its training exercises under the mitigation procedures adopted in conjunction with the exemption from the MMPA. The CEQ also imposed additional notice, research, and reporting requirements.

In light of these actions, the Navy then moved to vacate the District Court's injunction with respect to the 2,200–yard shutdown zone and the restrictions on training in surface ducting conditions. The District Court refused to do so, and the Court of Appeals affirmed. . . .

We granted certiorari, and now reverse and vacate the injunction.

---

3. That provision states in full: "Where emergency circumstances make it necessary to take an action with significant environmental impact without observing the provisions of these regulations, the Federal agency taking the action should consult with the Council about alternative arrangements. Agencies and the Council will limit such arrangements to actions necessary to control the immediate impacts of the emergency. Other actions remain subject to NEPA review."

III

A

A plaintiff seeking a preliminary injunction must establish that he is likely to succeed on the merits, that he is likely to suffer irreparable harm in the absence of preliminary relief, that the balance of equities tips in his favor, and that an injunction is in the public interest.

The District Court and the Ninth Circuit concluded that plaintiffs have shown a likelihood of success on the merits of their NEPA claim. The Navy strongly disputes this determination, arguing that plaintiffs' likelihood of success is low because the CEQ reasonably concluded that "emergency circumstances" justified alternative arrangements to NEPA compliance....

The District Court and the Ninth Circuit also held that when a plaintiff demonstrates a strong likelihood of prevailing on the merits, a preliminary injunction may be entered based only on a "possibility" of irreparable harm. The lower courts held that plaintiffs had met this standard because the scientific studies, declarations, and other evidence in the record established to "a near certainty" that the Navy's training exercises would cause irreparable harm to the environment.

The Navy challenges these holdings, arguing that plaintiffs must demonstrate a likelihood of irreparable injury—not just a possibility—in order to obtain preliminary relief. On the facts of this case, the Navy contends that plaintiffs' alleged injuries are too speculative to give rise to irreparable injury, given that ever since the Navy's training program began 40 years ago, there has been no documented case of sonar-related injury to marine mammals in SOCAL. * * *

We agree with the Navy that the Ninth Circuit's "possibility" standard is too lenient. Our frequently reiterated standard requires plaintiffs seeking preliminary relief to demonstrate that irreparable injury is *likely* in the absence of an injunction. *Los Angeles v. Lyons,* 461 U.S. 95, 103 (1983) * * *. Issuing a preliminary injunction based only on a possibility of irreparable harm is inconsistent with our characterization of injunctive relief as an extraordinary remedy that may only be awarded upon a clear showing that the plaintiff is entitled to such relief.

It is not clear that articulating the incorrect standard affected the Ninth Circuit's analysis of irreparable harm. Although the court referred to the "possibility" standard, and cited Circuit precedent along the same lines, it affirmed the District Court's conclusion that plaintiffs had established a "near certainty" of irreparable harm. At the same time, however, the nature of the District Court's conclusion is itself unclear. The District Court originally found irreparable harm from sonar-training exercises generally. But by the time of the District Court's final decision, the Navy challenged only two of six restrictions imposed by the court. The District Court did not reconsider the likelihood of irreparable harm in light of the four restrictions not challenged by the Navy. This failure is significant in light of the District Court's own statement that the 12–mile exclusion zone from the coastline—one of the unchallenged mitigation restrictions—"would bar the use of MFA sonar in a significant portion of important marine mammal habitat." 530 F. Supp. 2d, at 1119.

We also find it pertinent that this is not a case in which the defendant is conducting a new type of activity with completely unknown effects on the environment. * * * Part of the harm NEPA attempts to prevent in requiring an EIS is that, without one, there may be little if any information about prospective environmental harms and potential mitigating measures. Here, in contrast, the plaintiffs are seeking to enjoin—or substantially restrict—training exercises that have been taking place in SOCAL for the last 40 years. And the latest series of exercises were not approved until after the defendant took a hard look at environmental consequences, as evidenced by the issuance of a detailed, 293–page EA.

As explained in the next section, even if plaintiffs have shown irreparable injury from the Navy's training exercises, any such injury is outweighed by the public interest and the Navy's interest in effective, realistic training of its sailors. A proper consideration of these factors alone requires denial of the requested injunctive relief. For the same reason, we do not address the lower courts' holding that plaintiffs have also established a likelihood of success on the merits.

B

A preliminary injunction is an extraordinary remedy never awarded as of right. In each case, courts "must balance the competing claims of injury and must consider the effect on each party of the granting or withholding of the requested relief." *Amoco Production Co.,* 480 U.S., at 542. "In exercising their sound discretion, courts of equity should pay particular regard for the public consequences in employing the extraordinary remedy of injunction." *Romero–Barcelo,* 456 U.S., at 312. In this case, the District Court and the Ninth Circuit significantly understated the burden the preliminary injunction would impose on the Navy's ability to conduct realistic training exercises, and the injunction's consequent adverse impact on the public interest in national defense.

This case involves "complex, subtle, and professional decisions as to the composition, training, equipping, and control of a military force," which are "essentially professional military judgments." *Gilligan v. Morgan,* 413 U.S. 1, 10 (1973). We "give great deference to the professional judgment of military authorities concerning the relative importance of a particular military interest." *Goldman v. Weinberger,* 475 U.S. 503, 507 (1986). * * *

Here, the record contains declarations from some of the Navy's most senior officers, all of whom underscored the threat posed by enemy submarines and the need for extensive sonar training to counter this threat. * * * Several Navy officers emphasized that realistic training cannot be accomplished under the two challenged restrictions imposed by the District Court—the 2,200—yard shutdown zone and the requirement that the Navy power down its sonar systems during significant surface ducting conditions. We accept these officers' assertions that the use of MFA sonar under realistic conditions during training exercises is of the utmost importance to the Navy and the Nation.

These interests must be weighed against the possible harm to the ecological, scientific, and recreational interests that are legitimately before this Court. Plaintiffs have submitted declarations asserting that they take whale watching trips, observe marine mammals underwater, conduct scientific research on marine mammals, and photograph these animals in their natural habitats. Plaintiffs contend that the Navy's use of MFA sonar will injure marine mammals or alter their behavioral patterns, impairing plaintiffs' ability to study and observe the animals.

While we do not question the seriousness of these interests, we conclude that the balance of equities and consideration of the overall public interest in this case tip strongly in favor of the Navy. For the plaintiffs, the most serious possible injury would be harm to an unknown number of the marine mammals that they study and observe. In contrast, forcing the Navy to deploy an inadequately trained antisubmarine force jeopardizes the safety of the fleet. Active sonar is the only reliable technology for detecting and tracking enemy diesel-electric submarines, and the President—the Commander in Chief—has determined that training with active sonar is "essential to national security."

The public interest in conducting training exercises with active sonar under realistic conditions plainly outweighs the interests advanced by the plaintiffs. Of course, military interests do not always trump other considerations, and we have not held that they do. In this case, however, the proper determination of where the public interest lies does not strike us as a close question.

C

* * *

The Court of Appeals held that the balance of equities and the public interest favored the plaintiffs, largely based on its view that the preliminary injunction would not in fact impose a significant burden on the Navy's ability to conduct its training exercises and certify its strike groups. The court deemed the Navy's concerns about the preliminary injunction "speculative" because the Navy had not operated under similar procedures before. But this is almost always the case when a plaintiff seeks injunctive relief to alter a defendant's conduct. The lower courts failed properly to defer to senior Navy officers' specific, predictive judgments about how the preliminary injunction would reduce the effectiveness of the Navy's SOCAL training exercises.

* * *

The Court of Appeals concluded its opinion by stating that "the Navy may return to the district court to request relief on an emergency basis" if the preliminary injunction "actually result[s] in an inability to train and certify sufficient naval forces to provide for the national defense." This is cold comfort to the Navy. The Navy contends that the injunction will hinder efforts to train sonar operators under realistic conditions, ultimately leaving strike groups more vulnerable to enemy submarines. Unlike the Ninth Circuit, we do not think the Navy is required to wait until the injunction "actually result[s] in an inability to train … sufficient naval forces for the national defense" before seeking its dissolution. By then it may be too late.

IV

As noted above, we do not address the underlying merits of plaintiffs' claims. While we have authority to proceed to such a decision at this point, doing so is not necessary here. In addition, reaching the merits is complicated by the fact that the lower courts addressed only one of several issues raised, and plaintiffs have largely chosen not to defend the decision below on that ground.

At the same time, what we have said makes clear that it would be an abuse of discretion to enter a permanent injunction, after final decision on the merits, along the same lines as the preliminary injunction. An injunction is a matter of equitable discretion; it does not follow from success on the merits as a matter of course.

The factors examined above—the balance of equities and consideration of the public interest—are pertinent in assessing the propriety of any injunctive relief, preliminary or permanent. Given that the ultimate legal claim is that the Navy must prepare an EIS, not that it must cease sonar training, there is no basis for enjoining such training in a manner credibly alleged to pose a serious threat to national security. This is particularly true in light of the fact that the training has been going on for 40 years with no documented episode of harm to a marine mammal. A court concluding that the Navy is required to prepare an EIS has many remedial tools at its disposal, including declaratory relief or an injunction tailored to the preparation of an EIS rather than the Navy's training in the interim. In the meantime, we see no basis for jeopardizing national security, as the present injunction does.

* * *

■ JUSTICE BREYER, with whom JUSTICE STEVENS joins as to Part I, concurring in part and dissenting in part.

* * *

Respondents' (hereinafter plaintiffs) argument favoring the District Court injunction is a strong one. As Justice Ginsburg well points out, the very point of NEPA's insistence upon the writing of an EIS is to force an agency "carefully" to "consider … detailed information concerning significant environmental impacts," while "giv[ing] the public the assurance that the agency has indeed considered environmental concerns in its decision-making process." *Robertson v. Methow Valley Citizens Council*, 490 U.S. 332, 349 (1989). NEPA seeks to assure that when Government officials consider taking action that may affect the environment, they do so fully aware of the relevant environmental considerations. An EIS does not force them to make any particular decision, but it does lead them to take environmental considerations into account when they decide whether, or how, to act. Thus, when a decision to which EIS obligations attach is made without the informed environmental consideration that NEPA requires, much of the harm that NEPA seeks to prevent has already taken place. In this case, for example, the *absence* of an injunction means that the Navy will proceed with its exercises in the absence of the fuller consideration of environmental effects that an EIS is intended to bring. The absence of an injunction thereby threatens to cause the very environmental harm that a full preaction EIS might have led the Navy to avoid (say, by adopting the two additional mitigation measures that the NRDC proposes). Consequently, if the exercises are to continue, conditions designed to mitigate interim environmental harm may well be appropriate.

On the other hand, several features of this case lead me to conclude that the record, as now before us, lacks adequate support for an injunction imposing the two controverted requirements. *First,* the evidence of need for the two special conditions is weak or uncertain. The record does show that the exercises as the Navy originally proposed them could harm marine mammals. The District Court found (based on the Navy's study of the matter) that the exercises might cause 466 instances of Level A harm and 170,000 instances of Level B harm. * * *

The raw numbers seem large. But the parties argue about the extent to which they mean likely harm. The Navy says the classifications and estimates err on the side of caution. The Navy also points out that, by definition, mammals recover from Level B injuries, often very quickly. It notes that, despite 40 years of naval exercises off the southern California coast, no injured marine mammal has ever been found. At the same time, plaintiffs point to instances where whales have been found stranded. They add that scientific studies have found a connection between those beachings and the Navy's use of sonar, and the Navy has even acknowledged one stranding where "U.S. Navy mid-frequency sonar has been identified as the most plausible contributory source to the stranding event."

Given the uncertainty the figures create in respect to the harm caused by the Navy's original training plans, it would seem important to have before us at least some estimate of the harm likely avoided by the Navy's decision not to contest here *four of the six mitigating conditions* that the District Court ordered. Without such evidence, it is difficult to assess the *relevant* harm—that is, the environmental harm likely caused by the Navy's exercises with the four uncontested mitigation measures (but without the two contested mitigation measures) in place.

Second, the Navy has filed multiple affidavits from Navy officials explaining in detail the seriousness of the harm that the delay associated with completion of this EIS (approximately one year) would create in respect to the Navy's ability to maintain an adequate national defense. * * *

Third, and particularly important in my view, the District Court did not explain *why* it rejected the Navy's affidavit-supported contentions. * * *

I would thus vacate the preliminary injunction imposed by the District Court to the extent it has been challenged by the Navy. Neither the District Court nor the Court of Appeals has adequately explained its conclusion that the balance of the equities tips in favor of plaintiffs. Nor do those parts of the record to which the parties have pointed supply the missing explanation.

Nonetheless, as the Court of Appeals held when it first considered this case, the Navy's past use of mitigation conditions makes clear that the Navy can effectively train under *some* mitigation conditions. In the ordinary course, I would remand so the District Court could, pursuant to the Court of Appeals' direction, set forth mitigation conditions that will protect the marine wildlife while also enabling the Navy to carry out its exercises. But, at this point, the Navy has informed us that this set of exercises will be complete by January, at the latest, and an EIS will likely be complete at that point, as well. Thus, by the time the District Court would have an opportunity to impose new conditions, the case could very well be moot.

In February of this year, the Court of Appeals stayed the injunction imposed by the District Court—*but only pending this Court's resolution of the case.* The Court of Appeals concluded that "[i]n light of the short time before the Navy is to commence its next exercise, the importance of the Navy's mission to provide for the national defense and the representation by the Chief of Naval Operations that the district court's preliminary injunction in its current form will unacceptably risk effective training and strike group certification and thereby interfere with his statutory responsibility to organize, train, and equip the Navy, interim relief was appropriate, and the court then modified the two mitigation conditions at issue.

With respect to the 2,200 yard shutdown zone, it required the Navy to suspend its use of the sonar if a marine mammal is detected within 2,200 yards, *except* when sonar is being used at a "critical point in the exercise," in which case the amount by which the Navy must power down is proportional to the mammal's proximity to the sonar. With respect to surface ducting, the Navy is only required to shut down sonar altogether when a marine mammal is detected within 500 meters and the amount by which it is otherwise required to power down is again proportional to the mammal's proximity to the sonar source. The court believed these conditions would permit the Navy to go forward with its imminently planned exercises while at the same time minimizing the harm to marine wildlife.

In my view, the modified conditions imposed by the Court of Appeals in its February stay order reflect the best equitable conditions that can be created in the short time available before the exercises are complete and the EIS is ready. The Navy has been training under these conditions since February, so allowing them to remain in place will, in effect, maintain what has become the status quo. Therefore, I would modify the Court of Appeals'

February 29, 2008, order so that the provisional conditions it contains remain in place until the Navy's completion of an acceptable EIS.

■ JUSTICE GINSBURG, with whom JUSTICE SOUTER joins, dissenting.

The central question in this action under the National Environmental Policy Act of 1969 (NEPA) was whether the Navy must prepare an environmental impact statement (EIS). The Navy does not challenge its obligation to do so, and it represents that the EIS will be complete in January 2009—one month after the instant exercises conclude. If the Navy had completed the EIS before taking action, as NEPA instructs, the parties and the public could have benefited from the environmental analysis—and the Navy's training could have proceeded without interruption. Instead, the Navy acted first, and thus thwarted the very purpose an EIS is intended to serve. To justify its course, the Navy sought dispensation not from Congress, but from an executive council that lacks authority to countermand or revise NEPA's requirements. I would hold that, in imposing manageable measures to mitigate harm until completion of the EIS, the District Court conscientiously balanced the equities and did not abuse its discretion.

* * *

The EIS is NEPA's core requirement. This Court has characterized the requirement as "action-forcing." *Andrus v. Sierra Club,* 442 U.S. 347, 350 (1979). Environmental concerns must be "integrated into the very process of agency decisionmaking" and "interwoven into the fabric of agency planning." *Id.,* at 350–351. In addition to discussing potential consequences, an EIS must describe potential mitigation measures and alternatives to the proposed course of action. The EIS requirement ensures that important effects will not be overlooked or underestimated only to be discovered after resources have been committed or the die otherwise cast.

"Publication of an EIS ... also serves a larger informational role." *Ibid.* It demonstrates that an agency has indeed considered environmental concerns, and "perhaps more significantly, provides a springboard for public comment." *Ibid.* At the same time, it affords other affected governmental bodies "notice of the expected consequences and the opportunity to plan and implement corrective measures in a timely manner." *Id.,* at 350.

In light of these objectives, the timing of an EIS is critical. CEQ regulations instruct agencies to "integrate the NEPA process with other planning at the earliest possible time to insure that planning and decisions reflect environmental values." 40 CFR § 1501.2 (1987). An EIS must be prepared "early enough so that it can serve practically as an important contribution to the decisionmaking process and will not be used to rationalize or justify decisions already made." *Andrus,* 442 U.S., at 351–352, n. 3.

The Navy's publication of its EIS in this case, scheduled to occur *after* the 14 exercises are completed, defeats NEPA's informational and participatory purposes. The Navy's inverted timing, it bears emphasis, is the very reason why the District Court had to confront the question of mitigation measures at all. Had the Navy prepared a legally sufficient EIS before beginning the SOCAL exercises, NEPA would have functioned as its drafters intended: The EIS process and associated public input might have convinced the Navy voluntarily to adopt mitigation measures, but NEPA itself would not have impeded the Navy's exercises.

The Navy had other options. Most importantly, it could have requested assistance from Congress. The Government has sometimes obtained congressional authorization to proceed with planned activities without fulfilling NEPA's requirements. * * *

Flexibility is a hallmark of equity jurisdiction. Consistent with equity's character, courts do not insist that litigants uniformly show a particular, predetermined quantum of probable success or injury before awarding equitable relief. Instead, courts have evaluated claims for equitable relief on a "sliding scale," sometimes awarding relief based on a lower likelihood of harm when the likelihood of success is very high. This Court has never rejected that formulation, and I do not believe it does so today.

Equity's flexibility is important in the NEPA context. Because an EIS is the tool for *uncovering* environmental harm, environmental plaintiffs may often rely more heavily on their probability of success than the likelihood of harm. The Court is correct that relief is not warranted simply to prevent the possibility of some remote future injury. However, the injury need not have been inflicted when application is made or be certain to occur; a strong threat of irreparable injury before trial is an adequate basis. I agree with the District Court that NRDC made the required showing here.

The Navy's own EA predicted substantial and irreparable harm to marine mammals. Sonar is linked to mass strandings of marine mammals, hemorrhaging around the brain and ears, acute spongiotic changes in the central nervous system, and lesions in vital organs. * * *[4]

In my view, this likely harm—170,000 behavioral disturbances, including 8,000 instances of temporary hearing loss; and 564 Level A harms, including 436 injuries to a beaked whale population numbering only 1,121—cannot be lightly dismissed, even in the face of an alleged risk to the effectiveness of the Navy's 14 training exercises. There is no doubt that the training exercises serve critical interests. But those interests do not authorize the Navy to violate a statutory command, especially when recourse to the Legislature remains open. * * *

In light of the likely, substantial harm to the environment, NRDC's almost inevitable success on the merits of its claim that NEPA required the Navy to prepare an EIS, the history of this litigation, and the public

---

4. The majority reasons that the environmental harm deserves less weight because the training exercises "have been taking place in SOCAL for the last 40 years," such that "this is not a case in which the defendant is conducting a new type of activity with completely unknown effects on the environment." But the EA explains that the proposed action is not a continuation of the "status quo training." Instead, the EA is based on the Navy's proposal to employ a "surge" training strategy, in which the commander "would have the option to conduct two concurrent major range events."

interest, I cannot agree that the mitigation measures the District Court imposed signal an abuse of discretion. * * *

NOTES AND QUESTIONS

1. *What does Winter hold?* Did the Supreme Court disagree with the Ninth Circuit on the law, the facts, or both? Does the decision change the law of NEPA injunctions? Is it limited to the facts of this unusual case, and if so what are the key facts?

2. *Sliding scales.* The Court in *Winter* wrote that "A plaintiff seeking a preliminary injunction must establish that he is likely to succeed on the merits, that he is likely to suffer irreparable harm in the absence of preliminary relief, that the balance of equities tips in his favor, and that an injunction is in the public interest." Prior to this decision, the lower courts had looked to the same four elements, but had generally used a kind of amorphous balancing test, allowing a stronger showing on one element (such as likelihood of success) to compensate for a weaker showing on another (such as likelihood of irreparable harm).

Justice Ginsburg, in her dissent, says that she does not believe the Court's decision rejects this "sliding scale" approach. Do you agree? Doesn't the majority explicitly reject at least one aspect of the "sliding scale" test? It disapproves of the lower courts' formulation of the relevant test as allowing injunctive relief based on the "possibility" of irreparable harm and a strong showing of likelihood of success on the merits. According to the Court: "Issuing a preliminary injunction based only on a possibility of irreparable harm is inconsistent with our characterization of injunctive relief as an extraordinary remedy that may only be awarded upon a clear showing that the plaintiff is entitled to such relief." How certain must the showing of harm be? Note that in a NEPA case, as Justice Ginsburg argues in dissent, the environmental analysis itself will often be the key to demonstrating that a threatened environmental injury is both likely and serious.

Must the extent of the harm exceed some threshold level? In *Alliance for the Wild Rockies v. Cottrell*, 632 F.3d 1127 (9th Cir. 2011), the Ninth Circuit rejected the Forest Service's argument that plaintiffs had not shown a likelihood of sufficient harm due to post-fire logging because the challenged project involved only a small proportion of the total area affected by fire, and plaintiffs could continue to use and observe the remaining area:

> This argument proves too much. Its logical extension is that a plaintiff can never suffer from irreparable injury resulting from environmental harm in a forest area as long as there are other areas of the forest that are not harmed. The Project will prevent the use and enjoyment by AWR members of 1,652 acres of the forest. This is hardly a de minimus injury.

3. *"Serious questions"*. Prior to *Winter*, the lower courts had applied the "sliding scale" test in another way as well, authorizing injunctive relief when the balance of hardships tips sharply toward the plaintiff and "serious questions" are raised on the merits. Does the *Winter* decision call into question this use of "sliding scale" approach? Three circuits have held that the "serious questions" test survives *Winter*. Alliance for the Wild Rockies v. Cottrell, 632 F.3d 1127 (9th Cir. 2011); Hoosier Energy Rural Elec. Co-op. v. John Hancock Life Ins. Co., 582 F.3d 721 (7th Cir. 2009); Citigroup Global Mkts v. VCG Special Opportunities Master Fund, 598 F.3d 30 (2d Cir. 2010). The Fourth Circuit, however, has held that *Winter* replaced a balancing test based on "flexible interplay" among the four factors with a requirement that each of the four elements "must be satisfied as articulated." Real Truth About Obama Inc. v. Federal Election Comm'n, 575 F.3d 342, 347 (4th Cir. 2009), *vacated on other grounds*, ___ U.S. ___, 130 S.Ct. 2371 (2010). Who has the better of this circuit split? Is there a good reason for treating the likelihood of success on the merits differently than the likelihood of irreparable harm? District Judge Michael Mosman, sitting by designation on the Ninth Circuit panel, explained why he thinks there is:

> As between the two, a district court at the preliminary injunction stage is in a much better position to predict the likelihood of harm than the likelihood of success. In fact, it is not unusual for the parties to be in rough agreement about what will follow a denial of injunctive relief. * * *
>
> But predicting the likelihood of success is another matter entirely. * * * [T]he whole question of the merits comes before the court on an accelerated schedule. The parties are often mostly guessing about important factual points * * *. The arguments that flow from the facts, while not exactly half-baked, do not have the clarity and development that will come later at summary judgment or trial. In this setting, it can seem almost inimical to good judging to hazard a prediction about which side is likely to succeed. There are, of course, obvious cases. But in many, perhaps most cases, the *better* question to ask is whether there are serious questions going to the merits. That question has a legitimate answer. Whether plaintiffs are likely to prevail often does not.

Alliance for the Wild Rockies, 632 F.3d at 1139–1140.

4. *NEPA exceptionalism?* Should courts be more willing to issue permanent injunctions, after resolving the merits, in NEPA cases than in others? Do you agree with the *Winter* majority that other tools can effectively enforce NEPA's environmental analysis requirements? Until recently, some lower courts had believed that injunctive relief was generally appropriate in any NEPA case, absent unusual circumstances. The Supreme Court rejected that formulation in Monsanto Co. v. Geertson Seed Farms, ___ U.S. ___, 130 S.Ct. 2743 (2010). According to the Court, no "thumb on the scales [in favor of injunctive relief] is warranted" in NEPA cases. Rather, the same test applies as in other contexts. An injunction should issue only if the plaintiff demonstrates that it has suffered irreparable injury, that legal remedies such as monetary damages are inadequate, that the balance of hardships favors the plaintiff, and that an injunction would be consistent with the public interest.

Do you agree? In *Monsanto*, the majority simply asserted that NEPA cases must be judged by the traditional test. It offered no analysis specific to NEPA's purposes or its strictly procedural nature. Justice Stevens, the lone dissenter, argued that the injunction challenged in that case was within the district court's discretion. He agreed with the majority that "a court may not presume that a NEPA violation requires an injunction," but argued that NEPA endorses a cautious approach that a court could take into account in shaping a remedy.

5. *A NEPA national security exemption?* As Chief Justice Roberts notes in *Winter*, the Marine Mammal Protection Act explicitly allows the Secretary of Defense to exempt actions "necessary for national defense" from the prohibition on taking marine mammals, and the Coastal Zone Management Act allows the President to exempt federal activities which are "in the paramount interest of the United States." Many other environmental statutes include some form of national security exemption process. NEPA does not. Does that make sense? Does the Court's opinion in *Winter* effectively create a national security exemption? If so, is it appropriate for the Court to create an exemption where Congress did not? As Chief Justice Roberts points out, federal courts are often at their most deferential when dealing with the military. Why were the lower courts so unreceptive to the Navy's claims that it needed to use active sonar in its Southern California training exercises?

6. *Emergencies and NEPA.* The CEQ NEPA Guidelines include the following provision:

> Where emergency circumstances make it necessary to take an action with significant environmental impact without observing the provisions of these regulations, the Federal agency taking the action should consult with the Council about alternative arrangements. Agencies and the Council will limit such arrangements to actions necessary to control the immediate impacts of the emergency. Other actions remain subject to NEPA review.

40 C.F.R. 1506.11. This provision has rarely been invoked, and, until this dispute, only when events outside the agency's control had created a need for quick action. CEQ and the Navy asserted that it could be used to justify going ahead with the contested Southern California training exercises before a full EIS was prepared. The District Court and Ninth Circuit rejected that claim because the Navy itself had created the "emergency" by failing to comply with NEPA in a timely manner. Natural Resources Defense Council v. Winter, 518 F.3d 658 (9th Cir. 2008), *overruled on other grounds*, Winter v. NRDC, 555 U.S. 7 (2008).

SECTION 5.   EVALUATING NEPA

Perhaps the strongest evidence of NEPA's success is the progeny it has spawned. At least 15 states and the District of Columbia have some form of environmental policy act modeled after NEPA, as do many foreign nations. Some commentators now recognize environmental impact assessment as an emerging principle of international law. See William L. Andreen, Environmental Law and International Assistance: The Challenge of Strengthening Environmental Law in the Developing World, 25 Columbia J. Envtl. L. 17, 40–41 (2000); Philippe Sands, Principles of International Environmental Law 799–825 (2d ed. 2003).

NEPA has also shown remarkable political stability. Title I (sections 2—105) has been amended only once, to add section 102(D), which allows states to take the lead in preparing EISs for certain actions. CEQ's implementing regulations have shown similar durability.

Of course, imitation and durability do not necessarily equate with success. Here are some possible yardsticks for evaluating NEPA:

1) Has it produced decisions that are substantively more environmentally protective than they otherwise would have been?

2) Has it ensured that agencies make decisions with better understanding of their environmental consequences?

3) Has it changed the culture of single-minded, mission-oriented federal agencies, making them more sensitive to environmental concerns?

4) Has it increased public awareness of, and involvement in, agency decisions with environmental consequences?

5) Are the costs of NEPA compliance justified by its benefits?

It is difficult to obtain reliable answers to any of these questions. Lynton Caldwell, a political scientist who was the primary architect of NEPA, believes the law has been successful in "forcing government agencies to ascertain the probable environmental consequences of their actions," but has failed to induce those agencies to act in accordance with the principles set forth in § 101(b). Lynton K. Caldwell, A Constitutional Law for the Environment: 20 Years with NEPA Indicates the Need, Environment, Dec. 1989, at 6, 10. Many observers agree that NEPA has forced mission-oriented agencies to diversify their staffs, bringing in environmental specialists or assigning their core staff to understand and communicate environmental concerns. That increased diversity, in turn, is thought to have produced greater environmental sensitivity. See, e.g., Paul J. Culhane, NEPA's Impacts on Federal Agencies, Anticipated and Unanticipated, 20 Envtl. L. 681, 690–91 (1990). Nonetheless, Culhane concludes that NEPA has not led to truly "rational" decisionmaking because agencies do not consider alternatives antithetical to their primary mission, EISs often do not reflect state-of-the-art scientific understanding, and the forecasts of impacts made in EISs are often wrong. Id. at 693–94.

Some commentators believe the openness required by NEPA has led to substantively better decisions:

> NEPA, and its requirement of an environmental impact statement open to public view and comment, ventilated the planning processes of federal agencies in a way that had never occurred before. The citizen, once only a nosy intruder, became a legitimate participant. [L]egitimating public participation, and demanding openness in planning and decisionmaking, has been indispensable to a permanent and powerful increase in environmental protection * * *.

Joseph Sax, Introduction to Symposium: Environmental Law: More Than Just a Passing Fad, 19 U. Mich. J. L. Ref. 797, 804 (1986).

Others, however, are more skeptical. In the absence of substantive requirements, solicitation of public input may be cynically viewed as a ploy to defuse public opposition. Furthermore, NEPA may be geared toward a one-way exchange of information from the government to the public, rather than a truly deliberative exchange. Jonathan Poisner, A Civic Republican Perspective on the National Environmental Policy Act's Process for Citizen Participation, 26 Envtl. L. 53 (1996). Does NEPA adequately encourage public input? Does it force agencies to take that input seriously? Poisner suggests the use of lay "juries," randomly selected from the community, to oversee the preparation of EISs. What do you think of that proposal? Is it feasible? Would it be desirable?

NEPA (and its state analogues) can play an important role in achieving environmental justice, which depends in large part upon providing members of the relevant community with reasonable access to the decisionmaking process. In 1994, President Clinton issued Executive Order 12898, requiring each federal agency to make environmental justice a part of its mission. A memorandum accompanying Executive Order 12898 specifically directed federal agencies to examine environmental effects on minority and low-income communities in their NEPA documents. In 1998, relying in part on the Executive Order, the Nuclear Regulatory Commission found that a preliminary decision to issue a permit for a uranium enrichment plant required additional environmental analysis. The Commission ruled that the EIS must more carefully evaluate the disparate impacts the plant might have on nearby minority-dominated communities, but at the same time rejected the argument that the EIS must closely examine the role intentional racial discrimination may have played in the siting decision. In the Matter of Louisiana Energy Services, L.P. (Claiborne Enrichment Center), 47 N.R.C. 77 (1998).

In some circumstances, however, NEPA may stand as an obstacle to environmental justice. Wealthy communities are far more likely than poor ones to be able to make effective use of NEPA's avenues for public participation. Indeed, NEPA may amplify NIMBY (not in my backyard) reactions in wealthy communities, pushing environmentally undesirable facilities toward lower-income, often minority, communities.

NOTES AND QUESTIONS

1. *The forest and the trees.* Does NEPA as currently implemented focus too much on the details of individual projects, and too little on articulating a true national environmental policy? Richard Andrews suggests that NEPA has been least effective at the broadest policy levels, such as the determination of overall energy, logging, and appropriation decisions, where the most pervasive environmental impacts are set in motion. Richard N.L. Andrews, The Unfinished Business of National Environmental Policy, in Environmental Policy and NEPA: Past, Present, and Future 85 (Ray Clark and Larry Canter eds., 1997). Andrews attributes this failure to two aspects of NEPA. First, the EIS requirement is not readily applied to this most fundamental level of decisionmaking. Second, the lofty-sounding principles articulated in NEPA sections 2 and 101 are not useful guides for decisions because they

> require unspecified trade-offs against other "essential considerations of national policy," and they contain no specific objectives, criteria, or benchmarks by which their achievement might be measured.

Id. at 93.

How could greater substantive guidance be provided? Andrews suggests defining a set of specific environmental "benchmarks" or indicators with deadlines for their achievement. Several substantive federal environmental laws set benchmarks. The Clean Air Act, for example, calls for achievement of national ambient air quality standards that protect the public health and welfare with an adequate margin of safety.

Should EPA (or some other body) be directed to draft detailed operational benchmarks for the condition of the nation's air, water, and land that would fulfill NEPA's directives to assure safe, healthful, productive, and aesthetically and culturally pleasing surroundings; attain the widest range of beneficial uses of the environment without degradation; and achieve a balance between population and resource use? Suppose you were the EPA administrator charged with that task. How would you begin to approach it?

2. *Avoiding environmental impairment where feasible.* In the absence of comprehensively rational benchmarks, are there other ways to give NEPA greater substantive content? Many state NEPA equivalents require that adverse environmental impacts be avoided if possible. Minnesota's, for example, forbids state action "likely to cause pollution, impairment, or destruction of the air, water, land or other natural resources located within the state, so long as there is a feasible and prudent alternative * * *." Minn. Stat. Ann. § 116D.04(6). California's requires that significant adverse impacts be avoided or mitigated if feasible, and any remaining significant impacts be justified by "[s]pecific overriding economic, legal, social, technological, or other benefits." Cal. Pub. Res. Code § 21081(a)(3). Should NEPA be amended to impose this type of requirement?

3. *The interplay of NEPA and substantive environmental laws.* A complex web of federal environmental statutes post-dating NEPA regulates air pollution, water pollution, hazardous waste disposal, and harm to natural resources. NEPA can help make those laws effective by exposing the potential for federal actions to lead to violations of their standards. Does the existence of background standards obviate the need for NEPA to play a substantive role? Should environmental changes within the boundaries permitted by those substantive laws be deemed "insignificant" for NEPA purposes? In the *Calvert Cliffs* decision, Judge Wright argued against that interpretation:

> Certification by another agency that its own environmental standards are satisfied involves an entirely different kind of judgment. Such agencies, without overall responsibility for the particular federal action in question, attend only to one aspect of the problem: the magnitude of certain environmental costs. They simply determine whether those costs exceed an allowable amount. Their certification does not mean that they found no environmental damage whatever. In fact, there may be significant environmental damage (e.g., water pollution), but not quite enough to violate applicable (e.g., water quality) standards. Certifying agencies do not attempt to weigh that damage against the opposing benefits. Thus the balancing analysis remains to be done. It may be that the environmental costs, though passing prescribed standards, are nonetheless great enough to outweigh the particular economic and technical benefits involved in the planned action. The only agency in a position to make such a judgment is the agency with overall responsibility for the proposed federal action—the agency to which NEPA is specifically directed.

Calvert Cliffs Coordinating Comm. v. U.S. Atomic Energy Comm'n, 449 F.2d 1109, 1123 (D.C. Cir. 1971). Do you agree? In 1998 the California Resources Agency, which implements California's NEPA-analogue, the California Environmental Quality Act, adopted a rule providing that an environmental impact would not be considered significant provided it was within the boundaries permitted by applicable substantive environmental standards. What arguments could you make in favor of this policy choice? Is it consistent with the purposes of environmental impact assessment requirements? The California Court of Appeal ultimately determined that the rule was invalid, and that the determination of significance could not be so constrained. Communities for a Better Environment v. California Resources Agency, 103 Cal.App.4th 98, 126 Cal.Rptr.2d 441 (Cal. App. 2002).

4. *Limiting reliance on outside consultants.* NEPA documents are often prepared by environmental consultants under contract. Should that practice be forbidden? Does reliance on outsiders decrease the probability that environmental concerns will play an important role in the actual decision process? Does it reduce the "agency culture-forcing" effect of NEPA? See Ray Clark, The National Environmental Policy Act and the Role of the President's Council on Environmental Quality, 15 Envtl. Prof. 4 (1993).

5. *Monitoring project impacts.* Should agencies be required to monitor project impacts subsequent to EIS approval and project implementation? If those impacts exceed estimates in the EIS, should the project be halted?

Should the agency be required to keep a record comparing projected with actual impacts? See Council on Environmental Quality, The National Environmental Policy Act: A Study of Its Effectiveness after Twenty–Five Years 31–33 (1997); Bradley C. Karkkainen, Toward a Smarter NEPA: Monitoring and Managing Government's Environmental Performance, 102 Colum. L. Rev. 903 (2002).

6. *A constitutional right to environmental protection?* Several state constitutions include environmental rights in some form. The Illinois Constitution, for example, provides:

> Each person has the right to a healthful environment. Each person may enforce this right against any party, governmental or private, through appropriate legal proceedings subject to reasonable limitation and regulation as the General Assembly may provide by law.

Ill. Const. art. XI, § 2. Would you support a similar amendment to the federal constitution? To what extent does the Illinois provision permit or require courts to determine what is a "healthful environment"? Are the courts in a position to make that determination?

SECTION 6. BEYOND NEPA: INFORMATION AND THE MARKET

NEPA rests on the assumption (or at least hope) that requiring federal agencies to gather and make public information about the environmental impacts of their actions will encourage more environmentally responsible decisions. Information disclosure might have similar effects in private settings. Consumers, for example, might want to base their purchasing decisions on environmental impacts, but lack the information necessary to do so.

A variety of information disclosure strategies have been employed in efforts to reduce pollution, inform consumer choices, and facilitate political pressures. They include:

Publicly accessible databases. The best known example is the Toxics Release Inventory (TRI) prescribed by the Emergency Planning and Community Right-to-Know Act of 1986 (EPCRA). Section 313 of EPCRA, codified at 42 U.S.C. § 11023, requires certain industrial facilities to annually report releases to air, water, and soil of listed chemicals they manufactured, processed, or used in quantities exceeding a threshold amount. EPA must make those reports available to the public through a computer data base.

Warnings of hazardous exposures. Perhaps the broadest warning requirement is found in California's Safe Drinking Water and Toxic Enforcement Act, popularly known as Proposition 65. It requires that businesses with more than 10 employees provide "clear and reasonable" warning before exposing individuals to chemicals listed by the state as carcinogens or reproductive toxicants. Cal. Health & Safety Code § 25249.6.

Environmental labeling. A variety of voluntary or required labeling programs provide consumers with environmental information. Examples include: the use of terms such as "recycled" or "organic," or logos such as the "dolphin-friendly tuna" seal; environmental certification or seals of approval such as Germany's Blue Angel; and "report cards" such as the Energy Guide energy efficiency ratings on new household appliances.

Bradley C. Karkkainen, Information as Environmental Regulation: TRI and Performance Benchmarking, Precursor to a New Paradigm?

89 Georgetown L. J. 257, 287–333 (2000).

Mandatory production and disclosure of TRI information has prompted many firms to undertake ambitious voluntary emission reduction programs, often far beyond the levels required under current regulations. * * * Since TRI reporting began in 1988, reported releases of TRI-listed pollutants have dropped by nearly half, with the sharp downward trend continuing steadily year after year. * * * According to one EPA survey, some seventy percent of TRI reporting facilities indicate that they have intensified their waste reduction efforts under the influence of TRI.

* * *

TRI places information in the hands of corporate managers in the first instance. Consequently, it might be analogized to a private sector version of the National Environmental Policy Act, requiring a process—the production and disclosure of environmental information relevant to decisionmaking—rather than substantive outcomes. In neither case does the regulatory approach require that anything in particular be done with the information once it is produced. But by compelling managers to examine environmental outcomes, it may influence their decisionmaking. * * *

Many top corporate managers, previously unaware of the volumes of toxic pollutants their firms were generating, were indeed surprised by the information produced in the first rounds of TRI. In many cases, that knowledge prompted a swift and decisive response, as firms adopted ambitious improvement targets far above the levels required for compliance with regulatory requirements, often in the range of fifty, seventy, or even ninety percent reductions from initial TRI-reported levels. * * *

TRI-generated performance data are readily available to regulators, as well as to environmentalists and other citizen-critics of regulatory policy. Regulators can use TRI data to establish baselines, profiles, and trends in the pollution performance of facilities, firms, industrial sectors, communities, and states, and to make benchmarking comparisons among them. Moreover, the data provide some indication of the effectiveness of regulatory and non-regulatory environmental policies, providing the basis for comparative analysis and benchmarking of program outcomes. TRI data thus help regulators identify regulatory gaps and shortcomings, set research priorities, and identify the most effective programs so as to replicate or expand them. * * *

Simultaneously, citizen-critics of governmental policies can use TRI-derived information to criticize or support current policies and programs, propose new ones, and benchmark and evaluate the achievements of regulated entities and regulators alike. Thus, TRI-generated information holds great potential to alter the level of political demand for environmental regulation, and to redirect that demand toward perceived "problem" firms, industries, pollutants or communities as identified by TRI-generated criteria.

Adverse facility-, firm-, or industry-level TRI data thus carry the implicit threat that regulatory action may follow, whether at the initiative of regulators themselves or in response to rising political demand for regulatory action. But precisely because forward-thinking firms and investors anticipate that additional regulatory requirements may prove burdensome and costly, firms may come under self-imposed and market-driven pressures to undertake cost-effective, voluntary, pollution prevention measures. According to the CEO of a leading chemical manufacturer, pollution prevention becomes a matter of "hard, cold, economics . . . pay now or pay a whole lot more later."

* * *

In the absence of a broader and more comprehensive set of metrics, many users of TRI information are tempted to use it as a proxy for the overall environmental performance of a facility or firm simply because it is the most visible and accessible source of comparable, quantifiable data. But TRI information provides, at best, one narrow and potentially highly misleading indicator of environmental performance, measuring releases from major point sources of substances on a short and far-from-complete EPA-compiled list of toxic pollutants.

A firm with superior TRI data might nonetheless produce large volumes of conventional pollutants or solid waste, or recklessly despoil valuable wildlife habitats—all beyond TRI's purview—while a firm with poor TRI data could nonetheless be a superior environmental performer along these other dimensions. Nor can we safely assume that every improvement in TRI data counts as an environmental gain because, in some cases, it might reflect a shift to activities that cause equal or greater environmental harm that is not reflected in TRI data. To that extent, TRI's very power to drive performance improvements *as measured by the TRI metric* makes it potentially misleading and possibly counterproductive if it is not matched and counterbalanced by a set of equally powerful metrics for other important dimensions of environmental performance.

Similarly, because all reported TRI releases are measured uniformly in pounds, regardless of the relative toxicity of the pollutant, a firm or facility might cut its reported emissions and transfers without reducing—and possibly even while increasing—health and environmental risks by substituting lower-volume, higher-toxicity pollutants. * * *

In addition, because TRI measures only the quantity of the pollutant released without factoring in proximity to population, exposure route, dispersion, persistence, sensitivity of exposed populations, or other important risk-related factors, it does not provide a very good guide to actual human and environmental risks. While TRI data may be combined with other information to provide a richer and more nuanced picture of risk, such information is often not available, and is rarely provided in a form readily accessible to non-expert users. Many users are tempted to rely on TRI data as a handy proxy for the environmental and health risks associated with toxic pollutants. In short, they use TRI as an indicator of environmental *quality* (which it is not), rather than as an indicator of the environmental *performance* of a limited class of sources (the only use the data can fairly support). But to do so may lead to serious overestimation or underestimation of risk.

Clifford Rechtschaffen, The Warning Game: Evaluating Warnings Under California's Proposition 65

23 Ecology L.Q. 303, 313–48 (1996).

Laws utilizing information disclosure requirements—warnings, informational labeling, worker training and notification, and community reporting and disclosure—are based on several important, albeit diverse, rationales. The most common rationale is that such laws improve the efficient functioning of the market. Traditional microeconomic theory assumes consumers have perfect information. Where such information is lacking and will not be produced by the market, disclosure laws help insure that the market functions properly by bridging the information gap. * * * Relying on the power of the market, economists tout information disclosure laws as more efficient and less constraining than direct regulation, imposing lower costs on both business and regulators.

In addition, information disclosure laws are also premised on an entitlement rationale, as reflected in the title of recent "right-to-know" laws. The underlying notion is that members of the public have a "fundamental right to know" what chemicals are "out there" and the chemicals to which they are being exposed. Information promotes individual autonomy by providing individuals with knowledge of the risks involved in their choices and allowing them to decide whether or not to encounter these risks.

Information disclosure laws also promote citizen power and advance democratic decisionmaking. * * * Armed with more information, citizens can make better-informed decisions and are thus in a better position to bargain with private corporations and government.

* * * Information disclosure laws have inherent limitations as well. The marketplace model assumes markets in which there is an elastic demand for products and there are readily available product substitutes. It is also premised on the existence of perfectly rational consumers who seek

information regarding alternatives when making decisions, make trade-offs that allow them to compute utilities for every alternative, and select the alternatives that maximize utility. However, these conditions are often not satisfied. Consumers may lack the time or interest to seek out information. Many may have difficulty understanding certain information, especially information about risks. In particular, less educated and limited-English speaking individuals are less likely to be able to read, understand, and use warning information. Even when individuals read and comprehend warnings, they often do not change their behavior in response to the information they receive. * * *

[Most consumer product warnings under Proposition 65] have been located on product labels. * * * Although the regulations state that warnings must be presented with "such conspicuousness as to render them likely to be read and understood by an ordinary individual under customary conditions of purchase or use," in practice this general requirement has imposed few limitations on businesses and has done little to insure that warnings are noticed. Many Proposition 65 warnings are inadequately designed to attract attention. * * *

Research shows that numerous design features can make warnings more conspicuous, such as using a high color contrast relative to the background; using large, legible, bold-face characters; placing warnings prominently; using symbols or icons; and using signal words. However, except for employing the signal word "WARNING," the great majority of Proposition 65 warnings have none of these characteristics. * * *

Proposition 65 warnings have appeared on the back of product labels, on the underside of product cans, or on the inside of lids covering product cans and boxes. Some have been in small print and dull type, sometimes squeezed onto labels already crowded with information. * * *

Proposition 65 does not require any specific warning language, but the regulations do set forth "safe harbor" warning messages, which have been used on virtually all consumer product warnings. The basic safe harbor message for a consumer product warning states: "WARNING: This product contains a chemical known to the State of California to cause cancer [birth defects or other reproductive harm]." The warning message does not use symbols, despite a great deal of evidence that in addition to increasing the attractiveness of a warning, symbols facilitate the ability of consumers to process warning information. Symbols are especially desirable given the substantial portion of the population that cannot read, is functionally illiterate, or cannot read English.

The safe harbor warning statement also does not inform individuals that use of the product will expose them to a listed chemical. Rather, it simply contains the less informative message that the product *contains* a listed chemical. This inadequacy directly hinders communication of the statute's central message. It also makes the warning less personally relevant to recipients and more likely to be overlooked, since, not surprisingly, consumers are more likely to attend to warnings that they find personally relevant.

* * *

A Proposition 65 warning essentially warns that there is some level of risk associated with a product. However, the safe harbor warning message does not provide the consumer with any basis for evaluating the level or nature of the risk posed by individual exposures. The consumer knows only that the product contains a chemical known to cause cancer or reproductive toxicity. * * *

Despite the prevalence of poor warnings, Proposition 65's warning requirement has stimulated significant consumer-product reformulation, due to a combination of industry concerns about liability and consumer reaction to warnings. In some instances, the reformulations have been close to industry-wide, reflecting the competitive pressures that arise once a portion of the industry alters its products. Almost all the reformulated products are being sold nationwide, giving the statute national effect. * * *

Enforcement actions have triggered many product reformulations. Nearly forty manufacturers of glazed ceramicware (china) have agreed to reduce lead levels in their flatware by fifty percent and in their hollowware by twenty-five percent within five years. Two companies have become entirely lead-free. * * *

A large segment of the nail polish industry agreed to remove toluene from dozens of consumer and professional nail polish products. Manufacturers have agreed to reformulate dozens of automobile paints, coatings, adhesives, and related products. Approximately three hundred wineries, representing a large share of the domestic wine industry, agreed to phase out their use of lead foil caps on wine bottles. * * *

Other reported instances of product reformulation have occurred absent direct enforcement. Old El Paso canned foods eliminated its use of lead-soldered cans, as did a Mexican canner/importer. Major Paint removed methylene chloride from forty-five of its Xynolyte Brand products. Sunoco reformulated the inks in plastic grocery bags to eliminate listed chemicals. Sara Lee's Kiwi Brand Products reformulated its shoe-waterproofing sprays to remove listed chemicals. Sears Roebuck & Company reported that its supplier reformulated dozens of products, including car wax and carburetor cleaner. An herbicide manufacturer altered its products to remove arsenic, a listed chemical.

The extraordinary steps taken by businesses to avoid consumer product warnings can be partially explained by liability concerns. In Proposition 65 enforcement suits, the California Attorney General's Office and private parties have been willing to forego imposing civil fines on defendant companies in exchange for product reformulation, and indeed have made this a goal of their enforcement policies. Facing statutory fines that can be enormous, many companies have consented to reformulate their products in order to reduce their potential liability. Other companies have reformulated as a prophylactic measure to avoid the possibility of a lawsuit entirely, given the statute's large penalties and the relatively unpredictable nature of citizen enforcement. * * *

More significant than the desire to minimize liability is corporate concern over consumer reaction to product warnings, and the power of green consumerism in the marketplace. Consumer demand can be extremely sensitive to the disclosure of adverse health and safety product information, particularly in food products. Businesses perceive the possibility of significant sales losses by disclosing toxic chemical presence in certain consumer products, and warnings for these products have, consequently, become anathema to business. * * *

Proposition 65 has had notable success in reducing toxics in consumer products, although two caveats should be noted. First, reformulation may not always be completely beneficial. Products that are reformulated may substitute chemicals that pose other risks of equal or greater dimension than the Proposition 65 chemicals they replace. Likewise, a product may pose risks marginally above the warning threshold yet have important benefits that would be impaired by removing a listed chemical. From a risk/benefit perspective, reformulation in this instance would not be desirable. Second, reformulation may constrain the choices of consumers who would otherwise be willing to incur the added risk posed by a product.

From a policy perspective, these examples are most troubling if driven by exaggerated consumer fears of the risks posed by products, rather than consumers' deliberate and well-informed decisionmaking. If the latter mechanism is responsible, then businesses are simply responding, appropriately, to the collectively expressed preferences of the market.

The above discussion has focused on products for which substitutes exist. Where there are no available substitutes, the marketplace has fared poorly as a mechanism for achieving toxics reductions. In these situations, businesses have provided warnings that exact little or no cost in terms of reduced consumer demand. Thus, gas stations throughout California contain warnings that "chemicals known to the state to cause cancer, birth defects, or other reproductive harm are found in gasoline, crude oil and many other petroleum products, and ether vapors, or result from their use." Consumers do not have the option of using a "safer" gasoline, since all brands contain benzene, a listed carcinogen. Similarly, all mothball deodorizers sold contain paradichlorobenzene, a listed carcinogen. Without the availability of alternative products, consumers most likely "filter out [these warnings] from their field of vision."[243]

NOTES AND QUESTIONS

1. *Information and regulation.* What advantages do information mandates enjoy over command-and-control regulation? What disadvantages? How much environmental protection will they produce? How efficient will that

---

243. See [John P.] Dwyer, [Innovative Risk Regulation Under Proposition 65, Prop 65 News, Feb. 1992], at 31. * * *

improvement be? Are disclosure mandates likely to be less politically controversial than substantive mandates? Could disclosure requirements such as the TRI help overcome some of the difficulties with toxic tort suits described in Chapter 2?

2. *Simplifying without over-simplifying.* What are the shortcomings of TRI disclosures and Proposition 65 warnings? Can consumers be provided with enough information to help them make sound environmental decisions without swamping them with data? Will consumers correctly interpret the information they are given? What consequences might misinterpretation have? Are labels likely to be helpful where alternative products are characterized by complex environmental trade-offs, as in the case of cloth versus disposable diapers? Consider electricity generation. Several suppliers now market "green" electricity. The environmental impacts of electricity production, however, take many forms. Nuclear power creates radioactive waste. Fossil fuel combustion causes air pollution and accelerates global warming. Hydropower dams are a major threat to certain fish species, and wind turbines kill birds and bats. How should "green" power be defined? Should consumers control the trade-offs between global warming, nuclear waste production, and endangered fish, or should those trade-offs be made through the political process?

3. *Markets as drivers of information production.* As the green electricity example in the note above shows, market forces sometimes drive firms to generate and disclose information about the environmental impacts of their activities even without any regulatory requirements. A conspicuous recent example is WalMart's announcement in July 2009 that it will develop a "worldwide sustainable product index." As WalMart explains the initiative, it will survey its suppliers about greenhouse gas emission, material efficiency and solid waste production, raw materials purchasing guidelines, sources of their supply chains, and community development investments. It will use the information it gathers to create a life-cycle analysis database and, eventually, "provide customers with information about products in a simple, easy-to-understand manner, helping them save money while they help their families, and the world, live better." Walmart, Sustainability Index, http://walmartstores.com/Sustainability/9292.aspx.

One concern about such voluntary efforts is overseeing the truthfulness, reliability, and transparency of environmental claims. Environmental marketing (or "greenwashing," as it is sometimes disparagingly called by skeptics) is potentially subject to regulation by the Federal Trade Commission, which has issued a regulatory "green guide." 16 C.F.R. Part 260. The green guide has not been updated since 1998. Prodded by states and environmental groups concerned about misleading claims in the market for (voluntary) carbon offsets, such as those offered by computer manufacturers and airlines, the FTC proposed revisions in 2010. 75 Fed. Reg. 63552 (Oct. 15, 2010). The FTC also recently stepped up its enforcement efforts, filing complaints against several large companies that were allegedly making false claims that their products are biodegradable or environmentally friendly. Gabriel Nelson, FTC Moves May Signal Start of "Greenwashing" Crackdown, N.Y. Times, Feb. 3, 2010.

Another concern has to do with follow-through. WalMart got a great deal of positive publicity simply for announcing that it was going to survey its suppliers on sustainability. Sending around a survey, by itself, however, has no environmental or even consumer information benefits. Some skeptics worry that WalMart will be able to coast on the announcement alone, and that the media, shareholders, and customers will not track the continued development or use of the index over time. They may have a point. As of July 2011, nearly two years after the survey, it is not clear that any progress has been made on the index. No customer information tools have yet been announced.

CHAPTER SIX

Public and Quasi-Public Resources

Many natural resources have traditionally been fully available for private ownership and trading in ordinary markets. Most land falls in that category, as do oil and other minerals. Some resources, however, have long been considered unsuitable for ordinary private ownership due to special public importance or special obstacles to exclusive possession. This chapter examines the treatment of two such resources, wildlife and wetlands, for which the question of where to draw the line between public and private control is highly controversial.

SECTION 1. BIODIVERSITY PROTECTION

The term biodiversity refers to the entire range of living creatures, from microscopic bacteria to enormous whales. Estimates of the number of species on earth range from 3 million to 100 million. Bruce A. Stein et al., A Remarkable Array: Species Diversity in the United States, *in* Precious Heritage: The Status of Biodiversity in the United States 58 (Stein et al. eds. 2000). The United States harbors a substantial portion of the world's biotic diversity, including ten percent of the world's mammal species, and seven percent of its flowering plants. Id. at 67.

Worldwide, biodiversity is disappearing at an unprecedented rate. The International Union for the Conservation of Nature reported in 2000 that one in every four mammal species and one in eight bird species face significant risk of extinction. In the United States, as much as one-third of the native flora and fauna may be at risk. *See* Lawrence L. Master et al., Vanishing Assets: Conservation Status of U.S. Species, *in* Precious Heritage, *supra* at 101–04.

As you read the materials that follow, consider not only why we should care about threats to biodiversity, but to what extent those threats can and should be addressed by law. If law is not the entire answer, what else should we do, individually and as a society, to improve future prospects for biodiversity?

A. HISTORICAL BACKGROUND

In Roman law, wild animals were unowned until captured or killed by human enterprise. The only restriction on hunting was that landowners had the exclusive right to take wildlife on their property.

English law was quite different. The Crown held complete authority over hunting and wildlife management, even on private lands. The Crown, and later Parliament, jealously guarded the right to hunt, reserving it to landed gentry in part to restrict the spread of weapons among the lower classes but also as a signal of elite status.

In the United States, the states succeeded to the sovereign's broad authority to regulate with respect to wildlife management. *See* Martin v. Waddell's Lessee, 41 U.S. (16 Pet.) 367 (1842). Nonetheless, until the middle of the 19th century, free taking of wildlife was the general rule. The apparent inexhaustibility of wildlife resources, coupled with resistance to the English class structure, discouraged states from using their authority aggressively to protect wildlife. Instead, early colonial and state laws facilitated the capture of wildlife by opening private lands to public hunting and fishing. *See* Hope M. Babcock, Should *Lucas v. South Carolina Coastal Council* Protect Where the Wild Things Are? Of Beavers, Bob–O–Links, and Other Things That Go Bump in the Night, 85 Iowa L. Rev. 849, 883 (2000). Many states also offered bounties to encourage killing of predators such as wolves. *See* Dale D. Goble, Of Wolves and Welfare Ranching, 16 Harv. Envtl. L. Rev. 101, 104 (1992).

Restrictions on the taking of wildlife gained importance in the second half of the 19th century, as the mammals and birds that once dominated the continent fell to the guns of market hunters. In the 1850s, states began to enact bag limits and restrict hunting seasons. Karin P. Sheldon, Overview of Wildlife Law, *in* Environmental Law: From Resources to Recovery 204 (1993). It soon became clear, however, that state action alone was insufficient to stem the rapid decline of wildlife populations. Poachers could effectively evade state restrictions by removing their illegally-taken bounty from the state or claiming to have caught it legally in another state. Robert S. Anderson, The Lacey Act: America's Premier Weapon in the Fight Against Unlawful Wildlife Trafficking, 16 Pub. Land L. Rev. 27, 38 (1995).

The cautious first federal foray into wildlife law, the Lacey Act, currently codified at 16 U.S.C. §§ 3371–3378, addressed both of these problems, making it a federal crime to transport wildlife taken in violation of state law across state lines and subjecting imported game to state law as if it had been killed there.

At the time the Lacey Act was passed, it was widely believed that federal power did not extend to direct wildlife management. Judicial interpretation of state power over wildlife had given rise to a fiction of state "ownership" which seemed to preclude federal intervention. *See* Geer v. Connecticut, 161 U.S. 519 (1896); The Vessel 'Abby Dodge' v. United States, 223 U.S. 166 (1912).

The Supreme Court finally repudiated the state ownership doctrine as a special limitation on federal power over wildlife in Hughes v. Oklahoma, 441 U.S. 322, 326 n.2 (1979). Long before then, however, Congress, relying on the treaty power and the New Deal-era expansion of the commerce power, had greatly expanded federal wildlife law.

In 1913, the Migratory Bird Act imposed federal restrictions on hunting of migratory birds. After two federal courts declared the Act unconstitutional, the executive branch quickly negotiated a migratory bird treaty with Great Britain (acting for Canada). Congress then re-enacted essentially the same provisions as the Migratory Bird Treaty Act (currently codified at 16 U.S.C. §§ 703–712). The Supreme Court upheld the new law under the Treaty Power. Missouri v. Holland, 252 U.S. 416 (1920).

Emboldened by the Supreme Court's clear declaration that state power over wildlife did not exclude federal authority, Congress expanded federal regulation from hunting restrictions designed to ensure continuing availability of game for harvest to conservation for esthetic and other noneconomic purposes. By 1973, federal regulation had reached its zenith with passage of the Endangered Species Act (ESA), 16 U.S.C. §§ 1531–1544, which prohibits the taking of any animal species federally designated as endangered.

Legal protection of plants remains far weaker than legal protection of animals. At common law, ownership of plants followed ownership of the soil in which they grew. With the exception of scattered limitations on timber harvest, the law provided virtually no protection for plants until the second half of the 20th century. Today, the ESA and the Convention on International Trade in Endangered Species restrict commerce in declining plant species, and the ESA prohibits removal or destruction of listed plants on federal property.

Despite the great expansion of federal wildlife regulation since 1900, state law remains important and, in light of the judicial trend toward a narrower interpretation of federal power, may become more so. States provide the primary source of hunting and fishing regulations, even on federal lands. Although the state ownership doctrine has been discredited, states are still considered trustees of fish and wildlife resources on behalf of their citizens, giving them broad power to impose regulations consistent with, or more protective than, federal law. *See*, e.g., Babcock, *supra*, at 886–89. Many states have statutes protecting species recognized as endangered or threatened within the state, although most lack at least some of the protections of the federal law. *See* Dale D. Goble et al., Local and National Protection of Endangered Species: An Assessment, 2 Envtl. Sci. & Pol'y 43, 50 (1999). These laws are particularly crucial to protection of endangered plants. The federal ESA prohibits the taking of listed plants on private property "in knowing violation of any law or regulation of any State or in the course of any violation of a State criminal trespass law." 16 U.S.C. § 1538(a)(2)(B). Thus, landowners can legally destroy federally listed plants on their property unless forbidden to do so by state law. According to a recent study, only seven states and two federal territories prohibit the killing of protected plants on private property. Jeffrey J. Rachlinski, Protecting Endangered Species Without Regulating Private Landowners: The Case of Endangered Plants, 8 Cornell J.L. & Pub. Pol'y 1, 12 (1998).

Native American rights play a special role in wildlife law. Traditional tribal cultures were heavily dependent on local wildlife resources. *See*

United States v. Winans, 198 U.S. 371, 381 (1905) ("Salmon were not much less necessary to the existence of the Indians than the atmosphere they breathed."). Consequently, numerous treaties between tribes and the United States include provisions protecting tribal hunting and fishing practices, both on and off reservations. Exercise of these rights remains important, both economically and culturally, to many tribes. States can impose conservation restrictions on Indian hunting and fishing, but those restrictions must not have the effect of discriminating against Indians. Any available harvest must be "fairly apportioned" between Indians and non-Indians. Department of Game v. Puyallup Tribe, 414 U.S. 44, 48 (1973). In a long-running dispute over salmon fishing rights in the state of Washington, the Supreme Court eventually held that the tribe was entitled to roughly half the harvest. Washington v. Washington State Commercial Passenger Fishing Vessel Ass'n, 443 U.S. 658 (1979).

Congress retains the power to abrogate Indian treaties. Subsequent federal law, therefore, can change established Indian treaty rights to wildlife if the legislation clearly shows congressional intent to do so. In United States v. Dion, 476 U.S. 734 (1986), the Supreme Court held that the Bald Eagle Protection Act abrogated treaty rights to hunt eagles on a reservation. Lower courts have split on whether the Endangered Species Act applies to non-commercial hunting by Native Americans. Compare United States v. Billie, 667 F.Supp. 1485 (S.D. Fla. 1987), with United States v. Dion, 752 F.2d 1261 (8th Cir. 1985) (en banc), *rev'd on other grounds*, 476 U.S. 734 (1986).

Wildlife and wildlife parts are associated with many Native American religious practices. The Free Exercise clause is sometimes asserted as a defense to prosecution for wildlife violations. Although that defense has occasionally proven successful, it has typically been rejected. *See* United States v. Abeyta, 632 F.Supp. 1301 (D. N.M. 1986) (dismissing prosecution of Indian who killed golden eagle for religious purposes); United States v. Jim, 888 F.Supp. 1058 (D. Or. 1995) (upholding restrictions on hunting of bald and golden eagles, despite substantial burden on religious freedom).

B.   JUSTIFICATIONS FOR BIODIVERSITY PROTECTION

Holly Doremus, Patching the Ark: Improving Legal Protection of Biological Diversity

18 Ecology L. Q. 265, 269–81 (1991).

* * * [T]he arguments for preservation of biological diversity can be divided into three categories: utilitarian, esthetic, and moral. * * *

The Utilitarian Basis for Preservation of Diversity

* * * Individual species provide us with a number of direct benefits. For example, we have domesticated our food crops, both plant and animal, from wild species. Other species might provide new crops. Wild relatives of current crop species can also provide a source of useful genetic traits. * * *

Biological diversity is also a useful source of new medicinal drugs. Chemicals derived from higher plants form the major ingredient in about a quarter of all prescriptions written in the United States; chemicals derived from lower plants and microbes account for another eighth. Many of these drugs can be produced more cheaply by extraction than by chemical synthesis. Numerous species have yet to be examined for their medicinal properties. Thus, many undiscovered medicinally useful chemicals may exist in the natural world.

A number of animal species serve another important function in medicine as model systems for the study of human diseases. For obvious reasons, researchers cannot deliberately infect human subjects to facilitate laboratory study of the progress and properties of a disease. However, they can and do use animals as laboratory subjects. Examples include the use of desert pupfish to study kidney disease and of armadillos to study leprosy. * * *

Besides the direct benefits described above, ecosystems provide a number of indirect benefits to humanity. These "ecosystem services" include climate control, oxygen production, removal of carbon dioxide from the atmosphere, soil generation, nutrient cycling, and purification of fresh-water supplies. Some of these functions could probably be performed by managed systems, at least on a small scale, but management of such systems on a global scale is presently beyond our technological capability. Moreover, some of these processes, such as nutrient cycling, are highly complex and not yet fully understood.

* * *

The Esthetic Basis for Preservation of Diversity

Many people find beauty in the natural world, viewing natural objects, both living and nonliving, with a sense of admiration, wonder, or awe. Esthetic interest in nature is demonstrated in a variety of ways. For example, millions of Americans visit national parks and wildlife refuges every year. Some sixty million Americans participate in bird watching, and millions more engage in other forms of wildlife-related recreation. * * *

Individual species and specific natural areas may also come, over time, to be imbued with powerful symbolic value. They may embody the cultural or political identity of a people. The bald eagle is one such symbolic species * * *.

The interest that the biota holds for scientists and natural historians also has esthetic overtones. For example, one may appreciate the beauty of the interactions among species, or of the construction of an organism to function optimally in its environment. * * *

The esthetic value of diversity extends to ecosystem, species, and genetic diversity. * * * Ecosystems have esthetic value beyond that of the species they contain because the interactions that occur among species, and the way the system as a whole responds to perturbations, are themselves interesting. And genetic diversity is esthetically valuable both because the differences among individuals may fascinate us (as in the case of our own species), and because it provides the building blocks from which new manifestations of nature's wonder can be constructed. * * *

The Ethical Basis for Preservation of Diversity

In 1949, Aldo Leopold advocated the extension of ethical obligations to the relations between man and nature, calling for the development of an "ecological conscience" reflecting "a conviction of individual responsibility for the health of the land." Since then, several commentators have argued that nonhuman organisms, and even nonliving natural objects, have or should have rights based on their intrinsic value. Under such a view, human beings have an ethical obligation not to destroy these creatures and objects, at least in the absence of a strong countervailing value.

An ethical obligation to "nature" could conceivably be directed primarily to individuals, species, ecosystems, or the global environment as a whole. Human beings find it easiest to empathize and identify with individual beings and with vertebrate animals * * *. Therefore, people may most readily accept a moral obligation toward individual "higher" animals. Animal liberation philosophers have proposed ethical obligations toward all creatures able to experience pain, or capable of valuing their lives. * * *

Taking a different approach than animal rights proponents, a number of philosophers have expressed the view that man's ethical obligation to nature extends not primarily to individuals but to species or natural systems. This view echoes Leopold's famous statement: "A thing is right when it tends to preserve the integrity, stability, and beauty of the biotic community. It is wrong when it tends otherwise." Those espousing this view have emphasized the importance of the continuation of the biotic community, and the moral considerability of ecosystems and species. Some commentators have argued that species have a right to function normally in their ecosystems * * *.

Ethical obligations to nature need not rest on such a nonanthropocentric foundation. Several philosophers and theologians, while not granting "rights" similar to those held by human beings to other species or to natural systems, have appealed to a tradition of human responsibility for stewardship of the Earth. The theological argument for stewardship proceeds from the premise that God created nature in part for his own enjoyment. The nature of the creation gives rise to a three-fold role for man with respect to nature: man is both overlord, wondering onlooker, and caretaker. The combination of these roles requires that man, insofar as possible, allow nature to flourish and to continue in its place. This duty to nature is not absolute, however; it occupies a position secondary to man's duty to his fellow man. * * *

Public Policy Consequences of the Various Arguments For Preservation

Acceptance of any of the arguments given above for the preservation of biological diversity leads to the conclusion that preservation of some part of our biota is desirable as a matter of public policy. The different bases for preservation do not, however, necessarily justify protection of the same proportion of the total, nor of the same resources. * * *

Utilitarian grounds have been most often cited in and to Congress as justifying a national policy of protection of biological resources, although esthetic and ethical arguments have also been made. Utilitarian appeals may be most common because the people seeking protection of plants and animals believe that these justifications will have a greater appeal to the public than will other arguments. * * *

Although the utilitarian argument may be the easiest to sell to the public, it does not, by itself, provide a basis for preservation of the full spectrum of biological diversity. One common utilitarian argument is that, since most species have not been investigated with an eye to their exploitability, it would be foolhardy to allow them to become extinct before such an investigation has been made. This argument provides a solid basis for preservation of tropical systems, where little or nothing is known about a vast number of species, but is less applicable to developed countries like the United States, where, although large gaps in our knowledge remain, much of the flora and fauna has been at least cursorily investigated. Many species may have little or no utilitarian value, either individually or as components of an ecosystem. If utilitarian reasons are the only basis for preservation, we need not preserve these species. * * *

A strict utilitarian view would also justify extermination of a species or an ecosystem to serve a human purpose, even a fairly limited purpose. Although few would argue that a starving man might not maintain his life by eating the only available food source even if it was the last example of an endangered species, many choices are less stark. As an example, the bark of the Pacific yew (*Taxus brevifolia*), a tree found in oldgrowth forests of the Pacific Northwest, contains taxol, a chemical which can act as an anticancer drug. The tree is rare and slow-growing, the bark contains only a low concentration of the chemical, and high doses are needed to inhibit the growth of cancer cells. A utilitarian view might sanction the use of all specimens of the Pacific yew in destructive experiments if there were a good chance that such a course would allow scientists to develop a synthesis for taxol.

* * *

The esthetic argument * * * could allow the extermination of species and ecosystems which most people do not find appealing. For example, although many biologists would disagree, most people find swamps esthetically distasteful. Unless a scientific elite is made the arbiter of esthetic value, swamps might properly be turned into esthetically preferable meadows.

Similarly, if the purpose of preservation is primarily esthetic, people may demand that their esthetic experience be given first priority even when it conflicts with the health of the species or ecosystem. Such conflicts currently occur, for example, with respect to whale watching off the California coast. Because tourists demand the best possible view of the sounding whales, tour boats endeavor to get as close as possible. Some marine scientists believe that these intrusions have caused the whales to alter their migratory path significantly. If the primary basis for preservation of biological wonders such as whales is esthetic, perhaps they are not worth preserving unless they can be viewed at close range during their migration.

* * *

By contrast, nonanthropocentric moral arguments provide a basis for preservation of the entire range of biological diversity, at least if the ethical obligation runs primarily to species or natural systems rather than to individual creatures. An ethical obligation directed at individual organisms might lead indirectly to the protection of genetic diversity, but would not, in principle, allow one to distinguish between individuals of rare and abundant species. For example, under a view that primarily values individual creatures, it would be difficult to justify removal of feral goats or sheep from an island where they are eating the last examples of a rare plant.

Other factors also limit the reach of an ethical obligation running to individual organisms. Many (probably most) of the current threats to nonhuman species come from indirect causes, such as elimination of habitat, rather than from direct exploitation. Human activities causing these indirect threats are morally ambiguous compared to actions such as the clubbing of baby seals, as they often do not result in immediately apparent harm to individual animals. * * *

Only a moral obligation extending to ecosystems or even to the global biota as a whole provides a reason to preserve the full range of biological diversity. Such an obligation could be based on the rareness of life in the universe, the complexity of the systems which have evolved on the Earth, and the unique nature of human consciousness. Leopold and others have viewed the diversity of natural systems as a good in itself; the apparent rarity of life beyond our planet may enhance the value of that diversity.

Furthermore, *Homo sapiens*, as a species uniquely capable of appreciating the effects of its actions, may have a special obligation to see that those actions do not unnecessarily impinge on the biota. Humans are capable both of appreciating the range of life that has developed on Earth, and of modifying the environment in ways that threaten much of that range. This combination of awareness and power may carry with it a special responsibility to preserve, to the extent compatible with human survival, the other biological resources of the planet.

NOTES AND QUESTIONS

1. *Why protect biodiversity?* Should we strive to protect biodiversity, and if so to what extent? Which arguments do you find most persuasive, utilitarian, esthetic, or moral? What level should be the focus of our concern? Should we be concerned about old-growth forest as a community or about the individual plant and animal species that make up that community? If the community, how should we decide how much to protect? If the species, should we be satisfied to save a gene bank if we believed frozen embryos or cells could regenerate those plants and animals long into the future? Or should we seek to reintroduce species to areas from which they have been lost? Wolves, for example, once roamed much of North America. They have been successfully returned to a few areas, including Yellowstone National Park, and seem to be relatively tolerant of human impacts. Should we also try to bring wolves back to metropolitan Denver or the northeast corridor?

2. *The value of ecosystem services.* Much of the utilitarian value provided by nature lies outside the market system, and is therefore difficult to measure. No one currently pays for plants to replace carbon dioxide in the atmosphere with oxygen, for example, or for wetlands to filter water. Concerned that these services are not adequately considered in public and private decisions, economists have tried to estimate their monetary value. Based on willingness-to-pay studies and other data, one widely-circulated report places the global value of ecosystem services somewhere between $16 and $54 trillion annually (in 1994 dollars), compared to global gross national product totals of $18 trillion per year. Robert Costanza et al., The Value of the World's Ecosystem Services and Natural Capital, 387 Nature 252 (1997).

3. *The precautionary principle and burdens of proof.* Because extinction is irreversible, many commentators urge application of the "precautionary principle," which, in the spirit of "better safe than sorry," calls for action to protect the environment to precede certainty of harm. Developed to insure that scientific uncertainty does not unduly stall protective efforts, the precautionary principle essentially places the burden of proof on those who would change the environmental status quo.

The precautionary principle, in one form or another, has been incorporated into several recent international agreements. The 1992 Rio Declaration on Environment and Development, for example, provides:

> In order to protect the environment, the precautionary approach shall be widely applied by States according to their capabilities. Where there are threats of serious or irreversible damage, lack of full scientific certainty shall not be used as a reason for postponing cost-effective measures to prevent environmental degradation.

Preamble, Principle 15. Some observers argue that the precautionary principle has become a general principle of international law, although others disagree. *See* James Cameron & Juli Abouchar, The Status of the Precautionary Principle in International Law, *in* The Precautionary Principle and International Law: The Challenge of Implementation 29, 36–50 (David Freestone & Ellen Hey, eds. 1996).

Should the precautionary principle apply to biodiversity protection, either internationally or within the United States? How should it be operationalized? In other words, how strong a suspicion of potential harm should be sufficient to halt development, and how certain must it be that harm will not be serious or irreversible before development is permitted?

4. *Taxol update.* Demand for taxol no longer threatens the Pacific yew. Taxol and several closely related compounds can now be synthesized starting with needles of various common yew species. Hedge clippings which were once a disposal problem for gardeners now provide a renewable and economical source of these useful drugs. *See* Sarah Lonsdale, Shoots of Recovery, Daily Telegraph (London), May 13, 2000, at 17.

C.   THE ENDANGERED SPECIES ACT: THE FLAGSHIP BIODIVERSITY STATUTE

The most celebrated and controversial biodiversity protection measure in the United States is the federal Endangered Species Act (ESA). This section begins with a brief overview of the law, then considers listing, the prohibition on take, and the incidental take permit provision in greater detail.

1.   OVERVIEW

The U.S. Fish & Wildlife Service (FWS) of the Department of Interior is primarily responsible for implementing the ESA, although the National Marine Fisheries Service, an agency of the Department of Commerce, is responsible for protection of marine species and anadromous fish (fish that migrate from fresh water to the ocean during their life cycle). FWS maintains a list of species determined by regulation to be endangered or threatened. ESA § 4, 16 U.S.C. § 1533. The Services are supposed to designate "critical habitat" concurrent with species listing. Id.

Listed species are protected by two key regulatory provisions. Section 7 applies only to federal agencies. It imposes a duty to carry out programs for the conservation of listed species. ESA § 7(a)(1), 16 U.S.C. § 1536(a)(1). This provision allows agencies to use their existing authorities to assist listed species, but leaves them considerable discretion in choosing how to do so. *See* Carson–Truckee Water Conservancy Dist. v. Clark, 741 F.2d 257 (9th Cir. 1984); Pyramid Lake Paiute Tribe v. United States Dept. of the Navy, 898 F.2d 1410 (9th Cir. 1990).

Section 7 also requires federal agencies to ensure that actions they carry out, authorize, or fund are not likely to jeopardize the continued existence of any listed species or adversely modify or destroy its critical habitat. ESA § 7(a)(2), 16 U.S.C. § 1536(a)(2). This duty is fulfilled through a three-step process. First, the agency asks the appropriate Service whether any listed species are in the project area. Next, the agency undertakes a "biological assessment" to determine if the project is likely to affect any of those species. If so, the agency initiates formal consultation with the Service on the impacts of the project. Formal consultation culminates in issuance by the Service of a biological opinion as to whether the proposed action is likely to jeopardize the species or adversely modify its critical habitat. 16 U.S.C. § 1536(b)(3)(A). An action fails the jeopardy test if it "reasonably would be expected, directly or indirectly, to reduce appreciably the likelihood of both the survival and recovery of a listed species in the wild by reducing the reproduction, numbers, or distribution of that species." 50 C.F.R. § 402.02. It has impermissible impacts on critical habitat if it would appreciably diminish the value of that habitat for survival and recovery. Id. If the Service finds jeopardy or adverse modification of critical habitat, it must suggest "reasonable and prudent alternatives" that would allow the project to proceed without impermissibly harming the species. 16 U.S.C. § 1536(b)(3)(A). "No jeopardy" biological opinions are accompanied by incidental take statements which protect the action agency against liability under section 9.

In practice, section 7 consultation rarely halts projects. One study found that FWS conducted more than 94,000 informal and 2,700 formal consultations between 1987 and 1992. Those consultations produced 352 jeopardy opinions and actually blocked only 54 actions. World Wildlife Fund, For Conserving Listed Species, Talk is Cheaper than We Think: The Consultation Process Under the Endangered Species Act (Nov. 1994). Of course, the key statistic may not be the number of actions blocked but the value or potential benefits of those actions.

The other important regulatory provision of the ESA is section 9, which imposes a series of prohibitions applicable to all persons. With respect to endangered plants, section 9 forbids shipment or receipt in interstate or foreign commerce; removal from or malicious destruction on federal land; and removal or destruction from other lands in knowing violation of state law or in the course of a violation of state criminal trespass law. ESA § 9(a)(2), 16 U.S.C. § 1538(a)(2). Endangered animals receive stronger protection; no person may "take" an endangered animal within the United States or on the high seas. ESA § 9(a)(1), 16 U.S.C. § 1538(a)(1).

Knowing violation of the ESA is punishable by civil penalties of up to $25,000 per violation or criminal penalties of up to $50,000 per violation and imprisonment for up to one year. ESA § 11(a), (b), 16 U.S.C. § 1540(a), (b). Citizen suits are available to enjoin violations, and successful citizen plaintiffs can recover attorney fees. ESA § 11(g), 16 U.S.C. § 1540(g).

2. FEDERAL ACTIVITIES

Excerpts From the Endangered Species Act

16 U.S.C. § 1531–1544.

Sec. 7 Interagency cooperation.

(a)(1) The Secretary shall review other programs administered by him and utilize such programs in furtherance of the purposes of this chapter. All other Federal agencies shall, in consultation with and with the assistance of the Secretary, utilize their authorities in furtherance of the purposes of this chapter by carrying out programs for the conservation of endangered species and threatened species listed pursuant to section 1533 of this title.

(2) Each Federal agency shall, in consultation with and with the assistance of the Secretary, insure that any action authorized, funded, or carried out by such agency (hereinafter in this section referred to as an "agency action") is not likely to jeopardize the continued existence of any endangered species or threatened species or result in the destruction or adverse modification of habitat of such species which is determined by the Secretary, after consultation as appropriate with affected States, to be critical, unless such agency has been granted an exemption for such action by the Committee pursuant to subsection (h) of this section. In fulfilling the requirements of this paragraph each agency shall use the best scientific and commercial data available.

* * *

Tennessee Valley Authority v. Hill

United States Supreme Court, 1978.
437 U.S. 153.

■ MR. CHIEF JUSTICE BURGER delivered the opinion of the Court.

* * *

The Little Tennessee River originates in the mountains of northern Georgia and flows through the national forest lands of North Carolina into Tennessee, where it converges with the Big Tennessee River near Knoxville. The lower 33 miles of the Little Tennessee takes the river's clear, free-flowing waters through an area of great natural beauty. Among other environmental amenities, this stretch of river is said to contain abundant trout. * * *

In this area of the Little Tennessee River the Tennessee Valley Authority, a wholly owned public corporation of the United States, began constructing the Tellico Dam and Reservoir Project in 1967, shortly after Congress appropriated initial funds for its development. Tellico is a multi-purpose regional development project designed principally to stimulate shoreline development, generate sufficient electric current to heat 20,000 homes, and provide flatwater recreation and flood control, as well as improve economic conditions in "an area characterized by underutilization of human resources and outmigration of young people." Hearings on Public Works for Power and Energy Research Appropriation Bill, 1977, before a Subcommittee of the House Committee on Appropriations, 94th Cong., 2d Sess., pt. 5, p. 261 (1976). Of particular relevance to this case is one aspect of the project, a dam which TVA determined to place on the Little Tennessee, a short distance from where the river's waters meet with the Big Tennessee. When fully operational, the dam would impound water covering some 16,500 acres—much of which represents valuable and productive farmland—thereby converting the river's shallow, fast-flowing waters into a deep reservoir over 30 miles in length.

The Tellico Dam has never opened, however, despite the fact that construction has been virtually completed and the dam is essentially ready for operation. * * *

[In 1973], a discovery was made in the waters of the Little Tennessee which would profoundly affect the Tellico Project. Exploring the area around Coytee Springs, which is about seven miles from the mouth of the river, a University of Tennessee ichthyologist, Dr. David A. Etnier, found a previously unknown species of perch, the snail darter, or *Percina (Imostoma) tanasi.* This three-inch, tannish-colored fish, whose numbers are estimated to be in the range of 10,000 to 15,000, would soon engage the attention of environmentalists, the TVA, the Department of the Interior, the Congress of the United States, and ultimately the federal courts, as a new and additional basis to halt construction of the dam.

Until recently the finding of a new species of animal life would hardly generate a cause célèbre. This is particularly so in the case of darters, of which there are approximately 130 known species, 8 to 10 of these having been identified only in the last five years.[7] The moving force behind the snail darter's sudden fame came some four months after its discovery, when the Congress passed the Endangered Species Act of 1973 (Act), 16 U.S.C. § 1531 *et seq.* (1976 ed.). * * *

[The Secretary of Interior listed the snail darter as an endangered species in October 1975, after concluding] that the snail darter apparently lives only in that portion of the Little Tennessee River which would be completely inundated by the reservoir created as a consequence of the Tellico Dam's completion.[12] The Secretary went on to explain the significance of the dam to the habitat of the snail darter:

"[T]he snail darter occurs only in the swifter portions of shoals over clean gravel substrate in cool, low-turbidity water. Food of the snail darter is almost exclusively snails which require a clean gravel substrate for their survival. *The proposed impoundment of water behind the proposed Tellico Dam would result in total destruction of the snail darter's habitat." Ibid.* (emphasis added).

---

7. In Tennessee alone there are 85 to 90 species of darters, of which upward of 45 live in the Tennessee River system. New species of darters are being constantly discovered and classified—at the rate of about one per year. This is a difficult task for even trained ichthyologists since species of darters are often hard to differentiate from one another.

12. Searches by TVA in more than 60 watercourses have failed to find other populations of snail darters. The Secretary has noted that "more than 1,000 collections in recent years and additional earlier collections from central and east Tennessee have not revealed the presence of the snail darter outside the Little Tennessee River." 40 Fed. Reg. 47505 (1975). It is estimated, however, that the snail darter's range once extended throughout the upper main Tennessee River and the lower portions of its major tributaries above Chattanooga—all of which are now the sites of dam impoundments.

Subsequent to this determination, the Secretary declared the area of the Little Tennessee which would be affected by the Tellico Dam to be the "critical habitat" of the snail darter. * * *

[Despite the snail darter's listing, the House Committee on Appropriations recommended that an additional $29 million be appropriated for the Tellico project.] Congress then approved the TVA general budget, which contained funds for continued construction of the Tellico Project.[14] In December 1975, one month after the snail darter was declared an endangered species, the President signed the bill into law.

In February 1976, pursuant to § 11(g) of the Endangered Species Act, 16 U.S.C. § 1540(g) (1976 ed.), respondents filed the case now under review, seeking to enjoin completion of the dam and impoundment of the reservoir on the ground that those actions would violate the Act by directly causing the extinction of the species *Percina (Imostoma) tanasi.* * * * [The District Court declined to enjoin completion of the dam. The Sixth Circuit reversed.

During the litigation, Congress again passed TVA budgets, with the Appropriations Committees in both the House and Senate endorsing continued funding for the Tellico Project.]

II

We begin with the premise that operation of the Tellico Dam will either eradicate the known population of snail darters or destroy their critical habitat. Petitioner does not now seriously dispute this fact. * * *

It may seem curious to some that the survival of a relatively small number of three-inch fish among all the countless millions of species extant would require the permanent halting of a virtually completed dam for which Congress has expended more than $100 million. The paradox is not minimized by the fact that Congress continued to appropriate large sums of public money for the project, even after congressional Appropriations Committees were apprised of its apparent impact upon the survival of the snail darter. We conclude, however, that the explicit provisions of the Endangered Species Act require precisely that result.

One would be hard pressed to find a statutory provision whose terms were any plainer than those in § 7 of the Endangered Species Act. Its very words affirmatively command all federal agencies "to *insure* that actions *authorized, funded,* or *carried out* by them do not *jeopardize* the continued existence" of an endangered species or "*result* in the destruction or modification of habitat of such species...." 16 U.S.C. § 1536 (1976 ed.). (Emphasis added.) This language admits of no exception. Nonetheless, petitioner urges, as do the dissenters, that the Act cannot reasonably be interpreted as applying to a federal project which was well under way when Congress passed the Endangered Species Act of 1973. To sustain that

---

14.   TVA projects generally are authorized by the Authority itself and are funded—without the need for specific congressional authorization—from lump-sum appropriations provided in yearly budget grants.

position, however, we would be forced to ignore the ordinary meaning of plain language. It has not been shown, for example, how TVA can close the gates of the Tellico Dam without "carrying out" an action that has been "authorized" and "funded" by a federal agency. Nor can we understand how such action will *"insure"* that the snail darter's habitat is not disrupted. Accepting the Secretary's determinations, as we must, it is clear that TVA's proposed operation of the dam will have precisely the opposite effect, namely the *eradication* of an endangered species.

Concededly, this view of the Act will produce results requiring the sacrifice of the anticipated benefits of the project and of many millions of dollars in public funds. But examination of the language, history, and structure of the legislation under review here indicates beyond doubt that Congress intended endangered species to be afforded the highest of priorities.

* * *

The legislative proceedings in 1973 are, in fact, replete with expressions of concern over the risk that might lie in the loss of *any* endangered species. Typifying these sentiments is the Report of the House Committee on Merchant Marine and Fisheries on H.R. 37, a bill which contained the essential features of the subsequently enacted Act of 1973; in explaining the need for the legislation, the Report stated:

> As we homogenize the habitats in which these plants and animals evolved, and as we increase the pressure for products that they are in a position to supply (usually unwillingly) we threaten their—and our own—genetic heritage.
>
> *The value of this genetic heritage is, quite literally, incalculable.*

* * *

> Who knows, or can say, what potential cures for cancer or other scourges, present or future, may lie locked up in the structures of plants which may yet be undiscovered, much less analyzed? . . . Sheer self-interest impels us to be cautious.
>
> *The institutionalization of that caution* lies at the heart of H.R. 37. . . .

H.R. Rep. No.93–412, pp. 4–5 (1973). (Emphasis added.)

As the examples cited here demonstrate, Congress was concerned about the *unknown* uses that endangered species might have and about the *unforeseeable* place such creatures may have in the chain of life on this planet.

* * *

It is against this legislative background that we must measure TVA's claim that the Act was not intended to stop operation of a project which, like Tellico Dam, was near completion when an endangered species was discovered in its path. While there is no discussion in the legislative history of precisely this problem, the totality of congressional action makes it abundantly clear that the result we reach today is wholly in accord with both the words of the statute and the intent of Congress. The plain intent of Congress in enacting this statute was to halt and reverse the trend toward species extinction, whatever the cost. This is reflected not only in the stated policies of the Act, but in literally every section of the statute. All persons, including federal agencies, are specifically instructed not to "take" endangered species, meaning that no one is "to harass, harm,[30] pursue, hunt, shoot, wound, kill, trap, capture, or collect" such life forms. 16 U.S.C. §§ 1532(14), 1538(a)(1)(B) (1976 ed.). Agencies in particular are directed by §§ 2(c) and 3(2) of the Act to "use ... *all methods* and procedures which are necessary" to preserve endangered species. 16 U.S.C. §§ 1531(c), 1532(2) (emphasis added) (1976 ed.). In addition, the legislative history undergirding § 7 reveals an explicit congressional decision to require agencies to afford first priority to the declared national policy of saving endangered species. The pointed omission of the type of qualifying language previously included in endangered species legislation reveals a conscious decision by Congress to give endangered species priority over the "primary missions" of federal agencies.

* * *

One might dispute the applicability of these examples to the Tellico Dam by saying that in this case the burden on the public through the loss of millions of unrecoverable dollars would greatly outweigh the loss of the snail darter. But neither the Endangered Species Act nor Art. III of the Constitution provides federal courts with authority to make such fine utilitarian calculations. On the contrary, the plain language of the Act, buttressed by its legislative history, shows clearly that Congress viewed the value of endangered species as "incalculable." Quite obviously, it would be difficult for a court to balance the loss of a sum certain—even $100 million—against a congressionally declared "incalculable" value, even assuming we had the power to engage in such a weighing process, which we emphatically do not.

* * *

Notwithstanding Congress' expression of intent in 1973, we are urged to find that the continuing appropriations for Tellico Dam constitute an implied repeal of the 1973 Act, at least insofar as it applies to the Tellico Project. * * *

There is nothing in the appropriations measures, as passed, which states that the Tellico Project was to be completed irrespective of the

---

30. We do not understand how TVA intends to operate Tellico Dam without "harming" the snail darter. The Secretary of the Interior has defined the term "harm" to mean "an act or omission which actually injures or kills wildlife, including acts which annoy it to such an extent as to significantly disrupt essential behavioral patterns, which include, but are not limited to, breeding, feeding or sheltering; significant environmental modification or degradation which has such effects is included within the meaning of 'harm.' " 50 CFR § 17.3 (1976) (emphasis added).

requirements of the Endangered Species Act. These appropriations, in fact, represented relatively minor components of the lump-sum amounts for the *entire* TVA budget. To find a repeal of the Endangered Species Act under these circumstances would surely do violence to the "cardinal rule ... that repeals by implication are not favored." *Morton v. Mancari,* 417 U.S. 535, 549 (1974). * * *

The doctrine disfavoring repeals by implication "applies with full vigor when ... the subsequent legislation is an *appropriations* measure." *Committee for Nuclear Responsibility v. Seaborg,* 463 F.2d 783, 785 (1971) (emphasis added). This is perhaps an understatement since it would be more accurate to say that the policy applies with even *greater* force when the claimed repeal rests solely on an Appropriations Act. We recognize that both substantive enactments and appropriations measures are "Acts of Congress," but the latter have the limited and specific purpose of providing funds for authorized programs. When voting on appropriations measures, legislators are entitled to operate under the assumption that the funds will be devoted to purposes which are lawful and not for any purpose forbidden. Without such an assurance, every appropriations measure would be pregnant with prospects of altering substantive legislation, repealing by implication any prior statute which might prohibit the expenditure. * * *

Perhaps mindful of the fact that it is "swimming upstream" against a strong current of well-established precedent, TVA argues for an exception to the rule against implied repealers in a circumstance where, as here, Appropriations Committees have expressly stated their "understanding" that the earlier legislation would not prohibit the proposed expenditure. We cannot accept such a proposition. Expressions of committees dealing with requests for appropriations cannot be equated with statutes enacted by Congress, particularly not in the circumstances presented by this case.

* * *

Having determined that there is an irreconcilable conflict between operation of the Tellico Dam and the explicit provisions of § 7 of the Endangered Species Act, we must now consider what remedy, if any, is appropriate. It is correct, of course, that a federal judge sitting as a chancellor is not mechanically obligated to grant an injunction for every violation of law. * * *

But these principles take a court only so far. Our system of government is, after all, a tripartite one, with each branch having certain defined functions delegated to it by the Constitution. While "[i]t is emphatically the province and duty of the judicial department to say what the law is," *Marbury v. Madison,* 1 Cranch 137, 177 (1803), it is equally—and emphatically—the exclusive province of the Congress not only to formulate legislative policies and mandate programs and projects, but also to establish their relative priority for the Nation. Once Congress, exercising its delegated powers, has decided the order of priorities in a given area, it is for the Executive to administer the laws and for the courts to enforce them when enforcement is sought.

Here we are urged to view the Endangered Species Act "reasonably," and hence shape a remedy "that accords with some modicum of common sense and the public weal." But is that our function? We have no expert knowledge on the subject of endangered species, much less do we have a mandate from the people to strike a balance of equities on the side of the Tellico Dam. Congress has spoken in the plainest of words, making it abundantly clear that the balance has been struck in favor of affording endangered species the highest of priorities, thereby adopting a policy which it described as "institutionalized caution."

Our individual appraisal of the wisdom or unwisdom of a particular course consciously selected by the Congress is to be put aside in the process of interpreting a statute. Once the meaning of an enactment is discerned and its constitutionality determined, the judicial process comes to an end.
* * *

■ JUSTICE POWELL, with whom JUSTICE BLACKMUN joins, dissenting.

The Court today holds that § 7 of the Endangered Species Act requires a federal court, for the purpose of protecting an endangered species or its habitat, to enjoin permanently the operation of any federal project, whether completed or substantially completed. This decision casts a long shadow over the operation of even the most important projects, serving vital needs of society and national defense, whenever it is determined that continued operation would threaten extinction of an endangered species or its habitat. This result is said to be required by the "plain intent of Congress" as well as by the language of the statute.

In my view § 7 cannot reasonably be interpreted as applying to a project that is completed or substantially completed when its threat to an endangered species is discovered. Nor can I believe that Congress could have intended this Act to produce the "absurd result"—in the words of the District Court—of this case. If it were clear from the language of the Act and its legislative history that Congress intended to authorize this result, this Court would be compelled to enforce it. It is not our province to rectify policy or political judgments by the Legislative Branch, however egregiously they may disserve the public interest. But where the statutory language and legislative history, as in this case, need not be construed to reach such a result, I view it as the duty of this Court to adopt a permissible construction that accords with some modicum of common sense and the public weal.

* * *

* * * Under the Court's reasoning, the Act covers every existing federal installation, including great hydroelectric projects and reservoirs, every river and harbor project, and every national defense installation—however essential to the Nation's economic health and safety. The "actions" that an agency would be prohibited from "carrying out" would include the continued operation of such projects or any change necessary to preserve their continued usefulness. The only precondition, according to respondents, to thus destroying the usefulness of even the most important

federal project in our country would be a finding by the Secretary of the Interior that a continuation of the project would threaten the survival or critical habitat of a newly discovered species of water spider or amoeba.[13]

* * * The result that will follow in this case by virtue of the Court's reading of § 7 makes it unreasonable to believe that Congress intended that reading. Moreover, § 7 may be construed in a way that avoids an "absurd result" without doing violence to its language.

The critical word in § 7 is "actions" and its meaning is far from "plain." It is part of the phrase: "actions authorized, funded or carried out." In terms of planning and executing various activities, it seems evident that the "actions" referred to are not all actions that an agency can ever take, but rather actions that the agency is *deciding whether* to authorize, to fund, or to carry out. In short, these words reasonably may be read as applying only to *prospective actions, i.e.,* actions with respect to which the agency has reasonable decisionmaking alternatives still available, actions *not yet* carried out. At the time respondents brought this lawsuit, the Tellico Project was 80% complete at a cost of more than $78 million. * * * Thus, under a prospective reading of § 7, the action already had been "carried out" in terms of any remaining reasonable decisionmaking power.

* * *

I have little doubt that Congress will amend the Endangered Species Act to prevent the grave consequences made possible by today's decision. * * *

* * * If Congress acts expeditiously, as may be anticipated, the Court's decision probably will have no lasting adverse consequences. But I had not thought it to be the province of this Court to force Congress into otherwise unnecessary action by interpreting a statute to produce a result no one intended.

■ JUSTICE REHNQUIST, dissenting.

In the light of my Brother Powell's dissenting opinion, I am far less convinced than is the Court that the Endangered Species Act of 1973 was intended to prohibit the completion of the Tellico Dam. But the very difficulty and doubtfulness of the correct answer to this legal question convinces me that the Act did *not* prohibit the District Court from refusing,

---

13. Under the Court's interpretation, the prospects for such disasters are breathtaking indeed, since there are hundreds of thousands of candidates for the endangered list:

> The act covers every animal and plant species, subspecies, and population in the world needing protection. There are approximately 1.4 million full species of animals and 600,000 full species of plants in the world. Various authorities calculate as many as 10% of them—some 200,000—may need to be listed as Endangered or Threatened. When one counts in subspecies, not to mention individual populations, the total could increase to three to five times that number.

Keith Shreiner, Associate Director and Endangered Species Program Manager of the U. S. Fish and Wildlife Service, quoted in Wood, On Protecting an Endangered Statute: The Endangered Species Act of 1973, 37 Federal B. J. 25, 27 (1978).

in the exercise of its traditional equitable powers, to enjoin petitioner from completing the Dam. * * *

* * * Here the District Court recognized that Congress, when it enacted the Endangered Species Act, made the preservation of the habitat of the snail darter an important public concern. But it concluded that this interest on one side of the balance was more than outweighed by other equally significant factors. These factors * * * satisfy me that the District Court's refusal to issue an injunction was not an abuse of its discretion. * * *

National Association of Home Builders v. Defenders of Wildlife

United States Supreme Court, 2007.
551 U.S. 644.

■ JUSTICE ALITO delivered the opinion of the Court.

* * *

I

The Clean Water Act of 1972 (CWA), 86 Stat. 816, 33 U.S.C. § 1251 *et seq.*, established a National Pollution Discharge Elimination System (NPDES) that is designed to prevent harmful discharges into the Nation's waters. The Environmental Protection Agency (EPA) initially administers the NPDES permitting system for each State, but a State may apply for a transfer of permitting authority to state officials. See 33 U.S.C. § 1342. If authority is transferred, then state officials—not the federal EPA—have the primary responsibility for reviewing and approving NPDES discharge permits, albeit with continuing EPA oversight.

Under § 402(b) of the CWA, "the Governor of each State desiring to administer its own permit program for discharges into navigable waters within its jurisdiction may submit to [the EPA] a full and complete description of the program it proposes to establish and administer under State law or under an interstate compact," as well as a certification "that the laws of such State . . . provide adequate authority to carry out the described program." 33 U.S.C. § 1342(b). The same section provides that the EPA "shall approve each submitted program" for transfer of permitting authority to a State "unless [it] determines that adequate authority does not exist" to ensure that nine specified criteria are satisfied. *Ibid.* These criteria all relate to whether the state agency that will be responsible for permitting has the requisite authority under state law to administer the NPDES program.[2] If the criteria are met, the transfer must be approved.

---

2. The State must demonstrate that it has the ability: (1) to issue fixed-term permits that apply and ensure compliance with the CWA's substantive requirements and which are revocable for cause; (2) to inspect, monitor, and enter facilities and to require reports to the extent required by the CWA; (3) to provide for public notice and public hearings; (4) to ensure that the EPA receives notice of each permit application; (5) to ensure that any other State

The Endangered Species Act of 1973 (ESA), 87 Stat. 884, as amended, 16 U.S.C. § 1531 *et seq.,* is intended to protect and conserve endangered and threatened species and their habitats. * * *

Section 7 of the ESA prescribes the steps that federal agencies must take to ensure that their actions do not jeopardize endangered wildlife and flora. Section 7(a)(2) provides that "[e]ach Federal agency shall, in consultation with and with the assistance of the Secretary [of Commerce or the Interior], insure that any action authorized, funded, or carried out by such agency (hereinafter in this section referred to as an 'agency action') is not likely to jeopardize the continued existence of any endangered species or threatened species." 16 U.S.C. § 1536(a)(2).

Once the consultation process contemplated by § 7(a)(2) has been completed, the Secretary is required to give the agency a written biological opinion "setting forth the Secretary's opinion, and a summary of the information on which the opinion is based, detailing how the agency action affects the species or its critical habitat." § 1536(b)(3)(A). If the Secretary concludes that the agency action would place the listed species in jeopardy or adversely modify its critical habitat, "the Secretary shall suggest those reasonable and prudent alternatives which he believes would not violate [§ 7(a)(2)] and can be taken by the Federal agency ... in implementing the agency action." 16 U.S.C. § 1536(b)(3)(A). * * * Following the issuance of a "jeopardy" opinion, the agency must either terminate the action, implement the proposed alternative, or seek an exemption from the Cabinet-level Endangered Species Committee pursuant to 16 U.S.C. § 1536(e). The regulations also provide that "Section 7 and the requirements of this part apply to all actions in which there is discretionary Federal involvement or control." 50 CFR § 402.03.

In February 2002, Arizona officials applied for EPA authorization to administer that State's NPDES program. The EPA initiated consultation with the FWS to determine whether the transfer of permitting authority would adversely affect any listed species.

The FWS regional office concluded that the transfer of authority would not cause any direct impact on water quality that would adversely affect listed species. However, the FWS office was concerned that the transfer could result in the issuance of more discharge permits, which would lead to more development, which in turn could have an indirect adverse effect on the habitat of certain upland species, such as the cactus ferruginous pygmy-owl and the Pima pineapple cactus. Specifically, the FWS feared that,

---

whose waters may be affected by the issuance of a permit may submit written recommendations and that written reasons be provided if such recommendations are not accepted; (6) to ensure that no permit is issued if the Army Corps of Engineers concludes that it would substantially impair the anchoring and navigation of navigable waters; (7) to abate violations of permits or the permit program, including through civil and criminal penalties; (8) to ensure that any permit for a discharge from a publicly owned treatment works includes conditions requiring the identification of the type and volume of certain pollutants; and (9) to ensure that any industrial user of any publicly owned treatment works will comply with certain of the CWA's substantive provisions. §§ 1342(b)(1)–(9).

because § 7(a)(2)'s consultation requirement does not apply to permitting decisions by state authorities, the transfer of authority would empower Arizona officials to issue individual permits without considering and mitigating their indirect impact on these upland species. * * *

The EPA disagreed, maintaining that "its approval action, which is an administrative transfer of authority, [would not be] the cause of future non-discharge-related impacts on endangered species from projects requiring State NPDES permits." As a factual matter, the EPA believed that the link between the transfer of permitting authority and the potential harm that could result from increased development was too attenuated. And as a legal matter, the EPA concluded that the mandatory nature of CWA § 402(b)—which directs that the EPA "shall approve" a transfer request if that section's nine statutory criteria are met—stripped it of authority to disapprove a transfer based on any other considerations.

Pursuant to procedures set forth in a memorandum of understanding between the agencies, the dispute was referred to the agencies' national offices for resolution. [At that level, FWS adopted EPA's view that the transfer would not be the legally-relevant cause of any harm to listed species. EPA then approved the transfer of permitting authority.]

III

We turn now to the substantive statutory question raised by the petitions, a question that requires us to mediate a clash of seemingly categorical—and, at first glance, irreconcilable—legislative commands. Section 402(b) of the CWA provides, without qualification, that the EPA "shall approve" a transfer application unless it determines that the State lacks adequate authority to perform the nine functions specified in the section. 33 U.S.C. § 1342(b). By its terms, the statutory language is mandatory and the list exclusive; if the nine specified criteria are satisfied, the EPA does not have the discretion to deny a transfer application. * * *

The language of § 7(a)(2) of the ESA is similarly imperative: it provides that "[e]ach Federal agency shall, in consultation with and with the assistance of the Secretary, insure that any action authorized, funded, or carried out by such agency ... is not likely to jeopardize" endangered or threatened species or their habitats. 16 U.S.C. § 1536(a)(2). This mandate is to be carried out through consultation and may require the agency to adopt an alternative course of action. * * *

While a later enacted statute (such as the ESA) can sometimes operate to amend or even repeal an earlier statutory provision (such as the CWA), "repeals by implication are not favored" and will not be presumed unless the "intention of the legislature to repeal [is] clear and manifest." *Watt v. Alaska,* 451 U.S. 259, 267 (1981). We will not infer a statutory repeal "unless the later statute expressly contradict[s] the original act" or unless such a construction "is absolutely necessary ... in order that [the] words [of the later statute] shall have any meaning at all." *Traynor v. Turnage,* 485 U.S. 535, 548 (1988). Outside these limited circumstances, "a statute dealing with a narrow, precise, and specific subject is not submerged by a later enacted statute covering a more generalized spectrum." *Radzanower, supra,* at 153.

Here, reading § 7(a)(2) as the Court of Appeals did would effectively repeal § 402(b)'s statutory mandate by engrafting a tenth criterion onto the CWA. Section 402(b) of the CWA commands that the EPA "shall" issue a permit whenever all nine exclusive statutory prerequisites are met. Thus, § 402(b) does not just set forth *minimum* requirements for the transfer of permitting authority; it affirmatively mandates that the transfer "shall" be approved if the specified criteria are met. The provision operates as a ceiling as well as a floor. By adding an additional criterion, the Ninth Circuit's construction of § 7(a)(2) raises that floor and alters § 402(b)'s statutory command.

The Ninth Circuit's reading of § 7(a)(2) would not only abrogate § 402(b)'s statutory mandate, but also result in the implicit repeal of many additional otherwise categorical statutory commands. Section 7(a)(2) by its terms applies to "any action authorized, funded, or carried out by" a federal agency-covering, in effect, almost anything that an agency might do. Reading the provision broadly would thus partially override every federal statute mandating agency action by subjecting such action to the further condition that it pose no jeopardy to endangered species. * * *

The agencies charged with implementing the ESA have attempted to resolve this tension through regulations implementing § 7(a)(2). The NMFS and FWS, acting jointly on behalf of the Secretaries of Commerce and the Interior and following notice-and-comment rulemaking procedures, have promulgated a regulation stating that "Section 7 and the requirements of this part apply to all actions in which there is *discretionary* Federal involvement or control." 50 CFR § 402.03 (emphasis added). Pursuant to this regulation, § 7(a)(2) would not be read as impliedly repealing nondiscretionary statutory mandates, even when they might result in some agency action. Rather, the ESA's requirements would come into play only when an action results from the exercise of agency discretion. This interpretation harmonizes the statutes by giving effect to the ESA's no-jeopardy mandate whenever an agency has discretion to do so, but not when the agency is forbidden from considering such extrastatutory factors.

We have recognized that "[t]he latitude the ESA gives the Secretary in enforcing the statute, together with the degree of regulatory expertise necessary to its enforcement, establishes that we owe some degree of deference to the Secretary's reasonable interpretation" of the statutory scheme. *Babbitt v. Sweet Home Chapter, Communities for Great Ore.,* 515 U.S. 687, 703 (1995). But such deference is appropriate only where "Congress has not directly addressed the precise question at issue" through the statutory text. *Chevron U.S.A. Inc. v. Natural Resources Defense Council, Inc.,* 467 U.S. 837, 843 (1984).

* * * In making the threshold determination under *Chevron,* "a reviewing court should not confine itself to examining a particular statutory provision in isolation." *FDA v. Brown & Williamson Tobacco Corp.,* 529 U.S. 120, 132 (2000). Rather, "[t]he meaning—or ambiguity—of certain

words or phrases may only become evident when placed in context.... It is a fundamental canon of statutory construction that the words of a statute must be read in their context and with a view to their place in the overall statutory scheme." *Id.,* at 132–133.

We must therefore read § 7(a)(2) of the ESA against the statutory backdrop of the many mandatory agency directives whose operation it would implicitly abrogate or repeal if it were construed as broadly as the Ninth Circuit did below. When § 7(a)(2) is read this way, we are left with a fundamental ambiguity that is not resolved by the statutory text. An agency cannot simultaneously obey the differing mandates set forth in § 7(a)(2) of the ESA and § 402(b) of the CWA, and consequently the statutory language—read in light of the canon against implied repeals—does not itself provide clear guidance as to which command must give way.

In this situation, it is appropriate to look to the implementing agency's expert interpretation, which cabins § 7(a)(2)'s application to "actions in which there is discretionary Federal involvement or control." 50 CFR § 402.03. This reading harmonizes the statutes by applying § 7(a)(2) to guide agencies' existing discretionary authority, but not reading it to override express statutory mandates.

We conclude that this interpretation is reasonable in light of the statute's text and the overall statutory scheme, and that it is therefore entitled to deference under *Chevron*. Section 7(a)(2) requires that an agency "insure" that the actions it authorizes, funds, or carries out are not likely to jeopardize listed species or their habitats. To "insure" something—as the court below recognized—means "[t]o make certain, to secure, to guarantee (some thing, event, etc.)." 420 F.3d, at 963 (quoting 7 Oxford English Dictionary 1059 (2d ed.1989)). The regulation's focus on "discretionary" actions accords with the commonsense conclusion that, when an agency is *required* to do something by statute, it simply lacks the power to "insure" that such action will not jeopardize endangered species.

* * *

The court below simply disregarded § 402.03's interpretation of the ESA's reach, dismissing "the regulation's reference to discretionary involvement" as merely "congruent with the statutory reference to actions authorized, funded, or carried out by the agency." 420 F.3d, at 968. But this reading cannot be right. Agency discretion presumes that an agency can exercise "judgment" in connection with a particular action. As the mandatory language of § 402(b) itself illustrates, not every action authorized, funded, or carried out by a federal agency is a product of that agency's exercise of discretion.

* * *

In short, we read § 402.03 to mean what it says: that § 7(a)(2)'s no-jeopardy duty covers only discretionary agency actions and does not attach to actions (like the NPDES permitting transfer authorization) that an agency is *required* by statute to undertake once certain specified triggering events have occurred. This reading not only is reasonable, inasmuch as it gives effect to the ESA's provision, but also comports with the canon against implied repeals because it stays § 7(a)(2)'s mandate where it would effectively override otherwise mandatory statutory duties.

Respondents argue that our opinion in *TVA v. Hill,* 437 U.S. 153 (1978), supports their contrary position. * * *

TVA v. Hill, however, had no occasion to answer the question presented in these cases. That case was decided almost a decade before the adoption in 1986 of the regulations contained in 50 CFR § 402.03. And in any event, the construction project at issue in *TVA v. Hill,* while expensive, was also discretionary. The TVA argued that by continuing to make lump-sum appropriations to the TVA, some of which were informally earmarked for the Tellico Dam project, Congress had implicitly repealed § 7's no-jeopardy requirement as it applied to that project. The Court rejected this argument, concluding that "[t]he Appropriations Acts did not themselves identify the projects for which the sums had been appropriated" and that reports by congressional committees allegedly directing the TVA to complete the project lacked the force of law. *Id.,* at 189, n. 35. Central to the Court's decision was the conclusion that Congress did not *mandate* that the TVA put the dam into operation; there was no statutory command to that effect; and there was therefore no basis for contending that applying the ESA's no-jeopardy requirement would implicitly repeal another affirmative congressional directive.

* * *

IV

Finally, respondents and their *amici* argue that, even if § 7(a)(2) is read to apply only to "discretionary" agency actions, the decision to transfer NPDES permitting authority to Arizona represented such an exercise of discretion. They contend that the EPA's decision to authorize a transfer is not entirely mechanical; that it involves some exercise of judgment as to whether a State has met the criteria set forth in § 402(b); and that these criteria incorporate references to wildlife conservation that bring consideration of § 7(a)(2)'s no-jeopardy mandate properly within the agency's discretion.

The argument is unavailing. While the EPA may exercise some judgment in determining whether a State has demonstrated that it has the authority to carry out § 402(b)'s enumerated statutory criteria, the statute clearly does not grant it the discretion to add another entirely separate prerequisite to that list. Nothing in the text of § 402(b) authorizes the EPA to consider the protection of threatened or endangered species as an end in itself when evaluating a transfer application. And to the extent that some of the § 402(b) criteria may result in environmental benefits to marine species, there is no dispute that Arizona has satisfied each of those statutory criteria. * * *

■ JUSTICE STEVENS, with whom JUSTICE SOUTER, JUSTICE GINSBURG, and JUSTICE BREYER join, dissenting.

These cases present a problem of conflicting "shalls." On the one hand, § 402(b) of the Clean Water Act (CWA) provides that the Environmental Protection Agency (EPA) "shall" approve a State's application to administer a National Pollution Discharge Elimination System (NPDES) permitting program unless it determines that nine criteria are not satisfied. 33 U.S.C. § 1342(b). On the other hand, shortly after the passage of the CWA, Congress enacted § 7(a)(2) of the Endangered Species Act of 1973 (ESA), which commands that federal agencies "shall" insure that their actions do not jeopardize endangered species. 16 U.S.C. § 1536(a)(2).

* * *

In the celebrated "snail darter" case, *TVA v. Hill,* 437 U.S. 153 (1978), we held that the ESA "reveals a conscious decision by Congress to give endangered species priority over the 'primary missions' of federal agencies," *id.,* at 185. Consistent with that intent, Chief Justice Burger's exceptionally thorough and admirable opinion explained that § 7 "admits of no exception." *Id.,* at 173. Creating precisely such an exception by exempting nondiscretionary federal actions from the ESA's coverage, the Court whittles away at Congress' comprehensive effort to protect endangered species from the risk of extinction and fails to give the Act its intended effect. * * *

II

Given our unequivocal holding in *Hill* that the ESA has "first priority" over all other federal action, 437 U.S., at 185, if any statute should yield, it should be the CWA. But no statute must yield unless it is truly incapable of coexistence. Therefore, assuming that § 402(b) of the CWA contains its own mandatory command, we should first try to harmonize that provision with the mandatory requirements of § 7(a)(2) of the ESA.

The Court's solution is to rely on 50 CFR § 402.03, which states that "Section 7 and the requirements of this part apply to all actions in which there is discretionary Federal involvement or control." The Court explains that this regulation "harmonizes the statutes by giving effect to the ESA's no-jeopardy mandate whenever an agency has discretion to do so, but by lifting that mandate when the agency is forbidden from considering such extrastatutory factors." This is not harmony, and it certainly isn't effect. Rather than giving genuine effect to § 7(a)(2), the Court permits a wholesale limitation on the reach of the ESA. Its interpretation of § 402.03 conflicts with the text and history of the regulation, as well as our interpretation of § 7 in the "snail darter" case.

To begin with, the plain language of § 402.03 does not state that its coverage is limited to discretionary actions. Quite the opposite, the most natural reading of the text is that it confirms the broad construction of § 7 endorsed by our opinion in *Hill.* Indeed, the only way to read § 402.03 in accordance with the facts of the case and our holding that § 7 "admits of no exception[s]," 437 U.S., at 173, is that it eliminates any possible argument that the ESA does not extend to situations in which the discretionary federal involvement is only marginal.

The Court is simply mistaken when it says that it reads § 402.03 "to mean what it says: that § 7(a)(2)'s no-jeopardy duty covers *only* discretionary agency actions...." (emphasis added). That is not, in fact, what § 402.03 says. The word "only" is the Court's addition to the text, not the agency's. Moreover, that text surely does not go on to say (as the Court does) that the duty "does not attach to actions (like the NPDES permitting transfer authorization) that an agency is *required* by statute to undertake once certain specified triggering events have occurred." If the drafters of the regulation had intended such a far-reaching change in the law, surely they would have said so by using language similar to that which the Court uses today.

* * *

IV

As discussed above, I believe that the Court incorrectly restricts the reach of § 7(a)(2) to discretionary federal actions. Even if such a limitation were permissible, however, it is clear that EPA's authority to transfer permitting authority under § 402(b) *is* discretionary.

* * *

[Section] 402(b) is a perfect example of why our analysis should not end simply because a statute uses the word "shall." Instead, we must look more closely at its listed criteria to determine whether they allow for discretion, despite the use of "shall." In these cases, there is significant room for discretion in EPA's evaluation of § 402(b)'s nine conditions. The first criterion, for example, requires the EPA Administrator to examine five other statutes and ensure that the State has adequate authority to comply with each. 33 U.S.C. § 1342(b)(1)(A). One of those five statutes, in turn, expressly directs the Administrator to exercise his "judgment." § 1312. Even the Court acknowledges that EPA must exercise "some judgment in determining whether a State has demonstrated that it has the authority to carry out § 402(b)'s enumerated statutory criteria."

■ JUSTICE BREYER, dissenting.

I join Justice Stevens' dissent, while reserving judgment as to whether § 7(a)(2) of the Endangered Species Act of 1973 really covers every possible agency action even of totally unrelated agencies—such as, say, a discretionary determination by the Internal Revenue Service whether to prosecute or settle a particular tax liability.

At the same time I add one additional consideration in support of his (and my own) dissenting views. The Court emphasizes that "[b]y its terms, the statutory language [of § 402(b) of the Clean Water Act, 33 U.S.C. § 1342(b)] is mandatory and the list exclusive; if the nine specified criteria are satisfied, the EPA does not have the discretion to deny a transfer application." (emphasis added). My own understanding of agency action leads me to believe that the majority cannot possibly be correct in concluding that the structure of § 402(b) precludes application of § 7(a)(2) to the EPA's discretionary action. That is because grants of discretionary authority always come with some implicit limits attached. And there are likely numerous instances in which, prior to, but not after, the enactment of § 7(a)(2), the statute might have implicitly placed "species preservation" outside those limits.

To take one example, consider the statute that once granted the old Federal Power Commission (FPC) the authority to grant a "certificate of public convenience and necessity" to permit a natural gas company to operate a new pipeline. See 15 U.S.C. § 717f(c)(1)(A). It says that "a certificate shall be issued to any qualified applicant therefor ... if it is found that the applicant is able and willing properly to do the acts and to perform the service proposed ... and that the proposed service ... is or will be required by the present or future public convenience and necessity." § 717f(e).

Before enactment of the Endangered Species Act of 1973, it is at least uncertain whether the FPC could have withheld a certificate simply because a natural gas pipeline might threaten an endangered animal, for given the Act's language and history, species preservation does not naturally fall within its terms. But we have held that the Endangered Species Act changed the regulatory landscape, "indicat[ing] beyond doubt that Congress intended endangered species to be afforded the highest of priorities." TVA v. Hill, 437 U.S. 153, 174 (1978). * * * And given a new pipeline's potential effect upon habitat and landscape, it seems reasonable to believe, once Congress enacted the new law, the FPC's successor (the Federal Energy Regulatory Commission) would act within its authority in taking species-endangering effects into account.

* * *

NOTES AND QUESTIONS

1. *TVA v. Hill.* Before the Court granted certiorari in *TVA v. Hill* the justices discussed whether to summarily reverse the case without argument. Five justices favored summary reversal, but by convention they do not take that step unless six justices agree. After oral argument, Justice Byron White, who had initially favored reversal, changed his mind and voted to affirm. Chief Justice Burger then reversed as well, voting to affirm and assigning himself the majority opinion. For more on the background of the case, see Holly Doremus, The Story of TVA v. Hill: A Narrow Escape for a Broad New Law, in Oliver A. Houck & Richard J. Lazarus, eds., Environmental Law Stories: An In–Depth Look at Ten Leading Cases on Environmental Law 109–140 (2005)

2. *Interbranch dynamics.* Congress reacted to the *TVA* decision by creating a narrow exception from the no-jeopardy provision of section 7. The Endangered Species Committee, often called the "God squad," made up of seven cabinet-level officials, can grant an exemption if it finds by a super-majority vote that: there are no reasonable and prudent alternatives to the proposed action; the benefits of the action clearly outweigh those of alternatives consistent with conserving the species; the action is of regional or national significance; and there has been no irreversible commitment of resources pending the application for an exemption. ESA § 7(h) (16 U.S.C. § 1536(h)). The Committee does not necessarily have the last word, however. After it refused to grant an exemption for Tellico Dam, Congress passed an appropriations rider exempting the dam from the ESA. After the dam was completed, the snail darter was found in a handful of other streams in the region and was downlisted to threatened.

Is it ever appropriate for courts to look beyond the apparent plain meaning of a statute if they believe that plain meaning, in the context of a particular set of facts, conflicts with Congressional intent? In enacting the ESA, do you think Congress intended to halt ongoing projects like construction of the Tellico Dam? If not, where could the line be drawn? Does (and should) the ESA apply to continuing operation of federal dams constructed decades before the ESA was enacted? The Supreme Court has not addressed that question, but the lower federal courts have consistently held that ESA § 7 does apply to ongoing dam operations. See, e.g., National Wildlife Federation v. NMFS, 481 F.3d 1224 (9th Cir. 2007).

3. *ESA litigation.* The plaintiffs in *TVA v. Hill* (led by University of Tennessee law student Hiram Hill and his professor, Zygmunt Plater) had opposed construction of Tellico Dam before the ESA was enacted. They worried about the potential impact of their lawsuit on the new law, but decided to go ahead anyway. From that lawsuit forward, ESA plaintiffs have often been accused of misusing the law to block projects they oppose for other reasons. Does that strike you as a legitimate criticism? What are the risks of aggressive litigation under the ESA? What are the risks of holding back from litigation when government enforcement seems less than enthusiastic? Was it a good idea for Hill to challenge TVA over the Tellico Dam? For Defenders of Wildlife to challenge the transfer of CWA permitting authority to Arizona?

4. *Statutory interpretation.* Is the decision in *NAHB* consistent with *TVA v. Hill*? Can the two be distinguished? If not, which is the better interpretation of the ESA? Is the *NAHB* majority right that reading the ESA as Defenders of Wildlife proposed would amount to an implied repeal of the CWA? Does the answer depend upon how important you think the goal of turning responsibility over to the states is to the CWA? Do you think Congress, in adopting the 1973 ESA intended to add a new condition for the transfer of NPDES permitting authority? Is that a different question than whether ESA § 7 applies in Justice Breyer's pipeline example?

5. *Chevron deference.* Is the view of deference to agency views articulated in *NAHB* consistent with Massachusetts v. EPA, 549 U.S. 497 (2007), excerpted in Chapter 10, Section 3? On what grounds did the Court defer to the FWS regulation defining agency action? Was it appropriate to consider statutes other than the ESA in deciding whether the ESA is ambiguous for

Chevron purposes? Is it possible to harmonize the ESA and the CWA? If not, which should prevail and why?

6. *Discretion and the ESA.* How much discretion did EPA have in deciding whether or not to transfer permitting authority to Arizona? After *NAHB*, how much discretion must an agency have before section 7 of the ESA applies? Is federal action under any statute that uses the word "shall" outside the reach of the ESA? Can non-statutory constraints on discretion, such as contracts to deliver water from federal irrigation projects, free an agency from the obligations of section 7? According to the Ninth Circuit, "When an agency, acting in furtherance of a broad Congressional mandate, chooses a course of action which is not specifically mandated by Congress and which is not specifically necessitated by the broad mandate, that action is, by definition, discretionary and is thus subject to Section 7 consultation." National Wildlife Fed'n v. NMFS, 524 F.3d 917 (9th Cir. 2008).

In Florida Key Deer v. Paulison, 522 F.3d 1133 (11th Cir. 2008), the Eleventh Circuit held that the Federal Emergency Management Agency was required to consult with FWS on its administration of the National Flood Insurance Program. FEMA claimed its issuance of flood insurance was non-discretionary, but the court disagreed. FEMA must offer flood insurance in areas with adequate land use and control measures, but FEMA itself determines which areas qualify, applying criteria it develops under a general mandate to encourage the adoption of state and local measures which will reduce development of flood-prone land and "otherwise improve the long-range land management and use of flood-prone areas." 42 U.S.C. § 4102(c). The Eleventh Circuit found that mandate sufficiently broad to give FEMA the discretion to consider the protection of listed species in deciding which communities qualify for flood insurance. It therefore concluded that ESA § 7(a)(2) applied.

7. *Remedies.* If a court finds a violation of the ESA, must it always grant equitable relief? Does *NAHB* cast doubt on *TVA*'s holding with respect to remedies?

8. *The ESA by the numbers.* As of July 2011, 1058 U.S. species were listed as endangered and 314 as threatened. (The "box-score" of listed species, updated monthly, is available on the FWS web site, at http://ecos.fws.gov/tess_public/Boxscore.do.) The listing of another 264 species has been found to be "warranted but precluded" by work on higher priority species. *See* 16 U.S.C. § 1533(b)(3)(B)(iii). This backlog persists because the Services are chronically short of funds for listing activities. Many other species may be at significant risk but are not listed either because of lack of information or because of political opposition to listing.

9. *Science and listing decisions.* ESA section 4(b)(1) requires that listing decisions be made "solely on the basis of the best scientific . . . information available." Congress intended listing decisions to be entirely scientific and objective. Is that possible? Listing requires two major determinations: 1) delineation of a group meeting the statutory definition of "species;" and 2) determination that the group is at sufficient risk of extinction to qualify as "endangered" or "threatened." Neither is entirely scientific. The first requires identification of the purposes for which species should be saved, and evaluation of the extent to which individual groups serve those purposes. The second requires choices about acceptable extinction risk. For an argument that hiding these policy choices behind a curtain of scientific objectivity has undesirable consequences, see Holly Doremus, Listing Decisions Under the Endangered Species Act: Why Better Science Isn't Always Better Policy, 75 Wash. U. L.Q. 1029 (1997).

10. *Critical habitat.* Concurrent with listing, to the maximum extent prudent and determinable, the ESA directs the Services to designate critical habitat. ESA § 4(a)(3), 16 U.S.C. § 1533(a)(3). Critical habitat includes areas containing physical or biological features essential to the conservation of the species which may require special management protection. ESA § 3(5), 16 U.S.C. § 1532(5). Areas outside the species' range at listing may be included only if the Services determine they are essential for the conservation of the species. In determining critical habitat, the Services must consider economic and other impacts. ESA § 4(b)(2), 16 U.S.C. § 1533(b)(2). Once critical habitat has been designated, federal agencies must ensure that their actions do not destroy or adversely modify critical habitat. The Services have treated destruction or adverse modification of critical habitat as essentially coextensive with jeopardy to the species. See 50 C.F.R. § 402.02 (defining the two in nearly identical terms). Two federal circuits have held that the Services have defined destruction or adverse modification of critical habitat in an unlawfully narrow way. Gifford Pinchot Task Force v. US FWS, 378 F.3d 1059 (9th Cir. 2004); Sierra Club v. US FWS, 245 F.3d 434 (5th Cir. 2001). FWS has not yet formally revised the definitions.

11. *Climate change and ESA consultation.* The ESA's consultation provision was developed with direct effects on habitat, like logging and water diversions, in mind, but by its terms it applies to any action with a federal nexus that may jeopardize a listed species or adversely modify designated critical habitat. While many listed species are likely to be affected by climate change, the issue of how § 7 consultation duties should apply to actions a long way from the habitat of a listed species that might increase greenhouse gas emissions came to a head with the listing of the polar bear (73 Fed. Reg. 28211 (May 15, 2008)), a species threatened primarily by the disappearance of the Arctic sea ice upon which it depends.

Just before President George W. Bush left office, FWS finalized revisions to the consultation regulations providing (among other things) that federal agencies would not be required to consult on actions "not anticipated to result in take" the effects of which "are manifested through global processes" and "[c]annot be reliably predicted or measured at the scale of a listed species' current range," or pose only a remote or insignificant threat to a listed species. 73 Fed. Reg. 76272 (Dec. 16, 2008). The Bush rule was criticized not just for its treatment of global warming but for a variety of other provisions that appeared to weaken regulatory protections. Early in 2009, Congress authorized withdrawal of the Bush rules without following the usual APA notice and comment process. The Obama administration followed that script, formally withdrawing the Bush rules in May 2009 (74 Fed. Reg. 20421 (May 4, 2009)). At the same time, the administration sought comment on "ways to improve the section 7 regulations while retaining the purposes and policies of the ESA." As of July 2011, no proposal for new rulemaking had been issued.

The Obama administration has shown no signs of trying to use the ESA aggressively as a weapon against climate change. David Hayes, Deputy Secretary of Interior, and Tom Strickland, Assistant Secretary of Interior for Fish, Wildlife, and Parks, both testified at their confirmation hearings that the ESA is ill-suited to addressing the problem of climate change. For two views of the role the ESA might play in dealing with the causes and consequences of climate change, see J.B. Ruhl, Climate Change and the Endangered Species Act: Building Bridges to the No–Analog Future, 88 Boston U. L. Rev. 1 (2008); John Kostyack and Dan Rohlf, Conserving Endangered Species in an Era of Global Warming, 38 Envtl. L. Rep. 10203 (2008).

3.   THE PROHIBITION ON TAKE

Excerpts From the Endangered Species Act
16 U.S.C. § 1531–1544.

Sec. 3   Definitions

* * *

(19) The term "take" means to harass, harm, pursue, hunt, shoot, wound, kill, trap, capture, or collect, or to attempt to engage in any such conduct.

* * *

Sec. 9   Prohibited Acts

(a)(1) Except as provided in [section 10], with respect to any endangered species of fish or wildlife * * * it is unlawful for any person subject to the jurisdiction of the United States to—

* * *

   (B) take any such species within the United States or the territorial
       sea of the United States;

* * *

(g) It is unlawful for any person subject to the jurisdiction of the United States to attempt to commit, solicit another to commit or cause to be committed, any offense defined in this section.

Excerpts From Fish and Wildlife Service Regulations
50 C.F.R. Part 17.

Sec. 17.3   Definitions

* * *

Harm in the definition of "take" in the Act means an act which actually kills or injures wildlife. Such act may include significant habitat modification or degradation where it actually kills or injures wildlife by significantly impairing essential behavioral patterns, including breeding, feeding or sheltering.

* * *

Babbitt v. Sweet Home Chapter of Communities for a Great Oregon

United States Supreme Court, 1995.
515 U.S. 687.

■ JUSTICE STEVENS delivered the opinion of the Court.

The Endangered Species Act of 1973 (ESA or Act) contains a variety of protections designed to save from extinction species that the Secretary of the Interior designates as endangered or threatened. Section 9 of the Act makes it unlawful for any person to "take" any endangered or threatened species. The Secretary has promulgated a regulation that defines the statute's prohibition on takings to include "significant habitat modification or degradation where it actually kills or injures wildlife." This case presents the question whether the Secretary exceeded his authority under the Act by promulgating that regulation.

I

* * *

Respondents in this action are small landowners, logging companies, and families dependent on the forest products industries in the Pacific Northwest and in the Southeast, and organizations that represent their interests. They brought this declaratory judgment action against petitioners, the Secretary of the Interior and the Director of the Fish and Wildlife Service, in the United States District Court for the District of Columbia to challenge the statutory validity of the Secretary's regulation defining "harm," particularly the inclusion of habitat modification and degradation in the definition. Respondents challenged the regulation on its face. Their complaint alleged that application of the "harm" regulation to the red-cockaded woodpecker, an endangered species, and the northern spotted owl, a threatened species, had injured them economically.

Respondents advanced three arguments to support their submission that Congress did not intend the word "take" in § 9 to include habitat modification, as the Secretary's "harm" regulation provides. First, they correctly noted that language in the Senate's original version of the ESA would have defined "take" to include "destruction, modification, or curtailment of [the] habitat or range" of fish or wildlife, but the Senate deleted that language from the bill before enacting it. Second, respondents argued that Congress intended the Act's express authorization for the Federal

Government to buy private land in order to prevent habitat degradation in § 5 to be the exclusive check against habitat modification on private property. Third, because the Senate added the term "harm" to the definition of "take" in a floor amendment without debate, respondents argued that the court should not interpret the term so expansively as to include habitat modification.

The District Court considered and rejected each of respondents' arguments, finding "that Congress intended an expansive interpretation of the word 'take,' an interpretation that encompasses habitat modification." The court noted that in 1982, when Congress was aware of a judicial decision that had applied the Secretary's regulation, it amended the Act without using the opportunity to change the definition of "take." The court stated that, even had it found the ESA "silent or ambiguous" as to the authority for the Secretary's definition of "harm," it would nevertheless have upheld the regulation as a reasonable interpretation of the statute. The District Court therefore entered summary judgment for petitioners and dismissed respondents' complaint.

A divided panel of the Court of Appeals initially affirmed the judgment of the District Court. After granting a petition for rehearing, however, the panel reversed. Although acknowledging that "[t]he potential breadth of the word 'harm' is indisputable," the majority concluded that the immediate statutory context in which "harm" appeared counseled against a broad reading; like the other words in the definition of "take," the word "harm" should be read as applying only to "the perpetrator's direct application of force against the animal taken." * * *

The Court of Appeals' decision created a square conflict with a 1988 decision of the Ninth Circuit that had upheld the Secretary's definition of "harm." *See* Palila v. Hawaii Dept. of Land and Natural Resources, 852 F.2d 1106 (1988) (*Palila II*). The Court of Appeals neither cited nor distinguished *Palila II*, despite the stark contrast between the Ninth Circuit's holding and its own. We granted certiorari to resolve the conflict. Our consideration of the text and structure of the Act, its legislative history, and the significance of the 1982 amendment persuades us that the Court of Appeals' judgment should be reversed.

II

* * *

The text of the Act provides three reasons for concluding that the Secretary's interpretation is reasonable. First, an ordinary understanding of the word "harm" supports it. The dictionary definition of the verb form of "harm" is "to cause hurt or damage to: injure." In the context of the ESA, that definition naturally encompasses habitat modification that results in actual injury or death to members of an endangered or threatened species.

Respondents argue that the Secretary should have limited the purview of "harm" to direct applications of force against protected species, but the dictionary definition does not include the word "directly" or suggest in any way that only direct or willful action that leads to injury constitutes "harm." Moreover, unless the statutory term "harm" encompasses indirect as well as direct injuries, the word has no meaning that does not duplicate the meaning of other words that § 3 uses to define "take." A reluctance to treat statutory terms as surplusage supports the reasonableness of the Secretary's interpretation.

Second, the broad purpose of the ESA supports the Secretary's decision to extend protection against activities that cause the precise harms Congress enacted the statute to avoid. In *TVA v. Hill*, 437 U.S. 153 (1978), we described the Act as "the most comprehensive legislation for the preservation of endangered species ever enacted by any nation." Whereas predecessor statutes enacted in 1966 and 1969 had not contained any sweeping prohibition against the taking of endangered species except on federal lands, the 1973 Act applied to all land in the United States and to the Nation's territorial seas. As stated in § 2 of the Act, among its central purposes is "to provide a means whereby the ecosystems upon which endangered species and threatened species depend may be conserved...." 16 U.S.C. § 1531(b).

In *Hill*, we construed § 7 as precluding the completion of the Tellico Dam because of its predicted impact on the survival of the snail darter. Both our holding and the language in our opinion stressed the importance of the statutory policy. "The plain intent of Congress in enacting this statute," we recognized, "was to halt and reverse the trend toward species extinction, whatever the cost. This is reflected not only in the stated policies of the Act, but in literally every section of the statute." Although the § 9 "take" prohibition was not at issue in *Hill*, we took note of that prohibition, placing particular emphasis on the Secretary's inclusion of habitat modification in his definition of "harm." In light of that provision for habitat protection, we could "not understand how TVA intends to operate Tellico Dam without 'harming' the snail darter." Congress' intent to provide comprehensive protection for endangered and threatened species supports the permissibility of the Secretary's "harm" regulation.

Respondents advance strong arguments that activities that cause minimal or unforeseeable harm will not violate the Act as construed in the "harm" regulation. Respondents, however, present a facial challenge to the regulation. Thus, they ask us to invalidate the Secretary's understanding of "harm" in every circumstance, even when an actor knows that an activity, such as draining a pond, would actually result in the extinction of a listed species by destroying its habitat. Given Congress' clear expression of the ESA's broad purpose to protect endangered and threatened wildlife, the Secretary's definition of "harm" is reasonable.

Third, the fact that Congress in 1982 authorized the Secretary to issue permits for takings that § 9(a)(1)(B) would otherwise prohibit, "if such taking is incidental to, and not the purpose of, the carrying out of an otherwise lawful activity," strongly suggests that Congress understood § 9(a)(1)(B) to prohibit indirect as well as deliberate takings. * * * No one could seriously request an "incidental" take permit to avert § 9 liability for direct, deliberate action against a member of an endangered or threatened species, but respondents would read "harm" so narrowly that the permit procedure would have little more than that absurd purpose. "When Congress acts to amend a statute, we presume it intends its amendment to have real and substantial effect." Congress' addition of the § 10 permit provision supports the Secretary's conclusion that activities not intended to harm an endangered species, such as habitat modification, may constitute unlawful takings under the ESA unless the Secretary permits them.

* * *

We need not decide whether the statutory definition of "take" compels the Secretary's interpretation of "harm," because our conclusions that Congress did not unambiguously manifest its intent to adopt respondents' view and that the Secretary's interpretation is reasonable suffice to decide this case. *See* generally Chevron U.S.A. Inc. v. Natural Resources Defense Council, Inc., 467 U.S. 837 (1984). The latitude the ESA gives the Secretary in enforcing the statute, together with the degree of regulatory expertise necessary to its enforcement, establishes that we owe some degree of deference to the Secretary's reasonable interpretation.

III

Our conclusion that the Secretary's definition of "harm" rests on a permissible construction of the ESA gains further support from the legislative history of the statute. The Committee Reports accompanying the bills that became the ESA do not specifically discuss the meaning of "harm," but they make clear that Congress intended "take" to apply broadly to cover indirect as well as purposeful actions. The Senate Report stressed that " '[t]ake' is defined ... in the broadest possible manner to include every conceivable way in which a person can 'take' or attempt to 'take' any fish or wildlife." The House Report stated that "the broadest possible terms" were used to define restrictions on takings. The House Report underscored the breadth of the "take" definition by noting that it included "harassment, *whether intentional or not*." (emphasis added) The Report explained that the definition "would allow, for example, the Secretary to regulate or prohibit the activities of birdwatchers where the effect of those activities might disturb the birds and make it difficult for them to hatch or raise their young." These comments, ignored in the dissent's welcome but selective foray into legislative history, support the Secretary's interpretation that the term "take" in § 9 reached far more than the deliberate actions of hunters and trappers.

* * *

The definition of "take" that originally appeared in S. 1983 differed from the definition as ultimately enacted in one other significant respect: It included "the destruction, modification, or curtailment of [the] habitat or range" of fish and wildlife. Respondents make much of the fact that the Commerce Committee removed this phrase from the "take" definition before S. 1983 went to the floor. We do not find that fact especially significant. The legislative materials contain no indication why the habitat protection provision was deleted. That provision differed greatly from the regulation at issue today. Most notably, the habitat protection in S. 1983 would have applied far more broadly than the regulation does because it made adverse habitat modification a categorical violation of the "take" prohibition, unbounded by the regulation's limitation to habitat modifications that actually kill or injure wildlife. The S. 1983 language also failed to qualify "modification" with the regulation's limiting adjective "significant." We do not believe the Senate's unelaborated disavowal of the provision in S. 1983 undermines the reasonableness of the more moderate habitat protection in the Secretary's "harm" regulation.

* * *

IV

When it enacted the ESA, Congress delegated broad administrative and interpretive power to the Secretary. The task of defining and listing endangered and threatened species requires an expertise and attention to detail that exceeds the normal province of Congress. Fashioning appropriate standards for issuing permits under § 10 for takings that would otherwise violate § 9 necessarily requires the exercise of broad discretion. The proper interpretation of a term such as "harm" involves a complex policy choice. When Congress has entrusted the Secretary with broad discretion, we are especially reluctant to substitute our views of wise policy for his. *See Chevron*, 467 U.S. at 865–866. In this case, that reluctance accords with our conclusion, based on the text, structure, and legislative history of the ESA, that the Secretary reasonably construed the intent of Congress when he defined "harm" to include "significant habitat modification or degradation that actually kills or injures wildlife."

In the elaboration and enforcement of the ESA, the Secretary and all persons who must comply with the law will confront difficult questions of proximity and degree; for, as all recognize, the Act encompasses a vast range of economic and social enterprises and endeavors. These questions must be addressed in the usual course of the law, through case-by-case resolution and adjudication.

■ JUSTICE O'CONNOR, concurring.

My agreement with the Court is founded on two understandings. First, the challenged regulation is limited to significant habitat modification that causes actual, as opposed to hypothetical or speculative, death or injury to identifiable protected animals. Second, even setting aside difficult questions of scienter, the regulation's application is limited by ordinary principles of proximate causation, which introduce notions of foreseeability. These limitations, in my view, call into question Palila v. Hawaii Dept. of Land and Natural Resources, 852 F.2d 1106 (CA 9 1988)(*Palila II*), and with it, many of the applications derided by the dissent. Because there is no need to strike a regulation on a facial challenge out of concern that it is susceptible of erroneous application, however, and because there are many habitat-related circumstances in which the regulation might validly apply, I join the opinion of the Court.

* * *

As an initial matter, I do not find it as easy as Justice Scalia does to dismiss the notion that significant impairment of breeding injures living creatures. To raze the last remaining ground on which the piping plover currently breeds, thereby making it impossible for any piping plovers to reproduce, would obviously injure the population (causing the species' extinction in a generation). But by completely preventing breeding, it would also injure the individual living bird, in the same way that sterilizing the creature injures the individual living bird. To "injure" is, among other things, "to impair." One need not subscribe to theories of "psychic harm" to recognize that to make it impossible for an animal to reproduce is to impair its most essential physical functions and to render that animal, and its genetic material, biologically obsolete. This, in my view, is actual injury.

* * *

In my view, then, the "harm" regulation applies where significant habitat modification, by impairing essential behaviors, proximately (foreseeably) causes actual death or injury to identifiable animals that are protected under the Endangered Species Act. Pursuant to my interpretation, *Palila II*—under which the Court of Appeals held that a state agency committed a "taking" by permitting mouflon sheep to eat mamane-naio seedlings that, when full-grown, might have fed and sheltered endangered palila—was wrongly decided according to the regulation's own terms. Destruction of the seedlings did not proximately cause actual death or injury to identifiable birds; it merely prevented the regeneration of forest land not currently sustaining actual birds.

This case, of course, comes to us as a facial challenge. We are charged with deciding whether the regulation on its face exceeds the agency's statutory mandate. I have identified at least one application of the regulation (*Palila II*) that is, in my view, inconsistent with the regulation's *own* limitations. That misapplication does not, however, call into question the validity of the regulation itself. One can doubtless imagine questionable applications of the regulation that test the limits of the agency's authority. However, it seems to me clear that the regulation does not on its terms exceed the agency's mandate, and that the regulation has innumerable valid habitat-related applications. Congress may, of course, see fit to revisit this issue. And nothing the Court says today prevents the agency itself from narrowing the scope of its regulation at a later date.

With this understanding, I join the Court's opinion.

■ JUSTICE SCALIA, with whom THE CHIEF JUSTICE and JUSTICE THOMAS join, dissenting.

I think it unmistakably clear that the legislation at issue here (1) forbade the hunting and killing of endangered animals, and (2) provided federal lands and federal funds *for the acquisition of private lands*, to preserve the habitat of endangered animals. The Court's holding that the hunting and killing prohibition incidentally preserves habitat on private lands imposes unfairness to the point of financial ruin—not just upon the rich, but upon the simplest farmer who finds his land conscripted to national zoological use. I respectfully dissent.

* * *

The Endangered Species Act is a carefully considered piece of legislation that forbids all persons to hunt or harm endangered animals, but places upon the public at large, rather than upon fortuitously accountable individual landowners, the cost of preserving the habitat of endangered species. There is neither textual support for, nor even evidence of congressional consideration of, the radically different disposition contained in the regulation that the Court sustains. For these reasons, I respectfully dissent.

Defenders of Wildlife v. Bernal

United States Court of Appeals, Ninth Circuit, 2000.
204 F.3d 920.

■ HUG, CHIEF JUDGE:

* * *

Factual and Procedural Background

In 1994, the School District paid $1.78 million to purchase a 73 acre site in northwest Tucson, upon which a new high school would be built. The high school complex is intended to accommodate 2,100 students and is composed of several buildings, athletic fields and parking areas for students, faculty and visitors. In December 1994, after the purchase of the school site, the United States Fish and Wildlife Service (FWS) formally published a proposed rule to list the pygmy-owl as an endangered species under the ESA. On March 10, 1997, after the required procedures and commentary period, the FWS listed the pygmy-owl as an endangered species under the ESA.

The pygmy-owl is a small reddish brown owl known for its relatively long tail and monotonous call which is heard primarily at dawn and dusk. The pygmy-owl nests in a cavity of a large tree or large columnar cactus. Its diverse diet includes birds, lizards, insects, and small mammals and frogs. The pygmy-owl occurs from lowland central Arizona south through portions of western Mexico and from southern Texas south through other portions of Mexico on down through portions of Central America.[11] The FWS indicates that there are a total 54,400 acres of suitable pygmy-owl habitat in northwest Tucson, which includes the 73 acre school site. The

---

11. The cactus ferruginous pygmy-owl is one of four subspecies of the ferruginous pygmy-owl. It is the cactus ferruginous pygmy-owl that we are concerned with in this case, and the term "pygmy-owl" as used in this opinion refers to that subspecies.

school site falls within the area designated by the FWS as critical habitat for the pygmy owl. *See* 64 Fed. Red. 37,419 (1999).

Within the 73 acre parcel acquired by the School District in 1994, there are three "arroyos," defined as "dry washes" or "ephemeral desert waterways." The U.S. Army Corps of Engineers designated the arroyos as "jurisdictional waters" pursuant to the Clean Water Act, 33 U.S.C. § 1251 *et seq.* The original design of the School District complex called for some construction within the "jurisdictional waters," thereby requiring the School District to obtain a permit under the Clean Water Act. Because a federal permit was at issue, the FWS informed the Corps that "formal consultation" pursuant to section 7 of the ESA was required to assess the impact of the proposed project on the pygmy-owl. Consultation was initiated, but before completion of the process the School District withdrew its application for the permit because it had redesigned the project so that construction would not affect the jurisdictional waterways. As a result of the redesigned project, no development is planned for the 30 acres containing the arroyos in the western portion of the property. The School District has acquired or will acquire 17 acres to the east of the initially acquired property for utilization in the redesigned school project. Thus, the entire school site is 90 acres, including the 30 acres containing the arroyos. The 30 acre parcel will remain undeveloped and fenced off. For ease in identification in this opinion, the entire 90 acre parcel will be referred to as the "school site." The 60 acres upon which the school complex is designed to be built will be referred to as the "60 acre parcel." The undeveloped 30 acre parcel, which contains the arroyos, will be referred to as the "30 acre parcel."

In March 1998, the School District began plant salvaging operations as a precursor to beginning construction. Defenders immediately filed suit seeking a temporary restraining order and a preliminary injunction against the School District to prevent any action on the school site. Defenders alleged that the proposed construction violated Section 9 of the ESA because it was likely to harm or harass a pygmy-owl, which Defenders assert inhabit or use the site. * * *

Statutory Framework

* * *

Harming a species may be indirect, in that the harm may be caused by habitat modification, but habitat modification does not constitute harm unless it "actually kills or injures wildlife." The Department of Interior's definition of harm was upheld against a facial challenge to its validity in the case of *Babbitt v. Sweet Home Chapter of Communities for a Great Oregon,* 515 U.S. 687 (1995). In upholding the definition of "harm" as encompassing habitat modification, the Supreme Court emphasized that "every term in the regulation's definition of harm is subservient to the phrase 'an act which actually kills or injures wildlife.'" *Id.* at 700 n. 13.

Three months prior to the *Sweet Home* decision we held in *Forest Conservation Council v. Rosboro Lumber Co.,* 50 F.3d 781, 783 (9th Cir. 1995), that habitat modification that is reasonably certain to injure an endangered species by impairing their essential behavioral patterns satisfied the actual injury requirement and was sufficient to justify a permanent injunction. In a subsequent action, it was contended that *Sweet Home* had overruled *Rosboro* and that an actual violation of the ESA was required before an injunction could issue. However, in *Marbled Murrelet v. Babbitt,* 83 F.3d 1060, 1066 (9th Cir. 1996), we held that the Supreme Court's decision in *Sweet Home* does not overrule *Rosboro* and that a reasonably certain threat of imminent harm to a protected species is sufficient for issuance of an injunction under section 9 of the ESA.

III.

Harm and Harassment Claims

In order to prevail in this action Defenders had to prove that the School District's actions would result in an unlawful "take" of a pygmy-owl. * * * Defenders had the burden of proving by a preponderance of the evidence that the proposed construction would harm a pygmy-owl by killing or injuring it, or would more likely than not harass a pygmy-owl by annoying it to such an extent as to disrupt its normal behavioral patterns. The district court's final order was a thorough, detailed and carefully reasoned discussion and analysis of the testimony of the expert witnesses and other evidence produced at the trial. The judge framed his discussion and analysis as follows:

> In this case, there are primarily two material factual questions: 1) Does a pygmy-owl use or occupy any part of the school site? 2) Will the construction and operation of the site result in a § 9 "take" through the "harm" or "harassment" of a pygmy-owl? The Court has concluded that the evidence supports a finding that an owl or owls use a portion of the site which the Defendants do not intend to develop. Accordingly, the Court's inquiry has further devolved into two remaining questions: 1) whether clearing the unused portion of the property could "take" the owl, in spite of what the FWS has concluded in the Final Rule,[4] and 2) what proof is offered that the construction and operation of the school will harm or harass the owl.

The district judge first discussed his factual findings as to the territory that was occupied or used by the pygmy-owls. He found from the expert testimony and other evidence produced that the pygmy-owls used territory to the north of the boundary and the west of the boundary of the school site and that no pygmy-owl had been detected anywhere within the school site itself. However, he found that there was a reasonable inference that one or more pygmy-owls used the area of the arroyos between the north boundary and west boundary of the school site. These arroyos are within

---

4. The FWS said in its Final Rule that the clearing of unoccupied habitat would not be a § 9 take, whereas the "clearing or significant modification of occupied habitat" could potentially harm, harass, or otherwise take the pygmy owl. 62 Fed. Reg. 10746 (1997).

the 30 acre parcel that will remain undeveloped. He also found that there was insufficient evidence to prove that a pygmy-owl used any portion of the 60 acre parcel upon which the school complex is to be built.

The judge explained at some length what evidence he relied on to support his findings. The judge stated that the opinion of scientific experts, the evidence of the habits of the pygmy-owl, and the recent aural detection of the bird, supports a logical inference that the bird or birds currently use the areas where they have been detected near the north and west boundaries of the site, and the area between those two points within the arroyo. He noted that because habitat within this arroyo area is suitable for pygmy-owls, provides cover and prey for birds, provides a natural corridor for the owl to travel from the north boundary to the west boundary where it has been frequently sited, an inference can be drawn that the owl uses this area. The judge then contrasted the 30 acre parcel, which he refers to as "the Area", with the rest of the school site:

> Contrarily, there have been no sightings of the owl beyond the clusters of detections near the north and west boundaries of the property and extensive surveys of the entire property have failed to produce one single detection of a pygmy-owl. A search of 361 cavities of saguaro cacti on the site, in which pygmy owls prefer to nest, produced no pygmy-owls. There is therefore little factual basis to conclude that the owl uses the rest of the school site, outside of the Area. . . . Because owls display site fidelity and have been seen near the Area but never detected on the school site outside of the Area, in spite of concentrated efforts to find them there, a logical inference can be made that the owl is not using the remainder of the site. . . . Finally, the heaviest concentrations of sitings confirmed by the [Arizona Game and Fish Department] near the site are in residential areas west of the school site where there is low impact housing (one house on a 3–5 acre plot with minimal disturbance to native vegetation). . . . This supports the inference that the "core" of the owl's activity may not be in the Area but may be west of the school site, and that the 30 acre Area may be the outer fringe of the territory the bird uses.

The district court next discussed the basis for his finding that harm to the pygmy owl was not proven. He observed that while the inference that an owl uses the 30 acre parcel is based on solid factual premises and well-founded expert opinion, the allegation that the construction of the high school will harm the owl lacks this support and is weakened by seemingly inconsistent facts. The judge noted that although he gives weight to the opinions of the experts, he cannot blindly rely on their opinions and must consider how the conclusions were reached and whether they are relevant and reliable, citing *Daubert v. Merrell Dow Pharmaceuticals, Inc.,* 509 U.S. 579 (1993). One of Defenders' experts had testified that a school would increase the amount of human activity on the school site and that although pygmy-owls can tolerate some level of human activity, he suspected that level would be enough to render or cause a pygmy-owl not to occupy the area. The judge noted that in contradiction to the expert's suspicions that the owl would be harmed by human activity associated with the high school, there was evidence that pygmy-owls can tolerate a fairly high degree of human presence. The Arizona Game and Fish Department had reported that "pygmy-owls are not intimidated by the presence of people or can acclimate to low density urbanization and associated activities." In 1995–96, a K–8 school was constructed and has been operating a short distance north of the proposed school site. One neighbor testified that she had chased an owl shouting at it and waving a broom, but the owl had returned to the residence. At one residence, an owl family was found in a grapefruit tree close to the house and was inspected at close range for weeks on end by the resident and his guests.

The judge stated that the facts do not support a finding that the owl will be harassed. He noted that there was evidence that the owl can tolerate and even benefit from human activity, and that Defenders have only offered speculation that the activity associated with the school would harass the owl. He observed that the experts made little or no attempt to support their opinions with recorded observations of pygmy owls in similar circumstances or to draw analogies from other similar birds. The judge found that this failure to support opinion with fact seriously degraded the value of the expert opinions. He stated "the limited data about the owls which was presented did not show with clarity that breeding, feeding, and sheltering would be adversely impacted by the construction or operation of the school." The judge summarized his findings as follows:

> The contradictory facts presented by Plaintiffs and assumptions about what will harm the bird cannot support a conclusion that the owl will actually be injured or will likely be harassed. Finally, the FWS has concluded that clearing of unoccupied habitat will not "take" an owl and the Court has concluded that construction of the school, as planned, will not involve clearing of occupied habitat.

We review a district court's finding of fact under the clearly erroneous standard. The well supported factual findings of the district judge are not clearly erroneous, and we affirm the conclusion of the district court that the construction of the school complex will not "take" a pygmy-owl.

* * *

■ FLETCHER, CIRCUIT JUDGE, concurring:

I concur in the opinion but make these observations to clarify the limited precedential value of our opinion * * *. Future cases that involve action or contemplated action in pygmy owl habitat in Arizona will be informed by the critical habitat designation and accompanying explanation in the new Final Rule. At the time this case was tried and argued to us on appeal no final designation of critical habitat had been made. We concluded that the critical habitat designation had no legal significance in this action brought under Section 9 which involves private land. We concluded that the critical habitat designation did not alter the outcome in this case because, in the end, this case turned on the sufficiency of plaintiffs' evidence, not on the inclusion or exclusion of the school site from critical habitat. * * * We do not hold that the designation of critical habitat will never have any bearing on actions on private lands within designated critical habitat, and thus, our decision has limited value for any other case involving either the pygmy owl or private lands that lie within the mapped boundary of designated critical habitat.

NOTES AND QUESTIONS

1. *Meaning of "harm."* In *Sweet Home*, the majority expressly declined to decide whether the term "harm" within the statutory definition of "take" *must* be construed to include any significant habitat modification that kills or injures wildlife. Suppose the Department of Interior were to revise the definition of harm to include only direct application of force against an animal. Would that definition survive judicial review? How would *Chevron* apply?

2. *Habitat acquisition.* Habitat loss is widely agreed to be the single greatest current threat to dwindling species. *See*, e.g., David S. Wilcove et al., Quantifying Threats to Imperiled Species in the United States, 48 BioScience 607 (1998). Much of the habitat those species need is found on privately-owned lands. *See* General Accounting Office, Endangered Species Act: Information on Species Protection on Nonfederal Lands (1995).

Although plaintiffs in *Sweet Home* agreed that habitat protection plays a key role in species conservation, they argued that Congress intended to protect habitat primarily by purchasing it under authority granted in ESA section 5. What should be the relative roles of regulation and habitat acquisition in endangered species policy? Is it unfair to prohibit development of property occupied by endangered species without compensating the landowner? On the other hand, is it unfair for landowners to assume that title to land carries with it the right to exterminate a species? Will regulations without compensation encourage landowners to conceal the presence of endangered species on their property or surreptitiously eliminate those species? Will political barriers to taxation prevent acquisition of sufficient habitat even if there is strong support for endangered species protection?

3. *Proving take.* What evidence is needed to establish a violation of ESA § 9? Why did the evidence proffered by plaintiffs in *Bernal* fall short? What else could they have done to prove their case? Must an ESA plaintiff show that the landowner knew or should have known of occupancy and the potential for harm? Does designation of critical habitat have any relevance to a § 9 claim?

4. *Incidental take statements.* Biological opinions issued under ESA § 7 include "incidental take statements" specifying the amount of incidental taking that will result from the action, and listing reasonable and prudent measures that can be taken to minimize the impact of the taking. ESA § 7(b)(4); 50 C.F.R. § 402.14(i). Actions taken in accordance with an incidental take statement do not violate § 9.

5. *Third-party take.* In Strahan v. Coxe, 127 F.3d 155 (1st Cir. 1997), after three endangered northern right whales were found entangled in fishing gear deployed in Massachusetts waters, the First Circuit held that Massachusetts authorities had violated the ESA by licensing the use of gillnets and lobster pots without imposing sufficient restrictions to protect the whales. See also Defenders of Wildlife v. EPA, 882 F.2d 1294 (8th Cir. 1989) (EPA violated ESA by registering pesticides containing strychnine which killed endangered species). As a matter of statutory interpretation, do you agree that regulators violate the ESA by affirmatively permitting actions that harm endangered species? Would the result be the same if the regulators simply failed to exercise authority they might have to outlaw harmful actions? In *Strahan*, for example, does it matter that NMFS could have imposed the protective regulations plaintiffs sought? Was NMFS guilty of take? Could Massachusetts deflect liability by adding a prominent statement to all fishing licenses reading: "THIS LICENSE DOES NOT EXEMPT YOU FROM COMPLIANCE WITH THE FEDERAL ENDANGERED SPECIES ACT. YOU ARE RESPONSIBLE FOR ENSURING THAT YOU COMPLY WITH ALL APPLICABLE STATE AND FEDERAL LAWS"?

Does the ESA regulate not only the adoption of regulations but their enforcement? Could Massachusetts be liable for take if whales became entangled in illegally set gear? Under what circumstances? *See* Loggerhead Turtle v. County Council of Volusia County, 92 F. Supp. 2d 1296 (M.D. Fla. 2000) (holding county which had adopted ordinance forbidding harmful beach lighting not liable for take of endangered turtles by lighting which violated the ordinance).

6. *Remedies.* Once a court has found a violation of the take prohibition, is an injunction automatic? Does it matter how likely the take is to recur? *See* National Wildlife Fed'n v. Burlington Northern R.R., 23 F.3d 1508 (9th Cir. 1994). How much of a threat the take poses to survival of the species?

7. *Hypotheticals.* In each of the following hypothetical situations, has a take been committed? If so, by whom? How likely is an enforcement action by the government or a citizen suit to be effective?

(a) Jane Doe is driving 45 mph in a 35 mph zone on a county road in the Florida keys, when a Key deer (an endangered species) leaps in front of her car. Unable to stop, Jane hits and kills the deer. County officials, who are responsible for setting and enforcing the speed limit, are aware that dozens of Key deer have been killed in recent years by speeding cars.

(b) John Farmer owns land along a creek in the northwest. John maintains a small dam to divert water for irrigation purposes. The dam, constructed in 1955 with all required permits, has no fish passage facilities. Chinook salmon once spawned in the creek both above and below the dam, but because of John's dam and others like it, only a handful now return each year. In 2006, fourteen chinook were seen at the base of John's dam. None were counted above the dam. The next year, state and federal officials removed four dams downstream from John's. In 2008, the creek below John's dam teemed with thousands of chinook. Experts concluded that many of these salmon were unable to spawn because there was insufficient spawning habitat for the large number of fish. Is John liable for take in 2006? In 2008? Does your answer depend upon the condition of upstream spawning habitat?

(c) The threatened red-cockaded woodpecker hollows out nests in live pine trees. It prefers trees at least 60 years old, in stands relatively clear of hardwoods. Historically, periodic fire maintained southern pine forests in a state suitable for the red-cockaded woodpecker. Fire suppression and even-aged timber management together have caused its decline. Southern Timber Corp. owns thousands of acres of pine plantations inhabited by a handful of red-cockaded woodpeckers. It refuses to institute a program of prescribed burning, fearing that doing so will increase the population of woodpeckers, leading to tighter restrictions on timber harvest.

(d) The polar bear is listed as a threatened species. According to FWS, the most important threat to the polar bear is loss of its sea ice habitat due to global warming. A utility in Kansas proposes to construct a new coal-fired power plant, which will emit about 6.6 million tons of carbon dioxide annually. The Center for Biological Diversity threatens to bring a citizen suit under the ESA against the utility for "take" of polar bears. Should the utility be worried? Is it in any way relevant that the utility asserts that this plant will help promote future wind energy development, because the new plant will be accompanied by new transmission lines running through Kansas to Colorado, opening up opportunities for wind energy facilities along the way?

Now add one more fact to this hypothetical. FWS has issued a "special rule" under ESA § 4(d), 16 U.S.C. § 1533(d), which provides that, for threatened species, FWS "shall issue such regulations as [it] deems necessary and advisable to provide for the conservation" of the species. The statute defines "conservation" as "the use of all methods and procedures which are necessary to bring any endangered species or threatened species to the point at which the measures provided pursuant to this chapter are no longer necessary." 16 U.S.C. § 1532(3). The polar bear special rule provides in part that "incidental take of polar bears resulting from activities outside the bear's current range is not prohibited under the ESA." Can FWS lawfully define greenhouse gas emissions as outside the reach of § 9? Is that consistent with providing for the conservation of the polar bear?

CLASS DISCUSSION PROBLEM: SONAR AND WHALES

The United States Navy has spent more than ten years and $350 million developing a highly sensitive submarine detection system using low frequency active sonar (LFAS) technology. The system uses underwater speakers towed behind ships to generate extremely loud low frequency sound waves, which travel great distances underwater, bouncing back from objects in their path. By sweeping the ocean with intense, low frequency sonar, the Navy can detect modern quiet submarines over vast areas.

The Navy is now ready to deploy up to four ships towing LFAS arrays, but the proposal has run into considerable controversy. A recent test of a mid-frequency sonar near the Bahamas coincided with a rash of whale beachings. Autopsies on several whales revealed inner ear damage which could have been caused by exposure to high-intensity underwater sound. The Navy proposes to deploy the LFAS system world-wide; several endangered whale and sea turtle species live in waters where LFAS might be used.

If the Navy simply deploys the LFAS system, will it violate the ESA? What, if anything, must it do to satisfy the ESA? Who could challenge deployment? What would a plaintiff have to prove? What relief would be available?

Under the Coastal Zone Management Act, federal actions affecting the coastal zone of a state with an approved coastal zone management plan must be consistent with that approved plan. The federal agency must submit a consistency determination to the state coastal management body. *See* 16 U.S.C. § 1456. If the state body does not respond within 60 days, it is presumed to concur with the consistency determination. If the state objects, the federal agency may proceed at risk of a judicial finding of inconsistency, enter into mediation of the disagreement, or seek a presidential exemption.

The Navy has submitted a consistency determination to the California Coastal Commission for LFAS operations off the California coast. If the Commission concurs with that determination, does it risk ESA liability?

4. PERMITTING TAKE: HABITAT CONSERVATION PLANS

Excerpts From the Endangered Species Act

16 U.S.C. § 1531–1544.

Sec. 10. Exceptions

(a)(1) The Secretary may permit, under such terms and conditions as he shall prescribe—

* * *

(B) any taking otherwise prohibited by section 1538(a)(1)(B) of this title if such taking is incidental to, and not the purpose of, the carrying out of an otherwise lawful activity.

(2)(A) No permit may be issued by the Secretary authorizing any taking referred to in paragraph (1)(B) unless the applicant therefor submits to the Secretary a conservation plan that specifies—

(i) the impact which will likely result from such taking;

(ii) what steps the applicant will take to minimize and mitigate such impacts, and the funding that will be available to implement such steps;

(iii) what alternative actions to such taking the applicant considered and the reasons why such alternatives are not being utilized; and

(iv) such other measures that the Secretary may require as being necessary or appropriate for purposes of the plan.

(B) If the Secretary finds, after opportunity for public comment, with respect to a permit application and the related conservation plan that—

(i) the taking will be incidental;

(ii) the applicant will, to the maximum extent practicable, minimize and mitigate the impacts of such taking;

(iii) the applicant will ensure that adequate funding for the plan will be provided;

(iv) the taking will not appreciably reduce the likelihood of the survival and recovery of the species in the wild; and

(v) the measures, if any, required under subparagraph (A)(iv) will be met;

and he has received such other assurances as he may require that the plan will be implemented, the Secretary shall issue the permit. The permit shall contain such terms and conditions as the Secretary deems necessary or appropriate to carry out the purposes of this paragraph, including, but not limited to, such reporting requirements as the Secretary deems necessary for determining whether such terms and conditions are being complied with.

(C) The Secretary shall revoke a permit issued under this paragraph if he finds that the permittee is not complying with the terms and conditions of the permit.

Robert D. Thornton, Searching for Consensus and Predictability: Habitat Conservation Planning Under the Endangered Species Act of 1973

21 Envtl. L. 605, 621–24 (1991).

Section 10(a) of the ESA grew out of a multi-year conflict between a proposed development project and two species of endangered butterflies. In early 1976, the local board of supervisors ended a decade-long dispute over the appropriate level of development at San Bruno Mountain on the San Francisco Peninsula in Northern California by requiring the landowner to dedicate two-thirds of the mountain as a park. Two weeks after the final conveyance of the property to the state parks foundation, the FWS proposed to list the Callippe Silverspot butterfly as an endangered species and to designate critical habitat on the mountain. The critical habitat proposal substantially overlapped all of the remaining areas on the mountain designated for development by the County.

The proposed listing initiated a three-year planning process involving the environmental community, the landowners and developers, and local, state and federal agencies. After two years of intensive negotiation, the parties agreed on a habitat conservation plan which allowed the proposed development to proceed, but which also established a long-term program for the protection of the butterflies and several other species of concern.

The San Bruno Mountain plan addresses the ecological community on the mountain as a single unit. Although the plan focused on the conflict between development and the preservation of the butterflies, the plan also sought to preserve the diversity of species and their habitat on the mountain. The plan reflected a conscious attempt by its drafters to anticipate and resolve any conflicts that might develop over other biological resources on the mountain.

Under the plan, private development becomes a source of funds for acquiring habitat and for funding the needed habitat management measures. The plan's drafters carefully selected sites for private development using criteria reflecting the biological requirements of the species on the mountain. The plan establishes rigorous procedures to ensure that any land development occurs in conformity with the plan.

Two of the participants in the plan's development described its significant elements as follows:

1. *Protection of Open Space.* The plan preserves in open space 80 percent of the mountain; all but 2.7 percent of this total is preserved in an undisturbed condition. Approximately 90 percent of the habitat of the Mission Blue and Callippe Silverspot butterflies is protected under the plan.

2. *Diversity of Habitat Protected.* An essential feature of the plan is the preservation of the diversity of habitat on the mountain, including hilltops and valleys, north- and south-facing slopes, grasslands, brush, and other habitats. The effort was to protect the butterflies by protecting the diversity of the mountain's ecological community.

* * *

4. *Funding of Plan Activities.* The plan provides a source of permanent funding to carry out conservation activities through assessments (which will be imposed through recorded covenants and restrictions) that will raise approximately $60,000 per year, which is in addition to substantial, interim funding provided by the developers. The agreement provides that the permanent funding will be adjusted annually for inflation to insure an inflation-free source of funding. The level of ongoing private support for endangered species conservation is unprecedented.

5. *Ongoing Management of Public and Private Habitat.* The plan establishes the County as the ongoing manager of the habitat throughout the mountain and insures a uniformity of management within the various jurisdictional areas on the mountain. One of the key components of the plan is that it subjects both public and private activities within conserved habitat areas to the conservation principles enunciated in the plan. Thus, county and state parklands on the mountain are required to be managed in

the interest of habitat conservation to the same extent as privately held habitat.

6. *Assurances to Private Sector.* The implementing agreement includes unprecedented provisions that assure the private sector landowners and developers that, except as specifically set forth in the agreement, no further mitigation or compensation will be required in the interest of wildlife or their habitat on the mountain.

* * *

Despite the consensus between the developer and the leading environmental group concerning the plan's terms, the plan suffered from the absence of any specific ESA provision authorizing the FWS to permit the incidental taking contemplated by the conservation plan. As a result, the plan's proponents sought, and in 1982 Congress adopted, an amendment authorizing the FWS to issue incidental take permits in accordance with the terms of an HCP. Section 10(a)'s legislative history indicates that the San Bruno Mountain HCP is the model for the ESA's new provision and is also the standard against which similar conservation plans will be measured. * * *

National Wildlife Federation v. Babbitt

United States District Court, Eastern District of California, 2000.
128 F. Supp. 2d 1274.

■ LEVI, DISTRICT JUDGE.

Plaintiffs challenge the United States Fish and Wildlife Service's issuance of an incidental take permit [to the City of Sacramento] to allow development in the Natomas Basin, a 53,000 acre tract of largely undeveloped land * * *.

The Natomas Basin HCP is intended "to promote biological conservation along with economic development and the continuation of agriculture within the Natomas Basin." The HCP lists 26 species that are "potentially subject to take," and which are to "be included in the state and federal permits issued in accordance with the Plan." The proposed permit authorizes incidental take resulting from urban development, as well as any incidental take that may occur through rice-farming or result from management of the Plan's reserve lands. The HCP was developed as a regional conservation plan for the entire Natomas Basin, and was intended for use in connection with [Incidental Take Permit (ITP)] applications for each of the municipalities and water companies with interests in the Basin * * *. [Relying on the plan, FWS issued a permit to the City of Sacramento. No other permit applications had yet been filed.]

The Plan is administered by the Natomas Basin Conservancy ("NBC") which has the responsibility to establish and oversee "a concerted Basin-wide program for acquiring and managing mitigation lands on behalf of the permittees." * * *

The Plan calls upon the NBC to assemble connected 400 acre blocks of reserve lands—with one block of at least 2500 acres—for the benefit of the Giant Garter Snake and to protect Swainson's hawk habitat and nesting areas. The HCP states that "to the maximum extent practicable, the [Natomas Basin] HCP will ensure that habitat acquisition will be provided *in advance* of habitat conversion resulting from urban development in the Natomas Basin." Funding for land acquisition, however, is derived from the collection of mitigation fees for development. Thus, with regard to the phasing of land acquisition, the HCP actually requires only that, after an initial acquisition of 400 acres, which is to be made "as soon as possible," "no more than one year shall elapse between receipt of a fee and expenditure of that fee in the purchase or other acquisition of mitigation land."

The Plan is based on certain key principles and assumptions. First, the Plan assumes that only 17,500 acres of Basin land will be developed over the 50 year life of the permit, and that a substantial proportion of the undeveloped land will remain in agriculture, particularly rice, which is believed to have unique value as habitat for the [Giant Garter Snake (GGS)]. The Plan's conclusion that a ratio of .5 acres of reserve lands for each 1 acre of developed land will ensure the biological needs of the protected species is based on the assumption that a considerable portion of the undeveloped and agricultural lands in the Basin will remain undeveloped, thereby augmenting the habitat value of the reserve lands.

Second, the Plan pursues a regional approach to conservation. Whereas without the Plan, individual landowners could pursue separate permit applications, or develop their land without securing an ITP, the HCP is intended to provide a consolidated approach under which resources may be pooled and conservation lands may be purchased throughout the Basin. Third, the HCP treats all Basin lands as fungible, as equally valuable habitat. Thus, the HCP requires developers to "mitigate" for the anticipated take of individuals or habitat by payment of a fee for each acre developed. Rather than differentiating among lands according to their value as habitat for protected species, the HCP requires all landowners within the Permit area to pay a mitigation fee for developing their land, regardless of whether any particular parcel has or lacks habitat value. Depending on one's point of view, this uniform treatment is either a strength or a weakness of the Plan. It is a strength because mitigation fees are to be collected on all acreage and are used "to set aside 0.5 acres of habitat land for each 1.0 acres of gross development that occurs in the Basin." It is a potential weakness because the Plan does not attempt to identify, prior to intensified development under the ITP, particular parcels for acquisition as reserves, based upon the importance of those parcels as habitat, but simply specifies acquisition criteria, and leaves specific reserve acquisition to the future decisionmaking of the NBC.

* * *

IV. Endangered Species Act Claims

* * * [P]laintiffs' ESA claims fall into two categories. First, plaintiffs challenge as arbitrary the Service's findings as to the adequacy of the Plan's provisions, particularly those related to funding and mitigation; second, plaintiffs contend that the Service's findings regarding the biological effects of the Plan on covered species are arbitrary and capricious. As explained below, under the APA's deferential standard of review, the Service's findings largely pass muster with respect to the Plan as a whole; however, with respect to the City's Permit, the Service's findings do not. * * *

A. ESA § 10(a)(2)(A)—minimum criteria for a habitat conservation plan

Plaintiffs argue that the Service's approval of the HCP is improper because the HCP does not adequately disclose its impacts on covered species and their habitat. ESA § 10(a)(2)(A) states that no incidental take permit may be issued unless the applicant submits an HCP that meets certain requirements. One such requirement is that the HCP specify "the impact which will likely result from such taking." * * * [T]he HCP does discuss the impact that will likely result from development activities, rice farming, and operation of water conveyance systems in the Natomas Basin. While the Plan and associated supporting documents do not make specific quantitative estimates of take, they do make general assessments of the effect of development under the Plan as to the various species affected, particularly the GGS and the Swainson's hawk. Plaintiffs argue, however, that the ESA requires precise quantitative measures of take. According to plaintiffs, the HCP must estimate the number of individual members of a species within the Permit area and must then estimate the number of members of the species that will be taken. Plaintiffs cite no authority for this interpretation of the ESA. The Secretary's contrary interpretation of the statute is entitled to deference. The court finds that the HCP meets the minimum requirements for a habitat conservation plan.

B. ESA § 10(a)(2)(B)(ii)—minimize and mitigate the impact of permitted takings "to the maximum extent practicable"

Plaintiffs argue that the Service's (B)(ii) finding, that the Plan will minimize and mitigate takings to the maximum extent practicable, is arbitrary and capricious because the Service failed to consider any alternatives involving greater mitigation measures. * * * The linchpin of the HCP is the .5 to 1 preserved to developed acre ratio and the mitigation fee that is based on this ratio. Thus, to consider an alternative providing greater mitigation, in the context of this HCP, the record should provide some basis for concluding, not just that the chosen mitigation fee and land preservation ratio are practicable, but that a higher fee ratio would be impracticable.

The Secretary does not appear to disagree with the above analysis but rather argues that the record does adequately demonstrate that the HCP provides for the maximum practicable mitigation fee and reserve land ratio. However, the record is nearly non-existent on this matter. There are conclusory statements in the record to the effect that "the common and local wisdom is that a fee in the range from $2000 to $2500 per acre is practicable," but the record is devoid of evidence that the Service subjected this assumption to any examination or attempted to determine if a higher base fee would also be practicable. There is no economic analysis, discussion of mitigation fees in similar plans and circumstances, or even representations from particular landowners. * * * The plain language of the statutory provision requiring that the Plan minimize and mitigate its effects "to the maximum extent practicable" is not satisfied by a fee set, as here, at the minimum amount necessary to meet the minimum biological necessities of the covered species. The record lacks adequate evidence and analysis of whether a fee higher than that initially proposed by the working group would be economically practicable.

The Secretary finds support for the (B)(ii) finding in part in the Plan's provision allowing increases in the mitigation fee as necessary to cover increased costs. But increases over the life of the Plan are capped at 50% of the initial base fee for most, although not all, types of expenditures.[18] Moreover, because fee increases are not applied retroactively, the Plan's provisions for fee increases can be expected to produce revenue only if and to the extent that future developers are willing to participate in the HCP. The problem that this mitigation structure presents is particularly acute for the City's Permit, given the relatively small portion of the Basin within the City and the pace at which development of the City's land is expected. Thus, it is possible, even likely, that City developers will avoid the future substantial increases in the mitigation fee that will be borne by out of City developers. While this structure may make sense, at least without analysis and explanation, it is not obvious how the Secretary concluded that City developers would pay a fee that is the maximum practicable, particularly when later developers are expected to pay a much larger fee. In short, the Secretary's conclusion that $2240 per acre is the maximum practicable initial base mitigation fee is unsupported by substantial evidence in the record, and therefore is arbitrary and capricious.

* * *

For these reasons, the Service's (B)(ii) finding is arbitrary and capricious considering the HCP as a whole and the City's Permit in particular.

C.   *ESA § 10(a)(2)(B)(iii)—adequate funding*

Plaintiffs argue that the Service's finding that the City would "ensure" adequate funding for the Plan is arbitrary, for two reasons. First, plaintiffs contend that the initial mitigation fee, even in light of the Plan's provisions for fee increases, is inadequate to cover the costs of the various components of the mitigation program. The record, however, provides an adequate basis for the Secretary's conclusion to the contrary. The initial fee was set based on the estimated needs of the NBC prepared by experts * * *. Although plaintiffs point to evidence in the record suggesting that the fee was deemed inadequate by some, the Service's decision to rely on [expert] analysis is entitled to deference.

---

18.   Most significantly, the cap does not apply to fee increases necessitated by increased land acquisition costs.

Second, plaintiffs argue that the (B)(iii) finding was arbitrary and capricious with respect to the City's permit, in light of the City's explicit refusal to "ensure" funding in the event of a shortfall. This argument has merit. Plaintiffs argue that nothing in the record supports the HCP's assertion * * * that:

> The [Natomas Basin] HCP can be implemented independently by some individual permittees, but not by others, without adversely affecting the conservation program as a whole. This is because each land use agency is responsible under the Plan for mitigating the effects of urban development occurring within its respective permit area, regardless of the actions of other agencies.

Indeed, the record suggests a much more complicated picture than the Plan depicts concerning the consequences of nonparticipation by the other land-use agencies with jurisdiction over parts of the Basin. Given that the Plan does not permit retroactive fee increases, increases in the mitigation fee will be applied only to land developed after the need for a greater fee becomes apparent and the fee increase is approved. Thus, the Plan's funding mechanism depends on continual infusions of new developable land to provide funding for mitigation necessitated by previous development. Regardless of the City's incentives, if most or all of the City's land has been developed by the time the need for additional mitigation funding becomes apparent—a likelihood if the City lands are rapidly developed under the current fee—there may simply be no land left to which an increased fee could be applied. Given the Plan's acknowledgment that it is uncertain whether land-use agencies other than the City will submit applications, the statement that "each land use agency is *responsible* under the Plan for mitigating the effects of urban development occurring within its respective permit area," is not accurate with respect to the City, which refused to "ensure" funding for the mitigation necessitated by development under its permit.

* * *

It is not clear that a funding mechanism that is not backed by the applicant's guarantee could ever satisfy the requirement of § 1539(a)(2)(B)(iii) that the applicant "ensure" funding for the Plan. Assuming, however, that a cost shifting mechanism "ensures" funding within the meaning of § 1539(a)(2)(B)(iii), in these circumstances, where the adequacy of funding depends on whether third parties decide to participate in the Plan, the statute requires the applicant's guarantee.

* * * [W]hile the Service's (B)(iii) finding is not arbitrary with respect to the Plan as a whole, it is arbitrary and capricious with respect to the City's Permit.

D. ESA § 10(a)(2)(B)(iv)—Survival and Recovery, and § 7(a)(2)—No Jeopardy

Plaintiffs argue that in making the findings required by ESA §§ 10(a)(2)(B)(iv) and 7(a)(2) (collectively, the "no jeopardy" findings), the Service failed adequately to explain how habitat loss authorized by the

HCP would avoid jeopardizing the continued survival of the Giant Garter Snake, Swainson's hawk, and other covered species. * * * The no jeopardy findings, like the (B)(ii) and (B)(iii) findings, are undermined by the administrative record's focus on the regional HCP. Although the no jeopardy findings are adequately supported by the record if the Service's assumption that Sacramento and Sutter Counties will seek ITPs under the Plan is valid, the Service failed adequately to consider whether the findings could be made with respect to the issuance of an ITP to the City alone. In short, while the no jeopardy findings are not arbitrary with respect to the Plan, they are arbitrary with respect to the Permit.

(1) The Plan

Plaintiffs argue that the Service's no jeopardy findings are arbitrary and capricious for five reasons: (1) The Service "failed to articulate a rational connection between [the findings] and the fact that tens of thousands of acres of habitat will be destroyed and degraded under the HCP"; (2) the Service failed to explain its change in policy position on the habitat protections needed by covered species; (3) the Service "improperly ignored, and failed to explain its departure from, uncontradicted expert evidence regarding the survival and recovery needs of the imperiled species"; (4) the Service's no jeopardy findings are based on improper speculation; and (5) the Service failed to articulate a rational connection between the no jeopardy findings and the "admitted fact that the HCP's initial conservation strategy is highly uncertain to succeed."

As to plaintiffs' first argument, plaintiffs' principal contention is that the Service's reliance on the HCP's forecast of 17,500 acres of development over the 50 year term of the ITP is arbitrary. Plaintiffs argue that "up to 32,000 acres of habitat in the Natomas Basin" will be destroyed under the HCP. Plaintiffs have not established, however, that the Service's reliance on the 17,500 acre figure is unreasonable, and the Service adequately articulated its basis for the estimate.[24] Moreover, there are two important safeguards that justify reliance on the 17,500 acre figure. First, the HCP calls for a review at 9,000 acres, with a moratorium on development past 12,000 acres pending completion of the review. If the pace of development at that point exceeds expectations, various modifications may be requested or required, including a revocation of the permit. And second, because the 17,500 acre assumption is so central to the HCP, any significant departure from that figure would require reinitiation of consultation, again possibly leading to revocation or substantial modification of the permit. Based on the forecast of 17,500 acres, and using the 1:.5 development to preservation ratio, the Service concurred with the HCP's estimate that 8750 acres of reserve land would be protected under the Plan, and that most of the remainder of the Basin would be in agricultural lands, which frequently provide excellent habitat. The Service concluded that the reserve lands,

---

24. The 1997 Biological Opinion explains that the 17,500 acre figure is a prediction based on the City's and Counties' General Plans, which the Service deemed to provide "a reasonable basis for predicting the extent and location of future urban development."

together with undeveloped land kept in agriculture, would suffice to maintain, and in some cases increase, the Basin's populations of covered species.

Plaintiffs argue, in addition, that the Service's failure to include "basic information," such as the baseline condition and conservation needs of the species, and the effects of the HCP, undermines the "rational connection" between the no jeopardy findings and the record. * * * Plaintiffs' contention appears to be that the ESA requires detailed quantitative information as to each of these factors prior to the issuance of a permit, but plaintiffs cite no authority for such a requirement, and such a requirement would not be reasonable. For the Giant Garter Snake, for example, a reclusive species, it would be extraordinarily difficult to count the number of individual snakes, determine their habitat and habits, and reach conclusions as to their genetic makeup and variability. Instead, the 1997 Biological Opinion makes certain assumptions about the species based upon potential loss of habitat, which is a reasonable approach. Moreover, the Plan overprotects by assuming that any acre lost to development is potential habitat requiring the 1:.5 mitigation.

* * *

Plaintiffs' fourth contention is that the Service improperly speculated as to the likely success of the Plan's conservation measures. The subjects of "speculation" that plaintiffs identify include: (1) that habitat areas will be available for acquisition; [and] (2) that local governments and landowners will cooperate in the NBC's efforts to acquire reserve lands * * *.

The uncertainties to which plaintiffs object do not undermine the "rational connection" between the no jeopardy findings and the evidence in the record. Plaintiffs' first, second, and fifth charges of "speculation" are concerned with the uncertainties inherent in the market-based mitigation mechanism employed by the HCP. The NBC is given funds and acquisition criteria, and permitted to compete in the marketplace for land and for water rights. In the absence of any identified "critical habitat" in the Basin, or substantial evidence in the record that the market for land and water rights will not function—that is, that land and water rights will be unavailable to the NBC even if the Plan provides adequate funding—the adoption of such a market-based mitigation structure is not an arbitrary or otherwise impermissible exercise of the Secretary's discretion. * * *

As to plaintiffs' final challenge to the no jeopardy findings, which concerns the allegedly uncertain success of the HCP's initial conservation strategy, plaintiffs appear to contend that, in the face of incomplete data as to species' recovery needs and uncertainty as to the efficacy of the HCP, the Service's issuance of the ITP is arbitrary and capricious. Plaintiffs provide no authority for the duty they seek to impose on the Secretary, the resolution of all uncertainties before proceeding with a Plan, nor is any such duty apparent from the text of the ESA or case law. A certain degree of what plaintiffs label "speculation" and "uncertainty" is inevitable in any decisionmaking process, particularly one as complicated as that which led to the issuance of the ITP. The law does not require that the Secretary achieve certainty before acting.

(2) The Permit

Although the Service's no jeopardy findings are not arbitrary and capricious with respect to the Plan as a whole—that is, assuming that Sacramento and Sutter Counties will seek permits under the Plan—the record is startlingly devoid of support for the findings with respect to the possibility that only the City would participate in the Plan. This is understandable, perhaps, given the regional approach of the HCP which is its greatest strength. But the court does not have before it what the drafters of the Plan apparently envisioned, a permit or permits for all of the jurisdictions within the Basin; rather, the court has for review only a permit for the City, and may not assume that other jurisdictions will also join in the HCP.

The Service's expert analysis of the likely impacts of the Plan assumes that all Basin development occurs under the HCP subject to the mitigation fee. As discussed above, the record provides insufficient consideration by the Service of whether funding for mitigation would be adequate if only the City's lands were developed under the Plan. Moreover, the record contains little or no analysis of the effect on the species of the City's permit considered on its own. Thus, there is no analysis of the importance of the City's lands as habitat for covered species. At oral argument, counsel for the Secretary asserted that the court could assume that the City's lands were less valuable habitat than other Basin lands, but the court cannot so assume; it must rely on the considered judgment of the Service and the record. * * *

Furthermore, there is little discussion of the effect on the GGS if the Plan's goal of large connected blocks of reserve lands cannot be met because only the City participates in the Plan. Such a fundamental change in the Plan's conservation strategy requires discussion. Yet the Service merely acknowledges the problem without explaining how the reserves set aside by the City's development will be adequate to protect the GGS and the other affected species.

The problem of the reserve lands is just an example of a larger problem when the Plan is applied only to the City's Basin lands. The Secretary concedes that the ITP will result in take of threatened species, including between 14 and 37% of the Basin population of the GGS, but relies on certain features of the Plan, including the monitoring, adaptive management, and 9,000 acre review provisions, to adequately mitigate the impact of the take. The Secretary's emphasis on these provisions, however, only underscores the tension between the HCP's regional nature and the local focus of the ITP and the Service's biological findings. Based on the projected development in City's area of the Basin, the midcourse review will come too late to result in any change with respect to the City's permit. The record shows that the portion of the Basin with approved development plans, most of which is in the City, is expected to be developed quickly, while the pace of development in the Counties is largely unknown. Thus, the halfway point moratorium and opportunity for mid-course correction, so important to the HCP, are irrelevant to the City's permit, which contains no analogous features for correction and reconsideration. Similarly, the record does not suggest that the Service considered whether the monitoring and adaptive management provisions of the regional Plan could be effective if the City is the sole permittee. Given the evidence that the City's lands will be developed quite quickly, the Service's failure to consider whether the survival of the species will be put at risk by the City's permit, if the regional mitigation approach of the HCP is not available, is arbitrary and capricious.

* * *

NOTES AND QUESTIONS

1. *National Wildlife Federation v. Babbitt.* What precisely is the holding of *NWF v. Babbitt*? On remand, what changes or additional analysis must FWS do to reissue the permit? What problems would be remedied, and to what extent, if neighboring jurisdictions participated? What does it mean to minimize and mitigate the impacts of the permitted taking "to the maximum extent practicable"? Does the extent of required mitigation depend upon the extent of take authorized, or only upon the financial resources of the permittee? In a subsequent decision, the same judge held that a permittee need not do more than mitigate the actual effects of its activities.

> Thus, if a permit authorized the destruction of one acre of habitat that normally supports one individual member of a protected species, it would not be necessary for the applicant to create 100 acres of new habitat that would support some 100 individuals of the species, even if the particular developer could afford to do so.

National Wildlife Federation v. Norton, 306 F. Supp. 2d 920, 928 (E.D. Cal. 2004).

2. *HCP requirements.* In *NWF v. Babbitt*, do you agree that the Plan itself met the requirements of section 10, with the exception of the funding mechanism? Were the "no jeopardy" findings adequately supported? Who bears the burden of proof on that issue? Does section 10 permit "market-based" HCP approaches, relying on acquisition of reserves from willing sellers as development proceeds? What evidence is required to support those findings? Must FWS evaluate the importance of specific lands to the species?

3. *HCPs by the numbers.* By 1992, a decade after enactment of the incidental take provision, only fourteen HCPs had been approved, and by the end of 1994 there were only 25 more. At that point, however, the program took off. By February 2001, 341 HCPs covering 30 million acres had been approved. As of July 2009, 670 HCPs had been approved, and 782 incidental take permits issued on the basis of those plans. The plans range in size from 0.1 acre to more than 10 million acres. Some cover all the endangered, threatened and candidate species within a large area, such as

Clark County, Nevada, or San Diego County, California. Others cover a single species over entire states, such as the Wisconsin Karner Blue Butterfly Plan, or particular activities, such as the state of Washington Forest Practices Plan. Local governments are often the permit holders for large regional HCPs, as in the Natomas plan.

4. *Pros and cons of HCPs.* Advocates of the HCP process contend that it offers the opportunity to move away from reactive, species-specific conservation toward a more efficient and effective forward-looking, ecosystem-based approach. In some respects, HCPs effectively expand the protections of section 9. HCPs can cover species not listed, and because issuance of an incidental take permit is a federal action subject to section 7 they must protect against the possibility of jeopardy to listed plants. Large-scale plans can produce large contiguous reserves more likely to protect species in the long run but impossible or exceedingly difficult to create in response to piece-meal individual development projects. Finally, proponents claim, the program reduces political pressure on the ESA itself by accommodating some development while protecting species.

Not everyone is enthusiastic about HCPs, however. Many environmentalists are concerned that development may not turn out to be compatible with conservation. They assert that incidental take should be permitted only if the plan will provide a net benefit to the species, helping it move toward recovery and eventual delisting. Even those who support the concept of HCPs are concerned about its implementation, fearing that development pressure will encourage the Services to approve plans supported by insufficient data. Barriers to public participation at the early stages of plan drafting and judicial inclinations toward deference to agency decisions feed these fears.

5. *No surprises.* Of particular concern to HCP critics is a policy first adopted by FWS in 1994, and subsequently formalized as a regulation, that limits the responsibility of permittees for unforeseen shortcomings of HCPs. The "no surprises" rule provides that a permittee who is in compliance with a plan that adequately covered a species will not be required to provide additional financing or land for conservation if additional measures are subsequently deemed necessary to protect the species. 50 C.F.R. § 17.22(b). FWS regards "no surprises" assurances as central to the increase in permit applications after 1994. The associated "permit revocation rule" implements the Service's view that HCPs need not provide for recovery by forbidding revocation of the permit absent an uncorrected violation unless the continuation of the permit will cause jeopardy to the species. Id (b)(8). A federal district court upheld both rules against a facial challenge. Spirit of the Sage Council v. Kempthorne, 511 F. Supp. 2d 31 (D.D.C. 2007).

D.   OTHER BIODIVERSITY PROVISIONS

Many other federal and state laws protect biodiversity in one way or another. Economic incentives and market mechanisms form one part of the biodiversity protection picture. Habitat acquisition and management for wildlife purposes are authorized under several federal laws, and supported by federal taxes under the Pittman–Robertson Wildlife Restoration Act, 16 U.S.C. §§ 669–669k, and Migratory Bird Hunting and Conservation Stamp Act, 16 U.S.C. §§ 718–718k. Several programs provide subsidies to farmers who manage their lands for wildlife, or deny subsidies to farmers whose practices are harmful. *See* J.B. Ruhl, Farms, Their Environmental Harms, and Environmental Law, 27 Ecology L.Q. 325–27 (2000).

A large number of state and federal regulatory statutes also contribute to biodiversity protection. Some of the most important federal provisions include the Migratory Bird Treaty Act, 16 U.S.C. §§ 703–712; Bald and Golden Eagle Protection Act, 16 U.S.C. §§ 668–668d; Wild Free–Roaming Horses and Burros Act, 16 U.S.C. §§ 1331–1340; Marine Mammal Protection Act, 16 U.S.C. §§ 1371–1389; and Magnuson–Stevens Fishery Conservation and Management Act, 16 U.S.C. §§ 1802–1883. For comprehensive discussions of federal biodiversity law, *see* Bradley C. Karkkainen, Biodiversity and Land, 83 Cornell L. Rev. 1 (1997) and J.B. Ruhl, Biodiversity Conservation and the Ever–Expanding Web of Federal Laws Regulating Non–Federal Lands: Time for Something Completely Different?, 66 U. Colo. L. Rev. 555 (1995).

A number of international agreements are also relevant to biodiversity protection. There are treaties specifically focused on wildlife protection, such as the Convention for the Protection of Migratory Birds, Aug. 16–Dec. 8, 1916, U.S.–Gr. Brit., 39 Stat. 1702, and the International Convention for the Regulation of Whaling, Dec. 2, 1946, 62 Stat. 1716, 161 U.N.T.S. 72. There are also many agreements on habitat protection, including the Ramsar Convention on wetlands protection, Convention on of International Importance Especially as Waterfowl Habitat, Feb. 2, 1971, 996 U.N.T.S. 245, 11 I.L.M. 969, and the Convention for the Protection of the World Cultural and Natural Heritage, Nov. 23, 1972, 27 U.S.T. 37, 1037 U.N.T.S. 151. The 1992 Convention on Biological Diversity, 31 I.L.M. 818 (1992), sets the international framework for protection and exploitation of biotic resources. *See*, e.g., Michael A. Bowman and Catherine Redgwell, eds., International Law and the Conservation of Biological Diversity (1996); Lakshman Guruswamy & Jeffrey A. McNeely, eds., Protection of Global Biodiversity: Converging Strategies (1998). The United States is one of the few major nations not to have ratified this convention.

SECTION 2.   WETLANDS PROTECTION

A.   INTRODUCTION

Wetlands form the interface between terrestrial and aquatic habitats. They include such diverse areas as bogs, marshes, wet meadows, play lakes, prairie potholes and, in Alaska, tundra wetlands. Wetlands may be tidal or freshwater, seasonal or year-round, and inundated from above through flooding or rain, or from below through a high groundwater table.

Wetlands were once regarded as places to avoid or eliminate. Nearly ten percent of the land area of the continental United States, over 220 million acres, was wetlands at the time of European colonization. By the 1980s, more than half of these wetlands acres had been destroyed, primarily by drainage, and converted to agriculture. National Research Council, Wetlands: Characteristics and Boundaries 16 (1995). California and the farm belt of the midwest suffered especially high losses. *See* Thomas E. Dahl, Wetlands Losses in the United States, 1780s to 1980s, at 6 (1991).

We now recognize that wetlands perform many ecological functions. They are highly productive ecosystems, harboring a wide variety of plant and animal species. More than one-third of the threatened and endangered species in the U.S. live only in wetlands. Many commercially-harvested fish and shellfish breed in wetlands. A large number of migratory bird species, including many popular with hunters and birdwatchers, rest, forage or nest in wetlands. These areas also serve crucial hydrologic functions, moderating floods and reducing their erosive impact by slowing surface waters. In addition, they filter wastes from surface waters, contribute to nutrient cycling, and can remove the greenhouse gas carbon dioxide from the atmosphere. *See* U.S. Environmental Protection Agency, Office of Water, Office of Wetlands, Oceans and Watersheds, America's Wetlands: Our Vital Link Between Land and Water (undated) (available at http://www.epa.gov/owow/wetlands/ vital/toc.html).

Federal efforts to protect wetlands began in 1934 with the Duck Stamp Program, which imposed a tax on migratory bird hunting to support acquisition of waterfowl habitat. Nonetheless, the Department of Agriculture continued to subsidize wetland conversion, and wetland losses accelerated. By the 1960s, growing awareness of the ecological importance of wetlands and of their rapid disappearance created pressure for regulatory wetlands protection. A few states and localities began to require permits for wetland destruction. Finally, in 1972, Congress passed the Clean Water Act, section 404 of which authorized the issuance of permits for the discharge of fill to "navigable waters," defined elsewhere in the Act as "waters of the United States." The Army Corps of Engineers, which historically had been responsible for preventing obstructions to navigation under the Rivers and Harbors Act, 33 U.S.C. §§ 401–418, was given responsibility for this permitting program. Not entirely trusting the Corps to give proper weight to environmental values, however, Congress also gave EPA a significant role in the section 404 program.

Initially, the Corps narrowly construed its section 404 authority. By 1975, however, several courts had ruled that the Clean Water Act applied well beyond navigable waters as traditionally defined. *See* United States v. Holland, 373 F.Supp. 665 (M.D. Fla. 1974); Natural Resources Defense Council v. Callaway, 392 F.Supp. 685 (D.D.C. 1975); Conservation Council of North Carolina v. Costanzo, 398 F.Supp. 653 (E.D.N.C. 1975). In response to these decisions, EPA and the Corps issued new regulations extending section 404 to wetlands.

Today, the section 404 program is the centerpiece of federal wetlands policy, but both land acquisition and economic incentives also play a role. Federal acquisition of wetlands continues, particularly for national wildlife refuges. Federal agricultural law includes both positive economic incentives for wetlands protection, under the Wetlands Reserve Program, and penalties for wetlands destruction, under the "Swampbuster" program. *See* 16 U.S.C. § 3801–3824.

In 1989, President George H. W. Bush set a national goal of "no net loss" of wetlands. Between 1986 and 1997, annual wetland losses in the continental United States averaged 58,500 acres, eighty percent less than the average annual loss in the preceding decade. Thomas E. Dahl, Status and Trends of Wetlands in the Conterminous United States, 1986 to 1997, at 9–11 (2000). By 2004, wetland acreage in the United States was actually increasing by 32,000 acres annually. Those statistics may be misleading, however. The recent gains were attributable to increases in freshwater pond acreage. Other types of wetlands continued to be destroyed, albeit at steadily declining rates. Overall, open water ponds are replacing vegetated wetlands, with accompanying changes in ecosystem values and functions. Thomas E. Dahl, Status and Trends of Wetlands in the Conterminous United States, 1998 to 2004, at 16–17. Urban and rural development is now the primary threat to wetlands, accounting for sixty percent of recent freshwater wetlands losses, but agriculture and silviculture are also key threats. Although the Fish and Wildlife Service tracks wetlands acreage nationwide, there is no systematic measure of the quality or ecological functioning of those wetlands.

CLASS DISCUSSION PROBLEM: THE LOVELY HARBOR COMPANY DEVELOPS WETLANDS

In 1963 the Lovely Harbor Company (LHC) purchased approximately 350 acres of vacant land on the shores of Folly Beach Sound for $300,000. Sheltered by Folly Beach Island from the storm waves of the Atlantic Ocean, Folly Beach Sound is a beautiful, quiet area of tidal marshes and wetlands, teeming with aquatic life and water birds. LHC's land is the last large, privately-owned undeveloped parcel on Folly Beach sound. There are other large coastal parcels nearby, but they do not enjoy the same favorable weather conditions.

LHC plans to develop a golf course and housing complex on 250 acres of its Folly Beach Sound land. LHC does not plan to develop the remaining 100 acres of land immediately, but would like to clear it and plant it with soybeans to bring in some immediate income. LHC expects to develop this remaining land for single family residential use in a few years, assuming market conditions remain favorable.

In preparation for its contemplated development, LHC hired consultants to survey its remaining land for wetlands. Twenty-five acres bordering Folly Beach Sound are regularly subject to shallow flooding by the tides. Another 6–acre parcel, well back from the coast, contains several depressions in which water pools following heavy rains. This area is surrounded by low hills, and there is no obvious surface drainage from it to the sound. Although the rest of the land is usually dry, a biologist has warned the company that as many as 125 acres are covered with "hydrophytic plants" capable of growing in wetland areas.

An appraisal by a reputable expert has determined that the twenty-five tideland acres would be worth as much as $250,000 per acre as waterfront lots for homes. If they cannot be filled for development, however, these tidelands would be worth no more than a few hundred dollars per acre. Furthermore, LHC's plans for the entire 250–acre tract hinge on gaining permission to dredge and fill in the tidelands. LHC plans an upscale, water-oriented development with a series of canals providing each lot with water access to Folly Beach Sound. If the company cannot dredge and fill in the tidelands, it will have to abandon its canal project, substantially reducing the value of the entire parcel for residential development. The six-acre ponding area is also important to LHC's plans; it happens to lie precisely where LHC would like to put the clubhouse for its golf course.

In preliminary discussions, state and federal officials indicated that they would not grant a permit for any dredging or filling on LHC's land. They explained that LHC's tidelands include the "most important salt water marsh area remaining in Folly Beach Sound." They also cited the presence of a rare 20–acre coastal woodlot on the uplands portion of LHC's land, which would be destroyed if LHC's development proceeds as planned. LHC believes its development would provide substantial economic benefits to the region without disrupting the local ecology. Consequently, the company has strongly objected to the suggestion that it might not qualify for a permit.

Federal and state authorities now propose a compromise. They will issue a permit allowing dredging and filling on thirty of the 125 acres that support hydrophytic plants if LHC agrees to transfer the twenty-five tideland acres to the state by quitclaim deed (the state claims it already holds title to these lands under the public trust doctrine), and to preserve both the ponding area and the coastal woodlot in their natural state.

As you read the following materials, try to determine what legal rights LHC has in this situation. Should the company accept the offered deal?

B.   SCOPE OF FEDERAL WETLANDS AUTHORITY

Excerpts From the Clean Water Act

33 U.S.C. §§ 1251–1387.

Sec. 404   Permits for dredged or fill material

(a) The Secretary [of the Army] may issue permits, after notice and opportunity for public hearings for the discharge of dredged or fill material into the navigable waters at specified disposal sites. * * *

(b) Subject to subsection (c) of this section, each such disposal site shall be specified for each such permit by the Secretary (1) through the application of guidelines developed by the Administrator [of the Environmental Protection Agency], in conjunction with the Secretary * * *, and (2) in any case where such guidelines under clause (1) alone would prohibit the specification of a site, through the application additionally of the economic impact of the site on navigation and anchorage.

(c) The Administrator is authorized to prohibit the specification (including the withdrawal of specification) of any defined area as a disposal site, and he is authorized to deny or restrict the use of any defined area for specification (including the withdrawal of specification) as a disposal site, whenever he determines, after notice and opportunity for public hearings, that the discharge of such materials into such area will have an unacceptable adverse effect on municipal water supplies, shellfish beds and fishery areas (including spawning and breeding areas), wildlife, or recreational areas.

* * *

(f)(1) Except as provided in paragraph (2) of this subsection, the discharge of dredged or fill material—

(A) from normal farming, silviculture, and ranching activities such as plowing, seeding, cultivating, minor drainage, harvesting for the production of food, fiber, and forest products, or upland soil and water conservation practices;

* * *

is not prohibited by or otherwise subject to regulation under this section * * *.

(2) Any discharge of dredged or fill material into the navigable waters incidental to any activity having as its purpose bringing an area of the navigable waters into a use to which it was not previously subject, where the flow or circulation of navigable waters may be impaired or the reach of such waters be reduced, shall be required to have a permit under this section.

* * *

Excerpts From Corps of Engineers Regulations

33 C.F.R. Part 328.

Sec. 328.3   Definitions

(a) The term *waters of the United States* means

(1) All waters which are currently used, or were used in the past, or may be susceptible to use in interstate or foreign commerce * * *;

(2) All interstate waters including interstate wetlands;

(3) All other waters such as * * * wetlands, sloughs, prairie potholes, wet meadows, playa lakes, or natural ponds, the use, degradation or destruction of which could affect interstate or foreign commerce * * *;

(4) All impoundments of waters otherwise defined as waters of the United States * * *;

(5) Tributaries of waters identified in paragraphs (a)(1) through (4) of this section;

(6) The territorial seas;

(7) Wetlands adjacent to waters (other than waters that are themselves wetlands) identified in paragraphs (a)(1) through (6) of this section.

(b) The term *wetlands* means those areas that are inundated or saturated by surface or ground water at a frequency and duration sufficient to support, and that under normal circumstances do support, a prevalence of vegetation typically adapted for life in saturated soil conditions. Wetlands generally include swamps, marshes, bogs, and similar areas.

(c) The term *adjacent* means bordering, contiguous, or neighboring. Wetlands separated from other waters of the United States by man-made dikes or barriers, natural river berms, beach dunes and the like are "adjacent wetlands."

1. "WATERS OF THE UNITED STATES"

The extent of the "waters of the United States" is discussed in detail in Chapter 11, Section 2A.

2. IDENTIFYING WETLANDS

The regulatory definition of wetlands as "areas that are inundated or saturated . . . at a frequency and duration sufficient to support . . . vegetation typically adapted for life in saturated soil conditions" leaves many details unresolved. In practice, wetland delineation is carried out by examination of the vegetation, soils, and hydrology of the area, under the guidance of a Wetlands Delineation Manual produced in 1987 by the Corps of Engineers, supplemented by a variety of national and regional guidance documents. The manual defines as diagnostic features of wetlands: vegetation in which more than half the dominant species of plants are obligate wetland species, species found primarily in wetlands, or species which grow equally well in both wetlands and uplands; soils which are classified as hydric or show reducing (anaerobic) conditions; and inundation or soil saturation for about one-eighth or more of the growing season.

In 1989 the Corps, together with the other three agencies with some responsibility for identifying wetlands under federal law (EPA, the Fish and Wildlife Service, and the Natural Resources Conservation Service), produced a Joint Manual intended to provide a unified standard for wetlands delineation. Critics charged that the Joint Manual would greatly expand federal wetlands jurisdiction, and Congress barred its use, or the use of any subsequent manual not produced through notice and comment rulemaking. *See* Energy and Water Development Appropriations Act of 1992, Pub. L. No. 102–104, 105 Stat. 510 (1991). As a result, all four agencies currently rely on the 1987 Corps of Engineers Manual.

3. REGULATED ACTIVITIES

Section 404 regulates only the discharge of dredged or fill material. It does not, by its terms, address the draining of wetlands. In Save Our Community v. EPA, 971 F.2d 1155 (5th Cir. 1992), the Fifth Circuit agreed with EPA and the Corps that section 404 does not prohibit the removal of water from wetlands by pumping. Most wetland draining, however, is accomplished by dredging drainage ditches, a process that generally produces at least "incidental fallback," that is the redeposit of small quantities of dirt disturbed by a shovel or backhoe to approximately the same location. Ditching may also be accompanied by "sidecasting," the piling of removed soil alongside the ditch. Deciding whether and to what extent incidental fallback and sidecasting are regulated by CWA § 404 has proven difficult and controversial.

Borden Ranch Partnership v. United States Army Corps of Engineers

United States Court of Appeals, Ninth Circuit, 2001.
261 F.3d 810.

■ MICHAEL DALY HAWKINS, CIRCUIT JUDGE:

This appeal concerns the authority of the U.S. Army Corps of Engineers ("the Corps") and the Environmental Protection Agency ("EPA") over a form of agricultural activity called "deep ripping" when it occurs in wetlands. We conclude that the Clean Water Act applies to this activity and affirm the district court's findings that Borden Ranch violated the Act by deep ripping in protected wetland swales. * * *

Facts and Procedural Background

In June of 1993, Angelo Tsakopoulos, a Sacramento real estate developer, purchased Borden Ranch, an 8400 acre ranch located in California's Central Valley. Prior to Tsakopoulos's purchase, the relevant areas of the ranch had been used primarily as rangeland for cattle grazing. The ranch contains significant hydrological features including vernal pools, swales, and intermittent drainages. Vernal pools are pools that form during the rainy season, but are often dry in the summer. Swales are sloped wetlands that allow for the movement of aquatic plant and animal life, and that filter water flows and minimize erosion. Intermittent drainages are streams that transport water during and after rains. All of these hydrological features depend upon a dense layer of soil, called a "restrictive layer" or "clay pan," which prevents surface water from penetrating deeply into the soil.

Tsakopoulos intended to convert the ranch into vineyards and orchards and subdivide it into smaller parcels for sale. Vineyards and orchards, however, require deep root systems, much deeper than the restrictive layer in the relevant portions of Borden Ranch permitted. For vineyards and orchards to grow on this land, the restrictive layer of soil would first need to be penetrated. This requires a procedure known as "deep ripping," in which four- to seven-foot long metal prongs are dragged through the soil behind a tractor or a bulldozer. The ripper gouges through the restrictive layer, disgorging soil that is then dragged behind the ripper.

Under the Clean Water Act, an individual seeking to fill protected wetlands must first obtain a permit from the Corps. Since 1993, Tsakopoulos and the Corps have disagreed about the Corps' authority to regulate deep ripping in wetlands. Tsakopoulos initiated deep ripping without a permit in the fall of 1993, and the Corps granted him a retrospective permit in the spring of 1994, when Tsakopoulos agreed to various mitigation requirements. In the fall of 1994, the Corps and the EPA informed Tsakopoulos that he could deep rip in uplands and that he could drive over swales with the deep ripper in its uppermost position, but that he could not conduct any deep ripping activity in vernal pools. The next spring, the Corps discovered that deep ripping had occurred in protected wetlands and promptly issued a cease and desist order. From July 1995 through November 1995, Tsakopoulos again initiated deep ripping on various parcels of land without a permit. The Corps concluded that more protected wetlands had been ripped and again issued a cease and desist order.

In May of 1996, the Corps and the EPA entered into an Administrative Order on Consent with Tsakopoulos that was intended to resolve his alleged Clean Water Act violations. Under the agreement, Tsakopoulos set aside a 1368-acre preserve and agreed to refrain from further violations.

* * *

In March of 1997 the Corps concluded that Tsakopoulos had continued to deep rip wetlands without permission. That April, EPA investigators visited the ranch and observed fully engaged deep rippers passing over jurisdictional wetlands. EPA then issued an Administrative Order to Tsakopoulos.

Tsakopoulos responded by filing this lawsuit, challenging the authority of the Corps and the EPA to regulate deep ripping. The United States filed a counterclaim seeking injunctive relief and civil penalties for Tsakopoulos's alleged violations of the Clean Water Act.

Both parties filed motions for summary judgment. The district court ruled that the Corps has jurisdiction over deep ripping in jurisdictional waters. However, the court found disputed facts with respect to whether such deep ripping had actually occurred. These facts were litigated in a bench trial that began on August 24, 1999, and concluded on September 16, 1999. The district court heard evidence from over twenty witnesses and received hundreds of documentary exhibits.

The district court subsequently entered findings of fact and conclusions of law determining that Tsakopoulos had repeatedly violated the Clean Water Act. The court found 348 separate deep ripping violations in

29 drainages, and 10 violations in a single vernal pool. The district court gave Tsakopoulos the option of paying a $1.5 million penalty or paying $500,000 and restoring four acres of wetlands. Tsakopoulos chose the latter option. * * *

The Clean Water Act prohibits "the discharge of any pollutant" into the nation's waters. 33 U.S.C. § 1311(a). The nation's waters have been interpreted to include wetlands adjacent to navigable waters. The Act defines discharge as "any addition of any pollutant to navigable waters from any point source." 33 U.S.C. § 1362(12). A point source is "any discernible, confined and discrete conveyance . . . from which pollutants are or may be discharged." 33 U.S.C. § 1362(14). A pollutant is defined, *inter alia,* as "dredged spoil, . . . biological materials, . . . rock, sand, [and] cellar dirt." 33 U.S.C. 1362(6). It is unlawful to discharge pollutants into wetlands without a permit from the Army Corps of Engineers. 33 U.S.C. § 1344(a), (d).

Tsakopoulos initially contends that deep ripping cannot constitute the "addition" of a "pollutant" into wetlands, because it simply churns up soil that is already there, placing it back basically where it came from. This argument is inconsistent with Ninth Circuit precedent and with case law from other circuits that squarely hold that redeposits of materials can constitute an "addition of a pollutant" under the Clean Water Act. Rybachek v. United States Envtl. Prot. Agency, 904 F.2d 1276 (9th Cir. 1990), considered a claim that placer mining activities were exempt from the Act. We held that removing material from a stream bed, sifting out the gold, and returning the material to the stream bed was an "addition" of a "pollutant." *Id.* at 1285. The term "pollutant" encompassed "the materials segregated from gold in placer mining." *Id.*

Our reasoning in *Rybachek* is similar to that of the Fourth Circuit in United States v. Deaton, 209 F.3d 331 (4th Cir. 2000). In *Deaton,* a property owner alleged that the Corps could not regulate "sidecasting," which is "the deposit of dredged or excavated material from a wetland back into that same wetland." *Id.* at 334. The property owner asserted that "sidecasting results in no net increase in the amount of material present in the wetland" and therefore could not constitute the "addition of a pollutant." *Id.* at 335. The Fourth Circuit squarely rejected this argument, in language that is worth quoting in full:

> Contrary to what the Deatons suggest, the statute does not prohibit the addition of material; it prohibits the "addition of any pollutant." The idea that there could be an addition of a pollutant without an addition of material seems to us entirely unremarkable, at least when an activity transforms some material from a nonpollutant into a pollutant, as occurred here. . . . Once [earth and vegetable matter] was removed [from the wetland], that material became "dredged spoil," a statutory pollutant and a *type* of material that up until then was not present on the Deaton property. It is of no consequence that what is now dredged spoil was previously present on the same property in the less threatening form of dirt and vegetation in an undisturbed state.

What is important is that once that material was excavated from the wetland, its redeposit in that same wetland *added* a pollutant where none had been before.

Id. at 335–36. As the court concluded, "Congress determined that plain dirt, once excavated from waters of the United States, could not be redeposited into those waters without causing harm to the environment." *Id.* at 336.

These cases recognize that activities that destroy the ecology of a wetland are not immune from the Clean Water Act merely because they do not involve the introduction of material brought in from somewhere else. In this case, the Corps alleges that Tsakopoulos has essentially poked a hole in the bottom of protected wetlands. That is, by ripping up the bottom layer of soil, the water that was trapped can now drain out. While it is true, that in so doing, no new material has been "added," a "pollutant" has certainly been "added." Prior to the deep ripping, the protective layer of soil was intact, holding the wetland in place. Afterwards, that soil was wrenched up, moved around, and redeposited somewhere else. We can see no meaningful distinction between this activity and the activities at issue in *Rybachek* and *Deaton*. We therefore conclude that deep ripping, when undertaken in the context at issue here, can constitute a discharge of a pollutant under the Clean Water Act.[2]

* * *

Tsakopoulos next contends, that even if deep ripping constitutes a discharge of pollutants, it is nonetheless exempt from regulation under the "farming exceptions," which state that discharges "from normal farming . . . and ranching activities, such as plowing" are not subject to the Clean Water Act. 33 U.S.C. § 1344(f)(1)(A). The section of the statute containing the farming exceptions, however, includes a significant qualifying provision:

> Any discharge of dredged or fill material into the navigable waters incidental to any activity having as its purpose bringing an area of the navigable waters into a use to which it was not previously subject, where the flow or circulation of navigable waters may be impaired or the reach of such waters be reduced, shall be required to have a permit under this section.

33 U.S.C. § 1344(f)(2). Thus, even normal plowing can be regulated under the Clean Water Act if it falls under this so-called "recapture" provision.

We conclude that the deep ripping at issue in this case is governed by the recapture provision. Converting ranch land to orchards and vineyards is clearly bringing the land "into a use to which it was not previously subject," and there is a clear basis in this record to conclude that the

---

2. National Mining Assoc. v. U.S. Army Corps of Eng'rs, 145 F.3d 1399 (D.C. Cir. 1998), upon which Tsakopoulos heavily relies, does not persuade us to the contrary. That case distinguished "regulable redeposits" from "incidental fallback." Here, the deep ripping does not involve mere incidental fallback, but constitutes environmental damage sufficient to constitute a regulable redeposit.

destruction of the soil layer at issue here constitutes an impairment of the flow of nearby navigable waters.

Although the Corps cannot regulate a farmer who desires "merely to change from one wetland crop to another," activities that require "substantial hydrological alterations" require a permit. As we have explained, "the intent of Congress in enacting the Act was to prevent conversion of wetlands to dry lands," and we have classified "as non-exempt those activities which change a wetland's hydrological regime." United States v. Akers, 785 F.2d 814, 822 (9th Cir. 1986). In this case, Tsakopoulos's activities were not intended simply to substitute one wetland crop for another; rather they radically altered the hydrological regime of the protected wetlands. Accordingly, it was entirely proper for the Corps and the EPA to exercise jurisdiction over Tsakopoulos's activities.

* * *

■ GOULD, CIRCUIT JUDGE, dissenting:

I respectfully dissent. The crux of this case is that a farmer[1] has plowed deeply to improve his farm property to permit farming of fruit crops that require deep root systems, and are more profitable than grazing or other prior farm use. Farmers have been altering and transforming their crop land from the beginning of our nation, and indeed in colonial times. Although I have no doubt that Congress could have reached and regulated the farming activity challenged, that does not in itself show that Congress so exercised its power. I conclude that the Clean Water Act does not prohibit "deep ripping" in this setting.

I would follow and extend National Mining Association v. U.S. Army Corps of Engineers, 145 F.3d 1399 (D.C. Cir. 1998), and hold that the return of soil in place after deep plowing is not a "discharge of a pollutant." In *National Mining*, the court held that the Corps exceeded its authority under section 404 of the Clean Water Act by regulating the redeposit of dredged materials that incidentally fall back in the course of dredging operations. The court explained that "the straightforward statutory term 'addition' cannot reasonably be said to encompass the situation in which material is removed from the waters of the United States and a small portion of it happens to fall back." *Id.* at 1404. The court rejected the agencies' primary argument that incidental fallback constitutes an "addition" because once dredged the material becomes a pollutant:

---

1. Appellant, Angelo Tsakopoulos, is referred to by the majority as a "real estate developer." As the owner of Borden Ranch, which apparently engaged in both farming and ranching activities, it seems to me correct to refer to him as a farmer or a rancher, in addition to being a developer. Whether viewed as a farmer, rancher, or developer, his rights as a citizen are the same. Because the challenged activities in this case arise on land previously used for rangeland for cattle grazing, and his deep ripping was converting the land for orchard and vineyard farming, I consider him as a farmer and rancher, and the issues raised by his position in this litigation may impact farmers and ranchers regardless of whether they plan to sell portions of improved land.

Regardless of any legal metamorphosis that may occur at the moment of dredging, we fail to see how there can be an addition of dredged material when there is no addition of material. Although the Act includes "dredged spoil" in its list of pollutants, Congress could not have contemplated that the attempted removal of 100 tons of that substance could constitute an addition simply because only 99 tons of it were actually taken away.

Id. at 1404 (emphasis omitted).

Those considerations are persuasive here as deep ripping does not involve any significant removal or "addition" of material to the site. The ground is plowed and transformed. It is true that the hydrological regime is modified, but Congress spoke in terms of discharge or addition of pollutants, not in terms of change of the hydrological nature of the soil. If Congress intends to prohibit so natural a farm activity as plowing, and even the deep plowing that occurred here, Congress can and should be explicit. Although we interpret the prohibitions of the Clean Water Act to effectuate Congressional intent, it is an undue stretch for us, absent a more clear directive from Congress, to reach and prohibit the plowing done here, which seems to be a traditional form of farming activity.

Rybachek v. United States Environmental Protection Agency, 904 F.2d 1276 (9th Cir. 1990), in my view, is distinguishable. In *Rybachek,* we held that placer mining, "a process in which miners excavate dirt and gravel in and around waterways and, after extracting the gold, discharge the leftover material back into the water," fell within the scope of section 404 of the Clean Water Act. *Id.* at 1285. There, the *Rybachek* court identified the regulable discharge as the discrete act of dumping *leftover* material into the stream after it had been processed. * * * Because deep ripping does not move any material to a substantially different geographic location and does not process such material for any period of time, *Rybachek* is not controlling.

* * *

I would hold that the district court erred in finding that the activities here required a permit and otherwise violated the Clean Water Act. The problem of interpretation here arises because Congress prohibited the discharge or addition of any pollutant to navigable waters from any point source. It did not literally prohibit any conduct by farmers or ranchers that changes the hydrological character of their land. The majority opinion, motivated perhaps by the purposes of the statute, makes new law by concluding that a plow is a point source and that deep ripping includes discharge of pollutants into protected waters. The policy decision involved here should be made by Congress, which has the ability to study and the power to make such fine distinctions. * * *

NOTES AND QUESTIONS

1. *The Supreme Court anticlimax.* The Supreme Court granted certiorari in *Borden Ranch*, but in the end did not review the merits of the case. With

Justice Kennedy recused because of connections to the Tsakopoulos family, an evenly divided Court affirmed without opinion. 537 U.S. 99 (2002).

2.   *Incidental fallback versus regulated redeposit.* The Corps and EPA have long maintained that "sidecasting" is regulated under § 404, but have waffled on "incidental fallback." Regulations adopted in 1977 covered "any addition of dredged material into the waters of the United States." 42 Fed. Reg. 37,145 (July 19, 1977). In 1986, however, new regulations exempted "*de minimis*, incidental soil movement during normal dredging operations." 51 Fed. Reg. 41,232 (Nov. 13, 1986). In 1993, prompted by a lawsuit over development of more than 700 acres of wetlands using sophisticated techniques, such as welding shut openings in backhoe buckets, to minimize fallback, the agencies reversed course again, defining the "discharge of dredged material" to include "any addition of dredged material into, including any redeposit of dredged material within, the waters of the United States" 58 Fed. Reg. 45,008, 45,035 (Aug. 25, 1993). In the preamble to the 1993 rule, known as the Tulloch Rule after the litigation that inspired it, the agencies explained that "it is virtually impossible to conduct mechanized landclearing, ditching, channelization, or excavation in waters of the United States without causing incidental redeposition of dredged material (however small or temporary) in the process." 58 Fed. Reg. 45,017. The Tulloch Rule did exempt activities that would not destroy or degrade the waters of the United States, but placed the burden of proof on that issue on the person engaged in the activity.

The D.C. Circuit invalidated the Tulloch Rule in National Mining Association v. U.S. Army Corps of Engineers, 145 F.3d 1399 (D.C. Cir. 1998). The court explained:

> We agree with the plaintiffs, and with the district court, that the straightforward statutory term "addition" cannot reasonably be said to encompass the situation in which material is removed from the waters of the United States and a small portion of it happens to fall back. Because incidental fallback represents a net withdrawal, not an addition, of material, it cannot be a discharge. * * * The agencies' primary counterargument—that fallback constitutes an "addition of any pollutant" because material becomes a pollutant only upon being dredged—is ingenious but unconvincing. Regardless of any legal metamorphosis that may occur at the moment of dredging, we fail to see how there can be an addition of dredged material when there is no addition of material. Although the Act includes "dredged spoil" in its list of pollutants, 33 U.S.C. § 1362(6), Congress could not have contemplated that the attempted removal of 100 tons of that substance could constitute an addition simply because only 99 tons of it were actually taken away. * * *

> [The National Wildlife Federation] complains that our understanding of "addition" reads the regulation of dredged material out of the statute. They correctly note that since dredged material comes from the waters of the United States, any discharge of such material into those waters could technically be described as a "redeposit," at least on

a broad construction of that term. * * * But we do not hold that the Corps may not legally regulate some forms of redeposit under its § 404 permitting authority. We hold only that by asserting jurisdiction over "any redeposit," including incidental fallback, the Tulloch Rule outruns the Corps's statutory authority. Since the Act sets out no bright line between incidental fallback on the one hand and regulable redeposits on the other, a reasoned attempt by the agencies to draw such a line would merit considerable deference. But the Tulloch Rule makes no effort to draw such a line, and indeed its overriding purpose appears to be to expand the Corps's permitting authority to encompass incidental fallback and, as a result, a wide range of activities that cannot remotely be said to "add" anything to the waters of the United States.

Id. at 1404–05.

Three days before the inauguration of George W. Bush, the Corps and EPA issued a new regulation responding to *National Mining Association*. The new regulation provides:

> The Corps and EPA regard the use of mechanized earth-moving equipment to conduct landclearing, ditching, channelization, in-stream mining or other earth-moving activity in waters of the United States as resulting in a discharge of dredged material unless project-specific evidence shows that the activity results in only incidental fallback. This paragraph does not and is not intended to shift any burden in any administrative or judicial proceeding under the CWA.
>
> *Incidental fallback* is the redeposit of small volumes of dredged material that is incidental to excavation activity in waters of the United States when such material falls back to substantially the same place as the initial removal. Examples of incidental fallback include soil that is disturbed when dirt is shoveled and the back-spill that comes off a bucket when such small volume of soil or dirt falls into substantially the same place from which it was initially removed.

66 Fed. Reg. 4550, 4575 (Jan. 17, 2001). Is the new regulation valid? In 2007, a district court held that it is not. National Association of Home Builders v. U.S. Army Corps of Engineers, 2007 WL 259944 (D. D.C. 2007) (unpublished decision).

Did the D.C. Circuit correctly interpret the Clean Water Act in *National Mining Association*? If dredging stirs up the mud, making materials that once were bound up in the soil biologically available, why isn't that the "addition" of dredged material to the waters of the United States? On the other hand, do you agree that the agencies can regulate sidecasting? Is the movement of soil a small distance within a wetland the addition of dredged material?

Is *Borden Ranch* consistent with the D.C. Circuit decision in *National Mining Association*? Would Tsakopoulos' activities constitute "incidental fallback" under the Corps' 2001 regulations? Did Congress intend to regulate the types of activities that produce fallback when it enacted section 404? If so, why didn't it explicitly require a permit for dredging or draining as well as filling? Might legislators have assumed, as the regulatory agencies now assert, that such activities almost always add dredged material to the waters? Or did Congress intend only to regulate wetlands alteration to the extent it threatens water quality and assume that draining did not pose such a threat? What can (and should) regulatory agencies do when technological advances create what seem to be "loopholes" in the law?

3. *The "normal farming" exception.* Section 404 excepts from its permit requirement discharges resulting from "normal farming, silviculture, and ranching activities, such as plowing...." Why do you think Congress included this exception? Why did it not apply in *Borden Ranch*? Is it relevant that, according to the court, Tsakopoulos intended not only to convert his ranch to vineyards but to subdivide it into smaller parcels? Does a change in crops constitute a new use, depriving the farmer of the normal farming exception? Does changing the hydrology of the site constitute a change in use?

C.   Wetlands Permit Decisions

The Army Corps of Engineers and EPA share responsibility for implementing the § 404 program. The Corps bears the primary responsibility for evaluating permit applications. It must ensure that the action permitted complies with regulatory Guidelines (excerpted below) developed primarily by EPA, in consultation with the Corps. Even if the application meets the requirements of the Guidelines, the Corps may still deny a permit if, following consideration of a wide range of factors, it concludes that the proposed activity would be contrary to the public interest. 33 C.F.R. § 320.4(a)(1).

Although receipt of a Corps permit is necessary for a regulated project to proceed, it is not sufficient to ensure that the project can go ahead. EPA may veto any Corps-issued permit that would cause "an unacceptable adverse effect" on water supplies, fisheries, wildlife, or recreation. 33 U.S.C. § 1344(c).

Excerpts From Environmental Protection Agency Regulations

40 C.F.R. Part 230.

Sec. 230.10   Restrictions on Discharge

(a) Except as provided under section 404(b)(2), no discharge of dredged or fill material shall be permitted if there is a practicable alternative to the proposed discharge which would have less adverse impact on the aquatic ecosystem, so long as the alternative does not have other significant adverse environmental consequences.

(1) For the purpose of this requirement, practicable alternatives include, but are not limited to:

(i) Activities which do not involve a discharge of dredged or fill material into the waters of the United States or ocean waters;

(ii) Discharges of dredged or fill material at other locations in waters of the United States or ocean waters;

(2) An alternative is practicable if it is available and capable of being done after taking into consideration cost, existing technology, and logistics in light of overall project purposes. If it is otherwise a practicable alternative, an area not presently owned by the applicant which could reasonably be obtained, utilized, expanded or managed in order to fulfill the basic purpose of the proposed activity may be considered.

(3) Where the activity associated with a discharge which is proposed for a special aquatic site* does not require access or proximity to or siting within the special aquatic site in question to fulfill its basic purpose (i.e., is not "water dependent"), practicable alternatives that do not involve special aquatic sites are presumed to be available, unless clearly demonstrated otherwise. In addition, where a discharge is proposed for a special aquatic site, all practicable alternatives to the proposed discharge which do not involve a discharge into a special aquatic site are presumed to have less adverse impact on the aquatic ecosystem, unless clearly demonstrated otherwise.

* * *

(c) Except as provided under section 404(b)(2), no discharge of dredged or fill material shall be permitted which will cause or contribute to significant degradation of the waters of the United States. * * *

(d) Except as provided under section 404(b)(2), no discharge of dredged or fill material shall be permitted unless appropriate and practicable steps have been taken which will minimize potential adverse impacts of the discharge on the aquatic ecosystem.

National Wildlife Federation v. Whistler

United States Court of Appeals, Eighth Circuit, 1994.
27 F.3d 1341.

■ JOHN R. GIBSON, SENIOR CIRCUIT JUDGE.

The Turnbow Development Corporation sought permission from the United States Army Corps of Engineers to make several changes necessary to provide water access to a planned residential development. The Corps issued the permit * * *. The National Wildlife Federation and Michael Donahue, a Federation member and an owner of property adjacent to the mitigation area, brought this action before the district court seeking to suspend the permit. The district court denied the requested relief and

---

* [Wetlands are among the areas considered "special aquatic sites." *See* 40 C.F.R. §§ 230.3(q–1); 230.41.—Eds.]

granted summary judgment for the defendants. Donahue appeals from the district court's judgment. We affirm.

The planned housing development is located just south of Bismarck, North Dakota, on uplands on the east side of the Missouri River. The requested permit would allow Turnbow to provide these lots with boat access to the Missouri River by re-opening an old river channel adjacent to the planned development, thereby destroying the channel's existing wetlands status. * * * In total, approximately 14.5 acres of wetlands would be converted to deep water habitat.

As required by 33 C.F.R. § 325.2–.3, the Corps gave public notice of the application and solicited comments from several state and federal agencies. These agencies suggested that the Corps condition the permit on a mitigation plan to offset the loss of wetlands, but lodged no further objections. Turnbow responded with a plan to enhance an existing twenty-acre wetlands area by providing it with year-round water and saturated soil conditions. After additional public notice and comment, the Corps issued an environmental assessment and decision document containing the agency's determination that the permit should be issued. The Corps concluded that the project's purpose was to provide boat access to the Missouri River from Turnbow's planned development. Given this purpose, the Corps considered the project water-dependent and site-specific. No other alternative, the Corps stated, would serve Turnbow's purpose. "A boat access area located elsewhere," the agency reasoned, "would not be functional for the applicant's needs." The Corps concluded that the permit did not conflict with the public interest and satisfied the Clean Water Act section 404(b)(1) guidelines. * * * The agency issued the permit subject to forty-two conditions, including the requirement that Turnbow complete the enhancements to the mitigation area prior to any construction on the wetlands.

Donahue and the Federation sought a temporary restraining order and preliminary injunction to suspend the permit. The court denied the request for a temporary order and, after a two-day evidentiary hearing on the preliminary injunction issue, granted the Corps' motion for summary judgment. * * *

Donahue argues on appeal that the Corps failed to perform an adequate alternatives analysis, as required by 40 C.F.R. § 230.10, before issuing the permit. In particular, Donahue argues that the Corps completely failed to consider the feasibility of a nearby public boat ramp as a means of water access to residents. * * *

* * * "It would hardly be putting the case too strongly to say that the Clean Water Act and the applicable regulations do not contemplate that wetlands will be destroyed simply because it is more convenient than not to do so." Buttrey v. United States, 690 F.2d 1170, 1180 (5th Cir. 1982). Thus, where "there is a *practicable alternative* . . . which would have less adverse impact on the aquatic ecosystem," the Corps cannot issue a dredge or fill permit. 40 C.F.R. § 230.10(a) (1993) (emphasis added). Moreover, if a dredge or fill permit application does not concern a water-dependent project, the Corps assumes that practicable alternatives exist unless the

applicant "clearly demonstrated otherwise." 40 C.F.R. § 230.10(a)(3). This presumption of practicable alternatives "is *very* strong," *Buttrey,* 690 F.2d at 1180 (emphasis in original), "creat[ing] an incentive for developers to avoid choosing wetlands when they could choose an alternative upland site," *Bersani v. Robichaud,* 850 F.2d 36, 44 (2d Cir. 1988).

Despite these protections, Donahue faces an uphill road. When the Corps has followed the proper procedure, as here, a court may reverse only if the Corps' decision to issue the permit was an abuse of discretion, contrary to law, or arbitrary and capricious. 5 U.S.C. § 706(2)(A) (1988). * * *

Donahue argues that the Corps failed to even consider the availability of a local public boat ramp as an adequate alternative to Turnbow's proposal. The Corps explicitly acknowledged the existence of the boat ramp in its decision document, concluding that this access area was not "functional for the applicant's needs." In light of the Corps' determination of the project's purpose, the boat dock was, at best, an alternative. Our review of the record convinces us that the Corps considered the boat dock, but dismissed it as inadequate.

Donahue also argues that to the extent that the Corps did conduct an alternatives analysis, it reached an arbitrary and capricious result. Central to evaluating practicable alternatives is the determination of a project's purpose. Donahue suggests that the project's purpose is to build a residential or "high-end" residential development. Donahue relies on decisions by other courts that have rejected attempts by developers to build housing developments and adjacent boat docks on wetlands. In Shoreline Associates v. Marsh, 555 F. Supp. 169 (D. Md. 1983), for example, the court rejected one such attempt, stating that the "primary aspect of the proposed project is the construction of a townhouse community, not the construction of a boat storage facility and launch, which are incidental to it." *Id.* at 179. Similarly, in Korteweg v. Corps of Engineers of the United States Army, 650 F. Supp. 603, 606 (D. Conn. 1986), the court also upheld the denial of a permit for a riverside residential development. Although "the ability to tie one's boat at an adjacent dock would make the [lots] more valuable . . ., the docks are neither essential to the [lots] nor are they integral to their residential use." *Id.* at 605. Thus, each of these courts concluded that the housing project was not water-dependent and applied the regulatory presumption that practicable alternatives exist.

The Corps, however, began its analysis of Turnbow's application by stating that the planned housing development site was located on uplands and therefore could proceed without a permit. The Corps limited its alternatives analysis to the boat access area. This exclusion of the residential portion of the project led the Corps to conclude that the "project's purpose is to provide boat access to the Missouri River from lots Mr. Turnbow proposes to develop adjacent to the project area." The Corps did not consider the uplands housing development to be part of the project for which Turnbow requested a permit. The project, so defined, is clearly water-dependent. Moreover, insofar as the project contemplated immediate boat access to Turnbow's residential development, it was also site-specific. Turnbow's locating of the planned residential buildings on the surrounding uplands distinguishes this case from both *Shoreline* and *Korteweg,* where the developers sought to build their planned residential buildings on the wetlands. In those cases, the developers could have presumably relocated the entire developments to other locations. Here, the Corps found that Turnbow's development would proceed on the uplands residences even if the Corps denied the permit.

* * *

* * * "Obviously, an applicant cannot define a project in order to preclude the existence of any alternative sites and thus make what is practicable appear impracticable." *Sylvester II,* 882 F.2d at 409. The cumulative destruction of our nation's wetlands that would result if developers were permitted to artificially constrain the Corps' alternatives analysis by defining the projects' purpose in an overly narrow manner would frustrate the statute and its accompanying regulatory scheme. We do not believe the case before us raises these concerns. Moreover, our standard of review is a limited one. We conclude that neither the Corps' project definition nor its decision that no practicable alternatives existed was arbitrary and capricious. * * *

Bersani v. Robichaud

United States Court of Appeals, Second Circuit, 1988.
850 F.2d 36.

■ TIMBERS, CIRCUIT JUDGE.

Appellants John A. Bersani, the Pyramid Companies, Newport Galleria Group and Robert J. Congel ("Pyramid", collectively) appeal from a judgment * * * granting summary judgment in favor of appellees, the United States Environmental Protection Agency ("EPA"), [and] the United States Army Corps of Engineers (the "Corps") * * *.

I.

* * * Sweedens Swamp is a 49.5 acre wetland which is part of an 80 acre site near Interstate 95 in South Attleboro, Massachusetts. Although some illegal dumping and motorbike intrusions have occurred, these activities have been found to have had little impact on the site which remains a "high-quality red maple swamp" providing wildlife habitat and protecting the area from flooding and pollution.

The effort to build a mall on Sweedens Swamp was initiated by Pyramid's predecessor, the Edward J. DeBartolo Corporation ("DeBartolo"). DeBartolo purchased the Swamp some time before April 1982. At the time of this purchase an alternative site was available in North Attleboro (the "North Attleboro site"). * * *

Pyramid took over the project in 1983 * * *.

One of the key issues in dispute in the instant case is just when did Pyramid begin searching for a suitable site for its mall. EPA asserts that Pyramid began to search in the Spring of 1983. Pyramid asserts that it began to search several months later, in September 1983. The difference is crucial because on July 1, 1983—a date between the starting dates claimed by EPA and Pyramid—a competitor of Pyramid, the New England Development Co. ("NED"), purchased options to buy the North Attleboro site. This site was located upland and could have served as a "practicable alternative" to Sweedens Swamp, *if* it had been "available" at the relevant time. * * *

In December 1983, Pyramid purchased Sweedens Swamp from DeBartolo. In August 1984, Pyramid applied under § 404(a) to the New England regional division of the Corps (the "NE Corps") for a permit. It sought to fill or alter 32 of the 49.6 acres of the Swamp; to excavate nine acres of uplands to create artificial wetlands; and to alter 13.3 acres of existing wetlands to improve its environmental quality. Later Pyramid proposed to mitigate the adverse impact on the wetlands by creating 36 acres of replacement wetlands in an off-site gravel pit.

* * *

In January 1985, the NE Corps hired a consultant to investigate the feasibility of Sweedens Swamp and the North Attleboro site. The consultant reported that either site was feasible but that from a commercial standpoint only one mall could survive in the area. On February 19, 1985, the NE Corps advised Pyramid that denial of its permit was imminent. On May 2, 1985, the NE Corps sent its recommendation to deny the permit to the national headquarters of the Corps. Although the NE Corps ordinarily makes the final decision on whether to grant a permit, in the instant case, because of widespread publicity, General John F. Wall, the Director of Civil Works at the national headquarters of the Corps, decided to review the NE Corps' decision. Wall reached a different conclusion. He decided to grant the permit after finding that Pyramid's offsite mitigation proposal would reduce the adverse impacts sufficiently to allow the "practicable alternative" test to be deemed satisfied. * * *

Although he did not explicitly address the issue, Wall apparently assumed that the relevant time to determine whether there was a practicable alternative was the time of the application, not the time the applicant entered the market. In other words, Wall appears to have assumed that the market entry theory was not the correct approach. For example, while addressing the traditional "practicable alternatives" analysis as an alternative ground for his decision, Wall found that the North Attleboro site was unavailable "because it has been optioned by another developer." Since the site was not optioned at the time EPA argues Pyramid entered the market, this language suggests (to Pyramid at least) that Wall could not have been employing the market entry approach.

On May 31, 1985, Wall ordered the NE Corps to send Pyramid, EPA and FWS a notice of its intent to grant the permit. The NE Corps complied on June 28, 1985.

[Following notice and two public hearings, EPA vetoed the Corps' decision.] It found (1) that the filling of the Swamp would adversely affect wildlife; (2) that the North Attleboro site could have been available to Pyramid at the time Pyramid investigated the area to search for a site; (3) that considering Pyramid's failure or unwillingness to provide further materials about its investigation of alternative sites, it was uncontested that, at best, Pyramid never checked the availability of the North Attleboro site as an alternative; (4) that the North Attleboro site was feasible and would have a less adverse impact on the wetland environment; and (5) that the mitigation proposal did not make the project preferable to other alternatives because of scientific uncertainty of success. In the second of these findings, EPA used what Pyramid calls the "market entry" approach.

* * *

II.

One of Pyramid's principal contentions is that the market entry approach is inconsistent with [the 404(b)(1) guidelines].

* * * Pyramid reasons that the 404(b)(1) guidelines are framed in the present tense, while the market entry approach focuses on the *past* by considering whether a practicable alternative *was* available at the time the applicant entered the market to search for a site. To support its argument that the 404(b)(1) guidelines are framed in the present tense, Pyramid quotes the following language:

"An alternative is practicable if it *is* available.... If it is otherwise a practicable alternative, an area not *presently* owned by the applicant which *could* reasonably *be* obtained, utilized, expanded or managed in order to fulfill the basic purpose of the proposed activity *may be* considered."

40 C.F.R. § 230.10(a)(2). It then argues that EPA says "is" means "was." * * *

While this argument has a certain surface appeal, we are persuaded that it is contrary to a common sense reading of the regulations; that it entails an overly literal and narrow interpretation of the language; and that it creates requirements not intended by Congress.

First, while it is true that the language is in the present tense, it does not follow that the most natural reading of the regulations would create a time-of-application rule. As EPA points out, "the regulations do not indicate *when* it is to be determined whether an alternative 'is' available," i.e., the "present" of the regulations might be the time the application is submitted; the time it is reviewed; or any number of other times. Based upon a reading of the language in the context of the controlling statute and the regulations as a whole, moreover, we conclude that when the agencies drafted the language in question they simply were not thinking of the specific issues raised by the instant case, in which an applicant had available alternatives at the time it was selecting its site but these alternatives had evaporated by the time it applied for a permit. We therefore agree with the district court that the regulations are essentially silent on the issue of timing and that it would be appropriate to consider the objectives of the Act and the intent underlying the promulgation of the regulations.

Second, as EPA has pointed out, the preamble to the 404(b)(1) guidelines states that the purpose of the "practicable alternatives" analysis is to * * * create an incentive for developers to avoid choosing wetlands when they could choose an alternative upland site. Pyramid's reading of the regulations would thwart this purpose because it would remove the incentive for a developer to search for an alternative site at the time such an incentive is needed, i.e., at the time it is making the decision to select a particular site. If the practicable alternatives analysis were applied to the time of the application for a permit, the developer would have little incentive to search for alternatives, especially if it were confident that alternatives soon would disappear. Conversely, in a case in which alternatives were not available at the time the developer made its selection, but became available by the time of application, the developer's application would be denied even though it could not have explored the alternative site at the time of its decision.

* * *

IV.

[Pyramid argues that the market entry theory is too vague to provide adequate notice to the regulated community, because] any number of points in time could constitute "entry" into the market. It speculates whether market entry occurs "from the time the first internal memorandum is written," or the time "the first consultant [is] hired," or the time the "first negotiation for a site [is] conducted." We are persuaded, however, that EPA is correct in asserting that it is unnecessary to pin down the standard to such a degree and that it would confuse things further to attempt to do so. Since the point of "entry" necessarily will vary from case to case, we believe the concept of "market entry" is the best method and is specific enough to put a developer on notice of when it should be considering alternative sites.

* * *

[W]e believe the extensive administrative record supports a finding that the North Attleboro site was available to Pyramid when it entered the market. Even if Pyramid were found not to have entered the market until September 1983, after NED had acquired options to purchase the North Attleboro site, it does not necessarily follow that the site was unavailable. Aside from the fact that NED did not acquire all the options for the North Attleboro site until June 1984, it also was possible for Pyramid to attempt to purchase the options from NED. The record shows no such attempts to purchase the site, or even to investigate its availability. Alternatively, even though the district court apparently was not persuaded by it, there also is evidence in the record to show that Pyramid actually entered the market in the Spring of 1983, before NED had purchased its options. Finally, the evidence shows that the North Attleboro site had been available to DeBartolo, Pyramid's predecessor. EPA could reasonably have determined that Pyramid should be held to "stand in the shoes" of DeBartolo * * *.

■ George C. Pratt, Circuit Judge, dissenting.

* * * In this case I have no problem with EPA's basic approach. It conscientiously attempted to weigh the economic advantages against the ecological disadvantages of developing Sweedens Swamp and, in approaching this determination, it properly looked to alternate available sites. However, EPA went wrong—seriously wrong—when it adopted the market entry theory to decide whether an alternate site was available. By focusing on the decisionmaking techniques and tactics of a particular developer, instead of the actual alternatives to disturbing the wetland, EPA ignored the statute's central purpose.

The market entry theory in effect taints a particular developer with respect to a particular site, while ignoring the crucial question of whether the site itself should be preserved. Under the market entry theory, developer A would be denied a permit on a specific site because when he entered the market alternatives were available, but latecomer developer B, who entered the market after those alternatives had become unavailable, would be entitled to a permit for developing the same site. In such a case, the theory no longer protects the land, but instead becomes a distorted punitive device: it punishes developer A by denying him a permit, but grants developer B a permit for the same property—and the only difference between them is when they "entered the market."

* * *

Furthermore, in a business that needs as much predictability as possible, the market entry theory will regrettably inject exquisite vagueness. When does a developer enter the market? When he first contemplates a development in the area? If so, in what area—the neighborhood, the village, the town, the state or the region? Does he enter the market when he first takes some affirmative action? If so, is that when he instructs his staff to research possible sites, when he commits money for more intensive study of those sites, when he contacts a real estate broker, when he first visits a site, or when he makes his first offer to purchase? Without answers to these questions a developer can never know whether to proceed through the expense of contracts, zoning proceedings, and EPA applications. * * *

Since congress delegated to EPA the responsibility for striking a difficult and sensitive balance among economic and ecological concerns, EPA should do so only after considering the circumstances which exist, not when the developer first conceived of his idea, nor when he entered the market, nor even when he submitted his application; rather, EPA, like a court of equity, should have the full benefit of, and should be required to consider, the circumstances which exist at the time it makes its decision. This is the only method which would allow EPA to make a fully informed decision—as congress intended—based on whether, at the moment, there is available a site which can provide needed economic and social benefits to the public, without unnecessarily disturbing valuable wetlands.

NOTES AND QUESTIONS

1. *Practicable alternatives analysis.* The § 404 guidelines prohibit the issuance of a permit to fill wetlands unless there is no practicable alternative that would have less adverse impact. The Corps adjusts the stringency of the practicable alternatives test based on the expected impact of the proposed project. Regulatory Guidance Letter 93–02.

What is the purpose of the practicable alternatives test? What constitutes a practicable alternative? Does it depend on the resources of the individual developer seeking a permit? *See* Regulatory Guidance Letter 93–02 ("[T]he nature of the applicant may also be a relevant consideration in determining what constitutes a practicable alternative. It is important to emphasize, however, that it is not a particular applicant's financial standing that is the primary consideration for determining practicability, but rather characteristics of the project and what constitutes a reasonable expense for these projects that are most relevant to practicability determinations.").

Does it depend on who owns land that might offer a practicable alternative? Consider a hypothetical. Suppose Mall Development, Inc. proposes to build a mall on Dismal Swamp, a wetland. Five miles away, Supermalls Co. owns Dry Meadow, a site that contains no wetlands. Both companies acknowledge that Dry Meadow is suitable for a mall. Indeed, Supermalls has begun the preliminary process of planning one. Mall Development offers to purchase Dry Meadow, but Supermalls refuses to sell at the price offered. Shortly thereafter, Mall Development applies for a section 404 permit to fill Dismal Swamp in order to construct a mall. Is Dry Meadow a practicable alternative? Does it matter whether the area can support more than one mall?

2. *Timing.* At what point in time is the alternatives analysis conducted? The Corps has never endorsed the market entry approach, and continues to evaluate the existence of practicable alternatives as of the time the permit application is processed. Which is the better approach? What impact would the "market entry" approach have on developers' future choices of sites for non-water-dependent activities? Would it allow a subsequent developer to obtain a permit to develop Sweedens Swamp after Bersani had been denied a permit? If so, is that appropriate or not?

3. *Project purposes and the § 404 guidelines.* Identification of the purposes of the proposed project affects evaluation under the guidelines in two ways. First, if the project is not water-dependent, the Corps must presume that less damaging alternatives are available. Second, the project purpose strongly affects the identification of alternatives.

Was the project in *Whistler* water-dependent? How did the court distinguish other decisions holding that water-oriented housing developments were not water-dependent? Is some or all of the project proposed by Lovely Harbor Company in the Class Discussion Problem water-dependent? What alternatives must the Corps consider in evaluating LHC's permit application?

4. *General permits.* Section 404(e) authorizes the Corps of Engineers to issue "general" permits on a nationwide, regional, or statewide basis for categories of activities it finds will have minimal individual and cumulative adverse effects on the environment. Notice and an opportunity for comment must be provided before general permits, which must be re-issued every five years, can become effective. No individual permit is needed for activities covered by a general permit; the discharger must simply comply with the general permit regulations. Many, but not all, of the nationwide permits allow landowners to undertake the authorized activity without notifying the Corps. There are currently 50 nationwide permits, authorizing activities from buoy placement to cranberry production. See 72 Fed. Reg. 11092 (Mar. 12, 2007). One, authorizing the discharge of spoil from surface coal mining, was suspended in 2010. 75 F.R. 34711 (June 18, 2010).

5. *EPA's veto power.* Why do you think Congress gave EPA veto power over Corps-issued permits? What does the veto add to allowing judicial review of Corps permit decisions? On what basis did the EPA justify its veto in *Bersani*? Can EPA veto a permit if it concedes that no practicable alternative exists? *See* James City County v. Environmental Protection Agency, 12 F.3d 1330 (4th Cir. 1993) (upholding veto of permit for construction of a dam and reservoir based on environmental consequences alone).

EPA has used its § 404 veto power only thirteen times, and only twice since 1989. Most recently, in January 2011, EPA vetoed a permit issued to Mingo Coal for the Spruce No. 1 surface mining project in West Virginia. The permit issued by the Corps authorized six valley fills; it would have allowed the coal company to bury seven and a half miles of streams under 110 million cubic yards of mining spoil. EPA concluded that the permit would have unacceptable adverse impacts on wildlife through habitat destruction and degradation of downstream aquatic ecosystems. 76 Fed. Reg. 3126 (Jan. 19, 2011).

EPA has never lost a legal challenge to a veto. Yet the veto power remains highly controversial. In July 2011, the House passed H.R. 2018, which would allow the state in which the discharge would originate to override any § 404 veto. The White House quickly threatened a presidential veto. See http://www.whitehouse.gov/sites/default/files/omb/legislative/sap/ 112/saphr2018r_20110712.pdf. Would you favor requiring state concurrence in EPA vetoes? Other constraints on EPA's veto power?

6. *Penalties.* Under Clean Water Act section 309, 33 U.S.C. § 1319, violations of section 404 are punishable by civil penalties of up to $25,000 per day of violation. In addition to penalties, the government often seeks an order requiring restoration of the wetlands to its original condition, or as near that condition as feasible. Where restoration is not possible, the government may seek alternative environmental benefits, such as dedication of wildlife habitat. Criminal penalties are also available. 33 U.S.C. § 1319(c). Criminal prosecution of wetlands cases has aroused considerable political controversy. In general, the government does not seek criminal sanctions unless the defendants have been notified of the violation and persisted.

7. *"Mountaintop removal" mining.* In the 1990s, a coal mining technique known as "mountaintop removal" became increasingly prevalent. The Department of Interior's Office of Surface Mining defines mountaintop removal mining as: "surface mining activities, where the mining operation removes an entire coal seam or seams running through the upper fraction of a mountain, ridge, or hill * * * by removing substantially all of the overburden off the bench and creating a level plateau or a gently rolling contour." 30 C.F.R. § 785.14(b). More graphically, it is "a type of strip mining that utilizes explosives to blast as much as 800 to 1,000 feet off of the tops of mountains to access underlying coal deposits." Mark Baller and Leor Joseph Pantilat, Defenders of Appalachia: The Campaign to Eliminate Mountaintop Removal Coal Mining and the Role of Public Justice, 37 Envtl. L. 629, 631 (2007). Once the coal is removed, the mining companies are left with massive volumes of rock and dirt. Their preferred method of disposing of this material has been to fill nearby valleys and streams.

In 2000, the Corps of Engineers issued a § 404 permit to Martin County Coal Corporation, authorizing the company to place overburden in 27 valleys, burying 6.3 miles of streams. At the time, the Corps' regulatory definition of "fill material" did not mention mining overburden, but specifically excluded "trash or garbage," effectively prohibiting the Corps from authorizing the filling of wetlands with trash. An environmental group challenged the permit, arguing that disposal of mining waste required a permit under CWA § 402 (the NPDES program, discussed in depth in Chapter 11), rather than under § 404. During the litigation, the Corps and EPA amended their regulations, adopting a new definition of fill material that includes "overburden from mining or other excavation activities." 33 C.F.R. 323.2(e)(1); 40 C.F.R. § 232.2. The District Court ruled that § 404 precludes the issuance of permits for the purpose of waste disposal. The Fourth Circuit reversed in Kentuckians for the Commonwealth, Inc. v. Rivenburgh, 317 F.3d 425 (4th Cir. 2003), holding that the Corps' could reasonably interpret § 404 to govern disposal of mining overburden, and subsequently reaffirmed that view in Ohio Valley Envtl. Coalition v. Bulen, 429 F.3d 493 (4th Cir. 2005).

Although Coeur Alaska v. Southeast Alaska Conservation Council, 557 U.S. 261 (2009), was not a mountaintop removal case, it is significant to the validity of § 404 permits allowing disposal of mine spoils in waters of the United States. The first issue in *Coeur Alaska* was whether a § 404 permit could authorize placement of a slurry of wastewater and crushed rock from a gold mine in a nearby lake. Over time, the tailings would completely fill the lake, turning it into a wider, shallower, waterway and killing most of the lake's aquatic life. Deferring to the regulatory definition of fill material, a majority of the Court ruled that § 404, rather than § 402, was the proper permitting provision. The second issue was whether the § 404 permit must include the technology-based New Source Performance Standard that would apply to a § 402 permit for this type of source. Deferring to an internal agency memorandum, the Court concluded that the New Source Performance Standard did not apply.

The Obama administration has moved cautiously toward restricting mountaintop removal mining. In 2009, EPA began more carefully reviewing § 404 permits authorizing the practice. EPA got the Corps' attention by objecting to a handful of permits, demanding additional mitigation and suggesting the possibility of a veto. Although EPA soon approved 42 of 48 permits under review, in January 2011 it vetoed the Spruce No. 1 permit, as explained in note 5, above. A good place to follow developments on mountaintop removal mining is the Charleston (WV) Gazette's blog, Coal Tattoo, http://blogs.wvgazette.com/coaltattoo/.

8. *State wetland programs.* Section 404 authorizes delegation to state authorities of responsibility for permits "for the discharge of dredged or fill material into the navigable waters (other than those waters which are presently used, or are susceptible to use in their natural condition or by reasonable improvement as a means to transport interstate or foreign commerce * * *)" within their jurisdiction. 33 U.S.C. § 1344(g). To date only Michigan and New Jersey have assumed section 404 authority.

Even without delegated authority, states have considerable leverage over the section 404 permit process. Section 401 of the Clean Water Act, discussed in more detail in Chapter 11, allows states to veto or impose conditions on federally-permitted activities involving discharges to the waters of the United States that are inconsistent with state water quality standards. In twenty-one states, section 401 certification is the only non-federal mechanism for protecting wetlands. Environmental Law Institute, State Wetland Program Evaluation, Phase IV at 6 (October 2007). Others have their own state or local wetland permitting programs, overlapping to various degrees with section 404. Obtaining federal authorization under section 404 does not obviate the requirement of a separate state permit. *See* 33 U.S.C. § 1344(t) ("Nothing in this section shall preclude or deny the right of any State or interstate agency to control the discharge of dredged or fill material in any portion of the navigable waters within the jurisdiction of such State.").

D. MITIGATION

The Section 404 Guidelines prohibit any discharge of fill "unless appropriate and practicable steps have been taken which will minimize potential adverse impacts of the discharge on the aquatic ecosystem." 40 C.F.R. § 230.10(d). The Guidelines have been construed to require mitigation of impacts, not only through proper management of the permitted project, but also by compensating for destroyed wetlands.

The Guidelines do not make clear, however, to what extent mitigation can be used as a justification for approving a permit which otherwise would not be granted. EPA and the Corps long disagreed on the appropriate role of mitigation in permit decisions. In *Bersani*, for example, the Corps decided to grant the permit in part on the theory that creation of replacement wetlands in an abandoned gravel pit would reduce the adverse impacts of the project to or below those of the alternative uplands site. EPA's disagreement with that conclusion was reason for its veto.

In 1990, EPA and the Corps reached an agreement on mitigation, memorialized in the following Memorandum of Agreement.

Memorandum of Agreement Between the Environmental Protection Agency and the Department of the Army Concerning the Determination of Mitigation Under the Clean Water Act Section 404(b)(1) Guidelines

55 Fed. Reg. 9210 (Mar. 12, 1990).

* * *

II. Policy

A. The Council on Environmental Quality (CEQ) has defined mitigation in its regulations at 40 CFR 1508.20 to include: avoiding impacts, minimizing impacts, rectifying impacts, reducing impacts over time, and compensating for impacts. The Guidelines establish environmental criteria which must be met for activities to be permitted under Section 404. The types of mitigation enumerated by CEQ are compatible with the requirements of the Guidelines; however, as a practical matter, they can be combined to form three general types: avoidance, minimization and compensatory mitigation. The remainder of this MOA will speak in terms of these more general types of mitigation.

B. The Clean Water Act and the Guidelines set forth a goal of restoring and maintaining existing aquatic resources. The Corps will strive to avoid adverse impacts and offset unavoidable adverse impacts to existing aquatic resources, and for wetlands, will strive to achieve a goal of no overall net loss of values and functions. * * * However, the level of mitigation determined to be appropriate and practicable under Section 230.10(d) may lead to individual permit decisions which do not fully meet this goal because the mitigation measures necessary to meet this goal are not feasible, not practicable, or would accomplish only inconsequential reductions in impacts. Consequently, it is recognized that no net loss of wetlands functions and values may not be achieved in each and every permit action. * * *

C. * * * The Corps, except as indicated below, first makes a determination that potential impacts have been avoided to the maximum extent practicable; remaining unavoidable impacts will then be mitigated to the extent appropriate and practicable by requiring steps to minimize impacts, and, finally, compensate for aquatic resource values. * * * It may be appropriate to deviate from the sequence when EPA and the Corps agree the proposed discharge is necessary to avoid environmental harm (e.g., to protect a natural aquatic community from saltwater intrusion, chemical contamination, or other deleterious physical or chemical impacts), or EPA and the Corps agree that the proposed discharge can reasonably be expected to result in environmental gain or insignificant environmental losses.

* * *

1. *Avoidance.* Section 230.10(a) allows permit issuance for only the least environmentally damaging practicable alternative. The thrust of this section on alternatives is avoidance of impacts. Section 230.10(a) requires that no discharge shall be permitted if there is a practicable alternative to the proposed discharge which would have less adverse impact to the aquatic ecosystem, so long as the alternative does not have other significant adverse environmental consequences. In addition, Section 230.10(a)(3) sets forth rebuttable presumptions that 1) alternatives for non-water dependent activities that do not involve special aquatic sites are available and 2) alternatives that do not involve special aquatic sites have less adverse impact on the aquatic environment. Compensatory mitigation may not be used as a method to reduce environmental impacts in the evaluation of the least environmentally damaging practicable alternatives for the purposes of requirements under Section 230.10(a).

2. *Minimization.* Section 230.10(d) states that appropriate and practicable steps to minimize the adverse impacts will be required through project modifications and permit conditions. * * *

3. *Compensatory Mitigation.* Appropriate and practicable compensatory mitigation is required for unavoidable adverse impacts which remain after all appropriate and practicable minimization has been required. Compensatory actions (e.g., restoration of existing degraded wetlands or creation of man-made wetlands) should be undertaken, when practicable, in areas adjacent or contiguous to the discharge site (on-site compensatory mitigation). If on-site compensatory mitigation is not practicable, off-site compensatory mitigation should be undertaken in the same geographic area if practicable (i.e., in close physical proximity and, to the extent possible, the same watershed). In determining compensatory mitigation, the functional values lost by the resource to be impacted must be considered. Generally, in-kind compensatory mitigation is preferable to out-of-kind. There is continued uncertainty regarding the success of wetland creation or other habitat development. Therefore, in determining the nature and extent of habitat development of this type careful consideration should be given to its likelihood of success. Because the likelihood of success is greater and the impacts to potentially valuable uplands are reduced, restoration should be the first option considered.

In the situation where the Corps is evaluating a project where a permit issued by another agency requires compensatory mitigation, the Corps may consider that mitigation as part of the overall application for purposes of public notice, but avoidance and minimization shall still be sought.

Mitigation banking may be an acceptable form of compensatory mitigation under specific criteria designed to ensure an environmentally successful bank. * * * Simple purchase or "preservation" of existing wetlands resources may in only exceptional circumstances be accepted as compensatory mitigation. * * *

III. Other Procedures

* * *

* * * The objective of mitigation for unavoidable impacts is to offset environmental losses. Additionally for wetlands, such mitigation should provide, at a minimum, one for one functional replacement (i.e., no net loss of values), with an adequate margin of safety to reflect the expected degree of success associated with the mitigation plan, recognizing that this minimum requirement may not be appropriate and practicable, and thus may not be relevant in all cases, as discussed in Section II.B of this MOA.[7] In the absence of more definitive information on the functions and values of specific wetlands sites, a minimum of 1 to 1 acreage replacement may be used as a reasonable surrogate for no net loss of functions and values. However, this ratio may be greater where the functional values of the area being impacted are demonstrably high and the replacement wetlands are of lower functional value or the likelihood of success of the mitigation project is low. Conversely, the ratio may be less than 1 to 1 for areas where the functional values associated with the area being impacted are demonstrably low and the likelihood of success associated with the mitigation proposal is high.

* * *

Monitoring is an important aspect of mitigation, especially in areas of scientific uncertainty. Monitoring should be directed toward determining whether permit conditions are complied with and whether the purpose intended to be served by the condition is actually achieved. * * * Monitoring should not be required for purposes other than these, although information for other uses may accrue from the monitoring requirements. For projects to be permitted involving mitigation with higher levels of scientific uncertainty, such as some forms of compensatory mitigation, long term monitoring, reporting and potential remedial action should be required. * * *

Mitigation requirements shall be conditions of standard Section 404 permits. * * * This ensures legal enforceability of the mitigation conditions and enhances the level of compliance. If the mitigation plan necessary to ensure compliance with the Guidelines is not reasonably implementable or enforceable, the permit shall be denied.

NOTES AND QUESTIONS

1. *Mitigation and "no net loss."* Is the policy on mitigation announced in the 1990 Memorandum of Agreement consistent with the goal of "no net

---

7. For example, there are certain areas where, due to hydrological conditions, the technology for restoration or creation of wetlands may not be available at present, or may otherwise be impracticable. In addition, avoidance, minimization, and compensatory mitigation may not be practicable where there is a high proportion of land which is wetlands. * * *

loss" of wetlands? Under what circumstances does it permit net loss? Many observers have been critical of compensatory mitigation, particularly off-site. Critics cite concerns with loss of site specific wetland values, technical difficulties in creating certain types of wetlands, and the temptation to rely on wetlands creation rather than rigorously requiring avoidance and minimization of impacts. *See*, e.g., Michael C. Blumm, The Clinton Wetlands Plan: No Net Gain in Wetlands Protection, 9 J. Land Use Envtl. L. 203, 226–28 (1994). A National Research Council panel reported in 2001 that created wetlands often do not effectively replace the ecological functions of natural wetlands. National Research Council, Compensating for Wetland Losses Under the Clean Water Act (2001). How well does the 1990 Memorandum of Agreement address these concerns?

In 2004, Congress directed the Corps of Engineers to issue regulations establishing performance standards for compensatory mitigation measures. Pub. L. 108–136, § 314. The Corps and EPA jointly proposed rules to meet that requirement in 2006, and finalized them in 2008. 73 Fed. Reg. 19594 (Apr. 10, 2008); 40 C.F.R. § 230.91–230.98. The 2008 rules govern all forms of compensatory mitigation, subjecting in-lieu fee programs, after a five-year transition period, to the same standards as mitigation banks. They set up a preference for mitigation within the same watershed as the impact, at a site "likely to successfully replace lost functions and services, taking into account such watershed scale features as aquatic habitat diversity, habitat connectivity, relationships to hydrologic sources (including the availability of water rights), trends in land use, ecological benefits, and compatibility with adjacent land uses." 40 C.F.R. § 230.93(b)(1). They require mitigation in-kind, unless the district engineer determines "that out-of-kind compensatory mitigation will serve the aquatic resource needs of the watershed." *Id.* § 230.93(e)(2). The permit must require "sufficient financial assurances to ensure a high level of confidence that the compensatory mitigation project will be successfully completed, in accordance with applicable performance standards." *Id.* § 230.93(n)(1). Every mitigation plan must include ecological performance standards that are "objective and verifiable," and based on "the best available science that can be measured or assessed in a practicable manner." *Id.* § 230.95(b). Monitoring must be conducted for at least five years or as long as needed to ensure that the performance standards are met. *Id.* § 230.96(b).

2. *Preservation as compensatory mitigation.* Is it ever appropriate to allow preservation of an existing wetland, through purchase or a conservation easement, to serve as mitigation for a project that will destroy wetlands? Is the use of preservation as mitigation consistent with the goal of "no net loss"? How effectively does § 404 alone protect wetlands? Can the added security of a formal preservation agreement compensate for losses at other sites? What ratio of preserved to destroyed wetlands would you consider adequate? As of 2003, nearly 15% of compensatory wetlands mitigation requirements nationwide were satisfied by preservation measures. Environmental Law Institute, Mitigation of Impacts to Fish and Wildlife Habitat: Estimating Costs and Identifying Opportunities 29 (Oct. 2007).

3. *The costs of mitigation.* A 2007 report by the Environmental Law Institute estimates annual expenditures for wetland mitigation efforts at somewhere between $1.7 and $3.1 billion. ELI, supra, at 3.

4. *Mitigation banks.* Mitigation banking has become a popular tool for wetlands protection, as well as a profitable business enterprise. Mitigation banking offers several potential advantages over individual mitigation at each project site. Banks may be well developed before credits are sold, providing greater assurance of long-term success. They can produce larger, more biologically valuable, mitigation sites. Mitigation banks may also be economically preferable to project-by-project mitigation. They offer economies of scale, decreasing per-acre costs and thereby increasing the extent of "practicable" mitigation. Where active management may be necessary, banks can offer greater assurance of long-term financial viability.

5. *Fee-based mitigation and valuing wetlands.* If a local mitigation bank is not available, and on-site mitigation is impractical, should payment of a fee to a non-profit or public fund for the purpose of creating, restoring, or preserving wetlands be acceptable as mitigation? Should fee-based mitigation ever be permitted when a local mitigation bank is available?

6. *Mitigation banking and takings.* Does the potential for private, for-profit mitigation banks reduce the possibility that government regulations which preclude development of a wetland area will be deemed an unconstitutional taking?

7. *The mix of mitigation methods.* Although individual mitigation by the permittee has declined in importance with the rise of mitigation banking and in-lieu fee payments, it remains common. For fiscal year 2003, permittees accounted for about 60% of compensatory mitigation nationwide. Mitigation banks were responsible for 31.4%, and in-lieu fees for 8.4%. ELI, supra, at 27.

PART III

TOXICS AND WASTE

CHAPTER SEVEN

Toxic Substances

Toxins are substances that are poisonous, at some exposure level, to persons or the environment. The key policy questions with respect to toxic substances are what risks they pose, what risks are acceptable, and what steps should be taken to reduce the risks. Risk assessment and risk management are the primary analytic tools used to answer those questions. Given the high degree of uncertainty typically associated with both exposures and hazards, there is often strong disagreement about what regulatory action, if any, to take.

SECTION 1.   RISK ASSESSMENT AND MANAGEMENT

The term "risk" has many meanings. In environmental law, risk usually refers to both the probability of a harm occurring and the magnitude of that potential harm.

As explained in Chapter 2, the common law typically responds to manifest harm, rather than risk. The next case, *Ethyl Corp. v. EPA*, was one of the first significant judicial examinations of the authority to regulate risk prior to the occurrence of harm. In that case, the D.C. Circuit reviewed en banc EPA's ability to regulate lead in gasoline under a provision of the Clean Air Act authorizing regulation of additives that "will endanger the public health or welfare." As you read the case and the excerpts that follow, reflect on the concept of risk and on the amount of risk that ought to be required to justify regulation.

Ethyl Corp. v. EPA

United States Court of Appeals, District of Columbia Circuit, 1976.
541 F.2d 1.

■ J. Skelly Wright, Circuit Judge.

Section 211(c)(1)(A) of the Clean Air Act authorizes the Administrator of EPA to regulate gasoline additives whose emission products "will endanger the public health or welfare...." Acting pursuant to that power, the Administrator, after notice and comment, determined that the automotive emissions caused by leaded gasoline present "a significant risk of harm" to the public health. Accordingly, he promulgated regulations that reduce, in step-wise fashion, the lead content of leaded gasoline. We must decide whether the Administrator properly interpreted the meaning of Section 211(c)(1)(A) and the scope of his power thereunder[.] * * *

Petitioners argue that the "will endanger" standard requires a high quantum of factual proof, proof of actual harm rather than of a "significant risk of harm." Since, according to petitioners, regulation under Section 211(c)(1)(A) must be premised upon factual proof of actual harm, the Administrator has, in their view, no power to assess risks or make policy judgments in deciding to regulate lead additives. * * *

Simply as a matter of plain meaning, we have difficulty crediting petitioners' reading of the "will endanger" standard. The meaning of "endanger" is not disputed. Case law and dictionary definition agree that endanger means something less than actual harm. When one is endangered, harm is threatened; no actual injury need ever occur. Thus, for example, a town may be "endangered" by a threatening plague or hurricane and yet emerge from the danger completely unscathed. A statute allowing for regulation in the face of danger is, necessarily, a precautionary statute. Regulatory action may be taken before the threatened harm occurs; indeed, the very existence of such precautionary legislation would seem to demand that regulatory action precede, and, optimally, prevent, the perceived threat. As should be apparent, the "will endanger" language of Section 211(c)(1)(A) makes it such a precautionary statute.

* * *

* * * [Petitioner Ethyl] argues that even if actual harm is not required for action under Section 211(c)(1)(A), the occurrence of the threatened harm must be "probable" before regulation is justified. While the dictionary admittedly settles on "probable" as its measure of danger, we believe a more sophisticated case-by-case analysis is appropriate. Danger, the Administrator recognized, is not set by a fixed probability of harm, but rather is composed of reciprocal elements of risk and harm, or probability and severity. That is to say, the public health may properly be found endangered both by a lesser risk of a greater harm and by a greater risk of a lesser harm. Danger depends upon the relation between the risk and harm presented by each case, and cannot legitimately be pegged to "probable" harm, regardless of whether that harm be great or small. * * *

Questions involving the environment are particularly prone to uncertainty. Technological man has altered his world in ways never before experienced or anticipated. The health effects of such alterations are often unknown, sometimes unknowable. While a concerned Congress has passed legislation providing for protection of the public health against gross environmental modifications, the regulators entrusted with the enforcement of such laws have not thereby been endowed with a prescience that removes all doubt from their decision making. Rather, speculation, conflicts in evidence, and theoretical extrapolation typify their every action. How else can they act, given a mandate to protect the public health but only a slight or nonexistent data base upon which to draw? * * *

Undoubtedly, certainty is the scientific ideal to the extent that even science can be certain of its truth. But certainty in the complexities of environmental medicine may be achievable only after the fact, when scientists have the opportunity for leisurely and isolated scrutiny of an entire mechanism. Awaiting certainty will often allow for only reactive, not preventive, regulation. Petitioners suggest that anything less than certainty, that any speculation, is irresponsible. But when statutes seek to avoid environmental catastrophe, can preventive, albeit uncertain, decisions legitimately be so labeled?

* * *

* * * Where a statute is precautionary in nature, the evidence difficult to come by, uncertain, or conflicting because it is on the frontiers of scientific knowledge, the regulations designed to protect the public health, and the decision that of an expert administrator, we will not demand rigorous step-by-step proof of cause and effect. Such proof may be impossible to obtain if the precautionary purpose of the statute is to be served. Of course, we are not suggesting that the Administrator has the power to act on hunches or wild guesses. However, we do hold that in such cases the Administrator may assess risks. He must take account of available facts, of course, but his inquiry does not end there. The Administrator may apply his expertise to draw conclusions from suspected, but not completely substantiated, relationships between facts, from trends among facts, from theoretical projections from imperfect data, from probative preliminary data not yet certifiable as "fact," and the like. We believe that a conclusion so drawn—a risk assessment—may, if rational, form the basis for health-related regulations under the "will endanger" language of Section 211.[58]

---

58. It bears emphasis that what is herein described as "assessment of risk" is neither unprecedented nor unique to this area of law. To the contrary, assessment of risk is a normal part of judicial and administrative fact-finding. Thus EPA is not attempting to expand its powers; rather, petitioners seek to constrict the usual flexibility of the fact-finding process. Petitioners argue that the Administrator must decide that lead emissions "will endanger" the public health solely on "facts," or, in the words of the division majority, by a "chain of scientific facts or reasoning leading (the Administrator) ineluctably to this conclusion...." Petitioners demand sole reliance on scientific facts, on evidence that reputable scientific techniques certify as certain. Typically, a scientist will not so certify evidence unless the probability of error, by standard statistical measurement, is less than 5%. That is, scientific fact is at least 95% certain.

Such certainty has never characterized the judicial or the administrative process. It may be that the "beyond a reasonable doubt" standard of criminal law demands 95% certainty. But the standard of ordinary civil litigation, a preponderance of the evidence, demands only 51% certainty. A jury may weigh conflicting evidence and certify as adjudicative (although not scientific) fact that which it believes is more likely than not. Inherently, such a standard is flexible; inherently, it allows the fact-finder to assess risks, to measure probabilities, to make subjective judgments. Nonetheless, the ultimate finding will be treated, at law, as fact and will be affirmed if based on substantial evidence, or, if made by a judge, not clearly erroneous.

The standard before administrative agencies is no less flexible. Agencies are not limited to scientific fact, to 95% certainties. Rather, they have at least the same fact-finding powers as a jury, particularly when, as here, they are engaged in rule-making * * *

All of this is not to say that Congress left the Administrator free to set policy on his own terms. To the contrary, the policy guidelines are largely set, both in the statutory term "will endanger" and in the relationship of that term to other sections of the Clean Air Act. These prescriptions direct the Administrator's actions. Operating within the prescribed guidelines, he must consider all the information available to him. Some of the information will be factual, but much of it will be more speculative scientific estimates and "guesstimates" of probable harm, hypotheses based on still-developing data, etc. Ultimately he must act, in part on "factual issues," but largely "on choices of policy, on an assessment of risks, (and) on predictions dealing with matters on the frontiers of scientific knowledge...." *Amoco Oil Co. v. EPA*, [501 F.2d 722 (D.C. Cir. 1974)]. A standard of danger—fear of uncertain or unknown harm—contemplates no more.

* * *

NOTE ON THE BASICS OF RISK ASSESSMENT

Risk assessment was first developed in the 1960s to estimate the cancer risks posed by certain chemicals. That remains its paradigmatic use, although it is also used to predict neurotoxicity, reproductive toxicity, mutagenicity, and ecological risk. The goal of risk assessment is to synthesize available evidence in order to produce quantitative estimates of the probability and magnitude of harm from an activity, event, or substance. The process is conceptually simple, but in practice fraught with difficulty.

The process of risk assessment for regulatory purposes first became formalized in the 1980s. The National Research Council published a report in 1983 on *Risk Assessment in the Federal Government*; many of the recommendations in that report were adopted in EPA's initial 1986 *Guidelines for Carcinogen Risk Assessment* and parallel guidelines for other types of risk assessment. EPA extensively revised its *Guidelines* in 2005; the new Guidelines are available on the web at http://cfpub.epa.gov/ncea/raf/recor display.cfm?deid=116283. The 2005 Guidelines leave the basic risk assessment framework developed in the 1980s undisturbed.

That framework includes four steps: hazard identification, dose-response assessment, exposure assessment, and risk characterization. In hazard identification, the regulatory agency determines whether the substance in question is capable of causing specific adverse effects, such as cancer or birth defects. Essentially, hazard identification is a threshold screening step to determine whether a closer look is needed. For carcinogens, EPA currently characterizes this step as a "weight-of-the-evidence evaluation of all pertinent information" to determine if it is biologically plausible that the substance might be carcinogenic to humans. Obviously, the outcome of this step depends fundamentally upon the end point(s) selected for examination. The fact that a chemical is not a carcinogen does not guarantee that it poses no health or environmental hazards.

If a hazard is identified, the next two steps attempt to measure toxicity and likely exposure levels in order to quantify the overall risk. In dose-response assessment, all available relevant data, including the results of epidemiological studies and laboratory animal experiments, and information regarding the mechanism of toxicity, are used to assess the probability and magnitude of injury at various potential exposure levels.

Almost invariably, major extrapolations are required, from high-dose to low-dose conditions and from non-human to human subjects. Epidemiological studies of exposed and unexposed human populations will not unequivocally reveal carcinogenicity unless the risk is high or involves a form of cancer with very low background rates. Animal studies can provide additional information, but in order to save time and money those studies typically involve relatively small numbers of animals exposed to concentrations much higher than the expected environmental dose. Frequently, scientists do not know whether people respond the same way to a substance as rats or mice do. The use of susceptible strains of rodents in laboratory tests further complicates that extrapolation.

Extrapolation from high to low doses, though, is often the most controversial aspect of dose-response assessment. Typically, even if there is consensus that a particular compound is capable of inducing cancer, little is known about the mechanism by which it does so. Lacking that information, risk assessors are forced to rely on models, but have little basis to choose between models that can give radically different answers. A linear model, which assumes some risk from any non-zero concentration of the toxin, will frequently fit the observed data just as well as a threshold model, which assumes no risk below a certain threshold concentration.

In the absence of evidence it deems reliable concerning the mechanisms of carcinogenesis, EPA generally applies the conservative default presumptions that animal carcinogens are also human carcinogens and that low-dose responses are linear.

Another challenge for dose-response assessment is that different populations may respond differently. Young children, for example, are often more sensitive than adults to toxins. EPA, responding to a 1997 Executive Order, tries to evaluate risks to children separately in its cancer risk assessments, but acknowledges that good data on the effects of childhood exposure are often lacking. Other populations may be more susceptible to certain types of cancer because of genetics, other medical conditions, or voluntary behaviors (smoking, for example, can increase the risk of lung cancer from exposure to other hazards).

Finally, it is exceptionally difficult to model potential synergistic effects of multiple toxins. People are constantly exposed to a multitude of chemicals, not to one at a time. Harm from multiple exposures may be additive or multiplicative. There is rarely sufficient information available to predict the effects of such multiple exposures.

The third step in a quantitative risk assessment is exposure assessment, which evaluates the extent to which the relevant population is likely to be exposed to the hazardous substance. Exposure to toxic substances may occur through a variety of routes, including inhalation, ingestion, and contact with the skin. Exposure assessments typically concentrate on routes associated with an identified hazard. So, for example, asbestos fibers can cause lung diseases if inhaled; a risk assessment for those fibers would need to evaluate exposure through the air. Some types of fibers may also be connected to non-lung cancers if ingested with water or food; those routes would also be considered in a complete exposure assessment.

The intensity, frequency, and duration of exposure are predicted rather than actually measured. Exposure assessment includes a number of difficult steps. The risk assessor must, for example, understand the magnitude of emissions and their fate in the environment. The most controversial aspect of exposure assessment, however, is predicting the human choices that may bring people into contact with a hazardous substance.

In order to avoid the difficulties of predicting real human behavior and of understanding in detail the likely fate of a hazardous substance, a risk assessment may focus on the theoretical "maximum exposed individual" (MEI). For an air toxin, for example, the MEI would be a person who takes every breath throughout her life just outside the factory fence or right next to an exhaust pipe. Use of the MEI is intended to be a conservative approach, ensuring that regulation will protect every real exposed person, since by definition a person's actual exposure cannot exceed that of the MEI.

Like any conservative assumption, however, use of the MEI has the potential to encourage over-regulation, which would increase economic costs to society without producing countervailing health benefits. Critics believe that the maximum theoretical exposure may exceed by orders of magnitude the actual exposure to any real person. For example, an EPA assessment of the hazards of air emissions from municipal incinerators reportedly assumed that the MEI was a child living about one-quarter mile downwind from the incinerator who consumed primarily vegetables grown in the family garden, fish caught in a local pond, milk produced by a family cow, and sizeable quantities of dirt from the family yard. In addition to relying on unlikely assumptions, an MEI may overlook the potential for toxic chemicals to be broken down in the environment. Dennis J. Paustenback, Health Risk Assessments: Opportunities and Pitfalls, 14 Colum. J. Envtl. L. 397 (1989).

In order to avoid excessive regulation, therefore, the risk assessor might concentrate on the average or typical exposed individual. That approach, of course, carries its own problems. In particular, it may mask or implicitly devalue potential harm to subpopulations whose behavior or cultural practices lead to exposures (and therefore risks) substantially higher than those of the general population. For example, a number of toxins, including mercury and PCBs, bioaccumulate in fish tissues through aquatic food chains. Fish consumption is a major route of human exposure to these toxins. But the amount of fish Americans eat varies widely, often making up a much larger proportion of the diet for Native Americans in coastal communities (and some immigrant groups) than for most Americans. Regulations based on average fish consumption will fail to protect high fish consumers, and reducing consumption may not be a plausible response, given language barriers and the importance of fish as a source of affordable protein or as a significant cultural element. See Catherine A. O'Neill, Variable Justice: Environmental Standards, Contaminated Fish, and "Acceptable" Risk to Native Peoples, 19 Stan. Envtl. L. J. 3 (2000). One way to deal with high levels of variation in exposure between different subpopulations is to produce an exposure assessment that explicitly acknowledges the existence of different exposure groups, the basis for the behavioral differences, and the approximate size of the subpopulation. Risks can then be calculated separately for distinct groups, and a deliberate decision made as to whether to adopt more protective regulations to protect a more exposed subgroup or to try to persuade the group to change its behavior.

In the final step, risk characterization, the risk assessor combines the estimates of toxicity and exposure to produce a description of the nature and extent of the risk. The risk is generally expressed as the number of excess cancers (or other adverse effects) expected over a period of time or the increased lifetime cancer risk to a typical or maximally exposed individual. The risk characterization is supposed to summarize the assessment in a way that is clear and understandable to the public and those charged with making choices about how to respond to the risk. It should include not just a single number quantifying the risk, but a range of estimates, together with some discussion of the uncertainties in the analysis, the assumptions upon which it is based and the sensitivity of the outcome to those assumptions, and the degree of confidence the assessor places on the risk estimates. In a 1994 study of EPA's risk assessment practice, the National Research Council criticized the agency for its failure to explain its use of default assumptions and departures from those assumptions in specific cases. National Research Council, Science and Judgment in Risk Assessment 7–8 (1994).

More recently, the National Research Council sketched out a new approach to toxicity testing that would take advantage of emerging technologies in molecular biology and toxicology. National Research Council, Toxicity Testing in the 21st Century (2007). To identify and evaluate potential toxins, this new approach would rely heavily on *in vitro* testing, preferably using human cells, cell lines, or cellular components. If such tests reveal changes in biologic processes, the substance in question would undergo targeted testing to gather more information about toxicity pathways. Information developed through testing would be used to build dose-response models, which could then serve as the basis for risk management decisions. The proposed approach would also make greater use of biomonitoring and human surveillance studies to gather information on exposure to a substance and the effects of such exposure. The new approach, if adopted, would involve less animal experimentation, and thus offers the prospect of faster, less costly, and more accurate assessment of toxic risks. Such an approach, however, would require a significant investment of resources to develop adequate *in vitro* tests, perform those tests on a widespread basis, and conduct follow-up surveillance studies.

———————

Risk assessment is often distinguished from risk management, the process of deciding how to respond to information generated by risk assessment. Risk management is a policymaking process that incorporates various factors—including public perceptions, political factors, costs, and distributional effects—into the decisionmaking process. Although risk management is clearly driven by values, it is important to realize that risk assessment is not a purely scientific, values-free process. As the preceding discussion suggests, the available data frequently do not address all uncertainties, and the assumptions made and inferences drawn during the risk assessment process necessarily involve judgment calls based on values. Decisionmakers using risk assessment should be aware of these assumptions, as well as the limitations of risk assessment and lingering uncertainties.

Public perceptions of risk, which influence legislative and regulatory priorities, often differ dramatically from the data generated by risk assessments. Studies have identified a number of factors that tend to make a given level of risk less tolerable. In general, lay people are less tolerant of risks if:

- the benefits of the risky activity are *inadequate, unclear or unevenly distributed*;

- the risks are *imposed,* rather than voluntarily assumed;

- the risks are *beyond the risk bearer's personal control*;

- distribution of the burdens is seen as *unethical or unfair*;

- the risks are *artificial* as opposed to natural;

- the risks are *insidious,* meaning that they cause harm in ways that are not readily apparent (e.g. poisoning);

- the risks are of *unknown time duration,* especially if they may affect subsequent generations;

- the risks are *unfamiliar*; and

- the risks are *associated with memorable events* such as disasters.

John M. Stonehouse and John D. Mumford, Science, Risk Analysis, and Environmental Policy Decisions 42–43 (1994).

One approach to bridging the discrepancy between expert assessments and public perceptions of risk has been to focus on improving risk communication. Risk management can be made more rational, some suggest, if the public can be properly informed about the "real risks." The following passage, however, calls that approach into question.

Paul Slovic, The Risk Game

86 J. Hazardous Materials 17 (2001).

Public perceptions of risk have been found to play an important role in determining the priorities and legislative agendas of regulatory bodies such as the Environmental Protection Agency (EPA), much to the distress of agency technical experts who argue that other hazards deserve higher priority. The bulk of EPA's budget in recent years has gone to hazardous waste primarily because the public believes that the cleanup of Superfund sites is the most serious environmental threat that the country faces. Hazards such as indoor air pollution are considered more serious health risks by experts but are not perceived that way by the public.

Great disparities in monetary expenditures, designed to prolong life, may also be traced to public perceptions of risk. As noteworthy as the large sums of money devoted to preventing a statistical fatality from exposure to radiation and chemical toxins are the relatively small sums expended to prevent a fatality from mundane hazards such as automobile accidents. Other studies have shown that serious risks from national disasters such as floods, hurricanes, and earthquakes generate relatively little public concern and demand for protection.

Such discrepancies are seen as irrational by many harsh critics of public perceptions. These critics draw a sharp dichotomy between the experts and the public. Experts are seen as purveying risk assessments, characterized as objective, analytic, wise, and rational—based upon the *real risks*. In contrast, the public is seen to rely upon *perceptions of risk* that are subjective, often hypothetical, emotional, foolish, and irrational. * * *

In sum, polarized views, controversy, and overt conflict have become pervasive within risk assessment and risk management. Frustrated scientists and industrialists castigate the public for behaviors they judge to be based on irrationality or ignorance. Members of the public feel similarly antagonistic toward industry and government. A desperate search for salvation through risk-communication efforts began in the mid–1980s—yet, despite some localized successes, this effort has not stemmed the major conflicts or reduced much of the dissatisfaction with risk management. This dissatisfaction can be traced, in part, to a failure to appreciate the complex and socially determined nature of the concept "risk". * * *

Attempts to manage risk must confront the question: "What is risk?" The dominant conception views risk as "the chance of injury, damage, or loss." The probabilities and consequences of adverse events are assumed to be produced by physical and natural processes in ways that can be objectively quantified by risk assessment. Much social science analysis rejects this notion, arguing instead that risk is inherently subjective. In this view, risk does not exist "out there," independent of our minds and cultures, waiting to be measured. Instead, human beings have invented the concept risk to help them understand and cope with the dangers and uncertainties of life. Although these dangers are real, there is no such thing as "real risk" or "objective risk." * * *

One way in which subjectivity permeates risk assessments is in the dependence of such assessments on judgments at every stage of the process, from the initial structuring of a risk problem to deciding which endpoints or consequences to include in the analysis, identifying and estimating exposures, choosing dose-response relationships, and so on.

For example, even the apparently simple task of choosing a risk measure for a well-defined endpoint such as human fatalities is surprisingly complex and judgmental. Table 1 shows a few of the many different ways that fatality risks can be measured. How should we decide which measure to use when planning a risk assessment, recognizing that the choice is likely to make a big difference in how the risk is perceived and evaluated?

* * * * *

Table 1

Some ways of expressing mortality risks
Deaths per million people in the population
Deaths per million people within x miles of the source of exposure
Deaths per unit of concentration
Deaths per facility
Deaths per ton of air toxic released
Deaths per ton of air toxic absorbed by people
Deaths per ton of chemical produced
Deaths per million dollars of product produced
Loss of life expectancy associated with exposure to the hazard

Numerous research studies have demonstrated that different (but logically equivalent) ways of presenting the same risk information can lead to different evaluations and decisions. One dramatic example of this comes from a study [which] asked people to imagine that they had lung cancer and had to choose between two therapies, surgery or radiation. The two therapies were described in some detail. Then one group of subjects was presented with the cumulative probabilities of surviving for varying lengths of time after the treatment. A second group of subjects received the same cumulative probabilities framed in terms of dying rather than surviving * * *. Framing the statistics in terms of dying changed the percentage of subjects choosing radiation therapy over surgery from 18 to 44%. The effect was as strong for physicians as for laypeople.

Equally striking changes in preference result from framing the information about consequences in terms of either lives saved or lives lost or from describing an improvement in a river's water quality as a *restoration* of lost quality or an *improvement* from the current level.

We now know that every form of presenting risk information is a frame that has a strong influence on the decision maker. Moreover, when we contemplate the equivalency of lives saved versus lives lost, mortality rates versus survival rates, restoring lost water quality versus improving water quality, and so forth, we see that there are often no "right frames" or "wrong frames"—just "different frames."

As noted above, research has also shown that the public has a broad conception of risk, qualitative and complex, that incorporates considerations such as uncertainty, dread, catastrophic potential, controllability, equity, risk to future generations, and so forth, into the risk equation. In contrast, experts' perceptions of risk are not closely related to these dimensions or the characteristics that underlie them. Instead, studies show that experts tend to see riskiness as synonymous with expected mortality, consistent with the dictionary definition given above and consistent with the ways that risks tend to be characterized in risk assessments. As a result of these different perspectives, many conflicts over "risk" may result from experts and laypeople having different definitions of the concept. In this light, it is not surprising that expert recitations of "risk statistics" often do little to change people's attitudes and perceptions.

There are legitimate, value-laden issues underlying the multiple dimensions of public risk perceptions, and these values need to be considered in risk-policy decisions. For example, is risk from cancer (a dread disease) worse than risk from auto accidents (not dreaded)? Is a risk imposed on a child more serious than a known risk accepted voluntarily by an adult? Are the deaths of 50 passengers in separate automobile accidents equivalent to the deaths of 50 passengers in one aeroplane crash? Is the risk from a polluted Superfund site worse if the site is located in a neighborhood that has a number of other hazardous facilities nearby? The difficult questions multiply when outcomes other than human health and safety are considered.

* * * [T]he traditional view of risk characterized by the event probabilities and consequences treats subjective and contextual factors such as those described above as secondary or accidental dimensions of risk, just as coloration might be thought of as a secondary or accidental dimension of an eye. [A]ccidental dimensions do not serve as criteria for determining whether someone is or is not at risk, just as coloration is irrelevant to whether something is or is not an eye.

I believe that the multidimensional, subjective, value-laden, frame-sensitive nature of risky decisions, as described above, supports a very different view—* * * "the contextualist conception." This conception places probabilities and consequences on the list of relevant risk attributes along with voluntariness, equity, and other important contextual parameters. On the contextualist view, the concept of risk is more like the concept of a game than the concept of the eye. Games have time limits, rules of play, opponents, criteria for winning or losing, and so on, but none of these attributes is essential to the concept of a game, nor is any of them characteristic of all games. Similarly, a contextualist view of risk assumes that risks are characterized by some combination of attributes such as voluntariness, probability, intentionality, equity, and so on, but that no one of these attributes is essential. The bottom line is that, just as there is no universal set of rules for games, there is no universal set of characteristics for describing risk. The characterization must depend on which risk game is being played.

* * *

Whoever controls the definition of risk (i.e. determines the rules of the risk game) controls the rational solution to the problem at hand. If you define risk one way, then one option will rise to the top as the most cost-effective or the safest or the best. If you define it another way, perhaps incorporating qualitative characteristics and other contextual factors, you will likely get a different ordering of your action solutions. Defining risk is thus an exercise in power.

The limitations of risk science, the importance and difficulty of maintaining trust, and the subjective and contextual nature of the risk game point to the need for a new approach—one that focuses upon introducing more public participation into both risk assessment and risk decision making in order to make the decision process more democratic, improve the relevance and quality of technical analysis, and increase the legitimacy and public acceptance of the resulting decisions.

* * *

NOTE ON NONLINEAR MODELS

The conventional risk assessment model for carcinogens is a linear no-threshold model that assumes there is no dosage that has no risk of causing cancer and that the probability of adverse health effects increases with dosage. This model, however, has been challenged by data suggesting that the model may overstate the risks in some instances and understate the risks in others. One critique of the linear no-threshold model relies on the theory of hormesis, which suggests that human exposure to a substance at low levels might be beneficial even if exposures at higher levels might be extremely hazardous. The hormesis hypothesis proposes that as a dose of a hazardous substance rises from zero there are initially positive or beneficial effects until a "tipping point" is reached, with additional exposures resulting in increasingly negative consequences. An example of a substance that may have a hormetic effect is alcohol, the modest consumption of which may reduce cancer and cardiovascular disease, according to some studies, while excessive consumption increases the likelihood of various diseases.

Whether or how regulation should take hormesis into account presents difficult and controversial policy questions. While acknowledging that the evidence supporting the hormesis thesis is not conclusive, Frank Cross nevertheless posits that "the scientific data-base is sufficient to incorporate hormesis into regulation, and the quantity of data is such that hormesis could become a default assumption of risk assessment, presumed until disproven in a particular circumstance." Frank B. Cross, Incorporating Hormesis in Risk Regulation, 30 Envtl. L. Rep. 10778 (2000). See also Ralph Cook & Edward J. Calabrese, The Importance of Hormesis to Public Health, 114 Envtl. Health Persp. 1631 (2006) (contending that hormesis is a "ubiquitous natural phenomenon," that the hormetic model is testable and allows consideration of potential benefits as well as risks, and that the hormetic model should be incorporated into risk assessment processes). Other scholars, however, contend that the concept of hormesis oversimplifies complex biological processes and that "even if certain low-dose effects were sometimes determined to be beneficial, this finding should not be used to influence regulatory decisions to increase environmental exposures to toxic agents, given factors such as variability in individual susceptibility, variability in individual exposures, and the public's regular exposure to complex mixtures." Kristina A. Thayer et al., Fundamental Flaws of Hormesis for Public Health Decisions, 113 Envtl. Health Persp. 1271 (2005).

The linear no-threshold model is also challenged by a class of chemicals, endocrine disruptors, which interfere with the hormone signals that regulate human organ development, metabolism, reproduction, and other functions. Suspected endocrine disruptors include chemicals that are widely used in pesticides, plastic bottles, detergents, cosmetics, and toys. Although there is not yet conclusive evidence to prove that low-dose exposures to endocrine disruptors are causing adverse human health effects, studies of animals have found reductions in male and female fertility, abnormalities in reproductive organs, and increases in mammary, ovarian, and prostate cancer. Mounting concern regarding the effects on fetal and infant development of one particular endocrine disruptor, bisphenol A (BPA), has led some states and localities to ban the sale of baby bottles and similar products containing BPA and prompted some manufacturers to phase out such products.

Some endocrine disruptors exhibit a U-shaped curve of toxicity: exposure at very low levels or at very high levels results in more adverse effects than exposure at moderate levels. Scientists hypothesize that the endocrine system's extreme sensitivity makes it susceptible to low levels of endocrine disruptors, but that higher doses of chemicals may simply overwhelm endocrine receptors. For more information, see, e.g., International Programme on Chemical Safety, Global Assessment on the State-of-the-Science of Endocrine Disruptors, WHO/PCS/EDC/02.2 (2002); Common Industrial Chemicals in Tiny Doses Raise Health Issue, Wall St. J., July 25, 2005, at A1.

What role, if any, should findings regarding hormesis and U-shaped toxicity curves play in risk assessment and health and environmental regulation? How much data should EPA have regarding these phenomena before incorporating them into its regulatory standard setting practices?

NOTE ON "SOUND SCIENCE"

EPA's risk assessment methods and risk-based regulations have long been subject to challenge by critics. Some critics have focused on the total costs of regulatory "burdens," while others have attacked individual regulations as not cost effective. See, e.g., John D. Graham, Legislative Approaches to Achieving More Protection Against Risk at Less Cost, 1997 U. Chi. Legal F. 13 (1997) (arguing that current public health and safety regulations reflect "a syndrome of paranoia and neglect"); John F. Morrall III, A Review of the Record, Regulation 25 (Nov./Dec. 1986) (noting costs-per-life saved of various risk-reducing regulations); Stephen Breyer, Breaking the Vicious Circle: Toward Effective Risk Regulation (1993) (arguing that our regulatory priorities are random and irrational); but see Lisa Heinzerling, Regulatory Costs of Mythic Proportions, 107 Yale L.J. 1981 (1998) (criticizing Morrall's analysis and noting that government agencies rejected many of the more costly rules cited by Morrall).

In recent years, critics have used arguments about "sound science" to attack agency regulation and to justify regulatory inaction. Typically, advocates of a policy position use the phrase "sound science" to characterize the basis for their own position and the term "junk science" to describe the evidence relied on by their opponents. Understanding the potential appeal of the "sound science" argument requires a basic understanding of the nature of scientific inquiry.

Science is a continual process of discovering knowledge through observation, experimentation, and peer review; it is an inductive process that inherently involves uncertainty. Scientific knowledge is incomplete and subject to revision, as our experience with chemical substances illustrates. Of the approximately 70,000 chemicals in industrial and commercial use in North America, only 3,500 have been studied sufficiently for a human health risk assessment to be conducted, and scientists sometimes discover unanticipated health effects even for chemicals that have previously been studied. Despite such limitations, science is often portrayed in the media and understood by the public as rational, objective, and definitive. In this context, agency regulation of health and environmental risks that are suggested by evidence, but not definitively demonstrated, can be vulnerable to the charge that such regulation is not based on "sound science." Furthermore, an insistence on "sound science," if interpreted to require the resolution of all doubts, can delay or block new regulation.

Is it legal or appropriate for agencies to promulgate rules without producing or relying on definitive scientific studies that demonstrate harms to human health? Shouldn't regulatory decisions be based on reliable and comprehensive scientific data?

Sound science advocates have sought to influence the regulatory process in various ways, two of which are discussed below.

The Data Quality Act. This statute directs the Office of Management and Budget (OMB) to issue "guidance to Federal agencies for ensuring and maximizing the quality, objectivity, utility, and integrity of information ... disseminated by Federal agencies." All agencies are to issue their own guidelines to the same effect and "establish administrative mechanisms allowing affected persons to seek and obtain correction of information maintained and disseminated by the agency that does not comply." See Treasury and General Government Appropriation Act for Fiscal Year 2001, Pub. L. No. 106–554, § 515, 114 Stat. 2763A–153 (2000), reprinted in 44 U.S.C.A. § 3516 nt. The guidelines issued by OMB essentially direct agencies, *inter alia*, to use "the best available, peer-reviewed science and supporting studies conducted in accordance with sound and objective scientific practices."

Who is most likely to seek correction of information under the Act? Analyses of government records have found that industry has filed the majority of petitions, many of which are aimed at health and safety regulations. Those petitions include a challenge by the American Chemistry Council to data used to support a ban on wood treated with heavy metals and arsenic in playground equipment, and challenges by the sugar industry to government dietary recommendations to limit sugar intake. See Rick Weiss, "Data Quality" Law Is Nemesis of Regulation, Wash. Post, Aug. 16, 2004, at A1. Could the law serve as a useful tool for environmental groups as well?

To what extent is the Act judicially enforceable? Are courts qualified to review the "quality, objectivity, utility, and integrity" of information? See Salt Institute v. Leavitt, 440 F.3d 156 (4th Cir. 2006) (affirming dismissal of case for lack of standing and stating that the Data Quality Act "does not create any legal right to information or its correctness").

Guidance from OMB on Risk Analysis. In 1995, OMB issued a set of principles to guide policymakers in addressing environmental, health, and safety risks. OMB's Principles for Risk Analysis instructed agencies to establish "a clear distinction" between techniques for assessing risks and methods for managing risks. OMB recommended that risk assessments encompass all appropriate hazards and explicitly identify underlying assumptions and uncertainties. In managing risks, "agencies should seek to offer the greatest net improvement in total societal welfare, accounting for a broad range of relevant social and economic considerations...." OMB also advocated that risk communication involve an "open, two-way exchange of information between professionals, including both policy makers and 'experts' in relevant disciplines, and the public."

As part of its continuing efforts to supervise regulatory science, OMB issued in 2006 a "Proposed Risk Assessment Bulletin" for public comment. The bulletin proposed one set of risk assessment standards for regulatory analyses and an even more stringent set of standards for risk assessments expected to have a "clear and substantial impact on important public policies or private sector decisions." The bulletin was controversial, as one of its primary effects would have been to impose significant new burdens on agency rulemaking based on risk assessments.

The National Research Council, an arm of the National Academy of Sciences, issued a highly critical peer review of the proposed bulletin:

> The committee * * * is concerned that the bulletin is inconsistent with previous recommendations in a number of ways, including its presentation of a new definition of risk assessment, its omission of discussion of the important role of default assumptions and clear criteria to modify or depart from defaults, its proposal of risk *assessment* standards related to activities traditionally regarded as risk *management* activities, and its requirement for formal analyses of uncertainty and pres-

entation of "central" or "expected" risk estimates. In several respects, the bulletin attempts to move standards for risk assessment into territory that is beyond what previous reports have recommended and beyond the current state of the science. Such departures from expert studies are of serious concern, because any attempt to advance the practice of risk assessment that does not reflect the state of the science is likely to produce the opposite effect.

Committee to Review the OMB Risk Assessment Bulletin, National Research Council, Scientific Review of the Proposed Risk Assessment Bulletin from the Office of Management and Budget 3 (2007). The Council "conclude[d] that the OMB bulletin is fundamentally flawed and recommend[ed] that it be withdrawn." Id. at 6.

Although OMB withdrew the proposed bulletin, it subsequently issued a memorandum,"Updated Principles for Risk Analysis," to supplement the text of OMB's 1995 Principles. The memorandum, while of limited legal force, has the potential to impede the regulatory process by pushing agencies towards discussion of "different scientifically plausible endpoints" and "associated uncertainties" and towards greater use of quantitative analyses and cost-benefit analysis.

Should there be a uniform standard governing how risk assessments are performed? In cases involving significant uncertainty, shouldn't agencies be expected to qualify or describe as much uncertainty as they can?

The controversy over sound science is partly a dispute over burdens of proof. Who should have the burden of proof—the regulators or the chemical manufacturers and users? Who bears the costs of uncertainty if the burden of proof is not met?

SECTION 2.   INTRODUCTION TO REGULATING TOXIC RISKS

How should the law respond to the results of risk analysis and the need to control exposure to hazardous substances? A wide variety of legal tools for addressing the risks posed by toxics—including tort liability, permits, taxes, and labeling requirements—have been employed in this area. In Chapter 2, we explored the common law's approach to toxic risks, an approach that relies on *ex post* liability to compensate toxic tort victims and to deter against dangerous exposure. As the readings in that section illustrated, toxic tort plaintiffs often are unable to prove that their injuries were caused by chemicals released by defendants.

To address toxic risks, Congress has relied primarily on command and control regulation. Such regulation may incorporate health-based standards, technology-based standards, or standards that balance the economic and social costs of controls against health and safety benefits. The following case explores issues raised by the Occupational Safety and Health Act, the regulatory scheme that governs exposure to toxic substances in the workplace. These issues—the showing a regulatory agency must make before it can regulate, the information it may or must consider, and how much weight the agency should give to different kinds of information—arise repeatedly in regulatory statutes.

Excerpts From the Occupational Safety and Health Act

29 U.S.C. §§ 655, 652(8).

OSHA § 6 Standards

(b) Procedure for promulgation, modification, or revocation of standards

The Secretary may by rule promulgate, modify, or revoke any occupational safety or health standard in the following manner:

* * *

(5) The Secretary, in promulgating standards dealing with toxic materials or harmful physical agents under this subsection, shall set the standard which most adequately assures, to the extent feasible, on the basis of the best available evidence, that no employee will suffer material impairment of health or functional capacity even if such employee has regular exposure to the hazard dealt with by such standard for the period of his working life. Development of standards under this subsection shall be based upon research, demonstrations, experiments, and such other information as may be appropriate. In addition to the attainment of the highest degree of health and safety protection for the employee, other considerations shall be the latest available scientific data in the field, the feasibility of the standards, and experience gained under this and other health and safety laws. Whenever practicable, the standard promulgated shall be expressed in terms of objective criteria and of the performance desired.

OSHA § 3 Definitions

(8) The term "occupational safety and health standard" means a standard which requires conditions, or the adoption or use of one or more practices, means, methods, operations, or processes, reasonably necessary or appropriate to provide safe or healthful employment and places of employment.

Industrial Union Department, AFL–CIO v. American Petroleum Institute [The Benzene Case]

United States Supreme Court, 1980.
448 U.S. 607.

■ MR. JUSTICE STEVENS announced the judgment of the Court and delivered an opinion, in which THE CHIEF JUSTICE and MR. JUSTICE STEWART joined and in Parts I, II, III–A, III–B, III–C and III–E of which MR. JUSTICE POWELL joined.

The Occupational Safety and Health Act of 1970 (Act), 84 Stat. 1590, 29 U.S.C. § 651 et seq., was enacted for the purpose of ensuring safe and healthful working conditions for every working man and woman in the Nation. This litigation concerns a standard promulgated by the Secretary of Labor to regulate occupational exposure to benzene, a substance which has been shown to cause cancer at high exposure levels. The principal question is whether such a showing is a sufficient basis for a standard that places the most stringent limitation on exposure to benzene that is technologically and economically possible.

* * *

Wherever the toxic material to be regulated is a carcinogen, the Secretary has taken the position that no safe exposure level can be determined and that § 6(b)(5) requires him to set an exposure limit at the lowest technologically feasible level that will not impair the viability of the industries regulated. In this case, after having determined that there is a causal connection between benzene and leukemia (a cancer of the white blood cells), the Secretary set an exposure limit on airborne concentrations of benzene of one part benzene per million parts of air (1 ppm), regulated dermal and eye contact with solutions containing benzene, and imposed complex monitoring and medical testing requirements on employers whose workplaces contain 0.5 ppm or more of benzene.

* * *

I.

* * * Benzene is used in manufacturing a variety of products including motor fuels (which may contain as much as 2 percent benzene), solvents, detergents, pesticides, and other organic chemicals.

The entire population of the United States is exposed to small quantities of benzene, ranging from a few parts per billion to 0.5 ppm, in the ambient air. Over one million workers are subject to additional low-level exposures as a consequence of their employment. The majority of these employees work in gasoline service stations, benzene production (petroleum refineries and cooking operations), chemical processing, benzene transportation, rubber manufacturing, and laboratory operations.

Benzene is a toxic substance. Although it could conceivably cause harm to a person who swallowed or touched it, the principal risk of harm comes from inhalation of benzene vapors. When these vapors are inhaled, the benzene diffuses through the lungs and is quickly absorbed into the blood. Exposure to high concentrations produces an almost immediate effect on the central nervous system. Inhalation of concentrations of 20,000 ppm can be fatal within minutes; exposures in the range of 250 to 500 ppm can cause vertigo, nausea, and other symptoms of mild poisoning. Persistent exposures at levels above 25–40 ppm may lead to blood deficiencies and diseases of the blood-forming organs, including aplastic anemia, which is generally fatal.

* * *

In its published statement giving notice of the proposed permanent standard, OSHA did not ask for comments as to whether or not benzene presented a significant health risk at exposures of 10 ppm or less. Rather, it asked for comments as to whether 1 ppm was the minimum feasible exposure limit. As OSHA's Deputy Director of Health Standards, Grover Wrenn, testified at the hearing, this formulation of the issue to be considered by the Agency was consistent with OSHA's general policy with respect to carcinogens. Whenever a carcinogen is involved, OSHA will presume that no safe level of exposure exists in the absence of clear proof establishing such a level and will accordingly set the exposure limit at the lowest level feasible. The proposed 1 ppm exposure limit in this case thus was established not on the basis of a proven hazard at 10 ppm, but rather on the basis of "OSHA's best judgement at the time of the proposal of the feasibility of compliance with the proposed standard by the [a]ffected industries." Given OSHA's cancer policy, it was in fact irrelevant whether there was any evidence at all of a leukemia risk at 10 ppm. The important point was that there was no evidence that there was not some risk, however small, at that level. The fact that OSHA did not ask for comments on whether there was a safe level of exposure for benzene was indicative of its further view that a demonstration of such absolute safety simply could not be made.

* * *

As presently formulated, the benzene standard is an expensive way of providing some additional protection for a relatively small number of employees. According to OSHA's figures, the standard will require capital investments in engineering controls of approximately $266 million, first-year operating costs * * * of $187 million to $205 million and recurring annual costs of approximately $34 million. The figures outlined in OSHA's explanation of the costs of compliance to various industries indicate that only 35,000 employees would gain any benefit from the regulation in terms of a reduction in their exposure to benzene. * * *

Although OSHA did not quantify the benefits to each category of worker in terms of decreased exposure to benzene, it appears from the economic impact study done at OSHA's direction that those benefits may be relatively small. * * *

II.

* * *

Any discussion of the 1 ppm exposure limit must, of course, begin with the Agency's rationale for imposing that limit. The written explanation of the standard fills 184 pages of the printed appendix. Much of it is devoted to a discussion of the voluminous evidence of the adverse effects of exposure to benzene at levels of concentration well above 10 ppm. This discussion demonstrates that there is ample justification for regulating occupational exposure to benzene and that the prior limit of 10 ppm, with a ceiling of 25 ppm (or a peak of 50 ppm) was reasonable. It does not, however, provide direct support for the Agency's conclusion that the limit should be reduced from 10 ppm to 1 ppm.

* * *

In the end OSHA's rationale for lowering the permissible exposure limit to 1 ppm was based, not on any finding that leukemia has ever been caused by exposure to 10 ppm of benzene and that it will not be caused by exposure to 1 ppm, but rather on a series of assumptions indicating that some leukemias might result from exposure to 10 ppm and that the number of cases might be reduced by reducing the exposure level to 1 ppm. In reaching that result, the Agency first unequivocally concluded that benzene is a human carcinogen. Second, it concluded that industry had failed to prove that there is a safe threshold level of exposure to benzene below which no excess leukemia cases would occur. In reaching this conclusion OSHA rejected industry contentions that certain epidemiological studies indicating no excess risk of leukemia among workers exposed at levels below 10 ppm were sufficient to establish that the threshold level of safe exposure was at or above 10 ppm. It also rejected an industry witness' testimony that a dose-response curve could be constructed on the basis of the reported epidemiological studies and that this curve indicated that reducing the permissible exposure limit from 10 to 1 ppm would prevent at most one leukemia and one other cancer death every six years.[38]

Third, the Agency applied its standard policy with respect to carcinogens, concluding that, in the absence of definitive proof of a safe level, it must be assumed that any level above zero presents some increased risk of cancer. As the federal parties point out in their brief, there are a number of scientists and public health specialists who subscribe to this view, theorizing that a susceptible person may contract cancer from the absorption of even one molecule of a carcinogen like benzene.

Fourth, the Agency reiterated its view of the Act, stating that it was required by § 6(b)(5) [of OSHA] to set the standard either at the level that has been demonstrated to be safe or at the lowest level feasible, whichever is higher. If no safe level is established, as in this case, the Secretary's interpretation of the statute automatically leads to the selection of an exposure limit that is the lowest feasible. Because of benzene's importance to the economy, no one has ever suggested that it would be feasible to eliminate its use entirely, or to try to limit exposures to the small amounts that are omnipresent. Rather, the Agency selected 1 ppm as a workable exposure level and then determined that compliance with that level was technologically feasible and that "the economic impact of . . . (compliance) will not be such as to threaten the financial welfare of the affected firms or

38. OSHA rejected this testimony in part because it believed the exposure data in the epidemiological studies to be inadequate to formulate a dose-response curve. It also indicated that even if the testimony was accepted—indeed as long as there was any increase in the risk of cancer—the Agency was under an obligation to "select the level of exposure which is most protective of exposed employees."

the general economy." It therefore held that 1 ppm was the minimum feasible exposure level within the meaning of § 6(b)(5) of the Act.

* * *

III.

Our resolution of the issues in these cases turns, to a large extent, on the meaning of and the relationship between § 3(8), which defines a health and safety standard as a standard that is "reasonably necessary and appropriate to provide safe or healthful employment," and § 6(b)(5), which directs the Secretary in promulgating a health and safety standard for toxic materials to "set the standard which most adequately assures, to the extent feasible, on the basis of the best available evidence, that no employee will suffer material impairment of health or functional capacity...."

In the Government's view, § 3(8)'s definition of the term "standard" has no legal significance or at best merely requires that a standard not be totally irrational. It takes the position that § 6(b)(5) is controlling and that it requires OSHA to promulgate a standard that either gives an absolute assurance of safety for each and every worker or reduces exposures to the lowest level feasible. The Government interprets "feasible" as meaning technologically achievable at a cost that would not impair the viability of the industries subject to the regulation. The respondent industry representatives, on the other hand, argue that the Court of Appeals was correct in holding that the reasonably necessary and appropriate language of § 3(8), along with the feasibility requirement of § 6(b)(5), requires the Agency to quantify both the costs and the benefits of a proposed rule and to conclude that they are roughly commensurate.

In our view, it is not necessary to decide whether either the Government or industry is entirely correct. For we think it is clear that § 3(8) does apply to all permanent standards promulgated under the Act and that it requires the Secretary, before issuing any standard, to determine that it is reasonably necessary and appropriate to remedy a significant risk of material health impairment. Only after the Secretary has made the threshold determination that such a risk exists with respect to a toxic substance, would it be necessary to decide whether § 6(b)(5) requires him to select the most protective standard he can consistent with economic and technological feasibility, or whether, as respondents argue, the benefits of the regulation must be commensurate with the costs of its implementation. Because the Secretary did not make the required threshold finding in these cases, we have no occasion to determine whether costs must be weighed against benefits in an appropriate case.

A

Under the Government's view, § 3(8), if it has any substantive content at all, merely requires OSHA to issue standards that are reasonably calculated to produce a safer or more healthy work environment. Apart from this minimal requirement of rationality, the Government argues that § 3(8) imposes no limits on the Agency's power, and thus would not prevent it from requiring employers to do whatever would be "reasonably necessary" to eliminate all risks of any harm from their workplaces. With respect to toxic substances and harmful physical agents, the Government takes an even more extreme position. Relying on § 6(b)(5)'s direction to set a standard "which most adequately assures ... that no employee will suffer material impairment of health or functional capacity," the Government contends that the Secretary is required to impose standards that either guarantee workplaces that are free from any risk of material health impairment, however small, or that come as close as possible to doing so without ruining entire industries.

If the purpose of the statute were to eliminate completely and with absolute certainty any risk of serious harm, we would agree that it would be proper for the Secretary to interpret §§ 3(8) and 6(b)(5) in this fashion. But we think it is clear that the statute was not designed to require employers to provide absolutely risk-free workplaces whenever it is technologically feasible to do so, so long as the cost is not great enough to destroy an entire industry. Rather, both the language and structure of the Act, as well as its legislative history, indicate that it was intended to require the elimination, as far as feasible, of significant risks of harm.

By empowering the Secretary to promulgate standards that are "reasonably necessary or appropriate to provide safe or healthful employment and places of employment," the Act implies that, before promulgating any standard, the Secretary must make a finding that the workplaces in question are not safe. But "safe" is not the equivalent of "risk-free." There are many activities that we engage in every day—such as driving a car or even breathing city air—that entail some risk of accident or material health impairment; nevertheless, few people would consider these activities "unsafe." Similarly, a workplace can hardly be considered "unsafe" unless it threatens the workers with a significant risk of harm.

Therefore, before he can promulgate any permanent health or safety standard, the Secretary is required to make a threshold ruling that a place of employment is unsafe—in the sense that significant risks are present and can be eliminated or lessened by a change in practices. * * * [Section 6(b)(5)] repeatedly uses the term "standard" without suggesting any exception from, or qualification of, the general definition [found in § 3(8)]; on the contrary, it directs the Secretary to select "the standard"—that is to say, one of various possible alternatives that satisfy the basic definition in § 3(8)—that is most protective. Moreover, requiring the Secretary to make a threshold finding of significant risk is consistent with the scope of the regulatory power granted to him by § 6(b)(5), which empowers the Secretary to promulgate standards, not for chemicals and physical agents generally, but for "toxic materials" and "harmful physical agents."[48]

---

48. * * * Mr. Justice Marshall states that our view of § 3(8) would make the first sentence in § 6(b)(5) superfluous. We disagree. The first sentence of § 6(b)(5) requires the Secretary to select a highly protective standard once he has determined that a standard should be promulgated. The threshold finding that there is a need for such a standard in the sense that there is a significant risk in the workplace is not unlike the threshold finding that a

* * * In the absence of a clear mandate in the Act, it is unreasonable to assume that Congress intended to give the Secretary the unprecedented power over American industry that would result from the Government's view of §§ 3(8) and 6(b)(5), coupled with OSHA's cancer policy. Expert testimony that a substance is probably a human carcinogen either because it has caused cancer in animals or because individuals have contracted cancer following extremely high exposure would justify the conclusion that the substance poses some risk of serious harm no matter how minute the exposure and no matter how many experts testified that they regarded the risk as insignificant. That conclusion would in turn justify pervasive regulation limited only by the constraint of feasibility. In light of the fact that there are literally thousands of substances used in the workplace that have been identified as carcinogens or suspect carcinogens, the Government's theory would give OSHA power to impose enormous costs that might produce little, if any, discernible benefit.

If the Government was correct in arguing that neither § 3(8) nor § 6(b)(5) requires that the risk from a toxic substance be quantified sufficiently to enable the Secretary to characterize it as significant in an understandable way, the statute would make such a "sweeping delegation of legislative power" that it might be unconstitutional under the Court's reasoning in A.L.A. Schechter Poultry Corp. v. United States, 295 U.S. 495, 539, and Panama Refining Co. v. Ryan, 293 U.S. 388. A construction of the statute that avoids this kind of open-ended grant should certainly be favored.

* * *

Given the conclusion that the Act empowers the Secretary to promulgate health and safety standards only where a significant risk of harm exists, the critical issue becomes how to define and allocate the burden of proving the significance of the risk in a case such as this, where scientific knowledge is imperfect and the precise quantification of risks is therefore impossible. The Agency's position is that there is substantial evidence in the record to support its conclusion that there is no absolutely safe level for a carcinogen and that, therefore, the burden is properly on industry to prove, apparently beyond a shadow of a doubt, that there is a safe level for benzene exposure. The Agency argues that, because of the uncertainties in this area any other approach would render it helpless, forcing it to wait for the leukemia deaths that it believes are likely to occur before taking any regulatory action.

We disagree. As we read the statute, the burden was on the Agency to show, on the basis of substantial evidence, that it is at least more likely than not that long-term exposure to 10 ppm of benzene presents a significant risk of material health impairment. Ordinarily, it is the proponent of a rule or order who has the burden of proof in administrative proceedings.

---

chemical is toxic or a physical agent is harmful. Once the Secretary has made the requisite threshold finding, § 6(b)(5) directs him to choose the most protective standard that still meets the definition of a standard under § 3(8), consistent with feasibility.

See 5 U.S.C. § 556(d). In some cases involving toxic substances, Congress has shifted the burden of proving that a particular substance is safe onto the party opposing the proposed rule. The fact that Congress did not follow this course in enacting the Occupational Safety and Health Act indicates that it intended the Agency to bear the normal burden of establishing the need for a proposed standard.

* * *

Contrary to the Government's contentions, imposing a burden on the Agency of demonstrating a significant risk of harm will not strip it of its ability to regulate carcinogens, nor will it require the Agency to wait for deaths to occur before taking any action. First, the requirement that a "significant" risk be identified is not a mathematical straitjacket. It is the Agency's responsibility to determine, in the first instance, what it considers to be a "significant" risk. Some risks are plainly acceptable and others are plainly unacceptable. If, for example, the odds are one in a billion that a person will die from cancer by taking a drink of chlorinated water, the risk clearly could not be considered significant. On the other hand, if the odds are one in a thousand that regular inhalation of gasoline vapors that are 2 percent benzene will be fatal, a reasonable person might well consider the risk significant and take appropriate steps to decrease or eliminate it. Although the Agency has no duty to calculate the exact probability of harm, it does have an obligation to find that a significant risk is present before it can characterize a place of employment as "unsafe."

Second, OSHA is not required to support its finding that a significant risk exists with anything approaching scientific certainty. Although the Agency's findings must be supported by substantial evidence, § 6(b)(5) specifically allows the Secretary to regulate on the basis of the "best available evidence." * * * [T]his provision requires a reviewing court to give OSHA some leeway where its findings must be made on the frontiers of scientific knowledge. Thus, so long as they are supported by a body of reputable scientific thought, the Agency is free to use conservative assumptions in interpreting the data with respect to carcinogens, risking error on the side of overprotection rather than underprotection.[61]

It should also be noted that, in setting a permissible exposure level in reliance on less-than-perfect methods, OSHA would have the benefit of a backstop in the form of monitoring and medical testing. Thus, if OSHA properly determined that the permissible exposure limit should be set at 5 ppm, it could still require monitoring and medical testing for employees exposed to lower levels. By doing so, it could keep a constant check on the

---

61. Mr. Justice Marshall states that, under our approach, the Agency must either wait for deaths to occur or must "deceive the public" by making a basically meaningless determination of significance based on totally inadequate evidence. Mr. Justice Marshall's view, however, rests on the erroneous premise that the only reason OSHA did not attempt to quantify benefits in this case was because it could not do so in any reasonable manner. As the discussion of the Agency's rejection of an industry attempt at formulating a dose-response curve demonstrates, however, the Agency's rejection of methods such as dose-response curves was based at least in part on its view that nothing less than absolute safety would suffice.

validity of the assumptions made in developing the permissible exposure limit, giving it a sound evidentiary basis for decreasing the limit if it was initially set too high. Moreover, in this way it could ensure that workers who were unusually susceptible to benzene could be removed from exposure before they had suffered any permanent damage.

* * *

■ Justice Powell, concurring in part and concurring in the judgment.

For the reasons stated by the plurality, I agree that §§ 6(b)(5) and 3(8) of the Occupational Safety and Health Act of 1970 must be read together. They require OSHA to make a threshold finding that proposed occupational health standards are reasonably necessary to provide safe workplaces. When OSHA acts to reduce existing national consensus standards, therefore, it must find that (i) currently permissible exposure levels create a significant risk of material health impairment; and (ii) a reduction of those levels would significantly reduce the hazard.

* * *

* * * But even if one assumes that OSHA properly met this burden, I conclude that the statute also requires the agency to determine that the economic effects of its standard bear a reasonable relationship to the expected benefits. An occupational health standard is neither "reasonably necessary" nor "feasible," as required by statute, if it calls for expenditures wholly disproportionate to the expected health and safety benefits.

OSHA contends that § 6(b)(5) not only permits but actually requires it to promulgate standards that reduce health risks without regard to economic effects, unless those effects would cause widespread dislocation throughout an entire industry. Under the threshold test adopted by the plurality today, this authority will exist only with respect to "significant" risks. But the plurality does not reject OSHA's claim that it must reduce such risks without considering economic consequences less serious than massive dislocation. In my view, that claim is untenable.

Although one might wish that Congress had spoken with greater clarity, the legislative history and purposes of the statute do not support OSHA's interpretation of the Act. It is simply unreasonable to believe that Congress intended OSHA to pursue the desirable goal of risk-free workplaces to the extent that the economic viability of particular industries—or significant segments thereof—is threatened. * * *

In these cases, OSHA did find that the "substantial costs" of the benzene regulations are justified. But the record before us contains neither adequate documentation of this conclusion, nor any evidence that OSHA weighed the relevant considerations. The agency simply announced its finding of cost-justification without explaining the method by which it determines that the benefits justify the costs and their economic effects. No rational system of regulation can permit its administrators to make policy judgments without explaining how their decisions effectuate the purposes of the governing law, and nothing in the statute authorizes such laxity in these cases. * * *

■ JUSTICE REHNQUIST, concurring in the judgment, would have ruled that the relevant provisions of the OSH Act unconstitutionally delegated legislative power to the agency.

■ MR. JUSTICE MARSHALL with whom MR. JUSTICE BRENNAN, MR. JUSTICE WHITE, and MR. JUSTICE BLACKMUN join, dissenting.

The plurality ignores the plain meaning of the Occupational Safety and Health Act of 1970 in order to bring the authority of the Secretary of Labor in line with the plurality's own views of proper regulatory policy. The unfortunate consequence is that the Federal Government's efforts to protect American workers from cancer and other crippling diseases may be substantially impaired.

* * * I do not pretend to know whether the test the plurality erects today is, as a matter of policy, preferable to that created by Congress and its delegates: the area is too fraught with scientific uncertainty, and too dependent on considerations of policy, for a court to be able to determine whether it is desirable to require identification of a "significant" risk before allowing an administrative agency to take regulatory action. But in light of the tenor of the plurality opinion, it is necessary to point out that the question is not one-sided, and that Congress' decision to authorize the Secretary to promulgate the regulation at issue here was a reasonable one.

In this case the Secretary found that exposure to benzene at levels above 1 ppm posed a definite albeit unquantifiable risk of chromosomal damage, nonmalignant blood disorders, and leukemia. The existing evidence was sufficient to justify the conclusion that such a risk was presented, but it did not permit even rough quantification of that risk. Discounting for the various scientific uncertainties, the Secretary gave "careful consideration to the question of whether the[ ] substantial costs" of the standard "are justified in light of the hazards of exposure to benzene," and concluded that "these costs are necessary in order to effectuate the statutory purpose ... and to adequately protect employees from the hazards of exposure to benzene."

In these circumstances it seems clear that the Secretary found a risk that is "significant" in the sense that the word is normally used. There was some direct evidence of chromosomal damage, nonmalignant blood disorders, and leukemia at exposures at or near 10 ppm and below. In addition, expert after expert testified that the recorded effects of benzene exposure at higher levels justified an inference that an exposure level above 1 ppm was dangerous. The plurality's extraordinarily searching scrutiny of this factual record reveals no basis for a conclusion that quantification is, on the basis of "the best available evidence," possible at the present time. If the Secretary decided to wait until definitive information was available, American workers would be subjected for the indefinite future to a possibly substantial risk of benzene-induced leukemia and other illnesses. It is unsurprising, at least to me, that he concluded that the statute authorized him to take regulatory action now.

Under these circumstances, the plurality's requirement of identification of a "significant" risk will have one of two consequences. If the plurality means to require the Secretary realistically to "quantify" the risk in order to satisfy a court that it is "significant," the record shows that the plurality means to require him to do the impossible. But the regulatory inaction has very significant costs of its own. The adoption of such a test would subject American workers to a continuing risk of cancer and other serious diseases; it would disable the Secretary from regulating a wide variety of carcinogens for which quantification simply cannot be undertaken at the present time.

There are encouraging signs that today's decision does not extend that far.* * * The plurality * * * indicates that it would not prohibit the Secretary from promulgating safety standards when quantification of the benefits is impossible. The Court might thus allow the Secretary to attempt to make a very rough quantification of the risk imposed by a carcinogenic substance, and give considerable deference to his finding that the risk was significant. If so, the Court would permit the Secretary to promulgate precisely the same regulation involved in these cases if he had not relied on a carcinogen "policy," but undertaken a review of the evidence and the expert testimony and concluded, on the basis of conservative assumptions, that the risk addressed is a significant one. Any other interpretation of the plurality's approach would allow a court to displace the agency's judgment with its own subjective conception of "significance," a duty to be performed without statutory guidance.

The consequences of this second approach would hardly be disastrous; indeed, it differs from my own principally in its assessment of the basis for the Secretary's decision in these cases. It is objectionable, however, for three reasons. First, the requirement of identification of a "significant" risk simply has no relationship to the statute that the Court today purports to construe. Second, if the "threshold finding" requirement means only that the Secretary must find "that there is a need for such a standard," the requirement was plainly satisfied by the Secretary's express statement that the standard's costs "are necessary in order to effectuate the statutory purpose ... and to adequately protect employees from the hazards of exposure to benzene." Third, the record amply demonstrates that in light of existing scientific knowledge, no purpose would be served by requiring the Secretary to take steps to quantify the risk of exposure to benzene at low levels. Any such quantification would be based not on scientific "knowledge" as that term is normally understood, but on considerations of policy. For carcinogens like benzene, the assumptions on which a dose-response curve must be based are necessarily arbitrary. To require a quantitative showing of a "significant" risk, therefore, would either paralyze the Secretary into inaction or force him to deceive the public by acting on the basis of assumptions that must be considered too speculative to support any realistic assessment of the relevant risk. * * *

In passing the Occupational Safety and Health Act of 1970, Congress was aware that it was authorizing the Secretary to regulate in areas of scientific uncertainty. But it intended to require stringent regulation even when definitive information was unavailable. In reducing the permissible level of exposure to benzene, the Secretary applied proper legal standards. His determinations are supported by substantial evidence. The Secretary's decision was one, then, which the governing legislation authorized him to make.

In recent years there has been increasing recognition that the products of technological development may have harmful effects whose incidence and severity cannot be predicted with certainty. The responsibility to regulate such products has fallen to administrative agencies. Their task is not an enviable one. Frequently no clear causal link can be established between the regulated substance and the harm to be averted. Risks of harm are often uncertain, but inaction has considerable costs of its own. The agency must decide whether to take regulatory action against possibly substantial risks or to wait until more definitive information becomes available—a judgment which by its very nature cannot be based solely on determinations of fact.

Those delegations, in turn, have been made on the understanding that judicial review would be available to ensure that the agency's determinations are supported by substantial evidence and that its actions do not exceed the limits set by Congress. In the Occupational Safety and Health Act, Congress expressed confidence that the courts would carry out this important responsibility. But in these cases the plurality has far exceeded its authority. The plurality's "threshold finding" requirement is nowhere to be found in the Act and is antithetical to its basic purposes. * * *

NOTES AND QUESTIONS

1. *OSHA's analysis.* What rationale did OSHA use to justify its new rule? What are the costs and benefits of lowering the exposure limit for benzene to 1 ppm? Are the benefits worth the costs?

2. *Statutory interpretation.* In your opinion, did OSHA properly interpret its authority under the Occupational Safety and Health Act? Does OSHA have the authority to build a margin of safety into its regulatory standards? How clear is the statutory language? What evidence is there of Congress' intent?

3. *Understanding the opinions.* In the plurality's view, what was wrong with OSHA's rule? What, according to Justice Stevens, must OSHA do in order to justify its rule? How does Justice Powell's view differ from the plurality's? Why would Justice Marshall uphold the rule?

4. *A postscript to Benzene.* Following the *Benzene* decision, OSHA confirmed through further epidemiological tests that benzene poses very serious risks to workers. OSHA compiled a 36,000-page record, held hearings, and promulgated a new PEL in September 1987. The new PEL lowered the eight-hour average exposure limit from 10 ppm to 1 ppm. The new PEL was based upon OSHA's determination that the old PEL of 10 ppm posed a risk of 95 additional leukemia deaths per 1000 workers, that this risk was significant, and that the new PEL would save many lives. 52 Fed. Reg. 34,460 (1987).

Note that the new PEL is identical to the PEL promulgated in 1977 and struck down in the *Benzene* decision. What was gained by forcing OSHA to carry out additional tests, compile a more extensive record, and hold public hearings? What were the costs? Is judicial review worth the costs?

5. *Whether the OSH Act requires cost-benefit analysis.* In *American Textile Manufacturers Institute v. Donovan (The Cotton Dust Case),* 452 U.S. 490 (1981), the Supreme Court returned to an issue left undecided in the *Benzene* case: whether § 6(b)(5) or § 3(8) of the Occupational Safety and Health Act requires cost-benefit analysis. The case involved a challenge to a standard limiting occupational exposure to cotton dust. Turning first to § 6(b)(5), the Court explained that the provision's critical phrase, "to the extent feasible," plainly mandated feasibility analysis rather than cost-benefit analysis. Although the Court acknowledged that the "reasonably necessary or appropriate" language of § 3(8) might be construed to contemplate some balancing of costs and benefits, the Court found the feasibility language of § 6(b)(5) dispositive:

> * * * Congress specifically chose in § 6(b)(5) to impose separate and additional requirements for issuance of a subcategory of occupational safety and health standards dealing with toxic materials and harmful physical agents: it required that those standards be issued to prevent material impairment of health to the extent feasible. Congress could reasonably have concluded that health standards should be subject to different criteria than safety standards because of the special problems presented in regulating them.
>
> Agreement with petitioners' argument that § 3(8) imposes an additional and overriding requirement of cost-benefit analysis on the issuance of § 6(b)(5) standards would eviscerate the "to the extent feasible" requirement. Standards would inevitably be set at the level indicated by cost-benefit analysis, and not at the level specified by § 6(b)(5). For example, if cost-benefit analysis indicated a protective standard of 1,000 ug/m³ PEL, while feasibility analysis indicated a 500 ug/m³ PEL, the agency would be forced by the cost-benefit requirement to choose the less stringent point. We cannot believe that Congress intended the general terms of § 3(8) to countermand the specific feasibility requirement of § 6(b)(5). Adoption of petitioners' interpretation would effectively write § 6(b)(5) out of the Act.

452 U.S. at 512–13.

6. *The influence of the Benzene decision.* Justice Stevens' plurality opinion in the *Benzene* case has been very influential. The Courts of Appeals have generally concluded that the plurality opinion in *Benzene* was adopted by a majority of the Supreme Court in *American Textile Manufacturers Institute*. See, e.g., AFL–CIO v. OSHA, 965 F.2d 962 (11th Cir. 1992) (vacating and remanding OSHA's Air Contaminants Standard, a set of permissible exposure limits (PELs) for 428 toxic substances); Asarco, Inc. v. OSHA, 746 F.2d 483 (9th Cir. 1984).

7. *Determining the extent of regulatory control.* There are three basic approaches for determining the extent of regulatory control: health-based standards, cost-benefit balancing, and technology-based standards.

Statutes incorporating health-based standards focus on health protection without regard to cost (or at least without open reference to cost). The Clean Air Act, for example, directs EPA to set ambient air quality standards that, "allowing an adequate margin of safety, are requisite to protect the public health." 42 U.S.C. § 7409(b)(1). Pesticide tolerances under the Food Quality Protection Act, discussed later in this chapter, must provide "a reasonable certainty that no harm will result from aggregate exposure." 21 U.S.C. § 346a(b)(2)(A)(ii). Such health-based standards finesse tricky cost-benefit analysis issues, and can help correct political power imbalances between well-organized industry interests who stand to bear concentrated costs and the diffuse general public which benefits from regulation. But because health and environmental impacts are frequently uncertain, their use as a basis for standards can cause "paralysis by analysis" if the regulatory agency must bear the burden of proving a significant threat of harm, or produce unnecessary over-regulation if that burden is placed on the regulated community.

Other statutory provisions require some kind of comparison of the costs and benefits of regulations. The Federal Insecticide, Fungicide, and Rodenticide Act (FIFRA), for example, requires that EPA find, before registering a pesticide for use, that it will not cause "unreasonable adverse effects on the environment." 7 U.S.C. § 136a(c)(5). The statute defines an unreasonable adverse effect as "any unreasonable risk to man or the environment, taking into account the economic, social, and environmental costs and benefits" of the pesticide. As these provisions suggest, balancing standards are often murky. Analysts tend to interpret them in light of their own attitudes and preferences. Some characterize FIFRA as prohibiting regulation unless benefits justify costs, while others see a more open-ended balancing process. Balancing requirements recognize that society is often trying to effectuate multiple conflicting goals. A formal cost-benefit test, however, imposes substantial burdens on regulatory agencies, particularly when industry sources have better access than regulators to information about the costs of compliance.

Still other statutes focus not on the extent of risk reduction but instead on what is technologically feasible. The Clean Water Act and the Clean Air Act, among others, rely in part on standards mandating use of the best available pollution control technology. Technology-based standards have frequently been criticized as rigid and economically inefficient. As Wendy Wagner points out, however, they have their benefits. They save regulatory agencies from the informational challenges of both cost-benefit analysis and health risk demonstration. Although identifying the best available technology is not without its own difficulties, in practice technology-based regulations have been developed much more rapidly than either health-based or cost-benefit balancing standards. The Clean Air Act toxics provision offers a striking example of this advantage. For its first twenty years, the Clean Air Act directed EPA to issue health-based standards for toxic air pollutants. In that time, the agency managed to issue regulations for only seven pollutants. Switching to a technology-based approach in the 1990 Clean Air Act Amendments produced a dramatic turn-around. In the next ten years, EPA issued standards for nearly all major sources of toxic air pollution. In addition, by requiring that regulated facilities "do their best" to reduce environmental harms, technology-based standards communicate a message of moral responsibility while acknowledging the importance of industry to the nation's overall welfare. They may also provide greater predictability for regulated entities and be easier for regulatory agencies to monitor and enforce. Finally, technology-based standards can, at least in theory, be designed to easily ratchet up the level of regulation as technology improves, and to provide incentives for the development of new pollution control technologies. Wendy E. Wagner, The Triumph of Technology–Based Standards, 2000 U. Ill. L. Rev. 83 (2000).

SECTION 3. APPROACHES TO REGULATING TOXIC RISKS

Legislators can choose from a wide variety of mechanisms to regulate toxic risks, ranging from product bans to ambient standards to information disclosure requirements. As you learn in this section about some of the approaches that have been used, consider their relative strengths and weaknesses.

A. CONGRESS' ATTEMPT AT A COMPREHENSIVE APPROACH: THE TOXIC SUBSTANCES CONTROL ACT (TSCA)

The Toxic Substances Control Act (TSCA), 15 U.S.C. §§ 2601–2692, was enacted in 1976 to provide EPA broad regulatory authority over the manufacture, processing, distribution, use, and disposal of chemical substances both before and after their introduction into commerce.

TSCA provides EPA with regulatory authority in three key areas: regulating chemicals that present health or environmental risks; screening new chemicals and significant new uses of existing chemicals; and testing chemicals whose risks are unknown. First, under Section 6 of TSCA, EPA has the authority to regulate the manufacture, processing, distribution, use, or disposal of any chemical substance if it finds that there is a "reasonable basis to conclude" that such an activity "presents or will present an unreasonable risk of injury to health or the environment." Second, for new chemicals, Section 5 of TSCA requires manufacturers to provide a premanufacture notice ("PMN") and to submit any available health and safety data to EPA. EPA may take action to control unreasonable risks, but if EPA takes no action on the PMN within ninety days, manufacture of the chemical can proceed. Section 5 also gives EPA the authority to evaluate significant new uses of existing chemicals. EPA must promulgate a rule determining that there is a significant new use, and a company subject to such a rule must provide a significant new use notice ("SNUN"), which is similar to a PMN. Third, although TSCA itself does not require manufacturers to conduct testing that would generate any health and safety data, Section 4 of TSCA authorizes EPA to require such testing to be done. EPA must make certain statutory findings—that a chemical "may present an unreasonable risk of injury to health or the environment," or that a chemical "will be produced in substantial quantities," resulting in substantial human exposure or entry of substantial quantities into the environment—and EPA must promulgate a rule to require such testing. The EPA can promulgate a test rule without direct evidence of human exposure and even where potential exposure is brief and non-recurrent. See Chemical Manufacturers Association v. U.S. Environmental Protection Agency, 859 F.2d 977 (D.C. Cir. 1988).

Excerpts From the Toxic Substances Control Act

15 U.S.C. § 2605.

§ 6 Regulation of hazardous chemical substances and mixtures

(a) Scope of regulation

If the Administrator finds that there is a reasonable basis to conclude that the manufacture, processing, distribution in commerce, use, or disposal of a chemical substance or mixture, or that any combination of such activities, presents or will present an unreasonable risk of injury to health or the environment, the Administrator shall by rule apply one or more of the following requirements to such substance or mixture to the extent necessary to protect adequately against such risk using the least burdensome requirements:

(1) A requirement (A) prohibiting the manufacturing, processing, or distribution in commerce of such substance or mixture, or (B) limiting the amount of such substance or mixture which may be manufactured, processed, or distributed in commerce.

(2) A requirement—

(A) prohibiting the manufacture, processing, or distribution in commerce of such substance or mixture for (i) a particular use or (ii) a particular use in a concentration in excess of a level specified by the Administrator in the rule imposing the requirement, or

(B) limiting the amount of such substance or mixture which may be manufactured, processed, or distributed in commerce for (i) a particular use or (ii) a particular use in a concentration in excess of a level specified by the Administrator in the rule imposing the requirement.

(3) A requirement that such substance or mixture or any article containing such substance or mixture be marked with or accompanied by clear and adequate warnings and instructions with respect to its use, distribution in commerce, or disposal or with respect to any combination of such activities. The form and content of such warnings and instructions shall be prescribed by the Administrator.

(4) A requirement that manufacturers and processors of such substance or mixture make and retain records of the processes used to manufacture or process such substance or mixture and monitor or conduct tests which are reasonable and necessary to assure compliance with the requirements of any rule applicable under this subsection.

(5) A requirement prohibiting or otherwise regulating any manner or method of commercial use of such substance or mixture.

(6)(A) A requirement prohibiting or otherwise regulating any manner or method of disposal of such substance or mixture, or of any article containing such substance or mixture, by its manufacturer or processor or by any other person who uses, or disposes of, it for commercial purposes.

(B) A requirement under subparagraph (A) may not require any person to take any action which would be in violation of any law or requirement of, or in effect for, a State or political subdivision, and shall require each person subject to it to notify each State and political subdivision in which a required disposal may occur of such disposal.

(7) A requirement directing manufacturers or processors of such substance or mixture (A) to give notice of such unreasonable risk of injury to distributors in commerce of such substance or mixture and, to the extent reasonably ascertainable, to other persons in possession of such substance or mixture or exposed to such substance or mixture, (B) to give public notice of such risk of injury, and (C) to replace or repurchase such substance or mixture as elected by the person to which the requirement is directed.

* * *

Corrosion Proof Fittings v. Environmental Protection Agency

United States Court of Appeals, Fifth Circuit, 1991.
947 F.2d 1201.

■ Jerry E. Smith, Circuit Judge:

Asbestos is a naturally occurring fibrous material that resists fire and most solvents. Its major uses include heat-resistant insulators, cements, building materials, fireproof gloves and clothing, and motor vehicle brake linings. Asbestos is a toxic material, and occupational exposure to asbestos dust can result in mesothelioma, asbestosis, and lung cancer.

The EPA began these proceedings in 1979, when it issued an Advanced Notice of Proposed Rulemaking announcing its intent to explore the use of

TSCA "to reduce the risk to human health posed by exposure to asbestos." *See* 54 Fed. Reg. 29,460 (1989). While these proceedings were pending, other agencies continued their regulation of asbestos uses, in particular the Occupational Safety and Health Administration (OSHA), which in 1983 and 1984 involved itself with lowering standards for workplace asbestos exposure.

An EPA-appointed panel reviewed over one hundred studies of asbestos and conducted several public meetings. Based upon its studies and the public comments, the EPA concluded that asbestos is a potential carcinogen at all levels of exposure, regardless of the type of asbestos or the size of the fiber. The EPA concluded in 1986 that exposure to asbestos "poses an unreasonable risk to human health" and thus proposed at least four regulatory options for prohibiting or restricting the use of asbestos, including a mixed ban and phase-out of asbestos over ten years; a two-stage ban of asbestos, depending upon product usage; a three-stage ban on all asbestos products leading to a total ban in ten years; and labeling of all products containing asbestos.

Over the next two years, the EPA updated its data, received further comments, and allowed cross-examination on the updated documents. In 1989, the EPA issued a final rule prohibiting the manufacture, importation, processing, and distribution in commerce of most asbestos-containing products. Finding that asbestos constituted an unreasonable risk to health and the environment, the EPA promulgated a staged ban of most commercial uses of asbestos. The EPA estimates that this rule will save either 202 or 148 lives, depending upon whether the benefits are discounted, at a cost of approximately $450–800 million, depending upon the price of substitutes.

The rule is to take effect in three stages, depending upon the EPA's assessment of how toxic each substance is and how soon adequate substitutes will be available.[2] The rule allows affected persons one more year at each stage to sell existing stocks of prohibited products. The rule also imposes labeling requirements on stage 2 or stage 3 products and allows for exemptions from the rule in certain cases.

* * *

A. *Standard of Review*

* * *

Contrary to the EPA's assertions, the arbitrary and capricious standard found in the APA and the substantial evidence standard found in

---

2. The main products covered by each ban stage are as follows:

(1) Stage 1: August 27, 1990: ban on asbestos-containing floor materials, clothing, roofing felt, corrugated and flat sheet materials, pipeline wrap, and new asbestos uses;

(2) Stage 2: August 25, 1993: ban on asbestos-containing "friction products" and certain automotive products or uses;

(3) Stage 3: August 26, 1996: ban on other asbestos-containing automotive products or uses, asbestos-containing building materials including non-roof and roof coatings, and asbestos cement shingles.

See 54 Fed. Reg. at 29,461–62.

TSCA are different standards, even in the context of an informal rulemaking. Congress specifically went out of its way to provide that "the standard of review prescribed by paragraph (2)(E) of section 706 [of the APA] shall not apply and the court shall hold unlawful and set aside such rule if the court finds that the rule is not supported by substantial evidence in rulemaking record ... taken as a whole." 15 U.S.C. § 2618(c)(1)(B)(i). "The substantial evidence standard mandated by [TSCA] is generally considered to be more rigorous than the arbitrary and capricious standard normally applied to informal rulemaking," Environmental Defense Fund v. EPA, 636 F.2d 1267, 1277 (D.C. Cir. 1980), and "afford[s] a considerably more generous judicial review" than the arbitrary and capricious test. The test "imposes a considerable burden on the agency and limits its discretion in arriving at a factual predicate."

"Under the substantial evidence standard, a reviewing court must give careful scrutiny to agency findings and, at the same time, accord appropriate deference to administrative decisions that are based on agency experience and expertise." Environmental Defense Fund, 636 F.2d at 1277. * * *

The recent case of Chemical Mfrs. Assn. v. EPA, 899 F.2d 344 (5th Cir. 1990), provides our basic framework for reviewing the EPA's actions. In evaluating whether the EPA has presented substantial evidence, we examine (1) whether the quantities of the regulated chemical entering into the environment are "substantial" and (2) whether human exposure to the chemical is "substantial" or "significant." *Id.* at 359. An agency may exercise its judgment without strictly relying upon quantifiable risks, costs, and benefits, but it must "cogently explain why it has exercised its discretion in a given matter."

* * *

B. *The EPA's Burden Under TSCA*

TSCA provides, in pertinent part, as follows:

(a) Scope of regulation. If the Administrator finds that there is a *reasonable basis* to conclude that the manufacture, processing, distribution in commerce, use, or disposal of a chemical substance or mixture, or that any combination of such activities, presents or will present an *unreasonable risk of injury* to health or the environment, the Administrator shall by rule apply one or more of the following requirements to such substance or mixture to the extent necessary *to protect adequately* against such risk using the *least burdensome* requirements. [15 U.S.C. § 2605(a)] (emphasis added). As the highlighted language shows, Congress did not enact TSCA as a zero-risk statute. The EPA, rather, was required to consider both alternatives to a ban and the costs of any proposed actions and to "carry out this chapter in a reasonable and prudent manner [after considering] the environmental, economic, and social impact of any action." 15 U.S.C. § 2601(c).

We conclude that the EPA has presented insufficient evidence to justify its asbestos ban. We base this conclusion upon two grounds: the failure of the EPA to consider all necessary evidence and its failure to give adequate weight to statutory language requiring it to promulgate the least burdensome, reasonable regulation required to protect the environment adequately. Because the EPA failed to address these concerns, and because the EPA is required to articulate a "reasoned basis" for its rules, we are compelled to return the regulation to the agency for reconsideration.

1.

Least Burdensome and Reasonable

TSCA requires that the EPA use the least burdensome regulation to achieve its goal of minimum reasonable risk. This statutory requirement can create problems in evaluating just what is a "reasonable risk." Congress's rejection of a no-risk policy, however, also means that in certain cases, the least burdensome yet still adequate solution may entail somewhat more risk than would other, known regulations that are far more burdensome on the industry and the economy. The very language of TSCA requires that the EPA, once it has determined what an acceptable level of non-zero risk is, choose the least burdensome method of reaching that level.

In this case, the EPA banned, for all practical purposes, all present and future uses of asbestos—a position the petitioners characterize as the "death penalty alternative," as this is the *most* burdensome of all possible alternatives listed as open to the EPA under TSCA. TSCA not only provides the EPA with a list of alternative actions, but also provides those alternatives in order of how burdensome they are. The regulations thus provide for EPA regulation ranging from labeling the least toxic chemicals to limiting the total amount of chemicals an industry may use. Total bans head the list as the most burdensome regulatory option.

By choosing the harshest remedy given to it under TSCA, the EPA assigned to itself the toughest burden in satisfying TSCA's requirement that its alternative be the least burdensome of all those offered to it. Since, both by definition and by the terms of TSCA, the complete ban of manufacturing is the most burdensome alternative—for even stringent regulation at least allows a manufacturer the chance to invest and meet the new, higher standard—the EPA's regulation cannot stand if there is any other regulation that would achieve an acceptable level of risk as mandated by TSCA.

The EPA considered, and rejected, such options as labeling asbestos products, thereby warning users and workers involved in the manufacture of asbestos-containing products of the chemical's dangers, and stricter workplace rules. EPA also rejected controlled use of asbestos in the workplace and deferral to other government agencies charged with worker and consumer exposure to industrial and product hazards, such as OSHA * * *. The EPA determined that deferral to these other agencies was inappropriate because no one other authority could address all the risks posed "throughout the life cycle" by asbestos, and any action by one or more of the other agencies still would leave an unacceptable residual risk.

Much of the EPA's analysis is correct, and the EPA's basic decision to use TSCA as a comprehensive statute designed to fight a multi-industry problem was a proper one that we uphold today on review. What concerns us, however, is the manner in which the EPA conducted some of its analysis. TSCA requires the EPA to consider, along with the effects of toxic substances on human health and the environment, "the benefits of such substance[s] or mixture[s] for various uses and the availability of substitutes for such uses," as well as "the reasonably ascertainable economic consequences of the rule, after consideration for the effect on the national economy, small business, technological innovation, the environment, and public health." *Id.* § 2605(c)(*l*)(C–D).

The EPA presented two comparisons in the record: a world with no further regulation under TSCA, and a world in which no manufacture of asbestos takes place. The EPA rejected calculating how many lives a less burdensome regulation would save, and at what costs. Furthermore the EPA, when calculating the benefits of its ban, explicitly refused to compare it to an improved workplace in which currently available control technology is utilized. This decision artificially inflated the purported benefits of the rule by using a baseline comparison substantially lower than what currently available technology could yield.

Under TSCA, the EPA was required to evaluate, rather than ignore, less burdensome regulatory alternatives. TSCA imposes a least-to-most-burdensome hierarchy. In order to impose a regulation at the top of the hierarchy—a total ban of asbestos—the EPA must show not only that its proposed action reduces the risk of the product to an adequate level, but also that the actions Congress identified as less burdensome also would not do the job. The failure of the EPA to do this constitutes a failure to meet its burden of showing that its actions not only reduce the risk but do so in the Congressionally-mandated *least burdensome* fashion.

Thus it was not enough for the EPA to show, as it did in this case, that banning some asbestos products might reduce the harm that could occur from the use of these products. If that were the standard, it would be no standard at all, for few indeed are the products that are so safe that a complete ban of them would not make the world still safer.

This comparison of two static worlds is insufficient to satisfy the dictates of TSCA. While the EPA may have shown that a world with a complete ban of asbestos might be preferable to one in which there is only the current amount of regulation, the EPA has failed to show that there is not some intermediate state of regulation that would be superior to both the currently regulated and the completely-banned world. * * *

Upon an initial showing of product danger, the proper course for the EPA to follow is to consider each regulatory option, beginning with the least burdensome, and the costs and benefits of regulation under each option. The EPA cannot simply skip several rungs, as it did in this case, for in doing so, it may skip a less-burdensome alternative mandated by TSCA. Here, although the EPA mentions the problems posed by intermediate levels of regulation, it takes no steps to calculate the costs and benefits of these intermediate levels. Without doing this it is impossible, both for the EPA and for this court on review, to know, that none of these alternatives was less burdensome than the ban in fact chosen by the agency.

* * *

2.

The EPA's Calculations

Furthermore, we are concerned about some of the methodology employed by the EPA in making various of the calculations that it did perform. In order to aid the EPA's reconsideration of this and other cases, we present our concerns here.

First, we note that there was some dispute in the record regarding the appropriateness of discounting the perceived benefits of the EPA's rule. In choosing between the calculated costs and benefits, the EPA presented variations in which it discounted only the costs, and counter-variations in which it discounted both the costs and the benefits, measured in both monetary and human injury terms. As between these two variations, we choose to evaluate the EPA's work using its discounted benefits calculations.

Although various commentators dispute whether it ever is appropriate to discount benefits when they are measured in human lives, we note that it would skew the result to discount only costs without according similar treatment to the benefits side of the equation. Adopting the position of the commentators who advocate not discounting benefits would force the EPA similarly not to calculate costs in present discounted real terms, making comparisons difficult. Furthermore, in evaluating situations in which different options incur costs at varying time intervals, the EPA would not be able to take into account that soon-to-be-incurred costs are more harmful than postponable costs. Because the EPA must discount costs to perform its evaluations properly, the EPA also should discount benefits to preserve an apples-to-apples comparison, even if this entails discounting benefits of a non-monetary nature.

When the EPA does discount costs or benefits, however, it cannot choose an unreasonable time upon which to base its discount calculation. Instead of using the time of injury as the appropriate time from which to discount, as one might expect, the EPA instead used the time of exposure.

The difficulties inherent in the EPA's approach can be illustrated by an example. Suppose two workers will be exposed to asbestos in 1996, with worker X subjected to a tiny amount of asbestos that will have no adverse health effects, and worker Y exposed to massive amounts of asbestos that quickly will lead to an asbestos-related disease. Under the EPA's approach, which takes into account only the time of exposure rather than the time at which any injury manifests itself, both examples would be treated the same. The EPA's approach implicitly assumes that the day on which the risk of injury occurs is the same day the injury actually occurs. Such an approach might be proper when the exposure and injury are one and the same, such as when a person is exposed to an immediately fatal poison, but is inappropriate for discounting toxins in which exposure often is followed by a substantial lag time before manifestation of injuries.

Of more concern to us is the failure of the EPA to compute the costs and benefits of its proposed rule past the year 2000, and its double-counting of the costs of asbestos use. In performing its calculus, the EPA only included the number of lives saved over the next thirteen years, and counted any additional lives saved as simply "unquantified benefits." The EPA and intervenors now seek to use these unquantified lives saved to justify calculations as to which the benefits seem far outweighed by the astronomical costs. For example, the EPA plans to save about three lives with its ban of asbestos pipe, at a cost of $128–227 million (*i.e.*, approximately $43–76 million per life saved). Although the EPA admits that the price tag is high, it claims that the lives saved past the year 2000 justify the price.

Such calculations not only lessen the value of the EPA's cost analysis, but also make any meaningful judicial review impossible. While TSCA contemplates a useful place for unquantified benefits beyond the EPA's calculation, unquantified benefits never were intended as a trump card allowing the EPA to justify any cost calculus, no matter how high.

The concept of unquantified benefits, rather, is intended to allow the EPA to provide a rightful place for any remaining benefits that are impossible to quantify after the EPA's best attempt, but which still are of some concern. But the allowance for unquantified costs is not intended to allow the EPA to perform its calculations over an arbitrarily short period so as to preserve a large unquantified portion.

Unquantified benefits can, at times, permissibly tip the balance in close cases. They cannot, however, be used to effect a wholesale shift on the balance beam. Such a use makes a mockery of the requirements of TSCA that the EPA weigh the costs of its actions before it chooses the least burdensome alternative.

* * *

3.

Reasonable Basis

In addition to showing that its regulation is the least burdensome one necessary to protect the environment adequately, the EPA also must show that it has a reasonable basis for the regulation. 15 U.S.C. § 2605(a). To some extent, our inquiry in this area mirrors that used above, for many of the methodological problems we have noted also indicate that the EPA did not have a reasonable basis. We here take the opportunity to highlight some areas of additional concern.

Most problematical to us is the EPA's ban of products for which no substitutes presently are available. In these cases, the EPA bears a tough burden indeed to show that under TSCA a ban is the least burdensome alternative, as TSCA explicitly instructs the EPA to consider "the benefits of such substance or mixture for various uses and the availability of substitutes for such uses." *Id.* § 2605(c)(1)(C). These words are particularly appropriate where the EPA actually has decided to ban a product, rather than simply restrict its use, for it is in these cases that the lack of an adequate substitute is most troubling under TSCA.

As the EPA itself states, "[w]hen no information is available for a product indicating that cost-effective substitutes exist, the estimated cost of a product ban is very high." Because of this, the EPA did not ban certain uses of asbestos, such as its use in rocket engines and battery separators. The EPA, however, in several other instances, ignores its own arguments and attempts to justify its ban by stating that the ban itself will cause the development of low-cost, adequate substitute products.

As a general matter, we agree with the EPA that a product ban can lead to great innovation, and it is true that an agency under TSCA, as under other regulatory statutes, "is empowered to issue safety standards which require improvements in existing technology or which require the development of new technology." As even the EPA acknowledges, however, when no adequate substitutes currently exist, the EPA cannot fail to consider this lack when formulating its own guidelines. Under TSCA, therefore, the EPA must present a stronger case to justify the ban, as opposed to regulation, of products with no substitutes.

We note that the EPA does provide a waiver provision for industries where the hoped-for substitutes fail to materialize in time. Under this provision, if no adequate substitutes develop, the EPA temporarily may extend the planned phaseout.

The EPA uses this provision to argue that it can ban any product, regardless of whether it has an adequate substitute, because inventive companies soon will develop good substitutes. The EPA contends that if they do not, the waiver provision will allow the continued use of asbestos in these areas, just as if the ban had not occurred at all.

The EPA errs, however, in asserting that the waiver provision will allow a continuation of the status quo in those cases in which no substitutes materialize. By its own terms, the exemption shifts the burden onto the waiver proponent to convince the EPA that the waiver is justified. *See id.* As even the EPA acknowledges, the waiver only "may be granted by [the] EPA in very limited circumstances."

The EPA thus cannot use the waiver provision to lessen its burden when justifying banning products without existing substitutes. While TSCA gives the EPA the power to ban such products, the EPA must bear its heavier burden of justifying its total ban in the face of inadequate substitutes. Thus, the agency cannot use its waiver provision to argue that the ban of products with no substitutes should be treated the same as the ban of those for which adequate substitutes are available now.

We also are concerned with the EPA's evaluation of substitutes even in those instances in which the record shows that they are available. The EPA explicitly rejects considering the harm that may flow from the increased use of products designed to substitute for asbestos, even where the probable substitutes themselves are known carcinogens. The EPA justifies this by stating that it has "more concern about the continued use and exposure to asbestos than it has for the future replacement of asbestos in the products subject to this rule with other fibrous substitutes." The agency thus concludes that any "[r]egulatory decisions about asbestos which poses well-recognized, serious risks should not be delayed until the rise of all replacement materials are fully quantified."

This presents two problems. First, TSCA instructs the EPA to consider the relative merits of its ban, as compared to the economic effects of its actions. The EPA cannot make this calculation if it fails to consider the effects that alternate substitutes will pose after a ban.

Second, the EPA cannot say with any assurance that its regulation will increase workplace safety when it refuses to evaluate the harm that will result from the increased use of substitute products. While the EPA may be correct in its conclusion that the alternate materials pose less risk than asbestos, we cannot say with any more assurance than that flowing from an educated guess that this conclusion is true.

Considering that many of the substitutes that the EPA itself concedes will be used in the place of asbestos have known carcinogenic effects, the EPA not only cannot assure this court that it has taken the least burdensome alternative, but cannot even prove that its regulations will increase workplace safety. Eager to douse the dangers of asbestos, the agency inadvertently actually may increase the risk of injury Americans face. The EPA's explicit failure to consider the toxicity of likely substitutes thus deprives its order of a reasonable basis.

Our opinion should not be construed to state that the EPA has an affirmative duty to seek out and test every workplace substitute for any product it seeks to regulate. TSCA does not place such a burden upon the agency. We do not think it unreasonable, however, once interested parties introduce credible studies and evidence showing the toxicity of workplace substitutes, or the decreased effectiveness of safety alternatives such as non-asbestos brakes, that the EPA then consider whether its regulations are even increasing workplace safety, and whether the increased risk occasioned by dangerous substitutes makes the proposed regulation no longer reasonable. * * *

In short, a death is a death, whether occasioned by asbestos or by a toxic substitute product, and the EPA's decision not to evaluate the toxicity of known carcinogenic substitutes is not a reasonable action under TSCA. Once an interested party brings forth credible evidence suggesting the toxicity of the probable or only alternatives to a substance, the EPA must consider the comparative toxic costs of each. Its failure to do so in this case thus deprived its regulation of a reasonable basis, at least in regard to those products as to which petitioners introduced credible evidence of the dangers of the likely substitutes.

4.

Unreasonable Risk of Injury

The final requirement the EPA must satisfy before engaging in any TSCA rulemaking is that it only take steps designed to prevent "unreasonable" risks. In evaluating what is "unreasonable," the EPA is required to consider the costs of any proposed actions and to "carry out this chapter in a reasonable and prudent manner (after considering) the environmental, economic, and social impact of any action." 15 U.S.C. § 2601(c).

As the District of Columbia Circuit stated when evaluating similar language governing the Federal Hazardous Substances Act, "[t]he requirement that the risk be 'unreasonable' necessarily involves a balancing test like that familiar in tort law: The regulation may issue if the severity of the injury that may result from the product, factored by the likelihood of the injury, offsets the harm the regulation itself imposes upon manufacturers and consumers." Forester v. CPSC, 559 F.2d 774, 789 (D.C. Cir. 1977). * * *

That the EPA must balance the costs of its regulations against their benefits further is reinforced by the requirement that it seek the least burdensome regulation. While Congress did not dictate that the EPA engage in an exhaustive, full-scale cost-benefit analysis, it did require the EPA to consider both sides of the regulatory equation, and it rejected the notion that the EPA should pursue the reduction of workplace risk at any cost. *See* American Textile Mfrs. Inst., 452 U.S. at 510 n.30 ("unreasonable risk" statutes require "a generalized balancing of costs and benefits"). * * *

Even taking all of the EPA's figures as true, and evaluating them in the light most favorable to the agency's decision (non-discounted benefits, discounted costs, analogous exposure estimates included), the agency's analysis results in figures as high as $74 million per life saved. For example, the EPA states that its ban of asbestos pipe will save three lives over the next thirteen years, at a cost of $128–227 million ($43–76 million per life saved), depending upon the price of substitutes; that its ban of asbestos shingles will cost $23–34 million to save 0.32 statistical lives ($72–106 million per life saved); that its ban of asbestos coatings will cost $46–181 million to save 3.33 lives ($14–54 million per life saved); and that its ban of asbestos paper products will save 0.60 lives at a cost of $4–5 million ($7–8 million per life saved). *See* 54 Fed. Reg. at 29,484–85. * * *

While we do not sit as a regulatory agency that must make the difficult decision as to what an appropriate expenditure is to prevent someone from incurring the risk of an asbestos-related death, we do note that the EPA, in its zeal to ban any and all asbestos products, basically ignored the cost side of the TSCA equation. The EPA would have this court believe that Congress, when it enacted its requirement that the EPA consider the economic impacts of its regulations, thought that spending $200–300 million to save approximately seven lives (approximately $30–40 million per life) over thirteen years is reasonable.

As we stated in the OSHA context, until an agency "can provide substantial evidence that the benefits to be achieved by [a regulation] bear a reasonable relationship to the costs imposed by the reduction, it cannot show that the standard is reasonably necessary to provide safe or healthful workplaces." *American Petroleum Inst.*, 581 F.2d at 504. Although the OSHA statute differs in major respects from TSCA, the statute does require substantial evidence to support the EPA's contentions that its regulations both have a reasonable basis and are the least burdensome means to a reasonably safe workplace.

The EPA's willingness to argue that spending $23.7 million to save less than one-third of a life reveals that its economic review of its regulations, as required by TSCA, was meaningless. As the petitioners' brief and our review of EPA caselaw reveals, such high costs are rarely, if ever, used to support a safety regulation. If we were to allow such cavalier treatment of the EPA's duty to consider the economic effects of its decisions, we would have to excise entire sections and phrases from the language of TSCA. Because we are judges, not surgeons, we decline to do so.

NOTES AND QUESTIONS

1. *Asbestos regulation.* The Fifth Circuit went on to invalidate EPA's bans on asbestos use as to most subcategories of products, but upheld EPA's ban on products that no longer were being produced in the United States. Corrosion Proof Fittings, 947 F.2d at 1228–29. Although EPA has not sought to reestablish a general ban on asbestos, its use has declined as a result of concerns about potential tort liability and the application of regulatory schemes other than TSCA. See Charles G. Garlow, Asbestos—The Long–Lived Mineral, Nat. Res. & Env't, Spr. 2005, at 36 (noting that asbestos is regulated in part by Section 112 of the Clean Air Act and other statutes).

2. *EPA's authority under Section 6 of TSCA.* What does the plain language of Section 6 of TSCA suggest about EPA's authority to regulate asbestos and other hazardous substances? Why wasn't EPA's analysis sufficient to support its staged ban on the use of asbestos? Does this decision suggest anything about the usefulness of Section 6 in regulating toxic substances? If EPA decided to try to reinstate the ban, what would it have to do?

3. *Judicial review of TSCA regulation. Corrosion Proof Fittings* illustrates the difficulty of imposing a categorical ban on substances widely used in commerce. Consider the following questions with respect to the language and structure of TSCA: Why did Congress insert the "substantial evidence" test into the law rather than the usual "arbitrary and capricious" standard for reviewing administrative action? What are the social costs and benefits of the "least burdensome regulation" and the "reasonable basis" requirements? And why was this case litigated in the Fifth Circuit?

4. *Costs versus lives saved.* According to the Fifth Circuit, the ban on asbestos in certain products would have cost as much as $74 million per life saved. Would this amount be too great a cost to impose on manufacturers and consumers of asbestos products?

5. *Discounting human lives.* The Fifth Circuit suggests that it would be inappropriate for EPA to discount the costs of its ban without also discounting the benefits measured in human lives. Whether lives should be discounted, however, is a controversial issue. Criticizing the Fifth Circuit's analysis, Lisa Heinzerling disputes the fungibility of monetary costs and lives:

> In the asbestos case, the costs were dollars and the benefits were lives. These costs and benefits are the same only if dollars and lives are the same. Again, therefore, it turns out that the implicit premise of an argument in favor of discounting is that lives can be measured in dollars. Far from being a "value-free and good workable rule," * * * the decision to treat future costs and benefits the same—to discount them both and to discount them at the same rate—silently resolves one of the central moral questions of the modern regulatory state.

Lisa Heinzerling, Regulatory Costs of Mythic Proportions, 107 Yale L.J. 1981, 2053 (1998).

Richard Revesz defends the discounting of the value of life in certain circumstances and suggests the following distinction:

> The valuations of human life used in regulatory analyses are from threats of instantaneous death in workplace settings. Discounting, to reflect that in the case of latent harms the years lost occur later in a person's lifetime, is appropriate in these circumstances. Upward adjustments of the value of life need to be undertaken, however, to account for the dread and involuntary nature of environmental carcinogens as well as for higher income levels of the victims. By not performing these adjustments, the regulatory process may be undervaluing lives by as much as a factor of six.
>
> In contrast, in the case of harms to future generations, discounting is ethically unjustified. It is simply a means of privileging the interests of the current generation.

Richard Revesz, Environmental Regulation, Cost–Benefit Analysis, and the Discounting of Human Lives, 99 Colum. L. Rev. 941, 941 (1999). Does the rationale for discounting future costs and benefits apply to human lives? If discounting of human lives is appropriate, what discount rate should be used?

6. *EPA review of toxicity under TSCA.* TSCA was intended to allow EPA to exercise oversight over the introduction of new chemicals and to review potential hazards of chemicals already in use at the time of TSCA's enactment.

With respect to new chemicals, EPA receives a premanufacture notice and performs at least some review of the potential risks posed by such chemicals. TSCA does not require chemical companies, however, to test new chemicals for toxicity or to gauge exposure levels before they are submitted for EPA's review. Instead, EPA relies heavily on scientific models to predict potential toxicity based on comparisons with existing chemicals having similar molecular structures. According to a 2005 Government Accountability Office (GAO) report, EPA review has resulted in some action being taken to reduce the risks of approximately 3,500 of the 32,000 new chemicals that chemical companies have submitted for review. The actions taken include the voluntary withdrawal by companies of their notices of intent to manufacture new chemicals, companies entering into consent orders to produce a chemical under specified conditions, and the promulgation of significant new use rules requiring companies to notify EPA of their intent to manufacture or process certain chemicals for new uses prior to manufacturing or processing the chemicals for such uses.

With respect to existing chemicals, the GAO report found that "EPA does not routinely assess existing chemicals, has limited information on their health and environmental risks, and has issued few regulations controlling such chemicals." U.S. Government Accountability Office, Chemical Regulation: Options Exist to Improve EPA's Ability to Assess Health Risks and Manage Its Chemical Review Program 18 (2005).

In order to encourage the development of additional data on the potential risks posed by existing chemicals, EPA implemented the High Production Volume (HPV) Challenge Program in the late 1990s. Under the program, EPA invited chemical companies to voluntarily sponsor the approximately 2,800 chemicals produced or imported in amounts of 1 million pounds or more a year. Sponsors were to submit data summaries of existing information, along with a test plan that proposes a strategy to fill data gaps for individual chemicals or for a category of chemicals. Although the program led to the disclosure of a significant amount of existing and previously unpublished health and environmental data, some chemicals were left unsponsored and substantial data gaps remain to be filled. See id. at 4–5; Richard A. Denison (Environmental Defense), High Hopes, Low Marks: A Final Report Card on the High Production Volume Chemical Challenge (2007).

Faced with the challenge of obtaining data on tens of thousands of chemicals and of assessing complex issues such as cumulative exposures and varying genetic susceptibilities, EPA is moving towards a new approach to toxicity testing and risk assessment. As described in the agency's 2009 "Strategic Plan for Evaluating the Toxicity of Chemicals," this approach seeks to take advantage of advances in molecular biology and computational sciences to more efficiently prioritize chemicals for further assessment and reduce reliance on animal testing. In contrast to conventional toxicity testing, which concentrates on analyzing ultimate disease endpoints as expressed in animals, the new approach would focus on "toxicity pathways"—how exposure to chemicals can perturb normal biological processes and ultimately lead to adverse health effects. Much work remains to be done, however, in identifying toxicity pathways and predicting human responses that might result from pathway perturbations.

B.   LICENSING AND REGISTRATION SCHEMES

1.   PESTICIDE REGULATION UNDER THE FEDERAL INSECTICIDE, FUNGICIDE AND RODENTICIDE ACT (FIFRA)

Pesticides and herbicides are intended to have toxic effects—their purpose is to kill or retard the growth of living organisms such as weeds, insects, and vermin. Given their known and desired toxic properties, it should not be surprising that these chemicals are subject to a regulatory scheme that differs substantially from TSCA. Under the Federal Insecticide, Fungicide, and Rodenticide Act (FIFRA), 7 U.S.C. §§ 136–136y, pesticides (defined broadly to include herbicides, fungicides, insecticides, and rodenticides) are subject to a licensing scheme that requires such chemicals to be registered before they may be sold or distributed. *See* FIFRA § 3, 7 U.S.C. § 136a. Each pesticide is registered for an approved use, and a new use of an already registered pesticide requires additional registration. For example, a fungicide registered for use on apples may not be used legally on grapes or other crops, and an insecticide registered for outdoor use may not be used inside buildings. Use of a registered pesticide may also be restricted to pesticide applicators with special training.

An application for registration includes the chemical formula of the pesticide; a copy of the proposed product labeling, claims to be made for the product, and directions for use; and test data regarding product chemistry and safety. FIFRA § 3(c)(1). EPA "shall register a pesticide if":

(A) its composition is such as to warrant the proposed claims for it;

(B) its labeling and other material required to be submitted comply with the requirements of [FIFRA];

(C) it will perform its intended function without unreasonable adverse effects on the environment; and

(D) when used in accordance with widespread and commonly recognized practice it will not generally cause unreasonable adverse effects on the environment.

FIFRA § 3(c)(5). The statute defines the term "unreasonable adverse effects on the environment" as "(1) any unreasonable risk to man or the environment, taking into account the economic, social, and environmental costs and benefits of the use of any pesticide, or (2) a human dietary risk from residues that result from a use of a pesticide in or on any food inconsistent with the standard under section 346a of Title 21...." FIFRA § 2(bb).

Generally, EPA exercises its protective function under FIFRA by denying new pesticide registrations or by placing protective conditions on them. EPA continues to evaluate the safety of pesticides after they are registered as new information becomes available. Registrants must report new evidence of adverse effects of pesticide exposure, and EPA may also require registrants to conduct new studies to provide additional risk data. FIFRA § 3(c)(2)(B). Safety is reevaluated on both an ad hoc basis and a periodic basis. EPA may order ad hoc review, known as "special review," when EPA determines that a validated test or other significant evidence indicates that a registered pesticide may pose an unreasonable adverse risk to humans or the environment. FIFRA § 3(c)(8); 40 C.F.R. Part 154.

Periodic safety reviews occur pursuant to Section 3(g), added as an amendment to FIFRA in 1996. Section 3(g) directs EPA to establish procedures for reviewing pesticide registrations, with a goal of reviewing each pesticide's registration every 15 years. This review includes an assessment of changes since the pesticide's last registration decision, additional data collection and risk assessments if needed, and public comment. The purpose of registration review is to determine whether a pesticide continues to meet the standard for registration in FIFRA. See 71 Fed. Reg. 45,719 (2006) (final rule establishing procedures for registration review).

Once registered under FIFRA, a pesticide may lose its registration by suspension or cancellation. EPA may immediately suspend a registration, pending cancellation proceedings, if a pesticide poses an "imminent hazard." FIFRA § 6(c). EPA may cancel a registration if "a pesticide or its labeling or other material required to be submitted does not comply with [FIFRA] or, when used in accordance with widespread and commonly recognized practice, generally causes unreasonable adverse effects on the environment." FIFRA § 6(b). Cancellation must be preceded by a notice of intent either to cancel a pesticide's registration or to hold a hearing to determine whether it should be cancelled. FIFRA § 6(b)(1), (2). Cancellation typically triggers a lengthy adjudicatory hearing and scientific review process during which the pesticide remains on the market. FIFRA § 6(d).

NOTES AND QUESTIONS

1. *Comparing FIFRA and TSCA.* What is the basis for determining the extent of regulatory control under FIFRA: health-based, technology-based, or balancing? In what significant ways does FIFRA differ from TSCA? Are these differences appropriate in light of the substances regulated by each statute? What are the advantages and disadvantages of a licensing approach? Does FIFRA adequately address the problems of incomplete information and scientific uncertainty?

2. *Sources of data.* Consider the importance of technical information in the FIFRA registration process. Data contained in registration applications is submitted by the pesticide manufacturer, not by EPA. What might be the impact of this fact on the licensing system? One commentator writes:

> Another [data] quality issue is the source of the data, especially in the uncertain science of long-latency toxic illnesses in which inference and interpretation are always open to debate. The inevitably conflict-

ing interests between EPA and the industries it regulates invite the withholding or slanting of data submissions. The conflict rarely results in outright concealment, falsification, or deliberate misstatement of results (though this unfortunately is not unknown). Rather, every stage of the investigation process, from experimental design to execution to interpretation of results, is subject to judgment and inference and to bias. A screening or approval system may magnify the bias problem by casting EPA and industry in more obviously adversarial roles. A National Academy of Sciences study of EPA decision making warned about dependence on regulated industries for data and analysis and suggested a number of remedial measures, including reduced use of consulting firms that also work for industry, peer review, review by other agencies, stringent guidelines and protocols, certification of laboratories, and a strong in-house research capability. * * *

John S. Applegate, The Perils of Unreasonable Risk: Information, Regulatory Policy, and Toxic Substances Control, 91 Colum. L. Rev. 261, 311 (1991).

3. *Preemption of State and Local Regulation of Pesticides.* Does FIFRA preempt state and local regulation of pesticides? FIFRA § 24(a) provides that states "may regulate the sale or use of any federally registered pesticide . . ., but only if and to the extent the regulation does not permit any sale or use prohibited by this subchapter." This provision recognizes state authority to impose stricter regulation on pesticide uses than what FIFRA requires. Cf. Wisconsin Public Intervenor v. Mortier, 501 U.S. 597 (1991) (holding that a town ordinance requiring a special permit for aerial spraying was not preempted because there was no actual conflict between FIFRA and the local ordinance).

In an effort to have uniform pesticide product labeling, however, FIFRA also provides that states "shall not impose or continue in effect any requirements for labeling or packaging in addition to or different from those required under this subchapter." FIFRA § 24(b). Does this express preemption provision extend to tort and contract claims under state law?

Consider the factual circumstances of *Bates v. Dow Agrosciences LLC,* 544 U.S. 431 (2005). The plaintiffs alleged that their crops were severely damaged by the application of defendant's pesticide, whose label failed to warn against its use in soils with high pH levels. The plaintiffs brought claims for defective design, defective manufacture, negligent testing, breach of express warranty, fraud, negligent failure to warn, and violation of a state consumer protection statute. The defendant contended that FIFRA preempted all these claims. The Supreme Court rejected the defendant's broad argument, holding that for a state rule to be preempted by Section 24(b), it must be a requirement "for labeling or packaging" that is "in addition to or different from those required under" FIFRA. As the Court explained:

> Rules that require manufacturers to design reasonably safe products, to use due care in conducting appropriate testing of their products, to market products free of manufacturing defects, and to honor their express warranties or other contractual commitments plainly do not

qualify as requirements for "labeling or packaging." None of these common-law rules requires that manufacturers label or package their products in any particular way.

Bates, 544 U.S. at 444. The Court accordingly held that the plaintiffs' claims for defective design, defective manufacture, negligent testing, and breach of express warranty (including violation of the state consumer protection statute) were not preempted. The other two claims—for fraud and negligent failure to warn—were premised on common law rules that qualify as "requirements for labeling or packaging." These claims, the Court held, would be preempted only if they imposed requirements "in addition to or different from" what FIFRA requires.

2. CHEMICAL REGULATION IN THE EUROPEAN UNION

The European Union adopted a new comprehensive approach to regulating chemical substances in 2006: the Registration, Evaluation, and Authorization of Chemicals (REACH). Under the program, producers and importers of chemicals must register the properties of those chemicals with the European Chemicals Agency, a new agency that has the power to ban chemicals that pose significant health threats. Thirty thousand chemicals are expected to be covered by the registration process, which is slated to take eleven years. As you read the following description of REACH, consider whether the United States should adopt a similar program.

John S. Applegate, Synthesizing TSCA and REACH: Practical Principles for Chemical Regulation Reform
35 Ecol. L.Q. 721, 741–43, 760–61 (2007).

REACH was designed to correct weaknesses in the existing chemical regulatory system in Europe. Some of the weaknesses were distinct to the European system. For example, prior to REACH, an array of complicated directives and regulations covered the chemical industry, and the public expressed a widespread desire to reduce animal testing. However, REACH was also designed to correct the weaknesses apparent in the U.S. experience [with chemical regulation under TSCA].

* * *

While it simplified the existing regulatory structure for chemicals, REACH is by no means a simple piece of legislation. For present purposes, the basic regulatory process breaks down into four constituent parts, reflected in the elements of the REACH acronym: registration, evaluation, authorization, and restrictions. The first phase, registration, is primarily a data-gathering procedure. It covers all chemicals produced or imported in quantities above one metric ton per year, both new and existing (or "phase-in"), as well as certain substances found in other products. There are various exemptions for low-risk chemicals and polymers, but the ECHA [European Chemicals Agency] expects to need to register thirty thousand chemicals and review eighty thousand dossiers by 2011.

Applications for the registration of any chemical must include a technical dossier, which is comprehensive information on the chemical's inherent properties, including a base set of toxicological information, graduated by production volume. For chemicals produced in quantities above ten metric tons, a much more extensive Chemical Safety Report is required, which includes toxicology and exposure data, as well as measures to reduce risks from the chemical. Chemical data, including those obtained in registration, is shared up and down the supply chain to avoid unnecessary testing.

The second phase, evaluation, involves three basic steps: an automatic "completeness check" for technical compliance with the REACH requirements; a dossier evaluation, which is essentially a quality control effort to assure that objectives like avoidance of animal testing and data sharing have occurred; and substance evaluation, which examines the risks posed by a substance and the measures taken to control the risks. Evaluation leads to the two final phases.

Authorization applies to substances "of very high concern" (VHC). VHC substances include carcinogens, mutagens, and reproductively toxic (CMR) substances; persistent, bioaccumulative, or toxic (PBT) substances; very persistent or very bioaccumulative (vPvB) substances; persistent organic pollutants (POPs); and other chronic hazards. Authorization is not limited to chemicals that meet the registration threshold amount of one metric ton. The primary objective of authorization is to ensure the progressive replacement of VHCs with safer alternatives; therefore, the centerpiece of the process is analysis of substitute substances. Each proponent of a VHC chemical must present a replacement chemical or at least a research plan for alternatives; if no alternatives are in prospect, then the chemical's use must be justified under a cost-benefit test. In addition, authorization requires that the substance be "adequately controlled," and if it cannot be adequately controlled (CMR substances, by definition, cannot be), then, again, its benefits must outweigh its risks. ECHA expects that about 1,500 substances will require authorization. It is expected that VHC substances will be banned entirely, authorized for a limited period, or authorized for very specific uses and conditions.

The final phase is restriction. While the objective of authorization is replacement, substances that are not subject to authorization but nevertheless pose hazards in their manufacture or use may have European Community-wide restrictions imposed on them to assure that health and environmental risks remain at acceptable levels. Such restrictions may be imposed centrally if the Commission, in cooperation with the member states, determines that the risk is not adequately controlled and that it needs to be addressed at the Community-wide level. The legal standard for acceptability is not stated other than a general commitment to a "high level of protection." Restrictions represent REACH's "safety net," or last resort, for ensuring chemical safety.

* * *

[Although the two regimes are marked by substantial differences,] REACH and TSCA bear important and fundamental similarities in their approaches to chemicals regulation. Both balance protection of human health and promotion of the chemical industry, they regulate chemicals as such to supplement the media-based statutes, they seek to prevent toxic harm before it occurs, they regulate on the basis of a risk characterized by less-than-absolute safety and modified by cost and other non-health considerations, they are information-intensive in that they aspire to fill the data gap (albeit in different ways), and each is committed to a comprehensive, analytical approach to regulation.

Taken together, the areas of commonality between TSCA and REACH, the widely acknowledged failures of TSCA, and the regulatory innovations in REACH, suggest four interrelated principles for improvement of chemicals regulation:

1. Chemical regulation should be preventive and its restrictions proportionate to the risk presented;

2. Chemical regulation should aim for progressive improvement in chemical safety;

3. Regulation should be based on all currently available information, and lack of full information should not be a barrier to regulatory action;

4. The regulatory process should be as transparent and as simple as possible.

* * *

NOTES AND QUESTIONS

1. *Comparing REACH with TSCA and FIFRA.* REACH, like TSCA, purports to be a comprehensive scheme for addressing the toxic risks of chemicals. How is REACH similar to TSCA? How does REACH differ from TSCA? How does REACH compare with TSCA (or FIFRA) in terms of the amount of information that will be generated, and the burdens of producing that information? What are the advantages and disadvantages of REACH's approach? Should TSCA or FIFRA be amended to incorporate some of REACH's features?

2. *Evaluating REACH.* REACH replaced a regulatory system that was perceived as hampering innovation and as slow to identify and assess risks. Yet REACH has been criticized by industry for being too complicated and burdensome, and by environmentalists for having too many loopholes. Are these criticisms warranted? In what ways might REACH be improved?

3. *Approaches to risk.* The United States and the European Union are often described as taking two different approaches to environmental risks: the United States is generally characterized as employing a strict risk-assessment approach, whereas the European Union is often said to apply a precautionary approach in which regulatory action may be taken even in the absence of a quantifiable risk. *See* Philippe Sands, Principles of International Environmental Law (2d ed. 2003). Do you agree with these characterizations? Does REACH reflect a precautionary approach, a strict risk-assessment approach, or something in between?

4. *TSCA Reform.* In January 2009, the Government Accountability Office issued a report identifying EPA's chemical risk assessment and management process as being at high risk for waste, fraud, abuse, and mismanagement:

> EPA does not have sufficient chemical assessment information to determine whether it should establish controls to limit public exposure to many chemicals that may pose substantial health risks. Actions are needed to streamline and increase the transparency of the Integrated Risk Information System and to enhance EPA's ability under the Toxic Substances Control Act to obtain health and safety information from the chemical industry.

Government Accountability Office, High–Risk Series: An Update, GAO–09–271 (2009).

Such criticisms of TSCA, as well as the enactment of REACH, have prompted proposals for TSCA reform. In April 2011, Sen. Frank Lautenberg introduced legislation entitled the Safe Chemicals Act, S.847, 112th Cong. (2011). Patterned after REACH, the legislation would make a number of significant changes to TSCA. Specifically, the bill would require manufacturers to develop and submit a minimum data set for each chemical they produce, require EPA to use that information to categorize chemicals according to their likely risk, place the burden on chemical manufacturers to prove that a chemical used in commerce is safe, and establish a public database of chemical information submitted to EPA.

5. *State-level chemical regulation.* In the wake of TSCA's weaknesses and the uncertainties surrounding TSCA reform, various states have taken a more active role in chemical regulation. California's Green Chemistry Initiative, for example, requires the state's Department of Toxic Substances Control to identify and prioritize chemicals of concern, evaluate alternatives, specify potential regulatory responses, and create an online, information clearinghouse for chemical hazard data. Is it appropriate for states to regulate chemical substances in this manner?

C.   PROHIBITION

Instead of trying to fine-tune the regulation of toxics by applying standards that balance costs and benefits, as TSCA and FIFRA do, one alternative would be to simply ban chemicals found to pose toxic risks. The Delaney Clause of the Food, Drug, and Cosmetic Act (FDCA) provides an example of such an approach. Under the FDCA, the Secretary of Health and Human Services may issue regulations allowing a substance to be used as a food additive only if the proposed use of the food additive will be "safe." 21 U.S.C. § 348(c)(3). The Delaney Clause provides, however, that "no additive shall be deemed to be safe if it is found to induce cancer when ingested by man or animal, or if it is found, after tests which are appropriate for the evaluation of the safety of food additives, to induce cancer in man or animal. . . ." Id. Parallel and virtually identical versions of the Delaney Clause apply to color additives and drugs for food-producing animals as well. 21 U.S.C. § 379e(b)(5)(B); 21 U.S.C. § 360b(d)(1)(I).

In *Les v. Reilly*, the Ninth Circuit reviewed an EPA order permitting the residue of four pesticides to remain in processed foods even though the pesticides had been found to induce cancer. EPA had found that the pesticides posed only a de minimis risk of causing cancer and contended that the Delaney Clause permitted the use of such additives. To support its view that the FDCA implicitly contemplated a de minimis risk standard, the EPA pointed to FDCA provisions allowing carcinogenic pesticide residues below EPA-designated levels to be present in unprocessed foods. The Ninth Circuit rejected EPA's view:

> The language is clear and mandatory. The Delaney clause provides that no additive shall be deemed safe if it induces cancer. 21 U.S.C. § 348(c)(3). The EPA states in its final order that appropriate tests have established that the pesticides at issue here induce cancer in humans or animals. 56 Fed. Reg. at 7774–75. The statute provides that once the finding of carcinogenicity is made, the EPA has no discretion.
> * * *
>
> [T]he EPA argues that a de minimis exception to the Delaney clause is necessary in order to bring about a more sensible application of the regulatory scheme. It relies particularly on a recent study suggesting that the criterion of concentration level in processed foods may bear little or no relation to actual risk of cancer, and that some pesticides might be barred by rigid enforcement of the Delaney clause while others, with greater cancer-causing risk, may be permitted through [FDCA provisions allowing pesticide residues in raw foods to "flow through" to processed foods so long as they do not become more concentrated as a result]. The EPA in effect asks us to approve what it deems to be a more enlightened system than that which Congress established. * * * Revising the existing statutory scheme, however, is neither our function nor the function of the EPA.

Les v. Reilly, 968 F.2d 985, 988–90 (9th Cir. 1992).

In 1996, Congress enacted the Food Quality Protection Act (FQPA), Pub. L. No. 104–170 (1996) (codified as amended in sections of 7 U.S.C. and 21 U.S.C.), to deal with issues of food safety and to address concerns that the *Les v. Reilly* decision might result in the unavailability of critical pesticides. The FQPA amended the Delaney Clause to make clear that it does not apply to pesticide residues in food. The FQPA requires that pesticide tolerances for food be "safe" and defines "safe" with respect to pesticide residues as "a reasonable certainty that no harm will result from aggregate exposure." 21 U.S.C. § 346a(b)(2)(A)(ii). In other words, the FQPA establishes a single, health-based standard for all pesticide residues in all types of food, replacing the sometimes conflicting standards in the old law. In certain narrow circumstances, the FQPA allows pesticide tolerances that would not otherwise meet the safety standard, if necessary to prevent even greater health risks to consumers or to avoid "a significant disruption in domestic production of an adequate, wholesome, and economical food supply." For more on the Food Quality Protection Act, see Thomas O. McGarity, Politics by Other Means: Law, Science, and Policy in EPA's Implementation of the Food Quality Protection Act, 53 Admin. L. Rev. 103 (2001); James Smart, All the Stars in the Heavens Were in the Right Places: The Passage of the Food Quality Protection Act of 1996, 17 Stan. Envt'l L. J. 273 (1998).

What are the advantages and disadvantages to a blanket prohibition such as the Delaney Clause?

D. INFORMATIONAL REGULATION

As noted in Chapter 5, information disclosure strategies have been employed in a variety of contexts, including toxics regulation.

1. *Occupational Safety and Health Act.* The OSH Act's Hazard Communication Standard requires manufacturers and importers of chemicals to determine if such chemicals are hazardous and to develop (or obtain) a Material Safety Data Sheet (MSDS) for each hazardous chemical. 29 C.F.R. § 1910.1200. The MSDSs are intended to provide companies and workers with available information on hazardous ingredients in products they handle and to educate them on safe handling practices. MSDSs must be provided to distributors of such chemicals and to employers whenever those chemicals are used in the workplace. Employers are required to develop a written hazard communication program that includes provisions for safety training and making MSDSs accessible to employees.

2. *Emergency Planning and Community Right-to-Know Act (EPCRA),* 42 U.S.C. §§ 11001–11050. EPCRA imposes reporting requirements that provide state and local authorities, as well as the public, with information concerning the use, storage, and release of chemicals. This information is designed to facilitate community emergency preparedness and public decisionmaking. EPCRA imposes several distinct reporting requirements:

1. Planning Notification (EPCRA § 302): facilities that have "extremely hazardous substances" in an amount greater than a designated threshold planning quantity must notify state and local emergency planning authorities.

2. Emergency Notification (EPCRA § 304): facilities must report the release of an extremely hazardous substance or a substance listed as hazardous under CERCLA § 102 to state and local emergency planning authorities if the release exceeds a threshold amount.

3. Inventory Reporting (EPCRA §§ 311, 312): for all chemicals for which a facility is required by the Occupational Safety and Health Act to prepare or have available an MSDS, such facility must provide an annual inventory of such chemicals to state and local emergency planning authorities and to the local fire department.

4. Toxics Release Reporting (EPCRA § 313): facilities must submit annual reports on the amounts of listed toxic chemicals their facilities release into the environment, either routinely or as a result of an accident. These reports, which are available to the public, are used by EPA to compile the Toxics Release Inventory (TRI), a powerful tool for pressuring factories to reduce pollution. See supra Chapter 5, Section 5.

3. *Securities Laws*. Regulation S–K, promulgated by the Securities and Exchange Commission (SEC), requires all publicly held companies to disclose the material effects of compliance with environmental laws, any material pending legal proceedings, including environmental litigation, and any known trends, demands, commitments, events, or uncertainties that are reasonably likely to have a material effect on financial conditions or results of operations. Such disclosures must be made in a company's Annual Report (10K) and Quarterly Reports (10Q), as well as in other SEC filings.

E.   Discussion Problem: Nanotechnology

As new substances are developed and introduced into commerce at an increasingly rapid pace, the toxics problem is becoming more complicated. The following excerpt discusses nanotechnology, which is expected to revolutionize manufacturing processes and materials engineering in the coming years, but which also may pose substantial risks.

Albert C. Lin, Size Matters: Regulating Nanotechnology

31 Harv. Envtl. L. Rev. 349, 352–61 (2007).

The Promise of Nanotechnology

Nanotechnology is the science of manipulating matter at the nanometer scale. Broadly speaking, nanotechnology includes both traditional "top-down" manufacturing methods, such as those used to manufacture nanoscale electronic components, as well as "bottom-up" methods of building things on an atom-by-atom or molecule-by-molecule basis. The promise of nanotechnology is that its precise methods will serve as the basis of a manufacturing technology that is cleaner and more efficient than the relatively crude, top-down methods that dominate industrial processes today. Materials produced via nanotechnology—nanomaterials—are manufactured from conventional chemical substances. What makes these materials of particular interest is that they often behave very differently from the conventional materials from which they are derived. The small size and high surface-area-to-mass ratio of nanosized particles enhance the mechanical, electrical, optical, catalytic, and/or biological activity of a substance. These characteristics make nanomaterials potentially desirable as drug delivery devices, chemical catalysts, and various other purposes.

Nanomaterials are already being used in medical diagnosis and treatment, cosmetics, sunscreens, stain-resistant clothing, paints and coatings, electronics, tires, tennis rackets, and foods. The commercial potential of nanotechnology is tremendous, with some calling it the foundation for the "next industrial revolution." * * *

Health and Environmental Concerns

* * *As engineered nanomaterials come into wider use, the nature of exposure to nanomaterials will change, and the degree of exposure will increase. Free nanoparticles are of particular concern because they are most likely to enter the body, react with cells, and cause tissue damage. Even embedded nanomaterials may be released as free particles as the products into which they are incorporated wear out.

Intake of engineered nanomaterials is likely to occur through various routes, including inhalation, ingestion, absorption through the skin, and injection. The nature of the hazard posed by exposure to engineered nanomaterials may differ from that caused by naturally occurring nanoparticles. Engineered nanoparticles may be better able to evade the body's defenses because of their size or protective coatings. Moreover, the health and environmental risks that accompany exposure to engineered nanomaterials are not well understood. Little information on the risks is currently known, and the most rudimentary toxicological data is unlikely to be available for many years. Making the question particularly difficult is the wide variety of nanomaterials: there are many different types and sizes, and they possess unique characteristics and different surface coatings. Because the surface coatings of nanoparticles appear critical to their penetration rate and distribution in the body, toxicity may vary greatly from one type of particle to the next.

Notwithstanding the lack of firm health data specific to nanomaterials, there are reasons for serious concern. First, the same properties that make nanoparticles useful for certain products and processes—their small size, chemical composition, surface structure, solubility, shape, and aggregative tendencies—may also make them harmful when taken into the body. The small size of nanoparticles, for instance, corresponds to a greater surface area for a given mass of material, and hence a greater number of reactive groups at the surface. Surface reactive groups, scientists believe, play an important role in toxic reactions by generating reactive oxygen species that may damage DNA, proteins, and cell membranes. Consistent with this theory, experimental results suggest that tissue injury from exposure to nanoparticles is correlated with surface area rather than mass. Small size also enables some nanoparticles to move into and within the body in ways that bulkier materials made of the same chemical substance cannot. When inhaled, nanoparticles are deposited more efficiently and deeply into the respiratory tract and may evade defense mechanisms that trap larger particles. Nanoparticles that come in contact with the skin, such as nanomaterials incorporated into sunscreens, may penetrate the epidermis when the skin is flexed or damaged, and then pass further into the body through the lymphatic system. And unlike most contaminants, nanoparticles may cross the blood-brain barrier and enter the central nervous system through neuronal pathways leading from the respiratory tract to the brain.

Health and safety concerns arise not only because of the physical characteristics of engineered nanomaterials, but also because of what we know from studies of ambient ultrafine particles. Scientists have found, for example, that exposure to mineral dust particles, which are the same size as engineered nanoparticles, induces pulmonary inflammation, oxidative injury, and other damage. Exposure to such particles has also been associated with heart attacks and cardiac rhythmic disturbances.

The limited studies that have been done on engineered nanoparticles are similarly troubling. *In vivo* and *in vitro* studies of cells exposed to engineered nanoparticles have found adverse effects such as structural damage and oxidative stress. And consistent with what we know about nanoparticles, studies in lab animals suggest that nanoparticles can penetrate the body more readily and more deeply than larger particles. * * *

Nanotechnology companies, government agencies, and public interest groups recognize the urgent need for further research in nanotoxicology. Over time, such research will reduce at least some of the uncertainty of health and environmental effects. At present, however, we know very little. Risk assessment of nanotechnology is simply not possible, and evidence suggestive of potential dangers falls short of establishing that exposure to nanoparticles is harmful. The critical question concerns what to do in the meantime as scientists gather risk information.

NOTES AND QUESTIONS

1. *Using existing tools to address nanotechnology.* How might existing statutory authorities such as TSCA be used to address the potential risks posed by nanotechnology? Are such authorities adequate? What role might common law tort doctrines play?

2. *Other options for addressing nanotechnology.* Given the vast uncertainty surrounding the potential risks, a few commentators have called for a moratorium on the commercial use of nanotechnology until more health and safety data become available. See, e.g., Friends of the Earth, Nanomaterials, Sunscreens and Cosmetics: Small Ingredients, Big Risks 17 (2006). What are the advantages and disadvantages of a moratorium or even a blanket prohibition? How might information regulation be applied to nanotechnology? Could economic incentives be used to generate more information on the risks posed by nanotechnology and to internalize any costs that do materialize? What about voluntary initiatives? See, e.g., Gary E. Marchant et al., "A New Soft Law Approach to Nanotechnology Oversight: A Voluntary Product Certification Scheme," 28 UCLA J. Envtl. L. & Pol'y 135 (2010). For a general discussion of various tools that could be incorporated into a nanotechnology oversight system, see J. Clarence Davies, EPA and Nanotechnology: Oversight for the 21st Century (2007), http://www.nanotechproject.org/124/52307–epa-and-nanotechnology-oversight-for-the–21st-century.

3. *A proposal for bonding.* The author of the excerpt goes on to propose a regulatory scheme for nanomaterials. In addition to notification and labeling requirements that would apply to all products containing nanomaterials, the author also proposes a bonding requirement that would apply to products containing nanomaterials in a free form, which are believed to pose the greatest potential for negative health and environmental effects:

> The most important component of the proposal, with respect to internalizing potential costs, is the bonding requirement. Under this requirement, any manufacturer or distributor introducing into commerce a product containing free nanomaterials would be required to post a dated assurance bond that would cover damages that may arise as a result of the company's operations for each year. EPA would set the value of the bond at an amount adequate to cover the most damaging scenario deemed plausible under a worst-case analysis. Such an analysis, which would be assigned to an independent scientific advisory board, would consider factors such as possible routes and levels of exposure, and similarities between the material in question and substances with known toxicology. The term of the bond would be fifteen years, or a period long enough to generate a reasonable amount of short-term and long-term toxicity information, and its value could be revised upward or downward periodically to reflect new information. The bond would be refundable in whole or part, with interest, at the end of the term if the company could demonstrate lower damages, or lower expected damages, than those estimated by EPA in setting the bond. The unrefunded portion of the bond, intended to cover expected damages that have not yet occurred, would be deposited in a trust fund that the proposal would establish.

31 Harv. Envtl. L. Rev. at 397–98. What would a bonding requirement accomplish? Should such a requirement be used in conjunction with, or in place of, tort liability? What are the advantages and disadvantages of a bonding requirement? How much information would be required to carry out the scheme? How difficult would it be to administer such a scheme, and how costly would it be? What incentives and disincentives would it create?

CHAPTER EIGHT

WASTES, RECYCLING, AND RESOURCE CONSERVATION

Until the 1940s, most solid waste generated in the United States consisted of ashes from coal burning furnaces and food wastes. Scrap metals and other materials were routinely recycled, in many cases by scavengers. There was relatively little chemical waste. With increasing urbanization and industrialization in the second half of the twentieth century, the situation has changed dramatically. The United States generates hundreds of millions of tons of solid waste each year. Careless treatment of wastes, especially if they contain hazardous materials, can present major threats to human health and the environment. Discarding materials that could be reused or recycled also may unnecessarily waste resources.

The primary federal legislation dealing with waste management is the Resource Conservation and Recovery Act of 1976 (RCRA). RCRA was intended to close "the last remaining loophole in environmental law, that of unregulated land disposal of discarded materials and hazardous waste." H.R. Rep. No. 94–1491, pt. 1, at 4, reprinted in 1976 U.S.C.C.A.N. 6238, 6241. Radioactive wastes are treated separately, under a series of specific federal statutes. State and local law also plays an important role in regulating disposal of non-hazardous wastes.

SECTION 1. MANAGEMENT OF MUNICIPAL SOLID WASTE

Municipal solid waste (MSW) is a fancy term for the garbage generated by households, commercial facilities, and schools and other institutions. It includes everything from grass clippings to furniture, clothing, food scraps, newspapers, appliances, and batteries. In 2009, the United States produced 243 million tons of MSW, or roughly 4.3 pounds per person per day. EPA, Municipal Solid Waste in the United States: 2009 Facts and Figures 1 (Dec. 2010). MSW contains such potentially hazardous substances as paints, solvents, batteries, and pesticides. Although the proportion of hazardous materials is small, because the total volume of MSW is very large, the absolute quantities of hazardous substances are substantial. As a result, improperly managed municipal solid waste can pose a serious threat to the environment.

A. LANDFILLS

Landfilling remains the primary disposal strategy, accounting for 54% of U.S. municipal solid waste in 2009. *Id.* at 2.

Although states are primarily responsible for dealing with MSW, federal regulations set minimum standards for landfills. Subtitle D of the Resource Conservation and Recovery Act (RCRA) prohibits open dumping of municipal waste, 42 U.S.C. § 6945(a), and sets minimum siting and design criteria for landfills, 42 U.S.C. § 6944, 40 C.F.R. Pt. 258. Those standards prescribe liners, leachate collection systems, and groundwater monitoring wells to minimize the possibility that toxic substances leached from a landfill might contaminate groundwater. Landfill owners and operators must demonstrate financial responsibility, assuring that landfills will be properly closed and adequately cared for after closure. 40 C.F.R. §§ 258.71 to 258.73.

B. INCINERATION

About 12% of the municipal solid waste in the United States is incinerated. *Id.* at 14. Incineration greatly decreases the volume of waste, but it leaves a residue of ash that may be hazardous. Incineration also generates air pollutants that must be controlled to comply with the Clean Air Act.

Burning does offer the advantage that it can produce electricity at the same time it disposes of waste. In the late 1970s and early 1980s, the combination of the energy crisis and the search for landfill alternatives produced a wave of enthusiasm for garbage incineration. Waste-to-energy generation skyrocketed in the 1980s and continued to grow, although more slowly, in the 1990s. The enthusiasm for incineration proved short-lived, however, because low prices for oil and natural gas, combined with the high costs of controlling hazardous air emissions, made waste-to-energy facilities economically unattractive by comparison to landfilling in most locations. Since 2000, incineration of MSW for energy production has decreased by about 15%. *Id.* at 14. That may change again in the future, if the costs of fossil fuels rise.

C. RECYCLING

Familiar recyclable materials in municipal solid waste include paper, some plastics, and yard waste, which can be composted to produce garden mulch. Before the industrial age, the high costs of many raw materials encouraged both recycling and source reduction. Until the mid–19th century, for example, paper was made from rags, that is, recycled fabric, rather than new wood fibers. Recycling in the U.S. faded with industrialization, briefly rose again as a patriotic endeavor during World War II, then subsided again.

Today, recycling is enjoying a renaissance, fueled by environmental rather than economic concerns. Recycling levels have risen steeply over the past fifty years. In 1960, only six percent of the total municipal solid waste generated, less than six million tons, was recycled. Recycling efforts received a boost in the late 1980s from rising landfill tipping fees and the perception that landfill capacity would soon be exhausted. EPA adopted a national goal of reducing or recycling at least twenty-five percent of municipal solid waste. By 1994, forty-four states had announced similar or more stringent reduction and recycling targets. Frank Ackerman, Why Do We Recycle? 19 (1997).

The much-feared landfill crisis never materialized, although landfill space remains limited in a few areas of the country, including the urban northeast. Diversion efforts are only partially responsible for the fading of the landfill crisis. The fear that landfill space was running out had always been exaggerated, fueled by statistics showing a rapid decline in the number of landfill facilities nationwide. Many small landfills did close, but they were replaced by a smaller number of much larger facilities. Nonetheless, efforts to increase recycling continue. By 2009, just over one-third of the nation's municipal waste stream was recycled or composted. EPA, Municipal Solid Waste in the United States: 2009 Facts and Figures 2 (Dec. 2010). In 2005, EPA set a national recycling goal of thirty-five percent of MSW.

The European Community has experimented with building the costs of recycling into the initial purchase price of consumer items. Germany has been a leader in these efforts. In 1991, Germany adopted a law requiring retailers to install bins where consumers could dispose of product packaging free of charge. The law allowed an alternative for "primary packaging," such as the tube that holds toothpaste, as opposed to "secondary packaging" that can be removed and discarded immediately after sale, such as the paper carton holding the toothpaste tube. Retailers did not have to take back primary packaging if effective industry-wide systems for collection and recycling were available. As expected, retailers leaned on product manufacturers, who reduced secondary packaging and collaboratively established a number of collection and recovery initiatives for primary packaging. The best known is the "green dot" program run by a private company, Duales System Deutschland (DSD). Product manufacturers pay a fee, which varies with the type and extent of packaging, in return for the right to place a green dot on their packaging. DSD provides curbside collection facilities for green dot packaging, which is then sorted and recycled. Manufacturers pass the green dot fee on to consumers in the price of the product. This system has both increased recycling and decreased packaging waste. As one observer explains:

> If a company can manage the take-back and valorization of its product more cheaply than others through such innovations as packaging design, it gains a competitive advantage. As a result of this dynamic, a stroll through a German supermarket today shows a far different shelf than just five years ago. There are more concentrated products, lightweight bottles, refills, and far less outer packaging and

plastic than before. Toothpaste, for example, is no longer sold with an outer carton.

James Salzman, Sustainable Consumption and the Law, 27 Envtl. L. 1243, 1273 (1997).

There are some difficulties with the green dot system, however:

DSD's waste management costs have exceeded estimates, partially because the public puts non-recyclable material in the curbside recyclable bins. In addition, while 90 percent of the primary packages carried the green dot, only 60 percent of the companies paid the required licensing fee, leaving DSD in financial straits. Third, DSD does not have the capacity to recycle all the materials collected, forcing the company to store many recycled materials or export them for processing.

Germany's Polluter Pays Concept Could Be Applied to U.S. Industry, 17 Int'l Env't Rptr. (BNA) 368 (1994).

A few years after instituting packaging "take-back" requirements, Germany extended the idea from packaging to a wide variety of products, requiring that manufacturers provide for their recycling or incineration in a waste-to-energy facility. The European Union has even adopted a requirement that auto makers take back cars that no longer have resale value and ensure that 85% of the material in the cars is recovered for future use. *See* Carol J. Williams, EU Sees to It That When Cars Die, They Meet Their Maker, L.A. Times, Feb. 26, 2000, at A2.

Enthusiasm for recycling is not universal. In a 1996 cover article in the Sunday New York Times magazine, John Tierney argued that recycling was economically nonsensical. "Recycling," he wrote, "may be the most wasteful activity in modern America: a waste of time and money, a waste of human and natural resources." John Tierney, Recycling is Garbage, New York Times, June 30, 1996, Sec. 6, at 24. Tierney argued primarily that the economic costs of recycling exceeded its economic benefits. He pointed out that collecting recyclable items in New York City was more expensive than collecting garbage, and that the City often also had to pay recyclers to accept the material after collection. Tierney went so far as to calculate the costs to New Yorkers of recycling their garbage by multiplying the time it took a local college student to sort, rinse, and deliver his recyclables to a basement collection point—eight minutes per week—times the standard hourly wage for a janitor in New York City. His calculation yielded a whopping $792 in additional labor costs per ton of collected material, not counting the cost of the space in which recyclables are stored. He argued that the market should determine whether and to what extent recycling would occur. The easiest way to assure that, he suggested, would be to institute volume-based pricing for garbage collection (sometimes called "pay-as-you-throw") instead of covering waste disposal costs through property or other general taxes. If recycling proved more economically attractive than waste disposal for some or all wastes, consumers would naturally prefer it.

Tierney's article brought a spate of responses. Many critics pointed out that the economic costs of recyclables collection vary with the collection system and the amount collected. The more successful the recycling program, the less the per-unit collection costs tend to be. At least in large cities, diverting a high volume of material to recycling is likely to reduce the costs of garbage collection. Furthermore, where tipping fees are high, savings may more than cover any extra costs of collecting recyclables. Recycling advocates also questioned Tierney's claim that the time spent by homeowners in sorting recyclables should be counted as economic costs, noting that we do not pay people for performing other civic duties.

The economic and environmental benefits of recycling are often difficult to quantify. In part that is because they vary with the costs of disposal in the local area. But there are other complications. Markets for recycled materials take time to develop, and may fluctuate widely even when mature. The environmental impacts of production of new goods from either virgin or recycled materials can be hidden.

How to achieve the optimum level of recycling is also a knotty issue. Although no one argues against the theory of pay-as-you-throw, even such a seemingly obvious step turns out to have significant drawbacks. One reason most communities in the U.S. have traditionally financed waste disposal from general taxes is to encourage appropriate disposal. Disposal charges, even at levels below the true costs of disposal, encourage illegal dumping, which may be quite costly to prevent or correct. *See* Don Fullerton and Thomas C. Kinnaman, Household Responses to Pricing Garbage by the Bag, 86 Am. Econ. Rev. 971 (1996).

D. WASTE MINIMIZATION

Another strategy to reduce disposal is waste minimization, also known as source reduction. The best way to handle waste may be not to produce it in the first place. Reducing packaging and consuming less are two ways to minimize waste production. Mandatory recycling schemes, such as the German green dot program, may encourage waste minimization if the costs of recycling are high.

The Pollution Prevention Act of 1990, 42 U.S.C. §§ 13101–13109, gives the force of federal law to waste reduction efforts. The Act authorizes the EPA to encourage pollution prevention efforts, requires companies to provide information on source reduction and recycling activities, and requires the EPA to review its regulations to determine their potential for encouraging source reduction.

NOTES AND QUESTIONS

1. *Federalism and waste disposal.* What, if anything, justifies federal regulation of solid waste disposal? Would federal imposition of recycling or waste minimization mandates be justifiable?

2. *Evaluating recycling.* How should a community, state, or nation determine the appropriate level of recycling? Should recycling pay for itself in the short term? Why or why not? If recycling must be subsidized, what is the appropriate source of funds? A surcharge on landfill tipping fees? Increased property taxes?

Given the questionable economic justifications in many locations, what explains the high popularity of recycling among citizens? Does recycling simply provide a means of expiating our guilt for other environmental sins, perhaps allowing us to evade feelings of responsibility for more serious problems? Or does it provide indirect or non-monetary benefits that might justify financial subsidies?

EPA asserts that recycling: provides jobs, reduces the need for landfilling and incineration, prevents pollution, saves energy, reduces greenhouse gas emissions, conserves natural resources, and helps protect the environment for future generations. Environmental Protection Agency, Puzzled About Recycling's Value? Look Beyond the Bin, January 1998, at 1. Do you agree with these claims? Are any of these benefits likely to be missed by the market? Can you think of any other benefits from recycling? Might recycling increase awareness of wasteful consumption? Would that be valuable?

3. *Strategies to encourage recycling or source reduction.* If recycling is desirable, what strategy or combination of strategies should be used to encourage it? Considering equity, administrative costs, and feasibility, what role would you assign to: subsidies for recycled products; other positive economic incentives (one example is a contest in which waste management officials in Berkeley, California, periodically examine the garbage of volunteers, awarding cash prizes if the amount of recyclable material is below a certain threshold); surcharges on waste disposal; surcharges on consumption of virgin materials; or recycling mandates imposed on individuals or local governments? Should federal law more directly address recycling, or should it be left to state and local governments?

If mandates are part of the strategy, how should they be enforced? California's Integrated Waste Management Act, for example, permits the imposition of fines up to $10,000 per day on communities which fail to meet the diversion goals, with the money used to boost diversion rates in the jurisdiction. Cal. Pub. Res. Code § 41850(a). Are such penalties appropriate? Will they prove politically difficult to impose?

4. *Developing markets for recycled materials.* RCRA directs the Department of Commerce to encourage the development of markets for recycled materials by identifying barriers to the use of recycled materials and encouraging the development of new uses for such materials. 42 U.S.C. § 6953. A recent Government Accountability Office report noted that the Department was "not taking any actions to stimulate domestic markets and, therefore, is not fully meeting its responsibilities under RCRA." GAO, Recycling: Additional Efforts Could Increase Municipal Recycling, GAO–07–37 (Dec. 2006). Should government agencies (federal or state) work to stimulate markets for recycled products? What steps might they take to do so?

Section 2.   Management of Hazardous Waste

RCRA sets up a "cradle-to-grave" system for regulation of hazardous wastes from their generation to their ultimate disposal. RCRA does not deal with the clean-up of inactive hazardous waste disposal sites, which is covered instead by the Comprehensive Environmental Response, Compensation and Liability Act (CERCLA, covered in detail in Chapter 9). States remain primarily responsible for the difficult task of siting new hazardous waste facilities, and may regulate hazardous waste management more stringently than RCRA mandates.

A.   Subtitle C of the Resource Conservation and Recovery Act

RCRA's principal thrust is oversight of hazardous wastes from generation to disposal in order to protect human health and the environment. To that end, Subtitle C of RCRA, 42 U.S.C. §§ 6921 to 6939e, regulates the generation, transport, treatment, storage, and disposal of hazardous wastes. The Subtitle C program covers an enormous number of facilities and entities, including about 1,700 treatment, storage and disposal facilities (often referred to by the acronym TSDFs), 16,000 transporters, 17,000 large-quantity generators of hazardous waste, and more than 150,000 small-quantity generators.

1.   A BRIEF OVERVIEW OF SUBTITLE C

The requirements of Subtitle C apply only to "solid waste" identified as "hazardous." A preliminary, and highly contentious, issue is whether the material is a solid waste. If so, it is considered a hazardous waste if it has been specifically identified by EPA as hazardous or if it is ignitable, corrosive, reactive, or toxic under prescribed test conditions. *See* 40 C.F.R. Part 261. Radioactive wastes are excluded from RCRA's coverage. 42 U.S.C. § 6903(27). Medical wastes are subject to the special regulations of Subtitle J, 42 U.S.C. §§ 6992 to 6992k.

Generators of hazardous waste are subject to RCRA section 3002, 42 U.S.C. § 6922. EPA defines as "generators" persons who produce hazardous waste or cause a hazardous waste to become subject to regulation. 40 C.F.R. § 260.10. Generators must keep accurate records of the waste they generate, prepare a manifest to accompany waste sent off-site for disposal, and submit periodic reports to EPA. Manifests for off-site treatment, storage, or disposal must certify that the generator has a waste minimization program in place, and that the proposed method of treatment, storage, or disposal minimizes present and future hazards to human health and the environment to the extent practicable. "Small" generators, who produce no more than 100 kilograms of hazardous waste per month, are exempt from many of these requirements. *See* 40 C.F.R. 261.5(b).

Transporters are regulated under RCRA section 3003, 42 U.S.C. § 6923. They must keep adequate records, accept only properly labeled waste, and comply with the manifest system by delivering the waste and its accompanying manifest to the designated facility. Hazardous waste transporters are also regulated by the Department of Transportation under the Hazardous Materials Transportation Act, 49 U.S.C. §§ 5101–5127.

Treatment, storage, and disposal facilities (TSDFs) must obtain a permit under RCRA section 3005, 42 U.S.C. § 6925, and meet detailed record-keeping, design, operation, and financial responsibility standards promulgated under section 3004, 42 U.S.C. § 6924. These standards are intended to assure that TSDFs are operated safely and eventually closed in a manner that protects public and environmental health. TSDFs must comply with limitations on the methods of disposal or treatment of specific hazardous wastes. RCRA establishes a conditional "land ban," prohibiting landfilling of hazardous wastes unless EPA finds that human health and the environment will be adequately protected. The standards for waiver of the land ban have been hotly contested.

RCRA allows EPA to delegate to the states authority to administer and enforce approved state hazardous waste programs in lieu of the federal program. RCRA § 3006, 42 U.S.C. § 6926(b). To gain approval, state programs must be equivalent to, consistent with, and no less stringent than the federal program. As of 2005, 50 states and territories had gained approval to implement basic hazardous waste programs. Authority to implement programs added in the 1984 Hazardous and Solid Waste Amendments, including land disposal restrictions, corrective action, and toxicity characteristic testing, is delegated separately. Most states have been delegated authority only to implement selected parts of the overall RCRA program.

CLASS DISCUSSION PROBLEM: THE PHELPS–LEE FOUNDRY

The Phelps–Lee Foundry uses sand for mold liners and core butts in its casting operations. During use, the sand becomes contaminated with small amounts of copper, chromium, brass, tin, lead and other metals. According to EPA regulations, a solid waste exhibits the characteristic of toxicity if, under standard testing conditions, an extract of the waste contains chromium or lead at levels of 5 mg/l or above. Phelps–Lee has not tested its waste sand. Phelps–Lee has developed a new process for reconditioning used sand for reuse and recovering the contaminating metals, which have significant commercial value. The process separates the metals from the sand at high efficiency. The products are clean sand, which Phelps–Lee returns to its process, and purified metals. Phelps–Lee reuses some of the metals in its foundry operations, and sells others.

Phelps–Lee has patented this process and now uses it routinely. Prior to reclamation, the used sand is piled near the reclamation plant on a liner designed to protect the ground from contact with the sand or water leaching through the sand. All sand is reclaimed within a day or two of its use in casting.

The Phelps–Lee reclamation process uses large amounts of water and produces a large volume of effluent, which contains unspecified amounts of metals. Phelps–Lee pumps the effluent into a holding pond. The company contends that it is not necessary to treat the water, since it evaporates naturally or seeps down into the soil, which acts as a natural filter removing the metals from the water. Periodically, a metal reclamation company removes the residue or "sludge" that collects on the bottom of the pond, and hauls it away to a reclamation plant. Phelps–Lee does not charge for the sludge.

(a) Recently Phelps–Lee received a letter from the EPA stating that the company may be subject to RCRA's regulatory requirements as a waste treatment, storage, and disposal facility. Is Phelps–Lee in violation of RCRA?

(b) Suppose Phelps–Lee tested its used sand using EPA's prescribed toxicity characteristic leaching procedure, and determined that the extract contained only 0.4 mg/l chromium and 0.3 mg/l lead. Could EPA list the used sand as a hazardous waste? Must it do so?

2. IDENTIFYING "SOLID WASTE"

Excerpts From the Resource Conservation and Recovery Act

42 U.S.C. §§ 6901–6992k.

Sec. 1004   Definitions

(27) The term "solid waste" means any garbage, refuse, sludge from a waste treatment plant, water supply treatment plant, or air pollution control facility and other discarded material, including solid, liquid, semi-solid, or contained gaseous material resulting from industrial, commercial, mining, and agricultural operations, and from community activities, but does not include solid or dissolved material in domestic sewage, or solid or dissolved materials in irrigation return flows or industrial discharges which are point sources subject to permits under [section 402 of the Clean Water Act], or source, special nuclear, or byproduct material as defined by the Atomic Energy Act of 1954, as amended.

Excerpts From Environmental Protection Agency Regulations

40 C.F.R. Part 261.

Sec. 261.2   Definition of solid waste.

(a)(1) A *solid waste* is any discarded material that is not excluded by § 261.4(a) or that is not excluded by variance granted under §§ 260.30 and 260.31 or that is not excluded by a non-waste determination under §§ 260.30 and 260.34.

(2)(i) A *discarded material* is any material which is:

    (A) *Abandoned*, as explained in paragraph (b) of this section; or

    (B) *Recycled*, as explained in paragraph (c) of this section; or

    (C) *Considered inherently waste-like*, as explained in paragraph (d) of this section * * *.

  (ii) A hazardous secondary material is not discarded if it is generated and reclaimed under the control of the generator as defined in § 260.10, it is not speculatively accumulated as defined in § 261.1(c)(8), it is handled only in non-land-based units and is contained in such units, it is generated and reclaimed within the United States and its territories, it is not otherwise subject to material-specific management conditions under § 261.4(a) when reclaimed * * *, and the reclamation of the material is legitimate, as specified under § 260.43.

(b) Materials are solid waste if they are *abandoned* by being:

  (1) Disposed of; or

  (2) Burned or incinerated; or

  (3) Accumulated, stored, or treated (but not recycled) before or in lieu of being abandoned by being disposed of, burned, or incinerated.

(c) Materials are solid wastes if they are *recycled*—or accumulated, stored, or treated before recycling—as specified in paragraphs (c)(1) through (4) of this section.

  (1) *Used in a manner constituting disposal.*

    (i) Materials noted with a " * " in Column 1 of Table I are solid wastes when they are:

      (A) Applied to or placed on the land in a manner that constitutes disposal; or

      (B) Used to produce products that are applied to or placed on the land or are otherwise contained in products that are applied to or placed on the land (in which cases the product itself remains a solid waste).

    (ii) However, commercial chemical products listed in § 261.33 are not solid wastes if they are applied to the land and that is their ordinary manner of use.

  (2) *Burning for energy recovery.*

    (i) Materials noted with a " * " in column 2 of Table 1 are solid wastes when they are:

      (A) Burned to recover energy;

(B) Used to produce a fuel or are otherwise contained in fuels (in which cases the fuel itself remains a solid waste).

(ii) However, commercial chemical products listed in § 261.33 are not solid wastes if they are themselves fuels.

(3) *Reclaimed.* Materials noted with a "—" in column 3 of Table 1 are not solid wastes when reclaimed. Materials noted with an " * " in column 3 of Table 1 are solid wastes when reclaimed unless they meet the requirements of §§ 261.2(a)(2)(ii), or 261.4(a)(17), or 261.4(a)(23), or 261.4(a)(24) or 261.4(a)(25).

(4) *Accumulated speculatively.* Materials noted with a " * " in column 4 of Table 1 are solid wastes when accumulated speculatively.

(d) *Inherently waste-like materials.* [Specified materials] are solid wastes when they are recycled in any manner * * *.

(3) The Administrator will use the following criteria to add wastes to [the list of inherently waste-like materials]:

(i)(A) The materials are ordinarily disposed of, burned or incinerated; or

(B) The materials contain toxic constituents listed in appendix VIII of part 261 and these constituents are not ordinarily found in raw materials or products for which the materials substitute (or are found in raw materials or products in smaller concentration) and are not used or reused during the recycling process; and

(ii) The material may pose a substantial hazard to human health and the environment when recycled.

(e) *Materials that are not solid waste when recycled.*

(1) Materials are not solid wastes when they can be shown to be recycled by being:

(i) Used or reused as ingredients in an industrial process to make a product, provided the materials are not being reclaimed; or

(ii) Used or reused as effective substitutes for commercial products; or

(iii) Returned to the original process from which they are generated, without first being reclaimed or land disposed. The material must be returned as a substitute for feedstock materials. * * *

(2) The following materials are solid wastes, even if the recycling involves use, reuse, or return to the original process * * *:

(i) Materials used in a manner constituting disposal, or used to produce products that are applied to the land; or

(ii) Materials burned for energy recovery, used to produce a fuel, or contained in fuels; or

(iii) Materials accumulated speculatively * * *.

(f) *Documentation of claims that materials are not solid wastes or are conditionally exempt from regulation.* Respondents in actions to enforce regulations implementing subtitle C of RCRA who raise a claim that a certain material is not a solid waste, or is conditionally exempt from regulation, must demonstrate that there is a known market or disposition for the material, and that they meet the terms of the exclusion or exemption. In doing so, they must provide appropriate documentation (such as contracts showing that a second person uses the material as an ingredient in a production process) to demonstrate that the material is not a waste, or is exempt from regulation. In addition, owners or operators of facilities claiming that they actually are recycling materials must show that they have the necessary equipment to do so.

TABLE 1

	Use constituting disposal (§ 261.2(c)(1)) 1	Energy recovery/fuel (§ 261.2(c)(2)) 2	Reclamation (§ 261.2(c)(3)) except as provided in §§ 261.2(a)(2)(ii), 261.4(a)(17), 261.4(a)(23), 261.4(a)(24), or 261.4(a)(25) 3	Speculative accumulation (§ 261.2(c)(4)) 4
Spent Materials	(*)	(*)	(*)	(*)
Sludges (listed in 40 CFR 261.31 or 261.32)	(*)	(*)	(*)	(*)
Sludges exhibiting a characteristic of hazardous waste	(*)	(*)	---	(*)
By-products (listed in 40 CFR 261.31 or 261.32)	(*)	(*)	(*)	(*)
By-products exhibiting a characteristic of hazardous waste	(*)	(*)	---	(*)
Commercial chemical products listed in 40 CFR 261.33	(*)	(*)	---	---
Scrap metal that is not excluded under § 261.4(a)(13)	(*)	(*)	(*)	(*)

Note: The terms "spent materials," "sludges," "by-products," and "scrap metal" and "processed scrap metal" are defined in § 261.1.

Sec. 260.30 Non-waste determinations and variances from classification as a solid waste.

In accordance with the standards and criteria in § 260.31 and § 260.34 and the procedures in § 260.33, the Administrator may determine on a case-by-case basis that the following recycled materials are not solid wastes:

(a) Materials that are accumulated speculatively without sufficient amounts being recycled (as defined in § 261.1(c)(8) of this chapter);

(b) Materials that are reclaimed and then reused within the original primary production process in which they were generated;

(c) Materials that have been reclaimed but must be reclaimed further before the materials are completely recovered.

(d) Hazardous secondary materials that are reclaimed in a continuous industrial process; and

(e) Hazardous secondary materials that are indistinguishable in all relevant aspects from a product or intermediate.

FIGURE 1
DEFINITION OF A SOLID WASTE

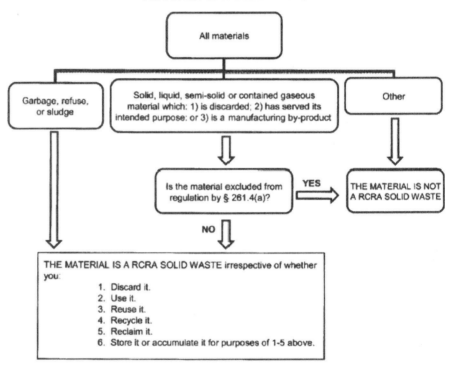

American Petroleum Institute v. United States Environmental Protection Agency

United States Court of Appeals, District of Columbia Circuit, 2000.
216 F.3d 50.

■ PER CURIAM:

* * *

RCRA is a comprehensive environmental statute granting EPA authority to regulate solid and hazardous wastes. "Solid wastes" are governed by Subtitle D of RCRA, and are generally subject to less stringent management standards than "hazardous wastes" which are regulated under Subtitle C. For purposes of RCRA, Congress defined solid waste as follows:

The term "solid waste" means any garbage, refuse, sludge from a waste treatment plant, water supply treatment plant, or air pollution control facility and other discarded material, including solid, liquid, semisolid, or contained gaseous material resulting from industrial, commercial, mining, and agricultural operations, and from community activities. . . .

42 U.S.C. § 6903(27).

In pursuit of its congressionally conferred duty and authority to regulate solid waste under RCRA, the EPA has adopted regulations defining solid waste for purposes of its hazardous waste regulations: "A solid waste is any discarded material," 40 C.F.R. § 261.2(a)(1) (1999), subject to a number of exclusions enumerated in § 261.4(a) and case-by-case variances under §§ 260.30 and 260.31. The term "discarded material" for purposes of the regulation means any material which is abandoned, recycled, or considered inherently wastelike. 40 C.F.R. § 261.2(a)(2).

In 1994 and 1998 rulemakings in pursuit of its RCRA obligations, the EPA examined the production processes of the petroleum refining industry. As pertinent to the issue before us, EPA considered whether to exclude from the definition of solid waste two secondary materials: oil-bearing wastewaters generated by the petroleum refining industry and recovered oil produced by the petrochemical manufacturing industry. EPA determined that oil-bearing wastewaters are solid waste for purposes of RCRA regulation * * *. Industry petitioners challenge [this conclusion].

In petroleum refining, impurities are removed and usable hydrocarbon fractions are isolated from crude oil feedstock. Large quantities of water are used, and the resulting wastewaters contain a small percentage of residual oil. These "oilbearing wastewaters" are destined for ultimate discharge, but only after a three-step treatment process is first applied. The first phase of treatment, known as "primary treatment," removes certain materials including the oil. This phase has at least two beneficial consequences: (1) it meets a Clean Water Act requirement that refineries remove oil from their wastewater, and (2) it allows refineries to recover a not insignificant quantity of oil (which industry claims can range up to 1,000 barrels a day at certain refineries) which is cycled back into the refinery production process.

Industry petitioners and EPA disagree over when these wastewaters become discarded for purposes of the solid waste definition. While no one disputes that discard has certainly occurred by the time the wastewaters move into the later phases of treatment, the question is whether discard happens before primary treatment, allowing regulation of wastewater as solid waste at that point, or not until primary treatment is complete and oil has been recovered for further processing.

EPA's initial proposal excluded oil-bearing wastewaters. However, it changed its mind in 1994 and concluded that even before the oil is recovered in primary treatment, "the wastewaters are discarded materials and hence solid wastes subject to regulation under RCRA." 59 Fed. Reg. 38,540/1. EPA stated: "Primary wastewater treatment operations exist to treat plant wastewaters." *Id.* at 38,539/3. It noted that the percentage of oil in the wastewater is very small and "not significant in the context of a refinery's overall production activities," and that the Clean Water Act mandates such treatment. *Id.* For these stated reasons, EPA concluded that "[c]learly, wastewater treatment is the main purpose of the systems in question, and any oil recovery is of secondary import." 59 Fed. Reg. at 38,539/3.

EPA restated its conclusion in its subsequent 1995 Proposed Rule and retained it in the Final Rule. *See* 63 Fed. Reg. at 42,184 (codified at 40 C.F.R. § 261.4(a)(12)(ii)). The actual regulation does not mention wastewaters. But by not being excluded, all wastewaters including oil-bearing wastewaters are considered to fall under EPA's general regulatory definition of solid waste.

Whether a material has been "discarded," subjecting it to RCRA regulation, is a question we have considered in four prior cases. First, in *American Mining Congress v. EPA*, 824 F.2d 1177 (D.C. Cir. 1987) ("*AMC I*"), we held that the term "discarded" conforms to its plain meaning. Thus, items that are "disposed of, abandoned, or thrown away" are discarded. *AMC I* concluded that "in-process secondary materials," that is, materials "destined for immediate reuse in another phase of [an] industry's ongoing production process," are not discarded under RCRA. *Id.* at 1185, 1193. We recently reaffirmed that holding in *Association of Battery Recyclers, Inc. v. U.S. EPA*, 208 F.3d 1047 (D.C. Cir. 2000), where we reiterated that EPA cannot regulate as solid waste secondary materials "destined for reuse as part of a continuous industrial process" that is therefore "not abandoned or thrown away." *Id.* at 1056.

At the other end of the spectrum we have held that a material that has been "indisputably discarded" can, of course, be subjected to regulation as solid waste. *API v. EPA*, 906 F.2d 729, 741 (D.C. Cir. 1990). Where a material was "delivered to [a metals reclamation] facility not as part of an *ongoing* manufacturing or industrial process within the generating industry, but as part of a mandatory waste treatment plan prescribed by EPA," we concluded that a material was not precluded from being classified by EPA as a solid waste. *Id.*

A material somewhere between the extremes of ongoing production and indisputable discard was addressed in *American Mining Congress v. EPA*, 907 F.2d 1179 (D.C. Cir. 1990) ("*AMC II*"). Industry petitioners claimed that sludges from wastewater stored in surface impoundments, which "may" later be reclaimed for treatment, could not be regulated. *Id.* at 1186. We disagreed and deferred to EPA's determination that such sludges have been discarded. Nothing, we reasoned, prevents EPA from regulating as "solid wastes" materials managed in land disposal units which are no longer part of an industrial process.

* * *

Industry petitioners * * * contend that * * * oil-bearing wastewaters cannot be regulated because they are unquestionably in-process materials not yet discarded. Alternately, even if the status of oil-bearing wastewaters is not so plain, petitioners assert that EPA's conclusion is arbitrary and capricious because it is not based on reasoned decisionmaking. Petitioners emphasize that primary treatment yields valuable oil that is reinserted into the refining processes in a continuous operation. They also claim that oil recovery operations began long before Clean Water Act regulations required it. In sum, they contend that oil recovery in primary treatment is a part of in-process oil production.

At bottom, the parties disagree over the proper characterization of primary treatment. Is it simply a step in the act of discarding? Or is it the last step in a production process before discard? Our prior cases have not had to draw a line for deciding when discard has occurred. While the issue was closest in *AMC II,* the sludges in dispute there were described as being stored in surface impoundments "that may at some time in the future be reclaimed." *AMC II,* 907 F.2d at 1186. We concluded that EPA's interpretation of "discarded" as including the sludges was reasonable and entitled to deference under Chevron U.S.A. Inc. v. Natural Resources Defense Council, Inc., 467 U.S. 837, 842–45 (1984). * * *

It may be permissible for EPA to determine that the predominant purpose of primary treatment is discard. Legal abandonment of property is premised on determining the intent to abandon, which requires an inquiry into facts and circumstances. Where an industrial by-product may be characterized as discarded or "in process" material, EPA's choice of characterization is entitled to deference. However, the record must reflect that EPA engaged in reasoned decisionmaking to decide which characterization is appropriate. The record in this case is deficient in that regard. EPA has noted two purposes of primary treatment and concludes, "[c]learly, wastewater treatment is the main purpose." 1994 Rule, 59 Fed. Reg. 38,539/3. As English teachers have long taught, a conclusion is not "clear" or "obvious" merely because one says so.

EPA points out that primary treatment only recovers a small amount of oil relative to the entire output of a typical refining facility. However, the oil is still valuable and usable, so that reason alone cannot show discard. The rock of a diamond mine may only contain a tiny portion of precious carbon, but that is enough to keep miners busy. According to claims by the refining industry, the net amount of oil recovered may reach 1,000 barrels a day for certain refineries. It is plausible to claim, as industry petitioners do, that refiners engage in primary treatment first and foremost to recover this usable resource. At the very least, EPA cannot merely rely on the small relative amount of oil recovered from primary treatment without further explanation.

EPA also notes that the Clean Water Act requires primary treatment before discharge. If refiners got nothing from primary treatment, this might be a compelling rationale because it would be hard to explain why, other than to discard, refiners would engage in a costly treatment activity with no economic benefits. However, petitioners claim they would engage in primary treatment regardless of the treatment standards in order to recover the desired oil. EPA does not explain why this possibly valid motivation is not compelling. EPA makes no attempt to balance the costs and benefits of primary treatment, or otherwise to explain why the Clean Water Act requirements are the real motivation behind primary treatment. Indeed, without further explanation, it is not inherently certain why a substance is definitively "discarded" if its possessor is continuing to process it, even though the possessor's decision to continue processing may have been influenced, or even predominantly motivated, by some external factor. Otherwise put, it is not so obvious as EPA would have us hold that if the industry petitioners conceded that their overriding motivation in further processing the wastewaters was compliance with Clean Water Act regulations that they would then conclusively be discarding the material in question even while further processing it. If the non-Clean Water Act benefits of the initial treatment are enough to justify firms' incurring the costs (petitioners point to material in the record that may support such a proposition), the EPA would have to reconcile that fact with any conclusion that the Clean Water Act purpose was primary.

In short, EPA has not set forth why it has concluded that the compliance motivation predominates over the reclamation motivation. Perhaps equally importantly it has not explained why that conclusion, even if validly reached, compels the further conclusion that the wastewater has been discarded. Therefore, because the agency has failed to provide a rational explanation for its decision, we hold the decision to be arbitrary and capricious. We therefore vacate the portion of EPA's decision declining to exclude oil-bearing wastewaters from the statutory definition of solid waste, and remand for further proceedings. We do not suggest any particular result on remand, only a reasoned one demonstrating when discard occurs if EPA wishes to assert jurisdiction.

NOTES AND QUESTIONS

1. *Identifying solid waste.* RCRA and its implementing regulations have been described as mind-numbingly complex. That complexity begins with the definition of "solid waste." Even experienced environmental lawyers struggle to understand whether a particular material is a solid waste for RCRA purposes. That question is crucial, because only solid wastes are potentially subject to the detailed requirements of Subtitle C.

How helpful is the flowchart EPA provides (reproduced with slight modifications at Figure 1) for determining whether a material qualifies as "solid waste"? Must the material be solid? Are the particles in diesel exhaust, which range in size from 0.1 to 10 micrometers (from 500 to 5 times smaller than the diameter of a human hair) and which include a number of toxic metals and other hazardous substances, "solid waste" for RCRA purposes? NRDC thinks so. In June 2011, it filed a notice of intent to sue two railroads for violating RCRA by improperly disposing of diesel particulate matter at railyards.

Must "solid waste" be waste, as that term is ordinarily understood? Are all wastes included?

Why is it so difficult to produce a simple definition of the term solid waste? What tensions do the statutory and regulatory definitions struggle to resolve? What do you suppose accounts for the statutory exemptions?

2. *Statutory and regulatory definitions.* The regulatory definition of "solid waste" in 40 C.F.R. § 261.2, excerpted above, "applies only to wastes that are also hazardous for purposes of the regulations implementing subtitle C of RCRA." 40 C.F.R. § 261.1(b)(1).

Only materials meeting the regulatory definition of solid waste, which EPA considers somewhat narrower than the statutory definition, can be hazardous wastes subject to the cradle-to-grave regulatory and record-keeping requirements of subtitle C. The statutory definition governs actions to abate imminent and substantial endangerment to health or the environment caused by the treatment, storage, or disposal of solid wastes. Such actions need not involve industrial processes at all. For example, in Safe Air for Everyone v. Meyer, 373 F.3d 1035 (9th Cir. 2004), plaintiffs who sought to block the open burning of the residues left in agricultural fields after the harvest of commercial grass seed alleged that the residue was "solid waste" for RCRA purposes. A divided panel of the Ninth Circuit disagreed. The majority concluded that the residue was "reused" by burning because the burning returned nutrients to the soil and helped to reduce pest infestations. Dissenting, Judge Paez agreed with plaintiffs that the residue was "discarded" because the primary purpose of burning was to remove it from the fields.

Does a shooting range need a RCRA TSDF permit because lead from spent ammunition is "disposed of" at the site? In Cordiano v. Metacon Gun Club, 575 F.3d 199 (2d Cir. 2009), the court rejected that argument, deferring to EPA's view that spent ammunition is not "discarded" but rather comes to rest on land "as a result of [its] proper and expected use." *Id.* at 207. Is EPA's interpretation reasonable? Does it make sense to distinguish between discarding and intended use, when the end result of either is that the product is left lying on the ground?

3. *Recycling versus waste.* One of the most difficult aspects of identifying solid waste is distinguishing materials that are truly waste from those undergoing recycling or further processing for the extraction or production of useful materials. Early identification of waste materials serves RCRA's goal of tracking hazardous wastes from their production to their ultimate disposal in order to ensure appropriate treatment at every step in between. However, as the *American Petroleum Institute* excerpt demonstrates, it is not always easy to determine where processing, reprocessing or recycling end and disposal or treatment of waste begins. How did EPA attempt to draw that line for oil-bearing wastewaters? What flaws did the court find in EPA's analysis? What explanation would be required to convince the court that treatment was the predominant purpose of wastewater processing? If EPA could make that showing, would that automatically make the waste-waters "solid waste" for RCRA purposes? If not, what else would be required?

Can materials be both waste and raw materials? Suppose the Acme Corporation purchases lead plates which have been removed from used batteries, removes the lead from those plates and produces lead ingots, which it then sells. Are the plates Acme uses as its raw material "solid waste"? *See* United States v. ILCO, 996 F.2d 1126 (11th Cir. 1993) (holding that EPA could classify the plates as solid waste even if they had monetary value to the reclaimer). What about sludge from an air pollution control device if sold for use as a feedstock for fertilizer production? *See* Safe Food and Fertilizer v. EPA, 350 F.3d 1263 (D.C. Cir. 2003) (upholding EPA's conclusion that the sludge was not solid waste because it had market value and presented no greater environmental or health risk than the virgin materials for which it substituted). Potassium hydroxide which has been used to clean metal castings, and when it is too contaminated to do that effectively is shipped to a fertilizer manufacturer for incorporation, without any processing, in fertilizers? See Howmet Corp. v. EPA, 614 F.3d 544 (D.C. Cir. 2010) (deferring to EPA's view that the potassium hydroxide was solid waste because it was no longer useful for its original intended purpose).

4. *Is fine-tuning needed?* RCRA allows material falling outside the definition of "solid waste" to essentially escape regulation, while imposing requirements viewed by industry as extremely burdensome on those solid wastes that are also hazardous. RCRA therefore may under-regulate hazardous materials that are not "solid waste." On the other hand, imposition of additional regulations on materials that are destined for reuse, reclamation, or recycling may discourage practices that are environmentally desirable in the sense that they conserve natural resources. Would a regulatory scheme less dependent on whether the material is waste and more finely tuned to the particular hazards posed by the material in a particular process be preferable to the current scheme? Could such a scheme be designed and implemented, or would it be too complex to be practical?

In 2008, after conducting studies of recycling practices and the hazards posed by recycling, EPA revised the definition of solid waste to exclude: (1) hazardous materials that are legitimately reclaimed (and not speculatively accumulated) under the control of the generator; and (2) hazardous materials transferred to another entity for the purpose of reclamation, provided a number of conditions intended to ensure the legitimacy of the transaction and the safety of the reclamation process are met. 73 Fed. Reg. 64668 (Oct. 30, 2008). It also provided a test for determining when recycling efforts are legitimate, as opposed to a sham. "Legitimate recycling must involve a hazardous secondary material that provides a useful contribution to the recycling process or to a product or intermediate of the recycling process, and the recycling process must produce a valuable product or intermediate." 40 C.F.R. § 260.43(b). In determining whether recycling is legitimate, the agency considers: whether the hazardous secondary material is managed as a valuable commodity, meaning primarily that it is contained; whether the product of the recycling process contains more hazardous constituents or exhibits more hazardous characteristics than analogous products; and other relevant factors. *Id.* § 260.43(c).

In July 2011, EPA proposed to further revise the definition of solid waste to increase oversight of reclamation by generators of hazardous materials, limit the exclusion of hazardous materials transferred to another entity for purposes of reclamation and reduce flexibility in the identification legitimate recycling. 76 Fed. Reg. 44094 (July 22, 2011). The agency is concerned that the 2008 exclusions are not adequately protective of human health and the environment.

3.   IDENTIFYING "HAZARDOUS WASTE"

Excerpts From the Resource Conservation and Recovery Act

42 U.S.C. §§ 6901–6992k.

Sec. 1004   Definitions

(5) The term "hazardous waste" means a solid waste, or combination of solid wastes, which because of its quantity, concentration, or physical, chemical, or infectious characteristics may—

> (A) cause, or significantly contribute to an increase in mortality or an increase in serious irreversible, or incapacitating reversible, illness; or

> (B) pose a substantial present or potential hazard to human health or the environment when improperly treated, stored, transported, or disposed of, or otherwise managed.

* * *

Sec. 3001   Identification and listing of hazardous waste

(a) Not later than eighteen months after October 21, 1976, the Administrator shall, after notice and opportunity for public hearing, and after consultation with appropriate Federal and State agencies, develop and promulgate criteria for identifying the characteristics of hazardous waste, and for listing hazardous waste, which should be subject to the provisions of this subchapter, taking into account toxicity, persistence, and degradability in nature, potential for accumulation in tissue, and other related factors such as flammability, corrosiveness, and other hazardous characteristics. Such criteria shall be revised from time to time as may be appropriate.

(b)(1) Not later than eighteen months after October 21, 1976, and after notice and opportunity for public hearing, the Administrator shall promulgate regulations identifying the characteristics of hazardous waste, and listing particular hazardous wastes (within the meaning of section 6903(5) of this title), which shall be subject to the provisions of this subchapter. Such regulations shall be based on the criteria promulgated under subsection (a) of this section and shall be revised from time to time thereafter as may be appropriate. * * *

Under RCRA, only solid wastes can be hazardous wastes, but not all solid wastes are hazardous wastes. EPA regulations specifically exclude some solid wastes, including household wastes, agricultural wastes used as fertilizers, and drilling wastes from oil and natural gas exploration, from hazardous waste classification. *See* 40 C.F.R. § 261.4(b). Solid wastes not excluded by § 261.4(b) are hazardous wastes if they qualify as either *characteristic wastes* or *listed wastes*.

Solid wastes are characteristic wastes if they exhibit any of four hazardous characteristics: ignitability, corrosivity, reactivity, or toxicity. Ignitable wastes burn easily, posing a threat of fire. Corrosive wastes are strong acids and bases, capable of eating through metals. Reactive wastes are unstable, with the potential to explode, react violently with water, or produce toxic fumes when exposed to water or strong acid or base. Toxic wastes have the potential to release toxic substances to the environment in toxic concentrations if handled improperly. EPA regulations further define these characteristics, and prescribe tests for determining if a particular solid waste exhibits them. *See* 40 C.F.R. Part 261, Subpart C.

Of the four characteristics, toxicity is the most important and the most controversial. EPA has prescribed a test, known as the Toxicity Characteristic Leaching Procedure (TCLP), intended to simulate the leaching process in a landfill. *See* 40 C.F.R. § 261.24. The TCLP rule was upheld against an industry challenge in Edison Electric Institute v. U.S. EPA, 2 F.3d 438 (D.C. Cir. 1993). In a 1996 study, EPA acknowledged some shortcomings of the TCLP. *See* U.S. Environmental Protection Agency, Hazardous Waste Characteristics Scoping Study (1996). But the agency has been unable to identify a better method for accurately predicting the toxicity characteristics of leachate.

Waste generators are responsible for determining if their wastes are characteristic hazardous wastes. EPA regulations give generators the option of undertaking the prescribed tests (or their functional equivalent) or "[a]pplying knowledge of the hazard characteristic of the waste in light of the materials or the processes used." 40 C.F.R. § 262.11(c).

Solid wastes are also hazardous for RCRA purposes if EPA has listed them as hazardous. The agency currently maintains three separate lists. The first includes hazardous wastes from non-specific sources (40 C.F.R. § 261.31). These wastes, known as "F wastes" because their EPA identification numbers begin with F, include spent solvents and wastes from chemical processes. The second list (40 C.F.R. § 261.32) is "K wastes," hazardous wastes from specific manufacturing processes, such as wood preserving and the chemical production. The third list (40 C.F.R. § 261.33) consists of discarded commercial chemicals or chemical intermediates that are hazardous ("U wastes") or acutely hazardous ("P wastes").

Generators of a listed waste who believe the waste from their facility is relatively innocuous can petition for exclusion of their waste from the list through a process known as "delisting." To obtain an exclusion, the generator must demonstrate that the facility's waste does not exhibit the criteria for which the waste category as a whole was listed. *See* 40 C.F.R.

§ 260.22. If a petition succeeds, the waste from that facility is no longer considered a listed waste. Waste generators view the delisting process as slow, expensive, and uncertain. *See*, e.g., Jeffrey M. Gaba, The Mixture and Derived-from Rules Under RCRA: Once a Hazardous Waste Always a Hazardous Waste?, 21 Envtl. L. Rep. 10033 (1991).

Excerpts From Environmental Protection Agency Regulations

40 C.F.R. Part 261.

Sec. 261.11 Criteria for listing hazardous waste.

(a) The Administrator shall list a solid waste as a hazardous waste only upon determining that the solid waste meets one of the following criteria:

(1) It exhibits any of the characteristics of hazardous waste identified in subpart C.

(2) It has been found to be fatal to humans in low doses or, in the absence of data on human toxicity, it has been shown in studies to have an oral LD 50 toxicity (rat) of less than 50 milligrams per kilogram, an inhalation LC 50 toxicity (rat) of less than 2 milligrams per liter, or a dermal LD 50 toxicity (rabbit) of less than 200 milligrams per kilogram or is otherwise capable of causing or significantly contributing to an increase in serious irreversible, or incapacitating reversible, illness. (Waste listed in accordance with these criteria will be designated Acute Hazardous Waste.)

(3) It contains any of the toxic constituents listed on appendix VIII and, after considering the following factors, the Administrator concludes that the waste is capable of posing a substantial present or potential hazard to human health or the environment when improperly treated, stored, transported or disposed of, or otherwise managed:

(i) The nature of the toxicity presented by the constituent.

(ii) The concentration of the constituent in the waste.

(iii) The potential of the constituent or any toxic degradation product of the constituent to migrate from the waste into the environment under the types of improper management considered in paragraph (a)(3)(vii) of this section.

(iv) The persistence of the constituent or any toxic degradation product of the constituent.

(v) The potential for the constituent or any toxic degradation product of the constituent to degrade into non-harmful constituents and the rate of degradation.

(vi) The degree to which the constituent or any degradation product of the constituent bioaccumulates in ecosystems.

(vii) The plausible types of improper management to which the waste could be subjected.

(viii) The quantities of the waste generated at individual generation sites or on a regional or national basis.

(ix) The nature and severity of the human health and environmental damage that has occurred as a result of the improper management of wastes containing the constituent.

(x) Action taken by other governmental agencies or regulatory programs based on the health or environmental hazard posed by the waste or waste constituent.

(xi) Such other factors as may be appropriate.

Substances will be listed on Appendix VIII only if they have been shown in scientific studies to have toxic, carcinogenic, mutagenic or teratogenic effects on humans or other life forms. (Wastes listed in accordance with these criteria will be designated Toxic Wastes.)

(b) The Administrator may list classes or types of solid waste as hazardous waste if he has reason to believe that individual wastes, within the class or type of waste, typically or frequently are hazardous under the definition of hazardous waste found in Section 1004(5) of the Act.

* * *

Dithiocarbamate Task Force v. Environmental Protection Agency

United States Court of Appeals, District of Columbia Circuit, 1996.
98 F.3d 1394.

■ Stephen F. Williams, Circuit Judge.

This consolidated case concerns four classes of carbamate compounds—carbamates proper, carbamoyl oximes, thiocarbamates and dithiocarbamates (collectively "carbamates")—whose similar names reflect similarities in their chemical origins and structures. All are derivatives of carbamic acid. Carbamates and derivative products are used as pesticides, herbicides and fungicides; they are also used in various ways by the rubber, wood and textile industries. In the rulemaking giving rise to this lawsuit the Environmental Protection Agency listed many of these carbamate-based products, as well as waste streams generated in carbamate-based production processes, as hazardous wastes under the Resource Conservation and Recovery Act, 42 U.S.C. §§ 6901–6992k ("RCRA") (1994). Petitioners, the Dithiocarbamate Task Force (treated collectively with intervenor Uniroyal Chemical Co. as "DTF" or the "Task Force"), Zeneca Inc., and Troy Chemical Corp., are (or represent) manufacturers who make various carbamate-based products or use carbamates in their production processes. They challenge a portion of these listings as arbitrary and capricious.

* * *

Once the EPA decides to list a waste as hazardous, the substance is assigned a particular code and included in the appropriate lists in Subpart D of Part 261. Wastes generated by manufacturing processes are listed as K wastes. Chemical products or manufacturing chemical intermediates that are hazardous if they are discarded or intended to be discarded are listed as P or U wastes, the P designation being reserved for "acute hazardous wastes" of this type.

* * *

The Present Rulemaking: [In this rulemaking,] 40 carbamate industry products received U listings * * *. In addition, manufacturers involved in each of the four classes of carbamates had at least one production waste stream listed as a K waste.

The U Listings: * * *

[P]etitioners argue that in making the determination necessary in the second step of a § 261.11(a)(3) listing—determining "that the waste is capable of posing a substantial present or potential hazard to human health or the environment when improperly treated, stored, transported or disposed of or otherwise managed"—EPA did not consider all of the 11 specified factors. (There are really only ten, since the final factor is a catch-all, allowing the Administrator to consider any other factor she finds relevant.) EPA argues both that § 261.11(a)(3) does not require the Administrator to consider all ten factors, and that in any event she did consider them.

The theory that § 261.11(a)(3) does not require consideration of the ten factors defies the language of the rule, which we have already quoted. * * *

Accordingly, despite the great deference we owe an agency in the interpretation of its own regulations, we must apply the regulation's specific language over the agency's current interpretation.

If EPA finds a factor to be irrelevant or unimportant in a particular listing, of course, that finding would be subject to very deferential review. But with no such finding, the court has no reason to suppose that the agency considered each factor, as required by its own regulation.

Almost as an afterthought, EPA argues in its brief that it did consider all the factors in § 261.11(a)(3). At oral argument, counsel for EPA acknowledged that EPA did not consider each factor for each of the products listed, but at most considered them in the aggregate, for each of the four classes of chemicals. Where it is reasonable to consider the factors in relation to a class of chemicals, EPA may do so. As we develop below * * *, that means essentially that if the known similarities of members of a class are such that it is reasonable to infer the presence of a disputed characteristic throughout the class (not just among members for which it has been shown), the EPA is free to draw that inference. * * *

Underlying all of EPA's generalizations is the premise that within the four groups, the chemicals have similar structures and therefore similar toxicological effects. At least at some level of generality, we do not understand petitioners to quarrel with the principle that structural similarities in chemicals imply at least some probability of similar attributes. What they do challenge is the legitimacy of the class-wide inferences that EPA makes in considering virtually every factor.

* * *

EPA's class-based approach allowed it successfully to consider two of the listed factors, "nature of the toxicity" and "concentration," factors (i) and (ii), and petitioners offer no convincing reason to doubt that these may be considered across all products * * *. As to quantities of U wastes generated, factor (viii), EPA addressed it only in a discussion of the economic impact of the rule, referring to a total quantity of 40 metric tons, which compares with 841,000 metric tons of waste generated as K wastes. Its discussion of other regulatory controls, factor (x), is exceptionally sketchy, considering that most of the substances listed as U wastes are extensively regulated under the Federal Insecticide Fungicide and Rodenticide Act ("FIFRA"), 7 U.S.C. § 136 (1995). Although EPA pointed out that RCRA regulation will not totally duplicate FIFRA regulation, since RCRA regulation exempts *household* users while FIFRA causes the issuance of disposal instructions "to *all* users," the agency's response leaves unclear what the advantage is in covering non-household users twice.

Foremost in our review, however, is EPA's consideration of mismanagement, the defects of which, as we shall see, interact with, and aggravate, the meagerness of the discussion of non-RCRA regulatory controls. Mismanagement is not only specifically listed among the numbered factors, "plausible types of improper management to which the waste could be subjected," factor (vii), but is also an aspect of two others: "[t]he potential of the constituent or any toxic degradation product . . . to migrate . . . into the environment" under improper management, factor (iii), and the "nature and severity of the human health and environmental damage . . . as a result of the improper management of wastes . . .," factor (ix). More important, the very question that the ten factors of § 261.11(a)(3) are supposed to help answer—the hazard posed by the substance—is explicitly phrased in terms of improper management. That language in turn echoes the statutory definition, which (in one of its aspects) looks to whether the substance will "pose a . . . substantial present or potential hazard to human health or the environment when *improperly* treated, stored, transported, or disposed of, or otherwise managed." 42 U.S.C. § 6903(5)(B) (emphasis added). * * *

Most of what the EPA had to say on the subject of mismanagement regarding the U wastes seemed to amount to an assertion of the obvious: accidents will happen. Of course—but if that constituted "plausible mismanagement," *see* § 261.11(a)(3)(vii), it would be ubiquitous and therefore unnecessary to be considered in a listing, contrary to the express language of § 261.11(a)(3). For specifics, EPA relied heavily on a train wreck in California that spilled a dithiocarbamate (metam-sodium) into a river and so caused environmental destruction. DTF argues that listing would have no *direct* effect on the likelihood of such spills, because the train's handling would in any event have been governed by Department of Transportation regulations. EPA resists that claim, arguing that under § 261.11(a)(3), "[T]he proper inquiry is not whether Subtitle C or other regulatory controls would prevent environmental harm, but whether the substances are *capable* of posing a hazard *if* improperly treated, stored, transported, disposed of or otherwise managed." But even if that be the correct reading of the express reference to mismanagement in § 261.11(a)(3)(vii), DTF's argument would necessarily come back in through factor (x), which looks to the relationship between RCRA regulation and the existing regulatory matrix, presumably with the intention of assuring that products will be listed only where doing so will yield some incremental benefit.

EPA further argues that accidents such as the metam-sodium train spill are relevant to RCRA because listing a product as a hazardous waste is likely to make handlers more careful. Perhaps, but not necessarily. The EPA itself noted in another context that RCRA listing might actually result in a stigma, leading to subterfuge of regulations, and a commenter in this rulemaking made the same point. As EPA never responded, we have no clue as to its official view of the matter.

* * *

EPA's effort to generalize from its best evidence of mismanagement, its discussion of bird kills resulting from the "use or possible misuse" of carbofuran, a carbamate proper, is more convincing. Most of these products are herbicides, fungicides and insecticides spread into the environment for agricultural purposes * * *. But EPA's own formulation here, alluding equally to "use or possible misuse," indicates that EPA has expanded the concept of mismanagement to embrace any uses of the chemical, such as spraying on crops. Again factor (x)'s reference to other regulatory measures is pertinent. Hazards from the proper use of such chemicals might justify a ban under FIFRA, 7 U.S.C. § 136a(c)(5)(D), but that is not the purpose of RCRA. Outside the area of increases in mortality or serious illnesses, *see* 42 U.S.C. § 6903(5)(A), which EPA does not appear to invoke here, the statute is concerned with the hazards of a substance when "*improperly* treated, stored, transported, or disposed of, or otherwise managed." *Id.* at § 6903(5)(B) (emphasis added).

To summarize: EPA's discussion of the quantities of waste is slight and oblique, but we need not consider whether such an inadequacy would require us to vacate the rule. Where EPA falls down completely is on the interlocked topics of other regulatory controls (factor (x)) and mismanagement (factor (vii)). It is tempting to say that the toxicity of these chemicals alone marks them as hazardous, and, of course, in one of the purely colloquial senses of the word, they are. But 40 CFR § 261.11(a)(2) gives explicit toxicity benchmarks that are not satisfied here. That relationship underscores what would be true anyway—that a failure on EPA's part to give serious consideration to the "softer" variables of § 261.11(a)(3) tends to turn its application of that section into an exercise in totally standardless discretion. Accordingly, we vacate the challenged U listings as arbitrary and capricious.

The K–Wastes: * * *

K160: Zeneca, the only maker of thiocarbamates, challenges the K160 listing for solid thiocarbamate wastes * * * as being based on an arbitrary mismanagement premise. * * *

EPA assumed that the solid thiocarbamate wastes would be dumped in unlined landfills, even though its understanding at the time was that Zeneca was putting its waste in lined landfills meeting the requirements of Subtitle C of RCRA. EPA defends this mismanagement scenario as plausible, arguing that unlined landfills had been used in the past and that it had no way of knowing if Zeneca would continue to ship its waste to lined landfills.

Of course complete certainty is not possible. But on a parallel issue, deciding not to list wastewaters from the production of thiocarbamates and dithiocarbamates, regardless of past disposal practices, EPA reasoned "that since the carbamate manufactures [sic] have already made a considerable investment in wastewater treatment systems using tanks, [EPA believes] they will continue to use them." Final Rule, 60 Fed. Reg. at 7831/3. The Agency also stated that the past management practice is unlikely to be repeated as "permitting authorities are strongly biased against" it. *Id*. EPA has sought to distinguish that reasoning, on the ground that here the use of high-quality landfills may not represent any capital investment by Zeneca. But the probative fact for the thiocarbamate and dithiocarbamate wastewater was surely not the sunk costs, which cannot properly guide a firm's future allocation of resources, but the fact that its behavior showed that, without a hazardous waste listing, the relevant firms had found it sensible, taking into account all relevant costs and benefits (including litigation risks averted), to adopt adequate disposal methods. The point is equally probative that Zeneca will continue in its practice, and that, if new firms enter the industry, they will follow suit. Because EPA failed to identify a plausible mismanagement scenario, we vacate the listing of K160.

NOTES AND QUESTIONS

1. *The significance of listing.* RCRA subtitle C applies to all solid wastes that exhibit the characteristics of ignitability, corrosivity, reactivity, or toxicity. In light of that background coverage, what is the purpose and significance of the regulatory lists of hazardous wastes?

2. *The listing decision.* What findings must EPA make in order to justify listing a solid waste, or class of solid wastes, as hazardous? Must EPA list any waste that generally exhibits one of the characteristics? Must a waste exhibit one or more characteristics in order to be listed? If not, is there a threshold level of hazard below which EPA may not list a waste?

With respect to wastes containing toxic constituents, how should the agency balance the various factors listed in 40 C.F.R. § 261.11? In particular, how should it identify "plausible types of improper management," and what weight should it give to other regulatory programs? In *Dithiocarbamate Task Force*, did the court hold that EPA could not base a listing on observed spills of carbamate materials in train accidents? What additional findings might support such a listing? Can EPA consider the extent to which listing as a hazardous waste might increase compliance with other legal requirements, such as Department of Transportation regulations? Must EPA provide data showing that increased compliance is likely? Why did petitioner Zeneca, which was disposing of its waste in landfills meeting Subtitle C requirements, object to listing of that waste as hazardous? Is EPA foreclosed from listing Zeneca's waste because Zeneca is currently managing that waste responsibly? Suppose Zeneca's profits fall in the future. Might it cut costs by disposing of its waste in a non-Subtitle C landfill? Must EPA constantly monitor the industry to ensure that proper management continues?

3. *The mixture and derived-from rules.* Characteristic hazardous wastes remain hazardous for regulatory purposes only as long as they exhibit a hazardous characteristic. *See* 40 C.F.R. § 261.3(d)(1). Under the mixture and derived-from rules, however, listed hazardous wastes remain hazardous until they are explicitly delisted. The mixture rule states that a solid waste becomes a hazardous waste if it is mixed with a listed waste, unless the listing was based solely on a characteristic that the mixture no longer exhibits, 40 C.F.R. § 261.3(a)(2)(iii), or the mixture has been delisted, 40 C.F.R. § 261.3(a)(2)(iv). The derived-from rule provides that listed hazardous wastes remain hazardous, even after treatment, until they are specifically delisted. *See* 40 C.F.R. § 261.3(c). Under the derived-from rule, residues from treatment of hazardous wastes, such as ash from hazardous waste incinerators, must be treated and disposed of as a hazardous waste.

The mixture and derived-from rules were first promulgated in 1980. In response to an industry challenge, the D.C. Circuit vacated the rules, holding that they had been promulgated in violation of the procedural requirements of the APA. Shell Oil Co. v. EPA, 950 F.2d 741 (D.C. Cir. 1991). The court suggested that EPA might want to consider reinstating the rules on an interim basis pending full notice and comment. EPA took this suggestion, temporarily reissuing the rules in 1992. Significant controversy ensued, leading Congress to forbid the issuance of new rules before October 1, 1993 and require that the interim rule remain in effect until replaced. Pub. L. No. 102–389, 106 Stat. 1571. The legislation set a deadline of October 1, 1994. When EPA did not meet that deadline, industry groups filed suit to enforce it. The suit was settled by consent decree requiring issuance of a final rule by December 1996. Again EPA failed to meet the deadline, which the court extended. The agency finally issued a new Hazardous Waste Identification Rule in 2001. 66 Fed. Reg. 27266 (May 16, 2001), 66 Fed. Reg. 50379 (Oct. 3, 2001). The rule retains both the mixture and derived-from rules, excluding both mixtures and derivatives of wastes listed solely on the basis of ignitability, corrosivity, or reactivity which no longer exhibit those characteristics.

What justifies the mixture and derived-from rules? EPA has explained:

> The mixture and derived-from rules are necessary to regulate hazardous wastes in a way that protects human health and the environment. Mixtures and residuals of hazardous waste represent a large and varied universe. Many hazardous wastes continue to be toxic after they have been mixed with other waste or have been treated.
> * * *
>
> We believe that without the mixture and derived-from rules, some generators would alter their waste to the point it no longer meets the listing description without detoxifying, immobilizing, or otherwise actually treating the waste. For example, without a "mixture" rule, generators of hazardous wastes could escape regulatory requirements by mixing listed hazardous wastes with other hazardous wastes or nonhazardous solid wastes to create a "new" waste that arguably no longer meets the listing description, but continues to pose a serious hazard. Similarly, without a "derived-from" rule, hazardous waste generators could potentially evade regulation by minimally processing or managing a hazardous waste and claiming that the resulting residue is no longer the listed waste, despite the continued hazards of the residue. * * *

64 Fed. Reg. 63382, 63389 (Nov. 19, 1999). Is this reasoning persuasive? Won't truly hazardous mixtures be captured by the characteristic waste rules? Should mixing that dilutes a waste until it no longer exhibits any of the characteristics be discouraged? Why? Are toxic wastes different than ignitable, corrosive, or reactive wastes for this purpose?

The mixture and derived-from rules were upheld in American Chemistry Council v. EPA, 337 F.3d 1060 (D.C. Cir. 2003). Applying *Chevron* analysis, the court reasoned that "Congress wanted the EPA, in deciding which substances to regulate as 'hazardous' under the RCRA, to err on the side of caution; the Final Rule is a reasonable exercise of such caution."

4. *Conditional exemptions.* RCRA draws a sharp line between ordinary solid waste and hazardous waste. The former is almost entirely left to state regulation, while the latter is subject to cradle-to-grave federal controls. In reality, however, the degree of hazard generally falls on a continuum, so that harmless wastes cannot be cleanly distinguished from potentially harmful ones. What should EPA do about materials that fall in the gray area? One approach, known as conditional exemption or contingent management, exempts solid wastes from hazardous classification if they are managed in compliance with specific regulatory requirements. Conditional exemption allows EPA to tailor management requirements to the realistic hazards associated with the waste. In its 1999 proposed Hazardous Waste Identification Rule, for example, EPA suggested that it might exempt certain low-risk wastes on condition that they be disposed of in a solid waste landfill. *See* 64 Fed. Reg. 63382, 63405 (Nov. 19, 1999). In support of this approach, EPA relied on the listing criteria in 40 C.F.R. § 261.11, including the risk of plausible mismanagement and existence of other regulatory controls. Is conditional exemption lawful? Is it desirable? For a critical discussion, *see* Jeffrey M. Gaba, Regulation by Bootstrap: Contingent Management of Hazardous Wastes Under the Resource Conservation and Recovery Act, 18 Yale J. Reg. 85 (2001).

5. *The household waste exclusion.* EPA's first RCRA regulations, issued in 1980, excluded a number of solid wastes, including household waste, from the definition of hazardous waste. *See* 40 C.F.R. § 261.4(b)(1). Household waste can contain small amounts of hazardous substances, such as cleaning fluids, pesticides, and discarded batteries. The preamble to the regulations declared that residues remaining after treatment, including incineration, of household wastes also would not be regulated as hazardous wastes. *See* 45 Fed. Reg. 33099 (May 19, 1980).

In 1984, Congress enacted RCRA § 3001(i), 42 U.S.C. § 6921(i), to "clarify" the household waste exclusion. Section 3001(i) provides that a "resource recovery facility recovering energy from the mass burning of municipal solid waste shall not be deemed to be treating, storing, disposing of, or otherwise managing hazardous wastes" provided it receives and burns only household waste and non-hazardous commercial or industrial waste. In City of Chicago v. Environmental Defense Fund, 511 U.S. 328 (1994), the Supreme Court ruled that this statute does not exempt the ash remaining after incineration of household wastes in waste-to-energy facilities from regulation as hazardous waste. The Court explained:

> The plain meaning of this language is that so long as a facility recovers energy by incineration of the appropriate wastes, *it* (*the facility*) is not subject to Subtitle C regulation as a facility that treats, stores, disposes of, or manages hazardous waste. The provision quite clearly does *not* contain any exclusion for the *ash itself.* Indeed, the waste the facility produces (as opposed to that which it receives) is not even mentioned.

Id. at 334–35.

Waste-to-energy operators were concerned that the *City of Chicago* decision would greatly increase the costs of managing ash. Subtitle C hazardous waste must be disposed of in licensed hazardous waste landfills with special design characteristics and operating procedures. Disposal of ash as hazardous waste can cost ten to fifteen times as much as disposal in a solid waste landfill. Some cities feared they might have to close their incinerators as a result of these increased costs. A study five years after the decision, however, found that most of the waste from incinerators passed the toxicity characteristic test, and therefore was not deemed hazardous. In part, that result is due to EPA's decision to allow combustors to combine relatively non-toxic "bottom ash," the larger unburned particles that remain on the grate after combustion, with "fly ash," the lighter particles that are suspended in the gas stream and collected in the air pollution control equipment, which tends to have higher concentrations of metals and organic materials. *See* Markus G. Puder, Trash, Ash, and the Phoenix: A Fifth Anniversary Review of the Supreme Court's *City of Chicago* Waste-to-Energy Combustion Ash Decision, 26 B.C. Envtl. Aff. L. Rev. 473, 510 (1999).

6. *A way out?* Currently, listed hazardous wastes remain subject to the burdensome requirements of subtitle C until they are delisted, a slow, expensive process which must be completed individually for each facility. Is a simpler exit procedure needed for low-risk wastes? EPA has been exploring the possibility of self-implementing (that is, not requiring individual EPA review or action) risk-based exemptions from subtitle C for years. So far, however, the agency has been stymied by its inability to assess the risks precisely enough to specify exemption levels. For a discussion of a framework under which low risk wastes could be exempted from subtitle C, *see* 64 Fed. Reg. 63382 (Nov. 19, 1999).

7. *Coal ash.* Coal ash, also known as coal combustion waste (CCW), is the ash left after coal is burned in industrial facilities and the residue from air pollution scrubbers. Roughly 120 million tons of coal ash are produced every year in the United States, enough to fill a million railroad cars. Coal ash contains a variety of toxic constituents, including arsenic, cadmium, mercury, selenium, lead, and other heavy metals. Up to 40% of coal ash is recycled into products like cement, wallboard, and highway pavement, but the rest is disposed of in landfills, surface impoundments, or abandoned mines.

EPA has been spent decades studying whether or not to regulate coal ash as a hazardous waste. Congress initially granted a short-term exemption for coal ash from treatment as hazardous waste, directing EPA to study the matter and decide whether coal ash should be regulated under Subtitle C (as hazardous waste) or Subtitle D (as ordinary solid waste). In 1993 and again in 2000, the agency determined that coal ash should be managed as solid waste rather than as hazardous waste, leaving primary regulatory authority and responsibility to the states. In reaching that conclusion in 2000, EPA acknowledged that the decision "was a difficult one," and promised to revisit the question as more information developed and if Subtitle D regulation proved insufficient. 65 Fed. Reg. 32214 (May 22, 2000).

Subsequently, a risk assessment prepared for EPA found that unlined coal ash ponds, a common means of disposal, are particularly dangerous, posing cancer risks of up to 1 in 50 for nearby residents through groundwater and well contamination. RTI, Human and Ecological Risk Assessment of Coal Combustion Wastes (Draft), Aug. 6, 2007. That risk assessment did not consider the additional risk of impoundment failure. Late in 2008, a coal ash holding pond at a Tennessee Valley Authority power plant near Kingston, Tennessee, breached after a month of heavy rains, spilling nearly 5.4 million cubic yards of ash, burying about 300 acres to depths of up to six feet, damaging two dozen homes, and raising concern for the safety of Chattanooga's water supply. TVA, which has agreed that it is responsible for financing the cleanup, estimates that it will cost $1.2 billion. In a report prepared for a congressional hearing on the Kingston spill, TVA's inspector general concluded that the utility knew of safety concerns but did not take corrective action, in part because "Ash was relegated to the status of garbage at a landfill rather than treating it as a potential hazard to the public and the environment." Tennessee Valley Authority, Office of the Inspector General, Inspection Report, Review of the Kingston Fossil Plant Ash Spill Root Cause Study and Observations About Ash Management, July 23, 2009.

The Kingston spill brought renewed attention to the coal ash problem. A coalition of more than 100 environmental groups sent a letter to EPA, pointing out that they had petitioned for stronger regulation in 2004 and were still awaiting a response. Based on the statutory definition of hazardous waste, and EPA's regulatory criteria for listing hazardous waste, should it list CCW? Would a CCW listing survive a lawsuit like *Dithiocarbamate Task Force*?

After considerable back-and-forth with the White House's Office and Management and Budget, EPA issued a proposed coal ash regulation in 2010. 75 Fed. Reg. 35128 (June 21, 2010). Unlike most proposed rules, this one did not articulate a preferred strategy. Instead, the agency sought comment on two proposals: to list coal ash as a hazardous waste and regulate it under Title C when it is destined for landfills or impoundments; or to continue to treat it as a non-hazardous solid waste under Title D, with tighter regulation of impoundments and landfills. The chief differences between the proposals are that under Title D EPA can only regulate disposal, not generation, treatment, or storage prior to disposal; and enforcement of Title D regulations is left to the states. Under the Title C proposal, coal ash placed in old mines or used for "beneficial uses" such as pavement, would not be considered hazardous waste.

4. LAND DISPOSAL RESTRICTIONS

Excerpts From the Resource Conservation and Recovery Act

42 U.S.C. §§ 6901–6992k.

Sec. 1002 Congressional findings

* * *

(b) The Congress finds with respect to the environment and health, that—

* * *

(2) disposal of solid waste and hazardous waste in or on the land without careful planning and management can present a danger to human health and the environment;

* * *

(5) the placement of inadequate controls on hazardous waste management will result in substantial risks to human health and the environment;

(6) if hazardous waste management is improperly performed in the first instance, corrective action is likely to be expensive, complex, and time consuming;

(7) certain classes of land disposal facilities are not capable of assuring long-term containment of certain hazardous wastes, and to avoid substantial risk to human health and the environment, reliance on land disposal should be minimized or eliminated, and land disposal, particularly landfill and surface impoundment, should be the least favored method for managing hazardous wastes * * *.

Sec. 3004 Standards applicable to owners and operators of hazardous waste treatment, storage, and disposal facilities

* * *

(d) Prohibitions on land disposal of specified wastes

(1) Effective 32 months after November 8, 1984 * * *, the land disposal of the hazardous wastes referred to in paragraph (2) is prohibited unless the Administrator determines the prohibition on one or more methods of land disposal of such waste is not required in order to protect human health and the environment for as long as the waste remains hazardous, taking into account—

(A) the long-term uncertainties associated with land disposal,

(B) the goal of managing hazardous waste in an appropriate manner in the first instance, and

(C) the persistence, toxicity, mobility, and propensity to bioaccumulate of such hazardous wastes and their hazardous constituents. * * *

(e)(1) Effective twenty-four months after November 8, 1984 * * *, the land disposal of the hazardous wastes referred to in paragraph (2) is prohibited unless the Administrator determines the prohibition of one or more methods of land disposal of such waste is not required in order to protect human health and the environment for as long as the waste remains hazardous, taking into account the factors referred to in subparagraph (A) through (C) of subsection (d)(1) of this section. For the purposes of this paragraph, a method of land disposal may not be determined to be protective of human health and the environment for a hazardous waste referred to in paragraph (2) (other than a hazardous waste which has complied with the pretreatment regulations promulgated under subsection (m) of this section), unless upon application by an interested person it has been demonstrated to the Administrator, to a reasonable degree of certainty, that there will be no migration of hazardous constituents from the disposal unit or injection zone for as long as the wastes remain hazardous.

(2) The hazardous wastes to which the prohibition under paragraph (1) applies are as follows—

(A) dioxin-containing hazardous wastes numbered F020, F021, F022, and F023 (as referred to in the proposed rule published by the Administrator in the Federal Register for April 4, 1983) * * *

(g)(1) Not later than twenty-four months after November 8, 1984, the Administrator shall submit a schedule to Congress for—

(A) reviewing all hazardous wastes listed (as of November 8, 1984) under section 6921 of this title other than those wastes which are referred to in subsection (d) or (e) of this section; and

(B) taking action under paragraph (5) of this subsection with respect to each such hazardous waste.

(2) The Administrator shall base the schedule on a ranking of such listed wastes considering their intrinsic hazard and their volume * * *.

(4) The schedule under this subsection shall require that the Administrator shall promulgate regulations in accordance with paragraph

(5) or make a determination under paragraph (5)—

(A) for at least one-third of all hazardous wastes referred to in paragraph (1) by the date forty-five months after November 8, 1984;

(B) for at least two-thirds of all such listed wastes by the date fifty-five months after November 8, 1984; and

(C) for all such listed wastes and for all hazardous wastes identified under [RCRA § 3001] by the date sixty-six months after November 8, 1984.

In the case of any hazardous waste identified or listed under section 6921 of this title after November 8, 1984, the Administrator shall determine whether such waste shall be prohibited from one or more methods of land disposal in accordance with paragraph (5) within six months after the date of such identification or listing.

(5) Not later than the date specified in the schedule published under this subsection, the Administrator shall promulgate final regulations prohibiting one or more methods of land disposal of the hazardous wastes listed on such schedule except for methods of land disposal which the Administrator determines will be protective of human health and the environment for as long as the waste remains hazardous, taking into account the factors referred to in subparagraphs (A) through (C) of subsection (d)(1) of this section. * * *

(6)* * *

(C) If the Administrator fails to promulgate regulations, or make a determination under paragraph (5) for any hazardous waste referred to in paragraph (1) within 66 months after November 8, 1984, such hazardous waste shall be prohibited from land disposal.

* * *

(j) Storage of hazardous waste prohibited from land disposal

In the case of any hazardous waste which is prohibited from one or more methods of land disposal under this section (or under regulations promulgated by the Administrator under any provision of this section) the storage of such hazardous waste is prohibited unless such storage is solely for the purpose of the accumulation of such quantities of hazardous waste as are necessary to facilitate proper recovery, treatment or disposal.

(k) "Land disposal" defined

For the purposes of this section, the term "land disposal," when used with respect to a specified hazardous waste, shall be deemed to include, but not be limited to, any placement of such hazardous waste in a landfill, surface impoundment, waste pile, injection well, land treatment facility, salt dome formation, salt bed formation, or underground mine or cave.

* * *

(m) Treatment standards for wastes subject to land disposal prohibition

(1) Simultaneously with the promulgation of regulations under subsection (d), (e), (f), or (g) of this section prohibiting one or more methods of land disposal of a particular hazardous waste, and as appropriate thereafter, the Administrator shall, after notice and an opportunity for hearings and after consultation with appropriate Federal and State agencies, promulgate regulations specifying those levels or methods of treatment, if any, which substantially diminish the toxicity of the waste or substantially reduce the likelihood of migration of hazardous constituents from the waste so that short-term and long-term threats to human health and the environment are minimized.

(2) If such hazardous waste has been treated to the level or by a method specified in regulations promulgated under this subsection, such waste or residue thereof shall not be subject to any prohibition promulgated under subsection (d), (e), (f), or (g) of this section and may be disposed of in a land disposal facility which meets the requirements of this subchapter. Any regulation promulgated under this subsection for a particular hazardous waste shall become effective on the same date as any applicable prohibition promulgated under subsection (d), (e), (f), or (g) of this section.

Environmental Protection Agency, Office of Solid Waste and Emergency Response, Introduction to Land Disposal Restrictions (40 CFR Part 268)

EPA530–K–05–013 (Sept. 2005).

* * *

A large part of the hazardous waste management regulatory program, including the LDR program, is designed to protect groundwater. Hazardous waste can pollute groundwater through a process known as leaching, in which precipitation percolating through the ground draws contaminants out of buried waste and carries them into groundwater. Congress understood that hazardous waste could be made less dangerous to groundwater in two main ways: by reducing a waste's toxicity through destruction or removal of harmful contaminants, or by reducing a waste's leachability by immobilizing hazardous contaminants. As a result, EPA created a tiered approach to the protection of groundwater by attempting to prevent leachability of harmful constituents at three levels: [Land Disposal Restrictions

(LDR)], [regulation of land disposal units (landfills)], and groundwater monitoring. The first tier of the approach, LDR, regulates what kind of waste can be placed on the land or in land disposal units. * * *

LDR requires that hazardous wastes undergo fundamental physical or chemical changes so that they pose less of a threat to groundwater. When directing EPA to establish the LDR program in RCRA § 3004(m), Congress specified that EPA should "promulgate regulations specifying those levels or methods of treatment, if any, which substantially diminish the toxicity of the waste or substantially reduce the likelihood of migration of hazardous constituents from the waste." To implement that goal, Congress gave EPA very specific directions for establishing the LDR program. In particular, Congress required EPA to specify how hazardous wastes should be treated to satisfy LDR's goal of groundwater protection. The rules EPA promulgated governing how different hazardous wastes must be treated are known as treatment standards. Treatment standards are simply instructions on how a hazardous waste should be treated.

For example, many of the chemicals capable of contaminating groundwater are organic compounds. Incineration or burning can destroy these organic compounds, usually breaking them down into less dangerous byproducts like carbon dioxide and water. Thus, incineration of organic-bearing hazardous wastes can protect groundwater by destroying organic contaminants before they have a chance to enter underground water supplies. The obvious advantage of such hazardous waste treatment is that it provides a more permanent and lasting form of groundwater protection than hazardous waste containment. Structural barriers separating hazardous contaminants from groundwater may eventually break down or leak. In contrast, treatment that destroys harmful contaminants or reduces a waste's toxicity before it enters the environment is a permanent groundwater protection solution.

Treatment, however, cannot destroy all types of contaminants found in hazardous waste. In particular, metal elements, which are common toxic contaminants, cannot be broken down through combustion. Treatment techniques other than incineration, however, can be used for such wastes. For example, through a process called stabilization or immobilization, metal contaminants can be chemically and physically bound into the wastes that contain them. Although this treatment method does not reduce the overall concentration of toxic metals in a hazardous waste, it does immobilize these constituents, making them less likely to leach from the waste. Reducing the mobility or leachability of hazardous constituents in a waste is another means of achieving LDR's groundwater protection goal.

Randolph L. Hill, An Overview of RCRA: The "Mind–Numbing" Provisions of the Most Complicated Environmental Statute

21 Envtl. L. Rep. 10254, 10268–69 (1991).

The land disposal restrictions (LDRs, or the land ban) are the centerpiece of the 1984 Amendments to RCRA. The land ban reflects a significant change in the focus of the subtitle C regulatory program: from one oriented toward preventing hazardous waste releases to one that encourages minimization and treatment of hazardous wastes. The land ban also incorporates the "hammer" concept.

"Land ban" is a misnomer for the program. The LDRs restrictions do not prohibit all hazardous wastes from land disposal. Rather, they represent a creative statutory method for ensuring that EPA establish standards for hazardous wastes destined for land disposal.

* * *

The statute provides four ways to avoid the prohibition against land disposal. First, under § 3004(m), EPA may establish treatment standards for the waste "which substantially diminish the toxicity of the waste or substantially reduce the likelihood of migration of hazardous constituents from the waste so that short-term and long-term threats to human health and the environment are minimized." Wastes that meet the treatment standards set by EPA under § 3004(m) may be disposed of in a land disposal unit. EPA sets § 3004(m) standards in one of two ways: (1) EPA establishes a maximum concentration level for hazardous constituents in the waste (for wastewaters) or the waste extract using the new TCLP (for nonwastewaters); or (2) EPA specifies a particular treatment technology to be used on the waste.

The relationship between § 3004(m) and the other LDR provisions is referred to as the statutory hammer in the LDR. It is so called because if EPA were to fail to promulgate § 3004(m) standards by the required date, all land disposal of that waste would be prohibited on that date (even wastes that had been treated to levels similar to those EPA might set). The hammers provide a strong incentive for EPA to develop and promulgate the required standards on time to avoid the serious disruptions in the economy that would result from an inability to legally dispose of any hazardous wastes. They were indeed effective; EPA issued all of its § 3004(m) regulations on time.

The second method for avoiding the land ban is through a "no-migration" petition. Hazardous wastes, whether treated or untreated, may be disposed of in any land disposal unit if "it has been demonstrated to [EPA], to a reasonable degree of certainty, that there will be no migration of hazardous constituents from the disposal unit or [for deep injection wells] injection zone for as long as the wastes remain hazardous."

Third, EPA may grant a "national capacity variance" for up to two years after the statutory ban would otherwise take effect based on when "adequate alternative treatment, recovery, or disposal capacity ... will be available." In other words, if the capacity does not exist to treat all the wastes to the § 3004(m) level using the § 3004(m) method at the time EPA issues the § 3004(m) standards, EPA can allow up to two additional years to allow that capacity to develop.

Finally, EPA can grant an individual capacity variance for up to one additional year if the facility has contracted to construct a treatment unit or arrange for treatment but cannot yet have the waste treated.

* * *

EPA must set § 3004(m) standards for newly identified or newly listed hazardous wastes within six months of when the wastes become hazardous; there is, however, no hammer or other prohibition on land disposal if EPA fails to do so. * * *

Hazardous Waste Treatment Council v. United States Environmental Protection Agency

United States Court of Appeals, District of Columbia Circuit, 1989.
886 F.2d 355.

■ PER CURIAM.

In 1984, Congress amended the Resource Conservation and Recovery Act ("RCRA"), to prohibit land disposal of certain hazardous solvents and wastes containing dioxins except in narrow circumstances to be defined by Environmental Protection Agency ("EPA") regulations. *See* 42 U.S.C. § 6924(e). In these consolidated cases, petitioners seek review of EPA's final "solvents and dioxins" rule published pursuant to Congress' 1984 mandate. We conclude that the rule under review is consistent with RCRA, but remand one aspect of the rulemaking to the agency for further explanation.

I. A. Statutory Scheme

The Hazardous and Solid Waste Amendments of 1984 ("HSWA"), Pub. L. No. 98–616, 98 Stat. 3221 (1984), *inter alia,* substantially strengthened EPA's control over the land disposal of hazardous wastes regulated under RCRA's "cradle to grave" statutory scheme. In preambular language to the HSWA, Congress, believing that "land disposal facilities were not capable of assuring long-term containment of certain hazardous wastes," expressed the policy that "reliance on land disposal should be minimized or eliminated." 42 U.S.C. § 6901(b)(7). In order to effectuate this policy, HSWA amended section 3004 of RCRA to prohibit land disposal of hazardous waste unless the waste is "pretreated" in a manner that minimizes "short-term and long-term threats to human health and the environment," *id.* § 6924(m), or unless EPA can determine that the waste is to be disposed of in such a fashion as to ensure that "there will be no migration of hazardous constituents from the disposal [facility]...." *Id.* § 6924(d)(1), (e)(1), & (g)(5).

As amended, RCRA requires EPA to implement the land disposal prohibition in three phases, addressing the most hazardous "listed" wastes first. In accordance with strict statutory deadlines, the Administrator is obligated to specify those methods of land disposal of each listed hazardous waste which "will be protective of human health and the environment." In addition, "[s]imultaneously with the promulgation of regulations ... prohibiting ... land disposal of a particular hazardous waste, the Administrator" is required to

> promulgate regulations specifying those levels or methods of treatment, if any, which substantially diminish the toxicity of the waste or substantially reduce the likelihood of migration of hazardous constituents from the waste so that short-term and long-term threats to human health and the environment are minimized.

Id. § 6924(m).

Respecting two categories of hazardous wastes, including the solvents and dioxins at issue here Congress, however, declined to wait for phased EPA implementation of the land disposal prohibition. For these wastes, Congress imposed earlier restrictions, prohibiting land disposal after dates specified in the HSWA except in accordance with pretreatment standards or pursuant to regulations specifying "protective" methods of disposal. *Id.* § 6924(e)(1). These prohibitions, as applied to the solvents and dioxins listed in the HSWA, were to take effect November 8, 1986. *Id.*

* * *

1. *Section 3004(m) Treatment Standards.*

In the Proposed Rule, EPA announced its tentative support for a treatment regime embodying both risk-based and technology-based standards. The technology-based standards would be founded upon what EPA determined to be the Best Demonstrated Available Technology ("BDAT"); parallel risk-based or "screening" levels were to reflect "the maximum concentration [of a hazardous constituent] below which the Agency believes there is no regulatory concern for the land disposal program and which is protective of human health and the environment." The Proposed Rule provided that these two sets of standards would be melded in the following manner:

First, if BDAT standards were more rigorous than the relevant health-screening levels, the latter would be used to "cap the reductions in toxicity and/or mobility that otherwise would result from the application of BDAT treatment[.]" Thus, "treatment for treatment's sake" would be avoided. Second, if BDAT standards were less rigorous than health-screening levels, BDAT standards would govern and the screening level would be used as "a goal for future changes to the treatment standards as new and more efficient treatment technologies become available." Finally, when EPA determined that the use of BDAT would pose a greater risk to human health and the environment than land disposal, or would provide insufficient safeguards against the threats produced by land disposal, the screening level would actually become the 3004(m) treatment standard.

EPA invited public comment on alternative approaches as well. The first alternative identified in the Proposed Rule (and the one ultimately selected by EPA) was based purely on the capabilities of the "best demonstrated available technology." Capping treatment levels to avoid treatment for treatment's sake, according to EPA, could be accomplished under this technology-based scheme by "the petition process":

> Under this approach, if a prescribed level or method of treatment under section 3004(m) resulted in concentration levels that an owner/operator believed to be overly protective, the owner/operator could petition the Agency to allow the use of an alternative treatment level or method or no treatment at all by demonstrating that less treatment would still meet the petition standard of protecting human health and environment.

* * *

The Agency received comments supporting both approaches, but ultimately settled on the pure-technology alternative. Of particular importance to EPA's decision were the comments filed by eleven members of Congress, all of whom served as conferees on the 1984 RCRA amendments. As EPA recorded in the preamble to the Final Rule:

> [these] members of Congress argued strongly that [the health screening] approach did not fulfill the intent of the law. They asserted that because of the scientific uncertainty inherent in risk-based decisions, Congress expressly directed the Agency to set treatment standards based on the capabilities of existing technology.
>
> The Agency believes that the technology-based approach adopted in [the] final rule, although not the only approach allowable under the law, best responds to the above stated comments.

Final Rule at 40,578.

EPA also relied on passages in the legislative history supporting an approach under which owners and operator [sic] of hazardous waste facilities would be required to use "the best [technology] that has been demonstrated to be achievable." *Id.* (quoting 103 Cong. Rec. S9178) (daily ed. July 25, 1984) (statement of Senator Chaffee). And the agency reiterated that the chief advantage offered by the health-screening approach—avoiding "treatment for treatment's sake"—could "be better addressed through changes in other aspects of its regulatory program." *Id.* As an example of what parts of the program might be altered, EPA announced that it was "considering the use of its risk-based methodologies to characterize wastes as hazardous pursuant to section 3001 [of RCRA]." *Id.*

Petitioner CMA [Chemical Manufacturers Association] challenges this aspect of the rule as an unreasonable construction of section 3004(m)'s mandate to ensure that "short-term and long-term threats to human health and the environment are minimized." 42 U.S.C. § 6924(m) (1982 & Supp. IV 1986). In the alternative, CMA argues that EPA has failed to explain the basis—in terms of relevant human health and environmental considerations—for its BDAT regime, which allegedly requires treatment in some circumstances to levels far below the standards for human exposure under other statutes administered by EPA. Thus, CMA claims that EPA's action in promulgating a technology-based rule is arbitrary and capricious.

* * *

II.   Section 3004(m) Treatment Standards

CMA challenges EPA's adoption of BDAT treatment standards in preference to the approach it proposed initially primarily on the ground that the regulation is not a reasonable interpretation of the statute. CMA obliquely, and Intervenors Edison Electric and the American Petroleum Institute explicitly, argues in the alternative that the agency did not adequately explain its decision to take the course that it did. We conclude, as to CMA's primary challenge, that EPA's decision to reject the use of screening levels is a reasonable interpretation of the statute. We also find, however, that EPA's justification of its choice is so fatally flawed that we cannot, in conscience, affirm it. We therefore grant the petitions for review to the extent of remanding this issue to the agency for a fuller explanation.

A.   *The Consistency of EPA's Interpretation with RCRA.*

Our role in evaluating an agency's interpretation of its enabling statute is as strictly circumscribed as it is simply stated: We first examine the statute to ascertain whether it clearly forecloses the course that the agency has taken; if it is ambiguous with respect to that question, we go on to determine whether the agency's interpretation is a reasonable resolution of the ambiguity. *Chevron v. Natural Resources Defense Council,* 467 U.S. 837, 842–45 (1984).

1.   *Chevron Step I: Is the Statute Clear?*

We repeat the mandate of § 3004(m)(1): the Administrator is required to promulgate "regulations specifying those levels or methods of treatment, if any, which substantially diminish the toxicity of the waste or substantially reduce the likelihood of migration of hazardous constituents from the waste so that short-term and long-term threats to human health and the environment are minimized." 42 U.S.C. § 6924(m)(1).

CMA reads the statute as requiring EPA to determine the levels of concentration in waste at which the various solvents here at issue are "safe" and to use those "screening levels" as floors below which treatment would not be required. CMA supports its interpretation with the observation that the statute directs EPA to set standards only to the extent that "threats to human health and the environment are minimized." We are unpersuaded, however, that Congress intended to compel EPA to rely upon screening levels in preference to the levels achievable by BDAT.

The statute directs EPA to set treatment standards based upon either "levels or methods" of treatment. Such a mandate makes clear that the choice whether to use "levels" (screening levels) or "methods" (BDAT) lies within the informed discretion of the agency, as long as the result is "that short-term and long-term threats to human health and the environment are minimized." To "minimize" something is, to quote the Oxford English Dictionary, to "reduce [it] to the smallest possible amount, extent, or degree." But Congress recognized, in the very amendments here at issue, that there are "long-term uncertainties associated with land disposal," 42 U.S.C. § 6924(d)(1)(A). In the face of such uncertainties, it cannot be said that a statute that requires that threats be minimized unambiguously requires EPA to set levels at which it is conclusively presumed that no threat to health or the environment exists.

* * *

This is not to say that EPA is free, under § 3004(m), to require generators to treat their waste beyond the point at which there is no "threat" to human health or to the environment. That Congress's concern in adopting § 3004(m) was with health and the environment would necessarily make it unreasonable for EPA to promulgate treatment standards wholly without regard to whether there might be a threat to man or nature. That concern is better dealt with, however, at *Chevron*'s second step; for, having concluded that the statute does not unambiguously and in all circumstances foreclose EPA from adopting treatment levels based upon the levels achievable by BDAT, we must now explore whether the particular levels established by the regulations supply a reasonable resolution of the statutory ambiguity.

2. *Chevron Step II: Is EPA's Interpretation Reasonable?*

The screening levels that EPA initially proposed were not those at which the wastes were thought to be entirely safe. Rather, EPA set the levels to reduce risks from the solvents to an "acceptable" level, and it explored, at great length, the manifest (and manifold) uncertainties inherent in any attempt to specify "safe" concentration levels. The agency discussed, for example, the lack of any safe level of exposure to carcinogenic solvents; the extent to which reference dose levels (from which it derived its screening levels) understate the dangers that hazardous solvents pose to particularly sensitive members of the population; the necessarily artificial assumptions that accompany any attempt to model the migration of hazardous wastes from a disposal site; and the lack of dependable data on the effects that solvents have on the liners that bound disposal facilities for the purpose of ensuring that the wastes disposed in a facility stay there. * * *

CMA suggests, despite these uncertainties, that the adoption of a BDAT treatment regime would result in treatment to "below established levels of hazard." It relies for this proposition almost entirely upon a chart in which it contrasts the BDAT levels with (1) levels EPA has defined as "Maximum Contaminant Levels" (MCLs) under the Safe Drinking Water Act; (2) EPA's proposed "Organic Toxicity Characteristics," threshold levels below which EPA will not list a waste as hazardous by reason of its having in it a particular toxin; and (3) levels at which EPA has recently granted petitions by waste generators to "delist" a particular waste, that is, to remove it from the list of wastes that are deemed hazardous. CMA points out that the BDAT standards would require treatment to levels that are, in many cases, significantly below these "established levels of hazard."

If indeed EPA had determined that wastes at any of the three levels pointed to by CMA posed no threat to human health or the environment, we would have little hesitation in concluding that it was unreasonable for EPA to mandate treatment to substantially lower levels. In fact, however, none of the levels to which CMA compares the BDAT standards purports to establish a level at which safety is assured or "threats to human health and the environment are minimized." Each is a level established for a different purpose and under a different set of statutory criteria than concern us here; each is therefore irrelevant to the inquiry we undertake today.

The drinking water levels, for example, are established under a scheme requiring EPA to set "goals" at a level at which "no known or anticipated adverse effects on the health of persons occur." 42 U.S.C. § 300g–1(b)(4). EPA is then to set MCLs as close to its goals as "feasible," taking into account, among other things, treatment costs. 42 U.S.C. §§ 300g–1(b)(4), (5). Since SDWA goals are set only to deal with "known or anticipated" adverse health effects, a mere "threat" to human health is not enough in that context. Moreover, SDWA levels are set without reference to threats to the environment. Finally, EPA must consider costs in setting its MCLs; there is no similar limitation in § 3004 of RCRA.

Similarly, in promulgating the OTC levels, EPA made clear that, "[i]n establishing a scientifically justifiable approach for arriving at [OTC levels], EPA wanted to assure a high degree of confidence that a waste which releases toxicants at concentrations above the [OTC level] would pose a hazard to human health." EPA Hazardous Waste Management System; Identification and Listing of Hazardous Waste, Proposed Rule, 51 Fed. Reg. 21,648, 21,649 (1986). Thus it is clear that wastes with toxicant levels below the OTC thresholds may still pose "threats to human health [or] the environment." Id. at 21,648.

Finally, CMA points to the "delisting levels" as appropriate points of comparison. The term is a bit misleading, however. EPA delists particular wastes in response to individual petitions, see, e.g., 42 U.S.C. § 6921(f)(1), and it has not adopted formal, or even *de facto,* levels below which any waste will be delisted. That EPA has delisted, in particular circumstances, wastes containing concentrations of solvents higher than those called for by the BDAT standards adds nothing to CMA's argument. The treatment standards establish a generic approach, requiring that all wastes deemed to be hazardous be treated to a set level in order to minimize threats to health and to the environment. If a waste is listed as hazardous, and an individual generator wants to dispose of it without meeting the BDAT standards, it may petition to have its particular waste delisted. If the agency grants the delisting petition, only the petitioner is affected; the generally required level of treatment remains the same. Hence, there is no inconsistency between a "delisting level," accepted in particular circumstances, that permits a higher level of a particular contaminant then the BDAT level otherwise generally applicable.

* * *

B. *Was EPA's Explanation Adequate?*

[I]n order to determine whether we can affirm EPA's action here, we must parse the language of the Final Rule to see whether it can be interpreted to make a sensible argument for the approach EPA adopted. We find that it cannot.

As we have said, EPA, in its Proposed Rule, expressed a tentative preference for an approach that combined screening levels and BDAT. It indicated that it thought either that approach or BDAT alone was consistent with the statute, and recognized that there were myriad uncertainties inherent in any attempt to model the health and environmental effects of the land disposal of hazardous wastes. It initially concluded, however, that despite those uncertainties, the better approach was to adopt the combination of screening levels and BDAT. Nevertheless, in the Final Rule, it rejected its earlier approach, and adopted a regime of treatment levels defined by BDAT alone.

* * *

[A]fter EPA issued the Proposed Rule, some commenters, including eleven members of Congress, chastised the agency on the ground that the use of screening levels was inconsistent with the intent of the statute. They stated that because of the uncertainties involved, Congress had mandated that BDAT alone be used to set treatment standards. EPA determined that the "best respon[se]" to those comments was to adopt a BDAT standard. It emphasized, however, that either course was consistent with the statute (and that it was therefore not *required* to use BDAT alone). Finally, it asserted, without explanation, that its major purpose in initially proposing screening levels "may be better addressed through changes in other aspects of its regulatory program," and gave an example of one such aspect that might be changed.

This explanation is inadequate. It should go without saying that members of Congress have no power, once a statute has been passed, to alter its interpretation by post-hoc "explanations" of what it means * * *.

It is unclear whether EPA recognized this fundamental point. On the one hand, it suggested that the adoption of a BDAT-only regime "bestrespond[ed]" to the comments suggesting that the statute required such a rule. On the other hand, EPA went on at some length to establish that the comments were in error, in that screening levels are permissible under the statute. * * *

Nor is anything added by EPA's bald assertion that its reason for initially preferring Result B (screening levels) "may be" better served by other changes in the statutory scheme. In its Proposed Rule, EPA had, after extensive analysis of the various alternatives, come to the opposite conclusion. It is insufficient, in that context, for EPA to proceed in a different direction simply on the basis of an unexplained and unelaborated statement that it might have been wrong when it earlier concluded otherwise.

* * *

V. Conclusion

We conclude that the solvents and dioxins rule is not arbitrary, capricious, or contrary to RCRA in any of the respects argued by petitioners, but remand the matter for the EPA to clarify its reasons for adopting the Final Rule in preference to the Proposed Rule. In order to avoid disrupting EPA's regulatory program, we will withhold issuance of our mandate for 90 days, during which the agency may either withdraw the Final Rule or publish an adequate statement of basis and purpose.

■ SILBERMAN, CIRCUIT JUDGE, concurring in part and concurring in the result.

I concur in all of the majority's *per curiam* opinion but its purported resolution of the *Chevron* "Step II" question concerning the reasonableness of BDAT treatment standards as a construction or application of RCRA. * * * I do not believe it proper for the court to have reached the Step II question as to whether the selection of BDAT treatment levels was "a reasonable policy choice for the agency to make." *Chevron U.S.A. Inc. v. Natural Res. Defense Council,* 467 U.S. 837, 845 (1984). In the absence of a valid *agency* explanation as to how it has attempted to accommodate the competing interests Congress has committed to its care via RCRA, it is in my view inappropriate (perhaps analytically impossible) even to address, much less resolve, CMA's challenge to the reasonableness of EPA's treatment regime under the statute. Because the court today remands for further EPA explanation of its adoption of BDAT standards, the majority's *Chevron* Step II discussion should be considered *dicta.*

* * *

NOTES AND QUESTIONS

1. *Judicial review and agency explanations.* Was it inconsistent for the *Hazardous Waste Treatment Council* majority to both uphold the agency's technology-based standards as a reasonable interpretation of the statute and remand them for further explanation? What purpose is served by the remand? Would you expect the agency to withdraw or significantly modify its rule? If you were general counsel for EPA, how would you draft the agency's response?

Shortly after the decision, EPA published a supplemental explanation for its adoption of standards based solely on the best demonstrated available technology (BDAT). The agency expressed its intention ultimately to use threshold levels of hazardous constituents to cap technology-based treatment requirements, but explained that it was "presently unable to promulgate such levels" because of the kinds of uncertainties noted by the

Hazardous Waste Treatment Council majority. *See* 55 Fed. Reg. 6640, 6641 (Feb. 26, 1990). EPA concluded that it would "retain treatment standards that are based on performance of BDAT until it develops acceptably certain threshold concentration levels." Id. at 6642. EPA's efforts to identify risk-based threshold levels continue, but the goal is as elusive as ever.

2. *Technology-based versus risk-based standards.* What are the advantages and disadvantages of a technology-based as opposed to a risk-based approach to hazardous waste treatment? Is one necessarily more protective than the other, or is their relative stringency context-specific? Is it easier to develop one type of standard than the other? Is one likely to be easier to enforce?

3. *The "land ban."* To what extent does RCRA § 3004 prohibit land disposal of hazardous wastes? What routes does the statute offer for overcoming the prohibition? Note the statute permits both nationwide and individual variances. The rationale for allowing variances and the challenges they pose are discussed in more detail in connection with the Clean Water Act, in Chapter 11, Section 2C.

4. *Treatment standards versus hazardous waste identification.* EPA has consistently taken the position that it may require treatment to risk levels below those needed to justify identification as a hazardous waste. Compare the language and purposes of the relevant statutory provisions. Do you agree with EPA? The D.C. Circuit upheld EPA's authority to require treatment beyond the level needed to remove hazardous characteristics in Chemical Waste Management v. United States Environmental Protection Agency, 976 F.2d 2 (D.C. Cir. 1992). In *Hazardous Waste Treatment Council*, the Chemical Manufacturers Association argued that EPA could not set treatment standards more severe than the levels at which it had delisted certain wastes. Why did the court reject this argument?

5. *RCRA's "hammer."* In the 1984 amendments to § 3004, Congress created a detailed scheme directing EPA to issue land disposal restrictions and accompanying treatment standards in phases, beginning with the most hazardous wastes. The amendments included a "hammer," § 3004(g)(6), providing that land disposal would be flatly prohibited if EPA failed to meet its deadlines. What effect would that prohibition have on generators? Could they simply store their waste pending development of treatment standards? Why do you suppose Congress included the hammer provision?

6. *"No migration."* Section 3004 allows EPA to permit land disposal, without pretreatment, by methods it determines are protective of human health and the environment. *See* § 3004(d), (e), (g). No land disposal method can be approved unless the person seeking approval demonstrates, "to a reasonable degree of certainty, that there will be no migration of hazardous constituents from the disposal unit or injection zone for as long as the wastes remain hazardous." Must the disposal method ensure containment of every single molecule of every hazardous material in the waste? In Natural Resources Defense Council v. United States Environmental Protection Agency, 907 F.2d 1146 (D.C. Cir. 1990), a panel of the D.C. Circuit, over the vigorous dissent of Judge Wald, upheld EPA's reading of the "no migration" standard to bar only migration of hazardous constituents in sufficient concentration to qualify as hazardous wastes.

7. *RCRA and cleanup of contaminated sites.* In general, RCRA is a forward-looking statute, requiring proper handling of newly generated hazardous wastes in order to prevent contamination. In order to minimize contamination threats, it takes a cautious approach. Besides ensuring environmental protection, that caution is intended to discourage the generation of hazardous wastes. But different incentives may be desirable in the context of remediation of existing contaminated sites. Under EPA's "contained-in" policy, soils containing hazardous wastes above certain minimum concentrations are themselves considered hazardous wastes. Faced with complaints that RCRA's regulations, particularly limitations on land disposal and burdensome permitting requirements for treatment, storage and disposal facilities, were delaying remediation efforts, EPA has developed special rules to streamline the permit process and permit on-site storage of remediation wastes. 63 Fed. Reg. 65874 (Nov. 30, 1998). The agency acknowledges that RCRA compliance continues to complicate many state remediation efforts.

5.   CORRECTIVE ACTION AND ENFORCEMENT

(a) *Corrective Action.* The EPA may issue a corrective action administrative order or file a civil suit for injunctive relief to require clean up of any release of hazardous waste at a permitted treatment, storage or disposal facility. Corrective action orders can compel cleanup of past as well as current releases, including releases of materials that were not considered hazardous at the time of release. The agency can even require corrective action beyond the boundary of the facility. *See* RCRA §§ 3004(u), (v) and 3008(h), 42 U.S.C. §§ 6924(u), (v), and 6928(h). Violation of a corrective action order may lead to suspension or revocation of authority to operate and a civil penalty of up to $25,000 per day. The corrective action program is intended to prevent currently operating facilities from requiring future cleanup at federal expense.

(b) *Enforcement.* Like other environmental laws, RCRA authorizes administrative, civil, and criminal enforcement options, and allows citizen suits. *See* RCRA §§ 3008, 7002; 42 U.S.C. §§ 6928, 6972. Enforcement of environmental laws is considered in detail in Chapter 12.

(c) *Imminent and Substantial Endangerment.* RCRA § 7003, 42 U.S.C. § 6973, gives EPA broad authority to issue an administrative order or file a judicial action against any person who has contributed to past or present handling, storage, treatment, transportation, or disposal of solid or hazardous waste which "may present an imminent and substantial endangerment to health or the environment." Citizen suits are also available to remedy imminent and substantial endangerment. RCRA § 7002(A)(1)(B), 42 U.S.C. § 6972(a)(1)(B). This section further provides that the court shall have jurisdiction to restrain any person who has contributed to the imminent and substantial endangerment, or order them to take such other action as may be necessary.

RCRA's imminent and substantial endangerment provision is the primary route for forcing cleanup of petroleum and other materials outside the reach of the Comprehensive Environmental Response, Compensation, and Liability Act (covered in Chapter 9). It requires only "a reasonable prospect of future harm ... so long as the threat is near-term and involves potentially serious harm." Maine People's Alliance v. Mallinckrodt, Inc., 471 F.3d 277, 296 (1st Cir. 2006). It may not, however, be used to recover the monetary costs of a clean-up that has been completed. Meghrig v. KFC Western, Inc., 516 U.S. 479, 485 (1996).

B. SITING HAZARDOUS WASTE FACILITIES: ENVIRONMENTAL JUSTICE

Americans enjoy the benefits of a consumptive, resource-intensive lifestyle, but all too often object to dealing with the consequences of that lifestyle. This is particularly true of the siting of "locally undesirable land uses," or LULUs. Hazardous waste treatment and disposal facilities, which impose focused costs on near neighbors while spreading their benefits to the community at large, are classic LULUs.

Controversies over the siting of hazardous waste facilities sparked the modern environmental justice movement, which focuses on the vulnerability of poor and minority neighborhoods to concentration of environmental hazards. Environmental justice encompasses much more than siting decisions; environmental justice claims have been raised in connection with enforcement, cleanup of contaminated sites, and the setting of general environmental standards such as acceptable toxin levels in fish. *See*, e.g., Eileen Gauna, Fairness in Environmental Protection, 31 Envtl. L. Rep. 10528, 10530 (2001). Nonetheless, siting decisions provide a useful lens through which to examine the concerns for distributional equity that underlie the quest for environmental justice or, to put it in stronger terms, the battle against environmental racism.

CLASS DISCUSSION PROBLEM: AN INCINERATOR FOR SMALLVILLE?

Smallville is a poor rural community in southwestern Georgia. About 45% of the residents of Smallville are African–American, compared to 35% in the county, 27% statewide, and roughly 12% nationwide. Twenty percent of Smallville's population is unemployed.

American Waste Disposal, Inc. (AWD) has announced plans to site a hazardous waste incinerator in Smallville. The incinerator would accept waste from throughout the southeastern United States. AWD considers Smallville an ideal site because it is centrally located, sparsely populated, and has a large available unskilled labor force. AWD will need zoning approval from the county, a Clean Air Act permit, and a RCRA permit to construct the incinerator. The latter two permits would be issued by the state under delegated authority.

Smallville residents are divided on the desirability of the incinerator. Some see it as a source of employment and economic growth. Construction of the facility will employ about 500 workers for three years. Operations thereafter will employ 200, most of them unskilled. Other residents worry about air emissions and possible spills of the toxic materials that will be brought to the incinerator for disposal.

As a resident of Smallville, would you support or oppose the AWD incinerator? Would your opinion change if AWD committed to hiring at least half its work force from the local area? If the state offered to provide funding for a new park or to modernize the local schools in return for the community accepting the incinerator? What steps might opponents take to block the facility?

1. DEVELOPMENT OF THE ENVIRONMENTAL JUSTICE MOVEMENT

As early as 1972, the Green Power Foundation issued a report on environmental conditions in Los Angeles, drawing attention to the special environmental problems of urban areas, and noting that those areas contained high proportions of non-white residents. Perhaps the first organized resistance to perceived environmental injustice occurred in 1982, when the Commission for Racial Justice of the United Church of Christ helped poor African–American residents of Warren County, North Carolina, mount protests against the siting of a hazardous waste landfill. Although unsuccessful in their immediate goal, these protests drew attention to the vulnerability of poor minority communities to LULU siting, and suggested that the techniques of the civil rights movement could help protect those communities.

The Warren County experience also led to demographic studies of hazardous waste sites. In 1983, the General Accounting Office found that three of the four largest hazardous waste facilities in the southeastern U.S. were in predominately African–American communities. In 1987, the Commission for Racial Justice released a national study on the racial and socioeconomic characteristics of areas near hazardous waste sites, concluding that community racial composition was closely correlated with the presence of toxic waste facilities, due to "an insidious form of racism." United Church of Christ, Commission for Racial Justice, Toxic Wastes and Race in the United States ix (1987).

The Commission for Racial Justice report triggered the environmental justice movement, which combines civil rights and environmental activism. In 1991, the First National People of Color Environmental Leadership Summit, organized by the Commission for Racial Justice, produced a statement of Principles of Environmental Justice, including universal rights to clean air, land, water and food, safe workplaces, and equality of participation at all levels of decisionmaking. *See* Proceedings, First National People of Color Environmental Leadership Summit xiii-xiv (1991). By the mid–1990s, ensuring environmental justice had become official federal policy. EPA established an Office of Environmental Justice in 1992. In

1994, President Clinton issued Executive Order 12898, directing each federal agency, "[t]o the greatest extent practicable and permitted by law," to "make achieving environmental justice part of its mission by identifying and addressing, as appropriate, disproportionately high and adverse human health or environmental effects of its programs, policies, and activities on minority populations and low-income populations in the United States."

2. DECIPHERING THE DATA

The nationwide study by the Commission for Racial Justice examined the racial and socioeconomic characteristics of communities, defined as 5–digit ZIP code areas, around all operating commercial hazardous waste treatment, storage and disposal facilities in the United States. Using 1980 census data, the Commission found that "the ZIP code areas with the highest number of commercial hazardous waste facilities also had the highest mean percentage of residents who belong to a [non-white] racial and ethnic group." Commission for Racial Justice, United Church of Christ, Toxic Wastes and Race in the United States 13 (1987).

> Specifically, in communities with one operating commercial hazardous waste facility, the mean minority percentage of the population was approximately twice that of communities without facilities (24 percent vs. 12 percent). In communities with two or more operating commercial hazardous waste facilities or one of the five largest landfills, the mean minority percentage of the population was more than three times that of communities without facilities (38 percent vs. 12 percent).

> The analysis also revealed that mean household income and the mean value of owner-occupied homes were not as significant as the mean minority percentage of the population in differentiating residential ZIP codes with lesser numbers of hazardous waste facilities versus those with greater numbers and the largest landfills. After controlling for regional differences and urbanization, the mean value of owner-occupied homes in a community was a significant discriminator, but less so than the minority percentage of the population.

Id.

Since that study, the extent and causes of inequities in the siting of hazardous waste facilities have been hotly debated. The evidence can be difficult to decipher because different studies use different datasets. Some large-scale studies have looked at siting at the scale of entire counties. Those studies may be revealing about political dynamics, but they do not provide much information about the characteristics of the populations most strongly affected by siting decisions, those immediately around the facility. At a local scale, some studies (like the original United Church of Christ study) have used ZIP codes as a proxy for neighborhood effects, while others have focused on census tracts. The use of proxies allows investigators to take advantage of the wealth of demographic data that has already been compiled. If proxies must be used, which is more appropriate for this type of study? Census tracts are generally smaller than ZIP codes, so their use may reveal more localized distributional patterns. They also have the advantages of being roughly comparable in population numbers, and drawn with the intention of reflecting neighborhood divisions. On the other hand, they may not fully capture the impacts of hazardous waste facilities. Because many waste facilities are located at the edge of a census tract, near the highways or rail lines that often form tract boundaries, their impacts may be felt more strongly in neighboring tracts than in the host tract. Vicki Been & Francis Gupta, Coming to the Nuisance or Going to the Barrio, 24 Ecology L.Q. 1, 13 (1997).

Other methodological sources of disagreement include what constitutes a "minority community" for purposes of identifying disparate impacts, what should be accepted as persuasive evidence of such impacts, and whether any observed effects are attributable to discrimination (intentional or otherwise) at the time of siting or to movement thereafter.

> While acknowledging these disputes, Professor Alice Kaswan concludes: the vast majority of the studies demonstrate some degree of inequity in the distribution of LULUs on the basis of race and/or income, with race being the more frequently relevant factor. While these studies do not prove anything about the presence of distributive injustice in every locality, they do support the "broad" claim of distributive injustice—that the overall pattern of LULU distribution is unequal.

Alice Kaswan, Distributive Justice and the Environment, 81 N.C. L. Rev. 1031, 1076 (2003). Rachel Godsil points out that most studies have focused on easily-measured environmental inequities, particularly the siting of LULUs and toxic emissions as reported to the federal Toxic Release Inventory. She argues that such studies are likely to underestimate environmental inequities because they do not consider the cumulative effects of exposure to multiple hazards, including small and mobile sources of air pollution. Rachel D. Godsil, Environmental Justice and the Integration Ideal, 49 N.Y. L. Sch. L. Rev. 1109, 1121 (2005).

NOTES AND QUESTIONS

1. *Terminology.* Various terms have been used to describe the inequitable distribution of environmental hazards. Dr. Benjamin Chavis, longtime civil rights activist, former executive director of the National Association for the Advancement of Colored People, and co-author of the 1987 Commission for Racial Justice report, coined the term "environmental racism" to describe the situation depicted by that report. Those who describe themselves as members of the movement also speak of environmental justice or injustice, terms they describe as broader, encompassing socioeconomic as well as racial disparities. Industries seeking permits sometimes prefer to talk about environmental equity, and seek to focus that term on demonstrable environmental risks. *See* Luke W. Cole & Sheila R. Foster, From the Ground

Up: Environmental Racism and the Rise of the Environmental Justice Movement 15 (2001).

What term do you think best captures the problem? How does the choice of terms affect perceptions of the problem and the search for solutions? According to Professor Richard Lazarus, "If environmental justice had not been so cast in terms of race, it is quite doubtful that the movement would have enjoyed such a strong political half-life." Richard J. Lazarus, "Environmental Racism! That's What It Is.", 2000 U. Ill. L. Rev. 255, 259. Another commentator, more sympathetic to the nationwide need for facilities, suggests that the use of strong rhetoric on both sides of the siting debate poses an unnecessary barrier to effective resolution of the problem. Lisa A. Binder, Religion, Race and Rights: A Rhetorical Overview of Environmental Justice Disputes, 6 Wis. Envtl. L. J. 1 (1999).

2. *Identifying environmental racism.* Because resources are unequally distributed by race, operation of the market economy often has unequal racial impacts. Should those unintentional effects be classified as "environmental racism"? Does the extent to which that background distribution has been shaped by past intentional discrimination matter? Consider the views of Professor Gerald Torres:

> The term racism draws its contemporary moral strength by being clearly identified with the history of the structural oppression of African–American and other people of color in this society. * * * When seeking to determine whether an activity is racist, the one characteristic that must be present is one of domination and subordination. The action need not necessarily be one of intention, but it may be both intentional and dominating.

> In analyzing environmental policies and activities from the perspective of their subordinating impact on racial groups we are led inexorably to examine the distributional impacts of environmental rules. We can examine both the substantive distributional impact of those rules in practice and the substantive blindness in the production of rules that lead to racially subordinating activities. In short, when we label an environmental practice as an example of environmental racism we are saying that the predictable distributional impact of that decision contributes to the structure of racial subordination and domination that has similarly marked many of our public policies in this country. We might also be saying that excluding considerations of racial impact in constructing the substantive environmental rules contributes to the subordination of identifiable racial groups. In many cases, this subordinating impact will be the result of an unconscious process. Regardless of how unconscious the process may be, however, if the perception of the affected class is that the impact is fundamentally racially targeted then we must assume that the substantive effect is racist unless a better or different justification can be put forward.

Gerald Torres, Introduction: Understanding Environmental Racism, 63 U. Colo. L. Rev. 839, 839–40 (1992). Do you agree? Must the racial impact be objectively identifiable, or does it depend solely on the perception of the minority group? How significant must the impact be? What justifications, if any, can remove the taint of racism from a siting decision?

3. *Defining environmental justice.* The Environmental Protection Agency defines environmental justice as "the fair treatment and meaningful involvement of all people regardless of race, color, national origin, or income with respect to the development, implementation, and enforcement of environmental laws, regulations, and policies." Under the Clinton administration, EPA went on to say that "Fair treatment means that no group of people, including a racial, ethnic, or socioeconomic group, should bear a disproportionate share of the negative environmental consequences resulting from industrial, municipal, and commercial operations or the execution of federal, state, local, and tribal programs and policies." In the Bush administration, it replaced that language with the statement that environmental justice "will be achieved when everyone enjoys the same degree of protection from environmental and health hazards and equal access to the decision-making process to have a healthy environment in which to live, learn, and work."

Is EPA's definition adequate to guide decisions? What is "meaningful involvement," and how can it be assured? Are affirmative efforts to build community political capacity a necessary element of environmental justice? Will those efforts simply expand the NIMBY (Not In My Back Yard) syndrome to include poor minority neighborhoods as well as wealthy white ones? Is opposition to hazardous waste TSDFs justified in poor neighborhoods, which receive less benefit from the activities that generate hazardous waste?

What impacts are unfair or "disproportionate"? Should hazardous waste facilities and other LULUs be distributed evenly across the entire landscape? How should population density be factored in? Should some places be off-limits to hazardous waste facilities? How should those areas be identified? Should the calculation of proportionality include local economic benefits, such as jobs, provided by a facility? Do impacts resulting from market dynamics after siting count? Does the law have a role to play in remedying those impacts?

4. *Facility presence and environmental risk.* Many studies rely entirely on the presence or absence of hazardous waste TSDFs as an indicator of environmental justice. While it is easy to measure, the presence of a facility does not necessarily correlate with environmental risk. The level of risk presumably depends upon the design and operation of the facility as well as the mix of materials it accepts. If a facility complies with all applicable state and federal regulations, does its siting raise no environmental equity concerns? Or are significant impacts, environmental or economic, not addressed by environmental laws?

5. *National data and local decisions.* Much of the evidence of environmental racism rests on a limited number of nationwide and local studies. What role should this data play in a local siting dispute in an area that has not been closely studied? Should it matter to local decisionmakers in Smallville, or to a judge reviewing their decision, that siting decisions nationwide or in

Detroit appear to be discriminatory? As an advocate for incinerator opponents in Smallville, what benefits and risks would you see in linking the local controversy to the broader environmental justice movement?

3.   THE LAW OF ENVIRONMENTAL JUSTICE

a.   *Civil Rights Litigation*

It is not surprising that the environmental justice movement, with its close ties to civil rights activism, looked to civil rights law for vindication. Early environmental justice litigation concentrated on allegations of racial discrimination in permitting decisions, seeking relief under the equal protection clause of the federal constitution. These claims face high evidentiary burdens. Establishing an equal protection violation requires proof of discriminatory intent. Washington v. Davis, 426 U.S. 229 (1976). Direct evidence of discriminatory purpose is extremely difficult to produce. Permitting bodies simply do not proclaim that racial animus motivates their decisions. Although the Supreme Court has made it clear that circumstantial evidence can be sufficient to establish discriminatory intent, *see* Village of Arlington Heights v. Metropolitan Housing Development Corp., 429 U.S. 252, 266–268 (1977), persuasive circumstantial evidence of discriminatory purpose is also difficult to find. Disparate impacts due to existing structural segregation or discrimination typically cannot be tied to current discriminatory intent. The number of siting decisions in any local jurisdiction is typically small, making it hard to obtain statistically significant data on disparate impacts and even harder to demonstrate a pattern suggesting racial animus. Moreover, permitting agencies typically react to applications brought forward by private parties, rather than initiating proposals. If the only applications for hazardous waste facilities are in areas with substantial minority applications, it is difficult to accuse the permitting body of targeting those neighborhoods.

Finding equal protection claims unpromising, environmental justice advocates turned to Title VI of the Civil Rights Act of 1964. Section 601 of Title VI provides:

> No person in the United States shall, on the ground of race, color or national origin, be excluded from participation in, be denied the benefits of, or be subjected to discrimination under any program or activity receiving Federal financial assistance.

42 U.S.C. § 2000d. Section 601 has been interpreted to proscribe only intentional discrimination. *See* Alexander v. Choate, 469 U.S. 287, 293 (1985). Section 602, however, which directs federal agencies to issue regulations to prevent discrimination, permits regulations covering disparate impacts as well as intentional discrimination. *See* 42 U.S.C. § 2000d–1; Alexander, 469 U.S. at 292–94.

EPA regulations implementing section 602 provide:

> (b) A recipient [of federal funds] shall not use criteria or methods of administering its program which have the effect of subjecting

individuals to discrimination because of their race, color, national origin or sex, or have the effect of defeating or substantially impairing accomplishment of the objectives of the program with respect to individuals of a particular race, color, national origin, or sex.

(c) A recipient shall not choose a site or location of a facility that has the purpose or effect of excluding individuals from, denying them the benefits of, or subjecting them to discrimination under any program to which this part applies on the grounds of race, color, or national origin or sex; or with the purpose or effect of defeating or substantially impairing the accomplishment of the objectives of this subpart.

40 C.F.R. § 7.35. Title VI and its implementing regulations apply only to programs receiving federal funding, but that includes many environmental permitting programs. The federal government provides significant funding to states under the majority of the federal environmental laws, including the Clean Air Act, Clean Water Act, and RCRA. The Supreme Court sharply limited the usefulness of section 602 in civil rights litigation in 2001, when it ruled by a 5–4 vote that there is no private right of action to enforce regulations issued under section 602. Alexander v. Sandoval, 532 U.S. 275 (2001).

b. Environmental Litigation

Environmental justice advocates have been understandably skeptical of the ability of environmental laws to advance their cause. Substantive environmental laws tend to set uniform acceptable levels of pollution or environmental hazards, disregarding the distribution of hazards across the landscape. Although they often provide avenues for public participation, effective use of those avenues requires sophistication, time, and money. Given the unequal distribution of those resources, opportunities for public input may exacerbate environmental injustices by enhancing the power of wealthy communities to engage in NIMBY politics.

Nonetheless, environmental laws have in some circumstances proven effective tools for combating environmental injustice. Perhaps the best known example comes from attempts to site a hazardous waste incinerator in Kettleman City, California. Although nearly 40% of the residents of Kettleman City spoke only Spanish, the County prepared the environmental review documents only in English. A state trial court ruled that the County had violated the California Environmental Quality Act (California's NEPA analogue) by effectively precluding meaningful community involvement. El Pueblo Para El Aire y Agua Limpio v. County of Kings, 22 Envtl. L. Rep. 20,357 (Cal. Super. Ct. 1991). That may be an isolated success. No court has ever ruled that NEPA required translation of environmental review documents to facilitate local participation. Some states mandate translation of information about certain hazards, *see*, e.g., N.J. Stat. Ann. 34:5A–4(c); Or. Rev. Stat. 654.770, but many others do not.

c. Administrative Remedies

The power of litigation under either civil rights or environmental laws to remedy environmental injustice faces two major limitations: difficulties of proof, and a poor fit between the aims of the environmental justice movement and legislation developed with other aims in mind. Federal legislation specific to environmental justice could reduce these barriers, but has not been forthcoming. In the 1990s, the Clinton administration sought to reduce the gap between environmental justice concerns and existing law through administrative initiatives.

Executive Order 12898: Federal Actions to Address Environmental Justice in Minority Populations and Low–Income Populations

59 Fed. Reg. 7629 (Feb. 11, 1994).

Section 1–1. Implementation

1–101. *Agency Responsibilities*. To the greatest extent practicable and permitted by law * * * each Federal agency shall make achieving environmental justice part of its mission by identifying and addressing, as appropriate, disproportionately high and adverse human health or environmental effects of its programs, policies, and activities on minority populations and low-income populations in the United States * * *.

* * *

Section 2–2. Federal Agency Responsibilities for Federal Programs

Each Federal agency shall conduct its programs, policies, and activities that substantially affect human health or the environment, in a manner that ensures that such programs, policies, and activities do not have the effect of excluding persons (including populations) from participation in, denying persons (including populations) the benefits of, or subjecting persons (including populations) to discrimination under, such programs, policies, and activities, because of their race, color, or national origin.

* * *

Section 6–6. General Provisions

* * *

6–608. *General*. Federal agencies shall implement this order consistent with, and to the extent permitted by, existing law.

6–609. *Judicial Review*. This order is intended only to improve the internal management of the executive branch and is not intended to, nor does it create any right, benefit, or trust responsibility, substantive or procedural, enforceable at law or equity by a party against the United States, its agencies, its officers, or any person. This order shall not be construed to create any right to judicial review involving the compliance or noncompliance of the United States, its agencies, its officers, or any other person with this order.

William J. Clinton, Memorandum on Environmental Justice

30 Weekly Comp. Pres. Doc. 279 (1994).

Today I have issued an Executive Order on Federal Actions to Address Environmental Justice in Minority Populations and Low–Income Populations. * * *

The purpose of this separate memorandum is to underscore certain provisions of existing law that can help ensure that all communities and persons across this Nation live in a safe and healthful environment. Environmental and civil rights statutes provide many opportunities to address environmental hazards in minority communities and low-income communities. Application of these existing statutory provisions is an important part of this Administration's efforts to prevent those minority communities and low-income communities from being subject to disproportionately high and adverse environmental effects.

I am therefore today directing that all department and agency heads take appropriate and necessary steps to ensure that the following specific directives are implemented immediately:

In accordance with Title VI of the Civil Rights Act of 1964, each Federal agency shall ensure that all programs or activities receiving Federal financial assistance that affect human health or the environment do not directly, or through contractual or other arrangements, use criteria, methods, or other arrangements that discriminate on the basis of race, color, or national origin.

Each Federal agency shall analyze the environmental effects, including human health, economic and social effects, of Federal actions, including effects on minority communities and low-income communities, when such analysis is required by the National Environmental Policy Act of 1969. Mitigation measures outlined or analyzed in an environmental assessment, environmental impact statement, or record of decision, whenever feasible, should address significant and adverse environmental effects of proposed Federal actions on minority communities and low-income communities.

* * *

Luke W. Cole and Caroline Farrell, Structural Racism, Structural Pollution and the Need for a New Paradigm

20 Wash. U. J. L. & Pol'y 265, 268–273 (2006).

Camden, New Jersey, is an economically depressed community across the Delaware River from Philadelphia. Following the collapse of its industrial base, Camden became one of the most blighted areas of the northeastern United States; when its manufacturing jobs disappeared, all that was left were heavily polluted industrial sites and abandoned factories. Camden became the poorest city in the state, and one of the poorest in the nation, with a per capita income of less than $8000 in 2002.

One Camden neighborhood is even more devastated and environmentally degraded than the rest—Waterfront South, a neighborhood of less than a square mile in South Camden between the river and an interstate. Waterfront South contains the South Jersey Port Corporation, which used to be a major shipbuilder, homes, boarded up stores, two federal Superfund sites, thirteen other known contaminated sites, four junkyards, a petroleum coke transfer station, a scrap metal recycling plant, numerous auto body shops, a paint company, a chemical company, three food processing plants, and other heavy industrial use sites. The huge U.S. Gypsum plant abuts the neighborhood to the north.

Despite this concentration of polluting facilities—and the attendant diesel truck traffic they require—decision-makers in Camden County and at the state level continue to target Waterfront South for undesirable land uses. The County chose Waterfront South as the site of a sewage treatment plant that serves thirty-five municipalities, and of an open-air sewage-sludge-composting facility next to the treatment plant. They also chose to put the garbage incinerator for the entire County's trash in Waterfront South, followed by a massive co-generation power plant. The New Jersey Department of Environmental Protection (DEP) granted permits for all of these projects, over local opposition.

* * *

Thus, in 1999, when the St. Lawrence Cement Company (SLC) announced plans to build a huge cement-grinding facility in Waterfront South that would emit an additional one hundred tons of air pollutants each year, local residents said "enough is enough." They mobilized to fight the plant, but their efforts were hampered by several factors. First, because SLC would construct and operate its plant within the boundaries of the South Jersey Port Corporation, a state agency, the plant was exempt from review by local Camden authorities. Thus, those decision makers closest to the residents—their own local elected officials—had no role in the permit approval process.

Second, under New Jersey law, companies that submit a completed permit application to the DEP may begin to construct their facility prior to its approval, "at risk," while the DEP processes the permit application. SLC completed its application and began construction in November, 1999, nine months before the first opportunity for public comment on the project. By the time of the only public hearing on the matter, in August, 2000, construction of the plant was more than half finished. The DEP made no changes whatsoever to the facility as a result of public input, and granted SLC its permit in October, 2000. New Jersey Governor Christine Todd Whitman attended the ribbon-cutting ceremony for the plant, which the DEP heralded as a much-needed new investment in Camden.

Local residents secured legal representation, and, with their lawyers, quickly realized that the new plant was "legal" under environmental law. The DEP had taken the necessary procedural steps in permitting the plant and would not be vulnerable to a legal challenge on environmental grounds.

The experience of Waterfront South residents illustrates the failure of environmental law to protect communities like Camden. Despite the overwhelming congregation of polluting industry in the neighborhood and the environmental health hazards faced by its residents, nothing in environmental law provided a means of stopping the facility. Under the law, the community's input was heard only after construction of the facility was underway, and the DEP did not alter a single permit provision in response to that input. Clearly, the old paradigm of environmental law did not work for Waterfront South.

There is another piece to the Camden picture: after thirty years of "white flight," the city is home to an almost exclusively African–American and Latino population. Ninety-four percent of Waterfront South's residents are people of color. * * *

Given the overwhelming concentration of polluting facilities permitted by the DEP in Waterfront South, it was not difficult for the community residents' experts to find that the DEP's actions had a disparate impact on the community. The expert's studies found disparate impact not only in Camden, but throughout New Jersey—black people bore more environmental burdens than white people. Professor Michel Gelobter, looking at the distribution of polluting facilities on a statewide basis, found that ZIP codes with higher than the state-wide average of 20.6% non-white residents had more than twice the air polluting facilities (13.7 facilities per ZIP code) than those with a below-average number of non-white residents. Waterfront South had 2.3 times as many polluting facilities as the average New Jersey ZIP code.

* * *

Facing a cement-grinding facility that was legal under environmental law, residents turned to the statutes ostensibly enacted to protect people of color—civil rights law. Their experience demonstrates the failure of the old paradigm of civil rights law, as well. The community sued SLC and the New Jersey DEP, alleging intentional discrimination under Title VI of the Civil Rights Act of 1964, and discriminatory effect, or disparate impact discrimination, under the Title VI regulations of the U.S. Environmental Protection Agency (EPA).

* * *

On April 19, 2001, Judge Orlofsky of the federal District Court in Camden issued an injunction against the cement plant prohibiting its operation. He found that there was indeed a disparate impact as prohibited by EPA regulations. * * *

The community's victory was short-lived. On April 24, 2001, the U.S. Supreme Court decided Alexander v. Sandoval (an unrelated case concerning drivers' licenses in Alabama), holding that there is no private right of action to enforce the disparate impact regulations promulgated by federal agencies under section 602 of Title VI. In response, the Third Circuit quickly lifted Judge Orlofsky's injunction, and, citing Sandoval, ruled that the Camden plaintiffs could not sue under a disparate impact theory. Although the district court found discriminatory impact as a result of DEP's decisions—factual findings not overturned on appeal—Camden residents were left without judicial recourse. * * *

The Supreme Court in Sandoval, in taking away the public's right to enforce disparate impact regulations promulgated under section 602 of Title VI, granted federal agencies the sole discretion to enforce these anti-discrimination measures. The experience of Camden residents illustrates the empty promise of the Supreme Court's decision.

Camden residents also filed an administrative complaint with the EPA under the agency's Title VI regulations. They might appear to have had an easy route to victory with this administrative complaint—after all, a federal judge had already found discriminatory disparate impact in violation of the EPA's own regulations. However, a unique political situation, combined with an utter failure by the EPA to enforce its own regulations, doomed the Camden residents' chances at redressing the civil rights violations in this manner.

It is instructive to remember the political circumstances that existed in early 2001. The newly-appointed EPA administrator, to whom Camden residents appealed, was, in an unfortunate coincidence, former New Jersey Governor Christine Todd Whitman. Thus, the residents asked the very governor whose DEP had approved the SLC permit, and who had attended the ribbon-cutting for the opening of the SLC plant, to now declare her own gubernatorial administration's actions a violation of civil rights. Given this situation, the residents were unlikely to prevail in their administrative complaint, and, to no one's surprise, they did not.

But it would be a mistake to ascribe the failure of EPA to act on the Camden residents' complaint to this unique circumstance. Indeed, their complaint fared no differently than almost 150 other civil rights complaints filed under Title VI with the EPA. Since 1992, when the first environmental justice Title VI complaints were filed with the agency, it has never ruled in favor of a complainant. It has dismissed a majority of the complaints on procedural grounds, sometimes appropriately, sometimes speciously. It has tortured its own regulations and policy to rule against the complainants in every case in which it has made a decision on the merits. And it has allowed cases to die from malnutrition, withering away for lack of attention over the years. Several cases filed in 1994 and 1995 have yet to be resolved. * * *

In re Chemical Waste Management of Indiana, Inc.

EPA Environmental Appeals Board, 1995.
6 E.A.D. 66.

■ Opinion of the Board by JUDGE REICH.

On March 1, 1995, U.S. EPA Region V issued a final permit decision approving the application of Chemical Waste Management of Indiana, Inc.

("CWMII") for the renewal of the federal portion[1] of a Resource Conservation and Recovery Act ("RCRA") permit and a Class 3 modification of the same permit for its Adams Center Landfill Facility in Fort Wayne, Indiana.
* * *

During the comment period * * *, Petitioners and other commenters raised what the parties refer to as "environmental justice" concerns. More specifically, issues were raised as to whether the operation of CWMII's facility will have a disproportionately adverse impact on the health, environment, or economic well-being of minority or low-income populations in the area surrounding the facility. * * *

During the pendency of CWMII's permit application, Executive Order 12898, relating to environmental justice, was issued. * * *

In response to the environmental justice concerns raised during the comment period on the draft modified permit, the Region held what was billed as an "informational" meeting in Fort Wayne, Indiana, on August 11, 1994. The meeting was attended by concerned citizens, and representatives of CWMII, the Indiana Department of Environmental Management, and the Region. The purpose of the meeting was to "allow representatives of all parties involved to freely discuss Environmental Justice and other key issues, answer questions and gain understanding of each party's concerns." The Region also performed a demographic analysis of census data on populations within a one-mile radius of the facility. The Region ultimately concluded that the operation of the facility would not have a disproportionately adverse health or environmental impact on minority or low-income populations living near the facility.

* * *

We believe it is useful to begin by considering the precise nature of Petitioners' environmental justice claim in the context of this RCRA proceeding and the effect, if any, the issuance of Executive Order 12898 should have on the way in which the Agency addresses such a claim.

"Environmental justice," at least as that term is used in the Executive Order, involves "identifying and addressing, as appropriate, disproportionately high and adverse human health or environmental effects of [Agency] programs, policies, and activities on minority populations and low-income populations...." 59 Fed. Reg. at 7629. Some of the commenters also believe that environmental justice is concerned with adverse effects on the *economic* well-being of such populations. Thus, when Petitioners couch their arguments in terms of environmental justice, they assert that the

---

1. The State of Indiana has received authorization to administer its own RCRA program, pursuant to section 3006 of RCRA, 42 U.S.C. § 6926. Indiana has not, however, received authorization to administer the requirements contained in the Hazardous and Solid Waste Amendments to RCRA ("HSWA"). Consequently, when a RCRA permit is issued in Indiana, the State issues the part of the permit relating to the non-HSWA requirements and EPA issues the part of the permit relating to the HSWA requirements.

issuance of the permit and the concomitant operation of the facility will have a disproportionately adverse impact not only on the health and environment of minority or low-income people living near the facility but also on economic growth and property values.

* * *

Although it is not made explicit in the petitions, it is nevertheless clear that Petitioners do not believe that the threats posed by the facility can be addressed through revision of the permit. Rather, it is apparent that Petitioners believe that their concerns can be addressed only by permanently halting operation of the facility at its present location or, at a minimum, preventing the Phase IV Expansion of the facility. Thus, Petitioners challenge the permit decision, including the modification, in its entirety, rather than any specific permit conditions.

At the outset, it is important to determine how (if at all) the Executive Order changes the way a Region processes a permit application under RCRA. For the reasons set forth below, we conclude that the Executive Order does not purport to, and does not have the effect of, changing the substantive requirements for issuance of a permit under RCRA and its implementing regulations. We conclude, nevertheless, that there are areas where the Region has discretion to act within the constraints of the RCRA regulations and, in such areas, as a matter of policy, the Region should exercise that discretion to implement the Executive Order to the greatest extent practicable.

Permit Issuance Under RCRA: While, as is discussed later, there are some important opportunities to implement the Executive Order in the RCRA permitting context, there are substantial limitations as well. As the Region notes in its brief, the Executive Order by its express terms is to be implemented in a manner that is consistent with existing law. Section 6–608. The Region correctly points out that under the existing RCRA scheme, the Agency is required to issue a permit to any applicant who meets all the requirements of RCRA and its implementing regulations. The statute expressly provides that:

> Upon a determination by the Administrator (or a State, if applicable), of compliance by a facility for which a permit is applied for under this section with the requirements of this section and section 3004, the Administrator (or the State) *shall issue* a permit for such facilities.

RCRA § 3005(c)(1), 42 U.S.C. § 6925 (emphasis added). * * * Accordingly, if a permit applicant meets the requirements of RCRA and its implementing regulations, the Agency *must* issue the permit, regardless of the racial or socio-economic composition of the surrounding community and regardless of the economic effect of the facility on the surrounding community.

Implementing the Executive Order: Nevertheless, there are two areas in the RCRA permitting scheme in which the Region has significant discretion, within the constraints of RCRA, to implement the mandates of the Executive Order. The first of these areas is public participation. [40 C.F.R.] Part 124 already provides procedures for ensuring that the public is afforded an opportunity to participate in the processing of a permit application. The procedures required under part 124, however, do not preclude a Region from providing other opportunities for public involvement beyond those required under part 124. We hold, therefore, that when the Region has a basis to believe that operation of the facility may have a disproportionate impact on a minority or low-income segment of the affected community, the Region should, as a matter of policy, exercise its discretion to assure early and ongoing opportunities for public involvement in the permitting process.

A second area in which the Region has discretion to implement the Executive Order within the constraints of RCRA relates to the omnibus clause under section 3005(c)(3) of RCRA. The omnibus clause provides that:

> Each permit issued under this section shall contain such terms and conditions as the Administrator (or the State) determines necessary to protect human health and the environment.

42 U.S.C. § 6925(c)(3). Under the omnibus clause, if the operation of a facility would have an adverse impact on the health or environment of the surrounding community, the Agency would be required to include permit terms or conditions that would ensure that such impacts do not occur. Moreover, if the nature of the facility and its proximity to neighboring populations would make it impossible to craft a set of permit terms that would protect the health and environment of such populations, the Agency would have the authority to deny the permit. In that event, the facility would have to shut down entirely. Thus, under the omnibus clause, if the operation of a facility truly poses a threat to the health or environment of a low-income or minority community, the omnibus clause would require the Region to include in the permit whatever terms and conditions are necessary to prevent such impacts. This would be true even without a finding of disparate impact.

There is nothing in section 3005(c)(3) to prevent the Region from taking a more refined look at its health and environmental impacts assessment, in light of allegations that operation of the facility would have a disproportionately adverse effect on the health or environment of low-income or minority populations. Even under the omnibus clause some judgment is required as to what constitutes a threat to human health and the environment. It is certainly conceivable that, although analysis of a broad cross-section of the community may not suggest a threat to human health and the environment from the operation of a facility, such a broad analysis might mask the effects of the facility on a disparately affected minority or low-income segment of the community. (Moreover, such an analysis might have been based on assumptions that, though true for a broad cross-section of the community, are not true for the smaller minority or low-income segment of the community.) A Region should take this under consideration in defining the scope of its analysis for compliance with § 3005(c)(3).

Of course, an exercise of discretion under section 3005(c)(3) would be limited by the constraints that are inherent in the language of the omnibus clause. In other words, in response to an environmental justice claim, the Region would be limited to ensuring the protection of the health or environment of the minority or low-income populations. The Region would not have discretion to redress impacts that are unrelated or only tenuously related to human health and the environment, such as disproportionate impacts on the economic well-being of a minority or low-income community. With that qualification in mind, we hold that when a commenter submits at least a superficially plausible claim that operation of the facility will have a disproportionate impact on a minority or low-income segment of the affected community, the Region should, as a matter of policy, exercise its discretion under section 3005(c)(3) to include within its health and environmental impacts assessment an analysis focusing particularly on the minority or low-income community whose health or environment is alleged to be threatened by the facility. In this fashion, the Region may implement the Executive Order within the constraints of RCRA and its implementing regulations.

* * *

Reviewing Challenges Based on the Executive Order: As a threshold matter, the Region suggests that claims relating to the implementation of the Executive Order are not subject to review. In support of this argument, the Region points out that the Executive Order itself expressly provides that it does not create any substantive or procedural rights that could be enforced through litigation. * * * However, while the Region is correct that section 6–609 precludes judicial review of the Agency's efforts to comply with the Executive Order, it does not affect implementation of the Order *within* an agency. More specifically, it does not preclude the *Board*, in an appropriate circumstance, from reviewing a Region's compliance with the Executive Order as a matter of policy or exercise of discretion to the extent relevant under section 124.19(a). Section 124.19(a) authorizes the Board to review any condition of a permit decision (or as here, the permit decision in its entirety). Accordingly, the Board can review the Region's efforts to implement the Executive Order in the course of determining the validity or appropriateness of the permit decision at issue. With that in mind, we turn to the specific challenges raised by Petitioners in this case.

* * *

The Region's Demographic Study: Petitioners * * * question the Region's efforts to determine whether operation of the facility will have a disproportionate impact on a minority or low-income community. To assess whether there would indeed be a disproportionate impact on low-income or minority populations, the Region performed a demographic study, based on census figures, of the racial and socio-economic composition of the community surrounding the facility. The Region concluded that no minority or low-income communities will face a disproportionate impact from the facility. Petitioners argue that, in arriving at this conclusion, the Region erred by ignoring available census and other information submitted during the comment period that allegedly demonstrate a disproportionate impact of the facility on minority or low-income populations, particularly those at distances greater than one mile. Petitioners particularly criticize the Region's decision to restrict the focus of its study to the community living within a one-mile radius of the facility. Petitioners contend that the facility adversely affects citizens who live further than one mile away from the facility. * * *

As explained above, the Region can and should consider a claim of disproportionate impact in the context of its health and environmental impacts assessment under the omnibus clause at section 3005(c)(3) of RCRA. The proper scope of a demographic study to consider such impacts is an issue calling for a highly technical judgment as to the probable dispersion of pollutants through various media into the surrounding community. This is precisely the kind of issue that the Region, with its technical expertise and experience, is best suited to decide. In recognition of this reality, the procedural rules governing Appeals of permitting decisions place a heavy burden on petitioners who seek Board review of such technical decisions. To carry that burden in this case, Petitioners would need to show either that the Region erred in concluding that the permit would be protective of populations within one mile of the facility, or that, even if it were protective of such close-in populations, it for some reason would not protect the health or environment of citizens who live at a greater distance from the facility. We believe that Petitioners have failed to demonstrate that the Region erred in either of these respects.

The petition mentions two parts of the administrative record in support of its claim. First, it refers to the comments of Fort Wayne City Councilman Cletus Edmonds, who contends that the facility will adversely affect the economic growth and housing of some 13,500 of his African–American constituents. As noted above, however, neither RCRA nor its implementing regulations requires the Agency to consider the economic effects of a facility.

Second, the petition mentions an environmental impact study submitted by the City of New Haven. That study indicates that particulates from the facility "could" affect an African–American community living as far as two miles away from the facility * * *. This conclusion, however, is stated in a very tentative fashion and provides no indication of the probabilities involved or the adverse effects, if any, increased exposure might cause. It does not show why the Region's conclusions as to the protectiveness of the permit were erroneous or why, if the population within one mile of the facility is protected (as the Region concludes), there would nonetheless be impacts beyond one mile cognizable under section 3005(c)(3). We conclude, therefore, that Petitioners have failed to carry their burden of demonstrating that the Region's technical judgment in this case does not deserve the same deference that the Board normally accords to such judgments. Review of this issue is therefore denied.

NOTES AND QUESTIONS

1. *Litigation and political action.* To date, environmental justice litigation, under either civil rights or environmental laws, has achieved few direct victories. It is important to keep in mind, however, that litigation is not pursued in isolation. Protests and political organizing have been crucial to the environmental justice movement, and frequently have succeeded in blocking siting. Indeed, a knowledgeable commentator argues that "taking environmental problems out of the streets and into the courts" is often "a tactical mistake." Luke W. Cole, Empowerment as the Key to Environmental Protection: The Need for Environmental Poverty Law, 19 Ecology L.Q. 619, 650 (1992). On the other hand, Richard Lazarus notes that civil rights suits have substantial symbolic value. Richard J. Lazarus, Pursuing 'Environmental Justice': The Distributional Effects of Environmental Protection, 87 Nw. U. L. Rev. 787, 829 (1993). What is the appropriate role of litigation (and lawyers) in the struggle for environmental justice? What can political action achieve that litigation cannot, and vice versa?

2. *Administrative appeals.* Although they are generally not required to do so, many administrative agencies provide an internal appeal process for persons dissatisfied with decisions. Unless agency regulations or the applicable statute makes the agency appeal process mandatory, a dissatisfied party has the choice of seeking review through the agency process or resorting directly to federal court. *See* Darby v. Cisneros, 509 U.S. 137 (1993).

Details of agency appeals processes vary widely. EPA permit decisions under RCRA, and certain permit decisions under the Clean Water and Clean Air Acts, are appealable to a specialized review body, the Environmental Appeals Board. *See* 40 C.F.R. § 124.19(a). The Board may also decide on its own initiative to review any condition in such permits. Id., § 124.19(b). Where available, appeal to the Board is mandatory prior to resort to federal court. Id., § 124.19(e). The Board consists of four career EPA employees appointed by the Administrator; it sits in panels of three, which decide cases by majority vote. *See* 40 C.F.R. § 1.25(e)(1). The Board cannot hear appeals from permits issued under authorized state RCRA programs. Where the state has partial authorization, the Board can hear appeals from conditions imposed under federal, but not state, authority. See In re Great Lakes Chemical Corp. Main Plant, 5 E.A.D. 395 (EAB 1994).

3. *Executive Order 12898.* Shortly after President Clinton issued Executive Order 12898, an observer derided it as "nothing but fluff." David Schoenbrod, Environmental 'Injustice' Is About Politics, Not Racism, Wall St. J., Feb. 23, 1994, at A21. Is that an accurate assessment? What, if anything, does the Executive Order add to the law of environmental justice? Note that the Executive Order does not provide grounds for judicial review. Are administrative appeals an effective mechanism to address environmental justice concerns?

4. *Siting and environmental law.* In what respects do Cole and Farrell think that environmental law failed the people of Waterfront South? Do you agree? Is the environmental justice problem primarily one of the cumulative impacts of multiple decisions, rather than the impacts of each individual decision? Does environmental law provide tools intended to incorporate such cumulative impacts into decisions? Why might those tools not work effectively? Note that in this case a state agency controlled the siting decision, rather than local authorities. What problems does that pose for local communities? Are there any circumstances in which it is legitimate to give local or even national authorities control over LULU siting decisions?

5. *Environmental justice considerations in RCRA permitting decisions.* In *Chemical Waste Management*, precisely what did the Board hold with respect to the consideration of environmental justice in the RCRA permitting process? Can a permit be denied for environmental justice reasons alone? To what extent can or must socioeconomic impacts and equity considerations play a role in the permitting decision? Can EPA consider the aggregate effects of the facility in combination with other existing facilities? For a careful analysis of EPA's authority to include environmental justice considerations in a variety of permit decisions, *see* Richard J. Lazarus & Stephanie Tai, Integrating Environmental Justice into EPA Permitting Authority, 26 Ecology L.Q. 617 (1999).

6. *Siting and racial discrimination.* In 1997, the Atomic Safety and Licensing Board of the Nuclear Regulatory Commission denied a license for a uranium enrichment facility in Louisiana because evidence presented by siting opponents, "the most significant portions of which are largely unrebutted or ineffectively rebutted," raised a reasonable inference "that racial considerations played some part in the site selection process." In the Matter of Louisiana Energy Servs., L.P., LBP–97–8 (Atomic Safety and Licensing Board, May 1, 1997). The Board concluded that the NEPA analysis was defective, and that "a thorough Staff investigation of the site selection process is needed in order to comply with the President's nondiscrimination directive in Executive Order 12898." On appeal, however, the Commission ruled (over a dissent) that the Executive Order provided no basis for mandating additional inquiry beyond "what NEPA has traditionally been interpreted to require." In the Matter of Louisiana Energy Services, L.P. (Claiborne Enrichment Center), 47 N.R.C. 77 (1998). The Commission did agree with the Board, however, that additional NEPA analysis was needed with respect to the effects of the proposed facility on pedestrian traffic in the area, and on local property values. To what extent is NEPA likely to be useful in effectuating the goals of Executive Order 12898? In what ways might the NEPA process exacerbate environmental injustice?

7. *Federal environmental justice legislation?* Is a new federal statute needed or desirable to combat environmental injustice? Or is environmental justice best addressed at the state or local level, or perhaps best addressed using tools other than law? If you would favor a federal statute, what form should it take? Should it be modeled on civil rights laws or environmental laws? What precisely would be the goals of such a law? What provisions should it include? Are procedural mandates sufficient, or is some substantive mandate necessary? Is it possible to frame a substantive mandate applicable to all federal actions that may raise environmental justice concerns?

8. *Climate change and environmental justice.* Global warming is a phenomenon caused largely by wealthy nations and people, who burn vast quantities of fossil fuels per capita to support high-consumption life styles. Its impacts, however, fall most heavily on the poor, who are least able to adapt to higher sea levels, stronger storms, and other changes. Indigenous peoples in Pacific island states and the Arctic are also at high risk. They are beginning to assert claims under international human rights and environmental law, but those claims face substantial barriers.

The highest profile effort so far has been the Inuit petition against the United States in the Inter–American Commission on Human Rights, an investigative arm of the Organization of American States. The petition, available at http://www.earthjustice.org/library/legal_docs/petition-to-the-inter-american-commission-on-human-rights-on-behalf-of-the-inuit-circumpolar-conference.pdf, alleges that global warming is already affecting the health and welfare of the Inuit people in many ways, and that those impacts are projected to become much worse. It blames the U.S., which was the largest greenhouse gas emitter in the world at the time the petition was filed, for refusing to take any steps to control it greenhouse gas emissions. The Inuit assert that intransigence on greenhouse gas emissions violates obligations the U.S. has assumed under a number international treaties and instruments.

The Commission initially rejected the petition without prejudice. It later granted the Inuit an opportunity to provide testimony on the link between global warming an human rights. Since then, it has not acted on, or even formally accepted, the petition. Nonetheless, the Center for International Environmental Law, which together with EarthJustice represents the Inuit, says that the petition "has helped change the tenor of the debate about global warming by introducing a moral and human rights dimension. Whereas the debate was previously limited almost exclusively to economic and environmental impacts, it is now common to hear climate protection and avoidance of its damaging consequences characterized as a human right. Additionally, the extensive media attention given to the petition helped to bring pressure to bear on the U.S. Government, and many legal, academic, and environmental organizations also took note of the petition." CIEL, Human Rights and Environment: Advocacy and Investigations, http://www.ciel.org/Hre/hrecomponent2.html. In 2008, the United Nations Human Rights Council asked the U.N. High Commissioner for Human Rights to prepare an analysis "of the relationship between climate change and human rights." U.N. Human Rights Council Res. 7/23, U.N. Doc. A/HRC/7/78 (Mar. 28, 2008). That study concluded that climate change has direct and indirect implications for the enjoyment of human rights, but

> The physical impacts of global warming cannot easily be classified as human rights violations, not least because climate change-related harm often cannot clearly be attributed to acts or omissions of specific

States. Yet, addressing that harm remains a critical human rights concern and obligation under international law. . . .

Report of the Office of the United Nations High Commissioner for Human Rights on the Relationship Between Climate Change and Human Rights, Jan. 15, 2009, available at http://daccessdds.un.org/doc/UNDOC/GEN/G09/103/44/PDF/G0910344.pdf?OpenElement

For contrasting views of what justice requires of the United States in terms of controlling greenhouse gas emissions, compare Eric A. Posner and Cass R. Sunstein, Climate Change Justice, 96 Georgetown L. J. 1565 (2008) (arguing that "distributive and corrective justice fail to provide strong justifications for imposing special obligations for greenhouse gas reductions on the United States") with Daniel A. Farber, The Case for Climate Compensation: Justice for Climate Change Victims in a Complex World, 2008 Utah L. Rev. 377 (2008) (responding that "the United States has a moral obligation to be accountable for its contribution to the climate change problem").

CHAPTER NINE

SUPERFUND AND HAZARDOUS WASTE LIABILITY

SECTION 1. INTRODUCTION

The Comprehensive Environmental Response, Compensation, and Liability Act (CERCLA), also known as the Superfund law, is the federal law that imposes liability for improper disposal of hazardous materials. CERCLA is conceptually simple, but in practice it has given rise to convoluted, drawn-out proceedings involving scores of parties and hundreds of millions of dollars. This chapter will focus on the extent to which CERCLA expands common-law liability for environmental contamination, and the extent to which it has been an invitation to courts to create a new form of common law filling the gaps and addressing the confusion caused by its incomplete and sometimes contradictory statutory language.

A. FROM POLLUTION CONTROL TO REMEDIATION

Modern federal environmental legislation began in the early 1970s with the passage of the National Environmental Policy Act (NEPA) and the Clean Air and Water Acts. The approach taken during this formative period was prospective—NEPA (discussed in detail in Chapter 5) required that federal agencies explicitly evaluate the environmental impacts before committing to action; and the Clean Air and Clean Water Acts (discussed in detail in Chapters 10 and 11 respectively) set regulatory standards for the level of acceptable pollution, primarily from industrial activities. This regulatory structure endures, and continues to form the core of federal (and state) environmental law.

Prospective regulation, however, cannot prevent all pollution problems. CERCLA addresses the retrospective problems of cleaning up hazardous waste when prospective measures either fail or are adopted too late. Congress had spent several years working on hazardous waste cleanup bills without success when in 1980 two events converged to spur passage of CERCLA: an election that meant the political landscape would soon change drastically, and a "shockwave of publicity" about chemical contamination at Love Canal in Niagara Falls, New York. Marc K. Landy, Marc J. Roberts, and Stephen R. Thomas, The Environmental Protection Agency: Asking the Wrong Questions from Nixon to Clinton 138 (expanded edition 1994).

> From the middle of May to the middle of June of 1980, Love Canal was virtually a daily feature of network newscasts. In addition, it was

featured on the news programs "Today," "The MacNeil–Lehrer Report," "Sixty Minutes," and "Good Morning America." Phil Donahue devoted a full hour of his talk show to the story, busing forty area residents to Chicago for the taping . . ."

Id. at 138–139.

Love Canal was the result of a failed nineteenth-century scheme to divert the flow of the Niagara River before the falls to generate electricity. Before he gave up, William Love dug a canal some sixty feet wide, 10 feet deep, and about half a mile long. Adeline Gordon Levine, Love Canal: Science, Politics, and People 9 (1982). Decades later, the canal became a dumping site for wastes produced by Hooker Chemicals & Plastics Corporation. Hooker (which later became a division of Occidental Petroleum) dramatically increased production at its Niagara Falls plant during World War II to satisfy the demands of the U.S. government and defense contractors. As the company's production grew, so did its need to dispose of chemical wastes. In 1942 the Niagara Power and Development Company, owners of Mr. Love's empty canal, gave Hooker permission to dispose of wastes in the canal. Later, the land was sold to Hooker. In 1953, after filling the canal with more than 21,000 tons of chemical wastes, Hooker covered it with a layer of clay and deeded the land to the Niagara Falls Board of Education for $1. Landy et al., *supra*, at 134. The deed included a disclaimer stating that the Board had been advised that the land was filled with industrial waste and agreed to assume all liability for any resulting harm. Levine, *supra*, at 11. An elementary school was constructed on the site. Over the years, the surrounding area sprouted a neighborhood of modest homes.

Love Canal residents occasionally complained about odors, irritation of the feet of children who played barefoot near the school, and "rocks from the fields [that] would often explode if they were dropped or thrown." Levine, *supra*, at 14. In the mid–1970s, with several years of heavy rains and progressively deteriorating buried drums, the situation worsened dramatically. By the spring of 1978, under pressure from local residents, newspapers, and elected officials, the state of New York formed an Interagency Task Force to decide on a course of remedial action. The Task Force visited Love Canal in April of 1978 and found the following situation.

> * * * [A] rainfall left the area quite muddy. In the southern sector a heavy chemical odor pervaded, and pools of water containing a black, oily substance rested on the surface. Boards were placed across some of these puddles to permit walking in the area. There was very little vegetation. The surface area around the school "was relatively intact except for a number of drums that appeared to be surfacing through the underlying vegetation." In the center was a baseball diamond.

United States v. Hooker Chemicals & Plastics Corp., 850 F.Supp. 993, 1040 (W.D. N.Y. 1994).

On August 2, 1978, the New York State Health Commissioner declared a public health emergency at Love Canal. He ordered the school temporarily closed, directed local government to stop migration of toxic substances at the site, and recommended that pregnant women and young children living closest to the school relocate as soon as possible. In the end, numerous houses immediately adjacent to the canal were destroyed and hundreds of families were relocated and compensated by federal and state governments for their losses.

The Love Canal episode focused attention on the problem of hazardous waste dumps across the nation, and on the lack of effective legal authorities for cleanup and cost recovery. At the federal level, RCRA § 7003 (42 U.S.C. § 6973) gave EPA the authority to seek injunctive relief including the cleanup of hazardous waste that presented "an imminent and substantial endangerment to health," but did not provide government funding for the cleanup of sites where those responsible for the contamination were unavailable or lacked the financial resources to respond. Clean Water Act § 311 (33 U.S.C. § 1321), which became the model for CERCLA, set up a fund for government cleanup with provisions for cost recovery, but applied only to spills of oil and hazardous substances into waterways.

In 1979, the Carter Administration submitted to Congress its proposal for new legislation authorizing federal cleanup of hazardous waste sites, paid for by a revolving fund initially funded by a tax on the chemical industry and replenished by imposing liability on those responsible for the contamination. The legislative process, as it typically does, worked slowly. In late September 1980, the House passed its version of a Superfund bill. The Senate, however, did not act until after the 1980 election, which would shortly bring not only a new President but a very different Congress into office. "Faced with loss of the entire effort," the Senate convened a lame-duck session at which it passed its own hurriedly negotiated compromise bill. Frank P. Grad, A Legislative History of the Comprehensive Environmental Response, Compensation and Liability ("Superfund") Act of 1980, 8 Columbia Journal of Environmental Law 1, 19 (1982). On December 3, 1980, the House agreed to the Senate bill, and on December 11 President Carter signed it. Although "hastily assembled" and "with virtually no legislative history at all," id., CERCLA has persisted with remarkably little change since its adoption. It remains the mainstay of federal law governing hazardous waste cleanup, and it has encouraged states to adopt their own state law versions.

B. OVERVIEW OF CERCLA

CERCLA is far less detailed and prescriptive than most of the federal environmental laws. There are many gaps and ambiguities in the statutory language, leaving courts to develop a body of common law interpreting the statute. That body of law has only recently begun to mature. Although CERCLA is nearly 30 years old, the typical CERCLA case is so complex that it may take decades to work its way through the courts. The courts have tended to construe the law broadly in favor of liability and cleanup, leading to results that sometimes seem unfair to individuals caught with a tenuous relationship to contaminated property. Congress has stepped in to soften liability in some respects for some people, but CERCLA remains a powerful legal weapon reaching a great deal of conduct that was not illegal or considered antisocial when it occurred.

The lack of statutory clarity begins with the law's goals. Unlike most federal environmental statutes, CERCLA does not include a statement of its purposes. The federal courts agree, however, that it has two primary purposes: "prompt cleanup of hazardous waste sites and imposition of all cleanup costs on the responsible party." General Electric Co. v. Litton Indus. Automation Systems, 920 F.2d 1415 (8th Cir. 1990), abrogated on other grounds by Key Tronic Corp. v. United States, 511 U.S. 809 (1994). Although CERCLA is primarily a remedial statute, its harsh liability scheme also provides incentives for those who handle and dispose of hazardous materials to prevent releases to the environment.

Cleanup authority. CERCLA § 104 (42 U.S.C. § 9604) authorizes the federal government to undertake cleanups in response to any release or substantial threat of release of hazardous substances to the environment. The definition of "hazardous substances," CERCLA § 101(14) (42 U.S.C. § 9601(14)), includes substances recognized as hazardous under RCRA, the Clean Water Act, the Clean Air Act, or the Toxic Substances Control Act, as well as substances specifically recognized as hazardous pursuant to CERCLA. It specifically excludes oil and natural gas, but does not exclude oil if it is mixed with other hazardous substances. Tosco Corp. v. Koch Industries Inc., 216 F.3d 886, 892 (10th Cir. 2000).

Cleanups are carried out, to the extent practicable, with the National Contingency Plan (NCP), a blueprint that provides procedures and standards for evaluating hazards, determining what actions are required, and carrying out those actions in a cost-effective manner. CERCLA § 121(a) (42 U.S.C. § 9621(a)); 40 CFR Part 300. The NCP includes a National Priorities List (NPL) of the sites that pose the most serious hazards. Cleanups occur in two stages. *Removal actions* are short-term responses intended to protect human health or the environment from immediate threats. *Remedial actions* are longer-term cleanup steps. Both terms are defined in the statute at §§ 101(23) and 101(24). These two categories should be viewed as a chronological sequence of cleanup activities although the exact boundary between the two concepts is not clear. A removal is a short term or emergency response activity "necessary to prevent, minimize, or mitigate damages to the public health or welfare or to the environment." CERCLA § 101(23). Examples of such actions include providing fences around a site, alternative water supplies, temporary evacuation and housing and the removal of leaking sources of contamination. A "remedial action" contemplates a long term, permanent remedy to neutralize the threat from the site and to protect the public health and the environment. The statute contains an extensive list of examples of "remedies" and these include removing and disposing of contaminated soil, pumping out polluted groundwater, building dikes or other barriers around the site, installing clay covers, and collecting leachate and runoff. These extensive and complex remedial responses usually take many years and millions of dollars to accomplish. EPA may engage in remedial actions only at sites listed on the NPL, but may undertake removal actions anywhere it finds an imminent threat to human health or the environment. Remedial actions which permanently reduce toxicity and mobility of the hazardous substances are preferred over others, such as the disposal of those substances offsite without treatment. CERCLA § 121(b) (42 U.S.C. § 9621(b)). Ultimately, contaminated sites are to be cleaned up to a level which assures protection of human health and the environment. CERCLA § 121(d) (42 U.S.C. § 9621(d)). It must meet the standards of all "applicable or relevant and appropriate requirements" (ARARs) of federal or state law. Id.

Federal response actions are financed by the Hazardous Substance Superfund Trust Fund, a revolving fund originally financed by taxes imposed on the petroleum and chemical industries, and replenished by cost recovery from liable parties. Authority for the taxes expired in 1995, and has not been renewed. The Fund balance fell rapidly, from about $4 billion in 1995 to essentially zero by 2004 because responsible parties cannot be identified for all contaminated sites. Currently, the burden of paying for the cleanup of "orphan" sites (those for which responsible parties cannot be identified or cannot finance the cleanup) falls on general revenues, meaning that it is shared by all federal taxpayers. Appropriations have fallen short of program needs, so that a number of cleanups have been slowed by lack of funds. James E. McCarthy, Superfund Taxes or General Revenues: Future Funding Options for the Superfund Program, CRS Report for Congress 8–9 (2005).

As an alternative to cleaning up at federal expense, if it finds that a contaminated site presents an imminent and substantial endangerment to health or the environment, EPA may order a responsible party to undertake the cleanup, or may seek a court order requiring cleanup. CERCLA § 106 (42 U.S.C. § 9606).

Liability. The liability provision, CERCLA § 107 (42 U.S.C. § 9607), is the heart of CERCLA. It imposes strict liability for cleanup costs on "Potentially Responsible Parties" (PRPs) including owners or operators of contaminated sites, those who arrange for disposal of hazardous substances, and certain transporters. PRPs are liable for: response costs incurred by federal or state government or an Indian tribe that are "not inconsistent" with the NCP; the response costs of other entities "consistent with the NCP;" damages for injury to natural resources; and the costs of health assessments deemed necessary by federal authorities. Liability is joint and several unless a defendant provides a basis for apportionment.

Information and investigation. CERCLA's cleanup and liability provisions are supported by information disclosure requirements and authority to investigate. CERCLA § 103 (42 U.S.C. § 9603) requires immediate notification of the National Response Center upon the release of a reportable quantity (specified by regulations issued under § 102) of a hazardous substance, on pain of civil penalties or criminal sanctions. Where there is reasonable basis to believe that there may be a release or substantial threat of release of hazardous substances, federal authorities may demand access to the site and relevant documents under CERCLA § 104(e) (42 U.S.C. 9604(e)).

SECTION 2.   LIABILITY

The heart of CERCLA is § 107 (42 U.S.C. § 9607), which imposes liability for cleanup costs. CERCLA deliberately expands common law liability in an effort to ensure that contaminated states are cleaned up, and that the parties responsible for contamination bear the costs. As you read the materials that follow, evaluate the wisdom and effectiveness of that approach.

CLASS DISCUSSION PROBLEM: CONTAMINATION IN SPRINGFIELD

Acme, Inc. (Acme) is a high-tech research company which has developed a new type of semi-conductor based on gallium arsenide rather than silicon. TechCo supplies Acme with gallium and arsenic. Acme turns those raw materials into semi-conductors, which it ships back to TechCo for use in TechCo products. TechCo knows that there is some inevitable loss of raw materials in the manufacturing process.

Acme's production process requires large amounts of water, which picks up small amounts of gallium and arsenic. Used water is cycled through a filtering system that removes most of the gallium and arsenic, which are returned to the production process. The remaining water, which generally contains concentrations of arsenic less than the 0.01 mg/l permitted by EPA regulations in drinking water, is stored in a tank on Acme's property for further purification prior to reuse. Occasionally, when purification must be delayed because the equipment is out of commission, the tank becomes too full. For those occasions, Acme has installed an overflow valve which runs from the tank to the storm drain, which leads into a storm sewer system constructed, owned, and maintained by the City of Springfield

Arsenic is a naturally occurring compound found in many soils, but it is toxic in certain concentrations. It is considered a characteristic hazardous waste under RCRA at concentrations above 5 mg/l. It has also been designated as a hazardous pollutant under the Clean Air Act.

Just to the east of Acme's plant is the former site of Slobbo Metal Plating Company. Slobbo, which operated from 1963 until it dissolved in 1995, was a cut-rate chrome plating business which did everything on the cheap. Slobbo's employees, under orders from their managers, regularly dumped barrels of plating solution containing chromium and cyanide (both listed as hazardous substances under a variety of federal laws) in a shallow open pond on the property to dispose of them. When the pond was full, employees occasionally dumped barrels directly into the nearest storm drain.

Slobbo rented its site from Sheila Clayton, a wealthy doctor who lives several hundred miles away. The lease included the following language:

> Lessee will, during the whole of the lease term, keep the premises in a strictly clean and sanitary condition and comply with all applicable laws, ordinances, rules and regulations, and will indemnify Lessor against all actions, suits, damages, and claims by whomsoever made by reason of the nonobservance of this covenant.

When Slobbo went out of business it stopped paying rent to Clayton, who in turn stopped paying property taxes on the parcel. The City of Springfield, foreclosed for non-payment of taxes in 2002. Shortly after foreclosure, the City discovered chemical residue around the pond and began an investigation, which revealed that toxic materials including chromium had leached into the surrounding soil and groundwater. A plume of contamination has spread east from the pond under the next parcel, which was purchased in 1999 by Mr. Clean's Organic Car Wash ("Mr. Clean") from Speculator Properties. Speculator had owned the property since 1955 but never found a good use for it. Mr. Clean advertises that it offers "a guaranteed non-toxic car wash, inside and out, using only 100% organically produced natural compounds." Mr. Clean has never used any toxic chemicals in its operations.

The storm drain and the storm sewer system to which it leads also turned out to be contaminated with chromium and cyanide. Sewer pipes, as any competent city engineer knows, are porous. The soil for several feet around the sewer pipes on the Slobbo and Mr. Clean properties contains significant levels of chromium and traces of arsenic. The soil in this area does not naturally contain arsenic.

The Slobbo property has been placed on the National Priorities List, and EPA and the state environmental agency are cooperating on cleaning it up. Who is liable for the costs of that cleanup, and to what extent?

Excerpts From the Comprehensive Environmental Compensation, Response, and Liability Act

42 U.S.C. §§ 9601–9662.

Sec. 101 Definitions

* * *

(9) The term "facility" means (A) any building, structure, installation, equipment, pipe or pipeline (including any pipe into a sewer or publicly owned treatment works), well, pit, pond, lagoon, impoundment, ditch, landfill, storage container, motor vehicle, rolling stock, or aircraft, or (B) any site or area where a hazardous substance has been deposited, stored, disposed of, or placed, or otherwise come to be located; but does not include any consumer product in consumer use or any vessel.

* * *

(14) The term "hazardous substance" means (A) any substance designated pursuant to section 1321(b)(2)(A) of Title 33, (B) any element, compound, mixture, solution, or substance designated pursuant to section 9602 of this title, (C) any hazardous waste having the characteristics identified under or listed pursuant to section 3001 of the Solid Waste Disposal Act [42 U.S.C.A. § 6921] * * *, (D) any toxic pollutant listed under section 1317(a) of Title 33, (E) any hazardous air pollutant listed under section 112 of the Clean Air Act [42 U.S.C.A. § 7412], and (F) any imminently hazardous chemical substance or mixture with respect to which the Administrator has taken action pursuant to section 2606 of Title 15 [the Toxic Substances Control Act]. The term does not include petroleum, including crude oil or any fraction thereof which is not otherwise specifically listed or designated as a hazardous substance under subparagraphs (A) through (F) of this paragraph, and the term does not include natural gas, natural gas liquids, liquefied natural gas, or synthetic gas usable for fuel (or mixtures of natural gas and such synthetic gas).

* * *

(22) The term "release" means any spilling, leaking, pumping, pouring, emitting, emptying, discharging, injecting, escaping, leaching, dumping, or disposing into the environment (including the abandonment or discarding of barrels, containers, and other closed receptacles containing any hazardous substance or pollutant or contaminant), but excludes (A) any release which results in exposure to persons solely within a workplace, with respect to a claim which such persons may assert against the employer of such persons, (B) emissions from the engine exhaust of a motor vehicle, rolling stock, aircraft, vessel, or pipeline pumping station engine, (C) release of source, byproduct, or special nuclear material from a nuclear incident, as those terms are defined in the Atomic Energy Act of 1954 [42 U.S.C.A. § 2011 et seq.] * * * and (D) the normal application of fertilizer.

(29) The terms "disposal", "hazardous waste", and "treatment" shall have the meaning provided in section 1004 of [RCRA, 42 U.S.C. § 6903].

(32) The terms "liable" or "liability" under this subchapter shall be construed to be the standard of liability which obtains under section 311 of the Federal Water Pollution Control Act [33 U.S.C. § 1321].

Sec. 107 Liability

(a) Covered persons; scope; recoverable costs and damages

Notwithstanding any other provision or rule of law, and subject only to the defenses set forth in subsection (b) of this section—

(1) the owner and operator of a vessel or a facility,

(2) any person who at the time of disposal of any hazardous substance owned or operated any facility at which such hazardous substances were disposed of,

(3) any person who by contract, agreement, or otherwise arranged for disposal or treatment, or arranged with a transporter for transport for disposal or treatment, of hazardous substances owned or possessed by such person, by any other party or entity, at any facility or incineration vessel

owned or operated by another party or entity and containing such hazardous substances, and

(4) any person who accepts or accepted any hazardous substances for transport to disposal or treatment facilities, incineration vessels or sites selected by such person, from which there is a release, or a threatened release which causes the incurrence of response costs, of a hazardous substance, shall be liable for—

(A) all costs of removal or remedial action incurred by the United States Government or a State or an Indian tribe not inconsistent with the national contingency plan;

(B) any other necessary costs of response incurred by any other person consistent with the national contingency plan;

(C) damages for injury to, destruction of, or loss of natural resources, including the reasonable costs of assessing such injury, destruction, or loss resulting from such a release; and

(D) the costs of any health assessment or health effects study carried out under section 9604(i) of this title.

* * *

(b) Defenses

There shall be no liability under subsection (a) of this section for a person otherwise liable who can establish by a preponderance of the evidence that the release or threat of release of a hazardous substance and the damages resulting therefrom were caused solely by—

(1) an act of God;

(2) an act of war;

(3) an act or omission of a third party other than an employee or agent of the defendant, or than one whose act or omission occurs in connection with a contractual relationship, existing directly or indirectly, with the defendant (except where the sole contractual arrangement arises from a published tariff and acceptance for carriage by a common carrier by rail), if the defendant establishes by a preponderance of the evidence that (a) he exercised due care with respect to the hazardous substance concerned, taking into consideration the characteristics of such hazardous substance, in light of all relevant facts and circumstances, and (b) he took precautions against foreseeable acts or omissions of any such third party and the consequences that could foreseeably result from such acts or omissions; or

(4) any combination of the foregoing paragraphs.

A. THE ELEMENTS OF LIABILITY

United States v. Alcan Aluminum Corp.

United States Court of Appeals, Third Circuit, 1992.
964 F.2d 252.

■ GREENBERG, CIRCUIT JUDGE.

This matter is before the court on appeal by Alcan Aluminum Corporation ("Alcan") from a summary judgment entered in favor of the United

States (the "Government") for response costs incurred by the Government in cleaning the Susquehanna River.

* * *

Virtually all of the facts in this case to the extent developed at this point are undisputed. The Butler Tunnel Site (the "Site") is listed on the National Priorities List established by the Environmental Protection Agency ("EPA") under section 105 of CERCLA, 42U.S.C. § 9605. The Site includes a network of approximately five square miles of deep underground mines and related tunnels, caverns, pools and waterways bordering the east bank of the Susquehanna River in Pittston, Pennsylvania. The mine workings at the Site are drained by the Butler Tunnel (the "Tunnel"), a 7500 foot tunnel which feeds directly into the Susquehanna River.

The mines are accessible from the surface by numerous air shafts or boreholes. One borehole (the "Borehole") is located on the premises of Hi–Way Auto Service, an automobile fuel and repair station situated above the Tunnel. The Borehole leads directly into the mine workings at the Site.

In the late 1970s, the owner of Hi–Way Auto Service permitted various liquid waste transport companies, including those owned and controlled by Russell Mahler (the "Mahler Companies"), to deposit oily liquid wastes containing hazardous substances into the Borehole. The Mahler Companies collected the liquid wastes from numerous industrial facilities located in the northeastern United States and, in total, disposed of approximately 2,000,-000 gallons of oily wastes containing hazardous substances through the Borehole. Apparently, it was contemplated that the waste would remain at the Site indefinitely.

Alcan is an Ohio corporation which manufactures aluminum sheet and plate products in Oswego, New York. From 1965 through at least 1989, Alcan's manufacturing process involved the hot-rolling of aluminum ingots. To keep the rolls cool and lubricated during the hot-rolling process, Alcan circulated an emulsion through the rolls, consisting of 95% deionized water and 5% mineral oil. At the end of the hot-rolling process, Alcan removed the used emulsion and replaced it with unused emulsion.

During the rolling process, fragments of the aluminum ingots, which also contained copper, chromium, cadmium, lead and zinc, hazardous substances under CERCLA, broke off into the emulsion. In an effort to remove those fragments, Alcan then filtered the used emulsion prior to disposing of it, but the filtering process was imperfect and hence some fragments remained. According to Alcan, however, the level of these compounds in the post-filtered, used emulsion was "far below the EP toxic or TCLP toxic levels and, indeed, orders of magnitude below ambient or naturally occurring background levels. * * *" The Government does not specifically challenge Alcan's assertion that the used emulsion contained only low levels of these metallic compounds, as it contends that this fact is irrelevant to Alcan's liability under CERCLA.

From mid–1978 to late 1979, Alcan contracted with the Mahler Companies to dispose of at least 2,300,950 gallons of used emulsion from its Oswego, New York, facility. During that period, the Mahler Companies disposed of approximately 32,500–37,500 gallons (or five 6500–7500 gallon loads) of Alcan's liquid waste through the Borehole into the Site.[3]

In September 1985, approximately 100,000 gallons of water contaminated with hazardous substances were released from the Site into the Susquehanna River. It appears that this discharge was composed of the wastes deposited into the Borehole in the late 1970's. Between September 28, 1985, and January 7, 1987, EPA incurred significant response costs due to the release and the threatened release of hazardous substances from the Site. * * *

[EPA sought recovery from a number of potentially responsible parties, including Alcan. By the time of this decision, all except Alcan had settled. The government sought to recover the remainder of its response costs from Alcan.]

CERCLA FRAMEWORK:

In response to widespread concern over the improper disposal of hazardous wastes, Congress enacted CERCLA, a complex piece of legislation designed to force polluters to pay for costs associated with remedying their pollution. As numerous courts have observed, CERCLA is a remedial statute which should be construed liberally to effectuate its goals.

CERCLA, as amended by the Superfund Amendments and Reauthorization Act of 1986, Pub. L. No. 99–499, 100 Stat. 1613 (Oct. 17, 1986), grants broad authority to the executive branch of the federal government to provide for the clean-up of hazardous substance sites. Specifically, section 104 authorizes the President to respond to a release or substantial threat of a release of hazardous substances into the environment by: (1) removing or arranging for the removal of hazardous substances; (2) providing for remedial action relating to such hazardous substances; and (3) taking any other response measure consistent with the National Contingency Plan that the President deems necessary to protect the public health or welfare or the environment. 42 U.S.C. § 9604(a). The President has delegated most of his authority under CERCLA to EPA.

CERCLA's bite lies in its requirement that responsible parties pay for actions undertaken pursuant to section 104. Under section 107, CERCLA liability is imposed where the plaintiff establishes the following four elements:

(1) the defendant falls within one of the four categories of "responsible parties";

(2) the hazardous substances are disposed at a "facility";[8]

---

3. Alcan asserts that it was not aware that Mahler was disposing of the oily waste in this fashion, but the Government does not contend otherwise, and in any event Alcan does not contend that this should affect our result.

8. * * * The parties have agreed that the Site is a "facility" within the meaning of CERCLA.

(3) there is a "release" or threatened release of hazardous substances from the facility into the environment;[9]

(4) the release causes the incurrence of "response costs".

* * *

Finally, and of great significance in this case, CERCLA imposes strict liability on responsible parties. 42 U.S.C. § 9601(32).[11] See New York v. Shore Realty Corp., 759 F.2d 1032, 1042 (2d Cir. 1985) ("Congress intended that responsible parties be held strictly liable, even though an explicit provision for strict liability was not included in the compromise....").

CERCLA CONTAINS NO QUANTITATIVE REQUIREMENT IN ITS DEFINITION OF "HAZARDOUS SUBSTANCE":

Alcan argues that it should not be held liable for response costs incurred by the Government in cleaning the Susquehanna River because the level of hazardous substances in its emulsion was below that which naturally occurs and thus could not have contributed to the environmental injury. It asserts that we must read a threshold concentration requirement into the definition of "hazardous substances" for the term "hazardous" to have any meaning. The United States Chamber of Commerce (the "Chamber") as amicus curiae agrees, observing that "Congress took pains to define 'hazardous substance'.... Congress clearly never intended to abandon altogether the requirement that the substance at issue be hazardous." The Chamber further states that "the uncontested facts show that Alcan's waste contained less of these [hazardous] elements than can be found in clean dirt." For these reasons it too claims that Alcan should not be held liable for any environmental injury to the Susquehanna River.

The Government responds that under a plain reading of the statute, there is no quantitative requirement in the definition of "hazardous substance." Therefore, the Government asserts that Alcan's argument that substances containing below-ambient levels of hazardous substances are not really "hazardous" is properly directed at Congress, not the judiciary.

* * *

Section 9601(14) sets forth CERCLA's definition of "hazardous substance" as:

'hazardous substance' means (A) any substance designated pursuant to section 1321(b)(2)(A) of Title 33, (B) any element, compound, mixture, solution, or substance designated pursuant to section 9602 of this title, (C) any hazardous waste having the characteristics identified under or listed pursuant to section 3001 of the Solid Waste Disposal Act [42 U.S.C.A. § 6921] (but not including any waste the regulation of which under the Solid Waste Disposal Act [42 U.S.C.A. § 6901 et seq.] has

---

9. * * * The parties in this suit have also agreed that a "release" has occurred.

11. That section provides that CERCLA liability "shall be construed to be the standard of liability" under section 311 of the Clean Water Act, 33 U.S.C. § 1321; section 1321 liability is strict.

been suspended by Act of Congress), (D) any toxic pollutant listed under section 1317(a) of Title 33, (E) any hazardous air pollutant listed under section 112 of the Clean Air Act [42 U.S.C.A. § 7412], and (F) any imminently hazardous chemical substance or mixture with respect to which the Administrator has taken action pursuant to section 2606 of Title 15. The term does not include petroleum, including crude oil or any fraction thereof which is not otherwise specifically listed or designated as a hazardous substance under subparagraphs (A) through (F) of this paragraph. . . .

Hence, the statute does not, on its face, impose any quantitative requirement or concentration level on the definition of "hazardous substances." Rather, the substance under consideration must simply fall within one of the designated categories.

Since the statute is plain on its face, we need not resort to legislative history to uncover its meaning. In any event, the legislative history is barren of any remarks directly revealing Congress' intent vis-a-vis a threshold requirement on the definition of hazardous substances. Significantly, however, the available legislative history of CERCLA does indicate that Congress created the statute to force all polluters to pay for their pollution. It is difficult to imagine that Congress intended to impose a quantitative requirement on the definition of hazardous substances and thereby permit a polluter to add to the total pollution but avoid liability because the amount of its own pollution was minimal.

In addition, courts that have addressed this issue have almost uniformly held that CERCLA liability does not depend on the existence of a threshold quantity of a hazardous substance. * * *

It may be that Congress did not intend such an all-encompassing definition of "hazardous substances," but this argument is best directed at Congress itself. If Congress had intended to impose a threshold requirement, it could easily have so indicated. We should not rewrite the statute simply because the definition of one of its terms is broad in scope.[13]

[The court went on to determine that the fragments of metal in Alcan's waste did not have to be present in quantities that require the reporting of a release under CERCLA § 104, nor did they have to exhibit any hazardous characteristic under RCRA to impose liability under CERCLA § 107, since

---

13. EPA's statement that it does not consider a waste to be "hazardous" for purposes of the Resource Conservation and Recovery Act ("RCRA") unless that waste exists in a form "capable of causing substantial harm if mismanaged," 57 Fed. Reg. 1, 12 (January 2, 1992), does not alter our conclusion. * * * RCRA's goals differ from CERCLA's, and we do not construe EPA's comments as indicating that the Agency also imputes a threshold concentration requirement into the definition of hazardous substance under section 101(14) of CERCLA, especially in the face of plain statutory language indicating otherwise.

There is some force to Alcan's argument that this definition of "hazardous substances" is so broad that it encompasses virtually everything and thereby eviscerates the meaning of "hazardous." However, our holding with respect to divisibility of harm as discussed below should assuage Alcan's fear that liability under CERCLA will be as far-reaching as the definition of hazardous substances.

they were listed as hazardous substances under both CERCLA and the Clean Water Act.]

* * *

In Alcan's view, the district court's construction of the statute is at odds with environmental policy because it imposes liability on generators of allegedly "hazardous" substances although the substances pose no real threat to the environment. Alcan's argument, though superficially appealing, is flawed. First, as noted above, the Government responds to "releases" that threaten environmental safety. Thus, it is the release alone that must justify the response costs, not the particular waste generated by one given defendant. Here, there is no question but that a release occurred. Second, the fact that a single generator's waste would not in itself justify a response is irrelevant in the multi-generator context, as this would permit a generator to escape liability where the amount of harm it engendered to the environment was minimal, though it was significant when added to other generators' waste. Accordingly, we find that the district court's construction of the statute furthers important environmental goals.

CAUSATION:

Alcan maintains that, if we decline to construe the determination of "hazardous substance" to encompass a concentration threshold, we must at least require the Government to prove that Alcan's emulsion caused or contributed to the release or the Government's incurrence of response costs. The Government contends * * * that the statute imposes no such causation requirement, but rather requires that the plaintiff in a CERCLA proceeding establish that the release or threatened release caused the incurrence of response costs; it underscores the difficulty CERCLA plaintiffs would face in the multi-generator context if required to trace the cause of the response costs to each responsible party.

The plain meaning of the statute supports the Government's position. As noted above, section 107 imposes liability upon a generator of hazardous substances who contracts with another party to dispose of the hazardous substances at a facility "from which there is a *release, or threatened release which causes the incurrence of response costs.*" 42 U.S.C. § 9607 (emphasis supplied). The statute does not, on its face, require the plaintiff to prove that the generator's hazardous substances themselves caused the release or caused the incurrence of response costs; rather, it requires the plaintiff to prove that the release or threatened release caused the incurrence of response costs, and that the defendant is a generator of hazardous substances at the facility.

The legislative history also supports the Government's position that CERCLA does not require the plaintiff to establish a specific causal relationship between a generator's waste and the release or the plaintiff's incurrence of response costs. It appears that the early House of Representatives' version of CERCLA imposed liability upon those persons who "caused or contributed to the release or threatened release." H.R. 7020, 96th Cong.,

2d Sess. § 3071(a)(D), 126 Cong. Rec. 26,779. However, the version ultimately passed by Congress deleted the causation requirement and instead imposed liability upon a class of responsible persons without regard to whether the person specifically caused or contributed to the release and the resultant response costs. Moreover, Congress added three limited defenses to liability based on causation which are contained in 42 U.S.C. § 9607(b): acts of God, acts of war, and acts or omissions of a contractually unrelated third party when the defendant exercised due care and took appropriate responses. Imputing a specific causation requirement would render these defenses superfluous.

* * *

Further, virtually every court that has considered this question has held that a CERCLA plaintiff need not establish a direct causal connection between the defendant's hazardous substances and the release or the plaintiff's incurrence of response costs. * * *

Despite Alcan's assertion, Amoco Oil Co. v. Borden, Inc., 889 F.2d 664, is not to the contrary. There, the Court of Appeals for the Fifth Circuit held that the plaintiff may not recover response costs unless the release posed a threat to the public or the environment. In the court's view, "the question of whether a release has caused the incurrence of response costs should rest upon a factual inquiry into the circumstances of a case and the relevant factual inquiry should focus on whether the particular hazard justified any response actions." Id. at 670. The court did not hold, as Alcan suggests, that the factual investigation would concern whether the defendant's waste caused the incurrence of response costs. Moreover, the environmental injury at issue in Amoco resulted from one generator's pollution, and the court expressly noted that other courts have concluded that, "in cases involving multiple sources of contamination, a plaintiff need not prove a specific causal link between costs incurred and an individual generator's waste." Id. at 670 n. 8. This distinction is significant for, in the single generator context, if the response costs were justified, the defendant necessarily caused the incurrence of those costs. However, in the multigenerator context, the fact that the response costs were justified would not per force signify that each generator's waste caused the release and the resultant response costs.

Decisions rejecting a causation requirement between the defendant's waste and the release or the incurrence of response costs are well-reasoned, consistent with the plain language of the statute and consistent with the legislative history of CERCLA. Accordingly, we reject Alcan's argument that the Government must prove that Alcan's emulsion deposited in the Borehole caused the release or caused the Government to incur response costs. Rather, the Government must simply prove that the defendant's hazardous substances were deposited at the site from which there was a release and that the release caused the incurrence of response costs.

PETROLEUM EXCLUSION:

Alcan further argues that its emulsion constitutes "petroleum" within the meaning of 42 U.S.C. § 9601 and is thus excluded from CERCLA liability. * * * According to Alcan, EPA has interpreted the petroleum exclusion to extend to "used oil" containing concentrations of hazardous substances at levels equal to or less than that found in virgin oil. Alcan contends that its emulsion is "used oil" with concentration levels of cadmium, chromium, copper, lead and zinc that are lower than the levels of these compounds in virgin oil and therefore falls within the petroleum exclusion. Although this argument has superficial appeal, it cannot withstand close scrutiny.

First, and most importantly, EPA has distinguished between oil that naturally contains low levels of hazardous substances and oil to which hazardous substances have been added through use. Although EPA has extended the petroleum exclusion to the former category of oily substances, it has specifically declined to extend such protection to the latter category. In EPA's words: "EPA does not consider materials such as waste oil to which listed CERCLA substances have been added to be within the petroleum exclusion." 50 Fed. Reg. 13,460 (1985). * * * EPA's interpretation of the petroleum exclusion comports with the relevant legislative history which indicates that the exclusion was intended for oil spills, not for releases of oil which has become infused with hazardous substances through use. See S. Rep. No. 848, 96th Cong., 2d Sess. 30–31 (1980).

Alcan has admitted that the hot-rolling process adds hazardous substances to the emulsion. Thus, it has effectively conceded that its emulsion does not fall within the scope of the petroleum exclusion as construed by EPA.

DIVISIBILITY OF HARM:

The foregoing conclusions that (1) there is no quantitative threshold in the definition of hazardous substances and (2) the plaintiff need not establish a causal connection between a given defendant's waste and the release or the incurrence of response costs would initially appear to lead to unfair imposition of liability. As Alcan asserts, this definition of "hazardous substances" effectively renders everything in the universe hazardous, including, for example, federally approved drinking water. When this definition is read in conjunction with the rule that specific causation is not required, CERCLA seemingly would impose liability on every generator of hazardous waste, although that generator could not, on its own, have caused any environmental harm.

While Alcan's assertion is of considerable strength, the Government's rebuttal is equally forceful. It notes that individual defendants must be held responsible for environmental injury brought about by the actions of multiple defendants, even if no single defendant itself could have produced the harm, for otherwise "each defendant in a multi-defendant case could avoid liability by relying on the low concentrations of hazardous substances in its waste, while the plaintiff is left with the substantial clean-up costs associated with the defendant's accumulated wastes." The Government reasons that this strong public interest in forcing polluters in the multi-generator context to pay outweighs a defendant's interest in avoiding liability even if that defendant has not acted in an environmentally unsound fashion when its actions are viewed without regard to the actions of others.

We find some merit in the arguments advanced by both the Government and Alcan. Accordingly, in our view, the common law principles of joint and several liability provide the only means to achieve the proper balance between Alcan's and the Government's conflicting interests and to infuse fairness into the statutory scheme without distorting its plain meaning or disregarding congressional intent.

CERCLA does not specifically provide for joint and several liability in a case involving multiple defendants. Further, both the House and Senate deleted provisions imposing joint and several liability from their respective versions of the statute before its enactment. However, as the court explained in United States v. Chem–Dyne Corp., 572 F. Supp. 802, 808 (S.D. Ohio 1983), at the conclusion of an exhaustive review of statements made by the legislation's sponsors concerning the deletion of joint and several liability,

> the scope of liability and term joint and several liability were deleted to avoid a mandatory legislative standard applicable in all situations which might produce inequitable results in some cases. The deletion was not intended as a rejection of joint and several liability. Rather, the term was omitted in order to have the scope of liability determined under common law principles, where a court performing a case by case evaluation of the complex factual scenarios associated with multiple-generator waste sites will assess the propriety of applying joint and several liability on an individual basis.

* * * In determining whether the imposition of joint and several liability upon Alcan is proper, so that it may be held liable for the Government's full response costs less what had been recovered from the settling defendants, we turn to the Restatement (Second) of Torts for guidance.

Section 433A of the Restatement provides that, when two or more joint tortfeasors acting independently cause a distinct or single harm for which there is a reasonable basis for division according to the contribution of each, each is subject to liability only for the portion of the harm that the individual tortfeasor has caused. It states,

(1) Damages for harm are to be apportioned among two or more causes where

(a) there are distinct harms, or

(b) there is a reasonable basis for determining the contribution of each cause to a single harm.

(2) Damages for any other harm cannot be apportioned among two or more causes.

* * *

Obviously, of critical importance in this analysis is whether a harm is divisible and reasonably capable of apportionment, or indivisible, thereby subjecting the tortfeasor to potentially far-reaching liability.

Under the Restatement, where a joint tortfeasor seeks to apportion the full amount of a plaintiff's damages according to that tortfeasor's own contribution to the harm, it is the tortfeasor's burden to establish that the damages are capable of such apportionment. As the comments concerning this issue explain, the burden of proving that the harm is capable of apportionment is placed on the tortfeasor to avoid:

> the injustice of allowing a proved wrongdoer who has in fact caused harm to the plaintiff to escape liability merely because the harm which he has inflicted has combined with similar harm inflicted by other wrongdoers, and the nature of the harm itself has made it necessary that evidence be produced before is can be apportioned. In such a case the defendant may justly be required to assume the burden of producing that evidence, or if he is not able to do so, of bearing full responsibility. As between the proved tortfeasor who has clearly caused some harm, and the entirely innocent plaintiff, any hardship due to lack of evidence as to the extent of the harm should fall upon the former.

Comment on Section 433 B subsection (2).

These provisions underscore the intensely factual nature of the "divisibility" issue and thus highlight the district court's error in granting summary judgment for the full claim in favor of EPA without conducting a hearing. For this reason, we will remand this case for the court to determine whether there is a reasonable basis for limiting Alcan's liability based on its personal contribution to the harm to the Susquehanna River.

* * * We observe in this regard that Alcan's burden in attempting to prove the divisibility of harm to the Susquehanna River is substantial, and the analysis will be factually complex as it will require an assessment of the relative toxicity, migratory potential and synergistic capacity of the hazardous waste at issue. But Alcan should be permitted this opportunity to limit or avoid liability. If Alcan succeeds in this endeavor, it should only be liable for that portion of the harm fairly attributable to it.

Alcan maintains that there is no need for a hearing because, not only is the harm divisible, but its relative contribution to the injury to the Susquehanna River is zero. According to Alcan, "[i]t is technically impossible to have a release or threatened release such that a clean-up would be authorized or justified under the National Contingency Plan as a result of the addition of the metal compounds in the Alcan emulsion to the Butler Site. When one adds two materials that have the same concentrations of an element or compound, the net result is the same concentration. It can never result in a higher concentration." Alcan's Reply Brief similarly asserts that "below ambient levels of any substance can never cause or contribute to a release or response costs."

* * * However, we are not the proper forum to consider Alcan's argument as we have no way of determining whether the trace levels of metallic compounds in Alcan's used emulsion became concentrated and thereby posed an environmental threat. Furthermore, there may be other circumstances bearing on this issue of which we are not even aware. Thus, the district court should re-evaluate Alcan's contention in light of the facts developed in the hearing on this issue.[29]

In sum, on remand, the district court must permit Alcan to attempt to prove that the harm is divisible and that the damages are capable of some reasonable apportionment. We note that the Government need not prove that Alcan's emulsion caused the release or the response costs. On the other hand, if Alcan proves that the emulsion did not or could not, when mixed with other hazardous wastes, contribute to the release and the resultant response costs, then Alcan should not be responsible for any response costs. In this sense, our result thus injects causation into the equation but, as we have already pointed out, places the burden of proof on the defendant instead of the plaintiff. We think that this result is consistent with the statutory scheme and yet recognizes that there must be some reason for the imposition of CERCLA liability. Our result seems particularly appropriate in light of the expansive meaning of "hazardous substance." Of course, if Alcan cannot prove that it should not be liable for any response costs or cannot prove that the harm is divisible and that the damages are capable of some reasonable apportionment, it will be liable for the full claim of $473,790.18.

---

29. In this vein, we also reject the Government's argument that a hearing is unnecessary because Alcan has admitted that its emulsion was "commingled" with the other generators' waste: "commingled" waste is not synonymous with "indivisible" harm. We observe that some courts have held that a generator may present evidence that it has paid more than its "fair share" in a contribution proceeding, expressly permitted under 42 U.S.C. § 9613(f)(2). In a sense, the "contribution" inquiry involves an analysis similar to the "divisibility" inquiry, as both focus on what harm the defendant caused. However, we believe that this inquiry, to the extent that it is the same as that discussed in above-noted cases, is best resolved at the initial liability phase and not at the contribution phase since it involves precisely relative degrees of liability. Thus, if the defendant can prove that the harm is divisible and that it only caused some portion of the injury, it should only be held liable for that amount. In our view, the logical consequence of delaying the apportionment determination may well be drastic, for it seems clear that a defendant could easily be strong-armed into settling where other defendants have settled in order to avoid being held liable for the remainder of the response costs. Indeed, in this case the court determined that Alcan, one of 20 defendants, was liable for $473,790.18 in response costs, although the total response costs amounted to $1,302,290.18. Thus, although Alcan comprised only 5% of the defendant pool, it was required by the court to absorb over 36% of the costs. Furthermore, Alcan's share of the liability seems to be disproportionate on a volume basis as well. We also point out that contribution will probably not be available from a settling defendant in an action by the United States. 42 U.S.C. § 9613(f)(2).

We note, of course, that a determination in a given case that harm is indivisible will not negate a defendant's right to seek contribution from other non-settling defendants, as the contribution proceeding is an equitable one in which a court is permitted to allocate response costs based on factors it deems appropriate, whereas the court is not vested with such discretion in the divisibility determination.

NOTES AND QUESTIONS

1. *CERCLA liability.* What are the elements of liability under CERCLA § 107? What are "hazardous substances"? Why doesn't the petroleum exclusion help Alcan? What is a "release" or "threatened release"?

What is the standard of liability? The courts are agreed that CERCLA imposes strict liability. What is the basis for that conclusion? Why might Congress, in the wake of Love Canal, have rejected a negligence standard for liability? Is that a sound policy choice? Why did Congress not explicitly state that it was imposing strict liability?

In what sense is causation an element of a claim for recovery under CERCLA § 107? Because it adopts such a broad approach to causation, CERCLA has been called a "super-strict liability" statute. Team Enterprises v. Western Investment Real Estate Trust, 721 F. Supp. 2d 898, 903 (E.D. Cal. 2010). Must the defendant's actions have caused harm to the environment or human health? Is it unfair to impose liability on defendants like Alcan? If a stricter standard of causation were used, would it be impossible to recover from defendants who should be required to pay? What, if anything, could Alcan have done to avoid liability?

2. *Retroactivity.* When did Alcan dispose of the wastes at issue in this case? Was there anything illegal about Alcan's conduct at the time? Is it improper or undesirable to subsequently impose liability on Alcan? Many sites that have become the subject of CERCLA cost recovery litigation include hazardous substances that were disposed of or released well before CERCLA's enactment in 1980. The courts have held that Congress intended to impose liability for the continuing effects of past disposal, and that such liability is constitutionally permissible because it rationally furthers the legitimate purpose of cleaning up abandoned hazardous waste sites. See, e.g., United States v. Dico, 266 F.3d 864, 880 (8th Cir. 2001); Franklin County Convention Facilities Auth. v. American Premier Underwriters, Inc., 240 F.3d 534, 551 (6th Cir. 2001); United States v. Northeastern Pharmaceutical & Chemical Co., 810 F.2d 726 (8th Cir. 1986).

3. *Joint and several liability.* Frequently many different entities have contributed hazardous substances to a site at which a release occurs. In such cases, how is liability for response costs allocated? The Supreme Court has not directly addressed this issue, but the lower courts have uniformly held that CERCLA § 107 imposes joint and several liability, so that a plaintiff can recover all its costs from any liable party unless that party can show that the harm is divisible. A PRP who is found jointly and severally liable is left with the remedy of seeking contribution from other PRPs. Contribution actions are discussed in more detail in Part D below.

Is joint and several liability justified in the CERCLA context? What difference does it make with respect to "orphan shares," the costs attributable to PRPs who are insolvent, defunct, or cannot be located? With respect to the incentives PRPs have to settle their liability following a government cleanup? With respect to the costs and complexity of litigation to recover cleanup costs? Both PRPs and their insurers remain staunchly opposed to joint and several liability. They argue that eliminating it would reduce the amount of money spent on litigation, leaving more for site cleanup work. Does this seem likely?

Is Alcan liable for all response costs not yet recovered at the Butler Tunnel Site? What must it show to limit its liability? According to the Eighth Circuit,

> The proper standard for determining divisibility * * * is that the defendant show either distinct harms or a reasonable basis for apportioning causation for a single harm. A defendant need not prove that its waste did not, or could not, contribute to any of the harm at a CERCLA site in order to establish divisibility, because it is also possible to prove divisibility of single harms based on volumetric, chronological or other types of evidence. A site may also be divisible if a defendant can establish that it consists of non-contiguous areas of contamination.

United States v. Hercules, Inc., 247 F.3d 706, 719 (8th Cir. 2001).

In practice, few PRPs have been able to meet the burden of proving divisibility. The Supreme Court recently reminded the lower courts that it is possible. In *Burlington Northern v. United States*, 556 U.S. 599 (2009) (excerpted later in this chapter), the Court reversed the Ninth Circuit's determination that damages were not divisible. The Court found that the record provided a reasonable basis for the District Court's conclusion that liability could be divided. *Burlington*, however, was an unusually simple contamination case, in which a single operator, an agricultural chemical formulator, was responsible for contamination of the site by a small number of hazardous compounds. The trial court found that the proportional responsibility of railroads which leased land to the operator could be determined based on the size of the leased area, duration of the lease, and chemicals used on that portion of the site. The Supreme Court ruled that the Ninth Circuit was wrong to demand a more precise accounting, but did not say that the trial court was required to find the harm divisible.

On remand in *Alcan*, the District Court found that Alcan had not shown that the harm was divisible or that damages could reasonably be apportioned. United States v. Alcan Aluminum Corp., 97 F. Supp. 2d 248 (N.D. N.Y. 2000). The evidence showed that Alcan's "emulsion had a mobilizing effect on other hazardous wastes," because it "absorbed the contaminants at the sites and facilitated their transport throughout." Id. at 270.

Note that in the *Alcan* case all other PRPs had settled with the United States. As discussed Part D below, PRPs cannot seek contribution against settling defendants. How should settlements by other defendants affect Alcan's liability? Should Alcan be responsible for all the costs not paid by the settling parties, or should the court try to determine the equitable share that should have been paid by the settlors, and charge Alcan only for the remainder? Would the former choice provide the United States too much leverage against parties that genuinely believe they have no responsibility for a cleanup? Would the latter undermine incentives to settle?

4. *Springfield contamination problem.* In the Class Discussion Problem, is Acme, Inc. liable for the costs of cleaning up the Slobbo Metal Plating and Mr. Clean parcels? Is it jointly and severally liable, or will it be able to provide a basis for dividing the response costs?

5. *Extraterritorial application of CERCLA.* In Arc Ecology v. U.S. Department of the Air Force, 411 F.3d 1092 (9th Cir. 2005), the Ninth Circuit held that the usual presumption against extraterritorial application of U.S. law applied to CERCLA, and precluded a suit by residents of the Philippines seeking to compel the Air Force to perform an assessment and cleanup at two former Air Force bases in the Philippines. The outcome is different, however, when action occurring beyond the U.S. border causes contamination within the U.S. In Pakootas v. Teck Cominco Metals Ltd., 452 F.3d 1066 (9th Cir. 2006), the Ninth Circuit ruled that there was no extraterritoriality problem in the application of CERCLA to require cleanup of slag in the Columbia River within the U.S. even though the initial source of the slag was a smelter in Canada. The court noted that the ongoing leaching of hazardous substances from the slag to the river constituted a continuing release within the terms of CERCLA § 107 entirely within the territory of the United States, making the original geographic source of the slag irrelevant.

6. *A feedback loop between CERCLA and the common law.* CERCLA § 107, despite its strength, does not provide full relief for those affected by environmental contamination. It allows recovery only for the costs of cleaning up, not for reductions in property value, lost profits, personal injury, or other damages. CERCLA suits are therefore frequently combined with state common-law actions. Although in other contexts many observers have found considerable judicial reluctance to expand the doctrine of strict liability, its statutory adoption in CERCLA may be encouraging a trend toward application of strict liability to common-law environmental contamination claims. A recent study finds that since 1980 the number of decisions applying strict liability to such claims has increased dramatically, and that courts often refer to CERCLA, analogous state laws, and the record built in Congress to justify CERCLA's liability standard to justify the imposition of strict liability. Alexandra B. Klass, From Reservoirs to Remediation: The Impact of CERCLA on Common Law Strict Liability Environmental Claims, 39 Wake Forest L. Rev. 903 (2004). Thus CERCLA, enacted to remedy a perceived shortcoming of the common law, may also be pushing the evolution of the common law towards more generous treatment of claims beyond those directly covered by CERCLA.

B.   Who Is Liable?

CERCLA § 107(a) (excerpted in Part A above) lists four categories of "covered persons" (PRPs) who "shall be liable for" hazardous waste site cleanup and response costs. Disputes about how broadly these categories sweep are common.

1. *Current owners and operators.* The first category of PRPs is "[t]he owner and operator of a vessel or a facility ... from which there is a release, or a threatened release." CERCLA § 101(20)(A) defines "owner or operator," but not in a very helpful manner. It simply say that the term means "any person owning or operating" a facility. As interpreted by the courts, this category of PRP includes anyone who is *either* an owner or an operator at the time litigation is commenced.

Holding a property interest in a site does not automatically make one an "owner." According to the Second Circuit, "the typical lessee should not be held liable as an owner." Commander Oil Corp. v. Barlo Equipment Corp., 215 F.3d 321, 329 (2d Cir. 2000). The court reasoned that the justification for imposing strict liability on owners—that they can be assumed to have benefitted from the conduct resulting in a release—does not typically apply to lessees, and that lessees are less likely to protect themselves against liability with a thorough environmental investigation before entering into the lease. It ruled that "owner" liability should only be imposed on lessees who qualify as "de facto owners," such as those who hold a very long lease that reserves essentially no rights to the owner during its term.

Even if a lessee is not liable as an "owner," she may face liability as an "operator." According to the Supreme Court,

> under CERCLA, an operator is simply someone who directs the workings of, manages, or conducts the affairs of a facility. To sharpen the definition for purposes of CERCLA's concern with environmental contamination, an operator must manage, direct, or conduct operations specifically related to pollution, that is, operations having to do with the leakage or disposal of hazardous waste, or decisions about compliance with environmental regulations.

United States v. Bestfoods, 524 U.S. 51, 66 (1998). The circuits are split on whether the authority to control operations related to contamination is sufficient to impose liability or whether that authority must actually be exercised. Compare K.C. 1986 Limited Partnership v. Reade Mfg., 472 F.3d 1009, 1020 (8th Cir. 2007) (operator liability requires both authority to control and exercise of that authority either personally or by directing others) with Nurad, Inc. v. William E. Hooper & Sons Co., 966 F.2d 837 (4th Cir. 1992) (authority to control suffices to impose operator liability). Which is the better rule?

2. *Past owners and operators.* In addition to current owners and operators, CERCLA § 107(a)(2) imposes liability on "any person who *at the time of disposal* of any hazardous substance owned or operated any facility at which such hazardous substances were disposed of" (emphasis added). While this might seem straightforward at first glance, its breadth turns on the statutory meaning of the term "disposal." CERCLA § 101(27) refers to RCRA for the definition of "disposal." RCRA, in turn, states that "disposal" means,

> the discharge, deposit, injection, dumping, spilling, leaking, or placing of any solid waste or hazardous waste into or on any land or water so

that such solid waste or hazardous waste or any constituent thereof may enter the environment. . . .

RCRA § 1004(3), 42 U.S.C. § 6903(3). Note that no release need have occurred during the defendant's ownership or operation, simply "disposal." Whether disposal encompasses the passive migration of wastes in soils or groundwater is discussed in depth below.

3. *Arrangers.* The third category of PRPs includes "any person who by contract, agreement, or otherwise arranged for" disposal, treatment, or transportation for disposal or treatment of hazardous substances they owned or possessed by a third party. CERCLA § 107(a)(3), 42 U.S.C. § 9607(a)(3). Most obviously, this category includes those who generate hazardous waste but do not dispose of it on their own property. In order to establish liability, a plaintiff need only prove that a generator (1) owned or possessed hazardous substances; (2) those substances were sent to the site in question; and (3) similar substances were found at the site. The generator need not have selected the facility, or even have known that the waste was being taken there. O'Neil v. Picillo, 883 F.2d 176, 182 (1st Cir. 1989). Imposing continuing responsibility on generators in this way gives them incentives to actively supervise the disposal of their wastes, and not to save money in the short run by choosing "fly-by-night" transporters or improperly operated disposal sites.

Arranger liability is not limited to those who create hazardous waste, however. It can potentially encompass anyone who comes into contact with hazardous waste and can be said to have some connection with its disposal. We consider in greater detail below the scope of arranger liability.

4. *Transporters.* The final category of PRPs includes "any person who accepts ... hazardous substances for transport to disposal or treatment facilities ... selected by such person ... from which there is a release, or a threatened release which causes the incurrence of response costs ..." CERCLA § 107(a)(4) (42 U.S.C. § 9607(a)(4)). The transporter must have been actively involved in site selection, but need not have made the final decision. The Third Circuit has explained that

> § 107(a)(4) applies if the transporter's advice was a *substantial contributing factor* in the decisions to dispose of the hazardous waste at a particular facility. As we interpret that section, a transporter selects the disposal facility when it *actively and substantially participates in the decision-making process* which ultimately identifies a facility for disposal.

Tippins, Inc. v. USX Corp., 37 F.3d 87 (3d Cir. 1994) (emphasis supplied).

Carson Harbor Village, Ltd. v. Unocal Corporation

United States Court of Appeals, Ninth Circuit, 2001 (en banc).
270 F.3d 863.

■ McKeown, Circuit Judge:

* * *

Carson Harbor owns and operates a mobile home park on seventy acres in the City of Carson, California. From 1977 until 1983, prior to

Carson Harbor's ownership, defendant Carson Harbor Village Mobile Home Park, a general partnership controlled by defendants Braley and Smith (the "Partnership Defendants"), owned the property. They, like Carson Harbor, operated a mobile home park on the property. Beginning over thirty years earlier, however, from 1945 until 1983, Unocal Corporation held a leasehold interest in the property and used it for petroleum production, operating a number of oil wells, pipelines, above-ground storage tanks, and production facilities.

* * *

While attempting to refinance the property in 1993, Carson Harbor discovered hazardous substances on the site. The prospective lender commissioned an environmental assessment, which revealed tar-like and slag materials in the wetlands area of the property. Subsequent investigation revealed that the materials were a waste or by-product of petroleum production and that they had been on the property for several decades prior to its development as a mobile home park.

Much of the tar-like and slag materials was covered with soil and vegetation. A portion of the tar-like material, however, was visible on the surface in an area measuring approximately twenty feet wide by thirty feet long. The slag material appeared to have been deposited on top of the tar-like material and was visible in an area approximately thirty feet by 170 feet. Subsequently, it was determined that the contaminated area covered an area approximately seventy-five feet wide by 170 feet long and extended from one to five feet below the surface. The material and surrounding soils contained elevated levels of petroleum hydrocarbons (measured in "total petroleum hydrocarbons" or "TPH") and lead; and soil samples upgradient of the materials also contained elevated levels of lead. These levels exceeded state reporting limits.

As required by law, Carson Harbor's environmental consultants reported their findings to the appropriate agencies. * * *

The tar-like and slag materials were removed from the property in 1995. * * *

In 1997, Carson Harbor brought suit against the Partnership Defendants * * *.

* * *

Carson Harbor argues that the Partnership Defendants fit within the second PRP category as owners of the property "at the time of disposal" under § 9607(a)(2).

CERCLA defines "disposal" for purposes of § 9607(a) with reference to the definition of "disposal" in RCRA, see 42 U.S.C. § 9601(29), which in turn defines "disposal" as follows:

The term "disposal" means the *discharge, deposit, injection, dumping, spilling, leaking, or placing* of any solid waste or hazardous waste into or on any land or water so that such solid waste or hazardous waste or any constituent thereof may enter the environment or be emitted into the air or discharged into any waters, including ground waters.

42 U.S.C. § 6903(3) (emphasis added). Under this definition, for the Partnership Defendants to be PRPs, there must have been a "discharge, deposit, injection, dumping, spilling, leaking, or placing" of contaminants on the property during their ownership.

* * *

"We begin, as always, with the language of the statute." Duncan, 121 S. Ct. at 2124. * * *

"When a statute includes an explicit definition, [however,] we must follow that definition, even if it varies from that term's ordinary meaning." Stenberg v. Carhart, 530 U.S. 914, 942. Therefore, we return to the definition of "disposal." Under § 6903(3), there is a "disposal" when there has been a

- discharge
- deposit,
- injection,
- dumping,
- spilling,
- leaking, or
- placing

of solid or hazardous wastes on the property. 42 U.S.C. § 6903(3). CERCLA does not define these terms, but we gain some insight into their statutory meaning by examining CERCLA's definition of "release," which includes some of the words used to define "disposal," as well as the word "disposing":

The term "release" means any *spilling, leaking, pumping, pouring, emitting, emptying, discharging, injecting, escaping, leaching, dumping, or disposing* into the environment (including the abandonment or discarding of barrels, containers, and other closed receptacles containing any hazardous substance or pollutant or contaminant)....

42 U.S.C. § 9601(22) (emphasis added).

"We must presume that words used more than once in the same statute have the same meaning." Boise Cascade Corp. v. United States Envtl. Prot. Agency, 942 F.2d 1427, 1432 (9th Cir.1991). Therefore, from these definitions, we can conclude that "release" is broader than "disposal," because the definition of "release" includes "disposing" (also, it includes "passive" terms such as "leaching" and "escaping," which are not included in the definition of "disposal"). But, at the same time, the definitions of "disposal" and "release" have several words in common:

"discharge"/"discharging"; "injection"/"injecting"; "dumping"; "spilling"; and "leaking."

We thus focus on the plain meanings of the terms used to define "disposal." We first note that one can find both "active" and "passive" definitions for nearly all of these terms in any standard dictionary. We therefore reject the absolute binary "active/passive" distinction used by some courts. Indeed, the substantial overlap in terms used to define "disposal" and "release" and the presence of both "active" and "passive" terms in both definitions suggests that something other than an active/passive distinction governs the terms.

Instead of focusing solely on whether the terms are "active" or "passive," we must examine each of the terms in relation to the facts of the case and determine whether the movement of contaminants is, under the plain meaning of the terms, a "disposal." Put otherwise, do any of the terms fit the hazardous substance contamination at issue?

Examining the facts of this case, we hold that the gradual passive migration of contamination through the soil that allegedly took place during the Partnership Defendants' ownership was not a "discharge, deposit, injection, dumping, spilling, leaking, or placing" and, therefore, was not a "disposal" within the meaning of § 9607(a)(2). The contamination on the property included tar-like and slag materials. * * * There was some evidence that the tar-like material moved through the soil and that lead and/or TPH may have moved from that material into the soil. If we try to characterize this passive soil migration in plain English, a number of words come to mind, including gradual "spreading," "migration," "seeping," "oozing," and possibly "leaching." But certainly none of those words fits within the plain and common meaning of "discharge, . . . injection, dumping, . . . or placing." 42 U.S.C. § 6903(3). Although these words generally connote active conduct, even if we were to infuse passive meanings, these words simply do not describe the passive migration that occurred here. Nor can the gradual spread here be characterized as a "deposit," because there was neither a deposit by someone, nor does the term deposit encompass the gradual spread of contaminants.[7] The term "spilling" is likewise inapposite. Nothing spilled out of or over anything. Unlike the spilling of a barrel or the spilling over of a holding pond, movement of the tar-like and slag materials was not a spill.

Of the terms defining "disposal," the only one that might remotely describe the passive soil migration here is "leaking." But under the plain and common meaning of the word, we conclude that there was no "leaking." The circumstances here are not like that of the leaking barrel or underground storage tank envisioned by Congress, or a vessel or some

---

7. The dissent's construction of "deposit" is so broad as to include virtually any contamination. As used in the statute, the term is akin to "putting down," or placement. Nothing in the context of the statute or the term "disposal" suggests that Congress meant to include chemical or geologic processes or passive migration. Indeed, where Congress intended such a meaning, it employed specific terminology, such as "leaching," see 42 U.S.C. § 9601(22).

other container that would connote "leaking." Therefore, there was no "disposal," and the Partnership Defendants are not PRPs. On this basis, we affirm the district court's grant of summary judgment to the Partnership Defendants on the CERCLA claim.

* * *

"CERCLA was enacted to protect and preserve public health and the environment by facilitating the expeditious and efficient cleanup of hazardous waste sites." Pritikin, 254 F.3d at 794–95. But CERCLA also has a secondary purpose—assuring that "responsible" persons pay for the cleanup:

> CERCLA was a response by Congress to the threat to public health and the environment posed by the widespread use and disposal of hazardous substances. Its purpose was (1) to ensure the prompt and effective cleanup of waste disposal sites, and (2) to assure that parties responsible for hazardous substances bore the cost of remedying the conditions they created.

Pinal Creek Group, 118 F.3d at 1300. We construe CERCLA liberally to achieve these goals. At the same time, we have cautioned that we must reject a construction that the statute on its face does not permit, and the legislative history does not support.

Our conclusion that "disposal" does not include passive soil migration but that it may include other passive migration that fits within the plain meaning of the terms used to define "disposal" is consistent with CERCLA's dual purposes. Holding passive owners responsible for migration of contaminants that results from their conduct and for passive migration ensures the prompt and effective cleanup of abandoned storage tanks, which is one of the problems Congress sought to address when enacting CERCLA. Indeed, if "disposal" is interpreted to exclude all passive migration, there would be little incentive for a landowner to examine his property for decaying disposal tanks, prevent them from spilling or leaking, or to clean up contamination once it was found.

Our plain-language interpretation of "disposal" also makes sense within the liability provisions of CERCLA—the sections identifying the parties that are "potentially responsible." * * * CERCLA creates four categories of PRPs: current owners or operators, owners or operators at the time of a disposal, arrangers, and transporters. This categorization makes the best sense only under a plain-meaning interpretation of "disposal;" the extreme positions on either side render the structure awkward. For example, had Congress intended all passive migration to constitute a "disposal," then disposal is nearly always a perpetual process. Hence, every landowner after the first disposal would be liable, and there would be no reason to divide owners and operators into categories of former and current. On the other extreme, had Congress intended "disposal" to include only releases directly caused by affirmative human conduct, then it would make no sense to establish a strict liability scheme assigning responsibility to "any person who at the time of disposal ... owned or operated any facility." 42 U.S.C.

§ 9607(a)(2). Rather, the statute would have a straightforward causation requirement.

Similarly, our interpretation of "disposal" is sensible in light of CERC-LA's twin concepts of "disposal," on one hand, and "release," on the other. * * * CERCLA holds a PRP liable for a disposal that "releases or threatens to release" hazardous substances into the environment. Some courts, examining this structure, note that it would be reasonable to conclude that Congress meant "disposal" and "release" to mean entirely different things—in other words, because "release" clearly requires no affirmative human conduct, "disposal" must be limited to affirmative human actions that make possible a "release."

Working on a blank slate, it might make sense to design a statute with such clear-cut, distinct, and interlocking concepts. Sadly, the words of the statute stand in the way of such an easy explanation. The definition of "disposal," as we have noted, includes the terms "discharge, deposit, injection, dumping, spilling, leaking, or placing." 42 U.S.C. § 6903(3). The definition of "release" includes "spilling, leaking, pumping, pouring, emitting, emptying, discharging, injecting, escaping, leaching, dumping, or disposing." 42 U.S.C. § 9601(22). Even a quick glance reveals two important aspects of these definitions. First, each term encompasses some form of five words: "dump," "spill," "discharge," "injection," and "leaking." Second, "release" even incorporates the term "disposing" itself.

This structure defeats the notion that the two terms are mutually exclusive, or that subtle differences between them mean that "disposal" always requires affirmative human conduct and "release" does not. With five terms in common, the definitions compel the conclusion that there is at least substantial overlap between "disposal" and "release," and the overlap includes some of those terms whose definitions do not necessarily require human conduct, such as "spilling" and "leaking." Thus, we reject the interpretation that the difference in the definitions requires us to put a gloss on "disposal" that would make the terms mutually exclusive.

This analysis suggests that the plain-meaning interpretation of "disposal" makes a good fit with the first part of CERCLA's overall structure—the assignment of presumptive liability to various parties.

* * *

■ B. FLETCHER, CIRCUIT JUDGE, with whom JUDGES PREGERSON and PAEZ, CIRCUIT JUDGES, join, Concurring in Part and Dissenting in Part.

I agree with the majority that CERCLA is not a model of legislative clarity. Inconsistencies and redundancies pervade the statute. As a result, our task in interpreting CERCLA is to search for a construction that produces the fewest inconsistencies and at the same time remains true to the statute's remedial purposes. In holding that passive migration of hazardous waste through soil in this case cannot constitute "disposal" under the Act, the majority misses the mark. If there is a plain meaning in CERCLA's definition of "disposal," it encompasses the sort of passive migration at issue here. * * *

CERCLA defines "disposal" as "the discharge, *deposit*, injection, dumping, spilling, leaking, or placing of any solid waste or hazardous waste into or on any land or water so that such solid waste or hazardous waste or any constituent thereof may enter the environment or be emitted into the air or discharged into any waters, including ground waters." 42 U.S.C. § 6903(3) (emphasis added). Although the majority recognizes that almost all of the terms defining "disposal" have both active and passive meanings, it concludes that these terms "simply do not describe the passive migration that occurred here." In reaching this conclusion, the majority purports to engage in a plain meaning analysis. However, the majority's analysis is nothing more than ipse dixit. Remarkably, nowhere does the majority consider the ordinary, contemporary, common meaning of the terms defining "disposal." Had it done so, the majority would have discovered that a common meaning of "deposit" exactly "fit[s] the hazardous substance contamination at issue" in this case.

The Oxford English Dictionary provides the following as one of the common definitions of the transitive form of the verb "deposit": "Said of the laying down of substances held in solution, and of similar operations wrought by natural agencies; to form as a natural deposit." IV The Oxford English Dictionary (OED) 482 (J.A. Simpson & E.S.C. Weiner, eds., 2d ed.1989). Webster's Dictionary offers a similar definition: "to lay down or let fall or drop by a natural process: foster the accretion or accumulation of as a natural deposit." Webster's Third New International Dictionary of the English Language (Webster's) 605 (Philip Babcock Gove, ed.-in-chief, Unabridged ed. 1993). In addition, both dictionaries state that an intransitive definition of "deposit" is "to be laid down or precipitated, to settle." IV OED 482; see Webster's 605.

The evidence in the record is that the slag and tar-like waste was located within a 17–acre open-flow wetlands area of the plaintiff's property. The evidence also indicates that the slag and tar-like substance had high concentrations of lead and TPH. In addition, there is evidence that water flowing through the wetlands carried lead and TPH and that these hazardous wastes settled in the soil throughout the wetlands. Thus, contrary to the majority's conclusory assertion, the plain meaning of "disposal" that includes "deposit" exactly describes the spread of hazardous waste throughout the wetlands: The wastes were carried by the water flowing through the wetlands and deposited in the surrounding soil.

The plain meaning of "deposit" applies to the soil contamination that occurred in this case. Thus, the Partnership Defendants were owners of the property "at the time of disposal." 42 U.S.C. § 9607(2). As a result, the Partnership Defendants are PRPs and the district court was wrong to grant them summary judgment dismissing Carson Harbor's CERCLA claim as to them.

II.

As we have noted, CERCLA has two central purposes: "to ensure the prompt and effective cleanup of waste disposal sites, and to assure that parties responsible for hazardous substances [bear] the cost of remedying the conditions they created." Pinal Creek Group v. Newmont Mining Corp., 118 F.3d 1298, 1300 (9th Cir. 1997). To effectuate the first purpose, Congress designed CERCLA to broadly define PRPs. To effectuate the second purpose, Congress created affirmative defenses to allow PRPs who bore no responsibility for the hazardous waste to avoid liability. Also in furtherance of the second purpose, Congress provided for the equitable distribution of cleanup costs among PRPs who cannot avail themselves of an affirmative defense. The majority's exclusion of parties such as the Partnership Defendants from the class of PRPs frustrates both of CERC-LA's central purposes.

a.   Prompt and Effective Cleanup

While it holds that the "passive soil migration" at issue in this case does not constitute "disposal," the majority also concludes that "disposal" may include other sorts of passive migration. Specifically, the majority opines that the passive spilling or leaking of hazardous wastes may count as "disposal." The majority notes that counting passive spilling or leaking as "disposal" furthers CERCLA's purpose to encourage prompt and effective cleanup of hazardous wastes. It also notes that were "disposal" read to exclude passive spilling or leaking, there would be little incentive for a landowner to examine her property for hazardous wastes and to clean up any contamination that was discovered. But, of course, counting the passive migration at issue in this case as "disposal" also would encourage prompt cleanup, and excluding it produces the decreased incentives about which the majority frets: The majority's holding would allow a property owner who discovers hazardous waste passively migrating through the soil to escape all CERCLA liability simply by selling the property to another.

The majority's parsimonious reading of "disposal" also leads to plainly nonsensical results. Hazardous waste that is placed directly on or in land and is actively discharging or depositing waste throughout the soil, as is the case here, is likely a more immediate and direct environmental threat than that which is placed into drums or containment pools which may or may not eventually leak. Under the majority's interpretation, however, CERC-LA gives the owner of land on which hazardous waste has previously been directly placed less of an incentive to clean up the waste than it does an owner whose land contains leaking drums. The failure to count the passive migration of contaminants through soil as "disposal" thus frustrates CERCLA's first central purpose.

* * *

b.   Fair Share of Remedial Costs

The majority's refusal to give full effect to the meaning of "deposit" and other terms also frustrates CERCLA's second central purpose: to ensure that the parties responsible for hazardous waste bear their fair share of cleanup costs.

This case presents a perfect illustration. The Partnership Defendants owned the property from 1977 until 1983, when they sold it to Carson Harbor. From 1945 until 1983, Unocal Corporation held a leasehold interest in the property. As the majority notes, Unocal used the property for petroleum production, operating a number of oil wells, pipelines, above-ground storage tanks, and production facilities. The evidence in the record indicates that the slag and tar-like material were placed on the property some time prior to the Partnership Defendant's ownership. Thus both the Partnership Defendants and Carson Harbor owned the property while lead and TPH from the tar and slag discharged into the wetlands. The only significant distinction between Carson Harbor and the Partnership Defendants is that during the latter's ownership, Unocal was actively engaged in petroleum production on the property. Thus, the Partnership Defendants had more reason to suspect the possibility of hazardous waste contamination than did Carson Harbor. But under the majority's interpretation of "disposal," the Partnership Defendants are completely exempt from liability for the cleanup costs incurred by Carson Harbor. This is an absurd result. By contrast, under the interpretation I urge, the Partnership Defendants would be PRPs and so liable for some of the cleanup costs unless they were able to establish an affirmative defense.

* * *

Burlington Northern and Santa Fe Railway Co. v. United States

United States Supreme Court, 2009.
556 U.S. 599.

■ Justice Stevens delivered the opinion of the Court.

* * *

I

In 1960, Brown & Bryant, Inc. (B & B), began operating an agricultural chemical distribution business, purchasing pesticides and other chemical products from suppliers such as Shell Oil Company (Shell). Using its own equipment, B & B applied its products to customers' farms. B & B opened its business on a 3.8 acre parcel of former farmland in Arvin, California, and in 1975, expanded operations onto an adjacent .9 acre parcel of land owned jointly by the Atchison, Topeka & Santa Fe Railway Company, and the Southern Pacific Transportation Company (now known respectively as the Burlington Northern and Santa Fe Railway Company and Union Pacific Railroad Company) (Railroads). Both parcels of the Arvin facility were graded toward a sump and drainage pond located on the southeast corner of the primary parcel. See Appendix, infra. Neither the sump nor the drainage pond was lined until 1979, allowing waste water and chemical runoff from the facility to seep into the ground water below.

During its years of operation, B & B stored and distributed various hazardous chemicals on its property. Among these were the herbicide dinoseb, sold by Dow Chemicals, and the pesticides D–D and Nemagon, both sold by Shell. Dinoseb was stored in 55–gallon drums and 5–gallon containers on a concrete slab outside B & B's warehouse. Nemagon was stored in 30–gallon drums and 5–gallon containers inside the warehouse. Originally, B & B purchased D–D in 55–gallon drums; beginning in the mid–1960's, however, Shell began requiring its distributors to maintain bulk storage facilities for D–D. From that time onward, B & B purchased D–D in bulk.[1]

When B & B purchased D–D, Shell would arrange for delivery by common carrier, f.o.b. destination.[2] When the product arrived, it was transferred from tanker trucks to a bulk storage tank located on B & B's primary parcel. From there, the chemical was transferred to bobtail trucks, nurse tanks, and pull rigs. During each of these transfers leaks and spills could—and often did—occur. Although the common carrier and B & B used buckets to catch spills from hoses and gaskets connecting the tanker trucks to its bulk storage tank, the buckets sometimes overflowed or were knocked over, causing D–D to spill onto the ground during the transfer process.

Aware that spills of D–D were commonplace among its distributors, in the late 1970's Shell took several steps to encourage the safe handling of its products. Shell provided distributors with detailed safety manuals and instituted a voluntary discount program for distributors that made improvements in their bulk handling and safety facilities. Later, Shell revised its program to require distributors to obtain an inspection by a qualified engineer and provide self-certification of compliance with applicable laws and regulations. B & B's Arvin facility was inspected twice, and in 1981, B & B certified to Shell that it had made a number of recommended improvements to its facilities.

Despite these improvements, B & B remained a sloppy operator. Over the course of B & B's 28 years of operation, delivery spills, equipment failures, and the rinsing of tanks and trucks allowed Nemagon, D–D and dinoseb to seep into the soil and upper levels of ground water of the Arvin facility. In 1983, the California Department of Toxic Substances Control (DTSC) began investigating B & B's violation of hazardous waste laws, and the United States Environmental Protection Agency (EPA) soon followed suit, discovering significant contamination of soil and ground water. Of particular concern was a plume of contaminated ground water located under the facility that threatened to leach into an adjacent supply of potential drinking water.

---

1. Because D–D is corrosive, bulk storage of the chemical led to numerous tank failures and spills as the chemical rusted tanks and eroded valves.

2. F.O.B. destination means "the seller must at his own expense and risk transport the goods to [the destination] and there tender delivery of them...." U.C.C. § 2–319(1)(b) (2001). The District Court found that B & B assumed "stewardship" over the D–D as soon as the common carrier entered the Arvin facility.

Although B & B undertook some efforts at remediation, by 1989 it had become insolvent and ceased all operations. That same year, the Arvin facility was added to the National Priority List, and subsequently, DTSC and EPA (Governments) exercised their authority under 42 U.S.C. § 9604 to undertake cleanup efforts at the site. By 1998, the Governments had spent more than $8 million responding to the site contamination; their costs have continued to accrue.

[The governments sought to recover their costs from both the Railroads and Shell. Four years after holding a 6–week bench trial, the District Court] held that both the Railroads and Shell were potentially responsible parties (PRPs) under CERCLA—the Railroads because they were owners of a portion of the facility, and Shell because it had "arranged for" the disposal of hazardous substances through its sale and delivery of D–D, see § 9607(a)(3). [Shell appealed, and the Ninth Circuit affirmed.]

* * *

To determine whether Shell may be held liable as an arranger, we begin with the language of the statute. As relevant here, § 9607(a)(3) applies to an entity that "arrange[s] for disposal . . . of hazardous substances." It is plain from the language of the statute that CERCLA liability would attach under § 9607(a)(3) if an entity were to enter into a transaction for the sole purpose of discarding a used and no longer useful hazardous substance. It is similarly clear that an entity could not be held liable as an arranger merely for selling a new and useful product if the purchaser of that product later, and unbeknownst to the seller, disposed of the product in a way that led to contamination. Less clear is the liability attaching to the many permutations of "arrangements" that fall between these two extremes—cases in which the seller has some knowledge of the buyers' planned disposal or whose motives for the "sale" of a hazardous substance are less than clear. In such cases, courts have concluded that the determination whether an entity is an arranger requires a fact-intensive inquiry that looks beyond the parties' characterization of the transaction as a "disposal" or a "sale" and seeks to discern whether the arrangement was one Congress intended to fall within the scope of CERCLA's strict-liability provisions.

Although we agree that the question whether § 9607(a)(3) liability attaches is fact intensive and case specific, such liability may not extend beyond the limits of the statute itself. Because CERCLA does not specifically define what it means to "arrang[e] for" disposal of a hazardous substance, we give the phrase its ordinary meaning. In common parlance, the word "arrange" implies action directed to a specific purpose. See Merriam–Webster's Collegiate Dictionary 64 (10th ed. 1993) (defining "arrange" as "to make preparations for: plan[;] . . . to bring about an agreement or understanding concerning"). Consequently, under the plain language of the statute, an entity may qualify as an arranger under § 9607(a)(3) when it takes intentional steps to dispose of a hazardous substance.

The Governments do not deny that the statute requires an entity to "arrang[e] for" disposal; however, they interpret that phrase by reference to the statutory term "disposal," which the Act broadly defines as "the discharge, deposit, injection, dumping, spilling, leaking, or placing of any solid waste or hazardous waste into or on any land or water." 42 U.S.C. § 6903(3). The Governments assert that by including unintentional acts such as "spilling" and "leaking" in the definition of disposal, Congress intended to impose liability on entities not only when they directly dispose of waste products but also when they engage in legitimate sales of hazardous substances knowing that some disposal may occur as a collateral consequence of the sale itself. Applying that reading of the statute, the Governments contend that Shell arranged for the disposal of D–D within the meaning of § 9607(a)(3) by shipping D–D to B & B under conditions it knew would result in the spilling of a portion of the hazardous substance by the purchaser or common carrier. Because these spills resulted in wasted D–D, a result Shell anticipated, the Governments insist that Shell was properly found to have arranged for the disposal of D–D.

While it is true that in some instances an entity's knowledge that its product will be leaked, spilled, dumped, or otherwise discarded may provide evidence of the entity's intent to dispose of its hazardous wastes, knowledge alone is insufficient to prove that an entity "planned for" the disposal, particularly when the disposal occurs as a peripheral result of the legitimate sale of an unused, useful product. In order to qualify as an arranger, Shell must have entered into the sale of D–D with the intention that at least a portion of the product be disposed of during the transfer process by one or more of the methods described in § 6903(3). Here, the facts found by the District Court do not support such a conclusion.

Although the evidence adduced at trial showed that Shell was aware that minor, accidental spills occurred during the transfer of D–D from the common carrier to B & B's bulk storage tanks after the product had arrived at the Arvin facility and had come under B & B's stewardship, the evidence does not support an inference that Shell intended such spills to occur. To the contrary, the evidence revealed that Shell took numerous steps to encourage its distributors to reduce the likelihood of such spills, providing them with detailed safety manuals, requiring them to maintain adequate storage facilities, and providing discounts for those that took safety precautions. Although Shell's efforts were less than wholly successful, given these facts, Shell's mere knowledge that spills and leaks continued to occur is insufficient grounds for concluding that Shell "arranged for" the disposal of D–D within the meaning of § 9607(a)(3). Accordingly, we conclude that Shell was not liable as an arranger for the contamination that occurred at B & B's Arvin facility.

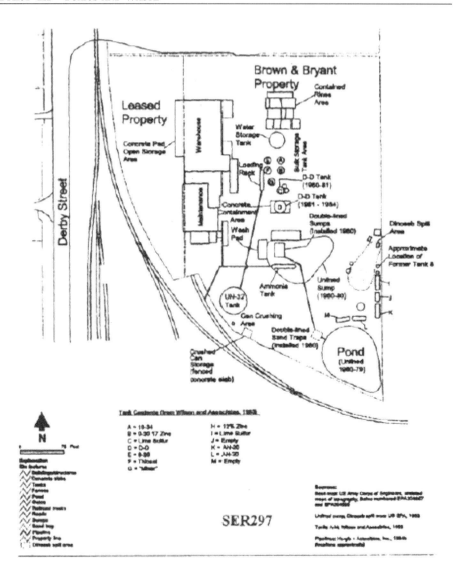

SER297

■ JUSTICE GINSBURG, dissenting.

Although the question is close, I would uphold the determinations of the courts below that Shell qualifies as an arranger within the compass of the Comprehensive Environmental Response, Compensation and Liability Act (CERCLA). See 42 U.S.C. § 9607(a)(3). * * *

In the 1950's and early 1960's, Shell shipped most of its products to Brown and Bryant (B & B) in 55–gallon drums, thereby ensuring against spillage or leakage during delivery and transfer. Later, Shell found it economically advantageous, in lieu of shipping in drums, to require B & B to maintain bulk storage facilities for receipt of the chemicals B & B purchased from Shell. By the mid–1960's, Shell was delivering its chemical to B & B in bulk tank truckloads. As the Court recognizes, "bulk storage of the chemical led to numerous tank failures and spills as the chemical rusted tanks and eroded valves."

Shell furthermore specified the equipment to be used in transferring the chemicals from the delivery truck to B & B's storage tanks.[2] In the process, spills and leaks were inevitable, indeed spills occurred every time deliveries were made.

That Shell sold B & B useful products, the Ninth Circuit observed, did not exonerate Shell from CERCLA liability, for the sales "necessarily and immediately result[ed] in the leakage of hazardous substances." 520 F.3d, at 950. The deliveries, Shell was well aware, directly and routinely resulted in disposals of hazardous substances (through spills and leaks) for more than 20 years. "[M]ere knowledge" may not be enough, but Shell did not simply know of the spills and leaks without contributing to them. Given the control rein held by Shell over the mode of delivery and transfer, the lower courts held and I agree, Shell was properly ranked an arranger. Relieving Shell of any obligation to pay for the cleanup undertaken by the United States and California is hardly commanded by CERCLA's text, and is surely at odds with CERCLA's objective-to place the cost of remediation on persons whose activities contributed to the contamination rather than on the taxpaying public.

NOTES AND QUESTIONS

1. *Past owners and passive migration.* The question of whether migration of hazardous substances through soil or groundwater without active human intervention constitutes "disposal" for purposes of establishing liability under CERCLA § 107 has vexed the courts, as the Ninth Circuit makes clear in *Carson Harbor.* On the facts as recited in that case, should the Partnership Defendants be liable for clean-up costs? What, if anything, could they have done to protect themselves against liability? What could Carson Harbor have done to protect itself? Note that the majority and dissent disagree on whether imposing or not imposing liability would better serve the purposes of liability. Which has the better argument? To what extent should the purpose of imposing costs on polluters be read to imply a second purpose of *not* imposing costs on people other than polluters? If costs cannot be imposed on those who actually caused the contamination, should they be borne by taxpayers or by those with some connection (however tenuous) to the site? If the goals of facilitating cleanup and imposing costs on polluters conflict, which should take priority?

---

2. Shell shipped the chemicals to B & B "F.O.B. Destination." At oral argument, the Court asked Shell's counsel: Suppose there had been "no transfer of ownership until the delivery [was] complete?" In that event, counsel responded, "Shell would have been the owner of the waste." The Court credits the fact that at the time of the spills, the chemicals, having been shipped "F.O.B. Destination," "had come under B & B's stewardship." In my view, CERCLA liability, or the absence thereof, should not turn, in any part, on such an eminently shipper-fixable specification as "F.O.B. Destination."

In *Carson Harbor*, the majority indicates that the presence or absence of direct human agency is not the key to determining what is a "disposal," and therefore which past owners or operators are liable. What is the key? Under what circumstances would the Ninth Circuit be prepared to impose liability on past owners who were not actively involved in disposal? Does that distinction serve the goals of CERCLA? Does it make sense to you, or would you draw a different line?

2. *Arranger liability.* The majority in *Burlington Northern* holds that "an entity may qualify as an arranger under § 9607(a)(3) when it takes intentional steps to dispose of a hazardous substance." Does Justice Ginsburg agree with that formulation, or would she frame it differently? Would the majority ever hold that a supplier of a hazardous substance is an "arranger" under CERCLA? Under what circumstances?

In United States v. Aceto Agricultural Chemicals, 872 F.2d 1373 (8th Cir. 1989) and Jones–Hamilton Co. v. Beazer Materials, 973 F.2d 688 (9th Cir. 1992), pesticide companies had contracted for formulation of their raw ingredients into commercial products for subsequent sale by the pesticide companies. In both cases, the courts ruled that the pesticide companies were potentially responsible as "arrangers" for cleanup of land the formulators had contaminated by spilling and improper disposal of wastes. In *Aceto*, the court noted that the complaint alleged that "the generation of pesticide-containing wastes through spills, cleaning of equipment, mixing and grinding operations, and production of batches which do not meet specifications is an 'inherent' part of the formulation process." 872 F.2d at 1375–76. In *Jones–Hamilton*, the contract with the formulator specifically allowed for up to 2% decrease in volume "by spillage or shrinkage." Are *Aceto* and *Jones–Hamilton* good law after *Burlington Northern*?

In *United States v. Cello–Foil*, 100 F.3d 1227 (6th Cir. 1996), the court held that the buyers of solvents might be liable for contamination caused by the seller's poor disposal practices. Thomas Solvent shipped solvents to customers in reusable 55–gallon drums, for which it charged a deposit. Customers returned the drums in exchange for new, full drums. "The contents of the returned drums varied. Some of the drums had been emptied as much as possible, some had been refilled with water, and some contained unused solvents of up to fifteen gallons." Thomas Solvent dumped the remaining contents on the ground and then rinsed and refilled the drums. The Sixth Circuit concluded that summary judgment should not have been granted for the buyers because the record revealed genuine issues of material fact regarding whether the buyers "returned solvents to Thomas Solvent with the additional purpose of disposal of unused solvents." How should a potential arranger's intent be evaluated? On what basis did the *Burlington Northern* majority decide that Shell lacked the intent to dispose of its products? How would it determine whether Thomas Solvent's customers had the requisite intent?

Did the *Burlington Northern* majority pay enough attention to CERCLA's purposes? Who set the terms of the relationship between Shell and B & B? Is that relevant? What could Shell have done to reduce the risk of spills? Would imposing liability on Shell help prevent future spills? Would it encourage the clean-up of this contaminated site? Would it fairly allocate the costs of that clean-up? Is the law of arranger liability clear enough to allow those who deal with hazardous materials to order their conduct? Is clarity necessarily a good thing in this context? Could it ever be a good thing to encourage "excessive" care in the handling of hazardous materials?

3. *Corporate and individual liability.* CERCLA § 101(21) (42 U.S.C. 9601(21)) defines person very broadly. PRPs can be individuals, any form of business entity, or any form of governmental entity. Many PRPs are corporations, partnerships, joint ventures, and the like. But of course individuals carry out the work of any business, serving as employees, managers, corporate officials and shareholders. Those individuals who meet CERCLA's definitions of owners, operators, arrangers, or transporters can find themselves on the hook in their individual capacity.

Shareholders are not considered "owners" for CERCLA purposes solely on the basis of their ownership of stock, but may be derivatively liable if the requirements for piercing the corporate veil are satisfied. It is unsettled whether the standard for veil-piercing in a CERCLA case is a matter of state or federal law. Browning–Ferris Indus. v. TerMaat, 195 F.3d 953, 959 (7th Cir. 1999); Carter Jones Lumber v. LTV Steel, 237 F.3d 745, 746 n.1 (6th Cir. 2001).

4. *Parent corporations.* In many cases, individual shareholders, officers, directors, or employees will not have sufficient assets to make tempting targets for CERCLA litigation. There may be much more incentive to try to hold a parent corporation liable for the CERCLA sins of its subsidiary. The same standard applies to parent corporations as to individual shareholders, officers, or directors. They may be held directly liable if they have sufficient involvement in and control over activities of the subsidiary connected to hazardous substances. See United States v. Bestfoods, 524 U.S. 51 (1998); United States v. Kayser–Roth Corp., 272 F.3d 89, 102 (1st Cir. 2001). Alternatively, a parent company is derivatively liable if the parent's corporate veil can be pierced. See United States v. Jon–T. Chemicals, Inc., 768 F.2d 686 (5th Cir. 1985).

5. *Successor corporations.* Changes in corporate ownership usually occur: 1) through the sale of stock to another corporation; 2) through a merger or consolidation with another corporation; or 3) through the sale of corporate assets to another corporation. Under general corporate law, in the first situation, stock sale to an acquiring firm, the corporate entity remains intact, retaining all its liabilities. In the second, merger or consolidation of one firm into another, the acquiring firm retains the legal liabilities of the predecessor. Only in the third context, the sale or transfer of corporate assets, is the acquiring firm not responsible for the liabilities of the predecessor.

Lest asset acquisition be used as a stratagem to escape liability, corporate law provides that acquisition of corporate assets carries with it acquisition of liabilities if:

1) the purchaser expressly or impliedly agrees to assume those liabilities;

2) the transaction amounts to a *de facto* merger or consolidation;

3) the purchaser is merely a continuation of the seller; or

4) the transaction is a fraudulent effort to escape liability.

Those concerns may be particularly acute in the CERCLA context. As the Eighth Circuit has pointed out:

> When including corporations within that set of entities which must bear the cost of cleaning up the hazardous conditions they have created, Congress could not have intended that those corporations be enabled to evade their responsibility by dying paper deaths, only to rise phoenix-like from the ashes, transformed, but free of their former liabilities.

United States v. Mexico Feed and Seed Co., 980 F.2d 478 (8th Cir. 1992). As a result, some federal courts have imposed an expanded version of successor liability, the "substantial continuity" test. First developed in the labor relations context, the substantial continuity test applies "in contexts where the public policy vindicated by recovery from the implicated assets is paramount to that supported by the traditional rules delimiting successor liability." Id. at 487. Under this test, liability is imposed upon "a showing that in substance, if not in form, the successor is a responsible party." Id. at 488. The Fourth Circuit has also applied the substantial continuity test to CERCLA cases, see United States v. Carolina Transformer Co., 978 F.2d 832, 837–838 (4th Cir. 1992), but the First, Second, Third, and Ninth Circuits have declined to do so, see United States v. Davis, 261 F.3d 1 (1st Cir. 2001); New York v. National Services Indust., 352 F.3d 682 (2d Cir. 2003); United States v. General Battery Corp., 423 F.3d 294 (3d Cir. 2005); Atchison, Topeka & Santa Fe Railway Co. v. Brown & Bryant, Inc., 159 F.3d 358 (9th Cir. 1997).

6. *Governmental entities.* Units of government are expressly included in the CERCLA's definition of a "person," CERCLA § 101(21) (42 U.S.C. § 9610(21)). At the federal level, CERCLA explicitly waives sovereign immunity. Section 120(a)(1) (42 U.S.C. § 9620(a)(1)) provides,

> Each department, agency, and instrumentality of the United States . . . shall be subject to, and comply with, this act in the same manner, and to the same extent, both procedurally and substantively as any non-governmental entity, including liability under Section 107 of this Act.

The federal government has frequently been a defendant in CERCLA cost-recovery and contribution suits, especially in connection with its operation of military bases and production of hazardous substances under military procurement contracts.

States are also included in CERCLA's definition of "person." In Pennsylvania v. Union Gas Co., 491 U.S. 1 (1989), the Supreme Court ruled that Congress had abrogated state sovereign immunity in CERCLA, and that the Commerce Clause gave it the power to do so. Subsequently, however, the Court overruled *Union Gas*, holding in Seminole Tribe v. Florida, 517 U.S. 44 (1996) that the Commerce Clause does not allow Congress to overcome state sovereign immunity. Following *Seminole Tribe*, states cannot be sued under CERCLA unless they waive their sovereign immunity. States do not waive immunity simply by accepting federal funds under CERCLA, Burnette v. Carothers, 192 F.3d 52, 60 (2d Cir. 1999), but they do waive immunity to counterclaims for contribution when they seek cost recovery. Local governments are not entitled to 11th Amendment immunity but, as the next section shows, they benefit from certain exemptions and defenses.

7. *Interpreting "covered persons".* Overall, how broadly or narrowly should CERCLA's list of responsible parties be construed? What are the benefits of a broad interpretation? What might be its shortcomings?

8. *Springfield contamination redux.* In the Class Discussion Problem at the start of this section, which of the following appears to be liable for cleanup costs, and on what basis: TechCo? Slobbo's employees? Slobbo's managers? Sheila Clayton? Mr. Clean? Speculator Properties? The City of Springfield?

C. DEFENSES AND EXEMPTIONS

The harshness of CERCLA's liability provision is tempered somewhat by a handful of defenses to and exemptions from liability. CERCLA § 107(b) has, from the outset, provided a defense if a release or threat of release is "caused solely by" an act of God, an act of war, or an act or omission of an independent third party. Subsequent amendments have gradually narrowed the universe of PRPs, adding protection for innocent purchasers or landowners, lenders, recyclers, generators of municipal solid waste, owners of contiguous property which becomes contaminated by passive migration, and those who purchase contaminated property to redevelop it.

1. The § 107(b) Defenses. The original statutory defenses, provided in CERCLA § 107(b), are difficult to satisfy but can potentially provide complete protection from liability. Reread § 107(b). It protects any "person otherwise liable" who can establish that a release or threatened release is *"caused solely by"* one or a combination of three sources: acts of war, acts of God, or acts of independent third parties.

a. *Acts of God.* CERCLA § 101(1) (42 U.S.C. § 9601(1)), defines an act of God as "an unanticipated grave natural disaster or other natural phenomena of an exceptional, inevitable, and irresistible character, the effects of which could not have been prevented or avoided by the exercise of due care or oversight." This defense has been narrowly construed. It does not apply where foreseeable natural events such as floods or strong winds trigger a release. What if a lightening bolt hits an industrial plant and sparks a fire that results in the release of hazardous substances? See Wagner Seed Co. v. Daggett, 800 F.2d 310 (2d Cir. 1986).

b. *Acts of war.* CERCLA does not define "act of war." The leading case is United States v. Shell Oil, 294 F.3d 1045 (9th Cir. 2002). Refusing to give the benefit of this defense to an oil company which had produced aviation gas under contract with the government during World War II, and dumped some of the wastes resulting from that process, the court noted that international law, legislative history, leading treatises, and case law from other contexts all supported a narrow construction of the term "acts of war," focused on "the use of force or other action by one state against another." Id. at 1061, citing James R. Fox, Dictionary of International and Comparative Law 6 (1992). Should the "act of war" defense be available to property owners when a release of hazardous substances occurs on their land as the result of an act of international terrorism? What about a riot or other civil disturbance? Should it matter how foreseeable the damage was, or what measures could have been taken to secure the site?

c. *Acts of independent third parties (the "innocent landowner" defense).* Under CERCLA § 107(b)(3), in order to qualify for this defense a PRP must prove:

1) the release was *solely caused* by a third party;

2) the release did not occur in connection with *a contractual relationship*, direct or indirect, between the PRP and the third party; and

3) the PRP exercised *due care* regarding the hazardous substance and took *precautions* against foreseeable conduct of the third party.

"Due care" requires that the PRP take reasonable steps after discovery of the contamination to contain it. See, e.g., Franklin County Convention Facilities Auth. v. American Premier Underwriters, 240 F.3d 534, 548 (6th Cir. 2001).

Because leases and deeds can be considered contracts, this defense did little to reassure those who became property owners or lessees after contamination. In 1986, Congress expanded it to protect some "innocent" landowners. Instead of amending § 107(b) (which might have been the most logical approach), Congress introduced this new defense by adding a definition of "contractual relationship" at § 101(35) (42 U.S.C. § 9601(35)). That section provides that the term includes "land contracts, deeds, easements, leases, or other instruments transferring title or possession," but provides protection for certain parties who acquire property "after the disposal or placement of the hazardous substance." It applies to government entities who acquire property involuntarily or by condemnation; those who acquire by inheritance or bequest; and those who acquire property voluntarily but who "did not know and had no reason to know" of the disposal. In order to establish that they had no reason to know, such "innocent purchasers" must show that they conducted "all appropriate inquiry" before acquiring the property.

The scope of appropriate inquiry depends on the context. Buyers of property once used a mercury mine, for example, can be expected to conduct substantial inquiry into possible contamination. McDonald v. Sun Oil Co., 423 F. Supp. 2d 1114, 1130 (D. Or. 2006). The requirement for all appropriate inquiry encourages prospective buyers to conduct environmental audits. A clean audit can provide the basis for later assertion of the innocent buyer defense against CERCLA liability. One which reveals contamination can lead to negotiation between buyer and seller over the terms of the sale. The buyer might insist, for example, on a price reduction sufficient to cover the costs of cleanup, or on the seller completing cleanup before closing. Maxine I. Lipeles, Environmental Law–Hazardous Waste 501 (3d ed. 1997). Because the innocent landowner defense left considerable uncertainty about the scope of inquiry necessary, in 2002 Congress directed EPA to issue regulations establishing standards and practices for that purpose. CERCLA § 101(35)(B)(ii). Those rules, which were issued in 2005 and became effective in November 2006, are codified at 40 C.F.R. Part 312.

Pre-acquisition environmental investigation can, however, carry its own CERCLA risks. Soil testing typically involves drilling and excavating, which can spread or move contaminating substances. Courts have split over whether testing firms and prospective purchasers who hire them are liable as operators or arrangers. Jennifer Scheller, No Good Deed Goes Unpunished: The CERCLA Liability Exposure Unfortunately Created by Pre–Acquisition Soil Testing, 103 Mich. L. Rev. 1930 (2005).

2. Lender liability. CERCLA's definition of "owner or operator," § 101(20) (42 U.S.C. § 9601(20)), excludes persons "who, without participating in the management of a . . . facility, hold[] indicia of ownership primarily to protect [a] security interest in the . . . facility." This language was initially intended to protect mortgage holders in those states where they nominally hold title to the property from being considered owners on that basis alone. It was not clear, however, what it meant for mortgage holders who foreclosed, or those who had some degree of authority or potential authority over a borrower's activities. In 1990, the Eleventh Circuit created panic in the banking community when it wrote in United States v. Fleet Factors, 901 F.2d 1550, 1557 (11th Cir. 1990):

> [A] secured creditor may incur section 9607(a)(2) liability, without being an operator, by participating in the financial management of a facility to a degree indicating a capacity to influence the corporation's treatment of hazardous waste.

EPA quickly responded with a rule providing that lenders would not become liable simply because they engaged in typical financial oversight practices, but the D.C. Circuit vacated that rule, concluding that CERCLA did not give EPA authority to define the limits of liability in private cost recovery actions. Kelley v. EPA, 15 F.3d 1100 (D.C. Cir. 1994). EPA reissued the rule as a policy statement indicating that it would not seek cost recovery from lenders who met the abortive rule's requirements, but that did not offer protection against private cost recovery actions.

In 1996, Congress stepped in, adding new provisions to § 101(20) to limit lender liability. These detailed provisions essentially codify EPA's short-lived lender liability rule. They protect lenders who actually exercise control only over the financial, rather than the operational, functions of the borrower. Lenders can take advantage of this exemption even if they foreclose, provided that they attempt to resell "at the earliest practicable, commercially reasonable time, on commercially reasonable terms, taking into account market conditions and legal and regulatory requirements." § 101(20)(E)(ii).

The 1996 amendments are not a complete panacea for lenders. They may still face liability if they take over a facility after the borrower has gone out of business in order to sell off valuable inventory, equipment and fixtures.

> Usually, there are barrels or drums of hazardous waste strewn about the facility and the equipment that is being auctioned off may even contain hazardous wastes. To avoid any suggestions that the bank or the auction had any control over hazardous wastes, the auctioneer often will rope off the area where the drums or barrels are found. In some cases, the bidders are actually allowed to cherry-pick barrels containing useful raw materials. After the auction is conducted, the drums and barrels are left in the abandoned facility. At some point, government authorities find out that there are abandoned drums at the facility and order the lender to pay for the removal of the materials. * * *

> However, the definition of "release" under CERCLA includes abandonment of drums. Thus, a lender who has taken control of a facility to conduct an auction and leaves behind drums or equipment containing hazardous wastes could be deemed to have caused a threatened release of hazardous substances.

Larry Schnapf, Congress Amends CERCLA to Expand Lender Liability Protection, Natural Resources and Environment, Spring 1997, at 70–71. In addition, lenders continue to face potential liability under state Superfund laws, other federal environmental laws, and the common law.

Of course, even if they are not potentially liable for response costs, lenders have financial incentives to ensure that they understand the risks of contamination when they make loans. Contaminated land is of little value as security.

> Lenders are therefore requiring environmental assessments before loans are made; they are including environmental compliance and monitoring obligations into loan contracts; and they are themselves policing the contracts. Where they discover contamination on collateral property, they are requiring the borrower to perform a cleanup, or are or themselves carrying out cleanups, in order to contain and correct the damage.

Walter E. Mugdan, Environmental Liability Under Superfund for Lenders and Fiduciaries, ALI–ABA Course of Study Materials, Feb. 11, 1998.

3. The Small Business Liability Relief and Brownfields Revitalization Act exemptions. Small business had long argued that it was unfairly burdened by CERCLA liability. After several years of lobbying by small business interests, in 2002, Congress enacted the Small Business

Liability Relief and Brownfields Revitalization Act, Pub. L. 107–118. The Act introduced four new exemptions from CERCLA liability.

a. *De micromis exemption.* The Act added § 107(*o*), exempting from liability arrangers or transporters responsible for less than 110 gallons of liquid or 200 pounds of solid material disposed of or treated at a facility from which there has been a release or threatened release. This exemption does not apply to owners or operators, and it applies only to disposals prior to April 1, 2001. It does not apply if EPA determines that the material has contributed or could contribute significantly to the costs of response. CERCLA § 107(*o*)(2) (42 U.S.C. § 9607(*o*)(2)). In a government cost recovery action, the PRP would have the burden of proving that it is entitled to this exemption. In a private cost recovery action, however, the plaintiff must prove that the PRP does not qualify. CERCLA § 107(*o*)(4) (42 U.S.C. § 9607(*o*)(4)). If the PRP is entitled to this exemption, the plaintiff is liable for the costs, including reasonable attorney fees, the PRP incurs in defending the action. CERCLA § 107(p)(7) (42 U.S.C. § 9607(p)(7)).

b. *Municipal solid waste exemption.* Under CERCLA § 107(p) (42 U.S.C. § 9607(p)), small businesses, households, and nonprofit organizations cannot be held liable as arrangers by reason of sending municipal solid waste to a facility, unless EPA finds that their waste has contributed or could contribute significantly to response costs. Municipal solid waste is defined for this purpose as ordinary household wastes and similar wastes containing no more hazardous waste than that produced by a typical household. The burden of proof rests with any party seeking recovery for disposal prior to April 1, 2001; for disposal after that date the burden rests with the PRP in government cost-recovery actions and with the plaintiff in private cost-recovery actions. No private contribution action can be brought against individual who contribute household waste to a facility at which a CERCLA response becomes necessary. Like *de micromis* contributors, the contributors of municipal solid waste are entitled to their costs and attorney fees if they prevail in a cost recovery suit. CERCLA § 107(p)(7) (42 U.S.C. § 9607(p)(7)).

c. *Contiguous property owner exemption.* The Act also added CERCLA § 107(q) (42 U.S.C. § 9607(q)), providing that the owners of property that is or may become contaminated by a release or threat of release from property owned by someone else shall not be liable as owners or operators if solely for that reason. In order to claim the benefit of this exemption, the property owner must not cause or contribute to the release, nor may it be affiliated with any PRP through a familial, contractual, corporate or financial relationship other than a contract for the sale of goods or services. The property owner must not have known or had reason to know of the contamination when it purchased its property, it must take reasonable steps to respond to the release, and it must cooperate with government authorities.

d. *Bona fide prospective purchaser.* Finally, the Act provides some protection for bona fide prospective purchasers of contaminated property. Such purchasers are not subject to liability so long as they do not impede a response action. The United States may have a "windfall lien" on the property for unrecovered response costs at the site up to the extent that the response increases the property's fair market value. CERCLA § 107(r) (42 U.S.C. § 9607(r)). In order to qualify as a bona fide prospective purchaser, the person must show that all disposal occurred prior to its acquisition, it conducted all appropriate inquiry, it is not affiliated with any PRP, and it has exercised due care and cooperated with any authorized response. CERCLA § 101(40) (42 U.S.C. § 9601(40)).

NOTES AND QUESTIONS

1. *Innocent landowners.* What is the scope of the "innocent landowner" protection? What is it intended to accomplish? What are the costs and benefits of removing this group from liability? Is the defense too broad, too narrow, or just about right? Does the language of CERCLA currently support the imposition of liability on soil testing firms and prospective purchasers who contract for soil testing? Can EPA protect against such liability in its regulations defining all appropriate inquiry? Is a legislative fix needed?

2. *Lenders.* To what extent are lenders protected against CERCLA liability? What are the costs and benefits of removing lenders from liability? Will the prospect of lender liability affect the likelihood of remediation and reuse of contaminated properties? Does the desirability of lender liability depend upon whether that liability is prospective or retrospective? Would it be unfair to hold lenders liable for future contamination at sites where they provide a loan secured by the property? Might such liability discourage loans to businesses that are likely to cause contamination, such as dry cleaners and plating businesses, or encourage lenders to require that such operations take precautions against contamination? Do lenders already have sufficient incentives to be careful about the environmental impacts of their borrowers?

3. *De micromis contributors.* The *de micromis* exemption was adopted in response to horror stories about small contributors caught in the web of CERCLA liability. Because the costs of CERCLA responses are so high, both those who undertake response actions and the large contributors that are typically the first targets of cost recovery actions have incentives to pursue anyone who might potentially share those costs. Without something like the *de micromis* exemption, any person who arranged for the disposal of any quantum of hazardous material at the site can potentially end up liable for all the costs of response. Although such small contributors may end up saddled with a relatively small proportion of the total costs after costs are allocated among PRPs (a process discussed in the next Part), litigation costs are typically high and the allocation of orphan shares can leave even very small contributors with a high bill.

Reportedly, roughly 80% of the PRPs at a typical contaminated site contribute less than 0.1% each of the total volume of hazardous substances. Lloyd S. Dixon, The Financial Implications of Releasing Small Firms and

Small–Volume Contributors from Superfund Liability 31 (2000), cited in Lance Schumacher, The Small Business Liability Relief and Brownfields Revitalization Act: Are We Any Closer to a Proper Allocation of Superfund Liability for Small Businesses?, 13 S. Cal. Interdisc. L.J. 331, 347 (2004). Many of those small contributors are small businesses. Note that the small contributors are not wholly "innocent;" their waste contributes to response costs. Is it appropriate to shift the proportion of costs for which the small contributors are responsible to larger contributors or the taxpayers? Why? Is it possible that eliminating small contributors from the litigation could save more in transaction costs than the loss in new "orphan shares"? Why does this exemption carry a cutoff date? If it is appropriate for wastes disposed of before 2001, why is it not appropriate for future disposal? Can small waste generators protect themselves against the prospect of future CERCLA liability?

Why is the burden of proof for this exemption placed on private parties trying to recover their costs from a small contributor, but not on the government when it seeks recovery? Why are attorney fees allowed to small contributors who prevail in a private cost recovery action?

4. *Municipal solid waste.* Why is the municipal solid waste exemption necessary? How much protection does it provide households? Who else does it protect?

5. *Contiguous property owners.* How is the exemption for contiguous property owners added in 2002 different than the established innocent landowner defense?

6. *Bona fide prospective purchasers.* What does the 2002 protection for bona fide prospective purchasers add? What purpose is it intended to serve? Why are bona fide prospective purchasers potentially subject to a lien in favor of the United States?

7. *Springfield contamination reconsidered.* Look again at the Springfield Class Discussion Problem. Do any of the parties have a viable defense to liability?

D.   RECOVERY BY LIABLE PARTIES

Much CERCLA litigation is between PRPs as one or more PRPs who have, voluntarily or under government order, undertaken a cleanup then seek to recover some or all of their costs from other PRPs. As initially enacted, CERCLA did not explicitly address claims by one PRP against another. It was not entirely clear whether § 107 allowed such claims, although most of the courts to address the issue ruled that it did. In 1986, Congress added § 113(f) (42 U.S.C. § 9613(f)), excerpted below.

Excerpts From the Comprehensive Environmental Compensation, Recovery, and Liability Act
42 U.S.C. §§ 9601–9662.

Sec. 113(f)   Contribution

(1) Contribution. Any person may seek contribution from any other person who is liable or potentially liable under section 9607(a) of this title,

during or following any civil action under section 9606 of this title or under section 9607(a) of this title. Such claims shall be brought in accordance with this section and the Federal Rules of Civil Procedure, and shall be governed by Federal law. In resolving contribution claims, the court may allocate response costs among liable parties using such equitable factors as the court determines are appropriate. Nothing in this subsection shall diminish the right of any person to bring an action for contribution in the absence of a civil action under section 9606 of this title or section 9607 of this title.

(2) Settlement. A person who has resolved its liability to the United States or a State in an administrative or judicially approved settlement shall not be liable for claims for contribution regarding matters addressed in the settlement. Such settlement does not discharge any of the other potentially liable persons unless its terms so provide, but it reduces the potential liability of the others by the amount of the settlement.

* * *

(3) Persons not party to settlement. * * *

(B) A person who has resolved its liability to the United States or a State for some or all of a response action or for some or all of the costs of such action in an administrative or judicially approved settlement may seek contribution from any person who is not party to a settlement referred to in paragraph (2).

---

1.   THE RELATIONSHIP BETWEEN § 107(a) AND § 113(f)

Cooper Industries, Inc. v. Aviall Services, Inc.

United States Supreme Court, 2004.
543 U.S. 157.

■ Thomas, Justice:

* * *

I

Under CERCLA, the Federal Government may clean up a contaminated area itself, see § 104, or it may compel responsible parties to perform the cleanup, see § 106(a). In either case, the Government may recover its response costs under § 107, 42 U.S.C. § 9607 (2000 ed. and Supp. I), the "cost recovery" section of CERCLA. Section 107(a) lists four classes of potentially responsible persons (PRPs) and provides that they "shall be liable" for, among other things, "all costs of removal or remedial action incurred by the United States Government ... not inconsistent with the national contingency plan." § 107(a)(4)(A). Section 107(a) further provides that PRPs shall be liable for "any other necessary costs of response incurred by any other person consistent with the national contingency plan." § 107(a)(4)(B).

After CERCLA's enactment in 1980, litigation arose over whether § 107, in addition to allowing the Government and certain private parties to recover costs from PRPs, also allowed a PRP that had incurred response costs to recover costs from other PRPs. More specifically, the question was whether a private party that had incurred response costs, but that had done so voluntarily and was not itself subject to suit, had a cause of action for cost recovery against other PRPs. Various courts held that § 107(a)(4)(B) and its predecessors authorized such a cause of action.

After CERCLA's passage, litigation also ensued over the separate question whether a private entity that had been sued in a cost recovery action (by the Government or by another PRP) could obtain contribution from other PRPs. As originally enacted in 1980, CERCLA contained no provision expressly providing for a right of action for contribution. A number of District Courts nonetheless held that, although CERCLA did not mention the word "contribution," such a right arose either impliedly from provisions of the statute, or as a matter of federal common law. That conclusion was debatable in light of two decisions of this Court that refused to recognize implied or common-law rights to contribution in other federal statutes. See Texas Industries, Inc. v. Radcliff Materials, Inc., 451 U.S. 630, 638–647 (1981); Northwest Airlines, Inc. v. Transport Workers, 451 U.S. 77, 90–99 (1981).

Congress subsequently amended CERCLA in the Superfund Amendments and Reauthorization Act of 1986 (SARA), 100 Stat. 1613, to provide an express cause of action for contribution, codified as CERCLA § 113(f)(1):

> "Any person may seek contribution from any other person who is liable or potentially liable under section 9607(a) of this title, during or following any civil action under section 9606 of this title or under section 9607(a) of this title. Such claims shall be brought in accordance with this section and the Federal Rules of Civil Procedure, and shall be governed by Federal law. In resolving contribution claims, the court may allocate response costs among liable parties using such equitable factors as the court determines are appropriate. Nothing in this subsection shall diminish the right of any person to bring an action for contribution in the absence of a civil action under section 9606 of this title or section 9607 of this title."

SARA also created a separate express right of contribution, § 113(f)(3)(B), for "[a] person who has resolved its liability to the United States or a State for some or all of a response action or for some or all of the costs of such action in an administrative or judicially approved settlement." In short, after SARA, CERCLA provided for a right to cost recovery in certain circumstances, § 107(a), and separate rights to contribution in other circumstances, §§ 113(f)(1), 113(f)(3)(B).

II

This case concerns four contaminated aircraft engine maintenance sites in Texas. Cooper Industries, Inc., owned and operated those sites until 1981, when it sold them to Aviall Services, Inc. Aviall operated the four sites for a number of years. Ultimately, Aviall discovered that both it and Cooper had contaminated the facilities when petroleum and other hazardous substances leaked into the ground and ground water through underground storage tanks and spills.

Aviall notified the Texas Natural Resource Conservation Commission (Commission) of the contamination. The Commission informed Aviall that it was violating state environmental laws, directed Aviall to clean up the site, and threatened to pursue an enforcement action if Aviall failed to undertake remediation. Neither the Commission nor the EPA, however, took judicial or administrative measures to compel cleanup.

Aviall cleaned up the properties under the State's supervision, beginning in 1984. Aviall sold the properties to a third party in 1995 and 1996, but remains contractually responsible for the cleanup. Aviall has incurred approximately $5 million in cleanup costs; the total costs may be even greater. In August 1997, Aviall filed this action against Cooper in the United States District Court for the Northern District of Texas, seeking to recover cleanup costs. The original complaint asserted a claim for cost recovery under CERCLA § 107(a), a separate claim for contribution under CERCLA § 113(f)(1), and state-law claims. Aviall later amended the complaint, combining its two CERCLA claims into a single, joint CERCLA claim. That claim alleged that, pursuant to § 113(f)(1), Aviall was entitled to seek contribution from Cooper, as a PRP under § 107(a), for response costs and other liability Aviall incurred in connection with the Texas facilities.[4] * * *

III

Section 113(f)(1) does not authorize Aviall's suit. The first sentence, the enabling clause that establishes the right of contribution, provides: "Any person *may* seek contribution ... *during or following* any civil action under section 9606 of this title or under section 9607(a) of this title," 42 U.S.C. § 9613(f)(1) (emphasis added). The natural meaning of this sentence is that contribution may only be sought subject to the specified conditions, namely, "during or following" a specified civil action.

Aviall answers that "may" should be read permissively, such that "during or following" a civil action is one, but not the exclusive, instance in which a person may seek contribution. We disagree. First, as just noted, the natural meaning of "may" in the context of the enabling clause is that it authorizes certain contribution actions—ones that satisfy the subsequent specified condition—and no others.

---

4. Aviall asserts that it framed its claim in the manner compelled by Fifth Circuit precedent holding that a § 113 claim is a type of § 107 claim.

Second, and relatedly, if § 113(f)(1) were read to authorize contribution actions at any time, regardless of the existence of a § 106 or § 107(a) civil action, then Congress need not have included the explicit "during or following" condition. In other words, Aviall's reading would render part of the statute entirely superfluous, something we are loath to do. Likewise, if § 113(f)(1) authorizes contribution actions at any time, § 113(f)(3)(B), which permits contribution actions after settlement, is equally superfluous. There is no reason why Congress would bother to specify conditions under which a person may bring a contribution claim, and at the same time allow contribution actions absent those conditions.

The last sentence of § 113(f)(1), the saving clause, does not change our conclusion. That sentence provides: "Nothing in this subsection shall diminish the right of any person to bring an action for contribution in the absence of a civil action under section 9606 of this title or section 9607 of this title." 42 U.S.C. § 9613(f)(1). The sole function of the sentence is to clarify that § 113(f)(1) does nothing to "diminish" any cause(s) of action for contribution that may exist independently of § 113(f)(1). In other words, the sentence rebuts any presumption that the express right of contribution provided by the enabling clause is the exclusive cause of action for contribution available to a PRP. The sentence, however, does not itself establish a cause of action; nor does it expand § 113(f)(1) to authorize contribution actions not brought "during or following" a § 106 or § 107(a) civil action; nor does it specify what causes of action for contribution, if any, exist outside § 113(f)(1). Reading the saving clause to authorize § 113(f)(1) contribution actions not just "during or following" a civil action, but also before such an action, would again violate the settled rule that we must, if possible, construe a statute to give every word some operative effect.

Our conclusion follows not simply from § 113(f)(1) itself, but also from the whole of § 113. As noted above, § 113 provides two express avenues for contribution: § 113(f)(1) ("during or following" specified civil actions) and § 113(f)(3)(B) (after an administrative or judicially approved settlement that resolves liability to the United States or a State). Section 113(g)(3) then provides two corresponding 3–year limitations periods for contribution actions, one beginning at the date of judgment, § 113(g)(3)(A), and one beginning at the date of settlement, § 113(g)(3)(B). Notably absent from § 113(g)(3) is any provision for starting the limitations period if a judgment or settlement never occurs, as is the case with a purely voluntary cleanup. The lack of such a provision supports the conclusion that, to assert a contribution claim under § 113(f), a party must satisfy the conditions of either § 113(f)(1) or § 113(f)(3)(B).

Each side insists that the purpose of CERCLA bolsters its reading of § 113(f)(1). Given the clear meaning of the text, there is no need to resolve this dispute or to consult the purpose of CERCLA at all. Section 113(f)(1) authorizes contribution claims only "during or following" a civil action under § 106 or § 107(a), and it is undisputed that Aviall has never been subject to such an action.[5] Aviall therefore has no § 113(f)(1) claim.

B

Aviall and amicus Lockheed Martin contend that, in the alternative to an action for contribution under § 113(f)(1), Aviall may recover costs under § 107(a)(4)(B) even though it is a PRP. The dissent would have us so hold. We decline to address the issue. * * *

"We ordinarily do not decide in the first instance issues not decided below." Adarand Constructors, Inc. v. Mineta, 534 U.S. 103, 109 (2001) (per curiam). Although we have deviated from this rule in exceptional circumstances, United States v. Mendenhall, 446 U.S. 544, 551–552, n. 5 (1980), the circumstances here cut against resolving the § 107 claim. Both the question whether Aviall has waived this claim and the underlying § 107 question (if it is not waived) may depend in part on the relationship between §§ 107 and 113. That relationship is a significant issue in its own right. It is also well beyond the scope of the briefing and, indeed, the question presented, which asks simply whether a private party "may bring an action seeking contribution pursuant to CERCLA Section 113(f)(1)." The § 107 claim and the preliminary waiver question merit full consideration by the courts below.

* * *

* * * Aviall itself recognizes the need for fuller examination of the § 107 claim; it has simply requested that we remand for consideration of that claim, not that we resolve the claim in the first instance.

In addition to leaving open whether Aviall may seek cost recovery under § 107, we decline to decide whether Aviall has an implied right to contribution under § 107. Portions of the Fifth Circuit's opinion below might be taken to endorse the latter cause of action; others appear to reserve the question whether such a cause of action exists. To the extent that Aviall chooses to frame its § 107 claim on remand as an implied right of contribution (as opposed to a right of cost recovery), we * * * note that, in enacting § 113(f)(1), Congress explicitly recognized a particular set (claims "during or following" the specified civil actions) of the contribution rights previously implied by courts from provisions of CERCLA and the common law. Nonetheless, we need not and do not decide today whether any judicially implied right of contribution survived the passage of SARA.

We hold only that § 113(f)(1) does not support Aviall's suit. We therefore reverse the judgment of the Fifth Circuit and remand the case for further proceedings consistent with this opinion.

■ JUSTICE GINSBURG, with whom JUSTICE STEVENS joins, dissenting.

---

5. Neither has Aviall been subject to an administrative order under § 106; thus, we need not decide whether such an order would qualify as a "civil action under section 9606 . . . or under section 9607(a)" of CERCLA. 42 U.S.C. § 9613(f)(1).

* * * In my view, the Court unnecessarily defers decision on Aviall's entitlement to recover cleanup costs from Cooper.

* * *

In its original complaint, Aviall identified § 107 as the federal-law basis for an independent cost-recovery claim against Cooper, and § 113 as the basis for a contribution claim. In amended pleadings, Aviall alleged both §§ 107 and 113 as the federal underpinning for its contribution claim. Aviall's use of §§ 113 and 107 in tandem to assert a contribution claim conformed its pleading to then-governing Fifth Circuit precedent, which held that a CERCLA contribution action arises through the joint operation of §§ 107(a) and 113(f)(1). A party obliged by circuit precedent to plead in a certain way can hardly be deemed to have waived a plea the party could have maintained had the law of the circuit permitted him to do so.

* * *

I see no cause for protracting this litigation by requiring the Fifth Circuit to revisit a determination it has essentially made already: Federal courts, prior to the enactment of § 113(f)(1), had correctly held that PRPs could "recover [under § 107] a proportionate share of their costs in actions for contribution against other PRPs," 312 F.3d, at 687;[2] nothing in § 113 retracts that right, ibid. (noting that § 113(f)'s saving clause preserves all preexisting state and federal rights of action for contribution, including the § 107 implied right this Court recognized in Key Tronic, 511 U.S., at 816). Accordingly, I would not defer a definitive ruling by this Court on the question whether Aviall may pursue a § 107 claim for relief against Cooper.

United States v. Atlantic Research Corp.

United States Supreme Court, 2007.
551 U.S. 128.

■ JUSTICE THOMAS delivered the opinion of the Court.

* * *

I

Courts have frequently grappled with whether and how PRPs may recoup CERCLA-related costs from other PRPs. The questions lie at the intersection of two statutory provisions—CERCLA §§ 107(a) and 113(f). Section 107(a) defines four categories of PRPs, 42 U.S.C. §§ 9607(a)(1)–(4), and makes them liable for, among other things:

---

2. The cases to which the Court refers, Texas Industries, Inc. v. Radcliff Materials, Inc., 451 U.S. 630 (1981), and Northwest Airlines, Inc. v. Transport Workers, 451 U.S. 77 (1981), do not address the implication of a right of action for contribution under CERCLA. Texas Industries concerned the Sherman and Clayton Acts, 451 U.S., at 639–646; Northwest Airlines, the Equal Pay Act of 1963 and Title VII of the Civil Rights Act of 1964, 451 U.S., at 90–99. A determination suitable in one statutory context does not necessarily carry over to a different statutory setting.

(A) all costs of removal or remedial action incurred by the United States Government or a State or an Indian tribe not inconsistent with the national contingency plan; [and]

(B) any other necessary costs of response incurred by any other person consistent with the national contingency plan." § 9607(a)(4)(A)–(B).

Enacted as part of the Superfund Amendments and Reauthorization Act of 1986 (SARA), § 113(f) authorizes one PRP to sue another for contribution in certain circumstances. 42 U.S.C. § 9613(f).[1]

Prior to the advent of § 113(f)'s express contribution right, some courts held that § 107(a)(4)(B) provided a cause of action for a private party to recover voluntarily incurred response costs and to seek contribution after having been sued. After SARA's enactment, however, some Courts of Appeals believed it necessary to "direc[t] traffic between" § 107(a) and § 113(f). As a result, many Courts of Appeals held that § 113(f) was the exclusive remedy for PRPs. But as courts prevented PRPs from suing under § 107(a), they expanded § 113(f) to allow PRPs to seek "contribution" even in the absence of a suit under § 106 or § 107(a).

In *Cooper Industries,* we held that a private party could seek contribution from other liable parties only after having been sued under § 106 or § 107(a). This narrower interpretation of § 113(f) caused several Courts of Appeals to reconsider whether PRPs have rights under § 107(a)(4)(B), an issue we declined to address in *Cooper Industries.* After revisiting the issue, some courts have permitted § 107(a) actions by PRPs. However, at least one court continues to hold that § 113(f) provides the exclusive cause of action available to PRPs. Today, we resolve this issue.

In this case, respondent Atlantic Research leased property at the Shumaker Naval Ammunition Depot, a facility operated by the Department of Defense. At the site, Atlantic Research retrofitted rocket motors for petitioner United States. Using a high-pressure water spray, Atlantic Research removed pieces of propellant from the motors. It then burned the propellant pieces. Some of the resultant wastewater and burned fuel contaminated soil and groundwater at the site.

Atlantic Research cleaned the site at its own expense and then sought to recover some of its costs by suing the United States under both § 107(a) and § 113(f). After our decision in *Cooper Industries* foreclosed relief under § 113(f), Atlantic Research amended its complaint to seek relief under § 107(a) and federal common law. The United States moved to dismiss, arguing that § 107(a) does not allow PRPs (such as Atlantic Research) to recover costs. The District Court granted the motion to dismiss, relying on a case decided prior to our decision in *Cooper Industries.*

The Court of Appeals for the Eighth Circuit reversed. Recognizing that *Cooper Industries* undermined the reasoning of its prior precedent, 459

---

1. Section 113(f)(1) permits private parties to seek contribution during or following a civil action under § 106 or § 107(a). 42 U.S.C. § 9613(f)(1). Section 113(f)(3)(B) permits private parties to seek contribution after they have settled their liability with the Government. § 9613(f)(3)(B).

F.3d, at 830, n. 4, the Court of Appeals joined the Second and Seventh Circuits in holding that § 113(f) does not provide "the exclusive route by which [PRPs] may recover cleanup costs." The court reasoned that § 107(a)(4)(B) authorized suit by any person other than the persons permitted to sue under § 107(a)(4)(A). Accordingly, it held that § 107(a)(4)(B) provides a cause of action to Atlantic Research. To prevent perceived conflict between § 107(a)(4)(B) and § 113(f)(1), the Court of Appeals reasoned that PRPs that "have been subject to §§ 106 or 107 enforcement actions are still required to use § 113, thereby ensuring its continued vitality." We granted certiorari, and now affirm.

II

The parties' dispute centers on what "other person[s]" may sue under § 107(a)(4)(B). The Government argues that "any other person" refers to any person not identified as a PRP in §§ 107(a)(1)–(4). In other words, subparagraph (B) permits suit only by non-PRPs and thus bars Atlantic Research's claim. Atlantic Research counters that subparagraph (B) takes its cue from subparagraph (A), not the earlier paragraph (1)–(4). In accord with the Court of Appeals, Atlantic Research believes that subparagraph (B) provides a cause of action to anyone except the United States, a State, or an Indian tribe—the persons listed in subparagraph (A). We agree with Atlantic Research.

Statutes must "be read as a whole." King v. St. Vincent's Hospital, 502 U.S. 215, 221 (1991). Applying that maxim, the language of subparagraph (B) can be understood only with reference to subparagraph (A). The provisions are adjacent and have remarkably similar structures. Each concerns certain costs that have been incurred by certain entities and that bear a specified relationship to the national contingency plan. Bolstering the structural link, the text also denotes a relationship between the two provisions. By using the phrase "other necessary costs," subparagraph (B) refers to and differentiates the relevant costs from those listed in subparagraph (A).

In light of the relationship between the subparagraph, it is natural to read the phrase "any other person" by referring to the immediately preceding subparagraph (A), which permits suit only by the United States, a State, or an Indian tribe. The phrase "any other person" therefore means any person other than those three. Consequently, the plain language of subparagraph (B) authorizes cost-recovery actions by any private party, including PRPs.

The Government's interpretation makes little textual sense. In subparagraph (B), the phrase "any other necessary costs" and the phrase "any other person" both refer to antecedents—"costs" and "person[s]"—located in some previous statutory provision. Although "any other necessary costs" clearly references the costs in subparagraph (A), the Government would inexplicably interpret "any other person" to refer not to the persons listed in subparagraph (A) but to the persons listed as PRPs in paragraphs (1)–(4). Nothing in the text of § 107(a)(4)(B) suggests an intent to refer to antecedents located in two different statutory provisions. Reading the statute in the manner suggested by the Government would destroy the symmetry of §§ 107(a)(4)(A) and (B) and render subparagraph (B) internally confusing.

Moreover, the statute defines PRPs so broadly as to sweep in virtually all persons likely to incur cleanup costs. Hence, if PRPs do not qualify as "any other person" for purposes of § 107(a)(4)(B), it is unclear what private party would. The Government posits that § 107(a)(4)(B) authorizes relief for "innocent" private parties—for instance, a landowner whose land has been contaminated by another. But even parties not responsible for contamination may fall within the broad definitions of PRPs in §§ 107(a)(1)–(4). The Government's reading of the text logically precludes all PRPs, innocent or not, from recovering cleanup costs. Accordingly, accepting the Government's interpretation would reduce the number of potential plaintiffs to almost zero, rendering § 107(a)(4)(B) a dead letter.[4]

According to the Government, our interpretation suffers from the same infirmity because it causes the phrase "any other person" to duplicate work done by other text. In the Government's view, the phrase "any other necessary costs" "already precludes governmental entities from recovering under" § 107(a)(4)(B). Even assuming the Government is correct, it does not alter our conclusion. The phrase "any other person" performs a significant function simply by clarifying that subparagraph (B) excludes the persons enumerated in subparagraph (A). In any event, our hesitancy to construe statutes to render language superfluous does not require us to avoid surplusage at all costs. It is appropriate to tolerate a degree of surplusage rather than adopt a textually dubious construction that threatens to render the entire provision a nullity.

The Government also argues that our interpretation will create friction between § 107(a) and § 113(f), the very harm courts of appeals have previously tried to avoid. In particular, the Government maintains that our interpretation, by offering PRPs a choice between § 107(a) and § 113(f), effectively allows PRPs to circumvent § 113(f)'s shorter statute of limitations. Furthermore, the Government argues, PRPs will eschew equitable apportionment under § 113(f) in favor of joint and several liability under § 107(a). Finally, the Government contends that our interpretation eviscerates the settlement bar set forth in § 113(f)(2).

We have previously recognized that §§ 107(a) and 113(f) provide two "clearly distinct" remedies. *Cooper Industries,* 543 U.S., at 163, n. 3. "CERCLA provide[s] for a *right to cost recovery* in certain circumstances, § 107(a), and *separate rights to contribution* in other circumstances,

---

4. Congress amended the statute in 2002 to exempt some bona fide prospective purchasers (BFPPs) from liability under § 107(a). The Government claims that these persons are non-PRPs and therefore qualify as "any other person" under its interpretation of § 107(a)(4)(B). Prior to 2002, however, the statute made this small set of persons liable as PRPs. Accordingly, even if BFPPs now give some life to the Government's interpretation of § 107(a)(4)(B), it would be implausible at best to conclude that § 107(a)(4)(B) lay dormant until the enactment of § 107(r)(1) in 2002.

§§ 113(f)(1), 113(f)(3)(B)." *Id.*, at 163 (emphases added). The Government, however, uses the word "contribution" as if it were synonymous with any apportionment of expenses among PRPs. This imprecise usage confuses the complementary yet distinct nature of the rights established in §§ 107(a) and 113(f).

Section 113(f) explicitly grants PRPs a right to contribution. Contribution is defined as the "tortfeasor's right to collect from others responsible for the same tort after the tortfeasor has paid more than his or her proportionate share, the shares being determined as a percentage of fault." Black's Law Dictionary 353 (8th ed. 1999). Nothing in § 113(f) suggests that Congress used the term "contribution" in anything other than this traditional sense. The statute authorizes a PRP to seek contribution "during or following" a suit under § 106 or § 107(a). 42 U.S.C. § 9613(f)(1). Thus, § 113(f)(1) permits suit before or after the establishment of common liability. In either case, a PRP's right to contribution under § 113(f)(1) is contingent upon an inequitable distribution of common liability among liable parties.

By contrast, § 107(a) permits recovery of cleanup costs but does not create a right to contribution. A private party may recover under § 107(a) without any establishment of liability to a third party. Moreover, § 107(a) permits a PRP to recover only the costs it has "incurred" in cleaning up a site. 42 U.S.C. § 9607(a)(4)(B). When a party pays to satisfy a settlement agreement or a court judgment, it does not incur its own costs of response. Rather, it reimburses other parties for costs that those parties incurred.

Accordingly, the remedies available in §§ 107(a) and 113(f) complement each other by providing causes of action "to persons in different procedural circumstances." *Consolidated Edison,* 423 F.3d, at 99. Section 113(f)(1) authorizes a contribution action to PRPs with common liability stemming from an action instituted under § 106 or § 107(a). And § 107(a) permits cost recovery (as distinct from contribution) by a private party that has itself incurred cleanup costs. Hence, a PRP that pays money to satisfy a settlement agreement or a court judgment may pursue § 113(f) contribution. But by reimbursing response costs paid by other parties, the PRP has not incurred its own costs of response and therefore cannot recover under § 107(a). As a result, though eligible to seek contribution under § 113(f)(1), the PRP cannot simultaneously seek to recover the same expenses under § 107(a). Thus, at least in the case of reimbursement, the PRP cannot choose the 6–year statute of limitations for cost-recovery actions over the shorter limitations period for § 113(f) contribution claims.[6]

---

6. We do not suggest that §§ 107(a)(4)(B) and 113(f) have no overlap at all. For instance, we recognize that a PRP may sustain expenses pursuant to a consent decree following a suit under § 106 or § 107(a). In such a case, the PRP does not incur costs voluntarily but does not reimburse the costs of another party. We do not decide whether these compelled costs of response are recoverable under § 113(f), § 107(a), or both. For our purposes, it suffices to demonstrate that costs incurred voluntarily are recoverable only by way of § 107(a)(4)(B), and costs of reimbursement to another person pursuant to a legal judgment or settlement are recoverable only under § 113(f). Thus, at a minimum, neither remedy swallows the other, contrary to the Government's argument.

For similar reasons, a PRP could not avoid § 113(f)'s equitable distribution of reimbursement costs among PRPs by instead choosing to impose joint and several liability on another PRP in an action under § 107(a).[7] The choice of remedies simply does not exist. In any event, a defendant PRP in such a § 107(a) suit could blunt any inequitable distribution of costs by filing a § 113(f) counterclaim. Resolution of a § 113(f) counter-claim would necessitate the equitable apportionment of costs among the liable parties, including the PRP that filed the § 107(a) action. 42 U.S.C. § 9613(f)(a) ("In resolving contribution claims, the court may allocate response costs among liable parties using such equitable factors as the court determines are appropriate").

Finally, permitting PRPs to seek recovery under § 107(a) will not eviscerate the settlement bar set forth in § 113(f)(2). That provision prohibits § 113(f) contribution claims against "[a] person who has resolved its liability to the United States or a State in an administrative or judicially approved settlement...." 42 U.S.C. § 9613(f)(2). The settlement bar does not by its terms protect against cost-recovery liability under § 107(a). For several reasons, we doubt this supposed loophole would discourage settlement. First, as stated above, a defendant PRP may trigger equitable apportionment by filing a § 113(f) counterclaim. A district court applying traditional rules of equity would undoubtedly consider any prior settlement as part of the liability calculus. Cf. Restatement (Second) of Torts § 886A(2), p. 337 (1977) ("No tortfeasor can be required to make contribution beyond his own equitable share of the liability"). Second, the settlement bar continues to provide significant protection from contribution suits by PRPs that have inequitably reimbursed the costs incurred by another party. Third, settlement carries the inherent benefit of finally resolving liability as to the United States or a State.[8]

NOTES AND QUESTIONS

1. *The distinction between § 107(a) and § 113(f).* Does it matter whether PRPs can seek cost recovery under § 107(a) or are instead relegated to § 113(f)? Section 107(a) is more generous to plaintiffs in several respects. First, it has been interpreted to impose joint and several liability on defendants. Second, the statute of limitations for a § 107(a) action extends three years from completion of a removal action or six years from initiation of physical on-site construction for a remedial action. CERCLA § 113(g)(2). The statute of limitations for a contribution action under § 113(f) is three years from the date of judgment in a cost-recovery action or the date of settlement with the United States or a state. CERCLA § 113(g)(3).

2. *The law after* <u>Atlantic Research</u>. Can PRPs get a judgment holding other PRPs jointly and severally liable in a § 107 cost recovery action? Why

---

7. We assume without deciding that § 107(a) provides for joint and several liability.

8. Because § 107(a) expressly permits PRPs to seek cost recovery, we need not address the alternative holding of the Court of Appeals that § 107(a) contains an additional implied right to contribution for PRPs who are not eligible for relief under § 113(f).

did the Court include footnote 7 in its opinion? Is it questioning whether § 107(a) imposes joint and several liability at all, or simply being careful not to decide questions not squarely presented in the case before it? Under what circumstances would a PRP be precluded from using § 107? Can a PRP who has performed a cleanup in response to a government order (the situation considered in footnote 6) choose between § 107(a) and § 113(f)? After *Atlantic Research*, what incentives do property owners have to clean up without awaiting government enforcement? What incentives do PRPs have to settle their liability with the government? Will settling PRPs be protected against subsequent § 107 cost-recovery suits?

3. *Why did the Supreme Court get involved?* Before the Court took up *Aviall*, most observers thought the law of CERCLA litigation by PRPs was reasonably well settled. Many, although not quite all, federal courts held prior to enactment of § 113(f) that § 107(a) provided an implied right of contribution for PRPs. After § 113(f) was added to the statute,

> every federal circuit court to consider the matter construed the newly added Section 113(f)(1) to permit contribution actions by PRPs, even in the absence of a civil action. Understandably, with the enactment of Section 113, the courts also concluded that Congress did not intend to allow liable parties to pursue at the same time what were essentially redundant Section 107 claims, which had been deemed *de facto* contribution claims.

David Ledbetter, Kathy Robb, and Andrew Skroback, *Cooper Industries v. Aviall: The Aftermath*, Andrews Environmental Litigation Reporter, July July 14, 2006, at 5. The Supreme Court upset that balance when it held that contribution actions could only be brought by a PRP who had been the subject of an enforcement or cost-recovery action. Because the lower courts had limited PRPs to § 113(f) contribution actions, that threw into doubt the ability of PRPs who voluntarily cleaned up their property to recover under any CERCLA mechanism. Does § 113 provide any way for such volunteers to gain access to court? *Atlantic Research* has now eased those concerns, by holding explicitly that PRPs who voluntarily clean up can seek cost recovery under § 107, but has opened up new questions about the relationship between §§ 107 and 113, and whether a cost recovery action by a PRP should be treated any differently than one brought by a non-liable party.

Why did the Supreme Court get involved, and should it have done so? One vision of the Supreme Court's role is to resolve splits among the circuit courts. Although the Fifth Circuit itself was not unanimous in its en banc decision allowing a contribution action in *Aviall*, the circuits were not split. Indeed, the Court created a split by failing to resolve in *Aviall* the question of whether PRPs could use § 107(a), making it necessary to later take up *Atlantic Research*. Another view is that the Supreme Court has a role when the lower courts, although united, have wrongly interpreted the law. Had the lower courts incorrectly read CERCLA? To the extent they were wrong, was the misinterpretation problematic for the goals of encouraging cleanup and the imposition of costs on responsible parties?

4. *The unique role of the United States in CERCLA litigation.* The United States plays a unique dual role in CERCLA litigation. It both seeks recovery from PRPs when it has used the Superfund to fund cleanups and is itself a frequent PRP because of its involvement at a large number of hazardous sites. The United States never faces the dilemma of a PRP who cleans up without waiting for a government enforcement action because § 107 unequivocally authorizes it (and states and Indian tribes) to recover its costs without regard to whether it is also a PRP, and under § 106 it can order other PRPs to clean up a site.

The United States urged the Supreme Court to take up the *Aviall* case, arguing that permitting contribution claims in the absence of litigation against or settlement with the government by a PRP would inhibit settlement. It also argued, both in *Aviall* and in *Atlantic Research*, that § 107 cost recovery actions should not be available to PRPs. The contrary conclusion, the government argued in its petition for certiorari in *Aviall*, would permit "errant CERCLA-based contribution suits, subject to no express limitation period, arising out of the many contaminated sites throughout the Nation." Although it argued to the Supreme Court primarily that such suits would unnecessarily burden the federal courts, the U.S. may also have been thinking that it would be a prime target of PRP cost-recovery suits at many of those contaminated sites.

2. ALLOCATING LIABILITY AMONG PRPS

Section 113(f)(1) provides that "in resolving contribution claims, the court may allocate response costs among liable parties using such equitable factors as the court determines are appropriate." Many courts have used six "Gore Factors" in determining how to allocate responsibility among PRPs. The Gore factors include:

> (1) the ability of the parties to demonstrate that their contribution to a discharge, release or disposal of a hazardous waste can be distinguished;
>
> (2) the amount of the hazardous waste involved;
>
> (3) the degree of toxicity of the hazardous waste involved;
>
> (4) the degree of involvement by the parties in the generation, transportation, treatment, storage, or disposal of the hazardous waste;
>
> (5) the degree of care exercised by the parties with respect to the hazardous waste concerned, taking into account the characteristics of such hazardous waste; and
>
> (6) the degree of cooperation by the parties with the Federal, State or local officials to prevent any harm to the public health or environment.

Id. at 354. The Gore factors are "neither an exhaustive nor exclusive list," United States v. Colorado & Eastern Railroad Co., 50 F.3d 1530, 1536 (10th Cir. 1995), but many courts have found them useful. They are derived from an amendment, proposed by (then) Congressman Al Gore of Tennessee, to the bill that became CERCLA. Gore's amendment would have allowed a court either to impose joint and several liability under § 107 or to apportion damages according to the six enumerated factors. The House passed Rep. Gore's amendment, but it ultimately was not included in the final version of CERCLA. Nonetheless, the list of Gore factors has been used as a starting point for the common law of liability allocation by courts dealing with contribution actions.

Action Manufacturing Co., Inc. v. Simon Wrecking Co.

United States District Court, Middle District of Pennsylvania, 2006.
428 F. Supp. 2d 288.

■ ANITA B. BRODY, DISTRICT JUDGE.

This is a contribution action brought under the Comprehensive Environmental Response, Compensation and Liability Act ("CERCLA") 42 U.S.C. § 9601 *et seq.* * * *. The litigation arises from the contamination of the Malvern TCE Superfund Site in Malvern, Pennsylvania. Chemclene Corporation processed and stored industrial solvents and other waste at the Site from approximately 1952 to 1992. By 1983, the Site was on the federal Environmental Protection Agency's ("EPA") National Priorities List. The EPA began considering the Site under the Superfund remedial program in 1993. In 1996, the EPA contacted all parties in the current suit to inform them that they were potentially responsible parties ("PRPs") under § 107(a) of CERCLA.

In 1999, plaintiffs, members of the Chemclene Site Defense Group ("CSDG"), entered a consent decree with the EPA and the Pennsylvania Department of Environmental Protection ("DEP") in which the CSDG promised to undertake the remediation of the Site. CERCLA allows PRPs that settle their liability with the EPA and incur response costs to collect money from other PRPs by bringing suit for contribution of amounts in excess of the plaintiff PRPs' fair share of cleanup costs. *See* CERCLA § 113, 42 U.S.C. § 9613. In 2002, the CSDG brought this contribution suit against seventy-four defendants. Only ["the Simon Entities," including Simon Wrecking Co. and its successors] remained active defendants by the time of trial. All other active parties have been dismissed or have settled with the plaintiffs.

* * *

[From 1974 through 1993, Chemclene received waste solvents at the site, distilled them, and delivered the clean solvents to customers. Some of the waste solvents contained hazardous substances, including trichloroethylene (TCE), trichloroethane (TCA), and methylene chloride. From 1974 to 1980, Simon Wrecking brought drums of waste solvent to Chemclene; some of the drums contained TCE, TCA, and methylene chloride. In at least some cases, Simon Wrecking made the decision to bring waste solvents to the Chemclene site, making it liable as a transporter. Remedial work began in 1997 and was ongoing at the time of trial. Approximately $4.2 million had already been spent on cleanup; the court estimated future costs at about $18.9 million, bringing the total cleanup costs for the site to $23,097,665. The CSDG had collected $6,630,670 in settlements from various PRPs.]

* * *

IV. *Equitable Allocation of Response Costs*

The allocation of response costs in a § 113 contribution case is governed by CERCLA's broad instruction that the court "may allocate response costs among liable parties using such equitable factors as the court determines are appropriate." 42 U.S.C. § 9613(f)(1). * * *

a. *Accounting for Settled Shares of Other PRPs*

All PRPs other than the Simon Entities have resolved their liability at the Site by settling with the EPA or the CSDG, and are thereby protected from further contribution liability to the CSDG. It is necessary to decide whether and how these prior settlements affect the allocation of costs between the CSDG and the Simon Entities. The CSDG urges me to use a *pro tanto* method of allocation, that is, to reduce the total to be allocated between the CSDG and the Simon Entities by the *dollar amount* of the CSDG's settlements with other defendants. The Simon Entities argue that fairness requires a *pro rata* allocation, which would reduce the amount to be allocated by the *proportionate share of fault* attributed to parties that have already settled with the CSDG. For the reasons that follow, the *pro tanto* approach is most appropriate in the present case.

The statute itself is silent on how to account for settlements in private PRP contribution suits, but mandates the *pro tanto* approach in government-initiated actions. When a party settles with the United States or a state, such settlement "does not discharge any of the other potentially liable persons unless its terms so provide, but it reduces the potential liability of the others *by the amount of the settlement." Id.* § 9613(f)(2) (emphasis added). In contrast, no method of allocating settlements is specified for private PRP actions such as the one before me, beyond directing the court to "allocate response costs among liable parties using such equitable factors as the court determines are appropriate." 42 U.S.C. § 9613(f)(1). The use of the *pro tanto* method in accounting for settlements in government-initiated suits demonstrates that it is at least a reasonable manner of allocating CERCLA liability. The broad discretion granted courts in § 113 allocations allows courts to decide whether to use the *pro tanto* approach or another, depending on the equitable considerations.

In general, the *pro tanto* approach, by placing the risk of lenient settlements on PRP hold-outs such as Simon Wrecking, facilitates CERCLA's goal of encouraging early settlement and private remediation. In a *pro rata* regime, PRPs such as the CSDG who assume responsibility for cleanup by signing consent decrees with the EPA will have no flexibility to negotiate in settlements. If they accept anything less from a PRP than what a court later determines to have been that PRP's proportionate share, they will have to pay for the difference out of their own pockets. Further, the defendant PRPs will have no incentive to settle early on, because the early settlements of other PRPs will have no effect on the potential liability of remaining PRPs. In such a regime, it would be more difficult to settle with contribution defendants. As a result, contribution plaintiffs would be forced to litigate against more PRPs, spending non-recoverable attorneys fees. Such a prospect would make it less likely that PRPs would be willing to sign consent decrees with EPA and voluntarily undertake remediation of polluted sites.

In contrast, under a *pro tanto* regime, contribution plaintiffs will have more flexibility in settling with defendant PRPs, because any potential shortfalls of early settlements can be shared by the contribution plaintiffs and non-settling PRPs in an equitable allocation at trial. In a *pro tanto* scheme, there is incentive for contribution defendants to settle early, because if they wait to settle and force plaintiff PRPs to litigate against them, they would likely face increased liability as a result of the favorable settlements of other PRPs. If it is easier for PRP groups to recover costs by settling early with other PRPs, they are more likely to come forward to settle with the EPA and take on the task of remediating contaminated sites, furthering CERCLA's goals of private party remediation and early settlement.

The *pro tanto* approach also has several advantages in this case specifically. First, it is better to compare the relative shares of parties with the opportunity to present evidence at trial. In this case, only the Simon Entities remained as viable defendants at trial, and the record was not adequately developed as to the liability of all the parties that settled with the CSDG before trial. The *pro tanto* method makes it possible to account for the settlements of PRPs not before the court, without having to determine their proportionate shares according to fault. Second, a good faith hearing is not required in this case to determine the fairness of the settlements. The *de minimis* settlements were based on the volumetric shares of the *de minimis* PRPs and the overall costs of cleanup calculated at the time, and there is no evidence in the record to indicate that the settlements the CSDG reached with the other parties, including Chemclene, were not negotiated in good faith. Therefore the settlement amounts presumably will not grossly underestimate the settling PRPs' liability. Finally, the *pro tanto* approach avoids having to determine the "orphan share," which would be impossible to determine in this case because there is no documentation for pre–1968 drums sent to the Site. Instead, the orphan share can be lumped in with the unrecovered costs to be allocated proportionately between the CSDG and the Simon Entities in proportion to their relative liabilities, as explained in the next subsection.

* * *

[T]he Site costs to be allocated between the CSDG and the Simon Entities will be reduced by the amounts of settlements the CSDG has received or expects from settled PRPs. All the settlement amounts are known except the amount that the CSDG will receive from its contingent settlement agreement with Chemclene, which I shall represent with the variable X. The other settlements provide the CSDG with $6,630,670. Thus the total amount of settlements with other PRPs equals ($6,630,670 + X). Subtracting this amount from the total expected cost of cleanup previously calculated, $23,097,665, yields the amount to be allocated, as follows:

$$\$23,097,665 - (\$6,630,670 + X) = (\$16,466,995 - X)$$

Therefore I will allocate the remaining ($16,466,995 − X) between the CSDG and Simon Wrecking.

b.   *The Orphan Share*

The share of waste from unidentifiable sources or insolvent PRPs is known as the "orphan share" at a CERCLA site. In this case, although the Site was in operation since the 1950s, there is no documentation of the origin of any waste sent to the Site before 1968. Some of the documentation of waste drop-offs that does exist links post–1968 waste to unidentifiable, insolvent, or defunct companies. The Site's orphan share is included in the remaining amount to be allocated ($16,466,995 − X) because the CSDG has not received any settlements to cover it. The Simon Entities argue that they should not be liable for any part of the orphan share. I disagree. Given the facts of this case, it is equitable to allocate the orphan share proportionally between the CSDG and the only remaining defendants.

Both the statute's language and goals support this decision. * * * It is undisputed that CERCLA gives federal courts broad discretion in the equitable apportionment of liability under § 113(f)(1). Nowhere in the statute is there a proscription against allocating part of an unrecoverable share to contribution action defendants as well as to PRP plaintiffs. * * * PRPs will be unlikely to fulfill the goals of CERCLA by settling early on and undertaking remediation of waste sites with an orphan share if they are unable to recover equitable contribution for the orphan share from other viable PRPs, and must instead add the entire amount to their own shares.

The Third Circuit has not addressed the issue of orphan share allocation in a CERCLA contribution action, but all the other federal courts of appeals to consider the issue have concluded or assumed that the orphan shares should be allocated equitably among plaintiff and defendant PRPs. * * *

Because the size of the orphan share is indeterminate, the fairest way to divide it is not to estimate what part of the remaining costs constitutes the orphan share and divide it separately, but instead to allocate the entire $(16,466,995 − X) between the CSDG and the Simon Entities, in proportion to their relative liability at the Site, as determined below.

c.   *Allocation Between the CSDG and Simon Wrecking*

To allocate the remaining ($16,466,995 − X) in Site costs, I must assess the relative responsibility of the CSDG and the Simon Entities, again "using such equitable factors as the court determines are appropriate." 42 U.S.C. § 9613(f)(1). An unsuccessful CERCLA amendment proposed by then-Representative Al Gore (referred to since as the "Gore Factors") is often cited as a non-exclusive list of appropriate considerations:

(i) the ability of the parties to demonstrate that their contribution to a discharge, release or disposal of a hazardous waste can be distinguished;

(ii) the amount of the hazardous waste involved;

(iii) the degree of toxicity of the hazardous waste involved;

(iv) the degree of involvement by the parties in the generation, transportation, treatment, storage, or disposal of the hazardous waste;

(v) the degree of care exercised by the parties with respect to the hazardous waste concerned, taking into account the characteristics of such waste; and

(vi) the degree of cooperation by the parties with Federal, State, or local officials to prevent any harm to the public health or the environment.

126 Cong. Rec. 26,779–81 (1980). While this list is not binding because the Gore Amendment was never passed, it provides some helpful guidance. The evidence presented at trial focused mostly on three of these factors: the amount of hazardous waste involved; "the degree of involvement by the parties in the generation, transportation, treatment, storage, or disposal of the hazardous waste"; and the degree of cooperation with federal officials.[33] I consider the amount of hazardous waste provided by each party and its involvement with the Site to be important, and do not find cooperation or recalcitrance to be a useful factor for allocation in this case.

i. *The Parties' Volumetric Shares*

Both the CSDG and the Simon Entities presented evidence and expert testimony as to the parties' relative volumetric shares, which is the proportion of barrels of waste each party is responsible for out of the total attributable to both the CSDG and the Simon Entities. The CSDG introduced and authenticated each document related to waste transported by Simon Wrecking to Chemclene. The CSDG's expert Dovell also included a database of each transaction involving members of the CSDG and Simon Wrecking, based on the EPA's Comprehensive Transaction Report, and taking into account more recently discovered documents. Based on his extensive documentation of the CSDG drum count, and the rational methods he employed in counting drums, as explained at trial, I adopt his calculation of 13,190.51 drums for the CSDG.

---

33. The other Gore factors are not useful in allocating costs in this case. The parties' contribution to the Site's contamination cannot be distinguished beyond the amount of waste that they introduced. There was no evidence presented on the degree of toxicity of the waste, beyond establishing that Simon Wrecking transported TCA and TCE, the primary contaminants necessitating the Site remediation. Finally, there was little evidence of Simon Wrecking's degree of care (only the letter from Lloyd Balderston certifying compliance with environmental laws and regulations), and no evidence of the degree of care exercised by the CSDG members.

* * * I assign Simon Wrecking only half of the drums it transported from Letterkenny Army Depot, because Letterkenny is a known PRP and the CSDG has already settled with the Department of the Army for those drums. I assign Simon Wrecking the full amount of drums it transported from unknown generators because there is no evidence that those parties had a relationship with Chemclene, and no expectation that those parties will contribute to the cost of remediating the Site. * * * Following these principles, Simon Wrecking's preliminary share is 976.51 drums.

Simon's preliminary share must be reduced by 10% to account for the evidence regarding the extent of Simon Wrecking's involvement in selecting the Site. As discussed above, there was sufficient evidence to conclude that Simon Wrecking had at least substantial participation in selecting the Site for disposal at least some of the time, but not enough to conclude that it always did so. The evidence indicated that at least once, waste generator Letterkenny consigned its waste directly to Chemclene, even though Simon Wrecking was to transport it. A 10% reduction in the amount of waste credited to Simon Wrecking reflects this uncertainty about how often it was substantially involved in site selection, and results in an adjusted share for Simon Wrecking of 878.86 drums.

The combined adjusted shares of the CSDG and Simon Wrecking amount to 14,069.37 drums. Of this total, the CSDG's 13,190.51 drums account for 93.75% and Simon Wrecking's 781.2 account for 6.25%. Therefore Simon Wrecking's preliminary share of the remaining estimated site costs is 6.25% x ($16,466,995 − X).

ii. *Recalcitrance*

I reject the CSDG's request to increase the Simon Entities' share based on their alleged non-cooperation, or recalcitrance, with the EPA and the CSDG. The CSDG illustrates the appropriateness of a recalcitrance multiplier by citing to *United States v. Consolidation Coal Co.*, 345 F.3d 409 (6th Cir. 2003). I find this case unpersuasive. The lone remaining defendant PRP in *Consolidation Coal* had declined to participate in the PRP investigation of that site, had violated county regulations in disposing of its waste, and did not cooperate at all with the state or federal EPA. The facts in *Consolidation Coal* are quite dissimilar from those in this case.

The evidence at trial showed that Simon Wrecking attempted to cooperate with the major PRPs and the EPA. Simon Wrecking joined the Chemclene Site Study Group and paid its dues. Indeed, Simon Wrecking was listed on the letterhead of the group's initial good faith offer to the EPA to conduct the clean up of the Site. Subsequently the CSDG unilaterally ejected Simon Wrecking, in violation of its internal rules, allegedly afraid that Simon Wrecking would use any consent decree as a shield against future lawsuits and then default on its obligations to the CSDG.

It is unfair to penalize Simon Wrecking for the CSDG's speculations about what Simon would do in the future. * * *

Unlike the defendant PRP in *Consolidation Coal,* the Simon Entities attempted to resolve their share of liability. They initiated a lawsuit against their insurers to obtain coverage for its liability at the Site. Simon Wrecking nevertheless attempted to settle with the CSDG, but was met with a demand of almost $8 million, far more than any liability it faced going to trial, and one third of the entire proposed site clean up costs. Therefore I do not find the Simon Entities' to have been recalcitrant, and their failure to settle with the CSDG before trial will not affect my equitable allocation of costs.

d.   *Uncertainty Multiplier*

Adding an uncertainty premium to Simon's preliminary share is appropriate in this case to account for the possibility that future costs could be higher than expected, and to maintain parity with earlier settlements. Testimony at trial established that the EPA charged a 50% premium in its settlements with *de minimis* parties in this case to cover uncertainty in future costs, and that it is likely that the costs of cleaning up the Site could be higher than expected. Courts routinely approve uncertainty premiums when signing consent decrees in CERCLA cases, to ensure that the parties assuming cleanup are not unduly burdened by unforeseen future costs, and to acknowledge the benefit settling parties receive in resolving their liability early. The rationales behind charging an uncertainty premium in voluntary settlements apply with equal force in an equitable allocation.

Evidence at trial indicated that costs may be higher than originally anticipated at the time of the Consent Decree. In the summer of 2005, additional drums were found at the MPA, causing the CSDG to extend the MPA cap to cover the area. In September 2005, the EPA's five-year review prompted the EPA to ask the CSDG to study vapor intrusion and 1,4 dioxane at the Site, two hazards that were not associated with the Site at the time the CSDG signed the Consent Decree. The EPA may force the CSDG to incur additional costs to remedy vapor intrusion or 1,4 dioxane contamination at the Site, even though any work that the CSDG does regarding these hazards would be in addition to the remedial action required by the original ROD. * * *

Additional cost variables are still unknown. The contaminant plume is not completely delineated yet, and so the cost of remediating it is still uncertain. Also, the costs are only projected for thirty years because that is as far as the EPA will predict. From the evidence at trial, it appears that cleaning up the site completely could take more than thirty years, adding significantly to the operation and maintenance components of the remedies.

Charging an uncertainty premium on a CERCLA defendant's preliminary share acknowledges the benefit that parties receive by resolving their liability long before the cleanup is completed. The CSDG, by agreeing with the EPA to remediate the Site, has assumed the risk that it may have to spend far more than expected before its responsibility has been fulfilled. Recognizing the benefits of a final settlement early on in a lengthy clean up process, the EPA charged *de minimis* PRPs an uncertainty premium of

50% to adjust for potential cost overruns in each of the three rounds of *de minimis* settlements in this case. Satisfaction of judgment in this case will likewise resolve the Simon Entities' liability at the Site, while the CSDG shoulders the uncertainty of costs in the years ahead. Therefore I will apply the same 50% premium for uncertainty to the Simon Entities' preliminary share. A 50% uncertainty premium for Simon would be 50% x [6.25% x ($16,466,995 − X)], or 3.13% x ($16,466,995 − X). The Simon Entities' equitable share including the uncertainty premium is thus 150% x [6.25% x ($16,466,995 − X)], which equals 9.38% x ($16,466,995 − X).

* * *

NOTES AND QUESTIONS

1. *Dividing costs among PRPs.* On what basis did the court divide responsibility for cleanup costs in *Action Manufacturing*? Which of the Gore factors did it find useful and why? Should it have considered any other factors? Why did it adopt an uncertainty multiplier? Was that appropriate? How did the court deal with the fact that the cleanup was not yet complete? Should cost allocation wait until the costs are known with certainty?

2. *Settlement.* How did the court account for settlements reached by the CSDG with other PRPs? The court considered *pro tanto* and *pro rata* approaches, choosing to adopt a *pro tanto* approach. Why did it make that choice, and what difference does it make? Which is the better approach, or does it depend on the circumstances? How does the statute treat settlements with the government differently than settlements (like the one in *Action Manufacturing*) with a private PRP or group of PRPs? Should settlements with the government be treated differently?

3. *Allocation and settlement in § 107 suits.* Following the Supreme Court's decision in *Atlantic Research*, PRPs will frequently have access to § 107, either in addition to or instead of § 113. Should courts apply the same approach to allocating liability among responsible parties under either section? Must a PRP who faces a § 107 claim by another PRP file a counterclaim in contribution? Should the effect of settlement on allocation of liability among non-settling parties be the same under either section?

4. *Orphan shares.* How did the court in *Action Manufacturing* deal with orphan shares? What other approaches might it have used? Who should be responsible for orphan shares? Should those shares be treated differently in cost recovery than in contribution actions?

E.   Natural Resource Damages

In addition to expanding the universe of liable parties beyond what the common law would have recognized, CERCLA expands the scope of recoverable damages. CERCLA § 107(a)(4) (42 U.S.C. § 9607(a)(4)) allows recovery not only of the costs of cleanup but also of "damages for injury to, destruction of, or loss of natural resources." CERCLA defines natural resources as "land, fish, wildlife, biota, air, water, ground water, drinking water supplies, and other such resources belonging to, managed by, held in trust by, appertaining to, or otherwise controlled by the United States, any State or local government, any foreign government, any Indian tribe, or, if such resources are subject to a trust restriction on alienation, any member of an Indian tribe." CERCLA § 101(16) (42 U.S.C. § 9601(16)). Only governments, federal, state, or tribal, can recover for natural resource damages. CERCLA § 107(f)(1) (42 U.S.C. § 9607(f)(1)). Any money recovered for natural resource damages must be used "only to restore, replace, or acquire the equivalent of such natural resources." Id.

CERCLA directs the Department of Interior to issue regulations for the assessment of natural resource damages. CERCLA § 301(c) (42 U.S.C. § 9651(c)). The regulations are required to identify the best available procedures to assess natural resource damages, "including both direct and indirect injury, destruction, or loss and shall take into consideration factors including, but not limited to, replacement value, use value, and ability of the ecosystem or resource to recover." Id. Interior's initial natural resource damage regulations led to the following decision.

State of Ohio v. U.S. Department of the Interior

United States Court of Appeals, District of Columbia Circuit, 1989.
880 F.2d 432.

■ WALD, CHIEF JUDGE, and SPOTTSWOOD W. ROBINSON III and MIKVA, CIRCUIT JUDGES:

I. BACKGROUND

* * *

Congress conferred on the President (who in turn delegated to Interior) the responsibility for promulgating regulations governing the assessment of damages for natural resource injuries * * *. CERCLA prescribed the creation of two types of procedures for conducting natural resources damages assessments. The regulations were to specify (a) "standard procedures for simplified assessments requiring minimal field observation" (the "Type A" rules), and (b) "alternative protocols for conducting assessments in individual cases" (the "Type B" rules). § 301(c)(2), 42 U.S.C. § 9651(c)(2). Both the Type A and the Type B rules were to "identify the best available procedures to determine such damages." Id. The regulations must be reviewed and revised as appropriate every two years. § 301(c)(3), 42 U.S.C. § 9651(c)(3). Under the Act, a trustee seeking damages is not required to resort to the Type A or Type B procedures, but CERCLA as amended provides that any assessment performed in accordance with the prescribed procedure is entitled to a rebuttable presumption of accuracy in a proceeding to recover damages from a responsible party. § 107(f)(2)(C), 42 U.S.C. § 9607(f)(2)(C).

In August 1986, Interior published a final rule containing the Type B regulations for natural resource damage assessments, the subject of this lawsuit. * * *

The August 1986 regulations were promptly challenged by state governments, environmental groups, industrial corporations and an industry group.

* * *

III. THE "LESSER–OF" RULE

The most significant issue in this case concerns the validity of the regulation providing that damages for despoilment of natural resources shall be "the *lesser of:* restoration or replacement costs; or diminution of use values." 43 C.F.R. § 11.35(b)(2) (1987) (emphasis added).

* * *

Although our resolution of the dispute submerges us in the minutiae of CERCLA text and legislative materials, we initially stress the enormous practical significance of the "lesser of" rule. A hypothetical example will illustrate the point: imagine a hazardous substance spill that kills a rookery of fur seals and destroys a habitat for seabirds at a sealife reserve. The lost use value of the seals and seabird habitat would be measured by the market value of the fur seals' pelts (which would be approximately $15 each) plus the selling price per acre of land comparable in value to that on which the spoiled bird habitat was located. Even if, as likely, that use value turns out to be far less than the cost of restoring the rookery and seabird habitat, it would nonetheless be the only measure of damages eligible for the presumption of recoverability under the Interior rule.

* * *

Interior's "lesser of" rule operates on the premise that, as the cost of a restoration project goes up relative to the value of the injured resource, at some point it becomes wasteful to require responsible parties to pay the full cost of restoration. The logic behind the rule is the same logic that prevents an individual from paying $8,000 to repair a collision-damaged car that was worth only $5,000 before the collision. Just as a prudent individual would sell the damaged car for scrap and then spend $5,000 on a used car in similar condition, DOI's rule requires a polluter to pay a sum equal to the diminution in the use value of a resource whenever that sum is less than restoration cost. What is significant about Interior's rule is the point at which it deems restoration "inefficient." Interior chose to draw the line not at the point where restoration becomes practically impossible, nor at the point where the cost of restoration becomes grossly disproportionate to the use value of the resource, but rather at the point where restoration cost exceeds—by any amount, however small—the use value of the resource. Thus, while we agree with DOI that CERCLA permits it to establish a rule exempting responsible parties *in some cases* from having to pay the full cost of restoration of natural resources,[7] we also agree with Petitioners that it does not permit Interior to draw the line on an automatic "which costs less" basis.

Interior's "lesser of" rule squarely rejects the concept of any clearly expressed congressional preference for recovering the full cost of restoration from responsible parties. The challenged regulation treats the two alternative measures of damages, restoration cost and use value, as though the choice between them were a matter of complete indifference from the statutory point of view: thus, in any given case, the rule makes damages turn solely on whichever standard is less expensive. If Congress, however, in enacting CERCLA, clearly expressed an intention that DOI's damage measurement rules incorporate a distinct preference for restoration cost over use value, then the "lesser of" rule is inconsistent with that intent. Congress' expressed preference would mean that restoration cost must normally be preferred over use value despite use value being the "lesser" figure, except in unusual situations where the disadvantages or expenses were extreme. Based on the discussion that follows, we conclude that CERCLA unambiguously mandates a distinct preference for using restoration cost as the measure of damages, and so precludes a "lesser of" rule which totally ignores that preference.

B. *Text and Structure of CERCLA*

* * *

The strongest linguistic evidence of Congress' intent to establish a distinct preference for restoration costs as the measure of damages is contained in § 107(f)(1) of CERCLA. That section states that natural resource damages recovered by a government trustee are "for use only to restore, replace, or acquire the equivalent of such natural resources." 42 U.S.C. § 9607(f)(1). It goes on to state: "The measure of damages in any action under [§ 107(a)(C)] shall not be limited by the sums which can be used to restore or replace such resources." *Id.*[8]

---

7. This can be inferred from § 301(c)(2) of CERCLA. First, that provision delegates to the President the duty to formulate a measure of damages, which suggests some degree of latitude in deciding what measure shall apply. Second, it states that the regulations "shall take into consideration factors including, but not limited to, replacement value, use value, and ability of the ecosystem or resource to recover." § 301(c)(2), 42 U.S.C. § 9651(c)(2). That suggests that DOI is permitted to apply use value in some cases and restoration cost in others (and both in yet others). * * * DOI obviously has some latitude in deciding which measure applies in a given case: the rule might for instance hinge on the relationship between restoration cost and use value (e.g., damages are limited to three-times the amount of use value), or it might hinge on the ability of the resource to recover (e.g., use value is the measure whenever restoration is infeasible). DOI has not, however, fashioned its rules along these lines.

8. Although at first glance these two sentences might seem inconsistent, a closer look reveals that the missing link is the absence of the phrase "or acquire the equivalent" in the latter sentence. This suggests (and the legislative history confirms) that damages recovered in excess of restoration or replacement costs must be spent on acquiring the equivalent of lost resources.

By mandating the use of all damages to restore the injured resources, Congress underscored in § 107(f)(1) its paramount restorative purpose for imposing damages at all. It would be odd indeed for a Congress so insistent that all damages be spent on restoration to allow a "lesser" measure of damages than the cost of restoration in the majority of cases. Only two possible inferences about congressional intent could explain the anomaly: Either Congress intended trustees to commence restoration projects only to abandon them for lack of funds, or Congress expected taxpayers to pick up the rest of the tab. The first theory is contrary to Congress' intent to effect a "make-whole" remedy of complete restoration, and the second is contrary to a basic purpose of the CERCLA natural resource damage provisions—that polluters bear the costs of their polluting activities. It is far more logical to presume that Congress intended responsible parties to be liable for damages in an amount sufficient to accomplish its restorative aims. Interior's rule, on the other hand, assumes that Congress purposely formulated a statutory scheme that would doom to failure its goals of restoration in a majority of cases.[11]

In this connection, it should be noted that Interior makes no claim that a "use value" measure will provide enough money to pay for *any* of the three uses to which all damages must be assigned: restoration, replacement *or acquisition of an equivalent resource*. Nor could Interior make such a claim, because its "lesser of" rule not only calculates use value quite differently from restoration or replacement cost but it also fails to link measurement of use value in any way to the cost of acquiring an equivalent resource. For example, Interior could not possibly maintain that recovering $15 per pelt for the fur seals killed by a hazardous substance release would enable the purchase of an "equivalent" number of fur seals.

The same section of CERCLA that mandates the expenditures of all damages on restoration (again a shorthand reference to all three listed uses of damages) provides that the measure of damages "shall not be limited by" restoration costs. § 107(f)(1), 42 U.S.C. § 9607(f)(1). This provision obviously reflects Congress' apparent concern that its restorative purpose for imposing damages not be construed as making restoration cost a damages ceiling. But the explicit command that damages "shall not be limited by" restoration costs also carries in it an implicit assumption that restoration cost will serve as the basic measure of damages in many if not most CERCLA cases. It would be markedly inconsistent with the restorative thrust of the whole section to limit restoration-based damages, as

---

11. DOI states that federal or state agencies "are not precluded from supplementing damage funds with other monies to restore, replace, or enhance the injured natural resource." 51 Fed. Reg. 27,705. Those "other monies," however, cannot come from Superfund, as the enactment of SARA in 1986 cut off the availability of Superfund money for restoration of injured natural resources. See SARA § 517(a), Pub.L. No. 99–499, 100 Stat. 1772 (1986), codified at 26 U.S.C. § 9507(c)(1)(A)(ii) (Superfund money to be available "only" to carry out the purposes of, inter alia, "section 111(c) of CERCLA . . . other than paragraphs (1) and (2) thereof").

Interior's rule does, to a minuscule number of cases where restoration is cheaper than paying for lost use.

* * *

The legislative history of CERCLA confirms that restoration costs were intended to be the presumptive measure of recovery. Senate proponents of the legislation, in the committee report and on the Senate floor, repeatedly emphasized that their primary objective in assessing damages for public resources was to achieve restoration.[26]

The history of the damages provision of CERCLA documents further Congress' intent to broaden government trustees' recovery beyond lost use value. As reported to the Senate floor, CERCLA's forerunner, S. 1480, allowed recovery for, *inter alia,* the following three categories of damages:

> (C) any injury to, destruction of, or loss of natural resources, including the reasonable costs of assessing such injury, destruction, or loss;

> (D) any *loss of use* of any natural resources, without regard to the ownership or management of such resources;

> (E) any *loss of income or profits or impairment of earning capacity* resulting from personal injury or from injury to or destruction of real or personal property or natural resources, without regard to the ownership of such property or resources. . . .

S. 1480, 96th Cong., 2d Sess. § 4(a)(2) (emphasis added). Although (D) and (E), which related to private party recovery, were later dropped from the bill, they evidence a sharp contrast with the language of (C), which governed recovery by public trustees (and which was retained in the enacted version of CERCLA). Private parties could recover damages only for lost use values, but public trustees were to be allowed under the language of (C) to recover for the loss of the natural resources themselves, based presumably on some measure other than lost use.

* * *

CERCLA's "shall not be limited by" language, its mandate that recovered funds be used solely for restoration activities, and the statements of its sponsors and supporters during its passage in 1980 all point in one direction: a distinct preference for restoration costs as the normative standard for damages. Congress' enactment of SARA in 1986 also provides strong evidence that a restoration measure of damages was the statute's original intent. Of controlling importance in the SARA phase is a House report indicating that, while the "shall not be limited by" language of the original statute would be retained, Interior's demonstrated "confusion" about what that phrase meant should be resolved in light of Congress' strong emphasis on restoration of resources.

While not altering the relevant phrases of § 107(f) in any basic way, SARA changed the permissible uses for damages from "restore, rehabili-

---

26. The House concurred in the Senate version of the bill without amendment. 126 Cong. Rec. 31981 (1980).

tate, or acquire the equivalent" to "restore, *replace,* or acquire the equivalent," in order to avoid the redundancy of "restore" and "rehabilitate," and to conform the exclusive use clause to the language of the "shall not be limited by" damages clause.

In the accompanying Report of the House Committee on Merchant Marine and Fisheries, explicating how the new § 107(f)(1) would work, its sponsors made their intent unmistakable that restoration costs were to be the preferred measure of damages. The committee report indicated that the "shall not be limited by" passage, while "essentially a restatement of the language of" the 1980 version, was aimed at ending what had been a "source of some confusion." H.R. Rep. No. 253(IV). "It is clear from [the] language [of § 107(f)(1)] that the *primary purpose* of the resource damage provisions of CERCLA is the *restoration or replacement of natural resources* damaged by unlawful releases of hazardous substances." *Id.* (emphasis added). Such an unequivocal statement of purpose is irreconcilable with DOI's "lesser of" rule, which would in a majority of cases risk underfunded, half-finished restoration projects.

The same House report went on to explain:

> [T]he final clause [dealing with use of damages to acquire a suitable equivalent resource] is necessary because a situation could arise in which the amount of damages caused by a release of hazardous substances *is in excess of the amount that could realistically or productively be used to restore or replace those resources. That is, the total amount of damages may include the costs of restoration and the value of all the lost uses of the damaged resources . . . from the time of the release up to the time of restoration. Since the damages contemplated by CERCLA include both, the total amount of damages recoverable would exceed the restoration costs alone.*

> The Committee therefore intends than [*sic:* probably should be "that"] any excess funds recovered shall be used, in such an instance, for the third purpose spelled out in the language of the amendment, which is to "acquire the equivalent of the damaged resource.

H.R. Rep. No. 253(IV) (emphasis added). The House report thus explicitly assumes that damages "contemplated by CERCLA" will normally include restoration costs at a minimum, plus interim lost-use value in appropriate cases. (This House amendment to § 107(f)(1) was adopted by the Conference Committee, H.R. Conf. Rep. No. 962, 99th Cong., 2d Sess. 204–05 (1986).)

* * *

CERCLA's legislative history undergirds its textual focus on recovering restoration costs as the primary aim of the natural resource damages provisions. Furthermore, it shows that Congress soundly rejected the two basic premises underlying Interior's "lesser of" rule-first, that the common-law measure of damages is appropriate in the natural resource context, and second, that it is economically inefficient to restore a resource whose use value is less than the cost of restoration.

DOI and Industry Intervenors argue that Congress intended that damages under CERCLA would be calculated according to traditional common-law rules. Accepting for the sake of argument the contention that the "lesser of" rule reflects the common law, support for the proposition that Congress adopted common-law damage standards wholesale into CERCLA is slim to nonexistent. DOI contends that Congress meant to adopt traditional methods of damage measurement, "[i]n the absence of clearly expressed Congressional intent to deviate from [the] common law rule." 51 Fed. Reg. at 27,705. The legislative history illustrates, however, that a motivating force behind the CERCLA natural resource damage provisions was Congress' dissatisfaction with the common law. Indeed, one wonders why Congress would have passed a new damage provision at all if it were content with the common law.

Alternatively, Interior justifies the "lesser of" rule as being economically efficient. Under DOI's economic efficiency view, making restoration cost the measure of damages would be a waste of money whenever restoration would cost more than the use value of the resource. Its explanation of the proposed rules included the following statement:

> [I]f use value is higher than the cost of restoration or replacement, then it would be more rational for society to be compensated for the cost to restore or replace the lost resource than to be compensated for the lost use. Conversely, if restoration or replacement costs are higher than the value of uses foregone, it is rational for society to compensate individuals for their lost uses rather than the cost to restore or replace the injured natural resource.

50 Fed. Reg. at 52,141.

This is nothing more or less than cost-benefit analysis: Interior's rule attempts to optimize social welfare by restoring an injured resource only when the diminution in the resource's value to society is greater in magnitude than the cost of restoring it. * * *

The fatal flaw of Interior's approach, however, is that it assumes that natural resources are fungible goods, just like any other, and that the value to society generated by a particular resource can be accurately measured in every case—assumptions that Congress apparently rejected. As the foregoing examination of CERCLA's text, structure and legislative history illustrates, Congress saw restoration as the presumptively correct remedy for injury to natural resources. To say that Congress placed a thumb on the scales in favor of restoration is not to say that it forswore the goal of efficiency. "Efficiency," standing alone, simply means that the chosen policy will dictate the result that achieves the greatest value to society. Whether a particular choice is efficient depends on *how the various alternatives are valued.* Our reading of CERCLA does not attribute to Congress an irrational dislike of "efficiency"; rather, it suggests that Congress was skeptical of the ability of human beings to measure the true "value" of a natural resource. Indeed, even the common law recognizes that restoration is the proper remedy for injury to property where measurement of damages by some other method will fail to compensate fully for the injury. Congress' refusal to view use value and restoration cost as having equal presumptive legitimacy merely recognizes that natural resources have value that is not readily measured by traditional means. Congress delegated to Interior the job of deciding at what point the presumption of restoration falls away, but its repeated emphasis on the primacy of restoration rejected the underlying premise of Interior's rule, which is that restoration is wasteful if its cost exceeds-by even the slightest amount-the diminution in use value of the injured resource.

* * *

Our reading of the complex of relevant provisions concerning damages under CERCLA convinces us that Congress established a distinct preference for restoration cost as the measure of recovery in natural resource damage cases. This is not to say that DOI may not establish some class of cases where other considerations—*i.e.,* infeasibility of restoration or grossly disproportionate cost to use value-warrant a different standard. We hold the "lesser of" rule based on comparing costs alone, however, to be an invalid determinant of whether or not to deviate from Congress' preference.

NOTES AND QUESTIONS

1. *What natural resources are covered?* CERCLA § 107(a)(4) (42 U.S.C. § 9607(a)(4)) seems to allow broadly for recovery of damages for loss of any natural resources, but the scope of that provision is narrowed by the statutes' definition of natural resources, which covers only resources "belonging to, managed by, held in trust by, appertaining to, or otherwise controlled by" the United States; a state, local, or foreign government; or an Indian tribe or the member of a tribe if the resources are held in trust. CERCLA § 101(16) (42 U.S.C. § 9601(16)). Damages to purely private resources are not recoverable, but damages to resources subject to a public trust, such as fish and wildlife, are recoverable, even if there is some private interest in those resources. To the extent that public and private interests in resource overlap, double recovery is not permitted. CERCLA § 107(f)(1) (42 U.S.C. § 9607(f)(1)). Trustees may not seek recovery of damages that have already been recovered by a private party in a tort action, therefore, and vice versa. See Alaska Sport Fishing Ass'n v. Exxon Corp., 34 F.3d 769 (9th Cir. 1994) (finding private claims for lost recreational use of Prince William Sound following the Exxon Valdez oil spill foreclosed by recovery of natural resource damages by federal and state trustees).

2. *Causation in natural resource damages actions.* CERCLA § 107 provides that PRPs are liable for natural resource damages "resulting from" a hazardous substance release. In a portion of the *Ohio* decision not reproduced above, the D.C. Circuit concluded that CERCLA "is at best ambiguous on the question of whether the causation-of-injury standard under § 107(a)(C) must be less demanding than that of the common law," 880 F.2d 472, and therefore upheld portions of Interior's assessment regulations that adopted traditional causation standards and imposed high evidentiary standards. Subsequently, the same court upheld "Type A" assessment rules, applicable to small releases, that allowed a conclusion that used computer models to establish injury and causation. National Association of Manufacturers v. U.S. Dept. of Interior, 134 F.3d 1095, 1105–1109 (D.C. Cir. 1998). The court noted that Type A assessments are intended to be rapid and cost-effective, and that a PRP who believes that Type A assessment overstates injury or damages can demand a more elaborate "Type B" assessment. Id. at 1108. The objecting PRP will be responsible for the reasonable costs of the more in-depth assessment. CERCLA § 107(a)(4)(C) (42 U.S.C. § 9607(a)(4)(C)).

3. *The role of Interior's regulations.* CERCLA directs the Department of Interior to issue regulations setting out procedures for the assessment of natural resource damages. Trustees are not required to follow those procedures, but they are encouraged to do so by CERCLA § 107(f)(2)(C) (42 U.S.C. § 9607(f)(2)(C)), which provides that assessments done in accordance with Interior's regulations are entitled to a "rebuttable presumption," presumably that they are accurate. At least some trustees prefer to use their own methodology to assess natural resource damages. The Commissioner of the New York Department of Environmental Conservation wrote in 1989:

> It appears, however, that the limited value of the "rebuttable presumption" is outweighed by many disadvantages inherent in the structure of the regulations, especially the low dollar value the regulations would assign to natural resource damages. More comprehensively, there are inherent limitations in the assessment methodologies, both scientific and economic, and significant procedural constraints in the regulations.
>
> In short, while the Department of Interior's regulations provide a useful starting point and helpful guidance for conducting natural resource damage assessments, strict adherence to them in order to gain the value of the "rebuttable presumption" is unwarranted.

Thomas C. Jorling, Commissioner, DEE–15, Natural Resource Damages Enforcement Policy (May 17, 1989).

4. *Economic efficiency and natural resource damages.* Interior justified the regulations reviewed in *Ohio* on the grounds that it would be economically inefficient to require PRPs to pay the full cost of restoring natural resources when restoration costs exceed the value of the resources lost. What did the D.C. Circuit find wrong with the that reasoning? Do you agree that it is precluded by CERCLA? Assuming it is, does that make CERCLA irrational?

In *Ohio*, the D.C. Circuit agreed with the Department of Interior that CERCLA "permits it to establish a rule exempting responsible parties *in some cases* from having to pay the full cost of restoration of natural resources." Is that a correct reading of the statute? Under what circumstances might the proper measure of damages be less than the restoration cost? In Kennecott Utah Copper Corp. v. U.S. Dept. of Interior, 88 F.3d

1191, 1218 (D.C. Cir. 1996), the court rejected an industry argument that the *Ohio* decision required Interior to adopt a standard precluding restoration "if its costs were grossly disproportionate to the use value of the injured resource." The current regulations direct trustees to consider a range of alternatives for restoration, rehabilitation, replacement or the acquisition of equivalent natural resources. In choosing among those alternatives, trustees are to consider a number of factors, including technical feasibility, the relationship of costs to expected benefits, and cost-effectiveness. 43 C.F.R. § 11.82(d). One of the alternatives considered must be natural recovery with minimal management actions. 43 C.F.R. § 11.82(c)(2). Presumably that will always be the least expensive alternative, but presumably it will also typically be the slowest and least effective. Should trustees ever be *required* to adopt the natural recovery alternative?

Section 3.   Cleanup and Reuse

Although the bulk of CERCLA litigation involves cost recovery, EPA regards the response and cleanup process as the heart of the CERCLA program. That process has also been at the center of much of the controversy over CERCLA, with critics complaining that it is both too slow and too costly. As of 2000, EPA reported that there had been over 6,400 removal actions taken at hazardous waste sites. One estimate sets the average cost of such removal actions at $500,000. James T. Hamilton and W. Kip Viscusi, Calculating Risks: The Spatial and Political Dimensions of Hazardous Waste Policy 8 (1999). Remedial actions, which are more complex, time-consuming and expensive, had been undertaken or were planned at nearly 1500 sites, at an average cost of $30 million.

Under CERCLA, cleanups are typically undertaken either directly by EPA using funds from the Superfund; by PRPs following an order to abate a hazard or a civil action under CERCLA § 106; or voluntarily by PRPs, often following protracted negotiation with EPA and the explicit or implicit threat of a § 106 action. The initial concept of the Superfund was "shovels first, lawyers later"—that the fund would allow the United States to resolve imminent hazards quickly, then engage in the protracted litigation necessary to recover costs. Fairly quickly, however, budget limitations led EPA to focus on encouraging privately-funded cleanups. Those incentives have become stronger with the expiration of the tax that replenished the Superfund. In addition, PRPs may have a strong incentive to take primary control of the cleanup process in order to minimize their costs.

No matter who does the cleanup, compliance with the National Contingency Plan is a prerequisite to cost recovery. The Plan prescribes the cleanup process, beginning with the discovery of a contaminated site, through statutorily required notification of a release, reports from the state or citizens, EPA investigation, or other means. Once discovered, sites are entered into a computerized inventory called the Comprehensive Environmental Response, Compensation, and Liability Information System (CERCLIS), and the process of evaluating them to determine what action is appropriate begins. Investigation and cleanup then proceed through the following steps:

Preliminary Assessment/Site Inspection (PA/SI). EPA undertakes a Preliminary Assessment (PA) at every CERCLIS site, reviewing available information to make rapid judgments about the extent of the hazard and the feasibility of response. "Typically, PA data collection includes a search of facility and regulatory agency files, 'desktop' data collection from reference materials and telephone interviews, a survey of the local environs, and a site reconnaissance." U.S. Dept. of Energy, Office of Environmental Guidance, Preliminary Assessments Under CERCLA, EH–231–016/0593 (May 1993).

The Preliminary Assessment may find no threat to health or the environment, in which case EPA takes no further action. If it finds an imminent hazard, EPA takes short-term response action to address that hazard. If it reveals a potential long-term risk, EPA performs a site inspection to determine the extent of the hazard. The site inspection provides the data needed to calculate a numeric hazard score using EPA's Hazard Ranking System, which considers the likelihood of release, the toxicity and quantity of hazardous substances, and the people or sensitive environments who could be affected by the release.

National Priorities List Designation. The Hazard Ranking System score determines whether a site should be listed on the NPL, and what priority it should be given for cleanup. NPL listing is done by notice and comment rulemaking. 40 C.F.R. § 300.425(d).

Remedial Investigation/Feasibility Study(RI/FS). After NPL listing, EPA undertakes a Remedial Investigation, a far more extensive information collection and investigation process than the Preliminary Assessment, and then a Feasibility Study, considering and evaluating alternative remedial approaches, which may include treatment, containment, removal of contaminated material, providing substitute water supplies, or controlling site use. After considering the alternatives, EPA issues a proposed cleanup plan which describes the remedial alternatives and selects a preferred remedy. Before it adopts the plan, EPA must provide notice, make the plan available, solicit public comment, and offer an opportunity for a public meeting near the cleanup site. CERCLA § 117(a) (42 U.S.C. § 9617(a)).

CERCLA provides that EPA "shall select a remedial action that is protective of human health and the environment, that is cost effective, and that utilizes permanent solutions ... to the maximum extent practicable." CERCLA § 121(b) (42 U.S.C. § 9621(b)). If any hazardous substances will remain after the cleanup, the site must be monitored every 5 years to assure that health and the environment are protected. The remedial action must achieve a level of control which meets all "legally applicable or relevant and appropriate" standards of state or federal law. Are these goals compatible? If not, which takes priority? How should cost effectiveness be evaluated in light of the preference for permanent solutions which significantly reduce the volume, toxicity or mobility of hazardous substances? Containment, through construction of an impermeable "cap," or removal of contaminated soil to a permitted disposal facility will often be less expensive than treating the soil in place until it poses no hazards. Under what circumstances should the cost differential be deemed sufficient to justify adopting a cap or remove strategy instead of treatment?

Record of Decision. The final step in the remedy selection process is the issuance of the Record of Decision (ROD). After considering all of the comments submitted to it, EPA reassesses the range of remedial alternatives, including its preferred remedy. The ROD outlines, in brief form, the nature of the contamination, the available remedial options, the reasons for selecting the preferred remedy, how that remedy meets the requirements of the NCP, and the anticipated post-cleanup site condition.

Remedial Action. Finally, the details of the plan are worked out and implemented through a contract with an engineering firm. Once any required physical construction is finished, EPA categorizes the site as "construction complete," even if cleanup has not been completed. EPA invented this category in 1990 in response to criticism about the slow pace of cleanups. It is intended to demonstrate progress before cleanups are fully complete. When all cleanup goals are met and no further response is needed to protect human health or the environment, the site can be proposed for deletion from the NPL. Deletion requires the agreement of the state and must be preceded by notice and opportunity for public comment.

A recent study found that it takes on average more than 11 years for a site to progress from proposed listing on the NPL to completion of remedial action. Katherine N. Probst et al., Res. for the Future, Superfund's Future: What Will It Cost? 47–52 (2001).

> Actually achieving final cleanup goals may take much longer in some cases; at sites with long term remedial actions such as bioremediation and soil vapor extraction final clean up can take twenty years or more. For the roughly 60 percent of sites where waste remains on site after completion of the remedy, monitoring and review are mandated for as long as contamination remains above a level that allows "unlimited use and unrestricted exposure." For some Department of Energy sites involving radioactive contaminants, the projected period of agency involvement extends for thousands of years.

Jonathan Z. Cannon, Adaptive Management in Superfund: Thinking Like a Contaminated Site, 13 N.Y.U. Envtl. L. J. 561, 592–593 (2005).

Hilary Sigman, The Pace of Progress at Superfund Sites: Policy Goals and Interest Group Influence

44 J. L. & Econ. 315 (2001).

Bureaucracies, like other organizations, must solve the problem of how to prioritize their workload. They may chose priorities that reflect social goals. However, concentrated private interest groups may also manage to manipulate agency agendas, as the capture theory articulated by George

Stigler and Sam Peltzman suggests. In addition, bureaucracies may respond to pressures imposed by legislators.

* * *

[A study of the time to NPL listing, issuance of a ROD, and construction completion at Superfund sites through 1997] provide[s] evidence that the EPA responds to interest groups in prioritizing its resources. Both the liable parties and the local communities get weight in the agency's priorities. Liable parties appear to delay progress at their sites. Sites without viable liable parties experienced 29 percent faster decision making than sites with viable liable parties. Sites with deep-pocketed liable parties (where the private financial stake in the site is likely to be large) have slower cleanup. Similarly, powerful communities manage to expedite progress. Sites in communities with higher voter turnout received faster cleanup of their sites, while higher-income communities receive faster listing.

This interest group influence may have a small but significant impact on social welfare. A rough calculation suggests that delays caused by liable parties may decrease Superfund's net benefits by 8 percent (about $.8 million per site or $1 billion in total). * * * [T]he results provide an argument for funding provision of environmental quality and other public goods from diffuse sources, such as broad-based taxes or general appropriations, to avoid the detrimental effects of interest group politics.

The agency does not appear to use broader social goals, such as health risks, to prioritize its workload. Sites' rate of progress is not materially affected by their hazardousness. In addition, sites in densely populated areas, where there may be greater human exposure, do not progress faster than other sites. Although contrary to social welfare, the irrelevance of exposure is not surprising because Superfund policy generally focuses on individual risk levels.

Despite the direct influence of interest groups such as the liable parties and local communities, the legislature does not have observable influence on cleanup speeds. Little evidence supports the frequent contention that powerful legislators (identified either by seniority or by serving on the Superfund authorizing subcommittee) significantly speed sites in their districts. * * *

Thus, eliminating liability funding [by which the author means cost recovery through CERCLA's liability provision] and moving to tax financing (as at orphan sites) might result in small gains from increased cleanup speeds. The policy implications of this result depend upon how these costs stack up against other costs and benefits of liability financing. On one hand, there are potential advantages of liability financing. Liability can provide incentives for precaution in managing potential contaminants. Liability financing and resulting PRP participation may also help control cleanup costs, as suggested above. On the other hand, liability may involve high transactions costs from legal expenses. Lloyd Dixon estimates that transactions costs will account for as much 30 percent of private spending on Superfund, so the delay costs would not loom large relative to these costs.

In summary, the empirical results suggest a few conclusions about bureaucratic priorities. First, although the EPA is widely viewed as being a highly ideological agency, it does not appear to prioritize resources on the basis of environmental goals. This evidence may weaken arguments for allowing bureaucracies discretion in setting their agendas. Second, the EPA is sensitive to concentrated private interests in its priorities, providing support for capture theories. Such responsiveness to private interests may be helpful if it encourages the agency to consider private costs and benefits in its calculations. However, it may also be harmful if it subverts broader social goals. Indeed, the empirical results presented here suggest that removing a set of concentrated interests by using a diffuse funding source (such as a broad-based tax) might increase welfare.

Jonathan Z. Cannon, Adaptive Management in Superfund: Thinking Like a Contaminated Site
13 N.Y.U. Envtl. L. J. 561 (2005).

* * *

Superfund sites represent a relatively small portion of the universe of contaminated sites in this country, but they include many if not most of the largest, environmentally most problematic, and politically most contentious sites, and thus have a policy importance disproportionate to their number. Although much progress has been made on the current inventory of Superfund sites, much work remains to be done. As of October 2005, EPA had placed 1547 sites on Superfund's National Priorities List (NPL). Of these, 308 had been deleted from the NPL, leaving 1239 on the current list. Of the total 1547 sites, construction of the remedy was complete at 966 (or about 60 percent). The term "construction complete" means that all physical construction for remedies at these sites is complete, but does not mean that long-term clean up goals have been met. Only 248 of the 1547 NPL sites, less than one-third of the "construction complete" sites, were in productive use.

* * *

The early implementation of Superfund heavily emphasized reducing the human health risks posed by contaminated sites to acceptable levels. Public debate focused on how quickly and effectively EPA was achieving that end, and for the most part it still does. As the program has matured, however, it is evident that other concerns and values have important bearing on the disposition of these sites, including values expressed through the market (e.g., market efficiency), through local government processes (e.g., community welfare), and through other non-market institutions such as local environmental groups (e.g., ecological sustainability) or neighborhood associations (e.g., neighborhood identity or amenities). Decisions by local stakeholders acting on these values can affect the long-term stability and effectiveness of federal remedy decisions and federal remedy decisions can affect the ability of these stakeholders to realize these values in the site's ultimate disposition.

* * *

All Superfund remedies must meet applicable or relevant and appropriate requirements ("ARARs") under other federal and state environmental laws and must also achieve EPA's more general requirement of "overall protection of human health and the environment." * * * EPA's regulations identify seven other decision criteria for Superfund remedy selection. Five of these are "balancing criteria": long-term effectiveness and permanence; reduction of toxicity, mobility, or volume through treatment; short-term effectiveness; implementability; and cost. The two remaining factors— acceptability of the remedy to the state and to the local community—are "modifying criteria." None of the balancing or modifying criteria may override the core requirement of protectiveness.

The general protectiveness criterion addresses the environmental benefits of cleanup. Environmental benefits include gains that relate directly to human health and those that do not, such as restoration of ecosystem services and protection of biodiversity. A 1995 study of Superfund remedial decisions found an "almost exclusive" reliance on human health considerations, to the exclusion of ecological concerns, but the Agency states that at present a number of its major clean up actions are driven by ecological protectiveness. * * * There is considerable play * * * in what protectiveness requires. For example, for carcinogenic contaminants, EPA's regulations require clean up to an individual excess cancer risk of no more than 10^{-4} (one in 10,000) to 10^{-6} (one in 1,000,000). * * * There is even broader discretion in determining the level of protectiveness required for ecological risks. EPA also has discretion in the application of ARARs, including the authority to waive ARARs under certain circumstances.

It is in this realm of discretion that a broader consideration of the public good may take place, including consideration of the non-environmental values associated with alternative remedial or reuse scenarios. * * *

1.   Reasonably Anticipated Future Land Use

As part of the remedial investigation, EPA conducts a baseline risk assessment, which includes the determination of a "reasonable maximum exposure [to contaminants on site] expected to occur under both current and future land use conditions."[57] In May 1995 guidance, the Agency stated that the "[f]uture use of the land will affect the types of exposures and the frequency of exposures that may occur to any residual contamination remaining on site, which in turn affects the nature of the remedy chosen."[58] * * *

---

57. U.S. EPA, Risk Assessment Guidance for Superfund, Human Health Evaluation Manual 6–4 (1989).

58. Memorandum from Elliott P. Laws, Assistant Administrator, U.S. EPA, to Regional Directors, Land Use in the CERCLA Remedy Selection Process (May 25, 1995). For an

The 1995 guidance concerning land use came in response to criticisms that the Agency's risk assessments and remedial decisions had reflexively assumed the future use would be residential. This assumption, critics argued, raised projected levels of exposure to contaminants left on site, leading to more aggressive clean up objectives and more expensive remedies. Although the directive does not explain it this way, by considering "reasonably anticipated future land use," EPA can avoid remedies whose incremental costs would not be justified by the incremental benefits, such as an aggressive remedy that made a site "safe" for residential use when only industrial use was likely.

* * *

Another related portal through which market considerations and other values important to the community may enter site deliberations along with environmental protection is the requirement that EPA solicit community views and consider the acceptability of the Agency's preferred remedy to the state and the community in selecting a remedy. The state and the local community typically have strong concerns about the environmental risks at a given site, but they also may have concerns about other issues. The state may be concerned about operation and maintenance costs that it will have to shoulder. The community may be concerned about the effects of the remedy and future uses of the site on jobs, property values, tax revenues, quality of life, the identity of the neighborhood, as well the environmental justice implications of such decisions. Under EPA regulations, acceptability of a remedy to the state and community is a consideration that comes relatively late in the process. As "modifying criteria," the acceptability of the remedy assumes, at least nominally, a less central role in EPA's deliberations than the "threshold" protectiveness criteria or even the "primary balancing criteria" such as effectiveness and implementability. Nevertheless, like consideration of land use, consultation with the state and local community on remedy selection provides a vehicle for a broader range of concerns to enter the process. In most cases, the local community is the primary if not the sole bearer of the environmental risks posted by the site, and its views will therefore bear importantly on the relative environmental value of various clean up scenarios. The local community also stands to reap a substantial portion of the non-environmental benefits of clean up, including the benefits that flow from reuse of the site, and may also be in the best position to assess those benefits.

* * *

NOTES AND QUESTIONS

1. *Judicial review of cleanup choices.* CERCLA § 113(h) (42 U.S.C. § 9613(h)) forbids judicial review of EPA's choice of a removal or remedial

---

excellent, detailed account of how land use is considered in the remedial process, see Robert Hersh et al., Res. for the Future, Linking Land Use and Superfund Clean Ups: Unchartered Territory 21–38 (1997).

action before that action is completed. Clinton County Commissioners v. EPA, 116 F.3d 1018 (3d Cir. 1997) (en banc). This provision was adopted to ensure that litigation did not delay site cleanup. Challenges to the selection of response actions can be raised in cost recovery actions after the cleanup. On the other hand, pre-implementation review is available in actions under § 106, when EPA seeks a court order forcing a PRP to undertake the response. To the extent that EPA relies on private clean-ups, as it has done more and more in recent years as the Superfund has dwindled, therefore, the result may be "lawyers first, shovels later."

2. *Compliance with the National Contingency Plan.* Compliance with the National Contingency Plan is essential to response cost recovery. The burden of proof of compliance depends upon whether the government or a private entity conducts the response. The United States, states, and Indian tribes are entitled to recover "all costs of removal or remedial action ... *not inconsistent with the national contingency plan*," while other entities may only recover "any other necessary costs of response ... *consistent with the national contingency plan*." What is the purpose of requiring consistency with the NCP as a condition of cost recovery? Should the NCP be regarded as a "floor" or a "ceiling" for cleanup features? In other words, is the consistency requirement intended to prevent shoddy, low-quality cleanups that could ultimately fail to achieve CERCLA's remedial goals, or is it intended to restrain wasteful and extravagant cleanups which exceed levels necessary for public health and environmental protection? Why is the burden of proof different for recovery of government and private response costs? Should consistency be evaluated solely in terms of substantive cleanup standards, or should it also consider the process followed? Several courts have held that failure to follow the public participation procedures prescribed in the NCP may limit or prevent recovery. See, e.g., United States v. Burlington Northern Railroad Co., 200 F.3d 679 (10th Cir. 1999).

3. *"Removal" versus "remedial" actions.* Distinguishing removal from remedial actions can be critical for cost recovery, because the NCP allows remedial action only after a site has been listed on the NPL and requires that EPA consider costs in selecting remedial, but not removal, actions. CERCLA defines "removal actions" and "remedial actions" in broad, partially overlapping, terms. See CERCLA 101(23) and 101(24). Finding that the plain language of the statute and its legislative history provided little help in distinguishing between removal and remedial actions, the Ninth Circuit in United States v. W.R. Grace & Co., 429 F.3d 1224, 1241 (9th Cir. 2005), deferred to EPA's interpretation, under which "the removal/remedial distinction boils down to whether the exigencies of the situation were such that the EPA did not have time to undertake the procedural steps required for a remedial action, and, in responding to such a time-sensitive threat, the EPA sought to minimize and stabilize imminent harms to human health and the environment." Under that standard, removal actions can occur over a protracted period of time, provided EPA can point to evidence of a substantial, continuing threat to health or the environment.

4. *Cost-benefit analysis of cleanup standards?* What role do costs play in the choice of remediation actions? Should explicit comparison of the costs and benefits of cleanup be required? James Hamilton and Kip Viscusi have argued that it should:

> The current policy approach used in the Superfund program is a peculiar halfway house. EPA devotes substantial effort to identifying chemicals at a site and ascertaining their potential risks. It also assesses costs of a range of remedies in considerable detail. However, many key elements are missing in the agency's analysis. There is no explicit consideration of the size of the population at risk in final remediation decisions. Risks to a single individual have the same weight as risks to a large exposed population. Actual and hypothetical exposures to chemicals receive equal weight so that risks to a person who, in the future, may choose to live near a currently uninhabited Superfund site receive the same weight as risks to large populations that are currently involuntarily exposed. EPA also reports the conservative risk assessment value for each site, without focusing its policy attention on the expected risk level or most likely risk scenarios. Finally, explicit trade-offs that balance benefits and costs do not enter remediation decisions. These problems arise in part because of decision-making constraints in the Superfund legislation and in part because of the way regulators have implemented the program.

* * *

> Sound risk analysis and benefit-cost analysis would force wiser spending and eliminate many of the problems that decrease the overall performance of * * * hazardous waste cleanup.

> Consider how benefit-cost analysis would help one answer how effectively EPA has targeted its expenditures to reduce risks. For the most effective 5 percent of cleanup expenditures, through remediation EPA eliminates 99.47 percent of the cancer risks averted. All expenditures beyond that level will have cleanup costs per discounted case of cancer averted in excess of $140 million. Potentially EPA can generate virtually all the wins in reduced risk at a fraction of the cleanup costs. At present, 95 percent of the expenditures at Superfund sites are devoted to eliminating only 0.5 percent of the cancer risk

> Under risk assessment and risk management reforms, EPA would assess population risks, rather than simply individual risks, from contamination at Superfund sites. The agency would present central tendency estimates so that analysts could see the range of risks at a site. More flexible remedy decisions based on risk levels rather than ARARs would reduce the costs associated with cleanup goals based on standards from other environmental programs. and costs based on the preference for permanent remedies.

> Risk reform is inevitably vulnerable to the fear that it will become a vehicle for ignoring environmental hazards rather than remediating them more efficiently. Our analysis shows, however, that there is a

wide zone within which risk reforms can improve efficiency without sacrificing human health considerations. In our analysis the shift toward site cleanups based on risk levels alone—rather than ARARs and calculations that include on-site future residents—would drop the number of sites remediated from 145 to 86 and site expenditures from $2.2 billion to $1.6 billion, but would reduce the number of cancer cases averted by only 21 (from 731 to 710) and the number of individuals protected from noncancer exposures by 16,000 (from 113,-000 to 97,000). Our analysis further indicates that calculation of risks based on central tendency would shift a substantial fraction of sites into the cleanup discretionary zone, where EPA site managers current-ly have the authority to decide whether or not to remediate a site. Removal of preference for permanence would also allow managers to consider more cost-effective alternatives.

The findings for minority populations are perhaps the most telling. * * * Sites with large minority populations had stronger benefit-cost performance. By focusing on objective measures of risk, benefit-cost analysis will highlight the policy importance of addressing the real risks that minorities may face from hazardous waste sites.

James T. Hamilton & W. Kip Viscusi, Calculating Risks: The Spatial and Political Dimensions of Hazardous Waste Policy 240–43 (The MIT Press, 1999). Do you agree? Is there any possible justification for not applying cost-benefit analysis to remedy selection? If it is applied, should future benefits in the form of human health protection be discounted to present value? How should the benefits of environmental restoration be calculated? Should cost-benefit analysis be used to set cleanup priorities even if it does not determine cleanup standards?

Consider, for example, the cleanup of the legacy of mining in Idaho's Coeur d'Alene Basin. "Perhaps the most intractable problem for ecological protection [in the Basin] is dissolved metals such as cadmium and zinc in surface water. Even with the most aggressive cleanup alternative, [which EPA projected would cost $2.6 billion,] computer modeling predicted that meeting federal water quality criteria for zinc would take at least 200 years." Clifford J. Villa, Superfund vs. Mega–Sites: The Couer d'Alene River Basin Story, 28 Colum. J. Envtl. L. 255, 302–303 (2003). Does Superfund require that level of cleanup, because water quality standards are an ARAR? Should it? The requirement that all ARARs be met can be waived, but the threshold requirement that cleanup protect health and the environment cannot. To the extent that water quality standards exist to protect aquatic life, it would seem that they could not be waived. Would spending $2.6 billion primarily to protect aquatic life in the Couer d'Alene Basin pass a cost-benefit test? Should it be required to do so?

5. *Funding cleanups.* Should the Superfund tax on oil and chemical producers be renewed? Is it fair to charge the "good actors" in those industries for contamination caused by others or contamination that occurs much later in the life-cycle of their products? Will the costs of the tax be passed on to the ultimate consumers of petroleum and chemical products, and if so is that appropriate? Or should the costs be spread to taxpayers at large? What should be the role of liability in financing cleanups? Sigman suggests that relying on liable parties to finance cleanups causes delays and increases transaction costs. Does that mean that CERCLA should move away from its focus on liability? On joint and several liability?

6. *The role of local communities.* What role do local communities play in determining CERCLA response actions, and through what procedural mechanisms? What are the benefits and costs of strong local involvement? Should the selection of response actions be informed at an early stage by likely future land use, or by the community's preferred land use? Or should the cost-effectiveness criterion for remedy selection be used to limit future uses where cleanup to a level that would permit them would be far more expensive than cleanup assuming a more restrictive future use?

7. *Risks created by remediation.* John Applegate and Steven Wesloh have noted that while remediation is being carried out, it may itself create or increase risks to health and the environment. They find that those risks are rarely explicitly considered when remedial actions are chosen, and that they may be exacerbated by the statutory preference for permanent treatment over capping or removal of contaminated soil. John S. Applegate & Steven M. Wesloh, Shortchanging Short–Term Risk: A Study of Superfund Remedy Selection, 15 Yale J. on Reg. 269 (1998). Should the NCP be revised to require explicit consideration of the risks posed by remediation activities? How should those risks be balanced against the long-term benefits of remediation?

PART IV

POLLUTION CONTROL

In this Part, we consider the complex statutes and regulations that have been developed to address air and water pollution. The two major federal anti-pollution laws, the Clean Air Act and the Clean Water Act, both rely primarily on "command and control" regulations. The Clean Air Act began with a primary focus on air quality and protecting human health, but has evolved more toward technology-based approaches. The Clean Water Act emphasized technology-based controls for many years, but is now moving haltingly toward a more water-quality-based regime. Their distinct trajectories demonstrate the need to combine technology-based and impact-based strategies. Experience with the federal pollution laws also shows the limits of command-and-control regulation. Under both the Clean Air and Clean Water Acts, efforts have been made in recent years to add market-based instruments and voluntary measures to the mix. Such non-traditional measures offer some advantages, but also pose their own distinct challenges.

CHAPTER TEN

Air Pollution Control

Section 1. Introduction and Overview

Air pollution presents one of the most serious environmental problems of the modern age. As Robert Arvill noted,

> [A]n average person requires over thirty pounds of air a day or about six pints every minute, and he has to take it as it comes. He would not readily stand in sewage or drink dirty water. Yet daily the individual draws 26,000 breaths, between 18 and 22 each minute, many of which—if not all in some cases—are of filthy air.

R. Arvill, *Man and Environment* 97 (1967).

The legal response to air pollution has evolved from reliance on the common law to remarkably detailed federal regulation. The federal Clean Air Act is important both for the specific ways that it approaches air quality protection and as an example of several key strategies and challenges for environmental regulation.

A. Historical Background

In pre-colonial North America, thanks to a variety of natural sources and the deliberate use of large-scale fire by some Native Americans, the air always had some pollutants. European settlement, though, followed by industrialization and urban growth, produced pollution on a far more dramatic scale. By the beginning of the 20th century, pollution from coal soot was so bad in industrial cities like Pittsburgh that "[e]pisodes would frequently blot out the sun, requiring gaslights at midday." John Bachmann, Will the Circle Be Unbroken: A History of the U.S. National Ambient Air Quality Standards, 57 Journal of the Air and Waste Management Association 652 (2007).

Legal authority to address smoke and soot was available, but not widely used. Early town planning made some effort to separate industrial activities from residential and commercial areas, as much for fire safety reasons as for concern over smoke pollution. The courts endorsed air pollution regulation as early as 1859, when a New Orleans ordinance regulating "dense smoke" was upheld, New Orleans v. Lambert, 14 La. Ann. 247 (1859), and the constitutionality of smoke abatement ordinances was firmly established against due process and equal protection challenges by the U.S. Supreme Court in 1916, in Northwestern Laundry v. Des Moines, 239 U.S. 486 (1916). But although everyone agreed that smoke and soot were a nuisance, their health impacts were not firmly established. As a result, not everyone agreed that pollution reduction was important, or that it should take priority over industrial expansion. Some industrial cities even prided themselves on their polluted air, which they saw as an indicator of the prosperity associated with a robust industrial economy. The lack of available substitutes for coal as an inexpensive power source both for industry and for residential heating in this era also contributed to reluctance to adopt strong pollution regulation.

Although a growing number of U.S. cities adopted "smoke ordinances" intended to limit pollution from large industrial sources and engineers worked to improve the technology of pollution control, air quality continued to deteriorate. Just after World War II, however, a series of dramatic events shifted the political landscape by making the health costs of air pollution apparent.

In 1948, as Pittsburgh was enjoying dramatic improvements from its smoke program, just 29 km away the small industrial community of Donora experienced an air pollution disaster that could not be ascribed solely to smoke. An unusual meteorological inversion resulted in a 4-day buildup of fog, PM [particulate matter], and SO_x [sulfur oxides] from steel and zinc smelters and sulfuric acid plant emissions. During the episode, 20 people died, and 6000 people (approximately 43% of the total Donora population) suffered respiratory problems described as "a gasping for air and complaints of unbearable chest pains." The Donora story made national headlines * * *.

The second transforming development was the unexplained occurrence of eye-burning smog events beginning in 1943 in Los Angeles, one of the major urban areas that used virtually no coal. Although it is called smog, it consisted neither of smoke nor fog, and it turned out to be a new form of air pollution that appeared as widespread haze that burned the eyes. * * *

Seeking expert advice, in 1946 the Los Angeles Times hired Raymond Tucker * * * to study the problem and recommend solutions. Tucker's recommendations focused on banning obvious sources of PM and SO_x emissions such as incinerators and fires at waste dumps, monitoring industrial emissions, and penalizing diesel truck drivers with smoky emissions. In 1947, California passed the first statewide legislation authorizing county air pollution regulations for anything other than smoke, and Los Angeles County immediately formed an Air Pollution Control District. But there was no "silver bullet" strategy * * *. When the kinds of sensible measures Tucker recommended were later adopted, dust fall was reduced, but the controls failed to address the main sources of the smog problem. In addition to initial regulatory activities, the city, industry, and the state mounted research and monitoring programs to better understand the nature, sources, and effects of smog. In this case, officials perceived the sudden and growing eye-stinging smog episodes as an economic threat to an area whose growth in part depended on the attraction of its warm, sunny skies to health seekers.

Near the end of 1952, (December 5–12), the worst air pollution disaster on record occurred in London, England. Initially, heavy fog obliterated visibility, causing traffic accidents and canceling events, but eventually official reports noted crowded hospitals and increased mortality. A year later, a report set the number of deaths at approximately 4000 (today estimates of the totals are as much as three times higher). This not only cemented the relationship between pollution and health, but also resulted in a substantial increase in research and monitoring, both in the United States and in Europe.

Bachmann, supra.

The Donora, Los Angeles, and London incidents brought attention to the health and economic costs of air pollution. They invigorated air pollution research and monitoring, notably through new commitments of federal funding. Regulatory authority remained with state and local governments, which moved at varying paces. California was the first to develop ambient air quality standards, although its standards were less strict than those LA authorities thought necessary. California's efforts accounted for fully 60% of the expenditures by state and local authorities to address air pollution during this period. Id.

In 1963, disappointed by the pace of state progress, Congress authorized federal action against some pollution sources, but only in narrowly defined circumstances and after byzantine procedural mazes were navigated. By 1966, little progress had been made at either the federal or the state and local level in developing air quality standards, much less in achieving those standards. In 1967, Congress directed the states to adopt air quality standards and develop plans to achieve those standards.

In the late 1960s, the environmental movement was in full swing. The public was focused on pollution problems, both air and water, and politicians were eager to respond. The ink was hardly dry on the 1967 version of the Clean Air Act before new federal air pollution legislation was being proposed. It was already clear that the process for implementing the 1967 law was cumbersome and time-consuming, and that technology-based emission limits might need to be combined with air quality standards. In 1970, prodded by a "race to the top" among politicians with national ambitions, Congress enacted the framework of the modern Clean Air Act. Despite two rounds of major amendments, in 1977 and 1990, that framework remains essentially intact today. It calls for national uniform air quality standards, primarily implemented by the states but backstopped by a variety of federal technology-based controls on both stationary and mobile sources. EPA, then only a month old itself, was given the daunting task of issuing the air quality and emission limitation regulations called for by the new law.

B. OVERVIEW OF THE CLEAN AIR ACT

1. *Ambient air quality standards.* The primary focus of the Clean Air Act at the outset was the identification and achievement of healthy air quality throughout the nation. To that end, § 108 directs EPA to identify

pollutants suitable for the issuance of national standards, and § 109 requires that EPA issue national ambient air quality standards (NAAQS) for those "criteria pollutants."

2. *State implementation plans and attainment of the standards.* Air quality standards, of course, do not by themselves produce clean air. They must be translated into controls on individual sources. Initially, the CAA relied entirely on the states to perform that translation step, requiring that they develop plans to achieve the national air quality standards within their borders, without contributing to air pollution problems elsewhere. When states failed to rapidly make progress toward cleaning up their skies, Congress added attainment deadlines and a variety of sanctions for non-attainment. It remains true today, however, that states have the primary responsibility for deciding what trade-offs to make to meet the national standards.

3. *Mobile source regulation.* The 1970 CAA introduced for the first time aggressive federal regulation of air pollution emissions from mobile sources (most importantly automobiles and trucks, but also trains, airplanes, and offroad vehicles). These national standards preempt state regulation in order to protect the national market in vehicles. Because California had adopted tailpipe emission controls before 1970, the CAA allows EPA to waive preemption of more stringent California standards. Other states may choose to adopt California's standards or EPA's, but may not develop their own. The mobile source regulations are detailed and complex, including regulation not only of engine emissions but of fuel composition. For our purposes, they are important primarily as the leading US example of an explicitly technology-forcing approach to pollution and as a current battleground over the extent of federal preemption of state standards.

4. *Federal stationary source regulation.* The CAA also creates an important federal role in the regulation of new and modified stationary sources. EPA sets industry-wide technology-based "new source performance standards" (NSPS). Potentially more stringent standards also apply specifically to new sources in clean-air and nonattainment areas. These special requirements for new or modified sources have significantly altered the economics of the electric power industry, encouraging utilities to continue using old plants well past what was expected to be the term of their useful life. They have also generated a series of disputes about exactly what it means for a source to be "new" or "modified." We will consider new source regulation in the context of the politics and environmental effects of "grandfathering" sources that predate regulation.

5. *Prevention of significant deterioration.* The primary thrust of the 1970 CAA was to clean up areas suffering from significant air pollution. The prevention of significant deterioration (PSD) program originated in a judicial mandate. In Sierra Club v. Ruckelshaus, 344 F.Supp. 253 (D.D.C. 1972), the district court, looking to the CAA's declared purpose of protecting and enhancing air quality, overturned EPA regulations allowing states to submit SIPS that would allow pollution levels in clean air areas to rise to

the level of the NAAQS. The D.C. Circuit and then the Supreme Court affirmed without opinion. 412 U.S. 541 (1973). EPA subsequently issued "non-degradation" regulations, but those were superseded in 1977 by amendments to the CAA creating what is now known as the PSD program. PSD requires a special sort of new source review for major new and modified stationary sources in areas that are in attainment of the relevant NAAQS. The new or modified facility must meet not only the category-wide NSPS, but also individually identified best available control technology. PSD also sets a type of air quality standards more stringent than the NAAQS for attainment areas, calling for EPA to set acceptable "increments," that is increases in pollution above baseline levels. The permissible increment levels vary with the designation of the area; many national park lands are by congressional fiat in the most protective class. States can also designate lands for strong PSD protection, but have not rushed to do so. Anyone seeking a permit for construction of a new or modified source in an attainment area must demonstrate, through air pollution modeling, that the new source will not cause a relevant increment to be exceeded. For a detailed description of the PSD program, see Craig N. Oren, Prevention of Significant Deterioration: Control–Compelling Versus Site–Shifting, 74 Iowa L. Rev. 1 (1988).

6. *Hazardous air pollutants.* As enacted in 1970, CAA § 112 (42 U.S.C. § 7412) called for EPA to identify, and develop health-based emission standards providing an ample margin of safety for, any air pollutant that might cause or contribute to serious adverse health effects. EPA found itself virtually paralyzed by this standard, unable to reliably identify safe levels of pollutants but unwilling to flatly prohibit their emission, at the potential cost of shutting down important industrial sectors. In twenty years, EPA listed only 8 substances as hazardous air pollutants. In the 1990 amendments to the CAA, Congress took control of the hazardous air pollutant program, ordering EPA to issue technology-based regulations for a list of 189 pollutants, and requiring EPA to add substances to the list if they may cause adverse human health effects. Within six years of promulgating technology-based standards, EPA was to evaluate any remaining health risks, report them to Congress, and issue additional regulations to reduce remaining health risks below a maximum cancer risk of 1 in 1 million based on maximum lifetime exposures. The hazardous air pollutant program, which continues to suffer from delays and high resource demands, illustrates the challenges of risk-based regulation. For a description of EPA's struggle to effectively implement the program, see Victor B. Flatt, Gasping for Breath: The Administrative Flaws of Federal Hazardous Air Pollution Regulation and What We Can Learn from the States, 34 Ecology L. Q. 107 (2007).

7. *Marketable emission permits for sulfur oxides.* In the 1990 CAA amendments, Congress adopted a system of tradable emission permits to address the problem of acid rain caused by emission of SO_x. Permits were distributed to major sources on the basis of past emissions. New sources, or those which want to increase emissions must acquire permits from existing sources. The number of available permits has also been gradually ramped

down over time, so that even existing sources must acquire additional permits if they want to continue emitting at a constant level. The SO_x permit program is the oldest and largest marketable pollution permit program in the United States. It provides lessons about such programs that may be useful for development and implementation of similar programs for greenhouse gas emissions, or for water pollution discharges. Marketable pollution allowances are considered in more detail in Section 5 of this chapter.

8. *Individual stationary source permits*. The CAA's focus on air quality is in some respects difficult to implement. While SIPs may allocate the available pollutant increment among the region's sources, it may be difficult for regulators, the interested public, or even the sources themselves to keep track of applicable requirements. The situation is further complicated by the plethora of different technology-based requirements that may apply to any one source under the NSPS, PSD, non-attainment and hazardous air pollutant programs. A mechanism is needed to oversee compliance with all these requirements and facilitate the imposition of sanctions on sources that exceed their authorized emissions. The 1990 CAA amendments provided that mechanism, mandating that each major stationary source have a permit incorporating all applicable operating requirements. CAA §§ 501–507 (42 U.S.C. §§ 7661–7661f). Title V also helps to make up for EPA's frequent delays in issuing category-wide emission limitations, requiring that where EPA has not issued limits applicable to the source category equivalent limitations must be determined and imposed, on a case-by-case basis, in each permit.

SECTION 2.   NATIONAL AMBIENT AIR QUALITY STANDARDS

The heart of the Clean Air Act is the federal definition of national ambient air quality standards and their implementation by the states. Defining an acceptable level of air pollution turns out to be a surprisingly difficult task. Achieving that level is even more challenging.

A.   SETTING NATIONAL AMBIENT AIR QUALITY STANDARDS

CLASS DISCUSSION PROBLEM: A NAAQS FOR CO_2?

In June 2003, the states of Massachusetts, Connecticut, and Maine filed suit against EPA, seeking an order compelling EPA to list CO_2 as a criteria pollutant and to develop a NAAQS for CO_2. The lawsuit is based on the dangers of global warming. The states point out that EPA has long recognized publicly, on its web site among other places, that CO_2 emissions from fossil-fuel burning power plants, automobiles, and a wide variety of other sources contribute to global warming, which may have a variety of serious impacts including raising sea level, altering precipitation patterns and water availability, and affecting human health as well as other species.

In 1998, Jonathan Cannon, then General Counsel for EPA, wrote a memorandum concluding that CO_2 was an "air pollutant" potentially subject to regulation under the CAA if it meets the definition of a "criteria" pollutant. In 2003, however, EPA reversed course, taking the position that it did not have the authority to regulate emissions of CO_2 or other greenhouse gases in order to address the problem of global climate change. EPA argued, among other things, that the NAAQS system is "fundamentally ill-suited to addressing global climate change" because actions taken by states and EPA cannot alone bring the U.S. into attainment with any NAAQS that might be set for CO_2. To support its position, EPA cited a Supreme Court decision holding that the grant of authority to the FDA to regulate "drugs" and "devices," broadly defined, did not authorize regulation of cigarettes. Food and Drug Administration v. Brown & Williamson Tobacco Corp., 529 U.S. 120 (2000). CO_2 regulation, EPA noted, would have broad impacts, "affecting every sector of the nation's economy and threatening its overall economic health."

In 2007, in a case dealing with the regulation of emissions from mobile sources, the Supreme Court ruled that CO_2 is an "air pollutant" under the Clean Air Act, making it eligible for regulation. Massachusetts v. EPA, 549 U.S. 497 (2007). Based on the material that follows, must EPA now set a NAAQS for CO_2? How would EPA determine the appropriate level of CO_2 in the atmosphere? What consequences would follow? Would the designation of a NAAQS for CO_2 help to address the problem of global warming?

Excerpts From the Clean Air Act

42 U.S.C. §§ 7401–7671q.

Sec. 108.   Air quality criteria and control techniques

(a) Air pollutant list; publication and revision by Administrator; issuance of air quality criteria for air pollutants

(1) For the purpose of establishing national primary and secondary ambient air quality standards, the Administrator shall within 30 days after December 31, 1970, publish, and shall from time to time thereafter revise, a list which includes each air pollutant—

(A) emissions of which, in his judgment, cause or contribute to air pollution which may reasonably be anticipated to endanger public health or welfare;

(B) the presence of which in the ambient air results from numerous or diverse mobile or stationary sources; and

(C) for which air quality criteria had not been issued before December 31, 1970, but for which he plans to issue air quality criteria under this section.

(2) The Administrator shall issue air quality criteria for an air pollutant within 12 months after he has included such pollutant in a list under paragraph (1). Air quality criteria for an air pollutant shall

accurately reflect the latest scientific knowledge useful in indicating the kind and extent of all identifiable effects on public health or welfare which may be expected from the presence of such pollutant in the ambient air, in varying quantities. * * *

Sec. 109. National primary and secondary ambient air quality standards

(a) Promulgation.

(1) The Administrator—

(A) within 30 days after December 31, 1970, shall publish proposed regulations prescribing a national primary ambient air quality standard and a national secondary ambient air quality standard for each air pollutant for which air quality criteria have been issued prior to such date; and

(B) after a reasonable time for interested persons to submit written comments thereon (but no later than 90 days after the initial publication of such proposed standards) shall by regulation promulgate such proposed national primary and secondary ambient air quality standards with such modifications as he deems appropriate.

(2) With respect to any air pollutant for which air quality criteria are issued after December 31, 1970, the Administrator shall publish, simultaneously with the issuance of such criteria and information, proposed national primary and secondary ambient air quality standards for any such pollutant. The procedure provided for in paragraph (1)(B) of this subsection shall apply to the promulgation of such standards.

(b) Protection of public health and welfare.

(1) National primary ambient air quality standards, prescribed under subsection (a) of this section shall be ambient air quality standards the attainment and maintenance of which in the judgment of the Administrator, based on such criteria and allowing an adequate margin of safety, are requisite to protect the public health. Such primary standards may be revised in the same manner as promulgated.

(2) Any national secondary ambient air quality standard prescribed under subsection (a) of this section shall specify a level of air quality the attainment and maintenance of which in the judgment of the Administrator, based on such criteria, is requisite to protect the public welfare from any known or anticipated adverse effects associated with the presence of such air pollutant in the ambient air. Such secondary standards may be revised in the same manner as promulgated.

* * *

(d) Review and revision of criteria and standards * * *.

(1) Not later than December 31, 1980, and at five-year intervals thereafter, the Administrator shall complete a thorough review of the criteria published under section 7408 of this title and the national ambient air quality standards promulgated under this section and shall make such revisions in such criteria and standards and promulgate such new standards as may be appropriate in accordance with section 7408 of this title and subsection (b) of this section. The Administrator may review and revise criteria or promulgate new standards earlier or more frequently than required under this paragraph.

(2)(A) The Administrator shall appoint an independent scientific review committee composed of seven members including at least one member of the National Academy of Sciences, one physician, and one person representing State air pollution control agencies.

(B) Not later than January 1, 1980, and at five-year intervals thereafter, the committee referred to in subparagraph (A) shall complete a review of the criteria published under section 7408 of this title and the national primary and secondary ambient air quality standards promulgated under this section and shall recommend to the Administrator any new national ambient air quality standards and revisions of existing criteria and standards as may be appropriate under section 7408 of this title and subsection (b) of this section.

* * *

Sec. 302. Definitions.

* * *

(g) The term "air pollutant" means any air pollution agent or combination of such agents, including any physical, chemical, biological, radioactive (including source material, special nuclear material, and byproduct material) substance or matter which is emitted into or otherwise enters the ambient air. * * *

(h) All language referring to effects on welfare includes, but is not limited to, effects on soils, water, crops, vegetation, manmade materials, animals, wildlife, weather, visibility, and climate, damage to and deterioration of property, and hazards to transportation, as well as effects on economic values and on personal comfort and well-being, whether caused by transformation, conversion, or combination with other air pollutants.

The main purpose of the Clean Air Act is to "to protect and enhance the quality of the Nation's air resources so as to promote the public health and welfare." CAA § 101(b)(1) (42 U.S.C. § 7401(b)(1)). The most important tool it provides for that purpose is the National Ambient Air Quality Standards (NAAQS), which are developed by EPA pursuant to CAA sections 108 and 109 (42 U.S.C. §§ 7408–7409). Section 108 directs EPA to identify air pollutants emitted from numerous or diverse sources that contribute to air pollution which may reasonably be anticipated to endanger public health or welfare. Those pollutants are called "criteria pollutants" because once it identifies them EPA must produce lengthy documents known as "air quality criteria" detailing current scientific understanding of their health and welfare effects. CAA § 109 then requires that EPA use those criteria to set primary and secondary NAAQS. The primary standards are intended to protect public health while the secondary standards protect the public welfare, expansively defined. Every five years both the criteria and the NAAQS are supposed to be reviewed and, if appropriate, revised.

Although the Clean Air Act anticipated that new NAAQS would be issued and existing standards would be revised as updated technical information became available, in fact there has been little change to the list of criteria pollutants since it was first issued in 1971. Before enactment of the 1970 CAA, the federal Department of Health, Education and Welfare had issued criteria for particulate matter, ozone, sulfur oxides, hydrocarbons, and nitrogen dioxide. Those criteria became the basis for the initial NAAQS, which were issued by EPA with remarkable rapidity, only four months after enactment of the CAA. They came with only a cursory explanation of how the scientific information in the criteria led EPA to its particular selection of substantive standard. Industry won a remand of the SO_x standard because the explanation was deemed insufficient. After discovering an embarrassing mistake in its analysis of the effects of SO_x on vegetation, EPA adopted much more formal administrative procedures for NAAQS adoption and revision. The process now is lengthy, time-consuming, and involves many layers of public comment and scientific advice.

Since those initial NAAQS were promulgated, the changes to the criteria pollutant list have been minor. EPA had projected in 1970 that it would add as many as 24 pollutants to the list over the course of a few years, but those listings never materialized. The separate hydrocarbon standard was revoked because its only purpose from the outset was to help with achievement of the ozone standard. Lead was added to the list in 1978 following litigation by environmental groups. NRDC v. Train, 545 F.2d 320 (2d Cir. 1976). Since then, the particulate matter standard has been broken into distinct standards for two size classes of particles but no additional substances have been added.

The NAAQS are codified at 40 C.F.R. Part 50. The current NAAQS cover carbon monoxide (CO); lead (Pb); nitrogen dioxide (NO_2); particulate matter, with separate standards for particles less than or equal to 10 micrometers in diameter (PM_{10}) and particles less than or equal to 2.5 micrometers in diameter ($PM_{2.5}$); ozone (O_3); and sulfur dioxide (SO_2). These are the pollutants EPA considers the "worst of the worst"—harmful to human health and the environment, and produced by many different sources. Their sources and health and environmental effects are briefly described in the next few paragraphs.

Carbon Monoxide (CO). Carbon monoxide (CO) is a colorless, odorless gas, formed when carbon-based fuels are incompletely burned. About 60%

of CO emissions nationwide are produced by motor vehicle exhaust. High concentrations of CO generally occur in areas with heavy traffic congestion. Other sources of CO emissions include industrial processes, nontransportation fuel combustion, and natural sources such as wildfires. By contrast to ozone, peak CO concentrations typically occur during the colder months of the year when automotive CO emissions are increased and weather conditions trap pollutants near the ground at night.

Carbon monoxide enters the bloodstream through the lungs. In the bloodstream it competes with oxygen for receptors, reducing the delivery of oxygen to organs and tissues. The health threat from lower levels of CO is most serious for those who suffer from cardiovascular disease. Visual impairment, reduced work capacity, reduced manual dexterity, poor learning ability, and difficulty in performing complex tasks are all associated with exposure to elevated CO levels. At high levels, CO can kill even healthy individuals by interfering with oxygen uptake and metabolism.

Lead (Pb). At one time, automotive sources were the major contributor of lead emissions to the atmosphere. Since leaded gasoline was banned, lead emissions from the transportation sector have substantially declined, although airplanes remain a major source of lead pollution. Today, industrial processes, primarily metals processing, are the major source of airborne lead pollution. The highest air concentrations of lead are found in the vicinity of smelters and battery manufacturers. Lead emitted into the air can settle on soil or in water, or become attached to atmospheric particles.

Exposure to lead occurs through its inhalation from the atmosphere or ingestion on food, soil, or dust, or in water. It accumulates in the blood, bones, and soft tissues. Lead can adversely affect the kidneys, liver, nervous system, and other organs. It can also cause neurological impairments including seizures, intelligence impairment, and behavioral disorders. Even at low doses, lead exposure is associated with damage to the nervous systems of fetuses and young children, resulting in learning deficits and lowered IQ. Through deposition on leaves, lead can pose a hazard to grazing animals.

Nitrogen oxides (NO_x). Nitrogen oxides (NO_x), which include NO, NO_2 and other oxides of nitrogen, play a major role in the formation of ozone, particulate matter, and acid rain. The major sources of man-made NO_x emissions are high-temperature combustion processes, like those which occur in automobiles and power plants. Home heaters and gas stoves also produce substantial amounts of NO_x in indoor settings.

Short-term exposures (e.g., less than 3 hours) to low levels of NO_x may lead to changes in airway responsiveness and lung function in individuals with pre-existing respiratory illnesses and increases in respiratory illnesses in children. Long-term exposures to NOx may increase susceptibility to respiratory infection and cause permanent lung damage. Nitrogen oxides also react in the air to form ground-level ozone and $PM_{2.5}$, with their associated health and welfare impacts.

Nitrogen oxides contribute to a wide range of environmental effects, including the formation of acid rain and the resulting acidification of waterways; and eutrophication, increases in the nutrient load of waterways connected with excessive algal growth and depletion of the oxygen needed by fish and other aquatic species.

Particulate Matter. Particulate matter (PM) refers to the mixture of solid particles and liquid droplets found in the air. Some particles are large or dark enough to be seen as soot or smoke. Others are so small they can be detected only with an electron microscope. $PM_{2.5}$ includes only particles less than or equal to 2.5 micrometers in diameter. PM_{10} refers to all particles less than or equal to 10 micrometers in diameter, about one seventh the diameter of human hair. It includes the fine $PM_{2.5}$ particles as well as the slightly larger particles that are 2.5 to 10 micrometers in diameter, sometimes called "coarse" particles.

Because it is often a product of incomplete combustion, PM is produced by many different stationary sources, mobile sources and natural sources. The finest particles come from motor vehicles, fossil fuel-burning power plants, various industrial facilities, residential fireplaces and wood stoves. Coarser particles are often connected to dust. They are produced by vehicles traveling on unpaved roads, materials handling, crushing and grinding operations, and various agricultural practices. Some particles are emitted directly from sources, such as smokestacks and cars. Others are the product of chemical reactions in which pollutants including SO_2, NO_X and VOCs interact with other compounds in the air to form fine particles. The chemical and physical composition of PM varies depending on location, time of year, and weather.

The human health effects of PM are typically related to respiratory functions and exposure through the lungs. Coarse particles are primarily associated with the aggravation of respiratory conditions such as asthma. Fine particles, which can lodge deeper in the lungs, are associated with heart disease, increased respiratory symptoms, decreased lung function, and premature death. Those at greatest risk include the elderly, individuals with cardiopulmonary disease, and children. Beyond its human health effects, PM is the major cause of reduced visibility in many parts of the United States. Airborne particles also can impact plants and wildlife, and can damage paints and building materials.

Ozone (O_3). Ozone occurs naturally in the stratosphere (6 to 30 miles above the surface), where it provides a protective layer insulating living organisms from the harmful effects of ultraviolet radiation from the sun. At the earth's surface, however, where it comes into direct contact with people, plants, and wildlife, ozone can be harmful. Ozone is not emitted directly into the air but is formed by the reaction of VOCs (Volatile Organic Compound) and NO_X in the presence of heat and sunlight. Ground-level ozone forms readily in the atmosphere, usually during hot summer weather. VOCs are emitted from a variety of sources, including motor vehicles, chemical plants, refineries, factories, consumer and commercial products, and other industrial sources. Nitrogen oxides are emitted from motor vehicles, power plants, and other sources of combustion. Changing weather patterns contribute to yearly differences in ozone concentrations from region to region. Ozone and the precursor pollutants that cause ozone can be transported hundreds of miles in the atmosphere.

Short-term (1–3 hours) and prolonged (6–8 hours) exposures to ambient ozone have been linked to a number of adverse health effects, including a variety of respiratory problems. Ozone effects are especially marked during exercise. Children, active outdoors during the summer when ozone levels are at their highest, are most at risk of experiencing such effects. Other at-risk groups include adults who are active outdoors (e.g., some outdoor workers) and individuals with pre-existing respiratory disease such as asthma. In addition, longer-term exposures to moderate levels of ozone may cause irreversible changes in the lungs which could worsen chronic respiratory illnesses.

Ozone also affects vegetation, leading to reductions in agricultural and forest yields, reduced growth and survival of some seedlings, and increased susceptibility to disease, pests, and environmental stresses (e.g., harsh weather). Ground-level ozone damage to foliage also can decrease the aesthetic value of gardens and the natural beauty of parks and recreation areas.

Sulfur oxides (SO$_x$). The major sources of sulfur oxides are combustion of fuels containing sulfur (most commonly coal and oil), metal smelting, and other industrial processes. High concentrations of SO$_x$ can impair breathing, particularly in asthmatics, children, and those who are active outdoors. Other effects associated with longer-term exposures to high concentrations of SOx in conjunction with high levels of PM include respiratory illness, alterations in the lungs' defenses, and aggravation of existing cardiovascular disease.

Together with NO$_x$, SO$_x$ is a major precursor to acid rain, which is associated with the acidification of soils, lakes, and streams, as well as accelerated corrosion of structures and paints. Sulfur dioxide also is a major precursor to PM$_{2.5}$.

The NAAQS are expressed in terms of concentration (micrograms per cubic meter or parts per million) and averaging time (varying from 1 hour to 1 year). For most of the criteria pollutants, EPA has set separate NAAQS for two or more averaging times.

Each NAAQS has four components: the indicator, the level, the averaging time, and the form. The "indicator" defines the parameters of the substance that the EPA will measure—for example, the size or composition of the particles to which a PM standard will apply. The "level" specifies the acceptable concentration of that indicator in the air. The "averaging time" specifies the span of time across which the amount of a pollutant in the air will be averaged. For example, some NAAQS require a certain average annual level, while others require a certain average daily level. The "form" of a NAAQS describes how compliance with the level will be determined within this averaging time. A NAAQS with a daily averaging time, for example, might require that the level not be exceeded on more than one day each year.

American Farm Bureau Federation v. EPA, 559 F.3d 512, 516 (D.C. Cir. 2009).

The following chart summarizes the NAAQS in effect as of July 2011.

Pollutant	Averaging time	Primary NAAQS	Secondary NAAQS
CO	8 hour	9 ppm (10 mg/m^3)	-------
	1 hour	35 ppm (40 mg/m^3)	-------
Pb	3 months	0.15 μg/m^3	same as primary
NO$_2$	annual	0.053 ppm (53 ppb)	same as primary
	1 hour	100 ppb	-------
PM$_{10}$	24 hour	150 μg/m3	same as primary
PM$_{2.5}$	annual	15 μg/m3	same as primary
	24 hour	35 μg/m3	same as primary
O$_3$	8 hour	0.075 ppm	same as primary
SO$_x$	annual	0.03 ppm	0.5 ppm, 3 hour averaging time
	24 hour	0.14 ppm	
	1 hour	75 ppb	

Whitman v. American Trucking Associations

United States Supreme Court, 2001.
531 U.S. 457.

■ JUSTICE SCALIA delivered the opinion of the Court.

* * *

I

Section 109(a) of the CAA, 42 U.S.C. § 7409(a), requires the Administrator of the EPA to promulgate NAAQS for each air pollutant for which "air quality criteria" have been issued under § 108, 42 U.S.C. § 7408. Once a NAAQS has been promulgated, the Administrator must review the standard (and the criteria on which it is based) "at five-year intervals" and make "such revisions ... as may be appropriate." CAA § 109(d)(1), 42 U.S.C. § 7409(d)(1). These cases arose when, on July 18, 1997, the Administrator revised the NAAQS for particulate matter and ozone. * * *

II

* * *

Section 109(b)(1) instructs the EPA to set primary ambient air quality standards "the attainment and maintenance of which ... are requisite to protect the public health" with "an adequate margin of safety." 42 U.S.C. § 7409(b)(1). Were it not for the hundreds of pages of briefing respondents have submitted on the issue, one would have thought it fairly clear that this text does not permit the EPA to consider costs in setting the standards. * * * The EPA, "based on" the information about health effects contained in the technical "criteria" documents compiled under § 108(a)(2), 42 U.S.C. § 7408(a)(2), is to identify the maximum airborne concentration of a pollutant that the public health can tolerate, decrease the concentration to provide an "adequate" margin of safety, and set the standard at that level. Nowhere are the costs of achieving such a standard made part of that initial calculation.

Against this most natural of readings, respondents make a lengthy, spirited, but ultimately unsuccessful attack. They begin with the object of § 109(b)(1)'s focus, the "public health." When the term first appeared in federal clean air legislation—in the Act of July 14, 1955 (1955 Act), 69 Stat. 322, which expressed "recognition of the dangers to the public health" from air pollution—its ordinary meaning was "[t]he health of the community." Webster's New International Dictionary 2005 (2d ed. 1950). Respondents argue, however, that § 109(b)(1), as added by the Clean Air Amendments of 1970, 84 Stat. 1676, meant to use the term's secondary meaning: "[t]he ways and means of conserving the health of the members of a community, as by preventive medicine, organized care of the sick, etc." *Ibid.* Words that can have more than one meaning are given content, however, by their surroundings, and in the context of § 109(b)(1) this second definition makes no sense. * * * We therefore revert to the primary definition of the term: the health of the public.

Even so, respondents argue, many more factors than air pollution affect public health. In particular, the economic cost of implementing a very stringent standard might produce health losses sufficient to offset the health gains achieved in cleaning the air—for example, by closing down whole industries and thereby impoverishing the workers and consumers dependent upon those industries. That is unquestionably true, and Congress was unquestionably aware of it. Thus, Congress had commissioned in the Air Quality Act of 1967 (1967 Act) "a detailed estimate of the cost of carrying out the provisions of this Act; a comprehensive study of the cost of program implementation by affected units of government; and a comprehensive study of the economic impact of air quality standards on the Nation's industries, communities, and other contributing sources of pollution." § 2, 81 Stat. 505. The 1970 Congress, armed with the results of this study, not only anticipated that compliance costs could injure the public health, but provided for that precise exigency. Section 110(f)(1) of the CAA permitted the Administrator to waive the compliance deadline for stationary sources if, *inter alia,* sufficient control measures were simply unavailable and "the continued operation of such sources is *essential ... to the public health* or welfare." 84 Stat. 1683 (emphasis added). Other provisions explicitly permitted or required economic costs to be taken into account in implementing the air quality standards. * * * Subsequent amendments to the CAA have added many more provisions directing, in explicit language, that the Administrator consider costs in performing various duties. * * * We have therefore refused to find implicit in ambiguous sections of the CAA an authorization to consider costs that has elsewhere, and so often, been expressly granted.

Accordingly, to prevail in their present challenge, respondents must show a textual commitment of authority to the EPA to consider costs in setting NAAQS under § 109(b)(1). And because § 109(b)(1) and the NAAQS for which it provides are the engine that drives nearly all of Title I of the CAA, that textual commitment must be a clear one. * * * Respondents' textual arguments ultimately founder upon this principle.

Their first claim is that § 109(b)(1)'s terms "adequate margin" and "requisite" leave room to pad health effects with cost concerns. * * * [W]e find it implausible that Congress would give to the EPA through these modest words the power to determine whether implementation costs should moderate national air quality standards.

The same defect inheres in respondents' next two arguments: that while the Administrator's judgment about what is requisite to protect the public health must be "based on [the] criteria" documents developed under § 108(a)(2), it need not be based *solely* on those criteria; and that those criteria themselves, while they must include "effects on public health or welfare which may be expected from the presence of such pollutant in the ambient air," are not necessarily *limited* to those effects. Even if we were to concede those premises, we still would not conclude that one of the unenumerated factors that the agency can consider in developing and applying the criteria is cost of implementation. That factor is *both* so indirectly related to public health *and* so full of potential for canceling the conclusions drawn from direct health effects that it would surely have been expressly mentioned in §§ 108 and 109 had Congress meant it to be considered. Yet while those provisions describe in detail how the health effects of pollutants in the ambient air are to be calculated and given effect, they say not a word about costs.

Respondents point, finally, to a number of provisions in the CAA that *do* require attainment cost data to be generated. Section 108(b)(1), for example, instructs the Administrator to "issue to the States," simultaneously with the criteria documents, "information on air pollution control techniques, which information shall include data relating to the cost of installation and operation." 42 U.S.C. § 7408(b)(*l*). And § 109(d)(2)(C)(iv) requires the Clean Air Scientific Advisory Committee to "advise the Administrator of any adverse public health, welfare, social, economic, or energy effects which may result from various strategies for attainment and maintenance" of NAAQS. 42 U.S.C. § 7409(d)(2)(C)(iv). Respondents argue that these provisions make no sense unless costs are to be considered in setting the NAAQS. That is not so. These provisions enable the Administrator to assist the States in carrying out their statutory role as primary *implementers* of the NAAQS. It is to the States that the CAA assigns initial and primary responsibility for deciding what emissions reductions will be required from which sources. It would be impossible to perform that task intelligently without considering which abatement technologies are most efficient, and most economically feasible—which is why we have said that "the most important forum for consideration of claims of economic and technological infeasibility is before the state agency formulating the implementation plan," *Union Elec. Co. v. EPA*, 427 U.S., at 266. * * *[3]

* * * The text of § 109(b), interpreted in its statutory and historical context and with appreciation for its importance to the CAA as a whole, unambiguously bars cost considerations from the NAAQS-setting process, and thus ends the matter for us as well as the EPA.[4] We therefore affirm the judgment of the Court of Appeals on this point.

Section 109(b)(1) of the CAA instructs the EPA to set "ambient air quality standards the attainment and maintenance of which in the judgment of the Administrator, based on [the] criteria [documents of § 108] and allowing an adequate margin of safety, are requisite to protect the public health." 42 U.S.C. § 7409(b)(1). The Court of Appeals held that this section as interpreted by the Administrator did not provide an "intelligible principle" to guide the EPA's exercise of authority in setting NAAQS. * * * We disagree.

In a delegation challenge, the constitutional question is whether the statute has delegated legislative power to the agency. Article I, § 1, of the Constitution vests "[a]ll legislative Powers herein granted . . . in a Congress of the United States." This text permits no delegation of those powers, and so we repeatedly have said that when Congress confers decisionmaking authority upon agencies *Congress* must "lay down by legislative act an intelligible principle to which the person or body authorized to [act] is directed to conform." *J.W. Hampton, Jr., & Co. v. United States*, 276 U.S. 394, 409 (1928). * * *

We agree with the Solicitor General that the text of § 109(b)(1) of the CAA at a minimum requires that "[f]or a discrete set of pollutants and based on published air quality criteria that reflect the latest scientific knowledge, [the] EPA must establish uniform national standards at a level that is requisite to protect public health from the adverse effects of the pollutant in the ambient air." Tr. of Oral Arg., p. 5. Requisite, in turn, "mean[s] sufficient, but not more than necessary." *Id.*, at 7. * * *

The scope of discretion § 109(b)(1) allows is in fact well within the outer limits of our nondelegation precedents. * * *

[Justice Thomas concurred separately. He agreed that the NAAQS decision was governed by an "intelligible principle" within the range of the Court's past decisions, but would "[o]n a future day," be willing to ask whether the non-delegation clause might bar even some delegations con-

---

3. Respondents scarcely mention in their arguments the secondary NAAQS required by § 109(b)(2), 42 U.S.C. § 7409(b)(2). For many of the same reasons described in the body of the opinion, as well as the text of § 109(b)(2), which instructs the EPA to set the standards at a level "requisite to protect the public welfare from any known or anticipated adverse effects associated with the presence of such air pollutant in the ambient air," we conclude that the EPA may not consider implementation costs in setting the secondary NAAQS.

4. Respondents' speculation that the EPA is secretly considering the costs of attainment without telling anyone is irrelevant to our interpretive inquiry. If such an allegation could be proved, it would be grounds for vacating the NAAQS, because the Administrator had not followed the law. It would not, however, be grounds for this Court's changing the law.

strained by such principles. Justice Stevens and Justice Souter also concurred separately. They would have the Court openly acknowledge that delegation of legislative authority is constitutionally permissible, provided it is constrained by sufficiently intelligible principles.]

■ JUSTICE BREYER, concurring in part and concurring in the judgment.

I join Parts I, III, and IV of the Court's opinion. I also agree with the Court's determination in Part II that the Clean Air Act does not permit the Environmental Protection Agency to consider the economic costs of implementation when setting national ambient air quality standards under § 109(b)(1) of the Act. But I would not rest this conclusion solely upon § 109's language or upon a presumption, such as the Court's presumption that any authority the Act grants the EPA to consider costs must flow from a "textual commitment" that is "clear." In order better to achieve regulatory goals—for example, to allocate resources so that they save more lives or produce a cleaner environment—regulators must often take account of all of a proposed regulation's adverse effects, at least where those adverse effects clearly threaten serious and disproportionate public harm. Hence, I believe that, other things being equal, we should read silences or ambiguities in the language of regulatory statutes as permitting, not forbidding, this type of rational regulation.

In these cases, however, other things are not equal. Here, legislative history, along with the statute's structure, indicates that § 109's language reflects a congressional decision not to delegate to the agency the legal authority to consider economic costs of compliance.

For one thing, the legislative history shows that Congress intended the statute to be "technology forcing." * * *

The Senate directly focused upon the technical feasibility and cost of implementing the Act's mandates. And it made clear that it intended the Administrator to develop air quality standards set independently of either. The Senate Report for the 1970 amendments explains:

"In the Committee discussions, considerable concern was expressed regarding the use of the concept of technical feasibility as the basis of ambient air standards. The Committee determined that 1) *the health of people is more important than the question of whether the early achievement of ambient air quality standards protective of health is technically feasible;* and, 2) the growth of pollution load in many areas, even with application of available technology, would still be deleterious to public health. . . .

"Therefore, the Committee determined that existing sources of pollutants either should meet the standard of the law or be closed down. . . ." S. Rep. No. 91–1196, pp. 2–3 (1970), 1 Leg. Hist. 402–403 (emphasis added).

Indeed, this Court, after reviewing the entire legislative history, concluded that the 1970 amendments were "expressly designed to force regulated sources to develop pollution control devices that *might at the time appear to be economically or technologically infeasible.*" *Union Elec. Co. v. EPA,* 427 U.S. 246, 257 (1976) (emphasis added). * * *

To read this legislative history as meaning what it says does not impute to Congress an irrational intent. Technology-forcing hopes can prove realistic. Those persons, for example, who opposed the 1970 Act's insistence on a 90% reduction in auto emission pollutants, on the ground of excessive cost, saw the development of catalytic converter technology that helped achieve substantial reductions without the economic catastrophe that some had feared.

At the same time, the statute's technology-forcing objective makes regulatory efforts to determine the costs of implementation both less important and more difficult. It means that the relevant economic costs are speculative, for they include the cost of unknown future technologies. It also means that efforts to take costs into account can breed time-consuming and potentially unresolvable arguments about the accuracy and significance of cost estimates. Congress could have thought such efforts not worth the delays and uncertainties that would accompany them. In any event, that is what the statute's history seems to say. And the matter is one for Congress to decide.

* * *

Finally, contrary to the suggestion of the Court of Appeals and of some parties, this interpretation of § 109 does not require the EPA to eliminate every health risk, however slight, at any economic cost, however great, to the point of "hurtling" industry over "the brink of ruin," or even forcing "deindustrialization." *American Trucking Assns., Inc. v. EPA,* 175 F.3d 1027, 1037, 1038, n. 4 (C.A.D.C. 1999). The statute, by its express terms, does not compel the elimination of *all* risk; and it grants the Administrator sufficient flexibility to avoid setting ambient air quality standards ruinous to industry.

Section 109(b)(1) directs the Administrator to set standards that are "requisite to protect the public health" with "an adequate margin of safety." But these words do not describe a world that is free of all risk-an impossible and undesirable objective. Nor are the words "requisite" and "public health" to be understood independent of context. We consider football equipment "safe" even if its use entails a level of risk that would make drinking water "unsafe" for consumption. And what counts as "requisite" to protecting the public health will similarly vary with background circumstances, such as the public's ordinary tolerance of the particular health risk in the particular context at issue. * * *

The statute also permits the Administrator to take account of comparative health risks. That is to say, she may consider whether a proposed rule promotes safety overall. A rule likely to cause more harm to health than it prevents is not a rule that is "requisite to protect the public health." For example, as the Court of Appeals held and the parties do not contest, the Administrator has the authority to determine to what extent possible health risks stemming from reductions in tropospheric ozone (which, it is claimed, helps prevent cataracts and skin cancer) should be taken into account in setting the ambient air quality standard for ozone.

* * * [T]he EPA, in setting standards that "protect the public health" with "an adequate margin of safety," retains discretionary authority to avoid regulating risks that it reasonably concludes are trivial in context. Nor need regulation lead to deindustrialization. Preindustrial society was not a very healthy society; hence a standard demanding the return of the Stone Age would not prove "requisite to protect the public health."

* * *

On remand from the Supreme Court, the D.C. Circuit issued the following decision:

American Trucking Associations v. EPA

United States Court of Appeals, District of Columbia Circuit, 2002.
283 F.3d 355.

■ TATEL, CIRCUIT JUDGE:

* * *

On July 18, 1997, EPA revised the primary and secondary NAAQS for particulate matter and ozone. For particulate matter, the Agency abandoned its approach of regulating both coarse and fine particles and droplets under the same standards. Observing that the "epidemiological evidence suggest[s] stronger associations of mortality and some morbidity effects with fine particles than with ... coarse particles," Nat'l Ambient Air Quality Standards for Ozone and Particulate Matter, Advance Notice of Proposed Rulemaking, 61 Fed. Reg. 29,719, 29,723 (June 12, 1996), the Agency adopted new, PM2.5–specific standards: an annual primary standard of 15 micrograms per cubic meter ("$\mu g/m^3$"); a daily primary standard of 65 $\mu g/m^3$; and secondary standards equal to the primary standards. Particulate Matter NAAQS, 62 Fed. Reg. at 38,652.

EPA also made significant changes to the ozone NAAQS. Citing new information that suggests a positive correlation between prolonged (six- to eight-hour) exposures to relatively low levels of ozone and "a wide range of health effects," Ozone NAAQS, 62 Fed. Reg. at 38,861, the Agency adopted new primary and secondary standards under which eight-hour-average ozone concentrations may not exceed 0.08 parts per million ("ppm"), in place of the old, one-hour-average standards of 0.12 ppm.

* * *

III.

We start with Petitioners' challenge to the $PM_{2.5}$ NAAQS. * * *

* * * EPA provided a lengthy explanation of its selection of these new standards, four aspects of which are relevant here: its discussions of (1) the need to revise the old NAAQS for particulate matter; (2) the reasons for adopting both annual and daily standards; (3) the grounds for choosing 15 and 65 μg/m³, respectively, as the levels for the new standards; and (4) the rationale behind the new daily standard's rather peculiar form.

Explaining the first point—the need for the new PM$_{2.5}$ NAAQS—EPA began by documenting evidence of the old PM standards' inadequacy. Examination of an "extensive ... epidemiological data base," EPA observed, showed that children, as well as the elderly and other "sensitive populations," were experiencing adverse, PM-related health effects—sometimes including mortality—even "in areas [and] at times when the levels of the [old] ... standards [were] met." [62 Fed. Reg.] at 38,657. In addition, a majority of [the members of the Clean Air Scientific Advisory Committee (CASAC)] recommended strengthening "the health protection[s] provided by the [old] PM standard[s]." *Id.* at 38,666. Finally, a majority of commenters agreed that "based on the available scientific information, the [old PM] standards [were] not of themselves sufficient to protect public health." *Id.* at 38,657.

* * *

Turning to the specific characteristics of the new PM$_{2.5}$ NAAQS, EPA gave only a brief explanation of its decision to adopt a primary standard with a twenty-four-hour averaging period: The standard is "consistent with [most] community epidemiological studies," which suggest that same-day and previous-day PM concentrations correlate positively with adverse health effects. EPA dismissed as insufficiently quantitative the few studies suggesting an association between health effects and shorter-term (minutes to hours) PM exposures, noting that in any case, regulating daily-average PM concentrations would also reduce shorter-term-average concentrations in most areas. * * *

EPA then discussed the annual NAAQS' one-year averaging time, explaining that it adopted the standard to reduce the likelihood of long-term and cumulative PM exposures, which "appear" to pose "larger" risks than shorter-term exposures. *Id.* * * *

Explaining its decision to establish both annual and daily standards, EPA indicated that although "either standard could be viewed as providing both short- and long-term protection" from PM$_{2.5}$, the use of two standards with very different averaging times would "serv[e] to address situations where the daily peaks and annual averages are not consistently correlated." Particulate Matter NAAQS, 62 Fed. Reg. at 38,669. In such situations, the annual standard would "lower[ ] both short and long-term PM$_{2.5}$ concentrations," while the daily standard would "protect[ ] against ... localized hot spots, and ... seasonal emissions," neither of which would be "well controlled by a national annual standard" alone. *Id.*

EPA next made a number of key points about the levels it selected for the new NAAQS. Implementing its view that the annual standard should do most of the work in mitigating the risks of PM$_{2.5}$, EPA selected the level of the standard "so as to protect against the range of effects associated with both short-and long-term exposures to PM." *Id.* at 38,675. In those studies reporting statistically significant correlations between health effects and PM exposures of *any* duration, the mean annual PM concentrations ranged from 16 to 21µg/m^3, while in those studies reporting nearly significant correlations, the mean annual concentrations ranged from 11 to 30 µg/m^3. *Id.* at 38,676. "[P]lacing greatest weight on those studies that were clearly statistically significant," therefore, the Agency adopted an annual standard level of 15 µg/m^3—just "below the range of annual data most strongly associated with both short and long-term exposure effects," *id.* * * * Although EPA acknowledged it could not rule out "the possibility of [health] effects at lower annual concentrations," it nevertheless decided not only that the evidence for such effects is "highly uncertain," but that "the likelihood of *significant* health risk" decreases as annual-average PM concentrations approach background levels. Particulate Matter NAAQS, 62 Fed. Reg. at 38,676 (emphasis added).

Having settled on a moderate level for the annual NAAQS, EPA selected the level of the daily standard "to provide supplemental protection against peak concentrations that might occur over limited areas and/or for limited time periods." *Id.* This selection process posed difficult questions because in all of the available studies in which short-term exposures correlated positively with adverse health effects, the long-term annual-average PM$_{2.5}$ concentration exceeded the new 15 µg/m^3 NAAQS. EPA thus had no way to evaluate the "incremental risk associated with single peak exposures to PM$_{2.5}$ in areas where the [new] annual standard is met." *Id.* at 38,677. Because it did not yet know how effective the new annual standard would be in reducing the risk of peak *short-term* exposures, therefore, EPA decided it could not justify a restrictive daily standard, instead selecting 65 µg/m^3—a level "at the upper end of the range recommended by [Agency] staff and most CASAC . . . members." *Id.*

In justifying the chosen levels for the new NAAQS, EPA made one final point relevant to these cases. Responding to commenters who advocated lower levels for both the daily and annual standards, EPA emphasized that considerable uncertainty remains about whether PM$_{2.5}$ is a threshold pollutant—that is, whether there is a concentration below which PM$_{2.5}$ is harmless. As a result, EPA could not be sure that lowering the NAAQS would produce corresponding reductions in health risks. "[T]he inherent scientific uncertainties are too great to support" lower levels for the NAAQS, the Agency explained. *Id.*

EPA also gave a lengthy explanation for the form of the primary standards. Only one aspect of that form is relevant here: the Agency's decision to base compliance with the daily standard on the average of the *98th percentile* of daily PM$_{2.5}$ concentrations at each monitoring station. This form permits monitoring stations to exceed the 65µg/m^3 level of the standard two percent of the time, or about seven days each year assuming the stations monitor PM levels every day. EPA justified these authorized exceedances on the ground that they will increase the "stability" of the standard by permitting States to design long-term PM$_{2.5}$ control programs without worrying about the effects of "single high exposure event[s] that may be due to unusual meteorological conditions alone." *Id.* at 38,673. * * * That said, EPA rejected alternative daily-standard forms (such as a 90th percentile form) that would have allowed more exceedances per year, on the ground that a daily standard that permitted such "a large number of days with peak $PM_{2.5}$ concentrations above the standard level" would not "serve as an effective supplement to the annual standard." *Id.*

Turning finally to the secondary $PM_{2.5}$ NAAQS, EPA focused primarily on the impact of particulate matter on visibility, "an important welfare effect [that] has direct significance to people's enjoyment of daily activities in all parts of the country." *Id.* at 38,680. EPA predicted that attainment of the new $PM_{2.5}$ primary standards would improve visibility in the eastern United States. Conceding that the new standards would have little or no effect in the west "except in and near certain urban areas," *id.* at 38,681, EPA observed that no single suite of secondary standards would solve visibility problems everywhere in the country because, due to regional differences in relative humidity, natural background PM levels, and other factors, "a national secondary standard intended to maintain or improve visibility conditions [in] . . . the West would have to be set at or even below natural background levels in the East," while a national secondary standard intended to "achieve an appropriate degree of visibility improvement in the East would permit further degradation in the West," *id.* at 38,680. * * *

State and Business Petitioners' Claims

State and Business Petitioners urge us to vacate the primary NAAQS because EPA "did not apply *any* legal standard, much less the correct standard." State & Bus. Pet'rs' Br. at 35. In support of this argument, they cite two passages in the final $PM_{2.5}$ rule. In one, Petitioners claim, EPA asserted that it had no obligation to determine a "safe level" of $PM_{2.5}$ prior to adopting a primary NAAQS. In the other, EPA allegedly acknowledged that "its approach might result in regulatory programs that go *beyond* those that are *needed* to effectively reduce risks to public health." As Petitioners see it, these "concessions" prove that EPA failed to set the primary NAAQS at levels "requisite—that is, not lower or higher than . . . necessary—to protect the public health with an adequate margin of safety," as mandated by *Whitman*, 531 U.S. at 475–76.

Petitioners' argument suffers from two significant flaws. First, the final PM rule makes neither alleged concession. In the first passage, which Petitioners cite as evidence that EPA failed to identify a "safe level" of $PM_{2.5}$, the Agency merely disclaimed any obligation to set primary NAAQS by means of a two-step process, identifying a "safe level" and then applying an additional margin of safety. Instead, EPA stated, it "may take into account margin of safety considerations throughout the process as long as such considerations are fully explained and supported by the record." Particulate Matter NAAQS, 62 Fed. Reg. at 38,688. * * *

Viewed in its proper context, EPA's other alleged "concession"—that the new NAAQS "go beyond" what is necessary to protect public health—

proves equally chimerical. In the final PM$_{2.5}$ rule, EPA said only that "a number of . . . commenters strongly supported standard levels more stringent than those proposed by" the Agency, but that "setting such [lower] standards . . . *might result in regulatory programs that go beyond those that are needed to effectively reduce risks to public health.*" *Id.* at 38,675 (emphasis added). This passage in no way supports Petitioners' argument that EPA failed to set the primary PM$_{2.5}$ NAAQS at levels requisite to protect the public health with an adequate margin of safety. Instead, the passage documents EPA's rejection of lower standards, demonstrating that the Agency not only recognized, but acted upon, its statutory obligation to set the primary NAAQS at levels no lower than necessary to reduce public health risks.

Petitioners' argument that EPA neither identified nor applied the proper legal standard also exaggerates the Agency's obligation to quantify its decisionmaking. * * *

Although we recognize that the Clean Air Act and circuit precedent require EPA qualitatively to describe the standard governing its selection of particular NAAQS, we have expressly rejected the notion that the Agency must "establish a measure of the risk to safety it considers adequate to protect public health every time it establishes a [NAAQS]." *Natural Res. Def. Council, Inc. v. EPA*, 902 F.2d 962, 973 (D.C. Cir. 1990). Such a rule would compel EPA to leave hazardous pollutants unregulated unless and until it completely understands every risk they pose, thus thwarting the Clean Air Act's requirement that the Agency err on the side of caution by setting primary NAAQS that "allow[ ] an adequate margin of safety[.]" 42 U.S.C. § 7409(b)(1). The Act requires EPA to promulgate protective primary NAAQS even where, as here, the pollutant's risks cannot be quantified or "precisely identified as to nature or degree," Particulate Matter NAAQS, 62 Fed. Reg. at 38,653. * * *

State and Business Petitioners' remaining substantive claims merit little discussion. They argue that EPA "failed to determine whether attainment of the [old particulate matter] standard would leave unacceptable public health risk." As EPA notes, however, the final PM rule explicitly states:

> [T]he extensive PM epidemiological data base provides evidence of serious health effects (e.g., mortality, exacerbation of chronic disease, increased hospital admissions) in sensitive populations (e.g., the elderly, individuals with cardiopulmonary disease), as well as significant adverse health effects (e.g., increased respiratory symptoms, school absences, and lung function decrements) in children. *Moreover, these effects associations are observed in areas or at times when the levels of the [old PM] standards are met.*

Particulate Matter NAAQS, 62 Fed. Reg. at 38,657 (emphasis added).

* * *

State and Business Petitioners' challenge to the secondary NAAQS hinges on the proposition that the identical primary NAAQS are arbitrary and capricious. Having just rejected the latter argument, we need not consider the former.

Environmental Petitioners' Claims

Environmental Petitioners' central argument regarding the primary NAAQS is straightforward: EPA should have set a stricter daily $PM_{2.5}$ NAAQS rather than relying almost exclusively on the stringent annual standard. Petitioners contend that because "adverse health effects [of] . . . $PM_{2.5}$ occur after single-day exposures[,] . . . the NAAQS must prevent most, if not all, such daily exposures in order to" reduce health risks. A strategy that focuses on the annual rather than the daily standard, Petitioners argue, will do little to prevent short-term pollution "events," in which $PM_{2.5}$ concentrations exceed healthy levels for days or weeks. * * *

Responding to these arguments, EPA observes that there are "significant uncertainties in identifying the extent of the incremental risk associated with single peak exposures to $PM_{2.5}$ in areas where the annual standard is met." Particulate Matter NAAQS, 62 Fed. Reg. at 38,677. As we understand the problem, existing data are insufficient to permit EPA to separate health effects of long-term-average $PM_{2.5}$ concentrations from those of short-term peak concentrations because in all cities in which the Agency found a positive correlation between short-term exposures and adverse health effects, the long-term-average $PM_{2.5}$ concentrations exceeded the new annual NAAQS. Thus, EPA cannot determine "what risks might have been associated with [short-term] peak [$PM_{2.5}$] levels had the long-term averages in these areas been below that selected for the [new] annual standard." *Id.* This uncertainty, together with evidence suggesting that "the . . . risk over the course of a year associated solely with a limited number of peak exposures is . . . considerably smaller than that associated with the entire air quality distribution," *id.* at 38,677, convinced EPA to focus its attention on the annual NAAQS. We think this expert judgment worthy of deference, at least until formerly polluted areas come into compliance with the new annual $PM_{2.5}$ standard and new health effects data from those areas become available.

* * *

IV.

Turning to the ozone standards, we again begin with a summary of the rulemaking process, and then consider Petitioners' challenges.

The Rulemaking

EPA first announced its plan to revise the ozone NAAQS in late 1996, issuing a public notice of proposed rulemaking. In that notice, EPA indicated that it intended to replace the existing, one-hour-average, primary ozone standard of 0.12 ppm with a new, eight-hour-average standard. It sought comments on this change and also on three possible levels for the new standard—0.09, 0.08, and 0.07 ppm. According to EPA, a level of 0.09 ppm would afford about the same protection as the old, one-hour-average standard; 0.08 would replicate the lowest exposure level actually tested in clinical studies; and 0.07 would be "highly precautionary in nature."

* * *

In the end, EPA adopted an eight-hour-average, 0.08 ppm standard. Ozone NAAQS, 62 Fed. Reg. at 38,856. Two aspects of this new standard require discussion here: averaging time and level.

Explaining its switch from a one to an eight-hour averaging time, EPA first noted that the one-hour-average standard reflected the belief—since refuted—that the most serious health effects of ozone result from short-term (one to three-hour) exposures. According to EPA, however, new studies clearly "demonstrate[ ] associations between a wide range of health effects and prolonged (... [six] to [eight]-hour) exposures" to concentrations less than that of the old standard. *Id.* at 38,861. * * * EPA indicated that an averaging time of eight hours not only reduces risk associated with short-term exposures, but also limits cumulative exposure. The longer averaging time, moreover, reduces variability in ozone levels across geographic areas. EPA also emphasized that CASAC unanimously agreed with the proposed change. * * * In EPA's opinion, "the fact that an averaging time of [eight] hours results in a significantly more uniformly protective national standard than the current [one]-hour standard is an important public health policy consideration that supports the selection" of the former averaging time. *Id.* at 38,862.

Turning to the 0.08 ppm level of the primary standard, EPA first explained that because ozone is—or is thought to be—a non-threshold pollutant, "it is not possible to select a level below which absolutely no [health] effects are likely to occur." *Id.* at 38,863. Nevertheless, EPA undertook to select a standard level that would "reduce risk sufficiently to protect public health with an adequate margin of safety." *Id.* In deciding among the proposed levels (0.09, 0.08, and 0.07 ppm), EPA took into account a number of "key observations and conclusions," *id.,* including:

- CASAC's conclusion that the old standard "provided little, if any, margin of safety," *id.;*

- Numerous epidemiological studies attributing "excess hospital admissions" to ozone exposure at concentrations below that of the old standard, *id.* at 38,864;

- Evidence that an eight-hour-average, 0.09 ppm standard would constitute only a modest improvement over the old standard, *id.;*

- "[C]lear evidence from human clinical studies" that prolonged exposure to 0.08 ppm of ozone, at moderate exertion, correlates positively with health effects like coughing, pain with inhalation, and reduced lung function, *id.* at 38,863–64;

- Clinical studies suggesting that "[w]hile group mean responses ... at ... 0.08 ppm"—the "lowest exposure level tested"—are usually "small or mild in nature, responses of some sensitive individuals are sufficiently severe ... to be considered adverse," *id.;*

- Indications from the nine area study that "statistically significant reductions in exposure and risk ... result from alternative [eight]-hour standards as the level [is lowered] from 0.09 ppm to ... 0.07 ppm," but that "there is no ... bright line that differentiates between acceptable and unacceptable risks within this range," *id.* at 38,864; and finally,

- Evidence from the same study that "a standard set at 0.09 ppm would allow approximately 40 percent to 65 percent more outdoor children to experience [decreases in lung function and pain with inhalation] than would a 0.08 ppm standard," *id.* at 38,868.

Despite some "inherent uncertainties," EPA viewed these observations and conclusions, taken together, as indicating that the "public health impacts" of ozone at levels lower than the one-hour, 0.12 ppm standard are "important and sufficiently large as to warrant a standard set at a level of 0.08 ppm." *Id.*

Acknowledging that numerous public comments advocated a level of 0.07 ppm, EPA offered several explanations for its decision to reject a more stringent standard. Most important, EPA pointed out that not one CASAC panel member "supported a standard set lower than 0.08 ppm, specifically after considering a range of alternative standards that included 0.07 ppm." Ozone NAAQS, 62 Fed. Reg. at 38,868. In addition, EPA contended that the "most certain" adverse health effects of ozone "are transient and reversible" at low ozone levels, while "the more serious ... impacts on health are less certain," *id.*—presumably in part because no human clinical studies have evaluated concentrations lower than 0.08 ppm. Finally, EPA noted that a 0.07 ppm standard "would be closer to peak background levels that infrequently occur in some areas due to nonanthropogenic sources of [ozone] precursors." *Id.*

One final aspect of EPA's discussion of the primary NAAQS level is relevant here: The Agency's response to certain comments questioning its reliance on specific field, epidemiological, and clinical studies. According to EPA, the comments "did not reflect an integrative assessment of the evidence—the approach CASAC has historically urged [the Agency] to follow—but rather a piecemeal look at each individual study." *Id.* at 38,866. EPA therefore dismissed the comments, arguing that such an incremental critique "tends to miss the strength of the entire body of evidence taken together." *Id.*

* * *

Ozone Petitioners' Claims

* * *

Petitioners raise two specific arguments regarding the primary ozone NAAQS. First, they assert that EPA "failed to determine whether attainment of the [old, one-hour-average, primary ozone] standard would leave unacceptable public health risk," and relatedly, that "none of the alternative [eight]-hour standards [considered by EPA] is significantly more protective of the public health than the [old] [one]-hour NAAQS." We disagree. As noted earlier, not only is the record replete with references to studies demonstrating the inadequacies of the old one-hour standard but EPA discussed at length the advantages of a longer averaging time, including reduced risk of prolonged exposures to unhealthy ozone levels and increased uniformity of protection across different urban areas. Moreover, EPA specifically cited CASAC's "consensus . . . that an [eight]-hour standard [is] more appropriate for a human health-based standard than a [one]-hour standard" and its recommendation that "the present . . . standard be eliminated and replaced with an [eight]-hour standard." Given this record evidence, our deferential standard of review, and the Clean Air Act's requirement that EPA must either follow CASAC's advice or explain why the proposed rule "differs . . . from . . . [CASAC's] recommendations," 42 U.S.C. § 7607(d)(3), Petitioners cannot seriously expect us to second-guess EPA's conclusion regarding the inadequacy of the old, one-hour-average standard.

Though somewhat more persuasive, Petitioners' second specific challenge also falls short. They argue that in selecting a level of 0.08 ppm rather than 0.09 or 0.07, EPA reached "inconsistent conclusions regarding specific health risks," thus "demonstrat[ing] that [the Agency's] decision to revise the NAAQS lacks a rational basis and therefore is arbitrary and capricious." In support of this point, Petitioners challenge EPA's three justifications for selecting 0.08 rather than 0.07: that no CASAC member supported a standard below 0.08; that health effects at ozone levels below 0.08 are transient and reversible; and that 0.07 would be too close to peak background levels. As to the first point, Petitioners observe that "most members of the CASAC panel who expressed an opinion on standard level supported a level *above* . . . 0.08 ppm," and that "CASAC ultimately concluded that there is no bright line distinguishing any of the alternative standards . . . as significantly more protective of public health." In addition, Petitioners point out, *ATA I* expressly discredits the contention that ozone health effects are more transient and reversible at concentrations below 0.08 ppm than at concentrations between 0.08 and 0.09. 175 F.3d at 1035 ("[The record evidence] does not make the categorical distinction the dissent says it does, and it is far from apparent that any health effects existing above [0.08 ppm] are permanent or irreversible."). Petitioners finally note that proximity to peak background levels is an indeterminate standard that points to no particular level for the primary NAAQS.

Although we think Petitioners' individual criticisms have some force, we are satisfied that in selecting a level of 0.08 rather than 0.07 (or, for that matter, 0.09), EPA "engage[d] in reasoned decision-making." *American Lung Ass'n,* 134 F.3d at 392. For one thing, CASAC's inability to reach consensus is hardly dispositive; EPA is entitled to give "significant weight" to the fact that no committee member advocated a level of 0.07 ppm, particularly as eight of the ten panel members who expressed opinions advocated a level of 0.08 ppm or greater, while the remaining two simply "endorsed the [0.07–0.09 ppm] range presented by the Agency . . . and stated that the [final] selection should be a policy decision." Also, although relative proximity to peak background ozone concentrations did not, in itself, necessitate a level of 0.08, EPA could consider that factor when choosing among the three alternative levels. Most convincing, though, is the absence of *any* human clinical studies at ozone concentrations below 0.08. This lack of data amply supports EPA's assertion that the most serious health effects of ozone are "less certain" at low concentrations, providing an eminently rational reason to set the primary standard at a somewhat higher level, at least until additional studies become available. Overall, therefore, we disagree with Petitioners that in selecting 0.08 ppm rather than a lower or higher level, EPA reached "inconsistent conclusions." The Agency could reasonably conclude that existing data support a standard below 0.09 but do not yet justify a standard below 0.08.

* * *

NOTES AND QUESTIONS

1. *Why national standards?* The NAAQS set minimal air quality standards that must be met nationwide. Does that make sense, or would it be more sensible to allow state or local governments to determine the appropriate level of air quality? What problems did determining national ozone and $PM_{2.5}$ standards pose for EPA? Why might Congress have demanded national standards? Do states retain any discretion with respect to air quality?

2. *Averaging times and exceedances.* The NAAQS set the allowable concentration of criteria pollutants in the ambient air based on specified averaging times. Note that for most criteria pollutants EPA has set multiple NAAQS employing different averaging times. Why does EPA believe that both short and longer-averaging-time standards are necessary? What does the 24–hour $PM_{2.5}$ standard, for example, accomplish that the annual standard does not? In addition to averaging times, the NAAQS must specify the number of permissible exceedances over a certain length of time. Why should any exceedances be permitted? With respect to the $PM_{2.5}$ standard, the D.C. Circuit deferred to EPA's judgment that it should permit exceedances of the daily standard up to 2% of the time, or roughly 7 days in a year. Could a court ever strike down EPA's choice of exceedance level? Under what circumstances?

3. *What can be the subject of a NAAQS?* In Massachusetts v. EPA, 549 U.S. 497 (2007) (excerpted in Section 3 below), the Supreme Court ruled that CO_2 is an "air pollutant" within the definition of the Clean Air Act. What, if anything, is left out of the statutory definition? Could EPA set NAAQS for heat, odors, light, or noise? What is "ambient" air? Could EPA set a § 108 standard for indoor air quality? For pollution in the stratosphere, for example with respect to chemicals capable of destroying stratospheric ("good") ozone? Does it matter whether the pollutant in question is initially emitted at ground level?

4. *What findings must be made?* What must EPA find in order to support a specific NAAQS level? If it finds no threshold "no effects" level, must the agency set a zero NAAQS? If not, how should it decide the appropriate non-zero level? How did it choose ozone and $PM_{2.5}$ levels in the revisions challenged in the *American Trucking Associations* litigation? Do you agree with the D.C. Circuit that those choices were entitled to deference? What other choices could EPA have made? What does it mean that the standard must be "requisite" to protect the public health? Under what circumstances would that foreclose an overly-protective standard?

Rejecting an industry claim that EPA's NAAQS for coarse PM was too stringent, the D.C. Circuit emphasized the precautionary nature of the NAAQS:

> Although the evidence of danger from coarse PM is, as the EPA recognizes, "inconclusive," the agency need not wait for conclusive findings before regulating a pollutant it reasonably believes may pose a significant risk to public health. * * * As this court has consistently reaffirmed, the CAA permits the Administrator to err on the side of caution in setting NAAQS.

American Farm Bureau Federation v. EPA, 559 F.3d 512, 533 (D.C. Cir. 2009).

5. *The role of costs.* In *American Trucking*, the Supreme Court unanimously concluded that the CAA does not permit consideration of costs in the setting of a NAAQS. Do you agree with that interpretation of the statute? Assuming it is correct, is it a justifiable policy choice? Can costs in fact be ignored? Is it irrational to bar their explicit consideration, or will that simply push their consideration underground? What goals might foreclosing explicit consideration of costs further? Justice Breyer reads the majority opinion as presuming, based on congressional silence, that the agency is not to consider costs. Is this a fair reading? If a statute is unclear or ambiguous, how should a court decide whether it allows consideration of costs? To what extent should it defer to the agency's view on that question?

Following *American Trucking*, what opportunities remain for consideration of costs? Are they sufficient? How feasible and useful would it be to estimate costs at the point of setting a NAAQS? Would that exercise be more appropriate at later regulatory points, such as implementation of the NAAQS or development of technology-based emission limits for new sources?

If the NAAQS were required to meet a cost-benefit test, it appears that they could do so. Because NAAQS are "major rules" with substantial economic impacts, they are routinely accompanied by cost-benefit analyses, even though EPA cannot consider those comparisons in setting the standards. In addition, EPA periodically prepares cost-benefit reviews of its standards for submission to Congress. CAA rules routinely pass those reviews, and in fact are responsible for the vast majority of the economic benefits from EPA's overall regulatory programs. EPA's most recent report, "The Benefits and Costs of the Clean Air Act: 1990 to 2020, Final

Report—Rev. A (Apr. 2011),"is available at http://www.epa.gov/air/sect812/feb11/fullreport.pdf. It estimates that the CAA provided net benefits between $110 billion and $3.7 trillion in 2010, and forecast that those benefits will be at least 50% higher in 2020.

6. *The role of science advisors.* What is the role of the Clean Air Scientific Advisory Committee (CASAC)? Would it ever be justifiable for EPA to reject CASAC's advice with respect to proposed NAAQS? To what extent are the judgments that must be made to arrive at a NAAQS scientific, and to what extent are they appropriately policy judgments? Should a reviewing court be more inclined to defer to a NAAQS decision if EPA follows CASAC's advice? Should it take an especially "hard look" if that advice is ignored?

The D.C. Circuit addressed those questions in a challenge to EPA's 2006 revisions of the PM NAAQS. The 1997 standards upheld in *American Trucking* sparked additional research and monitoring. New data and reanalysis of older studies led a majority (but not all) of the CASAC members to call for tightening of the 24–hour fine PM NAAQS to 30–35 μm^3 and the annual NAAQS to 13–14 μm^3. EPA career staff made similar recommendations. The agency ultimately followed CASAC's (and staff's) advice on the daily NAAQS, but not on the annual standard, which it set at 15 μm^3. 71 Fed. Reg. 61144 (Oct. 17, 2006). Environmentalists and a coalition of states challenged the rule, arguing in part that EPA should have set the annual standard at the levels recommended by CASAC and staff. The court remanded the annual standard, holding that EPA had not adequately explained its decision not to adopt the stricter recommendations. EPA announced in 2009 that it would reconsider the 2008 ozone NAAQS, which also were not as strict as CASAC recommended and which also had been challenged by environmental groups. 75 Fed. Reg. 2938 (Jan. 19, 2010).

7. *Compelling NAAQS establishment.* Can EPA be compelled to list additional criteria pollutants, such as CO_2? On what basis? *See* NRDC, Inc. v. Train, 545 F.2d 320 (2d Cir. 1976), requiring EPA to develop ambient air quality standards for lead.

8. *Secondary NAAQS.* The Clean Air Act directs EPA to set primary NAAQS to protect the public health, and secondary NAAQS to protect the public welfare. Currently only one secondary NAAQS, for SO_x, differs from the primary standard. In connection with the 2006 revision of the fine PM standards, EPA staff suggested that the agency adopt a secondary NAAQS for fine PM that would protect visibility at a target level between 40 and 60 kilometers, based on a number of research studies surveying public perceptions of the acceptable level of visibility. EPA rejected the staff recommendation, declining to set a specific target visibility range, but nonetheless deciding that the primary standard would adequately protect visibility. 71 Fed. Reg. 61144, 61207–61208 (Oct. 17, 2006). The D.C. Circuit remanded, holding that the EPA must decide what level of visibility protection is needed to protect the public welfare. American Farm Bureau Federation v. EPA, 559 F.3d 512 (D.C. Cir. 2009). How should EPA approach that determination? Does a national standard for visibility make sense? If so, how should the acceptable visibility level be identified? Should EPA be allowed to consider costs in setting secondary NAAQS?

9. *Risk assessment and the NAAQS.* EPA routinely prepares (or has consultants prepare) a quantitative risk assessment in the course of its periodic review of the NAAQS for each criteria pollutant. That risk assessment is not necessarily decisive, however. EPA is very aware of the limitations of risk assessments in this context, including uncertainties and untested assumptions. The D.C. Circuit is inclined to defer to EPA's views of the weight risk assessments deserve in NAAQS determinations. See American Trucking Associations v. EPA, 283 F.3d 355, 374 (D.C.Cir. 2002); American Farm Bureau Federation v. EPA, 559 F.3d 512, 527–28 (D.C. Cir. 2009).

B.   IMPLEMENTING THE NAAQS: STATE IMPLEMENTATION PLANS

The mere establishment of NAAQS does not purify the atmosphere. A mechanism is needed to translate the NAAQS into limitations on the emission of criteria pollutants from various sources. The Clean Air Act directs the states to issue "state implementation plans" (SIPs) to achieve the NAAQS within their borders.

SIPs combine two distinct functions. First, they serve as planning documents, assessing the state's air quality problem and determining in general terms the extent and nature of improvement needed to attain or maintain the NAAQS. This assessment requires not only the identification of current levels of criteria pollutants and the sources emitting those pollutants, but extensive computer modeling to determine what can be changed and what impacts alternative strategies would have on air pollution levels. Second, SIPs serve as regulatory instruments, allocating the acceptable level of emissions among the various sources, including both stationary and mobile sources, and accounting for new sources or increased emissions from existing sources over time. SIPs must be submitted to EPA for approval. Approved SIP provisions are enforceable under federal as well as state law.

Excerpts From the Clean Air Act

42 U.S.C. §§ 7401–7671q.

Sec. 101.   Congressional findings and declaration of purpose

(a) The Congress finds—

(1) that the predominant part of the Nation's population is located in its rapidly expanding metropolitan and other urban areas, which generally cross the boundary lines of local jurisdictions and often extend into two or more States;

* * *

(3) that air pollution prevention (that is, the reduction or elimination, through any measures, of the amount of pollutants produced or

created at the source) and air pollution control at its source is the primary responsibility of States and local governments; and

(4) that Federal financial assistance and leadership is essential for the development of cooperative Federal, State, regional, and local programs to prevent and control air pollution.

Sec. 110. State implementation plans for national primary and secondary ambient air quality standards

(a) Adoption of plan by State * * *

(1) Each State shall, after reasonable notice and public hearings, adopt and submit to the Administrator, within 3 years (or such shorter period as the Administrator may prescribe) after the promulgation of a national primary ambient air quality standard (or any revision thereof) under section 7409 of this title for any air pollutant, a plan which provides for implementation, maintenance, and enforcement of such primary standard in each air quality control region (or portion thereof) within such State. In addition, such State shall adopt and submit to the Administrator (either as a part of a plan submitted under the preceding sentence or separately) within 3 years (or such shorter period as the Administrator may prescribe) after the promulgation of a national ambient air quality secondary standard (or revision thereof), a plan which provides for implementation, maintenance, and enforcement of such secondary standard in each air quality control region (or portion thereof) within such State. * * *

(2) Each implementation plan submitted by a State under this chapter shall be adopted by the State after reasonable notice and public hearing. Each such plan shall—

(A) include enforceable emission limitations and other control measures, means, or techniques (including economic incentives such as fees, marketable permits, and auctions of emissions rights), as well as schedules and timetables for compliance, as may be necessary or appropriate to meet the applicable requirements of this chapter;

(B) provide for establishment and operation of appropriate devices, methods, systems, and procedures necessary to—

(i) monitor, compile, and analyze data on ambient air quality, and

(ii) upon request, make such data available to the Administrator;

(C) include a program to provide for the enforcement of the measures described in subparagraph (A), and regulation of the modification and construction of any stationary source within the areas covered by the plan as necessary to assure that national ambient air quality standards are achieved * * *;

(D) contain adequate provisions—

(i) prohibiting, consistent with the provisions of this title, any source or other type of emissions activity within the State from emitting any air pollutant in amounts which will—

(I) contribute significantly to non-attainment in, or interfere with maintenance by, any other State with respect to any such national primary or secondary ambient air quality standard, or

(II) interfere with measures required to be included in the applicable implementation plan for any other State under part C to prevent significant deterioration of air quality or to protect visibility,

(ii) insuring compliance with the applicable requirements of sections 7426 and 7415 of this title (relating to interstate and international pollution abatement);

(E) provide necessary assurances that the State * * * will have adequate personnel, funding, and authority under State law to carry out such implementation plan (and is not prohibited by any provision of Federal or State law from carrying out such implementation plan or portion thereof) * * * and necessary assurances that, where the State has relied on a local or regional government, agency, or instrumentality for the implementation of any plan provision, the State has responsibility for ensuring adequate implementation of such plan provision;

* * *

(H) provide for revision of such plan—

(i) from time to time as may be necessary to take account of revisions of such national primary or secondary ambient air quality standard or the availability of improved or more expeditious methods of attaining such standard, and

(ii) * * * whenever the Administrator finds on the basis of information available to the Administrator that the plan is substantially inadequate to attain the national ambient air quality standard which it implements or to otherwise comply with any additional requirements established under this Act;

* * *

(K) provide for—

(i) the performance of such air quality modeling as the Administrator may prescribe for the purpose of predicting the effect on ambient air quality of any emissions of any air pollutant for which the Administrator has established a national ambient air quality standard, and

(ii) the submission, upon request, of data related to such air quality modeling to the Administrator;

* * *

(M) provide for consultation and participation by local political subdivisions affected by the plan.

* * *

(c)(1) The Administrator shall promulgate a Federal implementation plan at any time within 2 years after the Administrator—

(A) finds that a State has failed to make a required submission * * *, or

(B) disapproves a State implementation plan submission in whole or in part, unless the State corrects the deficiency, and the Administrator approves the plan or plan revision, before the Administrator promulgates such Federal implementation plan.

* * *

(k) * * *

(2) Within 12 months of a determination by the Administrator * * * that a State has submitted a plan or plan revision [that is complete] the Administrator shall act on the submission in accordance with paragraph (3).

(3) In the case of any submittal on which the Administrator is required to act under paragraph (2), the Administrator shall approve such submittal as a whole if it meets all of the applicable requirements of this chapter. If a portion of the plan revision meets all the applicable requirements of this chapter, the Administrator may approve the plan revision in part and disapprove the plan revision in part. The plan revision shall not be treated as meeting the requirements of this chapter until the Administrator approves the entire plan revision as complying with the applicable requirements of this chapter.

(4) The Administrator may approve a plan revision based on a commitment of the State to adopt specific enforceable measures by a date certain, but not later than 1 year after the date of approval of the plan revision. Any such conditional approval shall be treated as a disapproval if the State fails to comply with such commitment.

(5) Whenever the Administrator finds that the applicable implementation plan for any area is substantially inadequate to attain or maintain the relevant national ambient air quality standard * * * or to otherwise comply with any requirement of this chapter, the Administrator shall require the State to revise the plan as necessary to correct such inadequacies. * * *

The process of developing a SIP is complex. The SIP must provide for attainment of each of the NAAQS in each air quality control region within the state. See CAA § 107, 42 U.S.C. § 7407. SIPs are typically developed region-by-region and pollutant-by-pollutant. Their preparation and implementation may be delegated to local bodies, but the state must ultimately remain responsible. Both the technical and the political decisions are challenging.

The following excerpt explains how a SIP for ozone attainment in California's San Joaquin Valley was developed in the 1990s.

James D. Fine and Dave Owen, Technocracy and Democracy: Conflicts Between Models and Participation in Environmental Law and Planning

56 Hastings L. J. 901, 949–965 (2005).

* * *

Air pollution problems in the Central Valley did not begin in the 1990s; early travelers noted the region's pervasive dust problems, and even in the late 1970s and early 1980s air quality measurements revealed that the region's air quality was frequently violating state and federal standards. Industry-funded air quality research commenced in the early 1980s, eventually leading to the San Joaquin Valley Air Quality Study (SJVAQS), an inter-agency, multi-stakeholder, well-funded study intended to produce a state-of-the-science air quality model and supporting observational database. Unfortunately, a lack of sufficient regulatory interest, as well as the need to gather more data to understand the problem, delayed early and effective regulation.

In 1990, Congress enacted major amendments to the Clean Air Act. By setting forth planning and air quality improvement deadlines for areas not meeting the ozone standard, these amendments mandated the planning processes of the 1990s. For "serious" nonattainment areas such as the SJV, an attainment plan was due by November 15, 1994, and the plan was to "demonstrate," through modeling, that the ozone standard would be achieved by 1999. Failure to meet the planning deadline meant costly sanctions, including the loss of federal funds for highway construction and stricter permitting rules for any industry with potential pollutant emissions.

Efforts to meet the 1994 planning deadline had, as a practical matter, begun with the 1980s air pollution studies and initial attainment plans, but the coordinated planning effort officially kicked off in 1991, when several county air districts merged to form the SJVUAPCD [San Joaquin Valley Unified Air Pollution Control District]. Working closely with CARB [the California Air Resources Board], the SJVUAPCD assembled the policy advisory and technical advisory committees that would oversee the research effort and subsequent planning process. Primary responsibility for planning rested with the SJVUAPCD itself, with substantial technical and policy assistance from CARB and some input from EPA.

Neither advisory committee was representative of the public as a whole. Both were composed exclusively of government employees and representatives of private industry; their membership did not include any representatives of public interest advocacy organizations. The technical advisory team was even less representative; it was composed exclusively of regulators and industry representatives.

With its research and planning teams in place, the SJVUAPCD began the process of developing its attainment plan. Sub-groups set about developing a modeling approach—which meant deciding on a modeling system to be used and on an ozone event to simulate—estimating emissions, identifying emissions reductions options, and simulating those reductions using the model.

Typically, modelers attempt to demonstrate future compliance by assessing how future air quality would fare if a past meteorological event repeated itself after implementation of proposed emissions controls. Modelers also use that same event to test the model itself; by improving the model's simulations of that past event, they attempt to assure themselves of its ability to predict future outcomes. The past event is generally an extended period of unfavorable weather for air quality—that is, weather that represents a worst-case scenario for generating ozone pollution. The planners settled upon a particularly severe week-long pollution event in August 1990, and then began preparing the input data to perform a modeling simulation of that event. The Technical Committee worked with planners to develop a modeling protocol that described the event and the modeling components to be used.

Once the simulation dates were specified, planners at the SJVUAPCD and CARB's Planning and Technical Support Division went about compiling baseline data for the modeling. They attempted to identify, locate, and quantify all emissions sources that had existed in 1990. They also attempted to do the same for all sources anticipated to exist, in the absence of further controls, in 1999. Once the sources were located and quantified, the group "mapped" them, translating emissions data, as well as information about ambient meteorological conditions, into geo-coded formats the model could accept as input.

The group's work involved constant dialogue and consultation with industry, local and state governments, and in some instances consultants. The inventory group also published and made publicly available its draft emissions inventory, and that draft inventory received careful scrutiny from regulated industries and the SJVAQS Technical Committee.

Somewhat concurrently, CARB and SJVUAPCD planners identified potential future emissions controls. Essentially, this group's task was to identify and develop potential new "rules" and to estimate resultant emissions reductions. The planners provided quantitative estimates of emissions reductions, timelines for when those reductions would be achieved, and estimates of how much the reductions would cost.

Once the modelers had chosen their modeling event, and once the planners believed they had run out of time to continue improving the emissions inventory, the modelers began executing the modeling simulations. Their first task was to determine the adequacy of the model itself, which they did by evaluating its ability to simulate observations gathered during the August 1990 ozone event. The modelers had not completed model performance evaluation to their satisfaction when time constraints necessitated initiating the planning simulations. The simulation was sufficiently accurate to meet EPA and CARB guidelines for model approval, however, and, with the knowledge that models necessarily do imperfect work, the modelers decided to proceed with simulating the 1999 predictions. Using the approved emissions inventories and the emissions reduction options developed by the control rules group, the modelers predicted air quality in the absence of additional emissions controls and using various combinations of proposed rules, with the goal of finding a set of rules sufficient to efficiently achieve compliance.

Again, regulated groups were heavily involved. The planners and modelers consulted the advisory committees throughout this process, and the Western States Petroleum Association requested specific modeling runs. When the modeling runs predicted compliance even without controls on petroleum facilities on the west side of the SJV, controls on those facilities were excluded from the plan.

The SJVUAPCD predicted that both existing and future rules would achieve substantial emissions reductions, and it identified several "contingency" measures. Nevertheless, a model attainment "demonstration" was not possible until modifications were made to boundary conditions values (i.e., assumptions about upwind air quality conditions). Few involved in plan development were particularly confident in this assertion; many were skeptical about the ultimate efficacy of the rules they had selected. With deadline pressure remaining intense, however, the planners felt obliged to use the modeling as the basis for their plan.

In October 1990, the SJVUAPCD made the draft plan available for public comment and held a public workshop. A hearing followed, but public comments, other than statements from those already involved to some extent in the process, did not. The minutes from subsequent board hearings reveal an almost complete absence of participation from public interest groups or from the general public, and very little specific criticism of the plan except from regulated industry. The interests involved in the hearings were similar to those already represented in the advisory and technical committees.

Following the public comment period, the SJVUAPCD made limited changes to the plan, submitting it on November 3, 1994, to the SJVUAPCD Board of Directors for final approval. Unlike the advisory committees, the Board of Directors is not a technical body; most of its members are locally elected political representatives. This non-technical review might have provided an opportunity for public advocacy, at least through representative proxies, but the board had little time to conduct a meaningful review. With the compliance deadline looming, and EPA and CARB reviews still pending, the technical staff urged a rapid approval in order to avoid the penalties that would result if the plan were not approved by November 15.

The Board held two meetings to discuss the plan, but the only public discussion came from regulators and industry representatives. Even the board's decision to exempt the west side petroleum facilities from regulation provoked no meaningful public comment.

The Board of Directors complied with the staff's request for a quick decision and approved the final attainment plan on November 14, 1994. CARB submitted the plan for EPA approval almost immediately thereafter.

Ultimately, the SJVUAPCD Attainment Plan called for a host of rule changes, and the SJVUAPCD predicted that those changes, in combination with existing rules and anticipated policy decisions by CARB and EPA, would meet the federal ozone standard by 1999. The planners sought to reduce both NOx and VOC emissions by regulating a wide range of industrial activities. The planners also placed heavy reliance upon emissions reductions from rules imposed by other regulatory entities, and in particular assumed that declining emissions from upwind areas would provide an important boost toward compliance.

The plan quite deliberately did not, however, provide for much margin of error. The SJVUAPCD exempted the petroleum facilities on the west side of the Valley from regulation under the SIP, believing that it could not legally justify controls that were not essential to obtaining a modeled attainment demonstration. Similarly, it did not impose any controls designed to provide a margin of error, instead describing controls beyond those necessary to achieve a hairs-breadth compliance margin as "excessive." The plan noted that efforts to improve the model would be ongoing, and included some contingency rules to be developed if further regulation proved necessary. Although the contingencies could provide some flexibility in the event that the plan did not succeed, the plan still created very little margin for error.

The attainment plan was based upon a host of uncertain model inputs. Because of deadlines and revisions to emissions estimates, the existing emissions inventory was known to have several uncertainties and omissions. Model predictions were known to be uncertain, but nobody knew how the uncertainties impacted predictions of future conditions. Together with assumptions about politics and engineering, unknowable future economic conditions introduced a further element of uncertainty; the planners simply had no way of predicting the economic boom that would create staggering levels of growth in upwind areas, and instead predicated their planning upon the assumption of declining levels of pollution from upwind activity. Additionally, like any model, SARMAP's usefulness could be compromised by erroneous or incomplete input data or by the inherent limitations created by basing a model upon just one potentially non-representative weather event.

On top of all of these uncertainties, the model itself, like all models, was a limited tool, and the Attainment Plan noted several ways in which the modelers viewed their tool as flawed. The modelers acknowledged that in the absence of tight deadlines they might have been able to generate a superior model.

All of these uncertainties threatened the reliability of the model prediction of attainment by 1999, but the plan's uncertainty discussions were far from comprehensive. The plan includes some blanket generalizations about the pervasiveness of uncertainty in modeling, but its discussion of particular sources of uncertainty was too general to allow a reader to discern how those uncertainties were managed or what economic and public health risks they might pose. The authors omitted discussion of some important sources of uncertainty, such as the contingent relationship between emissions reductions and rule enactment or economic growth. They addressed other sources of uncertainty in more detail, but without substantive discussion clarifying how those uncertainties might affect the result. A reader, even if able to understand the source of uncertainty, would have had no way of knowing whether it was likely to lead to overestimation or underestimation of actual pollutant levels, and a planner would have been without guidance about how to address model uncertainty when setting policy.

* * *

The Attainment Plan included a modeling prediction that the region would attain the federal ozone standard by 1999. The planning effort led to several effective emissions controls, and the region has achieved significant emissions reductions. Nevertheless, unhealthy levels of pollution remain. In 2000, the SJVUAPCD monitoring network measured ozone concentrations that exceeded the federal and state standards on 30 and 114 days, respectively. The region averaged over 30 annual violations of the federal standard from 1999 through 2002, despite the considerable emissions reductions.

* * *

In 2001, EPA reclassified part of the Valley as a "severe non-attainment area." In December, 2003, the SJVUAPCD Board went one step further and voted to request a voluntary reclassification to "extreme" nonattainment. EPA approved the request in April, 2004. This reclassification has several implications for the region, including a longer timeline to plan for and meet the ozone standard. Whereas the 1994 Attainment Plan claimed it would achieve the standard by 1999, this recent decision delays the attainment deadline until 2010.

Meanwhile, environmental activists, largely inactive in the 1990s planning efforts, have joined the San Joaquin Valley's air pollution planning debates. The Center for Race, Poverty, and the Environment has campaigned to increase environmental regulation of agriculture, and both the Sierra Club and the Earthjustice Legal Defense Fund have become active participants—and litigants—in San Joaquin Valley air quality controversies. Whether their involvement will make a significant difference in future planning efforts remains to be seen; the failure of the plans developed without public-interest-group participation does not imply success with their involvement. But at the very least, their presence should help ensure the inclusion of a broader diversity of viewpoints in the planning process.

Union Electric Co. v. Environmental Protection Agency

United States Supreme Court, 1976.
427 U.S. 246.

■ JUSTICE MARSHALL delivered the opinion of the Court.

* * *

We have addressed the history and provisions of the Clean Air Amendments of 1970 in detail in Train v. Natural Resources Defense Council (NRDC), 421 U.S. 60 (1975), and will not repeat that discussion here. Suffice it to say that the Amendments reflect congressional dissatisfaction with the progress of existing air pollution programs and a determination to "tak(e) a stick to the States," Id., at 64, in order to guarantee the prompt attainment and maintenance of specified air quality standards. The heart of the Amendments is the requirement that each State formulate, subject to EPA approval, an implementation plan designed to achieve national primary ambient air quality standards those necessary to protect the public health "as expeditiously as practicable but ... in no case later than three years from the date of approval of such plan." CAA § 110(a)(2)(A). The plan must also provide for the attainment of national secondary ambient air quality standards those necessary to protect the public welfare within a "reasonable time." Ibid. Each State is given wide discretion in formulating its plan, and the Act provides that the Administrator "shall approve" the proposed plan if it has been adopted after public notice and hearing and if it meets eight specified criteria.

On April 30, 1971, the Administrator promulgated national primary and secondary standards for six air pollutants he found to have an adverse effect on the public health and welfare. Included among them was sulfur dioxide, at issue here. After the promulgation of the national standards, the State of Missouri formulated its implementation plan and submitted it for approval. Since sulfur dioxide levels exceeded national primary standards in only one of the State's five air quality regions, the Metropolitan St. Louis Interstate region, the Missouri plan concentrated on a control strategy and regulations to lower emissions in that area. The plan's emission limitations were effective at once, but the State retained authority to grant variances to particular sources that could not immediately comply. The Administrator approved the plan on May 31, 1972.

Petitioner is an electric utility company servicing the St. Louis metropolitan area, large portions of Missouri, and parts of Illinois and Iowa. Its three coal-fired generating plants in the metropolitan St. Louis area are subject to the sulfur dioxide restrictions in the Missouri implementation plan. Petitioner did not seek review of the Administrator's approval of the plan within 30 days, as it was entitled to do under § 307(b)(1) of the Act, but rather applied to the appropriate state and county agencies for variances from the emission limitations affecting its three plants. Petitioner received one-year variances, which could be extended upon reapplication. The variances on two of petitioner's three plants had expired and petitioner was applying for extensions when, on May 31, 1974, the Administrator notified petitioner that sulfur dioxide emissions from its plants violated the emission limitations contained in the Missouri plan. Shortly thereafter petitioner filed a petition in the Court of Appeals for the Eighth Circuit for review of the Administrator's 1972 approval of the Missouri implementation plan.

* * *

[The Court held that Union Electric could raise its claim after expiration of the 30–day appeal period for SIP approvals only if it had new grounds for appeal that, had they been known at the time the plan was presented to the Administrator for approval, would have prevented the Administrator from approving the plan. Union Electric claimed that the SIP should have been disapproved because compliance with its terms was not economically or technologically feasible.]

* * * The Administrator's position is that he has no power whatsoever to reject a state implementation plan on the ground that it is economically or technologically infeasible, and we have previously accorded great deference to the Administrator's construction of the Clean Air Act. See Train v. NRDC, 421 U.S., at 75. After surveying the relevant provisions of the Clean Air Amendments of 1970 and their legislative history, we agree that Congress intended claims of economic and technological infeasibility to be wholly foreign to the Administrator's consideration of a state implementation plan.

As we have previously recognized, the 1970 Amendments to the Clean Air Act were a drastic remedy to what was perceived as a serious and otherwise uncheckable problem of air pollution. The Amendments place the primary responsibility for formulating pollution control strategies on the States, but nonetheless subject the States to strict minimum compliance requirements. These requirements are of a "technology-forcing character," *Train v. NRDC, supra,* at 91, and are expressly designed to force regulated sources to develop pollution control devices that might at the time appear to be economically or technologically infeasible.

This approach is apparent on the face of § 110(a)(2). The provision sets out eight criteria that an implementation plan must satisfy, and provides that if these criteria are met and if the plan was adopted after reasonable notice and hearing, the Administrator "shall approve" the proposed state plan. The mandatory "shall" makes it quite clear that the Administrator is not to be concerned with factors other than those specified, and none of the eight factors appears to permit consideration of technological or economic infeasibility. Nonetheless, if a basis is to be found for allowing the Administrator to consider such claims, it must be among the eight criteria, and so it is here that the argument is focused.

It is suggested that consideration of claims of technological and economic infeasibility is required by the first criterion that the primary air quality standards be met "as expeditiously as practicable but ... in no case later than three years ..." and that the secondary air quality standards be met within a "reasonable time." § 110(a)(2)(A). The argument is that what is "practicable" or "reasonable" cannot be determined without assessing whether what is proposed is possible. This argument does not survive analysis.

Section 110(a)(2)(A)'s three-year deadline for achieving primary air quality standards is central to the Amendments' regulatory scheme and, as both the language and the legislative history of the requirement make clear, it leaves no room for claims of technological or economic infeasibility. The 1970 congressional debate on the Amendments centered on whether technology forcing was necessary and desirable in framing and attaining air quality standards sufficient to protect the public health, standards later termed primary standards. The House version of the Amendments was quite moderate in approach, requiring only that health-related standards be met "within a reasonable time." H.R. 17255, 91st Cong., 2d Sess., § 108(c)(1)(C)(i) (1970). The Senate bill, on the other hand, flatly required that, possible or not, health-related standards be met "within three years." S. 4358, 91st Cong., 2d Sess., § 111(a)(2)(A) (1970).

The Senate's stiff requirement was intended to foreclose the claims of emission sources that it would be economically or technologically infeasible for them to achieve emission limitations sufficient to protect the public health within the specified time. As Senator Muskie, manager of the Senate bill, explained to his chamber:

> The first responsibility of Congress is not the making of technological or economic judgments or even to be limited by what is or appears to be technologically or economically feasible. Our responsibility is to establish what the public interest requires to protect the health of persons. This may mean that people and industries will be asked to do what seems to be impossible at the present time.

116 Cong. Rec. 32901–32902 (1970).

* * *

The Conference Committee and, ultimately, the entire Congress accepted the Senate's three-year mandate for the achievement of primary air quality standards, and the clear import of that decision is that the Administrator must approve a plan that provides for attainment of the primary standards in three years even if attainment does not appear feasible. In rejecting the House's version of reasonableness, however, the conferees strengthened the Senate version. The Conference Committee made clear that the States could not procrastinate until the deadline approached. Rather, the primary standards had to be met in less than three years if possible; they had to be met "as expeditiously as practicable." § 110(a)(2)(A). Whatever room there is for considering claims of infeasibility in the attainment of primary standards must lie in this phrase, which is, of course, relevant only in evaluating those implementation plans that attempt to achieve the primary standard in less than three years.

It is argued that when such a state plan calls for proceeding more rapidly than economics and the available technology appear to allow, the plan must be rejected as not "practicable." Whether this is a correct reading of § 110(a)(2)(A) depends on how that section's "as expeditiously as practicable" phrase is characterized. The Administrator's position is that § 110(a)(2)(A) sets only a minimum standard that the States may exceed in their discretion, so that he has no power to reject an infeasible state plan that surpasses the minimum federal requirements—a plan that reflects a state decision to engage in technology forcing on its own and to proceed more expeditiously than is practicable. On the other hand, petitioner and Amici supporting its position argue that § 110(a)(2)(A) sets a mandatory standard that the States must meet precisely and conclude that the Administrator may reject a plan for being too strict as well as for being too lax. * * *

Amici Appalachian Power Co. et al. * * * claim that the States are precluded from submitting implementation plans more stringent than federal law demands by § 110(a)(2)'s second criterion that the plan contain such control devices "as may be necessary" to achieve the primary and secondary air quality standards. § 110(a)(2)(B). The is that an overly restrictive plan is not "necessary" for attainment of the national standards and so must be rejected by the Administrator.

The principal support for this theory of Amici lies in the fact that while the House and Senate versions of § 110(a)(2) both expressly provided that the States could submit for the Administrator's approval plans that were stricter than the national standards required, the section as enacted contains no such express language. Amici argue that the Conference Committee must have decided to require state implementation plans simply and precisely to meet the national standards. The argument of Amici proves too much. A Conference Committee lacks power to make substantive changes on matters about which both Houses agree. Here the Conference Report expressly notes that both the Senate and House bills would allow States to submit plans more stringent than the national standards demand, and offers no suggestion that the Conference bill intended to change that result, even if it could. And while the final language of § 110(a)(2)(B) may be less explicit than the versions originally approved by the House and the Senate, the most natural reading of the "as may be necessary" phrase in context is simply that the Administrator must assure that the minimal, or "necessary," requirements are met, not that he detect and reject any state plan more demanding than federal law requires.

This reading is further supported by practical considerations. Section 116 of the Clean Air Act provides that the States may adopt emission standards stricter than the national standards. *Amici* argue that such standards must be adopted and enforced independently of the EPA-approved state implementation plan. This construction of §§ 110 and 116, however, would not only require the Administrator to expend considerable time and energy determining whether a state plan was precisely tailored to meet the federal standards, but would simultaneously require States desiring stricter standards to enact and enforce two sets of emission standards, one federally approved plan and one stricter state plan. We find no basis in the Amendments for visiting such wasteful burdens upon the States and the Administrator, and so we reject the argument of Amici.

We read the "as may be necessary" requirement of § 110(a)(2)(B) to demand only that the implementation plan submitted by the State meet the "minimum conditions" of the Amendments.[13] Beyond that, if a State makes the legislative determination that it desires a particular air quality by a certain date and that it is willing to force technology to attain it or lose a certain industry if attainment is not possible such a determination is fully consistent with the structure and purpose of the Amendments, and § 110(a)(2)(B) provides no basis for the EPA Administrator to object to the determination on the ground of infeasibility.

In sum, we have concluded that claims of economic or technological infeasibility may not be considered by the Administrator in evaluating a state requirement that primary ambient air quality standards be met in the mandatory three years. And, since we further conclude that the States may submit implementation plans more stringent than federal law requires and that the Administrator must approve such plans if they meet the minimum requirements of § 110(a)(2), it follows that the language of § 110(a)(2)(B) provides no basis for the Administrator ever to reject a state implementation plan on the ground that it is economically or technologically infeasible.

Our conclusion is bolstered by recognition that the Amendments do allow claims of technological and economic infeasibility to be raised in situations where consideration of such claims will not substantially interfere with the primary congressional purpose of prompt attainment of the national air quality standards. Thus, we do not hold that claims of infeasibility are never of relevance in the formulation of an implementation plan or that sources unable to comply with emission limitations must inevitably be shut down.

Perhaps the most important forum for consideration of claims of economic and technological infeasibility is before the state agency formulating the implementation plan. So long as the national standards are met, the State may select whatever mix of control devices it desires, and industries with particular economic or technological problems may seek special treatment in the plan itself. Moreover, if the industry is not exempted from, or accommodated by, the original plan, it may obtain a variance, as petitioner did in this case; and the variance, if granted after notice and a hearing, may be submitted to the EPA as a revision of the plan. Lastly, an industry denied an exemption from the implementation plan, or denied a subsequent variance, may be able to take its claims of economic or technological infeasibility to the state courts.

* * *

---

13. Economic and technological factors may be relevant in determining whether the minimum conditions are met. Thus, the Administrator may consider whether it is economically or technologically possible for the state plan to require more rapid progress than it does. If he determines that it is, he may reject the plan as not meeting the requirement that primary standards be achieved "as expeditiously as practicable" or as failing to provide for attaining secondary standards within "a reasonable time."

■ JUSTICE POWELL, with whom THE CHIEF JUSTICE joins, concurring.

I join the opinion of the Court because the statutory scheme and the legislative history, thoroughly described in the Court's opinion, demonstrate irrefutably that Congress did not intend to permit the Administrator of the Environmental Protection Agency to reject a proposed state implementation plan on the grounds of economic or technological infeasibility. Congress adopted this position despite its apparent awareness that in some cases existing sources that cannot meet the standard of the law must be closed down.

What this means in this case, if the allegations of Union Electric Co. prove to be correct, is that in the interest of public health the utility will be ordered to discontinue electric service to the public. As one cannot believe this would be allowed, I suppose that the State or Federal Government would find some basis for continuing to operate the company's facilities to serve the public despite noncompliance. But no such contingency program or authority therefor is found in the statute, and we must decide the case on the record before us.

The desire to impose strong incentives on industry to encourage the rapid development and adoption of pollution control devices is understandable. But it is difficult to believe that Congress would adhere to its absolute position if faced with the potentially devastating consequences to the public that this case vividly demonstrates.

Petitioner is an electric utility supplying power demands in the St. Louis metropolitan area, a large part of Missouri, and parts of Illinois and Iowa. It alleges that it cannot continue to operate if forced to comply with the sulfur dioxide restrictions contained in the Missouri implementation plan approved by the Administrator. Specifically, petitioner alleges that since the Administrator's approval of the plan, low-sulfur coal has become too scarce and expensive to obtain; reliable and satisfactory sulfur dioxide removal equipment that would enable it to comply with the plan's requirements simply has not been devised; the installation of the unsatisfactory equipment that is available would cost over $500 million, a sum impossible to obtain by bonds that are contingent on approval by regulatory bodies and public acceptance; and, even if the financing could be obtained, the carrying, operating, and maintenance costs of over $120 million a year would be prohibitive. Petitioner further alleges that recent evidence has disclosed that sulfur dioxide in the ambient air is not the hazard to public health that it was once thought to be, and that compliance with the sulfur regulation in the Missouri plan is not necessary to the attainment of national primary and secondary ambient air standards in the St. Louis area.

At the risk of civil and criminal penalties enforceable by both the State and Federal Governments, as well as possible citizens' suits, petitioner is being required either to embark upon the task of installing allegedly unreliable and prohibitively expensive equipment or to shut down. Yet the present Act permits neither the Administrator, in approving the state plan, nor the courts, in reviewing that approval even to consider petitioner's allegations of infeasibility.

Environmental concerns, long neglected, merit high priority, and Congress properly has made protection of the public health its paramount consideration. But the shutdown of an urban area's electrical service could have an even more serious impact on the health of the public than that created by a decline in ambient air quality. The result apparently required by this legislation in its present form could sacrifice the well-being of a large metropolitan area through the imposition of inflexible demands that may be technologically impossible to meet and indeed may no longer even be necessary to the attainment of the goal of clean air.

I believe that Congress, if fully aware of this Draconian possibility, would strike a different balance.

CLASS DISCUSSION PROBLEM: DESIGNING A STATE IMPLEMENTATION PLAN FOR $PM_{2.5}$

The current NAAQS for $PM_{2.5}$ are 15 $\mu g/m^3$ on an annual averaging basis and 35 $\mu g/m^3$ on a 24–hour basis. The 24–hour standards are considered to be met if the 98% percentile value for daily $PM_{2.5}$ over a period of 3 years is no greater than 35 $\mu g/m^3$. In other words, on average no more than 7 days per year may exceed the standard.

You are the Director of Air Pollution Programs for your state, and it is therefore your responsibility to prepare the SIP for $PM_{2.5}$. Preliminary technical information indicates that $PM_{2.5}$ is emitted from a range of sources including various industrial operations; motor vehicles and off-road vehicles; home fireplaces and woodstoves; agricultural operations (plowing and harvesting); and even portable diesel engines, which are used at large construction sites. There are also non-anthropogenic (natural) sources of $PM_{2.5}$; background levels from these sources vary, but can be as high 5 $\mu g/m^3$. Some of the anthropogenic sources are modern and state-of-the-art with respect to pollution control. Others (including the area's coal-fired electricity plant) are older, and their emissions are virtually uncontrolled. $PM_{2.5}$ is relatively immobile; once emitted it is not transported over great distances. Only one air quality control region in the state (the Jacksontown metropolitan area) is believed to be violating the new $PM_{2.5}$ standard. Monitoring over a three-year period in this region shows readings averaging 20 $\mu g/m^3$ on an annual basis, with spikes roughly 10 times per year of 35 $\mu g/m^3$ or more.

Based on this information, your staff has proposed a number of possible strategies around which to structure the SIP. Evaluate the following alternatives on the basis of ease of establishing standards; ease of enforcing standards; efficiency; fairness; political acceptability, and any other factors you believe are significant.

Option 1: Linear Relationship Approach. Since the current level of $PM_{2.5}$ in the Jacksontown air averages 20 $\mu g/m^3$ compared to the annual NAAQS of 15 $\mu g/m^3$, one alternative is to require that all sources uniformly reduce $PM_{2.5}$ emissions by 33% (if background, which we can assume can't be controlled, is roughly 5 $\mu g/m^3$, the concentration attributable to anthropogenic sources must fall from 15 $\mu g/m^3$ to 10 $\mu g/m^3$, a reduction of 33%).

Option 2: Focusing on industrial sources. Another alternative is to focus on the large industrial sources. Based on computer modeling that considers source location, elevation, emission rates, meteorological data, and other factors, staff believe that Jacksontown can achieve the annual NAAQS if all of the large industrial operations are required to reduce their PM2.5 emissions by 50%, or if the older installations are replaced with new, state-of-the-art plants. There is considerable uncertainty in the modeling. It is possible that the NAAQS could be attained with the equivalent of 40% reductions from all the large industrial sources, or that attainment might require 60% reductions.

Option 3: Job Preservation Approach. A third alternative, offered by staff in response to the requests of labor unions and major manufacturers would consider the impact of a range of proposed control measures on existing manufacturing jobs, with the goal of allocating emission reductions in such a way as to minimize adverse economic impact on the largest industrial sources. This strategy would shift control requirements to mobile sources, agricultural sources, and home fireplaces.

Option 4: The "Green" Approach. The governor of your state, who was elected on a platform emphasizing environmental protection, has instructed your agency to develop air pollution controls that are highly protective of health and welfare. Staff has therefore developed an alternative which will reduce annual $PM_{2.5}$ levels below the NAAQS, to 13 $\mu g/m^3$. This alternative would require extraordinarily stringent controls, including the closure of at least one and possibly several major manufacturing facilities or substantial reductions in the use of cars in the area.

Once you've identified a preferred alternative, how would you implement it? Is there a role for voluntary as well as regulatory measures? For public education?

The Jacksontown metropolitan area is projected to experience significant growth pressure over the next decade. In addition, it is just emerging from a recession; economic activity is expected to grow significantly over the next few years even if population does not. How should this information be factored into SIP development?

NOTES AND QUESTIONS

1. *Allocating authority and responsibility.* The CAA makes EPA responsible for establishing the NAAQS, but gives the states responsibility for achieving the NAAQS through the development and implementation of SIPs. Why do you think Congress chose to allocate responsibility that way?

What are the consequences if a state does not create approvable plans? What are the benefits to a state of developing a plan? What are the costs? Is EPA likely to be anxious to take on the responsibility of FIP preparation or enforcement?

2. *Deference to state judgments.* EPA must approve a state SIP that meets the requirements of CAA § 110. The Supreme Court's decision in *Union Electric* precludes EPA from reviewing the economic or technological feasibility of SIP measures, even if those measures are critical to the success of the SIP. Is that a good idea? What assurance does EPA have that Missouri will enforce its SIP, even if that means that Union Electric's plant must be shut down?

3. *Uncertainty and optimism.* In the San Joaquin example discussed by Fine and Owen, why did the SIP not produce the expected improvement in air quality? Are changes to the SIP preparation procedure or to the CAA needed to improve SIP performance? What changes would you recommend?

4. *Variances and discretion in SIPs.* In *Union Electric*, the utility had received a series of annual variances from the state before EPA notified it that its emissions exceeded the levels permitted by the SIP. What role should such variances play in SIPs and their implementation? EPA has long taken the position that variances are permitted only if they are adopted through the procedures applicable to SIP revisions and submitted to EPA for approval. Is that interpretation appropriate? Is it required by the CAA? Must EPA prohibit all discretionary provisions in a SIP? Is it possible to grant states the flexibility to respond to unexpected situations while ensuring that the SIP achieves compliance with the NAAQS?

5. *Whose SIP is it?* The SIP is a creature of both state and federal law, since it is prepared and implemented by a state agency but must be approved by EPA. When ambiguous provisions of a SIP must be interpreted, should courts defer to EPA's understanding of the meaning of those provisions, or the state's? The Ninth Circuit has explained that, because a SIP becomes federal law once approved by EPA, "the state's interpretation of the regulations incorporated into the SIP, even if binding as a matter of state law, is not directly dispositive of the meaning of the SIP." Safe Air for Everyone v. U.S. EPA, 475 F.3d 1096, 1105 (9th Cir. 2007).

6. *SIP indeterminacy.* As originally enacted, the CAA required that EPA annually assemble and publish a comprehensive document for each state setting forth all requirements of the state's SIP. The 1990 amendments soften that requirement a bit, allowing EPA three years between SIP compilations. CAA § 110(h)(1), 42 U.S.C. § 7410(h)(1). Still, EPA has not complied, and perhaps can not. SIPs are not prepared comprehensively by the states, nor are they static once prepared. They are documents in constant motion, as states or local air boards devise new rules and delete old ones, as the NAAQS change, and as EPA calls for changes in light of new information. The task of keeping track of the precise state of even a single state's SIP is well-nigh impossible. A top EPA official confessed as early as 1981 that no one at EPA could read the whole Illinois SIP, or knew what was in it. See William H. Rodgers, Jr., Environmental Law, 2d ed.,

209 (1994). The task has not gotten easier over the years. If no one at EPA even knows what an entire SIP says, how can the agency ever be sure that the SIP will achieve the NAAQS?

C. THE PROBLEM OF NON-ATTAINMENT

The 1970 CAA called for achievement of most of the NAAQS by 1975. Surprisingly, the 1970 Act did not state explicitly what would happen if that deadline was not met. As Professor William Rodgers explained, though,

> The predicted consequence of non-attainment under the 1970 amendments was a flat ban on new sources for the obvious reason, to put it starkly, that if prevailing air quality brought death and destruction, there was little to commend a move that would aggravate conditions already quite bad enough. The very real prospect, then, was a shutdown of industrial growth in many parts of the nation.

William H. Rodgers, Environmental Law, 2d ed., 210 (1994).

Of course, that did not happen. In 1977, Congress extended the NAAQS attainment dates, but also imposed an offset policy, requiring that the emissions of any new source in a non-attainment area be offset by reductions in existing sources, and introduced new requirements for SIPs in nonattainment areas. New deadlines were missed in 1982, and again in 1987. In 1990, Congress tried again, extending the deadlines once more, while adding even more SIP requirements for non-attainment areas, and stiff sanctions. Yet as of 2011, most major urban areas in the U.S. are in non-attainment for at least one of the NAAQS. The ozone NAAQS is the standard most commonly failed. The ozone non-attainment situation is going to get worse before it gets better. The current statistics reflect only non-attainment of the 1997 standards. EPA has yet to evaluate compliance with the stricter 2008 standards, which it has already proposed to tighten again. 75 Fed. Reg. 2938 (Jan. 19, 2010).

Thomas O. McGarity, Missing Milestones: A Critical Look at the Clean Air Act's VOC Emissions Reduction Program in Non-Attainment Areas

18 Virginia Environmental Law Journal 41 (1999).

* * *

One of the original pollutants for which the EPA established NAAQS was photochemical oxidants, commonly known as urban smog. Photochemical oxidants are formed when certain hydrocarbon compounds, also referred to as VOCs, combine with oxides of nitrogen (NO_x). As a measure of the concentration of photochemical oxidants in the atmosphere, regulatory agencies rely upon the more easily measured concentration of ozone.

* * *

By 1977, it had become clear that the statute's exceedingly ambitious goals for photochemical oxidants would not be met in most urban airsheds. To achieve the national primary standard for photochemical oxidants, as measured in concentrations of ozone, the states had to control emissions of VOCs and NO_x from a wide variety of sources, ranging from large refineries to individual automobiles. Although it was clear that VOCs and NO_x combined under sunlight to produce photochemical oxidants, the mechanisms were poorly understood. It was therefore unclear whether the states should have focused upon reducing emissions of VOCs or NO_x or some combination of the two. It also became apparent that not all VOCs were "anthropogenic" in origin—that is, generated by human activity. In some cities like Houston, almost one third of daily VOC emissions were "biogenic," generated from trees and other vegetation. * * *

Recognizing that the goals of the 1970 amendments had not been achieved for photochemical oxidants, Congress in 1977 amended the CAA to establish a specific "nonattainment" program for achieving the primary ambient air quality standards in areas where the states had previously failed. * * * The amendments required the states to submit a new SIP for nonattainment areas demonstrating that they would attain the primary standards by 1983. [That deadline was extendable to 1987 for ozone.]

* * *

As the 1987 deadline passed, it once again became painfully clear that dozens of nonattainment areas had not achieved the primary standard for photochemical oxidants * * *. Moreover, it was clear that some areas had not adopted the most effective measures available, but had allowed regulated sources to get by with only very modest improvements. * * *

Nevertheless, the EPA refused to impose the statutory sanctions on states that had obviously failed to attain the standards by the statutory deadline. Instead, the agency took the position that it would impose sanctions only if the state failed to carry out its SIP commitments in good faith or if the plan was inadequate on its face. In other words, absent bad faith on a state's part, the EPA would impose no sanctions so long as the SIP appeared to demonstrate attainment by the 1987 deadline, even though the deadline had passed and the area remained out of attainment. The EPA proposed sanctions for eleven areas with deficient SIPs in July 1987, but Congress immediately came to the rescue with legislation extending the deadlines for a year and prohibiting the EPA from carrying out sanctions.

* * *

At the end of three years of contentious debate, Congress enacted the 1990 Amendments to the CAA. * * *

The 1990 amendments divided the existing photochemical oxidant nonattainment areas into five categories, depending upon the degree to which the maximum concentration of ozone or "design value" for the area exceeded the primary ambient air quality standard. The five ozone nonattainment areas were named "marginal, moderate, serious, severe, and extreme." Areas with more serious pollution problems were given longer to attain the primary standards, but they were subject to increasingly stringent implementation plan requirements.

A. The Statutory Requirements

Like the 1970 and 1977 amendments, the 1990 amendments gave the states flexibility to promulgate and implement individual control measures for existing sources of VOCs and NO_x. The amendments retained the requirement of the 1977 Amendments that nonattainment plans implement "reasonably available control measures" including "reasonably available control technology" ("RACT") for existing stationary sources. This time, however, Congress required the EPA to promulgate control techniques guidelines ("CTGs") for stationary sources of VOCs according to a specific statutory timetable so that states would have uniform guidance for establishing RACT for categories of such sources.

Implementation plans for severe and extreme areas were required to identify and adopt "specific enforceable transportation control strategies" and particular transportation control measures sufficient to offset any growth in emissions from corresponding growth in automobile use. In addition, particular transportation control measures were required to be sufficient to represent "reasonable further progress" when added to SIP requirements for stationary sources. * * *

If a state failed to submit a plan that met the minimal criteria for plan submission, submitted an inadequate plan, or failed to implement any provision of an approved SIP, the EPA could elect one of two sanctions. As under the 1977 amendments, the EPA could cut off certain federal highway funds for the offending area. In addition, the Administrator could limit the construction or modification of major new sources in the area by requiring them to offset any additional emissions on a two-for-one basis. The 1990 amendments, however, required the EPA to give the affected state 18 months to cure any defects before invoking the sanctions. As an additional sanction, any areas (other than severe areas) that failed to attain the standards by the new statutory deadlines would be automatically "bumped up" to the next higher classification and would be obliged to implement all additional requirements applicable to that category.

SIPs still had to demonstrate that the areas were making "reasonable further progress" toward attainment, and that term was again defined to prevent any temporary increases in pollution and to require "annual incremental reductions" in emissions as needed to achieve the standards by the relevant deadlines. SIPs for moderate, serious, severe, and extreme areas had to provide for "specific annual reductions in emissions" of VOCs and NO_x "as necessary to attain" the primary standard for ozone by the applicable attainment date. * * *

The amendments went beyond the essentially media quality-based "reasonable further progress" requirement of the 1977 Amendments, however, to add an emissions reduction "milestones" program for heavily polluted nonattainment areas. This new program had to be implemented and monitored no matter how rapidly ambient ozone concentrations declined. In particular, the plans had to demonstrate that between 1990 and 1996, there would be a fifteen percent reduction in anthropogenic VOC emissions in moderate, serious, severe, and extreme areas. Moreover, the fifteen percent reduction target had to account for any additional emissions caused by growth in the number of stationary sources and in the number of vehicle miles traveled. * * * For serious and above areas, the "rate-of-progress" SIPs had to come up with an additional three percent reduction in VOC emissions per year until the ozone standard was attained.

* * *

IV.   State Implementation of the Fifteen Percent VOC Reduction Requirements

As the Texas Natural Resources Conservation Commission (the "TNRCC") began the difficult task of drafting its nonattainment SIP revisions in light of the 1990 CAA Amendments, it was building upon a history of failure to attain the standards by the 1977 and 1987 deadlines in the Houston/Galveston nonattainment area—an area, which by 1990, was second only to Los Angeles in the frequency and severity of its violations of the standard for photochemical oxidants.

* * *

The starting point for the fifteen percent reduction rate-of-progress SIP was the 1990 baseline emissions inventory. The TNRCC developed emissions estimates for five broad categories of emissions sources: point sources, minor and area sources, on-road mobile sources, non-road mobile sources, and biogenics. After adjusting for noncreditable emissions and estimated future growth, the TNRCC then calculated the target daily tonnage of VOCs that would have to be removed prior to November 15, 1996. The goal of the rate-of-progress SIP was to prescribe regulations and control measures sufficiently stringent to achieve the targeted amount of VOC reductions prior to the deadline.

* * *

The TNRCC submitted its 1990 Base Year Inventories for Houston/Galveston and the other Texas nonattainment areas to the EPA on November 17, 1992, only two days after the statutory due date. Almost two years later, the EPA finally approved the inventory after having received no negative comments.

The TNRCC submitted its original rate-of-progress SIP to the EPA on May 13, 1994, before it could even be certain that the EPA would approve the 1990 base-year inventory. In that submission, the TNRCC promised to implement a number of new requirements for both mobile and stationary sources and maintained that these changes, along with projected emissions reductions from various new federal programs, would yield the necessary 232.24 tons of VOC reductions per day in the Houston/Galveston nonattainment area. On January 29, 1995, long after the submission and less than a year from the November 15, 1996, deadline, the EPA proposed to approve the control requirements contained in the Texas rate-of-progress SIP, but it also proposed a "limited disapproval" because the plan failed to demonstrate that the required fifteen percent reduction in VOC emissions would occur in the relevant areas by November 15, 1996. * * *

Fugitive emissions from refineries and other stationary sources comprised the largest source of emissions reductions identified in the Texas SIP revisions. Fugitive emissions are those that cannot reasonably be captured by a stack, chimney, vent, or similar opening. They typically come from leaking valves and flanges, and they are most effectively controlled by periodic inspections for and repairs to leaks that fail to pass a specified threshold. The TNRCC proposed to reduce fugitive emissions from plants involved in petroleum refining and natural gas, gasoline, and petrochemical processing by lowering the threshold for requiring a repair of a leak from 10,000 ppm to 500 ppm. When company officials detect leaks of greater than 500 ppm under the new rules, the company would have to arrange for repairs to fix the leaks within fifteen days, absent extenuating circumstances. The agency predicted that its new fugitive emissions reduction requirements would reduce emissions in the Houston/Galveston area by 34.61 TPD. * * *

The second largest contributor of additional VOC reductions in the TNRCC rate-of-progress SIP was the agency's proposed centralized automobile I/M [inspection and maintenance] program. Since Houston/Galveston was classified as a "severe" nonattainment area, it was required to implement an "enhanced" automobile I/M program by November 15, 1994. Congress required enhanced programs: to cover more of the vehicles in operation than the "basic" I/M programs in place in most urban areas; to employ more sophisticated inspection methods for finding high emitting vehicles; and to contain additional features to ensure that all vehicles were tested properly and effectively repaired. In particular, the amendments mandated that an enhanced I/M program operate "on a centralized basis, unless the State demonstrates to the satisfaction of the Administrator that a decentralized program will be equally effective."

After avoiding inspection and maintenance in the Houston/Galveston nonattainment area for more than a decade, Texas finally began in earnest to implement an enhanced program. The TNRCC decided to require a state-of-the-art centralized testing program featuring biennial testing with EPA's preferred "IM–240" testing technologies. To ensure against fraud and collusion, the testing program did not allow the testing facility to make any subsequently needed repairs.

* * *

On July 11, 1997, eight months after the fifteen percent emissions reductions were supposed to have been accomplished in the real world, the EPA approved the changes to the TNRCC's base-line 1990 emissions inventory and proposed to conditionally approve the Texas fifteen percent rate-of-progress SIP. Approval meant that the EPA was convinced that

VOC emissions reductions attributable to the various state and federal programs would bring about a fifteen percent reduction in anthropogenic emissions from the 1990 baseline in the Houston/Galveston nonattainment area by November 15, 1996. * * *

Like SIP approvals dating back to the early 1970s, this approval was based upon false assumptions and unfulfilled promises, and the EPA knew this at the time that it accepted the TNRCC plan. The EPA was aware that the emissions reductions attributable to the I/M regime for Houston/Galveston had not occurred because that program had not gone into effect as of November 15, 1996. The EPA could also be quite confident that the much less effective decentralized test-and-repair regime that would soon go into place would not achieve the emissions reductions that the TNRCC in "good faith" claimed, but it was prevented by [a congressional appropriations rider] from taking that into consideration. * * *

The TNRCC had originally claimed 8.56 TPD in emissions reductions due to enhanced enforcement efforts aimed at making its new rules more effective. The Fix–Up rate-of-progress SIP claimed even more ambitious rule effectiveness. Despite the fact that the rules were being applied to a somewhat smaller 1990 emissions baseline, the TNRCC again applied its own methodology (rather than the EPA's suggested methodology) to conclude that "significant increases" in regional office compliance and enforcement staff and a revision of its "upset/maintenance" rule would bring about VOC reductions of 12.82 TPD in the Houston/Galveston area alone. Without any additional elaboration on the TNRCC methodology or any inquiry into whether the promised staff increases in fact occurred, the EPA approved the claimed emissions reductions. In fact, the staff increases had not come about as of November 15, 1996, and there is little prospect that they ever will occur.

* * *

VI.   Why the Milestone Program Failed

* * *

It is difficult to avoid the conclusion that the EPA has not taken the milestones program seriously. [T]he agency has consistently approved VOC emissions reduction claims in rate-of-progress SIPS that cannot possibly be borne out in the real world. * * *

In the final analysis, the milestone program failed because the states once again were not held accountable for empty promises and overly optimistic projections in their rate-of-progress SIPs. * * *

The milestone program that Congress established in the 1990 CAA Amendments had the potential to address in a straightforward way past failures to achieve the NAAQS for photochemical oxidants. The milestone idea was a simple one. By setting clear near-term goals and periodically checking to see whether those goals have been achieved, environmental agencies can ensure real progress toward meeting more ambitious long-term goals. The process of setting goals and evaluating progress toward those goals was intended to bring an element of accountability into the implementation process that had previously been missing. Congress envisioned that the milestone demonstration requirement would bring failures to the public's attention relatively rapidly and would identify the persons or entities that were responsible for those failures in sufficient time to remedy the problems by the next milestone.

* * * Congress understood in 1990 that attaining the standard would require tough choices, and it was willing to let the states have the first cut at making those choices. States were given the flexibility to use technology-based requirements or market-based techniques like emissions trading and taxes to achieve needed VOC emissions reductions. The states could choose whether to increase control measures for large industrial sources, small mom-and-pop operations, or even existing federal facilities. States could elect to implement transportation controls or limit the construction of indirect sources like domed stadiums that attract large amounts of traffic. The milestones program provided the vehicle for holding the states accountable for choosing a workable mix of controls and incentives and for implementing those choices in an effective way. The collapse of the milestone program means that state failures have not been identified and responsibility for those failures has not been assigned. * * *

BCCA Appeal Group v. United States Environmental Protection Agency

United States Court of Appeals, Fifth Circuit, 2003.
355 F.3d 817.

■ DAVIS, CIRCUIT JUDGE, and RESTANI, JUDGE:

* * *

The Houston–Galveston area, a large geographic area consisting of eight counties, is one air quality control region in Texas. Houston–Galveston has one of the most serious ozone problems in the country. In order to comply with the CAA's requirement for attainment of the one-hour ozone standard by 2007, Texas adopted the attainment demonstration SIP at issue in this case, which the EPA approved in its final rule.

An "attainment demonstration SIP" has two components: (1) the attainment demonstration, which is based on computer modeling that predicts whether the area will meet the ozone standard by the statutory deadline of 2007; and (2) the state's control strategy, which is its plan for achieving the actual emissions reductions needed for attainment. Modeling efforts for the Houston–Galveston SIP were complicated by a number of unique environmental factors and a shortage of readily-available control options sufficient to provide the needed reductions.[1] Nevertheless, Texas

---

1. The Houston–Galveston area's unique "land-sea breeze" meteorological condition affects ozone formation and movement around the region, adding a "level of complexity ...

developed an attainment demonstration and control strategy that its analyses confirmed would reach attainment by 2007.

The EPA evaluated the State's modeling and associated analyses and determined that they were consistent with the CAA and EPA's implementing regulations. * * *

* * * Two petitioners, BCCA Appeal Group ("BCCA")[4] and Brazoria County,[5] essentially oppose the Houston SIP because they believe some of its control measures are too stringent and will nevertheless fail to attain the NAAQS for ozone.

Conversely, the environmental petitioners believe the Houston SIP does not go far enough in adopting sufficient control measures to achieve attainment by the statutory deadline. * * *

C. Whether EPA's Approval of Texas's Attainment Demonstration Is Supported by the Record and Consistent with the CAA

Section 182(c)(2)(A) of the CAA requires Texas to demonstrate that the Houston SIP will achieve attainment of the ozone NAAQS by the statutory deadline. 42 U.S.C. § 7511a(c)(2)(A). "This attainment demonstration must be based on photochemical grid modeling[12] or any other analytical method determined . . . to be at least as effective." * * *

Texas's attainment demonstration includes both photochemical grid modeling and supplemental analyses that EPA considered in its "weight-of-evidence" analysis. As an initial matter, BCCA contends that Texas's photochemical grid modeling was flawed because it failed to simulate rapidly-forming ozone peaks, known as "spikes," and overestimated ozone formation in other parts of the Houston–Galveston area. * * *

Texas used an EPA-approved photochemical grid model * * *. Texas applied the model to a large geographic region, covering over 220,000 square kilometers, to ensure that all the major emission sources were included in the model's results. Texas adjusted the model to account for the unique land-sea breeze phenomenon conducive to ozone formation in the region. Before using the model to predict future ozone concentrations,

---

not seen anywhere else in the country." 66 Fed. Reg. at 57,164. This condition causes emissions in the Houston–Galveston to begin to form ozone in the local atmosphere, "later emissions and ozone formed are transported out over the warm air over the Gulf of Mexico where the warmer temperatures further activate the chemistry to form more ozone which is then transported back inland over the area." Id. In addition to overcoming this meteorological complexity, the Houston SIP had to reduce nitrogen oxide ("NO_x") emissions by 71 percent to reach attainment by 2007, despite a shortage of control options.

4. BCCA Appeal Group is comprised of owners and operators of stationary sources of air pollution that are subject to Texas's control measures.

5. Brazoria County is one of eight counties within the Houston–Galveston area. * * *

12. Photochemical grid modeling is computerized air quality modeling "that evaluates how emissions from various sources combine in the atmosphere and predicts the concentration of pollutants that likely will result." 1000 Friends, 265 F.3d at 220 n. 4. This technique employs complex computer models that can predict ozone levels as of the statutory attainment date based on monitoring data, meteorology, the area's projected growth, planned emission reductions, and other factors. * * *

however, Texas validated the model by performing a test run ("the base case") that compared the model's predictions with actual air quality data for a chosen time period. The base time period covered four days, September 8–11, 1993, that featured both high ozone concentrations and the land-sea breeze weather patterns characteristic of the Houston–Galveston area. Following EPA-accepted protocols, Texas then entered emissions data into the model for the base time period, ran the model, and compared the predicted results with actual ozone concentrations measured at 34 air quality monitors in Houston–Galveston during the base time period. Texas then applied a battery of tests and analyses set forth in EPA guidance, including diagnostic and sensitivity analyses, graphical displays, and statistical tests, which collectively demonstrated that the model's base case performance was acceptable.

Once it validated the model, Texas used it to predict ozone concentrations for the 2007 attainment date based on anticipated changes in the number and type of emissions sources. The state then introduced its proposed control strategy and ran the model's "attainment test," which compared the predicted ozone levels to the NAAQS * * *. The model showed that Texas's proposed strategy would significantly reduce ozone concentrations in the Houston–Galveston area, but not enough to meet the applicable ozone standard.

In response, Texas, following an approach set forth in EPA guidance, estimated the additional emissions reductions necessary to bring the area into attainment, and adopted a revised control strategy that would provide for attainment by 2007. The revised control strategy includes additional control measures and an enforceable commitment to adopt even more control measures after a mid-course review in 2004 and submission of a SIP revision to the EPA. EPA approved the attainment demonstration * * *.

While photochemical grid models are imperfect tools for predicting future air quality, a modeled attainment demonstration "provide[s] a reasonable expectation that the measures and procedures outlined will result in attainment of the NAAQS by [the statutory deadline]." 1996 Modeling Guidance at 3. "[A] reviewing court must remember that the [agency] is making predictions, within its area of special expertise, at the frontiers of science. When examining this kind of scientific determination, as opposed to simple findings of fact, a reviewing court must generally be at its most deferential." *Baltimore Gas & Elec. Co. v. NRDC*, 462 U.S. 87, 103 (1983). * * *

The court finds that EPA's reliance on the model's results was not arbitrary, capricious, or contrary to law. In its final rule, the EPA addressed BCCA's concern that the model fails to account for ozone spikes. EPA explained that while air quality monitors measure ozone concentration at one fixed point in space, ozone concentrations can vary significantly over a grid cell. The photochemical grid model, by definition, averages natural conditions over the volume of each grid cell. As such, EPA does not expect comparisons between model predictions and monitor observations to exactly match. The EPA found that while the Texas model has difficulty replicating rapid increases in ozone, "[t]his is to be expected and does not necessarily call into question the model's utility as a tool to predict the level of emission reductions needed to reach attainment." EPA determined that the Texas model "provides reasonable predictions of ozone levels as confirmed by comparisons with monitoring data and therefore can provide an acceptable estimate of the amount of emissions needed for attainment." This explanation is reasonable and is supported by the record, and, therefore, EPA's determination is entitled to deference.

The EPA's final rule also addressed BCCA's concern that the photochemical grid model both over-and under-predicted ozone in some areas. EPA's final rule explains that the model was validated by a battery of diagnostic and sensitivity analyses and graphical and statistical performance measures. * * * EPA considered all model performance measures and concluded that the model performed well. While the EPA recognized that the graphical model performance for one day of the base period indicated that the model underestimated ozone at some locations and overestimated ozone at others, the EPA attributed the error to the model's difficulty replicating wind speed and direction due to the area's unique land-sea breeze phenomenon. Nevertheless, because the diagnostic and sensitivity tests revealed no flaws in model formulations, and statistical measures confirmed that the model generally predicted the right magnitude of ozone peaks, the EPA determined that the model provided an acceptable tool for estimating the amount of emissions reductions needed for attainment.

Because EPA considered BCCA's arguments during the administrative process and offered a rational explanation for its reliance on the model despite the model's inability to exactly replicate Houston–Galveston's unique meteorological conditions, the court upholds EPA's approval of Texas's photochemical grid model. EPA recognized the model's shortcomings in the final rule and provided plausible explanations that were supported by the record. In light of the reasonable explanation for the model's discrepancies, and given the fact that the model nevertheless performed well on the full battery of validation tests, EPA's acceptance of Texas's modeling was neither arbitrary nor capricious. * * *

The statute requires that an attainment demonstration be "based on photochemical grid modeling or any other analytical method determined ... to be at least as effective." 42 U.S.C. § 7511a(c)(2)(A). Due to the inherent uncertainties in air quality modeling, EPA has interpreted the statute to allow states to supplement their photochemical modeling results with additional evidence to demonstrate attainment. EPA's modeling guidance was updated in 1996, and again in 1999, to permit states to use the weight-of-evidence approach to assess additional emissions reductions that are part of its SIP but were not modeled. * * *

The statute requires that an attainment demonstration be "based on photochemical grid modeling;" the statute does not require that an attainment demonstration be based *solely* or *directly* on photochemical grid modeling. As such, the statute is ambiguous as to how the photochemical grid modeling may be used. As the statute does not specifically govern the precise question at issue, the court must determine whether EPA's interpretation of it is entitled to deference.

EPA's weight-of-evidence approach to approving the Houston SIP was set forth in notice-and-comment rulemaking, and as such it is entitled to deference if it is reasonable. *See Mead,* 533 U.S. at 227–31. EPA has interpreted the "based on" language to allow for the assessment of additional emissions controls, not modeled, as part of the weight-of-evidence analysis. The model's results are the "principal component" of EPA's weight-of-evidence determination, but the weight-of-evidence approach allows Texas to supplement the modeled results with additional control measures. Furthermore, because the statute also grants EPA the broad authority to approve equally effective alternatives to photochemical grid modeling, Congress could not have intended to bar EPA from considering data in addition to modeled results.[21] As such, EPA's conclusion that the weight-of-evidence approach to approving attainment demonstrations is consistent with the CAA is reasonable and is entitled to deference.

* * *

E. Whether EPA's Approval of the SIP's "Enforceable Commitment" to Adopt Additional Controls on a Fixed Schedule is Consistent with the CAA

The EPA-approved control measures in the Houston SIP achieve 94 percent of the NO_x reductions needed for attainment. The final element of Texas's control strategy is an enforceable commitment[25] to adopt and implement additional NO_x controls on a fixed schedule to achieve an additional 56 tons/day of NO_x reductions.[26] Thus, the commitment addresses only 6 percent of the emission reductions necessary to attain the NAAQS for ozone. * * *

Nothing in the CAA speaks directly to enforceable commitments. The CAA does, however, provide EPA with great flexibility in approving SIPs. A SIP may contain "*enforceable* emission limitations and other control measures, *means, or techniques* . . . as well as *schedules and timetables* for compliance, *as may be* necessary or *appropriate*" to meet the CAA's requirements. 42 U.S.C. § 7410(a)(2)(A) (emphasis added). * * * Because the statute is silent on the issue of whether enforceable commitments are

---

21. Environmental Defense asserts that the weight-of-evidence determination is an improper "other analytical method" under 42 U.S.C. § 7511a(c)(2)(A) because the EPA Administrator did not make a specific determination that this approach is "at least as effective" as photochemical grid modeling. Because weight-of-evidence analysis is based on photochemical grid modeling, EPA did not use an "other analytical method" that would have required the Administrator's effectiveness determination.

25. These commitments are enforced by the EPA and citizens under the CAA. See 42 U.S.C. §§ 7413 (federal enforcement) and 7604 (citizen suits). * * * Finally, if a state fails to meet its commitments, EPA could find a failure to implement the SIP under section 179(a) of the CAA, which would trigger an 18–month period for the state to begin implementation before mandatory sanctions are imposed.

26. Under the schedule, Texas was required to adopt additional controls to provide 25 percent of the reductions covered by the enforceable commitment, or 14 tons/day of NO_x, by December 2002. Texas must adopt the remainder of the necessary controls by May 1, 2004.

appropriate means, techniques, or schedules for attainment, EPA's interpretation allowing limited use of an enforceable commitment in the Houston SIP must be upheld if reasonable.

* * * EPA generally considers three factors in determining whether to approve a SIP's enforceable commitment: (1) whether the commitment addresses a limited portion of the statutorily-required implementation plan; (2) whether the state is capable of fulfilling its commitment; and (3) whether the commitment is for a reasonable and appropriate period of time.

In the present case, EPA determined that Texas's limited use of the enforceable commitment as part of its overall control strategy was appropriate * * *. In applying the three-factor test to the Houston SIP, the EPA found that the first factor supported the use of an enforceable commitment here because it only addressed a small portion of the overall plan. In fact, the enforceable commitment addresses only six percent of the total emission reductions needed to attain the standard. The second factor also weighed in favor of approving the commitment because Texas "provided EPA with sufficient information to assure EPA that it will be capable of adopting controls to achieve the necessary level of emission reductions." Texas provided EPA with a list of soon-to-be-available, cutting-edge technologies that would achieve *at least* 56 tons/day of NO_x emission reductions by the statutory deadline,[30] thereby justifying its use of the enforceable commitment as opposed to adopted control measures. Finally, because Texas was in the process of exploring, developing, and assessing the capabilities of those cutting-edge technologies, some of which were further along in the development process than others, EPA approved the two-tiered timetable for adopting the additional controls covered by the commitment. EPA considered this timetable to be as expeditious as possible given the technological circumstances, in addition to the time Texas would need to adopt the measures that would achieve the necessary emission reductions. * * *

G.   Whether EPA's Approval of the Texas Emissions Reduction Plan is Supported by the Record

The Texas Emissions Reduction Plan or TERP is a discretionary economic incentive program to reduce emissions. At issue is TERP's diesel emission reduction program that provides financial incentives to help private and public entities purchase or lease cleaner diesel technology for mobile sources. Texas's program is modeled after [a] program in California, which was very successful. Economic incentives, like TERP, are explicitly allowed under the Act as one tool to achieve attainment. *See* 42 U.S.C. § 7410(a)(2)(A). * * *

---

30. The developing technologies submitted to EPA included, for example, diesel emulsion, fuel cells, diesel NO_x reductions systems, energy efficiency measures, and several innovative ideas, such as marine loading operations and episodic emission controls, all of which required further scientific study.

In considering TERP, the EPA reviewed the state's estimated costs, funding mechanisms, funding allocations, and estimated emission reductions from this program. Texas's TERP program was designed to generate 18.9 tons/day of NO_x reductions at an estimated average cost of $5000 per ton. Funding was to be provided by various fees and surcharges on vehicles. It was ultimately determined that the Houston area would be allocated $25 million for its diesel emission reduction program for fiscal year 2002. The EPA determined that Texas would achieve at least 25 tons/day of NO_x reductions in Houston from TERP, an amount the EPA determined to be sufficient to offset the emission reduction shortfall created by the Texas legislature in enacting TERP. The EPA's past experience with this type of diesel emission program in California supported its conclusion that substantial NO_x reductions could be achieved with the allocated funds.

* * *

H.   Whether EPA Reasonably Interpreted the CAA as Allowing Emission Reductions from the Voluntary Mobile Emission Reduction Program to be Considered in Reaching Attainment, and Whether the Record Supports EPA's Approval of the Program in the Houston SIP

The EPA encourages states to develop voluntary measures to reduce air pollution caused by vehicle emissions, such as trip reduction programs or growth management strategies, by granting limited SIP credit in appropriate circumstances for Voluntary Mobile Emission Reduction Programs or VMEP. The EPA believes that such voluntary measures, which rely on the discretionary actions of public or private parties, can provide emissions reductions that would not be available through traditional state regulatory programs. The EPA's VMEP Guidance provides a framework for states to obtain credit for such emission reductions. States must identify and describe the voluntary measures in its VMEP and include supportable projections of emissions reductions associated with the measures. The state must also make an enforceable commitment to monitor, assess, and report on the implementation and emissions effects of the VMEPs, as well as to timely remedy any shortfall in emissions reductions that do not meet the projected levels. The EPA requires that VMEP emissions reductions be quantifiable, surplus (i.e., they are not credited twice), enforceable, permanent, and adequately supported by the states. If these requirements are met, the emission reductions that can reasonably be attributed to VMEPs are included in a state's control strategy.[31]

The EPA's authority for the VMEP program is § 7410(a)(2)(A), which, as previously discussed, allows "enforceable ... control measures, means or techniques ... as may be necessary or appropriate to meet the applicable requirements of this chapter." * * *

The Texas VMEP consists of 14 voluntary measures designed to achieve 23 tons/day of NOx reductions. The state's decision to use volun-

---

31. EPA's guidance limits the SIP credit to three percent of the total future year emissions necessary to reach attainment until EPA gains additional experience in calculating credits for such voluntary measures.

tary measures was necessary due to the large magnitude of reductions needed for attainment. Many of the measures in the VMEP were existing voluntary programs that the state wanted to take SIP credit for towards its attainment demonstration. The VMEP added a few new programs that were already in development by Houston–Galveston Area Council, the regional transportation agency.

* * *

The state provided supporting documentation for each voluntary measure that included a description of the measure, the identified or predicted participants, the basis for the quantified emission reductions, and commitments to monitor, assess, and report emission reductions for the voluntary measures. * * * Based on its review of each VMEP measure and the SIP's recognition of the state's commitment to "monitor, evaluate, and report" on the VMEP, as well as "to remedy in a timely manner any SIP credit shortfall if the VMEP program does not achieve projected emission reductions," the EPA believed that Texas had fulfilled its requirements for VMEP submissions. * * *

NOTES AND QUESTIONS

1. *The designation of nonattainment areas.* The attainment status of an area has significant implications under the Clean Air Act, bringing with it both stringent SIP requirements and "a full complement of distasteful growth restrictions." William H. Rodgers, Environmental Law, 2d ed. 214 (1994). Every air quality control region in the country has been given one of three designations—attainment, nonattainment, or unclassifiable—for each of the NAAQS. See CAA § 107 (42 U.S.C. § 7407). Either actual monitoring data or modeling projections may serve as the basis for nonattainment designation. EPA receives a great deal of deference from the courts with respect to its identification of nonattainment areas and, as the *BCCA* decision demonstrates, with respect to the evidence it chooses to accept as demonstrating that a SIP will achieve attainment or has done so.

EPA may periodically revise its designations, on its own initiative or at the request of the state. A state seeking redesignation to attainment must provide a maintenance plan demonstrating that the area will remain in attainment for at least ten years following redesignation. CAA § 175A (42 U.S.C. § 7505a).

2. *Attainment deadlines.* In general, the CAA requires that states achieve attainment of all primary NAAQS "as expeditiously as practicable," but no later than five years after the area was designated as nonattainment, with EPA allowed to extend that date another five years. CAA § 172(a)(2)(A) (42 U.S.C. § 7502(a)(2)(A)). Secondary NAAQS must be achieved "as expeditiously as practicable." CAA § 172(a)(2)(B). The 1990 Amendments introduced a graduated series of compliance deadlines (and special SIP requirements) based on the severity of the pollution problem with respect to ozone, carbon monoxide, and particulate matter. The ozone program is the most detailed, establishing five different designations (marginal, moderate, serious, severe, and extreme), each with its own attainment deadline, extending as far as 20 years from the date of designation for "extreme" ozone non-attainment areas. CAA § 181(a) (42 U.S.C. § 7511(a)).

3. *SIP requirements in nonattainment areas.* SIPs for all nonattainment areas must include:

(a) Provisions for the application of "all reasonably available control measures," including the application of "reasonably available control technology" to existing sources. CAA § 172(c)(1). EPA regulations define RACT to mean:

> devices, systems, process modifications, or other apparatus or techniques that are reasonably available taking into account: (1) The necessity of imposing such controls in order to attain and maintain a national ambient air quality standard; [and] (2) The social, environmental, and economic impact of such controls.

40 C.F.R. § 51.100(*o*). EPA identifies RACT on a case-by-case, rather than an industry-wide, basis. The agency has developed voluminous guidance documents, called "control techniques guidelines" (CTG) to assist the states in determining RACT in specific situations. States may deviate from EPA's CTGs, but only if they can justify that departure based upon the individual economic and technical circumstances of a particular source.

(b) Provisions that will insure "reasonable further progress" toward attainment, defined to mean "such annual incremental reductions in emissions * * * as may reasonably be required by the Administrator" to ensure attainment by the applicable deadline. CAA § 172(c)(2); § 171(1).

(c) An explicit quantitative budget for the emissions which will be permitted from new or modified stationary sources, CAA § 172(c)(4), and a permit requirement for construction and operation of such sources, CAA § 172(c)(5). Permits may not be granted unless five conditions are met: (1) before the new source begins operation, its owner or operator must obtain sufficient offsetting reductions in emissions from other sources within the same nonattainment area to ensure reasonable further progress; (2) the source must meet "the lowest achievable emission rate," defined as the most stringent emission limitation found in any SIP or the most stringent limit achieved in practice for that category of source; (3) all major stationary sources controlled by the permit applicant must be subject to emission limitations and either in compliance or on a schedule for compliance with those limitations; (4) EPA must not have determined that the state is not adequately implementing the SIP for this nonattainment area; and (5) analysis of alternative sites, sizes, processes, and pollution control techniques must show that the benefits of the new source outweigh its environmental and social costs. CAA § 173.

In addition, the 1990 Amendments added a series of progressively more onerous requirements for SIPs in progressively more polluted ozone nonattainment areas. Notably, offset requirements progressively increase, from 1.1 to 1 for new or modified facilities in marginal nonattainment areas to

1.5 to 1 in the worst, "extreme" areas. The "milestone" 15% reduction in VOC emissions from the baseline that Professor McGarity mentions in the article excerpted above kicks in for areas that are deemed moderate (the second level of pollution) and above, becoming more stringent as the level of nonattainment rises. The requirements for demonstrating "reasonable further progress" are also gradually tightened, as are the stringency of required inspection and maintenance programs, and transportation control measures. Why did Congress adopt this tiered approach, and why did it make the requirements so detailed and prescriptive? Why did it require emission reduction milestones in addition to air quality progress? Why have the milestones and the RFP requirement not been fully effective?

4. *Automobiles and the SIP.* The next Section addresses tailpipe emission controls for new cars and other vehicles, which are outside the control of local air planners. Even with tailpipe controls, many SIPs must significantly reduce vehicle emissions in order to achieve the NAAQS. SIPs may include provisions focused on reducing emissions per mile traveled, such as enhanced vehicle inspection and maintenance programs, and provisions intended to reduce the number of vehicle miles traveled, such as highway tolls, gas or parking taxes, limits on parking, carpooling incentives, addition of bicycle lanes, or mass transit subsidies.

The Clean Air Act mandates that EPA provide the states with detailed information about the emission reduction potential of a number of specific transportation control measures. CAA § 108(f) (42 U.S.C. § 7408(f)). The 1990 Amendments require states with ozone or carbon monoxide non-attainment areas to implement I/M programs. For severe and extreme ozone non-attainment areas, they must implement "transportation control measures" (TCMs) to offset any growth in vehicle miles traveled or vehicle trips.

In order to assist states in controlling vehicle emissions, the CAA prohibits federal agencies from supporting or approving any activity which does not conform to an approved SIP. CAA § 176(c)(1) (42 U.S.C. § 7506(c)(1)). Specifically, "[n]o federal agency may approve, accept or fund any transportation plan, program or project unless [it] has been found to conform to any applicable" approved implementation plan. CAA § 176(c)(2).

5. *Sanctions.* The CAA provides that if EPA disapproves or finds that a state has failed to submit a SIP and the state fails to correct the deficiency within 18 months, EPA shall implement one of two sanctions: (1) a prohibition on the award of highway funding by the federal Department of Transportation within the nonattainment area, with an exception for safety improvements and mass transit projects; or (2) an increase in the offset ratio for new sources to "at least 2 to 1." CAA § 179(b). If the deficiency is not corrected within six months of imposition of one sanction, both must be imposed. CAA § 179(a). Although these sanctions sound like they would provide powerful leverage, a 2000 report to Congress concluded:

The threat of sanctions is a powerful tool; but, perhaps because the threat is powerful, the imposition is a rare event. Since 1990, only 2 areas have had highway sanctions imposed.

James E. McCarthy, Clean Air Issues for the 106th Congress, Congressional Research Service Issue Brief (2000). Because EPA has been slow to impose sanctions, Professor David Driesen suggests that it might be preferable to have "a system that rewards states for doing well instead of depending on politically difficult punishment of those states who do badly. The states would not receive highway monies unless, and until, they met CAA obligations. States that met or exceeded the CAA's requirements would win that money. Non-performing states would have to rely on state rather than federal funds." David M. Driesen, Five Lessons from the Clean Air Act Implementation, 14 Pace Envtl. L. Rev. 51, 56 (1996).

6. *Nonattainment air quality planning in Houston.* How well has the SIP process worked in Houston? How good were the models used to evaluate attainment in the version of the SIP reviewed in the *BCCA* decision? Why was EPA permitted to approve the SIP, even though the modeling did not demonstrate attainment? Should nonattainment SIPs be allowed to include "enforceable commitments" to adopt additional control measures not specified at the time the SIP is reviewed? In what sense are those commitments "enforceable" and against whom? What precisely would be the consequences if Houston failed to meet the additional reductions it promised through those commitments on the prescribed timeline? The Fifth Circuit noted in *BCCA* that the enforceable commitments in the Houston SIP accounted for only 6% of the necessary emission reductions. Is there a quantitative limit to the extent to which states can rely on such unspecified commitments? How should EPA evaluate those commitments when, as in the Houston case, they depend on developing technologies which require further scientific study? Is Union Electric Co. v. EPA, 427 U.S. 246 (1976), excerpted in the previous section, relevant to this question?

What is the role of non-regulatory economic incentives and other voluntary measures in the Houston SIP? To what extent does the CAA allow states to rely on voluntary measures? How should EPA evaluate the projected emission reductions from such programs? Note in this regard that even the effectiveness of regulatory measures is difficult to estimate, because it depends on the extent and effectiveness of enforcement measures. Is it reasonable for EPA to assume that rules will only be 80% effective unless the state demonstrates otherwise? How convincingly, according to Professor McGarity, did Texas make that demonstration?

In 2004, EPA issued a guidance document titled "Incorporating Emerging and Voluntary Measures in a State Implementation Plan," available at http://www.epa.gov/ttncaaa1/t1/memoranda/evm_ievm_g.pdf. EPA explained that, "[i]n light of the increasing incremental cost associated with stationary source emission reductions and the difficulty of identifying additional stationary sources of emission reduction," innovative emission reduction approaches should be encouraged. It endorsed the use of both voluntary measures and new measures whose effectiveness could not yet be empirically verified. It established a presumptive limit of six percent of the necessary emission reductions on the total of all such measures. The limit can be exceeded if the state provides "a clear and convincing justification" for a higher limit.

7. *Update on Houston's ozone problem.* Although the number of ozone exceedances in Houston has steadily decreased, in 2007 it missed the deadline for attaining the 1–hour, 0.12 ppm, ozone NAAQS. At the same time, EPA was transitioning to its 1997 standard, 0.08 ppm on an 8–hour averaging basis. Houston was initially classified as "moderate" for this standard, and directed to meet it by 2010. In June 2007, however, Texas Governor Rick Perry sent a letter to EPA acknowledging that Houston would not meet that deadline. Perry requested reclassification to "severe" (the worst non-attainment category), which would bring an extension of the compliance deadline to 2019. EPA granted the request. 73 Fed. Reg. 56983 (Oct. 1, 2008).

Based on what you know of the problem, whose fault is it that Houston remains out of compliance with the ozone NAAQS?

SECTION 3.   AUTOMOBILE EMISSIONS AND TECHNOLOGY FORCING

Automobiles are responsible for a remarkably high percentage of criteria pollutant emissions, as much as half or more of the total carbon monoxide, VOC, and NO_x emissions in many polluted urban areas. The strategy for addressing automobile emissions under the Clean Air Act has been very different from that applied to stationary sources. Because automobiles are a consumer product, regulation has focused on tailpipe emissions at the time they roll off the assembly line. Because automobiles are marketed nationally and frequently cross state lines, tailpipe emission standards have been almost entirely federal. California has been allowed to maintain its own, more aggressive, emission limits because its program predated the national one. With continual prodding from California's standards, federal tailpipe emission regulation is the most aggressive example in American environmental law of an explicitly technology-forcing regulatory strategy, and an impressively successful one.

Nonetheless, automobile pollution remains a serious problem, contributing to nonattainment across the country. Automobile pollution is a function not just of tailpipe emissions per mile traveled but also of the aggregate number of miles traveled. While emissions have been aggressively regulated, vehicle miles traveled have continued to climb, with little federal or state response.

A.   THE HISTORY OF FEDERAL CONTROLS

America has had a love affair with the automobile since it was first introduced. High economic prosperity throughout the 20th century accounts in part for the high levels of automobile ownership in the United States, but that is not the whole story. Americans have long chosen to spend their discretionary dollars on cars rather than other goods or services. For example, "from the 1920s until about 1950, a higher percentage of American households owned an automobile than had telephones," even though the costs of automobile ownership far exceeded those of telephone service. Rudi Volti, A Century of Automobility, 37 Technology and Culture 663, 674 (1996). Cars provide not only mobility and freedom but privacy and a sense of personal control. By 2006, more than 90% of American households owned at least one vehicle; 20% had three or more. The 2000 census revealed that more than three-quarters of Americans commute to work by driving alone; less than 5% use any form of public transportation.

By the mid–1950s, research on the smog choking Los Angeles had produced agreement that automobiles were a major source of smog precursors. The problem was quickly framed as a technological one: insufficient pollution controls rather than too many cars or too much driving. George A. Gonzalez, Urban Growth and the Politics of Air Pollution: The Establishment of California's Automobile Emission Standards, 35 Polity 213, 227 (2002). As it had been for air quality, the initial federal response was to provide funding for research. The federal government first tried to address automobile pollution by providing funding to help automobile manufacturers voluntarily develop cleaner cars. California, plagued by terrible smog in Los Angeles but already addicted to the automobile, moved first to regulate emissions. In 1959, California passed a law calling on the state's Director of Public Health to set standards for maximum allowable emissions from motor vehicles. The standards were not to take regulatory effect, however, until the newly created Motor Vehicle Pollution Control Board certified two or more pollution control devices capable of achieving them. The requirement for two or more devices was adopted not simply to prevent monopolies but to encourage research and the development of a range of pollution control technologies. Harold W. Kennedy and Martin E. Weekes, Control of Automobile Emissions: California Experience and the Federal Legislation, 33 Law & Contemp. Probs. 297, 300 (1968). The law was subsequently amended to drop the "two device" requirement, because of concerns that it might block the introduction of effective pollution control technologies. California imposed the first emission control requirement effective with the 1963 model year, requiring crankcase ventilation to increase the efficiency of combustion. In 1966, California imposed the first tailpipe emission standards for new cars, effective with the 1968 model year.

In 1965 Congress, noting that 10 years of federally-funded research had produced little progress, enacted the Motor Vehicle Air Pollution Control Act, which authorized the Department of Health, Education and Welfare (EPA was not established until 1970) to set emissions standards for new cars, considering both technological feasibility and economic costs. The automobile manufacturers quietly supported the new federal law because California was moving toward more aggressive regulation and they were concerned that other states might follow California's example, leaving them subject to a multitude of disparate state standards. J.R. DeShazo and Jody Freeman, Timing and Form of Federal Regulation: The Case of Climate Change, 155 U. Pa. L. Rev. 1499, 1512 (2007).

The political momentum in favor of regulation continued to build. In 1970, with adoption of the Clean Air Act, Congress moved aggressively to tighten tailpipe emission standards. The CAA mandated a 90% reduction in tailpipe emissions of hydrocarbons and carbon monoxide within five years, and of NO_x within six years. The 90% figure came from a rough back-of-the-envelope calculation of what would be needed to protect human health. Ambient levels of hydrocarbons, CO and NO_x pollutants in Los Angeles were about five times the level thought to be safe. Therefore, the drafters guessed, in order to achieve safe air quality levels automobile emissions should be reduced by 80%. An additional 10% was tagged on to account for growth in vehicle use and the presence of older cars on the road. Frank P. Grad et al., The Automobile and the Regulation of Its Impact on the Environment 33–36 (1974).

The automobile manufacturers were horrified. They insisted in Congressional hearings that they could not possibly meet the deadlines. Congress was in no mood to listen. Proposals were floated to ban the internal combustion engine. The Clean Air Act was quite deliberately intended to be "technology-forcing," providing a strong incentive for the rapid development of more effective pollution control technology. It marked a radical departure from the conventional approach of requiring the use of "feasible" or "available" technology.

The ambitious standards of the 1970 CAA were not met within its stringent timelines. The statute provided EPA with the authority to extend the deadlines by a year, but EPA refused to do so until directed by the federal courts to reconsider. See International Harvester Co. v. Ruckelshaus, 478 F.2d 615 (D.C. Cir. 1973). Congress provided additional extensions. Despite the delays, federal tailpipe emission standards have produced dramatic decreases in automobile pollution. Between 1970 and 2000, NO_x and VOC emissions per mile from new cars were reduced more than 95%. Additional reductions of roughly 90% from those levels were phased in for model years 2004–2009.

Natural Resources Defense Council v. U. S. EPA

District of Columbia Circuit, 1981.
655 F.2d 318.

■ MIKVA, CIRCUIT JUDGE:

* * *

I. THE REGULATORY FRAMEWORK

The EPA is authorized by the Clean Air Act (Act) to regulate emissions of harmful pollutants from motor vehicles. * * * Section 202(a)(1) of the Act confers on the EPA Administrator the general power to prescribe by regulation "standards applicable to the emission of any air pollutant from any class or classes of new motor vehicles or new motor vehicle engines, which in his judgment cause, or contribute to, air pollution which may reasonably be anticipated to endanger public health or welfare." These provisions are supplemented and qualified by various specific provisions relating to particular classes of vehicles or pollutants.

* * *

The emission standards set by the EPA under its general regulatory power * * * are "technology-based;" the levels chosen must be premised on a finding of technological feasibility. Section 202(a)(2) of the Act provides that standards promulgated under section 202(a)(1) shall not take effect until "after such period as the Administrator finds necessary to permit the development and application of the requisite technology."

* * *

II. THE PARTICULATE STANDARDS

The EPA announced its intention to promulgate standards for particulate emissions from light-duty diesels on February 1, 1979. The proposed standards would have limited diesel particulates to 0.60 grams per vehicle mile (gpm) in model year 1981, and to 0.20 gpm in model year 1983. The agency concluded that a single standard, governing all light-duty vehicles, was the preferable regulatory strategy, although 1979 certification data indicated that diesel particulate performance among those vehicles ranged from the 0.23 gpm achieved by the Volkswagen Rabbit to the 0.84 gpm emitted by the Oldsmobile 350. Furthermore, these restrictions would have applied equally to light-duty vehicles and light-duty trucks.

After analyzing the comments elicited by its notice of proposed rule-making, the EPA promulgated as final standards a modification of the rules originally announced. The limit of 0.60 gpm was retained, but its effective date was postponed to model year 1982, because the rulemaking process had absorbed so much time that testing and certification of 1981 models was no longer feasible. The agency concluded that the technology necessary to make the 0.20 gpm standard feasible would probably not be developed in time for implementation in 1983 model vehicles; 1984 was a more likely goal, but the effective date was postponed to model year 1985 to give sufficient margin for error. Finally, the EPA believed that light-duty trucks would not be able to perform as well as light-duty vehicles, and the 1985 standard for light-duty trucks was therefore adjusted to 0.26 gpm.

* * *

B. *Technological Feasibility*

The EPA's choice of the 0.20 gpm standard for light-duty diesels in 1985 was the result of adjusting current diesel particulate emission data by the percentage of reduction expected from certain technological improvements, most notably the trap-oxidizer. The manufacturers' attack on the standard focuses on the EPA's prediction concerning the probable pace of development of trap-oxidizer technology. Before examining the details of the agency's reasoning and the industry challenges, however, we find it useful to discuss the legal standard that governs our inquiry.

1. The Standard of Review

The standard of review in this case is the traditional one for judicial scrutiny of agency rulemaking: we are to set aside any action found to be "arbitrary, capricious, an abuse of discretion, or otherwise not in accordance with law." § 307(d)(9)(A). * * *

In the present case, GM attacks the EPA's estimation of the period of time "necessary to permit the development and application of the requisite technology" to achieve compliance with the 1985 particulate standards, see Act s 202(a)(2). The agency has determined that the technology will be available in time, and now seeks to defend its conclusion as a product of reasoned decisionmaking. Such predictions inherently involve a greater degree of uncertainty than estimations of the effectiveness of current technology. If we judge the EPA's action by the standard of certainty appropriate to current technology, the agency will be unable to set pollutant levels until the necessary technology is already available.

* * *

This court has upheld the agency's power to make such projections, while recognizing that it is "subject to the restraints of reasonableness, and does not open the door to crystal ball inquiry." International Harvester Co. v. Ruckelshaus, 478 F.2d 615, 629 (D.C. Cir. 1973). The Clean Air Act requires the EPA to look to the future in setting standards, but the agency must also provide a reasoned explanation of its basis for believing that its projection is reliable. This includes a defense of its methodology for arriving at numerical estimates.

The thoroughness and persuasiveness of the explanation we can expect from the agency will, of course, vary with the nature of the prediction undertaken. "Where existing methodology or research in a new area of regulation is deficient, the agency necessarily enjoys broad discretion to attempt to formulate a solution to the best of its ability on the basis of available information." Industrial Union Dep't v. Hodgson, 499 F.2d 467, 474 n.18 (D.C. Cir. 1974). At one extreme, this court has recognized that the EPA's decision to regulate potentially harmful pollutants involves a large element of policy choice that cannot be demonstrably "correct," although it must have a genuine scientific basis. * * * Ethyl Corp. v. EPA, 541 F.2d 1, 28 (D.C. Cir. 1976). We have also acknowledged the necessarily speculative nature of agency predictions in the social sciences, including judgments of the competitive impact of regulatory decisions. At the other extreme, this court's inquiry into agency methodology in the physical sciences has been far more exacting "where the facts pertinent to (a) standard's feasibility are available and easily discoverable by conventional technical means." National Lime Ass'n v. EPA, 627 F.2d 416, 454 (D.C. Cir. 1980).

The present case lies between those two extremes. It does not involve questions at the frontier of physiological knowledge, but it does require a determination by the EPA of the likely sequence of further technological development. There is no known scientific technique for calculating when an as yet unsolved design problem will be ironed out. Thus, unlike the short-term feasibility assessments scrutinized in National Lime Association, the present determination presents the court with "the question how much deference is owed a judgment predicated on limited evidence when additional evidence cannot be adduced or adduced in the near future," id. at 454.

The time element in the EPA's prediction affects our reviewing task in three distinct ways. First, it introduces uncertainties in the agency's judgment that render that judgment vulnerable to attack. At the same time, however, the time element gives the EPA greater scope for confidence that theoretical solutions will be translated successfully into mechanical realizations, for "the question of availability is partially dependent on lead time, the time in which the technology will have to be available." Portland Cement Ass'n v. Ruckelshaus, 486 F.2d 375, 391 (D.C. Cir. 1973). Finally, the presence of substantial lead time for development before manufacturers will have to commit themselves to mass production of a chosen prototype gives the agency greater leeway to modify its standards if the actual future course of technology diverges from expectation.

* * *

Given this time frame, we feel that there is substantial room for deference to the EPA's expertise in projecting the likely course of development. The essential question in this case is the pace of that development, and absent a revolution in the study of industry, defense of such a projection can never possess the inescapable logic of a mathematical deduction. We think that the EPA will have demonstrated the reasonableness of its basis for prediction if it answers any theoretical objections to the trap-oxidizer method, identifies the major steps necessary in refinement of the device, and offers plausible reasons for believing that each of those steps can be completed in the time available. If the agency can make this showing, then we cannot say that its determination was the result of crystal ball inquiry, or that it neglected its duty of reasoned decisionmaking.

2. The Time "Necessary to Permit the Development and Application of the Requisite Technology"

* * * The EPA bases its prediction that the 1985 standard will be achieved on two factors: modifications decreasing the particulate output of diesel engines, and development of "aftertreatment" technology, that is, means by which the vehicle will remove particulate matter from its own exhaust. The larger proportion of the expected reduction in particulate emissions depends on aftertreatment, and it is the availability of that technology that provokes the major controversy in this case.

The EPA has identified a number of strategies for extracting particulates from diesel exhaust, but the 1985 standard was set in reliance on one preferred method and must stand or fall with the agency's prediction that that method will be available in time. This favored device is the trap-oxidizer, a mechanism that filters out particulates and then periodically incinerates its catch in order to maintain the trapping capacity of the filter.

* * *

The EPA has predicted that trap-oxidizers will be available for use in model year 1985 vehicles. As the agency has repeatedly observed, the trap-oxidizer is familiar and unobjectionable as a concept. It is not only theoretically sound, experimental data demonstrate that periodic incineration can maintain efficiency for over 10,000 miles. But to date, no filter material has been found that can withstand periodic incineration of the accumulated particulates throughout the 50,000–mile useful life of the vehicle while maintaining a high level of trapping efficiency. The agency noted that

> the best durability of a trap reported to EPA was a metal mesh trap on an Opel vehicle, run on a modified AMA driving schedule with no hard accelerations, hills, or speeds above 45 mph. The trap survived 12,800 miles and at that time had a collection efficiency similar to its zero-mile efficiency of 55 percent.

Understandably, the EPA has concluded that further research is needed before devices with the appropriate characteristics will be available for use:

> Clearly, more basic research still needs to be done in the areas of regeneration initiation and control, and trap durability. Enough progress has been achieved to convince EPA that a successful trap-oxidizer can be developed, but as of this time, no design has proven to have the required collection efficiency over the desired length of time.

Nevertheless, the agency concludes that it is merely a question of time before the trap-oxidizer is perfected. "The improvements that are necessary are engineering problems, and are more a function of the resources allocated to the problem than any scientific or technical breakthrough." 45 Fed. Reg. 14,496, 14,498 (1980). Based on the routine nature of most of the remaining problems, the rapid pace of progress in the field since 1978, and the industry's own forecasts of 1985 as a potential completion date, the agency has determined that the lead time remaining is sufficient for application of the requisite technology.

GM dismisses the agency's conclusion as baseless speculation and charges the EPA with naive optimism about the solution of myriad uncertainties, ranging from the development of a durable filter material to the proper location of the trap on the vehicle itself. GM regards the gaps in present knowledge as vitiating the entire standard-setting endeavor:

> Until further experimental knowledge on these major development needs is obtained, it is totally impossible to specify when a successful system will be developed for passenger cars and light-duty trucks. Thus, any particulate standard which contemplates use of a regenera-

tive trap-oxidizer must be judged premature and not technologically feasible.

Thus, GM believes that no standard can be promulgated, regardless of its effective date, on the current record.

Before analyzing GM's technical objections, we must reiterate the standard of review that governs this case. The EPA is not obliged to provide detailed solutions to every engineering problem posed in the perfection of the trap-oxidizer. In the absence of theoretical objections to the technology, the agency need only identify the major steps necessary for development of the device, and give plausible reasons for its belief that the industry will be able to solve those problems in the time remaining. The EPA is not required to rebut all speculation that unspecified factors may hinder "real world" emission control.

* * *

a.   Development of a Durable Filter

The most vigorously controverted issue in this case concerns durability, which the EPA has recognized as the key remaining problem. * * * Both parties focus on the GM Opel test, in which a metal mesh trap survived over 12,000 miles; the EPA views this test as a stirring demonstration of how far research had progressed in the brief springtime of trap-oxidizer research, while GM sees the 12,000–mile mark as insubstantial compared to the 50,000– to 100,000–mile goal.

The EPA has predicted that the necessary work can be accomplished in time for 1985 model year production. The agency points to the wide variety of materials that have demonstrated appropriate initial efficiencies; several of these are hybrids, suggesting that new combinations of present candidates, rather than hitherto untested substances, may provide the answer. The EPA noted the rapid pace of achievement since attention turned to trap-oxidizers:

> Considerable progress has occurred in the last 1 1/2 years. Initial aftertreatment research concentrated on the use of simple traps and gasoline engine catalytic converters, with basic problems of efficiency and backpressure. In the last 1 1/2 years we have seen marked improvements in efficiency and backpressure, and more importantly, a general consensus that the trap-oxidizer can periodically (and possibly even continually) incinerate the particulate matter. Methods for regeneration initiation and control have been investigated and repetitive incineration has been demonstrated for several trap-oxidizers.

45 Fed. Reg. 14,496, 14,498 (1980). The small number of successful tests reflected the recent focus on trap-oxidizers, not a persistent record of failure ... Finally, the manufacturers themselves had projected the possibility of introducing trap-oxidizers in 1985 models. The agency fully recognized that no durable, efficient filter material was presently available, but concluded that, based on current progress and past achievements, there

were sufficient grounds for believing that one would be developed in time for the 1985 standard.

We conclude that these are plausible reasons for a determination that the industry is capable of solving the durability problem in the allotted time. The EPA could reasonably refuse to be discouraged by the limited initial success, as the project is relatively young. The rapidity of recent progress is a factor that the agency may consider in making a prediction of future capabilities. And the industry's own predictions, while not determinative, support the view that success in this kind of research can realistically be expected within the proposed time frame. We conclude that the EPA's durability prediction, though uncertain, is no more uncertain than such estimates inherently must be, and that the EPA has met the requirement of "reasoned decisionmaking."

* * *

C. NRDC's Objections to the Particulate Standards

The NRDC, in contrast to GM, thinks that the EPA's standards for diesel particulates are too lax. * * *

The EPA defends its decision to promulgate a single particulate standard applicable to all light-duty diesel vehicles, rather than a number of standards applicable to various classes of diesels. One reason given is the absence of any apparent parameter on which to base such a classification. Another concern is the paradoxical result that graduated standards, by imposing stricter and more costly requirements on low-polluting vehicles, would skew competition in favor of the more loosely regulated, highly polluting models. Finally, Congress itself has taught this method by example, providing unitary emission standards for all passenger vehicles in both the 1970 and 1977 amendments. We conclude that the adoption of a single particulate standard for light-duty diesel vehicles was within the EPA's regulatory discretion.

Even if a single standard is proper, the NRDC asserts, it ought not to be one that every diesel can meet. The NRDC cites a favorable passage in *International Harvester*, in which this court agreed with the Administrator that the Act's technological feasibility provisions required only that the standards permit basic auto demand to be met, "even though this might occasion fewer models and a more limited choice of engine types." 478 F.2d at 640. In this case, however, the EPA viewed the legislative history of the 1977 amendments as justifying a more tolerant attitude toward diesel development in the near future. The availability of waivers of the 1.0 gpm oxides of nitrogen standard for "any class or category" of diesel vehicles that requires them, Act § 202(b)(6)(B), certainly suggests an interest in exploring the full range of potential benefits of diesel technology. We do not hold that the statute mandates such an approach, but it was well within the EPA's regulatory discretion to impose "standards which provide significant particulate reductions, but which do not force any diesel models out of production."

* * *

■ Robb, Circuit Judge, * * * dissenting in part:

* * * I must dissent * * * from that part of the opinion in which the court sustains the particulate standards for 1985. In my view the record does not support the EPA's prediction that the necessary technology will be available in time to meet the 1985 standard. My doubts focus in particular on the inability of the auto manufacturers to develop a filtering material for trap-oxidizers that possesses the durability needed to withstand periodic incineration of collected particulates for the useful life of the vehicle.

* * *

The record demonstrates that General Motors (GM) alone, which began its particulate control research program in 1974, has tested many different trap materials provided by at least 16 different manufacturers. Of these materials, 22 are characterized by GM as "the best materials" available, based on tests conducted with an Opel 2.1 liter diesel engine and an Oldsmobile 5.7 liter diesel engine. Yet the durability of even the best of these materials, the metal mesh, is far below what will be needed to meet the standard. * * *

After acknowledging the shortcomings of the Opel test, the EPA summarized the status of trap-oxidizer research as follows:

> Clearly, more basic research still needs to be done in the areas of regeneration initiation and control, and trap durability. Enough progress has been achieved to convince EPA that a successful trap-oxidizer can be developed, but as of this time, no design has proven to have the required collection efficiency over the desired length of time. With the research that has been, and is, going on with regards to trap-oxidizer development, and a determined broad-based effort by the manufacturers to comply with the final standards, EPA's technical staff has concluded that it is very likely that a successful trap-oxidizer design can be optimized within the next 1 1/2 to 2 years.

In my opinion, these exhortations to the manufacturers and the EPA's vaguely articulated faith that a "design can be optimized" soon do not amount to "plausible reasons for believing that each of (the necessary) steps can be completed in the time available," within the meaning of the majority's standard. Pious hope and speculation cannot take the place of evidence.

NOTES AND QUESTIONS

1. *The need for and politics of technology forcing.* Why hadn't manufacturers produced cleaner cars prior to 1970? Reduced pollution was surely a desirable performance characteristic at the time from society's point of view. Why then did the market not provide it? Are you surprised that Congress managed to enact such stringent technology-forcing provisions? Do you think the manufacturers believed those provisions would be literally enforced? Were they sufficiently anxious to pre-empt state regulation that they were willing to accept apparently very stringent federal regulation?

Was the political tenor of those times simply so strongly pro-environment that the manufacturers had no choice? What assumptions underlie the aggressive technology-forcing strategy adopted in the 1970 CAA? Why has no other environmental law adopted such an aggressive technology-forcing approach? Is there something unique about the automobile industry that made it especially amenable to this approach, or was it just a matter of the right political timing?

2. *Innovation versus technology diffusion.* The term "technology forcing" is not self-explanatory. It is commonly used to mean two quite different things. The first is mandating technological advancement or innovation. This is true technology forcing. A California court has described it as akin to "Captain Picard's line to his immediate subordinate in the second Star Trek series, 'Make it so, Number One!'" National Paint & Coatings Ass'n v. South Coast Air Quality Mgmt. Dist., 100 Cal.Rptr.3d 35 (App. 2009), rcv. granted, 104 Cal.Rptr.3d 131, 223 P.3d 2 (2010). Innovation mandates are rare in environmental law, in part because of the risk of shutting down economically important industries if it proves impossible to "make it so" despite best efforts. More commonly, the law mandates use of technology which is, rather than will be, available or achievable. "Best available" technology requirements are usually interpreted to mean that the technical means of compliance must demonstrably exist, although they need not yet have been adopted by all or even a majority of the market players, or even by the precise industry being regulated. In effect, best available technology mandates require that existing state of the art technology be adopted by more players or adapted to new uses, rather than that the art be raised to a new state.

3. *Technology forcing and cost distribution.* When society concludes that technology must be improved to meet societal goals, who should bear the costs of improvement? Should Congress provide funding for research and development efforts, through grants or tax credits? Should the imposition of regulatory standards be delayed until substitute technologies have been demonstrated to be effective? Is government or industry likely to have better access to information about potential technological improvement? Will industry have sufficient incentive to develop and implement new technologies without a heavy regulatory hammer?

4. *Choosing technology forcing standards.* Congress chose the level of emissions reduction called for in the 1970 Clean Air Act through a simplistic calculation, disregarding the industry's protests that it could not possibly meet the prescribed standards. In fact, although they did not meet Congress' ambitious initial timetable, automobile tailpipe emissions fell far more rapidly than the industry had suggested was possible. What might account for the difference between the industry's claims of what it could do and its actual performance? In general, industry will have better access than regulators do to information about the potential for improved technological performance. Given their lack of knowledge, and assuming they do not want to bankrupt or shut down key industrial segments, how should regulators choose technology-forcing targets?

5. *Delays.* When the auto industry did not meet the statutory deadlines, the courts and then Congress provided extensions. Was it ever likely that EPA or Congress would move to shut down the automobile industry? If not, why did the industry put any effort into reducing emissions? Note that the CAA provided for sanctions short of stopping automobile assembly lines. Penalties could be imposed for each violation, that is each car that did not meet the standards. In addition, manufacturers might have worried that a competitor would meet the standards (or come close), demonstrating that it could be done, or that openly defying a government order to reduce unhealthful emissions would be bad public relations. How should regulators respond when industry seeks delay of a technology-forcing requirement?

6. *The role of the courts.* The 1970 Clean Air Act authorized EPA to suspend the mandated emission reductions for one year if the industry could show that, despite it having made all good faith efforts to comply, the needed technology would not be available in time, and suspension would be in the public interest. Several manufacturers filed petitions for suspension in 1972, but EPA rejected them, finding that the manufacturers had not met their burden of showing that the necessary technology was unavailable. The D.C. Circuit remanded that decision to EPA for further consideration of the potential costs of denying the suspension, should EPA's technological forecast prove incorrect. The opinion noted that Congress was unlikely to put up with any decision that would actually shut down the automobile industry.

> If in 1974, when model year 1975 cars start to come off the production line, the automobiles of Ford, General Motors and Chrysler cannot meet the 1975 standards and do not qualify for certification, the Administrator of EPA has the theoretical authority, under the Clean Air Act, to shut down the auto industry, as was clearly recognized in Congressional debate. We cannot put blinders on the facts before us so as to omit awareness of the reality that this authority would undoubtedly never be exercised, in light of the fact that approximately 1 out of every 7 jobs in this country is dependent on the production of the automobile. Senator Muskie, the principal sponsor of the bill, stated quite clearly in the debate on the Act that he envisioned the Congress acting if an auto industry shutdown were in sight.

International Harvester Co. v. Ruckelshaus, 478 F.2d 615, 636 (D.C. Cir. 1973). Is it legitimate for courts to refuse to fully enforce legislation because they believe Congress does not really mean what it said? Or should courts put Congress to the test? After all, Congress can always suspend, repeal, or waive onerous regulatory requirements if it finds that the public interest so requires.

When reviewing a regulatory decision that technology will be available within the required time, as in *NRDC v. EPA*, how much deference should the court give to the agency's predictions and extrapolations from current technology? Should reviewing courts require more evidence that the technology in question is ready or nearly ready for commercial use if the consequences of mistakenly tough regulation are especially dire (as in

International Harvester v. Ruckelshaus) or the regulatory deadline is especially near? Did EPA in that case provide enough evidence to satisfy you that the emission reductions it mandated by 1985 were possible?

7. *The California ZEV experience.* In 1990, the California Air Resources Board imposed Zero Emission Vehicle (ZEV) quotas. The original quotas required that 2% of all vehicles offered for sale in the state be ZEVs (electric or hydrogen fuel cell cars that do not emit anything other than water vapor) by 1998, 5% by 2001, and 10% by 2003. Faced with limited options and sluggish sales of battery-powered cars, in 1996 the Board lifted the 1998 quota, and in 1998 it lifted the 2001 quota. In 2001, the board reaffirmed the 10% quota for 2003, and added a 16% quota for 2018. It significantly eased compliance with these quotas, however, by offering partial ZEV credits for very clean vehicles such as very low emission gas vehicles and gas-electric hybrids. Currently, the Board's regulations require only a small percentage of true ZEVs in a manufacturer's fleet, allowing the bulk of the quota to be met with gas/electric hybrids very low emission conventional vehicles. Alternatively, manufacturers can choose to satisfy the ZEV requirements by producing a relatively small number of fuel cell vehicles. For a description of California's program since its inception, see California Environmental Protection Agency, Air Resources Board, Status Report on the California Air Resources Board's Zero Emission Vehicle Program (April 20, 2007), http://www.arb.ca.gov/msprog/zevprog/zevreview/zev_review_staffreport.pdf.

Has the California automobile emission regulation experiment been a success? California's standards, which have always been tighter than the national standards, have helped ratchet those national standards down over time by proving that the manufacturers could do better. California's large share of the national market undoubtedly has played a role in the national effectiveness of its emission standards. The ZEV standards catalyzed the production of commercially successful gas-electric hybrids and very low emission gas vehicles; all-electric cars are just beginning to hit the commercial market. California is now betting that its program can help commercialize fuel cell vehicles over the next decade or two. How should California decide what technologies to emphasize in the future? Or should it leave those choices, to the extent possible, to manufacturers?

8. *No free lunch: the environmental impacts of zero-emission vehicles.* Zero-emission vehicles are by no means environmentally perfect. Current ZEV technologies do not eliminate emissions associated with automobile use. Instead, they shift those emissions in time and space. All-electric vehicles require electricity to charge their batteries; in most locations that electricity still comes from fossil-fuel burning power plants which emit criteria pollutants. The batteries used in electric vehicles contain heavy metals; production and recycling of those batteries produces substantial emissions of toxic substances. Fuel cell vehicles rely on hydrogen fuel, which is currently produced primarily from fossil fuels in a relatively inefficient process.

9. *Incentives and technology development.* Would you expect economic incentives to be more or less effective than regulations in forcing technology development? Could escalating taxes on automobile purchase or registration pegged to tailpipe emissions have driven the development of pollution control technology as rapidly as regulation did? Would such a tax system be politically acceptable? What advantages and disadvantages would a tax system have, compared to regulation?

10. *Technology-forcing versus behavior-forcing.* While tailpipe emissions of criteria pollutants per mile have dramatically decreased over the past thirty years, those gains are partially offset by the continued increase in vehicle miles traveled. Californians, for example, drove a total of 117 billion miles in 1970. That number increased to 306 billion miles in 2000, and 324 billion miles in 2009, according to Federal Highway Administration statistics (available at http://www.fhwa.dot.gov/policyinformation/statistics.cfm). Automobile emissions remain a very significant source of criteria pollutants. In order for the most polluted areas to attain the NAAQS, they will need to reduce aggregate hydrocarbon and NO_x emissions from all sources by 60–80% from 1990 levels. A substantial amount of that reduction will have to come from automobile emissions.

While the federal government (and California) control emission standards, control of vehicle miles traveled rests with the states in their SIPS. States have considered or adopted a wide variety of transportation controls in SIPs, including tolls, gas or parking taxes, limits on parking or auto use, incentives for carpooling or use of mass transit, high occupancy vehicle lanes, bicycle lanes, pedestrian or vehicle free zones, gas rationing, mass transit subsidies, and limits on driving licenses or vehicle ownership. The Clean Air Act requires EPA to make available detailed information to environmental and transportation agencies concerning at least 19 transportation control measures which can reduce pollution. CAA § 108(f). The decision to take any of these measures remains entirely voluntary, except in the worst non-attainment areas, which are required to adopt and implement "transportation control measures" (TCMs) designed to lessen vehicle emissions. Such TCMs could include programs to reduce work-related trips, to encourage the greater use of mass transit or carpooling. CAA § 182(d)(1).

Why has Congress been so tentative in addressing the driving habits of Americans, while aggressively attacking emissions per mile? Should that change? Can behavior be "forced" by regulation in the way that technology can? If you were made "transportation czar" of a state or the United States, and sincerely wanted to reduce vehicle miles traveled, what steps would you take? What authority would you need?

B.   THE CURRENT STATUTORY AND REGULATORY SCHEME

Since 1970, tailpipe emission controls have become progressively more stringent and more detailed. The general standard is found at CAA § 202(a), which directs the Administrator of EPA to prescribe emission limits from new motor vehicles for any pollutant which may reasonably be anticipated to endanger public health or welfare.

In the 1990 Clean Air Amendments, Congress prescribed detailed gram-per-mile emission standards for hydrocarbons, carbon monoxide, NO_x, and particulate matter from passenger cars and light trucks effective with the 1994 model year. § 202(g). Those represent minimum standards. EPA is authorized to issue more stringent standards to achieve "the greatest degree of emission reduction achievable through the application of technology which the Administrator determines will be available for the model year to which such standards apply, giving appropriate consideration to cost, energy, and safety factors associated with the application of such technology."

Under this authority, EPA issued regulations in 2000 which established, effective with the 2004 model year, a single set of tailpipe emission standards applicable to all passenger cars, vans, light trucks and sport utility vehicles. These "Tier 2" regulations are based on a combination of tailpipe technologies and a mandate for production of lower-sulfur gasoline. EPA, Control of Air Pollution from New Motor Vehicles: Tier 2 Motor Vehicle Emissions Standards and Gasoline Sulfur Control Requirements, 65 Fed. Reg. 6698 (Feb. 10, 2000). The 1990 Clean Air Act Amendments also required for the first time that EPA regulate emissions of hazardous air pollutants from motor vehicles to achieve "the greatest degree of emission reduction achievable through the application of technology which will be available, taking into consideration * * * the availability and costs of the technology * * * and lead time." § 202(l)(2).

Manufacturers must demonstrate that their new vehicles meet the applicable emission standards at the time they roll off the assembly line. They do so by delivering a prototype of the model to EPA for emission testing. Under the 1990 amendments, manufacturers must also show at the time the model is offered for sale that it will continue to meet the applicable emission requirements for its useful life, currently defined as 120,000 miles for passenger cars and light trucks. EPA's first attempt at prescribing these "durability" standards was remanded by the D.C. Circuit because it left too much discretion about testing methods in the hands of manufacturers. Ethyl Corp. v. EPA, 306 F.3d 1144 (D.C. Cir. 2002). In response to that decision, EPA issued new regulations prescribing test procedures. Manufacturers can choose between driving a test vehicle on a track or dynamometer for 120,000 miles, or artificially aging key emission components before testing emissions. EPA, Emission Durability Procedures for New Light–Duty Vehicles, Light–Duty Trucks and Heavy–Duty Vehicles, 71 Fed. Reg. 2809 (Jan. 17, 2006).

In the past, actual observed "in use" performance has deviated significantly from the new car standards. In part, that is because the tests EPA uses for emissions certification have tended to underestimate actual on-road emissions. In addition, cars may not wear as well in consumer use as they do under controlled test conditions. Finally, some people deliberately tamper with or disable emission controls in order to enhance performance.

Regular inspection and maintenance (I/M) is required in non-attainment areas, see CAA § 182, in order to ensure that aging cars continue to meet required standards and discourage consumers from tampering with the emission systems.

Under the Clean Air Act, EPA also regulates emissions from a variety of other mobile sources, including airplanes, see CAA §§ 231–234, locomotives, see CAA § 213(a)(5), and any other "nonroad vehicles" whose emissions cause or contribute to air pollution which may reasonably be anticipated to endanger public health or welfare, CAA § 213(a)(1), such as boats, tractors, personal watercraft, all-terrain vehicles, and snowmobiles.

C.   THE ROLE OF THE STATES

Congress has allowed the states only a limited role in mobile source emission regulation. The CAA establishes minimum vehicle emission standards effective throughout the nation. It generally preempts state regulation, but allows California, which was in the business of regulating automobile emissions before the federal government was, to apply for a waiver of preemption. Other states may not impose their own regulations on motor vehicle or nonroad engine emissions. Nonattainment states may, however, choose to opt in to California's standards, CAA § 177, and some fourteen states have done so. No state, including California, may regulate emissions from locomotives or airplanes; that authority is reserved to the federal government. CAA §§ 209(e)(1), § 233.

Excerpts From the Clean Air Act

42 U.S.C. §§ 7401–7671q.

Section 202.   Emission standards for new motor vehicles * * *.

(a) Except as otherwise provided in subsection (b) of this section—

(1) The Administrator shall by regulation prescribe (and from time to time revise) in accordance with the provisions of this section, standards applicable to the emission of any air pollutant from any class or classes of new motor vehicles or new motor vehicle engines, which in his judgment cause, or contribute to, air pollution which may reasonably be anticipated to endanger public health or welfare. Such standards shall be applicable to such vehicles and engines for their useful life * * *.

(2) Any regulation prescribed under paragraph (1) of this subsection (and any revision thereof) shall take effect after such period as the Administrator finds necessary to permit the development and application of the requisite technology, giving appropriate consideration to the cost of compliance within such period.

Section 209.   State standards.

(a) No State or any political subdivision thereof shall adopt or attempt to enforce any standard relating to the control of emissions from new motor vehicles or new motor vehicle engines subject to this part. No State shall require certification, inspection, or any other approval relating to the control of emissions from any new motor vehicle or new motor vehicle engine as condition precedent to the initial retail sale, titling (if any), or registration of such motor vehicle, motor vehicle engine, or equipment.

(b)(1) The Administrator shall, after notice and opportunity for public hearing, waive application of this section to any State which has adopted standards (other than crankcase emission standards) for the control of emissions from new motor vehicles or new motor vehicle engines prior to March 30, 1966, if the State determines that the State standards will be, in the aggregate, at least as protective of public health and welfare as applicable Federal standards. No such waiver shall be granted if the Administrator finds that—

(A) the determination of the State is arbitrary and capricious,

(B) such State does not need such State standards to meet compelling and extraordinary conditions, or

(C) such State standards and accompanying enforcement procedures are not consistent with section [202].

(2) If each State standard is at least as stringent as the comparable applicable Federal standard, such State standard shall be deemed to be at least as protective of health and welfare as such Federal standards for purposes of paragraph (1).

* * *

Massachusetts v. Environmental Protection Agency

United States Supreme Court, 2007.
549 U.S. 497.

■ JUSTICE STEVENS delivered the opinion of the Court.

* * *

Section 202(a)(1) of the Clean Air Act, 42 U.S.C. § 7521(a)(1), provides:

"The [EPA] Administrator shall by regulation prescribe (and from time to time revise) in accordance with the provisions of this section, standards applicable to the emission of any air pollutant from any class or classes of new motor vehicles or new motor vehicle engines, which in his judgment cause, or contribute to, air pollution which may reasonably be anticipated to endanger public health or welfare...."

The Act defines "air pollutant" to include "any air pollution agent or combination of such agents, including any physical, chemical, biological, radioactive ... substance or matter which is emitted into or otherwise enters the ambient air." § 7602(g). "Welfare" is also defined broadly:

among other things, it includes "effects on ... weather ... and climate."
§ 7602(h).

* * *

II

On October 20, 1999, a group of 19 private organizations filed a rulemaking petition asking EPA to regulate "greenhouse gas emissions from new motor vehicles under § 202 of the Clean Air Act." Petitioners maintained that 1998 was the "warmest year on record"; that carbon dioxide, methane, nitrous oxide, and hydrofluorocarbons are "heat trapping greenhouse gases"; that greenhouse gas emissions have significantly accelerated climate change; and that the [U.N. Intergovernmental Panel on Climate Change's] 1995 report warned that "carbon dioxide remains the most important contributor to [man-made] forcing of climate change." The petition further alleged that climate change will have serious adverse effects on human health and the environment. As to EPA's statutory authority, the petition observed that the agency itself had already confirmed that it had the power to regulate carbon dioxide. In 1998, Jonathan Z. Cannon, then EPA's General Counsel, prepared a legal opinion concluding that "CO_2 emissions are within the scope of EPA's authority to regulate," even as he recognized that EPA had so far declined to exercise that authority. Cannon's successor, Gary S. Guzy, reiterated that opinion before a congressional committee just two weeks before the rulemaking petition was filed.

Fifteen months after the petition's submission, EPA requested public comment on "all the issues raised in [the] petition," adding a "particular" request for comments on "any scientific, technical, legal, economic or other aspect of these issues that may be relevant to EPA's consideration of this petition." 66 Fed. Reg. 7486, 7487 (2001). EPA received more than 50,000 comments over the next five months.

Before the close of the comment period, the White House sought "assistance in identifying the areas in the science of climate change where there are the greatest certainties and uncertainties" from the National Research Council, asking for a response "as soon as possible." The result was a 2001 report titled Climate Change: An Analysis of Some Key Questions (NRC Report), which, drawing heavily on the 1995 IPCC report, concluded that "[g]reenhouse gases are accumulating in Earth's atmosphere as a result of human activities, causing surface air temperatures and subsurface ocean temperatures to rise. Temperatures are, in fact, rising."

On September 8, 2003, EPA entered an order denying the rulemaking petition. 68 Fed. Reg. 52922. The agency gave two reasons for its decision: (1) that contrary to the opinions of its former general counsels, the Clean Air Act does not authorize EPA to issue mandatory regulations to address global climate change; and (2) that even if the agency had the authority to set greenhouse gas emission standards, it would be unwise to do so at this time.

In concluding that it lacked statutory authority over greenhouse gases, EPA observed that Congress "was well aware of the global climate change issue when it last comprehensively amended the [Clean Air Act] in 1990," yet it declined to adopt a proposed amendment establishing binding emissions limitations. Congress instead chose to authorize further investigation into climate change. EPA further reasoned that Congress' "specially tailored solutions to global atmospheric issues," 68 Fed. Reg. 52926—in particular, its 1990 enactment of a comprehensive scheme to regulate pollutants that depleted the ozone layer, see 42 U.S.C. §§ 7671–7671q—counseled against reading the general authorization of § 202(a)(1) to confer regulatory authority over greenhouse gases.

EPA stated that it was "urged on in this view" by this Court's decision in *FDA v. Brown & Williamson Tobacco Corp.*, 529 U.S. 120 (2000). In that case, relying on "tobacco['s] unique political history," *id.*, at 159, we invalidated the Food and Drug Administration's reliance on its general authority to regulate drugs as a basis for asserting jurisdiction over an "industry constituting a significant portion of the American economy."

EPA reasoned that climate change had its own "political history": Congress designed the original Clean Air Act to address *local* air pollutants rather than a substance that "is fairly consistent in its concentration throughout the *world's* atmosphere," 68 Fed. Reg. 52927 (emphasis added); declined in 1990 to enact proposed amendments to force EPA to set carbon dioxide emission standards for motor vehicles; and addressed global climate change in other legislation. Because of this political history, and because imposing emission limitations on greenhouse gases would have even greater economic and political repercussions than regulating tobacco, EPA was persuaded that it lacked the power to do so. In essence, EPA concluded that climate change was so important that unless Congress spoke with exacting specificity, it could not have meant the agency to address it.

Having reached that conclusion, EPA believed it followed that greenhouse gases cannot be "air pollutants" within the meaning of the Act. The agency bolstered this conclusion by explaining that if carbon dioxide were an air pollutant, the only feasible method of reducing tailpipe emissions would be to improve fuel economy. But because Congress has already created detailed mandatory fuel economy standards subject to Department of Transportation (DOT) administration, the agency concluded that EPA regulation would either conflict with those standards or be superfluous.

Even assuming that it had authority over greenhouse gases, EPA explained in detail why it would refuse to exercise that authority. The agency began by recognizing that the concentration of greenhouse gases has dramatically increased as a result of human activities, and acknowledged the attendant increase in global surface air temperatures. EPA nevertheless gave controlling importance to the NRC Report's statement that a causal link between the two "cannot be unequivocally established." Given that residual uncertainty, EPA concluded that regulating greenhouse gas emissions would be unwise.

The agency furthermore characterized any EPA regulation of motor-vehicle emissions as a "piecemeal approach" to climate change, and stated that such regulation would conflict with the President's "comprehensive approach" to the problem. That approach involves additional support for technological innovation, the creation of nonregulatory programs to encourage voluntary private-sector reductions in greenhouse gas emissions, and further research on climate change—not actual regulation. According to EPA, unilateral EPA regulation of motor-vehicle greenhouse gas emissions might also hamper the President's ability to persuade key developing countries to reduce greenhouse gas emissions.

* * *

VI

On the merits, the first question is whether § 202(a)(1) of the Clean Air Act authorizes EPA to regulate greenhouse gas emissions from new motor vehicles in the event that it forms a "judgment" that such emissions contribute to climate change. We have little trouble concluding that it does. In relevant part, § 202(a)(1) provides that EPA "shall by regulation prescribe ... standards applicable to the emission of any air pollutant from any class or classes of new motor vehicles or new motor vehicle engines, which in [the Administrator's] judgment cause, or contribute to, air pollution which may reasonably be anticipated to endanger public health or welfare." 42 U.S.C. § 7521(a)(1). Because EPA believes that Congress did not intend it to regulate substances that contribute to climate change, the agency maintains that carbon dioxide is not an "air pollutant" within the meaning of the provision.

The statutory text forecloses EPA's reading. The Clean Air Act's sweeping definition of "air pollutant" includes "*any* air pollution agent or combination of such agents, including *any* physical, chemical ... substance or matter which is emitted into or otherwise enters the ambient air...." § 7602(g) (emphasis added). On its face, the definition embraces all airborne compounds of whatever stripe, and underscores that intent through the repeated use of the word "any." Carbon dioxide, methane, nitrous oxide, and hydrofluorocarbons are without a doubt "physical [and] chemical ... substance[s] which [are] emitted into ... the ambient air." The statute is unambiguous.[26]

---

26. In dissent, Justice Scalia maintains that because greenhouse gases permeate the world's atmosphere rather than a limited area near the earth's surface, EPA's exclusion of greenhouse gases from the category of air pollution "agent[s]" is entitled to deference under Chevron U.S.A. Inc. v. Natural Resources Defense Council, Inc. 467 U.S. 837 (1984). EPA's distinction, however, finds no support in the text of the statute, which uses the phrase "the ambient air" without distinguishing between atmospheric layers. Moreover, it is a plainly unreasonable reading of a sweeping statutory provision designed to capture "any physical, chemical ... substance or matter which is emitted into or otherwise enters the ambient air." 42 U.S.C. § 7602(g). * * * At any rate, no party to this dispute contests that greenhouse gases both "ente[r] the ambient air" and tend to warm the atmosphere. They are therefore unquestionably "agent[s]" of air pollution.

Rather than relying on statutory text, EPA invokes postenactment congressional actions and deliberations it views as tantamount to a congressional command to refrain from regulating greenhouse gas emissions. Even if such postenactment legislative history could shed light on the meaning of an otherwise-unambiguous statute, EPA never identifies any action remotely suggesting that Congress meant to curtail its power to treat greenhouse gases as air pollutants. That subsequent Congresses have eschewed enacting binding emissions limitations to combat global warming tells us nothing about what Congress meant when it amended § 202(a)(1) in 1970 and 1977. And unlike EPA, we have no difficulty reconciling Congress' various efforts to promote interagency collaboration and research to better understand climate change with the agency's pre-existing mandate to regulate "any air pollutant" that may endanger the public welfare. Collaboration and research do not conflict with any thoughtful regulatory effort; they complement it.

EPA's reliance on *Brown & Williamson Tobacco Corp.*, 529 U.S. 120, is similarly misplaced. In holding that tobacco products are not "drugs" or "devices" subject to Food and Drug Administration (FDA) regulation pursuant to the Food, Drug and Cosmetic Act (FDCA), we found critical at least two considerations that have no counterpart in this case.

First, we thought it unlikely that Congress meant to ban tobacco products, which the FDCA would have required had such products been classified as "drugs" or "devices." Here, in contrast, EPA jurisdiction would lead to no such extreme measures. EPA would only *regulate* emissions, and even then, it would have to delay any action "to permit the development and application of the requisite technology, giving appropriate consideration to the cost of compliance," § 7521(a)(2).

Second, in *Brown & Williamson* we pointed to an unbroken series of congressional enactments that made sense only if adopted "against the backdrop of the FDA's consistent and repeated statements that it lacked authority under the FDCA to regulate tobacco." *Id.*, at 144. We can point to no such enactments here: EPA has not identified any congressional action that conflicts in any way with the regulation of greenhouse gases from new motor vehicles. Even if it had, Congress could not have acted against a regulatory "backdrop" of disclaimers of regulatory authority. Prior to the order that provoked this litigation, EPA had never disavowed the authority to regulate greenhouse gases, and in 1998 it in fact affirmed that it *had* such authority. There is no reason, much less a compelling reason, to accept EPA's invitation to read ambiguity into a clear statute.

EPA finally argues that it cannot regulate carbon dioxide emissions from motor vehicles because doing so would require it to tighten mileage standards, a job (according to EPA) that Congress has assigned to DOT. But that DOT sets mileage standards in no way licenses EPA to shirk its environmental responsibilities. EPA has been charged with protecting the public's "health" and "welfare," 42 U.S.C. § 7521(a)(1), a statutory obligation wholly independent of DOT's mandate to promote energy efficiency. The two obligations may overlap, but there is no reason to think the two agencies cannot both administer their obligations and yet avoid inconsistency.

While the Congresses that drafted § 202(a)(1) might not have appreciated the possibility that burning fossil fuels could lead to global warming, they did understand that without regulatory flexibility, changing circumstances and scientific developments would soon render the Clean Air Act obsolete. The broad language of § 202(a)(1) reflects an intentional effort to confer the flexibility necessary to forestall such obsolescence. Because greenhouse gases fit well within the Clean Air Act's capacious definition of "air pollutant," we hold that EPA has the statutory authority to regulate the emission of such gases from new motor vehicles.

VII

The alternative basis for EPA's decision—that even if it does have statutory authority to regulate greenhouse gases, it would be unwise to do so at this time—rests on reasoning divorced from the statutory text. While the statute does condition the exercise of EPA's authority on its formation of a "judgment," that judgment must relate to whether an air pollutant "cause[s], or contribute[s] to, air pollution which may reasonably be anticipated to endanger public health or welfare." Put another way, the use of the word "judgment" is not a roving license to ignore the statutory text. It is but a direction to exercise discretion within defined statutory limits.

If EPA makes a finding of endangerment, the Clean Air Act requires the agency to regulate emissions of the deleterious pollutant from new motor vehicles. EPA no doubt has significant latitude as to the manner, timing, content, and coordination of its regulations with those of other agencies. But once EPA has responded to a petition for rulemaking, its reasons for action or inaction must conform to the authorizing statute. Under the clear terms of the Clean Air Act, EPA can avoid taking further action only if it determines that greenhouse gases do not contribute to climate change or if it provides some reasonable explanation as to why it cannot or will not exercise its discretion to determine whether they do. To the extent that this constrains agency discretion to pursue other priorities of the Administrator or the President, this is the congressional design.

EPA has refused to comply with this clear statutory command. Instead, it has offered a laundry list of reasons not to regulate. For example, EPA said that a number of voluntary executive branch programs already provide an effective response to the threat of global warming, that regulating greenhouse gases might impair the President's ability to negotiate with "key developing nations" to reduce emissions, and that curtailing motor-vehicle emissions would reflect "an inefficient, piecemeal approach to address the climate change issue."

Although we have neither the expertise nor the authority to evaluate these policy judgments, it is evident they have nothing to do with whether greenhouse gas emissions contribute to climate change. Still less do they amount to a reasoned justification for declining to form a scientific judgment. In particular, while the President has broad authority in foreign affairs, that authority does not extend to the refusal to execute domestic laws. * * *

Nor can EPA avoid its statutory obligation by noting the uncertainty surrounding various features of climate change and concluding that it would therefore be better not to regulate at this time. If the scientific uncertainty is so profound that it precludes EPA from making a reasoned judgment as to whether greenhouse gases contribute to global warming, EPA must say so. That EPA would prefer not to regulate greenhouse gases because of some residual uncertainty—which, contrary to Justice Scalia's apparent belief, is in fact all that it said—is irrelevant. The statutory question is whether sufficient information exists to make an endangerment finding.

In short, EPA has offered no reasoned explanation for its refusal to decide whether greenhouse gases cause or contribute to climate change. Its action was therefore "arbitrary, capricious, . . . or otherwise not in accordance with law." 42 U.S.C. § 7607(d)(9)(A). We need not and do not reach the question whether on remand EPA must make an endangerment finding, or whether policy concerns can inform EPA's actions in the event that it makes such a finding. We hold only that EPA must ground its reasons for action or inaction in the statute.

* * *

■ Justice Scalia, with whom the Chief Justice, Justice Thomas, and Justice Alito join, dissenting.

* * *

* * * As the Court recognizes, the statute "condition[s] the exercise of EPA's authority on its formation of a judgment." There is no dispute that the Administrator has made no such judgment in this case.

The question thus arises: Does anything *require* the Administrator to make a "judgment" whenever a petition for rulemaking is filed? Without citation of the statute or any other authority, the Court says yes. Why is that so? When Congress wishes to make private action force an agency's hand, it knows how to do so. Where does the CAA say that the EPA Administrator is required to come to a decision on this question whenever a rulemaking petition is filed? The Court points to no such provision because none exists.

* * *

* * * When the Administrator *makes* a judgment whether to regulate greenhouse gases, that judgment must relate to whether they are air pollutants that "cause, or contribute to, air pollution which may reasonably be anticipated to endanger public health or welfare." 42 U.S.C. § 7521(a)(1). But the statute says *nothing at all* about the reasons for which the Administrator may *defer* making a judgment—the permissible reasons for deciding not to grapple with the issue at the present time. Thus, the various "policy" rationales that the Court criticizes are not "divorced from the statutory text," except in the sense that the statutory text is silent, as texts are often silent about permissible reasons for the exercise of agency discretion. The reasons the EPA gave are surely considerations executive agencies *regularly* take into account (and *ought* to take into account) when deciding whether to consider entering a new field: the impact such entry would have on other Executive Branch programs and on foreign policy. There is no basis in law for the Court's imposed limitation.

EPA's interpretation of the discretion conferred by the statutory reference to "its judgment" is not only reasonable, it is the most natural reading of the text. The Court nowhere explains why this interpretation is incorrect, let alone why it is not entitled to deference under *Chevron U.S.A. Inc. v. Natural Resources Defense Council, Inc.*, 467 U.S. 837 (1984). * * *

Even on the Court's own terms, however, the same conclusion follows. As mentioned above, the Court gives EPA the option of determining that the science is too uncertain to allow it to form a "judgment" as to whether greenhouse gases endanger public welfare. But EPA *has* said precisely that—and at great length, based on information contained in a 2001 report by the National Research Council (NRC) * * *.

Even before reaching its discussion of the word "judgment," the Court makes another significant error when it concludes that "§ 202(a)(1) of the Clean Air Act *authorizes* EPA to regulate greenhouse gas emissions from new motor vehicles in the event that it forms a 'judgment' that such emissions contribute to climate change." For such authorization, the Court relies on what it calls "the Clean Air Act's capacious definition of air pollutant."

"Air pollutant" is defined by the Act as "any air pollution agent or combination of such agents, including any physical, chemical, . . . substance or matter which is emitted into or otherwise enters the ambient air." 42 U.S.C. § 7602(g). The Court is correct that "[c]arbon dioxide, methane, nitrous oxide, and hydrofluorocarbons," fit within the second half of that definition: They are "physical, chemical, . . . substance[s] or matter which [are] emitted into or otherwise ente[r] the ambient air." But the Court mistakenly believes this to be the end of the analysis. In order to be an "air pollutant" under the Act's definition, the "substance or matter [being] emitted into . . . the ambient air" must also meet the *first* half of the definition—namely, it must be an "air pollution agent or combination of such agents." The Court simply pretends this half of the definition does not exist.

* * *

* * * An air pollutant *can* be "any physical, chemical, . . . substance or matter which is emitted into or otherwise enters the ambient air," but only if it retains the general characteristic of being an "air pollution agent or combination of such agents." This is precisely the conclusion EPA reached. Once again, in the face of textual ambiguity, the Court's application of *Chevron* deference to EPA's interpretation of the word "including" is

nowhere to be found. Evidently, the Court defers only to those reasonable interpretations that it favors.

Using (as we ought to) EPA's interpretation of the definition of "air pollutant," we must next determine whether greenhouse gases are "agent[s]" of "air pollution." If so, the statute would authorize regulation; if not, EPA would lack authority.

Unlike "air pollutants," the term "air pollution" is not itself defined by the CAA; thus, once again we must accept EPA's interpretation of that ambiguous term, provided its interpretation is a "permissible construction of the statute." *Chevron,* 467 U.S., at 843. * * * EPA began with the commonsense observation that the "[p]roblems associated with atmospheric concentrations of CO_2," bear little resemblance to what would naturally be termed "air pollution":

> EPA's prior use of the CAA's general regulatory provisions provides an important context. Since the inception of the Act, EPA has used these provisions to address air pollution problems that occur primarily at ground level or near the surface of the earth. For example, national ambient air quality standards (NAAQS) established under CAA section 109 address concentrations of substances in the ambient air and the related public health and welfare problems. This has meant setting NAAQS for concentrations of ozone, carbon monoxide, particulate matter and other substances in the air near the surface of the earth, not higher in the atmosphere.... CO_2, by contrast, is fairly consistent in concentration throughout the world's atmosphere up to approximately the lower stratosphere.

Id., at 52926–52927.

In other words, regulating the buildup of CO_2 and other greenhouse gases in the upper reaches of the atmosphere, which is alleged to be causing global climate change, is not akin to regulating the concentration of some substance that is *polluting* the *air*.

* * *

The Court's alarm over global warming may or may not be justified, but it ought not distort the outcome of this litigation. This is a straightforward administrative-law case, in which Congress has passed a malleable statute giving broad discretion, not to us but to an executive agency. No matter how important the underlying policy issues at stake, this Court has no business substituting its own desired outcome for the reasoned judgment of the responsible agency.

NOTES AND QUESTIONS

1. *The aftermath.* More than two years after the decision in *Massachusetts v. EPA,* EPA issued a formal finding that greenhouse gas pollution, defined as aggregate emissions of six long-lived greenhouse gases that are well-mixed in the atmosphere, endangers both public health and public welfare, and that emissions from motor vehicles contribute to greenhouse gas pollution. 74 Fed. Reg. 66496 (Dec. 15, 2009). In reaching those conclusions, EPA considered current and future harms for the lifetime of the pollutant's effects, which for CO_2 is "at least the remainder of this century." It determined that relevant health effects need not be the direct result of exposure to the pollutant, meaning that the health effects of a changing climate could be counted in the determination. It rejected claims that the endangerment calculation should take into account the ability to adapt to a changing climate or the possibility of some beneficial effects in some places.

As EPA summed it up:

> The Administrator has determined that the body of scientific evidence compellingly supports this finding. The major assessments by the U.S. Global Climate Research Program (USGCRP), the Intergovernmental Panel on Climate Change (IPCC), and the National Research Council (NRC) serve as the primary scientific basis supporting the Administrator's endangerment finding. The Administrator reached her determination by considering both observed and projected effects of greenhouse gases in the atmosphere, their effect on climate, and the public health and welfare risks and impacts associated with such climate change.

* * * * *

> The Administrator recognizes that human-induced climate change has the potential to be far-reaching and multidimensional, and in light of existing knowledge, that not all risks and potential impacts can be quantified or characterized with uniform metrics. There is variety not only in the nature and potential magnitude of risks and impacts, but also in our ability to characterize, quantify and project such impacts into the future. The Administrator is using her judgment, based on existing science, to weigh the threat for each of the identifiable risks, to weigh the potential benefits where relevant, and ultimately to assess whether these risks and effects, when viewed in total, endanger public health or welfare.

> The Administrator has considered how elevated concentrations of the wellmixed greenhouse gases and associated climate change affect public health by evaluating the risks associated with changes in air quality, increases in temperatures, changes in extreme weather events, increases in food- and water-borne pathogens, and changes in aeroallergens. The evidence concerning adverse air quality impacts provides strong and clear support for an endangerment finding. Increases in ambient ozone are expected to occur over broad areas of the country, and they are expected to increase serious adverse health effects in large population areas that are and may continue to be in nonattainment. The evaluation of the potential risks associated with increases in ozone in non-attainment areas also supports such a finding.

The impact on mortality and morbidity associated with increases in average temperatures, which increase the likelihood of heat waves, also provides support for a public health endangerment finding. There are uncertainties over the net health impacts of a temperature increase due to decreases in cold-related mortality, but some recent evidence suggests that the net impact on mortality is more likely to be adverse, in a context where heat is already the leading cause of weather-related deaths in the United States.

The evidence concerning how human-induced climate change may alter extreme weather events also clearly supports a finding of endangerment, given the serious adverse impacts that can result from such events and the increase in risk, even if small, of the occurrence and intensity of events such as hurricanes and floods. Additionally, public health is expected to be adversely affected by an increase in the severity of coastal storm events due to rising sea levels.

* * *

Finally, the Administrator places weight on the fact that certain groups, including children, the elderly, and the poor, are most vulnerable to these climate-related health effects.

The Administrator has considered how elevated concentrations of the well-mixed greenhouse gases and associated climate change affect public welfare by evaluating numerous and far-ranging risks to food production and agriculture, forestry, water resources, sea level rise and coastal areas, energy, infrastructure, and settlements, and ecosystems and wildlife. For each of these sectors, the evidence provides support for a finding of endangerment to public welfare. The evidence concerning adverse impacts in the areas of water resources and sea level rise and coastal areas provides the clearest and strongest support for an endangerment finding, both for current and future generations. Strong support is also found in the evidence concerning infrastructure and settlements, as well ecosystems and wildlife. Across the sectors, the potential serious adverse impacts of extreme events, such as wildfires, flooding, drought, and extreme weather conditions, provide strong support for such a finding.

74 Fed. Reg. 66497–66498. The endangerment finding has been challenged by a number of industry groups; the U.S. Chamber of Commerce; the states of Virginia, Texas, and Alabama; conservative lawmakers; and others. Sixteen states have intervened to defend the endangerment finding. The D.C. Circuit consolidated the endangerment finding challenges with several other suits challenging other EPA greenhouse gas regulation initiatives. In its initial ruling on the case, the court declined to stay the rules pending appeal.

Based on the endangerment finding, EPA acknowledged an obligation to issue greenhouse gas emission standards for mobile sources. In 2010, EPA and the National Highway Transportation and Safety Administration issued joint regulations governing greenhouse gas emissions and fuel economy standards for new light duty vehicles. They have proposed similar rules for heavy-duty vehicles.

Although the endangerment finding by its terms applies only to mobile source emissions, the language of CAA § 202(a) is virtually identical to that of § 108(a). Must EPA now find that the six greenhouse gases are, individually or collectively, criteria pollutants? Would there be any point to setting a NAAQS for greenhouse gases?

2. *California greenhouse gas emission regulations.* In 2004, California adopted regulations limiting tailpipe emissions of greenhouse gases, effective with model year 2009. California filed a request for a waiver under CAA § 209 (42 U.S.C. § 7543) in December 2005. EPA denied that request on the grounds that California did not need the regulations to meet compelling and extraordinary conditions. EPA took the position that climate change is a global problem that affects California no differently than other states. 73 Fed. Reg. 12156 (Mar. 6, 2008).

Shortly after his inauguration, President Obama directed EPA to re-examine the waiver decision. After holding a hearing and taking public comments, EPA reversed its earlier decision and granted California's waiver request. 74 Fed. Reg. 32744 (July 8, 2009). In its new decision, EPA returned to its traditional interpretation that the "compelling and extraordinary circumstances" issue applies to whether or not California generally needs a separate mobile source pollution program, rather than to the details of that program. Even if the need for greenhouse gas standards were evaluated separately, EPA Administrator Lisa Jackson wrote, a waiver would be justified. She noted that climate change will exacerbate California's already severe ozone problem, and that the opponents of California's request had not met their burden of proof "to demonstrate that the impacts of global climate change in California are either not significant enough or are not different enough from the rest of the country to be considered compelling and extraordinary conditions." Id. at 32765.

When EPA and NHTSA issued federal greenhouse gas and fuel efficiency standards, California agreed to accept compliance with those standards as meeting its own requirements. The state is now working with the two federal agencies to develop the next generation of GHG emission standards. EPA, News Release, EPA, DOT and California Align Timeframe for Proposing Standards for Next Generation of Clean Cars (Jan. 24, 2011).

3. *Preemption?* When California first announced its greenhouse gas standards, automobile manufacturers and the Bush administration argued that those standards were preempted by the Energy Policy and Conservation Act, which provides in relevant part:

> When an average fuel economy standard prescribed under this chapter is in effect, a State or a political subdivision of a State may not adopt or enforce a law or regulation related to fuel economy standards or average fuel economy standards for automobiles covered by an average fuel economy standard under this chapter.

49 U.S.C. § 32919(a). After the Supreme Court's decision in *Massachusetts v. EPA*, two federal district courts ruled that the fuel economy law does not preempt California's standards. Central Valley Chrysler–Jeep v. Goldstene, 529 F. Supp. 2d 1151 (E.D. Cal. 2007); Green Mountain Chrysler Plymouth, et al. v. Crombie, 508 F.Supp.2d 295 (D. Vt. 2007). The automakers dropped their challenge to California's standards when the state agreed to align its program with EPA's national standards. The Chamber of Commerce and a car dealers' industry group sought to pursue the preemption claim, but the D.C. Circuit held that they lacked standing. Chamber of Commerce v. EPA, 642 F.3d 192 (D.C. Cir. 2011).

4. *Effectiveness.* In denying the petition at issue in *Massachusetts v. EPA*, EPA had argued, among other things, that regulation of motor vehicle CO_2 emissions would be both inefficient and ineffective against global warming. The Supreme Court majority concludes that is not a valid reason for refusing to regulate. Do you agree? Is it nevertheless, as Justice Scalia argues, a valid reason for declining to initiate a rulemaking proceeding, that is, for declining to decide whether to regulate? Should it be? Do you agree with EPA's premise that regulation of automobile CO_2 emissions would not be a useful way to address the problem of climate change? Is it relevant that, in the course of finding that petitioners had standing, the Court majority pointed out that the U.S. transportation sector accounts for some 6% of worldwide CO_2 emissions?

5. *To defer or not to defer.* In *Massachusetts v. EPA*, should the Court have deferred, under *Chevron v. NRDC*, to EPA's interpretation of its authority and the scope of its discretion? Is the statute ambiguous? In determining whether the statute is ambiguous, can (and should) courts look to the potential impacts of regulation? To other statutes that overlap with the one being interpreted? A different 5–4 majority (with Justice Kennedy joining the Court's conservative wing) took a very different view of the appropriate use of deference in National Association of Home Builders v. Defenders of Wildlife, 551 U.S. 644 (2007), an Endangered Species Act case decided a few months after *Massachusetts v. EPA*.

SECTION 4. NEW SOURCE REVIEW AND THE PROBLEM OF GRANDFATHERING

The CAA draws an important distinction between new stationary sources, which are subject to stringent regulation, and existing ones, which for the most part are not unless a state chooses to impose such regulations through its SIP. There are two distinct elements to new source regulation.

First, all new or modified sources are subject to federal technology-based regulation. CAA § 111 requires that EPA set "new source performance standards" (NSPS) for categories of stationary sources that may, in the judgment of the administrator, reasonably be anticipated to endanger public health or welfare. CAA § 111(b) (42 U.S.C. § 7411(b)). NSPS are emission standards which reflect the degree of emission limitation achievable through the application of the best system of emission reduction which (taking into account the cost of achieving such reduction and any nonair quality health and environmental impact and energy requirements) the Administrator determines has been adequately demonstrated.

CAA § 111(a)(1). NSPS apply to "new sources," defined as stationary sources "the construction or modification of which is commenced" after NSPS are proposed or finalized for the category. CAA § 111(a)(2). "Modification" is further defined as "any physical change in, or change in the method of operation of, a stationary source which increases the amount of any air pollutant emitted by such source or which results in the emission of any air pollutant not previously emitted." CAA § 111(a)(4).

Second, new stationary sources above certain threshold emission limits are subject to preconstruction "new source review" (NSR) either under the Prevention of Significant Deterioration (PSD) program (in attainment areas) or under the nonattainment program. Since the entire country is either in or not in attainment, all new sources are necessarily subject to some form of NSR. Furthermore, since attainment is evaluated separately for each criteria pollutant, a single proposed new source can be subject to NSR review under both the PSD and the nonattainment programs.

The major consequences of NSR in PSD areas are that a proposed new source must not cause or contribute to any NAAQS violation or exceedance of the allowable PSD increment, and it must install "best available pollution control technology" (BACT). BACT is a facility-specific standard "based on the maximum degree of reduction ... which the permitting authority, on a case-by-case basis, taking into account energy, environmental, and economic impacts and other costs, determines is achievable." CAA § 169(3) (42 U.S.C. § 7479(3)). BACT may not be less stringent than the NSPS, if there is one, applicable to the industrial category. Id. In nonattainment areas, NSR requires that new sources provide offsets sufficient to insure reasonable further progress, and comply with the "lowest achievable emission rate" (LAER). CAA § 173(a)(2), (c) (42 U.S.C. § 7503(a)(2), (c)). LAER, like BACT, is a facility-specific, technology-based standard which may be more, but not less, stringent than NSPS. CAA § 171(3) (42 U.S.C. § 7501(3)).

What might justify this multi-layered scheme for regulation of new sources? The categorical, technology-based NSPS provide nationwide uniformity. From the industry perspective, NSPS offers a single design objective for new facilities nationwide. From a state perspective, it takes advantage of regulatory economies of scale, and relieves state officials of the burdensome job of setting technology-based standards for every type of facility that might wish to locate within the state. Finally, from an environmental perspective, uniform national standards for new sources should prevent a "race to the bottom," in which states might compete for new industry by offering lax pollution control standards. Overlaying PSD and nonattainment new source review on the nationwide minimum standards of NSPS allows the imposition of more stringent controls where feasible, provides an opportunity to review the facility not just in the abstract but in the context of the proposed location, and ensures that there is some regulation of new sources that fall outside the relatively small number of categories for which EPA has issued NSPS.

That explanation begs an important question, though: Why focus on new or modified sources, regulating them more stringently than existing ones?

Shi–Ling Hsu, Reducing Emissions From the Electricity Generation Industry: Can We Finally Do It?

14 Tulane Envtl. L. J. 427 (2001).

* * *

Retiring coal-fired power plants in the United States is essential to reducing emissions of pollutants and greenhouse gases from the electricity generation industry. In 1999, coal-fired power plants in the United States emitted 11.3 million tons of SO_2, 6.5 million tons of nitrogen oxides (NO_x), 1.9 billion tons of carbon dioxide (CO_2), and 43 tons of mercury. This accounted for approximately 60% of all SO_2 emissions nationwide and 25% of all NO_x emissions nationwide. Coal-fired power plants also accounted for 32% of all CO_2 emissions nationwide and 21% of all airborne mercury emissions nationwide. * * *

There is now widespread agreement that the retirement of older coal-fired power plants would produce substantial health and environmental benefits well in excess of the costs imposed. Per unit of energy produced, natural gas-fired plants are considerably cleaner than coal-fired plants, emitting only 33% of the CO_2, 10% of the NO_x, and virtually none of the SO_2, particulate matter, and mercury emitted by coal-fired plants. Retiring 80% of the coal-fired power plants and replacing the lost generation capacity with natural gas-fired power plants, without any other policy measures, would accomplish the carbon dioxide emissions reductions necessary for the United States to meet its Kyoto Protocol targets of reducing emissions by 7% below 1990 levels.[19]

* * *

A new power plant constructed today is much more likely to utilize natural gas as a fuel source than coal. Apart from the environmental benefits of using natural gas instead of coal, natural gas-fired power plants present significant economic advantages for the electricity generation industry. Natural-gas fired power plants generally have a smaller generating capacity than coal-fired power plants, but on a per-megawatt capacity basis,

---

19. The Kyoto Protocol calls for the United States to reduce carbon emissions to 93% of the level of carbon emissions in 1990, which would be 5.08 billion tons. Meeting the Kyoto Protocol targets would require a reduction from 6.17 to 5.08 billion tons, a reduction of 1.09 billion tons. Conversion of all coal-fired plants to natural gas-fired plants alone would accomplish a reduction of 1.33 billion tons. * * *

are much less expensive to construct. * * * Moreover, the smaller natural gas-fired power plants, in requiring a fraction of the capital commitments, provide electricity generation firms with much more financial flexibility. While natural gas-fired plants still face hurdles, the economics of new plants clearly point to natural gas as the preferred fuel source. * * *

However, the happy coincidence of good business and good environmental policy has not resulted in a wholesale conversion of the fleet of coal-fired power plants into natural gas-fired power plants. In 1999, 51% of U.S. energy needs were met by coal-fired power plants, while natural gas-fired power plants accounted for only 15% of all U.S. energy needs. This is scarcely different than the energy picture ten years ago, when coal accounted for 53% of U.S. energy needs, and natural gas accounted for 13%. Worse still, most of the electricity produced by coal-fired power plants is produced by plants that were built before 1980, and emit more pollution than newer coal-fired power plants. What's the problem?

The problem is that environmental laws have "grandfathered" these older coal-fired power plants so that they do not have to comply with many stringent environmental regulations that apply to new plants. This provides a strong incentive to keep old coal-fired power plants operating. While these older plants are less efficient than newer plants being built today, the costs of inefficiency have not yet been enough of an incentive to induce firms to retire their older plants.

This situation derives from an assumption in U.S. environmental policy that there would inevitably occur a natural turnover of power plants. Power plants have typically been built to last thirty to forty years, and environmental policy has been developed with the assumption that thirty-year-old plants would be soon phased out of production. This assumption ignores the economics of operating these older plants, and the cost advantage enjoyed by continuing operation of these plants over building new ones. In 1977, the Clean Air Act was amended to provide for New Source Review standards, stringent emissions standards that apply to any new construction of a facility that emits criteria air pollutants. It was believed that the United States Environmental Protection Agency could insist upon stringent standards because new power plant construction was inevitable. This was not so, as coal-fired power plants persisted throughout the 1980s. In 1990, the Clean Air Act was amended again to include the Acid Rain Program, which provided for tradable permits for emissions of SO_2—permits to emit one ton of SO_2, tradable primarily among the electricity generation firms. It was expected that by sending a price signal to electricity generation firms, the firms would finally retire their coal-fired power plants. Instead, only seven of the original 263 coal-fired plants originally subject to the Acid Rain Program were retired in the entire decade of the 1990s. Evidently, the price signal was not strong enough.

An examination of the economics of power plant operation reveals why the expected retirement of old coal-fired power plants has not occurred. While natural gas-fired plants are much cheaper to build and only slightly more expensive to operate and maintain, older coal-fired plants have no capital costs at all because they have been fully amortized. Also, an unexpectedly low price and easy availability of low-sulfur coal, as well as some surprising advances in SO_2 emissions control technology and a variety of subsidies available to firms with coal-fired power plants have all kept operating costs low for electricity generation firms, and given them good reason to keep running their old coal-fired power plants. * * *

The relative prices of natural gas and coal fluctuate, and with them so do the market incentives for building different types of power plants. Based on current market conditions, the Energy Information Administration projects that few new coal-fired power plants will be constructed between now and 2035, even absent new greenhouse gas emission limits. Due to increased use of existing coal-fired capacity, however, the EIA projects that coal's share of the nation's electricity generation mix will fall only slightly, from 45% to 43% over that time. Energy Information Administration, Annual Energy Outlook 2010. EIA's projections for the future of coal-fired electricity generation are highly sensitive to whether new environmental regulations are imposed on existing coal-fired plants.

Under the current regulatory framework, whether a plant has been "modified" or not is a crucial threshold question for existing power plants, because it determines whether or not new source review and NSPS apply. Like NSPS, both PSD and nonattainment new source review cover modified as well as new sources. Both new source review provisions define modification by reference to the NSPS definition, CAA § 111(a)(4) (CAA § 7411(a)(4)). The meaning of that definition, not surprisingly, has been hotly contested.

Environmental Defense v. Duke Energy Corporation

United States Supreme Court, 2007.
549 U.S. 561.

■ JUSTICE SOUTER delivered the opinion of the Court.

* * *

I

The Clean Air Amendments of 1970, 84 Stat. 1676, broadened federal authority to combat air pollution and directed EPA to devise National Ambient Air Quality Standards (NAAQS) limiting various pollutants, which the States were obliged to implement and enforce. The amendments dealing with NSPS authorized EPA to require operators of stationary sources of air pollutants to use the best technology for limiting pollution, both in newly constructed sources and those undergoing "modification," 42 U.S.C. § 7411(a)(2). Section 111(a) of the 1970 amendments defined this term within the NSPS scheme as "any physical change in, or change in the method of operation of, a stationary source which increases the amount of any air pollutant emitted by such source or which results in the emission of any air pollutant not previously emitted," 42 U.S.C. § 7411(a)(4).

EPA's 1975 regulations implementing NSPS provided generally that "any physical or operational change to an existing facility which results in an increase in the emission rate to the atmosphere of any pollutant to which a standard applies shall be considered a modification within the meaning of [S]ection 111." 40 CFR § 60.14(a) (1976). Especially significant here is the identification of an NSPS "modification" as a change that "increase[s] ... the emission rate," which "shall be expressed as kg/hr of any pollutant discharged into the atmosphere." § 60.14(b).

NSPS, however, did too little to "achiev[e] the ambitious goals of the 1970 Amendments," R. Belden, Clean Air Act 7 (2001), and the Clean Air Act Amendments of 1977 included the PSD provisions, which aimed at giving added protection to air quality in certain parts of the country "notwithstanding attainment and maintenance of" the NAAQS. 42 U.S.C. § 7470(1). The 1977 amendments required a PSD permit before a "major emitting facility" could be "constructed" in an area covered by the scheme. § 7475(a). As originally enacted, PSD applied only to newly constructed sources, but soon a technical amendment added the following subparagraph: "The term 'construction' when used in connection with any source or facility, includes the modification (as defined in [S]ection 111(a)) of any source or facility." § 14(a)(54), 42 U.S.C. § 7479(2)(C). In other words, the "construction" requiring a PSD permit under the statute was made to include (though it was not limited to) a "modification" as defined in the statutory NSPS provisions.

In 1980, EPA issued PSD regulations, which "limited the application of [PSD] review" of modified sources to instances of "major" modification, defined as "any physical change in or change in the method of operation of a major stationary source that would result in a significant net emissions increase of any pollutant subject to regulation under the Act." 40 CFR § 51.166(b)(2)(i) (1987). Further regulations in turn addressed various elements of this definition, three of which are to the point here. First, the regulations specified that an operational change consisting merely of "[a]n increase in the hours of operation or in the production rate" would not generally constitute a "physical change or change in the method of operation." § 51.166(b)(2)(iii)(*f*). For purposes of a PSD permit, that is, such an operational change would not amount to a "modification" as the Act defines it. Second, the PSD regulations defined a "net emissions increase" as "[a]ny increase in actual emissions from a particular physical change or change in the method of operation," net of other contemporaneous "increases and decreases in actual emissions at the source." § 51.166(b)(3). "Actual emissions" were defined to "equal the average rate, in tons per year, at which the unit actually emitted the pollutant during a two-year period which precedes the particular date and which is representative of normal source operation." § 51.166(b)(21)(ii). "[A]ctual emissions" were to be "calculated using the unit's actual operating hours [and] production rates." *Ibid*. Third, the term "significant" was defined as "a rate of emissions that would equal or exceed" one or another enumerated threshold, each expressed in "tons per year." § 51.166(b)(23)(i).

It would be bold to try to synthesize these statutory and regulatory provisions in a concise paragraph, but three points are relatively clear about the regime that covers this case:

(a) The Act defines modification of a stationary source of a pollutant as a physical change to it, or a change in the method of its operation, that increases the amount of a pollutant discharged or emits a new one.

(b) EPA's NSPS regulations require a source to use the best available pollution-limiting technology only when a modification would increase the rate of discharge of pollutants measured in kilograms per hour.

(c) EPA's 1980 PSD regulations require a permit for a modification (with the same statutory definition) only when it is a major one and only when it would increase the actual annual emission of a pollutant above the actual average for the two prior years.

* * *

II

Respondent Duke Energy Corporation runs 30 coal-fired electric generating units at eight plants in North and South Carolina. The units were placed in service between 1940 and 1975, and each includes a boiler containing thousands of steel tubes arranged in sets. Between 1988 and 2000, Duke replaced or redesigned 29 tube assemblies in order to extend the life of the units and allow them to run longer each day.

The United States filed this action in 2000, claiming, among other things, that Duke violated the PSD provisions by doing this work without permits. Environmental Defense, North Carolina Sierra Club, and North Carolina Public Interest Research Group Citizen Lobby/Education Fund intervened as plaintiffs * * *.

The United States and intervenor-plaintiffs (collectively, plaintiffs) subsequently stipulated "that they do not contend that the projects at issue in this case caused an increase in the maximum hourly rate of emissions at any of Duke Energy's units." Rather, their claim "is based solely on their contention that the projects would have been projected to result in an increased utilization of the units at issue." * * *

[The District Court entered summary judgment for Duke and the Fourth Circuit affirmed, holding that Congress, by defining "modification" for the PSD program by reference to the NSPS definition, had mandated that the term be interpreted identically for the two programs.]

III

* * *

In applying the 1980 PSD regulations to Duke's conduct, the Court of Appeals thought that, by defining the term "modification" identically in its NSPS and PSD provisions, the Act required EPA to conform its PSD interpretation of that definition to any such interpretation it reasonably adhered to under NSPS. But principles of statutory construction are not so rigid. Although we presume that the same term has the same meaning when it occurs here and there in a single statute, the Court of Appeals mischaracterized that presumption as "effectively irrebuttable." We also understand that "[m]ost words have different shades of meaning and consequently may be variously construed, not only when they occur in different statutes, but when used more than once in the same statute or even in the same section." *Atlantic Cleaners & Dyers, Inc. v. United States,* 286 U.S. 427 (1932). Thus, the "natural presumption that identical words used in different parts of the same act are intended to have the same meaning . . . is not rigid and readily yields whenever there is such variation in the connection in which the words are used as reasonably to warrant the conclusion that they were employed in different parts of the act with different intent." *Ibid.* A given term in the same statute may take on distinct characters from association with distinct statutory objects calling for different implementation strategies.

* * *

It is true that the Clean Air Act did not merely repeat the term "modification" or the same definition of that word in its NSPS and PSD sections; the PSD language referred back to the section defining "modification" for NSPS purposes. 42 U.S.C. § 7479(2)(C). But * * * we do not see the distinction as making any difference here. Nothing in the text or the legislative history of the technical amendments that added the cross-reference to NSPS suggests that Congress had details of regulatory implementation in mind when it imposed PSD requirements on modified sources; the cross-reference alone is certainly no unambiguous congressional code for eliminating the customary agency discretion to resolve questions about a statutory definition by looking to the surroundings of the defined term, where it occurs. Absent any iron rule to ignore the reasons for regulating PSD and NSPS "modifications" differently, EPA's construction need do no more than fall within the limits of what is reasonable, as set by the Act's common definition.

The Court of Appeals's reasoning that the PSD regulations must conform to their NSPS counterparts led the court to read those PSD regulations in a way that seems to us too far a stretch for the language used. The 1980 PSD regulations on "modification" simply cannot be taken to track the agency's regulatory definition under the NSPS.

True, the 1980 PSD regulations may be no seamless narrative, but they clearly do not define a "major modification" in terms of an increase in the "hourly emissions rate." On its face, the definition in the PSD regulations specifies no rate at all, hourly or annual, merely requiring a physical or operational change "that would result in a significant net emissions increase of any" regulated pollutant. 40 CFR § 51.166(b)(2)(i). But even when a rate is mentioned, as in the regulatory definitions of the two terms, "significant" and "net emissions increase," the rate is annual, not hourly. Each of the thresholds that quantify "significant" is described in "tons per year," § 51.166(b)(23)(i), and a "net emissions increase" is an "increase in actual emissions" measured against an "average" prior emissions rate of so many "tons per year." §§ 51.166(b)(3) and (21)(ii). And what is further at odds with the idea that hourly rate is relevant is the mandate that "[a]ctual emissions shall be calculated using the unit's actual operating hours," § 51.166(b)(21)(ii), since "actual emissions" must be measured in a manner that looks to the number of hours the unit is or probably will be actually running. What these provisions are getting at is a measure of actual operations averaged over time, and the regulatory language simply cannot be squared with a regime under which "hourly rate of emissions" is dispositive.

The reasons invoked by the Court of Appeals for its different view are no match for these textual differences. * * * The [court] thought that an increase in the hourly emissions rate was necessarily a prerequisite to a PSD "major modification" because a provision of the 1980 PSD regulations excluded an "increase in the hours of operation or in the production rate" from the scope of "[a] physical change or change in the method of operation." 40 CFR §§ 51.166(b)(2)(iii)(*f*) and (3)(i)(*a*) (1987)). The [court] read this exclusion to require, in effect, that a source's hours of operation "be held constant" when preproject emissions are being compared with postproject emissions for the purpose of calculating the "net emissions increase."

We think this understanding of the 1980 PSD regulations makes the mistake of overlooking the difference between the two separate components of the regulatory definition of "major modification": "[1] any physical change in or change in the method of operation of a major stationary source that [2] would result in a significant net emissions increase of any pollutant subject to regulation under the Act." § 51.166(b)(2)(i). The exclusion of "increase in ... hours ... or ... production rate," § 51.166(b)(2)(iii)(*f*), speaks to the first of these components ("physical change ... or change in ... method,"), but not to the second ("significant net emissions increase"). As the preamble to the 1980 PSD regulations explains, forcing companies to obtain a PSD permit before they could simply adjust operating hours "would severely and unduly hamper the ability of any company to take advantage of favorable market conditions." 45 Fed. Reg. 52704. In other words, a mere increase in the hours of operation, standing alone, is not a "physical change or change in the method of operation."

But the [court] took this language a step further. It assumed that increases in operating hours (resulting in emissions increases at the old rate per hour) must be ignored even if caused or enabled by an independent "physical change ... or change in the method of operation." That reading, however, turns an exception to the first component of the definition into a mandate to ignore the very facts that would count under the second, which defines "net emissions increase" in terms of "actual emissions" during "the unit's actual operating hours," § 51.166(b)(21)(ii).

* * *

■ JUSTICE THOMAS, concurring in part.

* * * Section 7411(a) contains the NSPS definition of "modification," which the parties agree is the relevant statutory definition of the term for both PSD and NSPS. Because of the cross-reference, the definitions of "modification" in PSD and NSPS are one and the same. The term "modification" therefore has the same meaning despite contextual variations in the two admittedly different statutory schemes. Congress' explicit linkage of PSD's definition of "modification" to NSPS' prevents the Environmental Protection Agency (EPA) from adopting differing regulatory definitions of "modification" for PSD and NSPS.

* * *

Even if the cross-reference were merely the equivalent of repeating the words of the definition, we must still apply our usual presumption that the same words repeated in different parts of the same statute have the same meaning. That presumption has not been overcome here. While the broadly stated regulatory goals of PSD and NSPS differ, these contextual differences do not compel different definitions of "modification." EPA demonstrated as much when it recently proposed regulations that would unify the regulatory definitions of "modification." See 70 Fed. Reg. 61083, n. 3 (2005).

* * *

NOTES AND QUESTIONS

1. *Grandfathering and the goals of the Clean Air Act.* Why do you suppose Congress decided to impose technology-based pollution control standards on new stationary (and for that matter mobile) sources, while leaving it up to the states what to require of existing sources? Note that the nonattainment provisions do require that the states impose some controls on existing sources in attainment areas. Nonattainment SIPs must provide for implementation of "reasonably available control technology," by existing sources, CAA § 172(c)(1) (42 U.S.C. § 7502(c)(1)), and ozone nonattainment SIPs must include vehicle inspection and maintenance provisions. Nonetheless, states remain free to regulate existing sources much less stringently than new ones, a strategy known as "grandfathering" or "vintage-differentiated regulation." What is gained and lost by a grandfathering approach? Consider the following excerpt:

> The vintage-differentiated approach has long appealed to many participants in the policy community, for reasons associated with efficiency, equity, and simple politics. First, it is frequently more cost-effective—in the short term—to introduce new pollution-abatement technologies at the time that new plants are constructed than to retrofit older facilities with such technologies. Second, it seems more fair to avoid changing the rules of the game in midstream, and hence to apply new standards only to new plants. Third, political pressures

tend to favor easily identified existing facilities rather than undefined potential facilities.

On the other hand, [vintage differentiated regulations] VDRs can be expected—on the basis of standard investment theory—to retard turnover in the capital stock (of durable plants and equipment), and thereby to reduce the cost-effectiveness of regulation in the long term, compared with equivalent undifferentiated regulations. A further irony is that, when this slower turnover results in delayed adoption of new, cleaner technology, VDR can result in higher levels of pollutant emissions than would occur in the absence of regulation.

Robert N. Stavins, Vintage Differentiated Environmental Regulation, 25 Stan. Envtl. L. J. 29, 30 (2006).

2. *Grandfathering as transition relief.* Grandfathering is a specific example of transition relicf, which generally encompasses any strategy that shields existing participants from the full effects of newly adopted or modified legal rules. Transition relief is appealing for its apparent fairness and for political reasons, as Professor Stavins outlines in the excerpt above. Although transition relief is common, it is not necessarily good policy:

[R]elief from a transition in legal regimes is ordinarily inadvisable because it creates an incentive for societal actors not to anticipate changes in the governing law. As a general matter, societal actors are not afforded public relief from change. For example, a firm that uses a particular technology in its production process runs the risk that the technology will change. If that happens, the firm may lose profits and perhaps go out of business altogether if it does not modernize its production process; no legal relief shields the firm from the market pressure to adopt the technological change.

The possibility of a change in legal regime is simply a subclass of the larger set of risks that societal actors face. In general, the government does not provide protection against such risks. Absent special justification, a change in legal regime should be treated similarly to other types of changes societal actors face. Thus, as a general rule, legal transition relief is undesirable. The prospect of transition relief inefficiently discourages actors from anticipating legal change. In contrast, placing the risk of legal change on societal actors encourages them to anticipate legal change and to comply voluntarily and in advance. Societal actors who are governed by one legal regime and who foresee a coming change in that regime will be less likely to conform voluntarily to that change if they also foresee a likelihood that the government will afford them transition relief from it. Moreover, when the government enacts a new legal regime with transition relief, it sends a signal to society at large that, in general, changes in legal standards will not govern existing actors. Actors who lie beyond the scope of the particular regime will be less likely to anticipate or to comply voluntarily with new legal standards in the regime that governs their own behavior.

Jonathan Remy Nash & Richard L. Revesz, Grandfathering and Environmental Regulation: The Law and Economics of New Source Review, 101 Nw. U. L. Rev. 1677, 1724–1725 (2007).

3. *The scope of new source review.* Determining whether NSPS and new source review apply requires regulators first to identify a "source," and then to decide whether it is "new" or "modified."

The CAA contains two definitions of "stationary source." The Act's general definitions provision, CAA § 302, defines a stationary source as "any source of an air pollutant except those emissions resulting directly from an internal combustion engine * * *." CAA § 302(z) (42 U.S.C. § 7602(z)). The NSPS provision includes its own definition, under which a stationary source is "any building, structure, facility, or installation which emits or may emit any air pollutant." CAA § 111(a)(3) (42 U.S.C. § 7411(a)(3)). Is a highway tunnel ventilation structure, which does not generate emissions but serves to funnel emissions from the vehicles that pass through the tunnel to the outside atmosphere, a "stationary source" for purposes of NSR or NSPS? See Sierra Club v. Larson, 2 F.3d 462 (1st Cir. 1993) (deferring to EPA's view that a tunnel ventilation structure is not a stationary source).

In Chevron v. NRDC, 467 U.S. 837 (1984), the Supreme Court upheld EPA's use of a plant-wide definition of stationary source for NSR purposes. Under such a definition, an increase in emissions from one part of a plant or facility does not trigger NSR if it is canceled out by a compensating decrease from another part of the facility. EPA currently applies plantwide definitions both in nonattainment areas, see 40 C.F.R. § 51.165(a)(1)(ii), and in PSD areas, see 40 C.F.R. § 51.166(w).

Modified, as well as new, facilities are covered by NSPS and NSR. A modification is "any physical change in, or change in the method of operation of, a stationary source which increases the amount of any air pollutant emitted by such source or which results in the emission of any air pollutant not previously emitted." CAA § 111(a)(4) (42 U.S.C. § 7411(a)(4)). As the Supreme Court explained in *Duke Energy*, under NSPS, EPA considers a plant to be modified only if the change increases its rate of emissions per hour of operation. 40 C.F.R. § 60.14(b). NSR, by contrast, is currently triggered by an increase in annual emissions. 40 C.F.R. § 52.21(b)(23)(I). Under the G.W. Bush Administration, EPA proposed to adopt an hourly test for electric generating units, but that proposal was never finalized. See 72 Fed. Reg. 26202 (May 8, 2007); 70 Fed. Reg. 61081 (Oct. 20, 2005).

Why is this distinction important? Does the statutory language allow EPA to use either an hourly or an annual test? Does EPA have the authority to adopt different tests for these different programs? Is there a difference between the goals of the programs that could justify different interpretations?

4. *Routine maintenance, repair and replacement.* EPA's regulatory definition of modification for NSR purposes excludes "[r]outine maintenance, repair, and replacement." 40 C.F.R. § 52.21(b)(2)(iii)(a). In 2003, EPA finalized a regulation defining, for the first time, the scope of the routine maintenance exclusion. 68 Fed. Reg. 61248 (Oct. 27, 2003). Previously, EPA had implemented the exclusion through case-by-case determinations, "weighing the nature, extent, purpose, frequency, and cost of the work as well as other factors to arrive at a common sense finding." 67 Fed. Reg. 80290, 80292–93 (Dec. 31, 2002). The 2003 rule provided an automatic exclusion for replacement of equipment with components that are identical or serve the same purpose from NSR, so long as the cost does not exceed 20% of the current replacement cost of the process unit and does not "alter the basic design parameters" of the unit, regardless of whether the replacement increased emissions. Other activities remained subject to case-by-case review.

Shortly after EPA issued the routine maintenance rule, it was stayed by the D.C. Circuit pending judicial review. In New York v. EPA, 443 F.3d 880 (D.C. Cir. 2006), the court struck it down, holding that it was inconsistent with the unambiguous statutory definition of "modification," which encompasses "any physical change" that increases emissions.

5. *NSR and the economics of electric power production.* When the various new source review provisions of the CAA were adopted, it was widely assumed that within a short time all existing sources would be replaced by new ones. Instead, especially in the electric power generation industry, old sources were nursed along. There is no doubt that the NSR program, by creating a sizeable regulatory gap between old and new sources, has delayed the replacement of old power plants by new ones. According to some analysts, the stringency of the NSR rules may be part of the problem; demanding the greatest emission reductions feasible from new plants may have the counterintuitive effect of impeding the adoption of new technologies that are both cleaner and more efficient than current ones, but not clean enough to satisfy NSR requirements. Because modifications can trigger NSR, the program may also discourage upgrades of existing plants that would be both economically and environmentally beneficial. Finally, because pollution control facilities like SO_2 scrubbers increase operating costs, NSR can encourage utilities to run their older plants at higher capacity than their newer ones. See Robert N. Stavins, Vintage Differentiated Environmental Regulation, 25 Stan. Envtl. L. J. 29 50–52 (2006).

6. *The NSR enforcement initiative.* For two decades, NSR had almost no application to the electric power industry. When changes were made to power plants, their operators offset new emissions with greater control elsewhere within the plant, or segmented what was essentially one project into a number of small ones in order to claim the protection of the "routine maintenance" exception. Furthermore, utilities simply undertook retrofitting and modernization without regard to whether NSR was required. See Nathaniel Lord Martin, The Reform of New Source Review: Toward a More Balanced Approach, 23 Stan. Envtl. L. J. 351, 363 (2004). As a result, electric generating units, perhaps the most important single industrial source of criteria air pollutants, remained largely outside the new source requirements.

In 1999, New York, a handful of other states and EPA began an enforcement offensive, filing a series of lawsuits against utilities alleging violations of the NSR provisions. The utilities responded in court and in the political realm. With the election of George W. Bush, the latter efforts bore fruit. The Bush administration proposed legislation (dubbed "Clear Skies") that among other things would have limited the application of NSR to utilities. Congress declined to enact the legislation, but the administration, over the objections of then-EPA administrator Christine Todd Whitman, put forth new NSR regulations making many of the same changes. The new rules, finalized shortly after Whitman's resignation, attempted to legalize much of the conduct that formed the basis of the NSR enforcement initiative. The Department of Justice declined to drop the enforcement cases, but did take the new rules into account in setting its enforcement and settlement priorities. Many of the cases were settled, including one that produced the largest environmental settlement in U.S. history. In October 2007, American Electric Power agreeing to spend $4.6 billion over 12 years to install pollution control equipment. AEP also agreed to pay a $15 million fine and contribute $60 million to environmental mitigation projects. In return, EPA agreed not to take further enforcement action based on any modifications through 2018. Juliet Eilperin, EPA Joins Settlement of Lawsuit But Adds a Waiver, Washington Post, Oct. 11, 2003, at A3. The other plaintiffs did not promise not to bring future suits. The Obama Administration, in addition to reversing several Bush Administration regulatory efforts, renewed NSR enforcement efforts.

7. *Immortal grandfathers?* Must there be an end to grandfathering at some point? EPA's answer, at least in the Bush Administration, was no. In denying a petition for reconsideration of its 2003 routine maintenance exception, EPA said:

> We do not believe, however, the modification provisions of the CAA should be interpreted to ensure that all major facilities either must eventually trigger NSR or must degrade in performance, safety, and reliability. In fact, such an interpretation cannot be squared with the plain language of the CAA. An existing source triggers NSR only if it makes a physical or operational change that results in an emissions increase. Thus, a facility can conceivably continue to operate indefinitely without triggering NSR—making as many physical or operational changes as it desires—as long as the changes do not result in emissions increases. This outcome is an unavoidable consequence of the plain statutory language and is at odds with the notion that Congress intended that every major source would eventually trigger NSR or otherwise fall into disrepair. Moreover, there is nothing in the legislative history of the 1977 Amendments, which created the NSR program, to suggest that Congress intended to force all then-existing sources to go through NSR. To the extent that some members of Congress expressed that view during the debate over the 1990 amend-

ments, such statements are not probative of what Congress meant in 1977.

70 Fed. Reg. 33838, 33844 (June 10, 2005).

What do you suppose Congress (or more realistically individual legislators) did mean in 1977? To the extent that legislators simply did not anticipate the long lifespan of old generators, should they have done so? If they anticipated the problem, how might they have resolved it, while still avoiding immediately subjecting existing operations to intense regulation?

At this point, should Congress amend the CAA to change the grandfathering provisions? What changes would you recommend? Is there a better answer to the problem of the "big dirties" (the grandfathered power plants) than tweaking the NSR rules? Would an emissions tax provide better incentives? Would it be politically acceptable? Should grandfathering gradually be phased out, with the oldest sources (for which capital expenses have presumably been fully amortized) forced to modernize first? Will SIPs eventually have to control emissions from these sources?

8. *Power plants and carbon emissions.* Coal-based power generation accounts for a shockingly high proportion of greenhouse gas emissions in the United States. Coal-fired electric power plants account for nearly one-third of total anthropogenic CO_2 emissions in the United States. Energy Information Administration, Annual Energy Outlook 2011 (Apr. 2011).

It turns out that the Clean Air Act's grandfathering provisions do not necessarily shield existing power plants from regulation of greenhouse gas emissions. Section 111(d) of the Clean Air Act calls on EPA to establish a procedure requiring states to submit plans for establishing performance standards for emission of pollutants not regulated by NAAQS or the hazardous air pollutant provisions from existing sources if similar new sources would be subject to NSPS. EPA has agreed, in litigation settlements, both to develop NSPS for greenhouse gas emissions from electric power plants, and to issue a proposed § 111(d) rule for existing power plants. See www.epa.gov/airquality/pdfs/boilerghgsettlement.pdf.

SECTION 5.   TRADABLE EMISSION PERMITS: USING THE POWER OF THE MARKET

Economists have long touted the advantages of market forces over command-and-control regulatory approaches to air pollution. They argue that the market, when it is functioning well, is a far more efficient allocator of scarce resources (such as clean air) than is the government. Command-and-control approaches tend to treat all sources within a class alike, ignoring potentially substantial differences in compliance costs. The market can adjust for such differences. In addition, putting the market to work can encourage identification of viable pollution control techniques that may otherwise be overlooked. Under a command-and-control regimen which relies on regulators to identify control technologies, pollution sources may find it economically advantageous not to develop, or even to hide the existence of, such technologies. Market incentives put the profit motive to work, encouraging industry, which has the greatest access to knowledge of control technologies, to identify and improve those technologies. Furthermore, by making pollution control possible at less total cost to society, market forces should reduce political opposition and attempts to evade the law.

Two major approaches can bring market forces to bear on pollution or other environmental problems. The first is direct economic incentives in the form of taxes and subsidies, which encourage market actors to take into account the effects of their actions on environmental quality. Subsidies have long been a feature of pollution control policy, in the form of tax credits and federal grants to states or industries. Their effectiveness is obviously limited by the extent of the resources government is prepared to apply to the problem. Taxes have never been a significant aspect of U.S. pollution policy because, although they are theoretically a very efficient means of addressing the problem, they are (or at least are thought to be) politically unpalatable.

The second major approach is the creation of tradable property rights or entitlements. By the late 1980s, a number of economists had suggested that the air pollution problem could be addressed by creation of a market in rights to pollute. In theory, such a market would facilitate efficient reduction of air pollution, encouraging those who can control their pollution at least cost to sell pollution credits to those whose pollution is more difficult to control. Suppose, for example, that two electric utility plants, Plants A and B, each emit 110 tons annually of SO_2. Suppose further that Plant A could cut its emissions by acquiring and installing scrubbers at a cost of $1,000 annually per ton of emissions removed. Plant B, because it is newer, designed differently, or uses cleaner-burning fuel, can reduce its emissions at a cost of $500/ton. If the government imposes a command-and-control regulation limiting each plant to a maximum of 105 tons of SO_2 emissions, Plant A will spend $5,000 to achieve that reduction, and plant B will spend $2,500. The net result will be ten tons less SO_2 emitted annually, at a total pollution control cost of $7,500.

If, on the other hand, the government gives each source tradable allowances to emit 105 tons of SO_2, Plant B can cut back to 100 tons, at a total cost of $5,000, and sell its extra 5 tons of allowances to Plant A. Under this scenario, the total pollution control cost for removing the same 10 tons of SO_2 from the atmosphere is only $5,000. In effect, Plant A will pay some part of this cost by paying Plant B an amount between $2500 (the minimum B will accept) and $5000 (the maximum A will pay) for the 5 allowances it purchases.

Emission trading was used on a small scale prior to the 1990 Clean Air Act Amendments through application of the bubble, netting, and offset concepts to new source review. The 1990 Amendments, however, implemented the first large-scale test of this strategy through the Title IV acid rain control program. See CAA §§ 401–416 (42 U.S.C. § 7651–7651o).

Acid rain (more accurately termed acid deposition, since acid compounds can be deposited in dry as well as wet form) was first recognized as a serious problem in the 1970s, when its effects on vegetation, lake ecology, and building materials and paints became apparent in the northeastern United States and Canada. The problem was traced to emissions of SO_2 and NO_x originating in the midwestern states and transported in the atmosphere to the northeast. Electric utility plants, which burn large quantities of fossil fuels, were the primary source of those emissions. In 1985 electric utilities accounted for more than two-thirds of the total nationwide emissions of SO_2, and roughly 36% of the total emissions of NO_x.

Title IV of the 1990 Amendments established a nationwide cap on SO_2 and NO_x emissions from fossil-fuel-powered utilities, and created tradable allowances to emit SO_2. Each unit allowance permits the emission of one ton of SO_2 during or after the calendar year of issuance. The total number of allowances was limited, creating an emissions cap, and further reduced in 2000. Allowances were initially allocated to utilities based on past fuel consumption. See CAA § 402(4) (42 U.S.C. § 7651a(4)). Once issued, allowances are freely tradable.

The Title IV program reduced emissions from 1990 levels faster and at dramatically lower cost than anticipated. By 2005, SO_2 emissions from the power plants included in the program had fallen 35% from 1990 levels. EPA, Acid Rain Program, 2005 Progress Report 2 (October 2006). The program is generally regarded as a triumph of cost-effectiveness. A 2005 study estimated that the program would provide benefits worth $122 million annually at a cost of about $3 million annually when its reductions were fully implemented in 2010. Lauraine G. Chestnut and David M. Mills, A Fresh Look at the Benefits and Costs of the U.S. Acid Rain Program, 77 Envtl. Mgmt. 252 (2005). Some of the cost savings, however, may not be attributable to emission trading. At roughly the same time that the acid rain program was initiated, low sulfur coal became more widely available at lower cost, reducing the need to retrofit power plants with scrubbers. Curtis A. Moore, The 1990 Clean Air Act Amendments: Failing the Acid Test, 34 Envtl. L. Rep. 10366, 10379 (2004).

Despite substantial SO_2 emission reductions, acid rain remains a serious problem. A 2001 study by leading acid rain researchers concluded that power plants must cut SO_2 emissions an additional 80% in order to allow sensitive waters and soils in the northeast to recover from the effects of past acid rain. See Kevin Krajick, *Long–Term Data Show Lingering Effects from Acid Rain*, 292 SCIENCE 195 (2001). A substantial proportion of lakes in New England and the Adirondack Mountains of New York remain acidic; their recovery will, at best, take decades. Curtis A. Moore, The 1990 Clean Air Act Amendments: Failing the Acid Test, 34 Environmental Law Reporter (ELI) 10366, 10367 (2004). Moreover NO_x emissions, which also cause acid rain, continue to increase. The impacts of NO_x-driven acid rain are beginning to be noticeable in the west, once thought to be immune from the problem. EPA is studying the possibility of creating a secondary NAAQS covering oxides of nitrogen and sulfur to deal with acidifying deposition. EPA, Secondary National Ambient Air Quality Standards for Oxides of Nitrogen and Sulfur, 76 Fed. Reg. 46,084 (August 1, 2011).

There is also some evidence that trading has exacerbated other pollution problems. According to a report prepared for the Environmental Integrity Project in 2001, SO_2 trading, by allowing more than 40% of the power plants covered by the program to actually increase their emissions, has led to increased respiratory problems and even mortality in the vicinity of these plants. Abt Associates, Inc., Particulate–Related Health Impacts of Emissions in 2001 from 41 Major U.S. Power Plants (Nov. 2002). The health problems are linked to the fact that SO_2 and NO_x emissions from power plants react with ammonia in the atmosphere to create $PM_{2.5}$.

Although the acid rain program is the largest scale, and best known, trading program under the Clean Air Act, it is far from the only one. Trading programs were elements of the phase-outs of lead from gasoline and of ozone-depleting substances under the Montreal Protocol. Trading within and between firms, through bubbles, netting, and offsets, has long been a part of New Source Review. See EPA, Emissions Trading Policy Statement: General Principles for Creation, Banking, and Use of Emission Reduction Credits, 51 Fed. Reg. 43814 (Dec. 4, 1986). Trading programs can be created in state SIPs; the best-known experiment with trading to achieve the NAAQS is Southern California's Regional Clean Air Incentives Market (RECLAIM), discussed in more detail below.

Beyond the Clean Air Act, cap-and-trade has become a popular strategy for addressing a variety of environmental problems. The excerpts below explore its advantages and shortcomings.

David M. Driesen, Is Emissions Trading an Economic Incentive Program?: Replacing the Command and Control/Economic Incentive Dichotomy

55 Washington & Lee Law Review 289, 313–319, 324–338 (1998).

* * *

The literature often fails to address adequately the question of whether emissions trading, now almost two decades old, has, in fact, stimulated innovation or even produced the emission reductions that comparable traditional regulation would generate. Unfortunately, the history of emissions trading reveals no evidence that emissions trading and its precursors have stimulated innovation or environmental performance superior to comparable traditional regulation.

The empirical literature raises especially serious questions about whether bubbles have spurred adequate environmental performance. The few studies of bubble implementation reveal that polluters often could not document claims that they had made the emission reductions that regulatory requirements underlying bubbles had required. Polluters almost never undertook fresh pollution control projects to satisfy these regulations.

Instead, they claimed credits for incidental reductions that would have occurred without the regulation. For example, polluters often claimed credits for routine business decisions to slow down production or shut down facilities. Without the ability to trade, the underlying regulation would trigger a fresh reduction that would supplement any incidental reductions.

* * *

The 1990 Amendments to the Clean Air Act create a system of transferrable emissions allowances to reduce sulfur dioxide emissions from large electric utilities, the most prominent contributors to acid rain. Two features make the acid rain program far superior to EPA's bubbles. First, the program caps the number of allowances for large utility units at a number representing a large cut in emissions. * * * Second, the acid rain program requires the use of continuous emission monitoring. Because actual baseline emission rates in electric utilities are known, traded SO_2 allowances will likely reflect actual emission reductions. * * *

Thus far, the acid rain program has worked rather well. Plants use well-known methods of emission control to avoid exceeding allowances. The plants have not employed substantial innovation, but such widespread diffusion of standard technologies may represent a perfectly adequate way of meeting many environmental goals.

Actual compliance with the acid rain requirements has cost much less than government officials anticipated when Congress established the program. Economic incentive proponents credit the emissions trading mechanism for lowering costs. In fact, few trades occurred in the program's first years. Studies comparing the actual compliance costs of traditional regulation to pre-regulation estimates regularly show that regulators and industry greatly overestimate costs. Hence, the low cost of sulfur dioxide control relative to estimates at the time Congress adopted the acid rain program may reflect a common feature of all regulation rather than some unique attribute of emissions trading.

* * *

[T]raditional regulation failed to provide an incentive for continuous environmental improvement. Once a polluter complies with a traditional regulation (with an adequate cushion) no further incentive exists to make more reductions unless doing so saves money. * * *

An emissions trading program necessarily includes requirements for specific reductions from pollution sources within the trading program and allows sources to avoid the limits by trading with sources of credits. This means that some governmental body must set quantitative limits for specific pollution sources.

Once a pollution source has complied with the underlying limits, no further incentive exists to make additional reductions. The incentive to provide reductions, either by making them at the source or purchasing credits from elsewhere, continues throughout the compliance period defined by the underlying regulations. The incentive's duration precisely matches that of a traditional regulation with the same compliance period. Once the polluters regulated by a trading program have reached an equilibrium providing the reductions that the governmental body required, no incentive for further reductions exists.

* * *

Some commentators argue that emissions trading provides a continuing incentive to reduce because the number of permits remain limited. Hence, economic growth will increase the demand for permits, raise the price, and provide a greater incentive for polluters to reduce their emissions.

Limiting the number of permits does not create an incentive for continuous net emission reductions below the equilibrium level required by the program. The limit creates an incentive for permit holders to reduce emissions only to the extent that others will increase emissions. Net emissions would remain consistent with those authorized by the promulgated emission limits.

* * *

If an administrative body sets the limits underlying a trading program, then the problems of the complexity of administrative environmental decision making and the attendant delay may infect these decisions, just as they infect decision making in traditional programs. * * *

In addition to the usual issues that arise in a traditional regulation, such as how costly reductions will be, how much benefit they will yield, and whether they are technologically achievable, arcane disputes arise about baseline emission levels, creditable reductions and the like in emissions trading programs. Sources subject to trading have economic incentives to seek rules establishing the cheapest possible method of complying with a trading program. The cheapest methods involve claiming compliance without doing anything at all to reduce emissions. For example, a participant might claim compliance by claiming credits for reductions that already occurred or for reductions that can occur through normal events in the business cycle, such as production declines and plant shutdowns without accepting debits for other normal events. Demands to write rules that allow evasion of actual emission reductions can consume regulators designing programs, increase uncertainty, and delay progress.

Efforts to establish an international trading regime for greenhouse gases, for example, may generate fresh evasion problems. United States utilities would like to claim credit for activities abroad in order to justify avoiding potential limits on their greenhouse gas emissions at home. They may have incentives to claim credits for their role in projects that increase worldwide CO_2 emissions, principally construction of new coal burning power plants. Unless the underlying emissions trading rules prohibit this explicitly, they may claim a credit representing the difference between the project built and a dirtier project that could have been built if less modern equipment was used. * * *

Utilities also have an economic incentive to seek credits for helping forest protection efforts abroad. If the government allows them to substitute credits for inexpensive forestry projects for more expensive pollution control efforts, they will save money. Since forests do sequester carbon emissions that would otherwise warm the atmosphere this seems sensible at first glance. But will the protection of any given forest have any effect on global carbon levels? If demand simply shifts to other unprotected forests then the protection effort may not decrease net deforestation at all. Rather, the protection effort may protect one area while channeling more deforestation into areas open to logging. Hence, emissions trading may provide incentives not just to make reductions elsewhere, but to claim credits for other activities that do not have comparable value.

Increased reliance on emissions trading may create a fresh incentive to resist emission limitations. Polluters may want to avoid regulation of pollution sources they own in order to protect potential sources of future credits. Thus, emissions trading will offer less of an incentive for continuous improvement (i.e. beginning before and continuing after compliance deadlines in the regulation) than comparable traditional regulation. Emissions trading, rather than providing an antidote to the problems of complex decision making that plague traditional regulation, provides a layer of additional complications and occasions for dispute.

Emissions trading will contribute to quicker realization of environmental goals if regulators make the underlying emissions limitations more stringent than comparable traditional regulation. If emissions trading generates large cost savings, as proponents claim, program designers can demand more emission reductions than they could under a traditional regulation and still save polluters money.

Typically, cost considerations constrain the stringency of environmental regulation. If the sources with high marginal control costs need not pay that cost because they can pay facilities with lower marginal costs to reduce in their stead, then there is no justification for a standard driven by the high marginal costs of the polluters with high local costs or even by their technological inability to meet the standard at the source. * * * Using cost savings to increase stringency in this manner could speed achievement of environmental goals, but emissions trading without this feature does nothing to overcome delay.

* * *

A trading program's ability to motivate innovation and good environmental performance depends on at least three factors: (1) the stringency of the emission limitations governing pollution sources; (2) the size of possible monetary penalties; and (3) the likelihood that the government or citizens will catch non-complying polluters. If regulators use emissions trading as a means of providing the same total emission reductions as a traditional program, emissions trading may provide less potent negative economic incentives to reduce pollution than a comparable traditional regulation, because the emission reduction obligation and monetary penalties may remain the same while evading regulatory obligations becomes easier.

It is easier for polluters to evade regulatory obligations when the complexity of enforcement increases, thereby decreasing the chances that a government enforcer will have time to detect failures to provide contemplated real reductions. Emissions trading requires an enforcer wishing to determine whether a buyer of emissions credits has satisfied an obligation to verify the amount of reductions foregone at the buyer's plant (which requires knowledge of current and baseline emissions from the uncontrolled source) and to evaluate whether the claimed reductions occurred at the source of the credits. The enforcer must run numerous other checks to make sure that no double counting or other gaming is going on. Hence, agencies relying upon trading need more resources to verify compliance than agencies relying upon traditional regulation.

Evasion of real emission reductions is easier in programs that do not require strict monitoring of pollution from all potential sources of credits and debits. Facilities subject to an emissions trading regime without adequate monitoring may pollute more than the law permits, because no monitoring detects the exceedances, just as in traditional regulation. Moreover, these undetected noncompliant facilities may claim emission credits for emitting less than the standard requires. The sale of these credits will justify increased pollution at a second facility. Hence, inadequate monitoring may prove twice as detrimental in an emissions trading scheme because monitoring inadequacies tend to permit increased emissions at one facility and simultaneously justify a second increase at some other facility. This particular problem, however, may not apply to emissions trading programs that feature accurate, reliable monitoring.

* * *

Because a well designed trading program may induce pollution sources with low marginal control costs to go beyond regulatory limits to a greater degree than they would under a traditional regulation, commentators focusing only on the low-cost sources have argued that emissions trading creates greater incentives for technological innovation than traditional regulation. As some economists have realized, this argument ignores the incentive for high-cost sources to avoid pollution reduction activities. Trading reduces the incentive for high-costs sources to apply new technology.

In theory, emissions trading probably weakens net incentives for innovation. If a regulation allows facilities to use trading to meet standards, the low-cost facilities tend to provide more of the total reductions than they would provide under a comparable traditional regulation. Conversely, the high-cost facilities will provide less of the total required reductions than they would have under a comparable traditional regulation. The low-cost facilities probably have a greater ability to provide reductions without substantial innovation than high-cost facilities. A high-cost facility may need to innovate to escape the high costs of routine compliance; the low-cost facility does not have this same motivation. Hence, emissions trading, by shifting reductions from high-cost to low-cost facilities, may lessen the incentives for innovation.

* * *

These observations are not meant to suggest that emissions trading is bad. Lowering short-term costs is desirable. But, short-term savings do not necessarily coincide with the encouragement of technological advancement or long-term savings. Significant up-front investment and stringent technical demands often play an important role in stimulating technological advances.

* * *

Richard Toshiyuki Drury, Michael E. Belliveau, J. Scott Kuhn & Shipra Bansal, Pollution Trading and Environmental Injustice: Los Angeles' Failed Experiment in Air Quality Policy

9 Duke Envtl. L. & Pol'y Forum 231 (1999).

* * * The Los Angeles, California, region provides an ideal testing ground for environmental policies. Los Angeles' environmental problems are severe, its regulatory agencies are sophisticated, its resources are relatively ample, and the region's population is multi-racial and economically diverse. Los Angeles and the State of California continue to be national and international pacesetters for the development of new air pollution control policies and technologies. Thus, the effect of Los Angeles' pollution trading programs on air quality, public health, and environmental justice will help inform the future of this market-based approach.

The South Coast Air Basin, which includes the metropolitan Los Angeles area, suffers the worst air quality in the nation. For example, nearly 6,000 premature deaths caused by particulate air pollution occur in the Los Angeles area each year, representing about a tenth of such fatalities nationwide. Additionally, millions of residents of the region are exposed to unhealthy levels of ground level ozone, which causes aching lungs, wheezing, coughing, headache and permanent lung tissue scarring. Levels of toxic chemicals in the air pose significant risks for causing cancer and other chronic diseases. This dangerous mix of air pollutants, which are emitted by multitudes of factories, cars, and other sources, seriously threatens public health and well being.

A richly diverse, multi-racial and multi-ethnic population lives, works, and plays in the Los Angeles region, raising the environmental justice concern that people of color and poor people are unfairly exposed to more air pollution than others. Therefore, air pollution reduction strategies, including pollution trading programs, should be evaluated not only for their efficacy in reducing air pollution, but also for their effect on achieving environmental justice. * * *

A. Pollution Trading Comes of Age in Los Angeles: From Rule 1610 to RECLAIM and Beyond

* * * Following a pattern shaped by the policy agenda of the largest industrial polluters, a group of market-based regulations centered on pollution trading have been adopted for the South Coast Air Basin. In 1993, SCAQMD approved the first old vehicle pollution trading program in the country, known as Rule 1610 or the "car scrapping program". * * *

Under Rule 1610, "licensed car scrappers" can purchase and destroy old cars. SCAQMD then grants the scrapper emissions credits based on the projected emissions of the car had it not been destroyed, which may then be sold to stationary source polluters (e.g. factories). The stationary sources use the pollution credits to avoid on-site emission reductions that would be required under the technology-based regulatory regime. Rule 1610 requires polluters to purchase credits representing twenty percent more emission reductions than would be achieved through compliance with technology-based regulations for their plant. Although industrial plants avoid emission reductions, the scrapping of older, high polluting cars should result in greater air quality improvements at a lower cost than regulatory mandates.

SCAQMD then adopted the centerpiece of its pollution trading strategy, the Regional Clean Air Incentives Market (RECLAIM), the world's first urban smog trading program. RECLAIM replaced many of SCAQMD's technology-based regulations aimed at reducing emissions of sulfur oxides (SO_x) and nitrogen oxides (NO_x). RECLAIM, a "declining cap and trade" program, mandates annual emission reductions for industry but provides them the flexibility to achieve that goal by either purchasing emission reduction credits or by reducing their own pollution. Under RECLAIM, SCAQMD allocates pollution credits to each major source facility in the region based on its historic level of emissions. Each facility has three options: 1) it can use all of its credits and pollute up to the level they allow; 2) it can reduce its pollution and sell the excess credits to other facilities; or 3) it can increase emissions relative to its initial endowment of credits by buying credits from other facilities. Each year SCAQMD decreases the number of credits allocated by the program, forcing facilities either to decrease their pollution or purchase credits from other facilities. As the number of available credits decreases, their market price should rise, increasing the market incentive for companies to reduce pollution rather than purchase credits. According to its supporters, by 2003 RECLAIM should spur the lowest cost pollution reduction among individual industrial plants and slash aggregate emissions of NO_x by seventy-five percent and SO_x by sixty percent.

* * *

B. The Harsh Reality: Problems with Pollution Trading in Los Angeles

Evidence indicates that pollution trading programs in Los Angeles are plagued with problems. Although the programs have succeeded in saving money for industry, they have not effectively reduced emissions and have not promoted technology innovation or public participation. Instead, they have further concentrated the region's pollution in lower income communities and given industry a "free ride" from otherwise obligatory emissions reduction schedules.

1. Toxic Hot-spots and Environmental Injustice: The Mad Science of Pollution Trading

Pollution trading programs can unfairly concentrate pollution in communities where factories purchase emissions reduction credits rather than reduce actual emissions. These localized health risks from pollution sources, or "toxic hot-spots," tend to be overlooked by policy makers focused on regional air quality concerns. However, the disproportionate burden thrust on communities surrounding major pollution emitters takes its toll in the form of increased risks of toxic exposure and damage to human health. Furthermore, it is environmentally unjust when these communities enduring localized toxic hot-spots are overwhelmingly low income and populated by people of color. Such hot-spots can be worsened when pollution trading programs ignore the differences in chemical hazards posed by the pollutants reduced to earn credits and the pollutants emitted through the purchase of credits. The problem of hot-spots is further complicated by the emission of co-pollutants and precursors, which may increase exposure to certain types of chemicals in downwind communities where pollution is concentrated.

SCAQMD's pollution trading programs have resulted in the creation of toxic hot-spots by concentrating pollution in communities surrounding major sources of pollution. Rule 1610 provides the clearest example. SCAQMD studies indicate that cars destroyed through the Rule 1610 program were registered throughout the air quality management district, a four-county region. Air pollution from these automobiles would have also been distributed throughout this region. By contrast, stationary sources in Los Angeles are densely clustered in only a few communities in this four-county region. As a result of these distribution patterns, Rule 1610 effectively takes pollution formerly distributed throughout the region by automobiles, and concentrates that pollution in the communities surrounding stationary sources.

Most of the emissions credits purchased to avoid stationary source controls have been purchased by four oil companies: Unocal, Chevron, Ultramar and GATX. Of these four companies, three are located close together in the communities of Wilmington and San Pedro; the fourth facility, Chevron, is located nearby in El Segundo. These companies have used pollution credits to avoid installing pollution control equipment that captures toxic gases released during oil tanker loading at their marine terminals. When loading oil tankers, toxic gases are forced out of the tanker and into the air, exposing workers and nearby residents to toxic vapors, including benzene, a known human carcinogen. Thus, by using pollution credits, these companies are allowed to avoid reducing local emissions of hazardous chemicals in exchange for reducing regional auto emissions. As a result of Rule 1610, the four oil companies created a toxic chemical hot-spot around their marine terminals, exposing workers and nearby residents to elevated health risks.

* * *

The demographics of this hot-spot area starkly contrast with that of the metropolitan Los Angeles region. The residents living in San Pedro and Wilmington, which host a majority of the oil companies emitting hazardous toxic chemicals, are overwhelmingly Latino. Furthermore, the racial composition of communities living near three of the marine terminals ranges from 75 to 90 percent people of color, while the entire South Coast Air Basin has a population of only 36 percent people of color.

* * *

2. *Market Incentives Run Amok: Fraud and Manipulation*

* * *

The Los Angeles pollution trading experience with car scrapping has been plagued by a history of under-reporting of actual emissions from industry and an over-reporting of claimed emission reductions from cars.

* * *

Rather than measure actual emissions released, companies estimate emissions using emission factors developed by the Western States Petroleum Association. Emissions factors are surrogate estimates of emissions based on activity level. For example, engineers may estimate that a small industrial boiler will release so many pounds of NO_x for every barrel of fuel oil burned. Emission factors are hotly argued among technical specialists from different fields and change as new information becomes available. Emissions factors are poor surrogates for actual measurements. With margins of error ranging from fifty percent to one hundred percent, emissions factors are highly uncertain, making claimed emission reduction difficult to verify. They can readily be adjusted to report emissions as being higher or lower, since at best they represent educated guesses of actual emissions. Source testing, which measures actual emissions, was required to ensure compliance with the technology-based emission limits set under Rule 1142 for marine terminals.

Information recently obtained through the Freedom of Information Act reveals that the oil companies did, in fact, measure their emissions. When the actual measurements were compared to reported emissions based on industry emissions factors, striking differences were revealed. Oil companies under-reported their oil tanker emissions by factors between 10 and 1000. As a result, the oil companies purchased between 10 and 1000 times too few credits from scrapping old, high-polluting cars to offset their tanker pollution. * * *

Exacerbating the huge gap between actual emissions and credits purchased by polluters, credit generators—the car scrappers—have abused the system. Many of the cars allegedly destroyed through the Rule 1610 program were not, in fact, destroyed, according to Bruce Lohmann,

SCAQMD's Chief Inspector for the Rule 1610 program. While the car bodies were crushed, many of the engines which produce the pollution were not. Instead, many of those engines were sold for re-use, despite the fact that pollution credits for destroying the car had been granted by SCAQMD. EPA has refused to approve the Rule 1610 program precisely because car engines are not always destroyed.

Several assumptions underlying the Rule 1610 program are also dubious. In order to quantify the credits generated by scrapping a vehicle, SCAQMD assumes that the old cars would have been driven approximately 4,000 to 5,000 miles annually for an additional three years and that the owner of the car would replace it with a "fleet average" automobile. Although these assumptions were based on studies of old car driving patterns, they have not been borne out in reality.

According to Inspector Lohmann and an audit conducted by SCAQMD, many of the cars scrapped through the Rule 1610 program were at the end of their useful life, and would have been destroyed through natural attrition. Each year, between 100,000 to 200,000 old vehicles are naturally scrapped or abandoned without the intervention of the Rule 1610 trading programs. No "surplus" credits should be counted from scrapping one of those thousands of cars, since those reductions would have naturally occurred. Since less than 23,000 cars have been destroyed through the Rule 1610 program in its five-year life, most of these cars are probably among those that would have been destroyed even without the program. However, market forces encourage people who were planning to scrap an old car for its $50 value as scrap metal to obtain $600 for it through the Rule 1610 program instead. This practice is encouraged in Los Angeles because many licensed scrappers are operated jointly with junkyards, where people bring their old cars to be destroyed. While this is rational economic behavior for the car owner, it creates false emission credits.

According to Lohmann and SCAQMD, of the cars that were not at the end of their lives, many were not regularly driven and would not have been driven for another three years. The Rule 1610 formula, therefore, over-allocates emission credits generated by destroying these cars. Inspector Lohmann reported many cases in which inoperable cars were brought to the car scrapping facility and minor repairs were made solely for the purpose of obtaining the $600 payment from the scrapping program. Obviously, such inoperable cars were not generating any pollution at all, but were merely collecting dust in someone's garage. * * *

3. *Distortion of the Market: Hot Air and Phantom Reductions*

In addition to fraud by market participants, "cap and trade" strategies, like Los Angeles' RECLAIM program, are plagued by a broader form of institutional manipulation. This manipulation takes the form of 'phantom reductions' in air emissions—reductions that exist on paper only. Under RECLAIM, allowable emissions have declined each year as required by regulation. However, because emissions reduction credits were initially allocated in an amount significantly inflated above actual emissions, early 'reductions' in emissions were illusory. In the first three years of the

RECLAIM program, actual industrial NO_x emissions have declined by at most three percent, while allowable emissions have been reduced on paper by about thirty percent. In the global context, the term "hot air" has been used to describe the vesting of certain countries like Russia with excess credits. Not only does the trading in hot air credits represent illusory environmental gains, the excess allocation drives down the price of credits, reducing the motivation to invest in actual emission reductions or technological innovation.

By inflating the initial allocation of credits, pollution trading programs like RECLAIM tend to reward the worst polluters. Rather than allocate emissions credits based on current actual emissions levels, SCAQMD allocated its initial round of credits based on historic emissions levels. SCAQMD allowed polluters to base their credit allocation on the highest year of emissions out of the last five years, because industry successfully argued that emissions should not be capped at current levels due to an economic recession that affected California before the RECLAIM program's adoption.

* * *

With the supply of RECLAIM credits so far in excess of demand, more than eighty-five percent of the NO_x credits traded (in tons) were sold for $0. Therefore, no rational company would reduce emissions when other facilities are giving credits away for free. In fact, a company would be at a competitive disadvantage if it did invest in pollution control in such a market. * * *

Not only were the RECLAIM trading credits over-allocated, they were given away, or grandfathered. In contrast, to internalize the costs of air pollution and to create proper price signals, many economists have called for an auctioning off of pollution credits to the highest bidder. The fees paid for emission credits would function like pollution taxes to encourage further emission reductions thereby saving money. Revenues could be used to fund monitoring and enforcement of market trading rules and to compensate workers and consumers who are adversely effected by the pass-through costs of pollution permits. By giving away a public resource, pollution-free air, for free rather than charging the highest price the market will bear, SCAQMD has subsidized industrial pollution and missed an important opportunity to harness market forces for environmental improvement.

* * *

III. The Trouble With Trading

A. Morality and the 'Right' to Pollute

Although it appears to have become socially unacceptable to discuss the morality of public policy, this poses an important obstacle for pollution trading. Pollution trading removes the social stigma associated with pollution. Rather than treating pollution as a social ill that we should attempt to eliminate to the extent feasible, trading programs turn pollution into another commodity, to be traded when economically efficiency dictates. What is wrong with polluting, when only money for the required pollution credits stands between socially acceptable behavior and socially aberrant activity? * * *

Ultimately, no regulatory program can survive if it does not generate morally acceptable outcomes. Economic efficiency alone does not create a sound basis for public policy if it results in immoral results such as toxic hot-spots in disempowered communities, fraudulent emission reductions, or actual increases in pollution. As domestic environmental agencies and the international community consider expanding pollution trading to combat regional pollution and global climate change, the social and moral costs should be fully weighed, not just the economic benefits.

B. Environmental Injustice

* * * The Los Angeles experiment shows that emissions trading programs can exchange small reductions in widespread pollution for increased exposure to concentrated, and often more toxic, pollution in the neighborhoods surrounding large industrial facilities. The resulting exposures to low-income communities of color make this a matter of environmental injustice.

* * *

Only recently has EPA acknowledged the legitimacy of the environmental justice impacts associated with pollution trading. They concede that no proposed or existing pollution trading program contains appropriate safeguards against concentrating pollution in low-income communities of color. The concerns raised about hot-spots, environmental justice, and the efficacy of the Los Angeles trading programs have given pause to EPA's plans to grant the necessary approval for new emissions trading programs. Based on the Los Angeles experience, EPA has pledged to revise its guidance for Economic Incentive Programs to ensure that the environmental justice impacts of pollution trading are assessed in advance and prevented or mitigated.

Whether this can be achieved remains to be seen. Environmental injustice may be an institutional feature of emissions trading programs, because economic models do not have adequate means to quantify values such as justice and fairness.

C. Pollution Trading: Many Promises, Poor Results

* * *

Driesen argues that pollution trading will actually stifle innovation by encouraging pursuit of cheap fixes rather than innovative and enduring solutions. * * *

The RECLAIM program in Los Angeles provides a good example. The average cost of best available control technology for NO_x was about \$12,500 per ton at the time RECLAIM was adopted. That is more than fifty times the average price of current 1997 NO_x credits under RECLAIM's emissions trading program. Rather than innovate, many large and some small firms have chosen to purchase cheap credits. * * *

Public participation is a tenet of democratic government and environmental policy making. Some academics argue that pollution trading enhances meaningful public participation. Yet, existing pollution trading programs effectively exclude the public (and to a large extent, government agencies) from the decision making process about industrial pollution.

Most states have permitting procedures through which affected community members can advocate for pollution control requirements on facilities. However, pollution trading allows facilities to avoid those permit requirements—usually without the knowledge or involvement of the affected community. Pollution trades made pursuant to Rule 1610 and RECLAIM are not subject to public review or comment. * * *

* * * The RECLAIM program recognized the need to verify that trading credits represented real emission reductions, not just progress on paper. RECLAIM requires that major sources use continuous emissions monitors (CEMs) to measure NO_x and SO_x releases from industrial facilities. * * *

However, an audit of the RECLAIM program found that industry has been slow to comply with the CEM requirements. After the first year, thirty percent of the RECLAIM facilities had still not installed properly operating CEMs. Although most CEMs are now certified, electronic data reporting requirements were still being violated forty percent of the time by major sources, and eighty percent of the time by small sources. As a result of poor compliance with emissions reporting requirements and continued industry opposition to comprehensive monitoring, SCAQMD's ability to verify claimed emission reductions from large sources of NO_x and SO_x remains in doubt.

* * *

Under the command and control technology-based approach, emissions uncertainties are less relevant. The important question is whether the pollution control action was taken or not. Regardless of the pollution control strategy employed, it is a simple matter to verify whether equipment was installed and is properly operating, or a process changed or a raw material substituted. Although uncertainty remains over actual emissions, verification of compliance with technology-based pollution control requirements ensures that emissions have declined, usually by significant amounts.

* * *

NOTES AND QUESTIONS

1. *The morality of markets.* Some environmentalists have opposed emission trading programs on the ground that it is morally wrong to grant rights to pollute. Others question whether trading will reduce the moral force of pollution control efforts. Do you agree?

2. *Markets and environmental justice.* Another claim made in opposition to trading programs is that they may exacerbate environmental injustice. What evidence do Drury et al. offer in support of this claim? A report by an environmental advocacy group, the Environmental Integrity Project, supports Drury's argument. In a study of the SO_2 market, the group found that although emissions had fallen by 5 million tons nationwide they had risen sharply in some areas as power companies bought credits for a few large plants. Abt Associates, Inc., Particulate–Related Health Impacts of Emissions in 2001 from 41 Major U.S. Power Plants (Nov. 2002). The study also concluded that mortality rates in these emission "hot spots" were unusually high, although utility officials claim that mortality cannot be tied to their emissions. A more recent study of the acid rain market concluded that it did not concentrate SO_2 emissions in communities of color, but did lead to increased emissions in poorly educated communities. Evan J. Ringquist, Trading Equity for Efficiency in Environmental Protection? Environmental Justice Effects from the SO_2 Allowance Trading Program, 92 Social Science Quarterly 297 (2011).

What steps might be taken to assure that pollution credit trading schemes do not cause or exacerbate distributional inequities? Any limitation on the scope of a trading market is likely to reduce the efficiency gains from trading. How should environmental justice concerns be balanced with the economic efficiency concerns that typically drive trading programs?

3. *The costs of markets.* One attraction of marketable permit systems is that they reduce the private costs of compliance with pollution limits, by allowing the least-cost reducers to take up the bulk of the reductions. But private costs are not the entire story. Would you expect total monitoring and administrative costs to be higher or lower for a marketable permit program than for a traditional command-and-control program? Why? Will it depend on the pollutant, the source, or other contextual factors?

In a study comparing the acid rain and RECLAIM programs, Lesley McAllister found that the former seemed to realize the promise of reduced administrative costs and reduced acrimony between regulators and the regulated community. Emissions and trade tracking work well, and fines are automatic if, at the end of the year, the firm does not have enough allowances to cover its emissions. Compliance rates are close to 100%, in stark contrast with more traditional Clean Air and Clean Water Act regulatory programs, where non-compliance rates can run as high as 40–60%. Lesley K. McAllister, Beyond Playing "Banker": The Role of the Regulatory Agency in Emissions Trading, 59 Admin. L. Rev. 269, 284–287 (2007). The RECLAIM experience was very different, with poor tracking of emissions and trades, no automatic sanctions, and much higher administrative costs than the command-and-control regime it replaced. Id., 298–305. What differences between the two programs might account for these very different outcomes?

The RECLAIM experience also suggests that in at least some circumstances technology-based regulation may produce emissions reductions much more quickly than trading. California was hit by an energy crisis in 2000, which led power plants to ramp up production to the extent possible. That not only sent the price for NO_x allowances on the RECLAIM market through the roof, putting them beyond the reach of most non-utility sources, it led to the NO_x cap being exceeded by nearly 20%. As a result, power plants were essentially removed from the RECLAIM program and required to install "Best Available Retrofit Control Technology." Under the renewed command-and-control regulatory program, emissions from power plants were reduced more than 90% between 2000 and 2004. Id., 289–291.

4. *The acid rain permit market.* Prices in the annual Chicago Board of Trade auctions of acid rain SO_2 credits have consistently been considerably lower than the $1000/ton estimate routinely bandied about during debate on the 1990 Clean Air Act Amendments. In the March 2003 auction, for example, the average price for "spot" allowances (those that are immediately usable) was $172. Allowances for use in 2010 sold for as low as $80. Prices rose briefly from 2005 to 2007 but then collapsed, falling to $2 for spot allowances and a mere 16 cents for advance allowances in 2011. EPA, 2011 EPA Allowance Auction Results, http://www.epa.gov/airmarkets/trading/ 2011/11summary.html. What do you suppose accounts for the difference between prices and pre-program estimates? For the price fluctuations? Lesley McAllister suggests that over-allocation has been the main factor keeping prices low, and that the short-lived increase in the mid–2000s was due to a Bush administration interstate trading emission trading program discussed in more detail in Note 9, below. Lesley McAllister, The End of the Acid Rain Program, CPRBlog, July 12, 2011.

5. *Tradable permits and emission levels.* Could emissions trading have the perverse effect of increasing emissions? Trading schemes give facilities whose emissions would otherwise be below the legal limit the ability to make money by selling unused pollution rights. Doesn't that provide an economic incentive for emissions to be maintained at the maximum level permitted by law? An EPA report shows that emissions covered by the acid rain program fell dramatically between 1990 and 1995, with only small subsequent reductions (it is important to keep in mind, of course, that electricity generation *increased* during this period). EPA, Acid Rain Program: 2005 Progress Report (Oct. 2006), available at http://epa.gov/airmarkets/ progress/docs/2005report.pdf.

Does Title IV of the Clean Air Act or the RECLAIM program provide any means of counteracting this tendency? Trading proponents have often argued that trading programs would increase incentives to innovate. Some opponents, including both Driesen and Drury et al., contend that, to the contrary, trading programs actually reduce incentives for technological innovation. Which argument do you find more persuasive, and why?

6. *Permits and property.* What is the legal status of Title IV emission allowances? The Clean Air Act states that they do "not constitute a property right." CAA § 403(f) (42 U.S.C. § 7651b(f)). Why was that language included? Could it reduce the effectiveness of the trading program? How?

7. *Allocating permits.* How were emission credits initially allocated and distributed under Title IV of the Clean Air Act and under RECLAIM? Why do you think those allocation systems were chosen? One early study of emission trading programs in the United States reported that, as of 2000, all such programs had allocated permits "free of charge to existing pollution sources." Thomas W. Merrill, Explaining Market Mechanisms, 2000 U. Ill. L. Rev. 275, 284. Merrill attributes the prevalence of grandfathering to political forces, noting that existing polluters receive a form of wealth from permit allocation. How else might credits be allocated? What are the benefits and drawbacks of various allocation systems? The northeastern states' Regional Greenhouse Gas Initiative plans to depart from the standard model, auctioning at least 25% and perhaps all of its CO_2 allowances, using the revenue "to benefit consumers and to support strategic energy investments." Charles Holt et al., Auction Design for Selling CO_2 Emission Allowances Under the Regional Greenhouse Gas Initiative (Oct. 2007), available at http://www.rggi.org/docs/rggi_auction_final.pdf.

8. *Fitting the strategy to the problem.* What characteristics make the acid rain problem, and Southern California's SO_2 and NO_x problems, suitable for an emission trading approach? Are other air pollution problems likely to be amenable to such an approach or not?

Gary Bryner identifies the following elements as essential to an effective pollution trading market:

> an accurate emissions inventory in place for determining the allocation of allowances; the selection of a baseline that fairly reflects economic ups and downs, breakdowns and other problems with maintenance and operation, investments in and performance of pollution control equipment, and other factors; sufficient authority and resources for effective monitoring and enforcement; continuous and accurate emissions monitoring; determinations that emissions reductions are surplus, quantifiable, permanent, and enforceable; and allocation of extra allowances in the cap and trade system that allow policy makers to deal with distributional issues such as who would be responsible for making the reductions and to help overcome resistance from those who are responsible for cleanup costs.

Gary C. Bryner, Carbon Markets: Reducing Greenhouse Gas Emissions Through Emissions Trading, 17 Tul. Envtl. L. J. 267 (2004). Is anything missing from that list? Does it matter what the pollutant is? How many sources might participate in the market?

Consider EPA's 2005 rule establishing a cap-and-trade program for mercury emissions from power plants, instead of imposing industry-wide mercury-specific technology-based emission limits. Standards of Performance for New and Existing Sources: Electric Utility Steam–Generating Units, 70 Fed. Reg. 28606 (May 18, 2005). The mercury trading rule was struck down by the D.C. Circuit in New Jersey v. EPA, 517 F.3d 574 (D.C.

Cir. 2008), on the grounds that it was inconsistent with the Clean Air Act. The major concern of opponents of mercury trading is that mercury, unlike SO_2, is an acute human toxin. Without limits on the geographic distribution of trades, critics are concerned that the program will produce "hot spots" posing serious health threats. The mercury trading rule allowed trades between any affected sources, wherever located. Is an emission trading strategy appropriate for mercury or other toxic pollutants? What sorts of limits would have to be placed on the trading market?

What about other types of environmental problems, such as water pollution, wetlands loss, or biodiversity loss? Proposals for tradable water pollution permits have moved slowly because of the large number of pollutants and the differences in receiving waters. It may be feasible on a smaller scale, through a form of "bubbling." In 2004, for example, Oregon's Department of Environmental Quality issued a single permit covering four wastewater treatment facilities owned and operated by a single entity and located in a single watershed. The permit sets total allowable emission limits, and allows trading of "credits" among the four covered point sources. *First Watershed–Based Discharge Permit Issued to Water Treatment Utility in Oregon*, 72 U.S. Law Week 2543 (Mar. 16, 2004). EPA has a adopted a policy encouraging trading within watersheds. EPA, Final Water Quality Trading Policy (Jan. 13, 2003), http://water.epa.gov/type/water sheds/trading/ finalpolicy2003.cfm.

9. *Tradable permits and the SIP.* EPA encourages states to consider trading and other voluntary measures in their SIPs. How should EPA evaluate those programs in reviewing SIPs? What hurdles might states face in trying to get approval for emission trading programs? It may be difficult to quantify expected emission reductions from voluntary programs. Coupling trading with a regulatory emission cap, as the national acid rain program does, can address that problem.

The initial allocation level may also present a problem. By basing credit allocation on the highest production levels between 1989 and 1992, the RECLAIM program allows higher emissions during the first year of operation than actually occurred in any year prior to the program's initiation. Allocation problems led SCAQMD to drop its plans to include VOCs (volatile organic compounds, the precursors of ozone) in the RE-CLAIM program. In 1995, as SCAQMD was about to begin that program, it discovered that the allocation formula would have allowed a 71% increase over 1993 levels of VOC emissions in the first year of the program. The VOC proposal was withdrawn and has not been implemented.

The EPA under President George W. Bush was anxious to promote market mechanisms. In addition to the mercury rule mentioned in Note 8 above, EPA developed the Clean Air Interstate Rule, which authorized certain states in the east and midwest, where ozone and particulate pollution are interstate problems, to satisfy some of their SIP requirements by participating in regional emission trading markets for SO_2 and NO_x. The D.C. Circuit struck down the Clean Air Interstate Rule in North Carolina v. EPA, 531 F.3d 896 (D.C. Cir. 2008), holding that the rule was not consistent with the CAA's mandate that each individual state ensure that its emissions do not cause or contribute significantly to a NAAQS violation in any downwind state. The Obama administration issued a revised version, called the Cross–State Air Pollution Rule in 2011. 76 Fed. Reg. 48,208 (Aug. 8, 2011). The Cross–State rule sets individual pollution budgets for each upwind state, and creates an "air-quality assured" trading market for power plants in the region. That market will include many of the same sources covered by the acid rain program, but acid rain permits cannot be used to comply with the new rule.

10. *Broadening the market.* Can trades between mobile and stationary sources contribute to solving the air pollution problem? What problems do Drury et al. identify with the SCAQMD car-scrapping rule? What safeguards are needed to ensure that real emission reductions are gained? One study has called into question the value of programs that target older cars as a group. Through direct measurement of on-road vehicle emissions, the researchers found that cars of all ages exhibit a range of pollution characteristics. Although the worst polluters were found among pre–1980 vehicles, many cars of that age were not high emitters. The authors suggest that repair programs targeted at gross polluters may be more effective than scrapping older cars. Stuart P. Beaton et al., *On–Road Vehicle Emissions: Regulations, Costs, and Benefits*, 268 Science 991 (1995).

11. *Emission trading and climate change.* Emission trading is part of the strategy adopted in the Kyoto Protocol to the Convention on Climate Change finalized in December 1997, and signed but not ratified by the United States. The Protocol calls for the major industrialized nations to reduce greenhouse gas emissions (primarily CO_2) by an average of five percent from 1990 levels by 2012. It allows trading of emission reductions among those nations. Individual nations may, if they choose, also use domestic emissions trading strategies to achieve their own reductions. During the negotiations, China and India strongly opposed the inclusion of trading provisions. Their opposition was one reason why the details of trading were left for later clarification. Why do you suppose China and India were so firmly opposed to trading? Why was the United States so firmly committed to it? What difficulties does a global trading system in CO_2 emissions present? What benefits would it bring? Do the benefits outweigh the difficulties?

Greenhouse gas emission trading is also features prominently in domestic climate change policy efforts. The states have entered into several regional cap-and-trade agreements. In 2009, the House of Representatives passed a bill, H.R. 2454, that would have established a federal cap-and-trade program for greenhouse gas emissions, but the bill died in the Senate. In the absence of a federal carbon trading program, state efforts are moving forward. The Regional Greenhouse Gas Initiative, a carbon market covering the power sector, is up and running in the northeast. See www.rggi.org/home. RGGI is not without its problems, however. New Jersey announced its departure from the initiative in 2011. New Jersey's governor explained that "this program is not effective in reducing greenhouse gases and is unlikely to be in the future," because allowance prices are too low. Statement of New Jersey Governor Chris Christie, May 26, 2011, http:// www.nj.gov/governor/news/news/552011/approved/20110526a.html. California, which in 2006 passed a state law requiring reduction of greenhouse gas emissions by about 30% by 2020, plans to meet part of that goal through a carbon market which is expected to open in 2012. See http://www.arb.ca. gov/cc/capandtrade/capandtrade.htm.

One controversial issue for carbon markets is the extent to which they should recognize "offsets," credits for projects that sequester atmospheric carbon rather than reducing emissions. In theory, offsets offer exactly the same benefits as emission reductions—they reduce the greenhouse gas load in the atmosphere. But in practice, they present a host of measurement and oversight problems. The Clean Development Mechanism, the offset provision of the Kyoto Protocol, has been widely criticized as riddled with fraud and manipulation. See, e.g., Michael Wara, Measuring the Clean Development Mechanism's Performance and Potential, 55 UCLA L. Rev. 1759 (2008). Nonetheless, there is a great deal of political pressure to allow offsets in domestic climate legislation. Assuming that offsets in some form are inevitable, two key issues remain. The first is whether to set limits on the extent to which offsets can be used to achieve required emission reductions. Why might some limit be desirable? California regulators plan to cap offset use at no more than 8% of a covered business's emissions. Ann C. Mulkern, Fight Brews Over Offsets in Calif. Climate Law, N.Y. Times, July 25, 2011. The second key issue deals with implementation: offset programs need to ensure that credited greenhouse gas reductions are quantifiable, additional (meaning they would not otherwise have occurred), and permanent. One sticking point in development of California's program has to do with who bears the risk that an offset project does not work as intended. California's draft would put that risk on offset buyers, who would have to make up any emission reduction deficit. Potential market participants contend that once regulators approve an offset, buyers should be insulated from liability for future non-performance. Id.

12. *Emission taxes—the other economic incentive.* Economists have long argued that emission taxes can provide continual incentives to reduce the costs of pollution. Setting the appropriate tax rate is just as challenging as setting a regulatory emissions cap, because it requires a determination of the social costs of pollution or some other judgment about how much pollution should be reduced and how sensitive pollution rates are likely to be to taxes. See, e.g., Driesen, supra, at 340–342. Moreover, unlike a cap-and-trade system, taxes leave decisions about the level of acceptable pollution to private actors, so long as they are willing to pay the costs. Allowing private market actors to set pollution levels would mark a significant change from the current regulatory scheme, under which the federal government sets minimum standards of air quality to protect public health and welfare.

CHAPTER ELEVEN

WATER POLLUTION CONTROL

SECTION 1. INTRODUCTION AND OVERVIEW

Water is an indispensable natural resource. It is a necessity not only for biological and ecological processes, but also for a robust economy. Fresh water, either flowing in or diverted from rivers, is used for agriculture, manufacturing, energy production, mining, navigation, and recreational activities such as fishing, swimming, and boating.

Both the quantity and the quality of water resources are of vital importance to people and natural systems. The law of the two has traditionally been distinct, with water allocation dealt with through state water rights law and water quality addressed through state and federal pollution law. In this chapter, we explore the law of water pollution, concentrating on the federal Clean Water Act. Controlling water pollution poses significant challenges because a variety of substances, produced by disparate sources, affect the nation's waters and because those waters are themselves dynamic, crossing political and institutional boundaries.

A. THE DEVELOPMENT OF WATER POLLUTION LAW

Concern about water pollution dates to the rise of cities, and the associated rise of waterborne diseases. In the American colonial period,

> [h]uman waste was typically discharged into backyard privies that sometimes overflowed into drainage ditches that came to resemble open sewers. Although the privies were cleaned out on occasion, the scavengers who did this work often dumped the waste into empty lots or the nearest waterway. Hogs and other domestic animals roamed the streets, eating garbage and depositing additional waste. Tanneries, slaughterhouses, cloth-dyeing establishments, and small factories added to this noxious waste load. By 1730, the shallow drinking water wells in Manhattan had become so filthy that the water was scarcely fit to drink. Those who could afford to purchased spring water from water carriers.

William L. Andreen, The Evolution of Water Pollution Control in the United States: State, Local and Federal Efforts, 1789–1972, Part I, 22 Stan. Envtl. L. J. 145, 161 (2003).

Little was done about the problems of contaminated water until cholera epidemics killed thousands in the mid–19th century. The first response to the health hazards of urban water pollution was to build aqueducts and waterworks to bring clean drinking water in from unpopulated areas. Municipal sewer systems followed. Early sewer systems actually made water pollution worse. Rather than treat waste, they simply removed it from the urban center, discharging it into nearby lakes and streams, where it was carried to other communities.

> Stream pollution increased, and serious health problems were exported downstream. During the 1880s and 1890s, the number of deaths and illnesses caused by infectious waterborne diseases grew alarmingly in cities and towns that drew drinking water from streams contaminated by upstream neighbors. Ironically, many of these downstream communities themselves had spent considerable sums on the construction of new sewer systems and had expected to reap significant health benefits as a result. Instead, they suffered rising rates of infection and mortality from typhoid fever.

Id. at 168.

While a few cities began to regulate sewer discharges in the late 19th century, most chose instead to filter, and later chlorinate, their water supply. That addressed the obvious public health problem, but left many streams "little more than sewers carrying a noxious mix of sewage and industrial pollutants." Id. at 181.

During and following World War II, industrial pollution grew exponentially. A few states began to experiment with regulation, employing water quality standards, effluent limitations or both. Nonetheless, in many parts of the country discharge of raw or incompletely treated sewage and large volumes of industrial waste continued apace.

> The implications for water quality were appalling. In the 1960s, Lake Erie was experiencing accelerated eutrophication—a process that also adversely affected a number of other American waters including Lake Tahoe, the Great South Bay on Long Island, Lake Oneida in New York, and a number of bays along the southern shore of Lake Ontario. In 1968, the Buffalo River was described as "a repulsive holding basin for industrial and municipal wastes under the prevalent sluggish flow conditions. It [was] devoid of oxygen and almost sterile. Oil, phenols, color, oxygen-demanding materials, iron, acid, sewage, and exotic organic compounds [we]re present in large amounts."[298] The Cuyahoga was described in equally graphic terms in 1968: "The lower Cuyahoga River and navigation channel throughout the Cleveland area is a waste treatment lagoon. At times, the river is choked with debris, oils, scums, and floating globs of organic sludge. Foul smelling gases can be seen rising from decomposing materials on the river's bottom."[299] While these two rivers were among the most polluted in the United States in

---

298. U.S. Dep't of Interior, FWPCA Lake Erie Report: A Plan for Water Pollution Control 50 (Aug. 1968).

299. [Arnold W. Reitze, Jr., Wastes, Water, and Wishful Thinking: The Battle of Lake Erie, 20 Case W. Res. L. Rev. 5, 7 (1968) (quoting a statement of George Harlow, Director of the Lake Erie Program Office of the Federal Water Pollution Control Administration)].

the late 1960s, appalling conditions afflicted countless streams and lakes across the country.

Andreen, Evolution of Water Pollution Control, Part I, at 197–198.

The first major federal water pollution statute was the Rivers and Harbors Act of 1899 (Act of Mar. 3, 1899, ch. 425, § 13, 30 Stat. 1152 (codified as amended at 33 U.S.C. § 407)), also known as the Refuse Act, which prohibited the discharge of "any refuse matter of any kind or description whatever" other than liquid discharges from streets and sewers into "any navigable water of the United States" without a permit from the U.S. Army Corps of Engineers. Although the Refuse Act might have been interpreted broadly, until the 1960s the Army Corps read it as only applying to discharges of solid materials that could cause a problem for navigation. William L. Andreen, The Evolution of Water Pollution Control in the United States–State, Local, and Federal Efforts, 1789–1972: Part II, 22 Stan. Envtl. L. J. 215, 221 (2003). In the late 1930s, Congress passed a federal water pollution bill, only to see President Roosevelt veto it over concerns that it went too far.

Federal water pollution legislation was enacted in 1948, but it had little effect. The Federal Water Pollution Control Act (FWPCA), ch. 758, Pub. L. No. 845, 62 Stat. 1155 (1948), "took modest steps toward establishing a regulatory program." Mark Squillace, From "Navigable Waters" to "Constitutional Waters": The Future of Federal Wetlands Regulation, 40 U. Mich. J. L. Reform 799, 812 (2007). The new law primarily provided funding and technical assistance to the states. Regulatory intervention was permitted in a narrow class of interstate pollution cases, but even in those cases was hobbled by a series of procedural hurdles.

Amendments in 1965 strengthened federal enforcement authority and required the states to adopt water quality standards subject to federal approval. Water Quality Act of 1965, Pub. L. No. 89–234, 79 Stat. 903 (1965). All the states met a 1967 deadline for adopting water quality standards, but those standards proved very difficult to enforce. "Perhaps the most fundamental weakness of the reliance upon water quality standards was the fact that the federal government was required to show which polluter caused the violation of ambient standards." Andreen, Evolution of Water Pollution Control, Part II, at 253. In addition, federal intervention was still limited to interstate pollution and courts hearing abatement actions were required to give "due consideration to the practicability and to the physical and economic feasibility" of compliance with the standards. Pub. L. No. 89–234, § 5.

Frustrated by the difficulties of enforcing the FWPCA, a number of U.S. Attorneys began filing suits against industrial polluters under the Refuse Act in 1969. The Corps of Engineers and EPA developed a permit program under the Refuse Act, but "the task of setting permit levels that would protect water quality standards was nearly hopeless." Andreen, Evolution of Water Pollution Control Law, Part II, at 259.

Spurred by the Refuse Act lawsuits and permit program efforts, late in 1972 Congress overwhelmingly passed the modern Clean Water Act, replacing the fledgling Refuse Act permit program with a detailed new program for permits for point source dischargers and adding several other new regulatory requirements. President Nixon, concerned about the federal budget deficit, vetoed the bill because it provided generous funding for construction of local wastewater treatment plants. Congress quickly overrode that veto, and the Clean Water Act became law.

B. THE MODERN WATER POLLUTION PROBLEM

William L. Andreen, Water Quality Today—Has the Clean Water Act Been a Success?
55 Ala. L. Rev. 537 (2004).

* * *

The surface water resources in the United States are immense. They consist of 3.5 million miles of rivers and streams—enough, in fact, to extend from the Earth to the Moon more than twelve times. The five Great Lakes occupy 94,000 square miles, and there are another 100,000 lakes which exceed 100 acres in size excluding Alaska, which alone has several million such lakes. We also enjoy 58,000 miles of ocean shoreline that is punctuated by magnificent estuaries such as San Francisco Bay, Puget Sound, Chesapeake Bay, Long Island Sound, Tampa Bay, and Mobile Bay. And between these open waters and dry land lies some 278 million acres of wetlands.

This abundant resource has been an important factor in building and sustaining a healthy economy. Our surface waters provide drinking water for approximately half of the nation's population, and more than 13 trillion gallons of water are used every year to manufacture goods and process food in the United States. The nation's beaches, lakes, and rivers are also the number one vacation destination for Americans who make an estimated 1.8 billion trips every year to swim or fish, boat, or simply relax around the water. And the American fishing industry produces over 10 billion pounds of fish and shellfish each year, the current value of which is estimated at $3.4 billion, while irrigated agriculture produces about $70 billion of crops every year. * * *

Hundreds of different kinds of pollutants can harm or destroy aquatic life, threaten human health, or simply foul water to such an extent that recreation and aesthetic appreciation are impaired. Some of these pollutants have been studied for years and are well understood. Conventional pollutants such as oxygen-depleting substances, suspended solids, fecal coliform (bacteria), pH (acids and alkalines), and oil and grease fit into this category. * * * Toxic pollutants include solvents, heavy metals, organic chemicals such as polychlorinated bipheyls (PCBs) and dioxins, and various pesticides. Another group of pollutants—including such substances as ammonia, chlorides, nitrates, color, and iron—while not toxic, are not as well understood as the conventional pollutants and are therefore referred to as nonconventional pollutants (or gray-area pollutants) since they are neither toxic nor conventional. * * * There are also a number of activities like water diversions and dredging, and structures such as dams, which can adversely affect aquatic habitat and hydrology.

1.   Oxygen–Depleting Substances

The ability of a water body to support fish and higher forms of aquatic life depends upon adequate levels of dissolved oxygen. Most fish and beneficial aquatic insects need oxygen in order to survive. * * * Prolonged exposure to low levels of dissolved oxygen can suffocate mature fish, eggs, and larvae and can starve fish by killing insect larvae.

Oxygen levels can fluctuate under natural conditions. Lengthy periods of hot, dry weather, for example, can depress in-stream oxygen levels, sometimes so severely that fish kills result. More often, however, serious cases of oxygen depletion result from the discharge and subsequent decomposition of biodegradable organic material such as sewage, food processing wastes, discharges from pulp and paper facilities, and animal waste. Although water quality standards refer to minimum levels of dissolved oxygen as necessary to meet particular use classifications, NPDES permits generally refer to biochemical oxygen demand ("BOD")—the measure of how much oxygen is consumed by the breakdown of organic material and the oxidation of some inorganic material.

2.   Nutrients

Nutrients such as nitrogen and phosphorus are essential ingredients for healthy and productive aquatic habitats. Excessive amounts of these nutrients, however, can produce eutrophic conditions where the nutrients over-stimulate the growth of algae and various aquatic weeds, which later decay causing a steep decline in the amount of oxygen available to fish and other life forms. The most significant sources of waterborne nutrients are lawn and crop fertilizers containing phosphorus and nitrates that often run off into nearby waters, sewage, manure from fields and feedlots, and detergents that contain phosphorus. The deposition of atmospheric nitrogen is another significant source of waterborne nitrogen. * * * Airborne nitrogen is removed from the air by precipitation or when nitrogen particles settle out of the air and into water. Air pollutants like nitrogen can also enter lakes and streams indirectly, by first being deposited on land, and then being flushed into a waterbody through stormwater runoff or blown into waters as dust. * * *

3.   Bacteria and Pathogens

A number of waterborne viruses, bacteria, and protozoa can cause infections and other illnesses in humans ranging from typhoid fever and dysentery to minor skin diseases and eye, ear, nose, and throat infections. Waterborne microbes are responsible for over 900,000 infections in the United States every year. These microbes originate in the excreta of warm-blooded animals and human beings and enter our waterways through inadequately treated sewage, septic tanks, boats, stormwater discharges, and runoff from livestock feeding and grazing areas. Rather than sample for all of these pathogens, state and federal agencies measure particular indicator bacteria that are widely found in the intestines of animals and people. The presence of such bacteria—common indicator groups such as fecal coliform bacteria or *Escherichia coli*, for example—indicates that the lake or river is contaminated with untreated or inadequately treated human or animal waste and that there is a risk that other, more dangerous organisms, such as *Salmonella typhi*, may infect humans who rely upon the waterbody for recreation or who consume drinking water or shellfish from it.

4. Suspended and Settleable Solids

Suspended and settleable solids include a wide variety of pollutants that can adversely affect aquatic communities. These pollutants include eroded soil particles such as sand, gravel, clay, and silt—collectively referred to as sediment—and other solid particles that can be suspended in sewage and other liquid pollutants. The turbidity which results from sedimentation can clog or abrade fish gills, suffocate fish eggs and water insect larvae, damage invertebrate populations, and reduce the sunlight available to normal aquatic vegetation, thus lowering levels of dissolved oxygen. Turbid water conditions can also interfere with recreational activities due to the loss of water clarity, and suspended silt and sediment can clog mountain streams and choke impounded water bodies. Some solids—discharged, for example, through sewer overflows—may contain bacteria or toxics or oxygen-consuming nutrients. Even ordinary sediment may contain toxic and nutrient pollution since pesticides, other toxics, and nutrients like lawn or agricultural fertilizers may have adhered to or been absorbed by soil particles that are subsequently washed into a waterway.

Approximately three billion tons of sediment are washed into our lakes and streams every year. About half of this erosion is from agriculture where cultivated land is often left without a vegetative cover and is therefore extremely vulnerable to erosion. Significant amounts of erosion also occur at construction and logging sites, in urban areas and from strip-mined lands, and as a result of removing vegetation from streambanks.
* * *

5. pH

"pH" is a measure of the acidity or alkalinity of a particular water. A low pH value (less than five) indicates acidic conditions whereas a high value (over nine) indicates alkaline conditions. A number of biological processes such as reproduction cannot function in either acidic or alkaline waters, and at extreme levels fish kills can occur. Acidic water conditions can also aggravate toxic contamination because acidic conditions will release toxic materials that are present in stream or lake sediments. Mine acid drainage, runoff from mine tailings, and acid rain (resulting from the transformation of sulfur dioxide and nitrogen oxides into acids in the atmosphere) are among the primary sources of acidic water conditions.

6.   Toxic Substances and Metals

Conventional pollutants were the initial focus of most pollution control programs because they were so ubiquitous and because their effects were so obvious and immediate. * * * Toxic pollutants, by contrast, often have a more obscure impact on human health and the environment. Although the impacts were often serious—causing, for example, cancerous tumors in fish and birth defects among predators like birds—cause and effect was not necessarily clear. Many toxics are dangerous at extremely low concentrations; others have long latency periods before they cause harm; and still others, those which bioaccumulate in the tissue of living organisms, pose the greatest danger to predators at the top of the food chain. * * *

Toxic water pollutants include solvents such as toluene and benzene, pesticides such as DDT and chlordane, organic chemicals such as PCBs and dioxin, and metals such as lead and mercury. In most cases involving metals contamination, high concentrations tend to appear in fish tissue rather than the water column because heavy metals accumulate in the fatty tissue of organisms near the top of the food chain. A number of toxic organic chemicals—like PCBs, DDT, and dioxin—not only bioaccumulate in fatty tissue but persist and accumulate in the environment because they do not readily degrade under normal circumstances. The toxic substances and metals found in surface waters, fish tissue, shellfish, bottom sediments, and sediment-dwelling organisms come primarily from industrial and municipal discharges, agricultural runoff containing various pesticides, spills, and even air pollution.

7.   Thermal Pollution

Heat reduces the capacity of water to absorb oxygen, making it less efficient in assimilating oxygen-demanding materials and in supporting fish and aquatic life. A number of industries generate thermal pollution. The enormous quantities of hot water produced by a nuclear or coal-fired electric generating station, for example, can, unless cooled, seriously alter the ecology of a lake, a stream, or a coastal bay.

8.   Other Pollutants

Large amounts of oil can kill fish and other wildlife. Smaller, more persistent amounts, however, can decrease reaeration rates as well as damage the gills and exposed surface membranes of fish. Oil and grease problems normally result from spills associated with the operation or loading of oil tankers and barges and from pipeline breaks. Less dramatic problems can result from the improper disposal of used motor oil and generalized urban runoff. A number of other pollutants can also cause serious harm to fish and aquatic life. Among these are two non-conventional, gray-area pollutants, ammonia and chlorine, both of which can be toxic to fish.

9.   Habitat and Hydrologic Modifications

Habitat modifications include a number of activities that can harm aquatic life. Such modifications include the removal of vegetation from stream banks, an operation that increases water temperature and causes erosion; the actual burying of streams; dredging; the filling and draining of wetlands; and other development and construction activities that change normal drainage patterns and increase the amount and intensity of storm water runoff. Hydrologic modifications like dams and channelization alter the flow of water, and in many instances, have adverse impacts on fish and wildlife. Low instream flows below a dam, for instance, can jeopardize the health, even the existence, of downstream fisheries, and many large hydroelectric impoundments discharge water that is low in dissolved oxygen and high in minerals and nutrients during the warm summer months.

EPA periodically reports to Congress on the nation's water quality, based on information submitted by the states. The most recent report was released in 2009 but documents water quality conditions as of 2004. It reports that of the 16% of the nation's river miles that were assessed, nearly half were impaired. Nearly two-thirds of assessed lakes were found to be impaired, and one-third of assessed estuaries. EPA believes those figures may overestimate the extent of the water pollution problem, because states may target waters thought to be impaired for monitoring. The agency is encouraging states to sample a random subset of their waters in order to get a more accurate sense of water quality overall. EPA, National Water Quality Inventory: Report to Congress, 2004 Reporting Cycle 1–2 (Jan. 2009).

The leading causes of impairment reported included agriculture, hydrologic modification by dams and other water projects, atmospheric deposition, municipal sewage discharges, and unknown sources. Id. Direct industrial discharges to water, which have been subject to technology-based control since passage of the 1972 Clean Water Act, are no longer among the most important sources of water pollution.

C. AN OVERVIEW OF THE CLEAN WATER ACT

Goals. The objective of the Clean Water Act (CWA) is "to restore and maintain the chemical, physical, and biological integrity of the Nation's waters." CWA § 101(a) (33 U.S.C. § 1251(a)). In order to achieve that objective, Congress declared a national goal of eliminating the discharge of pollutants into navigable waters by 1985, and attaining water quality that protects aquatic life and allows recreation, where possible, by 1983. CWA § 101(a)(1), (2). Much as it did under the Clean Air Act, Congress also declared its intent in the CWA "to recognize, preserve, and protect the primary responsibilities and rights of States to prevent, reduce, and eliminate pollution," CWA § 101(b), and disavowed any intent to interfere with state authority over water allocation, CWA § 101(c).

The National Pollutant Discharge Elimination System. The centerpiece of the Clean Water Act is a permit system, called the "national pollutant discharge elimination system" (NPDES) designed to address the weaknesses of early federal water pollution law. CWA § 301 (33 U.S.C. § 1311) prohibits the discharge of any pollutant from a point source to the waters of the United States without a permit. Permits are issued by EPA or by state agencies under delegated authority. CWA § 402 (33 U.S.C. § 1342). Forty-six states have been delegated authority to implement at least some aspects of the NPDES permitting program. (The outliers are Idaho, Massachusetts, New Hampshire, New Mexico, and the District of Columbia.) The CWA requires that permits be renewed every five years, CWA § 402(b)(1)(B), but EPA and state backlogs mean that a significant percentage of permits are not renewed on time. Provided the permittee has filed a timely application for renewal, permits generally continue under the same terms pending review. 40 C.F.R. § 122.6.

EPA sets technology-based effluent limitations for categories of sources; those limits must be included in permits for every source in the category. CWA § 302 (33 U.S.C. § 1312). The extent of control demanded depends upon the pollutant; conventional pollutants are subject to the most relaxed standards, toxic pollutants to the most stringent. CWA §§ 301, 307 (33 U.S.C. §§ 1311, 1317). EPA also develops special standards for new sources. CWA § 306 (CWA § 1316). If no categorical standard has been issued, standards are imposed based on the permit writer's "best professional judgment." 40 C.F.R. § 125.3. Permits are supposed to contain numerical limits on discharges in order to facilitate oversight and enforcement. Permittees are required to monitor and file periodic reports on their discharges.

State water quality standards. The CWA directs states to develop water quality standards for all the waters within their borders. CWA § 303(c). Water quality standards are based on the designated uses of individual waters, which include such things as municipal, industrial, or agricultural use, recreation, fish production, and the like. State water quality standards are to be achieved in part through NPDES permits, which must include restrictions beyond the categorical technology-based effluent limitation standards if necessary to ensure compliance with water quality standards. CWA § 301(b)(1)(C) (33 U.S.C. § 1311(b)(1)(B)). In addition, applicants for any federal license or permit which may result in a discharge to navigable waters must obtain state certification that the activity will not cause a violation of state water quality standards. CWA § 401(a) (33 U.S.C. § 1341(a)).

Identification of impaired waters and TMDLs. States are required to periodically assess the quality of their waters, CWA § 305(b) (33 U.S.C. § 1315(b)), and to identify those that do not meet water quality standards despite technology-based limitations on point source dischargers. CWA § 303(d) (42 U.S.C. § 1313(d)). For those "impaired" waters, the states are directed to develop "total maximum daily loads" (TMDLs) identifying the amount of pollution the waters can tolerate and still meet water quality standards, and allocating that load among all contributing sources. CWA § 303(d).

Nonpoint source pollution. While point source pollution is subject to the NPDES permit requirement, control of nonpoint source pollution is left almost entirely to the states. First under CWA § 208 (33 U.S.C. § 1288) and then under CWA § 319 (33 U.S.C. § 1329), Congress has provided funding and tried to encourage states to develop nonpoint source controls, but with little success. As a result, while pollution from industrial sources has been substantially reduced, nonpoint source pollution has remained largely uncontrolled. The TMDL requirement, because it requires states to document all sources of discharges to impaired waters and allocate the acceptable load among point and nonpoint sources, should provide a stronger incentive for control of nonpoint source pollution.

Publicly owned treatment works (POTWs). The CWA contains special provisions for publicly owned wastewater treatment works, because those present special problems. Improperly treated wastewater has been a major contributor to the nation's water pollution problem since the colonial period. Politically difficult as it may be to shut down industrial operations if they produce unacceptable pollution, wastewater plants pose an even more difficult challenge. Shutting them down would make the pollution problem worse rather than better. Money to upgrade them, if it is not provided by the federal government, must come from local taxpayers. In addition, the operators of POTWs do not directly control the discharges to their system in the same way other permittees do. The CWA has provided substantial grants to construct and upgrade wastewater plants, but it also imposes regulatory standards directed at POTWs. POTW operators are required to perform secondary treatment (biological treatment to remove organic compounds that produce biological oxygen demand), CWA § 301(b)(1)(B) (33 U.S.C. § 1311(b)(1)(B)), and those who introduce pollutants into wastewater systems must meet pretreatment standards, CWA § 307 (33 U.S.C. § 1317(b)).

Dredge and fill permits. The CWA includes a direct successor to the Refuse Act's permit provision. Under CWA § 404 (33 U.S.C. § 1344), EPA and the Corps of Engineers jointly implement a program of permits for the discharge of dredged or fill material to navigable waters. Section 404 is the basis for the federal wetlands regulatory program, considered in more detail in Chapter 6.

SECTION 2.   CONTROL OF POINT-SOURCE POLLUTION: THE NPDES PROGRAM

Excerpts From the Clean Water Act
33 U.S.C. §§ 1251–1387.

Sec. 301.   Effluent limitations.

(a) Except as in compliance [with various sections of the Clean Water Act], the discharge of any pollutant by any person shall be unlawful.

* * *

Sec. 402.   National pollutant discharge elimination system.

(a) * * * [T]he Administrator may, after opportunity for public hearing, issue a permit for the discharge of any pollutant, or combination of pollutants, notwithstanding section 1311(a) of this title * * *.

Sec. 502.   Definitions.

* * *

(6) The term "pollutant" means dredged spoil, solid waste, incinerator residue, sewage, garbage, sewage sludge, munitions, chemical wastes, biological materials, radioactive materials, heat, wrecked or discarded equipment, rock, sand, cellar dirt and industrial, municipal, and agricultural waste discharged into water. This term does not mean (A) "sewage from vessels or a discharge incidental to the normal operation of a vessel of the Armed Forces" within the meaning of section 1322 of this title; or (B) water, gas, or other material which is injected into a well to facilitate production of oil or gas, or water derived in association with oil or gas production and disposed of in a well, if the well used either to facilitate production or for disposal purposes is approved by authority of the State in which the well is located, and if such State determines that such injection or disposal will not result in the degradation of ground or surface water resources.

(7) The term "navigable waters" means the waters of the United States, including the territorial seas.

* * *

(12) The term "discharge of a pollutant" and the term "discharge of pollutants" each means (A) any addition of any pollutant to navigable waters from any point source, (B) any addition of any pollutant to the waters of the contiguous zone or the ocean from any point source other than a vessel or other floating craft.

(14) The term "point source" means any discernible, confined and discrete conveyance, including but not limited to any pipe, ditch, channel, tunnel, conduit, well, discrete fissure, container, rolling stock, concentrated animal feeding operation, or vessel or other floating craft, from which pollutants are or may be discharged. This term does not include agricultural stormwater discharges and return flows from irrigated agriculture.

* * *

A.   COVERED WATERS

The first challenge for determining whether an NPDES permit is required is deciding whether the waters into which a pollutant is discharged fall within the CWA's definition of "navigable waters." Many of the key cases on this issue have come up in the context of regulation of discharges to wetlands under CWA § 404, but the same statutory definitions apply to the NPDES program.

United States v. Riverside Bayview Homes, Inc.

United States Supreme Court, 1985.
474 U.S. 121.

■ JUSTICE WHITE delivered the opinion of the Court.

This case presents the question whether the Clean Water Act (CWA), together with certain regulations promulgated under its authority by the Army Corps of Engineers, authorizes the Corps to require landowners to obtain permits from the Corps before discharging fill material into wetlands adjacent to navigable bodies of water and their tributaries.

The relevant provisions of the Clean Water Act originated in the Federal Water Pollution Control Act Amendments of 1972, and have remained essentially unchanged since that time. Under §§ 301 and 502 of the Act, 33 U.S.C. §§ 1311 and 1362, any discharge of dredged or fill materials into "navigable waters"—defined as the "waters of the United States"—is forbidden unless authorized by a permit issued by the Corps of Engineers pursuant to § 404, 33 U.S.C. § 1344. * * *

* * * Congress chose to define the waters covered by the Act broadly. Although the Act prohibits discharges into "navigable waters," the Act's definition of "navigable waters" as "the waters of the United States" makes it clear that the term "navigable" as used in the Act is of limited import. In adopting this definition of "navigable waters," Congress evidently intended to repudiate limits that had been placed on federal regulation by earlier water pollution control statutes and to exercise its powers under the Commerce Clause to regulate at least some waters that would not be deemed "navigable" under the classical understanding of that term.

* * *

Solid Waste Agency of Northern Cook County v. United States Army Corps of Engineers

United States Supreme Court, 2001.
531 U.S. 159.

■ CHIEF JUSTICE REHNQUIST delivered the opinion of the Court.

Section 404(a) of the Clean Water Act (CWA or Act) 33 U.S.C. § 1344(a), regulates the discharge of dredged or fill material into "navigable waters." The United States Army Corps of Engineers (Corps), has interpreted § 404(a) to confer federal authority over an abandoned sand and gravel pit in northern Illinois which provides habitat for migratory birds. We are asked to decide whether the provisions of § 404(a) may be fairly extended to these waters, and, if so, whether Congress could exercise such authority consistent with the Commerce Clause, U.S. Const., Art. I, § 8, cl. 3. We answer the first question in the negative and therefore do not reach the second.

Petitioner, the Solid Waste Agency of Northern Cook County (SWANCC), is a consortium of 23 suburban Chicago cities and villages that united in an effort to locate and develop a disposal site for baled nonhazardous solid waste. The Chicago Gravel Company informed the municipalities of the availability of a 533–acre parcel, bestriding the Illinois counties Cook and Kane, which had been the site of a sand and gravel pit mining operation for three decades up until about 1960. Long since abandoned, the old mining site eventually gave way to a successional stage forest, with its remnant excavation trenches evolving into a scattering of permanent and seasonal ponds of varying size (from under one-tenth of an acre to several acres) and depth (from several inches to several feet).

The municipalities decided to purchase the site for disposal of their baled nonhazardous solid waste. By law, SWANCC was required to file for various permits from Cook County and the State of Illinois before it could begin operation of its balefill project. In addition, because the operation called for the filling of some of the permanent and seasonal ponds, SWANCC contacted federal respondents (hereinafter respondents), including the Corps, to determine if a federal landfill permit was required under § 404(a) of the CWA, 33 U.S.C. § 1344(a).

Section 404(a) grants the Corps authority to issue permits "for the discharge of dredged or fill material into the navigable waters at specified disposal sites." *Ibid.* The term "navigable waters" is defined under the Act as "the waters of the United States, including the territorial seas." § 1362(7). The Corps has issued regulations defining the term "waters of the United States" to include

> "waters such as intrastate lakes, rivers, streams (including intermittent streams), mudflats, sandflats, wetlands, sloughs, prairie potholes, wet meadows, playa lakes, or natural ponds, the use, degradation or destruction of which could affect interstate or foreign commerce...." 33 CFR § 328.3(a)(3) (1999).

In 1986, in an attempt to "clarify" the reach of its jurisdiction, the Corps stated that § 404(a) extends to intrastate waters:

> "a. Which are or would be used as habitat by birds protected by Migratory Bird Treaties; or
>
> "b. Which are or would be used as habitat by other migratory birds which cross state lines; or
>
> "c. Which are or would be used as habitat for endangered species; or
>
> "d. Used to irrigate crops sold in interstate commerce."

51 Fed. Reg. 41217. This last promulgation has been dubbed the "Migratory Bird Rule."

The Corps initially concluded that it had no jurisdiction over the site because it contained no "wetlands," or areas which support "vegetation typically adapted for life in saturated soil conditions," 33 CFR § 328.3(b) (1999). However, after the Illinois Nature Preserves Commission informed the Corps that a number of migratory bird species had been observed at the site, the Corps reconsidered and ultimately asserted jurisdiction over the balefill site pursuant to subpart (b) of the "Migratory Bird Rule." The

Corps found that approximately 121 bird species had been observed at the site, including several known to depend upon aquatic environments for a significant portion of their life requirements. * * *

This is not the first time we have been called upon to evaluate the meaning of § 404(a). In *United States v. Riverside Bayview Homes, Inc.,* 474 U.S. 121 (1985), we held that the Corps had § 404(a) jurisdiction over wetlands that actually abutted on a navigable waterway. In so doing, we noted that the term "navigable" is of "limited import" and that Congress evidenced its intent to "regulate at least some waters that would not be deemed 'navigable' under the classical understanding of that term." *Id.,* at 133. But our holding was based in large measure upon Congress' unequivocal acquiescence to, and approval of, the Corps' regulations interpreting the CWA to cover wetlands adjacent to navigable waters. We found that Congress' concern for the protection of water quality and aquatic ecosystems indicated its intent to regulate wetlands "inseparably bound up with the 'waters' of the United States." *Id.,* at 134.

It was the significant nexus between the wetlands and "navigable waters" that informed our reading of the CWA in *Riverside Bayview Homes.* Indeed, we did not "express any opinion" on the "question of the authority of the Corps to regulate discharges of fill material into wetlands that are not adjacent to bodies of open water. . . ." *Id.,* at 131–132, n. 8. In order to rule for respondents here, we would have to hold that the jurisdiction of the Corps extends to ponds that are *not* adjacent to open water. But we conclude that the text of the statute will not allow this. * * *[2]

* * *

We thus decline respondents' invitation to take what they see as the next ineluctable step after *Riverside Bayview Homes*: holding that isolated ponds, some only seasonal, wholly located within two Illinois counties, fall under § 404(a)'s definition of "navigable waters" because they serve as habitat for migratory birds. As counsel for respondents conceded at oral argument, such a ruling would assume that "the use of the word navigable in the statute . . . does not have any independent significance." We cannot agree that Congress' separate definitional use of the phrase "waters of the United States" constitutes a basis for reading the term "navigable waters" out of the statute. We said in *Riverside Bayview Homes* that the word "navigable" in the statute was of "limited import" and went on to hold that § 404(a) extended to nonnavigable wetlands adjacent to open waters. But it is one thing to give a word limited effect and quite another to give it no effect whatever. The term "navigable" has at least the import of

---

2. Respondents refer us to portions of the legislative history that they believe indicate Congress' intent to expand the definition of "navigable waters." Although the Conference Report includes the statement that the conferees "intend that the term 'navigable waters' be given the broadest possible constitutional interpretation," S. Conf. Rep. No. 92–1236, p. 144 (1972), neither this, nor anything else in the legislative history to which respondents point, signifies that Congress intended to exert anything more than its commerce power over navigation. * * *

showing us what Congress had in mind as its authority for enacting the CWA: its traditional jurisdiction over waters that were or had been navigable in fact or which could reasonably be so made.

* * *

■ JUSTICE STEVENS, with whom JUSTICE SOUTER, JUSTICE GINSBURG, and JUSTICE BREYER join, dissenting.

* * *

The Court has previously held that the Corps' broadened jurisdiction under the CWA properly included an 80–acre parcel of low-lying marshy land that was not itself navigable, directly adjacent to navigable water, or even hydrologically connected to navigable water, but which was part of a larger area, characterized by poor drainage, that ultimately abutted a navigable creek. *United States v. Riverside Bayview Homes, Inc.*, 474 U.S. 121 (1985).[2] Our broad finding in *Riverside Bayview* that the 1977 Congress had acquiesced in the Corps' understanding of its jurisdiction applies equally to the 410–acre parcel at issue here. Moreover, once Congress crossed the legal watershed that separates navigable streams of commerce from marshes and inland lakes, there is no principled reason for limiting the statute's protection to those waters or wetlands that happen to lie near a navigable stream.

* * *

Rapanos v. United States

United States Supreme Court, 2006.
547 U.S. 715.

■ JUSTICE SCALIA announced the judgment of the Court, and delivered an opinion, in which the CHIEF JUSTICE, JUSTICE THOMAS, and JUSTICE ALITO join.

In April 1989, petitioner John A. Rapanos backfilled wetlands on a parcel of land in Michigan that he owned and sought to develop. This parcel included 54 acres of land with sometimes-saturated soil conditions. The nearest body of navigable water was 11 to 20 miles away. Regulators had informed Mr. Rapanos that his saturated fields were "waters of the United

---

2. The District Court in *Riverside Bayview* found that there was no direct "hydrological" connection between the parcel at issue and any nearby navigable waters. The wetlands characteristics of the parcel were due, not to a surface or groundwater connection to any actually navigable water, but to "poor drainage" resulting from "the Lamson soil that underlay the property." Nevertheless, this Court found occasional surface runoff from the property into nearby waters to constitute a meaningful connection. *Riverside Bayview,* 474 U.S., at 134. Of course, the *ecological* connection between the wetlands and the nearby waters also played a central role in this Court's decision. *Riverside Bayview,* 474 U.S., at 134–135. Both types of connection are also present in many, and possibly most, "isolated" waters. Indeed, although the majority and petitioner both refer to the waters on petitioner's site as "isolated," their role as habitat for migratory birds, birds that serve important functions in the ecosystems of other waters throughout North America, suggests that—ecologically speaking—the waters at issue in this case are anything but isolated.

States," 33 U.S.C. § 1362(7), that could not be filled without a permit. Twelve years of criminal and civil litigation ensued.

* * *

The enforcement proceedings against Mr. Rapanos are a small part of the immense expansion of federal regulation of land use that has occurred under the Clean Water Act—without any change in the governing statute— during the past five Presidential administrations. In the last three decades, the Corps and the Environmental Protection Agency (EPA) have interpreted their jurisdiction over "the waters of the United States" to cover 270 to 300 million acres of swampy lands in the United States—including half of Alaska and an area the size of California in the lower 48 States. And that was just the beginning. The Corps has also asserted jurisdiction over virtually any parcel of land containing a channel or conduit—whether manmade or natural, broad or narrow, permanent or ephemeral—through which rainwater or drainage may occasionally or intermittently flow. On this view, the federally regulated "waters of the United States" include storm drains, roadside ditches, ripples of sand in the desert that may contain water once a year, and lands that are covered by floodwaters once every 100 years. Because they include the land containing storm sewers and desert washes, the statutory "waters of the United States" engulf entire cities and immense arid wastelands. In fact, the entire land area of the United States lies in some drainage basin, and an endless network of visible channels furrows the entire surface, containing water ephemerally wherever the rain falls. Any plot of land containing such a channel may potentially be regulated as a "water of the United States."

* * *

The Rapanos petitioners contend that the terms "navigable waters" and "waters of the United States" in the Act must be limited to the traditional definition of *The Daniel Ball,* which required that the "waters" be navigable in fact, or susceptible of being rendered so. See 10 Wall., at 563. But this definition cannot be applied wholesale to the CWA. The Act uses the phrase "navigable waters" as a *defined* term, and the definition is simply "the waters of the United States." 33 U.S.C. § 1362(7). * * * We have twice stated that the meaning of "navigable waters" in the Act is broader than the traditional understanding of that term, *SWANCC,* 531 U.S., at 167; *Riverside Bayview,* 474 U.S., at 133. We have also emphasized, however, that the qualifier "navigable" is not devoid of significance, *SWANCC, supra,* at 172.

We need not decide the precise extent to which the qualifiers "navigable" and "of the United States" restrict the coverage of the Act. Whatever the scope of these qualifiers, the CWA authorizes federal jurisdiction only over "waters." 33 U.S.C. § 1362(7). The only natural definition of the term "waters," our prior and subsequent judicial constructions of it, clear evidence from other provisions of the statute, and this Court's canons of construction all confirm that "the waters of the United States" in § 1362(7) cannot bear the expansive meaning that the Corps would give it.

The Corps' expansive approach might be arguable if the CWA defined "navigable waters" as "water of the United States." But "the waters of the United States" is something else. The use of the definite article ("the") and the plural number ("waters") show plainly that § 1362(7) does not refer to water in general. In this form, "the waters" refers more narrowly to water "[a]s found in streams and bodies forming geographical features such as oceans, rivers, [and] lakes," or "the flowing or moving masses, as of waves or floods, making up such streams or bodies." Webster's New International Dictionary 2882 (2d ed. 1954) (hereinafter Webster's Second). On this definition, "the waters of the United States" include only relatively permanent, standing or flowing bodies of water.[5] The definition refers to water as found in "streams," "oceans," "rivers," "lakes," and "bodies" of water "forming geographical features." *Ibid.* All of these terms connote continuously present, fixed bodies of water, as opposed to ordinarily dry channels through which water occasionally or intermittently flows. Even the least substantial of the definition's terms, namely "streams," connotes a continuous flow of water in a permanent channel—especially when used in company with other terms such as "rivers," "lakes," and "oceans." None of these terms encompasses transitory puddles or ephemeral flows of water.

The restriction of "the waters of the United States" to exclude channels containing merely intermittent or ephemeral flow also accords with the commonsense understanding of the term. In applying the definition to "ephemeral streams," "wet meadows," storm sewers and culverts, "directional sheet flow during storm events," drain tiles, man-made drainage ditches, and dry arroyos in the middle of the desert, the Corps has stretched the term "waters of the United States" beyond parody. The plain language of the statute simply does not authorize this "Land Is Waters" approach to federal jurisdiction.

* * *

Moreover, only the foregoing definition of "waters" is consistent with the CWA's stated "policy of Congress to recognize, preserve, and protect the primary responsibilities and rights of the States to prevent, reduce, and eliminate pollution, [and] to plan the development and use (including restoration, preservation, and enhancement) of land and water resources...." § 1251(b). * * * [T]he expansive theory advanced by the Corps, rather than "preserv[ing] the primary rights and responsibilities of

---

5. By describing "waters" as "relatively permanent," we do not necessarily exclude streams, rivers, or lakes that might dry up in extraordinary circumstances, such as drought. We also do not necessarily exclude seasonal rivers, which contain continuous flow during some months of the year but no flow during dry months—such as the 290-day, continuously flowing stream postulated by Justice Stevens' dissent. Common sense and common usage distinguish between a wash and seasonal river.

Though scientifically precise distinctions between "perennial" and "intermittent" flows are no doubt available, we have no occasion in this litigation to decide exactly when the drying-up of a stream bed is continuous and frequent enough to disqualify the channel as a water of the United States. It suffices for present purposes that channels containing permanent flow are plainly within the definition, and that the dissent's "intermittent" and "ephemeral" streams are not.

the States," would have brought virtually all "plan[ning of] the development and use . . . of land and water resources" by the States under federal control. It is therefore an unlikely reading of the phrase "the waters of the United States."

* * *

[Justice Scalia further concluded that only "those wetlands with a continuous surface connection to bodies that are 'waters of the United States' in their own right" could be covered by the CWA.]

Respondents and their *amici* urge that such restrictions on the scope of "navigable waters" will frustrate enforcement against traditional water polluters under 33 U.S.C. §§ 1311 and 1342. Because the same definition of "navigable waters" applies to the entire statute, respondents contend that water polluters will be able to evade the permitting requirement of § 1342(a) simply by discharging their pollutants into noncovered intermittent watercourses that lie upstream of covered waters.

That is not so. Though we do not decide this issue, there is no reason to suppose that our construction today significantly affects the enforcement of § 1342, inasmuch as lower courts applying § 1342 have not characterized intermittent channels as "waters of the United States." The Act does not forbid the "addition of any pollutant *directly* to navigable waters from any point source," but rather the "addition of any pollutant *to* navigable waters." § 1362(12)(A) (emphasis added). Thus, from the time of the CWA's enactment, lower courts have held that the discharge into intermittent channels of any pollutant *that naturally washes downstream* likely violates § 1311(a), even if the pollutants discharged from a point source do not emit "directly into" covered waters, but pass "through conveyances" in between. * * *

In contrast to the pollutants normally covered by the permitting requirement of § 1342(a), "dredged or fill material," which is typically deposited for the sole purpose of staying put, does not normally wash downstream, and thus does not normally constitute an "addition . . . to navigable waters" when deposited in upstream isolated wetlands. §§ 1344(a), 1362(12). The Act recognizes this distinction by providing a separate permitting program for such discharges in § 1344(a). It does not appear, therefore, that the interpretation we adopt today significantly reduces the scope of § 1342 of the Act. * * *

■ JUSTICE KENNEDY, concurring in the judgment.

* * * In *Solid Waste Agency of Northern Cook Cty. v. Army Corps of Engineers*, 531 U.S. 159 (2001) *(SWANCC)*, the Court held, under the circumstances presented there, that to constitute "navigable waters" under the Act, a water or wetland must possess a "significant nexus" to waters that are or were navigable in fact or that could reasonably be so made. *Id.*, at 167. * * *

The plurality's opinion begins from a correct premise. As the plurality points out, and as *Riverside Bayview* holds, in enacting the Clean Water

Act Congress intended to regulate at least some waters that are not navigable in the traditional sense. * * *

From this reasonable beginning the plurality proceeds to impose two limitations on the Act; but these limitations, it is here submitted, are without support in the language and purposes of the Act or in our cases interpreting it. * * *

The plurality's first requirement—permanent standing water or continuous flow, at least for a period of "some months,"—makes little practical sense in a statute concerned with downstream water quality. The merest trickle, if continuous, would count as a "water" subject to federal regulation, while torrents thundering at irregular intervals through otherwise dry channels would not. Though the plurality seems to presume that such irregular flows are too insignificant to be of concern in a statute focused on "waters," that may not always be true. Areas in the western parts of the Nation provide some examples. The Los Angeles River, for instance, ordinarily carries only a trickle of water and often looks more like a dry roadway than a river. Yet it periodically releases water-volumes so powerful and destructive that it has been encased in concrete and steel over a length of some 50 miles. Though this particular waterway might satisfy the plurality's test, it is illustrative of what often-dry watercourses can become when rain waters flow.

To be sure, Congress could draw a line to exclude irregular waterways, but nothing in the statute suggests it has done so. * * *

The concerns addressed in *SWANCC* do not support the plurality's interpretation of the Act. In *SWANCC*, by interpreting the Act to require a significant nexus with navigable waters, the Court avoided applications—those involving waters without a significant nexus—that appeared likely, as a category, to raise constitutional difficulties and federalism concerns. Here, in contrast, the plurality's interpretation does not fit the avoidance concerns it raises. On the one hand, when a surface-water connection is lacking, the plurality forecloses jurisdiction over wetlands that abut navigable-in-fact waters—even though such navigable waters were traditionally subject to federal authority. On the other hand, by saying the Act covers wetlands (however remote) possessing a surface-water connection with a continuously flowing stream (however small), the plurality's reading would permit applications of the statute as far from traditional federal authority as are the waters it deems beyond the statute's reach. Even assuming, then, that federal regulation of remote wetlands and nonnavigable waterways would raise a difficult Commerce Clause issue notwithstanding those waters' aggregate effects on national water quality, the plurality's reading is not responsive to this concern. As for States' "responsibilities and rights," § 1251(b), it is noteworthy that 33 States plus the District of Columbia have filed an *amici* brief in this litigation asserting that the Clean Water Act is important to their own water policies. These *amici* note, among other things, that the Act protects downstream States from out-of-state pollution that they cannot themselves regulate.

* * *

B

While the plurality reads nonexistent requirements into the Act, the dissent reads a central requirement out—namely, the requirement that the word "navigable" in "navigable waters" be given some importance. * * *

Consistent with *SWANCC* and *Riverside Bayview* and with the need to give the term "navigable" some meaning, the Corps' jurisdiction over wetlands depends upon the existence of a significant nexus between the wetlands in question and navigable waters in the traditional sense. The required nexus must be assessed in terms of the statute's goals and purposes. Congress enacted the law to "restore and maintain the chemical, physical, and biological integrity of the Nation's waters," 33 U.S.C. § 1251(a), and it pursued that objective by restricting dumping and filling in "navigable waters," §§ 1311(a), 1362(12). With respect to wetlands, the rationale for Clean Water Act regulation is, as the Corps has recognized, that wetlands can perform critical functions related to the integrity of other waters—functions such as pollutant trapping, flood control, and runoff storage. 33 CFR § 320.4(b)(2). Accordingly, wetlands possess the requisite nexus, and thus come within the statutory phrase "navigable waters," if the wetlands, either alone or in combination with similarly situated lands in the region, significantly affect the chemical, physical, and biological integrity of other covered waters more readily understood as "navigable." When, in contrast, wetlands' effects on water quality are speculative or insubstantial, they fall outside the zone fairly encompassed by the statutory term "navigable waters."

* * *

When the Corps seeks to regulate wetlands adjacent to navigable-in-fact waters, it may rely on adjacency to establish its jurisdiction. Absent more specific regulations, however, the Corps must establish a significant nexus on a case-by-case basis when it seeks to regulate wetlands based on adjacency to nonnavigable tributaries. Given the potential overbreadth of the Corps' regulations, this showing is necessary to avoid unreasonable applications of the statute. Where an adequate nexus is established for a particular wetland, it may be permissible, as a matter of administrative convenience or necessity, to presume covered status for other comparable wetlands in the region. That issue, however, is neither raised by these facts nor addressed by any agency regulation that accommodates the nexus requirement outlined here.

* * *

In both the consolidated cases before the Court the record contains evidence suggesting the possible existence of a significant nexus according to the principles outlines above. Thus the end result in these cases and many others to be considered by the Corps may be the same as that suggested by the dissent, namely that the Corps' assertion of jurisdiction is valid. Given, however, that neither the agency nor the reviewing courts properly considered the issue, a remand is appropriate, in my view, for application of the controlling legal standard.

■ JUSTICE STEVENS, with whom JUSTICE SOUTER, JUSTICE GINSBURG, and JUSTICE BREYER join, dissenting.

In my view, the proper analysis is straightforward. The Army Corps has determined that wetlands adjacent to tributaries of traditionally navigable waters preserve the quality of our Nation's waters by, among other things, providing habitat for aquatic animals, keeping excessive sediment and toxic pollutants out of adjacent waters, and reducing downstream flooding by absorbing water at times of high flow. The Corps' resulting decision to treat these wetlands as encompassed within the term "waters of the United States" is a quintessential example of the Executive's reasonable interpretation of a statutory provision. See *Chevron U.S.A. Inc. v. Natural Resources Defense Council, Inc.,* 467 U.S. 837, 842–845 (1984).

Our unanimous decision in *United States v. Riverside Bayview Homes, Inc.,* 474 U.S. 121 (1985), was faithful to our duty to respect the work product of the Legislative and Executive Branches of our Government. Today's judicial amendment of the Clean Water Act is not.

* * *

The plurality imposes two novel conditions on the exercise of the Corps' jurisdiction that can only muddy the jurisdictional waters. * * * The impropriety of crafting these new conditions is highlighted by the fact that *no* party or *amicus* has suggested either of them.

First, ignoring the importance of preserving jurisdiction over water beds that are periodically dry, the plurality imposes a requirement that only tributaries with the "relatively permanent" presence of water fall within the Corps' jurisdiction. Under the plurality's view, then, the Corps can regulate polluters who dump dredge into a stream that flows year round but may not be able to regulate polluters who dump into a neighboring stream that flows for only 290 days of the year—even if the dredge in this second stream would have the same effect on downstream waters as the dredge in the year-round one.

To find this arbitrary distinction compelled by the statute, the plurality cites a dictionary for a proposition that it does not contain. The dictionary treats "streams" as "waters" but has nothing to say about whether streams must contain water year round to qualify as "streams." * * * But common sense and common usage demonstrate that intermittent streams, like perennial streams, are still streams. * * *

Most importantly, the plurality disregards the fundamental significance of the Clean Water Act. * * * The Corps has concluded that it must regulate pollutants at the time they enter ditches or streams with ordinary high-water marks—whether perennial, intermittent, or ephemeral—in order to properly control water pollution. Because there is ambiguity in the phrase "waters of the United States" and because interpreting it broadly to cover such ditches and streams advances the purpose of the Act, the Corps' approach should command our deference. Intermittent streams can carry pollutants just as perennial streams can, and their regulation may prove as important for flood control purposes. The inclusion of all identifiable tributaries that ultimately drain into large bodies of water within the mantle of federal protection is surely wise.

* * *

While I generally agree with Parts I and II–A of Justice Kennedy's opinion, I do not share his view that we should replace regulatory standards that have been in place for over 30 years with a judicially crafted rule distilled from the term "significant nexus" as used in *SWANCC*. * * *

Justice Kennedy's "significant nexus" test will probably not do much to diminish the number of wetlands covered by the Act in the long run. Justice Kennedy himself recognizes that the records in both cases contain evidence that "should permit the establishment of a significant nexus," and it seems likely that evidence would support similar findings as to most (if not all) wetlands adjacent to tributaries of navigable waters. But Justice Kennedy's approach will have the effect of creating additional work for all concerned parties. Developers wishing to fill wetlands adjacent to ephemeral or intermittent tributaries of traditionally navigable waters will have no certain way of knowing whether they need to get § 404 permits or not. And the Corps will have to make case-by-case (or category-by-category) jurisdictional determinations, which will inevitably increase the time and resources spent processing permit applications. * * *

I would affirm the judgments in both cases, and respectfully dissent from the decision of five Members of this Court to vacate and remand. I close, however, by noting an unusual feature of the Court's judgments in these cases. It has been our practice in a case coming to us from a lower federal court to enter a judgment commanding that court to conduct any further proceedings pursuant to a specific mandate. That prior practice has, on occasion, made it necessary for Justices to join a judgment that did not conform to their own views. In these cases, however, while both the plurality and Justice Kennedy agree that there must be a remand for further proceedings, their respective opinions define different tests to be applied on remand. Given that all four Justices who have joined this opinion would uphold the Corps' jurisdiction in both of these cases—and in all other cases in which either the plurality's or Justice Kennedy's test is satisfied—on remand each of the judgments should be reinstated if *either* of those tests is met.

NOTES AND QUESTIONS

1. *The rule of Rapanos.* Which opinion or set of opinions controls in *Rapanos*? What is the reach of the CWA's definition of "navigable waters"? Is the Act's reach different for purposes of the NPDES permit requirement than for purposes of the wetlands permit requirement? If Justice Kennedy's "significant nexus" test controls, what does it require?

In Marks v. United States, 430 U.S. 188, 193 (1977), the Supreme Court explained that "[w]hen a fragmented Court decides a case and no single rationale explaining the result enjoys the assent of five Justices, the

holding of the Court may be viewed as that position taken by those
Members who concurred in the judgments on the narrowest grounds."
Applying that rule, the Fourth, Seventh, Ninth, and Eleventh Circuits have
concluded that the significant nexus test articulated by Justice Kennedy is
the ruling standard of *Rapanos*. Precon Development Corp. v. U.S. Army
Corps of Engineers, 633 F.3d 278 (4th Cir. 2011); United States v. Gerke
Excavating Inc., 464 F.3d 723 (7th Cir. 2006); Northern California River
Watch v. City of Healdsburg, 496 F.3d 993 (9th Cir. 2007); United States v.
Robison, 505 F.3d 1208 (11th Cir. 2007). The First and Eighth Circuits
have accepted Justice Stevens's invitation to find CWA jurisdiction whenever either the plurality's or Justice Kennedy's test is satisfied because the
four dissenters would join in finding jurisdiction in either case. United
States v. Johnson, 467 F.3d 56 (1st Cir. 2006); United States v. Bailey, 571
F.3d 791 (8th Cir. 2009). The Eleventh Circuit has squarely rejected that
position. Robison, 505 F.3d at 1221. The other circuits have yet to directly
address it.

2. *Jurisdictional guidance.* Despite separate opinions by Chief Justice
Roberts and Justice Breyer urging them to do so speedily, EPA and the
Army Corps of Engineers have not launched a new rulemaking to define
the scope of "waters of the United States." Instead, they have proceeded
through a series of guidance documents. The first, issued in 2007, opined
that "regulatory jurisdiction under the CWA exists over a water body if
either the plurality's or Justice Kennedy's standard is satisfied." Benjamin
H. Grumbles & John Paul Woodley, Jr., Clean Water Act Jurisdiction
Following the U.S. Supreme Court's Decision in *Rapanos v. United States
& Carabell v. United States*, June 5, 2007, at 3. The 2007 Guidance went on
to explain that jurisdiction exists over traditional navigable waters, wetlands adjacent to those waters, and non-navigable tributaries of those
waters that "are relatively permanent ... or have continuous flow at least
seasonally (e.g., typically three months)." Id. at 1. It called for a case-by-
case decision on jurisdiction using the significant nexus test for "non-
navigable tributaries that are not relatively permanent," wetlands adjacent
to such tributaries, and wetlands not directly abutting permanent non-
navigable tributaries. Id. The 2007 Guidance was re-issued with minor
alterations   in   2008.   http://www.epa.gov/owow/wetlands/pdf/CWA_
Jurisdiction_Following_Rapanos120208.pdf.

In 2011, EPA and the Corps issued a new Draft Guidance on Identifying Waters Protected by the Clean Water Act. http://water.epa.gov/
lawsregs/guidance/wetlands/upload/wous_guidance_4–2011.pdf. Not surprisingly in light of the intervening change of administration, the 2011 Draft
Guidance takes a more expansive view of the extent of federal authority
than its predecessors.

> The agencies expect, based on relevant science and recent field
> experience, that under the understandings stated in this draft guid-
> ance, the extent of waters over which the agencies assert jurisdiction
> under the CWA will increase compared to the extent of waters over
> which jurisdiction has been asserted under existing guidance, though

certainly not to the full extent that it was typically asserted prior to the Supreme Court decisions in *SWANCC* and *Rapanos*.

Id. at 3. The Draft Guidance begins by setting out a broad view of "traditional navigable waters," including waters currently or historically used for commercial navigation including commercial recreation such as boat or canoe rentals and waters capable of that sort of use in the future. The Draft Guidance is consistent with EPA's 2010 determination that the Los Angeles River is a traditional navigable water for its entire length. That determination relied in part on "The Los Angeles River Expedition," a kayak and canoe trip in July 2008 (the dry season on the west coast) which was able to navigate about 90% of the river. It doesn't take a lot of water to float a kayak; the expedition observed that typical water depths for most of the river were about 8–12 inches. EPA Region IX, Special Case Evaluation Regarding Status of the Los Angeles River, California, as a Traditional Navigable Water 24 (July 1, 2010), available at http://www.epa. gov/region9/mediacenter/LA-river/LASpecialCaseLetterandEvaluation.pdf.

The Draft Guidance goes on to emphasize that all interstate waters and their adjacent wetlands are under federal jurisdiction. The earlier guidance did not mention interstate waters, but they have long been included in the regulatory definition of "waters of the United States." 40 C.F.R. § 122.2. Based on Justice Scalia's opinion, the Draft Guidance defines tributaries of traditional navigable waters as subject to federal jurisdiction if they have "at least seasonal flow," meaning that they predictably flow during the region's wet season in most years. Draft Guidance at 13. Wetlands with a continuous surface connection to traditional navigable waters or their tributaries would also be covered. Id. at 15.

Other waters are jurisdictional under the Draft Guidance if they meet Justice Kennedy's "significant nexus" test. That test is satisfied, according to the agencies, if the waters being evaluated, by themselves or with other waters of the same type in the same watershed have more than a "speculative or insubstantial" effect on the chemical, physical, or biological integrity of traditional navigable waters or interstate waters. Id. at 8. A hydrologic connection is not necessary; waters might affect traditional navigable waters by retaining floodwater or pollutants precisely because there is no hydrologic connection. Id. at 9.

In issuing the Draft Guidance, EPA and the Corps indicated that they expect to follow it with a rulemaking "to clarify further . . . the extent of Clean Water Act jurisdiction." Id. at 1.

In your view, which is more consistent with the Clean Water Act, the 2007 Guidance or the 2011 Draft Guidance? Which is more consistent with *Rapanos*? Is a rulemaking necessary or desirable? What benefits, if any, would it offer over continuing to rely on guidance documents?

3. *Rapanos and NPDES permitting.* Although both *SWANCC* and *Rapanos* involved disputes about the permitting authority of the Army Corps of Engineers under CWA § 404 (33 U.S.C. § 1344), the same definitions govern the scope of the NPDES program. Do you agree with the *Rapanos* plurality that jurisdiction can be successfully narrowed with respect to wetlands filling without freeing more traditional polluters from the strictures of the NPDES permit requirement? In San Francisco Baykeeper v. Cargill Salt Division, 481 F.3d 700 (9th Cir. 2007), the Ninth Circuit held that an NPDES permit was not required for disposal of salt processing residue in a non-navigable pond separated by an earthen levee from a navigable tributary of San Francisco Bay. The court concluded that even if a significant nexus was enough to permit regulation of waters other than wetlands on the basis of "adjacency" to navigable waters, plaintiffs had not established a significant nexus where they did not show that water ever flowed from the pond to the tributary. In Northern California River Watch v. City of Healdsburg, 496 F.3d 993 (9th Cir. 2007), on the other hand, the same court found that an NPDES permit was required for the discharge of treated wastewater to a quarry pit that had filled with water from the surrounding aquifer. The *River Watch* court concluded that a significant nexus with navigable waters was established by evidence that both water and pollutants from the quarry seeped into the nearby Russian River through surface wetlands and the underground aquifer. See also United States v. Chevron Pipe Line Co., 437 F. Supp. 2d 605 (N.D. Tex. 2006) (holding under the Oil Pollution Act, which also defines "navigable waters" as "waters of the United States," that Chevron could not be fined for spilling oil into intermittent stream at time when it contained no flowing water).

Does *Rapanos* appear to pose problems for the NPDES system?

4. *The CWA and the Commerce Clause.* The constitutional limits on federal regulation are discussed in detail in Chapter 4. Do you believe that Congress, in enacting the CWA, intended to push its authority to the constitutional limit? To what extent is it appropriate for the Court to interpret the CWA narrowly in order to avoid "difficult constitutional questions"? Might that unnecessarily restrict congressional authority, by reading out of the statute provisions Congress intended to include that would, if the Court directly addressed the issue, in fact survive constitutional review? Should the Court assume that Congress would not approach the constitutional boundary without a clear statement? Does it matter whether the prevailing constitutional interpretation was broader or narrower than the current one at the time the statute was adopted? Does it matter how important the interpretation the Court rejects is to achieving the statutory purpose?

B. COVERED ACTIVITIES

Identifying the waters which are subject to the CWA is only the beginning of understanding whether the NPDES permit provisions apply. The next question is whether there is a "discharge of a pollutant" to jurisdictional waters.

South Florida Water Management District v. Miccosukee Tribe of Indians

United States Supreme Court, 2004.
541 U.S. 95.

■ JUSTICE O'CONNOR delivered the opinion of the Court.

* * *

I

The Central and South Florida Flood Control Project (Project) consists of a vast array of levees, canals, pumps, and water impoundment areas in the land between south Florida's coastal hills and the Everglades. Historically, that land was itself part of the Everglades, and its surface and groundwater flowed south in a uniform and unchanneled sheet. Starting in the early 1900s, however, the State began to build canals to drain the wetlands and make them suitable for cultivation. These canals proved to be a source of trouble; they lowered the water table, allowing salt water to intrude upon coastal wells, and they proved incapable of controlling flooding. Congress established the Project in 1948 to address these problems. It gave the United States Army Corps of Engineers the task of constructing a comprehensive network of levees, water storage areas, pumps, and canal improvements that would serve several simultaneous purposes, including flood protection, water conservation, and drainage. These improvements fundamentally altered the hydrology of the Everglades, changing the natural sheet flow of ground and surface water. The local sponsor and day-to-day operator of the Project is the South Florida Water Management District (District).

Five discrete elements of the Project are at issue in this case. One is a canal called "C–11." C–11 collects groundwater and rainwater from a 104 square-mile area in south central Broward County. The area drained by C–11 includes urban, agricultural, and residential development, and is home to 136,000 people. At the western terminus of C–11 is the second Project element at issue here: a large pump station known as "S–9." When the water level in C–11 rises above a set level, S–9 begins operating and pumps water out of the canal. The water does not travel far. Sixty feet away, the pump station empties the water into a large undeveloped wetland area called "WCA–3," the third element of the Project we consider here. WCA–3 is the largest of several "water conservation areas" that are remnants of the original South Florida Everglades. The District impounds water in these areas to conserve fresh water that might otherwise flow directly to the ocean, and to preserve wetlands habitat.

Using pump stations like S–9, the District maintains the water table in WCA–3 at a level significantly higher than that in the developed lands drained by the C–11 canal to the east. Absent human intervention, that water would simply flow back east, where it would rejoin the waters of the canal and flood the populated areas of the C–11 basin. That return flow is prevented, or, more accurately, slowed, by levees that hold back the surface waters of WCA–3. Two of those levees, L–33 and L–37, are the final two elements of the Project at issue here. The combined effect of L–33 and L–37, C–11, and S–9 is artificially to separate the C–11 basin from WCA–3; left to nature, the two areas would be a single wetland covered in an undifferentiated body of surface and ground water flowing slowly southward.

As the above description illustrates, the Project has wrought large-scale hydrologic and environmental change in South Florida, some deliberate and some accidental. Its most obvious environmental impact has been the conversion of what were once wetlands into areas suitable for human use. But the Project also has affected those areas that remain wetland ecosystems.

Rain on the western side of the L–33 and L–37 levees falls into the wetland ecosystem of WCA–3. Rain on the eastern side of the levees, on the other hand, falls on agricultural, urban, and residential land. Before it enters the C–11 canal, whether directly as surface runoff or indirectly as groundwater, that rainwater absorbs contaminants produced by human activities. The water in C–11 therefore differs chemically from that in WCA–3. Of particular interest here, C–11 water contains elevated levels of phosphorous, which is found in fertilizers used by farmers in the C–11 basin. When water from C–11 is pumped across the levees, the phosphorous it contains alters the balance of WCA–3's ecosystem (which is naturally low in phosphorous) and stimulates the growth of algae and plants foreign to the Everglades ecosystem.

The phosphorous-related impacts of the Project are well known and have received a great deal of attention from state and federal authorities for more than 20 years. A number of initiatives are currently under way to reduce these impacts and thereby restore the ecological integrity of the Everglades. Respondents Miccosukee Tribe of Indians and the Friends of the Everglades (hereinafter simply Tribe), impatient with the pace of this progress, brought this Clean Water Act suit in the United States District Court for the Southern District of Florida. They sought, among other things, to enjoin the operation of S–9 and, in turn, the conveyance of water from C–11 into WCA–3.

Congress enacted the Clean Water Act (Act) in 1972. Its stated objective was "to restore and maintain the chemical, physical, and biological integrity of the Nation's waters." 33 U.S.C. § 1251. To serve those ends, the Act prohibits "the discharge of any pollutant by any person" unless done in compliance with some provision of the Act. § 1311(a). The provision relevant to this case, § 1342, establishes the National Pollutant Discharge Elimination System, or "NPDES." Generally speaking, the NPDES requires dischargers to obtain permits that place limits on the type and quantity of pollutants that can be released into the Nation's waters. The Act defines the phrase "discharge of a pollutant" to mean "any addition of any pollutant to navigable waters from any point source." § 1362(12). A "point source," in turn, is defined as "any discernible, confined and discrete conveyance," such as a pipe, ditch, channel, or tunnel, "from which pollutants are or may be discharged." § 1362(14).

According to the Tribe, the District cannot operate S–9 without an NPDES permit because the pump station moves phosphorous-laden water from C–11 into WCA–3. The District does not dispute that phosphorous is a pollutant, or that C–11 and WCA–3 are "navigable waters" within the meaning of the Act. The question, it contends, is whether the operation of the S–9 pump constitutes the "discharge of [a] pollutant" within the meaning of the Act.

* * *

II

The District and the Federal Government, as amicus, advance three separate arguments, any of which would, if accepted, lead to the conclusion that the S–9 pump station does not require a point source discharge permit under the NPDES program. * * *

In its opening brief on the merits, the District argued that the NPDES program applies to a point source "only when a pollutant originates from the point source," and not when pollutants originating elsewhere merely pass through the point source. * * * Although the Government rejects the District's legal position, it and the Tribe agree with the factual proposition that S–9 does not itself add any pollutants to the water it conveys into WCA–3.

This initial argument is untenable, and even the District appears to have abandoned it in its reply brief. A point source is, by definition, a "discernible, confined, and discrete *conveyance*." § 1362(14) (emphasis added). That definition makes plain that a point source need not be the original source of the pollutant; it need only convey the pollutant to "navigable waters," which are, in turn, defined as "the waters of the United States." § 1362(7). Tellingly, the examples of "point sources" listed by the Act include pipes, ditches, tunnels, and conduits, objects that do not themselves generate pollutants but merely transport them. § 1362(14). In addition, one of the Act's primary goals was to impose NPDES permitting requirements on municipal wastewater treatment plants. But under the District's interpretation of the Act, the NPDES program would not cover such plants, because they treat and discharge pollutants added to water by others. We therefore reject the District's proposed reading of the definition of "discharge of a pollutant" contained in § 1362(12). That definition includes within its reach point sources that do not themselves generate pollutants.

Having answered the precise question on which we granted certiorari, we turn to a second argument, advanced primarily by the Government as amicus curiae in merits briefing and at oral argument. For purposes of determining whether there has been "any addition of any pollutant to navigable waters from any point source," the Government contends that all the water bodies that fall within the Act's definition of "navigable waters" (that is, all "the waters of the United States, including the territorial seas,"

§ 1362(7)) should be viewed unitarily for purposes of NPDES permitting requirements. Because the Act requires NPDES permits only when there is an addition of a pollutant "to navigable waters," the Government's approach would lead to the conclusion that such permits are not required when water from one navigable water body is discharged, unaltered, into another navigable water body. That would be true even if one water body were polluted and the other pristine, and the two would not otherwise mix. Under this "unitary waters" approach, the S–9 pump station would not need an NPDES permit.

The "unitary waters" argument focuses on the Act's definition of a pollutant discharge as "any addition of any pollutant to navigable waters from any point source." § 1362(12). The Government contends that the absence of the word "any" prior to the phrase "navigable waters" in § 1362(12) signals Congress' understanding that NPDES permits would not be required for pollution caused by the engineered transfer of one "navigable water" into another. It argues that Congress intended that such pollution instead would be addressed through local nonpoint source pollution programs. * * *

We note, however, that * * * several NPDES provisions might be read to suggest a view contrary to the unitary waters approach. For example, under the Act, a State may set individualized ambient water quality standards by taking into consideration "the designated uses of the navigable waters involved." 33 U.S.C. § 1313(c)(2)(A). Those water quality standards, in turn, directly affect local NPDES permits; if standard permit conditions fail to achieve the water quality goals for a given water body, the State must determine the total pollutant load that the water body can sustain and then allocate that load among the permit-holders who discharge to the water body. § 1313(d). This approach suggests that the Act protects individual water bodies as well as the "waters of the United States" as a whole.

The Government also suggests that we adopt the "unitary waters" approach out of deference to a longstanding EPA view that the process of "transporting, impounding, and releasing navigable waters" cannot constitute an "addition" of pollutants to "the waters of the United States." But the Government does not identify any administrative documents in which EPA has espoused that position. Indeed, an amicus brief filed by several former EPA officials argues that the agency once reached the opposite conclusion. * * *

Finally, the Government and numerous amici warn that affirming the Court of Appeals in this case would have significant practical consequences. If we read the Clean Water Act to require an NPDES permit for every engineered diversion of one navigable water into another, thousands of new permits might have to be issued, particularly by western States, whose water supply networks often rely on engineered transfers among various natural water bodies. Many of those diversions might also require expensive treatment to meet water quality criteria. It may be that construing the NPDES program to cover such transfers would therefore raise the costs of water distribution prohibitively, and violate Congress' specific instruction that "the authority of each State to allocate quantities of water within its jurisdiction shall not be superseded, abrogated or otherwise impaired" by the Act. § 1251(g). On the other hand, it may be that such permitting authority is necessary to protect water quality, and that the States or EPA could control regulatory costs by issuing general permits to point sources associated with water distribution programs.[1] Indeed, that is the position of the one State that has interpreted the Act to cover interbasin water transfers.

Because WCA–3 and C–11 are both "navigable waters," adopting the "unitary waters" approach would lead to the conclusion that the District may operate S–9 without an NPDES permit. But despite its relevance here, neither the District nor the Government raised the unitary waters approach before the Court of Appeals or in their briefs respecting the petition for certiorari. Indeed, we are not aware of any reported case that examines the unitary waters argument in precisely the form that the Government now presents it. As a result, we decline to resolve it here. Because we find it necessary to vacate the judgment of the Court of Appeals with respect to a third argument presented by the District, the unitary waters argument will be open to the parties on remand.

In the courts below, as here, the District contended that the C–11 canal and WCA–3 impoundment area are not distinct water bodies at all, but instead are two hydrologically indistinguishable parts of a single water body. The Government agrees with the District on this point, claiming that because the C–11 canal and WCA–3 "share a unique, intimately related, hydrological association," they "can appropriately be viewed, for purposes of Section 402 of the Clean Water Act, as parts of a single body of water." The Tribe does not dispute that if C–11 and WCA–3 are simply two parts of the same water body, pumping water from one into the other cannot constitute an "addition" of pollutants. As the Second Circuit put it in *Trout Unlimited*, "[i]f one takes a ladle of soup from a pot, lifts it above the pot, and pours it back into the pot, one has not 'added' soup or anything else to the pot." 273 F.3d, at 492. What the Tribe disputes is the accuracy of the District's factual premise; according to the Tribe, C–11 and WCA–3 are two pots of soup, not one.

The record does contain information supporting the District's view of the facts. Although C–11 and WCA–3 are divided from one another by the L–33 and L–37 levees, that line appears to be an uncertain one. Because Everglades soil is extremely porous, water flows easily between ground and surface waters, so much so that "[g]round and surface waters are essential-

---

1. An applicant for an individual NPDES permit must provide information about, among other things, the point source itself, the nature of the pollutants to be discharged, and any water treatment system that will be used. General permits greatly reduce that administrative burden by authorizing discharges from a category of point sources within a specified geographic area. Once EPA or a state agency issues such a permit, covered entities, in some cases, need take no further action to achieve compliance with the NPDES besides adhering to the permit conditions. See 40 CFR § 122.28(b)(2)(v) (2003).

ly the same thing." C–11 and WCA–3, of course, share a common underlying aquifer. Moreover, the L–33 and L–37 levees continually leak, allowing water to escape from WCA–3. This means not only that any boundary between C–11 and WCA–3 is indistinct, but also that there is some significant mingling of the two waters; the record reveals that even without use of the S–9 pump station, water travels as both seepage and groundwater flow between the water conservation area and the C–11 basin.

The parties also disagree about how the relationship between S–9 and WCA–3 should be assessed. At oral argument, counsel for the Tribe focused on the differing "biological or ecosystem characteristics" of the respective waters, while counsel for the District emphasizes the close hydrological connections between the two. Despite these disputes, the District Court granted summary judgment to the Tribe. It applied a test that neither party defends; it determined that C–11 and WCA–3 are distinct "because the transfer of water or its contents from C–11 into the Everglades would not occur naturally." The Court of Appeals for the Eleventh Circuit endorsed this test. 280 F.3d, at 1368.

We do not decide here whether the District Court's test is adequate for determining whether C–11 and WCA–3 are distinct. Instead, we hold only that the District Court applied its test prematurely. Summary judgment is appropriate only where there is no genuine issue of material fact. The record before us leads us to believe that some factual issues remain unresolved. The District Court certainly was correct to characterize the flow through the S–9 pump station as a non-natural one, propelled as it is by diesel-fired motors against the pull of gravity. And it also appears true that if S–9 were shut down, the water in the C–11 canal might for a brief time flow east, rather than west, as it now does. But the effects of shutting down the pump might extend beyond that. The limited record before us suggests that if S–9 were shut down, the area drained by C–11 would flood quite quickly. That flooding might mean that C–11 would no longer be a "distinct body of navigable water," but part of a larger water body extending over WCA–3 and the C–11 basin. It also might call into question the Eleventh Circuit's conclusion that S–9 is the cause in fact of phosphorous addition to WCA–3. Nothing in the record suggests that the District Court considered these issues when it granted summary judgment. Indeed, in ordering later emergency relief from its own injunction against the operation of the S–9 pump station, the court admitted that it had not previously understood that shutting down S–9 would "literally ope[n] the flood gates."

We find that further development of the record is necessary to resolve the dispute over the validity of the distinction between C–11 and WCA–3. After reviewing the full record, it is possible that the District Court will conclude that C–11 and WCA–3 are not meaningfully distinct water bodies. If it does so, then the S–9 pump station will not need an NPDES permit. In addition, the Government's broader "unitary waters" argument is open to the District on remand. Accordingly, the judgment of the United States

Court of Appeals for the Eleventh Circuit is vacated, and the case is remanded for further proceedings consistent with this opinion.

■ JUSTICE SCALIA, concurring in part and dissenting in part.

I join Parts I and II–A of the Court's opinion, which hold that a point source is not exempt from the NPDES permit requirement merely because it does not itself add pollutants to the water it pumps. I dissent, however, from its decision to vacate the judgment below on another ground, Part II–C, and to invite consideration of yet another legal theory, Part II–B. Neither of those actions is taken in response to the question presented. I would affirm the Court of Appeals' disposition of the question presented without reaching other issues.

* * *

NOTES AND QUESTIONS

1. *Permitting as a pollution control strategy.* The NPDES permit program is the heart of the Clean Water Act. By contrast, the Clean Air Act focuses primarily on achieving nationally determined air quality standards. How do those strategies differ? Which is preferable, or do they work most effectively in tandem? Consider that the CAA added a permit requirement for all major stationary sources in 1990, and that (as we shall see later in this chapter) water quality is an increasingly important aspect of CWA implementation.

2. *The reach of the NPDES permit requirement.* The NPDES permit requirement applies to "any *addition* of any *pollutant* to navigable waters from any *point source.*" CWA § 502(12) (33 U.S.C. § 1362(12)). Each of the italicized terms can be contested.

    a. Any"addition." In *Miccosukee Tribe*, the key issue was whether the S–9 pump "added" pollutants to Water Conservation Area 3 when it transferred polluted water to that area. The plaintiffs sought to require a permit for the S–9 pump (and other Everglades pumps) as part of their overall strategy to reduce phosphorous inputs to the Everglades. Is it relevant to that question that historically the water on both sides of the pump was naturally connected? That is, if human action separates waters, then rejoins them, should an NPDES permit be required?

    Does a dam "add" pollutants to a river? EPA has taken the position, in litigation and in policy statements but not in any formal regulation, that hydroelectric dams do not require NPDES permits even though they cause water-quality changes and dead fish may be discharged from their turbines. The D.C. Circuit and Sixth Circuit agree. *National Wildlife Federation v. Gorsuch*, 693 F.2d 156, 174–45 (D.C. Cir. 1982); *National Wildlife Federation v. Consumers Power Co.*, 862 F.2d 580 (6th Cir. 1988). The Florida Department of Environmental Protection had relied on this position in rejecting the Tribe's argument that a permit was required for the S–9 pump. Does *Miccosukee Tribe* prohibit EPA or the state from requiring an NPDES permit for a dam?

b. Any "pollutant." The term "pollutant" is broadly defined in the statute. See Sierra Club v. Cedar Point Oil Co., 73 F.3d 546, 566 (5th Cir. 1996) ("the definition of 'pollutant' is meant to leave out very little."). The courts have struggled with the question of whether pesticides sprayed directly into water or into the air in places where they are likely to drift into water are "pollutants" for NPDES purposes. The Ninth Circuit finessed that question in Headwaters Inc. v. Talent Irrigation District, 243 F.3d 526 (9th Cir. 2001) ("Although it would seem absurd to conclude that a toxic chemical directly poured into water is not a pollutant, we need not decide that issue because we agree with the district court that the residual acrolein left in the water after its application qualifies as a chemical waste product and thus as a 'pollutant' under the CWA."), answered it in the affirmative in League of Wilderness Defenders v. Forsgren, 309 F.3d 1181, 1185 (9th Cir. 2002) ("the insecticides at issue meet the definition of 'pollutant' under the Clean Water Act"), but then answered it in the negative in Fairhurst v. Hagener, 422 F.3d 1146, 1150–51 (9th Cir. 2005) ("We conclude that pesticides that are applied to water for a beneficial purpose and in compliance with [the Federal Insecticide, Fungicide and Rodenticide Act], and that produce no residue or unintended effects, are not 'chemical wastes,' and thus are not 'pollutants' regulated by the CWA.").

In 2007, EPA adopted a rule excluding application of pesticides into or over waters from the NPDES permit requirements, provided that the application is "consistent with all relevant requirements under [the Federal Insecticide, Fungicide and Rodenticide Act] (i.e. those relevant to protecting water quality)." The Sixth Circuit held that rule unlawful in National Cotton Council of America v. U.S. EPA, 553 F.3d 927 (6th Cir. 2009). The court concluded that excess chemical pesticides, chemical pesticide residues, and biological pesticides all fall within the statute's unambiguous definition of "pollutant," and that pesticides applied to or over water are added from point sources.

EPA responded by proposing a general permit for pesticide application. 75 Fed. Reg. 31775 (June 4, 2010). EPA consulted with the National Marine Fisheries Service on the proposed pesticides general permit, as required by Endangered Species Act § 7 (discussed in Chapter 6). In a draft Biological Opinion, NMFS tentatively concludes that the proposed general permit is likely to jeopardize endangered aquatic species and destroy critical habitat because as proposed it is not fine-tuned to take into account the possible presence of listed species and the impacts of pesticides on those species. NMFS, Draft Endangered Species Act Section 7 Consultation Biological Opinion on the U.S. Environmental Protection Agency's Proposed Pesticides General Permit (June 17, 2011).

c. Any "point source." The Court in *Miccosukee Tribe* rejected the District's argument that a "point source" must itself produce or be the source of a pollutant, rather than a mere conduit for transfers. As a matter of statutory interpretation, do you agree? If the Court had accepted the District's argument, what would the implications have been for federal control of water pollution? What types of sources would have gone unregulated? Would other regulatory authorities be available to pick up the slack?

An astonishing variety of fact situations have given rise to litigation over whether a particular discharge is from a "point source." Courts have found the following, among others, to be point sources within the meaning of the CWA: a trap shooting range and its firing stations, Stone v. Naperville Park Dist., 38 F. Supp. 2d 651 (N.D. Ill. 1999); a landfill from which wastes flowed to a wetland, Dague v. City of Burlington, 732 F.Supp. 458 (D. Vt. 1989); a barge from which chunks of concrete and rebar were cut off and dumped in the waterway, United States v. West Indies Transp., Inc., 127 F.3d 299 (3d Cir. 1997); and a pile of spent mushroom substrate from which rain leached "a black oil-like liquid" into a stream, Reynolds v. Rick's Mushroom Service, 246 F. Supp. 2d 449 (E.D. Pa. 2003). Even a state trying to remediate an abandoned mine site may have to obtain an NPDES permit. West Virginia Highlands Conservancy v. Huffman, 625 F.3d 159 (4th Cir. 2010).

The definition of "point source" has been litigated frequently because (like the definition of "solid waste" for RCRA, discussed in Chapter 8) it is an important gatekeeper. Point sources must have an NPDES permit, while nonpoint sources are essentially free of federal regulation. The most difficult cases are those in which the pollutants are actually delivered to the waterway by rain or runoff, the paradigmatic example of nonpoint source pollution. In United States v. Earth Sciences, Inc., 599 F.2d 368, 373 (10th Cir. 1979), the Tenth Circuit concluded that the purposes of the CWA require a broad reading of "point source":

> Beginning with the Congressional intent to eliminate pollution from the nation's waters by 1985, the FWPCA was designed to regulate to the fullest extent possible those sources emitting pollution into rivers, streams and lakes. The touchstone of the regulatory scheme is that those needing to use the waters for waste distribution must seek and obtain a permit to discharge that waste, with the quantity and quality of the discharge regulated. The concept of a point source was designed to further this scheme by embracing the broadest possible definition of any identifiable conveyance from which pollutants might enter the waters of the United States. It is clear from the legislative history Congress would have regulated so-called nonpoint sources if a workable method could have been derived; it instructed the EPA to study the problem and come up with a solution.

> We believe it contravenes the intent of FWPCA and the structure of the statute to exempt from regulation any activity that emits pollution from an identifiable point.

Accordingly, the court held that a pool which collected wastewater from cyanide heap-leach gold mining was a point source when it overflowed into a nearby creek as a result of a heavy snowstorm. Id. See also Concerned Area Residents for the Environment v. Southview Farm, 34 F.3d 114 (2d Cir. 1994) (holding that vehicles which spread liquid manure on fields, from which it flowed into streams, were "point sources").

In United States v. Plaza Health Laboratories, 3 F.3d 643 (2d Cir. 1993), a divided panel of the Second Circuit ruled that a man who placed vials of human blood in a bulkhead crevice from which they were washed into the Hudson River by the rising tide was not a point source, and therefore had not committed a criminal violation of the CWA. Influenced by the criminal posture, the Second Circuit held that a human being cannot be a point source for CWA purposes. Dissenting, Judge Oakes argued that any source which is both identifiable and controllable should be considered a point source.

In short, the term "point source" has been broadly construed to apply to a wide range of polluting techniques, so long as the pollutants involved are not just humanmade, but reach the navigable waters by human effort or by leaking from a clear point at which waste water was collected by human effort. From these cases, the writers of one respected treatise have concluded that such a "man-induced gathering mechanism plainly is the essential characteristic of a point source" and that a point source, "[p]ut simply, . . . is an identifiable conveyance of pollutants." 5 Robert E. Beck, *Waters & Water Rights* § 53.01(b)(3) at 216–17 (1991). * * *

This broad reading of the term "point source" is essential to fulfill the mandate of the Clean Water Act. * * *

Nonetheless, the term "point source" sets significant definitional limits on the reach of the Clean Water Act. Fifty percent or more of all water pollution is thought to come from nonpoint sources. S. Rep. 99–50, 99th Cong., 1st Sess. 8 (1985). So, to further refine the definition of "point source," I consider what it is that the Act does not cover: nonpoint source discharges.

Nonpoint source pollution is, generally, runoff: salt from roads, agricultural chemicals from farmlands, oil from parking lots, and other substances washed by rain, in diffuse patterns, over the land and into navigable waters. The sources are many, difficult to identify and difficult to control. Indeed, an effort to greatly reduce nonpoint source pollution could require radical changes in land use patterns which Congress evidently was unwilling to mandate without further study. The structure of the statute—which regulates point source pollution closely, while leaving nonpoint source regulation to the states under the Section 208 program—indicates that the term "point source" was included in the definition of discharge so as to ensure that nonpoint source pollution would *not* be covered. Instead, Congress chose to regulate first that which could easily be regulated: direct discharges by identifiable parties, or point sources.

This rationale for regulating point and nonpoint sources different-ly—that point sources may readily be controlled and are easily attrib-utable to a particular source, while nonpoint sources are more difficult to control without radical change, and less easily attributable, once they reach water, to any particular responsible party—helps define what fits within each category. Thus, Professor Rodgers has suggested, "[t]he statutory 'discernible, confined and discrete conveyance' . . . can be understood as singling out those candidates suitable for control-at-the-source." 2 William H. Rodgers, Jr., *Environmental Law: Air and Water* § 4.10 at 150 (1986). And, as Professor Rodgers notes, "[c]ase law confirms the controllability theory, adding to it a responsibility component, so that 'point sources' are understood both as sources that can be cleaned up and as sources where fairness suggests the named parties should do the cleaning." *Id.*

Plaza Health, 651–653 (Oakes, J., dissenting). Does the Plaza Health dissent capture the key elements of the definition of "point source"? Is it overbroad? What does it leave out, if anything? Suppose that the rocks out of which a dam is constructed contain metals toxic to aquatic life, and those metals are leached into the waters downstream, either by water seeping through from behind the dam or by rainwater corroding the face of the dam. Is the dam a "point source" requiring an NPDES permit? Is the route by which the metals reach the stream relevant?

Some types of discharges that might otherwise appear to be from nonpoint sources are specifically swept into the NPDES permitting universe by the CWA. The statutory definition of point source includes "concentrated animal feeding operation," and CWA § 402(p), added in 1987, requires permits for industrial and municipal stormwater discharges. EPA regulations define industrial stormwater discharges to include discharges from construction sites that disturb one acre of land or more. 40 C.F.R. § 122.26(b)(15)(ii). Not surprisingly, regulation of discharges from CAFOs, construction sites, and storm sewer systems has proven both complex and controversial.

3. *"Unitary waters."* Although it constructed the Central and South Florida Project, the United States does not operate the pumps in question and was not a party to the *Miccosukee Tribe* case. Nonetheless, the U.S. is routinely asked by the Supreme Court to share its views on certiorari petitions that may affect its interests. In *Miccosukee Tribe*, the Solicitor General filed a brief in opposition to the petition for certiorari, arguing that the Eleventh Circuit decision did not merit review because it did not conflict with any other appellate decision and it was "unlikely to result in any change in the operation of the pumping station or to subject petitioner to additional pollution control requirements beyond those that are already required under Florida's recently amended Everglades Forever Act." Once certiorari was granted, however, the United States argued for reversal of the Eleventh Circuit's decision on the grounds that the Clean Water Act regulates only the initial discharge of pollutants into any navigable waters, not their subsequent transfer from one water to another (what the Court calls the "unitary waters" theory).

Two circuits had explicitly rejected the unitary waters argument prior to *Miccosukee Tribe. Dubois v. USDA*, 102 F.3d 1273 (1st Cir. 1996); *Catskill Mountains Chapter of Trout Unlimited v. City of New York*, 273 F.3d 481 (2d Cir. 2001). The Eleventh Circuit's decision in *Miccosukee Tribe* also appeared to reject the unitary waters claim. See Miccosukee

Tribe of Indians v. South Florida Management Dist., 280 F.3d 1364, 1368 ("When a point source changes the natural flow of a body of water which contains pollutants and causes that water to flow into another distinct body of navigable water into which it would not have otherwise flowed," a permit is required).

After the Supreme Court decided *Miccosukee Tribe*, EPA adopted what it calls the Water Transfers Rule. The Water Transfers Rule provides that conveyance of water from one water body to another and connection of previously separate waterways are not subject to NPDES regulation, so long as the transferred water is not subject to any intervening industrial, municipal, or commercial use. 73 Fed. Reg. 33,697 (June 13, 2008). In Friends of the Everglades v. South Florida Water Management District, 570 F.3d 1210 (11th Cir. 2009), the Eleventh Circuit upheld the water transfers rule, based on *Chevron* deference, despite noting that "all of the existing precedent [is] against the unitary waters theory." Is the Water Transfers Rule consistent with the CWA? Is it good policy?

4. *Surface water versus groundwater.* There is some doubt about how or if the NPDES program applies to discharges of groundwater. The courts and EPA agree that pollution of groundwater itself is not addressed by the CWA, because groundwater is not among the "navigable waters." See Exxon Corp. v. Train, 554 F.2d 1310 (5th Cir. 1977). The situation is more complicated where the groundwater in question is hydrologically connected to surface waters. Some courts have held that NPDES permits are required if pollutants reach surface waters through groundwater. Hernandez v. Esso Standard Oil, 599 F. Supp. 2d 175, 181 (D. P.R. 2009) (discharges to groundwater are covered if they "have an adverse impact" on jurisdictional surface waters); Idaho Rural Council v. Bosma, 143 F. Supp. 2d 1169, 1180 (D. Id. 2001) ("the CWA extends federal jurisdiction over groundwater that is hydrologically connected to surface waters that are themselves waters of the United States;" plaintiff must prove that pollutants reach covered surface waters). Others have concluded that discharges to groundwater are not covered, even if the groundwater is hydrologically connected to surface waters. Village of Oconomowoc Lake v. Dayton Hudson Corp., 24 F.3d 962 (7th Cir. 1994) ("Neither the Clean Water Act nor the EPA's definition asserts authority over ground waters, just because these may be hydrologically connected with surface waters."); Umatilla Waterquality Protective Association v. Smith Frozen Foods, 962 F.Supp. 1312, 1320 (D. Or. 1997) ("discharges of pollutants into groundwater are not subject to the CWA's NPDES permit requirement even if that groundwater is hydrologically connected to surface water"). Which is the better interpretation?

5. *Pollution from federal facilities.* CWA § 313(a) (42 U.S.C. § 1323(a)) requires that federal facilities comply with "all federal, state, interstate, and local requirements ... respecting the control and abatement of water pollution in the same manner and to the same extent as any nongovernmental entity." The President may exempt any source "if he determines it to be in the paramount interest of the United States to do so," id., but only for a year at a time. In Weinberger v. Romero–Barcelo, 456 U.S. 305 (1982), the Supreme Court ruled that although Navy weapons training in the waters off Puerto Rico was subject to the NPDES permit requirement because it resulted in the discharge of ordinance to coastal waters, the courts were not required to enjoin training operations while a permit was secured. The Navy proceeded to get a permit. That permit expired in 1989 by its terms, but because the Navy had applied for renewal it continued in effect. In Abreu v. United States, 468 F.3d 20, 28–29 (1st Cir. 2006), the court held that live fire exercises off the coast of Puerto Rico did not violate the CWA because they were within the terms of the 1989 permit.

C. EFFLUENT STANDARDS FOR POINT SOURCES

CLASS DISCUSSION PROBLEM: TROUBLE AT AJAX PAPERBOARD'S CENTRALIA PLANT

The city of Centralia and its surrounding suburbs has a population of 450,000. This growing community is located on the East River within 2 miles of the Atlantic Ocean. The city has a diversified economy composed of a mixture of service, manufacturing and governmental activities. The East River historically supported a wide variety of fish and other aquatic species, attracted large numbers of birds, and was used for swimming, boating, and fishing. Now it is degraded to the point that it supports only limited numbers of resilient "bottom fish" and the water is not suitable for water contact sports or domestic use. Recreational fishing continues, but several fishermen claim that a high proportion of fish recently have been deformed or have had unusual skin ulcers.

Upstream cities and factories discharge substantial quantities of pollutants to the East River before it reaches Centralia. Within the metropolitan area, Centralia's municipal sewer authority operates three treatment works which receive domestic as well as some industrial wastes, discharging treated effluent into the East River. Four major industrial plants treat their own process wastes (containing a range of pollutants) and discharge them to the river pursuant to permits issued by the State Water Board. Surface runoff caused by increasing land development, impervious land cover, and agricultural practices (pesticides and fertilizer applications) also affects water quality.

Citizen groups and the city have become increasingly disturbed about the deteriorating condition of the East River. Their attention has been focused on the local industries that discharge directly to the river. A pulp and paper mill operated by the Ajax Paperboard Company just upstream of Centralia has come in for particular criticism. The Ajax Centralia plant employs the Kraft process with conventional bleaching to produce pulp and paper products. Paper is created by extracting fibers, which requires digestion of the lignin. In the Kraft process, used for about 80% of paper production in the United States, lignin is broken down by heating wood chips under pressure in a solution of sodium sulfide and sodium hydroxide dissolved in water. The resulting pulp is then washed and, to make many products, bleached. Worldwide, pulp mills use three different technologies for bleaching: traditional bleaching, a process introduced in the 1950s using chlorine gas; elemental chlorine free ("ECF"), using chlorine dioxide; and total chlorine free ("TCF"), using ozone, hydrogen peroxide, or oxygen as a bleaching agent. Various combinations of bleaching technologies are also used.

The bleached Kraft process generates conventional (BOD, Total Suspended Solids, and pH) and toxic pollutants (chiefly chlorinated hydrocarbons, including dioxins). The levels of pollutants discharged depend on several factors, including: the type of wood used (pulping of softwoods leave more residual organic pollutants at the end of the cooking process than hardwoods); whether a second stage of oxygen-based delignification is added after the conventional digestion process (adding this process reduces both BOD and, because it leaves fewer aromatic hydrocarbons in the pulp at the bleaching stage, dioxins, but it requires significant capital investment, especially at older plants); and the bleaching process used (ECF bleaching reduces BOD and organic hydrocarbon discharges; TCF bleaching eliminates the discharge of organic hydrocarbons). In the United States, ECF was introduced about 1990 and spread rapidly in the industry. About 95% of US bleached pulp production currently relies on ECF. TCF is not widely used in the United States, but accounts for over 30% of pulp production in Scandinavia, another major pulp producing region.

Ajax Centralia currently uses softwoods, which are the predominant species in the Centralia region, does not have a second-stage digester, and uses conventional bleaching. ECF bleaching requires second-stage digestion. Switching to it is fairly straightforward for mills that have a second-stage digester, because the chemicals it requires are widely available and can be integrated without significant process changes. TCF bleaching requires substantial process modification, because the bleaching agents used tend to corrode metals and stimulate the formation of foams. It also increases production costs and the demand for wood chips, because it reduces the strength of paper with a constant fiber content.

Ajax has operated its Centralia facility for the last twenty-five years after acquiring it from the now defunct Diamond Paper Company. At its peak production in 1950, the mill employed 800 people; today it employs approximately 250. Ajax claims its mill is barely profitable. While the mill workers' union vigorously disputes that assertion, rumors that the mill might close or be taken over surface regularly.

You are an attorney representing the newly-formed group Citizens for a Clean Centralia (CCC). CCC has asked you to determine generally what avenues might be available to push for greater pollution control at the Ajax Centralia plant.

1. What authority does the CWA provide for EPA to establish water pollution control regulations for an existing industrial point source like Ajax Paperboard? What if Ajax were proposing to construct a new plant at the Centralia site? How will any regulations EPA issues be implemented?

2. You learn that EPA is considering revisions to the effluent limitations for pulp and paper mills. What kind(s) of information does EPA need in order to develop regulations? Where would it obtain this data? How does EPA identify the level or type of pollution control measures to require? What role do costs play in that decision? Should EPA recognize separate categories for plants with and without secondary digesting? Should it require secondary digesting for all plants as BAT? What bleaching technology should it require?

3. Suppose that EPA issues revised effluent standards grouping all Kraft process plants in a single category and setting effluent limits based on the levels of dioxin and BOD discharges achievable through ECF bleaching. Can the Ajax Centralia plant obtain a variance from those standards? How would you oppose a variance request?

Excerpts From the Clean Water Act

33 U.S.C. §§ 1251–1387.

Sec. 301.   Effluent limitations.

* * *

(b) In order to carry out the objective of this chapter there shall be achieved—

(1)(A) not later than July 1, 1977, effluent limitations for point sources, other than publicly owned treatment works, (i) which shall require the application of the best practicable control technology currently available as defined by the Administrator pursuant to section [304(b)], or (ii) in the case of a discharge into a publicly owned treatment works * * * which shall require compliance with any applicable pretreatment requirements and any requirements under section [307]; and

  (B) for publicly owned treatment works * * * effluent limitations based upon secondary treatment as defined by the Administrator pursuant to section [304(d)(1)]; or,

  (C) not later than July 1, 1977, any more stringent limitation, including those necessary to meet water quality standards, treatment standards, or schedules of compliance, established pursuant to any State law or regulations or any other Federal law or regulation, or required to implement any applicable water quality standard established pursuant to this chapter.

(2)(A) for [toxic pollutants and non-conventional pollutants], by no later than three years after standards are set under § 304(b)], effluent limitations for categories and classes of point sources, other than publicly owned treatment works, which (i) shall require application of the best available technology economically achievable for such category or class, which will result in reasonable further progress toward the national goal of eliminating the discharge of all pollutants, as determined in accordance with regulations issued by the Administrator pursuant to section

[304(b)(2)] of this title, which such effluent limitations shall require the elimination of discharges of all pollutants if the Administrator finds, on the basis of information available to him, that such elimination is technologically and economically achievable for a category or class of point sources * * *, or (ii) in the case of the introduction of a pollutant into a publicly owned treatment works * * * shall require compliance with any applicable pretreatment requirements and any other requirement under section [307];

* * *

(E) as expeditiously as practicable but in no case later than three years after the date such limitations are promulgated under section [304(b)] * * *, compliance with effluent limitations for categories and classes of point sources, other than publicly owned treatment works, which in the case of [conventional pollutants] shall require application of the best conventional pollutant control technology as determined in accordance with regulations issued by the Administrator pursuant to section [304(b)] * * *.

(c) The Administrator may modify the requirements of subsection (b)(2)(A) of this section with respect to any point source for which a permit application is filed after July 1, 1977, upon a showing by the owner or operator of such point source satisfactory to the Administrator that such modified requirements (1) will represent the maximum use of technology within the economic capability of the owner or operator; and (2) will result in reasonable further progress toward the elimination of the discharge of pollutants.

(d) Any effluent limitation required by paragraph (2) of subsection (b) of this section shall be reviewed at least every five years and, if appropriate, revised pursuant to the procedure established under such paragraph.

* * *

(n) Fundamentally different factors

(1) General rule. The Administrator, with the concurrence of the State, may establish an alternative requirement under subsection (b)(2) of this section or section [307(b)] of this title for a facility that modifies the requirements of national effluent limitation guidelines or categorical pretreatment standards that would otherwise be applicable to such facility, if the owner or operator of such facility demonstrates to the satisfaction of the Administrator that—

(A) the facility is fundamentally different with respect to the factors (other than cost) specified in section [304(b) or 304(g)] and considered by the Administrator in establishing such national effluent limitation guidelines or categorical pretreatment standards;

(B) the application—

(i) is based solely on information and supporting data submitted to the Administrator during the rulemaking for establishment of the applicable national effluent limitation guidelines or categorical pretreatment standard specifically raising the factors that are fundamentally different for such facility; or

(ii) is based on information and supporting data referred to in clause (i) and information and supporting data the applicant did not have a reasonable opportunity to submit during such rulemaking;

(C) the alternative requirement is no less stringent than justified by the fundamental difference; and

(D) the alternative requirement will not result in a non-water quality environmental impact which is markedly more adverse than the impact considered by the Administrator in establishing such national effluent limitation guideline or categorical pretreatment standard.

* * *

Sec. 304. Information and guidelines.

(a)(1) The Administrator, after consultation with appropriate Federal and State agencies and other interested persons, shall develop and publish, within one year after October 18, 1972 (and from time to time thereafter revise) criteria for water quality accurately reflecting the latest scientific knowledge (A) on the kind and extent of all identifiable effects on health and welfare including, but not limited to, plankton, fish, shellfish, wildlife, plant life, shorelines, beaches, esthetics, and recreation which may be expected from the presence of pollutants in any body of water, including ground water; (B) on the concentration and dispersal of pollutants, or their byproducts, through biological, physical, and chemical processes; and (C) on the effects of pollutants on biological community diversity, productivity, and stability, including information on the factors affecting rates of eutrophication and rates of organic and inorganic sedimentation for varying types of receiving waters.

(2) The Administrator, after consultation with appropriate Federal and State agencies and other interested persons, shall develop and publish, within one year after October 18, 1972 (and from time to time thereafter revise) information (A) on the factors necessary to restore and maintain the chemical, physical, and biological integrity of all navigable waters, ground waters, waters of the contiguous zone, and the oceans; (B) on the factors necessary for the protection and propagation of shellfish, fish, and wildlife for classes and categories of receiving waters and to allow recreational activities in and on the water; and (C) on the measurement and classification of water quality; and (D) for the purpose of section [303], on and the identification of pollutants suitable for maximum daily load measurement correlated with the achievement of water quality objectives.

* * *

(b) For the purpose of adopting or revising effluent limitations under this Act the Administrator shall, after consultation with appropriate Federal and State agencies and other interested persons, publish within one year of October 18, 1972, regulations, providing guidelines for effluent limitations, and, at least annually thereafter, revise, if appropriate, such regulations. Such regulations shall—

(1)(A) identify, in terms of amounts of constituents and chemical, physical, and biological characteristics of pollutants, the degree of effluent reduction attainable through the application of the best practicable control technology currently available for classes and categories of point sources (other than publicly owned treatment works); and

   (B) specify factors to be taken into account in determining the control measures and practices to be applicable to point sources (other than publicly owned treatment works) within such categories or classes. Factors relating to the assessment of best practicable control technology currently available to comply with subsection (b)(1) of section 1311 of this Act shall include consideration of the total cost of application of technology in relation to the effluent reduction benefits to be achieved from such application, and shall also take into account the age of equipment and facilities involved, the process employed, the engineering aspects of the application of various types of control techniques, process changes, non-water quality environmental impact (including energy requirements), and such other factors as the Administrator deems appropriate;

(2)(A) identify, in terms of amounts of constituents and chemical, physical, and biological characteristics of pollutants, the degree of effluent reduction attainable through the application of the best control measures and practices achievable including treatment techniques, process and procedure innovations, operating methods, and other alternatives for classes and categories of point sources (other than publicly owned treatment works); and

   (B) specify factors to be taken into account in determining the best measures and practices available to comply with subsection (b)(2) of section 1311 of this Act to be applicable to any point source (other than publicly owned treatment works) within such categories of classes. Factors relating to the assessment of best available technology shall take into account the age of equipment and facilities involved, the process employed, the engineering aspects of the application of various types of control techniques, process changes, the cost of achieving such effluent reduction, non-water quality environmental impact (including energy requirements), and such other factors as the Administrator deems appropriate. * * *

(4)(A) Identify, in terms of constituents and chemical, physical and biological characteristics of pollutants, the degree of effluent reduction attainable through the application of the best conventional pollutant control technology (including measures and practices) for classes and categories of point sources (other than publicly owned treatment works); and

   (B) specify factors to be taken into account in determining the best conventional pollutant control technology measures and practices to comply with section 1311(b)(2)(E) of this title to be applicable to any point source (other than publicly owned treatment works) within such categories or classes. Factors relating to the assessment of best conventional pollutant control technology (including measures and practices) include consideration of the reasonableness of the relationship between the costs of obtaining a reduction in effluents and the effluent reduction benefits derived, and the comparison of the cost and level of reduction of such pollutants from the discharge from publicly owned treatment works to the cost and level of reduction of such pollutants from a class or category of industrial sources, and shall take into account the age of equipment and facilities involved, the process employed, the engineering aspects of various types of control techniques, process changes, non-water quality environmental impact (including energy requirements), and such other factors as the Administrator deems appropriate.

* * *

(m)(1) Within 12 months after February 4, 1987, and biennially thereafter, the Administrator shall publish in the Federal Register a plan which shall—

(A) establish a schedule for the annual review and revision of promulgated effluent guidelines, in accordance with subsection (b) of this section;

(B) identify categories of sources discharging toxic or nonconventional pollutants for which guidelines under subsection (b)(2) of this section and section [306] have not previously been published; and

(C) establish a schedule for promulgation of effluent guidelines for categories identified in subparagraph (B), under which promulgation of such guidelines shall be no later than 4 years after February 4, 1987, for categories identified in the first published plan or 3 years after the publication of the plan for categories identified in later published plans.

* * *

OVERVIEW OF POINT SOURCE CONTROLS

The 1972 CWA specified two levels of pollution control—"best practicable control technology currently available" (BPT) was to be achieved by 1977, and the more demanding "best available technology economically achievable" (BAT) by 1983. Based on the CWA's goal of eliminating pollutant discharges to water by 1985, BAT is supposed to require zero discharge if that is technologically and economically achievable for the class of sources. E.I. DuPont de Nemours & Co. v. Train, 430 U.S. 112, 126 (1977).

In 1977 Congress created a more complex scheme of discharge regulations depending upon the type of pollutant. All of these standards, it should be noted, are set for classes and categories of sources, rather than on a source-by-source basis.

a. *Conventional pollutants.* CWA § 304(a)(4) identifies as "conventional pollutants" biological oxygen demand, suspended solids, fecal coliform, and pH (pollutants that are only problematic in large amounts and are typically associated with POTWs). As permitted by this section, EPA has added oil and grease to the list. See 40 C.F.R. § 401.16. Conventional pollutants are freed from the BAT requirement; instead, they are subject to the "best conventional pollutant control technology" or BCT.

b. *Toxic pollutants.* Before 1977, the CWA mandated development of risk-based standards for toxic pollutants, without regard to the cost of compliance. "As a result of the limited availability of data on the aquatic toxicology and the fate and transport of toxic water pollutants, the agency could not manage the task." Robert L. Glicksman, The Value of Agency–Forcing Citizen Suits to Enforce Nondiscretionary Duties, 10 Widener L. Rev. 353, 362–363 (2002). Environmentalists sued, resulting in a settlement under which EPA agreed to set technology-based standards for a list of 65 toxic substances. In the 1977 amendments to the CWA, Congress essentially endorsed the settlement, directing EPA to issue BAT standards for toxic pollutants. See CWA § 307 (33 U.S.C. § 1317).

c. *Nonconventional pollutants.* Pollutants (other than heat) not classified as conventional or toxic are considered nonconventional pollutants. CWA § 301(b)(2)(F) (33 U.S.C. § 1311(b)(2)(F)). Examples include ammonia, chlorides, nitrates, iron, and color. Nonconventional pollutants are subject to BAT standards, subject to the possibility of limited modifications under CWA § 301(g).

d. *Heat.* Thermal discharges are ostensibly regulated under the general technology-based structure of the Act. Most thermal discharge permits are issued, however, under the authority of CWA § 316(b) (33 U.S.C. § 1326(b)), which requires that the location, design, construction, and capacity of new cooling water intake structures reflect the best technology available for minimizing adverse environmental impact.

In addition, the CWA requires special standards for new sources, defined to mean those for which construction is begun after publication of the proposed standards. CWA § 306(a)(2) (33 U.S.C. § 1316(a)(2)). By contrast to the CAA, modification does not trigger the application of new source performance standards under the CWA. New sources must achieve "the greatest degree of effluent reduction which the Administrator determines to be achievable through application of the best available demonstrated control technology, processes, operating methods, or other alternatives, including, where practicable, a standard permitting no discharge of pollutants." CWA § 306(a)(1). This standard is typically abbreviated as BDT.

Finally, CWA § 301(b) requires that publicly owned treatment works (POTWs) comply with secondary treatment standards. Primary treatment is mechanical—floating material is skimmed off and heavy solids are settled out. Secondary treatment adds a biological step in which bacteria consume organic materials, reducing the biological oxygen demand in the wastewater. Tertiary treatment, which can remove nutrients, is typically not mandated.

Many POTWs receive substantial quantities of industrial wastewater. EPA has estimated that more than 60,000 industrial plants in 34 primary industrial groups discharge into POTWs. These effluent generators have been termed "indirect dischargers" since their wastes are not sent to directly to rivers or streams, but eventually reach those waters through discharges from wastewater treatment plants. CWA § 307 (33 U.S.C. § 1317) requires technology-based pretreatment, equivalent to BAT, before wastewaters are introduced to a public sewer system. EPA adopts nationally applicable, category-based, pretreatment standards for indirect dischargers which track the effluent standards set by the agency for direct dischargers under §§ 310 and 304.

CWA effluent standards typically establish the maximum quantity of pollutants which may be discharged for each unit of production. For instance, BAT limitations in the primary nickel and cobalt subcategory of the Non–Ferrous Metals Point Source Category state that a source may not discharge, on a daily average, more than 16.25 pounds of the pollutant copper for each million pounds of nickel produced. 40 C.F.R. § 421.233(c). In theory, as control technology improves the amounts of waste copper for each million pounds of nickel produced should approach zero. Alternatively, some effluent standards are expressed in terms of permissible pollutant concentrations in wastewater. Concentration-based effluent standards are stated in terms of milligrams of pollutant per liter of wastewater regardless of the amount of production. Although such limitations are acceptable to EPA in limited circumstances, they run afoul of the basic anti-pollution policy of the Act because a source could meet them by diluting its wastestream with water rather than reducing the production of pollutants.

EPA, Effluent Guidelines Plan
55 Fed. Reg. 80, 84–86 (1990).

* * * This section of the notice summarizes the various tasks which the Agency [EPA] must complete in a typical effluent guideline rulemaking.

Initially, the Agency must establish the scope of the rulemaking and the dimensions of the rulemaking project by defining the industry category. For some industry categories, such as the Inorganic Chemicals Manufacturing category (40 C.F.R. part 415), the Agency was able to use readily available tools such as the Standard Industrial Classification (SIC) Manual in defining the category to be addressed. For others, such as the Machinery Manufacturing and Rebuilding category ("MM & R"), the process has been more difficult. In defining the MM & R category, the Agency first examined what industrial activities had not been regulated in the "Machinery and Mechanical Products" category as identified in the 1976 consent decree. From that, the Agency identified approximately 89,000 facilities that manufacture or rebuild machinery but that were not covered by previously promulgated guidelines. The Agency then examined whether the Metal Finishing category (40 C.F.R. part 433) would cover these establishments and found that it did cover approximately 13,000 of the 89,000 identified. EPA then examined the products manufactured and processes employed by the remaining 76,000 facilities and by facilities with related processes and facilities. The Agency was unable, from a process or practical basis, to differentiate between manufacturing, maintenance and rebuilding. Accordingly, EPA determined these three classifications should be evaluated together.

Next, the Agency determines the size of the category as it has been defined, using all available sources. Given the diversity of regulatory categories, no one source suffices to establish size. At various times, EPA has used one or more of the following sources: standard published sources, information available through trade associations, data purchased from the Dun and Bradstreet, Inc. data base, other publicly available data bases, census data, other U.S. Government information and any available EPA data base. For MM & R, for example, the Agency found that its original estimate of 89,000 facilities had included only the larger manufacturing facilities. The Agency currently believes this category includes over 278,000 facilities with 10 or more employees, and totals approximately 970,000 facilities. If a category is very large, the Agency will determine whether it can be broken down into appropriate categories or subcategories. If more than one subcategory can be identified, the Agency may need to establish priorities for regulation.

Regulatory information about industry categories is obtained largely through survey questionnaires and on-site wastewater sampling. Survey questionnaires solicit detailed information necessary to assess the statutory rulemaking factors (particularly technological and economic achievability of available controls), water use, production processes, and wastewater treatment and disposal practices. A significant portion of the Agency's questionnaires typically seek information necessary to assess economic achievability.

If the survey questionnaire is expected to go to more than nine entities, clearance from the Office of Management and Budget (OMB) is required under the Paperwork Reduction Act (44 U.S.C. § 3501 et seq.). Typically, the Agency will construct a questionnaire and obtain public reaction on it. Often the Agency will pre-test the questionnaire by having one or more facilities complete the draft form. Formal submission to OMB will follow completion of these activities. OMB review can take up to 90 days from official submission of the questionnaire. * * *

Generally, the Agency is able to define its wastewater sampling effort based on information received in response to the questionnaires. While the questionnaire provides information about production processes, water uses and, in general terms, what is found in the industry's wastewater, on-site sampling is required to characterize specifically the pollutants found in discharges. This is because direct dischargers are ordinarily required to do limited, though regular, sampling under the monitoring provisions of their permits, and few indirect dischargers are required to do any frequent testing. Moreover, site visits are necessary to assess pollutant control technology. Scheduling of site visits depends on a number of factors. First, sampling is generally conducted by contractors selected by the strict standards of the government contracting process. The logistics of coordinating the sampling can be extensive. Second, successful site visits require the presence of knowledgeable plant personnel to answer pertinent questions and to assist the sampling team in various ways. Third, site visits are useful only if plants are operating under "normal" conditions; therefore, visits must be scheduled to avoid "down time" periods for maintenance or other interruptions. Finally, scheduling of a site visit may depend on plant production schedules, if a plant produces numerous products or changes its product mix as part of a production cycle.

Sampling and site visits and many other tasks related to the preparation of guidelines, including numerous efforts related to economic, statistical and environmental analyses, are generally accomplished with the assistance of EPA contractors under supervision of Agency program staff. In addition, contract laboratories, rather than EPA laboratories, ordinarily analyze these samples. (EPA laboratories generally are devoted to research and development.) Hiring contractors is a rigorous and somewhat protracted process that is dictated by Federal contracting requirements. * * *

Most of the effluent sampling and analysis that has supported effluent guideline regulations promulgated to date has been conducted and funded by EPA. On occasion, however, these activities have been pursued on a cooperative basis with industry parties. For example, EPA and numerous pulp and paper manufacturers participated in a cooperative effort to sample and analyze effluent, wastewater treatment sludge and pulp from domestic mills that bleach pulp in their production processes. Despite the obvious advantage that such a cooperative situation presents to the Agency in terms of reduced cost, it is not clear that such a process shortens the time required to promulgate a regulation. In fact, the negotiated nature of such a cooperative program may actually lengthen the analytical data collection phase of the regulation development process.

When sampling is completed, wastewater samples are sent to laboratories for analysis. * * *

Responses to questionnaires are generally written on the questionnaire form itself. Together with results from sampling and site visits, the information must be entered into computer files. This is a considerable task that generally precedes the major analytical work and must be performed according to quality assurance procedures. Frequently, this effort is slowed by the need to interpret the information as submitted by the respondent and to reconcile discrepancies. However, only when it is completed, can the Agency conduct the statistical, economic and engineering analyses necessary to develop treatment control options and to select one or more of these options tentatively as the basis for a rulemaking proposal.

Rulemaking proposals, as well as final rules and other rulemaking notices (such as notices of the availability of new data) all undergo thorough internal Agency review before publication in the Federal Register. The process of internal review is designed not only to ensure the quality and completeness of regulatory packages, but to expedite rulemaking by the early identification of issues and resolution of any disagreements among concerned EPA offices.

Within the Agency, an individual "work group" oversees the development of each effluent guideline and the supporting record. The purpose of work groups is to provide for full consultation and coordination on a rulemaking package among all EPA offices (often including regional offices) that participate in the rulemaking. After the work group develops treatment control options for a guideline, the options typically are presented to the Administrator as the basis for the proposed guideline. After "options selection", work groups must reach closure on a rulemaking package that implements the proposal of the selected treatment option before review of the package at higher levels. "Work Group Closure" on a regulatory package that proposes a guideline occurs when the work group concludes that the major issues presented by a rulemaking package are resolved and that the package is generally ready for consideration by the Agency's senior management. A closure meeting usually follows review and revision of several drafts of a rulemaking package. This can take many months.

Following Work Group Closure, several steps must be taken before publication of a proposed guideline. These steps usually begin with revision of the preamble, proposed rule and associated documents in response to the comments raised by concerned offices at Work Group Closure. After the completion of revisions to these documents, which can be quite lengthy, final review begins. This includes a review by senior Agency management known as the "Red Border" process, separate review by OMB under Executive Order 12291, formal recommendation by the Assistant Administrator for Water and signature by the Administrator. This final review is not a mere formality; the Agency usually allows about 4 months to accomplish these steps. Any unresolved issues that remain after Work Group Closure must be settled. Once the Administrator approves the proposal, the rulemaking proposal can be published in the Federal Register, opening the public comment period. Comment periods generally are set for 60 to 90 days, but sometimes extend beyond 90 days for particularly complicated proposals.

At the close of the comment period on the proposed rule, the work group reviews the comments to identify significant issues and to initiate the preparation of responses to comments. Responding to comments submitted in guidelines rulemaking is often an enormous task because of the variety of processes and pollutants covered by the proposal, the range of treatment technologies that may be required, the different types of manufacturers in the category to be covered, and the number of parties and citizens affected by the rule. (In the recent rulemaking setting guidelines for the Organic Chemicals, Plastics and Synthetic Fibers category (40 C.F.R. part 414), the Agency received over 15,000 pages of comments.) During this period, the Agency also revises the technical support documents and other analyses in light of comments received.

Ultimately the Agency must decide what modifications to the proposed rule must be made in response to the public comments or in response to new data developed by EPA itself since the proposal. Sometimes it is necessary to re-propose all or parts of a rule or to publish a supplemental notice or notice of data availability. For example, in the Organic Chemicals rulemaking, the Agency issued three notices and requests for comments after the original proposal. If any notices must be issued between the publication of the rulemaking proposal and the promulgation of the final rule, these notices undergo internal review with many of the same requirements before publication and are subject to comment by the public.

Finally, the Agency prepares a final rulemaking package. This package must reflect appropriate resolution of comments received and issues raised since the proposal. Typically, "Options Selection" at the Administrator's level again takes place. In addition, the rulemaking record, which often includes tens of thousands of pages, must be assembled. The final rule is subject to the same review process as rulemaking proposals, including Work Group Closure, review in Red Border, and separate review by OMB before signature by the Administrator.

After publication of a final rule, the Agency must continue to devote significant time and resources to the rulemaking project. For example, the project staff works with staff from EPA regional offices and States on implementation of the guideline. In the event of a challenge in the United States Court of Appeals, the project staff must spend a great deal of additional time assisting in the defense of the rule. Project staff sometimes also become involved in special studies relating to the published rule. Until these post-publication activities end, the resources involved frequently cannot be transferred to the preparation of other guidelines.

American Petroleum Institute v. U.S. EPA

United States Court of Appeals, Fifth Circuit, 1988.
858 F.2d 261.

■ JERRY E. SMITH, CIRCUIT JUDGE:

The American Petroleum Institute (API) and four individual oil companies petition us to invalidate Environmental Protection Agency (EPA) regulations imposing certain restrictions upon oil companies that drill offshore in Alaskan waters. We have previously upheld the criteria under which such permits are issued. API v. EPA, 787 F.2d 965, 975–77 (5th Cir. 1986). In that opinion, we ordered the EPA to substantiate further its pill-substitution[1] regulations. In response, EPA has reissued revised substantia-

---

1. Normally, thousands of barrels of "mud" lubricate the drilling pipe and bit and carry the drill cuttings to the surface. The industry is usually allowed to dispose of this mud in the

tion for BAT-level control of diesel oil, effectively requiring drillers to use mineral oil, rather than diesel oil, as a drilling additive to lubricant mud. * * *

Virtually conceding agency authority, API argues that EPA's permit scheme is flawed because, even if diesel oil may be characterized in such a way as to merit BAT treatment, EPA chose an improper method from among the alternative BAT-level technologies. The continuing controversy in this seven-year litigation is whether mineral oil pill-substitution is the appropriate BAT-level technology.

EPA determined that the best available technology for limiting diesel oil discharges is product substitution, so EPA required the industry to use mineral oil instead of diesel oil in the pills it circulates down wellheads being drilled. If industry prefers, it may continue to use diesel oil pills, but must barge the entire mud system for on-land disposal; while API asserts that the barge alternative is not realistic for Alaskan waters, water discharge is allowed so long as no diesel oil has been used in the pills.

API contends that EPA applied the wrong standard in determining that mineral oil was an appropriate product substitute. In arguing its position, API focuses upon which survey data the EPA relied in determining that mineral oil is an appropriate substitute for diesel oil in pills. EPA followed its regulations in ordering the substitution, and its interpretation of the various surveys and choice between indicated outcomes commands great deference.

Indeed, we review deferentially not only EPA's factual evaluations, but also its statutory and regulatory interpretation and application, and its policy determinations. * * * Certainly the data is subject to dispute, but we cannot say that EPA's conclusions are unfounded.

API also argues, without citation to authority, that the product substituted must be "operationally equivalent" to diesel oil before EPA may require the substitution. EPA counters that the substitution must be only "technologically and economically achievable." 33 U.S.C. § 1311(b)(2)(A). Our remand to the agency was confined to the diesel-oil provision, and EPA has now developed evidence to meet our concerns.

Upon remand, EPA considered survey data gathered from wells on which diesel oil and mineral oil pills were used and concluded that the substitution met the "achievability" standard. EPA is correct that API is without legal support for its contention that a technology must be widely used in the industry to be considered as an appropriate product substitute. While acknowledging that mineral oil is used for pills less frequently than

---

surrounding waters. When the pipe becomes stuck, however, additional lubrication is required. In these cases, a "pill" of oil or other additives is circulated down the drilling hole. Pills are made up of mud buffers on either end of a significant amount of diesel oil or mineral oil. These pills may not be discharged into the surrounding waters, and the industry is usually required to dispose of the pill in approved land hazardous materials management sites. This EPA permit for Alaskan waters effectively condemns the entire mud system to on-land disposal if diesel oil is used in the pill. * * *

is diesel oil, EPA argues that it is presently used in some circumstances and demonstrably can be used effectively in the future. Even if mineral oil is not the industry's choice as an additive for lubricant mud, and even if this plausible substitute is only most rarely seen in practice, studies support feasibility (at an added cost); thus, mineral oil replacement for toxic-carrying diesel oil is "technologically and economically achievable."[4]

However, under existing environmental legislation a process is deemed "available" even if it is not in use at all. Such an outcome is consistent with Congress' intent to "push pollution control technology." *Weyerhauser,* 590 F.2d at 1061.

One further concern motivated our inquiry here: API's repeated argument that toxic-carrying diesel pills pose no environmental threat when discharged in the relatively small volumes of mud typical of Alaskan operations.[5] However, the Clean Water Act permits blanket prohibitions and other "stringent pollution restrictions" to be imposed "even where the discharge caused no discernible harm to the environment." *API v. EPA,* 661 F.2d at 344.

---

4. API argues that the EPA's substitution of mineral oil for diesel oil is improper because EPA inadequately considered the statutory factors required for BAT-level limitations. Before EPA selects BAT-level limitations, it is required to address both (1) operational considerations, including "the process employed, the engineering aspects of the application of various types of control techniques [and] process changes," and (2) cost, including "the cost of achieving such effluent reduction[,] non-water quality, environmental impact [and] energy requirements." 33 U.S.C. § 1314(b)(2)(B).

In arguing this point, API asserts that mineral oil is not as effective as diesel oil for pill usage, indicating that the substitution does not meet operational standards. API estimates that the use of mineral oil pills could add as much as $30 million to the cost of drilling off the Alaskan coast over the next ten years. In addition, API argues that "one to three wells will be needlessly lost if only the Agency's product substitute (i.e., mineral oil) is used."

It is significant that API attacks the EPA's conclusions and the data upon which it is based in asserting that the EPA's action was arbitrary and capricious. EPA based its ruling on various surveys of pill usage in the Gulf of Mexico, and API disputes the agency's interpretation of that data. Neither the mineral oil evaluation nor EPA's rejection of (allegedly less costly) alternate or additional treatment processes are open for our reconsideration; as long as the policy choices reached are supported in the scientific record, we cannot second-guess the agency's decision. We note, however, that EPA's data and factfinding explicitly addressed the problem that "existing pill recovery techniques have not been shown to be effective in reducing the diesel oil content and toxicity of discharged muds."

* * *

5. Citing 40 years in which diesel oil has been discharged "without environmental damage" to the Outer Continental Shelf, API argues that "the discharge of approximately 24 barrels of diesel oil per year [into] the general permit areas encompass[ing] thousands of square miles of open ocean ... will be avoided at an annual cost of nearly $6,000,000.00"; this "infinitesimal" impact at a "monumental" cost is indicative of Region 10's administrators' "perverse" and "obsessive" disregard of correct agency decisionmaking in order to ban effluents with *de minimis* environmental harm and proves that "this limitation is not based upon any adverse impact to the receiving water." Under BCT-level control, EPA is not allowed to impose "treatment for treatment's sake [but must consider] 'the reasonableness of the relationship between the costs of attaining a reduction in effluents and the effluent reduction benefits derived.' " *API v. EPA,* 787 F.2d at 976 (quoting 33 U.S.C. § 1314(b)(4)(B)). However, BAT-level limitations are not subject to such a strict cost/benefit correlation.

"Analogous to a strict liability standard," *API v. EPA,* 661 F.2d at 344, BAT limitations properly may require industry, regardless of a discharge's effect on water quality, to employ defined levels of technology to meet effluent limitations; a direct cost/benefit correlation is not required, so even minimal environmental impact can be regulated, so long as the prescribed alternative is "technologically and economically achievable." 4 Leg. History of the Clean Water Act of 1977: A Continuation of the Leg. History of the Fed. Water Pollution Control Act, 95th Cong., 2d Sess. 1469–70 (1978). * * *

NOTES AND QUESTIONS

1. *The promise of technology-based standards.* The CWA requires various levels of technology-based controls, depending on the pollutant and the source. As the history of regulation of toxic water pollutants demonstrates, risk-based standards may be paralyzing, because they are so information-intensive and because they may threaten to shut down important industry sectors. Technology-based standards also require substantial amounts of information, as the Effluent Planning Guidelines illustrate, but there are fewer irresolvable uncertainties and, because they take economic and technological feasibility into account, they do not present the same threat to industry. In addition, because NPDES permits must be renewed every five years and effluent limitations must be reviewed periodically, the NPDES system should theoretically result in continual technological improvement until the CWA's zero-pollution goal, or something as close to it as feasible, is achieved.

Although it is simpler in some respects than setting risk-based standards, determining technology-based standards poses its own challenges. Why did Congress direct EPA to set uniform effluent standards on an industry-by-industry basis, and then create different levels of control for different pollutants? What challenges does this pose for EPA? Does the complex scheme serve a useful function, or is it needless micro management?

2. *Subcategorization.* To what extent does the CWA allow or require EPA to divide a single industry into subcategories for the purpose of setting effluent limitations? What is the purpose of industry subdivision? What effect does it have on the CWA's technology-forcing goal? EPA's effluent standards subcategorize industries to a remarkable degree. Within the Canned and Preserved Seafood Processing category, for example, EPA has set separate standards for thirty-two subcategories, including seven for different types of crab meat processing operations and five for shrimp processors. See 40 C.F.R. Part 408. Why would the question of subcategorization be important to a particular plant such as the Ajax facility? Should the agency be required to take into consideration regional differences, age, climate, and other factors? The courts have generally been quite deferential to EPA's categorization decisions.

3. *Technology transfer.* When establishing effluent standards under the CWA, EPA must determine that a pollution control technology exists which, if employed, would allow sources within the industrial category to meet the standard. Where would you look for such "model" pollution control technology? Would you try to find the least polluting facility in the country and use it as the norm? Should the agency be able to extrapolate from one industry or category to another? That sort of extrapolation is permitted if EPA shows that shows that the technology is transferable, and makes a reasonable prediction of how effective it will be in the new industry. See, e.g., Kennecott v. EPA, 780 F.2d 445, 453 (4th Cir. 1985).

4. *The role of costs.* As a general proposition, the marginal cost of removing a unit of pollutant from a waste stream increases as the percentage of pollutant removed rises. For example, it might be possible to reduce the level of BOD discharge from a factory by 80% at a cost of $0.25 per pound removed. The cost of the removing the next 10%, to get to a total control level of 90%, might rise to $0.75 per pound. Finally, the incremental costs of removing the last 10% could be much higher—as much as $2.50 or more per pound. How should EPA decide how far to go along the control spectrum? Recall that the CWA imposes uniform effluent standards without regard to the quality of the receiving water or the number of other sources.

What guidance does the statute provide with respect to consideration of costs? Do they play a different role in BPT, BCT, and BAT standards? In setting BPT and BCT standards, EPA must consider the relationship between costs and benefits. Such a comparison is not required for BAT, however. Costs are simply one of several factors EPA must consider, and benefits are not mentioned. BAT may be set at a level that will require some plants to close. Association of Pac. Fisheries v. EPA, 615 F.2d 794, 818 (9th Cir. 1980).

Are uniform technology-based effluent limitation standards irrational? Consider the following excerpt:

> Economists long have argued that technology-based controls, of which the Clean Water Act provides a nearly perfect example, waste money in two major ways. First, by imposing the same requirements on similar plants everywhere they run the risk of regulating too little to meet water quality goals in some areas and more than necessary in others. As a result, some bodies of water fail to improve in quality or to avoid deterioration. Other requirements are strict beyond any rational link to environmental improvements. The unimpressive overall ratio of benefits to expenditures since 1972 and the remaining cases of unarrested decline in water quality strongly suggest that this model of economically inefficient expenditures fits the Clean Water Act. What case studies there are tend to confirm that impression.

> Second, even if one assumes that the effluent load that technology-based standards produce for a body of water is somehow the load that best suits water quality, the industry-by-industry method by which these standards are set assures inefficiency in allocating the costs of

reaching that pollution level. Only rarely will the costs of restricting pollutant X in industry A to a specified level—as calculated by rule-making immersed in the details of determining the proper technology-based controls for that industry—equal the costs of restricting pollutant X to the level specified by similarly parochial rulemaking for industry B. Whenever those costs differ, the efficiency of pollution control for a given body of water will suffer to the extent that the overall reduction target could be met by substituting low-cost reductions at a plant in one industry for high-cost reductions at a plant in another. For example, if the cost of controlling a unit of pollution is ten percent less at plant A than at plant B, and the environmental benefits are the same, society will save resources if it shifts the burden from plant B to plant A until marginal control costs at the two plants are equal. * * *

William F. Pedersen, Jr., *Turning the Tide on Water Quality*, 15 ECOLOGY L.Q. 69, 82–83 (1988). We will see shortly how the CWA does (or at least tries to) take water quality into account. Putting that to one side, is there any justification for imposing uniform effluent standards even though sources face differential costs of control? Does the practice of subdividing industry categories address Pedersen's concerns? Would tradable allowances be a better way to address some water pollution problems? What shortcomings might trading have in this context?

5. *Cooling water intakes.* Many electric power plants are cooled by water taken in from nearby sources. For power plants which also are point sources requiring an NPDES permit, CWA § 316 (33 U.S.C. § 1326) mandates that EPA set standards requiring that "the location, design, construction, and capacity of cooling water intake structures reflect the best technology available for minimizing adverse environmental impact." Unlike the NPDES provisions, § 316 does not explain what factors the agency should take into account when identifying the "best technology available."

After long delays, and only when prompted by lawsuits, EPA adopted rules for water intake structures at large power plants, which together suck in more than 200 billion gallons of water every day, causing impingement and entrainment of over 3.4 billion aquatic organisms each year. EPA's standards required that facilities substantially reduce deaths of fish and shellfish. EPA refused to require that power plants convert to closed cycle cooling or meet equivalent standards for impacts on aquatic organisms, because it found that the additional costs would not significantly exceed the limited environmental benefits.

Environmental groups challenged the rules, asserting that CWA § 316 prohibits the use of that kind of cost-benefit analysis. In *Entergy Corp. v. Riverkeeper*, 556 U.S. 208 (2009), the Court upheld EPA's rules as a reasonable interpretation of § 316. Three dissenting justices, citing Whitman v. American Trucking, 531 U.S. 457 (2001) (excerpted in Chapter 10), would have read congressional silence in § 316 to forbid the use of cost-benefit analysis. Justice Breyer, concurring in part and dissenting in part,

thought the statute would allow EPA not to impose technological requirements if their cost was wholly disproportionate to the environmental
benefits.

How useful is cost-benefit analysis in this context? What is the value of
the 3.4 billion fish and shellfish that are killed in intake structures every
year? In crafting the rule upheld in *Entergy*, EPA decided it could only
monetize the value of "those species that are commercially or recreationally
harvested, a tiny slice (1.8 percent to be precise) of all impacted fish and
shellfish." Entergy v. Riverkeeper, 129 S. Ct. at 1516–1517 (Stevens, J.,
dissenting). Subsequently, EPA decided to revisit its analysis of the value of
the fish lost at cooling water intake structures. It has designed a survey
that will ask whether respondents would vote in favor of policies that
would increase their cost of living in exchange for reduced loss of fish at
intakes, increases in fish populations, or healthier aquatic ecosystems. 76
Fed. Reg. 3883 (Jan. 21, 2011). Should EPA rely on cost-benefit analysis in
deciding what technology to require at cooling water intakes? If so, how
should it estimate the benefits of reducing entrainment of fish and other
aquatic organisms?

6. *Fundamentally different factors variances.* Under what circumstances
does the CWA allow EPA to grant a variance from categorical effluent
standards? See CWA § 301(n), excerpted above. What purpose does this
provision serve? What must an applicant show in order to qualify for a
variance? The legislative history indicates that variances should be granted
"only rarely and only to create a separate standard for a facility so unique
that it would have required a separate subcategory had EPA given it
adequate attention in the national rulemaking." S. Rep. No. 99–50, at 19
(1985).

7. *Permit issuance in the absence of categorical standards.* If a source
must apply for or seek renewal of its NPDES permit before EPA issues
BAT standards for its industry, what standards would apply? The permit-
issuing agency (either the state or EPA) uses its best professional judgment
to set technology based requirements. See 33 U.S.C. § 1342(a)(1)(B); 40
C.F.R. § 125.3(c)(2). In doing so, the permit writer considers the same
factors EPA would consider in setting category-wide standards. See 40
C.F.R. § 125.3(d). It enjoys "considerable flexibility in establishing permit
terms and conditions," EPA, NPDES Permit Writers' Manual 69 (1996),
but must be prepared to show that the judgment "is reasonable and based
on sound engineering analysis." Id.

8. *The consequences of NPDES regulation.* Suppose that EPA revisits the
Water Transfers Rule mentioned in Section 1, and that the South Florida
Water Management District is required to obtain NPDES permits for the
Everglades pumps at issue in South Florida Water Management District v.
Miccosukee Tribe, 541 U.S. 95 (2004). Exactly what would the Tribe gain?
What conditions would have to be or might be imposed in an NPDES
permit? What exactly would the Water Management District lose? Why has
it so vigorously resisted applying for permits?

If the NPDES provisions do not apply, a source currently faces essentially no federal regulation although, as we shall see in Section 4, the TMDL program may eventually catalyze stronger state regulation of sources that escape the NPDES net. If an NPDES permit is required, it must require use of "best available technology" if EPA had set a categorical standard. There is currently no standard for phosphate discharges from pumping stations, nor is EPA likely to produce one. In the absence of such a rule, the permit writer (the state permitting agency) must apply its "best professional judgement" to determine what treatment technology would be available. In addition, the permit would have to include "any more stringent limitation . . . required to implement any applicable water quality standard." 33 U.S.C. § 1311(b)(1)(C).

Wastewater treatment plants have some experience with elimination of phosphate from their discharges. Most of them do not take special steps to remove phosphate, but they must do it where (as in the Everglades) the receiving waters are highly sensitive to phosphate contamination. Some phosphate can be removed by growing plants in the water to be treated. This is done at some wastewater treatment plants by incorporating wetlands into the process. But removing the amount of phosphate needed to meet water quality standards for the Everglades would almost certainly require chemical precipitation, which would have to be done in a very large settling tank. Whether or not that would be feasible for the Everglades pumps is an open question.

SECTION 3.   NONPOINT SOURCE POLLUTION

Nonpoint source pollution is any water pollution that does not come from a point source. It includes runoff from agricultural and urban areas, as well as deposition from the atmosphere.

> "The CWA has never addressed non-point source pollution in a straightforward comprehensive way. Instead, it has been treated as something of an afterthought, a troublesome area to be primarily left in the hands of state and local government. As a consequence, nonpoint source pollution has evolved into the largest single obstacle to improving water quality. Approximately 82% of the rivers and streams that fail to meet water quality standards and 77% of such lakes are impaired because of agricultural runoff and hydrological modifications."

William L. Andreen, Water Quality Today: Has the Clean Water Act Been a Success?, 55 Ala. L. Rev. 537, 593 (2004).

CWA sections 208 (33 U.S.C. § 1288) and 319 (33 U.S.C. § 1329) address nonpoint source pollution. Section 208, included in the 1972 CWA, directed states to identify areas with "substantial water quality control problems," CWA § 208(a)(2), and develop plans to correct those problems, CWA § 208(b). The plans were to identify nonpoint sources of pollution methods, "including land use requirements," to control those sources "to the extent feasible." CWA § 208(b)(2)(F)–(K). Although plans had to be submitted to EPA for approval, there was essentially no sanction for failure to create or implement a plan. As a result, although many plans were developed, they had little impact on the nonpoint source pollution problem. See David Zaring, Agriculture, Nonpoint Source Pollution, and Regulatory Control: The Clean Water Act's Bleak Present and Future, 20 Harv. Envtl. L. Rev. 515, 523–524 (1996). By the 1980s, the § 208 process had been essentially abandoned. See Robert W. Adler, Jessica C. Landman and Diane M. Cameron, the Clean Water Act Twenty Years Later 184 (1993).

> In 1987, Congress added a new program to address nonpoint source pollution [CWA § 319]. While requiring new lists of waters impaired by nonpoint sources of pollution, and new statewide plans to redress that pollution, section 319 adds little rigor to the Act's nonpoint source controls. The provision includes a general requirement that states develop new programs on a watershed-specific basis "to the maximum extent practicable." [CWA § 319(b)(4).] This requirement suggests the need for states to focus on specific water quality problems, including WQS violations, in individual watersheds. Aside from this vague admonition, however, section 319 did little to remedy the lack of a precise requirement for states to match specific management practices with the degree of control necessary (in combination with new and existing controls on point sources) to meet WQS. Moreover, although section 319 authorizes EPA to conduct listing and assessment if a state fails to do so, [CWA § 319(d)(3),] like section 208, it contains no express authority for EPA to prepare or implement a nonpoint source pollution control program if a state's program is nonexistent or inadequate.

Robert W. Adler, Integrated Approaches to Water Pollution: Lessons from the Clean Air Act, 23 Harv. Envtl. L. Rev. 203, 228 (1999). Not surprisingly, § 319, like § 208 before it, did little to solve the nonpoint source pollution problem.

By 1990, EPA recognized nonpoint source pollution as the biggest problem for water quality. Yet today, nonpoint source pollution remains virtually uncontrolled at the federal level, and barely addressed by most states. The following excerpts, the first from then-EPA Administrator William Reilly and the second from law professor and environmental advocate Oliver Houck, offer two views on the reasons for that gap.

William K. Reilly, The Issues and the Policy: View From EPA

EPA Journal, Nov./Dec. 1991, 20.

* * * Nonpoint-source pollution is runoff from rainwater or snow melt that picks up along the way soil, animal wastes, fertilizers, pesticides, used oil, toxic substances, and street debris. It comes from farms, cities, forests, mining operations, and construction sites. And it carries contaminants into

nearby surface or underground waterways—sometimes washing directly into lakes and streams, sometimes entering storm and sanitary sewer systems, where from EPA's regulatory perspective it becomes a point source. However it reaches our waterways, it originates, nonetheless, as nonpoint-source pollution. And almost always, it is subtle, it is diffuse, it is difficult to visualize.

Unlike dramatic scenes from an earlier era of belching smokestacks spewing black clouds skyward or sewer pipes disgorging viscous, green ooze seaward, nonpoint-source pollution conjures up no vivid images in the mind's eye. Unlike the mere mention of oil spills or beach closings or toxic waste dumps, nonpoint-source pollution fails to inflame or incite to action. Yet this "pointless" pollution is one of the most serious remaining threats to our nation's water quality—and its cumulative effects from many small sources and individual actions *are* visible and disturbing: algal blooms that choke lakes and aquatic life, fish kills, fishing bans, silt-covered spawning habitat along riverbeds.

* * *

Clearly, the problem is enormous. Yet because this type of pollution is so hard to pinpoint and because almost everybody contributes to the problem, it largely defies traditional command-and-control regulatory approaches that have brought so much success in curbing pollution from specific plants or pipes over the past 20 years.

* * *

I see three hurdles ahead in curbing nonpoint source pollution.

First, a national regulatory program similar to that to control point sources simply won't work. The challenge is, in part, one of promoting changes in longstanding habits and practices—at home, at work, in our communities, on farms, in mining, forestry, and construction operations. Education is key to influencing changes in lifestyles and behaviors to prevent this type of pollution. * * *

Farmers and other landowners, in particular, are understandably wary of intrusive government programs. No effective solutions will work without the whole-hearted involvement of farmers, whose stake in conservation is greater than that of virtually all others, whose very livelihood depends on productive soils and healthy natural systems. Their trust, and their interests, need to be protected.

Second, addressing nonpoint-source pollution effectively may require attention to land use planning. States and localities often find they can't protect water quality without planning for protection of their watersheds—and that means planning for growth. That, of course, is properly a matter for state and local governments, not the federal government. * * *

* * * The federal government has the responsibility to provide basic scientific information, incentives, technical expertise, and limited funding to state governments to develop effective programs. Research, information, education, technical assistance-all are reasonable federal rules. But it is

local building and land use decisions more than anything else that will help cut nonpoint-source pollution.

Third, in some instances—like our incipient efforts to regulate urban stormwater—the costs to control nonpoint-source pollution through traditional approaches are potentially enormous: tens of billions of dollars. I might add that on the stormwater permitting front, the Agency is hearing from states, municipalities, and industries alarmed at the cost and complexity of implementing statutory requirements to regulate stormwater as a point source. With all the concurrent demands on local governments for an entire array of environmental improvements, not to mention other worthy needs, financing nonpoint-source controls is a real challenge.

Oliver A. Houck, The Clean Water Act TMDL Program: Law, Policy, and Implementation

2d ed., 2002, at 87–92.

The history of nonpoint source pollution control since 1972 is of an attempt, to date largely unsuccessful, to find replacements for these features through voluntary, local programs. The rationales offered for treating nonpoint sources separately under the Act include

(1) the alleged "number and variety of nonpoint sources";

(2) the "site-specific nature" of the pollution; and

(3) the "lack of known control technologies."

One reflection, none of these reasons are terribly convincing, because

(1) we have a great number and variety of point sources as well; and

(2) each industrial discharge, too, has site-specific effects on its receiving water (effects that are irrelevant to the setting of technology-based guidelines); and

(3) the control technologies for nonpoint pollution (e.g., shelter-belts, nutrient caps, retention ponds) are anything but unknown, complex, technologically difficult, or even very costly.

In truth, we do not avoid regulating nonpoint source pollution because we are unable to figure out how to do it. Rather, we have deferred to the myth that its impacts are essentially local and of secondary importance, as we have deferred to legislatures dominated by rural constituencies unaccustomed to any regulation and ready to fight. Recently—albeit with glacial slowness—both the myth and the dominance have begun to melt, reopening the question of nonpoint source controls. One answer to the problem is simply to treat a greater number of dischargers as point sources, bringing them into the operational features of the Act.

EPA and Congress have been wrestling with the application of the NPDES program to agriculture, silviculture, and land-based pollution since the adoption of the Act in its modern form. In 1973, the Agency adopted a definition of point sources that included runoff collected or channeled virtually in any way, but then proceeded to exempt discharges from all silviculture, all urban storm sewers, and all but the largest agricultural operations. These exemptions were immediately challenged by a citizen suit and rejected by both the federal district and appellate courts of the District of Columbia. Facing EPA arguments—similar to those noted above—that nonpoint sources were too numerous, diffuse, and difficult to regulate, these courts suggested the use of alternative permit conditions and general permits, and concluded with the inspiration that "[i]magination conjoined with determination will likely give EPA capability for practical administration. If not the remedy lies with Congress." [NRDC v. Costle, 568 F.2d 1369, 1383 (D.C. Cir. 1977).]

NOTES AND QUESTIONS

1. *Statutory interpretation.* Should the lack of federal regulation of nonpoint sources inform agency and judicial interpretation of the NPDES point source provisions? If so, does it provide an argument for reading those provisions broadly, in order to further the goal of restoring and maintaining the nation's waters? Or for reading them narrowly, because Congress has made it clear that only some sources are subject to the NPDES process?

2. *The challenge of nonpoint source pollution.* Why has nonpoint source pollution proved so difficult to tackle? Is the problem primarily technical, political, or fiscal? What level of government should have the primary responsibility for controlling nonpoint source pollution? What regulatory, incentive, or other strategies would you regard as most promising? Might pollution allowance trading play a role? To what extent, and with what limits?

3. *Best management practices.* Nonpoint source pollution is not amenable to end-of-the-pipe technological pollution controls because, by definition, it does not pass through a pipe. Instead, it has to be addressed through "best management practices" which reduce pollution at the source or prevent it from reaching waterways. Examples include fencing riparian areas to keep livestock out, limiting pesticide spraying in windy or wet weather, and maintaining cover crops on fallow fields.

4. *State authority.* Although Congress has so far chosen not to aggressively regulate nonpoint source pollution, the states remain free to do so. The CWA generally preserves state authority to adopt more stringent water pollution requirements. CWA § 510 (33 U.S.C. § 1370). So far, few states have taken up the task of regulating nonpoint sources, but that is beginning to change. California's Central Coast Regional Water Quality Control Board, for example, now requires farmers who discharge waste to waters to attend educational programs, develop management plans for their farms, implement applicable best management practices, and monitor water quality, either individually or through a cooperative organization. See California Regional Water Quality Control Board, Central Coast Region, Order No. R3–2004–0117, Conditional Waiver of Waste Discharge Requirements for Discharges from Irrigated Lands (July 9, 2004). The next section considers whether the Total Maximum Daily Load program might strengthen the incentives for state regulation of nonpoint source pollution.

SECTION 4. WATER QUALITY STANDARDS

Although the CWA emphasizes technology-based effluent controls, it does not ignore water quality standards (WQSs). It requires states to set WQSs for their waters, and to identify waters that are not meeting the standards. It mandates that NPDES permits include effluent limitations sufficient to achieve WQSs, allows states to veto federal activities that would interfere with their achievement and, perhaps most importantly, requires that states develop total maximum daily loads (TMDLs).

CLASS DISCUSSION PROBLEM: UNIVERSAL WIDGET COMPANY AND WATER QUALITY STANDARDS

Universal Widget Company (UWC), a major widget manufacturer, wishes to construct a new manufacturing facility. UWC has identified Centralia as the perfect location based on its proximity to raw materials, ample skilled labor, abundant cheap electricity, and central location within the target marketing region. Since the UWC widget plant would benefit the local economy, state and local government officials support the project. After carefully examining the local market for industrially-zoned land, UWC has located a suitable site on the East River.

UWC prides itself on being a good corporate citizen and an environmental leader. It is committed to meeting EPA's effluent standards for the widget industry, which allow the discharge of up to 5 pounds of suspended solids and 0.5 pounds of copper per ton of widgets produced. The plant is capable of producing 200 tons of widgets per day if it operates at full capacity. Unfortunately, the East River currently does not meet water quality standards for either copper or suspended solids. Major sources of copper include drainage from an abandoned mine and Centralia's three POTWs (because the city's wells are in soils with high copper levels, and copper in the water supply passes through the sewage treatment plant). Major sources of suspended solids include the Ajax pulp and paper mill, other industrial sources, the POTWs, and agriculture, timber harvest, and construction activities. The East River in this location is on the most recent impaired waters list prepared by the state Department of Environmental Quality (DEQ). Because it regards other waters as higher priorities, DEQ has not yet produced any TMDLs for the East River. It intends to do so, but not for five years.

Can UWC get an NPDES permit for its proposed new widget plant? Must that permit include controls beyond the industry-wide effluent discharge standards set by EPA? Will anyone else have to change their discharges in order for UWC to get a permit?

Excerpts From the Clean Water Act

33 U.S.C. § 1251–1387.

Sec. 303 Water quality standards and implementation plans.

(a) Existing water quality standards

* * *

(3)(A) Any State which prior to October 18, 1972, has not adopted pursuant to its own laws water quality standards applicable to intrastate waters shall, not later than one hundred and eighty days after October 18, 1972, adopt and submit such standards to the Administrator.

(B) If the Administrator determines that any such standards are consistent with the applicable requirements of this Act as in effect immediately prior to October 18, 1972, he shall approve such standards.

(C) If the Administrator determines that any such standards are not consistent with the applicable requirements of this Act as in effect immediately prior to October 18, 1972, he shall, not later than the ninetieth day after the date of submission of such standards, notify the State and specify the changes to meet such requirements. If such changes are not adopted by the State within ninety days after the date of notification, the Administrator shall promulgate such standards * * *.

(c) Review; revised standard; publication

* * *

(2)(A) Whenever the State revises or adopts a new standard, such revised or new standard shall be submitted to the Administrator. Such revised or new water quality standard shall consist of the designated uses of the navigable waters involved and the water quality criteria for such waters based upon such uses. Such standards shall be such as to protect the public health or welfare, enhance the quality of water and serve the purposes of this chapter. * * *

(3) If the Administrator, within sixty days after the date of submission of the revised or new standard, determines that such standard meets the requirements of this chapter, such standard shall thereafter be the water quality standard for the applicable waters of that State. If the Administrator determines that any such revised or new standard is not consistent with the applicable requirements of this chapter, he shall not later than the ninetieth day after the date of submission of such standard notify the State and specify the changes to meet such requirements. If such changes are not adopted by the State within ninety days after the date of notification, the Administrator shall promulgate such standard * * *.

(d)(1)(A) Each State shall identify those waters within its boundaries for which the effluent limitations required by section [301(b)(1)(A)] and section [301(b)(1)(B)] are not stringent enough to implement any water quality standard applicable to such waters. The State shall establish a priority ranking for such waters, taking into account the severity of the pollution and the uses to be made of such waters.

* * *

(C) Each State shall establish for the waters identified in paragraph (1)(A) of this subsection, and in accordance with the priority ranking, the total maximum daily load, for those pollutants which the Administrator identifies under section [304(a)(2)] as suitable for such calculation. Such load shall be established at a level necessary to implement the applicable water quality standards with seasonal variations and a margin of safety which takes into account any lack of knowledge concerning the relationship between effluent limitations and water quality.

* * *

(2) Each State shall submit to the Administrator from time to time, with the first such submission not later than one hundred and eighty days after the date of publication of the first identification of pollutants under section 1314(a)(2)(D) of this title, for his approval the waters identified and the loads established under paragraphs [(1)(A) and (1)(C)] of this subsection. The Administrator shall either approve or disapprove such identification and load not later than thirty days after the date of submission. If the Administrator approves such identification and load, such State shall incorporate them into its current plan under subsection (e) of this section. If the Administrator disapproves such identification and load, he shall not later than thirty days after the date of such disapproval identify such waters in such State and establish such loads for such waters as he determines necessary to implement the water quality standards applicable to such waters and upon such identification and establishment the State shall incorporate them into its current plan under subsection (e) of this section.

* * *

(e) Continuing planning process

(1) Each State shall have a continuing planning process approved under paragraph (2) of this subsection which is consistent with this chapter.

(2) Each State shall submit not later than 120 days after October 18, 1972, to the Administrator for his approval a proposed continuing planning process which is consistent with this chapter. Not later than thirty days after the date of submission of such a process the Administrator shall either approve or disapprove such process. * * * The Administrator shall not approve any State [NPDES permit program] for any State which does not have an approved continuing planning process under this section.

(3) The Administrator shall approve any continuing planning process submitted to him under this section which will result in plans for all

navigable waters within such State, which include, but are not limited to, the following:

(A) effluent limitations and schedules of compliance at least as stringent as those required by section 1311(b)(1), section 1311(b)(2), section 1316, and section 1317 of this title, and at least as stringent as any requirements contained in any applicable water quality standard in effect under authority of this section;

(B) the incorporation of all elements of any applicable area-wide waste management plans under section 1288 of this title, and applicable basin plans under section 1289 of this title;

(C) total maximum daily load for pollutants in accordance with subsection (d) of this section;

(D) procedures for revision;

(E) adequate authority for intergovernmental cooperation;

(F) adequate implementation, including schedules of compliance, for revised or new water quality standards, under subsection (c) of this section;

(G) controls over the disposition of all residual waste from any water treatment processing;

(H) an inventory and ranking, in order of priority, of needs for construction of waste treatment works required to meet the applicable requirements of sections 1311 and 1312 of this title.

* * *

A. Setting Water Quality Standards

State water quality standards combine two elements: designated uses and water quality criteria. The process of setting standards begins with the establishment of use classifications for each of the state's surface waters, through a form of water zoning. Water uses can include such things as water supply for domestic, agricultural, or industrial uses; propagation of various species or types of fish, wildlife, or aquatic life; recreation that does or does not involve contact with the water; and navigation. All existing uses must be included. *See* 40 C.F.R. § 131.10(g)–(i). Waste assimilation or transport cannot be a designated use. Id. at 131.10(a).

The "criteria" portion of the water quality standards are water quality levels sufficient to protect designated uses. They may be expressed either as numerical values, that is, acceptable pollutant concentrations, or narrative descriptions. Examples of both can be found in Iowa's Water Quality Standards. There are numerical standards for pH values. For waters whose uses include contact recreation, for example, the pH must be "not less than 6.5 nor greater than 9.0," and no discharge may change that value by more than 0.5 pH units. Iowa Admin. Code, Division 567, § 61.3(3)(a)(2). Narrative standards cover both toxicity and esthetics. For example, waters designated for drinking supply or routinely used for fishing for human consumption "shall contain no substances in concentrations which will make fish or shellfish inedible due to undesirable tastes or cause a hazard to humans after consumption." Iowa Admin. Code, Division 567, § 61.3(3)(d). EPA encourages the adoption of numeric standards where feasible. Numeric criteria are statutorily required for certain toxic pollutants. CWA § 303(c)(2)(B) (33 U.S.C. § 1313(c)(2)(B)).

EPA has published recommended water quality criteria for about 150 pollutants, as required by CWA § 304(a). EPA, National Recommended Water Quality Criteria: 2002, EPA–822–R–02–047 (Nov. 2002). States may, but need not, follow these criteria. They are free to adopt their own criteria, so long as they can defend their scientific basis. See NRDC v. EPA, 16 F.3d 1395 (4th Cir. 1993) (upholding EPA approval of state criteria for dioxins more than 1000 times higher than EPA's recommended criteria).

Federally recognized Indian tribes may be treated as states under the CWA, with authority to set water quality standards and assume NPDES permitting authority. CWA § 518(e) (33 U.S.C. § 1377(e)). EPA is directed to provide a mechanism for resolving any "unreasonable consequences that may arise as a result of differing water quality standards that may be set by States and Indian tribes located on common bodies of waters." Id. In *Montana v. EPA*, 137 F.3d 1135 (9th Cir. 1998), the Ninth Circuit held that the Flathead Indian tribe could enforce water quality standards against all sources of pollutant discharge within the reservation's boundaries, including sources owned by non-Indians. In *City of Albuquerque v. Browner*, 97 F.3d 415, 423 (10th Cir. 1996), the Tenth Circuit upheld EPA's approval of stringent tribal water quality standards and application of those standards to upstream, nontribal, pollutant sources. Most recently, in Wisconsin v. EPA, 266 F.3d 741 (7th Cir. 2001), the court ruled that EPA could approve tribal water quality standards for a lake even though the state owned the bed of the lake.

B. THE SIGNIFICANCE OF WATER QUALITY STANDARDS

State water quality standards play two important roles in the CWA scheme. First, NPDES permits for point source dischargers must include "any more stringent limitation ... required to implement any applicable water quality standard." 33 U.S.C. § 1311(b)(1)(C). In the abstract, however, it is difficult to tie achievement of even numerical water quality standards to specific point sources, either for enforcement purposes or to establish individual effluent limitations. Narrative standards add another layer of difficulty. In a recent review of NPDES permits issued for surface coal mining operations by authorities in the Appalachian states, EPA found that many of the permits lacked any water-quality based limits, and none of them had limits implementing key narrative water quality standards. EPA, Review of Clean Water Act § 402 Permitting for Surface Coal Mines by Appalachian States: Findings & Recommendations (July 13, 2010). The TMDL program discussed in the next subsection is intended to provide the information base needed to translate water quality standards into effluent limitations applicable to specific sources (both point and nonpoint).

Second, water quality standards provide the basis for a state veto of federal approvals. Under CWA § 401(a)(1) (33 U.S.C. § 1341(a)(1)), an applicant for a federal license or permit "which may result in any discharge into the navigable waters" must obtain certification from the state in which the discharge will originate that it will not violate any state water quality standard. Section 401 requires only a "discharge," not a "discharge of a pollutant." Section 401 certification, therefore, is required even for federally-permitted activities that discharge only water, such as hydroelectric dams. See S.D. Warren Co. v. Maine Board of Environmental Protection, 547 U.S. 370 (2006); PUD No. 1 of Jefferson City v. Washington Dept. of Ecology, 511 U.S. 700 (1994).

C. TOTAL MAXIMUM DAILY LOADS

Pronsolino v. Nastri

United States Court of Appeals, Ninth Circuit, 2002.
291 F.3d 1123.

■ BERZON, CIRCUIT JUDGE.

* * *

Section 303(d)(1)(A) requires each state to identify as "areas with insufficient controls" "those waters within its boundaries for which the effluent limitations required by section [301(b)(1)(A)] and section [301(b)(1)(B)] of this title are not stringent enough to implement any water quality standard applicable to such waters." The CWA defines "effluent limitations" as restrictions on pollutants "discharged from point sources." CWA § 502(11), 33 U.S.C. § 1362(11). Section 301(b)(1)(A) mandates application of the "best practicable control technology" effluent limitations for most point source discharges, while § 301(b)(1)(B) mandates application of effluent limitations adopted specifically for secondary treatment at publicly owned treatment works. § 301(b)(1), 33 U.S.C. § 1311(b)(1).

For waters identified pursuant to § 303(d)(1)(A) (the "§ 303(d)(1) list"), the states must establish the "total maximum daily load" ("TMDL") for pollutants identified by the EPA as suitable for TMDL calculation. § 303(d)(1)(C). "A TMDL defines the specified maximum amount of a pollutant which can be discharged or 'loaded' into the waters at issue from all combined sources." *Dioxin/Organochlorine Center v. Clarke*, 57 F.3d 1517, 1520 (9th Cir. 1995). The TMDL "shall be established at a level necessary to implement the applicable water quality standards...." § 303(d)(1)(C).

Section 303(d)(2), in turn, requires each state to submit its § 303(d)(1) list and TMDLs to the EPA for its approval or disapproval. If the EPA approves the list and TMDLs, the state must incorporate the list and TMDLs into its "continuing planning process," the requirements for which are set forth in § 303(e). § 303(d)(2). If the EPA disapproves either the § 303(d)(1) list or any TMDLs, the EPA must itself put together the missing document or documents. *Id.* The state then incorporates any EPA-set list or TMDL into the state's continuing planning process. *Id.*

* * *

The final pertinent section of § 303, § 303(e), requiring each state to have a "continuing planning process," gives some operational force to the prior information-gathering provisions. The EPA may approve a state's continuing planning process only if it "will result in plans for all navigable waters within such State" that include, inter alia, effluent limitations, TMDLs, areawide waste management plans for nonpoint sources of pollution, and plans for "adequate implementation, including schedules of compliance, for revised or new water quality standards." § 303(e)(3).

The upshot of this intricate scheme is that the CWA leaves to the states the responsibility of developing plans to achieve water quality standards if the statutorily-mandated point source controls will not alone suffice, while providing federal funding to aid in the implementation of the state plans. TMDLs are primarily informational tools that allow the states to proceed from the identification of waters requiring additional planning to the required plans. As such, TMDLs serve as a link in an implementation chain that includes federally-regulated point source controls, state or local plans for point and nonpoint source pollution reduction, and assessment of the impact of such measures on water quality, all to the end of attaining water quality goals for the nation's waters.

II. Factual and Procedural Background

In 1992, California submitted to the EPA a list of waters pursuant to § 303(d)(1)(A). Pursuant to § 303(d)(2), the EPA disapproved California's 1992 list because it omitted seventeen water segments that did not meet the water quality standards set by California for those segments. Sixteen of the seventeen water segments, including the Garcia River, were impaired only by nonpoint sources of pollution. * * *

California did not, however, establish TMDLs for the segments added by the EPA. Environmental and fishermen's groups sued the EPA in 1995 to require the EPA to establish TMDLs for the seventeen segments, and in a March 1997 consent decree the EPA agreed to do so. [Pursuant to that decree, EPA established a TMDL for the Garcia River.]

The Garcia River TMDL for sediment is 552 tons per square mile per year, a sixty percent reduction from historical loadings. The TMDL allocates portions of the total yearly load among the following categories of nonpoint source pollution: a) "mass wasting" associated with roads; b) "mass wasting" associated with timber-harvesting; c) erosion related to road surfaces; and d) erosion related to road and skid trail crossings.

In 1960, appellants Betty and Guido Pronsolino purchased approximately 800 acres of heavily logged timber land in the Garcia River watershed. In 1998, after re-growth of the forest, the Pronsolinos applied for a harvesting permit from the California Department of Forestry ("Forestry").

In order to comply with the Garcia River TMDL, Forestry and/or the state's Regional Water Quality Control Board required, among other things, that the Pronsolino's harvesting permit provide for mitigation of 90% of controllable road-related sediment run-off and contain prohibitions on removing certain trees and on harvesting from mid-October until May 1. The Pronsolinos' forester estimates that the large tree restriction will cost the Pronsolinos $750,000.

* * *

III. Analysis

Section 303(d)(1)(A) requires listing and calculation of TMDLs for "those waters within [the state's] boundaries for which the effluent limitations required by section [301(b)(1)(A)] and section [301(b)(1)(B)] of this title *are not stringent enough to implement any water quality standard* applicable to such waters." § 303(d) (emphasis added). The precise statutory question before us is whether, as the Pronsolinos maintain, the term "not stringent enough to implement . . . water quality standard[s]" as used in § 303(d)(1)(A) must be interpreted to mean *both* that application of effluent limitations will not achieve water quality standards *and* that the waters at issue are subject to effluent limitations. As only waters with point source pollution are subject to effluent limitations, such an interpretation would exclude from the § 303(d)(1) listing and TMDL requirements waters impaired only by nonpoint sources of pollution.

The EPA, as noted, interprets "not stringent enough to implement . . . water quality standard[s]" to mean "not adequate" or "not sufficient . . . to implement any water quality standard," and does not read the statute as implicitly containing a limitation to waters initially covered by effluent limitations. According to the EPA, if the use of effluent limitations will not implement applicable water quality standards, the water falls within § 303(d)(1)(A) regardless of whether it is point or nonpoint sources, or a combination of the two, that continue to pollute the water.

Whether or not the appellants' suggested interpretation is entirely implausible, it is at least considerably weaker than the EPA's competing construction. The Pronsolinos' version necessarily relies upon: (1) understanding "stringent enough" to mean "strict enough" rather than "thorough going enough" or "adequate" or "sufficient"; and (2) reading the phrase "not stringent enough" in isolation, rather than with reference to the stated goal of implementing "any water quality standard applicable to such waters." Where the answer to the question "not stringent enough for what?" is "to implement any [applicable] water quality standard," the meaning of "stringent" should be determined by looking forward to the broad goal to be attained, not backwards at the inadequate effluent limitations. One might comment, for example, about a teacher that her standards requiring good spelling were not stringent enough to assure good writing, as her students still used bad grammar and poor logic. Based on the language of the contested phrase alone, then, the more sensible conclusion is that the § 303(d)(1) list must contain any waters for which the particular effluent limitations will not be adequate to attain the statute's water quality goals.

Placing the phrase in its statutory context supports this conclusion. Section 303(d) begins with the requirement that each state "identify those waters within its boundaries...." § 303(d)(1)(A). So the statute's starting point for the listing project is a compilation of each and every navigable water within the state. Then, only those waters that will attain water quality standards after application of the new point source technology are excluded from the § 303(d)(1) list, leaving all those waters for which that technology will not "implement any water quality standard applicable to such waters." § 303(d)(1)(A). The alternative construction, in contrast, would begin with a subset of all the state's waterways, those that have point sources subject to effluent limitations, and would result in a list containing only a subset of that subset-those waters as to which the applicable effluent limitations are not adequate to attain water quality standards.

The Pronsolinos' contention to the contrary notwithstanding, no such odd reading of the statute is necessary in order to give meaning to the phrase "for which the effluent limitations required by section [301(b)(1)(A)] and section [301(b)(1)(B)] ... are not stringent enough." The EPA interprets § 303(d)(1)(A) to require the identification of any waters not meeting water quality standards only if specified effluent limitations would not achieve those standards. 40 C.F.R. § 130.2(j). If the pertinent effluent limitations would, if implemented, achieve the water quality standards but are not in place yet, there need be no listing and no TMDL calculation.

* * *

Nothing in § 303(d)(1)(A) distinguishes the treatment of point sources and nonpoint sources as such; the only reference is to the "effluent limitations required by" § 301(b)(1). So if the effluent limitations required by § 301(b)(1) are "as a matter of law" "not stringent enough" to achieve the applicable water quality standards for waters impaired by point sources not subject to those requirements, then they are also "not stringent enough" to achieve applicable water quality standards for other waters not subject to those requirements, in this instance because they are impacted only by nonpoint sources. * * *

There is one final aspect of the Act's structure that bears consideration because it supports the EPA's interpretation of § 303(d): The list required by § 303(d)(1)(A) requires that waters be listed if they are impaired by a combination of point sources and nonpoint sources; the language admits of no other reading. Section 303(d)(1)(C), in turn, directs that TMDLs "shall be established at a level necessary *to implement* the applicable water quality standards...." *Id.* (emphasis added). So, at least in blended waters, TMDLs must be calculated with regard to nonpoint sources of pollution; otherwise, it would be impossible "to implement the applicable water quality standards," which do not differentiate sources of pollution. * * *

Nothing in the statutory structure—or purpose—suggests that Congress meant to distinguish, as to § 303(d)(1) lists and TMDLs, between waters with one insignificant point source and substantial nonpoint source pollution and waters with only nonpoint source pollution. Such a distinction would, for no apparent reason, require the states or the EPA to monitor waters to determine whether a point source had been added or removed, and to adjust the § 303(d)(1) list and establish TMDLs accordingly. There is no statutory basis for concluding that Congress intended such an irrational regime.

Looking at the statute as a whole, we conclude that the EPA's interpretation of § 303(d) is not only entirely reasonable but considerably more convincing than the one offered by the plaintiffs in this case.

The Pronsolinos finally contend that, by establishing TMDLs for waters impaired only by nonpoint source pollution, the EPA has upset the balance of federal-state control established in the CWA by intruding into the states' traditional control over land use. *See Solid Waste Agency of Northern Cook County v. United States Army Corps of Eng'rs,* 531 U.S. 159, 172–73 (2001). That is not the case.

The Garcia River TMDL identifies the maximum load of pollutants that can enter the Garcia River from certain broad categories of nonpoint sources if the river is to attain water quality standards. It does not specify the load of pollutants that may be received from particular parcels of land or describe what measures the state should take to implement the TMDL. Instead, the TMDL expressly recognizes that "implementation and monitoring" "are state responsibilities" and notes that, for this reason, the EPA did not include implementation or monitoring plans within the TMDL. EPA, *Garcia River Sediment Total Maximum Daily Load* 43 (Mar. 16, 1998).

Moreover, § 303(e) requires—separately from the § 303(d)(1) listing and TMDL requirements—that each state include in its continuing planning process "adequate implementation, including schedules of compliance, for revised or new water quality standards" "for all navigable waters within such State." § 303(e)(3). The Garcia River TMDL thus serves as an informational tool for the creation of the state's implementation plan, independently—and explicitly—required by Congress.

California chose both *if* and *how* it would implement the Garcia River TMDL. States must implement TMDLs only to the extent that they seek to avoid losing federal grant money; there is no pertinent statutory provision otherwise requiring implementation of § 303 plans or providing for their enforcement. *See* CWA § 309, 33 U.S.C. § 1319; CWA § 505, 33 U.S.C. § 1365.

Finally, it is worth noting that the arguments that the Pronsolinos raise here would apply equally to nonpoint source pollution controls for blended waters. Yet, as discussed above, Congress definitely required that the states or the EPA establish TMDLs for all pollutants in waters on § 303(d)(1) lists, including blended waters.

Friends of Pinto Creek v. U.S. EPA

United States Court of Appeals, Ninth Circuit, 2007.
504 F.3d 1007.

■ Hug, Circuit Judge:

* * *

Pinto Creek is a desert river located near Miami, Arizona, approximately 60 miles east of Phoenix. It has been listed by the American Rivers Organization as one of the country's most endangered rivers due to threats from proposed mining operations. Pinto Creek and its riparian environs are home to a variety of fish, birds, and other wildlife, some of which are specially protected. Due to excessive copper contamination from historical mining activities in the region, Pinto Creek is included on Arizona's list of impaired waters under § 303(d) of the Clean Water Act, 33 U.S.C. § 1313(d), as a water quality limited stream due to non-attainment of water quality standards for dissolved copper.

Carlota proposed to construct and operate an open-pit copper mine and processing facility approximately six miles west of Miami, Arizona, covering over 3000 acres while extracting about 100 million tons of ore. Part of the operation plan includes constructing diversion channels for Pinto Creek to route the stream around the mine, as well as groundwater cut-off walls to block the flow of groundwater into the mine.

* * * Because the proposed action would involve the discharge of pollutants into Pinto Creek, Carlota applied to the EPA for an NPDES permit under § 402 of the Clean Water Act, 33 U.S.C. § 1342, in 1996. The EPA ultimately issued the permit * * *.

[EPA published a draft NPDES permit in 1998. In response to comments, EPA amended the draft permit by adding two new conditions—(1) requiring additional groundwater discharges to augment the stream flow into Pinto Creek, and (2) an offset provision whereby Carlota would be required to remediate sources of copper loading from an upstream inactive mine site called the Gibson Mine. EPA issued an NPDES permit to Carlota on July 24, 2000. In response to Petitioners' argument that it was required to establish a TMDL for copper before issuing the permit, EPA withdrew the permit, completed a TMDL for dissolved copper in Pinto Creek, and reissued the permit.]

* * *

The Petitioners contend that as a "new discharger" Carlota's discharge of dissolved copper into a waterway that is already impaired by an excess of [copper] violates the intent and purpose of the Clean Water Act. Under the NPDES permitting program, 40 C.F.R. § 122.4(i) addresses the situation where a new source seeks to permit a discharge of pollutants into a stream already exceeding its water quality standards for that pollutant. Section 122.4 states in relevant part:

No permit may be issued: . . . (i) To a new source or a new discharger if the discharge from its construction or operation will cause or contribute to the violation of water quality standards. The owner or operator of a new source or new discharger proposing to discharge into a water segment which does not meet applicable water quality standards or is not expected to meet those standards . . . and for which the State or interstate agency has performed a pollutants load allocation for the pollutant to be discharged, must demonstrate, before the close of the public comment period, that:

(1) There are sufficient remaining pollutant load allocations to allow for the discharge; and

(2) The existing dischargers into that segment are subject to compliance schedules designed to bring the segment into compliance with applicable water quality standards.

40 C.F.R. § 122.4 (2000).

The plain language of the first sentence of the regulation is very clear that no permit may be issued to a new discharger if the discharge will contribute to the violation of water quality standards. This corresponds to the stated objectives of the Clean Water Act "to restore and maintain the chemical, physical, and biological integrity of the nation's waters." 33 U.S.C. § 1251(a) (1987). * * *

The EPA contends that the partial remediation of the discharge from the Gibson Mine will offset the pollution. However, there is nothing in the Clean Water Act or the regulation that provides an exception for an offset when the waters remain impaired and the new source is discharging pollution into that impaired water.

The regulation does provide for an exception where a TMDL has been performed and the owner or operator demonstrates that *before the close of the comment period* two conditions are met, which will assure that the impaired waters will be brought into compliance with the applicable water quality standards. The plain language of this exception to the prohibited discharge by a new source provides that the exception does not apply unless the new source can demonstrate that, under the TMDL, the plan is designed to bring the waters into compliance with applicable water quality standards.

The EPA argues that under the requirements of clause (1), there are sufficient remaining load allocations to allow for the discharge because the TMDL provides a method by which the allocations could be established to allow for the discharge. There is no contention, however, that these load allocations represent the amount of pollution that is currently discharged from the point sources and nonpoint sources, and there is no indication of any plan that will effectuate these load allocations so as to bring Pinto Creek within the water quality standards. The TMDL merely provides for the manner in which Pinto Creek *could* meet the water quality standards if all of the load allocations in the TMDL were met, not that there are sufficient remaining pollutant load allocations under existing circumstances.

With regard to the requirements of clause (2), the EPA argues that the requirement of "compliance schedules" pertains only to point sources for which there is a permit. This does not correspond to the plain language of clause (2), which provides "the existing discharges into that segment [of Pinto Creek] are subject to compliance schedules designed to bring the segment into compliance with applicable water quality standards." 40 C.F.R. § 122.4(i)(2) (2000).

We examine that language utilizing the definitions provided in the regulation. The term "discharge" is defined to mean "the discharge of a pollutant." 40 C.F.R. § 122.2 (2000). The term "discharge of a pollutant," is defined as any addition of any "pollutant" or combination of pollutants to "waters of the United States" from *any point source." Id.* at § 122.2(a) (emphasis added). Thus, under the plain language of the regulation, compliance schedules are not confined only to "permitted" point source discharges, but are applicable to "any" point source.

The EPA contends that this would amount to a complete ban of the discharge of pollution to impaired waters. This is based on its misreading of the plain language of the regulation to state that the remediation has to be *completed* before Carlota's discharge. The plain language of clause (2) of the regulation, instead, provides that existing discharges into that segment (of the waters) are "subject to *compliance schedules* designed to bring the segment into compliance with applicable water quality standards." 40 C.F.R. § 122.4(i)(2) (2000) (emphasis added). This is not a complete ban but a requirement of schedules to meet the objective of the Clean Water Act.

Here the existing discharges from point sources are not subject to compliance schedules designed to bring Pinto Creek into compliance with water quality standards. Thus, Carlota has not demonstrated that clause (2) of 40 C.F.R. § 122.4(i) has been met. This is the regulation upon which Carlota and the EPA rely for issuance of the permit.

* * *

The Respondents and Carlota rely on *Arkansas v. Oklahoma,* 503 U.S. 91 (1992) in support of their contentions. That case involved the issuance of a permit for a city in Arkansas to discharge effluent into a stream in Arkansas that entered a river that eventually flowed into Oklahoma. Oklahoma challenged the permit before the EPA, alleging that the discharge violated Oklahoma Water Quality Standards. In that case, the EPA found that the discharge would not lead to a "detectable change in water quality," which the Supreme Court held was supported by substantial evidence. *Arkansas,* 503 U.S. at 112. In the opinion, the Court stated that "the parties have pointed to nothing that mandates a complete ban on discharges into a waterway that is in violation of those standards. The statute does, however, contain provisions designed to remedy existing water quality violations and to allocate the burden of reducing undesirable

discharges between existing sources and new sources. See, e.g. § 1313(d)."
Id. at 108. Section 1313(d) of the Clean Water Act, referred to by the Court,
is the one that provides for the establishment of water quality standards
and TMDLs.

* * *

In Carlota's case, there are no plans or compliance schedules to bring
the Pinto Creek segment "into compliance with applicable water quality
standards," as required by § 122.4(I)(2) * * *. The error of both the EPA
and Carlota is that the objective of that section is not simply to show a
lessening of pollution, but to show how the water quality standard will be
met if Carlota is allowed to discharge pollutants into the impaired waters.

The EPA has the responsibility to regulate discharges from point
sources and the states have the responsibility to limit pollution coming into
the waters from non-point sources. If point sources, other than the permitted point source, are necessary to be scheduled in order to achieve the
water quality standard, then the EPA must locate any such point sources
and establish compliance schedules to meet the water quality standard
before issuing a permit. If there are not adequate point sources to do so,
then a permit cannot be issued unless the state or Carlota agrees to
establish a schedule to limit pollution from a nonpoint source or sources
sufficient to achieve water quality standards.

* * *

NOTES AND QUESTIONS

1. *Water quality standards.* What do water quality standards add to the
technology-based effluent limitations determined by the EPA? Why does
the CWA leave the primary role in setting WQSs to the states? What
constraints does it impose on state choices?

2. *Anti-degradation.* What if existing water quality meets or exceeds
water quality standards? Must water quality remain unchanged at this high
level indefinitely? If the state wants to encourage economic development
and attract industry, can it lower the use designations of waterways in
order to permit additional discharges? Should it be able to?

EPA regulations require that state water quality standards include an
anti-degradation policy. 40 C.F.R. § 131.12(a). That policy must, at a
minimum, maintain the level of water quality needed to support existing
uses in all the state's waters. § 131.12(a)(1). Where water quality currently
exceeds "fishable/swimmable" standards, it may be reduced only if the
state finds, after a public process, that "allowing lower water quality is
necessary to accommodate important economic or social development," and
implements "the highest statutory and regulatory requirements for all new
and existing point sources and all cost-effective and reasonable best management practices for nonpoint source control." § 131.12(a)(2). Finally,
waters designated as "outstanding national resource waters" (ONRWs) are

subject to a "no degradation" standard. See § 131.12(a)(3). Despite the terminology, states designate ONRWs. EPA has never been certain that it had the authority to do so. See Memorandum, EPA Designation of Outstanding National Resource Waters (May 25, 1989).

Congress attempted (rather cryptically) to codify EPA's antidegradation policy in 1987, when it added CWA § 303(d)(4)(B) (33 U.S.C. § 1313(d)(4)(B)), providing that TMDLs, water quality standards, and permitting standards for waters with quality above that required to protect designated uses may be revised "only if such revision is subject to and consistent with the antidegradation policy established under this section."

3. *Permits for discharges to impaired waters.* Should new discharges to waters already designated as impaired be prohibited? The Tenth Circuit held in Oklahoma v. EPA, 908 F.2d 595 (10th Cir. 1990), that the CWA prohibited new permits where WQSs were already violated, but the Supreme Court reversed. Arkansas v. Oklahoma, 503 U.S. 91, 107–108 (1992). Until the *Pinto Creek* decision, states and EPA had routinely issued new permits on impaired waters provided the permittee could arrange an offsetting reduction in pollution from some other source. On what basis did the Ninth Circuit reject that approach in *Pinto Creek*? Does EPA's regulation, as interpreted in *Pinto Creek*, ask too much of a new source? What would Carlota Copper have to do to qualify for a new NPDES permit?

As explained in Chapter 10, the Clean Air Act sets up a series of conditions that must be met before new pollution sources can be constructed in non-attainment areas. The requirements include that the new source must meet especially demanding technology-based standards; that it provide offsets sufficient to at least provide for "reasonable further progress" toward attainment, and for several pollutants increasing on a sliding scale with the magnitude of the non-attainment problem; and a showing that the benefits of the new source outweigh the environmental costs. In what ways does that scheme differ from the regulation interpreted in *Pinto Creek*? Should the Clean Air Act's scheme be imported into the CWA? Would that require statutory amendment, or could it be done by EPA through regulation?

4. *Mixing zones.* Pollutant concentrations are typically high at the precise point of discharge, falling off gradually as the discharge stream mixes with the receiving water. Strictly enforcing water quality standards at the point of discharge rather than at some distance from the discharge, therefore requires more stringent pollution reductions, perhaps for little health or welfare benefit.

> The size and configuration of the mixing zone is a crucial variable in determining whether or not a given effluent can be discharged. If the permitted mixing zone is tiny—say, one meter in diameter—any effluent whatever will violate water quality standards; if the permitted mixing zone is huge—say, 100 kilometers—a tremendously toxic effluent can be discharged without violating water quality standards.

Marathon Oil Co. v. EPA, 830 F.2d 1346, 1349 (5th Cir. 1987).

EPA permits states to allow WQSs to be exceeded within mixing zones provided that aquatic life, human health, and the esthetic qualities of the water are adequately protected. See 40 C.F.R. § 131.13; EPA, Water Quality Standards Handbook, § 5.1.1.

5. *Implementing water quality standards.* Media quality standards, in order to be effective, must be translated into limitations on discharges from specific sources. The TMDL program provides a mechanism for that translation. It requires first that states identify waters that do not meet water quality standards, and will not do so even if technology-based effluent standards are fully implemented. Which waters are most likely to fall in that category? Next, states must set priorities for addressing the problems of these waters, taking into account the severity of pollution and the uses of the waters. Finally, states must establish TMDLs, based on their priority schedule, at levels necessary to meet applicable water quality standards, accounting for seasonal variation and including a margin of safety. TMDLs are produced for each pollutant impairing each waterbody on the impaired list. A TMDL is essentially a pollution budget. It identifies the level of acceptable daily input of the pollutant into the waterbody, and allocates that load among all sources, including both point and nonpoint anthropogenic sources and any natural loading. It is analogous to a State Implementation Plan under the Clean Air Act, determining what reductions are needed to achieve acceptable environmental quality and how those reductions should be achieved.

6. *History of the TMDL program.* Although the TMDL provision was included in the 1972 CWA, it was essentially ignored for many years, as both EPA and the states concentrated on developing technology-based effluent standards. The first TMDLs were due in 1979, but most states submitted no TMDLs by that deadline. EPA, which did not even promulgate regulations for the TMDL program until 1985, showed little interest in pushing the states. Environmental groups took up that task, filing lawsuits in 38 states asserting that TMDLs were inadequate or that the protracted failure of states to file TMDLs amounted to constructive submission of inadequate TMDLs, invoking EPA's duty to prepare TMDLs for the state. Enough of these suits succeeded that by 2002 EPA was subject to court orders or consent decrees setting schedules for TMDL production in 22 states. Oliver A. Houck, The Clean Water Act TMDL Program: Law, Policy and Implementation 190 (2d ed. 2002).

At the same time, after years of ignoring the TMDL program, EPA undertook a major overhaul of its TMDL regulations in the late 1990s, culminating in the issuance of substantially revised TMDL regulations in July 2000. One of the most controversial aspects of those regulations was the explicit requirement that states prepare TMDLs for waters impaired only by non-point sources. They also would have required EPA approval not only of identification of the acceptable waste load and allocation of the waste load among sources, but also of an implementation plan for actually distributing the load among those sources. Congress halted implementation of the rules through a 2001 budget rider and the Bush administration later formally withdrew them, 68 Fed. Reg. 13608 (March 19, 2003), restoring the TMDL regulations which were in effect before 2000. Those regulations say very little about the content of TMDLs, and nothing about their implementation. See 40 C.F.R. § 130.7.

7. *The TMDL challenge.* Creating and implementing TMDLs has turned out to be a Herculean task. Since 1995, EPA has approved nearly 45,000 TMDLs, including more than 4000 per year between 2005 and 2009, although the rate of approval has fallen off noticeably in the Obama administration. Still, many thousands of impaired water segments do not yet have TMDLs. Lack of data about water quality needs, impairments, and the costs of addressing those impairments have complicated the process of producing TMDLs.

Individual TMDLs are as varied as the receiving waters, water quality standards, and pollutants they deal with. Most involve "common" pollutants such as mercury or other metals, sediment, oxygen depletion and the like. Others address more unusual concerns, such as noxious aquatic plants or radiation.

The Los Angeles River is the subject of a controversial TMDL for trash, intended to achieve narrative water quality standards providing that the River shall not contain floating, suspended, or settled materials "in concentrations that cause nuisance or adversely affect beneficial uses." Thousands of tons of trash wash out of the Los Angeles River onto the area's beaches every year, adversely affecting wildlife and recreational uses. In 2001, concluding that any level of trash can be detrimental, the Los Angeles Regional Water Quality Control Board set a progressively decreasing TMDL for trash discharge to the river, culminating in a zero discharge level by 2014. A group of affected cities and counties challenged the zero trash goal. In 2006, the California Court of Appeal upheld the goal, holding that the Board was not required to conduct a scientific study to determine if some level of trash was compatible with the designated uses of the river and coastal waters, or to do a cost-benefit analysis before adopting the TMDL. City of Arcadia v. State Water Resources Control Board, 135 Cal.App.4th 1392 (2006). Trash is carried to the Los Angeles River primarily by municipal storm drains, into which litter washes during storm events. As a result, the TMDL focuses on reducing the inflow of trash to storm sewers and the outflow from storm sewer systems to the River. So far the City has met each of the milestones in the plan, at a cost far less than originally projected.

8. *Nonpoint sources and TMDLs.* In *Pronsolino*, the Ninth Circuit held that TMDLs must be prepared for impaired waters even if the impairment is due entirely to nonpoint sources. Do you agree, as a matter of statutory interpretation?

Does it make sense, in light of both the goals of the CWA and the costs of TMDL development, to require TMDLs for these waters? What exactly is the benefit of such a TMDL? Does it mean that nonpoint source pollution *must* be controlled? Does it increase the likelihood that states will voluntarily impose such controls? Does the CWA give EPA the authority to oversee state TMDL implementation? If so, should EPA do so, as it had committed to do in the short-lived 2000 regulations?

9. *The costs of implementing TMDLs.* In 2001, EPA estimated that the implementing TMDLs that would achieve water quality standards for the 22,000 waters then identified as impaired would cost pollution sources between $900 million and $4.3 billion annually. Factoring control costs into pollution allocations and using allowance trading as one implementation mechanism would reduce compliance costs compared to uniform reduction requirements. Although there was a wide range of uncertainty, EPA estimated that it would be more cost-effective in many cases to focus control efforts on nonpoint sources. EPA, The National Costs to Implement TMDLs (Draft Report), Support Document #2 (Aug. 1, 2001). What role should trading play in achieving water quality standards? How might trading be incorporated into a TMDL? What limits should be imposed, on pollutants subject to trading or on the geographic scope of trades? EPA has issued a policy encouraging the use of trading within a defined watershed, to achieve water quality standards for nutrients and sediment. The policy indicates that EPA may approve trading of other pollutants on a case-by-case basis, but rules out trading of persistent bioaccumulative toxics. EPA, Office of Water, Water Quality Trading Policy (Jan. 13, 2003).

10. *Toxic water pollutants.* The 1987 CWA amendments added § 304(*l*) (33 U.S.C. § 1314(*l*)), which establishes a TMDL-like procedure for toxic pollutants. States must identify waters which are impaired by point source discharges of toxic substances, despite implementation of technology-based effluent controls, and develop "individual control strategies" to achieve the water quality standards within three years.

11. *TMDLs for the East River.* What kind of data would DEQ need to prepare TMDLs for copper and suspended solids for the East River near Centralia? Suppose that DEQ has determined that the East River can assimilate 250 pounds of copper and 3000 pounds of suspended solids per day and still meet water quality standards (with a margin of safety). The present loading is 300 pounds of copper (roughly 100 from the abandoned mine, 150 from the POTW, and 50 from unidentified sources) and 4000 pounds of suspended solids (roughly 3000 from various nonpoint sources, 500 from the Ajax mill, and 500 from other industrial sources). How should DEQ allocate the needed reductions? How should it implement, enforce, and monitor those reductions? How should it decide how to reduce existing loads sufficiently to allow UWC to open its proposed plant, or should that decision be made by the market?

CHAPTER TWELVE

ENVIRONMENTAL ENFORCEMENT

SECTION 1. INTRODUCTION

A. OVERVIEW

During the 1970s, EPA focused its energy on developing basic programs and setting standards authorized by the Clean Water Act, Clean Air Act, and other newly enacted or expanded environmental statutes. Although these statutes contained enforcement authorities, EPA devoted relatively little effort and resources to ensuring compliance with the emerging regulatory schemes. At the state level, the development of enforcement authority and capabilities lagged even further behind. Beginning in the 1980s, however, environmental enforcement became a higher priority at all levels of government and with citizens as well. It is important to understand the basic theories, techniques, and issues of environmental enforcement because many environmental lawyers work on regulatory compliance and enforcement matters as their primary function.

Environmental enforcement is important to the government, the public, and even the regulated community. First and foremost, enforcement reduces polluting activities and helps attain environmental goals. Active enforcement establishes and maintains the credibility of environmental regulations and institutions. Furthermore, by holding similar facilities within a given industry to the same standards, enforcement ensures that no individual company obtains a competitive advantage over its rivals through noncompliance with permits or other regulatory requirements. Enforcement also may generate long-term economic benefits to society and complying facilities by reducing public health costs and potential industry liability for damages and cleanup costs.

Traditional enforcement activities focus upon a determination of whether a regulated entity is in compliance with its permits and other regulatory requirements. EPA and state regulatory agencies collect source performance data to establish compliance status through source reporting, monitoring, inspections, and the receipt of citizen complaints. Because of their limited resources, government agencies must concentrate enforcement efforts on more serious or significant cases. EPA may make it a priority, for instance, to enforce against certain industries or with regard to certain media.

Once compliance data is collected and verified, problem cases are identified and a range of enforcement actions may be taken. EPA may resolve a case through more informal methods such as a warning letter or notice of violation. The agency may also use administrative complaints and penalty orders, and a case may be settled administratively after negotiations between EPA and the violator. These administrative actions, which are by far the most common techniques employed to assure compliance, offer several potential advantages over judicial enforcement. Administrative proceedings tend to be less costly, less time-consuming, and more flexible. Most administrative cases are settled, however, in a process that involves relatively little transparency and public visibility. See Ronald H. Rosenberg, Doing More or Doing Less for the Environment: Shedding Light on EPA's Stealth Method of Environmental Enforcement, 35 B.C. Envtl. Aff. L. Rev. 175 (2008). In some cases, judicial enforcement may be necessary to achieve compliance and deterrence objectives. In judicial enforcement, the government may seek an order to enforce a previously issued administrative order, other injunctive relief, or civil penalties. EPA refers several hundred cases per year to the U.S. Department of Justice for civil enforcement and a smaller number of cases for criminal prosecution. State agencies are important partners in environmental enforcement, particularly where a state has been delegated authority or authorized to implement a program under one of the major federal environmental statutes.

Private citizens, nonprofit organizations, and other entities also play an important role in environmental enforcement. Many federal environmental statutes contain citizen suit provisions authorizing actions that supplement governmental enforcement. Citizen enforcement may also involve lawsuits against the government when government agencies violate pollution standards or statutory requirements.

In recent years, EPA has emphasized compliance incentives and compliance assistance in conjunction with more traditional enforcement techniques. These efforts acknowledge that firms, particularly small businesses, sometimes need assistance in complying with complex environmental regulations. EPA's compliance assistance programs transfer information by way of on-site visits, compliance assistance hotlines, workshops/training presentations, informational websites, and the distribution of compliance checklists and guides. Additionally, EPA has encouraged voluntary auditing and disclosure of environmental violations through its Audit Policy. See Incentives for Self–Policing: Discovery, Disclosure, Correction, and Prevention of Violations, 65 Fed. Reg. 19,618 (Apr. 11, 2000). The Audit Policy provides incentives for companies to develop environmental audit and compliance management systems to detect, disclose, and correct violations. When firms voluntarily discover and promptly disclose environmental violations to EPA, the agency may waive or reduce the portion of the civil penalty based on the gravity of the violations. While the voluntary audit technique remains controversial, it does reflect the modern trend towards more firm-initiated compliance assurance techniques.

Measuring the effectiveness of enforcement efforts is complicated. EPA reports annually on the amounts of civil and criminal penalties assessed, the value of injunctive relief, and the quantity of pollution reduced as a result of its enforcement programs. A 2008 Government Accountability

Office study identified various shortcomings in EPA's calculations and measures, however, including the agency's reliance on formal judgments issued by courts, rather than actual penalties paid and pollution reduction measures implemented by violators. See Government Accountability Office, Environmental Enforcement: EPA Needs to Improve the Accuracy and Transparency of Measures Used to Report on Program Effectiveness (2008).

The materials in this chapter focus on issues that arise in the judicial enforcement of environmental law. Although many environmental statutes contain enforcement provisions specific to that statute, enforcement provisions from different statutes often share common features. This chapter relies primarily, but not exclusively, on the provisions of the Clean Water Act to illustrate many of these features.

B.   ENFORCEMENT THEORY

Clifford Rechtschaffen, Deterrence vs. Cooperation and the Evolving Theory of Environmental Enforcement

71 S. Cal. L. Rev. 1181, 1186–89 (1998).

The traditional practice of environmental enforcement is grounded in theory on a deterrence-based model of enforcement. It assumes that most regulated entities are rational economic actors that act to maximize profits. As such, decisions regarding compliance are based on self-interest. In short, businesses comply where the costs of noncompliance outweigh the benefits of noncompliance. The benefits of noncompliance consist of money saved by not purchasing pollution control equipment or taking other required measures. The costs of noncompliance include the costs of implementing control measures once a violation is detected, plus any additional penalties imposed for being found in violation, multiplied (discounted) by the probability that the violations will be detected. The task for enforcement agencies is to make penalties high enough and the probability of detection great enough that it becomes economically irrational for facilities to violate environmental requirements. The speed and the certainty with which sanctions are imposed are also important factors in obtaining compliance.

Deterrence may be achieved through civil or criminal sanctions. Criminal sanctions may be more appropriate where the amount of civil penalties needed to constitute an economic deterrent is unrealistic. Many also believe that the unique moral stigma and threat of jail time from criminal enforcement constitute the most powerful incentives to obey the law. But whether the penalty is civil or criminal, the essential inquiry turns on the same pleasure-pain calculus: make the penalty sufficiently painful so that rational actors will be deterred despite the benefits of noncompliance.

As a theoretical construct, a deterrence-based system has a number of distinctive features. A central concern regards the application of punishment for breaking a rule: if there is a breach of a legal requirement, it deserves punishment. Thus, there is a strong emphasis on detecting non-compliance and gathering evidence to prove it. Imposing fines is seen as a mark of success and serves notice that all violators will be treated similarly. Enforcement is also largely retrospective since it focuses on reacting to violations that have already occurred and penalizing violators as a means of deterring future violations.

By contrast, a "compliance" or cooperative system emphasizes securing compliance rather than sanctioning wrongdoing. Penalties are seen as threats rather than sanctions, and sanctions are typically withdrawn if compliance is achieved. Levying penalties is seen as a mark of the system's failure (to otherwise obtain compliance); compliance systems rely far more on rewards and incentives than penalties. Enforcement is primarily prospective, oriented toward inducing conditions that lead to conformity. The system focuses more on the underlying conditions or violations than on the violator.

Deterrence-based enforcement is the prevailing societal approach for controlling unlawful individual and corporate conduct. This theory underlies the EPA's current enforcement system. The agency's enforcement approach is legalistic, and its extensive enforcement policies stress the use of formal enforcement actions. Since the mid–1980s, one of its guiding principles has been ensuring "timely and appropriate responses" to observed violations, which involves applying a series of escalating actions once noncompliance is detected. The agency has traditionally measured the success of its program by the number of inspections conducted, the number of enforcement actions initiated, and the number and size of penalties assessed—all indicators that some type of formal enforcement action has been taken. State environmental agencies have generally followed the EPA's lead, especially when implementing federally-delegated programs that entail EPA oversight of their enforcement activities.

Although the theoretical underpinning of the current enforcement system relies largely on deterrence, in practice the process is much more flexible. Most enforcers use a hybrid strategy that includes elements of both coercion and cooperation; few rely on a strictly legalistic model. Most enforcement activity, particularly state enforcement, is aimed at bringing violators back into compliance rather than punishing or deterring. Most instances of noncompliance are met with either no sanctions or only minor, informal ones. Moreover, most regulatory officials do not rigidly adhere to legalistic procedures.

C. CLASS DISCUSSION PROBLEM: ENFORCEMENT OF THE CLEAN WATER ACT

The following class discussion problem introduces some of the major issues presented by environmental enforcement cases. To answer the questions in the problem, you should consider the government enforcement provisions of the Clean Water Act (CWA §§ 308, 309), as well as its citizen suit provisions (CWA § 505).

One of Centralia's oldest business firms is Wilson Foods (Wilson). Wilson operates a food processing, canning, and warehousing facility in Centralia. The wastewater generated by these activities is discharged into the East River. Wilson has obtained a discharge permit from the State of Euphoria's Department of Environmental Conservation (DEC), the agency authorized by EPA to administer the CWA National Pollutant Discharge Elimination System (NPDES) program. Under the terms of this permit, Wilson may discharge wastewater into the river at a specific outfall, but its discharged effluent must have characteristics that do not exceed numerical limits set by the permit. The permit also requires Wilson to monitor the nature of its wastewater, to keep records of its plant operation, and to report regularly its pollution control results to DEC in the form of Discharge Monitoring Reports (DMRs).

Recently, the DEC and EPA's regional office received an anonymous letter alleging that Wilson "is violating anti-pollution laws." Specifically, the letter alleges:

1. that the effluent monitoring device on Wilson's outfall has been intentionally miscalibrated to under-register effluent concentrations;

2. that Wilson filed its DMRs sporadically, and that they were often filed six months late;

3. that during peak production periods, Wilson discharged untreated effluent through an unlisted outfall point and through a sewer line that crosses the Wilson plant site; and

4. that, as reflected in the plant's DMRs, Wilson frequently violated the effluent limitations contained in its NPDES permit.

Although the letter was unsigned, it reflected a familiarity with the plant's design and operation that could only have come from first-hand experience, likely from a Wilson employee. Although the DEC found the letter credible, it merely placed the facility on its "careful watch" list because of a staffing shortage. EPA, on the other hand, took the matter so seriously that it assigned the case to a compliance team. Over the past two years, EPA had noticed significant variations in the discharge performance reported in Wilson's DMRs. In addition, ambient water quality in the vicinity of the Wilson plant continues to violate state water quality standards in spite of substantial point source and non-point source control on that East River segment.

Consider the following questions:

A. As a preliminary step, EPA intends to inspect the facility, its production processes, and its outfall, and to collect documentary evidence in Wilson's files concerning production and discharge practices. Is EPA authorized to enter the Wilson plant and attempt to recover this data? Can EPA enlist the services of a private engineering consultant to assist in the inspection or to conduct it under EPA's direction? Can the information derived from this inspection be made available to the public or can Wilson prevent EPA from disclosing it? See CWA § 308 (reproduced in Section 2.A of this chapter).

B. What enforcement options are available to EPA under § 309 of the CWA (reproduced in Section 2.B of this chapter)? If you were EPA's regional attorney, what would be the objectives of your enforcement strategy, and what enforcement options would you pursue?

1. Can EPA administratively order Wilson to comply with its permit conditions? How would such an order be enforced? Can EPA go directly to court to seek injunctive relief without first issuing an order?

2. Can EPA seek financial penalties against Wilson for any or all four of the violations alleged in the letter if they are corroborated with evidence? Can EPA assess penalties by itself, or must it go to court to obtain the penalties through a court order?

3. Can any individual be prosecuted for criminal violation of the CWA for the conduct described in the anonymous letter? What range of Wilson corporate officers and employees might be exposed to criminal sanctions? See CWA § 309 (c) (reproduced in Section 3.B of this chapter).

4. Assume that Sam, the Wilson employee who wrote the anonymous letter alerting EPA and DEC to Wilson's violations, is fired when his actions become known. Does Sam have any legal recourse under the CWA? See 33 U.S.C. § 1367.

C. What if the DEC begins investigating Wilson's compliance status? Would this state action displace EPA's power to enforce? What if the DEC commences an enforcement action against Wilson in state court or through state administrative means? Would this prevent EPA from taking its own action? Would EPA have any recourse against Wilson or against the state if the state settles the case on terms that EPA believes are unduly favorable to Wilson?

D. Can a private individual living close to the facility bring a citizen suit against Wilson? What about an individual living in another state? What prerequisites must the individual satisfy in order to sue? Does the ability to bring a citizen suit depend on whether EPA or the state has already commenced an enforcement action against Wilson? See CWA § 505 (reproduced in Section 4.A of this chapter).

SECTION 2. CIVIL ENFORCEMENT

A. INFORMATION GATHERING

EPA, Principles of Environmental Enforcement

6–1 to 6–18 (1992).

There are four primary sources of compliance information:

• Inspections conducted by program inspectors.

- Self-monitoring, self-recordkeeping, and self-reporting by the regulated community.

- Citizen complaints.

- Monitoring environmental conditions near a facility.

* * *

Inspections

Inspections are the backbone of most enforcement programs. Inspections are conducted by government inspectors, or by independent parties hired by and reporting back to the responsible agency. Inspectors plan inspections, gather data in and/or around a particular facility, record and report on their observations, and (sometimes) make independent judgments about whether the facility is in compliance. Inspections can be very resource-intensive, therefore they require careful targeting and planning. By standardizing inspection procedures, enforcement officials can help ensure that all facilities are treated equally and that all the appropriate information is gathered. * * *

Inspections may be routine (i.e., there is no reason to suspect that the facility is out of compliance), or "for cause" (i.e., a particular facility is targeted because there is reason to believe it is out of compliance). Inspectors may notify the facility prior to inspection or simply arrive unannounced.

* * *

During the inspection, the inspector records notes on every aspect of the inspection. The inspector may also gather additional evidence, such as physical samples, photographs, and copies of facility documents. As soon as possible following the inspection, the inspector prepares and files an inspection report, which references any additional evidence collected (photographs, documents, etc.). Any samples collected are sent to a laboratory for analysis. Analytical data are interpreted and presented in the final inspection report. This report serves as the basis for any testimony by the inspector and will likely be used as evidence should the case go to trial. * * *

Self–Monitoring, –Recordkeeping, and –Reporting by the Regulated Community

Self-monitoring, -recordkeeping, and -reporting are three ways in which sources can be required to track their own compliance and record or report the results for government review. Increasingly, self-monitoring, -recordkeeping, and -reporting are being recognized as providing essential data to supplement and support inspections.

In self-monitoring, sources measure an emission, discharge, or performance parameter that provides information on the nature of the pollutant discharges or the operation of control technologies. For example, sources may monitor groundwater quality, or may periodically sample and analyze effluent for the presence and concentration of particular pollutants. Sources may also be asked to monitor operating parameters on pollution control equipment (such as line voltage and electrical current used) that indicate how well the equipment itself is operating. Operating parameters are generally inexpensive to monitor and provide reliable data that give a more accurate and representative picture of emissions than occasional sampling and analysis of the emissions themselves. This type of monitoring has proven to be a cost-effective way for enforcement programs and sources to assure themselves that controls are operating correctly.

Self-recordkeeping means that sources are responsible for maintaining their own records of certain regulated activities (e.g., shipment of hazardous waste).

Self-reporting requires that sources provide the enforcement program with self-monitoring or recordkeeping data periodically and/or upon request.

Self-monitoring, -recordkeeping, and -reporting provide much more extensive information on compliance than can be obtained with periodic inspections. Self-monitoring, -recordkeeping, and -reporting requirements also shift some of the economic burden of monitoring to the regulated community, and they provide a mechanism for educating this community about the compliance requirements. Self-monitoring, recordkeeping, and -reporting may also increase the level of management attention devoted to compliance, and may inspire management to improve production efficiency and prevent pollution.

Self-monitoring requires that reliable and affordable monitoring equipment be available to the regulated community. Self-monitoring, -recordkeeping, and -reporting rely on the integrity and capability of the source to provide accurate data. The data will be misleading if the source either deliberately falsifies the information or lacks the technical capability to provide accurate data. Therefore, programs using self-monitoring, -reporting, and -recordkeeping will need to establish some way to help ensure accuracy, e.g., by requiring self-monitoring only in facilities with the appropriate technical capability, by developing quality control standards for monitoring and recordkeeping, etc.

[S]elf-monitoring, -recordkeeping, and -reporting are often required by environmental regulations. Enforcement officials translate these regulatory requirements to facility-specific requirements via permits. Information from self-monitoring, -recordkeeping, and -reporting is used primarily to target inspections. It is also sometimes used as a basis for enforcement actions. Usually, it is supplemented by inspections to corroborate the accuracy of the data.

* * *

Citizen Complaints

Citizen complaints are an important way of detecting violations that are unlikely to be detected through self-reporting or inspections. These include violations that take place in isolated areas, and illegal acts within an organization. Enforcement programs can help educate and train citizens to detect and report problems. * * *

Area Monitoring

Information on compliance status can be gained by area monitoring, i.e., monitoring environmental conditions near a facility. Area monitoring includes ambient monitoring, remote sensing, and overflights.

[Ambient monitoring] includes any monitoring to detect pollutant levels in the ambient air, ground, or surface waters near a facility. The main problem with ambient monitoring is that it can be difficult to demonstrate that the pollutants measured came from a particular facility. Ambient monitoring is most useful when a source is the only significant polluter in the area, or when its emissions have a characteristic composition that serves to "fingerprint" them. In these cases, ambient measurements clearly suggest potential violations at a facility, and can be used to target inspections. [A]mbient data are rarely used alone to prove a violation because of the difficulty of proving a connection with the source.

Remote-sensing techniques can provide positive proof from outside a facility's boundaries that the facility is violating an environmental requirement. The most developed remote-sensing technique is laser-beam radar, also known as "Lidar," for "light detection and ranging." This technique measures the density of a smoke plume by day or night. It is relatively inexpensive compared to other air monitoring methods such as stack tests.

Both satellites and aircraft can be used to measure ambient and source-specific conditions. Satellites have been useful for detecting large discharges of water pollutants and are most often used to trigger inspections. Satellite images are usually too coarse to calculate the magnitude of the violation. Aircraft overflights can be even more effective than satellites for compliance monitoring. Airborne cameras can detect and record the densities, temperatures, and area of air and water discharges. Even some biological effects in streams can be detected from the air. Perhaps most significantly, overflights can be used to observe the physical characteristics and work practices at a facility. For example, dikes and fences can be observed and checked against permit records for correct location and condition. Practices such as the loading and unloading of hazardous materials can be observed. Production levels can be estimated from the air and compared to assumptions used in permits or licenses.

Excerpt From the Clean Water Act
33 U.S.C. § 1318.

CWA § 308 Records and reports; inspections

(a) Maintenance; monitoring equipment; entry; access to information

Whenever required to carry out the objective of this chapter, including but not limited to (1) developing or assisting in the development of any effluent limitation, or other limitation, prohibition, or effluent standard, pretreatment standard, or standard of performance under this chapter; (2) determining whether any person is in violation of any such effluent limitation, or other limitation, prohibition or effluent standard, pretreatment standard, or standard of performance; (3) any requirement established under this section; or (4) carrying out sections 1315, 1321 (relating to State permit programs), 1345, and 1364 of this title—

(A) the Administrator shall require the owner or operator of any point source to (i) establish and maintain such records, (ii) make such reports, (iii) install, use, and maintain such monitoring equipment or methods (including where appropriate, biological monitoring methods), (iv) sample such effluents (in accordance with such methods, at such locations, at such intervals, and in such manner as the Administrator shall prescribe), and (v) provide such other information as he may reasonably require; and

(B) the Administrator or his authorized representative . . . , upon presentation of his credentials—

(i) shall have a right of entry to, upon, or through any premises in which an effluent source is located or in which any records required to be maintained under clause (A) of this subsection are located, and

(ii) may at reasonable times have access to and copy any records, inspect any monitoring equipment or method required under clause (A), and sample any effluents which the owner or operator of such source is required to sample under such clause.

(b) Availability to public; trade secrets exception; penalty for disclosure of confidential information

Any records, reports, or information obtained under this section (1) shall, in the case of effluent data, be related to any applicable effluent limitations, toxic, pretreatment, or new source performance standards, and (2) shall be available to the public, except that upon a showing satisfactory to the Administrator by any person that records, reports, or information, or particular part thereof (other than effluent data), to which the Administrator has access under this section, if made public would divulge methods or processes entitled to protection as trade secrets of such person, the Administrator shall consider such record, report, or information, or particular portion thereof confidential in accordance with the purposes of section 1905 of Title 18. Any authorized representative of the Administrator . . . who knowingly or willfully publishes, divulges, discloses, or makes known in any manner or to any extent not authorized by law any information which is required to be considered confidential under this subsection shall be fined not more than $1,000 or imprisoned not more than 1 year, or both. Nothing in this subsection shall prohibit the Administrator or an authorized representative of the Administrator . . . from disclosing records, reports, or information to other officers, employees, or authorized representatives of the United States concerned with carrying out this chapter or when relevant in any proceeding under this chapter.

NOTES AND QUESTIONS

1. Under the CWA, sources are usually required to report their pollution control performance in their regular discharge monitoring reports (DMRs). But as § 308 of the CWA makes clear, the DMR is not the only method available to EPA to obtain data. The CWA, like other federal environment statutes, vests significant authority in EPA to gather data concerning CWA compliance. Cf. 42 U.S.C. § 6927 (RCRA information gathering authority); 42 U.S.C. § 7414 (CAA information gathering authority). Sometimes, important compliance information can be acquired only by inspecting facilities themselves, and this can give rise to the need for a search warrant if the facility refuses to consent to inspection. See Marshall v. Barlow's, Inc., 436 U.S. 307, 312–13, 320 (1978) (holding that government agency conducting inspection for safety hazards and regulatory violations must obtain search warrant, unless business is "pervasively regulated," but that "probable cause justifying the issuance of a warrant may be based not only on specific evidence of an existing violation but also on a showing that reasonable legislative or administrative standards for conducting an inspection are satisfied with respect to a particular [establishment]"). However, no warrant is required if, as is often the case, a permit includes within its conditions a right of inspection. Cf. CAA § 504(c) (requiring that Title V permits "set forth inspection, entry, monitoring, compliance certification, and reporting requirements to assure compliance with permit terms and conditions"); CWA § 402(a)(2) (authorizing conditions in NPDES permits "to assure compliance . . . including conditions on data and information collection, reporting and such other requirements as [the Administrator] deems appropriate").

2. Must a warrant be procured or consent be granted for emissions observations taken outside of or above the facility itself? The Supreme Court has ruled in two air pollution cases that no warrant is required under these circumstances. See Dow Chemical Co. v. United States, 476 U.S. 227, 238–39 (1986) (holding that EPA's use of aerial overflights to examine and photograph defendant's facility did not violate Fourth Amendment); Air Pollution Variance Board v. Western Alfalfa Corp., 416 U.S. 861, 865 (1974) (holding that state inspector's observation and analysis of plume of smoke from outside of defendant's plant fell within "open fields" exception of Fourth Amendment).

3. What about legitimate business concerns about disclosure of operations? Could competitors review a company's NPDES permit application, its monitoring data, and inspection reports to acquire information about the business, such as trade secrets? On the other hand, could an individual or an environmental group have access to information gathered by EPA? See CWA § 308(b).

B. Civil Enforcement Options and Issues

1. CIVIL ENFORCEMENT AUTHORITIES

Section 309 of the Clean Water Act spells out various options for state and federal governments for enforcing the requirements of the statute. As you read § 309, consider what factors in a specific case might lead to choosing one option rather than another.

Excerpt From the Clean Water Act

33 U.S.C. §§ 1251–1387.

Sec. 309   Enforcement

(a) State enforcement; compliance orders

(1) Whenever, on the basis of any information available to him, the Administrator finds that any person is in violation of any condition or limitation which implements section 1311, 1312 of this title in a permit issued by a State under an approved permit program under section 1342 of this title, he shall proceed under his authority in paragraph (3) of this subsection or he shall notify the person in alleged violation and such State of such finding. If beyond the thirtieth day after the Administrator's notification the State has not commenced appropriate enforcement action, the Administrator shall issue an order requiring such person to comply with such condition or limitation or shall bring a civil action in accordance with subsection (b) of this section.

(2) Whenever, on the basis of information available to him, the Administrator finds that violations of permit conditions or limitations as set forth in paragraph (1) of this subsection are so widespread that such violations appear to result from a failure of the State to enforce such permit conditions or limitations effectively, he shall so notify the State. If the Administrator finds such failure extends beyond the thirtieth day after such notice, he shall give public notice of such finding. During the period beginning with such public notice and ending when such State satisfies the Administrator that it will enforce such conditions and limitations (hereafter referred to in this section as the period of "federally assumed enforcement"), except where an extension has been granted under paragraph (5)(B) of this subsection, the Administrator shall enforce any permit condition or limitation with respect to any person—

(A) by issuing an order to comply with such condition or limitation, or

(B) by bringing a civil action under subsection (b) of this section.

(3) Whenever on the basis of any information available to him the Administrator finds that any person is in violation of section 1311 of this title, or is in violation of any permit condition or limitation implementing any of such sections in a permit issued under section 1342 of this title by him or by a State or in a permit issued under section 1344 of this title by a State, he shall issue an order requiring such person to comply with such section or requirement, or he shall bring a civil action in accordance with subsection (b) of this section.

(4) A copy of any order issued under this subsection shall be sent immediately by the Administrator to the State in which the violation occurs and other affected States. * * *

(b) Civil actions

The Administrator is authorized to commence a civil action for appropriate relief, including a permanent or temporary injunction, for any violation for which he is authorized to issue a compliance order under subsection (a) of this section. Any action under this subsection may be brought in the district court of the United States for the district in which the defendant is located or resides or is doing business, and such court shall have jurisdiction to restrain such violation and to require compliance. Notice of the commencement of such action shall be given immediately to the appropriate State.

* * *

(d) Civil penalties; factors considered in determining amount

Any person who violates section 1311, 1312, 1316, 1317, 1318, 1328, or 1345 of this title, or any permit condition or limitation implementing any of such sections in a permit issued under section 1342 of this title by the Administrator, or by a State, or in a permit issued under section 1344 of this title by a State, or any requirement imposed in a pretreatment program approved under section 1342(a)(3) or 1342(b)(8) of this title, and any person who violates any order issued by the Administrator under subsection (a) of this section, shall be subject to a civil penalty not to exceed $25,000 per day for each violation. In determining the amount of a civil penalty the court shall consider the seriousness of the violation or violations, the economic benefit (if any) resulting from the violation, any history of such violations, any good-faith efforts to comply with the applicable requirements, the economic impact of the penalty on the violator, and such other matters as justice may require. For purposes of this subsection, a single operational upset which leads to simultaneous violations of more than one pollutant parameter shall be treated as a single violation.

NOTES AND QUESTIONS

1. *Enforcing administrative orders.* If a permit violator refuses to comply with an EPA administrative order to meet its permit conditions or to pay monetary penalties, how can EPA enforce the order? Can EPA go directly to court to seek injunctive relief or monetary penalties without first issuing an administrative order? If so, why should EPA bother with issuing an administrative order in the first instance?

If EPA has issued an administrative order but not sought judicial enforcement, can the recipient of the order nonetheless obtain judicial review of the order? Although federal courts of appeal have uniformly answered this question in the negative, the Supreme Court recently granted certiorari on the issue and took the opposite view. Sackett v. EPA, ___ U.S. ___, 132 S.Ct. 1367 (March 21, 2012). See also General Electric Co. v.

Jackson, 610 F.3d 110 (D.C. Cir. 2010); Laguna Gatuna, Inc. v. Browner, 58 F.3d 564 (10th Cir. 1995); Hoffman Group, Inc. v. EPA, 902 F.2d 567 (7th Cir. 1990); Lloyd A. Fry Roofing Co. v. EPA, 554 F.2d 885 (8th Cir. 1977).

2. *Penalty factors.* What factors must a court or EPA consider in setting penalties? Does the statute provide sufficient guidance as to how these factors are to be weighed?

3. *Enforcement provisions in other statutes.* Other pollution statutes contain similar government enforcement provisions. See CAA § 113, 42 U.S.C. § 7413 (enforcement authority under Clean Air Act for stationary source compliance with SIP and national emission limitations); RCRA § 3008, 42 U.S.C. § 6928 (RCRA enforcement authority).

2.   PENALTY POLICIES

Although the major environmental statutes contain provisions specifying the maximum penalty that can be assessed for each violation, the statutes give EPA and the courts broad discretion in determining the appropriate penalty in a particular case. To guide the exercise of discretion in administrative proceedings and in settlement negotiations, EPA has issued penalty policies for each statute. The penalty policies are intended to promote uniformity among cases, while giving violators an incentive to settle rather than litigate. Below is an excerpt from a penalty policy applicable to most violations of the Clean Water Act.

Environmental Protection Agency, Interim Clean Water Act Settlement Penalty Policy

(1995).

This Policy applies to civil judicial and administrative penalties sought under CWA § 309, including: violations of NPDES permit limits and conditions; discharges without an NPDES permit; violations of pretreatment standards and requirements (including local limits and pretreatment programs); violations of § 405 sludge use or disposal requirements; violations of § 308 information requests; and violations of § 309(a) compliance orders. * * *

This Policy sets forth how the Agency generally expects to exercise its enforcement discretion in deciding on an appropriate enforcement response and determining an appropriate settlement penalty. * * * This Policy only establishes how the Agency expects to calculate the minimum penalty for which it would be willing to settle a case. The development of the penalty amount to plead in an administrative or judicial complaint is developed independent of this Policy, except that the Agency may not seek a settlement penalty in excess of the statutory maximum penalty for the violations alleged in the complaint. This Policy is not intended for use by EPA, violators, courts, or administrative judges in determining penalties at a hearing or trial.

* * *

IV.   Penalty Calculation Methodology

* * *

The settlement penalty is calculated based on this formula:

Penalty = Economic Benefit + Gravity +/− Gravity Adjustment Factors − Litigation Considerations − Ability to Pay − Supplemental Environmental Projects.

Each component of the penalty calculation is discussed below.

A.   Economic Benefit

Consistent with EPA's February 1984 Policy on Civil Penalties, every effort should be made to calculate and recover the economic benefit of noncompliance. The objective of the economic benefit calculation is to place violators in the same financial position as they would have been if they had complied on time. Persons that violate the CWA are likely to have obtained an economic benefit as a result of delayed or completely avoided pollution control expenditures during the period of noncompliance. Commonly delayed and avoided CWA pollution control expenditures, include, but are not limited to:

- Monitoring and Reporting (including costs of the sampling and proper laboratory analysis);
- Capital equipment improvements or repairs, including engineering design, purchase, installation, and replacement;
- Operation and maintenance expenses (e.g., labor, power, chemicals) and other annual expenses; and
- One-time acquisitions (such as land purchase).

* * *

B.   Gravity Component

The gravity calculation methodology is based upon a logical scheme and criteria that quantifies the gravity of the violation based upon the CWA and its regulatory programs. Every reasonable effort must be made to calculate and recover a gravity component in addition to the economic benefit component. As EPA's February 1984 Policy on Civil Penalties states on page 4:

> The removal of the economic benefit of noncompliance only places the violator in the same position as he would have been if compliance had been achieved on time. Both deterrence and fundamental fairness require that the penalty include an additional amount to ensure that the violator is economically worse off than if [he] had obeyed the law.

The gravity component of the penalty is calculated for each month in which there was a violation. The total gravity component for the penalty calculation equals the sum of each monthly gravity component. The monthly gravity formula is:

Monthly gravity component = (1 + A + B + C + D) x $1,000.

The four gravity factors—A, B, C, and D—are considered for each month in which there were one or more violations. Values are assigned to each of the four factors as described in the text and tables below. In performing the gravity calculation, the monthly gravity component is calculated from the first date of noncompliance up to when the violations ceased or the date the complaint is expected to be filed, but EPA has the option to start the gravity calculation no more than five years prior to the date when the complaint should be filed. In cases with continuing violations, the gravity calculation should be revised periodically to include additional months of violations that have occurred since the previous calculation.

"A"—Significance of Violation (Monthly Range 0 to 20). This factor is based on the degree of exceedance of the most significant effluent limit violation in each month. Values for this factor are selected from within designated ranges; violations of toxic monthly effluent limits are weighted most heavily. Values are selected using the table below based on the effluent value which yields the highest factor A value. Regions select a particular value for factor A within the designated range. For purposes of this table conventional and nonconventional pollutants include biochemical oxygen demand, chemical oxygen demand, total oxygen demand, dissolved oxygen, total organic carbon, total suspended solids, total dissolved solids, inorganic phosphorous compounds, inorganic nitrogen compounds, oil and grease, calcium, chloride, fluoride, magnesium, sodium, potassium, sulfur, sulfate, total alkalinity, total hardness, aluminum, cobalt, iron, vanadium and temperature. Factor A values for fecal coliform and pH, which are calculated using logarithmic scales, are calculated using the special scales at the bottom of the table. All other pollutants are classified as toxic pollutants.

If there were no effluent limit violations in a particular month, but there were other violations, then factor A is assigned a value of zero in that month's gravity calculation. * * *

GRAVITY FACTOR A—SIGNIFICANCE OF THE VIOLATION
Select a value for factor A based on the effluent limit violated in the month which produces the highest range of values for factor A.

Percent by which daily effluent limit was exceeded:			Factor A Value Ranges:	
Monthly Average	7–day Average	Daily Maximum	Toxic Pollutants	Conventional & Nonconventional Pollutants
1–20	1–30	1–50	1–3	0–2
21–40	31–60	51–100	1–4	1–3

41–100	61–150	101–200	3–7	2–5
101–300	151–450	201–600	5–15	3–6
301–>	451–>	601–>	10–20	5–15

Percent Exceedance of Fecal Coliform Limit:	Standard Units above or below pH Limit:	Factor A Value Ranges:
0–100	0–.50	0–5
101–500	.51–2.0	2–8
501–5,000	2.01–3.0	4–10
5,000–>	3.01–4.0	6–12
	4.01–>	8–15

"B"—Health and Environmental Harm (Monthly Range 0 to 50). A value for this factor is selected for each month in which one or more violations present actual or potential harm to human health or to the environment. Values are selected using the table below based on the type of actual or potential harm that yields the highest factor value.

GRAVITY FACTOR B—HEALTH AND ENVIRONMENTAL HARM	
Type of Actual or Potential Harm	Factor B Value Ranges
Impact on Human Health (e.g., interference with drinking water supplies, harm or increased risks to subsistence fishing)	10–50
Impact on Aquatic Environment (or the POTW)	
Water quality-based effluent standard(s) or whole effluent toxicity limit violated	1–10
Fish kill, beach closing, restrictions on use of water body; or pass through interference at the POTW caused by the IU discharge.	4–50
Other impact on aquatic environment	2–25

"C"—Number of Effluent Limit Violations (Monthly Range 0 to 5). This factor is based on the total number of effluent limit violations each month.... In order to properly quantify the gravity of the violations, all effluent limit violations are considered and evaluated. Violations of different parameters at the same outfall are counted separately and violations of the same parameter at different outfalls are counted separately.... A minimum factor C value of 1 is generally appropriate whenever there are violations of two or more different pollutants. Values for this factor may be selected by comparing the number of effluent limits exceeded with the number of effluent limits in the permit: e.g., if all of the limits in the permit were violated in a month, a value of 5 would be appropriate; if 50 percent of the limits in the permit were violated, a factor of 2 or 3 would be appropriate.

"D"—Significance of Non-effluent Limit Violations. This factor has a value ranging from 0 (zero) to 70 and is based on the severity and number of the six different types of non-effluent limitation requirements violated each month. There are six types of non-effluent violations: 1) monitoring and reporting; 2) pretreatment program implementation; 3) sludge handling; 4) unauthorized discharges; 5) permit milestone schedules; and 6) other types of non-effluent violations. The value for factor D for each month in which there is a non-effluent limit violation is selected pursuant to the table on the next page. The factor D value for a given month is the sum of the highest value for each type of non-effluent limit violation.

* * *

GRAVITY FACTOR D—NON–EFFLUENT LIMIT VIOLATIONS

THE FACTOR D VALUE FOR A GIVEN MONTH IS THE SUM OF THE HIGHEST VALUE FOR EACH TYPE OF NON–EFFLUENT LIMIT VIOLATION.

Type and Extent of Violation	Factor D Value Ranges
1. Effluent Monitoring and Reporting Violations:	
Failure to conduct or submit adequate pollutant sampling data for 1 or more pollutant parameters (but not all parameters)	1 to 6
Failure to conduct or submit any required pollutant sampling data in a given month but with a reasonable belief that the facility was in compliance with applicable limits.	2 to 6
Failure to conduct or submit any required pollutant sampling data in a given month without a reasonable basis to believe that the facility was otherwise in compliance with applicable limits.	6 to 10
Failure to conduct or submit whole effluent toxicity sampling data	4 to 10
Delay in submitting sampling data	0 to 5
Failure to submit a pretreatment baseline report, 90–day compliance report, or periodic compliance report (40 CFR 403.12(b), (d), or (e), failure to sample again after finding a violation (40 CFR 403.12 (g)(2)).	2 to 8
Any other monitoring or reporting violation	0 to 10
2. Pretreatment Program Implementation Violations:	
All key program activities implemented, with some minor violations.	0 to 4
One or two key program activities not implemented	2 to 6
Many key program activities not implemented	4 to 8

Few if any key program activities implemented	6 to 10
3. Failure to properly control or treat sludge	1 to 10
4. Unauthorized discharge: e.g., discharge through an unpermitted outfall, discharge of a wastestream not identified in the permit, sewer overflows, or spill (other than oil or § 311 hazardous substance)	1 to 20
5. Violation of permit milestone schedule	1 to 10
6. Any other type of noneffluent limit violation	1 to 10

C.   Gravity Adjustment Factors

In certain circumstances as explained below, the total monthly gravity amount may be adjusted by three factors: flow reduction factor (to reduce gravity); history of recalcitrance (to increase gravity); and the quick settlement reduction factor (to reduce gravity). The resulting figure—benefit + (gravity +/− gravity adjustments)—is the preliminary penalty amount.

* * *

D.   Litigation Considerations (to decrease preliminary penalty amount)

1.   Overview. The government should evaluate every penalty with a view toward litigation and attempt to ascertain the maximum civil penalty the court or administrative judge is likely to award if the case proceeds to trial or hearing. Many enforcement cases may have mitigating factors, weaknesses or equitable problems that could be expected to persuade a court to assess a penalty less than the statutory maximum amount. The simple existence of weaknesses in a case, however, should not automatically result in a litigation consideration reduction of the preliminary bottom-line settlement penalty amount (economic benefit + gravity + gravity adjustment factors). The government may reduce the amount of the civil penalty it will accept at settlement to reflect weaknesses in its case where the facts demonstrate a substantial likelihood that the government will not achieve a higher penalty at trial.

* * *

E.   Ability to Pay (to decrease preliminary penalty amount)

* * *

The adjustment for ability-to-pay may be used to reduce the settlement penalty to the highest amount that the violator can reasonably pay and still comply with the CWA. The violator has the primary burden of establishing the claim of inability to pay. The violator must submit the necessary information demonstrating actual inability to pay as opposed to unwillingness to pay. Further, the claim of inability to pay a penalty should not be confused with a violator's aversion to make certain adjustment in its operations in order to pay the penalty.

* * *

NOTES AND QUESTIONS

1. *Applying the penalty policy.* Assume that Wilson Foods concedes the following violations: deliberately miscalibrating an effluent monitoring device on one occasion; failing to file three monthly DMRs because it neglected to conduct the necessary sampling; and exceeding the daily maximum effluent limit for total suspended solids by 50–200% on multiple occasions over a seven-month period. Using the penalty policy, and assuming an economic benefit of $10,000, calculate a reasonable penalty settlement offer on behalf of EPA.

2. *The purposes of penalty policies.* Recall that one of the main purposes of penalty policies is to guide EPA's exercise of discretion. Does the CWA penalty policy accomplish this purpose?

3. *The fate of penalties collected.* When EPA obtains a civil penalty through court action or administrative imposition, how does the environment benefit? Note that EPA does not retain penalties collected in civil or criminal enforcement actions. Because all of these funds are deposited into the U.S. Treasury, they do not yield direct environmental improvement. Furthermore, civil penalties are usually considered fines and are not tax-deductible for the firm paying them. While paying financial penalties may punish past misconduct and influence future behavior, greater benefit to the environment can result from the use of more flexible and creative remedies.

4. *Supplemental Environmental Projects.* In the 1980s, EPA began to seek alternatives to monetary penalties in enforcement actions that would provide an improvement in environmental quality. The Supplemental Environmental Project (SEP) is one important alternative to penalties. EPA has defined a SEP as "an environmentally beneficial project which a defendant/respondent agrees to undertake in settlement of an enforcement action, but which the defendant/respondent is not otherwise legally required to perform." EPA has issued a policy that reflects the agency's increased emphasis on environmentally beneficial projects as a part of case settlements. See Final EPA Supplemental Environmental Projects Policy Issued, 63 Fed. Reg. 24,796 (1998). For a proposed project to be approved as a SEP, it must benefit primarily the public health or the environment, and there must be a nexus, or relationship, between the project and the violation. The policy provides for a reduction in penalties in settlement for a violator who agrees to perform an acceptable SEP. While emphasizing pollution prevention and reduction, SEPs have included a range of projects such as funding for local emergency planning councils, an air toxics reduction demonstration study, environmental audits, process changes, energy conservation, enhanced training, and reclamation and recycling. See

U.S. EPA, Beyond Compliance: Supplemental Environmental Projects, EPA 325–R–01–001, http://www.epa.gov/compliance/resources/publications/civil/programs/sebrochure.pdf.

As an EPA enforcement attorney, how would you approach the SEP question in settlement negotiations? How might a defendant firm consider a SEP? What are the benefits to a firm of undertaking a SEP? What concerns might an environmental group have about SEPs? How should the use of SEPs be limited, if at all?

3. ENFORCEMENT ISSUES AND DEFENSES

a. Overfiling

Section 309 of the CWA provides for concurrent state and federal enforcement, even where the NPDES permitting authority has been transferred to the state. What exactly does this mean? What is the relationship between federal and state enforcement efforts? Should a state's exercise of CWA permitting and enforcement power prevent EPA from acting independently?

While state environmental enforcement duties have risen dramatically, the federal/state relationship is not always satisfactory to either party. The states often seek greater flexibility and independence in dealing with enforcement matters and may resent federal supremacy, which they believe undermines their credibility. One particular problem is the issue of federal "overfiling." Overfiling occurs when EPA determines that a state's enforcement action is inappropriate (e.g., a fine is inadequate) and EPA then steps in and files its own case. This practice has been criticized as duplicative, costly, time-consuming, and likely to create conflict. For regulated entities, the potential for separate enforcement actions may discourage settlement or lead to unanticipated liabilities.

The following case addresses the overfiling issue in the context of a RCRA prosecution.

Harmon Industries v. Browner

United States Court of Appeals, Eighth Circuit, 1999.
191 F.3d 894.

■ HANSEN, CIRCUIT JUDGE.

Harmon Industries operates a plant in Grain Valley, Missouri, which it utilizes to assemble circuit boards for railroad control and safety equipment. In November 1987, Harmon's personnel manager discovered that maintenance workers at Harmon routinely discarded volatile solvent residue behind Harmon's Grain Valley plant. This practice apparently began in 1973 and continued until November 1987. Harmon's management was unaware of its employees' practices until the personnel manager filed his report in November 1987. Following the report, Harmon ceased its disposal activities and voluntarily contacted the Missouri Department of Natural

Resources (MDNR). The MDNR investigated and concluded that Harmon's past disposal practices did not pose a threat to either human health or the environment. The MDNR and Harmon created a plan whereby Harmon would clean up the disposal area. Harmon implemented the clean up plan. While Harmon was cooperating with the MDNR, the EPA initiated an administrative enforcement action against Harmon in which the federal agency sought $2,343,706 in penalties. * * *

On March 5, 1993, while the EPA's administrative enforcement action was pending, a Missouri state court judge approved a consent decree entered into by the MDNR and Harmon. In the decree, MDNR acknowledged full accord and satisfaction and released Harmon from any claim for monetary penalties. MDNR based its decision to release Harmon on the fact that the company promptly self-reported its violation and cooperated in all aspects of the investigation. After the filing of the consent decree, Harmon litigated the EPA claim before an administrative law judge (ALJ). The ALJ found that a civil penalty against Harmon was appropriate in this case. The ALJ rejected the EPA's request for a penalty in excess of $2 million but the ALJ did impose a civil fine of $586,716 against Harmon. A three-person Environmental Appeals Board panel affirmed the ALJ's monetary penalty. Harmon filed a complaint challenging the EPA's decision in federal district court on June 6, 1997. In its August 25, 1998, summary judgment order, the district court found that the EPA's decision to impose civil penalties violated the Resource Conservation and Recovery Act and contravened principles of res judicata. The EPA appeals to this court.

Discussion

A.   The Permissibility of Overfiling

* * *

The Resource Conservation and Recovery Act (RCRA), 42 U.S.C. § 6901–6992K (1994), permits states to apply to the EPA for authorization to administer and enforce a hazardous waste program. *See* 42 U.S.C. § 6926(b). If authorization is granted, the state's program then operates "in lieu of" the federal government's hazardous waste program. *Id.* The EPA authorization also allows states to issue and enforce permits for the treatment, storage, and disposal of hazardous wastes. *Id.* "Any action taken by a State under a hazardous waste program authorized under [the RCRA] [has] the same force and effect as action taken by the [EPA] under this subchapter." 42 U.S.C. § 6926(d). Once authorization is granted by the EPA, it cannot be rescinded unless the EPA finds that (1) the state program is not equivalent to the federal program, (2) the state program is not consistent with federal or state programs in other states, or (3) the state program is failing to provide adequate enforcement of compliance in accordance with the requirements of federal law. *See* 42 U.S.C. § 6926(b). Before withdrawing a state's authorization to administer a hazardous waste program, the EPA must hold a public hearing and allow the state a reasonable period of time to correct the perceived deficiency. *See* 42 U.S.C. § 6926(e).

Missouri, like many other states, is authorized to administer and enforce a hazardous waste program pursuant to the RCRA. Despite having authorized a state to act, the EPA frequently files its own enforcement actions against suspected environmental violators even after the commencement of a state-initiated enforcement action. * * *

The EPA contends that the district court's interpretation runs contrary to the plain language of the RCRA. Specifically, the EPA cites section 6928 of the RCRA, which states that:

(1) Except as provided in paragraph (2), whenever on the basis of any information the [EPA] determines that any person has violated or is in violation of any requirement of this subchapter, the [EPA] may issue an order assessing a civil penalty for any past or current violation, requiring compliance immediately or within a specified time period, or both, or the [EPA] may commence a civil action in the United States district court in the district in which the violation occurred for appropriate relief, including a temporary or permanent injunction.

(2) In the case of a violation of any requirement of [the RCRA] where such violation occurs in a State which is authorized to carry out a hazardous waste program under section 6926 of this title, the [EPA] shall give notice to the State in which such violation has occurred prior to issuing an order or commencing a civil action under this section.

42 U.S.C. § 6928(a)(1) and (2).

The EPA argues that the plain language of section 6928 allows the federal agency to initiate an enforcement action against an environmental violator even in states that have received authorization pursuant to the RCRA. The EPA contends that Harmon and the district court misinterpreted the phrases "in lieu of" and "same force and effect" as contained in the RCRA. According to the EPA, the phrase "in lieu of" refers to which regulations are to be enforced in an authorized state rather than who is responsible for enforcing the regulations. The EPA argues that the phrase "same force and effect" refers only to the effect of state issued permits. The EPA contends that the RCRA, taken as a whole, authorizes either the state or the EPA to enforce the state's regulations, which are in compliance with the regulations of the EPA. The only requirement, according to the EPA, is that the EPA notify the state in writing if it intends to initiate an enforcement action against an alleged violator.

* * *

An examination of the statute as a whole supports the district court's interpretation. The RCRA specifically allows states that have received authorization from the federal government to administer and enforce a program that operates "in lieu of" the EPA's regulatory program. 42 U.S.C. § 6926(b). While the EPA is correct that the "in lieu of" language refers to the program itself, the administration and enforcement of the program are inexorably intertwined.

The RCRA gives authority to the states to create and implement their own hazardous waste program. The plain "in lieu of" language contained in the RCRA reveals a congressional intent for an authorized state program to supplant the federal hazardous waste program in all respects including enforcement. Specifically, the statute permits the EPA to repeal a state's authorization if the state's program "does not provide adequate enforcement of compliance with the requirements of" the RCRA. *Id.* This language indicates that Congress intended to grant states the primary role of enforcing their own hazardous waste program. Such an indication is not undermined, as the EPA suggests, by the language of section 6928. Again, section 6928(a)(1) allows the EPA to initiate enforcement actions against suspected environmental violators, except as provided in section 6928(a)(2). Section 6928(a)(2) permits the EPA to enforce the hazardous waste laws contained in the RCRA if the agency gives written notice to the state. Section 6928(a)(1) and (2), however, must be interpreted within the context of the entire Act. Harmonizing the section 6928(a)(1) and (2) language that allows the EPA to bring an enforcement action in certain circumstances with section 6926(b)'s provision that the EPA has the right to withdraw state authorization if the state's enforcement is inadequate manifests a congressional intent to give the EPA a secondary enforcement right in those cases where a state has been authorized to act that is triggered only after state authorization is rescinded or if the state fails to initiate an enforcement action. Rather than serving as an affirmative grant of federal enforcement power as the EPA suggests, we conclude that the notice requirement of section 6928(a)(2) reinforces the primacy of a state's enforcement rights under RCRA. Taken in the context of the statute as a whole, the notice requirement operates as a means to allow a state the first chance opportunity to initiate the statutorily-permitted enforcement action. If the state fails to initiate any action, then the EPA may institute its own action. Thus, the notice requirement is an indicator of the fact that Congress intended to give states, that are authorized to act, the lead role in enforcement under RCRA.

[The court found additional support for its interpretation in the "same force and effect" language of 42 U.S.C. § 6926(d), which states that "[a]ny action taken by a State under a hazardous waste program authorized under this section shall have the same force and effect as action taken by the [EPA] under this subchapter."]

* * * Without question, the EPA can initiate an enforcement action if it deems the state's enforcement action inadequate. Before initiating such an action, however, the EPA must allow the state an opportunity to correct its deficiency and the EPA must withdraw its authorization. *See* 42 U.S.C. § 6926(b) and (e). Consistent with the text of the statute and its legislative history, the EPA also may initiate an enforcement action after providing written notice to the state when the authorized state fails to initiate any enforcement action. *See* 42 U.S.C. § 6928(a)(2); 1976 U.S.C.C.A.N. 6270.

The EPA may not, however, simply fill the perceived gaps it sees in a state's enforcement action by initiating a second enforcement action without allowing the state an opportunity to correct the deficiency and then withdrawing the state's authorization.

A contrary interpretation would result in two separate enforcement actions. Such an interpretation, as explained above, would derogate the RCRA's plain language and legislative history. Companies that reach an agreement through negotiations with a state authorized by the EPA to act in its place may find the agreement undermined by a later separate enforcement action by the EPA. While, generally speaking, two separate sovereigns can institute two separate enforcement actions, those actions can cause vastly different and potentially contradictory results. Such a potential schism runs afoul of the principles of comity and federalism so clearly embedded in the text and history of the RCRA. * * *

B. Res Judicata

As an alternative basis to support its grant of summary judgment, the district court concluded that principles of res judicata also bar the EPA's enforcement action by reason of the Missouri state court consent decree. * * * In Missouri, res judicata requires "(1) [i]dentity of the thing sued for; (2) identity of the cause of action; (3) identity of the persons and parties to the action; and (4) identity of the quality of the person for or against whom the claim is made." * * * The only dispute is whether the parties are identical.

A party is identical when it is the same party that litigated a prior suit or when a new party is in privity with a party that litigated a prior suit. Privity exists when two parties to two separate suits have "a close relationship bordering on near identity." As the United States and the State of Missouri are not the same party, we must resolve whether their relationship in the enforcement action is nearly identical.

The statutory language of the RCRA provides the framework for the party identity analysis. Pursuant to 42 U.S.C. § 6926(b), the federal program operates "in lieu of" the state program. Section 6926(d) of the same statute mandates that "[a]ny action taken by a State under a hazardous waste program authorized under this section shall have the same force and effect as action taken by the [EPA] under this subchapter." 42 U.S.C. § 6926(d). As we determined [above], the plain language of the RCRA permits the State of Missouri to act in lieu of the EPA. When such a situation occurs, Missouri's action has the same force and effect as an action initiated by the EPA. Accordingly, the two parties stand in the same relationship to one another. The EPA argues that it has enforcement interests sufficiently distinct from the interests of the State of Missouri. We explained in *Hickman,* however, that privity under Missouri law is satisfied when the two parties represent the same legal right. *See Hickman,* 741 F.2d at 233. As the district court correctly indicated, privity is not dependent upon the subjective interests of the individual parties. *See Harmon,* 19 F. Supp. 2d at 998; *see also Hickman,* 741 F.2d at 233. In this case, the

State of Missouri advanced the exact same legal right under the statute as the EPA did in its administrative action. Accordingly, the identity of the parties requirement is satisfied.

* * *

NOTES AND QUESTIONS

1. *Overfiling.* The Tenth Circuit, when confronted with the overfiling issue presented in *Harmon*, reached the contrary conclusion that the language of RCRA does not bar EPA from bringing a civil enforcement action subsequent to state enforcement. See United States v. Power Eng'g, 303 F.3d 1232 (10th Cir. 2002). The court criticized the analysis in *Harmon*:

> While *Harmon* correctly states that section 6928(a) limits the EPA's right to bring an enforcement action to "certain circumstances," the only explicit limitation is that the EPA must provide prior notice to authorized states. 42 U.S.C. § 6928(a)(2). Withdrawal of authorization for a state program is an "extreme" and "drastic" step that requires the EPA to establish a federal program to replace the cancelled state program. Waste Mgmt., Inc. v. EPA, 714 F.Supp. 340, 341 (N.D. Ill. 1989). Nothing in the text of the statute suggests that such a step is a prerequisite to EPA enforcement or that it is the only remedy for inadequate enforcement.
>
> * * *
>
> In our judgment, limiting the "same force and effect" language to the issuance of permits is not "incongruous" with RCRA as a whole. Harmon, 191 F.3d at 900. It would be reasonable to conclude that Congress simply intended for section 6926(d) to clarify that recipients of state-issued permits need not obtain a permit from the EPA.

303 F.3d at 1238–39. Which court has the better argument?

2. *Overfiling in other statutes.* Although the Clean Air Act and Clean Water Act resemble RCRA in providing for state permitting and implementation under a cooperative federalism scheme, they do not contain the "in lieu of" and "same force and effect" language on which the *Harmon* court relied. Not surprisingly, courts have generally rejected overfiling arguments made by defendants with respect to these statutes. See United States v. City of Rock Island, 182 F. Supp. 2d 690, 694 (C.D. Ill. 2001) (distinguishing *Harmon* in case brought under Clean Water Act); United States v. City of Youngstown, 109 F. Supp. 2d 739, 741 (N.D. Ohio 2000) (same); United States v. Murphy Oil USA, Inc., 143 F. Supp. 2d 1054, 1090–91 (W.D. Wis. 2001) (distinguishing *Harmon* in case brought under Clean Air Act); United States v. LTV Steel Co., 118 F. Supp. 2d 827, 832–33 (N.D. Ohio 2000) (same).

3. *Res judicata.* While the overfiling doctrine has been confined to RCRA, the common law doctrine of res judicata has potentially broader application. Under res judicata, a final judgment on the merits of a claim precludes the parties from further litigation based on that claim. As the analysis in *Harmon* suggests, res judicata may bar an enforcement action by the federal government once judgment has been entered on a prosecution by the state, and it may bar a state prosecution once judgment has been entered on an enforcement action by the federal government. In *State Water Control Board v. Smithfield Foods, Inc.*, 261 Va. 209, 542 S.E.2d 766 (2001), the Virginia Supreme Court, applying res judicata, held that the state could not bring an enforcement action against the firm for alleged violations of state water pollution laws after EPA had successfully enforced in federal court. Privity was found even though the state did not participate in the federal action and even though EPA's case generally involved violations of different discharge limits than those alleged in the state suit. The *Smithfield Foods* case reveals how sympathetic some courts may be to company complaints of being surprised by a second enforcement case after a matter has apparently been settled.

b. Permit Shields

Piney Run Preservation Ass'n. v. County Commissioners

United States Court of Appeals, Fourth Circuit, 2001.
268 F.3d 255.

■ KING, CIRCUIT JUDGE:

The Piney Run Preservation Association sued the Commissioners of Carroll County, Maryland, claiming that a county-operated waste treatment plant was discharging warm water into a local stream, Piney Run, in violation of the Clean Water Act. The district court construed the plant's NPDES permit as not prohibiting the discharge of heat. Nonetheless, the court decided that the Commissioners were liable under the Clean Water Act for the discharge of pollutants not expressly authorized by the permit. On appeal, the Commissioners maintain that the "permit shield" defense, embodied in 33 U.S.C. § 1342(k), bars suit against a permit holder for the discharge of pollutants not expressly listed in the permit. Although we do not accept the Commissioners' position on the permit shield defense, we also disagree with the district court's interpretation of the Clean Water Act. Utilizing the two-part test spelled out in *Chevron, U.S.A., Inc. v. Natural Resources Defense Council*, 467 U.S. 837 (1984), we adhere to the interpretation provided by the EPA. We therefore view the NPDES permit as shielding its holder from liability under the Clean Water Act as long as (1) the permit holder complies with the express terms of the permit and with the Clean Water Act's disclosure requirements and (2) the permit holder does not make a discharge of pollutants that was not within the reasonable contemplation of the permitting authority at the time the permit was granted. Applying this rule, we conclude that the Commissioners did not violate the Clean Water Act because (1) they complied with the discharge limitations and reporting requirements of their permit, and (2) their discharges of heat were within the reasonable contemplation of the permitting authority at the time the permit was issued. Accordingly, we vacate the judgment of the district court, and we remand for entry of judgment in favor of the Commissioners.

* * *

* * * [T]he NPDES permit sets out the allowable departures from the CWA's baseline of total liability for discharges of effluent. Natural Res. Def. Council, Inc. v. Costle, 568 F.2d at 1374. It is clear, therefore, that if a permit holder discharges pollutants precisely in accordance with the terms of its permit, the permit will "shield" its holder from CWA liability. The permit shield defense, however, raises two additional questions that are slightly more difficult: (1) what comprises the scope or terms of an NPDES permit, and (2) whether the permit shield bars CWA liability for discharges not expressly allowed by the permit when the holder has complied with the permit's express restrictions. It is to these matters that we now turn.

The central issue in determining the scope of a NPDES permit is whether the permit implicitly incorporates pollutant discharges disclosed by the permit holder to the permitting authority that are not explicitly allowed in the permit. Put more simply, although an operator may report multiple discharges of pollutants to the licensing body, the permit may only contain explicit limitations for some of those pollutants. The question, in that circumstance, is whether the permit holder may continue to empty the unlisted pollutants into the water, or whether it may only discharge those pollutants that are specifically listed in the permit.

Determining the proper scope of an NPDES permit requires us to examine the language of the CWA. In construing the application of the CWA's provisions in this case, we find it necessary and appropriate to perform a *Chevron* analysis. *See* Chevron, U.S.A., Inc. v. Natural Res. Def. Council, Inc., 467 U.S. 837, 842–43 (1984). Under *Chevron*, we are required to apply a two-part test. First, we examine the language of the statute to see if "Congress has directly spoken to the precise question at issue." *Id.* at 842. If Congressional intent is clear, "that is the end of the matter; for the court, as well as the agency, must give effect to the unambiguously expressed intent of Congress." *Id.* at 843. If the statute is ambiguous, then we apply *Chevron's* second step, and we defer to the agency's interpretation of its governing statute and regulations, as long as (1) the agency has promulgated that interpretation pursuant to a notice-and-comment rule-making or a formal adjudication, and (2) the agency's interpretation is reasonable. *Id.* at 843. * * *

In applying step one of *Chevron*, we view the crucial language of the CWA as ambiguous. The permit shield provision, 33 U.S.C. § 1342(k), specifies that "compliance with a permit issued pursuant to this section shall be deemed compliance, for purposes of sections 1319 and 1365 of this title, with sections 1311, 1312, 1316, 1317, and 1343 of this title." Although this statutory language makes clear that compliance with a permit constitutes an exception to the general strict liability of the CWA, we must agree with the Second Circuit's conclusion that § 1342(k) does not explicitly explain the scope of permit protection. *See* Atlantic States Legal Found., 12 F.3d at 357–58 (concluding that permit shield language ambiguous with respect to scope of coverage). Therefore, because Congressional intent is not clear, we must turn to the second step of the *Chevron* analysis.

In applying step two of *Chevron,* we observe that the EPA has promulgated, pursuant to a formal adjudication, an interpretation of the permit shield provision that is reasonable. In a 1998 formal adjudication proceeding before the EPA's Environmental Appeals Board, *In re Ketchikan Pulp Co.,* the Board determined that the NPDES permit covers all pollutants disclosed to the permitting authority during the permit application process. 7 E.A.D. 605, 1998 WL 284964, at *12–13 (EPA 1998) ("[W]hen the permittee has made adequate disclosures during the application process regarding the nature of its discharges, unlisted pollutants may be considered to be within the scope of an NPDES permit, even though the permit does not expressly mention those pollutants."). In explaining this ruling, the *Ketchikan* Board observed that the EPA had already acknowledged that "it is impossible to identify and rationally limit every chemical or compound present in the discharge of pollutants" and that the EPA consequently had determined that the "goals of the CWA may be more effectively achieved by focusing on the chief pollutants and wastestreams established in effluent guidelines and disclosed by permittees in their permit applications." *Id.* at *11. The Board, adopting the reasoning of the Second Circuit in *Atlantic States Legal Foundation,* therefore held that "[t]he proper interpretation of the [CWA] regulations is that ... [w]ater quality based limits are established where the permitting authority reasonably anticipates the discharge of pollutants by the permittee at levels that have the reasonable potential to cause or contribute to an excursion above any state water quality criterion." *Id.* at *11 (quoting *Atlantic States Legal Found.,* 12 F.3d at 358).

The *Ketchikan* decision therefore made clear that a permit holder is in compliance with the CWA even if it discharges pollutants that are not listed in its permit, as long as it only discharges pollutants that have been adequately disclosed to the permitting authority. *Id.* at *17. To the extent that a permit holder discharges a pollutant that it did not disclose, it violates the NPDES permit and the CWA. *Id.* at *13.

The EPA in *Ketchikan* therefore outlined the proper structure for the permitting process. The applicant discloses the nature of its effluent discharges to the permitting authority. The permitting authority analyzes the environmental risk posed by the discharge, and places limits on those pollutants that, in the words of the Second Circuit and EPA, it "reasonably anticipates" could damage the environmental integrity of the affected waterway. *Id.* at *11; *Atlantic States Legal Found.,* 12 F.3d at 358 (internal citations omitted). Thus, as long as a permit holder complies with the CWA's reporting and disclosure requirements, it may discharge pollutants not expressly mentioned in the permit. The only other limitation on the permit holder's ability to discharge such pollutants is that the discharges must be reasonably anticipated by, or within the reasonable contemplation of, the permitting authority. Because the permitting scheme is dependent on the permitting authority being able to judge whether the discharge of a particular pollutant constitutes a significant threat to the environment, discharges not within the reasonable contemplation of the permitting authority during the permit application process, whether spills or otherwise, do not come within the protection of the permit shield. We see the EPA's interpretation of the permit shield as a rational construction of the CWA's statutory ambiguity; as such, we deem it "reasonable" within the meaning of a *Chevron* analysis. Therefore, because the CWA provision in question, § 1342(k), is ambiguous, and because the EPA's interpretation of this provision is reasonable, we must defer under *Chevron* to the EPA's interpretation of the scope of an NPDES permit.

[The Court went on to hold that the plant's NPDES permit did not specifically bar discharges of heat and that the Commissioners disclosed during the permit application process that the plant was discharging heat.]

NOTE ON CAA PERMIT SHIELD

Title V of the Clean Air Act provides for a limited permit shield under which compliance with the terms of a Title V permit constitutes compliance with Title V. See CAA § 504(f), 42 U.S.C. § 7661c(f). EPA regulations state, however, that in general, such a permit shield applies only if it is explicitly incorporated into a company's Title V permit. See 40 C.F.R. § 70.6(f).

  c. Fair Notice

United States v. Ohio Edison Co.

United States District Court, Southern District of Ohio, 2003.
276 F. Supp. 2d 829.

■ SARGUS, DISTRICT JUDGE

This case highlights an abysmal breakdown in the administrative process following the passage of the landmark Clean Air Act in 1970. For thirty-three years, various administrations have wrestled with and, to a great extent, have avoided a fundamental issue addressed in the Clean Air Act, that is, at what point plants built before 1970 must comply with new air pollution standards. The Clean Air Act requires plants constructed after 1970 to meet stringent air quality standards, but the Act exempts old facilities from compliance with the law, unless such sites undergo what the law identifies as a "modification." Decades later, the United States Environmental Protection Agency, together with the States of Connecticut, New Jersey and New York ask this Court to find that eleven construction projects undertaken between 1984 and 1998 on the seven electric generating units at the Sammis Plant constituted modifications, requiring Ohio

Edison to bring the units into compliance with current ambient air quality standards.

* * *

The issues presented in this lawsuit turn on an interpretation of the term "modification." Congress provided in the Clean Air Act that *any* modification of a plant triggered application of the Act and later amendments. * * * [T]he Administrator of the EPA has refined, by regulation, the definition of modification to include only activities which involve both a physical change to a unit and a resulting significant increase in emissions. Excluded from the definition of modification are projects involving only "routine maintenance, repair or replacement." 40 C.F.R. § 52.21(b)(2)(iii)(a).

* * *

Defendant Ohio Edison contends that it did not have fair notice of its obligations under the Clean Air Act. Specifically, Defendant contends that the definition of "routine maintenance, repair or replacement" has changed repeatedly, as has the method used to calculate emissions. As a consequence, Defendant argues that the tests for routineness and emissions were not "ascertainably certain" and therefore Ohio Edison lacked fair notice of the law. The Government disputes these contentions.

* * *

* * * The doctrine of fair notice, as applied in the context of a CAA civil enforcement action, was recently addressed by the United States District Court for the Southern District of Indiana in *United States v. Southern Indiana Gas and Electric Co.*, 245 F. Supp. 2d 994 (S.D. Ind. 2003). The court stated, in pertinent part:

> The fair notice doctrine ... prevents ... deference shown to agency interpretations from "validating the application of a regulation that fails to give fair warning of the conduct it prohibits or requires." Gates & Fox Co., Inc. v. Occupational Safety and Health Review Comm'n 790 F.2d 154, 156 (D.C. Cir. 1986). Though this principle arises most often in the criminal context, the fair notice concept has been recognized in the civil administrative context, and is now thoroughly incorporated into administrative law....

> The fair notice doctrine (also called fair warning) in the administrative context is a developing concept of relatively recent vintage. The Fifth Circuit began the line of case law on fair notice when it reversed an administrative court's conclusion that the defendant had violated an OSHA regulation, holding that the defendant did not have fair warning of how OSHA was interpreting the regulation at issue. *See Diamond Roofing,* 528 F.2d at 649–50. In an oft-cited passage, the court held, "If a violation of a regulation subjects private parties to criminal or civil sanctions, a regulation cannot be construed to mean what an agency intended but did not adequately express ... [the agency] has the responsibility to state with ascertainable certainty what is meant by

the standards he has promulgated." *Id.* at 649. The bulk of the fair warning case law comes from the D.C. Circuit, which stated the test this way: "If, by reviewing the regulations and other public statements issued by the agency, a regulated party acting in good faith would be able to identify, with 'ascertainable certainty,' the standards with which the agency expects parties to conform, then the agency has fairly notified a petitioner of the agency's interpretation." *Gen. Elec.,* 53 F.3d at 1329. The inquiry is taken from the perspective of the regulated party (not the agency) and analyzes whether that party could have predicted the agency's interpretation of the regulation at the time of the conduct at issue.

Id. at 1010–11.

As the district court in the *SIGECO* case noted, the degree of ambiguity required for a regulation to violate the fair notice doctrine is not subject to a clear standard. Consequently, courts have considered several factors in applying the fair notice doctrine. In some cases, the plain language of the regulation itself suffices to show that the defendant had fair notice or a lack of fair notice of the administrative agency's interpretation of the regulation. Public statements by the agency may also be relevant to the analysis. In addition, the consistency of such public statements may bear on whether or not the defendant had fair notice. Furthermore, confusion within an enforcing agency as to the proper interpretation of a regulation is an appropriate factor to consider. Finally, whether or not the defendant makes inquiry of the agency as to the meaning of a regulation is pertinent to the fair notice issue.

In this case, Defendant Ohio Edison contends that the EPA's interpretation of the "routine maintenance, repair or replacement" exemption has changed over time, preventing a regulated party from gleaning fair notice as to the meaning of the law. The Defendant bears the burden of establishing such a lack of notice as the issue is raised as an affirmative defense to liability.

Ohio Edison first contends that a narrow interpretation of the routine maintenance exemption is "expressly contradicted by USEPA's statements in the PSD and NSPS regulations' preambles." A reading of the preambles does not support this assertion.

The preamble to the 1980 regulations provides:

> With the final amendments announced here, the Part 51 and Part 52 PSD regulations now define "major modification" as any "physical change" or "change in the method of operation" at a major stationary source which would result in a "significant net emissions increase" in any pollutant subject to regulation under the Act. . . .

> While the new PSD regulations do not define "physical change" or "change in the method of operation," they provide that those phrases do not encompass certain specific types of events. Those types are: (1) routine maintenance, repair and replacement. . . .

45 Fed. Reg. 52676, 52698 (August 7, 1980).

The preamble to the WEPCO rule states, in relevant part:

> The EPA has always recognized that the definition of physical or operational change in section 111(a)(4) could, standing alone, encompass the most mundane activities at an industrial facility (even the repair or replacement of a single leaky pipe, or a change in the way that pipe is utilized). However, EPA has always recognized that Congress obviously did not intend to make every activity at a source subject to new source requirements.
>
> As a result, EPA has defined "modification" in the NSPS and NSR regulations to include common-sense exclusions from the "physical or operational change" component of the definition. For example, both sets of regulations contain similar exclusions for routine maintenance, repair and replacement; for increases in the hours of operation or in the production rate; and for certain types of fuel switches....

57 Fed. Reg. 32314, 32316 (July 21, 1992).

The Defendant, however, relies on the following portion of the 1992 WEPCO preamble in support of its contention that the narrowness of the exemption has not been ascertainably certain:

> EPA is today clarifying that the determination of whether the repair or replacement of a particular item of equipment is "routine" under the NSR regulations, while made on a case-by-case basis, must be based on the evaluation of whether that type of equipment has been repaired or replaced by sources within the relevant industrial category.

57 Fed. Reg. 32314, 32326 (July 21, 1992).

According to the Defendant, the preamble's reference to "sources within the relevant industrial category" supports the notion that an activity is routine if it has been performed with some frequency in the industry, as opposed to at a particular unit. The Court disagrees. The preamble followed the 1990 decision of the Seventh Circuit in *WEPCO*, which made it very clear that activities performed in the industry are relevant to one factor of the four-part test used by the EPA to determine whether an activity constitutes routine maintenance-the frequency factor. Reading the preamble with the *WEPCO* decision, it is unambiguous that the routine maintenance exemption is narrow and the analysis is to be made on a case-by-case basis, not elevating one factor of the analysis over another.

The Court further finds that the preambles reiterate the plain language of the statute and the regulation. The CAA states that "any physical change" constitutes a "modification" for purposes of statutory compliance. The language used is indeed broad and the word "any" must be given its plain meaning. To temper this expansive definition, the EPA promulgated a regulation providing an exemption for "routine maintenance, repair or replacement." The narrow extent of this exemption is apparent from the plain language of the regulation itself. The regulation does not exempt *any* maintenance, repair or replacement from statutory compliance—rather, only *routine* maintenance is exempted. In view of this language, it is hard to fathom that Ohio Edison did not have notice that the sorts of projects undertaken at the Sammis plant would not be considered as "routine." As described *supra,* it is undisputed that the projects were undertaken at a great expense (a capitalized expense), the projects lasted for months at a time, and the stated goal of the projects was to extend the useful lives of the units well into the future. Furthermore, at least one of the projects—the spiral furnace rebuild to Unit 5–was unprecedented in the industry. If any of the activities undertaken could be considered to be "routine mainte-nance," the regulation would vitiate the very language of the CAA itself. Such a result could not have been intended by Congress.

* * *

The Court concludes that Ohio Edison's assertion that it lacked fair notice of the interpretation of the routine maintenance exemption is unavailing.

d.   Other Defenses

i.   Statutes of Limitations

What is the relevant statute of limitations on government enforcement actions (as well as on citizen suits)? The enforcement provisions of environ-mental statutes generally do not contain an explicit limitation period. Courts often look to the five-year statute of limitations period contained in 28 U.S.C. § 2462, which provides:

> Except as otherwise provided by Act of Congress, an action, suit or proceeding for the enforcement of any civil fine, penalty, or forfeiture, pecuniary or otherwise, shall not be entertained unless commenced within five years from the date when the claim first accrued....

What types of actions are barred by § 2462? See United States v. Telluride, 146 F.3d 1241, 1245–48 (10th Cir. 1998) (holding that § 2462 does not bar claim for injunction that would require defendant to restore damaged wetlands). A key question in many cases involving statute of limitations defenses is "when does a claim first accrue?" The answer to this question may depend on the specific type of violation at issue. See, e.g., United States v. Duke Energy Corp., 278 F. Supp. 2d 619, 652 (M.D.N.C. 2003) (holding that failure to obtain CAA preconstruction permit was a continu-ing violation and therefore not barred by statute of limitations).

ii.   Upset Defense

Sometimes a defendant may try to have a violation excused as an "upset," which is defined by EPA as an exceptional and temporary state of violation which is beyond the control of the source. See 40 C.F.R. § 122.41(n)(1) (definition of upset with respect to Clean Water Act permit); 40 C.F.R. § 70.6(g) (describing emergency as an affirmative defense to certain actions for noncompliance with CAA Title V permit). The defense is generally a narrow one; under the Clean Water Act, for instance, the defense "does not include noncompliance to the extent caused by operational error, improperly designed treatment facilities, inadequate treatment facilities, lack of preventive maintenance, or careless or improper operation." See 40 C.F.R. § 122.41(n)(1).

iii. Laboratory Error Defense

Regulated entities are often responsible for measuring and reporting their compliance status. Such entities sometimes question the accuracy of data indicating a violation. Although courts generally are hostile to such challenges, evidence of laboratory error may undermine the presumption of correctness for data in self-monitoring reports reflecting a violation. Compare Sierra Club v. Union Oil Co., 813 F.2d 1480, 1492 (9th Cir. 1987) (holding, in light of importance of self-monitoring under CWA, that "permittee may not impeach its own reports by showing sampling error"); with United States v. Allegheny Ludlum Corp., 366 F.3d 164, 174–76 (3d Cir. 2004) (holding that defendant could raise lab error defense to CWA claim and that strict liability scheme of statute did not relieve government of obligation to show violative act).

SECTION 3. CRIMINAL ENFORCEMENT

A. INTRODUCTION

Although the major environmental statutes have contained criminal sanctions since the 1970s, the Department of Justice and EPA only began to allocate resources for criminal enforcement in the early 1980s. Prior to that time, environmental agencies relied almost exclusively on civil rather than criminal penalties to sanction polluters and to achieve compliance with anti-pollution regulations. In the 1980s and 1990s, criminal enforcement efforts increased after many environmental statutes were amended to elevate environmental crimes from misdemeanors to felonies. The majority of cases were brought under the Clean Water Act, RCRA, and CERCLA. Although criminal enforcement has largely remained a "poor stepchild" within EPA,[1] the environmental crimes program has grown in the last decade amidst a growing acceptance of criminal prosecution as a suitable remedy for serious environmental violations. See David M. Uhlmann, Environmental Crime Comes of Age: The Evolution of Criminal Enforcement in the Environmental Regulatory Scheme, 2009 Utah L. Rev. 1223, 1226 (2009).

Should polluters be subject to criminal punishment? This question presents issues of enforcement philosophy—will the threat of civil penalties alone deter non-compliant behavior, or is the additional threat of prison time necessary? These issues are discussed in the following excerpts.

---

1. See Steven P. Solow, *The State of Environmental Crime Enforcement: Survey of Developments in 2006,* 38 Env't Rep. (BNA), at 518 (Mar. 2, 2007) (noting recent developments "that have moved the criminal program from the status of a self-described 'poor stepchild' to a position of prominence").

Richard J. Lazarus, Meeting the Demands of Integration in the Evolution of Environmental Law: Reforming Environmental Criminal Law

83 Geo. L.J. 2407, 2423–38 (1995).

To the extent that a criminal enforcement program seeks to superimpose itself onto a pre-existing set of environmental protection laws, the features of those environmental protection laws themselves are relevant to the proper integration of environmental and criminal law. Indeed, as discussed below, the absence of any meaningful consideration of the distinct features of the environmental laws upon which the criminal provisions rely is the principal failing of current environmental criminal law.

Many significant features of environmental laws derive directly from the characteristics of environmental pollution just discussed. The laws seek to reduce risk to avoid possible catastrophic results and to compensate for the uncertainty of environmental science. Environmental standards are based on imprecise scientific information regarding cause and effect; and those standards apply to virtually every kind of human activity, including many socially desirable activities and the activities of the government itself. There are, however, further defining features of environmental law that emerge from the legislative and regulatory processes and are important in thinking about environmental crime. These include: (a) the aspirational quality of environmental law; (b) its dynamic and evolutionary tendency; and (c) its complexity.

a. Aspirational Quality. Environmental statutes reflect the nation's aspirations for environmental quality. They were not intended to codify existing norms of behavior, but to force dramatic changes in existing behavior. They supply an "inspirational and radical message."

* * *

These laws imposed hundreds of deadlines on EPA, state regulatory authorities, and industry. The Clean Air Act of 1970 mandated that states attain national ambient air quality standards necessary for the protection of public health and welfare by 1975. Achievement of those standards not only would require dramatic changes in the pollution control technology and industrial processes of 20,000 to 40,000 major stationary sources of air pollution, but would also mandate fundamental change in the driving habits of millions of Americans and a major retooling of motor vehicles.

The Clean Water Act was no less ambitious. The 1972 law sought to achieve fishable and swimmable waters everywhere by 1983, and zero discharge of pollutants into the waters of the United States by 1985. Attaining this goal would have required at least 68,000 existing dischargers to reduce their existing effluent pollution by several orders of magnitude to comply with a series of technology-forcing standards. All discharges of regulated pollutants into waters of the United States were made unlawful in the absence of a permit issued by EPA or an approved state program that affirmatively allowed the discharge. Similarly ambitious aspirational goals and demanding environmental standards are contained in the other environmental laws.

Not surprisingly, over two decades later, few of the above deadlines or environmental quality goals have been met. * * * This is not to detract from the vast accomplishments of these laws. The nation's waters, land, and air are no longer open dumping grounds. Strict regulation of air emissions, effluent discharges into waterways, and land disposal has resulted in significant improvements in the quality of the environment in many places. Perhaps more important, these laws have retarded serious further degradation that otherwise would have occurred in their absence as the nation's economy has grown. Pollution control technologies and industrial process changes have, in fact, been successfully "forced" by those laws.

Moreover, the aspirational quality of environmental laws—including their overly ambitious goals, unrealistic deadlines, and uncompromising and unduly rigid standards—doubtless deserves much of the credit for these environmental successes. But it does not inexorably follow that such aspirational laws are equally well suited to civil and criminal enforcement. The susceptibility of those environmental laws to criminal, rather that just civil, enforcement presents a distinct policy issue. * * *

b. Dynamic and Evolutionary Tendency. The only constant in environmental law is change. The field is marked by "dynamics and flux where a regulation is inseparable from a revision, a statute not far from an amendment." * * * This phenomenon of constant revision is endemic to environmental law, deeply rooted in the law's relationship to both science and politics.

The relationship between environmental law's dynamic quality and science (including technology) is straightforward. Much of environmental law, particularly the environmental standards themselves, are based on "scientifically informed value judgments." Scientific changes create pressure for legal redefinition. Moreover, because so much of the scientific information underlying environmental law is tentative and uncertain, the momentum towards change is constant. "Every solution seems provisional and subject to reevaluation as new information appears and old solutions are tested against experience."

* * *

[E]nvironmental law is the product of fiercely contested entrepreneurial politics within both the legislative and executive branches. The makeup of the significant congressional authorization and appropriation committees in both chambers and the constituencies of their members, as well as the relative power within the executive branch of various stakeholder agencies (most important EPA and the Office of Management and Budget), shape the result. Consequently, as the identity of the key players and the relative power of their respective institutions shift, pressure invariably increases in favor of revisiting and modifying the statutory and regulatory provisions. * * *

c. Complexity. * * *

Environmental law's complexity undoubtedly is attributable in large part to its dynamic tendency, especially the scientific and political roots of that dynamism. But, at bottom, this complexity has even more basic origins: environmental laws reflect the complexities of the ecosystem itself. Lawmakers cannot avoid those complexities; instead, they must ultimately subsume them within a regulatory scheme. Environmental law's complexity is therefore not merely the notion that the subject is "hard," "difficult," or "rigorous," but is far more multidimensional. It encompasses: (i) technicality; (ii) indeterminacy; (iii) obscurity; and (iv) differentiation. Each warrants separate discussion.

i. Technicality. Of the ways in which environmental law is complex, "technicality" is perhaps the most self-evident and, ultimately, the least problematic for the development of an environmental crimes program. Environmental law's "technicality" refers to the way in which environmental laws "require special sophistication or expertise on the part of those who wish to understand and apply them."

* * *

ii. Indeterminacy. "Indeterminate" laws are "open-textured, flexible, multifactored, and fluid"; "outcomes are hard to predict"—a description that fits many of environmental law's key provisions, especially the jurisdictional terms of art that determine the scope of the law's applicability. It also describes well many environmental protection standards. There are rarely any clear threshold levels at which environmental pollution becomes unacceptable. The legal system, therefore, draws lines that tend to be based on fairly arbitrary distinctions. The jurisdictional boundaries of most environmental laws, as well as the substantive environmental protection standards themselves, tend to turn on questions of degree that are, at best, gray at the border. It is rarely self-evident, on which side of the border one lies.

Environmental regulations rarely pose the question whether one can pollute, but instead precisely where, when, and how much one can pollute. The real-world difference in terms of the environmental impact of the various legal lines drawn to answer the where, when, and how much of environmental law—that is, the difference between being on just one side of the line rather than just on the other side—is likely to be negligible, if any at all. Indeed, the answers given are just as likely to be based (as they are in other areas of law) on political and economic clout as they are on environmental impact. Despite the lack of environmental consequences, however, the legal implications of being barely on one side of the law rather than barely on the other side can nonetheless be tremendous.

* * *

iii. Obscurity. Environmental law's "obscurity," while closely related to its indeterminacy, describes a slightly different feature. "Indeterminacy" focuses on the meaning of the law once it is located. "Obscurity" refers to the difficulty, in the first instance, of even locating the law. This obscurity stems from the sheer density of environmental rules and their obscure, often inaccessible source materials.

* * *

iv. Differentiation. "Differentiation" is a shorthand reference for "institutionally differentiated"; it is present when the law "contains a number of decision structures that draw upon different sources of legitimacy." This is a prominent feature of environmental law; indeed, when it comes to its role in environmental protection, the government exhibits both "multiple personality disorder" and "schizophrenia." Its multiple personalities are revealed in the many different governmental bodies with authority to regulate environmental pollution. Governmental schizophrenia derives from the government's dual role as both regulator and regulated in environmental protection.

* * *

David M. Uhlmann, Environmental Crime Comes of Age: The Evolution of Criminal Enforcement in the Environmental Regulatory Scheme

2009 Utah L. Rev. 1223, 1231–35 (2009).

[O]vercriminalization arguments about environmental crime do not account for the significant sociological changes that have occurred since the 1970s. In the nearly forty years since Congress enacted the environmental laws, an extensive waste management industry has developed. Environmental compliance has become a professional field. Climate change and the deterioration of the global environment have become pressing national and international concerns. In the process, a new generation has come of age, and a new set of societal norms has emerged, both emphasizing the need for greater stewardship of the environment and internalizing the notion that pollution is inherently wrong.

* * *

From a practical perspective, however, whether the complexity of environmental law raises problems for criminal enforcement depends upon whether prosecutors pursue cases that involve issues of regulatory uncertainty. Congress often uses broad statutory language to address white-collar crimes, because the sophistication of the regulated businesses makes it difficult, if not impossible, to anticipate all the scenarios where criminal prosecution might be appropriate. The relevant question thus becomes whether there are sufficient legal and prudential safeguards in the environmental context to ensure that prosecutors do not abuse their discretion by pursuing criminal charges against defendants who run afoul of complex regulations, which reasonably could be subject to conflicting or uncertain interpretations. While there may be circumstances where overreaching has occurred, a number of safeguards exist.

First, due process concerns preclude criminal prosecution when the meaning of the law is unclear. "A criminal statute must be sufficiently definite to give notice of the required conduct to one who would avoid its penalties...." Although fair notice requirements are more relaxed in the business context, statutory and regulatory requirements are "void for vagueness" if a reasonable person in the defendant's position would be unable to determine what conduct is forbidden by the law.

* * *

Second, the rule of lenity reinforces the void-for-vagueness doctrine by requiring courts in criminal cases to resolve ambiguities about the meaning of the law in favor of the defendant. The rule of lenity "is rooted in the concern of the law for individual rights, and in the belief that fair warning should be accorded as to what conduct is criminal and punishable by deprivation of liberty or property." As an example, in United States v. Plaza Health Laboratories, the Second Circuit vacated convictions under the Clean Water Act, concluding that it was not clear that a human being could be a point source under the Act. The Second Circuit's decision is one of the few times a defendant has prevailed on rule of lenity grounds, which could demonstrate that courts do not give sufficient weight to lenity arguments. On the other hand, the fact that prosecutors usually prevail could be another indication that prosecutors exercise their discretion to avoid cases where the underlying regulations are ambiguous. At the very least, the rule of lenity provides further doctrinal protection against government overreaching.

Third, the burden of proof in criminal cases counsels the government to avoid prosecution where the meaning of the law is difficult to ascertain. The government must prove a criminal defendant's guilt beyond a reasonable doubt, which is difficult to accomplish where the underlying regulations and definitions are confusing or unclear. There are limits to this argument; criminal trials can involve complex areas of proof and extensive instructions of law from the court. But the government's ability to convince a unanimous jury beyond a reasonable doubt is compromised if a criminal prosecution focuses on unduly complex statutory and regulatory concepts. Prosecutors have limited resources and tend not to pursue cases that are unwinnable. It is not surprising, therefore, that environmental crime prosecutors generally have left to their civil counterparts the more controversial enforcement issues.

Due process protections and the exercise of prosecutorial discretion do not invalidate the concerns that were raised prospectively about whether environmental law and criminal law could be integrated effectively. From a theoretical perspective, reconciling the vagaries of environmental law with the due process demands of criminal law presents challenges. A fair consideration of those challenges, however, requires evaluating the complexity of environmental law alongside the doctrinal protections of the void-for-vagueness doctrine and the rule of lenity. If those protections are given meaning by the courts, and if they are honored in the exercise of prosecutorial discretion, criminal enforcement should not involve issues of regulatory uncertainty. In addition, criminal enforcement under the environmental laws can be reserved for types of violations that are less likely to raise integration concerns.

B. ISSUES IN CRIMINAL ENFORCEMENT

Civil liability for violating environmental statutes may attach without any showing of intent or negligence. In contrast, criminal liability under environmental statutes, as in other substantive areas, generally requires proof of mens rea. As you read the Clean Water Act's criminal provisions, note the mens rea requirements and the corresponding punishments.

Excerpts From the Clean Water Act

33 U.S.C. §§ 1251–1387.

Sec. 309 Enforcement

(c) Criminal penalties

(1) Negligent violations

Any person who—

(A) negligently violates section 1311, 1312, 1316, 1317, 1318, 1321(b)(3), 1328, or 1345 of this title, or any permit condition or limitation implementing any of such sections in a permit issued under section 1342 of this title by the Administrator or by a State, or any requirement imposed in a pretreatment program approved under section 1342(a)(3) or 1342(b)(8) of this title or in a permit issued under section 1344 of this title by the Secretary of the Army or by a State; or

(B) negligently introduces into a sewer system or into a publicly owned treatment works any pollutant or hazardous substance which such person knew or reasonably should have known could cause personal injury or property damage or, other than in compliance with all applicable Federal, State, or local requirements or permits, which causes such treatment works to violate any effluent limitation or condition in any permit issued to the treatment works under section 1342 of this title by the Administrator or a State;

shall be punished by a fine of not less than $2,500 nor more than $25,000 per day of violation, or by imprisonment for not more than 1 year, or by both. If a conviction of a person is for a violation committed after a first conviction of such person under this paragraph, punishment shall be by a fine of not more than $50,000 per day of violation, or by imprisonment of not more than 2 years, or by both.

(2) Knowing violations

Any person who—

(A) knowingly violates section 1311, 1312, 1316, 1317, 1318, 1321(b)(3), 1328, or 1345 of this title, or any permit condition or limitation implementing any of such sections in a permit issued under section 1342 of this title by the Administrator or by a State, or any requirement imposed in a pretreatment program approved under section 1342(a)(3) or 1342(b)(8) of this title or in a permit issued under section 1344 of this title by the Secretary of the Army or by a State; or

(B) knowingly introduces into a sewer system or into a publicly owned treatment works any pollutant or hazardous substance which such person knew or reasonably should have known could cause personal injury or property damage or, other than in compliance with all applicable Federal, State, or local requirements or permits, which causes such treatment works to violate any effluent limitation or condition in a permit issued to the treatment works under section 1342 of this title by the Administrator or a State;

shall be punished by a fine of not less than $5,000 nor more than $50,000 per day of violation, or by imprisonment for not more than 3 years, or by both. If a conviction of a person is for a violation committed after a first conviction of such person under this paragraph, punishment shall be by a fine of not more than $100,000 per day of violation, or by imprisonment of not more than 6 years, or by both.

(3) Knowing endangerment

(A) General rule

Any person who knowingly violates section 1311, 1312, 1313, 1316, 1317, 1318, 1321(b)(3), 1328, or 1345 of this title, or any permit condition or limitation implementing any of such sections in a permit issued under section 1342 of this title by the Administrator or by a State, or in a permit issued under section 1344 of this title by the Secretary of the Army or by a State, and who knows at that time that he thereby places another person in imminent danger of death or serious bodily injury, shall, upon conviction, be subject to a fine of not more than $250,000 or imprisonment of not more than 15 years, or both. A person which is an organization shall, upon conviction of violating this subparagraph, be subject to a fine of not more than $1,000,000. If a conviction of a person is for a violation committed after a first conviction of such person under this paragraph, the maximum punishment shall be doubled with respect to both fine and imprisonment.

(B) Additional provisions

For the purpose of subparagraph (A) of this paragraph—

(i) in determining whether a defendant who is an individual knew that his conduct placed another person in imminent danger of death or serious bodily injury—

(I) the person is responsible only for actual awareness or actual belief that he possessed; and

(II) knowledge possessed by a person other than the defendant but not by the defendant himself may not be attributed to the defendant;

except that in proving the defendant's possession of actual knowledge, circumstantial evidence may be used, including evidence that the defendant took affirmative steps to shield himself from relevant information;

* * *

(iv) the term "serious bodily injury" means bodily injury which involves a substantial risk of death, unconsciousness, extreme physical pain, protracted and obvious disfigurement, or protracted loss or impairment of the function of a bodily member, organ, or mental faculty.

(4) False statements

Any person who knowingly makes any false material statement, representation, or certification in any application, record, report, plan, or other document filed or required to be maintained under this chapter or who knowingly falsifies, tampers with, or renders inaccurate any monitoring device or method required to be maintained under this chapter, shall upon conviction, be punished by a fine of not more than $10,000, or by imprisonment for not more than 2 years, or by both. If a conviction of a person is for a violation committed after a first conviction of such person under this paragraph, punishment shall be by a fine of not more than $20,000 per day of violation, or by imprisonment of not more than 4 years, or by both.

(5) Treatment of single operational upset

For purposes of this subsection, a single operational upset which leads to simultaneous violations of more than one pollutant parameter shall be treated as a single violation.

(6) Responsible corporate officer as "person"

For the purpose of this subsection, the term "person" means, in addition to the definition contained in section 1362(5) of this title, any responsible corporate officer.

* * *

NOTES AND QUESTIONS

1. *Mens rea.* The potential scope of criminal liability under the CWA is quite broad because a mens rea of negligence may suffice to establish liability. What might be the rationale for imposing criminal rather than civil liability in such instances?

2. *Other criminal provisions.* Environmental statutes other than the Clean Water Act also contain criminal provisions. See also 16 U.S.C. § 1540(b) (criminal provisions of ESA); 42 U.S.C. § 6928(d)–(f) (criminal provisions of RCRA); 42 U.S.C. § 7413(c) (criminal provisions of CAA). One should keep in mind that environmental criminal cases often involve the violation of more general criminal statutes as well. These more general statutes include federal provisions governing conspiracy (18 U.S.C. § 371), false statement (18 U.S.C. § 1001), obstruction of justice (18 U.S.C.

§§ 1503, 1505), perjury (18 U.S.C. § 1621), money laundering (18 U.S.C. § 1956), and mail fraud (18 U.S.C. § 1341). The defendant in *United States v. Protex Indus.*, for instance, was convicted of not only violating the substantive provisions of RCRA and the Clean Water Act, but also conspiring to violate those statutes, making false statements to federal and state environmental and health agencies, and conspiring to make false statements. United States v. Protex Indus., 874 F.2d 740, 741 n.1 (10th Cir. 1989).

3. *Economic punishments.* If a principal objective of environmental enforcement is to alter polluter behavior, why not appeal to the economic self-interest of the offending actor by cutting off lucrative business opportunities with a large purchaser? Section 306 of the Clean Air Act and § 508 of the Clean Water Act do just that by prohibiting the federal government from providing contracts, grants, or loans to a firm whose facilities criminally violated clear air or clean water standards. Effective automatically upon conviction, these facilities are listed by EPA until the agency determines they have corrected the conditions that led to the criminal convictions. At its discretion EPA can extend this ban to other facilities owned or operated by the firm. How significant would this contractor listing or debarment be? If you were an EPA enforcement attorney, how would you use this technique?

United States v. Weitzenhoff

United States Court of Appeals, Ninth Circuit, 1993
35 F.3d 1275.

■ FLETCHER, CIRCUIT JUDGE:

Michael H. Weitzenhoff and Thomas W. Mariani, who managed the East Honolulu Community Services Sewage Treatment Plant, appeal their convictions for violations of the Clean Water Act ("CWA"), 33 U.S.C. §§ 1251 et seq., contending that the district court misconstrued the word "knowingly" under section 1319(c)(2) of the CWA[.] * * *

We affirm the convictions and sentence.

In 1988 and 1989 Weitzenhoff was the manager and Mariani the assistant manager of the East Honolulu Community Services Sewage Treatment Plant ("the plant"), located not far from Sandy Beach, a popular swimming and surfing beach on Oahu. The plant is designed to treat some 4 million gallons of residential wastewater each day by removing the solids and other harmful pollutants from the sewage so that the resulting effluent can be safely discharged into the ocean. The plant operates under a permit issued pursuant to the National Pollution Discharge Elimination System ("NPDES"), which established the limits on the Total Suspended Solids ("TSS") and Biochemical Oxygen Demand ("BOD")-indicators of the solid and organic matter, respectively, in the effluent discharged at Sandy Beach. * * *

From March 1987 through March 1988, the excess WAS [waste activated sludge] generated by the plant was hauled away to another treatment plant, the Sand Island Facility. In March 1988, certain improvements were made to the East Honolulu plant and the hauling was discontinued. Within a few weeks, however, the plant began experiencing a buildup of excess WAS. Rather than have the excess WAS hauled away as before, however, Weitzenhoff and Mariani instructed two employees at the plant to dispose of it on a regular basis by pumping it from the storage tanks directly into the outfall, that is, directly into the ocean. The WAS thereby bypassed the plant's effluent sampler so that the samples taken and reported to Hawaii's Department of Health ("DOH") and the EPA did not reflect its discharge.

The evidence produced by the government at trial showed that WAS was discharged directly into the ocean from the plant on about 40 separate occasions from April 1988 to June 1989, resulting in some 436,000 pounds of pollutant solids being discharged into the ocean, and that the discharges violated the plant's 30–day average effluent limit under the permit for most of the months during which they occurred. Most of the WAS discharges occurred during the night, and none was reported to the DOH or EPA. DOH inspectors contacted the plant on several occasions in 1988 in response to complaints by lifeguards at Sandy Beach that sewage was being emitted from the outfall, but Weitzenhoff and Mariani repeatedly denied that there was any problem at the plant. In one letter responding to a DOH inquiry in October 1988, Mariani stated that "the debris that was reported could not have been from the East Honolulu Wastewater Treatment facility, as our records of effluent quality up to this time will substantiate." One of the plant employees who participated in the dumping operation testified that Weitzenhoff instructed him not to say anything about the discharges, because if they all stuck together and did not reveal anything, "they [couldn't] do anything to us."

Following an FBI investigation, Weitzenhoff and Mariani were charged in a thirty-one-count indictment with conspiracy and substantive violations of the Clean Water Act ("CWA"). At trial, Weitzenhoff and Mariani admitted having authorized the discharges, but claimed that their actions were justified under their interpretation of the NPDES permit. The jury found them guilty of six of the thirty-one counts.

Weitzenhoff was sentenced to twenty-one months and Mariani thirty-three months imprisonment. Each filed a timely notice of appeal.

DISCUSSION

Section 1311(a) of the CWA prohibits the discharge of pollutants into navigable waters without an NPDES permit. 33 U.S.C. § 1311(a). Section 1319(c)(2) makes it a felony offense to "knowingly violate [ ] section 1311, 1312, 1316, 1317, 1318, 1321(b)(3), 1328, or 1345 ..., or any permit condition or limitation implementing any of such sections in a permit issued under section 1342."

Prior to trial, the district court construed "knowingly" in section 1319(c)(2) as requiring only that Weitzenhoff and Mariani were aware that they were discharging the pollutants in question, not that they knew they were violating the terms of the statute or permit. According to appellants, the district court erred in its interpretation of the CWA and in instructing the jury that "the government is not required to prove that the defendant knew that his act or omissions were unlawful," as well as in rejecting their proposed instruction based on the defense that they mistakenly believed their conduct was authorized by the permit. * * *

As with certain other criminal statutes that employ the term "knowingly," it is not apparent from the face of the statute whether "knowingly" means a knowing violation of the law or simply knowing conduct that is violative of the law. We turn, then, to the legislative history of the provision at issue to ascertain what Congress intended.

In 1987, Congress substantially amended the CWA, elevating the penalties for violations of the Act. *See* H.R. Conf. Rep. No. 1004, 99th Cong., 2d Sess. 138 (1986). Increased penalties were considered necessary to deter would-be polluters. S. Rep. No. 50, 99th Cong., 1st Sess. 29 (1985). With the 1987 amendments, Congress substituted "knowingly" for the earlier intent requirement of "willfully" that appeared in the predecessor to section 1319(c)(2). The Senate report accompanying the legislation explains that the changes in the penalty provisions were to ensure that "[c]riminal liability shall . . . attach to any person who is not in compliance with all applicable Federal, State and local requirements and permits *and causes* a POTW [publicly owned treatment works] to violate any effluent limitation or condition in any permit issued to the treatment works." *Id.* (emphasis added). Similarly, the report accompanying the House version of the bill, which contained parallel provisions for enhancement of penalties, states that the proposed amendments were to "provide penalties for dischargers or individuals who knowingly or negligently violate *or cause the violation of* certain of the Act's requirements." H.R. Rep. No. 189, 99th Cong., 1st Sess. 29–30 (1985) (emphasis added). Because they speak in terms of "causing" a violation, the congressional explanations of the new penalty provisions strongly suggest that criminal sanctions are to be imposed on an individual who knowingly engages in conduct that results in a permit violation, regardless of whether the polluter is cognizant of the requirements or even the existence of the permit.

Our conclusion that "knowingly" does not refer to the legal violation is fortified by decisions interpreting analogous public welfare statutes. The leading case in this area is *United States v. International Minerals & Chem. Corp.,* 402 U.S. 558 (1971). In *International Minerals,* the Supreme Court construed a statute which made it a crime to "knowingly violate[ ] any . . . regulation" promulgated by the ICC pursuant to 8 U.S.C. § 834(a), a provision authorizing the agency to formulate regulations for the safe transport of corrosive liquids. *Id.* at 559. The Court held that the term "knowingly" referred to the acts made criminal rather than a violation of the regulation, and that "regulation" was a shorthand designation for the specific acts or omissions contemplated by the act. *Id.* at 560–62. "[W]here . . . dangerous or deleterious devices or products or obnoxious waste materials are involved, the probability of regulation is so great that anyone who is aware that he is in possession of them or dealing with them must be presumed to be aware of the regulation." *Id.* at 565.

This court followed *International Minerals* in *United States v. Hoflin,* 880 F.2d 1033 (9th Cir. 1989), when it held that knowledge of the absence of a permit is not an element of the offense defined by 42 U.S.C. § 6928(d)(2)(A), part of the Resource Conservation and Recovery Act ("RCRA"). *Id.* at 1039. "There can be little question that RCRA's purposes, like those of the Food and Drug Act, '. . . touch phases of the lives and health of people which, in the circumstances of modern industrialism, are largely beyond self-protection.' " *Id.* at 1038. * * *

Subsequent to the filing of the original opinion in this case, the Supreme Court decided two cases which Weitzenhoff contends call our analysis into question. *See* Ratzlaf v. United States, 510 U.S. 135, 114 S. Ct. 655 (1994); Staples v. United States, 511 U.S. 600, 114 S. Ct. 1793 (1994). We disagree.

The statute in *Ratzlaf* does not deal with a public welfare offense, but rather with violations of the banking statutes. The Court construed the term "willfully" in the anti-structuring provisions of the Bank Secrecy Act to require both that the defendant knew he was structuring transactions to avoid reporting requirements and that he knew his acts were unlawful. The Court recognized that the money structuring provisions are not directed at conduct which a reasonable person necessarily should know is subject to strict public regulation and that the structuring offense applied to all persons with more than $10,000, many of whom could be engaged in structuring for innocent reasons. *Ratzlaf,* 114 S. Ct. at 660–62. In contrast, parties such as Weitzenhoff are closely regulated and are discharging waste materials that affect public health. The *International Minerals* rationale requires that we impute to these parties knowledge of their operating permit. This was recognized by the Court in *Staples.*

The specific holding in *Staples* was that the government is required to prove that a defendant charged with possession of a machine gun knew that the weapon he possessed had the characteristics that brought it within the statutory definition of a machinegun. But the Court took pains to contrast the gun laws to other regulatory regimes, specifically those regulations that govern the handling of "obnoxious waste materials." *See Staples,* 114 S. Ct. at 1798. It noted that the mere innocent ownership of guns is not a public welfare offense. 114 S. Ct. at 1804. The Court focused on the long tradition of widespread gun ownership in this country and, recognizing that approximately 50% of American homes contain a firearm, 114 S. Ct. at 1801, acknowledged that mere ownership of a gun is not sufficient to place people on notice that the act of owning an unregistered firearm is not innocent under the law.

Staples thus explicitly contrasted the mere possession of guns to public welfare offenses, which include statutes that regulate " 'dangerous or deleterious devices or products or obnoxious waste materials,' " 114 S. Ct. at 1800, and confirmed the continued vitality of statutes covering public welfare offenses, which "regulate potentially harmful or injurious items" and place a defendant on notice that he is dealing with a device or a substance "that places him in 'responsible relation to a public danger.'" *Id.* "[I]n such cases Congress intended to place the burden on the defendant to ascertain at his peril whether [his conduct] comes within the inhibition of the statute." 114 S. Ct. at 1798.

* * *

■ KLEINFELD, CIRCUIT JUDGE, with whom CIRCUIT JUDGES REINHARDT, KOZINSKI, TROTT, and T.G. NELSON join, dissenting from the order rejecting the suggestion for rehearing en banc.

* * * In my view, this is a case of exceptional importance, for two reasons. First, it impairs a fundamental purpose of criminal justice, sorting out the innocent from the guilty before imposing punishment. Second, it does so in the context of the Clean Water Act. This statute has tremendous sweep. Most statutes permit anything except what is prohibited, but this one prohibits all regulated conduct involving waters and wetlands except what is permitted. 33 U.S.C. § 1311(a); *United States v. Riverside Bayview Homes, Inc.,* 474 U.S. 121 (1985). Much more ordinary, innocent, productive activity is regulated by this law than people not versed in environmental law might imagine.

The harm our mistaken decision may do is not necessarily limited to Clean Water Act cases. Dilution of the traditional requirement of a criminal state of mind, and application of the criminal law to innocent conduct, reduces the moral authority of our system of criminal law. If we use prison to achieve social goals regardless of the moral innocence of those we incarcerate, then imprisonment loses its moral opprobrium and our criminal law becomes morally arbitrary.

We have now made felons of a large number of innocent people doing socially valuable work. They are innocent, because the one thing which makes their conduct felonious is something they do not know. It is we, and not Congress, who have made them felons. The statute, read in an ordinary way, does not. If we are fortunate, sewer plant workers around the circuit will continue to perform their vitally important work despite our decision. If they knew they risk three years in prison, some might decide that their pay, though sufficient inducement for processing the public's wastes, is not enough to risk prison for doing their jobs. We have decided that they should go to prison if, unbeknownst to them, their plant discharges exceed permit limits. * * *

In this case, the defendants, sewage plant operators, had a permit to discharge sewage into the ocean, but exceeded the permit limitations. The legal issue for the panel was what knowledge would turn innocently or negligently violating a permit into "knowingly" violating a permit. Were the plant operators felons if they knew they were discharging sewage, but did not know that they were violating their permit? Or did they also have to know they were violating their permit? Ordinary English grammar, common sense, and precedent, all compel the latter construction.

* * *

The statute says "knowingly violate[s] . . . any permit condition or limitation." "Knowingly" is an adverb. It modifies the verb "violates." The object of the verb is "any permit condition or limitation." The word "knowingly" is placed before "violates" to "explain its meaning in the case at hand more clearly." 1 George O. Curme, A Grammar of the English Language 72 (1935). Congress has distinguished those who knowingly violate permit conditions, and are thereby felons, from those who unknowingly violate permit conditions, so are not. The panel reads the statute as though it says "knowingly discharges pollutants." It does not. If we read the statute on the assumption that Congress used the English language in an ordinary way, the state of mind required is knowledge that one is violating a permit condition.

This approach has the virtue of attributing common sense and a rational purpose to Congress. It is one thing to defy a permit limitation, but quite another to violate it without realizing that one is violating it. Congress promulgated a parallel statute making it a misdemeanor "negligently" to violate a permit condition or limitation. 33 U.S.C. § 1319(c)(1)(A). If negligent violation is a misdemeanor, why would Congress want to make it a felony to violate the permit without negligence and without even knowing that the discharge exceeded the permit limit? That does not make any sense. It would deter people from working in sewer plants, instead of deterring people from violating permits. All dischargers acting lawfully pursuant to a permit know that they are discharging pollutants. * * *

The panel reaches its surprising result in surprising ways. First, it says that the statute is ambiguous. * * * As explained above, a grammatical and sensible reading of the statute leaves no room for ambiguity. But for the sake of discussion, suppose that the statute is ambiguous, as the panel says. Then the rule of lenity requires that the construction allowing the defendant more liberty rather than less be applied by the courts. * * *

The panel * * * tries to bolster its construction by categorizing the offense as a "public welfare offense," as though that justified more aggressive criminalization without a plain statutory command. This category is a modernized version of "malum prohibitum." Traditionally the criminal law distinguishes between malum in se, conduct wrong upon principles of natural moral law, and malum prohibitum, conduct not inherently immoral but wrong because prohibited by law. Black's Law Dictionary 1112 (4th ed. 1951). To put this in plain, modern terms, any normal person knows murder, rape and robbery are wrong, and they would be wrong even in a place with no sovereign and no law. Discharging 6% more pollutants than one's permit allows is wrong only because the law says so. Substitution of the modern term "public welfare offense" for the traditional one, malum prohibitum, allows for confusion by rhetorical suggestion. The new term suggests that other offenses might merely be private in their impact, and therefore less serious. The older set of terms made it clear that murder was more vile than violating a federal regulation. The category of malum prohibitum, or public welfare offenses, makes the rule of lenity especially important, most particularly for felonies, because persons of good conscience may not recognize the wrongfulness of the conduct when they engage in it.

Staples v. United States reminds us that "offenses that require no *mens rea* generally are disfavored." 114 S. Ct. at 1797. *Mens rea* may be dispensed with in public welfare offenses, but the penalty is a "significant consideration in determining whether the statute should be construed as dispensing with *mens rea*." 114 S. Ct. at 1802.

* * *

* * * If Congress makes a crime a felony, the felony categorization alone is a "factor tending to suggest that Congress did not intend to eliminate a *mens rea* requirement. In such a case, the usual presumption that a defendant must know the facts that make his conduct illegal should apply." 114 S. Ct. at 1804. In the case at bar, "the facts that make his conduct illegal" are the permit violations, not the discharges of pollutants. Discharge of pollutants was licensed by the federal government in the NPDES permit. * * *

The panel cites *United States v. International Minerals & Chem. Corp.* in support of its reading. *International Minerals* expressly limits its holding to "dangerous or deleterious devices or products or obnoxious waste materials." 402 U.S. at 565. The Court distinguished materials not obviously subject to regulation:

> Pencils, dental floss, paper clips may also be regulated. But they may be the type of products which might raise substantial due process questions if Congress did not require . . . "*mens rea*" as to each ingredient of the offense. But where, as here . . ., dangerous or deleterious devices or products or obnoxious waste materials are involved, the probability of regulation is so great that anyone who is aware that he is in possession of them or dealing with them must be presumed to be aware of the regulation.

Id. at 564–65. *International Minerals* would have much persuasive force for *Weitzenhoff,* because of the grammatical similarity of the statute, if (1) the Clean Water Act limited pollutants to "dangerous or deleterious devices or products or obnoxious waste materials;" (2) the crime was only a misdemeanor; and (3) *Staples* had not come down this term. But all three of these conditions are contrary to fact. The pollutants to which the Clean Water Act felony statute applies include many in the "pencils, dental floss, paper clips" category. Hot water, rock, and sand are classified as "pollutants" by the Clean Water Act. *See* 33 U.S.C. § 1362(6). Discharging silt from a stream back into the same stream may amount to discharge of a pollutant. For that matter, so may skipping a stone into a lake. So may a cafeteria worker's pouring hot, stale coffee down the drain. Making these acts a misdemeanor is one thing, but a felony is quite another, as *Staples* teaches.

* * *

NOTES AND QUESTIONS

1. *Statutory interpretation.* As a matter of statutory interpretation, which opinion has the better argument? What is the public welfare offense doctrine? How does it affect the court's analysis?

2. *Policy concerns.* How concerned are you by the dangers identified in Judge Kleinfeld's dissent? How might Judge Fletcher respond to these concerns?

3. *"Knowingly."* The opinions in *Weitzenhoff* differ over whether the knowledge requirement in the statute applies to the illegality of the conduct. The issue of what a defendant must know to be convicted arises with some frequency. As in *Weitzenhoff*, most courts have held that the government does not need to prove that the defendant knew that his actions were illegal or that a permit was required. See, e.g., United States v. Cooper, 482 F.3d 658, 665–68 (4th Cir. 2007) (holding that prosecution need not prove that Clean Water Act criminal defendant had knowledge that pollutant was discharged to waters of the United States); United States v. Buckley, 934 F.2d 84 (6th Cir. 1991) (holding that Clean Air Act provision criminalizing knowing violation of air emission standard "requires knowledge only of the emissions themselves, not knowledge of the statute or of the hazards that emissions pose"); United States v. Hoflin, 880 F.2d 1033, 1038–39 (9th Cir. 1989) (holding that section 3008(d)(2)(A) of RCRA, 42 U.S.C. § 6928(d)(2)(A), which makes it a felony to "knowingly treat[], store[], or dispose[] of any hazardous waste . . . without a permit" does not require that the person charged have known that he lacked a required permit); but see United States v. Johnson & Towers, Inc., 741 F.2d 662, 668–69 (3d Cir. 1984) (holding that section 3008(d)(2)(A) of RCRA requires showing that defendants knew they were acting without a permit or in violation of the law).

4. *Criminal negligence.* The Clean Water Act is unusual, but not unique, in that it criminalizes negligent conduct. Compare 33 U.S.C. § 1319(c) with, e.g., 42 U.S.C. § 6928(c) (RCRA provisions criminalizing knowing violations of other substantive requirements); 42 U.S.C. § 7413(c) (Clean Air Act provisions criminalizing knowing violations of other substantive requirements, as well as negligent releases of hazardous air pollutants that negligently place another person in imminent danger). Courts have generally rejected defendants' contentions that the CWA requires a demonstration of gross negligence, noting the absence of specific language to that effect. See United States v. Hanousek, 176 F.3d 1116, 1121 (9th Cir. 1999) (concluding that § 309(c)(1)(A) of the Clean Water Act imposes criminal liability for ordinary negligence); United States v. Ortiz, 427 F.3d 1278, 1283 (10th Cir. 2005) (same).

5. *Mens rea requirements.* The issue of what mental state is required to show a criminal violation is primarily a question of statutory interpretation. Nevertheless, the Supreme Court has recognized the importance of common law principles, including the presumption of a mens rea requirement, in interpreting federal criminal statutes. See Staples v. United States, 511 U.S. 600, 605–06 (1994) (noting common law presumption that mens rea is required, even where not explicit in statute).

United States v. Iverson

United States Court of Appeals, Ninth Circuit, 1998.
162 F.3d 1015.

■ GRABER, CIRCUIT JUDGE:

Defendant was a founder of CH2O, Inc., and served as the company's President and Chairman of the Board. CH2O blends chemicals to create numerous products, including acid cleaners and heavy-duty alkaline compounds. The company ships the blended chemicals to its customers in drums.

CH2O asked its customers to return the drums so that it could reuse them. Although customers returned the drums, they often did not clean them sufficiently. Thus, the drums still contained chemical residue. Before CH2O could reuse the drums, it had to remove that residue.

To remove the residue, CH2O instituted a drum-cleaning operation, which in turn generated wastewater. In the early to mid–1980s, defendant approached the manager of the local sewer authority to see whether the sewer authority would accept the company's wastewater. The sewer authority refused, because the wastewater "did not meet the parameters we had set for accepting industrial waste. It had too high of a metal content." Thereafter, defendant and the general manager of CH2O made two other attempts to convince the sewer authority to accept the wastewater. Both times, it refused.

Beginning in about 1985, defendant personally discharged the wastewater and ordered employees of CH2O to discharge the wastewater in three places: (1) on the plant's property, (2) through a sewer drain at an apartment complex that defendant owned, and (3) through a sewer drain at defendant's home. (The plant did not have sewer access.) Those discharges continued until about 1988, when CH2O hired Bill Brady.

Brady initially paid a waste disposal company to dispose of the wastewater. Those efforts cost the company thousands of dollars each month. Beginning in late 1991, CH2O stopped its drum-cleaning operation and, instead, shipped the drums to a professional outside contractor for cleaning.

In April 1992, CH2O fired Brady. Around that same time, defendant bought a warehouse in Olympia. Unlike the CH2O plant, the warehouse had sewer access. After the purchase, CH2O restarted its drum-cleaning operation at the warehouse and disposed of its wastewater through the sewer. CH2O obtained neither a permit nor permission to make these discharges. The drum-cleaning operation continued until the summer of 1995, when CH2O learned that it was under investigation for discharging pollutants into the sewer.

A few months before CH2O restarted its drum-cleaning operation, defendant announced his "official" retirement from CH2O. Thereafter, he continued to receive money from CH2O, to conduct business at the company's facilities, and to give orders to employees. Moreover, the company continued to list him as the president in documents that it filed with the state, and the employee who was responsible for running the day-to-day aspects of the drum-cleaning operation testified that he reported to defendant.

During the four years of the operation at the warehouse, defendant was sometimes present when drums were cleaned. During those occasions, defendant was close enough to see and smell the waste.

In some instances, defendant informed employees that he had obtained a permit for the drum-cleaning operation and that the operation was on the "up and up." At other times, however, defendant told employees that, if they got caught, the company would receive only a slap on the wrist.

[T]he jury convicted defendant of violating the CWA, the WAC [Washington Administrative Code], and [the City of Olympia's Municipal Code.] The WAC and the Olympia code are not, by themselves, federal offenses. However, the CWA allows states to administer water pretreatment programs. 33 U.S.C. § 1342(b). If the Environmental Protection Agency (EPA) approves a state's regulations, violations of those regulations are treated as federal criminal offenses. 33 U.S.C. § 1319(c)(2). On September 30, 1986, the EPA approved the WAC.

Similarly, the CWA requires publicly owned treatment works (POTW) to create their own regulatory programs. 40 C.F.R. § 403.5(c). Those local regulations are deemed pretreatment standards under the CWA. 40 C.F.R. § 403.5(d). In 1994, the City of Olympia approved its regulatory code. Thus, its provisions state federal offenses. 33 U.S.C. § 1319(c)(2).

* * *

Defendant * * * argues that the district court erred in formulating its "responsible corporate officer" jury instruction. We are not persuaded.

* * *

The district court instructed the jury that it could find defendant liable under the CWA as a "responsible corporate officer" if it found, beyond a reasonable doubt:

1. That the defendant had knowledge of the fact that pollutants were being discharged to the sewer system by employees of CH2O, Inc.;

2. That the defendant had the authority and capacity to prevent the discharge of pollutants to the sewer system; and

3. That the defendant failed to prevent the on-going discharge of pollutants to the sewer system.

Defendant argues that the district court misinterpreted the scope of "responsible corporate officer" liability. Specifically, defendant suggests that a corporate officer is "responsible" only when the officer in fact exercises control over the activity causing the discharge or has an express corporate duty to oversee the activity. We have not previously interpreted the scope of "responsible corporate officer" liability under the CWA. We do so now and reject defendant's narrow interpretation.

When interpreting a statute, this court looks first to the words that Congress used. The CWA holds criminally liable "any person who ... knowingly violates" its provisions. *See* 33 U.S.C. § 1319(c)(2). The CWA defines the term "person" to include "any responsible corporate officer." *See* 33 U.S.C. § 1319(c)(6) ("For the purpose of this subsection, the term 'person' means, in addition to the definition contained in section 1362(5) of this title, any responsible corporate officer."). However, the CWA does not define the term "responsible corporate officer."

When a statute does not define a term, we generally interpret that term by employing the ordinary, contemporary, and common meaning of the words that Congress used. Using that meaning, "any corporate officer" who is "answerable" or "accountable" for the unlawful discharge is liable under the CWA.

The history of "responsible corporate officer" liability supports the foregoing construction. The "responsible corporate officer" doctrine originated in a Supreme Court case interpreting the Federal Food, Drug, and Cosmetic Act (FFDCA), *United States v. Dotterweich.*

In *Dotterweich,* the president and the general manager of a corporation each argued that he was not a "person" as that term is defined in the FFDCA. The Court disagreed, holding that "[t]he offense is committed ... by all who do have such a responsible share in the furtherance of the transaction which the statute outlaws." * * * Because Congress used a similar definition of the term "person" in the CWA, we can presume that Congress intended that the principles of *Dotterweich* apply under the CWA.

After Congress initially enacted the CWA in 1972, the Supreme Court further defined the scope of the "responsible corporate officer" doctrine under the FFDCA. In *United States v. Park,* 421 U.S. 658, 668 (1975), a corporate president argued that he could not be "responsible" under *Dotterweich,* because he had delegated decision-making control over the activity in question to a subordinate. The Court rejected that argument, holding that "the Government establishes a prima facie case when it introduces evidence sufficient to warrant a finding by the trier of the facts that the defendant had, by reasons of his position in the corporation, responsibility and authority either to prevent in the first instance or promptly to correct, the violation complained of, and that he failed to do so." Id. at 673–74. Stated another way, the question for the jury is whether the corporate officer had "authority with respect to the conditions that formed the basis of the alleged violations." The Court did not, however, require the corporate officer actually to exercise any authority over the activity.

In 1987, after the Supreme Court decided *Park,* Congress revised and replaced the criminal provisions of the CWA. (Most importantly, Congress made a violation of the CWA a felony, rather than a misdemeanor.) In replacing the criminal provisions of the CWA, Congress made no changes to its "responsible corporate officer" provision. That being so, we can presume that Congress intended for *Park*'s refinement of the "responsible corporate officer" doctrine to apply under the CWA.

* * *

Taken together, the wording of the CWA, the Supreme Court's interpretations of the "responsible corporate officer" doctrine, and this court's interpretation of similar statutory requirements establish the contours of the "responsible corporate officer" doctrine under the CWA. Under the CWA, a person is a "responsible corporate officer" if the person has authority to exercise control over the corporation's activity that is causing the discharges. There is no requirement that the officer in fact exercise such authority or that the corporation expressly vest a duty in the officer to oversee the activity.

NOTES AND QUESTIONS

1. *Responsible corporate officer.* What is the effect of the responsible corporate officer doctrine? What are the prerequisites for applying the doctrine? Are there limitations on where it might be applied?

The Clean Water Act expressly refers to a "responsible corporate officer," as the analysis in *Iverson* notes. The Clean Air Act contains similar language. 42 U.S.C. § 7413(c)(6). Courts nevertheless have applied the responsible corporate officer doctrine even to environmental statutes that lack such language. See Humboldt Baykeeper v. Simpson Timber Co., 2006 WL 3545014 (N.D. Cal. 2006) (denying motion to dismiss RCRA criminal charge where defendant alleged that he was merely in a position of authority at polluting company).

2. *Corporate liability.* The responsible corporate officer doctrine relates to the issue of when a corporate officer may be held liable for the misconduct of subordinates. Can the corporation be held criminally liable as well? Under principles of *respondeat superior*, a corporation may be held vicariously liable for criminal violations committed by an employee if the employee's acts were within the employee's scope of authority and were done with the intent to benefit the employer.

C.   SENTENCING

First promulgated in 1987, the federal Sentencing Guidelines provide detailed instructions to district judges regarding the appropriate sentencing ranges for persons convicted of federal crimes, including environmental crimes. Prior to establishment of the guidelines, sentencing judges' discretion was constrained only by statutory maximums. By taking account of the specific characteristics of an offense as well as an offender's criminal history, the guidelines are intended to ensure that similarly situated offenders are treated similarly and that sentences are proportional to the seriousness of the crimes committed.

The centerpiece of the guidelines is the Sentencing Table, a two-dimensional grid that spells out sentencing ranges dependent on the offense level involved in the case and the offender's criminal history. To calculate the offense level, a judge begins with the base offense level, which is determined by the type of crime the defendant committed. Environmental crimes involving the mishandling of hazardous or toxic substances or pesticides, for example, are assigned a base offense level of 8. See USSG § 2Q1.2. A judge then adds or subtracts points from the base offense level, depending on the factual circumstances the judge determines were present in a specific case, such as whether the offense resulted in a substantial likelihood of death or serious bodily injury. Further adjustments can be made based on other factors, such as assistance provided by the defendant to the government in resolving the case or in prosecuting other cases.

The Supreme Court held in United States v. Booker, 543 U.S. 220, 232–37 (2005), that the federal Sentencing Guidelines are unconstitutional to the extent that they are binding on district court judges. The Guidelines, the Court explained, violate a defendant's Sixth Amendment right to a jury trial because judges make factual determinations in applying the Guidelines. Although the Guidelines are no longer binding, district court judges may continue to consider them as advisory. *Id.* at 245–46.

For examples of cases applying Sentencing Guideline § 2Q1.2, see United States v. Van Loben Sels, 198 F.3d 1161 (9th Cir. 1999); United States v. Ferrin, 994 F.2d 658 (9th Cir. 1993); United States v. Rutana, 932 F.2d 1155 (6th Cir. 1991); United States v. Sellers, 926 F.2d 410 (5th Cir. 1991).

SECTION 4.   CITIZEN SUITS

A.   INTRODUCTION

Environmental enforcement is carried out not only by federal and state environmental and law enforcement agencies, but also by private citizens. Many federal environmental statutes contain citizen suit provisions authorizing "any citizen" or "any person" to sue for violations of the statute or of standards issued under the statute. Citizen suits tap into private citizens' interest, knowledge, and resources, and are an important means of supplementing government enforcement efforts. Although the citizen suit provision found in § 304 of the Clean Air Act has served as the model for most other citizen suit provisions, it is the citizen suit provision of the Clean Water Act, reproduced below, that has seen the most frequent use.

Excerpts From the Clean Water Act

33 U.S.C. §§ 1251–1387.

Sec. 505   Citizen suits

(a) Authorization; jurisdiction

Except as provided in subsection (b) of this section and section 1319(g)(6) of this title, any citizen may commence a civil action on his own behalf—

(1) against any person (including (i) the United States, and (ii) any other governmental instrumentality or agency to the extent permitted by the eleventh amendment to the Constitution) who is alleged to be in violation of (A) an effluent standard or limitation under this chapter or (B) an order issued by the Administrator or a State with respect to such a standard or limitation, or

(2) against the Administrator where there is alleged a failure of the Administrator to perform any act or duty under this chapter which is not discretionary with the Administrator.

The district courts shall have jurisdiction, without regard to the amount in controversy or the citizenship of the parties, to enforce such an effluent standard or limitation, or such an order, or to order the Administrator to perform such act or duty, as the case may be, and to apply any appropriate civil penalties under section 1319(d) of this title.

(b) Notice

No action may be commenced—

(1) under subsection (a)(1) of this section—

(A) prior to sixty days after the plaintiff has given notice of the alleged violation (i) to the Administrator, (ii) to the State in which the alleged violation occurs, and (iii) to any alleged violator of the standard, limitation, or order, or

(B) if the Administrator or State has commenced and is diligently prosecuting a civil or criminal action in a court of the United States, or a State to require compliance with the standard, limitation, or order, but in any such action in a court of the United States any citizen may intervene as a matter of right.

(2) under subsection (a)(2) of this section prior to sixty days after the plaintiff has given notice of such action to the Administrator, except that such action may be brought immediately after such notification in the case of an action under this section respecting a violation of sections 1316 and 1317(a) of this title. Notice under this subsection shall be given in such manner as the Administrator shall prescribe by regulation.

(c) Venue; intervention by Administrator; United States interests protected

(1) Any action respecting a violation by a discharge source of an effluent standard or limitation or an order respecting such standard or

limitation may be brought under this section only in the judicial district in which such source is located.

(2) In such action under this section, the Administrator, if not a party, may intervene as a matter of right.

(3) Protection of interests of United States

Whenever any action is brought under this section in a court of the United States, the plaintiff shall serve a copy of the complaint on the Attorney General and the Administrator. No consent judgment shall be entered in an action in which the United States is not a party prior to 45 days following the receipt of a copy of the proposed consent judgment by the Attorney General and the Administrator.

(d) Litigation costs

The court, in issuing any final order in any action brought pursuant to this section, may award costs of litigation (including reasonable attorney and expert witness fees) to any prevailing or substantially prevailing party, whenever the court determines such award is appropriate. The court may, if a temporary restraining order or preliminary injunction is sought, require the filing of a bond or equivalent security in accordance with the Federal Rules of Civil Procedure.

(e) Statutory or common law rights not restricted

Nothing in this section shall restrict any right which any person (or class of persons) may have under any statute or common law to seek enforcement of any effluent standard or limitation or to seek any other relief (including relief against the Administrator or a State agency).

(f) Effluent standard or limitation

For purposes of this section, the term "effluent standard or limitation under this chapter" means (1) effective July 1, 1973, an unlawful act under subsection (a) of section 1311 of this title; (2) an effluent limitation or other limitation under section 1311 or 1312 of this title; (3) standard of performance under section 1316 of this title; (4) prohibition, effluent standard or pretreatment standards under section 1317 of this title; (5) certification under section 1341 of this title; (6) a permit or condition thereof issued under section 1342 of this title, which is in effect under this chapter (including a requirement applicable by reason of section 1323 of this title); or (7) a regulation under section 1345(d) of this title.

(g) "Citizen" defined. For the purposes of this section the term "citizen" means a person or persons having an interest which is or may be adversely affected.

NOTES AND QUESTIONS

1. *Prerequisites to a citizen suit.* What statutory requirements must a plaintiff satisfy in order to bring a citizen suit? What is the purpose of these requirements? Are there any other safeguards in the statute to ensure that citizen suits are not abused?

2. *Attorneys fees and litigation expenses.* The citizen suit provisions of the Clean Water Act provide that courts may award the "costs of litigation (including reasonable attorney and expert witness fees) to any prevailing or substantially prevailing party, whenever the court determines such award is appropriate." CWA § 505(d); cf. 42 U.S.C. § 7002(e) (RCRA provision authorizing awards of costs, including attorney fees). Thus, a plaintiff who prevails in a citizen suit may file a petition, supported by well-documented contemporaneous records, for the award of litigation expenses. Attorney fee awards are based on a "lodestar" amount calculated by multiplying the reasonable number of hours expended on the matter by a reasonable hourly rate. See City of Burlington v. Dague, 505 U.S. 557, 562 (1992). Although the attorney fee provisions of some statutes, such as the Clean Air Act, authorize fee awards "to any party, whenever the court determines such award is appropriate," 42 U.S.C. §§ 7604(d), 7607(f), a fee applicant must demonstrate some success on the merits in order to recover fees even under these statutes. See Ruckelshaus v. Sierra Club, 463 U.S. 680 (1983).

B. JUSTICIABILITY DOCTRINES

Citizen suits depart significantly from traditional common law models of litigation between private parties. Unlike parties involved in a tort or contract action, a citizen suit plaintiff may not have a direct financial or proprietary stake in the litigation. Despite the presence of broad language in citizen suit provisions authorizing "any person" to bring suit, various jurisdictional barriers may prevent environmental citizen suit plaintiffs from obtaining a ruling on the merits of their case. The most important of these barriers is the constitutional requirement of standing, which is discussed in detail in Chapter 3, Section 2.C.

Other justiciability doctrines, including ripeness, finality, exhaustion, and mootness, also are litigated frequently in citizen suits. These doctrines are discussed in detail in Chapter 3, Section 2.D.

C. STATUTORY REQUIREMENTS

Citizen suit provisions usually contain two important limitations on the ability to bring a citizen suit: a notice requirement and a "diligent prosecution" restriction.

1. NOTICE

With respect to the notice requirement, a potential CWA citizen suit plaintiff must provide 60–day notice to the polluter and to the state and federal governments. See CWA § 505(b); cf. 42 U.S.C. § 7604(b) (notice requirement of Clean Air Act citizen suit provision); 42 U.S.C. § 6972(b) (notice requirement of RCRA citizen suit provision). What is the purpose of such a provision? What is the effect of failing to comply with the notice requirement? Is the notice requirement a prerequisite to obtaining federal jurisdiction? See Hallstrom v. Tillamook County, 493 U.S. 20, 26 (1989) ("compliance with the 60–day notice provision [under RCRA] is a mandatory, not optional, condition precedent for suit"). How does one comply with it? See 40 C.F.R. Part 54 (regulations specifying notice requirements under CAA); 40 C.F.R. Part 135 (regulations specifying notice requirements under CWA); San Francisco Baykeeper v. Tosco Corp., 309 F.3d 1153, 1155 (9th Cir. 2002) ("as long as a notice letter is reasonably specific as to the nature and time of the alleged violations, the plaintiff has fulfilled the notice requirement"). The notice requirement is strictly enforced, but plaintiffs fail to give it with surprising frequency.

2.   DILIGENT PROSECUTION

Karr v. Hefner

United States Court of Appeals, Tenth Circuit, 2007.
475 F.3d 1192.

■ HARTZ, CIRCUIT JUDGE.

Under [33 U.S.C.] § 1365(b)(1)(B) a citizen cannot bring a private action to enjoin violations of the CWA "if the [EPA] or State has commenced and is diligently prosecuting a civil or criminal action in a court of the United States, or a State to require compliance with the standard, limitation, or order." The district court ruled that the EPA's investigation and entry of a consent decree with two of the GHK Defendants qualified as diligent prosecution with respect to all the GHK Defendants.

Plaintiffs do not dispute that the EPA pursued enforcement of the CWA against GHK. But they urge four reasons why the EPA's actions do not foreclose their claims: (1) the EPA did not file its action within 60 days of Plaintiffs' notice; (2) the consent decree between the EPA and GHK did not address violations at all 37 well sites named in their complaint; (3) the consent decree addressed stormwater and wetlands violations but not point-source-discharge requirements under the CWA; and (4) the consent decree names only two of the GHK Defendants. We address each contention after a discussion of the diligence requirement.

1.   Diligence Under § 1365(b)(1)(B)

The CWA gives primary enforcement authority to the EPA and state enforcement agencies. Under § 1365(b)(1)(B), diligent prosecution of alleged CWA violations by these agencies may preclude the filing of a citizen CWA lawsuit. As the Supreme Court stated in Gwaltney of Smithfield v. Chesapeake Bay Found., 484 U.S. 49, 60 (1987), "[T]he citizen suit is meant to supplement rather than to supplant governmental action." Citizen lawsuits under the CWA have a merely "interstitial" role; Congress did not intend for them to be even "potentially intrusive" on agency discretion. Id. at 61.

Section 1365(b)(1)(B) does not require government prosecution to be far-reaching or zealous. It requires only diligence. Nor must an agency's prosecutorial strategy coincide with that of the citizen-plaintiff. As expressed by the Sixth Circuit, "[S]econd-guessing of the EPA's assessment of an appropriate remedy ... fails to respect the statute's careful distribution of enforcement authority among the federal EPA, the States and private citizens, all of which permit citizens to act where the EPA has 'failed' to do so, not where the EPA has acted but has not acted aggressively enough in the citizens' view." Ellis v. Gallatin Steel Co., 390 F.3d 461, 477 (6th Cir. 2004).

Particularly when the EPA chooses to enforce the CWA through a consent decree, failure to defer to its judgment can undermine agency strategy. If a defendant is exposed to a citizen suit whenever the EPA grants it a concession, defendants will have little incentive to negotiate consent decrees. The Supreme Court has recognized the importance of deference to the EPA's bargains:

> Suppose ... that the Administrator agreed not to assess or otherwise seek civil penalties on the condition that the violator take some extreme corrective action, such as to install particularly effective but expensive machinery, that it otherwise would not be obliged to take. If citizens could file suit ... in order to seek the civil penalties that the Administrator chose to forgo, then the Administrator's discretion to enforce the Act in the public interest would be curtailed considerably.

Gwaltney, 484 U.S. at 60–61. As one court nicely put it, "An Administrator unable to make concessions is unable to obtain them." *Heritage Group*, 973 F.2d at 1324. We should not interpret § 1365 in a manner that would undermine the EPA's ability to reach voluntary settlements with defendants.

Allowing the EPA to compromise does not strip citizens of their role in helping to bring about remedies for CWA violations. Indeed, the Department of Justice's regulations entitle citizens to comment on pending environmental consent decrees. *See* 28 C.F.R. § 50.7 ("It is hereby established as the policy of the Department of Justice to consent to a proposed judgment in an action to enjoin discharges of pollutants into the environment only after or on condition that an opportunity is afforded persons (natural or corporate) who are not named as parties to the action to comment on the proposed judgment prior to its entry by the court.").

2.   Enforcement Against the GHK Defendants

In light of our deferential review of the matter, we do not hesitate to hold that the EPA's prosecution against the GHK Defendants was diligent. The EPA chose to investigate and reach a settlement with GHK concerning essentially the same violations alleged in Plaintiffs' complaint. From the uncontested assertions of the GHK Defendants in district court, it appears that the prosecution was not only diligent but vigorous and thorough; indeed, in some respects the EPA appears to have accomplished more through its consent decree than Plaintiffs sought to achieve on their own. We reject Plaintiffs' four challenges to the district court's determination of diligence—delay, inadequate coverage of sites, inadequate coverage of violations, and inadequate coverage of defendants.

Plaintiffs argue that the EPA's action cannot bar their complaint because the EPA did not file its suit within 60 days of when they sent notice of their claims. But § 1365(b)(1) does not require the EPA to act within 60 days. Instead, it prevents *plaintiffs* from acting within 60 days of their own notice. Plaintiffs rely on *Chesapeake Bay Foundation v. American Recovery Co.,* 769 F.2d 207 (4th Cir. 1985); but it is not helpful to their position. In that case "the government did not act within the sixty-day waiting period *and it had not yet filed suit when plaintiffs filed their independent action." Id.* at 208 (emphasis added). In contrast, in this case the EPA *did* file its suit before Plaintiffs—even if only by a short time. Thus, as long as the EPA's prosecution was otherwise diligent, it does not matter that it commenced after the 60–day notice period provided by § 1365(b)(1)(A).

Plaintiffs contend that the EPA's enforcement action against GHK was not diligent because the consent decree addressed only between 19 and 21 of the 37 sites listed in Plaintiffs' complaint. As we have noted, however, we do not evaluate the EPA's diligence by requiring that its accomplishments track those sought by the citizen-plaintiffs.

In any event, Plaintiffs have not established that the EPA failed to pursue diligently all relevant sites named in their complaint. For example, regarding Plaintiffs' stormwater and point-source-discharge claims, the GHK Defendants asserted in their motion to dismiss, and Plaintiffs did not dispute, that the consent decree addresses all GHK-related sites governed by the CWA's stormwater and point-source-discharge regulations. As for the wetlands-permit claims, it was the GHK Defendants' uncontradicted assertion that the EPA found no violations at nine of the twelve GHK-related sites listed by Plaintiffs and that the consent decree required mitigation at the other three sites, as well as at several other sites, including sites not listed by Plaintiffs. Nothing in the record indicates that the district court clearly erred in its assessment of the consent decree's aim-that is, that the consent decree "has as its underlying purpose the resolution of all claims that GHK violated the CWA with respect to well sites in the Potato Hills area."

[The court declined to consider the argument that EPA's prosecution was not diligent because it did not cover violations of point source discharge requirements because the plaintiffs failed to make this argument before the district court.]

Plaintiffs also contend that the EPA's prosecution, which resulted in a consent decree against only two of the GHK Defendants, should not bar citizen lawsuits against the remaining GHK Defendants. We disagree.

The discretion we afford the EPA extends to its choice of defendants. Section 1365(b)(1)(B) does not speak of diligently prosecuting particular defendants but of "diligently prosecuting a civil or criminal action ... to require compliance." Even a diligent prosecutor may decide that the strategically appropriate course of action is to seek a consent decree against a particular set of parties rather than to pursue further action against all parties alleged to have violated provisions of the CWA. In this case, paragraph 4 of the consent decree suggests that GHK could adequately ensure compliance and that other entities who might be liable under the CWA had essentially passive, or at least subordinate, interests. Plaintiffs have not indicated why the EPA's choice of defendants showed that its prosecution of violations was less than diligent.

For the above reasons, we affirm the dismissal of all the GHK Defendants from Plaintiffs' action.

NOTES AND QUESTIONS

1. *Diligent prosecution.* The diligent prosecution requirement prohibits the filing of a citizen suit "if the Administrator or State has commenced and is diligently prosecuting a civil or criminal action in a court of the United States or a State to require compliance." See CWA § 505(b)(1)(B) (found in Section 4.A of this chapter); see also 42 U.S.C. § 7604(b)(1)(B) (Clean Air Act); 42 U.S.C. § 6972(b)(1)(B) (RCRA). What is the purpose of such a provision? Does the language of these provisions mean exactly what it says—the government action must be prosecuted "in a court" in order to bar citizen suits? What if the government is using an administrative rather than a judicial setting to seek compliance?

2. *Administrative diligent prosecution.* In addition to the judicial diligent prosecution bar found in § 505, the CWA (but not other federal environmental statutes) also contains an administrative diligent prosecution bar in § 309(g), 33 U.S.C. § 1319(g). Under this more limited bar, administrative action by EPA or a state may preclude a citizen suit for penalties. In order for a state administrative action to serve as a bar, three requirements must be satisfied: the state must have commenced an enforcement proceeding against the polluter; the state must be diligently prosecuting the enforcement proceedings; and the state's statutory enforcement scheme must be comparable to the federal administrative scheme promulgated under CWA § 309(g). To determine whether the state and federal administrative schemes are comparable, a court will carefully examine the specific provisions of each. See, e.g., McAbee v. City of Fort Payne, 318 F.3d 1248, 1256–57 (11th Cir. 2003) (holding that state scheme was not comparable to federal scheme because it provided for notice of the government enforcement action only after the fact and because opportunities for public involvement in the administrative enforcement process were far more limited). Moreover, the bar does not apply at all as long as the citizen suit is filed before the 120th day after the date on which the citizen provided notice to the violator. See CWA § 309(g)(6)(B).

3. *Res judicata.* Note that the diligent prosecution bar only prohibits commencement of a citizen suit; government prosecution after a citizen suit is filed does not divest a court of jurisdiction over the citizen suit. However, if the later-filed government action reaches a final judgment before the citizen suit, res judicata may bar the citizen suit. See Friends of Milwaukee's Rivers v. Milwaukee Metro. Sewerage Dist., 382 F.3d 743, 757–65 (7th Cir. 2004) (noting that final judgment in government enforcement action may serve as res judicata bar to earlier-filed citizen suit, but holding that bar did not apply because citizen suit plaintiffs were not in privity with state agency).

3.   "IN VIOLATION"

Gwaltney of Smithfield Ltd. v. Chesapeake Bay Foundation

United States Supreme Court, 1987.
484 U.S. 49.

■ JUSTICE MARSHALL delivered the opinion of the Court.

In this case, we must decide whether § 505(a) of the Clean Water Act . . . confers federal jurisdiction over citizen suits for wholly past violations.

The holder of a state NPDES permit is subject to both federal and state enforcement action for failure to comply. §§ 1319, 1342(b)(7). In the absence of federal or state enforcement, private citizens may commence civil actions against any person "alleged to be in violation of" the conditions of either a federal or state NPDES permit. § 1365(a)(1). If the citizen prevails in such an action, the court may order injunctive relief and/or impose civil penalties payable to the United States Treasury. § 1365(a).

The Commonwealth of Virginia established a federally approved state NPDES program administered by the Virginia State Water Control Board (Board). In 1974, the Board issued a NPDES permit to ITT–Gwaltney authorizing the discharge of seven pollutants from the company's meat-packing plant on the Pagan River in Smithfield, Virginia. The permit, which was reissued in 1979 and modified in 1980, established effluent limitations, monitoring requirements, and other conditions of discharge. In 1981, petitioner Gwaltney of Smithfield acquired the assets of ITT–Gwaltney and assumed obligations under the permit.

Between 1981 and 1984, petitioner repeatedly violated the conditions of the permit by exceeding effluent limitations on five of the seven pollutants covered. These violations are chronicled in the Discharge Monitoring Reports that the permit required petitioner to maintain. The most substantial of the violations concerned the pollutants fecal coliform, chlorine, and total Kjeldahl nitrogen (TKN). Between October 27, 1981, and August 30, 1984, petitioner violated its TKN limitation 87 times, its chlorine limitation 34 times, and its fecal coliform limitation 31 times. Petitioner installed new equipment to improve its chlorination system in March 1982, and its last reported chlorine violation occurred in October 1982. The new chlorination system also helped to control the discharge of fecal coliform, and the last recorded fecal coliform violation occurred in February 1984. Petitioner installed an upgraded wastewater treatment system in October 1983, and its last reported TKN violation occurred on May 15, 1984.

Respondents Chesapeake Bay Foundation and Natural Resources Defense Council, two nonprofit corporations dedicated to the protection of natural resources, sent notice in February 1984 to Gwaltney, the Administrator of EPA, and the Virginia State Water Control Board, indicating respondents' intention to commence a citizen suit under the Act based on petitioner's violations of its permit conditions. Respondents proceeded to file this suit in June 1984, alleging that petitioner "has violated . . . [and] will continue to violate its NPDES permit." Respondents requested that the District Court provide declaratory and injunctive relief, impose civil penalties, and award attorney's fees and costs. The District Court granted partial summary judgment for respondents in August 1984, declaring Gwaltney "to have violated and to be in violation" of the Act. The District Court then held a trial to determine the appropriate remedy.

Before the District Court reached a decision, Gwaltney moved in May 1985 for dismissal of the action for want of subject-matter jurisdiction under the Act. Gwaltney argued that the language of § 505(a), which permits private citizens to bring suit against any person "alleged to be in violation" of the Act, requires that a defendant be violating the Act at the time of suit. Gwaltney contended that because its last recorded violation occurred several weeks before respondents filed their complaint, the District Court lacked subject-matter jurisdiction over respondents' action.

The District Court rejected Gwaltney's argument, concluding that § 505 authorizes citizens to bring enforcement actions on the basis of wholly past violations. The District Court found that "[t]he words 'to be in violation' may reasonably be read as comprehending unlawful conduct that occurred solely prior to the filing of the lawsuit as well as unlawful conduct that continues into the present." 611 F. Supp. 1542, 1547 (ED Va. 1985). In the District Court's view, this construction of the statutory language was supported by the legislative history and the underlying policy goals of the Act. *Id.,* at 1550. The District Court held in the alternative that respondents satisfied the jurisdictional requirements of § 505 because their complaint alleged in good faith that Gwaltney was continuing to violate its permit at the time the suit was filed. *Id.,* at 1549, n. 8.

The Court of Appeals concluded that the "to be in violation" language of § 505 is ambiguous, whereas petitioner asserts that it plainly precludes the construction adopted below. We must agree with the Court of Appeals that § 505 is not a provision in which Congress' limpid prose puts an end to all dispute. But to acknowledge ambiguity is not to conclude that all interpretations are equally plausible. The most natural reading of "to be in violation" is a requirement that citizen-plaintiffs allege a state of either continuous or intermittent violation—that is, a reasonable likelihood that a past polluter will continue to pollute in the future. Congress could have phrased its requirement in language that looked to the past ("to have violated"), but it did not choose this readily available option.

Our reading of the "to be in violation" language of § 505(a) is bolstered by the language and structure of the rest of the citizen suit provisions in § 505 of the Act. These provisions together make plain that the interest of the citizen-plaintiff is primarily forward-looking.

One of the most striking indicia of the prospective orientation of the citizen suit is the pervasive use of the present tense throughout § 505. A citizen suit may be brought only for violation of a permit limitation "which is in effect" under the Act. 33 U.S.C. § 1365(f). Citizen-plaintiffs must give notice to the alleged violator, the Administrator of EPA, and the State in which the alleged violation "occurs." § 1365(b)(1)(A). A Governor of a State may sue as a citizen when the Administrator fails to enforce an effluent limitation "the violation of which is occurring in another State and is causing an adverse effect on the public health or welfare in his State." § 1365(h). The most telling use of the present tense is in the definition of "citizen" as "a person . . . having an interest which is or may be adversely affected" by the defendant's violations of the Act. § 1365(g). This definition makes plain what the undeviating use of the present tense strongly suggests: the harm sought to be addressed by the citizen suit lies in the present or the future, not in the past.

Any other conclusion would render incomprehensible § 505's notice provision, which requires citizens to give 60 days' notice of their intent to sue to the alleged violator as well as to the Administrator and the State. If the Administrator or the State commences enforcement action within that 60–day period, the citizen suit is barred, presumably because governmental action has rendered it unnecessary. It follows logically that the purpose of notice to the alleged violator is to give it an opportunity to bring itself into complete compliance with the Act and thus likewise render unnecessary a citizen suit. If we assume, as respondents urge, that citizen suits may target wholly past violations, the requirement of notice to the alleged violator becomes gratuitous. Indeed, respondents, in propounding their interpretation of the Act, can think of no reason for Congress to require such notice other than that "it seemed right" to inform an alleged violator that it was about to be sued.

Adopting respondents' interpretation of § 505's jurisdictional grant would create a second and even more disturbing anomaly. The bar on citizen suits when governmental enforcement action is under way suggests that the citizen suit is meant to supplement rather than to supplant governmental action. Permitting citizen suits for wholly past violations of the Act could undermine the supplementary role envisioned for the citizen suit. This danger is best illustrated by an example. Suppose that the Administrator identified a violator of the Act and issued a compliance order under § 309(a). Suppose further that the Administrator agreed not to assess or otherwise seek civil penalties on the condition that the violator take some extreme corrective action, such as to install particularly effective but expensive machinery, that it otherwise would not be obliged to take. If citizens could file suit, months or years later, in order to seek the civil penalties that the Administrator chose to forgo, then the Administrator's discretion to enforce the Act in the public interest would be curtailed considerably. The same might be said of the discretion of state enforcement authorities. Respondents' interpretation of the scope of the citizen suit would change the nature of the citizens' role from interstitial to potentially intrusive. We cannot agree that Congress intended such a result.

Our conclusion that § 505 does not permit citizen suits for wholly past violations does not necessarily dispose of this lawsuit, as both lower courts recognized. The District Court found persuasive the fact that "[respondents'] allegation in the complaint, that Gwaltney was continuing to violate its NPDES permit when plaintiffs filed suit[,] appears to have been made fully in good faith." 611 F. Supp., at 1549, n. 8. On this basis, the District Court explicitly held, albeit in a footnote, that "even if Gwaltney were correct that a district court has no jurisdiction over citizen suits based entirely on unlawful conduct that occurred entirely in the past, the Court would still have jurisdiction here." *Ibid.* The Court of Appeals acknowledged, also in a footnote, that "[a] very sound argument can be made that [respondents'] allegations of continuing violations were made in good faith," 791 F.2d, at 308, n. 9, but expressly declined to rule on this alternative holding. Because we agree that § 505 confers jurisdiction over citizen suits when the citizen-plaintiffs make a good-faith allegation of continuous or intermittent violation, we remand the case to the Court of Appeals for further consideration.

Petitioner argues that citizen-plaintiffs must prove their allegations of ongoing noncompliance before jurisdiction attaches under § 505. We cannot agree. The statute does not require that a defendant "be in violation" of the Act at the commencement of suit; rather, the statute requires that a defendant be *"alleged* to be in violation." Petitioner's construction of the Act reads the word "alleged" out of § 505. As petitioner itself is quick to note in other contexts, there is no reason to believe that Congress' drafting of § 505 was sloppy or haphazard. We agree with the Solicitor General that "Congress's use of the phrase 'alleged to be in violation' reflects a conscious sensitivity to the practical difficulties of detecting and proving chronic episodic violations of environmental standards." Our acknowledgment that Congress intended a good-faith allegation to suffice for jurisdictional purposes, however, does not give litigants license to flood the courts with suits premised on baseless allegations. Rule 11 of the Federal Rules of Civil Procedure, which requires pleadings to be based on a good-faith belief, formed after reasonable inquiry, that they are "well grounded in fact," adequately protects defendants from frivolous allegations.

NOTES AND QUESTIONS

1. *The meaning of "in violation."* In a concurring opinion, Justice Scalia criticized the majority's holding that good-faith allegations of ongoing violations would satisfy the "in violation" requirement:

> [T]he issue to be resolved by the Court of Appeals on remand of this suit is not whether the allegation of a continuing violation on the day suit was brought was made in good faith after reasonable inquiry, but whether petitioner was in fact "in violation" on the date suit was brought. The phrase in § 505(a), "to be in violation," unlike the phrase "to be violating" or "to have committed a violation," suggests a

state rather than an act—the opposite of a state of compliance. A good or lucky day is not a state of compliance. Nor is the dubious state in which a past effluent problem is not recurring at the moment but the cause of that problem has not been completely and clearly eradicated. When a company has violated an effluent standard or limitation, it remains, for purposes of § 505(a), "in violation" of that standard or limitation so long as it has not put in place remedial measures that clearly eliminate the cause of the violation.

Gwaltney, 484 U.S. at 69–70 (Scalia, J., concurring in part and concurring in the judgment). Despite some predictions that *Gwaltney* would severely limit CWA citizen suits, the consistent flow of § 505 cases decided since 1987 suggests that *Gwaltney* has not been the obstacle some had feared. In lower court cases following *Gwaltney,* courts have had relatively little difficulty applying its "good-faith allegations" and "ongoing violation" requirements. See, e.g., Sierra Club v. El Paso Gold Mines, Inc., 421 F.3d 1133, 1139–41 (10th Cir. 2005) (holding that plaintiffs' allegations that abandoned mine shaft was continuing to discharge pollutants into creek constituted good-faith allegations of continuous or intermittent violations); United States Pub. Interest Research Group v. Atlantic Salmon of Me., 339 F.3d 23, 33 (1st Cir. 2003) (holding that present violation requirement does not prevent court from ordering equitable relief to remedy the harm done in the past).

2. *Demonstrating an ongoing violation. Gwaltney* held that once jurisdiction attaches to a § 505 case, the plaintiff must prove its allegation that the CWA violation was "continuous or intermittent." 484 U.S. at 57. On remand from the Supreme Court, the Fourth Circuit held that a plaintiff may prove an ongoing violation either by 1) proving violations that continue on or after the date the complaint is filed, or 2) adducing evidence from which a reasonable trier of fact could find a continuing likelihood of a recurrence in intermittent or sporadic violations. Chesapeake Bay Foundation, Inc. v. Gwaltney, 844 F.2d 170, 171–72 (4th Cir. 1988). This test has been cited with approval and applied by the Second, Third, Fifth, Ninth, and Eleventh Circuits. See, e.g., Natural Resources Defense Council v. Southwest Marine, Inc., 236 F.3d 985, 998 (9th Cir. 2000).

3. *Gwaltney and standing doctrine.* What is the significance of *Gwaltney* in light of the standing jurisprudence set out in Chapter 3?

4. *Effect on government enforcement.* The decision in *Gwaltney* prevents CWA § 505 from being used to punish "wholly past" violations that are not ongoing at the time an action is filed. But what about governmental enforcement efforts aimed at such violations? Are they precluded by *Gwaltney?* Compare CWA § 505 with CWA § 309.

5. *Other environmental statutes.* Not all environmental citizen suit provisions contain the "in violation" language found in CWA § 505. The citizen suit provision of the Clean Air Act, for instance, was amended in 1990 to authorize citizen suits against persons "alleged to have violated . . . or to be in violation" of an emission standard or limitation. See 42 U.S.C. § 7604(a); cf. 42 U.S.C. § 11046(a)(1)(A) (authorizing citizen suits against owners or operators of facilities to do various acts required by EPCRA).

PART V

INTERNATIONAL ENVIRONMENTAL LAW

The environmental impacts of human activities have become increasingly global. In order to respond effectively to global problems, environmental law must transcend national boundaries. Chapter 13 provides a brief introduction to international environmental law. Rather than attempting to provide a comprehensive discussion of the field, the chapter considers the sources of international environmental law, how it is formed, and how it might be used to address the problem of climate change.

CHAPTER THIRTEEN

INTERNATIONAL ENVIRONMENTAL LAW

SECTION 1.   INTRODUCTION

The development of international environmental law parallels roughly the development of federal environmental law. Just as growing environmental concerns in the United States during the 1960s and 1970s led to the passage of the National Environmental Policy Act, Clean Air Act, Clean Water Act, and other comprehensive statutory schemes, growing global environmental concern over the past several decades has prompted the adoption of numerous treaties addressing transboundary and global environmental problems, as well as international conferences seeking to establish general principles of law with respect to the environment.

International environmental law is not a completely new field, however. Its origins lie in international law, including historic international agreements to address resource conflicts and customary principles governing fishing rights, navigation, and the like. These early efforts to protect the environment were largely ad hoc responses to specific local and regional problems. The health of the global environment as a whole did not become a prominent issue until the late 1960s, when increasing environmental awareness within industrialized countries and growing concern over transboundary pollution led to the first United Nations conference focused on the global environment, the 1972 Stockholm Conference. Notable accomplishments of the Stockholm Conference include the adoption of a formal statement of environmental principles, the Stockholm Declaration; the establishment of an agenda of issues to be addressed; and the creation of the United Nations Environment Program and the Environment Fund, institutions for addressing environmental protection at the international level. Subsequent years have witnessed the negotiation of a number of international environmental treaties, including a comprehensive regime governing the world's oceans (the 1982 United Nations Convention on the Law of the Sea), a regulatory regime to address the depletion of the ozone layer (the Montreal Protocol regime), a treaty to protect endangered species through trade restrictions (the 1973 Convention on International Trade in Endangered Species), and a treaty addressing biodiversity more generally (the 1992 Convention on Biological Diversity).

Although treaties have come to dominate international environmental law, it is important to understand that treaties are just one source of international law. Traditionally, sources of international law include treaties, international custom, general principles of law, and secondary sources such as judicial decisions and writings of publicists (i.e., international law experts). See Article 38(1) of the Statute of the International Court of Justice.

Treaties, agreements between states that create legal obligations, are the predominant form of binding international environmental law today. Treaties are analogous to contracts in that their obligations are contingent on the express consent of states. States most commonly express consent through ratification, which typically involves approval of a signed treaty through domestic political processes. Parties become bound to a treaty only when the treaty enters into force, which occurs when all signatory states have ratified the treaty or, if the treaty so provides, when a certain minimum number of states have ratified the treaty. Ratification by each state may be a laborious process, and many years may pass between the signing of a treaty and its entering into force.

Binding international obligations may also result from customary law, as reflected by the general practice of states. Customary law requires both the existence of a general state practice and evidence that the practice occurs out of a sense of legal obligation (known as *opinio juris*). Evidence of general practice need not be universal nor perfectly consistent, but conduct inconsistent with the practice must have been treated as a breach of the rule. The existence of *opinio juris* may be demonstrated through government policy statements, official legal opinions, national legislation and court decisions, international resolutions and declarations, and other official statements. An example of customary international environmental law is the principle that states have a duty not to cause environmental harm to other states. As you will learn, an international arbitration proceeding—the 1941 *Trail Smelter* arbitration—played an important role in establishing this principle.

The other source of binding international obligations is general principles, which refer to "rules accepted in the domestic law of all civilized states." Ian Brownlie, Principles of Public International Law 16 (6th ed. 2003). This category of law refers primarily to evidentiary or procedural rules used by international tribunals to fill formal gaps, although some commentators argue that general principles may also include substantive duties based on natural law. General principles have not served as a significant source of international environmental law, but some advocates have sought to ground environmental rights, such as a right to a clean environment, in general principles.

Judicial decisions and teachings of publicists, the other sources of law referred to in the International Court of Justice statute, may help states and courts to determine what the law is, but do not establish binding obligations in and of themselves. Although international courts are not bound by the doctrine of stare decisis, states, courts, and dispute resolution panels often look to such decisions for guidance.

This chapter will introduce the various sources of international environmental law, as well as a sampling of major issues in the field. After considering the decision of the *Trail Smelter* arbitral tribunal, we will examine the Rio Declaration on Environment and Development, an important source of nonbinding international norms sometimes referred to as "soft law." The next section of this chapter will discuss international responses to ozone depletion and climate change, and the last section will explore the potential conflict between trade and the environment.

The following excerpt comes from the *Trail Smelter* arbitration, an ad hoc tribunal decision that has played an influential role in international environmental law. The controversy concerned a smelter operated by a Canadian company in the town of Trail, British Columbia, approximately seven miles from the boundary between Canada and the United States. Sulfur dioxide emissions from the smelter traveled across the border and damaged apple farms and timberlands in Washington state. Canada and the United States agreed to submit the controversy to an arbitral tribunal after an unsuccessful attempt to have the matter resolved by a commission created by the 1909 Boundary Waters Treaty.

Trail Smelter Arbitration

United States v. Canada, Arbitral Tribunal.
3 U.N. Rep. Int'l Arb. Awards, reprinted in 35 Am. J. Int'l Law 684 (1941).

As between the two countries involved, each has an equal interest that if a nuisance is proved, the indemnity to damaged parties for proven damage shall be just and adequate and each has also an equal interest that unproven or unwarranted claims shall not be allowed. For, while the United States' interests may now be claimed to be injured by the operations of a Canadian corporation, it is equally possible that at some time in the future Canadian interests might be claimed to be injured by an American corporation. * * *

The duty imposed upon the Tribunal by the Convention was to "finally decide" the following questions:

(1) Whether damage caused by the Trail Smelter in the State of Washington has occurred since the first day of January, 1932, and, if so, what indemnity should be paid therefor?

(2) In the event of the answer to the first part of the preceding question being in the affirmative, whether the Trail Smelter should be required to refrain from causing damage in the State of Washington in the future and, if so, to what extent?

(3) In the light of the answer to the preceding question, what measures or régime, if any, should be adopted or maintained by the Trail Smelter?

* * *

[As to the first question, the Tribunal had previously found that the smelter caused damage in the State of Washington and awarded $78,000 in damages plus interest. As to the second question,] [t]he first problem which arises is whether the question should be answered on the basis of the law followed in the United States or on the basis of international law. The Tribunal, however, finds that this problem need not be solved here as the law followed in the United States in dealing with the quasi-sovereign rights of the States of the Union, in the matter of air pollution, whilst more definite, is in conformity with the general rules of international law.

* * *

As Professor Eagleton puts in (*Responsibility of States in International Law,* 1928, p.80): "A State owes at all times a duty to protect other States against injurious acts by individuals from within its jurisdiction." * * * But the real difficulty often arises rather when it comes to determine what, *pro subjecta materie,* is deemed to constitute an injurious act.

* * *

No case of air pollution dealt with by an international tribunal has been brought to the attention of the Tribunal nor does the Tribunal know of any such case. The nearest analogy is that of water pollution. But, here also, no decision of an international tribunal has been cited or has been found.

There are, however, as regards, both air pollution and water pollution, certain decisions of the Supreme Court of the United States which may legitimately be taken as a guide in this field of international law, for it is reasonable to follow by analogy, in international cases, precedents established by that court in dealing with controversies between States of the Union or with other controversies concerning the quasi-sovereign rights of such States, where no contrary rule prevails in international law and no reason for rejecting such precedents can be adduced from the limitations of sovereignty inherent in the Constitution of the United States.

* * *

In the matter of air pollution itself, the leading decisions are those of the Supreme Court in the State of Georgia v. Tennessee Copper Company and Ducktown Sulphur, Copper and Iron Company, Limited. Although dealing with a suit against private companies, the decisions were on questions cognate to those here at issue. Georgia stated that it had in vain sought relief from the State of Tennessee, on whose territory the smelters were located, and the court defined the nature of the suit by saying: "This is a suit by a State for an injury to it in its capacity of quasi-sovereign. In that capacity, the State has an interest independent of and behind the titles of its citizens, in all the earth and air within its domain."

On the question whether an injunction should be granted or not, the court said (206 U. S. 230):

> It (the State) has the last word as to whether its mountains shall be stripped of their forests and its inhabitants shall breathe pure air.... It is not lightly to be presumed to give up quasi-sovereign rights for pay and ... if that be its choice, it may insist that an infraction of

them shall be stopped. This court has not quite the same freedom to balance the harm that will be done by an injunction against that of which the plaintiff complains, that it would have in deciding between two subjects of a single political power. Without excluding the considerations that equity always takes into account ... it is a fair and reasonable demand on the part of a sovereign that the air over its territory should not be polluted on a great scale by sulphurous acid gas, that the forests on its mountains, be they better or worse, and whatever domestic destruction they may have suffered, should not be further destroyed or threatened by the act of persons beyond its control, that the crops and orchards on its hills should not be endangered from the same source.... Whether Georgia, by insisting upon this claim, is doing more harm than good to her own citizens, is for her to determine. The possible disaster to those outside the State must be accepted as a consequence of her standing upon her extreme rights.

Later on, however, when the court actually framed an injunction, in the case of the Ducktown Company (237 U. S. 474, 477) (an agreement on the basis of an annual compensation was reached with the most important of the two smelters, the Tennessee Copper Company), they did not go beyond a decree "adequate to diminish materially the present probability of damage to its (Georgia's) citizens."

Great progress in the control of fumes has been made by science in the last few years and this progress should be taken into account.

The Tribunal, therefore, finds that the above decisions, taken as a whole, constitute an adequate basis for its conclusions, namely, that, under the principles of international law, as well as of the law of the United States, no State has the right to use or permit the use of its territory in such a manner as to cause injury by fumes in or to the territory of another or the properties or persons therein, when the case is of serious consequence and the injury is established by clear and convincing evidence.

The decisions of the Supreme Court of the United States which are the basis of these conclusions are decisions in equity and a solution inspired by them, together with the regime hereinafter prescribed, will, in the opinion of the Tribunal, be "just to all parties concerned," as long, at least, as the present conditions in the Columbia River Valley continue to prevail.

Considering the circumstances of the case, the Tribunal holds that the Dominion of Canada is responsible in international law for the conduct of the Trail Smelter. Apart from the undertakings in the Convention, it is, therefore, the duty of the Government of the Dominion of Canada to see to it that this conduct should be in conformity with the obligation of the Dominion under international law as herein determined.

The Tribunal, therefore, answers Question No. 2 as follows: So long as the present conditions in the Columbia River Valley prevail, the Trail Smelter shall be required to refrain from causing any damage through fumes in the State of Washington; the damage herein referred to and its extent being such as would be recoverable under the decisions of the courts of the United States in suits between private individuals. The indemnity for such damage should be fixed in such manner as the Governments, acting under Article XI of the Convention, should agree upon.

The third question under Article III of the Convention is as follows: "In the light of the answer to the preceding question, what measures or régime, if any, should be adopted and maintained by the Trail Smelter?"

Answering this question in the light of the preceding one, since the Tribunal has, in its previous decision, found that damage caused by the Trail Smelter has occurred in the State of Washington since January 1, 1932, and since the Tribunal is of opinion that damage may occur in the future unless the operations of the Smelter shall be subject to some control, in order to avoid damage occurring, the Tribunal now decides that a régime or measure of control shall be applied to the operations of the Smelter and shall remain in full force unless and until modified * * *.

NOTES AND QUESTIONS

1. *Sources of law.* Why did the Tribunal look to U.S. law as precedent for settling this international dispute? How might this have affected the outcome of the case? Is this fair to Canada?

2. *State responsibility.* The Tribunal's declaration that "Canada is responsible in international law for the conduct of the Trail Smelter," while initially surprising, is consistent with the well-established principle of state responsibility, which provides that states are responsible for breaches of their obligations under international law. Is this fair to the state? To what extent should a state be liable for harm caused by multinational corporations or other private actors?

3. *The duty not to harm other states.* The Tribunal quoted Professor Eagleton for the premise that "[a] state owes at all times a duty to protect other states against injurious acts by individuals from within its jurisdiction." The significance of *Trail Smelter* lies in its application of this principle to transboundary pollution. However, in a portion of the opinion not included in the excerpt, the Tribunal notes the "relativity of the rule," as demonstrated by a case before the Federal Court of Switzerland. That court enjoined the use of a shooting range in the Canton of Argovia because it endangered the inhabitants of the neighboring Canton of Soleure. After certain improvements were made to the shooting range, the court granted Argovia's request to permit renewed use of the establishment: "The demand of the Government of Soleure that all endangerment be absolutely abolished apparently goes too far.... [N]o more precautions may be demanded for shooting ranges near the boundaries of two Cantons than are required for shooting ranges in the interior of a Canton." What does the outcome of this dispute suggest about the "relativity of the rule"?

4. *Tort litigation as an alternative to international arbitration.* Public international arbitration proceedings to address transboundary air pollution, such as *Trail Smelter*, are relatively uncommon. Did the United States (or its citizens whose property was damaged by smelter emissions) have alternative means of collecting damages or of enjoining the smelter from polluting further? What difficulties might plaintiffs in a tort action face? A common law rule in effect at the time required that complaints relating to property be brought in the jurisdiction where that property was located. However, personal jurisdiction over the smelter was not available in Washington courts at the time because the smelter did not have a physical presence in the state. See Pennoyer v. Neff, 95 U.S. 714 (1877). Given the expansion of constitutional limits on personal jurisdiction in the United States after *International Shoe Co. v. Washington*, 326 U.S. 310, 316 (1945), however, the analysis would likely be different today. Note that there is no international judicial mechanism analogous to domestic courts for private citizens to raise transboundary pollution problems. The International Court of Justice (also known as the World Court) resolves disputes between states, not private parties, and may do so only if the states involved in a dispute consent to the court's jurisdiction.

5. *Trail Smelter redux.* The smelter at issue in *Trail Smelter* continues to cause pollution problems today. In a recent decision, the Ninth Circuit held that the Canadian smelter owner was a potentially responsible party under CERCLA, where the waste it initially discharged into the Canadian portion of the Columbia River ultimately wound up in the United States' section of the river. Pakootas v. Teck Cominco Metals Ltd., 452 F.3d 1066 (9th Cir. 2006).

In addition to the "hard law" discussed above, international law also relies heavily on nonbinding norms referred to as "soft law." Sources of soft law include international resolutions and declarations, hortatory language of treaties, and guidelines and recommendations by international organizations. Although such declarations lack binding legal force, the care and attention surrounding their negotiation and approval suggest that they substantially influence state conduct. Repetition plays an important role in the process of making soft law. The reiteration of a principle, and cross-references to prior pronouncements, help establish its normative force, while furthering international understanding of what the principle may require. Soft law often represents a "half-way stage[] in the law-making process," a good-faith pledge by states to support and adhere to a norm, without a binding commitment. Patricia Birnie & Alan Boyle, International Law & the Environment 25 (2d ed. 2002). Soft law may eventually become hard law as soft law principles are incorporated into treaty commitments or as soft law norms become the basis of general state practice and give rise to a sense of legal obligation.

A leading example of a soft law instrument is the Rio Declaration on Environment and Development, a statement of environmental principles approved at the 1992 Earth Summit held in Rio de Janeiro. As you read the following excerpts from the declaration, consider how such soft law instruments might affect the behavior of nation-states, corporations, and individuals.

Rio Declaration on Environment and Development

(1992).

The United Nations Conference on Environment and Development,

Having met at Rio de Janeiro from 3 to 14 June 1992,

Reaffirming the Declaration of the United Nations Conference on the Human Environment, adopted at Stockholm on 16 June 1972, and seeking to build upon it,

With the goal of establishing a new and equitable global partnership through the creation of new levels of cooperation among States, key sectors of societies and people,

Working towards international agreements which respect the interests of all and protect the integrity of the global environmental and developmental system,

Recognizing the integral and interdependent nature of the Earth, our home,

Proclaims that:

Principle 1

Human beings are at the centre of concerns for sustainable development. They are entitled to a healthy and productive life in harmony with nature.

Principle 2

States have, in accordance with the Charter of the United Nations and the principles of international law, the sovereign right to exploit their own resources pursuant to their own environmental and developmental policies, and the responsibility to ensure that activities within their jurisdiction or control do not cause damage to the environment of other States or of areas beyond the limits of national jurisdiction.

Principle 3

The right to development must be fulfilled so as to equitably meet developmental and environmental needs of present and future generations.

Principle 4

In order to achieve sustainable development, environmental protection shall constitute an integral part of the development process and cannot be considered in isolation from it.

Principle 5

All States and all people shall cooperate in the essential task of eradicating poverty as an indispensable requirement for sustainable development, in order to decrease the disparities in standards of living and better meet the needs of the majority of the people of the world.

Principle 6

The special situation and needs of developing countries, particularly the least developed and those most environmentally vulnerable, shall be given special priority. International actions in the field of environment and development should also address the interests and needs of all countries.

Principle 7

States shall cooperate in a spirit of global partnership to conserve, protect and restore the health and integrity of the Earth's ecosystem. In view of the different contributions to global environmental degradation, States have common but differentiated responsibilities. The developed countries acknowledge the responsibility that they bear in the international pursuit to sustainable development in view of the pressures their societies place on the global environment and of the technologies and financial resources they command.

Principle 8

To achieve sustainable development and a higher quality of life for all people, States should reduce and eliminate unsustainable patterns of production and consumption and promote appropriate demographic policies.

Principle 9

States should cooperate to strengthen endogenous capacity-building for sustainable development by improving scientific understanding through exchanges of scientific and technological knowledge, and by enhancing the development, adaptation, diffusion and transfer of technologies, including new and innovative technologies.

Principle 10

Environmental issues are best handled with participation of all concerned citizens, at the relevant level. At the national level, each individual shall have appropriate access to information concerning the environment that is held by public authorities, including information on hazardous materials and activities in their communities, and the opportunity to participate in decision-making processes. States shall facilitate and encourage public awareness and participation by making information widely available. Effective access to judicial and administrative proceedings, including redress and remedy, shall be provided.

Principle 11

States shall enact effective environmental legislation. Environmental standards, management objectives and priorities should reflect the environmental and development context to which they apply. Standards applied by some countries may be inappropriate and of unwarranted economic and social cost to other countries, in particular developing countries.

Principle 12

States should cooperate to promote a supportive and open international economic system that would lead to economic growth and sustainable development in all countries, to better address the problems of environmental degradation. Trade policy measures for environmental purposes should not constitute a means of arbitrary or unjustifiable discrimination or a disguised restriction on international trade.

Unilateral actions to deal with environmental challenges outside the jurisdiction of the importing country should be avoided. Environmental measures addressing transboundary or global environmental problems should, as far as possible, be based on an international consensus.

Principle 13

States shall develop national law regarding liability and compensation for the victims of pollution and other environmental damage. States shall also cooperate in an expeditious and more determined manner to develop further international law regarding liability and compensation for adverse effects of environmental damage caused by activities within their jurisdiction or control to areas beyond their jurisdiction.

Principle 14

States should effectively cooperate to discourage or prevent the relocation and transfer to other States of any activities and substances that cause severe environmental degradation or are found to be harmful to human health.

Principle 15

In order to protect the environment, the precautionary approach shall be widely applied by States according to their capabilities. Where there are threats of serious or irreversible damage, lack of full scientific certainty shall not be used as a reason for postponing cost-effective measures to prevent environmental degradation.

Principle 16

National authorities should endeavour to promote the internalization of environmental costs and the use of economic instruments, taking into account the approach that the polluter should, in principle, bear the cost of pollution, with due regard to the public interest and without distorting international trade and investment.

Principle 17

Environmental impact assessment, as a national instrument, shall be undertaken for proposed activities that are likely to have a significant adverse impact on the environment and are subject to a decision of a competent national authority.

Principle 18

States shall immediately notify other States of any natural disasters or other emergencies that are likely to produce sudden harmful effects on the environment of those States. Every effort shall be made by the international community to help States so afflicted.

Principle 19

States shall provide prior and timely notification and relevant information to potentially affected States on activities that may have a significant adverse transboundary environmental effect and shall consult with those States at an early stage and in good faith.

* * *

NOTES AND QUESTIONS

1. *The legacy of Trail Smelter.* Is the central principle of the *Trail Smelter* decision, that "no State has the right to use or permit the use of its territory in such a manner as to cause injury by fumes in or to the territory of another or the properties or persons therein," reflected in any of the Rio Declaration's principles? How does the Rio Declaration expand on the teaching of *Trail Smelter*?

2. *Sustainable development.* The concept of sustainable development pervades the Rio Declaration and has become a common theme in international environmental discussions. What exactly is sustainable development? One of the leading articulations of the concept comes from *Our Common Future* (1987), also known as the Brundtland Report: "Sustainable development is development that meets the needs of the present without compromising the ability of future generations to meet their own needs." What is the Rio Declaration's understanding of sustainable development? Does sustainable development provide a meaningful criterion for formulating responses to specific environmental problems?

3. *The role of soft law.* What does the Rio Declaration accomplish? As a nonbinding instrument, what is its potential value in addressing international environmental problems? What are some possible advantages of a soft law approach over a hard law approach? Why has soft law played a prominent role in international law?

4. *The North–South divide.* With 178 nations in attendance, the 1992 Earth Summit presented an opportunity for establishing broad consensus on the need for global cooperation on sustainable development, climate change, and other issues. Discussions at the conference nevertheless were dominated by the divide between industrialized countries (commonly referred to as the North) and developing countries (the South). Industrialized countries were increasingly concerned about climate change, biodiversity conservation, and other environmental issues, and they sought the cooperation of developing countries in these matters. Developing countries, in contrast, focused on the need for development to grow their way out of poverty and feared that environmental protection would be used by the North as a means of suppressing their interests. Reexamine the Rio Declaration in light of these tensions and consider whether the tensions were resolved.

SECTION 2.   GLOBAL CHALLENGES

A.   OZONE DEPLETION

The regulatory regime established in response to the depletion of the ozone layer is one of international environmental law's most significant achievements. The Montreal Protocol and its subsequent revisions have eliminated almost all production of ozone-depleting substances and contain commitments to phase out remaining production and consumption of these substances by the year 2040. Such a comprehensive and widely accepted agreement was hardly preordained, given the challenges posed by ozone depletion. Ozone depletion posed a truly global threat to humans and the environment, requiring global participation for it to be addressed effectively. Yet in the mid–1980s, when the international community turned its attention to the issues, scientific uncertainty surrounded critical questions such as how much ozone had already been lost and how much ozone would be destroyed if no action were taken. In addition, ozone-depleting substances were widely used, representing billions of dollars in economic value and hundreds of thousands of jobs. As Richard Benedick, the chief negotiator for the United States, commented, "Knowledgeable observers had long believed that this particular agreement would be impossible to achieve because the issues were so complex and arcane and the initial positions of the negotiating parties so widely divergent." Richard Benedick, Ozone Diplomacy: New Directions in Safeguarding the Planet 1 (1998).

The relative success of the Montreal Protocol regime has led various commentators to hail the process of developing the regime as a role model for international cooperation. As you read the following account of ozone depletion and the accompanying international response, consider what lessons might be applicable to other global environmental challenges such as climate change.

John K. Setear, Ozone, Iteration, and International Law

40 Va. J. Int'l L. 193, 195–216 (1999).

The "ozone layer" is a colloquial expression for a portion of the atmosphere several miles above the surface of the earth and relatively rich in ozone, a molecule consisting of three atoms of oxygen. Ozone reflects ultra-violet radiation emitted by the sun. Ultra-violet radiation that strikes the earth can cause skin cancer and cataracts in humans, and, of indirect concern to humans, a wide variety of potentially harmful mutations in plants and animals. * * *

Certain substances containing atoms of chlorine or bromine serve as catalysts for chemical reactions in the atmosphere that lead to the destruction of stratospheric ozone. These ozone-depleting substances are man-made. They serve a wide variety of functions as (among other things) refrigerants, fire retardants and propellants. They are capable of being transported from the surface of the earth into the stratosphere by naturally occurring air currents. Once in the stratosphere, these molecules typically remain[] in the stratosphere to catalyze the destruction of ozone molecules for many years or even many decades.

In terms of international cooperation, the anthropogenic response to this anthropogenic problem has been the enactment of the series of international legal agreements that constitute the ozone-treaty regime.

The first such enactment was the Vienna Convention for the Protection of the Ozone Layer (the "Convention"), signed in 1985 and entered into force in late 1988. The Convention set forth some vague promises of international cooperation and some concrete procedural rules to govern future enactments.

The second enactment in the ozone-treaty regime was the Montreal Protocol on Substances that Deplete the Ozone Layer ("Original Protocol" or "Montreal Protocol"), signed in 1987 and entered into force in early 1989. This treaty set forth some concrete substantive obligations based on a core regulatory approach. * * * [The Montreal Protocol has since been followed by a number of revisions that "have broadened and deepened the core regulatory approach" of the Protocol.]

The core regulatory approach of the ozone-treaty regime establishes yearly per-nation quotas for the consumption or production of ozone-depleting substances. The per-nation quotas are set, for each "group" of chemicals of similar molecular composition, as a percentage of a given nation's consumption or production of that group compared to that nation's consumption or production in a baseline year. I refer to this percentage as the "Allowable Percentage." The Allowable Percentage may vary from group to group and from year to year, but the Allowable Percentage for a given group in a given year is the same for every nation. The baseline year remains constant across agreements for any given group of ozone-depleting substances. By applying a factor to each chemical's consumption or production that varies proportionally with the ozone-depleting potential ("ODP") of that chemical (as determined by the best scientific evidence), the relevant formulae in both the year of the quota and the baseline year account for the possibility that different chemicals within a group might differentially harm the ozone layer.

* * *

The set of treaties governing the production and consumption of ozone-depleting substances is generally considered to have been an extremely successful response to a problem of great scientific and political complexity. Although stratospheric diffusion ensures that the benefits of a thicker ozone layer will be a pure public good, and although anthropogenic ozone-depleting substances have long played a variety of important and low-cost roles in developed economies, dozens of developed nations have agreed to dramatic reductions in the use of such substances and well over one hundred developing nations have agreed to a more lenient schedule of reductions. In addition, in an unprecedented example of North–South redistribution, the developed nations as a group have agreed to pay 100% of the compliance costs incurred by their poorer counterparts.

Furthermore, the implementation of the relevant treaties has been nearly as successful as the formulation of the rules themselves. First, the formal assent of nations to the obligations of the treaties has been widespread, especially among the developed nations that currently produce the lion's share of the regulated substances. Second, disputes over interpretation of the treaties have been essentially non-existent. Third, and perhaps most importantly, compliance with both the letter and the spirit of the treaties appears to have been high. In terms of both promise and performance, therefore, the treaties on ozone-depleting substances appear to be a successful example of international cooperation.

Analysts offer a variety of explanations for the success of these treaties. Some argue that an early U.S. statutory ban on certain ozone-depleting substances in the U.S. marketplace pushed U.S. businesses to seek a global ban as a way to prevent foreign producers of ozone-depleting substances from gaining a competitive advantage. In this view, the U.S. chemical companies and the resulting pressure they placed on the U.S. government were responsible for allowing or compelling the U.S. government to push (successfully) for global reductions. Those who adopt a collective-action perspective might emphasize that, in an important sense, relatively few actors were truly relevant: only a handful of companies in a handful of countries produced ozone-depleting substances when international negotiations on the topic began. Those who emphasize the difficulties of redistributing wealth through bargaining might note that these companies were able to develop relatively low-cost alternatives as the international legal regulation of ozone unfolded. Still other analysts emphasize the role of an "epistemic community"—a transnational collection of scientists and policy-makers who, in the case of ozone, rapidly came to share a common perception of the causes of and a proper solution to the problem. For yet another school of thought, a straightforward calculation of benefits and risks is a sufficient explanation (at least in providing an account for the differential enthusiasm for the endeavor among different nations).

* * *

From the iterative perspective, * * * the success of the ozone treaties is the result of a series of policy choices that promote temporally well-defined iterations with clear mechanisms for signaling formal consent, and with clear rules for determining actual compliance by nation-states seeking a cooperative solution to a difficult international political problem.

The iterative perspective is distinctive in three ways from the typical explanations advanced to account for the success of the ozone treaties. The iterative perspective is a dynamic explanation of international cooperation with respect to ozone-depleting substances, in that it examines interactions through time and postulates increasing cooperation over time. It is a legalistic explanation of ozone-oriented international cooperation, in that it examines the general and specifically tailored rules of international law as factors in international politics. It is a textually oriented explanation of ozone-oriented cooperation, in that it takes seriously and examines closely the particular words set forth in the international legal enactments, which specifically address the problem of ozone depletion. In its focus on the text of the ozone treaties as an explanation for their success, the article takes seriously the notion that nations might take seriously their international legal obligations—although the article does not ignore the issue of actual compliance with the rules specified in the text of the ozone treaties.

* * *

Scholars of international law have noted the development in the late twentieth century of what one might call a "meta-treaty:" the "convention-protocol" approach to a particular subject matter of international cooperation. The convention-protocol approach involves at least two separate enactments, one "convention" and one or more "protocols." The convention sets forth vague substantive provisions that serve mainly to acknowledge that the subject of the treaty is a matter worthy of serious further consideration. The convention includes procedural provisions that, in contrast to its substantive terms, are quite specific. The convention contemplates that one or more subsequent protocols will be created and administered largely under the procedures set forth in the convention. The protocols provide the substantive detail of the treaty regime.

* * *

From an iterative perspective, the convention-protocol approach is sensible. Full and formal consent to a convention serves as a nation-state's cooperative response to an initial formalized interaction regarding a particular subject matter. The convention at least contemplates future iterations. Accordingly, it sets forth the procedural rules to be used in determining the substantive standards against which cooperation will be measured in future iterations, if any. To some extent, enthusiasm for the convention-protocol approach depends upon phenomena (such as the acquisition over time of scientific knowledge) that straightforward descriptions of the iterated Prisoner's Dilemma do not incorporate. Nonetheless, the general flavor of the convention-protocol approach contains more than a dash of the iterative perspective.

Proponents of the iterative perspective, however, would do well to note that a convention typically contains no more than a contingent specification of future iterations even as a matter of international law. A convention sets forth rules that will govern future protocols if the parties agree upon such protocols; a convention does not typically involve a promise that such interactions will occur. Nonetheless, from an iterative perspective, the convention-protocol approach is, as Maurice Chevalier said about old age, better than the alternative. In the international legal context, of course, the alternative is not death but rather the traditional treaty, which does not explicitly even contemplate the future construction of separate and more detailed agreements.

The Convention and the Original Protocol, true to their names, together embody a convention-protocol approach to ozone depletion. The Convention's chief substantive requirement is appropriately, perhaps even excessively, cautious about imposing particular duties upon its adherents: the parties pledge that, "in accordance with the means at their disposal and their capabilities," they will "adopt appropriate legislative or administrative measures [to] reduce or prevent human activities ... should it be found that these activities have or are likely to have adverse effects resulting from modification or likely modification of the ozone layer." The Convention also includes some promises of similar generality regarding scientific cooperation among the parties.

The drafters of the Convention expressly recognized the possibility of future protocols: Article 8 notes that the parties may "adopt protocols pursuant to" the above-described general provisions. Consistent with the formative role of a convention, the Convention also sets forth a variety of concrete procedural rules—applicable to both itself and future protocols—that govern dispute resolution, amendments, voting rights, and purely administrative aspects of the treaty such as the provision of notice for future meetings and the specification of a depositary for ratifications.

NOTES AND QUESTIONS

1. *International cooperation on ozone.* What factors led to the development of an international consensus on responding to ozone depletion and to the successful negotiation of a treaty regime?

2. *The iterative approach.* Why, or under what circumstances, might an iterative approach, such as that followed in negotiating first the Vienna Convention and then the Montreal Protocol, be more successful than traditional treaty negotiation? Are there certain characteristics of global environmental problems that lend themselves to an iterative approach?

3. *Methyl bromide.* Methyl bromide, a fumigant widely used in growing strawberries, tomatoes, and other crops, is an ozone-depleting substance estimated to be responsible for seven percent of ozone layer destruction. Although the chemical was not listed in the Montreal Protocol itself, subsequent adjustments to the Protocol provided for its phase-out in developed countries by 2005 and in developing countries by 2015. Parties can seek exemptions for the use of methyl bromide, however, for "critical" uses—where a party shows that "the lack of availability of methyl bromide for that use would result in a significant market disruption" and that "[t]here are no technically and economically feasible alternatives." Report of the Ninth Meeting of the Parties to the Montreal Protocol on Substances that Deplete the Ozone Layer, UN Doc. UNEP/OzL.Pro.9/12, Decision IX/6 (1997). The United States and other parties have continually sought and obtained exemptions to use methyl bromide, although in decreasing amounts. *See, e.g.*, EPA, Protection of Stratospheric Ozone: The 2011 Critical Use Exemption From the Phaseout of Methyl Bromide, 76 Fed. Reg. 23,769 (2011) (proposing to allocate consumption of two million kilograms of methyl bromide under critical use exemption for 2011).

B. GLOBAL CLIMATE CHANGE

As explained in the class discussion problem in Chapter 1, rising concentrations of greenhouse gases in the atmosphere are contributing to global climate change. Tackling climate change is a complicated matter technically, economically, and politically. For one, a wide variety of human activities—including fossil fuel combustion, deforestation, cattle and pork production, and cement manufacturing—generates greenhouse gas emissions. Because many of these activities play a critical role in the world economy and in daily life, curbing greenhouse gas emissions will require technological innovation, lifestyle changes, and economic restructuring. For another, the problem is truly global in that all nations generate greenhouse gases, albeit at varying rates and in varying amounts. China, the world's leading generator of greenhouse gases by total volume, has a per capita emission rate approximately one-quarter of that of the United States, the second greatest generator of greenhouse gases. Although climate change will affect all nations, effects will vary by region, giving some countries more of a stake in addressing the problem. Possible nonlinear effects, such as the melting of the Greenland ice shelf, and the uncertainty regarding specific effects on individual countries add to the potential for disagreement on how to respond.

International concern regarding climate change prompted the World Meteorological Organization and the United Nations Environment Programme to establish the Intergovernmental Panel on Climate Change (IPCC) in 1988. The IPCC's mission is to assess the scientific, technical, and socio-economic information relevant to understanding the risk of human-induced climate change, its potential impacts, and options for adaptation and mitigation. The IPCC has periodically issued reports on climate change, and its role in forging scientific consensus and promoting awareness of the problem led to it being awarded the 2007 Nobel Peace Prize with former Vice President Al Gore. The IPCC's first reports, issued in 1990, as well as international conferences on the climate change problem, led to the establishment of an ad hoc committee charged with producing an agreement to be signed at the 1992 Earth Summit in Rio de Janeiro. In talks preceding the Earth Summit, it became apparent that the United States held a different position from other industrialized nations in its reluctance to make binding commitments to address the problem. Rather than supporting targets and timetables for reducing emissions, the

United States advocated a "no regrets" policy that would promote only those actions that could be justified as economically or environmentally beneficial aside from any climate change benefits. See Donald Goldberg, As the World Burns: Negotiating the Framework Convention on Climate Change, 6 Geo. Int'l Envtl. L. Rev. 239, 245–52 (1993); Daniel Bodansky, The United Nations Framework Convention on Climate Change: A Commentary, 18 Yale J. Int'l L. 451, 478–79 (1993). Although the differences between the United States and other industrialized nations did not block agreement at Rio, they influenced the nature of the agreement as well as subsequent developments.

The approach taken towards negotiating an international response to climate change followed the framework-protocol model used to address depletion of the ozone layer. The Framework Convention on Climate Change, which was presented for signature at the Rio Summit, declares an "ultimate objective" of "stabiliz[ing] ... greenhouse gas concentrations in the atmosphere at a level that would prevent dangerous anthropogenic interference with the climate system." However, largely because of U.S. resistance, the Framework Convention does not contain explicit emission limits or targets, nor does it contain any timetables for stabilizing emissions. The Convention entered into force on March 21, 1994, and almost all nations—195 countries, as of 2011—have ratified it.

The Framework Convention, reproduced in part below, laid the foundation for the Kyoto Protocol and other future measures to address climate change. The Framework Convention defines three overlapping categories of signatories subject to differing obligations: all Parties, all industrialized countries ("Annex I" Parties), and industrialized countries other than former Soviet bloc countries undergoing economic transition ("Annex II" Parties).

United Nations Framework Convention on Climate Change

(1992).

The Parties to this Convention,

Acknowledging that change in the Earth's climate and its adverse effects are a common concern of humankind,

Concerned that human activities have been substantially increasing the atmospheric concentrations of greenhouse gases, that these increases enhance the natural greenhouse effect, and that this will result on average in an additional warming of the Earth's surface and atmosphere and may adversely affect natural ecosystems and humankind,

Noting that the largest share of historical and current global emissions of greenhouse gases has originated in developed countries, that per capita emissions in developing countries are still relatively low and that the share of global emissions originating in developing countries will grow to meet their social and development needs, * * *

Noting that there are many uncertainties in predictions of climate change, particularly with regard to the timing, magnitude and regional patterns thereof, * * *

Have agreed as follows: * * *

Article 2   Objective

The ultimate objective of this Convention and any related legal instruments that the Conference of the Parties may adopt is to achieve, in accordance with the relevant provisions of the Convention, stabilization of greenhouse gas concentrations in the atmosphere at a level that would prevent dangerous anthropogenic interference with the climate system. Such a level should be achieved within a time-frame sufficient to allow ecosystems to adapt naturally to climate change, to ensure that food production is not threatened and to enable economic development to proceed in a sustainable manner.

Article 3   Principles

In their actions to achieve the objective of the Convention and to implement its provisions, the Parties shall be guided, inter alia, by the following:

1.   The Parties should protect the climate system for the benefit of present and future generations of humankind, on the basis of equity and in accordance with their common but differentiated responsibilities and respective capabilities. Accordingly, the developed country Parties should take the lead in combating climate change and the adverse effects thereof.

2.   The specific needs and special circumstances of developing country Parties, especially those that are particularly vulnerable to the adverse effects of climate change, and of those Parties, especially developing country Parties, that would have to bear a disproportionate or abnormal burden under the Convention, should be given full consideration.

3.   The Parties should take precautionary measures to anticipate, prevent or minimize the causes of climate change and mitigate its adverse effects. Where there are threats of serious or irreversible damage, lack of full scientific certainty should not be used as a reason for postponing such measures, taking into account that policies and measures to deal with climate change should be cost-effective so as to ensure global benefits at the lowest possible cost. To achieve this, such policies and measures should take into account different socio-economic contexts, be comprehensive, cover all relevant sources, sinks and reservoirs of greenhouse gases and adaptation, and comprise all economic sectors. * * *

Article 4   Commitments

1.   All Parties, taking into account their common but differentiated responsibilities and their specific national and regional development priorities, objectives and circumstances, shall:

(a) Develop, periodically update, publish and make available to the Conference of the Parties, in accordance with Article 12, national inventories of anthropogenic emissions by sources and removals by sinks of all greenhouse gases not controlled by the Montreal Protocol, using comparable methodologies to be agreed upon by the Conference of the Parties;

(b) Formulate, implement, publish and regularly update national and, where appropriate, regional programmes containing measures to mitigate climate change by addressing anthropogenic emissions by sources and removals by sinks of all greenhouse gases not controlled by the Montreal Protocol, and measures to facilitate adequate adaptation to climate change;

(c) Promote and cooperate in the development, application and diffusion, including transfer, of technologies, practices and processes that control, reduce or prevent anthropogenic emissions of greenhouse gases not controlled by the Montreal Protocol in all relevant sectors, including the energy, transport, industry, agriculture, forestry and waste management sectors;

(d) Promote sustainable management, and promote and cooperate in the conservation and enhancement, as appropriate, of sinks and reservoirs of all greenhouse gases not controlled by the Montreal Protocol, including biomass, forests and oceans as well as other terrestrial, coastal and marine ecosystems;

(e) Cooperate in preparing for adaptation to the impacts of climate change; develop and elaborate appropriate and integrated plans for coastal zone management, water resources and agriculture, and for the protection and rehabilitation of areas, particularly in Africa, affected by drought and desertification, as well as floods;

* * *

(g) Promote and cooperate in scientific, technological, technical, socio-economic and other research, systematic observation and development of data archives related to the climate system and intended to further the understanding and to reduce or eliminate the remaining uncertainties regarding the causes, effects, magnitude and timing of climate change and the economic and social consequences of various response strategies;

* * *

(j) Communicate to the Conference of the Parties information related to implementation, in accordance with Article 12.

2.   The developed country Parties and other Parties included in annex I commit themselves specifically as provided for in the following:

(a) Each of these Parties shall adopt national policies and take corresponding measures on the mitigation of climate change, by limiting its anthropogenic emissions of greenhouse gases and protecting and enhancing its greenhouse gas sinks and reservoirs. These policies and measures will demonstrate that developed countries are taking the lead in modifying longer-term trends in anthropogenic emissions consistent with the objective of the Convention, recognizing that the return by the end of the present decade to earlier levels of anthropogenic emissions of carbon dioxide and other greenhouse gases not controlled by the Montreal Protocol would contribute to such modification, and taking into account the differences in these Parties' starting points and approaches, economic structures and resource bases, the need to maintain strong and sustainable economic growth, available technologies and other individual circumstances, as well as the need for equitable and appropriate contributions by each of these Parties to the global effort regarding that objective. These Parties may implement such policies and measures jointly with other Parties and may assist other Parties in contributing to the achievement of the objective of the Convention and, in particular, that of this subparagraph;

(b) In order to promote progress to this end, each of these Parties shall communicate, within six months of the entry into force of the Convention for it and periodically thereafter, and in accordance with Article 12, detailed information on its policies and measures referred to in subparagraph (a) above, as well as on its resulting projected anthropogenic emissions by sources and removals by sinks of greenhouse gases not controlled by the Montreal Protocol for the period referred to in subparagraph (a), with the aim of returning individually or jointly to their 1990 levels these anthropogenic emissions of carbon dioxide and other greenhouse gases not controlled by the Montreal Protocol. This information will be reviewed by the Conference of the Parties, at its first session and periodically thereafter, in accordance with Article 7;

* * *

3. The developed country Parties and other developed Parties included in Annex II shall provide new and additional financial resources to meet the agreed full costs incurred by developing country Parties in complying with their obligations under Article 12, paragraph 1. They shall also provide such financial resources, including for the transfer of technology, needed by the developing country Parties to meet the agreed full incremental costs of implementing measures that are covered by paragraph 1 of this Article and that are agreed between a developing country Party and the international entity or entities referred to in Article 11, in accordance with that Article. The implementation of these commitments shall take into account the need for adequacy and predictability in the flow of funds and the importance of appropriate burden sharing among the developed country Parties.

* * *

7. The extent to which developing country Parties will effectively implement their commitments under the Convention will depend on the effective implementation by developed country Parties of their commitments under the Convention related to financial resources and transfer of technology and will take fully into account that economic and social

development and poverty eradication are the first and overriding priorities of the developing country Parties.

* * *

Article 7 Conference of the Parties

1.   A Conference of the Parties is hereby established.

2.   The Conference of the Parties, as the supreme body of this Convention, shall keep under regular review the implementation of the Convention and any related legal instruments that the Conference of the Parties may adopt, and shall make, within its mandate, the decisions necessary to promote the effective implementation of the Convention. To this end, it shall:

(a) Periodically examine the obligations of the Parties and the institutional arrangements under the Convention, in the light of the objective of the Convention, the experience gained in its implementation and the evolution of scientific and technological knowledge;

(b) Promote and facilitate the exchange of information on measures adopted by the Parties to address climate change and its effects, taking into account the differing circumstances, responsibilities and capabilities of the Parties and their respective commitments under the Convention;

(c) Facilitate, at the request of two or more Parties, the coordination of measures adopted by them to address climate change and its effects, taking into account the differing circumstances, responsibilities and capabilities of the Parties and their respective commitments under the Convention;

(d) Promote and guide, in accordance with the objective and provisions of the Convention, the development and periodic refinement of comparable methodologies, to be agreed on by the Conference of the Parties, inter alia, for preparing inventories of greenhouse gas emissions by sources and removals by sinks, and for evaluating the effectiveness of measures to limit the emissions and enhance the removals of these gases;

(e) Assess, on the basis of all information made available to it in accordance with the provisions of the Convention, the implementation of the Convention by the Parties, the overall effects of the measures taken pursuant to the Convention, in particular environmental, economic and social effects as well as their cumulative impacts and the extent to which progress towards the objective of the Convention is being achieved;

* * *

Article 9 Subsidiary Body for Scientific and Technological Advice

1.   A subsidiary body for scientific and technological advice is hereby established to provide the Conference of the Parties and, as appropriate, its other subsidiary bodies with timely information and advice on scientific and technological matters relating to the Convention. This body shall be open to participation by all Parties and shall be multidisciplinary. It shall comprise government representatives competent in the relevant field of expertise. It shall report regularly to the Conference of the Parties on all aspects of its work.

2.   Under the guidance of the Conference of the Parties, and drawing upon existing competent international bodies, this body shall:

(a) Provide assessments of the state of scientific knowledge relating to climate change and its effects;

(b) Prepare scientific assessments on the effects of measures taken in the implementation of the Convention;

(c) Identify innovative, efficient and state-of-the-art technologies and know-how and advise on the ways and means of promoting development and/or transferring such technologies;

(d) Provide advice on scientific programmes, international cooperation in research and development related to climate change, as well as on ways and means of supporting endogenous capacity-building in developing countries; and

(e) Respond to scientific, technological and methodological questions that the Conference of the Parties and its subsidiary bodies may put to the body.

* * *

NOTES AND QUESTIONS

1. *Role of the Framework Convention.* As explained above, the Framework Convention did not establish any binding commitments regarding specific greenhouse gas emission levels. What, then, did the Framework Convention accomplish? What specific commitments exist in the Framework Convention, and how do they lay the foundation for further efforts to deal with climate change? How do the commitments of Annex II Parties differ from those of Annex I Parties, and from those of developing country Parties?

2. *Objective of the Convention.* Article 2 declares that "the ultimate objective" of the Convention "is to achieve, in accordance with the relevant provisions of the Convention, stabilization of greenhouse gas concentrations in the atmosphere at a level that would prevent dangerous anthropogenic interference with the climate system." How might the Conference of the Parties determine whether this objective is achieved? What might be advantages and disadvantages of defining the Convention's objective in this manner?

3. *The precautionary principle.* Consider the Framework Convention's articulation of the precautionary principle in Article 3.3: "Where there are threats of serious or irreversible damage, lack of full scientific certainty should not be used as a reason for postponing such measures, taking into account that policies and measures to deal with climate change should be cost-effective so as to ensure global benefits at the lowest possible cost." Compare this account of the precautionary principle with Judge Wright's discussion in *Ethyl Corp.*, excerpted in Chapter 7. Does the precautionary principle provide a useful basis for justifying or deciding upon a regulatory response? Given the current state of knowledge regarding anthropogenic climate change, does the adoption of policy measures to reduce greenhouse gas emissions necessarily rely on the precautionary principle? See Robert V. Percival, Who's Afraid of the Precautionary Principle?, 23 Pace Envtl. L. Rev. 21 (2005–06).

———————

Article 7 of the Framework Convention established a "Conference of the Parties," which is to conduct regular reviews of the Convention's implementation, including a review at its first session of the adequacy of industrialized countries' commitments. At this first meeting, held in Berlin, Germany, countries agreed to establish a process for negotiating binding commitments by industrialized countries to quantified targets and timetables. The result of this process, the Kyoto Protocol to the Framework Convention, emerged in December 1997 after two years of negotiations. The Protocol contains commitments by industrialized nations (Annex 1 Parties to the Framework Convention) collectively to reduce their greenhouse gas emissions in the period from 2008 to 2012 by five percent relative to 1990 levels, with varying individual country commitments. These commitments followed intensive negotiations and reflect a compromise between the position of the European Union, which advocated a 15 percent emissions reduction from 1990 levels by industrialized nations, and the position of the United States, which favored stabilization of emissions at 1990 levels by industrialized nations as well as a commitment by developing nations to constrain emissions in the future.

Whether the Protocol would ever enter into force was thrown in doubt, however, once it became clear that the United States would not ratify the agreement. By its terms, the Protocol would enter into force only if ratified by industrialized countries accounting for at least 55 percent of global carbon dioxide emissions. With the United States accounting for approximately one-fourth of global emissions, Russia's ratification of the Protocol was critical. For Russia, ratification was motivated largely by self-interest: economic contraction after the dissolution of the Soviet Union left its emission levels so low that it expected to have spare emissions credits to trade under Kyoto. Ultimately, the Protocol entered into force on February 16, 2005 and was ratified by a total of 193 nations. Notable sources of greenhouse gas emissions not subject to emission limits include the United States, which never ratified the Protocol, and China and India, which as developing country parties to the Protocol are not subject to binding emissions limits.

Kyoto Protocol to the United Nations Framework Convention on Climate Change

(1997).

Article 2

1. Each Party included in Annex I, in achieving its quantified emission limitation and reduction commitments under Article 3, in order to promote sustainable development, shall:

(a) Implement and/or further elaborate policies and measures in accordance with its national circumstances, such as:

(i) Enhancement of energy efficiency in relevant sectors of the national economy;

(ii) Protection and enhancement of sinks and reservoirs of greenhouse gases not controlled by the Montreal Protocol, taking into account its commitments under relevant international environmental agreements; promotion of sustainable forest management practices, afforestation and reforestation;

(iii) Promotion of sustainable forms of agriculture in light of climate change considerations;

(iv) Research on, and promotion, development and increased use of, new and renewable forms of energy, of carbon dioxide sequestration technologies and of advanced and innovative environmentally sound technologies;

(v) Progressive reduction or phasing out of market imperfections, fiscal incentives, tax and duty exemptions and subsidies in all greenhouse gas emitting sectors that run counter to the objective of the Convention and application of market instruments;

(vi) Encouragement of appropriate reforms in relevant sectors aimed at promoting policies and measures which limit or reduce emissions of greenhouse gases not controlled by the Montreal Protocol;

(vii) Measures to limit and/or reduce emissions of greenhouse gases not controlled by the Montreal Protocol in the transport sector;

* * *

Article 3

1.   The Parties included in Annex I shall, individually or jointly, ensure that their aggregate anthropogenic carbon dioxide equivalent emissions of the greenhouse gases listed in Annex A do not exceed their assigned amounts, calculated pursuant to their quantified emission limitation and reduction commitments inscribed in Annex B and in accordance with the provisions of this Article, with a view to reducing their overall emissions of such gases by at least 5 per cent below 1990 levels in the commitment period 2008 to 2012.

2.   Each Party included in Annex I shall, by 2005, have made demonstrable progress in achieving its commitments under this Protocol.

3.   The net changes in greenhouse gas emissions by sources and removals by sinks resulting from direct human-induced land-use change and forestry activities, limited to afforestation, reforestation and deforestation since 1990, measured as verifiable changes in carbon stocks in each commitment period, shall be used to meet the commitments under this Article of each Party included in Annex I. The greenhouse gas emissions by sources and removals by sinks associated with those activities shall be

reported in a transparent and verifiable manner and reviewed in accordance with Articles 7 and 8.

4. Prior to the first session of the Conference of the Parties serving as the meeting of the Parties to this Protocol, each Party included in Annex I shall provide, for consideration by the Subsidiary Body for Scientific and Technological Advice, data to establish its level of carbon stocks in 1990 and to enable an estimate to be made of its changes in carbon stocks in subsequent years. * * *

7. In the first quantified emission limitation and reduction commitment period, from 2008 to 2012, the assigned amount for each Party included in Annex I shall be equal to the percentage inscribed for it in Annex B of its aggregate anthropogenic carbon dioxide equivalent emissions of the greenhouse gases listed in Annex A in 1990, or the base year or period determined in accordance with paragraph 5 above, multiplied by five. Those Parties included in Annex I for whom land-use change and forestry constituted a net source of greenhouse gas emissions in 1990 shall include in their 1990 emissions base year or period the aggregate anthropogenic carbon dioxide equivalent emissions by sources minus removals by sinks in 1990 from land-use change for the purposes of calculating their assigned amount.

* * *

9. Commitments for subsequent periods for Parties included in Annex I shall be established in amendments to Annex B to this Protocol, which shall be adopted in accordance with the provisions of Article 21, paragraph 7. The Conference of the Parties serving as the meeting of the Parties to this Protocol shall initiate the consideration of such commitments at least seven years before the end of the first commitment period referred to in paragraph 1 above.

10. Any emission reduction units, or any part of an assigned amount, which a Party acquires from another Party in accordance with the provisions of Article 6 or of Article 17 shall be added to the assigned amount for the acquiring Party.

11. Any emission reduction units, or any part of an assigned amount, which a Party transfers to another Party in accordance with the provisions of Article 6 or of Article 17 shall be subtracted from the assigned amount for the transferring Party.

12. Any certified emission reductions which a Party acquires from another Party in accordance with the provisions of Article 12 shall be added to the assigned amount for the acquiring Party.

13. If the emissions of a Party included in Annex I in a commitment period are less than its assigned amount under this Article, this difference shall, on request of that Party, be added to the assigned amount for that Party for subsequent commitment periods.

* * *

Article 4

1. Any Parties included in Annex I that have reached an agreement to fulfil their commitments under Article 3 jointly, shall be deemed to have met those commitments provided that their total combined aggregate anthropogenic carbon dioxide equivalent emissions of the greenhouse gases listed in Annex A do not exceed their assigned amounts calculated pursuant to their quantified emission limitation and reduction commitments inscribed in Annex B and in accordance with the provisions of Article 3. The respective emission level allocated to each of the Parties to the agreement shall be set out in that agreement.

* * *

Article 5

1. Each Party included in Annex I shall have in place, no later than one year prior to the start of the first commitment period, a national system for the estimation of anthropogenic emissions by sources and removals by sinks of all greenhouse gases not controlled by the Montreal Protocol. Guidelines for such national systems, which shall incorporate the methodologies specified in paragraph 2 below, shall be decided upon by the Conference of the Parties serving as the meeting of the Parties to this Protocol at its first session.

* * *

Article 6

1. For the purpose of meeting its commitments under Article 3, any Party included in Annex I may transfer to, or acquire from, any other such Party emission reduction units resulting from projects aimed at reducing anthropogenic emissions by sources or enhancing anthropogenic removals by sinks of greenhouse gases in any sector of the economy, provided that:

(a) Any such project has the approval of the Parties involved;

(b) Any such project provides a reduction in emissions by sources, or an enhancement of removals by sinks, that is additional to any that would otherwise occur;

(c) It does not acquire any emission reduction units if it is not in compliance with its obligations under Articles 5 and 7; and

(d) The acquisition of emission reduction units shall be supplemental to domestic actions for the purposes of meeting commitments under Article 3.

* * *

Article 7

1. Each Party included in Annex I shall incorporate in its annual inventory of anthropogenic emissions by sources and removals by sinks of greenhouse gases not controlled by the Montreal Protocol, submitted in

accordance with the relevant decisions of the Conference of the Parties, the necessary supplementary information for the purposes of ensuring compliance with Article 3[.]

* * *

Article 8

1. The information submitted under Article 7 by each Party included in Annex I shall be reviewed by expert review teams pursuant to the relevant decisions of the Conference of the Parties and in accordance with guidelines adopted for this purpose by the Conference of the Parties serving as the meeting of the Parties to this Protocol under paragraph 4 below. The information submitted under Article 7, paragraph 1, by each Party included in Annex I shall be reviewed as part of the annual compilation and accounting of emissions inventories and assigned amounts. * * *

3. The review process shall provide a thorough and comprehensive technical assessment of all aspects of the implementation by a Party of this Protocol. The expert review teams shall prepare a report to the Conference of the Parties serving as the meeting of the Parties to this Protocol, assessing the implementation of the commitments of the Party and identifying any potential problems in, and factors influencing, the fulfilment of commitments. Such reports shall be circulated by the secretariat to all Parties to the Convention. The secretariat shall list those questions of implementation indicated in such reports for further consideration by the Conference of the Parties serving as the meeting of the Parties to this Protocol.

* * *

Article 12

1. A clean development mechanism is hereby defined.

2. The purpose of the clean development mechanism shall be to assist Parties not included in Annex I in achieving sustainable development and in contributing to the ultimate objective of the Convention, and to assist Parties included in Annex I in achieving compliance with their quantified emission limitation and reduction commitments under Article 3.

3. Under the clean development mechanism:

(a) Parties not included in Annex I will benefit from project activities resulting in certified emission reductions; and

(b) Parties included in Annex I may use the certified emission reductions accruing from such project activities to contribute to compliance with part of their quantified emission limitation and reduction commitments under Article 3, as determined by the Conference of the Parties serving as the meeting of the Parties to this Protocol.

4. The clean development mechanism shall be subject to the authority and guidance of the Conference of the Parties serving as the meeting of the

Parties to this Protocol and be supervised by an executive board of the clean development mechanism.

5. Emission reductions resulting from each project activity shall be certified by operational entities to be designated by the Conference of the Parties serving as the meeting of the Parties to this Protocol, on the basis of:

(a) Voluntary participation approved by each Party involved;

(b) Real, measurable, and long-term benefits related to the mitigation of climate change; and

(c) Reductions in emissions that are additional to any that would occur in the absence of the certified project activity.

6. The clean development mechanism shall assist in arranging funding of certified project activities as necessary.

7. The Conference of the Parties serving as the meeting of the Parties to this Protocol shall, at its first session, elaborate modalities and procedures with the objective of ensuring transparency, efficiency and accountability through independent auditing and verification of project activities.

8. The Conference of the Parties serving as the meeting of the Parties to this Protocol shall ensure that a share of the proceeds from certified project activities is used to cover administrative expenses as well as to assist developing country Parties that are particularly vulnerable to the adverse effects of climate change to meet the costs of adaptation.

9. Participation under the clean development mechanism, including in activities mentioned in paragraph 3(a) above and in the acquisition of certified emission reductions, may involve private and/or public entities, and is to be subject to whatever guidance may be provided by the executive board of the clean development mechanism.

* * *

Article 17

The Conference of the Parties shall define the relevant principles, modalities, rules and guidelines, in particular for verification, reporting and accountability for emissions trading. The Parties included in Annex B may participate in emissions trading for the purposes of fulfilling their commitments under Article 3. Any such trading shall be supplemental to domestic actions for the purpose of meeting quantified emission limitation and reduction commitments under that Article.

* * *

Annex B

Party	Quantified emission limitation or reduction commitment (percentage of base year or period)
Australia	108
Austria	92
Belgium	92

Party	Quantified emission limitation or reduction commitment (percentage of base year or period)
Bulgaria*	92
Canada	94
Croatia*	95
Czech Republic*	92
Denmark	92
Estonia*	92
European Community	92
Finland	92
France	92
Germany	92
Greece	92
Hungary*	94
Iceland	110
Ireland	92
Italy	92
Japan	94
Latvia*	92
Liechtenstein	92
Lithuania*	92
Luxembourg	92
Monaco	92
Netherlands	92
New Zealand	100
Norway	101
Poland*	94
Portugal	92
Romania*	92
Russian Federation*	100
Slovakia*	92
Slovenia*	92
Spain	92
Sweden	92
Switzerland	92
Ukraine*	100
United Kingdom	92
United States of America	93

* Countries that are undergoing the process of transition to a market economy.

NOTES AND QUESTIONS

1. *Treaty obligations.*

a. What did the industrialized (Annex I) parties commit to do by joining the Protocol? What did the developing country (non-Annex I) parties commit to? Among Annex I parties, how do the obligations of countries undergoing the process of transition to a market economy differ from other Annex I parties?

b.   Does Article 2 contain any enforceable commitments? If not, what is the purpose of including these provisions?

c.   What is the Clean Development Mechanism described in Article 12? What other market-based mechanisms are found in the Protocol? Do these mechanisms increase the probability that parties will meet their commitments under the Protocol?

d.   How does the Protocol lay the groundwork for future emissions limitations beyond those applicable in the commitment period from 2008 to 2012?

e.   What mechanisms does the Protocol include to verify or enforce emissions reductions?

f.   How, if at all, does the Protocol deal with the problem of uncertainty regarding contributions to climate change and impacts of climate change?

2.   *Additionality.* One of the critical requirements for projects incorporated within the Clean Development Mechanism is that emissions reductions resulting from such projects be "additional to any that would occur in the absence of the certified project activity." A similar requirement applies to joint implementation projects undertaken pursuant to Article 6. What is the purpose of this additionality requirement? What sort of analysis must be undertaken to demonstrate additionality?

3.   *The relationship between ozone depletion and climate change.* Although carbon dioxide is the primary greenhouse gas of concern, and although ozone depletion and climate change are distinct problems, ozone-depleting substances, as well as many of their substitutes, are in fact greenhouse gases. By eliminating CFCs and other ozone depleting substances, the Montreal Protocol helped to address climate change. Many of the substitutes promoted by the Montreal Protocol, however, may actually exacerbate climate change because of their greater global warming potential. For example, HCFC–22, which is not scheduled for phase-out in industrialized countries until 2020 and in developing countries until 2040, has a warming effect 1500 times greater than that of carbon dioxide. What might explain this apparently short-sighted feature of the Montreal Protocol regime?

The Kyoto Protocol left a number of important matters for future resolution, including how features such as emissions trading and the clean development mechanism would operate. These details were worked out in further negotiations that produced the Marrakesh Accords, which established a compliance regime for the Protocol.

Still other, even more significant, matters remain unresolved: What emissions limitations will apply to industrialized nations after 2012? What emissions limitations, if any, will apply to the United States? What emissions limitations, if any, will apply to developing nations? What should be the target limits for actual greenhouse gas concentrations in the atmosphere? And what role should mitigation and adaptation play in policy responses to climate change? Tackling these and other issues requires consideration of technologies to address climate change, as well as political obstacles to coordinated action.

In 2007, the parties to the Framework Convention agreed to work towards negotiating a revised, post-Kyoto international response to climate change, with such agreement to be finalized in Copenhagen in 2009. What emerged from frantic negotiations at Copenhagen was the Copenhagen Accord, a nonbinding agreement under which nations pledged to achieve voluntary emissions reduction targets. To date, 141 nations, representing over 80 percent of global greenhouse gas emissions, have indicated their association with, or support for, the Accord. The Accord establishes a long-term goal of limiting the increase in mean global temperature to below 2°C and contains a commitment by developed countries for new and additional financial assistance to assist developing countries in adaptation and mitigation efforts. The inability to agree on binding and more drastic emissions reductions, however, has led some observers to suggest that the negotiation process under the Framework Convention is too unwieldy. See, e.g., Robert N. Stavins & Robert C. Stowe, What Hath Copenhagen Wrought? A Preliminary Assessment, Environment Magazine, May/June 2010, at 8–14. Support is growing for a bifurcated approach under which major emitting countries would conduct negotiations focused on emissions reductions, and financial assistance and other issues would be addressed separately. Consistent with this approach, the 2010 Cancun Agreements affirmed commitments made under the Copenhagen Accord, created a Green Climate Fund to assist developing countries, and deferred to future negotiations any agreement on mandatory emissions reductions.

To help frame the technical challenges of reducing greenhouse gas emissions in sufficient quantities to make a difference, scientists Stephen Pacala and Robert Socolow developed the concept of "stabilization wedges" in a 2004 article. Each stabilization wedge represents a policy measure that would eventually reduce carbon emissions by one gigaton per year. Pacala and Socolow estimate that seven of these wedges will be necessary to stabilize atmospheric carbon dioxide concentration at 500 parts per million (ppm)—higher than the level some experts believe to be prudent and well above the preindustrial concentration of 280 ppm. The stabilization wedges identified include:

- doubling motor vehicle fuel economy;

- reducing miles driven per motor vehicle by half;

- applying existing energy efficiency strategies to all residential and commercial buildings;

- storing in underground reservoirs significant quantities of carbon generated by coal-fired power plants;

- quintupling electricity production from natural gas plants, and substituting these for coal-fired power plants;

- tripling electricity production by nuclear plants, and substituting these for coal-fired power plants;

- increasing electricity production from wind by 50–fold, and substituting this for electricity from coal-fired power plants;

- increasing electricity production from solar power by 700–fold (as compared to 2004 levels), and substituting this for electricity from coal-fired power plants; and

- eliminating clear-cutting of tropical forests, combined with aggressive reforestation.

See S. Pacala and R. Socolow, Stabilization Wedges: Solving the Climate Problem for the Next 50 Years with Current Technologies, 305 Science 968–72 (2004); Carbon Mitigation Initiative, Princeton University, Stabilization Wedge Game, http://cmi.princeton.edu/wedges/. What are the trade-offs involved with each of these options? Which options are more politically feasible? How should these options be integrated into a post-Kyoto accord?

What are some of the political obstacles to reducing carbon emissions? The following discussion suggests that national calculations of the costs and benefits of climate change are a critical factor.

Cass R. Sunstein, Of Montreal and Kyoto: A Tale of Two Protocols

31 Harv. Envtl. L. Rev. 1 (2007).

* * * [B]oth the success of the Montreal Protocol and the mixed picture for the Kyoto Protocol were largely driven by the decisions of the United States, and those decisions were driven in turn by a form of purely domestic cost-benefit analysis. To the United States, the monetized benefits of the Montreal Protocol dwarfed the monetized costs, and hence the circumstances were extremely promising for American support and even enthusiasm for the agreement. Remarkably, the United States had so much to lose from depletion of the ozone layer that it would have been worthwhile for the nation to act unilaterally to take the steps required by the Montreal Protocol. For the world as a whole, the argument for the Montreal Protocol was overwhelmingly strong.

The Kyoto Protocol presented a radically different picture. To the United States alone, prominent analyses suggested that the monetized benefits of the Kyoto Protocol would be dwarfed by the monetized costs. If the United States complied with the Kyoto Protocol on its own, those analyses suggested that it would spend a great deal and gain relatively little. If all parties complied, some of the most influential analyses suggested that the United States would nonetheless be a net loser. Because of the distinctive properties of the agreement, it was not at all clear that the world as a whole had more to gain than to lose from the Kyoto Protocol. Hence the circumstances were unpromising for a successful agreement—and they were especially unpromising for American participation, no matter the political affiliation of the relevant president. The different perceptions of costs and benefits, for the United States in particular but also for the world, provide the central explanation for the success of one agreement and the complex picture for the other. To make these points, it is unnecessary to accept any particular projection of costs and benefits, or to reach a final conclusion about whether ratification and compliance with the Kyoto Protocol might have been in the interest of the United States. The only suggestion is that on the basis of the understandings of the relevant actors at the relevant time—including public officials at many different points in the ideological spectrum—the Kyoto Protocol was taken to be a bad deal.

* * *

The implications of these points are simple. With respect to international environmental agreements in general, the participation of the United States, and of other nations as well, is greatly affected by perceived domestic consequences. To say this is not to deny that moral judgments may play some role and even a significant one—not only, but above all, if injured nations are in a position to punish those who do not diminish their injury. As we shall see, there are exceedingly good reasons, grounded in corrective justice, to ask the United States to assist those nations that are most vulnerable as a result of climate change. In addition, reputational incentives may matter, complicating the outcome of an unduly simple cost-benefit analysis. But if the United States is spending much more than it receives, it is unlikely to be an enthusiastic participant.

For climate change in particular, it is reasonable to predict that the United States will ratify an international agreement to reduce greenhouse gases only if the perceived domestic costs of the relevant reductions decrease, the perceived domestic benefits increase, or both. It is possible that the perceived cost-benefit ratio of aggressive controls will change significantly with new information, or with better understanding of old information. There is a still more general lesson. Without the participation of the United States, the success of any such agreement is likely to be limited, if only because the United States accounts for such a high percentage of the world's greenhouse gas emissions. Indeed, I have noted that China and India are anticipated to be increasingly large emitters in the near future, and they are most unlikely to participate if the United States does not. * * *

It is true that the United States accounts for only about one-fifth of global greenhouse gas emissions—a stunning per capita figure, but one that is not high enough to derail international action if other nations are willing to go forward without the United States. If the world were able to make significant cuts in what is 80% of total emissions, it could do a great deal about climate change. The problem is that if the United States stands to one side, it is almost certain that coordinated, aggressive action will be impossible. At Kyoto, China and India showed an unwillingness to commit to cuts even when the United States suggested that it would participate. Those nations, and other developing countries, will likely be reluctant to confer benefits on industrialized nations, including the United States, unless there is a degree of reciprocity and perhaps significant side payments as well (as in the Montreal Protocol).

* * *

Who has the most to lose from reductions in greenhouse gases, and who has the most to gain from such reductions? To understand the prospects for some kind of parallel to the Montreal Protocol, it is necessary to answer this question. Four possibilities can be imagined: some nations might both contribute substantially to the problem and stand to lose a great deal from it; some might contribute little while standing to lose little; some might contribute a great deal while standing to lose little; and some might contribute little while standing to lose a great deal. The most promising situation for an international accord would be one in which those who contribute most to the problem also have the most to lose. If so, they would face a strong incentive to scale back their emissions. The least promising situation would be one in which the major contributors have little to lose. If so, they would have a weak incentive to do anything about the problem.

Here as elsewhere, any particular figures must be taken as mere estimates and inevitably controversial estimates at that. But in order to begin discussion, here is a prominent projection of anticipated losses:

FIGURE 7: DAMAGES RESULTING FROM A 2.5° C WARMING AS A PERCENTAGE OF GDP

Country	Percent Loss of GDP
India	4.93
Africa	3.91
OECD Europe	2.83
High Income OPEC	1.95
Eastern Europe	0.71
Japan	0.50
United States	0.45
China	0.22
Russia	−0.65

It is important to underline the fact that these figures assume a 2.5° C warming. With a higher number, the damages would undoubtedly be higher as well. Indeed, higher damages are possible even with a 2.5° C warming. Whether or not these particular numbers are right, it is readily apparent that some nations are far more vulnerable than others. Strikingly, Russia stands to be a net gainer, with substantial benefits to agriculture. India is particularly vulnerable, primarily because it is expected to suffer devastating losses in terms of both public health and agriculture. African nations also stand to lose a great deal as a result of effects on public health, with a massive anticipated increase in climate-related diseases. In light of these figures, we might therefore expect that Russia would not be especially enthusiastic about controls of greenhouse gas emissions, except, perhaps, if an emissions trading system that ensured financial gain to Russia from those controls was established (as the Kyoto system in fact does). The

United States faces limited threats to agriculture and health. Like Russia, China is projected to benefit in terms of agriculture, and while it will suffer health losses, they are relatively modest, far below those expected in Africa and India. We might therefore expect that the United States and China would be unlikely to take a particular interest in reducing greenhouse gas emissions, at least on these figures. As shown above, their behavior is consistent with that prediction.

* * *

We can now see a real obstacle to an international agreement to control greenhouse gases. The United States and China are the largest emitters, and according to prominent projections, they also stand to lose relatively less from climate change. In terms of their own domestic self-interest, these projections weaken the argument for stringent controls. The nations of Africa stand to lose a great deal, but they are trivial greenhouse gas emitters. India is even more vulnerable, and its contribution, while not exactly trivial, is modest.

* * *

These are descriptive points, and none of them should be taken to suggest that the domestic cost-benefit analysis ought to be decisive in principle. In fact, it should not be. If one nation imposes significant harms on citizens of another, it should not continue to do so even if, or because, a purely domestic analysis suggests that emissions reductions are not justified from the point of view of the nation that is imposing those harms. As I have suggested, the problems of ozone depletion and climate change stem disproportionately from the actions of wealthy nations, above all the United States—actions from which citizens of wealthy nations, above all the United States, have disproportionately benefited. It is even possible to see the emission of greenhouse gases as a kind of tort, producing damage for which emitters, and those who gained from their actions, ought to pay. * * *

Whether nations as such should be held responsible, and what such responsibility should specifically entail, are complicated questions. But in view of the fact that Americans have gained so much from activities that impose risks on citizens of other nations, it seems clear that they have a special obligation to mitigate the harm, or to provide assistance to those who are likely to suffer. The assistance might take the form of financial or technological aid, making it easier to meet emissions targets, or monetary amounts designed to ease adaptation to hotter climates.

There is an additional problem. The citizens of Africa and India, the most vulnerable regions, are also disproportionately poor. The citizens of China, standing to lose a great deal from significant restrictions on greenhouse gases, are also relatively poor, and economic growth is contributing to significant reductions in their poverty. It is certainly plausible to think that the issue of relative wealth and poverty should play a role in distributing the costs of emissions reductions.

* * *

Nothing said here is inconsistent with the claim that an agreement to control greenhouse gases might be appealing or at least acceptable to the United States even if the cost-benefit calculation were fairly close, or perhaps mildly unfavorable to the deal. The Montreal Protocol and the Kyoto Protocol were at opposite extremes. Technocrats, both scientists and economists, seemed to demonstrate that the Montreal Protocol was a terrific bargain for the United States, while the Kyoto Protocol presented a much less favorable picture. The overwhelming votes in the Senate are at least suggestive on this count.

But for both agreements, the overall assessment would have been far more difficult if the relevant numbers had suggested a closer call—if the scientific and economic judgments, working together, suggested that reasonable people could differ. Even if the United States was a modest net loser, perhaps moral considerations might have tipped, or might in the future tip, the national calculus in favor of an agreement to control climate change. But it should be clear that in order for such an agreement to be acceptable to the United States, a method must be found to drive down the costs and to increase the benefits. Such a method would make the relevant agreement far more attractive to the world as well—and hence increase the likelihood of compliance by nations that are now skeptical about controls on greenhouse gases.

* * *

A useful step would involve a clear distinction between stocks and flows. To come to terms with past contributions, nations might participate in the creation of some kind of fund for climate change damages, with their participation reflecting their contributions to the total existing stock of emissions. India and China need not contribute much to such a fund; the United States and Europe would be required to contribute a great deal. A step of this kind would be a sensible response to the fact, shown by the above table of CO_2 emissions, that different nations have added dramatically different amounts to the current situation.

A separate step would involve the response to existing flows. Perhaps a "polluter-pays" principle could be made a part of an international agreement, so that nations would pay an amount to reflect their continuing contributions. In short, greenhouse gas emissions might be taxed, with the hope that the tax would lead to reductions. It would be easy to do something of this kind domestically, and an international agreement might form the basis for the imposition of greenhouse taxes. Alternatively, an understanding of past contributions and current emissions rates might be built into a structure closer to that of the Montreal Protocol, helping to serve as the foundation for both reduction requirements and economic transfers. In particular, the transfers might be designed to compensate for past and future contributions to the problem. If high contributors make significant cuts, perhaps their transfers need not be so large. If they continue to be high contributors, their transfers might be very high. If the goal is to ensure significant benefits, steps of this sort would be the place to start.

It is also possible that the overall benefits of greenhouse gas reductions are greater, domestically and for the world, than suggested by the most prominent analyses from several years ago. If the perceived damage from climate change increases, and if steps can be taken to reduce that damage, then the likelihood of a firm domestic response will of course increase.

On the cost side, two steps would be highly desirable. The first is to create an ambitious and reliable system for fully global emissions trading, which could make the cost-benefit ratio far more favorable for any agreement. The second is to produce better targets and requirements in a way that allows stringency to increase over time.

* * *

Do you agree with Sunstein's explanation as to why the Montreal Protocol has proven to be more successful than the Kyoto Protocol? Is securing the United States' cooperation primarily a matter of changing perceived costs and benefits, as Sunstein suggests, or more a matter of moral suasion?

NOTE ON LIABILITY REGIMES FOR CLIMATE CHANGE

International attention has focused on treaty-based approaches to climate change. Although both the Framework Convention and Kyoto Protocol reflect the disproportionate role of industrialized countries in contributing to climate change, neither explicitly imposes liability on industrialized countries for climate change damages. Under customary international law, the *Trail Smelter* principle that states are responsible for transboundary pollution might provide a basis for liability akin to public nuisance. See Katharine Q. Seelye, Global Warming May Bring New Variety of Class Action, N.Y. Times, Sept. 6, 2001, at A14 (discussing potential legal theories based on *Trail Smelter*). What international law options might be available to island and low-lying nations, which may bear the most devastating climate change impacts, against industrialized nations largely responsible for the climate change problem?

There is no international court with exclusive environmental jurisdiction. Although there are a number of international tribunals before which climate change-related claims may be brought, the prospects for securing effective relief are weak. Securing jurisdiction over the United States or any other potential defendant state is likely to be difficult, demonstrating causation not much easier, and obtaining substantial relief similarly challenging.

In 2005, a human rights petition was brought on behalf of the Inuit people against the United States in the Inter–American Commission, an arm of the Organization of American States. The petition alleged that harms from climate change violate the human rights of the Inuit because the retreat of sea ice, reduced access to vital resources, and loss of homes threaten Inuit culture and property. The Inter–American Commission, which lacks the authority to order compensatory or injunctive relief, rejected the petition in November 2006 on the grounds that "the information provided [in the petition] does not enable [the Commission] to determine whether the alleged facts would tend to characterize a violation of rights."

Another possible forum for raising climate change issues is the International Court of Justice (ICJ). Also referred to as the World Court, the ICJ adjudicates disputes between states and is the only international court of general jurisdiction. Given the principle of state sovereignty, however, jurisdiction in any international court exists only upon the consent of the parties to a dispute. The United States, for instance, has rescinded its general assent to ICJ jurisdiction, and is unlikely to consent to jurisdiction in a proceeding that might result in the imposition of liability for climate change harms. See Andrew L. Strauss, The Legal Option: Suing the United States in International Forums for Global Warming Emissions, 33 Envtl. L. Rep. 10,185 (2003). In addition to its capacity to adjudicate disputes, the ICJ also has the power to issue advisory opinions upon request by the General Assembly or Security Council of the United Nations, or by other UN organs when so authorized. The United States and other countries likely to be the subject of an advisory opinion on liability, however, would likely block a request for an advisory opinion. See id.

Given the limitations of international tribunals, why might states or nongovernmental organizations nevertheless pursue climate change actions in these forums?

SECTION 3.   TRADE AND THE ENVIRONMENT

International trade is a powerful force that permeates our daily lives, as reflected in the cars we drive, the clothes we wear, and the food we eat. Notwithstanding the tangible benefits of international trade, the liberalization and expansion of trade since World War II also have prompted concerns about inequality, economic dislocation, and environmental damage. What exactly is the relationship between international trade and the environment? As the following excerpt suggests, the relationship is a complex one whose effects are not always obvious.

Steve Charnovitz, Free Trade, Fair Trade, Green Trade: Defogging the Debate

27 Cornell Int'l L.J. 459, 462–65 (1994).

International trade is the exchange of ownership and the relocation of a good across a border. The exchange is motivated by a payment or by a barter. The relocation of the good could have environmental effects, although the payment probably has none.

One direct environmental impact of trade involves the transportation of goods. For example, the energy consumed, preservatives used, the port polluted, and the possibility of some hazardous spill are all potentially adverse environmental effects of transportation. The relocation of a good can also have a direct environmental impact. For example, imported fruit may allow a potentially hazardous animal to enter a country. Hazardous waste may be transferred to a country that does not dispose of it properly. Of course, not all locational effects are negative. Trade in environmental technology may eventuate cleaner production.

Trade may also involve economic changes that have indirect consequences for the environment or human health. These consequences can impact production or disposal of goods and materials. (In some cases, they are "externalities," but they can also be "internalities.") Many of the consequences would happen anyway as a result of domestic production. For example, the purchase of an imported car will lead to the burning of fossil fuels and will cause some auto pollution. But it is inappropriate to attribute these effects to international trade if autos would have otherwise been produced by domestic companies. Thus, if one is to analyze the indirect effects of trade, one must look for effects that would not have occurred from domestic production and commerce.

There are two main types of indirect effects—scale and structural. Scale effects result from the higher level of economic activity induced by trade. In other words, trade can accelerate the existing trends of production. For example, the increased air pollution in Mexico is a scale effect of NAFTA. Structural effects on the other hand result from changes in the patterns of production. In other words, trade can engender production that might not otherwise exist. For example, without the possibility of exporting ivory, less harvesting of African elephants would occur.

In summary, the direct effects of trade involve transportation and location. The indirect effects concern the scale and the structure of the economy. The effects of trade liberalization (or trade restrictions) can also be analyzed in these four categories: scale, structure, direct, and indirect effects.

Criticism over the effects of trade and trade liberalization on environmental quality has grown over the past few years. For example, Ravi Batra has written that "[i]nternational trade comes out as the worst villain in the destruction of the environment. It is the most diabolical polluter in the world and offers a precious lesson in the desirability of economic diversification versus specialization." Tim Lang and Colin Hines have written that "trade brings more of the problems the world needs less of: threats to the environment, uneven spread of employment, and widening gaps between rich and poor, both within societies and between societies." * * *

When firms compete for trade, those that use cleaner and healthier manufacturing techniques may put themselves at a competitive disadvantage. National environmental regulations establish a "level playing field" within a country. Yet very little international regulation exists. As Herman E. Daly explains:

> Economists rightly urge nations to follow a domestic program of internalizing costs into prices. They also wrongly urge nations to trade

freely with other countries that do not internalize their costs (and consequently have lower prices). If a nation tries to follow both those policies, the conflict is clear: free competition between different cost-internalizing regimes is utterly unfair. Furthermore, trade may entice governments to lower environmental standards (or taxes), or to refrain from raising them, in the presence of less-regulated foreign competition. To deal with this pressure, many commentators suggest the use of trade restrictions. For example, Frances Cairncross writes that "[f]ree-traders will fret. Yet green trade barriers may have a logic of their own. They may be the only way that one country can put real pressure on another to make sure its companies shoulder the costs they would otherwise impose on the environment."

Another concern about trade relates to the paradigm of "sustainable development." According to Daly, "[s]ustainable development means living within environmental constraints of absorptive and regenerative capacities.... Trade between nations or regions offers a way of loosening local constraints by importing environmental services (including waste absorption) from elsewhere." It is possible to disagree with Daly's policy conclusions but still recognize the quandary he identifies. Simply put, can a nation really be pursuing sustainable development if it imports environmental services from a nation that does not follow sustainable development?

Several responses have been made to this new critique. First, while countries may need harmonized environmental standards on certain global or regional issues, there are many topics of regulation that do not have significant transborder implications. For those issues, one might anticipate that national regulations would differ and such non-uniformity is proper since it reflects differing national values. Second, international trade could raise product standards as producers meet market demand for greener products. Third, greater competition could force firms to look for more efficient production methods, which may result in better pollution control technology. Fourth, there is also an "income effect" from economic growth: as countries become richer, citizens may demand more environmental quality. Yet as Gene Grossman notes, "even for those dimensions of environmental quality where growth seems to have been associated with improving conditions, there is no reason to believe that the process has been automatic." Fifth, the relocation of production to countries with lower environmental standards can be viewed as desirable, not undesirable. According to Martin Wolf, "Provided barriers to trade are small, polluting processes will move to the country with the more liberal regulations. In this case, the country that has imposed the tighter regulation loses the processes its people dislike, while still enjoying, through trade, the products they desire." * * *

NOTES AND QUESTIONS

1. *Trade and the environment.* Charnovitz lists a number of responses to the general environmentalist critique of free trade. Do you find his arguments persuasive?

2. *Trade as a tool for peace.* Liberalized trade has been promoted strongly since World War II as an important tool for reducing global conflict through increased economic interdependence. Does the recent trend toward the outsourcing of jobs (e.g., from the United States to India) and clashes between China and its trade partners (including the United States) over the safety of products made in China undermine this hypothesis?

3. *Trade and sustainable development.* How is international trade related to sustainable development? How can international trade, and particularly trade between industrialized and developing nations, promote sustainable development? How might such trade undermine sustainable development?

An important concern that the preceding excerpt mentions is the potential conflict between free trade regimes and measures to protect human health and the environment. The *Tuna/Dolphin* cases, which involved challenges to American restrictions on imported tuna, brought this conflict to international attention in the early 1990s.

In the Eastern Tropical Pacific Ocean (ETP), dolphins and tuna associate with each other, and fishermen locate and capture tuna by finding dolphins, pursuing them, and encircling them with nets to catch the tuna. In some years, this practice resulted in hundreds of thousands of dolphin injuries and deaths. The U.S. Marine Mammal Protection Act (MMPA) seeks to reduce dolphin mortality by requiring that U.S. tuna fishermen use certain techniques and by imposing a ceiling on the number of dolphins that can be killed or injured by the U.S. fishing fleet in the ETP. At the time of the Tuna/Dolphin dispute, the MMPA also banned the importation of fish caught with commercial fishing technology that resulted in the incidental killing or serious injury of ocean mammals in excess of U.S. standards. Each country seeking to export tuna to the United States had to have in place a regulatory regime comparable to that of the United States with respect to the taking of marine mammals. Specifically, the average rate of incidental taking of marine mammals by a foreign fleet could be no greater than 1.25 times the average incidental taking rate of U.S. vessels operating in the ETP during the same period. The United States imposed an embargo on tuna imports from countries that failed to make such a showing. The United States also banned tuna imports from "intermediary nations"—nations buying tuna from countries against whom the United States had imposed a primary embargo.

Pursuant to the MMPA, the United States imposed an embargo on tuna imports from Mexico. In *Tuna/Dolphin I*, Mexico challenged the embargo before a dispute settlement panel of the General Agreement on Tariffs and Trade (GATT). Formed shortly after World War II and now administered by the World Trade Organization, the GATT seeks to promote global security and political and economic interdependence by reducing trade barriers and promoting free trade. The central principles of the GATT include: (1) the Most Favored Nation obligation of Article I, which prohibits discrimination between like products of different states; (2) the National Treatment obligation of Article III, which prohibits discrimination between imported and domestically manufactured products that are alike; and (3) the general prohibition on quantitative restrictions of Article XI. Mexico contended that the embargo violated Article XI. The United States responded that the embargo was authorized under Article III as a permissible internal regulation, and alternatively, that the embargo fell within the environmental exceptions to the GATT found in Article XX.

The panel issued the report excerpted below. Although the report was never adopted (adoption required consensus of the parties), the case raised serious concerns about the potential of free trade regimes to undermine environmental protection.

General Agreement on Tariffs and Trade, Dispute Settlement Panel Report on United States Restrictions on Imports of Tuna

DS21/R (Sept. 3, 1991) (unadopted), reprinted in 30 I.L.M. 1594.

* * *

Categorization as internal regulations (Article III) or quantitative restrictions (Article XI)

5.8.   The Panel noted that Mexico had argued that the measures prohibiting imports of certain yellowfin tuna and yellowfin tuna products from Mexico imposed by the United States were quantitative restrictions on importation under Article XI, while the United States had argued that these measures were internal regulations enforced at the time or point of importation under Article III:4 and the Note Ad Article III, namely that the prohibition of imports of tuna and tuna products from Mexico constituted an enforcement of the regulations of the MMPA relating to the harvesting of domestic tuna.

5.9.   The Panel examined the distinction between quantitative restrictions on importation and internal measures applied at the time or point of importation, and noted the following. While restrictions on importation are prohibited by Article XI:1, contracting parties are permitted by Article III:4 and the Note Ad Article III to impose an internal regulation on products imported from other contracting parties provided that it: does not discriminate between products of other countries in violation of the most-favoured-nation principle of Article I:1; is not applied so as to afford protection to domestic production, in violation of the national treatment principle of Article III:1; and accords to imported products treatment no less favourable than that accorded to like products of national origin, consistent with Article III:4. The relevant text of Article III:4 provides:

> The products of the territory of any contracting party imported into the territory of any other contracting party shall be accorded treatment no less favourable than that accorded to like products of national

origin in respect of all laws, regulations and requirements affecting their internal sale, offering for sale, purchase, transportation, distribution or use.

The Note Ad Article III provides that:

Any internal tax or other internal charge, or any law, regulation or requirement of the kind referred to in [Article III:1] which applies to an imported product and the like domestic product and is collected or enforced in the case of the imported product at the time or point of importation, is nevertheless to be regarded as an internal tax or other internal charge, or a law, regulation or requirement of the kind referred to in [Article III:1], and is accordingly subject to the provisions of Article III.

5.10.   The Panel noted that the United States had claimed that the direct import embargo on certain yellowfin tuna and certain yellowfin tuna products of Mexico constituted an enforcement at the time or point of importation of the requirements of the MMPA that yellowfin tuna in the ETP be harvested with fishing techniques designed to reduce the incidental taking of dolphins. The MMPA did not regulate tuna products as such, and in particular did not regulate the sale of tuna or tuna products. Nor did it prescribe fishing techniques that could have an effect on tuna as a product. This raised in the Panel's view the question of whether the tuna harvesting regulations could be regarded as a measure that "applies to" imported and domestic tuna within the meaning of the Note Ad Article III and consequently as a measure which the United States could enforce consistently with that Note in the case of imported tuna at the time or point of importation. The Panel examined this question in detail and found the following.

5.11.   The text of Article III:1 refers to the application to imported or domestic products of "laws, regulations and requirements affecting the internal sale.... of products" and "internal quantitative regulations requiring the mixture, processing or use of products"; it sets forth the principle that such regulations on products not be applied so as to afford protection to domestic production. Article III:4 refers solely to laws, regulations and requirements affecting the internal sale, etc. of products. This suggests that Article III covers only measures affecting products as such. Furthermore, the text of the Note Ad Article III refers to a measure "which applies to an imported product and the like domestic product and is collected or enforced in the case of the imported product at the time or point of importation." This suggests that this Note covers only measures applied to imported products that are of the same nature as those applied to the domestic products, such as a prohibition on importation of a product which enforces at the border an internal sales prohibition applied to both imported and like domestic products.

* * *

5.14.   The Panel concluded from the above considerations that the Note Ad Article III covers only those measures that are applied to the product as such. The Panel noted that the MMPA regulates the domestic harvesting of yellowfin tuna to reduce the incidental taking of dolphin, but that these regulations could not be regarded as being applied to tuna products as such because they would not directly regulate the sale of tuna and could not possibly affect tuna as a product. Therefore, the Panel found that the import prohibition on certain yellowfin tuna and certain yellowfin tuna products of Mexico and the provisions of the MMPA under which it is imposed did not constitute internal regulations covered by the Note Ad Article III.

5.15. The Panel further concluded that, even if the provisions of the MMPA enforcing the tuna harvesting regulations (in particular those providing for the seizure of cargo as a penalty for violation of the Act) were regarded as regulating the sale of tuna as a product, the United States import prohibition would not meet the requirements of Article III. * * *Article III:4 calls for a comparison of the treatment of imported tuna as a product with that of domestic tuna as a product. Regulations governing the taking of dolphins incidental to the taking of tuna could not possibly affect tuna as a product. Article III:4 therefore obliges the United States to accord treatment to Mexican tuna no less favourable than that accorded to United States tuna, whether or not the incidental taking of dolphins by Mexican vessels corresponds to that of United States vessels.

* * *

Article XX

5.23. The Panel proceeded to examine whether Article XX(b) or Article XX(g) could justify the MMPA provisions on imports of certain yellowfin tuna and yellowfin tuna products, and the import ban imposed under these provisions. The Panel noted that Article XX provides that:

> Subject to the requirement that such measures are not applied in a manner which would constitute a means of arbitrary or unjustifiable discrimination between countries where the same conditions prevail, or a disguised restriction on international trade, nothing in this Agreement shall be construed to prevent the adoption or enforcement by any contracting party of measures . . .
>
> (b) necessary to protect human, animal or plant life or health; . . .
>
> (g) relating to the conservation of exhaustible natural resources if such measures are made effective in conjunction with restrictions on domestic production or consumption; . . . .

5.24. The Panel noted that the United States considered the prohibition of imports of certain yellowfin tuna and certain yellowfin tuna products from Mexico, and the provisions of the MMPA on which this prohibition is based, to be justified by Article XX(b) because they served solely the purpose of protecting dolphin life and health and were ''necessary'' within the meaning of that provision because, in respect of the protection of dolphin life and health outside its jurisdiction, there was no alternative measure reasonably available to the United States to achieve this objective.

Mexico considered that Article XX(b) was not applicable to a measure imposed to protect the life or health of animals outside the jurisdiction of the contracting party taking it and that the import prohibition imposed by the United States was not necessary because alternative means consistent with the General Agreement were available to it to protect dolphin lives or health, namely international co-operation between the countries concerned.

5.25. The Panel noted that the basic question raised by these arguments, namely whether Article XX(b) covers measures necessary to protect human, animal or plant life or health outside the jurisdiction of the contracting party taking the measure, is not clearly answered by the text of that provision. It refers to life and health protection generally without expressly limiting that protection to the jurisdiction of the contracting party concerned. The Panel therefore decided to analyze this issue in the light of the drafting history of Article XX(b), the purpose of this provision, and the consequences that the interpretations proposed by the parties would have for the operation of the General Agreement as a whole. * * *

5.27. The Panel further noted that Article XX(b) allows each contracting party to set its human, animal or plant life or health standards. The conditions set out in Article XX(b) which limit resort to this exception, namely that the measure taken must be "necessary" and not "constitute a means of arbitrary or unjustifiable discrimination or a disguised restriction on international trade," refer to the trade measure requiring justification under Article XX(b), not however to the life or health standard chosen by the contracting party. The Panel recalled the finding of a previous panel that this paragraph of Article XX was intended to allow contracting parties to impose trade restrictive measures inconsistent with the General Agreement to pursue overriding public policy goals to the extent that such inconsistencies were unavoidable. The Panel considered that if the broad interpretation of Article XX(b) suggested by the United States were accepted, each contracting party could unilaterally determine the life or health protection policies from which other contracting parties could not deviate without jeopardizing their rights under the General Agreement. The General Agreement would then no longer constitute a multilateral framework for trade among all contracting parties but would provide legal security only in respect of trade between a limited number of contracting parties with identical internal regulations.

5.28. The Panel considered that the United States' measures, even if Article XX(b) were interpreted to permit extrajurisdictional protection of life and health, would not meet the requirement of necessity set out in that provision. The United States had not demonstrated to the Panel—as required of the party invoking an Article XX exception—that it had exhausted all options reasonably available to it to pursue its dolphin protection objectives through measures consistent with the General Agreement, in particular through the negotiation of international cooperative arrangements, which would seem to be desirable in view of the fact that dolphins roam the waters of many states and the high seas. Moreover, even assuming that an import prohibition were the only resort reasonably available to the United States, the particular measure chosen by the United States could in the Panel's view not be considered to be necessary within the meaning of Article XX(b). The United States linked the maximum incidental dolphin taking rate which Mexico had to meet during a particular period in order to be able to export tuna to the United States to the taking rate actually recorded for United States fishermen during the same period. Consequently, the Mexican authorities could not know whether, at a given point of time, their policies conformed to the United States' dolphin protection standards. The Panel considered that a limitation on trade based on such unpredictable conditions could not be regarded as necessary to protect the health or life of dolphins.

5.29. On the basis of the above considerations, the Panel found that the United States' direct import prohibition imposed on certain yellowfin tuna and certain yellowfin tuna products of Mexico and the provisions of the MMPA under which it is imposed could not be justified under the exception in Article XX(b).

* * *

[The Panel proceeded to analyze the potential applicability of the Article XX(g) exception and, based on similar reasoning, found Article XX(g) to be inapplicable as well.]

6.1. The Panel wished to underline that its task was limited to the examination of this matter "in the light of the relevant GATT provisions," and therefore did not call for a finding on the appropriateness of the United States' and Mexico's conservation policies as such.

6.2. The Panel wished to note the fact, made evident during its consideration of this case, that the provisions of the General Agreement impose few constraints on a contracting party's implementation of domestic environmental policies. The Panel recalled its findings in paragraphs 5.10—5.16 above that under these provisions, a contracting party is free to tax or regulate imported products and like domestic products as long as its taxes or regulations do not discriminate against imported products or afford protection to domestic producers, and a contracting party is also free to tax or regulate domestic production for environmental purposes. As a corollary to these rights, a contracting party may not restrict imports of a product merely because it originates in a country with environmental policies different from its own.

* * *

NOTES AND QUESTIONS

1. *Like products.* Did the Panel decide whether tuna imported from Mexico and tuna harvested by the American fleet were "like products?" Subsequent cases have elaborated on the factors that may be relevant to determining whether products are "like": the physical properties of the products; the extent to which the products serve similar end uses; the extent to which consumers perceive the products as alternatives; and the international classification of the products for tariff purposes. The Appellate Body of the WTO applied these factors in *EC-Asbestos*, an influential decision that upheld a French regulation prohibiting the sale of chrysotile asbestos and products containing that type of asbestos. See European Communities–Measures Affecting Asbestos and Asbestos–Containing Products, Report of the Appellate Body, WT/DS135/AB/R, ¶¶ 101–02 (Mar. 12, 2001). The Appellate Body rejected the WTO panel's conclusion that the banned fibers and noncarcinogenic substitutes were "like products" primarily because they had the same end uses. In particular, the Appellate Body acknowledged that the carcinogenic character of the banned fibers was relevant to at least two factors in the likeness analysis—the physical properties of the products, and consumer perception of them:

> 114. Panels must examine fully the physical properties of products. In particular, panels must examine those physical properties of products that are likely to influence the competitive relationship between products in the marketplace. In the case of chrysotile asbestos fibres, their molecular structure, chemical composition, and fibrillation capacity are important because the microscopic particles and filaments of chrysotile asbestos fibres are carcinogenic in humans, following inhalation. * * * This carcinogenicity, or toxicity, constitutes, as we see it, a defining aspect of the physical properties of chrysotile asbestos fibres. The evidence indicates that PCG fibres [i.e., cellulose and glass fibers that are substitutes for asbestos], in contrast, do not share these properties, at least to the same extent. We do not see how this highly significant physical difference cannot be a consideration in examining the physical properties of a product as part of a determination of "likeness" under Article III:4 of the GATT 1994.

> * * *

> 121. Furthermore, in a case such as this, where the fibres are physically very different, a panel cannot conclude that they are "like products" if it does not examine evidence relating to consumers' tastes and habits. In such a situation, if there is no inquiry into this aspect of the nature and extent of the competitive relationship between the products, there is no basis for overcoming the inference, drawn from the different physical properties of the products, that the products are not "like."

> 122. In this case especially, we are also persuaded that evidence relating to consumers' tastes and habits would establish that the health risks associated with chrysotile asbestos fibres influence consumers' behaviour with respect to the different fibres at issue. We observe that, as regards chrysotile asbestos and PCG fibres, the consumer of the fibres is a manufacturer who incorporates the fibres into another product, such as cement-based products or brake linings. We do not wish to speculate on what the evidence regarding these consumers would have indicated; rather, we wish to highlight that consumers' tastes and habits regarding fibres, even in the case of commercial

parties, such as manufacturers, are very likely to be shaped by the health risks associated with a product which is known to be highly carcinogenic.

Id. ¶¶ 114, 121–22. The Appellate Body report in *EC–Asbestos* supports the efforts by some WTO members to promulgate domestic environmental regulations that distinguish between products based on health and safety risks.

2. *Processes and Production Methods (PPMs).* In *EC–Asbestos*, the Appellate Body concluded that the French regulation did not discriminate against like products because the products at issue were physically different. *Tuna/Dolphin I*, however, concerned physically similar products produced using different processes and production methods (PPMs). PPM-based measures, such as environmental taxes, are frequently used in environmental regulation because manufacturing processes, rather than goods themselves, are often the primary source of environmental impacts. Exporting countries argue that such measures constitute disguised protectionism, while importing countries respond that such distinctions are necessary to maintain domestic environmental standards and to prevent foreign competitors from gaining an unfair advantage. Under *Tuna/Dolphin I*, measures that discriminate between like products based on how they are made violate Article III of the GATT if foreign products receive less favorable treatment than domestic products.

3. *Environmental exceptions to the GATT.* Why did the Panel in *Tuna/Dolphin I* conclude that the environmental exceptions to the GATT did not apply? Could the United States achieve its goal of protecting dolphins through some other trade measure? Despite the relatively broad language of Article XX, GATT and WTO tribunals have generally rejected contentions that environmental trade restrictions are covered by Article XX. In the *Shrimp/Turtle* case, however, the WTO Appellate Body concluded that Article XX(g) applied to a U.S. law banning imports of shrimp caught without using a Turtle Excluder Device (TED). After finding sea turtles to be an exhaustible natural resource, the Appellate Body analyzed whether the law "related to" conservation of an exhaustible natural resource as follows:

> 135.   Article XX(g) requires that the measure sought to be justified be one which "relat[es] to" the conservation of exhaustible natural resources. In making this determination, the treaty interpreter essentially looks into the relationship between the measure at stake and the legitimate policy of conserving exhaustible natural resources. * * *
>
> 138.   Section 609(b)(1) imposes an import ban on shrimp that have been harvested with commercial fishing technology which may adversely affect sea turtles. This provision is designed to influence countries to adopt national regulatory programs requiring the use of TEDs by their shrimp fishermen. In this connection, it is important to note that the general structure and design of Section 609 cum implementing guidelines is fairly narrowly focused. There are two basic exemptions from the import ban, both of which relate clearly and directly to the policy

goal of conserving sea turtles. First, Section 609, as elaborated in the 1996 Guidelines, excludes from the import ban shrimp harvested "under conditions that do not adversely affect sea turtles." Thus, the measure, by its terms, excludes from the import ban: aquaculture shrimp; shrimp species (such as pandalid shrimp) harvested in water areas where sea turtles do not normally occur; and shrimp harvested exclusively by artisanal methods, even from non-certified countries. The harvesting of such shrimp clearly does not affect sea turtles. Second, under Section 609(b)(2), the measure exempts from the import ban shrimp caught in waters subject to the jurisdiction of certified countries.

* * *

141.   In its general design and structure, therefore, Section 609 is not a simple, blanket prohibition of the importation of shrimp imposed without regard to the consequences (or lack thereof) of the mode of harvesting employed upon the incidental capture and mortality of sea turtles. Focusing on the design of the measure here at stake, it appears to us that Section 609, cum implementing guidelines, is not disproportionately wide in its scope and reach in relation to the policy objective of protection and conservation of sea turtle species. The means are, in principle, reasonably related to the ends. The means and ends relationship between Section 609 and the legitimate policy of conserving an exhaustible, and, in fact, endangered species, is observably a close and real one * * *.

United States—Import Prohibition of Certain Shrimp and Shrimp Products, Report of the Appellate Body, WT/DS58/AB/R, reprinted in 38 I.L.M. 121, 157–59 (1999). Is *Shrimp/Turtle* consistent with *Tuna/Dolphin I*?

4. *Tuna/Dolphin II.* The European Community and the Netherlands challenged the intermediary embargo provisions of the MMPA in *Tuna/Dolphin II*. The panel in *Tuna/Dolphin II* concluded that the intermediary embargo, like the primary embargo considered in *Tuna/Dolphin I*, was inconsistent with Article XI of the GATT and did not fall within the environmental exceptions of Article XX. The panel differed from the *Tuna/Dolphin I* panel in its analysis of Article XX(g), however, explaining that this exception could be applied extraterritorially—i.e., to resources outside the jurisdiction of the regulating country. The panel nevertheless concluded that the embargo was too broad because it applied to all tuna from the intermediary nation, not just to tuna caught in a dolphin-unsafe manner. General Agreement on Tariffs and Trade: Dispute Settlement Panel Report on United States Restrictions on Imports of Tuna, 33 I.L.M. 839, 891–94 (1994).

INDEX

References are to pages.

NIMBY POLITICS—Cont'd
NEPA litigation, 309
Wealthy communities' advantages, 526

NONDELEGATION DOCTRINE
Administrative law, 102

NORTH AMERICAN FREE TRADE AGREEMENT (NAFTA)
NEPA duties, 270

NOTICES OF INTENT (NOI)
See National Environmental Policy Act, this index

NUISANCE
Generally, 41
Air pollution, 630
Balancing of utilities rule, private nuisance, 41
Causation issues
Expert testimony, 58
Toxic torts, 58
Damages, 56
Emotional distress damages, water pollution, 51
Expert testimony, causation issues, 58
Federal common law
Generally, 55
Erie doctrine, 70
Statutory remedies displacing, 80
Federal preemption of common law remedies, 82
Injunctions, 56
Latent injuries, causation issues, 62
Legal acts constituting, 80
Per se negligence, CWA violations as, 68
Permitted action defenses, 80, 83
Private nuisance
Generally, 41
Balancing of utilities rule, 41
Public nuisance
Generally, 42
Permitted action defenses, 80, 83
Transboundary pollution, 75
Remedies, 56
Standing to sue, 56
Stigma damages, 52
Transboundary pollution
Generally, 55
Public nuisance, 75
Trespass compared, 43
Water pollution
CWA violations as per se negligence, 68
Emotional distress damages, 51

OCCUPATIONAL SAFETY AND HEALTH ACT
Benzene, regulatory tools, 430
Material Safety Data Sheets, 467
Toxic substances, regulatory tools, 429

OCEAN RESOURCES
Tragedy of the commons, 13
Whale hunting, aboriginal subsistence exception, 249, 255

OFFICE OF INFORMATION AND REGULATORY AFFAIRS (OIRA)
Administrative agency oversight, 106

OFFICE OF MANAGEMENT AND BUDGET (OMB)
Risk assessment guidelines, 428

OFFICE OF TECHNOLOGY ASSESSMENT
Regulatory policy tools study, 32

OLD ECOLOGY
Generally, 10

OZONE DEPLETION
International environmental law, 919

PARENT AND SUBSIDIARY CORPORATIONS
Superfund liability, 579

PARETO EFFICIENCY
See also Economic Policy, this index
Cost-benefit analysis efficiency compared, 17

PERMIT SHIELD
Civil enforcement defenses, 865, 868
Nuisance claims, permitted action defenses, 80, 83

PERMITS
Administrative authority, 95
Civil enforcement permit shield defenses, 865, 868
Compliance defenses to common law claims, 80, 83
Cooperative federalism, state wetland programs, 406
CWA and CAA permit policies compared, 791
Design standards, 32
Environmental justice challenges
Generally, 525, 532
EPA authority, 538
EPA authority
Environmental justice challenges, 538
Vetoes of Corps permit decisions, 404
Equal protection challenges, 525
ESA
Generally, 367
Incidental take permits, 370
Mitigation requirements, 378
Individual stationary source permits, 635
Integrated permitting
Regulatory policy tools, 33
Mitigation
No net loss standard, wetlands protection, 409
Wetlands permits, 399, 406 et seq.
National Pollutant Discharge Elimination System (NPDES) permits
Generally, 767
See also Water Pollution, this index
NEPA, CWA exemptions, 267
No net loss mitigation standard, wetlands protection, 409

†